Revised Printing

MW01706146

Solutions Manual

Electric Circuits

Sixth Edition

James W. Nilsson ◆ Susan A. Riedel

Prentice Hall

Prentice Hall, Upper Saddle River, NJ 07458

Publisher: Tom Robbins
Supplement Editor: Jessie Power
Special Projects Manager: Barbara A. Murray
Production Editor: Barbara A. Till
Supplement Cover Manager: Paul Gourhan
Supplement Cover Designer: PM Workshop Inc.
Manufacturing Buyer: Lisa McDowell

Printed in the United States of America

10 9 8 7 6 5 4 3 2 1

ISBN 0-13-090867-3

Prentice-Hall International (UK) Limited, London
Prentice-Hall of Australia Pty. Limited, Sydney
Prentice-Hall Canada, Inc., Toronto
Prentice-Hall Hispanoamericana, S.A., Mexico
Prentice-Hall of India Private Limited, New Delhi
Pearson Education Asia Pte. Ltd., Singapore
Prentice-Hall of Japan, Inc., Tokyo
Editora Prentice-Hall do Brazil, Ltda., Rio de Janeiro

Contents

1

Circuit Variables

Drill Exercises

DE 1.1 $100 \text{ billion} = 100 \times 10^9$

$T_y = \text{ number of ms/year } = 365 \times 24 \times 3600 \times 1000 = 31{,}536 \times 10^6$

$\text{Dollars/ms} = 100 \times 10^9/(31.536 \times 10^9) = 3.17$

DE 1.2 $180\text{million} = 180 \times 10^6$

$\text{Energy stored} = 180 \times 440 \times 10^6 = 79.2 \times 10^9 = 79.2 \text{ GWh}$

DE 1.3 $\text{Number of megabytes} = \dfrac{1280 \times 1024 \times 24}{8 \times 10^6} = 3.93$

DE 1.4 $\text{Seconds/day} = (24)(60)(60) = 86{,}400$

$$\text{Cell lengths/day} = \frac{250 \times 10^{-3}}{10 \times 10^{-6}} = 25{,}000$$

$$\text{Cell length/second} = \frac{86{,}400}{25{,}000} = 3.46 \text{ s} \approx 3.5 \text{ s}$$

DE 1.5 $\text{Volume} = \text{area} \times \text{thickness}$

$10^6 = (10 \times 10^6)(\text{thickness})$

$$\Rightarrow \text{thickness} = \frac{10^6}{10 \times 10^6} = 0.10 \text{ mm}$$

DE 1.6 $(3 \times 10^8 \text{ m/s})(0.8)(10^{-9} \text{ s})(100 \text{ cm/m})(1 \text{ in}/2.54 \text{ cm}) = 9.45''$

DE 1.7 $$q = \int_0^\infty 20e^{-5000t}\,dt = 4000\,\mu\text{C}$$

DE 1.8 $$i = \frac{dq}{dt} = te^{-\alpha t}, \qquad \frac{di}{dt} = (1 - \alpha t)e^{-\alpha t}, \qquad \frac{di}{dt} = 0 \qquad \text{when } t = \frac{1}{\alpha};$$

$$\text{Therefore } i_{max} = \frac{1}{\alpha e} = \frac{1}{0.03679e} \cong 10 \text{ A}$$

DE 1.9 [a]

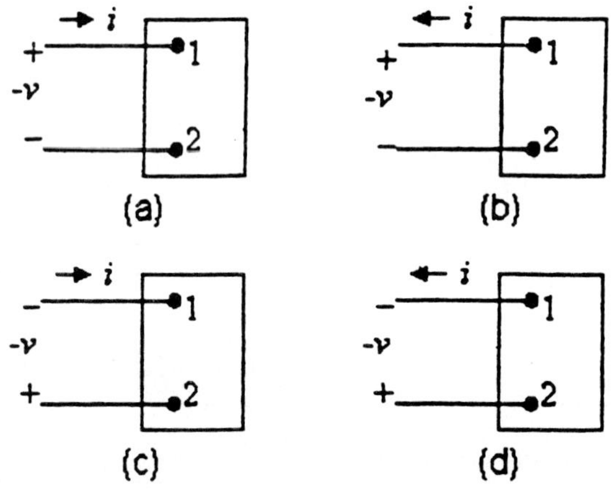

Therefore

(a) $v = -20\,\text{V}$, $i = -4\,\text{A}$; (b) $v = -20\,\text{V}$, $i = 4\,\text{A}$

(c) $v = 20\,\text{V}$, $i = -4\,\text{A}$; (d) $v = 20\,\text{V}$, $i = 4\,\text{A}$

[b] Using the reference system in Fig. 1.6(a), $p = vi = (-20)(4) = 80\,\text{W}$, so the box is absorbing power.

[c] The box is absorbing 80 W.

DE 1.10 $$p = vi = 20 \times 10^4 e^{-10{,}000t}\ \text{W}; \qquad w = \int_0^\infty 20 \times 10^4 e^{-10{,}000t}\,dt = 20 \text{ J}$$

DE 1.11 $$p = 800 \times 10^3 \times 1.8 \times 10^3 = 1440 \times 10^6 = 1440 \text{ MW}$$

from Oregon to California

Problems

P 1.1 $$\text{Time} = \frac{\text{distance}}{\text{velocity}} = \frac{(1100)(1609.35)}{2 \times 10^8} = 8.85 \text{ ms}$$

P 1.2 $$\text{No. of kilograms} = \frac{(845)(5280)(2.526)(4)}{2.2} = 20.49 \times 10^6 \text{ kg}$$

P 1.3 $$\text{Velocity} = \frac{\text{distance}}{\text{time}} = \frac{(1.5 \times 10^{-3})(4)(200 \times 10^9)}{(60)(60)(24)(365.25)}$$
$$= \frac{1.2 \times 10^9}{31{,}557{,}600} = 38 \text{ m/s}$$

P 1.4 $$\text{C/m}^3 = 1.6022 \times 10^{-19} \times 10^{29} = 1.6022 \times 10^{10}\,\text{C/m}^3$$

$$\text{C/m} = (1.6022 \times 10^{10})(5.4 \times 10^{-4}) = 8.65 \times 10^6\,\text{C/m}$$

$$\text{Therefore, } (8.65 \times 10^6)\frac{\text{C}}{\text{m}} \times \text{ave vel}\left(\frac{m}{s}\right) = i$$

$$\text{Thus, average velocity} = \frac{1400}{8.65} \times 10^{-6} = 161.85\,\mu\text{m/s}$$

P 1.5 $$\text{Width of track} = \frac{1\text{ in}}{77\text{ tracks}}\frac{25{,}400\mu\text{m}}{\text{in}} = 329.87\mu\text{m/track}$$

$$\text{Bits on a track} = \frac{1.4\text{ MB}}{2\text{ sides}}\frac{8\text{ bits}}{\text{byte}}\frac{1\text{ side}}{77\text{ tracks}} = 72{,}727.273\text{ bits/track}$$

$$\text{Circumference of inner track} = 2\pi(1/2'')(25{,}400\mu\text{m/in}) = 79{,}796.453\mu\text{m}$$

$$\text{Width of bit on inner track} = \frac{79{,}796.453\mu\text{m}}{72{,}727.273\text{ bits}} = 1.0972\mu\text{m/bit}$$

$$\text{Area of bit on inner track} = (1.0972)(329.87) = 361.934\mu\text{m}^2$$

P 1.6 [a] $$n = \frac{35 \times 10^{-6}}{1.6022 \times 10^{-19}} = 2.18 \times 10^{14}\text{ e/s}$$

[b] $$m = (7500)(1609) \times 10^6 = 12.0675 \times 10^{12}\text{ micrometers}$$

$$\text{Therefore, } \frac{n}{m} = 18.065$$

The number of electrons/second is approximately 18 times the number of microns between Sydney and San Francisco.

P 1.7 $$w = qV = (1.6022 \times 10^{-19})(6) = 9.62 \times 10^{-19} = 0.962\text{ aJ}$$

P 1.8 $$i = \frac{dq}{dt} = 24\cos 4000t$$

Therefore, $dq = 24\cos 4000t\,dt$

$$\int_{q(0)}^{q(t)} dx = 24\int_0^t \cos 4000y\,dy$$

$$q(t) - q(0) = 24\frac{\sin 4000y}{4000}\bigg|_0^t$$

But $q(0) = 0$ by hypothesis, i.e., the current passes through its maximum value at $t = 0$, so $q(t) = 6 \times 10^{-3}\sin 4000t$ C $= 6\sin 4000t$ mC

P 1.9 $p = (6)(100) \times 10^{-3} = 0.6$ W; $w = (0.6)(3)(60)(60) = 6480$ J

P 1.10 Assume we are standing at box A looking toward box B, then $p = vi$.

[a] $p = (120)(5) = 600$ W from A to B

[b] $p = (250)(-8) = -2000$ W from B to A

[c] $p = (-150)(16) = -2400$ W from B to A

[d] $p = (-480)(-10) = 4800$ W from A to B

P 1.11 [a]

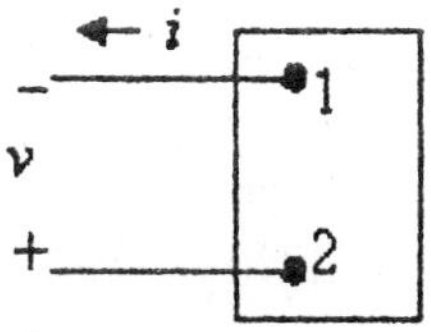

$p = vi = (40)(-10) = -400$ W
Power is being delivered by the box.

[b] Entering

[c] Gain

P 1.12 [a] $p = vi = (-60)(-10) = 600$ W, so power is being absorbed by the box.

[b] Leaving

[c] Lose

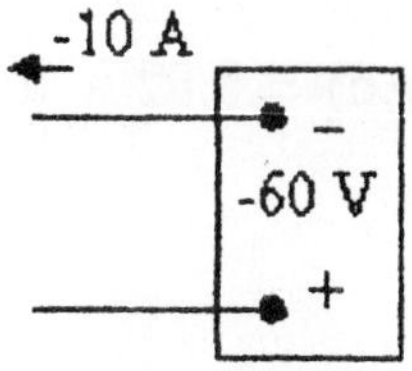

P 1.13 [a] Looking from A to B the current i is in the direction of the voltage rise across the 12 V battery, therefore $p = vi = -12(30) = -360$ W.
Thus the power flow is from B to A, and Car A has the "dead" battery.

[b]
$$w = \int_0^t p\,dx = \int_0^t 360\,dx$$
$$w = 360t = 360(1 \times 60) = 21.6 \text{ kJ}$$

P 1.14
$$p = vi; \qquad w = \int_0^t p\,dx$$

Since the energy is the area under the power vs. time plot, let us plot p vs. t.

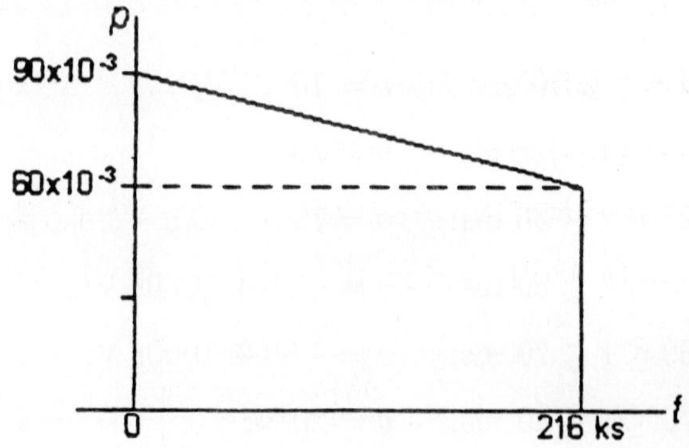

$$p(0) = (6)(15 \times 10^{-3}) = 90 \times 10^{-3} \text{ W}$$
$$p(216 \text{ ks}) = (4)(15 \times 10^{-3}) = 60 \times 10^{-3} \text{ W}$$
$$w = (60 \times 10^{-3})(216 \times 10^{3}) + \frac{1}{2}(216)(30) = 16.2 \text{ kJ}$$

Note: 60 hr $\equiv$ 216,000 s = 216 ks

P 1.15 [a] $p = vi = 30e^{-500t} - 30e^{-1500t} - 40e^{-1000t} + 50e^{-2000t} - 10e^{-3000t}$
$p(1 \text{ ms}) = 3.1$ mW

[b]
$$\begin{aligned} w(t) &= \int_0^t (30e^{-500x} - 30e^{-1500x} - 40e^{-1000x} + \\ &\quad 50e^{-2000x} - 10e^{-3000x})dx \\ &= 21.67 - 60e^{-500t} + 20e^{-1500t} + 40e^{-1000t} - \\ &\quad 25e^{-2000t} + 3.33e^{-3000t}\,\mu\text{J} \end{aligned}$$
$$w(1 \text{ ms}) = 1.24\mu\text{J}$$

[c] $w_{\text{total}} = 21.67\mu\text{J}$

P 1.16 [a] $v(20\text{ ms}) = 100e^{-1}\sin 3 = 5.19$ V

$i(20\text{ ms}) = 20e^{-1}\sin 3 = 1.04$ A

$p(20\text{ ms}) = vi = 5.39$ W

[b]

$$\begin{aligned}
p &= vi = 2000e^{-100t}\sin^2 150t \\
&= 2000e^{-100t}\left[\frac{1}{2} - \frac{1}{2}\cos 300t\right] \\
&= 1000e^{-100t} - 1000e^{-100t}\cos 300t \\
w &= \int_0^\infty 1000e^{-100t}\,dt - \int_0^\infty 1000e^{-100t}\cos 300t\,dt \\
&= 1000\left.\frac{e^{-100t}}{-100}\right|_0^\infty - 1000\left\{\frac{e^{-100t}}{(100)^2+(300)^2}[-100\cos 300t + 300\sin 3(\right. \\
&= 10 - 1000\left[\frac{100}{1\times 10^4 + 9\times 10^4}\right] = 10 - 1 \\
\text{w} &= 9 \text{ J}
\end{aligned}$$

P 1.17 [a]

$0 \le t \le 10$ ms:	$v = 1000t$ V;	$i = 0.6$ mA;	$p = 0.6t$ mW
$10 \le t \le 25$ ms:	$v = 10$ V;	$i = 0.6$ mA;	$p = 6$ mW
$25 \le t \le 35$ ms:	$v = 75 - 2500t$ V;	$i = 0$ mA;	$p = 0$ mW
$35 \le t \le 60$ ms:	$v = -50 + 1000t$ V;	$i = -0.4$ mA;	$p = 20 - 0.4t$ ı
$60 \le t \le 70$ ms:	$v = -50 + 1000t$ V;	$i = 0$ mA;	$p = 0$ mW
$70 \le t \le 80$ ms:	$v = 20$ V;	$i = -0.5$ mA;	$p = -10$ mW
$80 \le t \le 90$ ms:	$v = 180 - 2000t$ V;	$i = 0$ mA;	$p = 0$ mW
$90 \le t \le 95$ ms:	$v = 180 - 2000t$ V;	$i = 0.9$ mA;	$p = 162 - 1.8t$
$95 \le t \le 100$ ms:	$v = -200 + 2000t$ V;	$i = 0.9$ mA;	$p = -180 + 1.$

[b]

$$\begin{aligned}
w(25) &= \tfrac{1}{2}(6)(10) + (6)(15) = 120 \text{ mJ} \\
w(60) &= 120 + \tfrac{1}{2}(15)(6) - \tfrac{1}{2}(10)(4) = 145 \text{ mJ} \\
w(90) &= 145 - (10)(10) = 45 \text{ mJ} \\
w(100) &= 45 - \tfrac{1}{2}(10)(9) = 0 \text{ mJ}
\end{aligned}$$

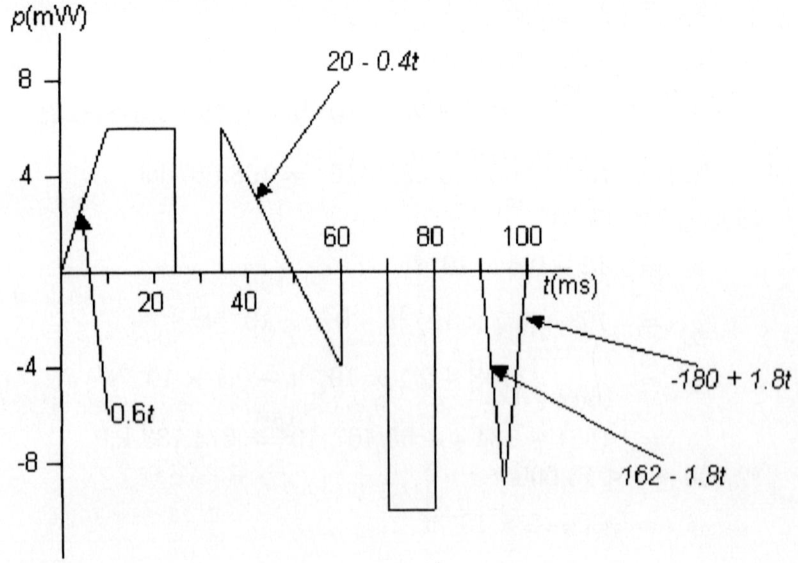

P 1.18 [a] $p = vi = (2e^{-500t} - 2e^{-1000t})$ W

$$\frac{dp}{dt} = -1000e^{-500t} + 2000e^{-1000t} = 0 \text{ at t} = 0 \text{ and at t} = 1.4 \text{ ms}$$

$$p_{\text{max}} = p(1.4 \text{ ms}) = 0.5 \text{ W}$$

[b] $$w = \int_0^\infty [2e^{-500t} - 2e^{-1000t}]\,dt = \left[\frac{2}{-500}e^{-500t} - \frac{2}{-1000}e^{-1000t}\Big|_0^\infty\right]$$

$$= 2 \text{ mJ}$$

P 1.19 [a] $p = vi = 900\sin(200\pi t)\cos(200\pi t) = 450\sin(400\pi t)$ W

Therefore, $p_{\text{max}} = 450$ W

[b] $p_{\text{max}}(\text{extracting}) = 450$ W

[c] $$p_{\text{avg}} = 200\int_0^{5\times10^{-3}} 450\sin(400\pi t)\,dt$$

$$= 9 \times 10^4 \left[\frac{-\cos 400\pi t}{400\pi}\Big|_0^{2.5\times10^{-3}}\right] = \frac{225}{\pi}[1 - \cos 2\pi] = 0$$

[d] $$p_{\text{avg}} = \frac{180}{\pi}[1 - \cos 2.5\pi] = \frac{180}{\pi} = 57.3 \text{ W}$$

P 1.20 [a] $$q = \text{area under } i \text{ vs. } t \text{ plot}$$

$$= \left[\tfrac{1}{2}(5)(4) + (10)(4) + \tfrac{1}{2}(8)(4) + (8)(6) + \tfrac{1}{2}(3)(6)\right] \times 10^3$$

$$= [10 + 40 + 16 + 48 + 9]10^3 = 123{,}000 \text{ C}$$

[b] $$w = \int p\,dt = \int vi\,dt$$

$$v = 0.2 \times 10^{-3}t + 9 \qquad 0 \le t \le 15 \text{ ks}$$

$0 \le t \le 4000s$

$$i = 15 - 1.25 \times 10^{-3}t$$

$$p = 135 - 8.25 \times 10^{-3}t - 0.25 \times 10^{-6}t^2$$

$$w_1 = \int_0^{4000} (135 - 8.25 \times 10^{-3}t - 0.25 \times 10^{-6}t^2)\, dt$$

$$= (540 - 66 - 53.333)10^3 = 468.667 \text{ kJ}$$

$4000 \le t \le 12{,}000$

$$i = 12 - 0.5 \times 10^{-3}t$$

$$p = 108 - 2.1 \times 10^{-3}t - 0.1 \times 10^{-6}t^2$$

$$w_2 = \int_{4000}^{12{,}000} (108 - 2.1 \times 10^{-3}t - 0.1 \times 10^{-6}t^2)\, dt$$

$$= (864 - 134.4 - 55.467)10^3 = 674.133 \text{ kJ}$$

$12{,}000 \le t \le 15{,}000$

$$i = 30 - 2 \times 10^{-3}t$$

$$p = 270 - 12 \times 10^{-3}t - 0.4 \times 10^{-6}t^2$$

$$w_3 = \int_{12{,}000}^{15{,}000} (270 - 12 \times 10^{-3}t - 0.4 \times 10^{-6}t^2)\, dt$$

$$= (810 - 486 - 219.6)10^3 = 104.4 \text{ kJ}$$

$$w_T = w_1 + w_2 + w_3 = 468.667 + 674.133 + 104.4 = 1247.2 \text{ kJ}$$

P 1.21 [a]

$$p = vi$$

$$= 400 \times 10^3 t^2 e^{-800t} + 700te^{-800t} + 0.25e^{-800t}$$

$$= e^{-800t}[400{,}000t^2 + 700t + 0.25]$$

$$\frac{dp}{dt} = \{e^{-800t}[800 \times 10^3 t + 700] - 800e^{-800t}[400{,}000t^2 + 700t + 0.25]\}$$

$$= 3{,}200{,}000t^2 - 2400t - 5$$

Therefore, $\frac{dp}{dt} = 0$ when $3{,}200{,}000t^2 - 2400t - 5 = 0$
so p_{max} occurs at $t = 1.68$ ms.

[b]

$$p_{max} = [400{,}000(.00168)^2 + 700(.00168) + 0.25]e^{-800(.00168)}$$

$$= 666 \text{ mW}$$

[c] $w = \int_0^t p\,dx$

$$w = \int_0^t 400{,}000x^2e^{-800x}\,dx + \int_0^t 700xe^{-800x}\,dx + \int_0^t 0.25e^{-800x}\,dx$$

$$= \frac{400{,}000e^{-800x}}{-512\times 10^6}[64\times 10^4x^2 + 1600x + 2]\Big|_0^t +$$

$$\frac{700e^{-800x}}{64\times 10^4}(-800x-1)\Big|_0^t + 0.25\frac{e^{-800x}}{-800}\Big|_0^t$$

When $t = \infty$ all the upper limits evaluate to zero, hence

$$w = \frac{(400{,}000)(2)}{512\times 10^6} + \frac{700}{64\times 10^4} + \frac{0.25}{800} = 2.97 \text{ mJ}.$$

P 1.22 [a]

$$p = 0 \quad t < 0, \qquad p = 0 \quad t > 3 \text{ s}$$

$$p = vi = t(3-t)(6-4t) = 18t - 18t^2 + 4t^3 \qquad 0 \le t \le 3 \text{ s}$$

$$\frac{dp}{dt} = 18 - 36t + 12t^2 = 12(t^2 - 3t + 1.5)$$

$$\frac{dp}{dt} = 0 \qquad \text{when } t^2 - 3t + 1.5 = 0$$

$$t = \frac{3\pm\sqrt{9-6}}{2} = \frac{3\pm\sqrt{3}}{2}$$

$$t_1 = 3/2 - \sqrt{3}/2 = 0.634 \text{ s}; \qquad t_2 = 3/2 + \sqrt{3}/2 = 2.366 \text{ s}$$

$$p(t_1) = 18(0.634) - 18(0.634)^2 + 4(0.634)^3 = 5.196 \text{ mW}$$

$$p(t_2) = 18(2.366) - 18(2.366)^2 + 4(2.366)^3 = -5.196 \text{ mW}$$

Therefore, maximum power is being delivered at $t = 0.634$ s.

[b] $p_{max} = 5.196$ mW (delivered)

[c] Maximum power is being extracted at $t = 2.366$ s.

[d] $p_{max} = 5.196$ mW (extracted)

[e] $w = \int_0^t p\,dx = \int_0^t (18x - 18x^2 + 4x^3)dx = 9t^2 - 6t^3 + t^4$

$$w(0) = 0 \text{ mJ} \qquad w(2) = 4 \text{ mJ}$$

$$w(1) = 4 \text{ mJ} \qquad w(3) = 0 \text{ mJ}$$

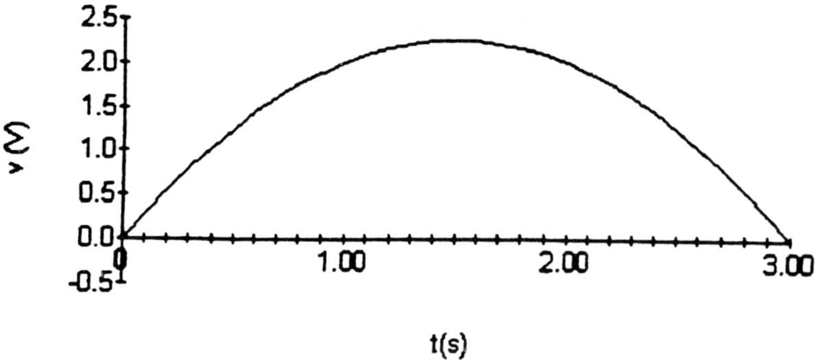
v (V)
2.5
2.0
1.5
1.0
0.5
0.0
-0.5
0
1.00
2.00
3.00
t(s)

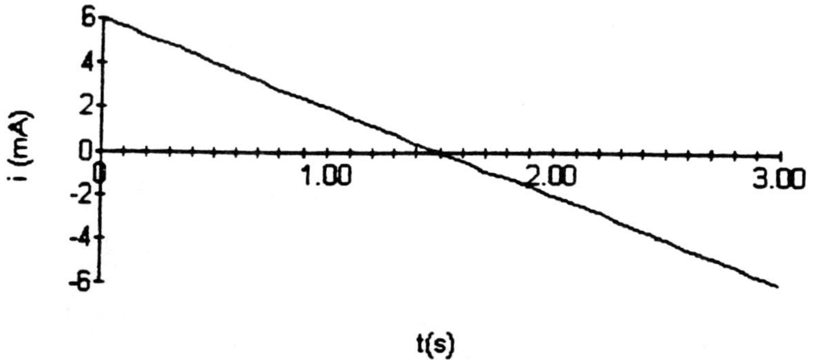
i (mA)
6
4
2
0
-2
-4
-6
0
1.00
2.00
3.00
t(s)

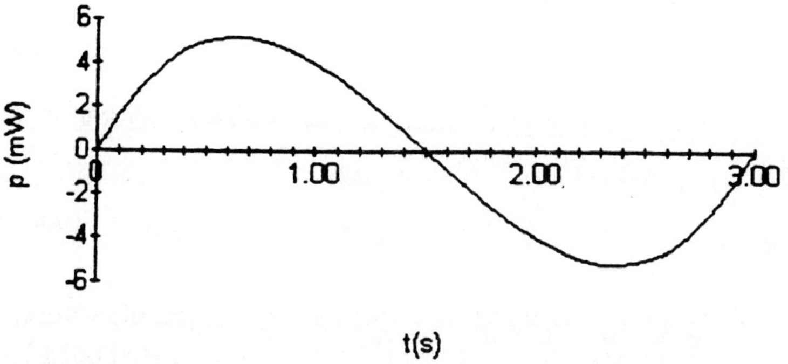
p (mW)
6
4
2
0
-2
-4
-6
0
1.00
2.00
3.00
t(s)

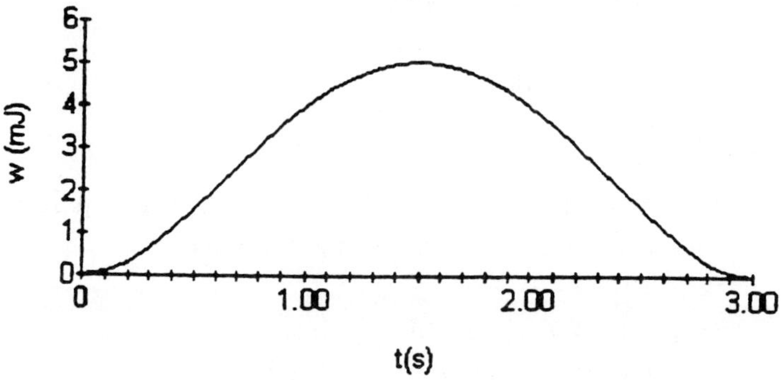
w (mJ)
6
5
4
3
2
1
0
0
1.00
2.00
3.00
t(s)

P 1.23 [a]

$$p = vi = 12 \times 10^5 t^2 e^{-1000t} \text{ W}$$

$$\frac{dp}{dt} = 12 \times 10^5[t^2(-1000)e^{-1000t} + e^{-1000t}(2t)]$$

$$= 12 \times 10^5 te^{-1000t}[t(2 - 1000t)]$$

$$\frac{dp}{dt} = 0 \text{ at } t = 0, \qquad t = 2 \text{ ms}$$

We know p is a minimum at $t = 0$ since v and i are zero at $t = 0$.

[b] $p_{max} = 12 \times 10^5(2 \times 10^{-3})^2 e^{-2} = 649.61$ mW

[c]

$$w = 12 \times 10^5 \int_0^\infty t^2 e^{-1000t}\, dt$$

$$= 12 \times 10^5 \left\{ \frac{e^{-1000t}}{(-1000)^3}[10^6 t^2 + 2{,}000t + 2]\Bigg|_0^\infty \right\} = 2.4 \text{ mJ}$$

P 1.24 [a] From the diagram and the table we have

$$p_a = -v_a i_a = -(46.16)(6) = -276.96 \text{ W} \qquad \text{(del)}$$

$$p_b = v_b i_b = (14.16)(4.72) = 66.8352 \text{ W} \qquad \text{(abs)}$$

$$p_c = v_c i_c = (-32)(-6.4) = 204.80 \text{ W} \qquad \text{(abs)}$$

$$p_d = -v_d i_d = -(22)(1.28) = -28.16 \text{ W} \qquad \text{(del)}$$

$$p_e = -v_e i_e = -(33.60)(1.68) = -56.448 \text{ W} \qquad \text{(del)}$$

$$p_f = v_f i_f = (66)(-0.4) = -26.40 \text{ W} \qquad \text{(del)}$$

$$p_g = v_g i_g = (2.56)(1.28) = 3.2768 \text{ W} \qquad \text{(abs)}$$

$$p_h = -v_h i_h = -(-0.4)(0.4) = 0.16 \text{ W} \qquad \text{(abs)}$$

$$\sum P_{del} = 276.96 + 28.16 + 56.448 + 26.40 = 387.9680 \text{ W}$$

$$\sum P_{abs} = 66.8352 + 204.80 + 3.2768 + 0.16 = 275.072 \text{ W}$$

Therefore, $\sum P_{del} \neq \sum P_{abs}$ and the subordinate engineer is correct.

[b] We can also check the data using Kirchhoff's laws.

From Fig. P1.24 the following equations should be satisfied:

$i_a - i_b - i_d = 0$ (ok)

$i_b + i_c - i_e = 0$ (no)

$i_f - i_a - i_c = 0$ (ok)

$i_d = i_g$ (ok)

$i_g + i_e + i_h = 0$ (no)

$i_h = -i_f$ (ok)

Using Kirchhoff's current law, it appears i_e is in error.

From Kirchhoff's voltage law we have

$v_b - v_a - v_c = 0$ (ok)

$-v_d - v_b + v_e + v_g = 0$ (ok)

$-v_e + v_c + v_f + v_h = 0$ (ok)

Therefore all the voltages are consistent with Kirchhoff's voltage law.
Assume i_e is in error. Therefore,
$i_e = i_b + i_c = -i_g - i_h = 4.72 - 6.40 = -1.28 - 0.4 = -1.68$ A
So the error is in the sign of i_e; i_e equals minus 1.68 A.
Correcting i_e leads to
$\sum P_{\text{del}} = \sum P_{\text{abs}} = 331.52$ W

P 1.25
$$
\begin{aligned}
p_a &= v_a i_a = (120)(8) = 960 \text{ W} \qquad \text{(abs)} \\
p_b &= -v_b i_b = -(120)(-5) = -600 \text{ W} \qquad \text{(del)} \\
p_c &= v_c i_c = (70)(-3) = -210 \text{ W} \qquad \text{(del)} \\
p_d &= v_d i_d = (80)(11) = 880 \text{ W} \qquad \text{(abs)} \\
p_e &= v_e i_e = (-30)(7) = -210 \text{ W} \qquad \text{(del)} \\
p_f &= v_f i_f = (-10)(-14) = 140 \text{ W} \qquad \text{(abs)} \\
p_g &= -v_g i_g = -(-60)(-10) = -600 \text{ W} \qquad \text{(del)} \\
p_h &= -v_h i_h = -(90)(4) = -360 \text{ W} \qquad \text{(del)}
\end{aligned}
$$
Therefore, $\sum P_{\text{abs}} = 1980$ W and $\sum P_{\text{del}} = 1980$ W so
$\sum P_{\text{abs}} = \sum P_{\text{del}}$, yes

P 1.26
$$
\begin{aligned}
p_a &= -v_a i_a = -(-18)(-51) = -918 \text{ W} \qquad \text{(dev)} \\
p_b &= v_b i_b = (-18)(45) = -810 \text{ W} \qquad \text{(dev)} \\
p_c &= v_c i_c = (2)(-6) = -12 \text{ W} \qquad \text{(dev)} \\
p_d &= -v_d i_d = -(20)(-20) = 400 \text{ W} \qquad \text{(abs)} \\
p_e &= -v_e i_e = -(16)(-14) = 224 \text{ W} \qquad \text{(abs)} \\
p_f &= v_f i_f = (36)(31) = 1116 \text{ W} \qquad \text{(abs)}
\end{aligned}
$$
$\sum P_{\text{dev}} = 1740$ W; $\sum P_{\text{abs}} = 1740$ W
Since $\sum P_{\text{dev}} = \sum P_{\text{abs}}$, Developed = 1740 W.

P 1.27 $p_a = v_a i_a = (48)(12) = 576$ W (abs)

$p_b = v_b i_b = (18)(-4) = -72$ W (del)

$p_c = -v_c i_c = -(30)(-10) = 300$ W (abs)

$p_d = v_d i_d = (36)(16) = 576$ W (abs)

$p_e = -v_e i_e = -(36)(8) = -288$ W (del)

$p_f = -v_f i_f = -(-54)(14) = 756$ W (abs)

$p_g = -v_g i_g = -(84)(22) = -1848$ W (del)

$\sum P_{\rm del} = 72 + 288 + 1848 = 2208$ W

$\sum P_{\rm abs} = 576 + 300 + 576 + 756 = 2208$ W

Therefore, $\sum P_{\rm del} = \sum P_{\rm abs} = 2208$ W

P 1.28 [a] From an examination of reference polarities, the following elements employ the passive convention: $a, c, e,$ and f.

[b] $p_a = -56$ W (del)

$p_b = -14$ W (del)

$p_c = 150$ W (abs)

$p_d = -50$ W (del)

$p_e = -18$ W (del)

$p_f = -12$ W (del)

$\sum P_{\rm abs} = 150$ W; $\sum P_{\rm del} = 56 + 14 + 50 + 18 + 12 = 150$ W.

2

Circuit Variables

Drill Exercises

DE 2.1 [a] $v_l - v_c + v_1 - v_s = 0, \qquad i_l R_l - i_c R_c + i_1 R_1 - v_s = 0$

$$i_s R_l + i_s R_c + i_s R_1 - v_s = 0$$

[b] $i_s = v_s/(R_l + R_c + R_1)$

DE 2.2 [a] $24 = v_2 + v_5 - v_1 = 3i_5 + 7i_5 - (-2i_5) = 12i_5$

Therefore $i_5 = 24/12 = 2$ A

[b] $v_1 = -2i_5 = -4$ V

[c] $v_2 = 3i_5 = 6$ V

[d] $v_5 = 7i_5 = 14$ V

[e] $p_{24} = -(24)(2) = -48$ W; therefore 24 V source is delivering 48 W.

DE 2.3

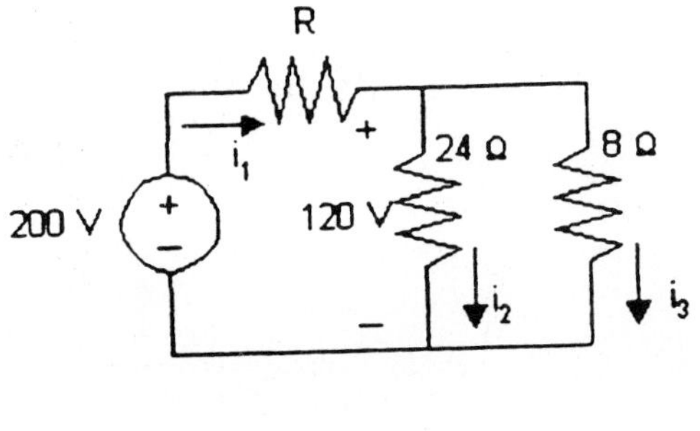

$$i_2 = 120/24 = 5 \text{ A}$$

$$i_3 = 120/8 = 15 \text{ A}$$

$$i_1 = i_2 + i_3 = 20 \text{ A}$$

$$-200 + 20R + 120 = 0$$

$$R = 80/20 = 4\,\Omega$$

DE 2.4 [a] Plotting a graph of v_t versus i_t gives

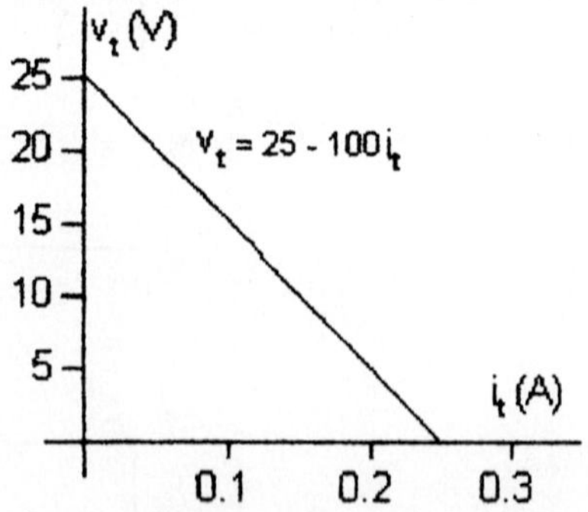

Note that when $i_t = 0$, $v_t = 25$ V; therefore the voltage source must be 25 V. When v_t is zero, $i_t = 0.25$ A, hence the resistor must be 25/0.25 or 100Ω.

A circuit model having the same $v - i$ characteristic is a 25 V source in series with a 100Ω resistor.

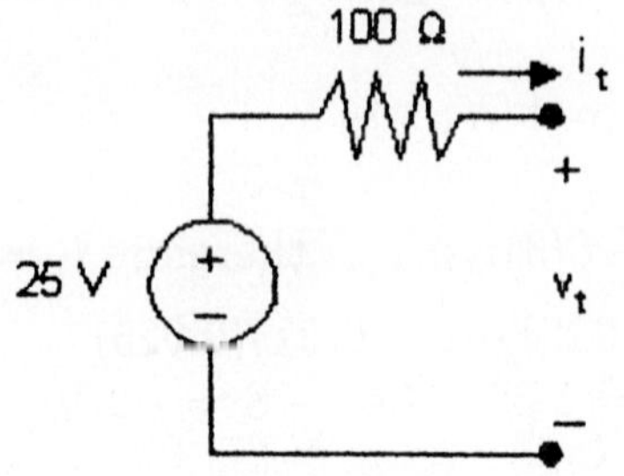

[b]

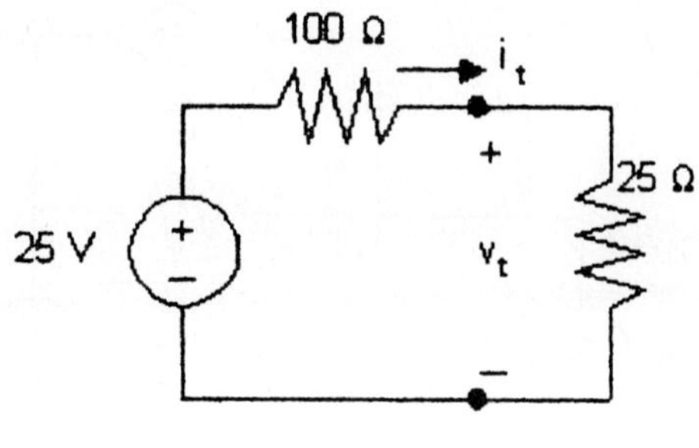

$$i_t = \frac{25}{125} = 0.2 \text{ A}; \qquad p = (0.2)^2(25) = 1 \text{ W}.$$

DE 2.5 [a] Since we are constructing the model from two elements, we have two choices on interconnecting them—series or parallel. From the $v-i$ characteristic we require $v_t = 25$ V when $i_t = 0$. The only way we can satisfy this requirement is with a parallel connection. The constraint that $v_t = 0$ when $i_t = 0.25$ A tells us the ideal current source must produce 0.25 A. Therefore the parallel resistor must be 25/0.25 or 100Ω.

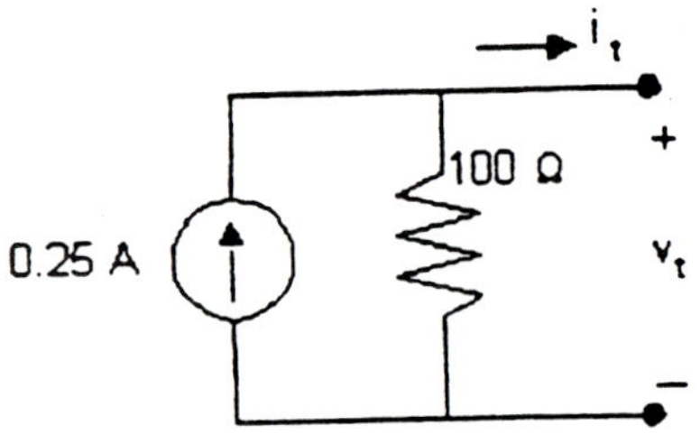

[b]

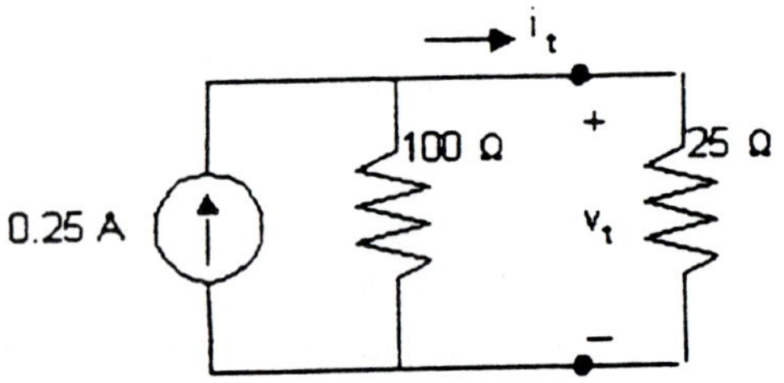

$$-0.25 + \frac{v_t}{100} + \frac{v_t}{25} = 0, \qquad 5v_t = 25, \qquad v_t = 5 \text{ V}$$

$$p = \frac{v_t^2}{25} = 1 \text{ W}.$$

DE 2.6 [a] $5 = 54i_1 - 1 + 6(31i_1)$; therefore $i_1 = 6/240 = 25\,\mu$A

[b] $8 = 1.8(30)(0.025) - v + 6(31)(0.025)$
Therefore $v = 1.35 + 4.65 - 8 = -2$ V

DE 2.7

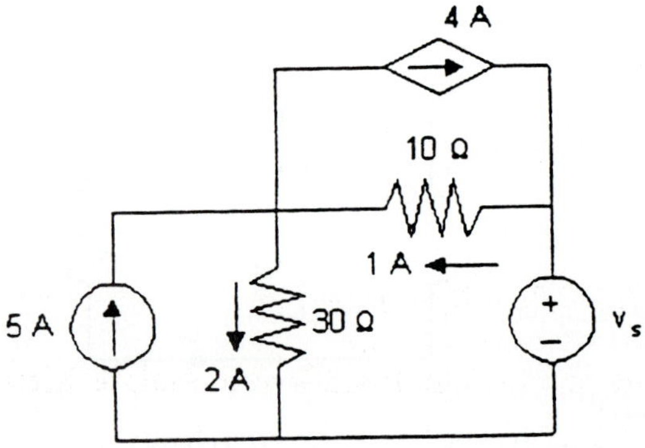

[a] $-I_{10\Omega} - 5 + i_\phi + 2i_\phi = 0$, therefore, $I_{10\Omega} = 2 + 4 - 5 = 1$ A
$v_s = 10(1) + 30(2) = 70$ V

[b] $p_{v_s} = 3v_s = 210$ W

[c] $p_{5A} = 5(60) = 300$ W. therefore, p_{5A} (del) $= -300$ W

[d] $p_{4A} = -4(10) = -40$ W. therefore, p_{4A} (del) $= 40$ W

[e] $p_{30\Omega} = (2)^2(30) = 120$ W; $p_{10\Omega} = (1)^2(10) = 10$ W
so $p_{\text{diss}} = 130$ W.

Problems

P 2.1

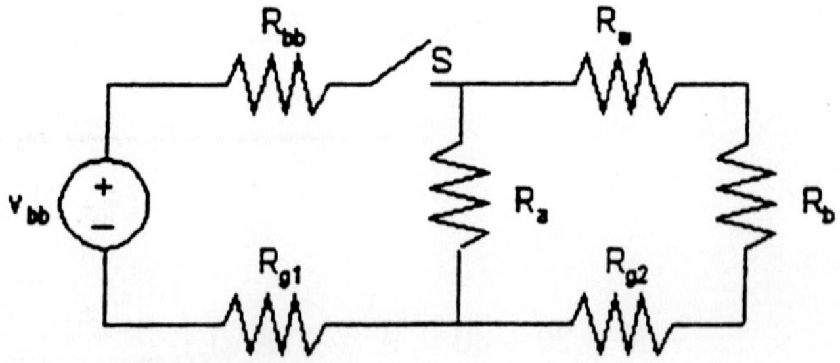

V_{bb} = no-load voltage of battery

R_{bb} = internal resistance of battery

R_a = resistance of lamp A

R_b = resistance of lamp B

R_w = resistance of wire between lamp A and lamp B

R_{g1} = resistance of frame between battery and lamp A

R_{g2} = resistance of frame between lamp A and lamp B

S = switch

P 2.2 (a) 9 (b) 7 (c) 4 (d) v_a–R_a, v_b–R_b, v_c–R_c (e) 6

(f) (1) $v_a - R_a - R_d - R_b - v_b$

(2) $R_d - R_f - R_e$

(3) $v_b - R_b - R_d - R_f - R_c - v_c$

(4) $v_c - R_c - R_f - R_a - v_a$

(5) $v_a - R_a - R_f - R_e - R_b - v_b$

P 2.3 The interconnect is valid since it does not violate Kirchhoff's laws.

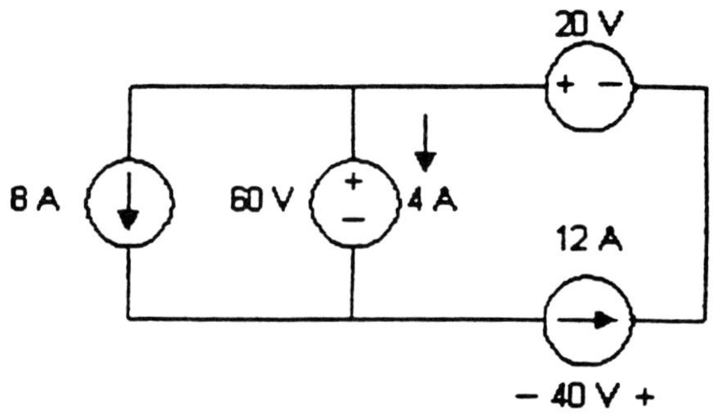

$$-60 + 20 + 40 = 0 \qquad \text{(KVL)}$$

$$10 + 4 + 12 = 0 \qquad \text{(KCL)}$$

$$\sum P_{\text{dev}} = 4(60) + 8(60) = 720 \text{ W}$$

$$\sum P_{\text{abs}} = 12(20) + 12(40) = 720 \text{ W}$$

$$\sum P_{\text{dev}} = \sum P_{\text{abs}} = 720 \text{ W}$$

P 2.4 [a] Yes, Kirchhoff's laws are not violated.

[b] No, because the voltages across the independent and dependent current sources are indeterminate. For example, define v_1, v_2, and v_3 as shown:

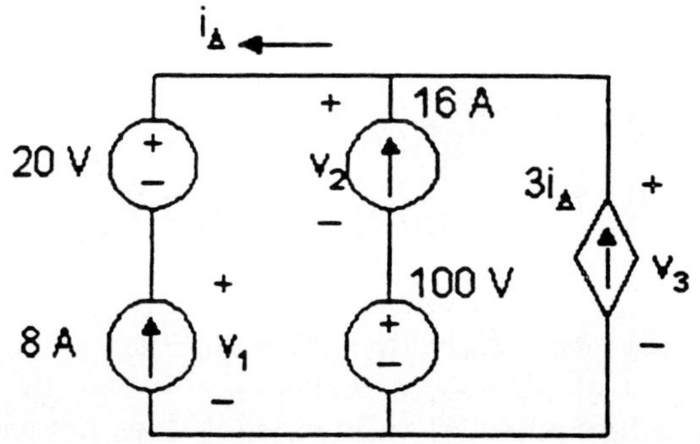

Kirchoff's voltage law requires

$$v_1 + 20 = v_3$$

$$v_2 + 100 = v_3$$

Conservation of energy requires

$$8(20) + 8v_i + 16v_2 + 1600 - 24v_3 = 0$$

or

$$v_1 + 2v_2 - 3v_3 = -220$$

Now arbitrarily select a value of v_3 and show the conservation of energy will be satisfied. Examples:
If $v_3 = 200$ V then $v_1 = 180$ V and $v_2 = 100$ V. Then

$$180 + 200 - 600 = -220 \text{ (CHECKS)}$$

If $v_3 = -100$ V, then $v_1 = -120$ V and $v_2 = -200$ V. Then

$$-120 - 400 + 300 = -220 \text{ (CHECKS)}$$

P 2.5 [a] Yes, independent voltage sources can carry whatever current is required by the connection; independent current source can support any voltage required by the connection.

[b] 30 V source: absorbing

10 V source: delivering

8 A source: delivering

[c]

$$P_{30V} = (30)(8) = 240 \text{ W} \quad \text{(abs)}$$

$$P_{10V} = -10(8) = -80 \text{ W} \quad \text{(del)}$$

$$P_{8A} = -20(8) = -160 \text{ W} \quad \text{(del)}$$

$$\sum P_{abs} = \sum P_{del} = 240 \text{ W}$$

[d] Yes, 30 V source is delivering, the 10 V source is delivering, and the 8 A source is absorbing

$$P_{30V} = -30(8) = -240 \text{ W} \quad \text{(del)}$$

$$P_{10V} = -10(8) = -80 \text{ W} \quad \text{(del)}$$

$$P_{8A} = +40(8) = 320 \text{ W} \quad \text{(abs)}$$

P 2.6 The interconnection is valid because it does not violate Kirchhoff's laws.

$$i_\Delta = -25 \text{ A}; \quad 6i_\Delta = -150 \text{ V}$$

$$-200 + 50 - (-150) = 0$$

But the power developed in the circuit cannot be determined, as the current in the 200 V source is unspecified.

P 2.7 The interconnection is not valid because it violates Kirchhoff's current law:

$$3 \text{ A} + (-5 \text{ A}) \neq 8 \text{ A}.$$

P 2.8

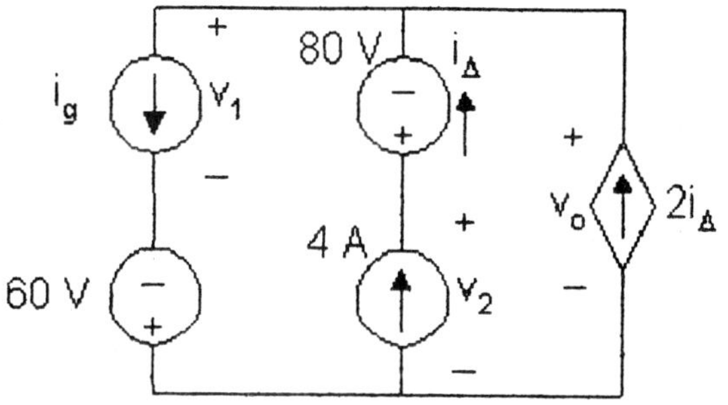

$i_\Delta = 4$ A so $i_g = 12$ A

$v_o = 100$ V

$-60 + v_1 = 100$, so $v_1 = 160$ V

$v_2 - 80 = 100$, so $v_2 = 180$ V

$$\sum P_{\text{dev}} = 180(4) + 100(8) + 60(12) = 2240 \text{ W}$$

$$\text{CHECK: } \sum P_{\text{diss}} = 160(12) + 80(4) = 1920 + 320$$
$$= 2240 \text{ W — CHECKS}$$

P 2.9 The interconnection is valid because it does not violate Kirchhoff's laws:

$$p_{V\text{-sources}} = -(100 - 60)(5) = -200 \text{ W}.$$

P 2.10 First there is no violation of Kirchhoff's laws, hence the interconnection is valid.
Kirchhoff's voltage law requires

$$v_1 + v_2 = 150 - 50 = 100 \text{ V}$$

The conservation of energy law requires

$$20v_1 - 10v_1 + 10v_2 + 500 - 1500 = 0$$

or

$$v_1 + v_2 = 100$$

Hence any combination of v_1 and v_2 that adds to 100 is a valid solution. For example if $v_1 = 80$ V and $v_2 = 20$ V

$$P_{abs} = 80(20) + 10(20) + 50(10) = 2300 \text{ W}$$

$$P_{dev} = 1500 + 80(10) = 2300 \text{ W}$$

If $v_1 = 60$ V and $v_2 = 40$ V

$$P_{abs} = 60(20) + 10(40) + 500 = 2100 \text{ W}$$

$$P_{dev} = 60(10) + 1500 = 2100 \text{ W}$$

If $v_1 = -100$ V and $v_2 = 200$ V

$$P_{abs} = 10(100) + 10(200) + 10(50) = 3500 \text{ W}$$

$$P_{dev} = 20(100) + 10(150) = 3500 \text{ W}$$

P 2.11 [a]

$$1.6 = i_a - i_g$$

$$80i_a = 1.6(30 + 90) = 192 \quad \text{therefore, } i_a = 2.4 \text{ A}$$

$$i_g = i_a + 1.6 - 2.4 + 1.6 = 4 \text{ A}$$

[b] $v_g = 90(1.6) = 144$ V

[c]

$$\sum P_{dis} = 2.4^2(80) + 1.6^2(120) = 768 \text{ W}$$

$$\sum P_{dev} = (4)(192) = 768 \text{ W}$$

Therefore, $\sum P_{dis} = \sum P_{dev} = 768$ W

P 2.12 [a]

$$v_o = 8i_a + 14i_a + 18i_a = 40(20) = 800 \text{ V}$$

$$800 = 10i_o$$

$$i_o = 800/10 = 80 \text{ A}$$

[b] $i_g = i_a + i_o = 20 + 80 = 100$ A

[c] $p_g(\text{delivered}) = (100)(800) = 80{,}000 \text{ W} = 80 \text{ kW}$

P 2.13 [a]

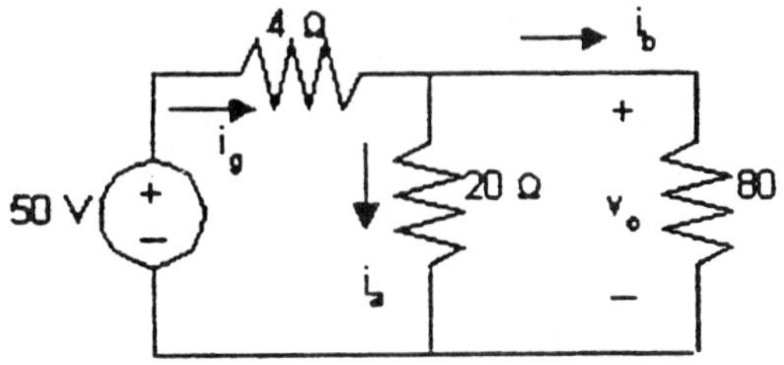

$$20i_a = 80i_b \qquad i_g = i_a + i_b = 5i_b$$

$$i_a = 4i_b$$

$$50 = 4i_g + 80i_b = 20i_b + 80i_b = 100i_b$$

$$i_b = 0.5 \text{ A, therefore, } i_a = 2 \text{ A}$$

[b] $i_b = 0.5$ A

[c] $v_o = 80i_b = 40$ V

[d] $p_{4\Omega} = i_g^2(4) = 6.25(4) = 25$ W

$p_{20\Omega} = i_a^2(20) = (4)(20) = 80$ W

$p_{80\Omega} = i_b^2(80) = 0.25(80) = 20$ W

[e] p_{5V} (delivered) $= 5i_g = 125$ W

Check:

$$\sum P_{dis} = 25 + 80 + 20 = 125 \text{ W}$$

$$\sum P_{del} = 125 \text{ W}$$

P 2.14 [a]

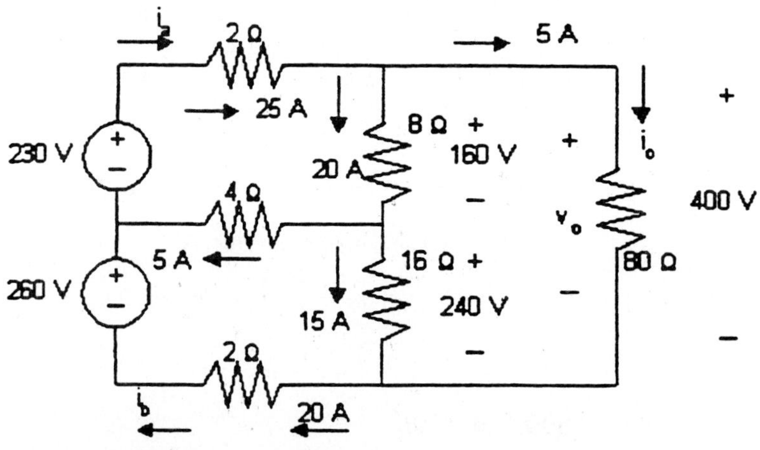

$$v_o = 20(8) + 16(15) = 400 \text{ V}$$

$$i_o = 400/80 = 5 \text{ A}$$

$$i_a = 25 \text{ A}$$

P_{230} (supplied) $= (230)(25) = 5750$ W

$i_b = 5 + 15 = 20$ A

P_{260} (supplied) $= (260)(20) = 5200$ W

[b] $$\sum P_{\text{dis}} = (25)^2(2) + (20)^2(8) + (5)^2(4) + (15)^2 16 + (20)^2 2 + (5)^2(80)$$
$$= 1250 + 3200 + 100 + 3600 + 800 + 2000 = 10{,}950 \text{ W}$$

$$\sum P_{\text{sup}} = 5750 + 5200 = 10{,}950 \text{ W}$$

Therefore, $\sum P_{\text{dis}} = \sum P_{\text{sup}} = 10{,}950$ W

P 2.15 [a]

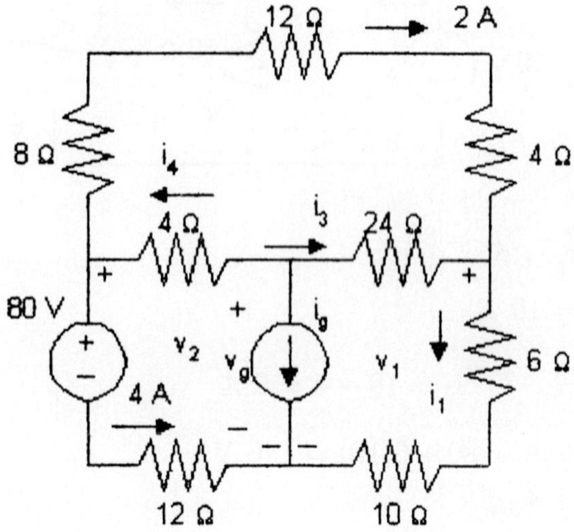

$$v_2 = 80 + 4(12) = 128 \text{ V}$$
$$v_1 = 128 - 24(2) = 80 \text{ V}$$
$$i_1 = \frac{v_1}{16} = \frac{80}{16} = 5 \text{ A}$$
$$i_3 = i_1 - 2 = 5 - 2 = 3 \text{ A}$$
$$v_g = v_1 + 24 i_3 = 80 + 72 = 152 \text{ V}$$
$$v_g - 4 i_4 = v_2$$
$$4 i_4 = v_g - v_2 = 152 - 128 = 24 \text{ V}$$
$$i_4 = 24/4 = 6 \text{ A}$$
$$i_g = -(i_3 + i_4) = -(3 + 6) = -9 \text{ A}$$

[b]

$p_{8\Omega} = (2)^2(8) = 32$ W		$p_{4\Omega} = (6)^2(4) = 144$ W	
$p_{12\Omega} = (2)^2(12) = 48$ W		$p_{6\Omega} = (5)^2(6) = 150$ W	
$p_{4\Omega} = (2)^2(4) = 16$ W		$p_{10\Omega} = (5)^2(10) = 250$ W	
$p_{24\Omega} = (3)^2(24) = 216$ W		$p_{12\Omega} = (4)^2(13) = 192$ W	

[c] $v_g = 152$ V

[d] $$\sum P_{\text{dis}} = 32 + 48 + 16 + 216 + 144 + 150 + 250 + 192 + 80(4) = 1368 \text{ W}$$

$$\sum P_{\text{del}} = (152)(9) = 1368 \text{ W}$$

Therefore, $\sum P_{\text{dis}} = \sum P_{\text{del}}$

Therefore, $\sum P_{\text{dis}} = \sum P_{\text{del}}$

P 2.16 [a]

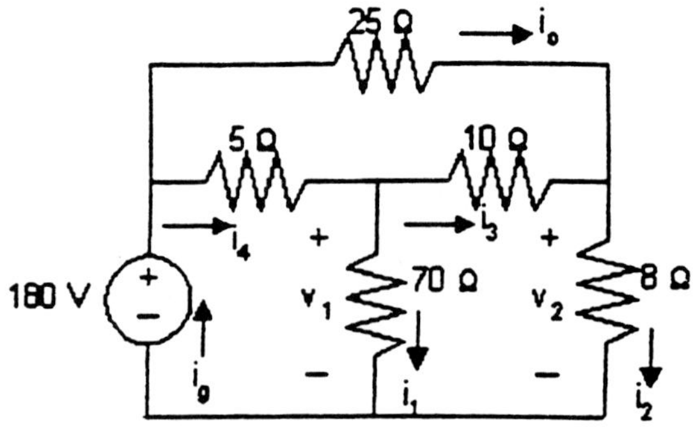

$$v_2 = 180 - 100 = 80 \text{ V}$$

$$i_2 = \frac{v_2}{8} = 10 \text{ A}$$

$$i_3 + 4 = i_2, \qquad i_3 = 10 - 4 = 6 \text{ A}$$

$$v_1 = v_2 + v_3 = 80 + 6(10) = 140 \text{ V}$$

$$i_1 = \frac{v_1}{70} = \frac{140}{70} = 2 \text{ A}$$

[b]

$$\begin{aligned} p_{5\Omega} &= 8^2(5) = 320 \text{ W} \\ p_{25\Omega} &= (4)^2(25) = 400 \text{ W} \\ p_{70\Omega} &= 2^2(70) = 280 \text{ W} \\ p_{10\Omega} &= 6^2(10) = 360 \text{ W} \\ p_{8\Omega} &= 10^2(8) = 800 \text{ W} \end{aligned}$$

[c]

$$\sum P_{\text{dis}} = 320 + 400 + 280 + 360 + 800 = 2160 \text{ W}$$

$$P_{\text{dev}} = 180 i_g = 180(12) = 2160 \text{ W}$$

P 2.17 [a]

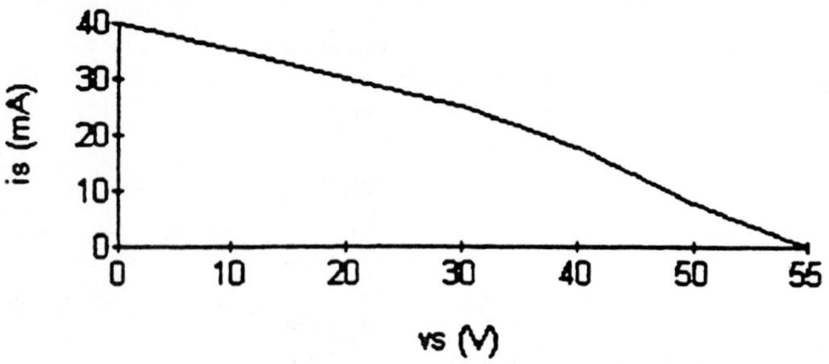

[b] $\Delta v = 20$ V; $\Delta i = 10$ mA; $R = \frac{\Delta v}{\Delta i} = 2$ kΩ

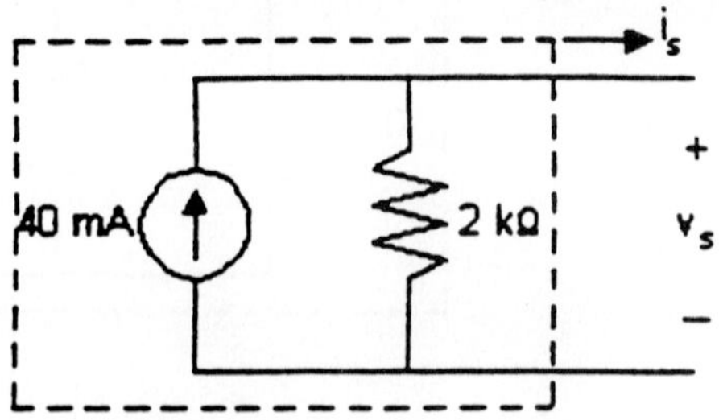

[c] $2i_1 = 3i_s, \qquad i_1 = 1.5i_s$

$40 = i_1 + i_s = 2.5i_s, \qquad i_s = 16$ mA

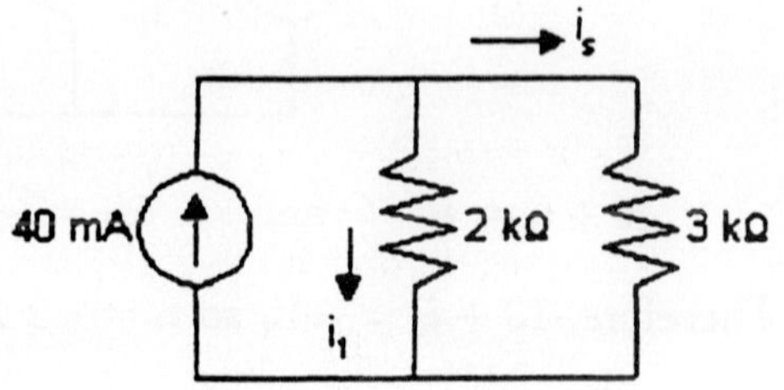

[d] v_s(open circuit) $= (40 \times 10^{-3})(2 \times 10^3) = 80$ V

[e] v_s(open circuit) $= 55$ V

[f] Linear model cannot predict the nonlinear behavior of the practical current source.

P 2.18 [a] Plot the $v - i$ characteristic

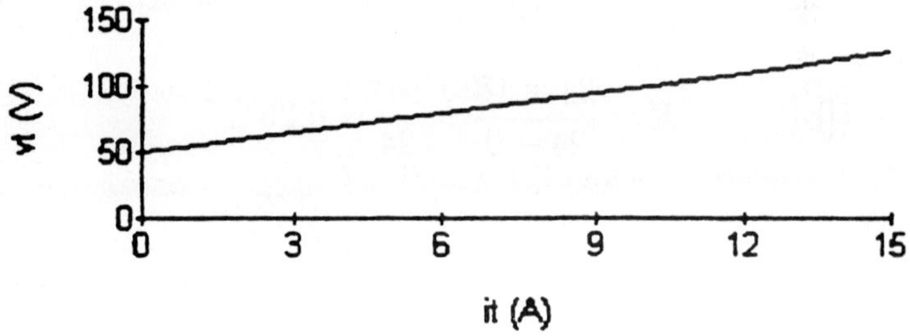

From the plot:

$$R = \frac{\Delta v}{\Delta i} = \frac{(125 - 50)}{(15 - 0)} = 5\,\Omega$$

When $i_t = 0$, $v_t = 50$ V; therefore the ideal current source has a current of 10 A

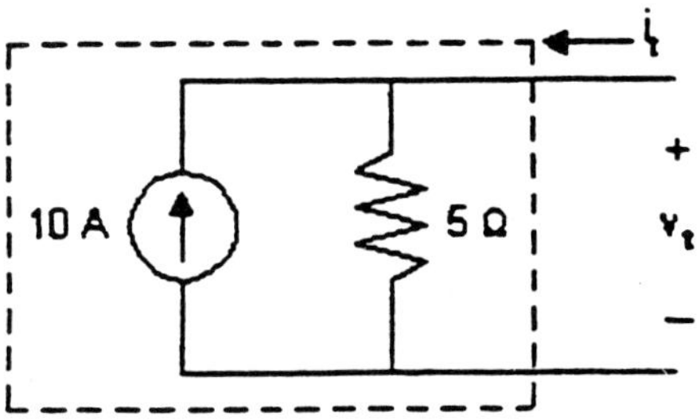

[b]

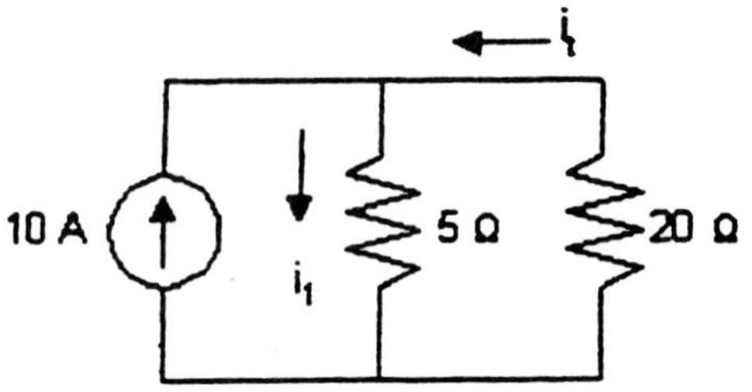

$$10 + i_t = i_1 \qquad \text{and} \qquad 5i_1 = -20i_t$$

Therefore, $10 + i_t = -4i_t$ so $i_t = -2$ A

P 2.19 [a]

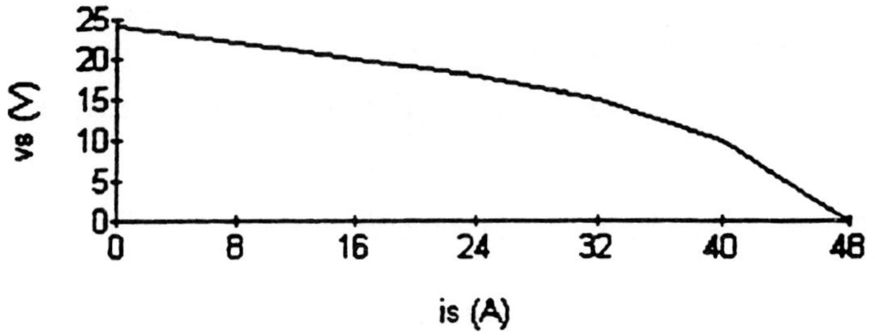

[b] $$R = \frac{24 - 18}{24 - 0} = \frac{6}{24} = 0.25\,\Omega$$

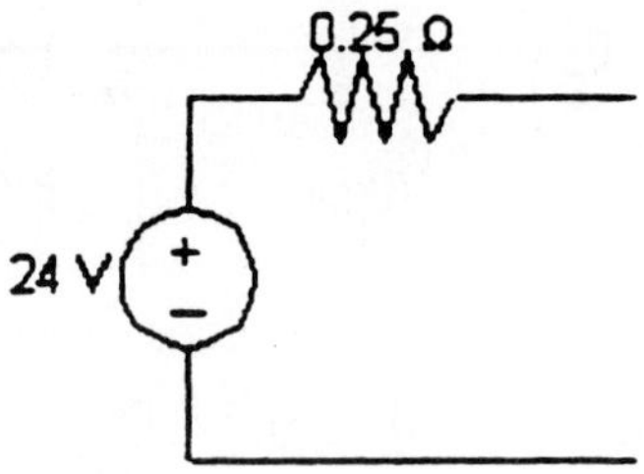

[c] $$i = \frac{24}{1.25} = 19.2 \text{ A}, \qquad v = 24 - 19.2(0.25) = 19.2 \text{ V}$$

[d] $$i_{sc} = \frac{24}{0.25} = 96 \text{ A}$$

[e] $i_{sc} = 48$ A (from graph)

[f] Linear model cannot predict nonlinear behavior of voltage source.

P 2.20 [a] Plot the v—i characteristic:

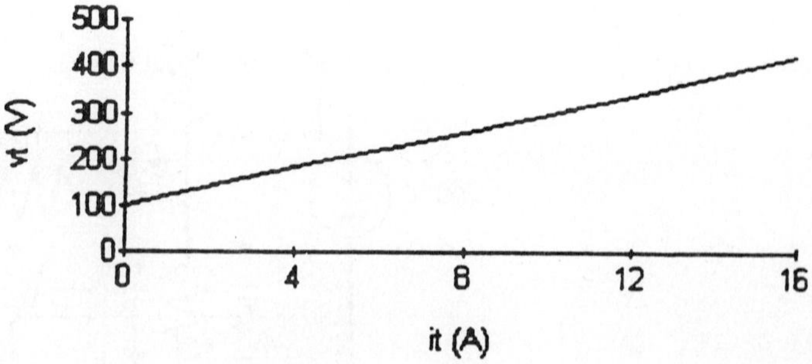

From the plot:

$$R = \frac{\Delta v}{\Delta i} = \frac{(420 - 100)}{(16 - 0)} = 20\,\Omega$$

When $i_t = 0$, $v_t = 100$ V; therefore the ideal voltage source has a voltage of 100 V

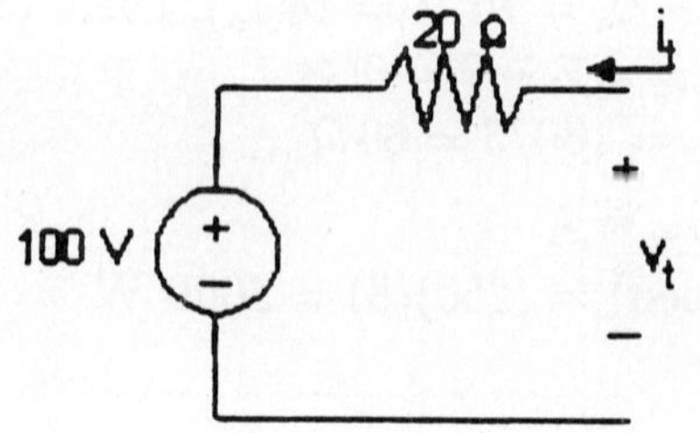

[b]

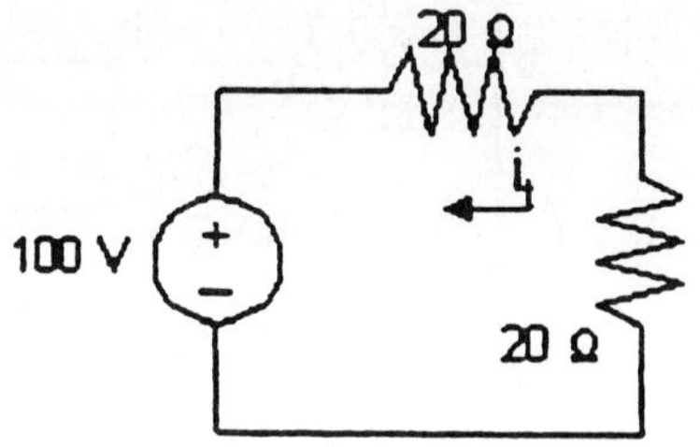

$i_t = 100/(20 + 20) = 2.5$ A; Therefore, $p_{20\Omega} = (2.5)^2(20) = 125$ W

P 2.21 [a]

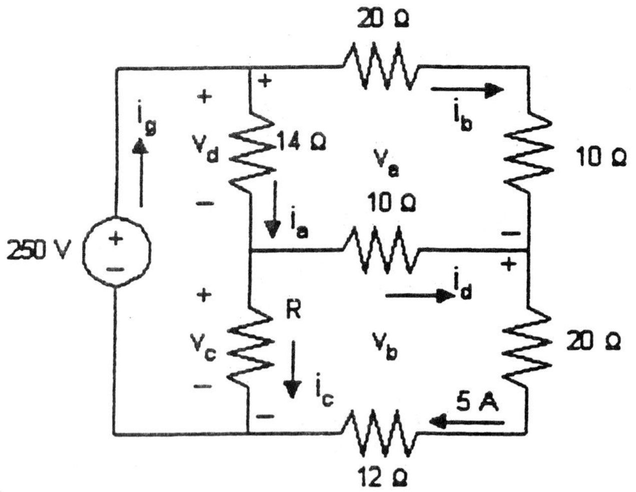

$v_b = 5(20 + 12) = 160$ V
$v_b + v_a = 250$ V, so $v_a = 90$ V
$i_b = 90/(20 + 10) = 3$ A
$i_d = 5 - i_b = 2$ A
$v_c = v_b + 10(i_d) = 180$ V
$v_d = 250 - v_c = 70$ V $= 14(i_a)$, therefore, $i_a = 5$ A
$i_c = i_a - i_d = 5 - 2 = 3$ A
$R = v_c/i_c = 180/3 = 60\,\Omega$

[b] $i_g = 5 + 3 = 8$ A
p_g (supplied) $= (250)(8) = 2000$ W

P 2.22

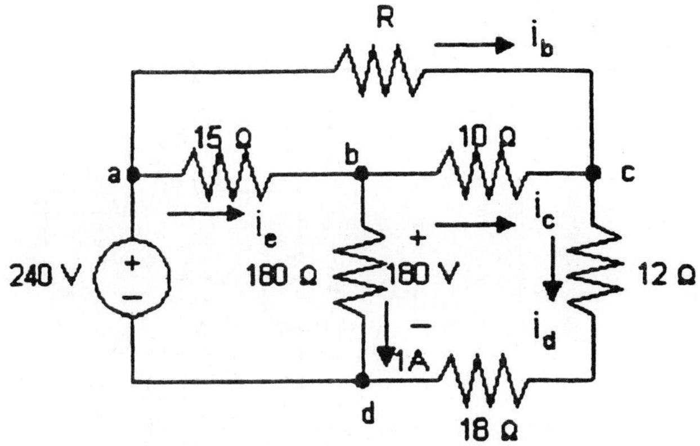

$v_{ab} = 240 - 180 = 60$ V; therefore, $i_e = 60/15 = 4$ A
$i_c = i_e - 1 = 4 - 1 = 3$ A; therefore, $v_{bc} = 10i_c = 30$ V
$v_{cd} = 180 - v_{bc} = 180 - 30 = 150$ V;
therefore, $i_d = v_{cd}/(12 + 18) = 150/30 = 5$ A
$i_b = i_d - i_c = 5 - 3 = 2$ A
$v_{ac} = v_{ab} + v_{bc} = 60 + 30 = 90$ V

$R = v_{ac}/i_b = 90/2 = 45\,\Omega$

CHECK: $i_g = i_b + i_e = 2 + 4 = 6$ A

$p_{dev} = (240)(6) = 1440$ W

$\sum P_{dis} = 1(180) + 4(45) + 9(10) + 25(12) + 25(18) + 16(15) = 1440$ W (CHEC

P 2.23 [a]

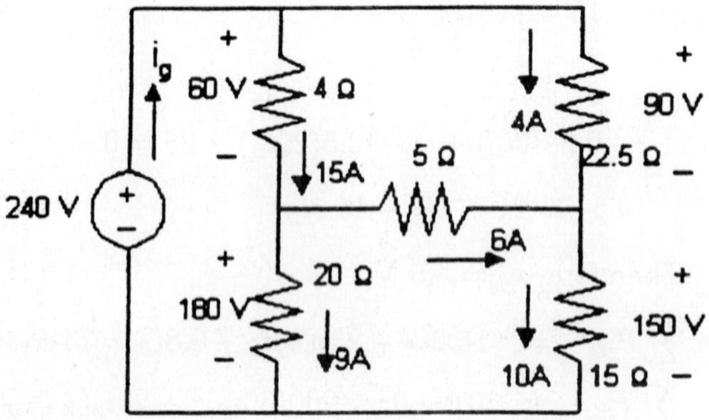

$p_{4\Omega} = 225(4) = 900$ W $\quad p_{20\Omega} = 81(20) = 1620$ W

$p_{5\Omega} = 36(5) = 180$ W $\quad p_{22.5\Omega} = 16(22.5) = 360$

$p_{15\Omega} = 100(15) = 1500$ W

[b] $i_g = 15 + 4 = 19$ A

$p_g = -240(19) = -9560$ W

p_g (supplied) $= 4560$ W

[c] $\sum P_{dis} = 900 + 1620 + 180 + 360 + 1500 = 4560$ W

Therefore,

$$\sum P_{supp} = \sum P_{dis}$$

P 2.24 $i_E - i_B - i_C = 0$

$i_C = \beta i_B$ therefore $i_E = (1 + \beta)i_B$

$i_2 = -i_B + i_1$

$V_o + i_E R_E - (i_1 - i_B)R_2 = 0$

$-i_1 R_1 + V_{CC} - (i_1 - i_B)R_2 = 0$ or $i_1 = \dfrac{V_{CC} - i_B R_2}{R_1 + R_2}$

$$V_o + i_E R_E + i_B R_2 - \frac{V_{CC} + i_B R_2}{R_1 + R_2} R_2 = 0$$

Now replace i_E by $(1+\beta)i_B$ and solve for i_B. Thus

$$i_B = \frac{[V_{CC}R_2/(R_1+R_2)] - V_o}{(1+\beta)R_E + R_1R_2/(R_1+R_2)}$$

P 2.25 [a]

$$15.2 = 10i_\beta - 0.80 + (0.2)30i_\beta$$

$$16 = (16)i_\beta$$

$$i_\beta = 1 \text{ mA}$$

$$0.2(30i_\beta) + v_y + 0.5(29i_\beta) - 25 = 0$$

$$v_y = 25 - 6i_\beta - 14.5i_\beta$$

Therefore, $v_y = 4.5$ V

[b]

$$\sum P_{\text{gen}} = 15.2i_\beta + 25(29)i_\beta + 0.8i_\beta = 741i_\beta = 741 \text{ mW}$$

$$\sum P_{\text{dis}} = 10^4(i_\beta)^2 + 200(30i_\beta)^2 + 29i_\beta(4.5) + 500(29i_\beta)^2$$

$$= 741 \text{ mW}.$$

P 2.26 [a] $i_2 = 0$ because no current can exist in a single conductor connecting two parts of a circuit.

[b]

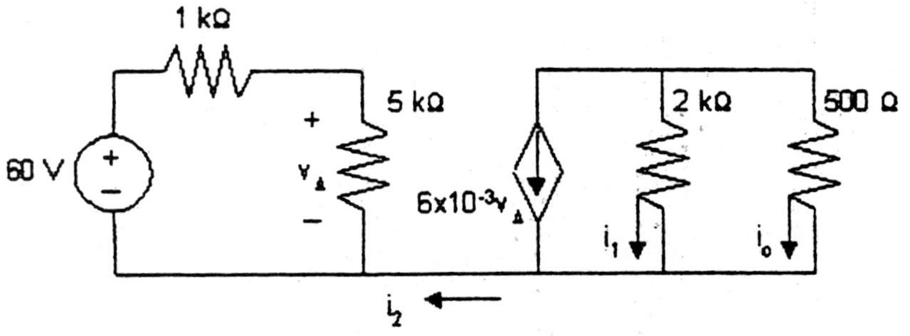

$$60 = 6000i_g \qquad i_g = 10 \text{ mA}$$

$$v_\Delta = 5000i_g = 50 \text{ V} \qquad 6\times10^{-3}v_\Delta = 300 \text{ mA}$$

$2000i_1 = 500i_o$, so $i_1 + 4i_1 = -300$ mA; therefore, $i_1 = -60$ mA

[c] $300 - 60 + i_2 = 0$, so $i_o = -240$ mA.

P 2.27 [a]

$$12 - 2i_\sigma = 5i_\Delta$$

$$5i_\Delta = 8i_\sigma + 2i_\sigma = 10i_\sigma$$

Therefore, $12 - 2i_\sigma = 10i_\sigma$, so $i_\sigma = 1$ A

$5i_\Delta = 10i_\sigma = 10$; so $i_\Delta = 2$ A

$$v_o = 2i_\sigma = 2 \text{ V}$$

[b] i_g = current out of the positive terminal of the 12 V source
v_d = voltage drop across the $8i_\Delta$ source

$$i_g = i_\Delta + i_\sigma + 8i_\Delta = 9i_\Delta + i_\sigma = 19 \text{ A}$$

$$v_d = 2 + 8 = 10 \text{ V}$$

$$\begin{aligned}
\sum P_{\text{gen}} &= 12i_g + 8i_\Delta(8) = 12(19) + 8(2)(8) = 356 \text{ W} \\
\sum P_{\text{diss}} &= 2i_\sigma i_g + 5i_\Delta^2 + 8i_\sigma(i\sigma + 8) + 2i_\sigma^2 + 8i_\Delta v_d \\
&= 2(1)(19) + 5(2)^2 + 8(1)(17) + 2(1)^2 + 8(2)(10) \\
&= 356 \text{ W; Therefore,} \\
\sum P_{\text{gen}} &= \sum P_{\text{diss}} = 356 \text{ W}
\end{aligned}$$

P 2.28

$$\frac{V_{CC}R_2}{R_1 + R_2} = \frac{(15)(80)}{100} = 12 \text{ V}$$

$$\frac{R_1R_2}{R_1 + R_2} = \frac{(20)(80)}{100} = 16 \text{ k}\Omega$$

$$i_B = \frac{12 - 0.2}{16 + 40(0.1)} = \frac{11.8}{20} = 0.59 \text{ mA}$$

$$i_C = \beta i_B = (39)(0.59) = 23.01 \text{ mA}$$

$$i_E = i_C + i_B = 23 + 0.59 = 23.6 \text{ mA}$$

$$v_{3d} = (23.6)(0.1) = 2.36 \text{ V}$$

$$v_{bd} = V_o + v_{3d} = 2.56 \text{ V}$$

$$i_2 = \frac{v_{bd}}{R_2} = \frac{2.56}{80} \times 10^{-3} = 32\,\mu\text{A}$$

$$i_1 = i_2 + i_B = 32 + 590 = 622\,\mu\text{A}$$

$$v_{ab} = 20(0.622) = 12.44 \text{ V}$$

$$i_{CC} = i_C + i_1 = 23.01 + 0.622 = 23.632 \text{ mA}$$

$$v_{13} + 23.01(0.5) + 2.36 = 15$$

$$v_{13} = 1.135 \text{ V}$$

P 2.29 $$50i_2 + \frac{250}{50} + \frac{250}{12.5} = 0; \quad i_2 = -0.5 \text{ mA}$$

$$v_1 = 100i_2 = -50 \text{ mV}$$

$$20i_1 + \frac{(-50)}{25} + (-0.5) = 0; \quad i_1 = 125\,\mu\text{A}$$

$$v_g = 10i_1 + 40i_1 = 50i_1$$

Therefore, $v_g = 6.25$ mV.

P 2.30 [a]

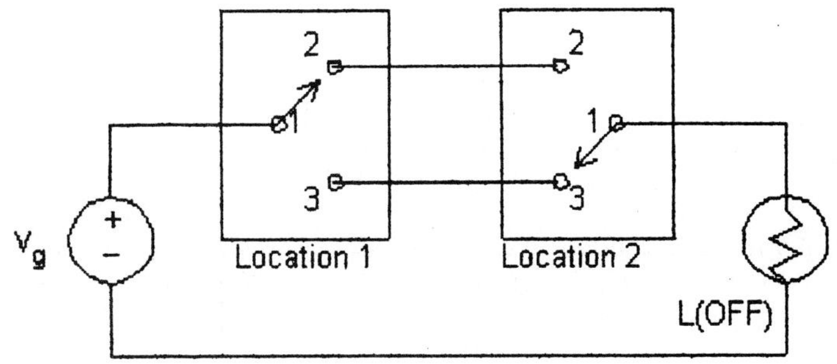

[b]

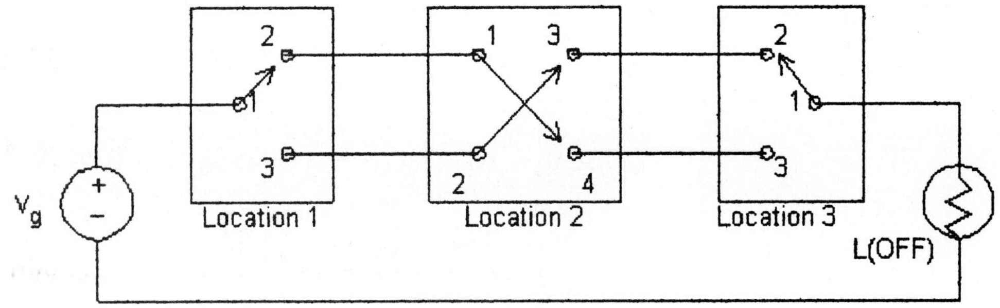

P 2.31

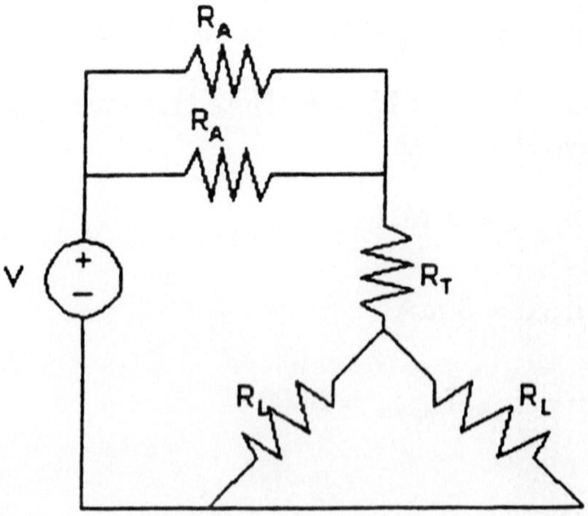

P 2.32 [a] $p = i^2 R$

$$p_{\text{arm}} = \left(\frac{250}{650}\right)^2 (400) = 59.17 \text{ W}$$

$$p_{\text{leg}} = \left(\frac{250}{650}\right)^2 (200) = 29.59 \text{ W}$$

$$p_{\text{trunk}} = \left(\frac{250}{650}\right)^2 (50) = 7.40 \text{ W}$$

[b] $$\left(\frac{dT}{dt}\right)_{\text{arm}} = \frac{2.39 \times 10^{-4} p_{\text{arm}}}{4} = 35.36 \times 10^{-4}\,^\circ\text{ C/s}$$

$$t_{\text{arm}} = \frac{5}{35.36} \times 10^4 = 1414.23 \text{ s or } 23.57 \text{ min}$$

$$\left(\frac{dT}{dt}\right)_{\text{leg}} = \frac{2.39 \times 10^{-4}}{10} P_{\text{leg}} = 7.07 \times 10^{-4}\,^\circ\text{ C/s}$$

$$t_{\text{leg}} = \frac{5 \times 10^4}{7.07} = 7{,}071.13 \text{ s or } 117.85 \text{ min}$$

$$\left(\frac{dT}{dt}\right)_{\text{trunk}} = \frac{2.39 \times 10^{-4}(7.4)}{25} = 0.71 \times 10^{-4}\,^\circ\text{ C/s}$$

$$t_{\text{trunk}} = \frac{5 \times 10^4}{0.71} = 70{,}677.37 \text{ s or } 1{,}177.96 \text{ min}$$

[c] They are all much greater than a few minutes.

P 2.33 [a]

$$R_{\text{arms}} = 400 + 400 = 800\Omega$$

$$i_{\text{letgo}} = 50 \text{ mA (minimum)}$$

$$v_{\text{min}} = (800)(50) \times 10^{-3} = 40 \text{ V}$$

[b] No, 12/800 = 15 mA. Note this current is sufficient to give a perceptible shock.

P 2.34

$$R_{\text{space}} = 1 \text{ M}\Omega$$

$$i_{\text{space}} = 3 \text{ mA}$$

$$v = i_{\text{space}} R_{\text{space}} = 3000 \text{ V}.$$

3

Simple Resistive Circuits

Drill Exercises

DE 3.1

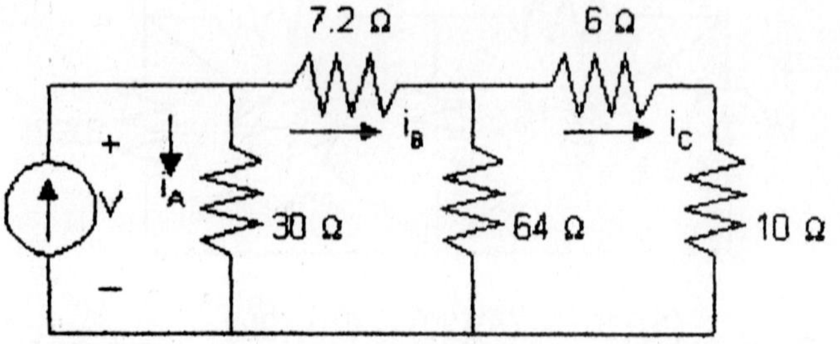

$16\|64 = 12.8\,\Omega, \qquad 12.8 + 7.2 = 20\,\Omega, \qquad 20\|30 = 12\,\Omega$

[a] $v = 5(12) = 60$ V

[b] $p_{5A}(\text{del}) = (5)(60) = 300$ W

[c] $i_A = 60/30 = 2$ A $\qquad i_C = 3(64)/(80) = 2.4$ A

$i_B = 5 - 2 = 3$ A $\qquad p_{10\Omega} = (2.4)^2 10 = 57.6$ W

DE 3.2 [a] $v_o(\text{no load}) = 200(75)/100 = 150$ V

[b] $75\|150 = 50$ kΩ, therefore $v_o = 200(50)/75 = 133.3$ V

[c] $i = 200/25 = 8$ mA, $\qquad p_{25k} = (8 \times 10^{-3})^2(25{,}000) = 1.6$ W

[d] Maximum dissipation at no load since v_o is maximum

$$p = \frac{v_o^2}{75{,}000} = 0.3 \text{ W}$$

DE 3.3 [a] $i = 1/100 = 10$ mA

[b] $i_{\text{meas}} = 1/105.555 = 9.474$ mA

DE 3.4 [a] $v = 60(75)/90 = 50$ V

[b] $R_m = 150/10^{-3} = 150$ kΩ, $\qquad 150\text{ k}\Omega\|75\text{ k}\Omega = 50$ kΩ

Therefore $v_{\text{meas}} = 50(60)/65 = 46.15$ V

DE 3.5 [a] $100R_x = (1000)(150), \qquad R_x = 1.5\ \text{k}\Omega$

[b] The current supplied by the 5 V source is

$$i_s = \frac{5}{250} + \frac{5}{2500} = 0.022\ \text{A} = 22\ \text{mA}$$

Therefore $p_{5V}(\text{delivered}) = 5(22) = 110\ \text{mW}$
Since total power delivered to bridge is less than 250 mW, bridge will not be damaged.

DE 3.6

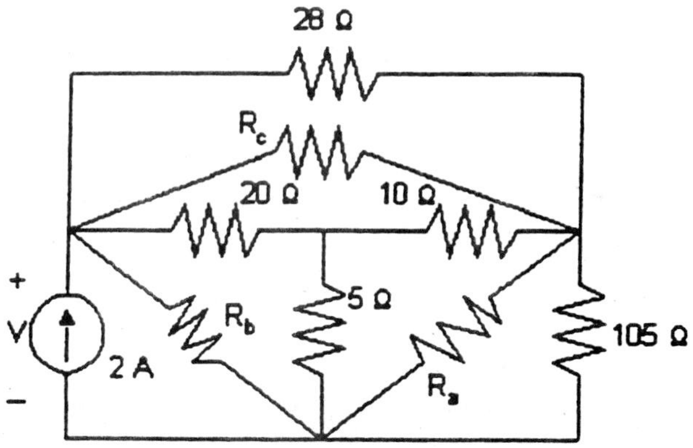

$$R_a = \frac{(5)(10)+(5)(20)+(10)(20)}{20} = 17.5\,\Omega$$
$$R_b = \frac{(5)(10)+(5)(20)+(10)(20)}{10} = 35\,\Omega$$
$$R_c = \frac{(5)(10)+(5)(20)+(10)(20)}{5} = 70\,\Omega$$

The resistance seen by the 2 A source is

$$R = 35\|(70\|28 + 17.5\|105)$$
$$= 35\|(20+15) = 17.5\,\Omega$$
$$v = (17.5)(2) = 35\ \text{V}$$

Problems

P 3.1 [a] $p_{4\Omega} = i_s^2 4 = (12)^2 4 = 576\ \text{W} \qquad p_{18\Omega} = (4)^2 18 = 288\ \text{W}$

$p_{3\Omega} = (8)^2 3 = 192\ \text{W} \qquad p_{6\Omega} = (8)^2 6 = 384\ \text{W}$

[b] $p_{120V}(\text{delivered}) = 120i_s = 120(12) = 1440$ W

[c] $p_{diss} = 576 + 288 + 192 + 384 = 1440$ W

P 3.2 [a] From Ex. 3-1: $i_1 = 4$ A, $i_2 = 8$ A, $i_s = 12$ A
at node x: $-12 + 4 + 8 = 0$, at node y: $12 - 4 - 8 = 0$

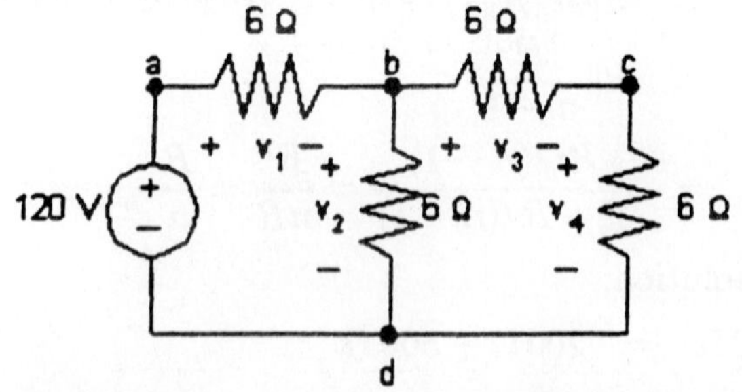

$$v_1 = 4i_s = 48 \text{ V} \qquad v_3 = 3i_2 = 24 \text{ V}$$
$$v_2 = 18i_1 = 72 \text{ V} \qquad v_4 = 6i_2 = 48 \text{ V}$$

loop abda: $-120 + 48 + 72 = 0$,
loop bcdb: $-72 + 24 + 48 = 0$,
loop abcda: $-120 + 48 + 24 + 48 = 0$

P 3.3 $$\frac{1}{R_{eq}} = \frac{1}{6} + \frac{1}{10} + \frac{1}{15} = \frac{10}{30} = \frac{1}{3}; \qquad R_{eq} = 3\,\Omega$$

$v_{(2+8+5)\Omega} = (20)(3) = 60$ V

$P_{5\Omega} = (4)^2(5) = 80$ W

P 3.4 [a]

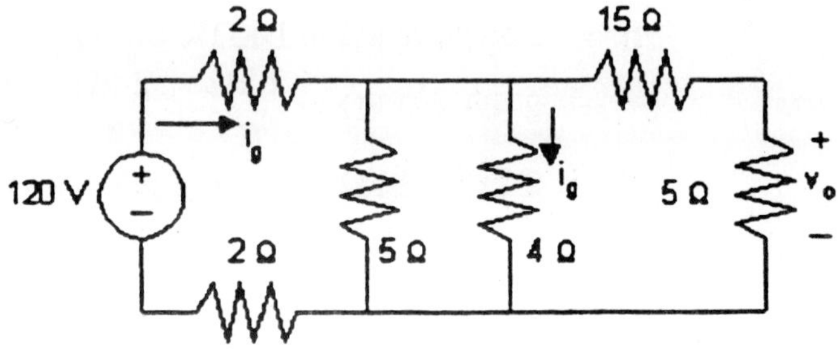

$R_{eq} = 2 + 2 + 1/4 + 1/5 + 1/20 = 6\,\Omega$

$i_g = 120/6 = 20$ A

$v_{4\Omega} = 120 - (2 + 2)20 = 40$ V

$i_o = 40/4 = 10$ A

$i_{(15+5)\Omega} = 40/(15 + 5) = 2$ A

$v_o = (5)(2) = 10$ V

[b] $i_{15\Omega} = 2$ A; $P_{15\Omega} = (2)^2(15) = 60$ W

[c] $P_{120V} = (120)(20) = 2.4$ kW

P 3.5 [a] $R_{eq} = R\|R = \frac{R^2}{2R} = \frac{R}{2}$

[b]
$$\begin{aligned} R_{eq} &= R\|R\|R\|\cdots\|R \qquad (n\ R\text{'s}) \\ &= R\|\frac{R}{n-1} \\ &= \frac{R^2/(n-1)}{R+R/(n-1)} = \frac{R^2}{nR} = \frac{R}{n} \end{aligned}$$

[c] One solution:

$$\begin{aligned} 700\,\Omega &= 200\,\Omega + 500\,\Omega \\ &= 1000/5 + 1000/2 \\ &= 1\ \text{k}\Omega\|1\ \text{k}\Omega\|1\ \text{k}\Omega\|1\ \text{k}\Omega\|1\ \text{k}\Omega + 1\ \text{k}\Omega\|1\ \text{k}\Omega \end{aligned}$$

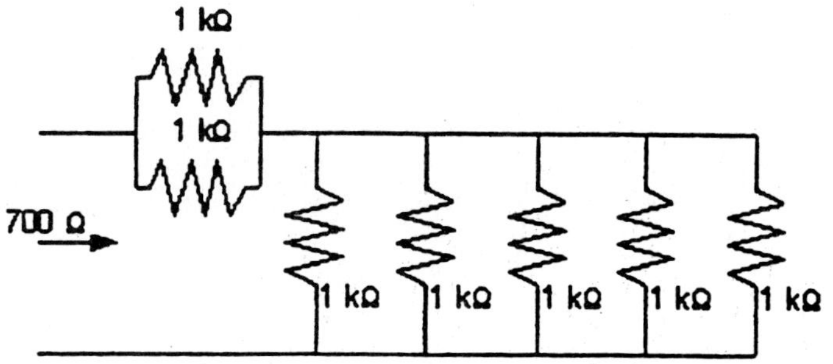

[d] One solution:

$$\begin{aligned} 5.5\ \text{k}\Omega &= 5\ \text{k}\Omega + 0.5\ \text{k}\Omega \\ &= 2\ \text{k}\Omega + 2\ \text{k}\Omega + 1\ \text{k}\Omega + 0.5\ \text{k}\Omega \\ &= 2\ \text{k}\Omega + 2\ \text{k}\Omega + \frac{2\ \text{k}\Omega}{2} + \frac{2\ \text{k}\Omega}{4} \\ &= 2\ \text{k}\Omega + 2\ \text{k}\Omega + 2\ \text{k}\Omega\|2\ \text{k}\Omega + 2\ \text{k}\Omega\|2\ \text{k}\Omega\|2\ \text{k}\Omega\|2\ \text{k}\Omega \end{aligned}$$

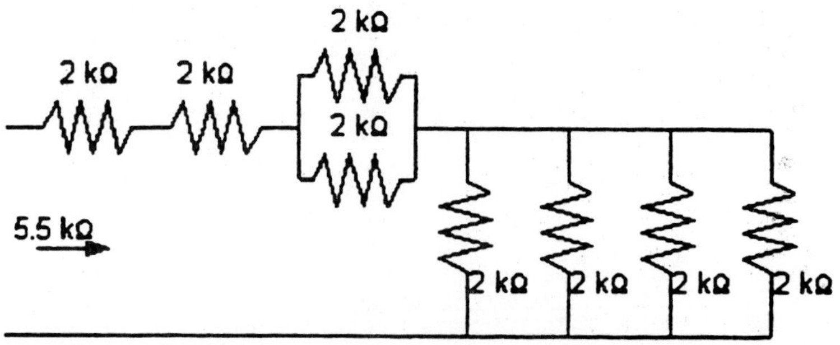

P 3.6 [a] $12\,\Omega\|24\,\Omega = 8\,\Omega$ Therefore, $R_{ab} = 8 + 2 + 6 = 16\,\Omega$

[b] $$\frac{1}{R_{eq}} = \frac{1}{24} + \frac{1}{30} + \frac{1}{20} = \frac{15}{120} = \frac{1}{8}$$

$$R_{eq} = 8\ \text{k}\Omega; \qquad R_{eq} + 7 = 15\ \text{k}\Omega$$

$$\frac{1}{R_{ab}} = \frac{1}{15} + \frac{1}{30} + \frac{1}{15} = \frac{5}{30} = \frac{1}{6}$$

$$R_{ab} = 6\ \text{k}\Omega$$

P 3.7 [a] For circuit (a)

$$R_{ab} = 15\|(18 + 48\|16) = 10\,\Omega$$

For circuit (b)

$$\frac{1}{R_e} = \frac{1}{20} + \frac{1}{15} + \frac{1}{20} + \frac{1}{4} + \frac{1}{12} = \frac{30}{60} = \frac{1}{2}$$

$$R_e = 2\,\Omega$$

$$R_e + 16 = 18\,\Omega$$

$$18\|18 = 9\,\Omega$$

$$R_{ab} = 10 + 8 + 9 = 27\,\Omega$$

For circuit (c)

$$48\|16 = 12\,\Omega$$

$$12 + 8 = 20\,\Omega$$

$$20\|30 = 12\,\Omega$$

$$12 + 18 = 30\,\Omega$$

$$30\|15 = 10\,\Omega$$

$$10 + 10 + 20 = 40\,\Omega$$

$$R_{ab} = 40\|60 = 24\,\Omega$$

[b] $$P_a = \frac{20^2}{10} = 40\ \text{W}$$

$$P_b = \frac{144^2}{27} = 768\ \text{W}$$

$$P_c = 6^2(24) = 864\ \text{W}$$

P 3.8 [a] $5\|20 = 100/25 = 4\,\Omega$ $\quad$ $5\|20 + 9\|18 + 10 = 20\,\Omega$

$9\|18 = 162/27 = 6\,\Omega$ $\quad$ $20\|30 = 600/50 = 12\,\Omega$

$R_{ab} = 5 + 12 + 3 = 20\,\Omega$

[b] $5 + 15 = 20\,\Omega$ $\quad$ $30\|20 = 600/50 = 12\,\Omega$

$20\|60 = 1200/80 = 15\,\Omega$ $\quad$ $3\|6 = 18/9 = 2\,\Omega$

$15 + 10 = 25\,\Omega$ $\quad$ $3\|6 + 30\|20 = 2 + 12 = 14\,\Omega$

$25\|75 = 1875/100 = 18.75\,\Omega$ $\quad$ $26\|14 = 364/40 = 9.1\,\Omega$

$18.75 + 11.25 = 30\,\Omega$ $\quad$ $R_{ab} = 2.5 + 9.1 + 3.4 = 15\,\Omega$

[c] $3 + 5 = 8\,\Omega$ $\quad$ $60\|40 = 2400/100 = 24\,\Omega$

$8\|12 = 96/20 = 4.8\,\Omega$ $\quad$ $24 + 6 = 30\,\Omega$

$4.8 + 5.2 = 10\,\Omega$ $\quad$ $30\|10 = 300/40 = 7.5\,\Omega$

$45 + 15 = 60\,\Omega$ $\quad$ $R_{ab} = 1.5 + 7.5 + 1.0 = 10\,\Omega$

P 3.9 [a]

$$R_{cond} = 845(0.0397) = 33.5465\,\Omega$$

$$R_{total} = 2(1/2)R_{cond} = 33.5465\,\Omega$$

$$P_{loss} = (2000)^2(33.5465) = 134.186 \text{ MW}$$

$$P_{calif} = 800(2) - 134.186 = 1465.814 \text{ MW}$$

$$\text{Efficiency} = (1465.814/1600) \times 100 = 91.61\%$$

[b]

$$P_{calif} = 2000 - 134.86 = 1865.814 \text{ MW}$$

$$\text{Efficiency} = 93.29\%$$

[c]

$$P_{loss} = (3000)^2 \cdot 2 \cdot (1/3) \cdot 845 \cdot (0.0397) = 201.279 \text{ MW}$$

$$P_{oregon} = 3000 \text{ MW}, \qquad P_{calif} = 3000 - 201.279 = 2798.7 \text{ MW}$$

$$\text{Efficiency} = (2798.70/3000) \times 100 = 93.29\%$$

P 3.10

$$i_{10k} = \frac{(18)(15)}{40} = 6.75 \text{ mA}$$

$$v_{15k} = -(6.75)(15) = -101.25 \text{ V}$$

$$i_{3k} = 18 - 6.75 = 11.25 \text{ mA}$$

$$v_{12k} = -(12)(11.25) = -135 \text{ V}$$

$$v_o = -101.25 - (-135) = 33.75 \text{ V}$$

P 3.11 [a] $$v_{1k} = \frac{1}{1+5}(30) = 5\text{ V}$$

$$v_{15k} = \frac{15}{15+60}(30) = 6\text{ V}$$

$$v_x = v_{15k} - v_{1k} = 6 - 5 = 1\text{ V}$$

[b] $$v_{1k} = \frac{v_s}{6}(1) = v_s/6$$

$$v_{15k} = \frac{v_s}{75}(15) = v_s/5$$

$$v_x = (v_s/5) - (v_s/6) = v_s/30$$

P 3.12 $$60\|30 = 20\,\Omega$$

$$i_{30\Omega} = \frac{(25)(75)}{125} = 15\text{ A}$$

$$v_o = (15)(20) = 300\text{ V}$$

$$v_o + 30i_{30} = 750\text{ V}$$

$$v_g - 12(25) = 750$$

$$v_g = 1050\text{ V}$$

P 3.13 $5\,\Omega\|20\,\Omega = 4\,\Omega$; $4\,\Omega + 6\,\Omega = 10\,\Omega$; $10\|40 = 8\,\Omega$;

Therefore, $i_g = \dfrac{125}{8+2} = 12.5\text{ A}$

$$i_{6\Omega} = \frac{(40)(12.5)}{50} = 10\text{ A}; \quad i_o = \frac{(5)(10)}{25} = 2\text{ A}$$

P 3.14 [a] $40\|10 = 8\,\Omega$ $\qquad i_{75V} = \dfrac{75}{10} = 7.5\text{ A}$

$8 + 7 = 15\,\Omega$ $\qquad i_{4+3\Omega} = 7.5\left(\dfrac{30}{45}\right) = 5\text{ A}$

$15\|30 = 10\,\Omega$ $\qquad i_o = -5\left(\dfrac{10}{50}\right) = -1\text{ A}$

[b] $$i_{10\Omega} = i_{4+3\Omega} + i_o = 5 - 1 = 4\text{ A}$$

$$P_{10\Omega} = (4)^2(10) = 160\text{ W}$$

P 3.15 [a]

$$v_{9\Omega} = (1)(9) = 9 \text{ V}$$

$$i_{2\Omega} = 9/(2+1) = 3 \text{ A}$$

$$i_{4\Omega} = 1 + 3 = 4 \text{ A};$$

$$v_{25\Omega} = (4)(4) + 9 = 25 \text{ V}$$

$$i_{25\Omega} = 25/25 = 1 \text{ A};$$

$$i_{3\Omega} = i_{25\Omega} + i_{9\Omega} + i_{2\Omega} = 1 + 1 + 3 = 5 \text{ A};$$

$$v_{40\Omega} = v_{25\Omega} - v_{3\Omega} = 25 - (-5)(3) = 40 \text{ V}$$

$$i_{40\Omega} = 40/40 = 1 \text{ A}$$

$$i_{5\|20\Omega} = i_{40\Omega} + i_{25\Omega} + i_{4\Omega} = 1 + 1 + 4 = 6 \text{ A}$$

$$v_{5\|20\Omega} = (4)(6) = 24 \text{ V}$$

$$v_{32\Omega} = v_{40\Omega} + v_{5\|20\Omega} = 40 + 24 = 64 \text{ V}$$

$$i_{32\Omega} = 64/32 = 2 \text{ A};$$

$$i_{10\Omega} = i_{32\Omega} + i_{5\|20\Omega} = 2 + 6 = 8 \text{ A}$$

$$v_g = 10(8) + v_{32\Omega} = 80 + 64 = 144 \text{ V}.$$

[b]

$$P_{20\Omega} = \frac{(v_{5\|20\Omega})^2}{20} = \frac{24^2}{20} = 28.8 \text{ W}$$

P 3.16

$$6 = \frac{18R_2}{(R_2 + 40)}; \qquad R_2 = 20\,\Omega$$

$$4 = \frac{18R_e}{(40 + R_e)}; \qquad R_e = \frac{80}{7}\,\Omega$$

$$\text{Therefore, } \frac{80}{7} = \frac{20R_L}{20 + R_L}; \qquad R_L = 26.67\,\Omega$$

P 3.17 [a]

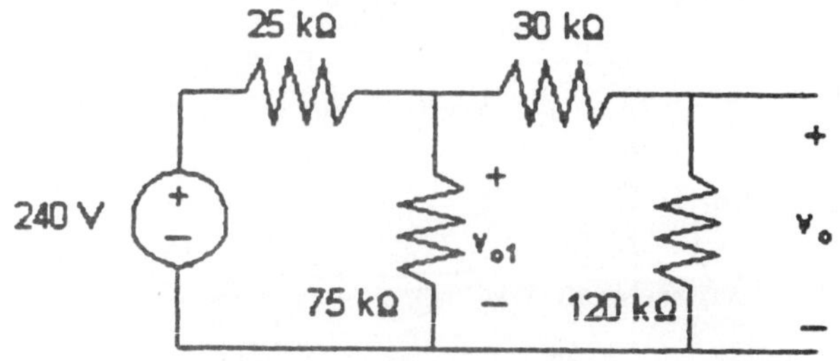

$$120 + 30 = 150 \text{ k}\Omega$$

$$75\|150 = 50 \text{ k}\Omega$$

$$v_{o1} = \frac{240}{(25+50)}(50) = 160 \text{ V}$$

$$v_o = \frac{v_{o1}}{(150)}(120) = 128 \text{ V}, \qquad v_o = 128 \text{ V}$$

[b]

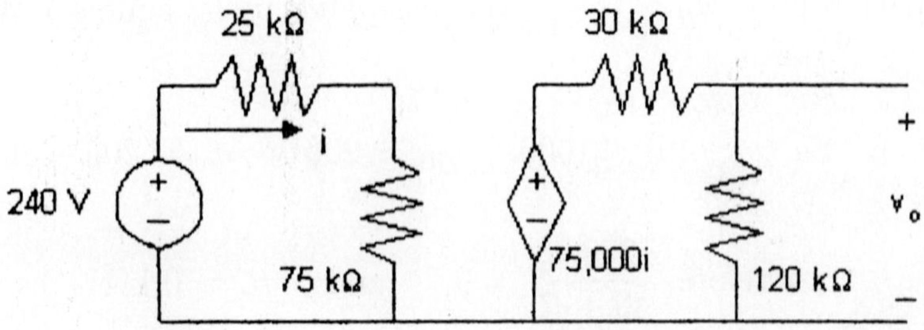

$$i = \frac{240}{100} = 2.4 \text{ mA}$$

$$75{,}000i = 180 \text{ V}$$

$$v_o = \frac{180}{150}(120) = 144 \text{ V}; \qquad v_o = 144 \text{ V}$$

[c] It removes loading effect of second voltage divider on the first voltage divider. Observe that the open circuit voltage of the first divider is

$$v'_{o1} = \frac{240}{(100)}(75) = 180 \text{ V}$$

Now note this is the input voltage to the second voltage divider when the current controlled voltage source is used.

P 3.18 [a] $v_o = \frac{200R_2}{(R_1+R_2)} =$ ~~40~~ 150; Therefore $R_2 = 3R_1$

$$\text{Let } R_e = R_2\|R_L = \frac{R_2 R_L}{R_2 + R_L}$$

$$v_o = \frac{200R_e}{R_1 + R_e} = 100; \qquad \text{Therefore } R_1 = R_e$$

$$\text{Thus, } R_2/3 = \frac{60R_2}{60 + R_2}$$

$$R_2 = 120 \text{ k}\Omega; \qquad R_1 = 40 \text{ k}\Omega$$

[b] Power dissipated in R_1 will be maximum when the voltage across R_1 is maximum. This will occur under load conditions.

$$v_{R_1} = 200 - 100 = 100 \text{ V}; \qquad P_{R_1} = \frac{(100)^2}{40 \times 10^3} = 250 \text{ mW}$$

So specify a 1/4 W power rating for the resistor.

P 3.19 Refer to the solution of Problem 3.18. The divider will reach its dissipation limit when the power dissipated in R_1 equals 1 W

$$\text{So } (v_{R_1}^2/40) = 1000; \quad v_{R_1} = 200 \text{ V} \quad v_o = 200 - 200 = 0 \text{ V}$$

$$\text{Therefore, } \frac{200R_e}{40 + R_e} = 0, \quad \text{and} \quad R_e = 0 \text{ k}\Omega$$

Thus, $R_L = 0$ kΩ (short circuit)

P 3.20 [a]

$$v_o = \frac{16(3.3)}{(4.7 + 3.3)} = 66 \text{ V}$$

[b]

$$i = 160/8 = 20 \text{ mA}$$

$$P_{R_1} = (400 \times 10^{-6})(4.7 \times 10^3) = 1.88 \text{ W}$$

$$P_{R_2} = (400 \times 10^{-6})(3.3 \times 10^3) = 1.32 \text{ W}$$

[c] Since R_1 and R_2 carry the same current and $R_1 > R_2$ to satisfy the voltage requirement, first pick R_1 to meet the 0.5 W specification

$$i_{R_1} = \frac{160 - 66}{R_1}, \qquad \text{Therefore, } \left(\frac{94}{R_1}\right)^2 R_1 \leq 0.5$$

$$\text{Thus, } R_1 \geq \frac{94^2}{0.5} \quad \text{or} \quad R_1 \geq 17{,}672\,\Omega$$

Now use the voltage specification:

$$\frac{R_2}{R_2 + 17{,}672}(160) = 66$$

Thus, $R_2 = 12{,}408\,\Omega$

P 3.21

$$\frac{(24)^2}{R_1 + R_2 + R_3} = 36, \qquad \text{Therefore, } R_1 + R_2 + R_3 = 16\,\Omega$$

$$\frac{(R_1 + R_2)24}{(R_1 + R_2 + R_3)} = 12$$

Therefore, $2(R_1 + R_2) = R_1 + R_2 + R_3$

Thus, $R_1 + R_2 = R_3$; $2R_3 = 16$; $R_3 = 8\,\Omega$

$$\frac{R_2(24)}{R_1 + R_2 + R_3} = 6$$

$4R_2 = R_1 + R_2 + R_3$ so $R_2 = R_3/2 = 4\,\Omega$

$R_2 = 4\,\Omega$; $R_1 = 16 - 8 - 4 = 4\,\Omega$

P 3.22 [a] At no load: $v_o = kv_s = \frac{R_2}{R_1 + R_2}v_s$.

At full load: $v_o = \alpha v_s = \frac{R_e}{R_1 + R_e}v_s$, where $R_e = \frac{R_o R_2}{R_o + R_2}$

$$\text{Therefore } k = \frac{R_2}{R_1 + R_2} \quad \text{and} \quad R_1 = \frac{(1-k)}{k}R_2$$

$$\alpha = \frac{R_e}{R_1 + R_e} \quad \text{and} \quad R_1 = \frac{(1-\alpha)}{\alpha}R_e$$

$$\text{Thus } \left(\frac{1-\alpha}{\alpha}\right)\left[\frac{R_2 R_o}{R_o + R_2}\right] = \frac{(1-k)}{k}R_2$$

Solving for R_2 yields $R_2 = \frac{(k-\alpha)}{\alpha(1-k)}R_o$

[b] $R_1 = \left(\frac{0.05}{0.68}\right)R_o = 2.5\text{ k}\Omega$

$R_2 = \left(\frac{0.05}{0.12}\right)R_o = 14.167\text{ k}\Omega$

[c]

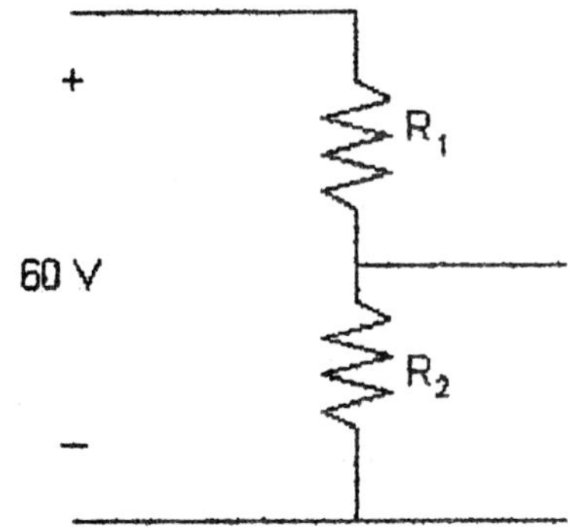

Maximum dissipation in R_2 occurs at no load, therefore,

$$P_{R_2(\max)} = \frac{[(60)(0.85)]^2}{14{,}167} = 183.6\text{ mW}$$

Maximum dissipation in R_1 occurs at full load.

$$P_{R_1(\max)} = \frac{[60 - 0.80(60)]^2}{2500} = 57.60 \text{ mA}$$

[d]

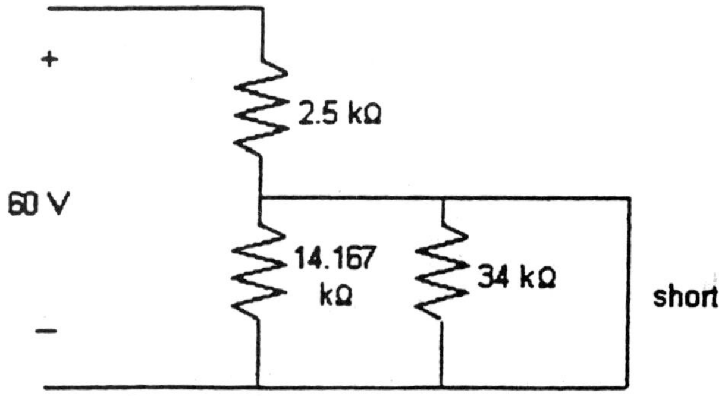

$$P_{R_1} = \frac{(60)^2}{2500} = 1.44 \text{ W} = 1440 \text{ mW}$$

$$P_{R_2} = \frac{(0)^2}{14{,}167} = 0 \text{ W}$$

P 3.23

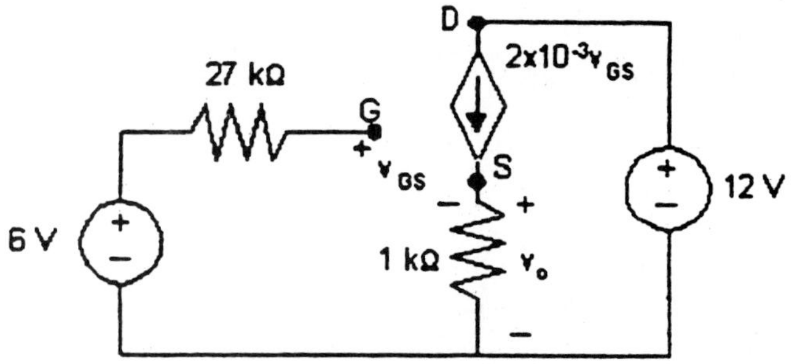

$6 = v_{GS} + 1000(2 \times 10^{-3} v_{GS}) = 3v_{GS}$, therefore, $v_{GS} = \frac{6}{3} = 2$ V

$v_o = 1000(2 \times 10^{-3})(2) = 4$ V

$v_{DS} + v_o = 12V$, so $v_{DS} = 8$ V

P 3.24 [a] Let v_o be the voltage across the parallel branches, positive at the upper terminal, then

$$i_g = v_oG_1 + v_oG_2 + \cdots + v_oG_N = v_o(G_1 + G_2 + \cdots + G_N)$$

It follows that $v_o = \dfrac{i_g}{(G_1 + G_2 + \cdots + G_N)}$

The current in the kth branch is $i_k = v_oG_k$; Thus,

$$i_k = \frac{i_gG_k}{[G_1 + G_2 + \cdot + G_N]}$$

[b] $$i_{6.25} = \frac{1142(0.16)}{[4 + 0.4 + 1 + 0.16 + 0.1 + 0.05]} = 32 \text{ mA}$$

P 3.25 $$R_e = \frac{4}{8} \times 10^3 = 500\,\Omega$$

$$\therefore \quad \sum G = \frac{1}{500} = 2 \text{ mmho}$$

$$i_1 = 2i_2 = 2(10i_3) = 20i_4$$

$$i_2 = 10i_3 = 10i_4$$

$$i_3 = i_4$$

$$8 = 20i_4 + 10i_4 + i_4 + i_4 = 32i_4$$

$$\therefore \quad i_4 = \frac{8}{32} = 0.25 \text{ mA}$$

$$R_4 = \frac{v_g}{i_4} = \frac{4}{0.25 \times 10^{-3}} = 16 \text{ k}\Omega$$

$$i_3 = i_4 = 0.25 \text{ mA}$$

$$\therefore \quad R_3 = 16 \text{ k}\Omega$$

$$i_2 = 10i_4 = 2.5 \text{ mA}$$

$$R_2 = \frac{v_g}{i_2} = \frac{4}{2.5 \times 10^{-3}} = 1.6 \text{ k}\Omega$$

$$i_1 = 20i_4 = 5 \text{ mA}$$

$$R_1 = \frac{v_g}{i_1} = \frac{4}{5 \times 10^{-3}} = 800\,\Omega$$

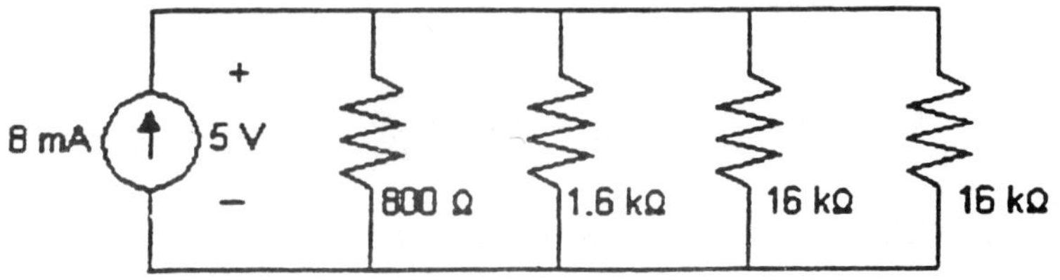

P 3.26

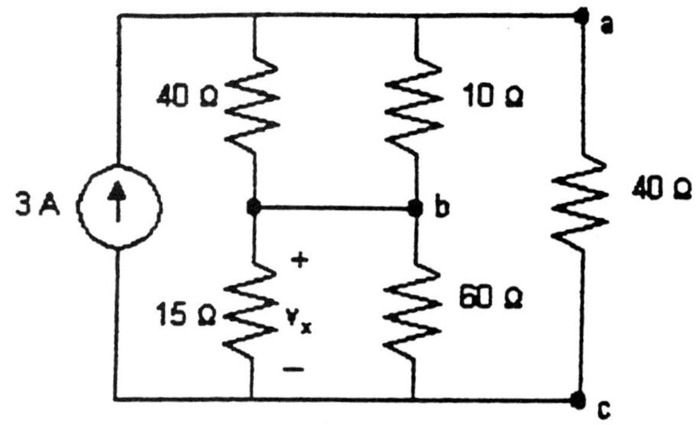

$40\|10 = 8\,\Omega \qquad 15\|60 = 12\,\Omega$

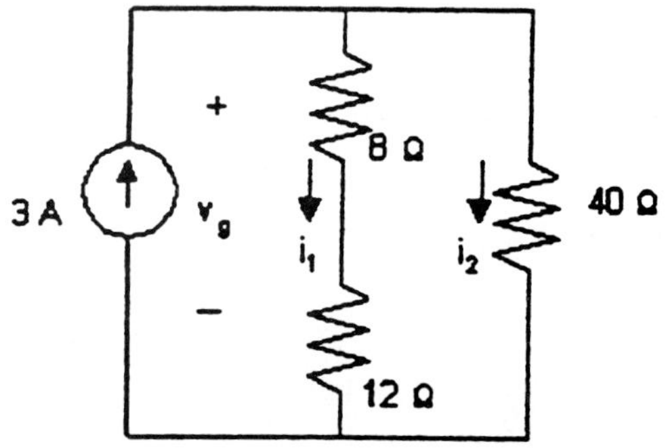

$$i_1 = \frac{(3)(40)}{(60)} = 2; \qquad v_x = 8i_1 = 16 \text{ V}$$

$$v_g = 20i_1 = 40 \text{ V}$$

$$v_{60} = v_g - v_x = 24 \text{ V}$$

$$P_{\text{device}} = \frac{24^2}{60} + \frac{16^2}{10} + \frac{40^2}{40} = 75.2 \text{ W}$$

P 3.27 [a] $$i_m = \frac{i_{\text{meas}}(10/3)}{30 + (10/3)} = \frac{10i_{\text{meas}}}{100} = \frac{1}{10}i_{\text{meas}}$$

[b] $$R_s = \frac{30}{1999}\,\Omega$$

$$i_m = \frac{i_{\text{meas}}(30/1999)}{30 + (30/1999)} = \frac{30i_{\text{meas}}}{60{,}000} = \frac{i_{\text{meas}}}{2000}$$

[c] Yes

P 3.28

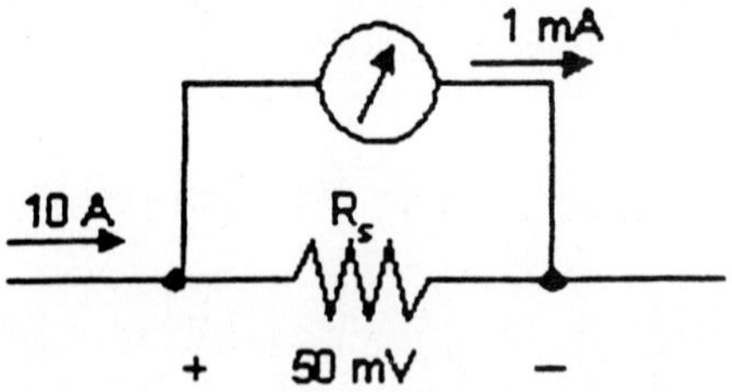

Original meter: $R_e = \dfrac{50 \times 10^{-3}}{10} = 0.005\,\Omega$

Modified meter: $R_e = \dfrac{(0.015)(0.005)}{0.02} = 0.00375\,\Omega$

$\therefore\ (I_{fs})(0.00375) = 50 \times 10^{-3}$

$\therefore\ I_{fs} = 13.33$ A

P 3.29 The current in the shunt resistor at full-scale deflection is

$$i_A = i_{\text{fullscale}} - 20 \times 10^{-6}$$

The voltage across R_A at full-scale deflection is always 10 mV, therefore

$$R_A = \frac{10 \times 10^{-3}}{i_{\text{fullscale}} - 2 \times 10^{-3}} = \frac{10}{1000 i_{fs} - 0.02}$$

[a] $R_A = \dfrac{10}{10{,}000 - 0.02} = 1\ \text{m}\Omega$

[b] $R_A = \dfrac{10}{1000 - 0.02} = 10\ \text{m}\Omega$

[c] $R_A = \dfrac{10}{100 - 0.02} = 1\,\Omega$

[d] $R_A = \dfrac{10}{0.1 - 0.02} = 125\,\Omega$

P 3.30 At full scale the voltage across the shunt resistor will be 100 mV; therefore the power dissipated will be

$$P_A = \frac{(100 \times 10^{-3})^2}{R_A}$$

Therefore $R_A \geq \dfrac{(100 \times 10^{-3})^2}{0.25} = 40\ \text{m}\Omega$

Otherwise the power dissipated in R_A will exceed its power rating of 0.25 W

When $R_A = 40$ mΩ, the shunt current will be

$$i_A = \frac{100 \times 10^{-3}}{40 \times 10^{-3}} = 2.5 \text{ A}$$

The measured current will be $i_{meas} = 2.5 + 0.001 = 2.501$ A

$\therefore$ Full-scale reading is for practical purposes is 2.5 A

P 3.31 Measured value: $60\|20.1 = 15.056\,\Omega$

$$i_g = \frac{50}{(15.056 + 10)} = 1.9955 \text{ A}; \qquad i_{meas} = (1.9955)\frac{60}{80.1} = 1.495 \text{ A}$$

True value: $60\|20 = 15\,\Omega$

$$i_g = \frac{50}{(15 + 10)} = \frac{50}{25} = 2.0 \text{ A}; \qquad i_{true} = (2)\left(\frac{60}{80}\right) = 1.5 \text{ A}$$

$$\% \text{ error} = \left[\frac{1.495}{1.5} - 1\right] \times 100 = -0.3488\%$$

P 3.32
$$i_{true} = \frac{(50)(15)}{60} = 12.5 \text{ mA}$$

$$i_{meas} = \frac{(50)(15)}{60.1} = 12.48 \text{ mA}$$

$$\% \text{ error} = \left[\frac{12.48}{12.5} - 1\right] 100 = -0.1664\%$$

P 3.33 For all full-scale readings the total resistance is

$$R_V + R_{movement} = \frac{\text{full-scale reading}}{10^{-3}}$$

$$\therefore \quad R_V = 1000 \text{ (full-scale reading)} - 50$$

[a] $R_V = 1000(100) - 50 = 99{,}950\,\Omega$

[b] $R_V = 1000(5) - 50 = 4950\,\Omega$

[c] $R_V = 100 - 50 = 50\,\Omega$

P 3.34 [a] $v_{meas} = (50 \times 10^{-3})(15\|45\|4950) = 0.5612$ V

[b] $v_{\text{true}} = (50 \times 10^{-3})(15\|45) = 0.5625$ V

$$\%\ \text{error} = \left(\frac{0.5612}{0.5625} - 1\right) \times 100 = -0.23\%$$

P 3.35 [a] $v_{\text{meter}} = 180$ V

[b] $R_{\text{meter}} = (100)(200) = 20$ kΩ

$$20\|70 = 15.56 \text{ k}\Omega$$

$$v_{\text{meter}} = \frac{180}{35.56} \times 15.56 = 78.76 \text{ V}$$

[c] $20\|20 = 10$ kΩ

$$v_{\text{meter}} = \frac{180}{80}(10) = 22.5 \text{ V}$$

[d] $v_{\text{meter a}} = 180$ V

$$v_{\text{meter b}} + v_{\text{meter c}} = 101.26 \text{ V}$$

No, because of the loading effect.

P 3.36 $R_{\text{meter}} = R_m + R_{\text{movement}} = 600$ kΩ

$$v_{\text{meas}} = \frac{R_e}{R_e + 300 + 100}(600)$$

$$R_e = 500 \text{ k}\Omega\|600 \text{ k}\Omega$$

$$v_{\text{meas}} = 243.24 \text{ V}$$

$$v_{\text{true}} = (2 \times 10^{-3})\frac{300}{300 + 600}(500 \times 10^3) = 333.33 \text{ V}$$

$$\%\ \text{error} = \left(\frac{243.24}{333.33} - 1\right) 100 = -27.03\%$$

P 3.37 [a] $R_{\text{movement}} = 5\,\Omega$

$$R_1 + R_{\text{movement}} = \frac{50}{2 \times 10^{-3}} = 25 \text{ k}\Omega \quad \therefore\ R_1 = 24{,}955\,\Omega$$

$$R_2 + R_1 + R_{\text{movement}} = \frac{100}{2 \times 10^{-3}} = 50 \text{ k}\Omega \quad \therefore\ R_2 = 25 \text{ k}\Omega$$

$$R_3 + R_2 + R_1 + R_{\text{movement}} = \frac{200}{2 \times 10^{-3}} = 100 \text{ k}\Omega$$

$$\therefore\ R_3 = 50 \text{ k}\Omega$$

[b]

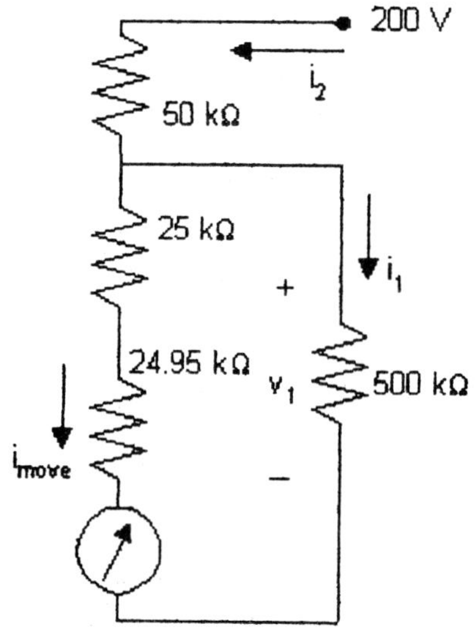

$$i_{\text{move}} = \frac{188}{200}(2) = 1.88 \text{ mA}$$

$$v_1 = (1.88)(50) = 94 \text{ V}$$

$$i_1 = \frac{94}{500} = 0.188 \text{ mA}$$

$$i_2 = i_{\text{move}} + i_1 = 1.88 + 0.188 = 2.068 \text{ mA}$$

$$v_{\text{meas}} = v_x = 94 + 50i_2 = 197.4 \text{ V}$$

[c] $v_1 = 100$ V $i_2 = 2 + 0.20 = 2.20$ mA

$i_1 = 100/500 = 0.20$ mA $v_{\text{meas}} = v_x = 100 + 50(2.20) = 210$ V

P 3.38 [a] $R_1 = (10)10^3 = 10 \text{ k}\Omega$

$R_2 = (5)10^3 = 5 \text{ k}\Omega$

$R_3 = (1)10^3 = 1 \text{ k}\Omega$

[b] Let i_a = actual current in the movement

i_d = design current in the movement

Then % error $= \left(\frac{i_a}{i_d} - 1\right) 100$

For the 10 V scale:

$$i_a = \frac{10}{10{,}000 + 100} = \frac{10}{10{,}100}, \qquad i_d = \frac{10}{10{,}000}$$

$$\frac{i_a}{i_d} = \frac{10{,}000}{10{,}100} \cong 0.9910 \qquad \% \text{ error} = (0.9910 - 1)100 = -0.9901\%$$

For the 5 V scale:

$$\frac{i_a}{i_d} = \frac{5{,}000}{5{,}100} \cong 0.98 \qquad \%\ \text{error} = (0.98 - 1.0)100 = -1.9608\%$$

For the 1 V scale:

$$\frac{i_a}{i_d} = \frac{1000}{1100} \cong 0.91 \qquad \%\ \text{error} = (0.91 - 1.0)100 = -9.0909\%$$

P 3.39 [a] $R_{\text{meter}} = 360\ \text{k}\Omega + 200\ \text{k}\Omega \| 50\ \text{k}\Omega = 400\ \text{k}\Omega$

$$400 \| 600 = 240\ \text{k}\Omega$$

$$V_{\text{meter}} = \frac{240}{300}(300) = 240\ \text{V}$$

[b] What is the percent error in the measured voltage?

$$\text{True value} = \frac{600}{660}(300) = 272.73$$

$$\%\ \text{error} = \left(\frac{240}{272.73} - 1\right)100 = -12\%$$

P 3.40 [a]

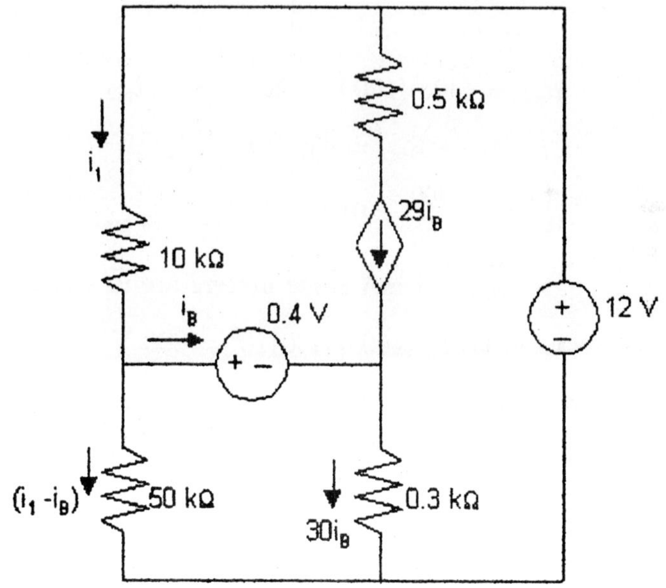

$$10 \times 10^3 i_1 + 50 \times 10^3(i_1 - i_B) = 12$$

$$50 \times 10^3(i_1 - i_B) = 0.4 + 30 i_B(0.3 \times 10^3)$$

$$\therefore \quad 60 i_1 - 50 i_B = 12 \times 10^{-3}$$

$$50 i_1 - 59 i_B = 0.4 \times 10^{-3}$$

Calculator solution yields $i_B = 553.85\,\mu\text{A}$

[b] With the insertion of the ammeter the equations become

$$60i_1 - 50i_B = 12 \times 10^{-3} \quad \text{(no change)}$$

$$50 \times 10^3(i_1 - i_B) = 2 \times 10^3 i_B + 0.4 + 30i_B(300)$$

$$50i_1 - 61i_B = 0.4 \times 10^{-3}$$

Calculator solution yields $i_B = 496.6\,\mu\text{A}$

[c] $$\%\ \text{error} = \left(\frac{496.6}{553.85} - 1\right) 100 = -10.34\%$$

P 3.41 [a] Since the unknown voltage is greater than either voltmeter's maximum reading, the only possible way to use the voltmeters would be to connect them in series.

[b]

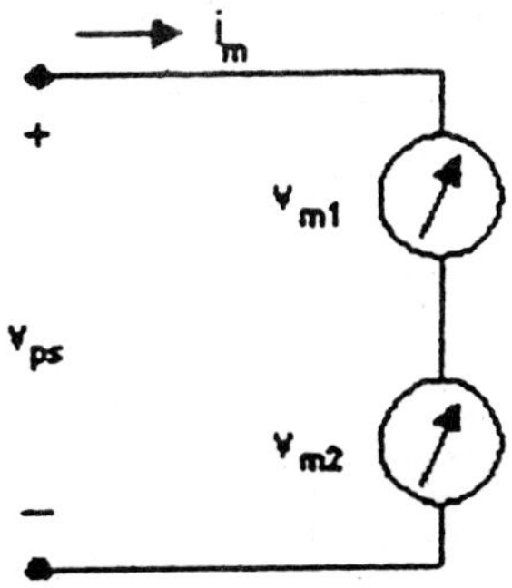

$$R_{m1} = (400)(1000) = 400\ \text{k}\Omega = R_{m2}$$

$$\therefore\ R_{m1} + R_{m2} = 800\ \text{k}\Omega$$

$$i_{1\ \text{max}} = \frac{400}{400} \times 10^{-3} = 1\ \text{mA} = i_{2\ \text{max}}$$

$$\therefore\ i_{\text{max}} = 1\ \text{mA since meters are in series}$$

$$v_{\text{max}} = 10^{-3}(400 + 400)10^3 = 800\ \text{V}$$

Thus the meters can be used to measure the voltage

[c] $$i_m = \frac{504}{800 \times 10^3} = 0.63\ \text{mA}$$

$$v_{m1} = (0.63)(400) = 252\ \text{V} = v_{m2}$$

P 3.42 The current in the series-connected voltmeters is

$$i_m = \frac{328}{400} = 0.82\ \text{mA}$$

$$v_{50\ \text{k}\Omega} = (0.82)(50) = 41\ \text{V}$$

$$V_{\text{power supply}} = 328 + 328 + 41 = 697\ \text{V}$$

P 3.43 From the problem statement we have

$$80 = \frac{V_s(10)}{10 + R_s} \quad (1) \quad V_s \text{ in mV}; \; R_s \text{ in M}\Omega$$

$$72 = \frac{V_s(5)}{5 + R_s} \quad (2)$$

[a] From Eq (1) $\quad 10 + R_s = 0.125V_s$

$$\therefore \; R_s = 0.125V_s - 10$$

Substituting into Eq (2) yields

$$72 = \frac{5V_s}{0.125V_s - 5} \quad \text{or} \quad V_s = 90 \text{ mV}$$

[b] From Eq (1)

$$80 = \frac{900}{10 + R_s} \quad \text{or} \quad 80R_s = 100$$

So $R_s = 1250$ kΩ

P 3.44 Since the bridge is balanced, we can remove the detector without disturbing the voltages and currents in the circuit.

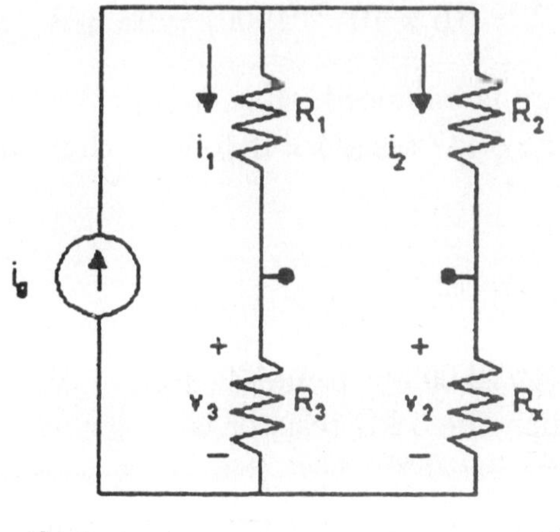

It follows that

$$i_1 = \frac{i_g(R_2 + R_x)}{R_1 + R_2 + R_3 + R_x} = \frac{i_g(R_2 + R_x)}{\sum R}$$

$$i_2 = \frac{i_g(R_1 + R_3)}{R_1 + R_2 + R_3 + R_x} = \frac{i_g(R_1 + R_3)}{\sum R}$$

$$v_3 = R_3 i_1 = v_x = i_2 R_x$$

$$\therefore \; \frac{R_3 i_g(R_2 + R_x)}{\sum R} = \frac{R_x i_g(R_1 + R_3)}{\sum R}; \quad \therefore \; R_3(R_2 + R_x) = R_x(R_1 + R_3)$$

From which $R_x = \dfrac{R_2 R_3}{R_1}$

P 3.45 [a]

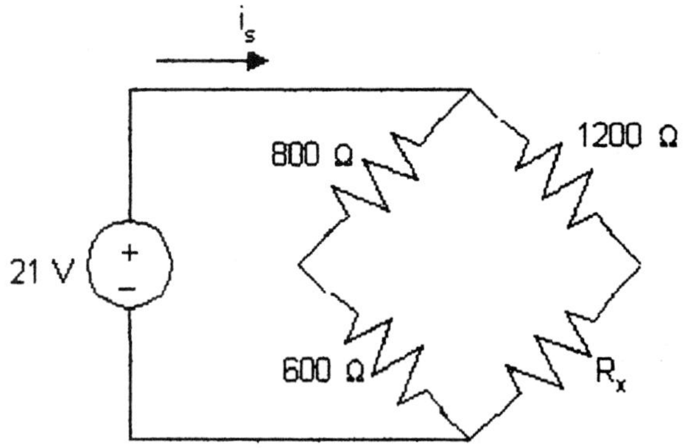

$$R_x = \frac{(1200)(600)}{800} = 900\,\Omega$$

[b] $$i_s = \frac{21}{1.4} + \frac{21}{2.1} = 15 + 10 = 25 \text{ mA}$$

[c] 800 Ω resistor $\quad P = 225 \times 10^{-6}(800) = 180$ mW

[d] 900 Ω resistor $\quad P = (10 \times 10^{-3})^2(900) = 90$ mW

P 3.46 Note the bridge structure is balanced, that is $15 \times 5 = 25 \times 3$, hence there is no current in the 5 kΩ resistor. It follows that the equivalent resistance of the circuit is

$$R_{eq} = 0.750 + 11.25 = 12 \text{ k}\Omega$$

The source current is 192/12,000 = 16 mA.
The current down through the 3 kΩ resistor is

$$i_{3k} = 16\frac{30}{48} = 10 \text{ mA}$$

$$\therefore \;\; p_{3k} = (10 \times 10^{-3})^2(3 \times 10^3) = 300 \text{ mW}$$

P 3.47 Redraw the circuit, replacing the detector branch with a short circuit.

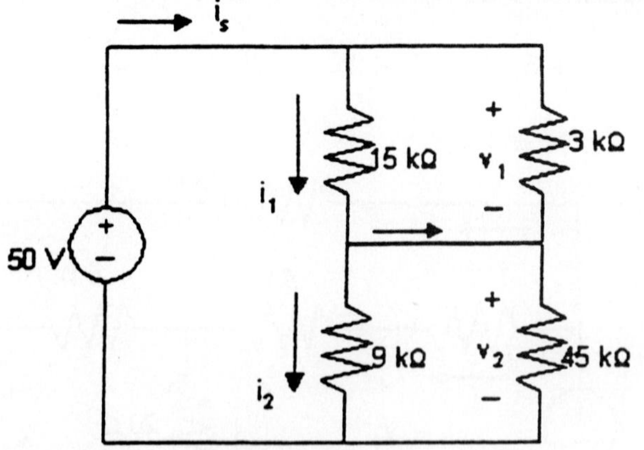

$15\ \text{k}\Omega \| 3\ \text{k}\Omega = 2.5\ \text{k}\Omega$

$9\ \text{k}\Omega \| 45\ \text{k}\Omega = 7.5\ \text{k}\Omega$

$$i_g = \frac{50}{10} = 5\ \text{mA}$$

$v_1 = 5(2.5) = 12.5\ \text{V}$

$v_2 = 5(7.5) = 37.5\ \text{V}$

$$i_1 = \frac{12.5}{15} = 833.3\,\mu\text{A}$$

$$i_2 = \frac{37.5}{9} = 4166.7\,\mu\text{A}$$

$i_d = i_1 - i_2 = -3333.4\,\mu\text{A}$

P 3.48 $R_1 = \dfrac{(40)(10)}{100} = 4\,\Omega$; $R_2 = \dfrac{(50)(10)}{100} = 5\,\Omega$; $R_3 = \dfrac{(40)(50)}{100} = 20\,\Omega$

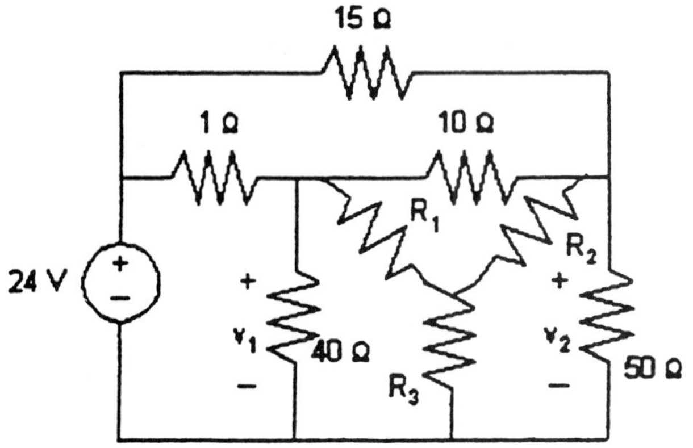

The resistance seen by the 24 V source is

$$= (15+5)\|(4+1)+20 = 20\|5+20 = 4+20 = 24\,\Omega$$

$$= 24/24 = 1 \text{ A}$$

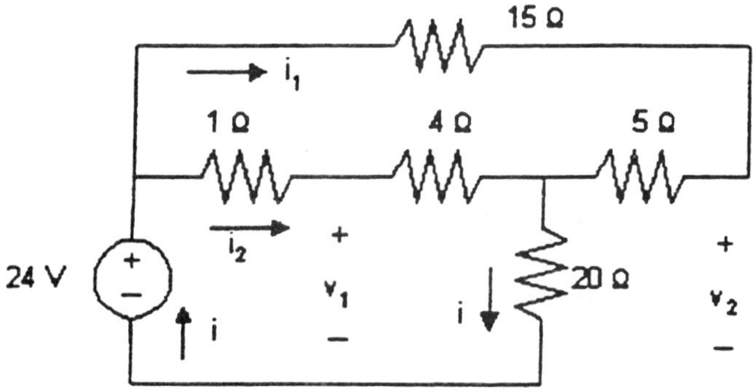

$$i_1 = (5/25)i = 0.2 \text{ A}, \qquad i_2 = 1 - 0.2 = 0.8 \text{ A}$$

$$v_1 = 4i_2 + 20i + 3.2 + 20 = 23.2 \text{ V}$$

$$v_2 = 5i_1 + 20i = 1.0 + 20 = 21.0 \text{ V}$$

P 3.49 In order that all four decades (1, 10, 100, 1000) that are used to set R_3 contribute to the balance of the bridge, the ratio R_2/R_1 should be set to 0.001.

P 3.50 [a] $$R_X = \frac{(20)(50)}{100} = 10\,\Omega; \qquad R_Y = \frac{(30)(20)}{100} = 6\,\Omega;$$

$$R_Z = \frac{(50)(30)}{100} = 15\,\Omega$$

Replacing the R_2—R_3—R_4 delta with its equivalent Y gives

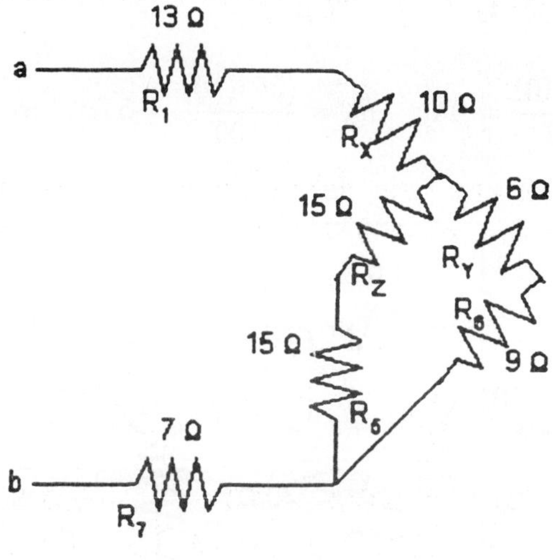

$$R_{ab} = 13 + 10 + 30\|15 + 7 = 40\,\Omega$$

[b] $R_X = \frac{(50)(30)+(50)(15)+(15)(30)}{15} = \frac{2700}{15} = 180\,\Omega$

$R_Y = \frac{2700}{50} = 54\,\Omega$

$R_Z = \frac{2700}{30} = 90\,\Omega$

Replacing the R_2, R_4, R_5 wye with its equivalent Δ gives

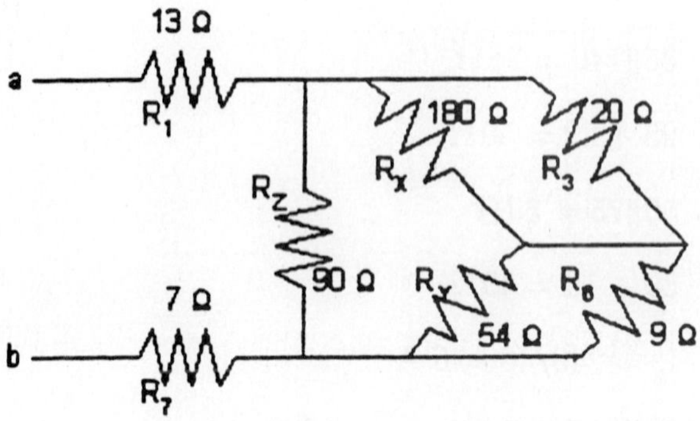

Now note that $180\|20 = 18\,\Omega$; $54\|9 = \frac{486}{63} = \frac{54}{7}\,\Omega$

$\therefore\ 180\|20 + 54\|9 = 18 + 54/7 = 180/7\,\Omega$

$\therefore\ \frac{180}{7}\|90 = \frac{(90)(180)}{7[90+(180/7)]} = 20\,\Omega$

$\therefore\ R_{ab} = 13 + 20 + 7 = 40\,\Omega$

[c] Convert the delta connection R_4—R_5—R_6 to its equivalent wye.
Convert the wye connection R_3—R_4—R_6 to its equivalent delta.

P 3.51 The top of the pyramid can be replaced by a resistor equal to

$$R_1 = \frac{(3.6)(1.8)}{5.4} = 1.2\ \text{k}\Omega$$

The lower left and right deltas can be replaced by wyes. Each resistance in the wye equals $600\,\Omega$. Thus our circuit can be reduced to

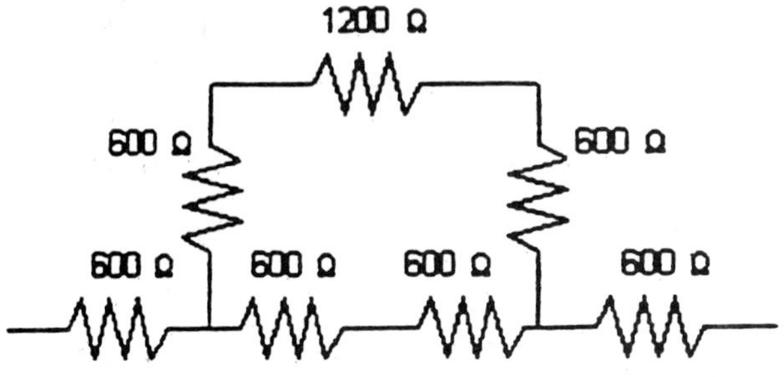

Now the 2400 Ω in parallel with 1200 Ω reduces to 800 Ω.

$$\therefore \quad R_{ab} = 600 + 800 + 600 = 2000 = 2\ \text{k}\Omega$$

P 3.52 $8 + 12 = 20\,\Omega$

$20\|60 = 15\,\Omega$

$15 + 20 = 35\,\Omega$

$35\|140 = 28\,\Omega$

$28 + 22 = 50\,\Omega$

$50\|75 = 30\,\Omega$

$30 + 10 = 40\,\Omega$

$i_g = 240/40 = 6$ A

$i_o = (6)(50)/125 = 2.4$ A

$i_{140\Omega} = (6 - 2.4)(35)/175 = 0.72$ A

$p_{30\Omega} = (0.72)^2(140) = 72.576$ W

P 3.53 Replace the upper and lower deltas with the equivalent wyes:

$$R_{1U} = \frac{(50)(10)}{100} = 5\,\Omega;\ R_{2U} = \frac{(50)(40)}{100} = 20\,\Omega;\ R_{3U} = \frac{(40)(10)}{100} = 4\,\Omega$$

$$R_{1L} = \frac{(60)(10)}{100} = 6\,\Omega;\ R_{2L} = \frac{(60)(30)}{100} = 18\,\Omega;\ R_{3L} = \frac{(30)(10)}{100} = 3\,\Omega$$

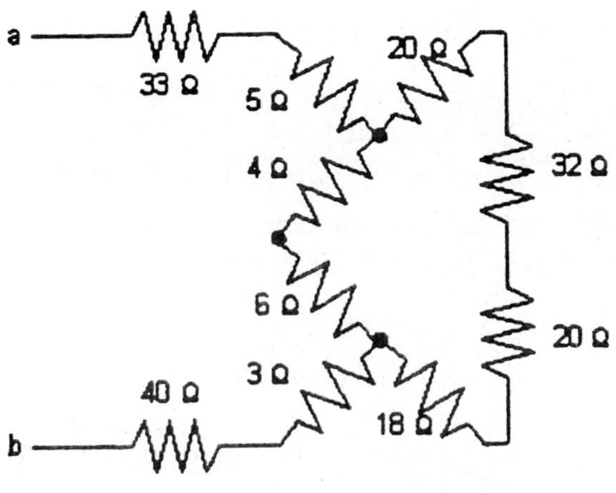

$(4 + 6)\|(20 + 32 + 20 + 18) = 10\|90 = 9\,\Omega$

$R_{ab} = 33 + 5 + 9 + 3 + 40 = 90\,\Omega$

P 3.54 [a] Convert the upper delta to a wye.

$$R_1 = \frac{(80)(200)}{400} = 40\,\Omega$$

$$R_2 = \frac{(80)(120)}{400} = 24\,\Omega$$

$$R_3 = \frac{(120)(200)}{400} = 60\,\Omega$$

Convert the lower delta to a wye.

$$R_4 = \frac{(60)(90)}{300} = 18\,\Omega$$

$$R_5 = \frac{(60)(150)}{300} = 30\,\Omega$$

$$R_6 = \frac{(90)(150)}{300} = 45\,\Omega$$

Now redraw the circuit using the wye equivalents.

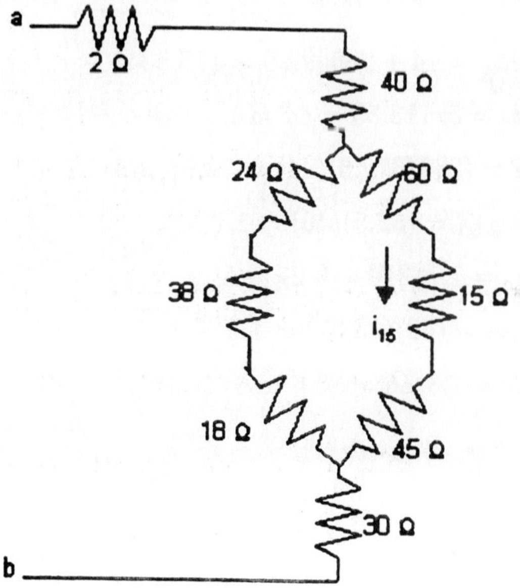

$$R_{ab} = 2 + 40 + \frac{(80)(120)}{200} + 30 = 42 + 48 + 30 = 120\,\Omega$$

[b] When $v_{ab} = 600$ V

$$i_g = \frac{600}{120} = 5 \text{ A}$$

$$i_{15} = \frac{(5)(80)}{200} = 2 \text{ A}$$

$$p_{15\Omega} = (4)(15) = 60 \text{ W}$$

P 3.55 [a] After the 20 Ω—80 Ω—40 Ω wye is replaced by its equivalent delta, the circuit reduces to

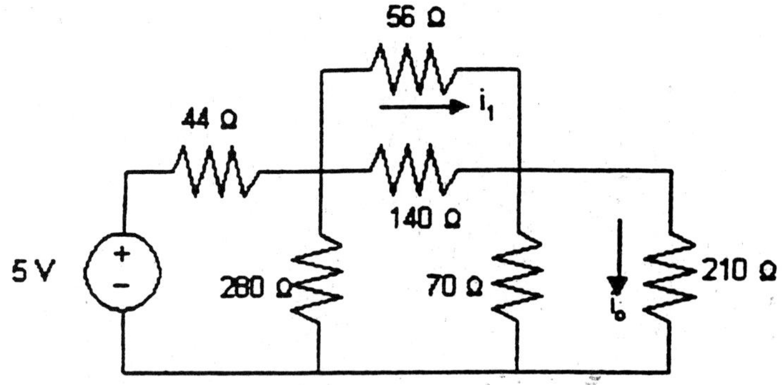

Now the circuit can be reduced to

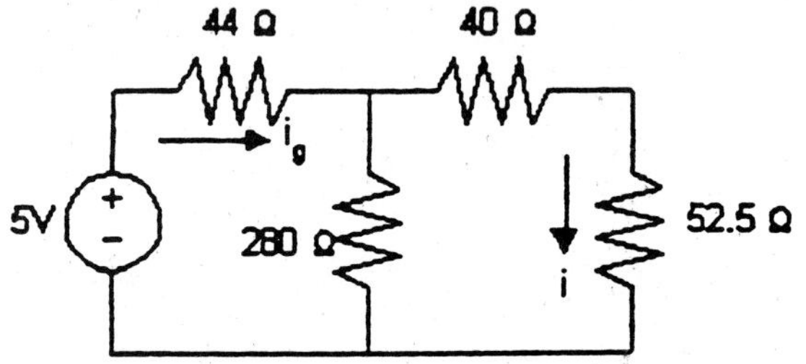

$$R_{eq} = 44 + 280\|92.5 = 113.53\,\Omega$$

$$i_g = 5/113.53 = 44 \text{ mA}$$

$$i = (280/372.5)(44) = 33.07 \text{ mA}$$

$$v_{52.5\Omega} = (52.5)(40) = 1.7 \text{ V}$$

$$i_o = 1.7/210 = 8.27 \text{ mA}$$

[b] $$v_{40\Omega} = (40)(33.07) = 1.3 \text{ V}$$

$$i_1 = 1.3/56 = 23.6 \text{ mA}$$

[c] Now that i_o and i_1 are known return to the original circuit

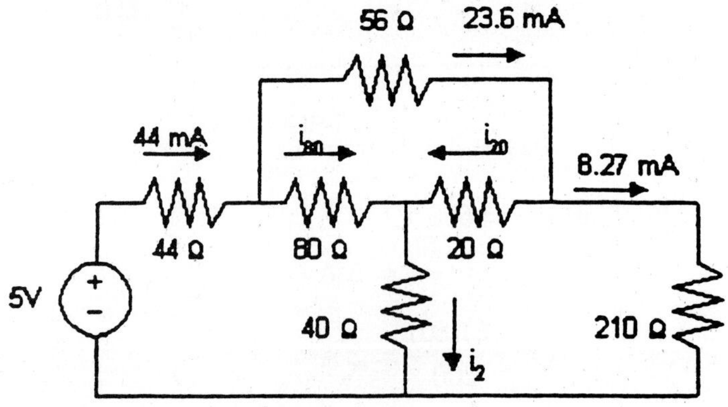

$$i_{80\Omega} = 44 - 23.6 = 20.4 \text{ mA}$$

$$i_{20\Omega} = 23.6 - 8.27 = 15.33 \text{ mA}$$

$$i_2 = i_{80\Omega} + i_{20\Omega} = 35.73 \text{ mA}$$

[d] $p_{\text{del}} = (5)(44) = 0.22$ W

P 3.56 [a] Replace the 30—60—10 Ω delta with a wye equivalent to get

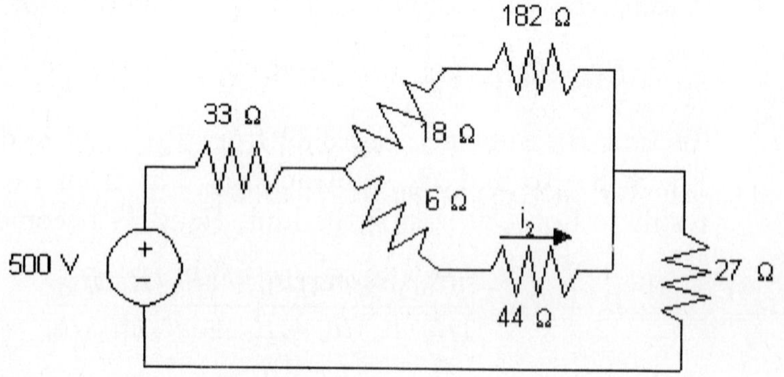

Using series/parallel reductions the circuit reduces to

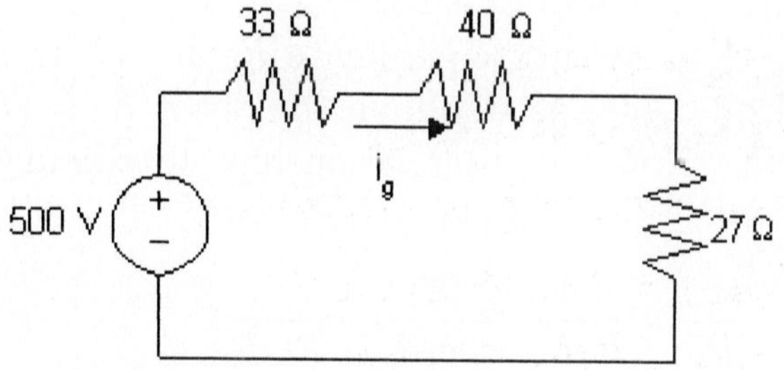

$$i_g = \frac{500}{100} = 5 \text{ A}$$

$$i_2 = \frac{200}{250}(5) = 4 \text{ A}$$

[b] $i_1 = 33/30 = 1.1$ A

Returning to the original circuit we have

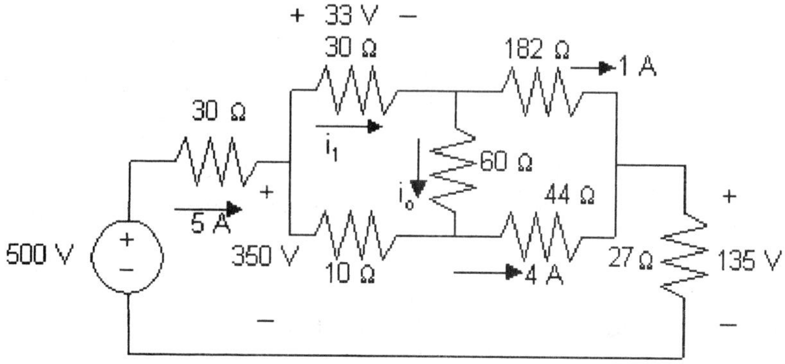

$$i_o = 1.1 - 1.0 = 0.1 \text{ A}$$

[c] $v = 60i_o = 6$ V

[d] $P_{\text{supplied}} = (500)(5.0) = 2500$ W

P 3.57 Subtracting Eq. 3.38 from Eq. 3.39 gives

$$R_1 - R_2 = (R_cR_b - R_cR_a)/(R_a + R_b + R_c).$$

Adding this expression to Eq. 3.37 and solving for R_1 gives

$$R_1 = R_cR_b/(R_a + R_b + R_c).$$

To find R_2, subtract Eq. 3.39 from Eq. 3.37 and add this result to Eq. 3.38. To find R_3, subtract Eq. 3.37 from Eq. 3.38 and add this result to Eq. 3.39. Using the hint, Eq. 3.39 becomes

$$R_1 + R_3 = \frac{R_b[(R_2/R_3)R_b + (R_2/R_1)R_b]}{(R_2/R_1)R_b + R_b + (R_2/R_3)R_b} = \frac{R_b(R_1 + R_3)R_2}{(R_1R_2 + R_2R_3 + R_3R_1)}$$

Solving for R_b gives $R_b = (R_1R_2 + R_2R_3 + R_3R_1)/R_2$. To find R_a: First use Eqs. 3.40–3.42 to obtain the ratios $(R_1/R_3) = (R_c/R_a)$ or $R_c = (R_1/R_3)R_a$ and $(R_1/R_2) = (R_b/R_a)$ or $R_b = (R_1/R_2)R_a$. Now use these relationships to eliminate R_b and R_c from Eq. 3.38. To find R_c, use Eqs. 3.40–3.42 to obtain the ratios $R_b = (R_3/R_2)R_c$ and $R_a = (R_3/R_1)R_c$. Now use the relationships to eliminate R_b and R_a from Eq. 3.37.

P 3.58
$$\begin{aligned} G_a &= \frac{1}{R_a} = \frac{R_1}{R_1R_2 + R_2R_3 + R_3R_1} \\ &= \frac{1/G_1}{(1/G_1)(1/G_2) + (1/G_2)(1/G_3) + (1/G_3)(1/G_1)} \\ &= \frac{(1/G_1)(G_1G_2G_3)}{G_1 + G_2 + G_3} = \frac{G_2G_3}{G_1 + G_2 + G_3} \end{aligned}$$

Similar manipulations generate the expressions for G_b and G_c.

P 3.59 [a]
$$R_{ab} = 2R_1 + \frac{R_2(2R_1 + R_L)}{2R_1 + R_2 + R_L} = R_L$$

Therefore $2R_1 - R_L + \dfrac{R_2(2R_1 + R_L)}{2R_1 + R_2 + R_L} = 0$

Thus $R_L^2 = 4R_1^2 + 4R_1R_2 = 4R_1(R_1 + R_2)$

When $R_{ab} = R_L$, the current into terminal a of the attenuator will be v_i/R_L

Using current division, the current in the R_L branch will be

$$\frac{v_i}{R_L} \cdot \frac{R_2}{2R_1 + R_2 + R_L}$$

Therefore $v_o = \dfrac{v_i}{R_L} \cdot \dfrac{R_2}{2R_1 + R_2 + R_L} R_L$ and $\dfrac{v_o}{v_i} = \dfrac{R_2}{2R_1 + R_2 + R_L}$

[b] $$(600)^2 = 4(R_1 + R_2)R_1$$

$$9 \times 10^4 = R_1^2 + R_1R_2$$

$$\frac{v_o}{v_i} = 0.6 = \frac{R_2}{2R_1 + R_2 + 600}$$

$$tdot1.2R_1 + 0.6R_2 + 360 = R_2$$

$$0.4R_2 = 1.2R_1 + 360$$

$$R_2 = 3R_1 + 900$$

$$\therefore \quad 9 \times 10^4 = R_1^2 + R_1(3R_1 + 900) = 4R_1^2 + 900R_1$$

$$\therefore \quad R_1^2 + 225R_1 - 22{,}500 = 0$$

$$R_1 = -112.5 \pm \sqrt{(112.5)^2 + 22{,}500} = -112.5 \pm 187.5$$

$$\therefore \quad R_1 = 75\,\Omega$$

$$\therefore \quad R_2 = 3(75) + 900 = 1125\,\Omega$$

P 3.60 [a] After making the Y-to-Δ transformation, the circuit reduces to

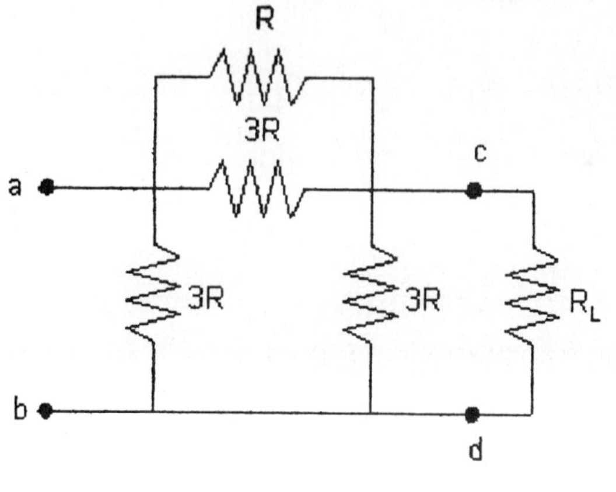

Combining the parallel resistors reduces the circuit to

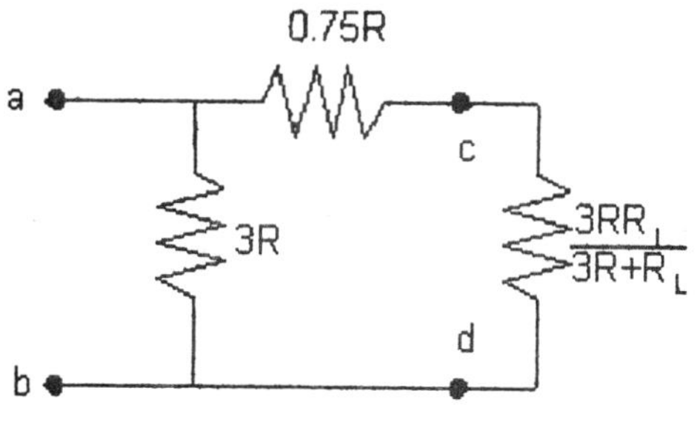

Now note: $$0.75R + \frac{3RR_L}{3R + R_L} = \frac{2.25R_L^2 + 3.75RR_L}{3R + R_L}$$

$$\text{Therefore} \quad R_{ab} = \frac{3R\left(\dfrac{2.25R_L^2 + 3.75RR_L}{3R + R_L}\right)}{3R + \left(\dfrac{2.25R_L^2 + 3.75RR_L}{3R + R_L}\right)} = \frac{3R(3R + 5R_L)}{15R + 9R_L}$$

When $R_{ab} = R_L$, we have $\quad 15RR_L + 9R_L^2 = 9R^2 + 15RR_L$

Therefore $\quad R_L^2 = R^2 \quad$ or $\quad R_L = R$

[b] When $R = R_L$, the circuit reduces to

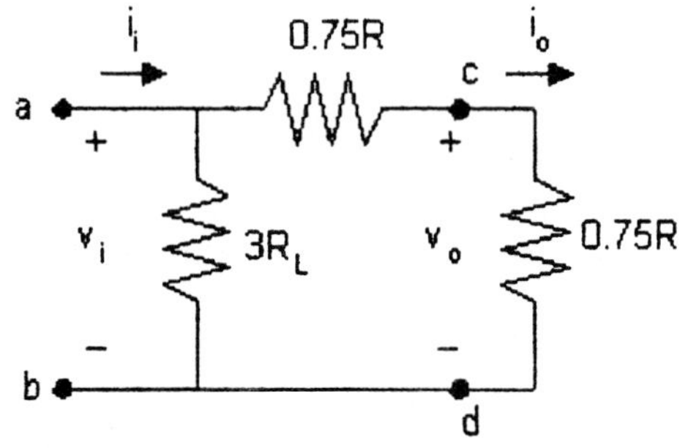

$$i_o = \frac{i(3R_L)}{4.5R_L} = \frac{1}{1.5}i = \frac{1}{1.5}\frac{v_i}{R_L}, \qquad v_o = 0.75R_L i_o = \frac{1}{2}v_i,$$

Therefore $\quad \dfrac{v_o}{v_i} = 0.5$

P 3.61 [a]

$$3(3R - R_L) = 3R + R_L$$

$$9R - 1800 = 3R + 600$$

$$6R = 2400, \qquad R = 400\,\Omega$$

$$R_2 = \frac{2(400)(600)^2}{3(400)^2 - (600)^2} = 2400\,\Omega$$

[b]

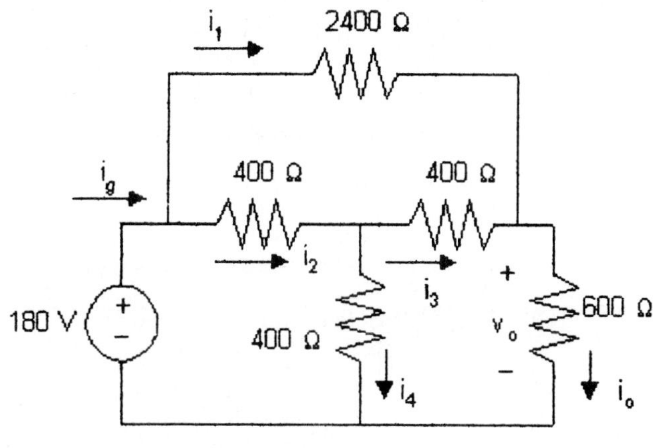

$$v_o = \frac{v_i}{3} = \frac{180}{3} = 60 \text{ V}$$

$$i_o = \frac{60}{600} = 100 \text{ mA}$$

$$i_1 = \frac{180 - 60}{2400} = \frac{120}{2400} = 50 \text{ mA}$$

$$i_g = \frac{180}{600} = 300 \text{ mA}$$

$$i_2 = 300 - 50 = 250 \text{ mA}$$

$$i_3 = 100 - 50 = 50 \text{ mA}$$

$$i_4 = 250 - 50 = 200 \text{ mA}$$

$$p_{2400 \text{ top}} = (50 \times 10^{-3})^2(2400) = 6 \text{ W}$$

$$p_{400 \text{ left}} = (250 \times 10^{-3})^2(400) = 25 \text{ W}$$

$$p_{400 \text{ right}} = (50 \times 10^{-3})^2(400) = 1 \text{ W}$$

$$p_{400 \text{ vertical}} = (200 \times 10^{-3})^2(400) = 16 \text{ W}$$

$$p_{600 \text{ load}} = (100 \times 10^{-3})^2(600) = 6 \text{ W}$$

The 400 Ω resistor carrying i_2

[c] $p_{400 \text{ left}} = 25$ W

[d] The 400 Ω resistor carrying i_3

[e] $p_{400 \text{ right}} = 1$ W

P 3.62 [a]

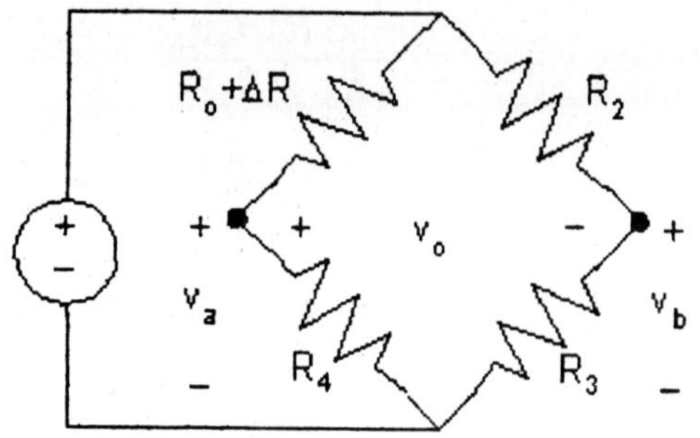

$$v_a = \frac{v_{\text{in}} R_4}{R_o + R_4 + \Delta R}$$

$$v_b = \frac{R_3}{R_2 + R_3} v_{\text{in}}$$

$$v_o = v_a - v_b = \frac{R_4 v_{\text{in}}}{R_o + R_4 + \Delta R} - \frac{R_3}{R_2 + R_3} v_{\text{in}}$$

When the bridge is balanced,

$$\frac{R_4}{R_o + R_4} v_{\rm in} = \frac{R_3}{R_2 + R_3} v_{\rm in}$$

$$\therefore \quad \frac{R_4}{R_o + R_4} = \frac{R_3}{R_2 + R_3}$$

Thus,

$$\begin{aligned} v_o &= \frac{R_4 v_{\rm in}}{R_o + R_4 + \Delta R} - \frac{R_4 v_{\rm in}}{R_o + R_4} \\ &= R_4 v_{\rm in}\left[\frac{1}{R_o + R_4 + \Delta R} - \frac{1}{R_o + R_4}\right] \\ &= \frac{R_4 v_{\rm in}(-\Delta R)}{(R_o + R_4 + \Delta R)(R_o + R_4)} \\ &\approx \frac{-(\Delta R) R_4 v_{\rm in}}{(R_o + R_4)^2} \end{aligned}$$

[b] $\Delta R = 0.03 R_o$

$$R_o = \frac{R_2 R_4}{R_3} = \frac{(1000)(5000)}{500} = 10{,}000\,\Omega$$

$$\Delta R = (0.03)(10^4) = 300\,\Omega$$

$$\therefore \quad v_o \approx \frac{-300(5000)(6)}{(15{,}000)^2} \approx= 40 \text{ mV}$$

[c]

$$\begin{aligned} v_o &= \frac{-(\Delta R) R_4 v_{\rm in}}{(R_o + R_4 + \Delta R)(R_o + R_4)} \\ &= \frac{-300(5000)(6)}{(15{,}300)(15{,}000)} \\ &= -39.2157 \text{ mV} \end{aligned}$$

P 3.63 [a]

$$\text{approx value} = \frac{-(\Delta R) R_4 v_{\rm in}}{(R_o + R_4)^2}$$

$$\text{true value} = \frac{-(\Delta R) R_4 v_{\rm in}}{(R_o + R_4 + \Delta R)(R_o + R_4)}$$

$$\therefore \quad \frac{\text{approx value}}{\text{true value}} = \frac{(R_o + R_4 + \Delta R)}{(R_o + R_4)}$$

$$\therefore \quad \%\text{ error} = \left[\frac{R_o + R_4 + \Delta R}{R_o + R_4} - 1\right] \times 100 = \frac{\Delta R}{R_o + R_4} \times 100$$

But $R_o = \dfrac{R_2 R_4}{R_3}$

$$\therefore \quad \%\text{ error} = \frac{R_3 \Delta R}{R_4(R_2 + R_3)}$$

[b] $$\% \text{ error } = \frac{(500)(300)}{(5000)(1500)} \times 100 = 2\%$$

P 3.64 $$\frac{\Delta R(R_3)(100)}{(R_2 + R_3)R_4} = 0.5$$

$$\frac{\Delta R(500)(100)}{(1500)(5000)} = 0.5$$

$$\therefore \quad \Delta R = 75\,\Omega$$

$$\% \text{ change } = \frac{75}{10{,}000} \times 100 = 0.75\%$$

P 3.65 [a] From Eq 3.60 we have

$$\left(\frac{i_1}{i_2}\right)^2 = \frac{R_2^2}{R_1^2(1+2\sigma)^2}$$

Substituting into Eq 3.59 yields

$$R_2 = \frac{R_2^2}{R_1^2(1+2\sigma)^2} R_1$$

Solving for R_2 yields

$$R_2 = (1+2\sigma)^2 R_1$$

[b] From Eq 3.63 we have

$$\frac{i_1}{i_b} = \frac{R_2}{R_1 + R_2 + 2R_a}$$

But $R_2 = (1+2\sigma)^2 R_1$ and $R_a = \sigma R_1$ therefore

$$\frac{i_1}{i_b} = \frac{(1+2\sigma)^2 R_1}{R_1 + (1+2\sigma)^2 R_1 + 2\sigma R_1} = \frac{(1+2\sigma)^2}{(1+2\sigma) + (1+2\sigma)^2} = \frac{1+2\sigma}{2(1+\sigma)}$$

It follows that

$$\left(\frac{i_1}{i_b}\right)^2 = \frac{(1+2\sigma)^2}{4(1+\sigma)^2}$$

Substituting into Eq 3.62 gives

$$R_b = \frac{(1+2\sigma)^2 R_a}{4(1+\sigma)^2} = \frac{(1+2\sigma)^2 \sigma R_1}{4(1+\sigma)^2}$$

P 3.66 From Eq 3.65

$$\frac{i_1}{i_3} = \frac{R_2 R_3}{D}$$

But $D = (R_1 + 2R_a)(R_2 + 2R_b) + 2R_bR_2$

$$\text{where } R_a = \sigma R_1; R_2 = (1+2\sigma)^2 R_1 \text{ and } R_b = \frac{(1+2\sigma)^2\sigma R_1}{4(1+\sigma)^2}$$

Therefore D can be written as

$$\begin{aligned}
D &= (R_1 + 2\sigma R_1)\left[(1+2\sigma)^2 R_1 + \frac{2(1+2\sigma)^2\sigma R_1}{4(1+\sigma)^2}\right] + \\
&\quad 2(1+2\sigma)^2 R_1\left[\frac{(1+2\sigma)^2\sigma R_1}{4(1+\sigma)^2}\right] \\
&= (1+2\sigma)^3 R_1^2\left[1 + \frac{\sigma}{2(1+\sigma)^2} + \frac{(1+2\sigma)\sigma}{2(1+\sigma)^2}\right] \\
&= \frac{(1+2\sigma)^3 R_1^2}{2(1+\sigma)^2}\{2(1+\sigma)^2 + \sigma + (1+2\sigma)\sigma\} \\
&= \frac{(1+2\sigma)^3 R_1^2}{(1+\sigma)^2}\{1 + 3\sigma + 2\sigma^2\}
\end{aligned}$$

$$D = \frac{(1+2\sigma)^4 R_1^2}{(1+\sigma)}$$

$$\begin{aligned}
\therefore \frac{i_1}{i_3} &= \frac{R_2R_3(1+\sigma)}{(1+2\sigma)^4 R_1^2} \\
&= \frac{(1+2\sigma)^2 R_1 R_3(1+\sigma)}{(1+2\sigma)^4 R_1^2} \\
&= \frac{(1+\sigma)R_3}{(1+2\sigma)^2 R_1}
\end{aligned}$$

When this result is substituted into Eq 3.65 we get

$$R_3 = \frac{(1+\sigma)^2 R_3^2 R_1}{(1+2\sigma)^4 R_1^2}$$

Solving for R_3 gives

$$R_3 = \frac{(1+2\sigma)^4 R_1}{(1+\sigma)^2}$$

P 3.67 From the solution to the rear-window defroster problem we have $i_b = 21$ A and $i_3 = 10$ A. By symmetry $i_c = 21$ A thus the total current supplied by the 12 V source is $21 + 21 + 10$ or 52 A. Therefore the total power delivered by the source is p_{12V} (del) $= (12)(52) = 624$ W. We also have from the solution that $p_a = p_b = p_c = p_d = 3$ W. Therefore the total power delivered to the vertical resistors is $p_V = (8)(3) = 24$ W. The total power delivered to the five horizontal resistors is $p_H = 5(120) =$ 600 W.

$$\therefore \sum p_{diss} = p_H + p_V = 624 \text{ W} = \sum p_{del}$$

P 3.68 [a] $\sigma = 0.05/1.25 = 0.04$

Since the power dissipation is 150 W/m the power dissipated in R_3 must be 150(1.25) or 187.5 W. Therefore

$$R_3 = \frac{12^2}{187.5} = 0.768\,\Omega$$

From Table 3.1 we have

$$R_1 = \frac{(1+\sigma)^2 R_3}{(1+2\sigma)^4} = 0.6106\,\Omega$$

$$R_a = \sigma R_1 = 0.0244\,\Omega$$

$$R_2 = (1+2\sigma)^2 R_1 = 0.7122\,\Omega$$

$$R_b = \frac{(1+2\sigma)^2 \sigma R_1}{4(1+\sigma)^2} = 0.0066\,\Omega$$

Therefore

$$R_4 = R_2 = 0.7122\,\Omega \qquad R_5 = R_1 = 0.6106\,\Omega$$

$$R_c = R_b = 0.0066\,\Omega \qquad R_d = R_a = 0.0244\,\Omega$$

[b] $D = 0.4877$

$$i_1 = \frac{V_{dc} R_2}{D} = 17.52 \text{ A}$$

$$i_1^2 R_1 = 187.5 \text{ W or } 150 \text{ W/m}$$

$$i_2 = \frac{R_1 + 2R_a}{D} V_{dc} = 16.23 \text{ A}$$

$$i_2^2 R_2 = 187.5 \text{ W or } 150 \text{ W/m}$$

$$i_1^2 R_a = 7.5 \text{ W or } 150 \text{ W/m}$$

$$i_b = \frac{R_1 + R_2 + 2R_a}{D} V_{dc} = 33.75 \text{ A}$$

$$i_b^2 R_b = 7.5 \text{ W or } 150 \text{ W/m}$$

$$i_{\text{source}} = 33.75 + 33.75 + \frac{12}{0.768} = 83.125 \text{ A}$$

$$p_{\text{del}} = 12(83.125) = 997.50 \text{ W}$$

$$p_H = 5(187.5) = 937.5 \text{ W}$$

$$p_V = 8(7.5) = 60 \text{ W}$$

$$\sum p_{\text{del}} = \sum p_{\text{diss}} = 997.50 \text{ W}$$

4

Techniques of Circuit Analysis

Drill Exercises

DE 4.1 [a] 11,8 resistors, 2 independent sources, 1 dependent source

[b] 9

[c] 9, $R_4 - R_5$ forms an essential branch as does $R_8 - 10$ V. The remaining seven branches contain a single element.

[d] 7 [e] 6 [f] 4 [g] 6

DE 4.2 Solution given in text.

DE 4.3 Solution given in text.

DE 4.4 Solution given in text.

DE 4.5 [a] The two node voltage equations are

$$-15 + \frac{v_1}{60} + \frac{v_1}{15} + \frac{v_1 - v_2}{5} = 0$$

$$5 + \frac{v_2}{2} + \frac{v_2 - v_1}{5} = 0$$

Solving, $v_1 = 60$ V and $v_2 = 10$ V;
Therefore, $i_1 = (v_1 - v_2)/5 = 10$ A

[b] p_{15A} (del) $= (-15)(60) = 900$ W

[c] $p_{5A} = 5(10) = 50$ W

DE 4.6 Use the lower node as the reference node. Let v_1 = node voltage across 1 Ω resistor and v_2 = node voltage across 12 Ω resistor. Then

$$\frac{v_1}{1} + \frac{v_1 - v_2}{8} = 4.5$$

$$\frac{v_2}{12} + \frac{v_2 - -v_1}{8} + \frac{v_2 - 30}{4} = 0$$

Solving, $v_1 = 6$ V $\quad v_2 = 18$ V Thus, $i = (v_1 - v_2)/8 = -1.5$ A
$v = v_2 + 2i = 15$ V

DE 4.7 Use the lower node as the reference node. Let v_1 = node voltage across the 8 Ω resistor, let v_2 = node voltage across the 4 Ω resistor. Then

$$\frac{v_1 - 50}{6} + \frac{v_1}{8} + \frac{v_1 - v_2}{2} - 3i_1 = 0$$

$$-5 + \frac{v_2}{4} + \frac{v_2 - v_1}{2} + 3i_1 = 0$$

$$i_1 = \frac{50 - v_1}{6}$$

Solving, $v_1 = 32$ V; $\quad v_2 = 16$ V; $\quad i_1 = 3$ A
$p_{50\text{V}} = -50i_1 = -150$ W (delivering)
$p_{5\text{A}} = -5(v_2) = -80$ W (delivering)
$p_{3i_1} = 3i_1(v_2 - v_1) = -144$ W (delivering)

DE 4.8 Use the lower node as the reference node. Let v_1 = node voltage across the 7.5 Ω resistor and v_2 = node voltage across the 2.5 Ω resistor. Place the dependent voltage source inside a supernode between the node voltages v and v_2. The node voltage equations are

$$\text{node 1:} \quad \frac{v_1}{7.5} + \frac{v_1 - v}{2.5} = 4.8$$

$$\text{supernode:} \quad \frac{v - v_1}{2.5} + \frac{v}{10} + \frac{v_2}{2.5} + \frac{v_2 - 12}{1} = 0$$

We also have: $v + i_x = v_2$ and $i_x = v_1/7.5$. Solving this set of equations for v gives $v = 8$ V

DE 4.9 $$\frac{v_1 - 60}{2} + \frac{v_1}{24} + \frac{v_1 - (60 + 6i_\phi)}{3} = 0, \qquad i_\phi = \frac{60 + 6i_\phi - v_1}{3}$$

Therefore $\quad v_1 = 48$ V

DE 4.10

$$\frac{v_o}{40} + \frac{v_o - 10}{10} + \frac{v_o + 20i_\Delta}{20} = 0, \qquad i_\Delta = \frac{10 - v_o}{10} + \frac{10 + 20i_\Delta}{30}$$

Therefore $\quad v_o = 24$ V

DE 4.11 Define three clockwise mesh currents i_1, i_2 And i_3 in the lower left, upper, and lower right windows. The three mesh-current equations are

$$80 = 31i_1 - 5i_2 - 26i_3$$
$$0 = -5i_1 + 125i_2 - 90i_3$$
$$0 = -26i_1 - 90i_2 + 124i_3$$

[a] Solving, $i_1 = 5$ A; therefore the 80 V source is delivering 400 W to the circuit.

[b] Solving, $i_3 = 2.5$ A; therefore $p_{8\Omega} = (6.25)(8) = 50$ W

DE 4.12 [a] $b = 8,\quad n = 6,\quad b - n + 1 = 3$

[b] Define three clockwise mesh currents i_1, i_2 And i_3 in the upper, lower left, and lower right windows. The three mesh-current equations are

$$-(-3v_\phi) + 19i_1 - 2i_2 - 3i_3 = 0$$
$$25 - 10 = -2i_1 + 7i_2 - 5i_3$$
$$10 = -3i_1 - 5i_2 + 9i_3$$

We also have $v_\phi = 3(i_3 - i_1)$
Solving for i_1 and i_3 gives $i_1 = -1$ A, $i_3 = 3$ A
Therefore $v_\phi = 12$ V and $p_{3v_\phi} = -(-3v_\phi)i_1 = -36$ W

DE 4.13 Let i_a = lower left mesh current cw, let i_b = upper mesh current cw, and i_c = lower right mesh current cw. Then

$$25 = 14i_a - 6i_b - 8i_c$$
$$0 = -6i_a + 16i_b - 8i_c$$
$$0 = -8i_a - 8i_b + 16i_c + 5i_\phi$$
$$i_\phi = i_a, \quad i_a = 4 \text{ A}, \quad i_c = 2A$$
$$v_o = 8(i_a - i_c) = 16 \text{ V}$$

DE 4.14 Define two mesh currents i_1 and i_2 (clockwise) in the left and center windows of the circuit. Then $30 = 11i_1 - 2i_2$ and $0 = -2i_1 + 19i_2 - 5(-16)$. Solving for i_1 and i_2 gives $i_1 = 2$ A and $i_2 = -4$ A. The current in the 2 Ω resistor is $i_1 - i_2 = 6$ A, therefore $p_{2\Omega} = (6)^2(2) = 72$ W.

DE 4.15 $$75 = (i_a + 10)2 + 5\left(i_a - 2v_\phi/5\right),$$

$$v_\phi = 5\left(i_a - 2v_\phi/5\right)$$

Therefore $v_\phi = \frac{5}{3}i_a, \quad i_a = 15$ A.

DE 4.16

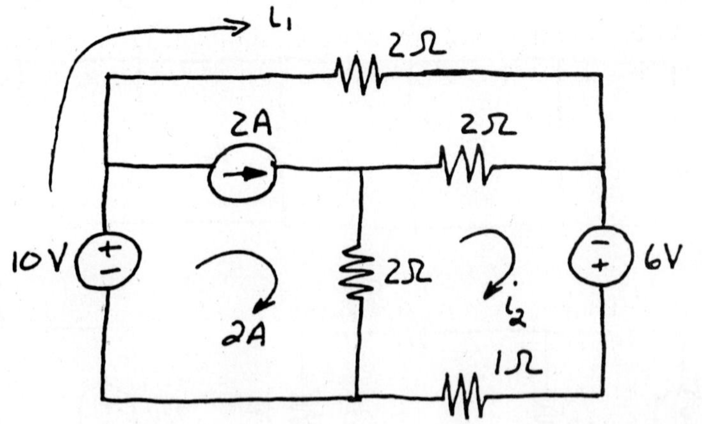

$$-10 + 2i_1 - 6 + 1(i_1 + i_2) = 0 \qquad \text{or} \qquad 3i_1 + i_2 = 16$$

$$2(i_2 - 2) + 2i_2 - 6 + 1(i_1 + i_2) = 0 \qquad \text{or } i_1 + 5i_2 = 10$$

Solving, $i_1 = 5$ A and $i_2 = 1$ A
Thus, $p_{1\Omega} = (i_1 + i_2)^2(1) = 36$ W

DE 4.17 Let v_1 denote the voltage across the 2 A source. Let v_1 be a voltage rise in the direction of the 2 A current.

$$\frac{v_1 - 20}{15} - 2 + \frac{v_1 - 25}{10} = 0, \qquad v_1 = 35 \text{ V}$$

$$p_{2A} = -35(2) = -70 \text{ W} \qquad p_{2A}(\text{del}) = 70 \text{ W}$$

DE 4.18 Define two clockwise mesh currents i_1 and i_2 in the lower left and lower right windows. The two mesh equations are $128 = 12i_1 - 6i_2 - 4(4)$ and $0 = -6i_1 + 14i_2 - 3(4) + 30(i_1 - 4)$. The solutions for i_1 and i_2 are $i_1 = 9$ A and $i_2 = -6$ A. The voltage drop across the 4 A source in the direction of the source current is $v_{4A} = 4(i_1 - 4) + 3(i_2 - 4) = 20 - 30 = -10$ V, therefore $p_{4A} = 4(-10) = -40$ W, therefore $p_{4A}(\text{del}) = 40$ W.

DE 4.19

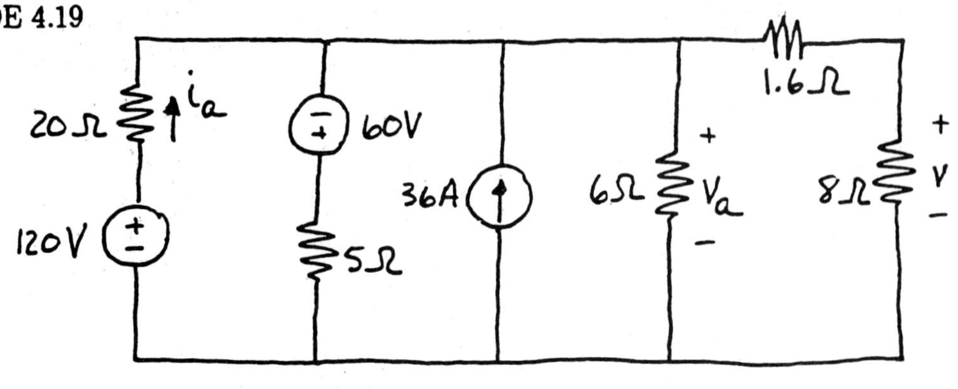

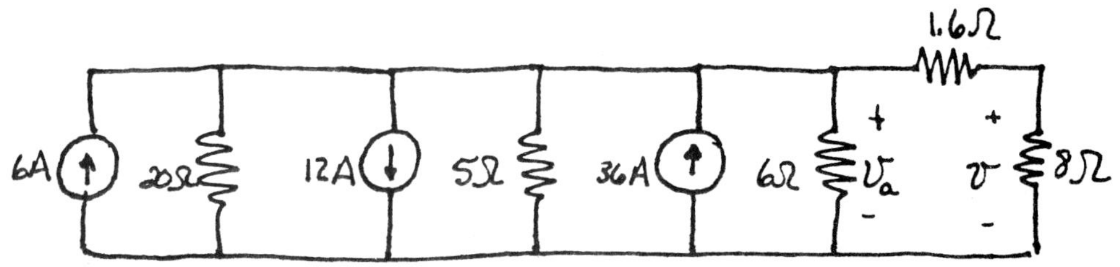

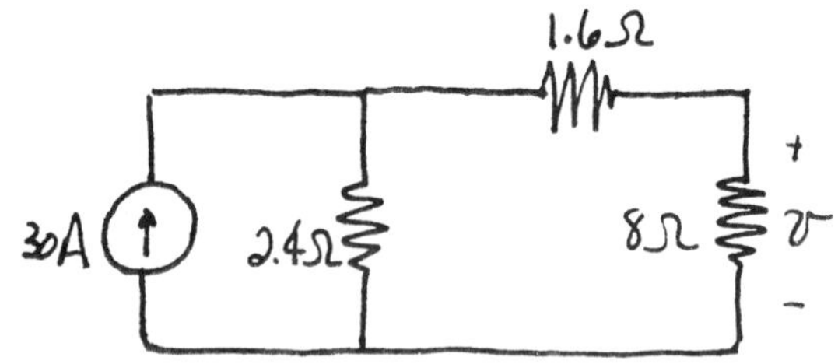

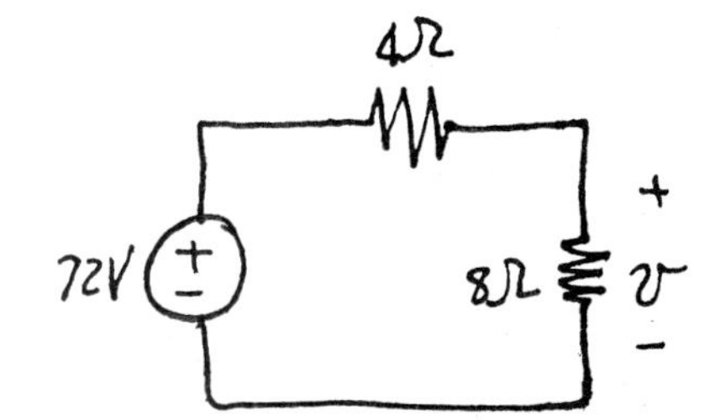

[a] $v = \frac{72}{12}(8) = 48$ V, $\quad i_a = \frac{120 - 57.6}{20} = 3.12$ A

[b] $v_a = 6(9.6) = 57.6$ V, $\quad p_{120V}(\text{del}) = 120i_a = 374.40$

DE 4.20 To find the Thévenin resistance, deactivate the independent voltage source and note that $R_{Th} = 8\|(12 + 10\|15) = 8\|24 = 6\,\Omega$. With the terminals a, b open, the current delivered by the 72 V source is 72/24 or 3 A. The current (left-to-right) in the 5 Ω resistor is (20/25)(3) = 2.4 A, and the current (left-to-right) in the 12 Ω resistor is (5/25)3 or 0.6 A. The Thévenin voltage $v_{Th} = v_{ab}$ is the drop across the 8 Ω resistor plus the drop across the 20 Ω resistor. Thus $v_{Th} = (8)(0.6) + (20)(3) = 64.8$ V.

DE 4.21 After one source transformation, the circuit becomes

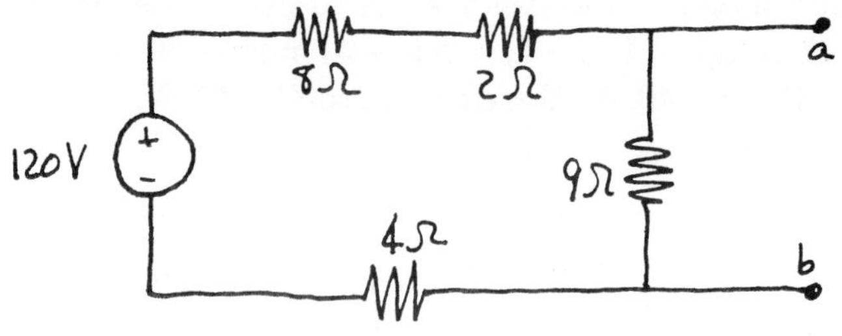

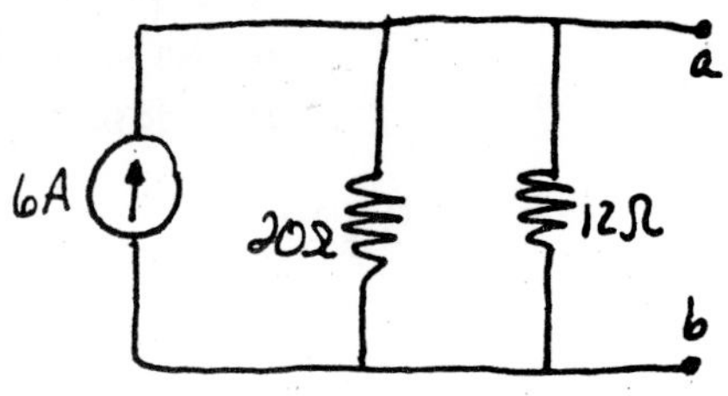

Therefore $I_N = 6$ A, $\quad R_N = 20\|12 = 7.5\,\Omega$

DE 4.22 Find the Thévenin equivalent with respect to A, B.

$$\frac{V_{Th} + 36}{12} + \frac{V_{Th}}{60} - 18 = 0, \qquad V_{Th} = 150 \text{ V}$$

$$R_{Th} = 15 + \frac{(60)(12)}{72} = 25 \text{ k}\Omega;$$

$$\text{Therefore, } v_{\text{meas}} = \frac{150}{125}(100) = 120 \text{ V}$$

DE 4.23 Summing the currents away from node a, where $v_{\text{Th}} = v_{ab}$ We have

$$\frac{v_{\text{Th}}}{8} + 4 + 3i_x + \frac{v_{\text{Th}} - 24}{2} = 0, \qquad i_x = \frac{v_{\text{Th}}}{8}$$

Solving for v_{Th} yields $v_{\text{Th}} = 8$ V

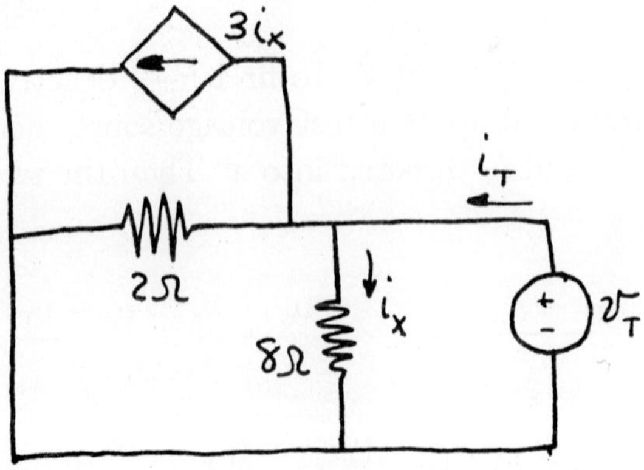

$$i_{\text{T}} = 4i_x + v_{\text{T}}/2, \qquad i_x = v_{\text{T}}/8$$

Therefore $\quad i_{\text{T}} = v_{\text{T}} \quad$ and $\quad R_{\text{Th}} = v_{\text{T}}/i_{\text{T}} = 1\,\Omega$

DE 4.24 Use the bottom node as the reference. Let v_1 be the node voltage across the 60 Ω resistor. Then

$$\frac{v_1}{60} + \frac{v_1 - (v_{\text{Th}} + 160i_\Delta)}{20} - 4 = 0,$$

$$\frac{v_{\text{Th}}}{40} + \frac{v_{\text{Th}}}{80} + \frac{v_{\text{Th}} + 160i_\Delta - v_1}{20} = 0$$

$$i_\Delta = \frac{v_{\text{Th}}}{40}, \quad \text{therefore} \quad v_{\text{Th}} = 30 \text{ V}$$

Let i_{T} be the test current into terminal a:

$$i_{\text{T}} = \frac{v_{\text{T}}}{80} + \frac{v_{\text{T}}}{40} + \frac{v_{\text{T}} + 160(v_{\text{T}}/40)}{80}, \qquad \frac{i_{\text{T}}}{v_{\text{T}}} = \frac{1}{10}$$

Therefore, $R_{\text{Th}} = 10\,\Omega$

DE 4.25 First find the Thévenin equivalent circuit. To find v_{Th}, use the bottom node as the reference. Let $v_{Th} = v_{ab}$ and v_1 = node voltage across the 20 V – 4 Ω branch. The two node Voltage equations are

$$\frac{v_{Th} - 100 - v_\phi}{4} + \frac{v_{Th} - v_1}{4} = 0, \qquad (v_\phi = v_1 - 20)$$

$$\frac{v_1 - 100}{4} + \frac{v_1 - 20}{4} + \frac{v_1 - v_{Th}}{4} = 0$$

Solving for v_{Th} gives $v_{Th} = 120$ V. To find R_{Th}, deactivate the two independent sources and apply a test voltage source across a, b. Let v_T be positive at a and i_T directed into a. Then the two node Voltage equations are

$$\frac{v_T - v_\phi}{4} + \frac{v_{Th} - v_\phi}{4} = i_T, \qquad \frac{v_\phi}{4} + \frac{v_\phi}{4} + \frac{v_\phi - v_T}{4} = 0$$

Therefore $v_\phi = v_T/3$ and $12i_T = 4v_T$
So $R_{Th} = v_T/i_T = 3\,\Omega$

[a] For maximum power transfer, $R_L = R_{Th} = 3\,\Omega$

[b] $p_{max} = (120/6)^2(3) = 1200$ W

DE 4.26 When $R_L = 3\,\Omega$, the voltage across R_L is 60 V. As before, let v_1 be the node voltage across the 20 V—4 Ω branch, then $v_\phi = v_1 - 20$ and

$$\frac{60}{3} + \frac{60 - v_1}{4} + \frac{60 - 100 - v_\phi}{4} = 0$$

Therefore $v_1 = 60$ V and $v_\phi = 40$ V. The current out of the plus terminal of the 100 V source is

$$i_1 = \frac{100 - 60}{4} + \frac{100 + 40 - 60}{4} = 10 + 20 = 30 \text{ A}$$

[a] Therefore 100 V is delivering 3000 W to the circuit.

[b] The current out of the plus terminal of the dependent source is 20 A. Therefore the dependent source is delivering 800 W to the circuit.

[c] The load power is (1200/3800)100 or 31.58% of this generated power.

DE 4.27 110 V source acting alone:

$$\frac{v'}{10} + \frac{v' - 110}{5} + \frac{v'}{14} = 0, \qquad v' = \frac{1540}{26}\ \text{V}$$

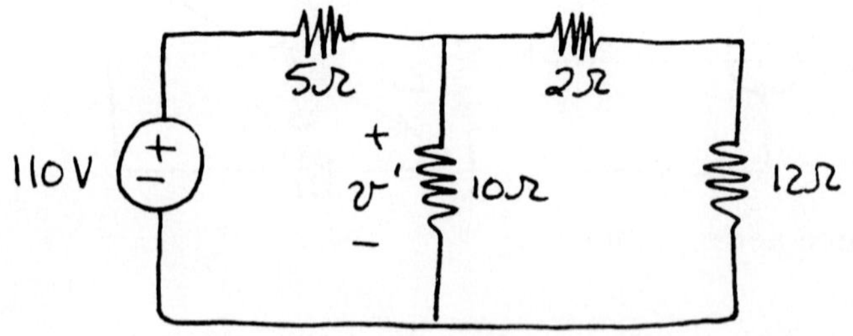

4 A source acting alone:

$$15i_1 - 10i_2 + 20 = 0$$

$$-10i_1 + 24i_2 + 8 = 0$$

Solving, $i_1 = -56/26$ A; $i_2 = -32/26$ A;
so $v'' = 10(i_1 - i_2) = -240/26$ V

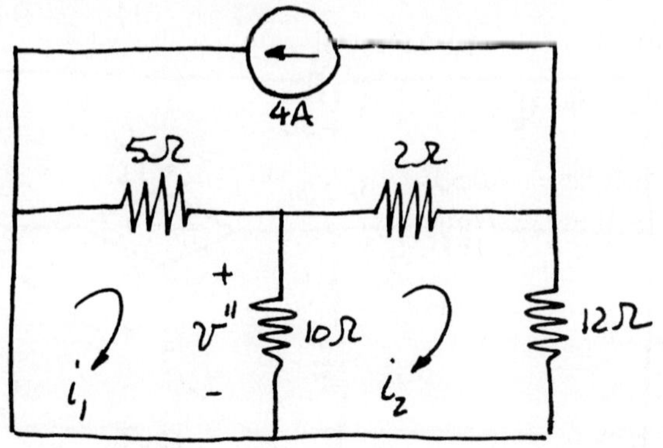

[a] $v = v' + v'' = 1540/26 - 240/26 = 1300/26 = 50$ V

[b] $p_{10\Omega} = \dfrac{(50)^2}{10} = 250$ W

DE 4.28 70 V source acting alone:

$$\frac{v' - 70}{4} + \frac{v'}{10} + \frac{v' - 2i_b'}{2} + \frac{v' - 2i_b' - 70}{20} = 0, \quad \therefore \quad 18v' - 22i_b' = 420$$

$$i_b = \frac{70 - v'}{4}$$

Combining, $18v' - 22\left(\dfrac{70 - v'}{4}\right) = 420 \quad \therefore \quad v' = \dfrac{3220}{94}$ V

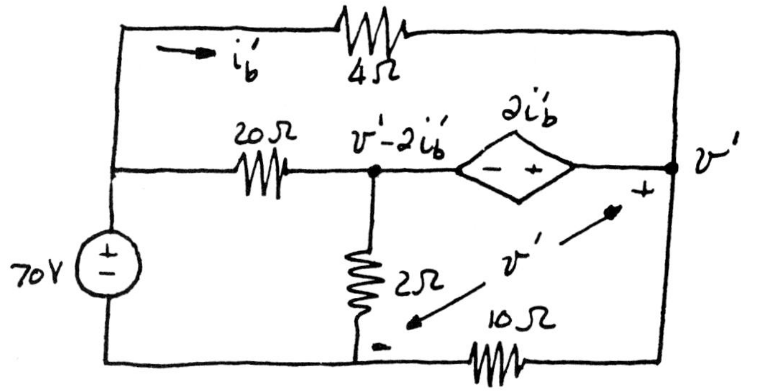

50 V source acting alone:

$$\frac{v''-2i_b''}{2}+\frac{v''-2i_b''}{20}+\frac{v''}{4}+\frac{v''+50}{10}=0, \quad \therefore \quad 18v''-22i_b''=-100$$

Also, $$i_b''=\frac{-v''}{4}$$

Combining, $$18v''+22v''/4=-100 \quad \therefore \quad v''=\frac{-400}{94}\text{ V}$$

Therefore $$v=v'+v''=\frac{3220}{94}-\frac{400}{94}=\frac{2820}{94}=30\text{ V}$$

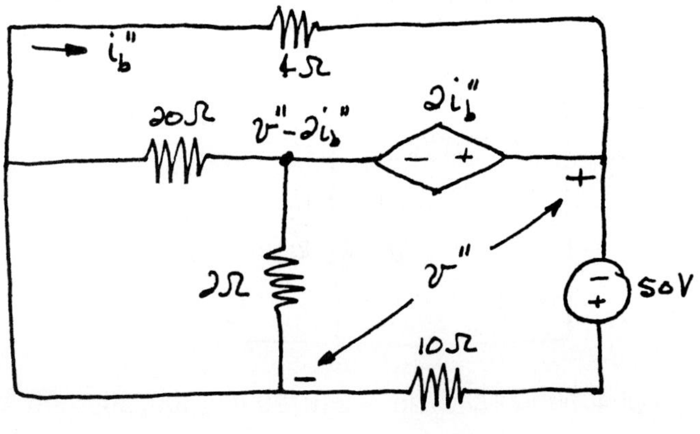

Problems

P 4.1 [a] Five

[b] Three

[c] Sum the currents at any three of the four essential nodes a, b, c, and d. Using nodes a, b, and c we get

$$-i_g + i_1 + i_2 = 0$$

$$-i_1 - i_4 + i_3 = 0$$

$$i_5 - i_2 - i_3 = 0$$

[d] Two.

[e] Sum the voltages around two independent closed paths, avoiding a path that contains the independent current source since the voltage across the current source is not known. Using the upper and lower meshes formed by the five resistors gives

$$R_1 i_1 + R_3 i_3 - R_2 i_2 = 0$$

$$R_3 i_3 + R_5 i_5 - R_4 i_4 = 0$$

P 4.2

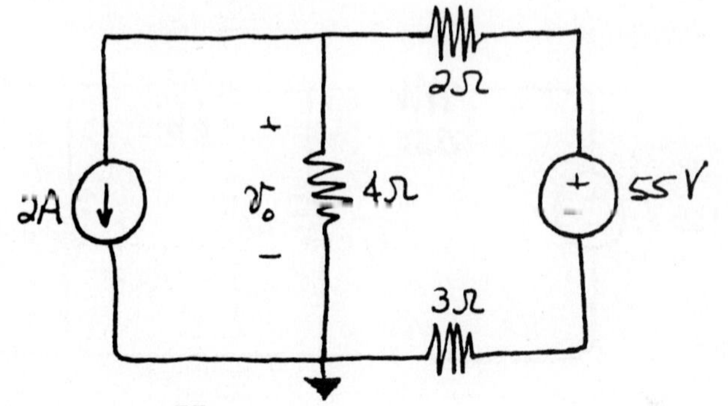

$$2 + \frac{v_o}{4} + \frac{v_o - 55}{5} = 0$$

$$40 + 5v_o + 4v_o - 220 = 0$$

$$9v_o = 180$$

$$v_o = 20 \text{ V}$$

$$p_{2A} = (20)(2) = 40 \text{ W} \quad \text{(absorbing)}$$

P 4.3 Let v_2 be the node voltage across the 80 Ω resistor, positive at the upper terminal.

$$\text{Then} \quad -4 + \frac{v_1}{20} + \frac{v_2}{80} + \frac{v_2}{40} = 0$$

(Note we have created a super node in writing this expression.)

$$-320 + 4v_1 + v_2 + 2v_2 = 0$$

$$4v_1 + 3v_2 = 320$$

$$v_1 + 60 = v_2$$

$$4v_1 + 3v_1 + 180 = 320$$

$$\therefore \quad v_1 = 20 \text{ V}$$

$$\therefore \quad v_2 = 80 \text{ V}$$

$p_{\text{del}} = 60 i_g$ where i_g is the current out of the positive terminal

$$4 = i_g + \frac{v_1}{20}; \qquad i_g = 3 \text{ A}$$

$$\therefore \quad p_{\text{del}} = 60(3) = 180 \text{ W}$$

P 4.4 [a]

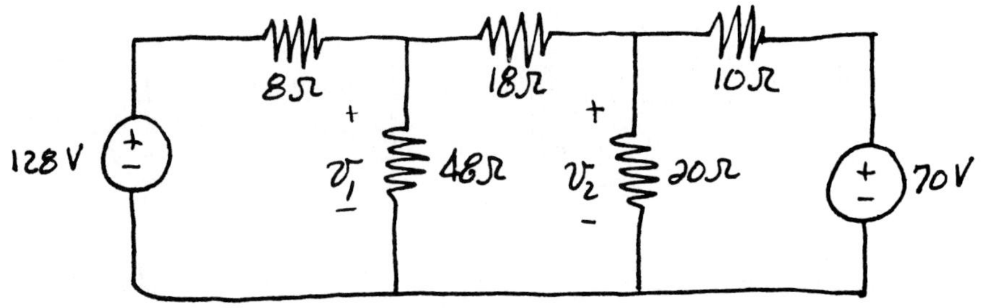

$$\frac{v_1}{48} + \frac{v_1 - 128}{8} + \frac{v_1 - v_2}{18} = 0 \quad \text{so} \quad 29v_1 - 8v_2 = 2304$$

$$\frac{v_2}{20} + \frac{v_2 - v_1}{18} + \frac{v_2 - 70}{10} = 0 \quad \text{so} \quad -10v_1 + 37v_2 = 1260$$

Solving, $v_1 = 96$ V; $\quad v_2 = 60$ V

$$i_a = \frac{128 - 96}{8} = 4 \text{ A}$$

$$i_b = \frac{96}{48} = 2 \text{ A}$$

$$i_c = \frac{96 - 60}{18} = 2 \text{ A}$$

$$i_d = \frac{60}{20} = 3 \text{ A}$$

$$i_e = \frac{60 - 70}{10} = -1 \text{ A}$$

[b] $p_{\text{dev}} = 128(4) + 70(1) = 582$ W

P 4.5 Use the lower terminal of the 80 Ω resistor as the reference node.

$$\frac{v_o - 60}{10} + \frac{v_o}{5} + 3 = 0$$

Solving, $\quad v_o = 10$ V

P 4.6 [a]

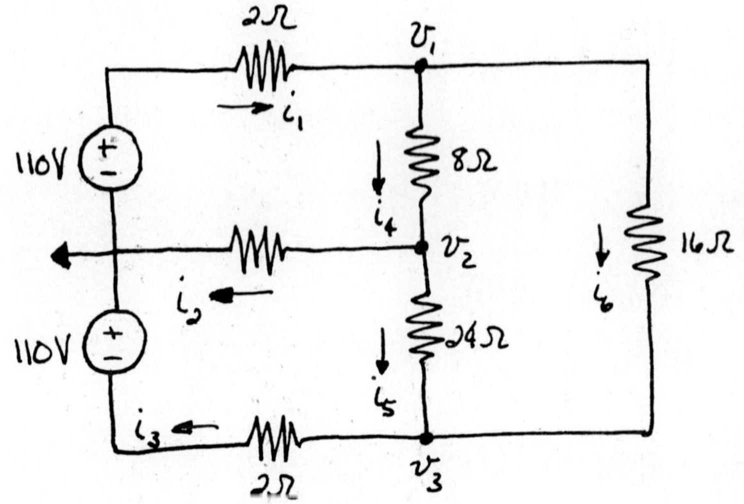

$$\frac{v_1 - 110}{2} + \frac{v_1 - v_2}{8} + \frac{v_1 - v_3}{16} = 0 \qquad \text{so} \qquad 11v_1 - 2v_2 - v_3 = 880$$

$$\frac{v_2 - v_1}{8} + \frac{v_2}{3} + \frac{v_2 - v_3}{24} = 0 \qquad \text{so} \qquad -3v_1 + 12v_2 - v_3 = 0$$

$$\frac{v_3 + 110}{2} + \frac{v_3 - v_2}{24} + \frac{v_3 - v_1}{16} = 0 \qquad \text{so} \qquad -3v_1 - 2v_2 + 29v_3 = -2640$$

Solving, $v_1 = 74.64$ V; $\quad v_2 = 11.79$ V; $\quad v_3 = -82.5$ V

Thus, $i_1 = \dfrac{110 - v_1}{2} = 17.68$ A $\qquad i_4 = \dfrac{v_1 - v_2}{8} = 7.86$ A

$i_2 = \dfrac{v_2}{3} = 3.93$ A $\qquad i_5 = \dfrac{v_2 - v_3}{24} = 3.93$ A

$i_3 = \dfrac{v_3 + 110}{2} = 13.75$ A $\qquad i_6 = \dfrac{v_1 - v_3}{16} = 9.82$ A

[b] $\quad \sum P_{\text{dev}} = 110i_1 + 110i_3 = 3457.3$ W

$$\sum P_{\text{dis}} = i_1^2(2) + i_2^2(3) + i_3^2(2) + i_4^2(8) + i_5^2(24) + i_6^2(16) = 3457.3 \text{ W}$$

P 4.7 $\qquad 2.4 + \dfrac{v_1}{125} + \dfrac{v_1 - v_2}{25} = 0$

$$\frac{v_2 - v_1}{25} + \frac{v_2}{250} + \frac{v_2}{375} - 3.2 = 0$$

Solving, $v_1 = 25$ V; $v_2 = 90$ V
CHECK:

$$p_{125\Omega} = \frac{(25)^2}{125} = 5 \text{ W}$$

$$p_{25\Omega} = \frac{(90-25)^2}{25} = 169 \text{ W}$$

$$p_{250\Omega} = \frac{(90)^2}{250} = 32.4 \text{ W}$$

$$p_{375\Omega} = \frac{(90)^2}{375} = 21.6 \text{ W}$$

$$p_{2.4\text{A}} = (25)(2.4) = 60 \text{ W}$$

$$\sum p_{\text{abs}} = 5 + 169 + 32.4 + 21.6 + 60 = 288 \text{ W}$$

$$\sum p_{\text{dev}} = (90)(3.2) = 288 \text{ W} \quad \text{(CHECKS)}$$

P 4.8 [a]

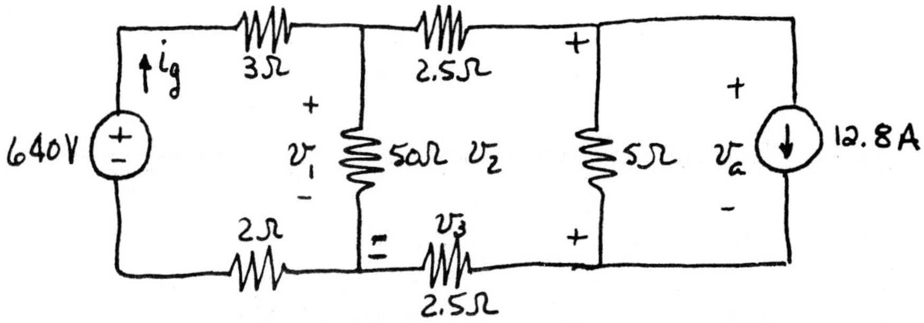

$$\frac{v_1}{50} + \frac{v_1 - 640}{5} + \frac{v_1 - v_2}{2.5} = 0 \quad \text{so} \quad 31v_1 - 20v_2 + 0v_3 = 6400$$

$$\frac{v_2 - v_1}{2.5} + \frac{v_2 - v_3}{5} + 12.8 = 0 \quad \text{so} \quad -2v_1 + 3v_2 - v_3 = -64$$

$$\frac{v_3}{2.5} + \frac{v_3 - v_2}{5} - 12.8 = 0 \quad \text{so} \quad 0v_1 - v_2 + 3v_3 = 64$$

Solving, $v_1 = 380\ V$; $v_2 = 269$ V; $v_3 = 111$ V,

[b] $$i_g = \frac{640 - 380}{5} = 52 \text{ A}$$

$$p_g(\text{del}) = (640)(52) = 33{,}280 \text{ W}$$

P 4.9

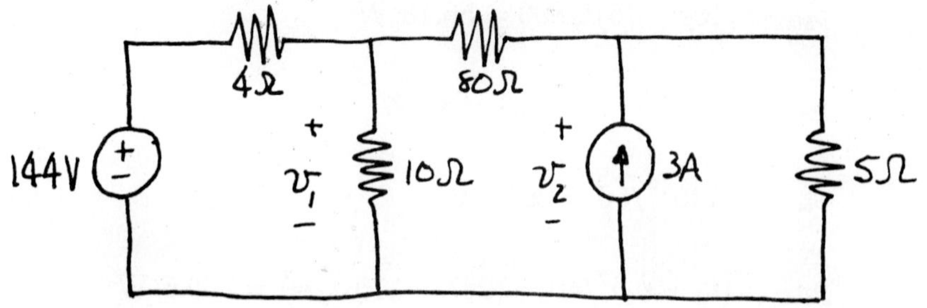

$$\frac{v_1 - 144}{4} + \frac{v_1}{10} + \frac{v_1 - v_2}{80} = 0 \qquad \text{so} \qquad 29v_1 - v_2 = 2880$$

$$-3 + \frac{v_2 - v_1}{80} + \frac{v_2}{5} = 0 \qquad \text{so} \qquad -v_1 + 17v_2 = 240$$

Solving, $v_1 = 100$ V; $\quad v_2 = 20$ V

P 4.10

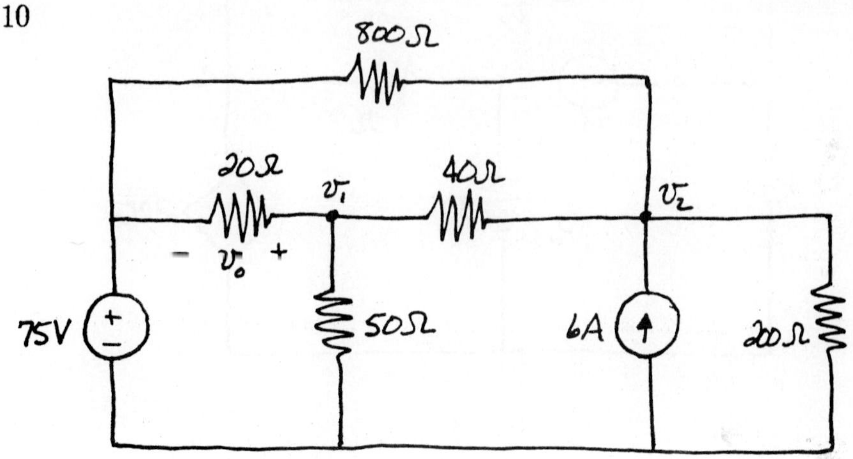

$$\frac{v_1 - 75}{20} + \frac{v_1}{50} + \frac{v_1 - v_2}{40} = 0$$

$$\frac{v_2 - v_1}{40} + \frac{v_2 - 75}{800} - 6 + \frac{v_2}{200} = 0$$

Solving, $v_1 = 115$ V; $\quad v_2 = 287$ V

$$\therefore \quad v_o = 115 - 75 = 40 \text{ V}$$

CHECK:

$$i_g = (75 - 115)/20 + (75 - 287)/800 = -2.265 \text{ A}$$

$$p_{75\text{V}} = -75i_g = 169.875 \text{ W} \quad \text{(abs)}$$

$$p_{6\text{A}} = -6v_2 = -6(287) = -1722 \text{ W} \quad \text{(del)}$$

$$p_{800\Omega} = (v_2 - 75)^2/800 = 56.18 \text{ W}$$

$$p_{20\Omega} = v_o^2/20 = 1600/20 = 80 \text{ W}$$

$$p_{50\Omega} = (115)^2/50 = 264.5 \text{ W}$$

$$p_{40\Omega} = (v_2 - v_1)^2/40 = (287 - 115)^2/40 = 739.6 \text{ W}$$

$$p_{200\Omega} = (287)^2/200 = 411.845 \text{ W}$$

$$\sum p_{\text{abs}} = 169.875 + 56.18 + 80 + 264.5 + 739.6 + 411.845 = 1722 \text{ W}$$

P 4.11

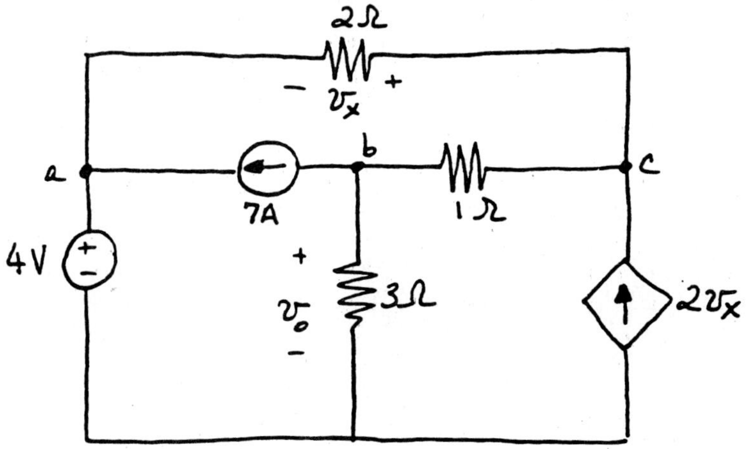

$$v_a = 4 \text{ V}$$

$$7 + \frac{v_b}{3} + \frac{v_b - v_c}{1} = 0$$

$$-2v_x + \frac{v_c - v_b}{1} + \frac{v_c - v_a}{2} = 0$$

$$v_x = v_c - v_a = v_c - 4$$

Solving, $v_o = v_b = 1.5$ V

P 4.12

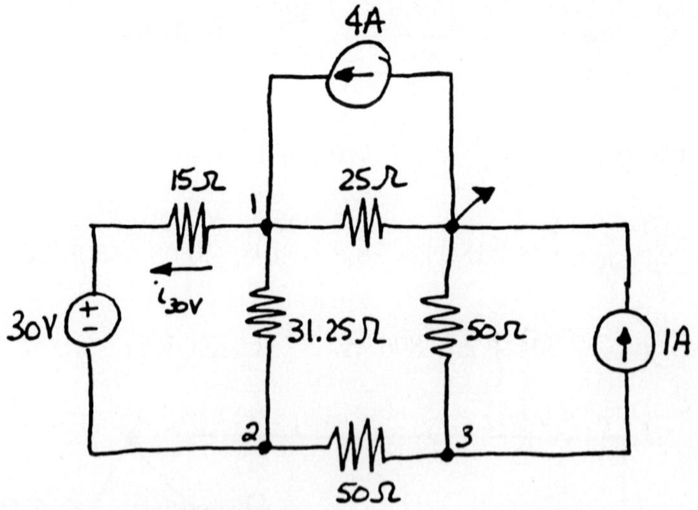

$$i_{30V} + \frac{v_1 - v_2}{31.25} + \frac{v_1}{25} - 4 = 0$$

$$-i_{30V} + \frac{v_2 - v_3}{50} + \frac{v_2 - v_1}{31.25} = 0$$

$$\frac{v_3 - v_2}{50} + \frac{v_3}{50} + 1 = 0$$

$$i_{30V} = \frac{v_1 - (v_2 + 30)}{15}$$

Solving, $v_1 = 76$ V; $v_2 = 46$ V; $v_3 = -2$ V; $i_{30V} = 0$ A

$p_{4A} = -4v_1 = -4(76) = -304$ W (del)

$p_{1A} = (1)(-2) = -2$ W (del)

$p_{30V} = 0$ W

$p_{15\Omega} = 0$ W

$$p_{25\Omega} = \frac{v_1^2}{25} = \frac{76^2}{25} = 231.04 \text{ W}$$

$$p_{31.25\Omega} = \frac{(v_1 - v_2)^2}{31.25} = \frac{30^2}{31.25} = 28.8 \text{ W}$$

$$p_{50\Omega}(\text{lower}) = \frac{(v_2 - v_3)^2}{50} = \frac{48^2}{50} = 46.08 \text{ W}$$

$$p_{50\Omega}(\text{right}) = \frac{v_3^2}{50} = \frac{4}{50} = 0.08 \text{ W}$$

$$\sum p_{\text{diss}} = 0 + 231.04 + 28.8 + 46.8 + 0.08 = 306 \text{ W}$$

$$\sum p_{\text{dev}} = 304 + 2 = 306 \text{ W} \qquad \text{(CHECKS)}$$

P 4.13

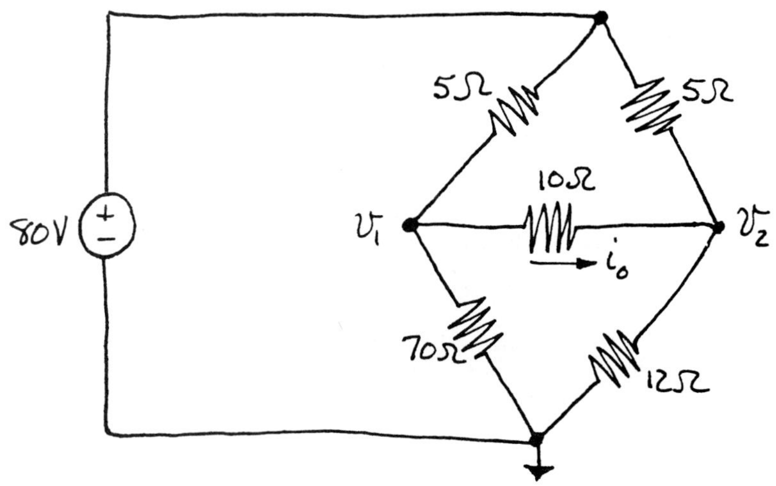

$$\frac{v_1}{70} + \frac{v_1 - v_2}{10} + \frac{v_1 - 80}{5} = 0 \qquad \text{so} \qquad 22v_1 - 7v_2 = 1120$$

$$\frac{v_2}{12} + \frac{v_2 - v_1}{10} + \frac{v_2 - 80}{5} = 0 \qquad \text{so} \qquad -6v_1 + 23v_2 = 960$$

Solving, $v_1 = 70$ V; $v_2 = 60$ V

Thus, $i_o = \dfrac{v_1 - v_2}{10} = 1$ A

P 4.14 [a] $\dfrac{v_0 - 60}{10} + \dfrac{v_o}{5} + 3 = 0; \quad v_o = 10$ V

[b] Let v_x = voltage drop across 3 A source

$$v_x = v_o - (100)(3) = -290 \text{ V}$$

$$p_{3\text{A}} \text{ (developed)} = (3)(-290) = -870 \text{ W}$$

[c] Let i_g = current into positive terminal of 60 V source

$$i_g = (10 - 60)/10 = -5 \text{ A}$$

$$p_{60\text{V}} \text{ (developed)} = (5)(60) = 300 \text{ W}$$

[d] $$\sum p_{\rm dis} = (5)^2(10) + (3)^2(100) + (10)^2/5 = 1170 \text{ W}$$

$$\sum p_{\rm dis} = 300 + 870 = 1170 \text{ W}$$

[e] v_o is independent of any finite resistance connected in series with the 3 A current source

P 4.15 [a] From the solution to Problem 4.5 we know $v_o = 10$ V, therefore

$$p_{3\rm A} = 3v_o = 30 \text{ W}$$

$$\therefore \quad p_{3\rm A} \text{ (dissipated)} = 30 \text{ W}$$

[b] The current into the negative terminal of the 60 V source is

$$i_g = \frac{60 - 10}{10} = 5 \text{ A}$$

$$p_{60\rm V} = -60(5) = -300 \text{ W}$$

$$\therefore \quad p_{60\rm V} \text{ (developed)} = 300 \text{ W}$$

[c] $$p_{10\Omega} = (5)^2(10) = 250 \text{ W}$$

$$p_{5\Omega} = (10)^2/5 = 20 \text{ W}$$

$$\sum p_{\rm dev} = |30 - 300| = 270 \text{ W}$$

$$\sum p_{\rm dis} = 250 + 20 = 270 \text{ W}$$

P 4.16 [a]

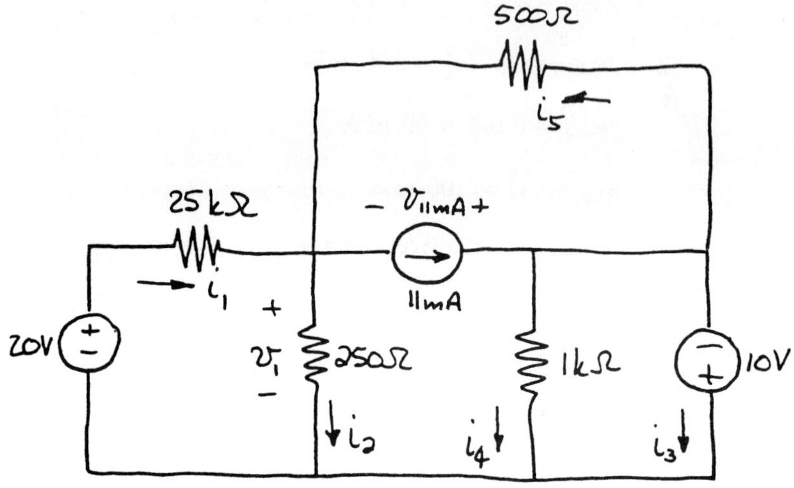

$$\frac{v_1 - 20}{25 \times 10^3} + \frac{v_1}{0.25 \times 10^3} + 11 \times 10^{-3} + \frac{v_1 + 10}{0.5 \times 10^3} = 0$$

$$v_1 - 20 + 100v_1 + 275 + 50v_1 + 500 = 0$$

$$151v_1 = -755$$

$$v_1 = -5 \text{ V}$$

$$i_1 = \frac{20+5}{25} = 1 \text{ mA}$$

$$i_2 = \frac{v_1}{0.25} = \frac{-5}{0.25} = -20 \text{ mA}$$

$$i_5 = \frac{-10+5}{0.5} = -10 \text{ mA}$$

$$i_4 = \frac{-10}{1} = -10 \text{ mA}$$

$$i_4 + i_3 - 11 + i_5 = 0$$

$$\therefore \quad i_3 = 11 - i_4 - i_5 = 11 + 10 + 10 = 31 \text{ mA}$$

[b] $$p_{20V} = 20i_1 = 20(1) = 20 \text{ mW}$$

$$p_{10V} = 10i_3 = 10(31) = 310 \text{ mW}$$

$$v_{11mA} + v_1 = -10, \quad v_{11mA} = -10 + 5 = -5 \text{ V}$$

$$p_{11mA} = -11v_{11mA} = -55 \text{ mW} \qquad \text{(del)}$$

$$\sum p_{dev} = 20 + 310 - 55 = 275 \text{ mW}$$

$$p_{25k} = 25i_1^2 = 25 \text{ mW}$$

$$p_{0.25k} = 0.25i_2^2 = 100 \text{ mW}$$

$$p_{0.5k} = 0.5i_5^2 = 50 \text{ mW}$$

$$p_{1k} = 1i_4^2 = 100 \text{ mW}$$

$$\sum p_{diss} = 25 + 100 + 50 + 100 = 275 \text{ mW}$$

$$\sum p_{diss} = \sum p_{dev} = 275 \text{ mW}$$

P 4.17 [a]

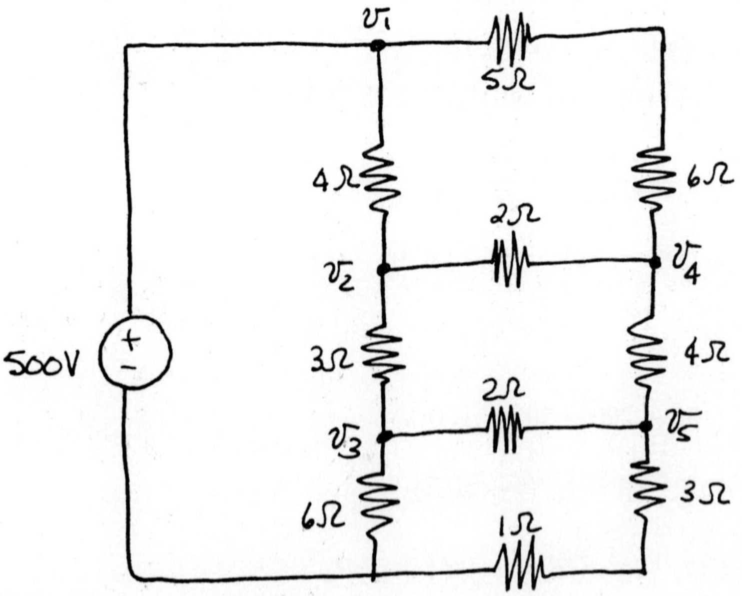

$$\frac{v_2 - 500}{4} + \frac{v_2 - v_4}{2} + \frac{v_2 - v_3}{3} = 0 \qquad \text{so} \qquad 13v_2 - 4v_3 - 6v_4 + 0v_5 = 1500$$

$$\frac{v_3 - v_2}{3} + \frac{v_3}{6} + \frac{v_3 - v_5}{2} = 0 \qquad \text{so} \qquad -2v_2 + 6v_3 + 0v_4 - 3v_5 = 0$$

$$\frac{v_4 - v_2}{2} + \frac{v_4 - 500}{11} + \frac{v_4 - v_5}{4} = 0 \qquad \text{so} \qquad -22v_2 + 0v_3 + 37v_4 - 11v_5 = 2000$$

$$\frac{v_5 - v_3}{2} + \frac{v_5}{4} + \frac{v_5 - v_4}{4} = 0 \qquad \text{so} \qquad 0v_2 - 2v_3 - v_4 + 4v_5 = 0$$

Solving, $v_2 = 300$ V; $\quad v_3 = 180$ V; $\quad v_4 = 280$ V; $\quad v_5 = 160$ V

$$i_{5\Omega} = \frac{500 - v_4}{11} = \frac{500 - 280}{11} = 20 \text{ A}$$

$$p_{5\Omega} = (20)^2(5) = 2000 \text{ W}$$

[b]
$$i_{500\text{V}} = \frac{v_1 - v_2}{4} + \frac{v_1 - v_4}{11}$$

$$= \frac{500 - 300}{4} + \frac{500 - 280}{11} = 50 + 20 = 70 \text{ A}$$

$$p_{500\text{V}} = 35{,}000 \text{ W}$$

Check:

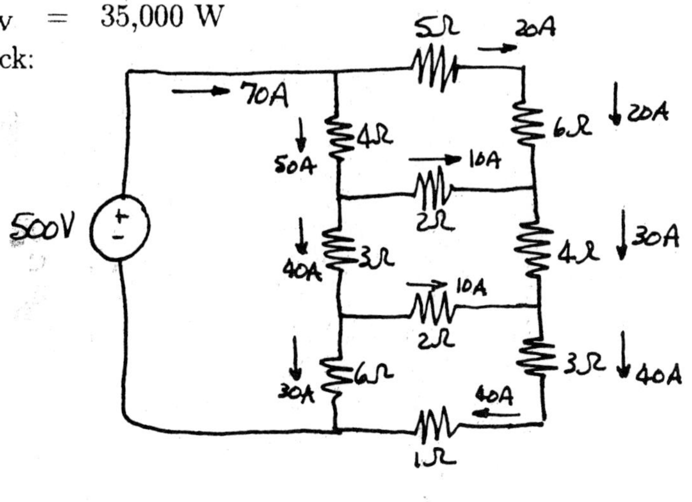

$$\sum P_{\text{dis}} = (50)^2(4) + (40)^2(3) + (30)^2(6) + (20)^2(11) + (10)^2(2) + (30$$
$$+(10)^2(2) + (40)^2(4) = 35{,}000 \text{ W}$$

P 4.18 [a]
$$\frac{v_o - v_1}{R} + \frac{v_o - v_2}{R} + \frac{v_o - v_3}{R} + \cdots + \frac{v_o - v_n}{R} = 0$$

$$\therefore \quad nv_o = v_1 + v_2 + v_3 + \cdots + v_n$$

$$\therefore \quad -v_o = \frac{1}{n}[v_1 + v_2 + v_3 + \cdots + v_n] = \frac{1}{n}\sum_{R=1}^{n} v_k$$

[b]
$$v_o = \frac{1}{3}(150 + 200 - 50) = 100 \text{ V}$$

P 4.19 From Eq. 4.16, $i_B = v_c/(1+\beta)R_E$

From Eq. 4.17, $i_B = (v_b - v_o)/(1+\beta)R_E$

From Eq. 4.19,
$$i_B = \frac{1}{(1+\beta)R_E}\left[\frac{V_{CC}(1+\beta)R_E R_2 + V_o R_1 R_2}{R_1R_2 + (1+\beta)R_E(R_1+R_2)} - v_o\right]$$

$$= \frac{V_{CC}R_2 - v_o(R_1+R_2)}{R_1R_2 + (1+\beta)R_E(R_1+R_2)} = \frac{[V_{CC}R_2/(R_1+R_2)] - v_o}{[R_1R_2/(R_1+R_2)] + (1+\beta)R_E}$$

P 4.20 Place $v_\Delta/5$ inside a supernode and use the lower node as a reference. Then

$$\frac{v_1 - 50}{10} + \frac{v_1}{30} + \frac{v_1 - v_\Delta/5}{39} + \frac{v_1 - v_\Delta/5}{78} = 0$$

$$134v_1 - 6v_\Delta = 3900; \qquad v_\Delta = 50 - v_1$$

Solving, $v_1 = 30$ V; $v_\Delta = 20$ V; $v_o = 30 - v_\Delta/5 = 30 - 4 = 26$ V

P 4.21 [a]

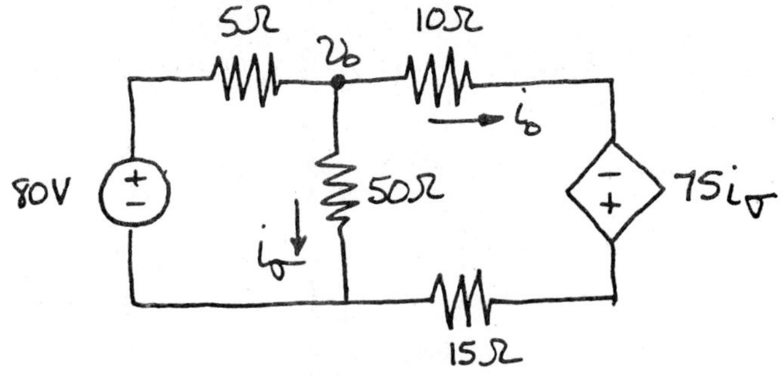

$$\frac{v_o - 80}{5} + \frac{v_o}{50} + \frac{v_o + 75i_\sigma}{25} = 0; \quad i_\sigma = \frac{v_o}{50}$$

Solving, $v_o = 50$ V; $\qquad i_\sigma = 1$ A

$$i_o = \frac{50 - (-75)(1)}{25} = 5 \text{ A}$$

$$p_{75i_\sigma} = 75 i_\sigma i_o = -375 \text{ W}$$

$\therefore$ The dependent voltage source delivers 375 W to the circuit.

P 4.22 $$-3 + \frac{v_o}{200} + \frac{v_o + 5i_\Delta}{10} + \frac{v_o - 80}{20} = 0; \quad i_\Delta = \frac{v_o - 80}{20}$$

[a] Solving, $v_o = 50$ V

[b] $$i_{\text{ds}} = \frac{v_o + 5i_\Delta}{10}$$

$$i_\Delta = (50 - 80)/20 = -1.5 \text{ A}$$

$$\therefore \; i_{\text{ds}} = 4.25 \text{ A}; \quad 5i_\Delta = -7.5 \text{ V}: \quad p_{\text{ds}} = (-5i_\Delta)(i_{\text{ds}}) = 31.875 \text{ W}$$

[c] $$p_{3\text{A}} = -3v_o = -3(50) = -150 \text{ W} \quad \text{(del)}$$

$$p_{80\text{V}} = 80 i_\Delta = 80(-1.5) = -120 \text{ W} \quad \text{(del)}$$

$$\sum p_{\text{del}} = 150 + 120 = 270 \text{ W}$$

CHECK:

$$p_{200\Omega} = 2500/200 = 12.5 \text{ W}$$

$$p_{20\Omega} = (80 - 50)^2/20 = 900/20 = 45 \text{ W}$$

$$p_{10\Omega} = (4.25)^2/10 = 180.625 \text{ W}$$

$$\sum p_{\text{diss}} = 31.875 + 180.625 + 12.5 + 45 = 270 \text{ W}$$

P 4.23 [a]

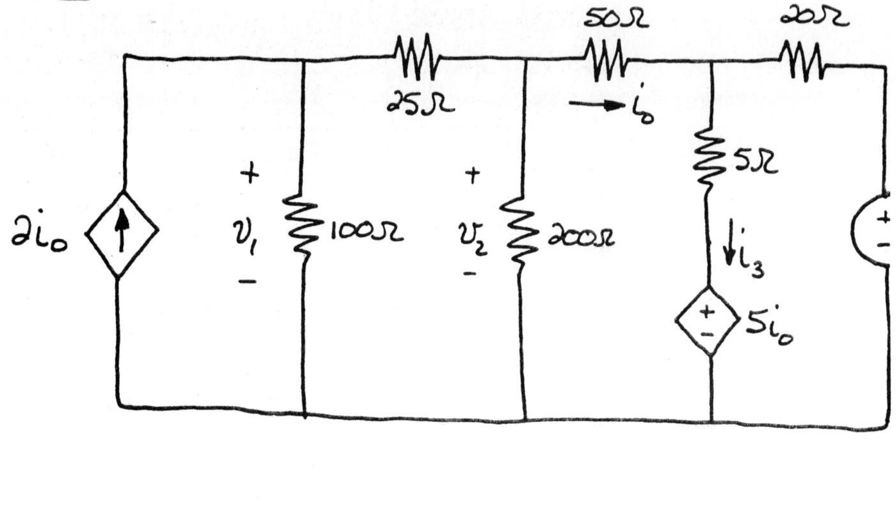

$$i_o = \frac{v_2 - v_3}{50}$$

$$-2i_o + \frac{v_1}{100} + \frac{v_1 - v_2}{25} = 0 \qquad \text{so} \qquad 5v_1 - 8v_2 + 4v_3 = 0$$

$$\frac{v_2 - v_1}{25} + \frac{v_2}{200} + \frac{v_2 - v_3}{50} \qquad \text{so} \qquad -8v_1 + 13v_2 - 4v_3 = 0$$

$$\frac{v_3 - v_2}{50} + \frac{v_3 - 5i_o}{5} + \frac{v_3 - 38.5}{20} = 0 \qquad \text{so} \qquad 0v_1 - 4v_2 + 29v_3 = 192.5$$

Solving, $v_1 = -50$ V; $v_2 = -30$ V; $v_3 = 2.5$ V

[b] $$i_o = \frac{v_2 - v_3}{50} = \frac{-30 - 2.5}{50} = -0.65 \text{ A}$$

$$i_3 = \frac{v_3 - 5i_o}{5} = \frac{2.5 - 5(-0.65)}{5} = 1.15 \text{ A}$$

$$i_g = \frac{38.5 - 2.5}{20} = 1.8 \text{ A}$$

$$\sum p_{\text{dis}} = \sum p_{\text{dev}}$$

Calculate $\sum p_{\text{dev}}$ because we don't know if the dependent sources are developing or absorbing power. Likewise for the independent source.

$$p_{2i_o} = -2i_o v_1 = -2(-0.65)(-50) = -65 \text{ W(dev)}$$

$$p_{5i_o} = 5i_o i_3 = 5(-0.65)(1.15) = -3.7375 \text{ W(dev)}$$

$$p_g = -38.5(1.8) = -69.30 \text{ W(dev)}$$

$$\sum p_{\text{dev}} = 69.3 + 65 + 3.7375 = 138.0375 \text{ W}$$

CHECK

$$\sum p_{\text{dis}} = \frac{2500}{100} + \frac{900}{200} + \frac{400}{25} + (0.65)^2(50) + (1.15)^2 5 + (1.8)^2(20)$$

$$= 138.0375 \text{ W}$$

$$\therefore \sum p_{\text{dev}} = \sum p_{\text{dis}} = 138.0375 \text{ W}$$

P 4.24 [a] $$-5 + \frac{v_1}{15} + \frac{v_1 - v_2}{5} = 0 \quad \text{so} \quad 4v_1 - 3v_2 + 0i_\Delta = 75$$

$$\frac{v_2 - v_1}{5} + \frac{v_2}{30} + \frac{v_2}{10} + \frac{v_2 + 5i_\Delta}{30} = 0 \quad \text{so} \quad -6v_1 + 11v_2 + 5i_\Delta = 0$$

$$i_\Delta = \frac{v_1 - v_2}{5} \quad \text{so} \quad v_1 - v_2 - 5i_\Delta = 0$$

Solving, $v_1 = 30$ V; $v_2 = 15$ V; $i_\Delta = 3$ A; $i_o = \dfrac{15 + 15}{30} = 1$ A

$$p_{5i_\Delta} = (-15)(1) = -15 \text{ W(del)}$$

$$p_{5\text{A}} = -5(30) = -150 \text{ W(del)}$$

$$\therefore p_{\text{dev}} = 165 \text{ W}$$

[b] $$\sum p_{\text{abs}} = \frac{(30)^2}{15} + \frac{(15)^2}{30} + \frac{(15)^2}{10} + (3)^2(5) + (1)^2(30) = 165 \text{ W}$$

$$\therefore \quad \sum p_{\text{dev}} = \sum p_{\text{abs}} = 165 \text{ W}$$

P 4.25 $$i_\phi = \frac{v_3 - v_4}{4} = \frac{235 - 222}{4} = 3.25 \text{ A}$$

$$\beta i_\phi = 30(3.25) = 97.5 \text{ V}$$

$$v_1 + \beta i_\phi = v_4$$

$$v_1 = v_4 - \beta i_\phi = 222 - 97.5 = 124.5 \text{ V}$$

$$v_3 + v_\Delta = 250$$

$$\therefore \quad v_\Delta = 250 - 235 = 15 \text{ V}$$

$$\alpha v_\Delta = (3.2)(15) = 48 \text{ A}$$

$$i_g = \frac{250 - 124.5}{2} + \frac{250 - 235}{1} = 77.75 \text{ A}$$

$$p_{250\text{V}} = -250 i_g = -250(77.75) = -19{,}437.5 \text{ W(del)}$$

$$i_{30i_\phi} - i_\phi + v_4/40 + 48 = 0$$

$$i_{30i_\phi} = i_\phi - 222/40 - 48 = 3.25 - 5.55 - 48 = -50.3 \text{ A}$$

$$p_{30i_\phi} = (30 i_\phi) i_{30i_\phi} = (97.5)(-50.3) = -4904.25 \text{ W(dev)}$$

$$p_{3.2v_\Delta} = (\alpha v_\Delta)(v_4) = (48)(22) = 10{,}656 \text{ W(abs)}$$

$$\therefore \quad \sum p_{\text{dev}} = 19{,}437.5 + 4904.25 = 24{,}341.75 \text{ W}$$

$$p_{10\Omega} = \frac{v_1^2}{10} = \frac{(124.5)^2}{10} = 1550.025 \text{ W}$$

$$p_{2\Omega} = \frac{(250 - 124.5)^2}{2} = 7875.125 \text{ W}$$

$$p_{1\Omega} = \frac{(250 - 235)^2}{1} = 225 \text{ W}$$

$$p_{20\Omega} = \frac{(235)^2}{20} = 2761.25 \text{ W}$$

$$p_{4\Omega} = (3.25)^2(4) = 42.25 \text{ W}$$

$$p_{40\Omega} = \frac{(222)^2}{40} = 1232.10 \text{ W}$$

$$\therefore \sum p_{\text{diss}} = 10{,}656 + 1550.025 + 7875.125 + 225 + 2761.250 + 42.25 + 1232.1 = 24{,}341.75 \text{ W}$$

Thus, $\sum p_{\text{dev}} = \sum p_{\text{diss}}$

P 4.26

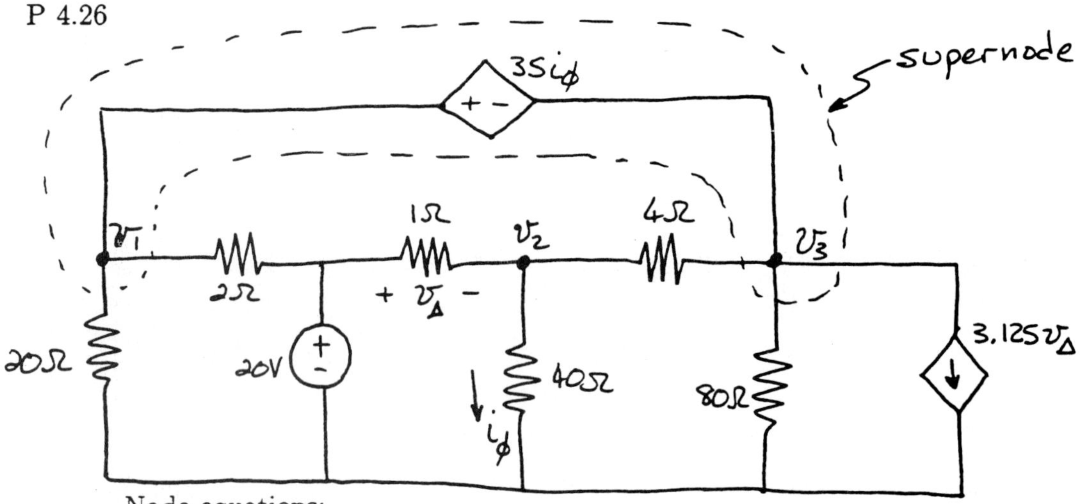

Node equations:

$$\frac{v_1}{20} + \frac{v_1 - 20}{2} + \frac{v_3 - v_2}{4} + \frac{v_3}{80} + 3.125 v_\Delta = 0$$

$$\frac{v_2}{40} + \frac{v_2 - v_3}{4} + \frac{v_2 - 20}{1} = 0$$

Constraint equations:

$$v_\Delta = 20 - v_2$$

$$v_1 - 35 i_\phi = v_3$$

$$i_\phi = v_2/40$$

Solving, $v_1 = -20.25$ V; $v_2 = 10$ V; $v_3 = -29$ V

Let i_g be the current delivered by the 20 V source, then

$$i_g = \frac{20 - (20.25)}{2} + \frac{20 - 10}{1} = 30.125 \text{ A}$$

$$p_g \text{ (delivered)} = 20(30.125) = 602.5 \text{ W}$$

P 4.27

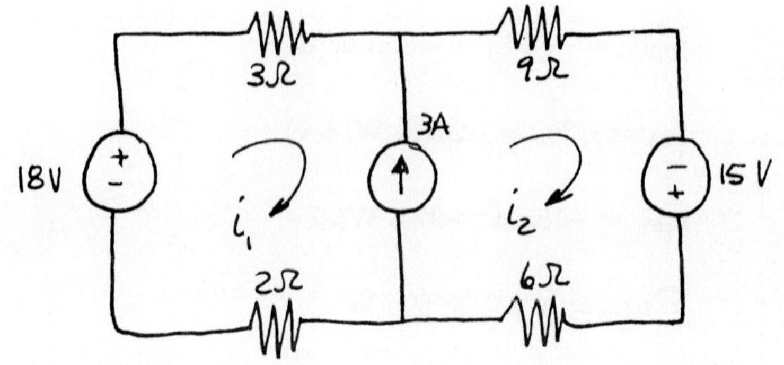

$$-18 + 3i_1 + 9i_2 - 15 + 6i_2 + 2i_1 = 0; \quad i_2 - i_1 = 3$$

Solving, $i_1 = -0.6$ A; $i_2 = 2.4$ A; $p_{18\text{V}} = -18i_1 = 10.8$ W

$$v_o = 15i_2 - 15 = 36 - 15 = 21 \text{ V}$$

$$p_{3\text{A}} = -3v_o = -63 \text{ W(dev)}$$

$$p_{15\text{V}} = -15i_2 = -36 \text{ W(dev)}$$

$$\sum p_{\text{dev}} = 99 \text{ W}$$

P 4.28

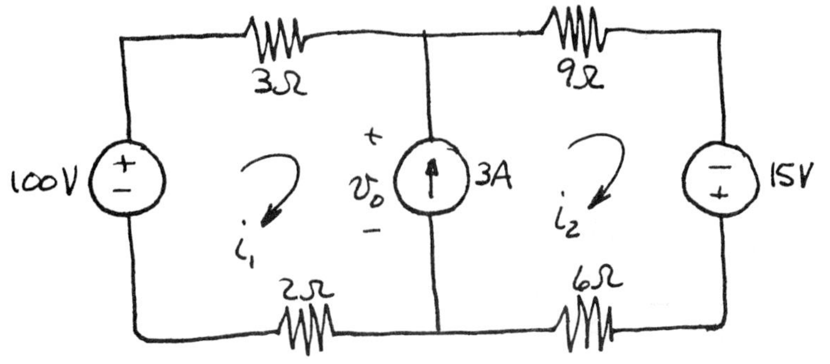

$$-100 + 5i_1 + 15i_2 - 15 = 0$$

$$5i_1 + 15i_2 = 115$$

$i_2 - i_1 = 3; \qquad i_2 = i_1 + 3; \qquad 15i_2 = 15i_1 + 45$

$\therefore \quad 20i_1 = 70$

$i_1 = 3.5 \text{ A}; \qquad i_2 = 6.5 \text{ A}$

$v_o = 15i_2 - 15 = 97.5 - 15 = 82.5 \text{ V}$

$p_{100V} = -100i_1 = -350 \text{ W(dev)}$

$p_{3A} = -3v_o = -247.5 \text{ W(dev)}$

$p_{15V} = -15i_2 = -97.5 \text{ W(dev)}$

$\sum p_{dev} = \sum p_{dis} = 695 \text{ W}$

Check: $\sum p_{dis} = (3.5)^2(5) + (6.5)^2(15) = 695 \text{ W}$

P 4.29 [a] Summing around the supermesh used in the solution to Problem 4.28 gives

$-5 + 5i_1 + 15i_2 = 0$

$i_2 = i_1 + 3$

$\therefore \quad i_1 = -2 \text{ A}; \qquad i_2 = 1 \text{ A}$

$p_{10V} = 10(-2) = -20 \text{ W (del)}$

$v_o = 15i_2 - 15 = 0 \text{ V}$

$p_{3A} = 3v_o = 0 \text{ W}$

$p_{15V} = -15i_2 = -15 \text{ W (del)}$

$\sum P_{dev} = 35 \text{ W} = \sum P_{diss}$

[b] With 3 A current source replaced with a short circuit

$i_1 = -2 \text{ A}, \qquad i_2 = 1 \text{ A}$

$\therefore \quad \sum P_{dis} = (-2)^2(5) + (1)^2(15) = 35 \text{ W}$

[c] A 3 A source with zero terminal voltage is equivalent to a short circuit carrying 3 A.

P 4.30 [a]

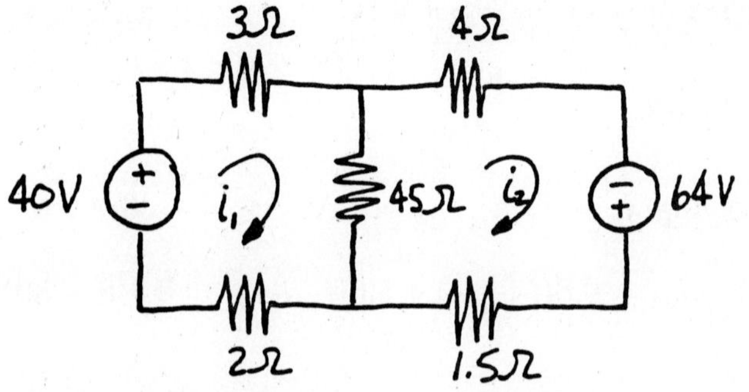

$40 = 50i_1 - 45i_2$

$64 = -45i_1 + 50.5i_2$

Solving, $i_1 = 9.8$ A; $i_2 = 10$ A

$i_a = i_1 = 9.8$ A; $i_b = i_1 - i_2 = -0.2$ A; $i_c = -i_2 = -10$ A

[b] If the polarity of the 64 V source is reversed, we have

$40 = 50i_1 - 45i_2$

$-64 = -45i_1 + 50.5i_2$

$\Delta = 500, \quad N_1 = -860, \quad N_2 = -1400$

$i_1 = -1.72$ and $i_2 = -2.8$ A

$i_a = i_1 = -1.72$ A; $i_b = i_1 - i_2 = 1.08$ A; $i_c = -i_2 = 2.8$ A

P 4.31

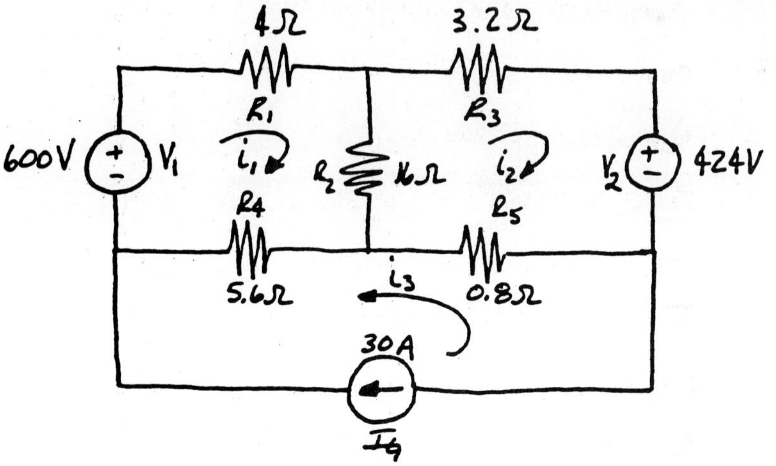

$600 = 25.6i_1 - 16i_2 + 5.6i_3$

$$-424 = -16i_1 + 20i_2 + 0.8i_3$$

$$-30 = i_3$$

Solving, $i_1 = 35$ A; $i_2 = 8$ A; $i_3 = -30$ A

[a] $$v_{30A} = 0.8(i_2 + i_3) + 5.6(i_1 + i_3) = 0.8(8 - 30) + 5.6(35 - 30) = 10.4$$

$$p_{30A} = 30v_{30A} = 30(10.4) = 312 \text{ W (abs)}$$

Therefore, the 30 A source delivers −312 W.

[b] $$p_{600V} = -600(35) = -21{,}000 \text{ W(del)}$$

$$p_{424V} = 424(8) = 3392 \text{ W(del)}$$

Therefore, the total power delivered is 21,000 W

[c] $$p_{4\Omega} = (35)^2(4) = 4900 \text{ W}$$

$$p_{3.2\Omega} = (8)^2(3.2) = 204.8 \text{ W}$$

$$p_{16\Omega} = (35 - 8)^2(16) = 11{,}664 \text{ W}$$

$$p_{5.6\Omega} = (35 - 30)^2(5.6) = 140 \text{ W}$$

$$p_{0.8\Omega} = (-30 + 8)^2(0.8) = 387.2 \text{ W}$$

$$\sum p_{\text{resistors}} = 17{,}296 \text{ W}$$

$$\sum p_{\text{abs}} = 17{,}296 + 312 + 3392 = 21{,}000 \text{ W (CHECKS)}$$

P 4.32 [a]

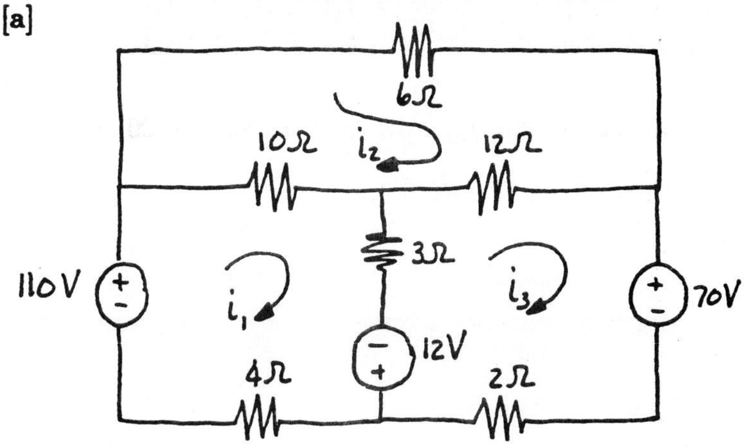

$110 + 12 = 17i_1 - 10i_2 - 3i_3$

$0 = -10i_1 + 28i_2 - 12i_3$

$-12 - 70 = -3i_1 - 12i_2 + 17i_3$

Solving, $i_1 = 8$ A; $\quad i_2 = 2$ A; $\quad i_3 = -2$ A

$p_{110} = -110i_1 = -880$ W(del)

$p_{12} = -12(i_1 - i_3) = -120$ W(del)

$p_{70} = 70i_3 = -140$ W(del)

$\therefore \quad \sum p_{\text{dev}} = 1140$ W

[b] $p_{4\Omega} = (8)^2(4) = 256$ W

$p_{10\Omega} = (6)^2(10) = 360$ W

$p_{12\Omega} = (-4)^2(12) = 192$ W

$p_{2\Omega} = (-2)^2(2) = 8$ W

$p_{6\Omega} = (2)^2(6) = 24$ W

$p_{3\Omega} = (10)^2(3) = 300$ W

$\therefore \quad \sum p_{\text{abs}} = 1140$ W

P 4.33 [a]

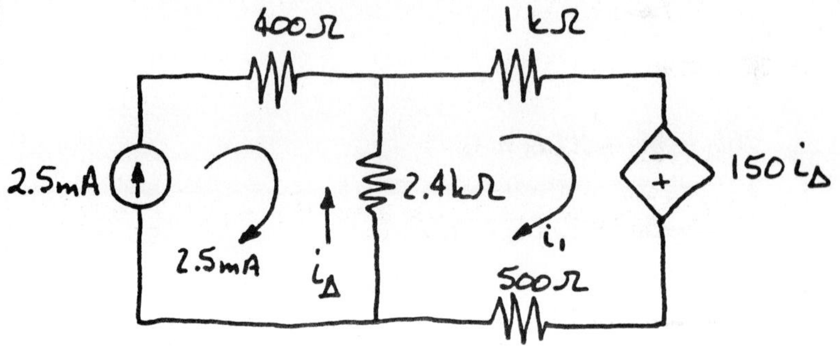

$2400(i_1 - 0.0025) + 1500i_1 - 150(i_1 - 0.0025) = 0$

$3750i_1 = 6 - 0.375 = 5.625$

$\therefore \quad i_1 = 1.5$ mA

$i_\Delta = i_1 - 2.5 = -1.0$ mA

[b] $v_o = 2.5(0.4) + 1(2.4) = 3.4$ V

$p_{2.5\text{mA}} = -3.4(2.5) = -8.5$ mW

$\therefore\ p_{2.5\text{mA}}$ (deliver) $= 8.5$ mW

[c] $150i_\Delta = 150(-1.0 \times 10^{-3}) = -0.15$ V

$p_{\text{dep source}} = 150i_\Delta i_1 = (0.15)(1.5) = 0.225$ mW

$p_{\text{dep source}}$ (delivered) $= 0.225$ mW

P 4.34

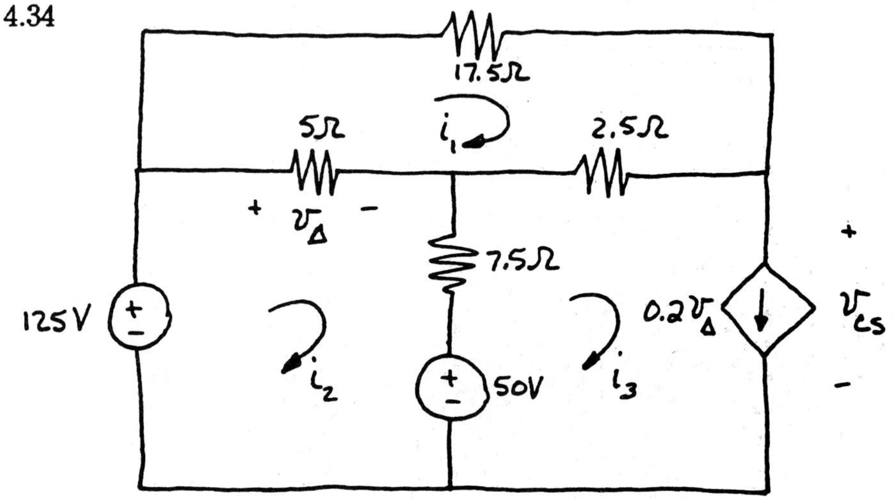

Mesh equations:

$$25i_1 - 5i_2 - 2.5i_3 = 0$$

$$75 = -5i_1 + 12.5i_2 - 7.5i_3$$

Constraint equations:

$$i_3 = 0.2v_\Delta$$

$$v_\Delta = 5(i_2 - i_1)$$

Solving, $i_1 = 3.6$ A; $i_2 = 13.2$ A; $i_3 = 9.6$ A

$$v_{cs} = 125 - v_\Delta - 2.5(i_3 - i_1) = 125 - 48 - 2.5(9.6 - 3.6) = 62 \text{ V}$$

$$p_{vc} = (62)(9.6) = 595.2 \text{ W (abs)}$$

$$p_{50V} = 50(i_2 - i_3) = 50(13.2 - 9.6) = 180 \text{ W (abs)}$$

$$p_{125V} = -125i_2 = -125(13.2) = -1650 \text{ W(del)}$$

Thus, the total power developed is 1650 W.
CHECK:

$$p_{17.5\Omega} = (3.6)^2(17.5) = 226.8 \text{ W}$$

$$p_{5\Omega} = (13.2 - 3.6)^2(5) = 460.8 \text{ W}$$

$$p_{2.5\Omega} = (9.6 - 3.6)^2(2.5) = 90 \text{ W}$$

$$p_{7.5\Omega} = (13.2 - 9.6)^2(7.5) = 97.2 \text{ W}$$

$$\therefore \sum p_{\text{abs}} = 226.8 + 460.8 + 90 + 97.2 + 180 + 595.2 = 1650 \text{ W}$$

P 4.35

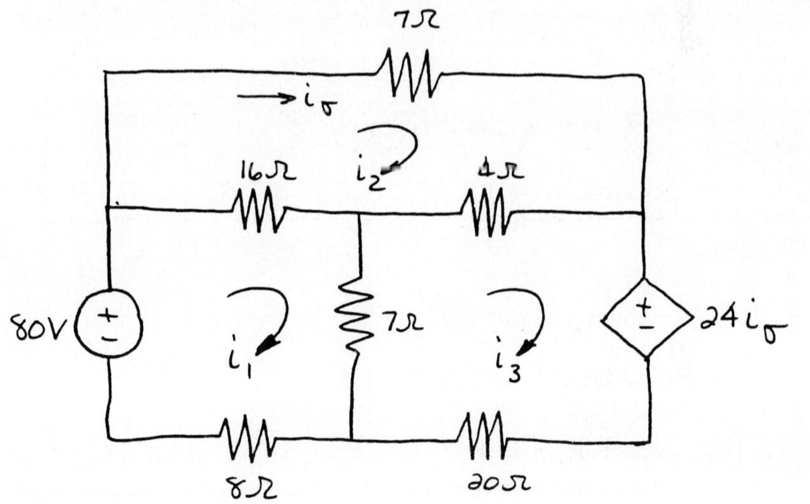

$$-80 + 31i_1 - 16i_2 - 7i_3 = 0$$

$$-16i_1 + 27i_2 - 4i_3 = 0$$

$$-7i_1 - 4i_2 + 31i_3 + 24i_2 = 0$$

Solving, $i_1 = 3.5$ A

$$p_{8\Omega} = (3.5)^2(8) = 98 \text{ W}$$

P 4.36 [a]

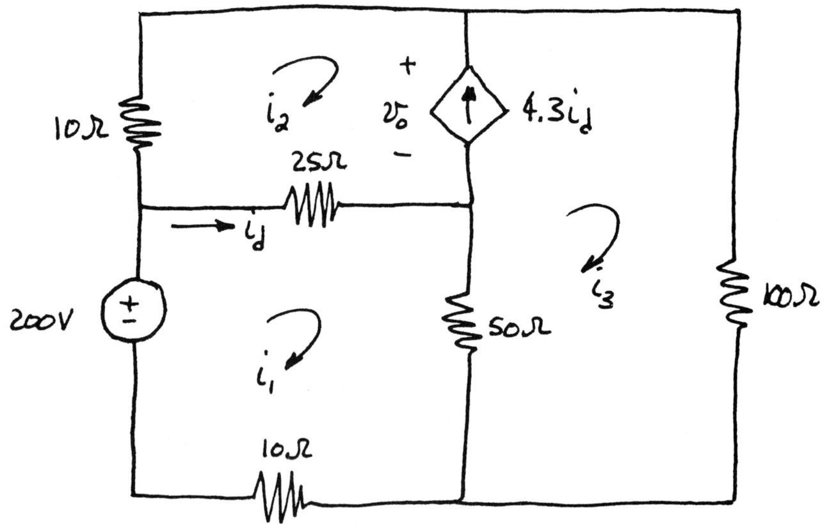

$$200 = 85i_1 - 25i_2 - 50i_3$$

$$0 = -75i_1 + 35i_2 + 150i_3$$

$$i_3 - i_2 = 4.3(i_1 - i_2)$$

Solving, $i_1 = 4.6$ A; $i_2 = 5.7$ A; $i_3 = 0.97$ A

$$i_a = i_2 = 5.7 \text{ A}; \qquad i_b = i_1 = 4.6 \text{ A}$$

$$i_c = i_3 = 0.97 \text{ A}; \qquad i_d = i_1 - i_2 = -1.1 \text{ A}$$

$$i_e = i_1 - i_3 = 3.63 \text{ A}$$

[b] $10i_2 + v_o + 25(i_2 - i_1) = 0$

$$\therefore \quad v_o = -57 - 27.5 = -84.5 \text{ V}$$

$$p_{4.3i_d} = -v_o(4.3i_d) = -(-84.5)(4.3)(-1.1) = -399.685 \text{ W(dev)}$$

$$p_{200V} = -200(4.6) = -920 \text{ W(dev)}$$

$$\sum P_{dev} = 1319.685 \text{ W}$$

$$\sum P_{dis} = (5.7)^2 10 + (1.1)^2(25) + (0.97)^2 100 + (4.6)^2(10) + (3.63)^2(50)$$

$$= 1319.685 \text{ W}$$

$$\therefore \quad \sum P_{dev} = \sum P_{dis} = 1319.685 \text{ W}$$

P 4.37

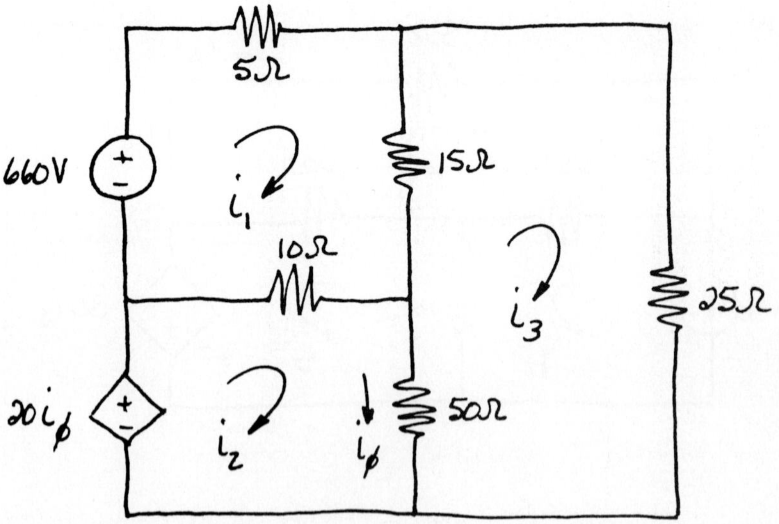

$$660 = 30i_1 - 10i_2 - 15i_3$$

$$20i_\phi = -10i_1 + 60i_2 - 50i_3$$

$$0 = -15i_1 - 50i_2 + 90i_3$$

$$i_\phi = i_2 - i_3$$

Solving, $i_1 = 42$ A; $i_2 = 27$ A; $i_3 = 22$ A; $i_\phi = 5$ A

$$20i_\phi = 100 \text{ V}$$

$$p_{20i_\phi} = -100i_2 = -100(27) = -2700 \text{ W}$$

$$\therefore \; p_{20i_\phi} \text{ (developed)} = 2700 \text{ W}$$

CHECK:

$$p_{660\text{V}} = -660(42) = -27{,}720 \text{ W (dev)}$$

$$\therefore \; \sum P_{\text{dev}} = 27{,}720 + 2700 = 30{,}420 \text{ W}$$

$$\sum P_{\text{dis}} = (42)^2(5) + (22)^2(25) + (20)^2(15) + (5)^2(50) + (15)^2(10)$$

$$= 30{,}420 \text{ W}$$

P 4.38

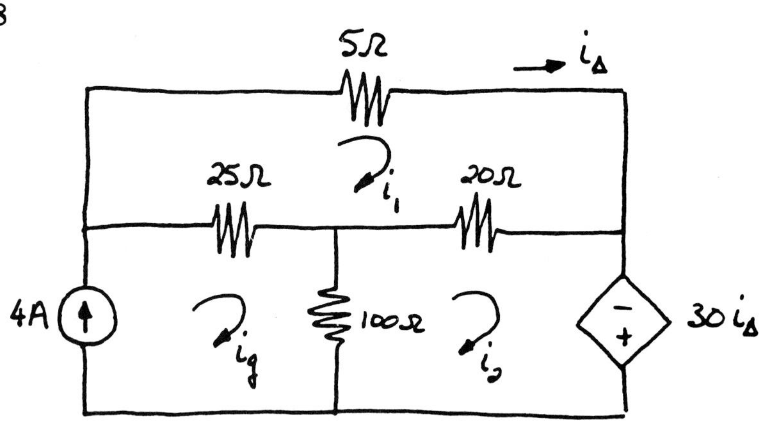

Mesh equations:

$$50i_1 - 20i_2 - 25i_g = 0$$

$$-20i_1 + 120i_2 - 30i_\Delta = 0$$

Constraint equations:

$$i_g = 4; \qquad i_\Delta = i_1$$

Solving, $i_1 = 4$ A; $\quad i_2 = 5$ A

$$i_{25\Omega} = 4 - i_1 = 0 \text{ A}$$

$$i_{20\Omega} = i_2 - i_1 = 1 \text{ A}$$

$$i_{100\Omega} = 4 - i_2 = -1 \text{ A}$$

$$i_{5\Omega} = i_1 = 4 \text{ A}$$

$$v_{4A} = 100(4 - i_2) = -100 \text{ V}$$

$$p_{4A} = -v_{4A}i_g = -(-100)(4) = 400 \text{ W (abs)}$$

$$v_{30i_\Delta} = 30i_\Delta = 3 - i_1 = 120 \text{ V}$$

$$p_{30i_\Delta} = -30i_\Delta i_2 = -120(5) = -600 \text{ W}$$

Therefore, the dependent source is developing 600 W, all other elements are absorbing power, and the total power developed is thus 600 W.
CHECK:

$$p_{5\Omega} = 16(5) = 80 \text{ W}$$

$$p_{25\Omega} = 0 \text{ W}$$

$$p_{20\Omega} = 1(20) = 20 \text{ W}$$

$$p_{100\Omega} = 1(100) = 100 \text{ W}$$

$$p_{4\text{A}} = 400 \text{ W}$$

$$\sum p_{\text{abs}} = 80 + 0 + 20 + 100 + 400 = 600 \text{ W (CHECKS)}$$

P 4.39 [a]

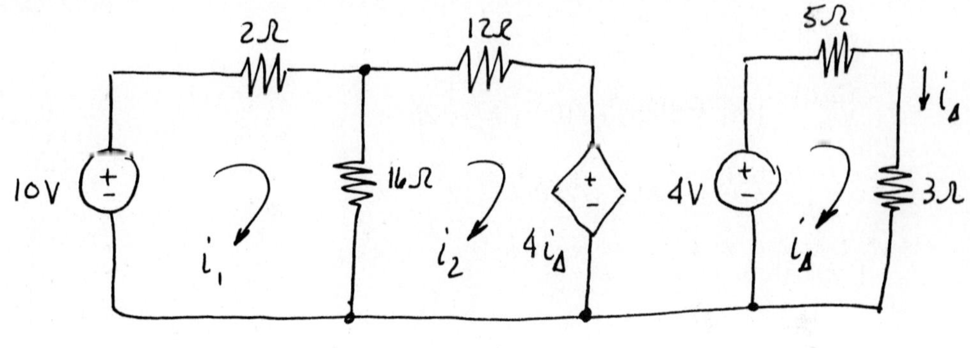

$$10 = 18i_1 - 16i_2$$

$$0 = -16i_1 + 28i_2 + 4i_\Delta$$

$$4 = 8i_\Delta$$

Solving, $i_1 = 1$ A; $\qquad i_2 = 0.5$ A

$$v_0 = 16(i_1 - i_2) = 16(0.5) = 8 \text{ V}$$

[b] $\qquad p_{4i_\Delta} = 4i_\Delta i_2 = (4)(0.5)(0.5) = 1 \text{ W (abs)}$

$$\therefore \; p_{4i_\Delta} \text{ (deliver) } = -1 \text{ W}$$

P 4.40

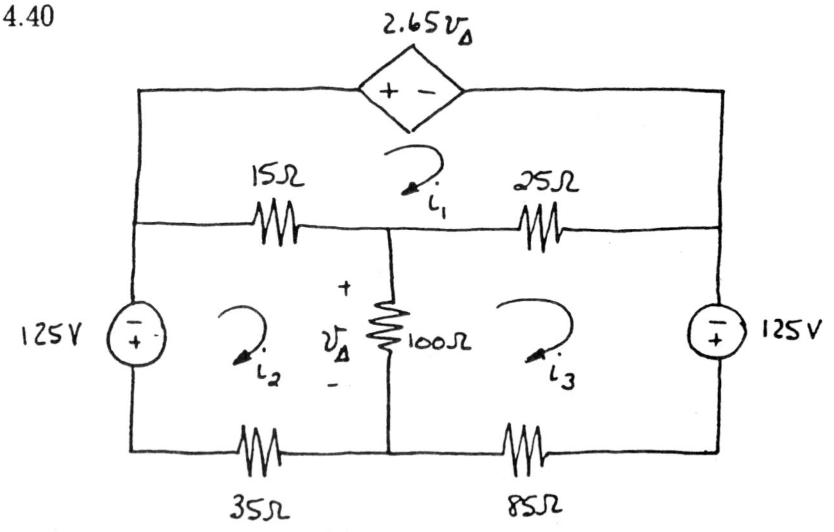

Mesh equations:

$$2.65v_\Delta + 40i_1 - 15i_2 - 25i_3 = 0$$

$$-15i_1 + 150i_2 - 100i_3 = -125$$

$$-25i_1 - 100i_2 + 210i_3 = 125$$

Constraint equations:

$$v_\Delta = 100(i_2 - i_3)$$

Solving, $i_1 = 7$ A; $i_2 = 1.2$ A; $i_3 = 2$ A

$$v_\Delta = 100(i_2 - i_3) = 100(1.2 - 2) = -80 \text{ V}$$

$$p_{2.65v_\Delta} = 2.65v_\Delta i_1 = -1484 \text{ W}$$

Therefore, the dependent source is developing 1484 W.
CHECK:

$$p_{125V} = 125i_2 = 150 \text{ W (left source)}$$

$$p_{125V} = -125i_3 = -250 \text{ W (right source)}$$

$$\sum p_{dev} = 1484 + 250 = 1734 \text{ W}$$

$$p_{35\Omega} = (1.2)^2(35) = 50.4 \text{ W}$$

$$p_{85\Omega} = (2)^2(85) = 340 \text{ W}$$

$$p_{15\Omega} = (7 - 1.2)^2(15) = 504.6 \text{ W}$$

$$p_{25\Omega} = (7 - 2)^2(25) = 625 \text{ W}$$

$$p_{100\Omega} = (1.2 - 2)^2(100) = 64 \text{ W}$$

$$\sum p_{\text{diss}} = 50.4 + 340 + 504.6 + 625 + 64 + 150 = 1734 \text{ W}$$

P 4.41 [a]

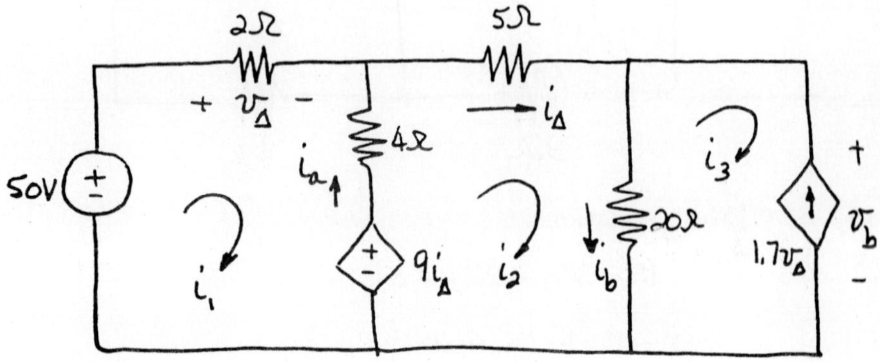

Mesh equations:

$$-50 + 6i_1 - 4i_2 + 9i_\Delta = 0$$

$$-9i_\Delta - 4i_1 + 29i_2 - 20i_3 = 0$$

Constraint equations:

$$i_\Delta = i_2; \qquad i_3 = -1.7v_\Delta; \qquad v_\Delta = 2i_1$$

Solving, $i_1 = -5$ A; $\quad i_2 = 16$ A; $\quad i_3 = 17$ A

$$9i_\Delta = 9(16) = 144 \text{ V}$$

$$i_a = i_2 - i_1 = 21 \text{ A}$$

$$i_b = i_2 - i_3 = -1 \text{ A}$$

$$v_b = 20i_b = -20 \text{ V}$$

$$p_{50\text{V}} = -50i_1 = 250 \text{ W (absorbing)}$$

$$p_{9i_\Delta} = -i_a(9i_\Delta) = -(21)(144) = -3024 \text{ W (delivering)}$$

$$p_{1.7\text{V}} = -1.7v_\Delta v_b = i_3 v_b = (17)(-20) = -340 \text{ W (delivering)}$$

[b] $\sum P_{\text{dev}} = 3024 + 340 = 3364$ W

$\sum P_{\text{dis}} = 250 + (-5)^2(2) + (21)^2(4) + (16)^2(5) + (-1)^2(20) = 3364$ W

P 4.42 [a]

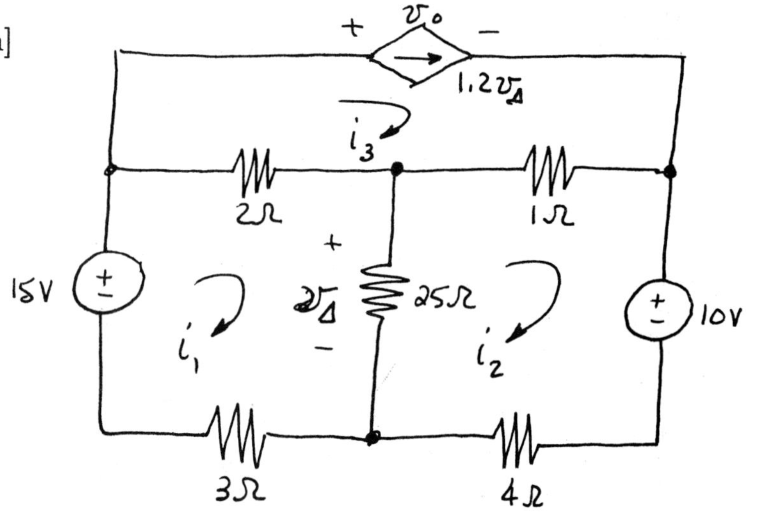

Mesh equations:

$$15 = 30i_1 - 25i_2 - 2i_3$$

$$-10 = -25i_1 + 30i_2 - i_3$$

Constraint equations:

$$i_3 = 1.2v_\Delta; \qquad v_\Delta = 25(i_1 - i_2)$$

Solving, $i_1 = 10$ A; $\quad i_2 = 9$ A; $\quad i_3 = 30$ A

$$i_{2\Omega} = i_1 - i_3 = 9 - 30 = -20 \text{ A}$$

$$p_{2\Omega} = (-20)^2(2) = 800 \text{ W}$$

[b] $p_{15V} = -15(10) = -150$ W(dev)

$$p_{10V} = 10i_2 = 10(9) = 90 \text{ W (abs)}$$

$$v_o = (i_1 - i_3)2 + (i_2 - i_3)1 = -40 - 21 = -61 \text{ V}$$

$$p_{1.2v_\Delta} = i_3 v_o = (30)(-61) = -1830 \text{ W (dev)}$$

$$\sum P_{\text{dev}} = 1830 + 150 = 1980 \text{ W}$$

$$\% \text{ delivered to } 2\Omega = \frac{800}{1980} \times 100 = 40.4\%$$

P 4.43 [a]

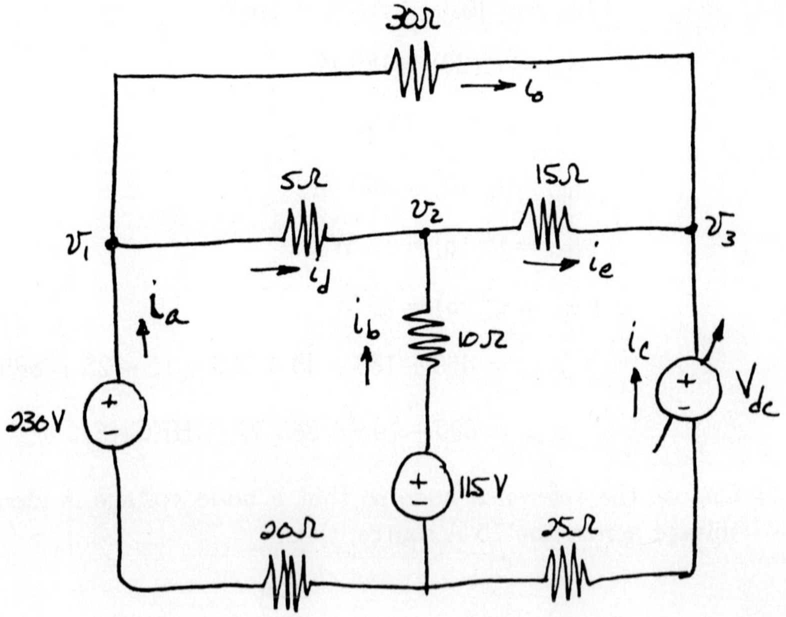

If $i_o = 0$ then $v_1 = v_3$; therefore,

$$\frac{v_1 - v_2}{5} + \frac{v_1 - 230}{20} = 0$$

$$\frac{v_2 - v_1}{5} + \frac{v_2 - v_3}{15} + \frac{v_2 - 115}{10} = 0$$

Solving, $v_1 = 170$ V $= v_3$; $\quad v_2 = 155$ V

$$\therefore \quad \frac{170 - 155}{15} + \frac{170 - v_{dc}}{25} = 0$$

Solving, $v_{dc} = 195$ V

[b]
$$i_a = \frac{230 - 170}{20} = 3 \text{ A}$$

$$i_b = \frac{115 - 155}{10} = -4 \text{ A}$$

$$i_c = \frac{195 - 170}{25} = 1 \text{ A}$$

$$i_d = \frac{170 - 155}{5} = 3 \text{ A}$$

$$i_e = \frac{155 - 170}{15} = -1 \text{ A}$$

$$p_{230\text{V}} = -230 i_a = -690 \text{ W (dev)}$$

$$p_{115\text{V}} = -115 i_b = 460 \text{ W (abs)}$$

$$p_{v_{dc}} = -v_{dc}i_c = -195 \text{ W (dev)}$$

$$p_{20\Omega} = i_a^2(20) = 180 \text{ W}$$

$$p_{5\Omega} = i_d^2(5) = 45 \text{ W}$$

$$p_{10\Omega} = i_b^2(10) = 160 \text{ W}$$

$$p_{15\Omega} = i_e^2(15) = 15 \text{ W}$$

$$p_{25\Omega} = i_c^2(25) = 25 \text{ W}$$

$$\sum p_{\text{diss}} = 460 + 180 + 45 + 160 + 15 + 25 = 885 \text{ W}$$

$$\sum p_{\text{dev}} = 690 + 195 = 885 \text{ W (CHECKS)}$$

P 4.44 Choose the reference node so that a node voltage is identical to the voltage across the 15 A source; thus:

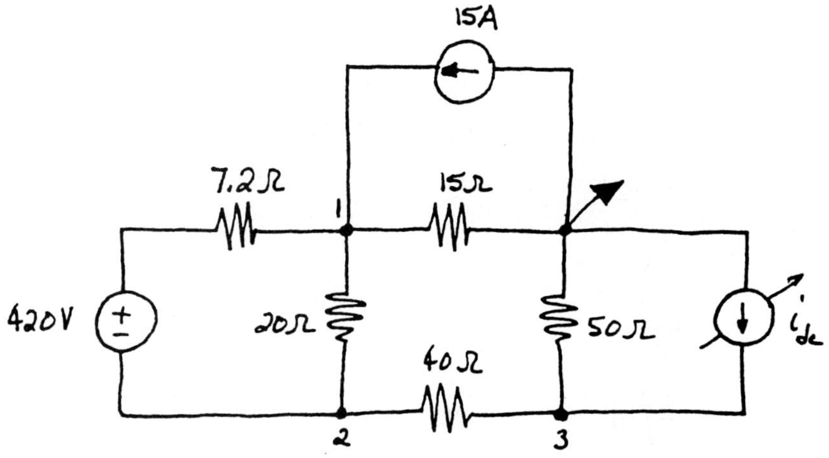

Since the 15 A source is developing 3750 W, v_1 must be 250 V.

Since v_1 is known, we can sum the currents away from node 1 to find v_2; thus:

$$\frac{250 - (420 + v_2)}{7.2} + \frac{250 - v_2}{20} + \frac{250}{15} - 15 = 0$$

$$\therefore \quad v_2 = -50 \text{ V}$$

Now that we know v_2 we sum the currents away from node 2 to find v_3; thus:

$$\frac{v_2 + 420 - 250}{7.2} + \frac{v_2 - 250}{20} + \frac{v_2 - v_3}{40} = 0$$

$$\therefore \quad v_3 = 50/3 \text{ V}$$

Now that we know v_3 we sum the currents away from node 3 to find i_{dc}; thus:

$$\frac{v_3}{50} + \frac{v_3 + 50}{40} = i_{dc}$$

$$\therefore \quad i_{dc} = 2 \text{ A}$$

P 4.45 [a]

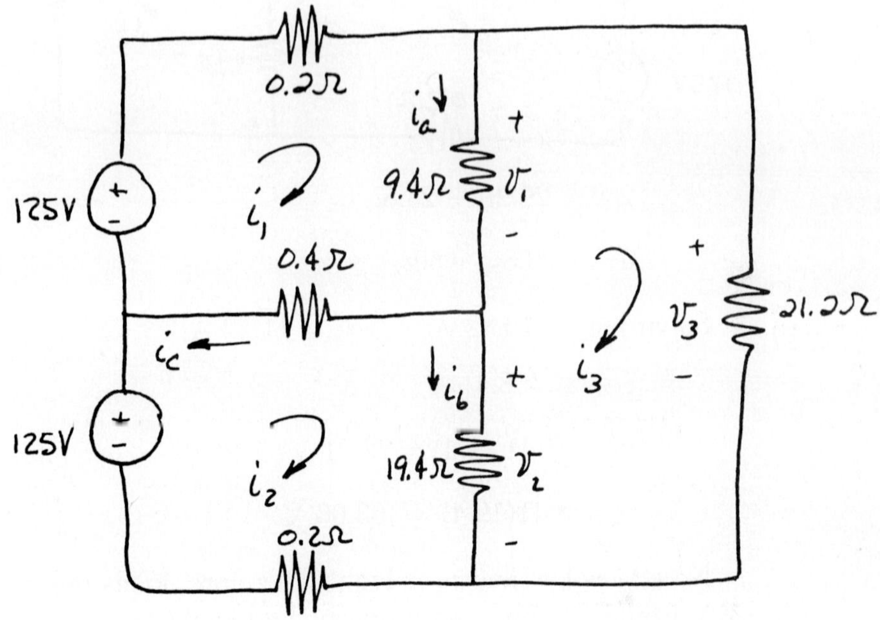

$$125 = 10i_1 - 0.4i_2 - 9.4i_3$$

$$125 = -0.4i_1 + 20i_2 - 19.4i_3$$

$$0 = -9.4i_1 - 19.4i_2 + 50i_3$$

Solving, $i_1 = 23.93$ A; $\quad i_2 = 17.79$ A; $\quad i_3 = 11.40$ A

$$v_1 = 9.4(i_1 - i_3) = 117.76 \text{ V}$$

$$v_2 = 19.4(i_2 - i_3) = 123.90 \text{ V}$$

$$v_3 = 21.2i_3 = 241.66 \text{ V}$$

[b]

$$P_{R1} = (i_1 - i_3)^2(9.4) = 1475.22 \text{ W}$$

$$P_{R2} = (i_2 - i_3)^2(19.4) = 791.29 \text{ W}$$

$$P_{R3} = i_3^2(21.2) = 2754.64 \text{ W}$$

[c] $\sum p_{\rm dev} = 125(i_1 + i_2) = 5213.99$ W

$\sum p_{\rm load} = 5021.15$ W

$$\% \text{ delivered } = \frac{5021.15}{5213.99} \times 100 = 96.3\%$$

[d]

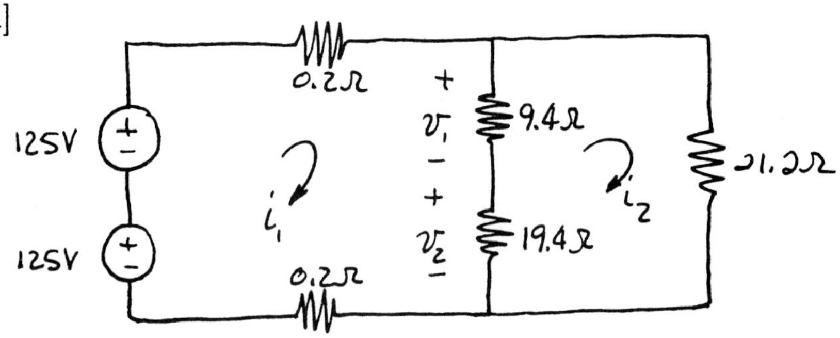

$$250 = 29.2i_1 - 28.8i_2$$

$$0 = -28.8i_1 + 50i_2$$

Solving, $i_1 = 19.82$ A; $\quad i_2 = 11.42$ A

$$i_1 - i_2 = 8.41 \text{ A}$$

$$v_1 = (8.41)(9.4) = 79.01 \text{ V}$$

$$v_2 = 8.41(19.4) = 163.06 \text{ V}$$

Note v_1 is low and v_2 is high. Therefore, loads designed for 125 V would not function properly, and could be damaged.

P 4.46

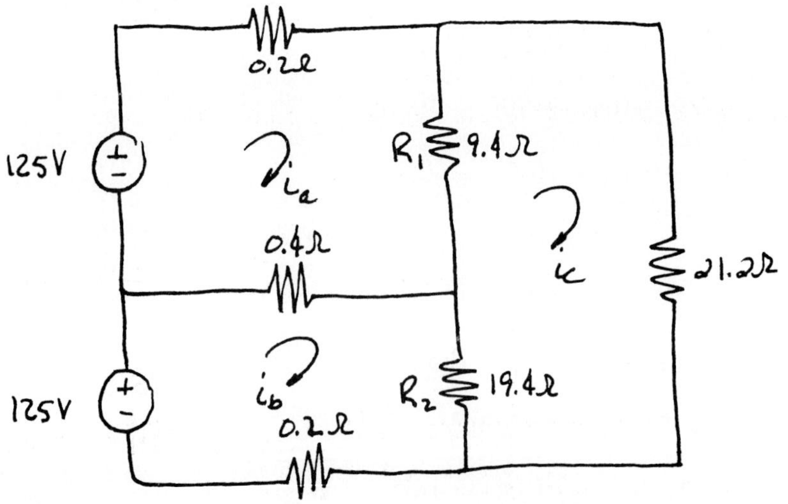

$$125 = (R_1 + 0.6)i_{\rm a} - 0.4i_{\rm b} - R_1 i_{\rm c}$$

$$125 = -0.4i_{\rm a} + (R_2 + 0.6)i_{\rm b} - R_2 i_{\rm c}$$

$$0 = -R_1 i_\mathrm{a} - R_2 i_\mathrm{b} + (R_1 + R_2 + 21.2) i_\mathrm{c}$$

$$\Delta = \begin{vmatrix} (R_1 + 0.6) & 0.4 & -R_1 \\ -0.4 & (R_2 + 0.6) & -R_2 \\ -R_1 & -R_2 & (R_1 + R_2 + 21.2) \end{vmatrix}$$

When $R_1 = R_2$, Δ reduces to

$$\Delta = 21.2R_1^2 + 25.84R_1 + 4.24.$$

$$\begin{aligned} N_\mathrm{a} &= \begin{vmatrix} 125 & -0.4 & -R_1 \\ 125 & (R_2 + 0.6) & -R_2 \\ 0 & -R_2 & (R_1 + R_2 + 21.2) \end{vmatrix} \\ &= 125\,[2R_1R_2 + R_1 + 22.2R_2 + 21.2] \end{aligned}$$

$$\begin{aligned} N_\mathrm{b} &= \begin{vmatrix} (R_1 + 0.6) & 125 & -R_1 \\ -0.4 & 125 & -R_2 \\ -R_1 & 0 & (R_1 + R_2 + 21.2) \end{vmatrix} \\ &= 125\,[2R_1R_2 + 22.2R_1 + R_2 + 21.2] \end{aligned}$$

$$i_\mathrm{a} = \frac{N_\mathrm{a}}{\Delta}, \qquad i_\mathrm{b} = \frac{N_\mathrm{b}}{\Delta}$$

$$i_\mathrm{neutral} = i_\mathrm{a} - i_\mathrm{b} = \frac{N_\mathrm{a} - N_\mathrm{b}}{\Delta} = \frac{125[(R_1 + R_2) + 22.2(R_2 - R_1)]}{\Delta}$$

Now note that when $R_1 = R_2$, i_neutral reduces to

$$i_\mathrm{neutral} = \frac{0}{\Delta} = 0$$

P 4.47 [a]

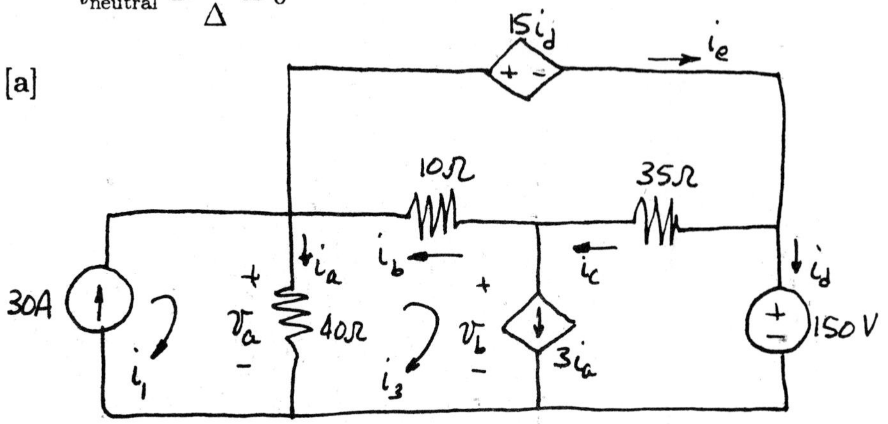

$$40(i_3 - 30) + 15i_4 + 150 = 0$$

$$40(i_3 - 30) + 10(i_3 - i_2) + 35(i_4 - i_2) + 150 = 0$$

$$i_a = 30 - i_3; \qquad 3i_a = i_3 - i_4$$

Solving, $i_1 = 30$ A; $\quad i_2 = 8$ A; $\quad i_3 = 24$ A; $\quad i_4 = 6$ A

$$i_a = 30 - 24 = 6\text{ A}; \quad i_b = 8 - 24 = -16\text{ A}; \quad i_c = 8 - 6 = 2\text{ A};$$

$$i_d = 6\text{ A}; \qquad i_e = i_c + i_d = 6 + 2 = 8\text{ A}$$

[b] $\quad v_a = 40i_a = 240$ V; $\qquad v_b = 150 - 35i_c = 80$ V

$$p_{30\text{A}} = -30v_a = -30(240) = -7200\text{ W (gen)}$$

$$p_{15i_d} = 15i_d i_e = 15(6)(8) = 720\text{ W (diss)}$$

$$p_{3i_a} = 3i_a v_b = 3(6)(80) = 1440\text{ W (diss)}$$

$$p_{150\text{V}} = 150i_d = 150(6) = 900\text{ W (diss)}$$

$$p_{40\Omega} = (6)^2(40) = 1440\text{ W (diss)}$$

$$p_{10\Omega} = (-16)^2(10) = 2560\text{ W (diss)}$$

$$p_{35\Omega} = (2)^2(35) = 140\text{ W (diss)}$$

$$\sum P_{\text{gen}} = 7200\text{ W}$$

$$\sum P_{\text{diss}} = 720 + 1440 + 900 + 1440 + 2560 + 140 = 7200\text{ W}$$

P 4.48 [a] The node voltage method requires summing the currents at two supernodes in terms of four node voltages and using two constraint equations to reduce the system of equations to two unknowns. If the connection at the bottom of the circuit is used as the reference node, then the voltages controlling the dependent sources are node voltages. This makes it easy to formulate the constraint equations. The current in the 5 V source is obtained by summing the currents at either terminal of the source.

The mesh current method requires summing the voltages around the two meshes not containing current sources in terms of four mesh currents. In addition the voltages controlling the dependent sources must be expressed in terms of the mesh currents. Thus the constraint equations are more complicated, and the reduction to two equations and two unknowns involves more algebraic manipulation. The current in the 5 V source is found by subtracting two mesh currents.

Because the constraint equations are easier to formulate in the node Voltage method, it is the preferred approach.

[b]

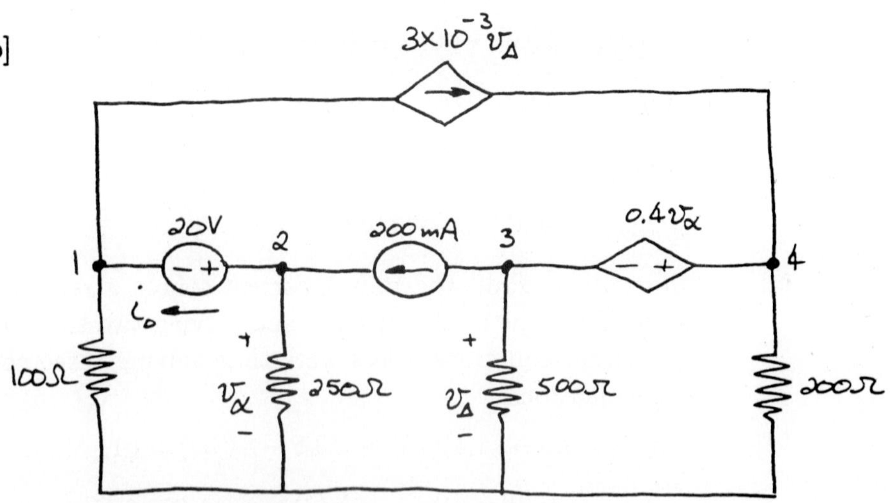

Node voltage equations:

$$\frac{v_1}{100} + \frac{v_2}{250} - 0.2 + 3\times10^{-3}v_3 = 0$$

$$\frac{v_3}{500} + \frac{v_4}{200} - 3\times10^{-3}v_3 + 0.2 = 0$$

Constraints:

$$v_2 - v_1 = 20; \qquad v_4 - v_3 = 0.4v_\alpha; v_\alpha = v_2$$

Solving, $v_2 = 44$ V

$$i_o = 200 - 44/0.25 = 24 \text{ mA}$$

$$p_{20\text{V}} = 20i_o = 480 \text{ mW (abs)}$$

P 4.49 [a] There are three unknown node voltages and only two unknown mesh currents. Use the mesh current method to minimize the number of simultaneous equations.

[b]

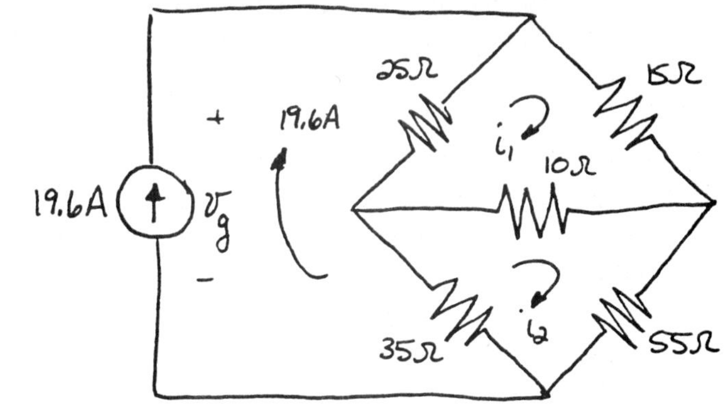

$$25(i_1 - 19.6) + 15i_1 + 10(i_1 - i_2) = 0$$

$$35(i_2 - 19.6) + 10(i_2 - i_1) + 55i_2 = 0$$

Solving, $i_1 = 11.4$ A; $\qquad i_2 = 8$ A

$$i_{10\Omega} = i_1 - i_2 = 3.4 \text{ A}$$

$$p_{10\Omega} = (3.4)^2(10) = 115.6 \text{ W}$$

[c] No, the voltage across the 19.6 A current source is readily available from the mesh currents, and solving two simultaneous mesh-current equations is less work than solving three node voltage equations.

[d] $$v_g = (19.6 - 11.4)(25) + (19.6 - 8)(35) = 611 \text{ V}$$

$$p_{19.6\text{A}} \text{ (developed)} = 19.6(611) = 11{,}975.6 \text{ W}$$

P 4.50 [a] There are three unknown node voltages and three unknown mesh currents, so the number of simultaneous equations required are the same for both methods. The node Voltage method has the advantage of having to solve the three simultaneous equations for one unknown voltage provided the connection at either the top or bottom of the circuit is used as the reference node. Therefore recommend the node Voltage method.

[b]

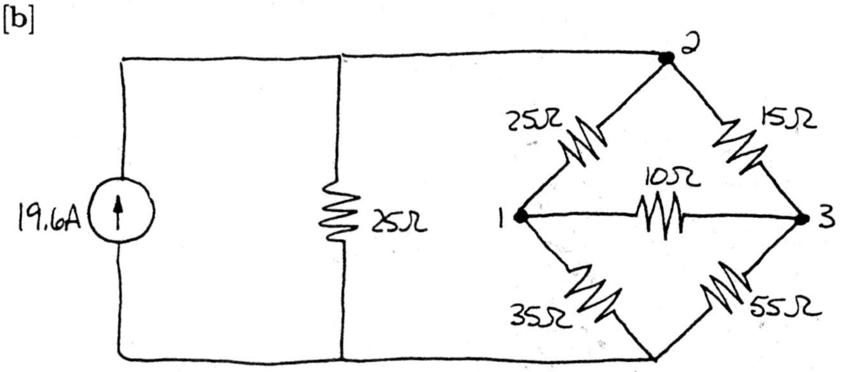

$$\frac{v_1}{35} + \frac{v_1 - v_2}{25} + \frac{v_1 - v_3}{10} = 0$$

$$\frac{v_2}{25} - 19.6 + \frac{v_2 - v_1}{25} + \frac{v_2 - v_3}{15} = 0$$

$$\frac{v_3 - v_1}{10} + \frac{v_3 - v_2}{15} + \frac{v_3}{55} = 0$$

Solving, $v_2 = 271.9255$ V

$$p_{19.6\text{A}} = -(19.6)(271.9255) = -5329.74 \text{ W(dev)}$$

$\therefore$ The 19.6 A source is developing 5329.74 W

P 4.51 [a]

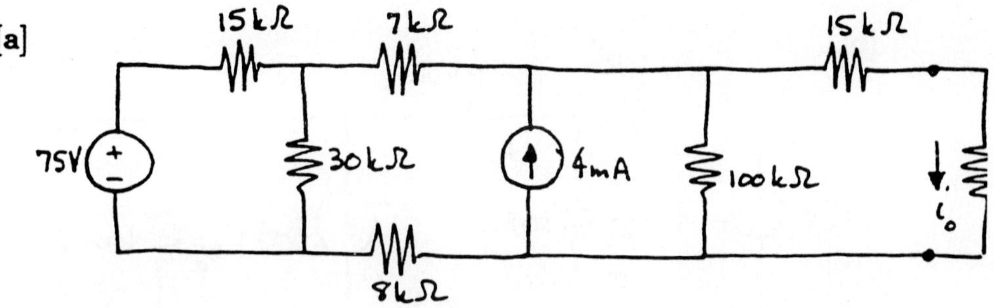

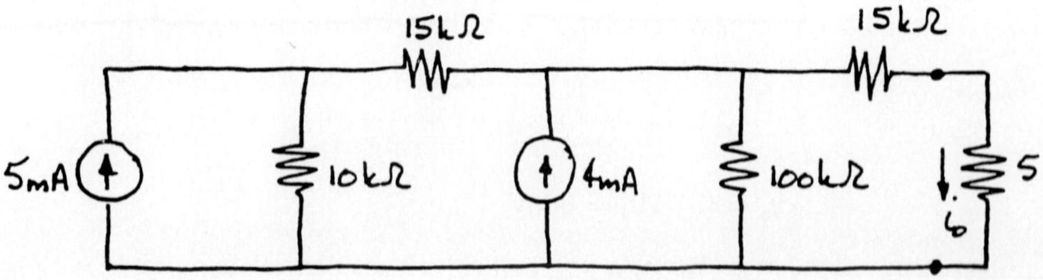

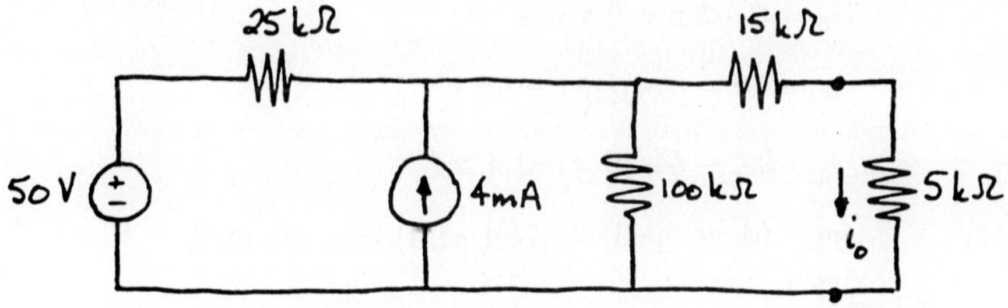

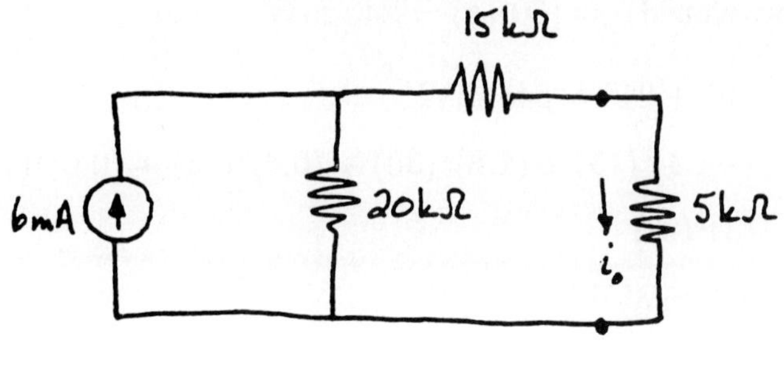

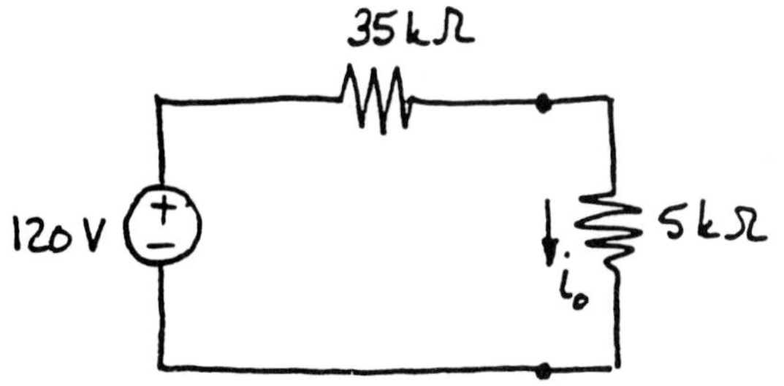

$i_o = 120/40 = 3$ mA

[b]

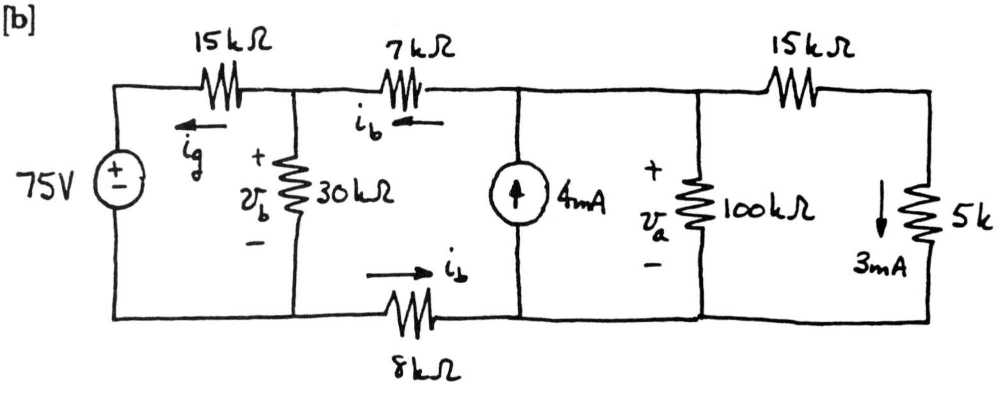

$v_a = (3)(20) = 60$ V

$i_a = \frac{v_a}{100} = 0.6$ mA

$i_b = 4 - 3.6 = 0.4$ mA

$v_b = 60 - (0.4)(15) = 54$ V

$i_g = 0.4 - 54/30 = -1.4$ mA

p_{75V} (developed) $= (75)(-1.4) = -105$ mW

Check:

p_{4mA} (developed) $= (60)(4) = 240$ mW

$$\sum P_{dev} = 105 + 240 = 345 \text{ mW}$$

$$\sum P_{dis} = (-1.4)^2(15) + (1.8)^2(30) + (0.4)^2(15) + (0.6)^2(100) + (3)^2(20) = 345 \text{ mW}$$

P 4.52 [a] Apply source transformations to both current sources to get

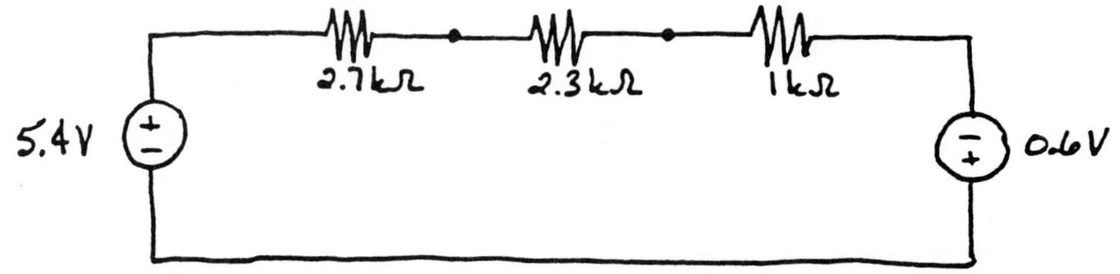

$i_o = \frac{-6}{6} = -1$ mA

[b]

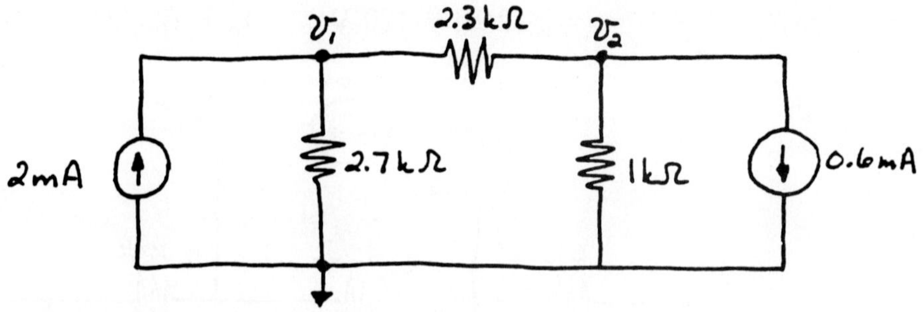

$$-2 + \frac{v_1}{2.7} + \frac{v_1 - v_2}{2.3} = 0$$

$$\frac{v_2}{1} + \frac{v_2 - v_1}{2.3} + 0.6 = 0$$

Solving, $v_1 = 2.7$ V; $\quad v_2 = 0.4$ V

$$\therefore\ i_o = \frac{v_2 - v_1}{2.3} = -1 \text{ mA}$$

P 4.53 [a]

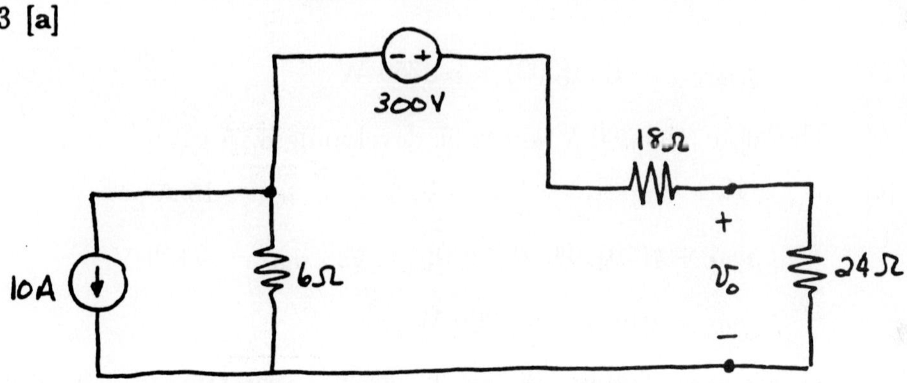

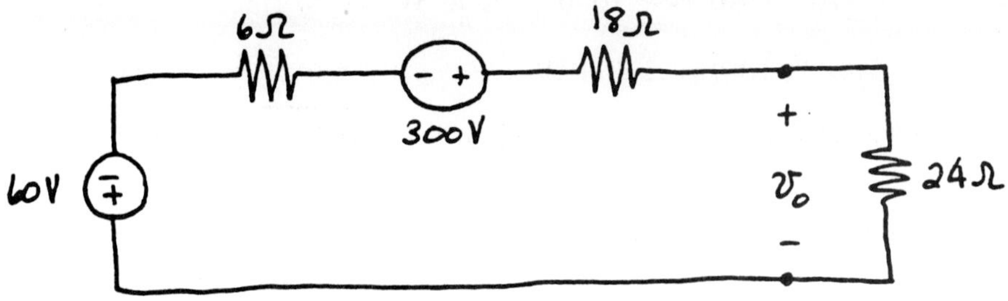

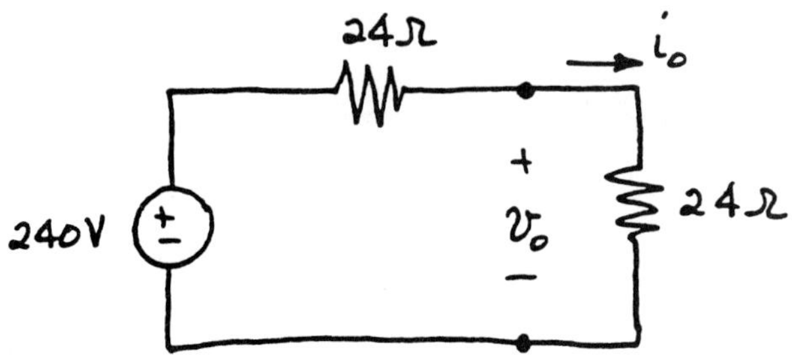

$$\therefore \quad v_o = \frac{1}{2}(240) = 120 \text{ V}; \qquad i_o = 120/24 = 5 \text{ A}$$

[b]

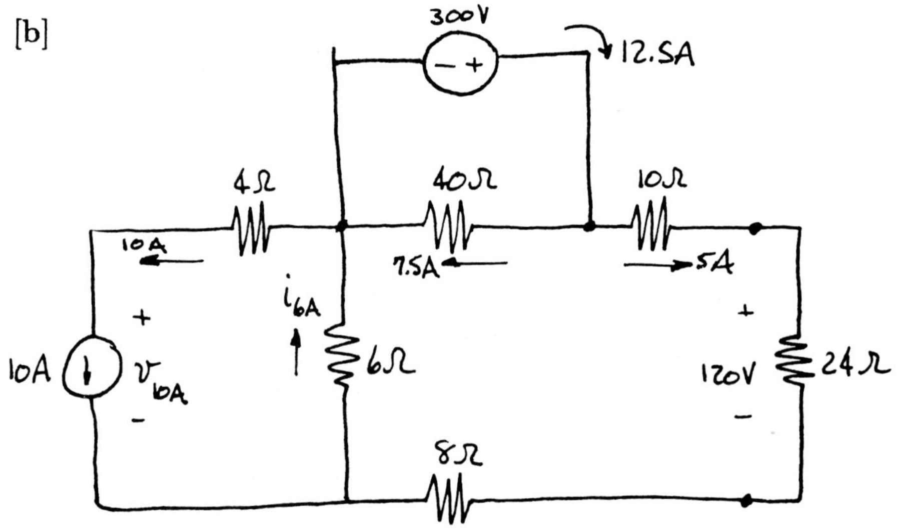

$$p_{300\text{V}} = -12.5(300) = -3750 \text{ W}$$

Therefore, the 300 V source is developing 3.75 kW.

[c] $$-10 + i_{6\Omega} + 7.5 - 12.5 = 0; \qquad \therefore \quad i_{6\Omega} = 15 \text{ A}$$

$$v_{10\text{A}} + 4(10) + 6(15) = 0; \qquad \therefore \quad v_{10\text{A}} = -130 \text{ V}$$

$$p_{10\text{A}} = 10v_{10\text{A}} = -1300 \text{ W}$$

Therefore the 10 A source is developing 1300 W.

[d] $$\sum p_{\text{dev}} = 3750 + 1300 = 5050 \text{ W}$$

$$p_{4\Omega} = 100(4) = 400 \text{ W}$$

$$p_{40\Omega} = (7.5)^2(40) = 2250 \text{ W}$$

$$p_{6\Omega} = (15)^2(6) = 1350 \text{ W}$$

$$p_{42\Omega} = (5)^2(42) = 1050 \text{ W}$$

$$\sum p_{\text{diss}} = 400 + 1350 + 2250 + 1050 = 5050 \text{ W (CHECKS)}$$

P 4.54 [a] Applying a source transformation to each current source yields

P 4.54 **[a]** Applying a source transformation to each current source yields

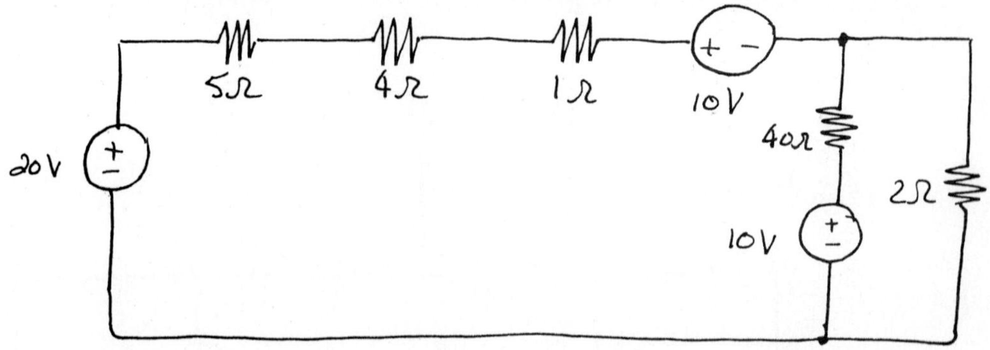

Now combine the 20 V and 10 V sources into a single voltage source and the 5 Ω, 4 Ω and 1 Ω resistors into a single resistor to get

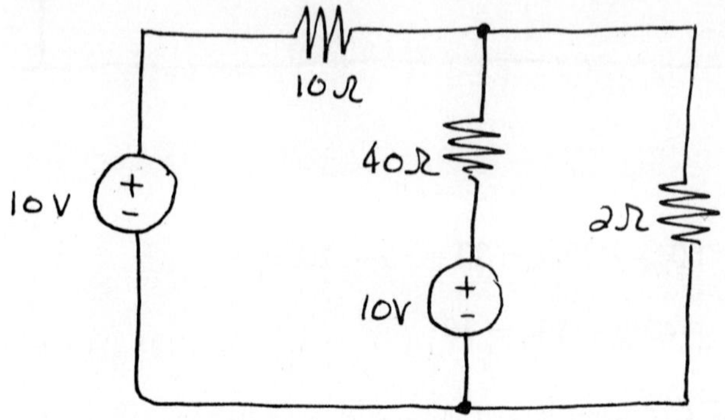

Now use a source transformation on each voltage source, thus

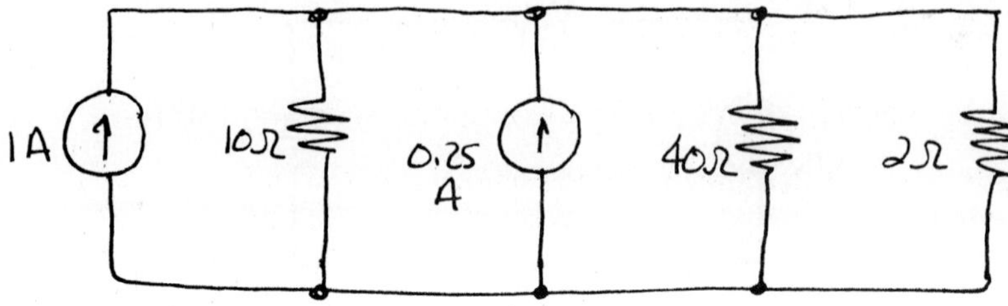

which can be reduced to

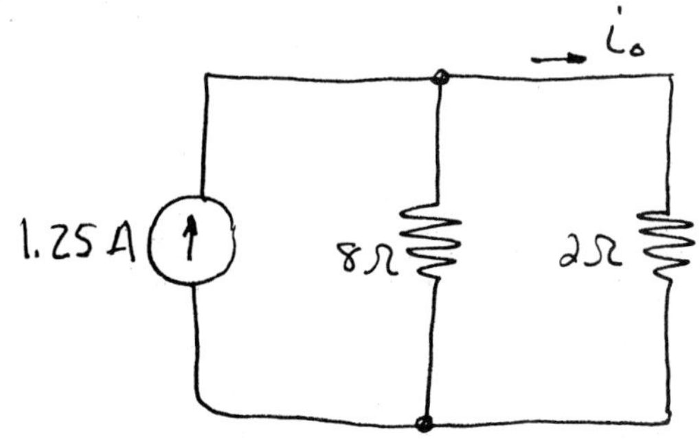

$$\therefore\; i_o = \frac{(1.25)(8)}{10} = 1 \text{ A}$$

[b]

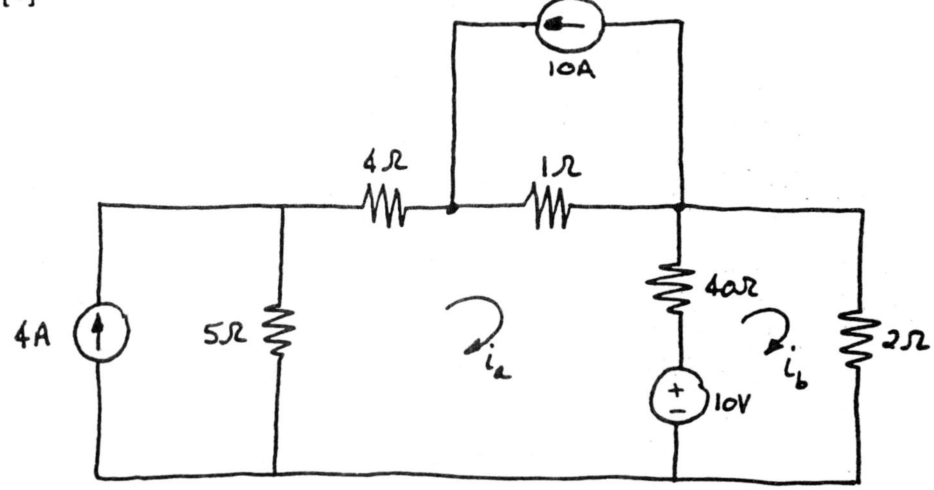

$$50i_a - 40i_b = 20 - 10 - 10 = 0$$

$$-40i_a + 42_b = 10$$

$$\text{Solving, } i_b = \frac{N_b}{\Delta} = 1 \text{ A} = i_o$$

P 4.55

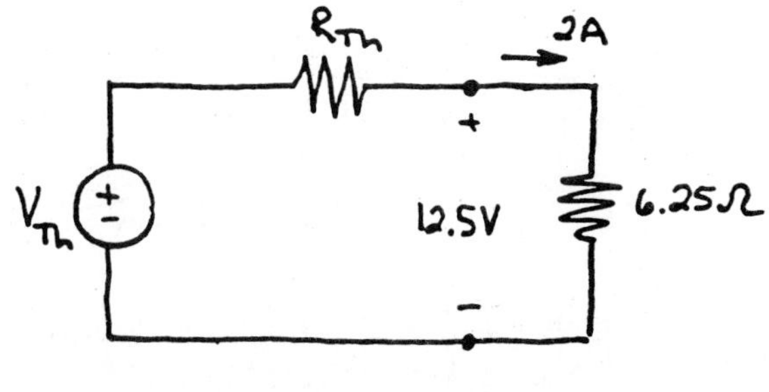

$$12.5 = V_{Th} - 2R_{Th}$$

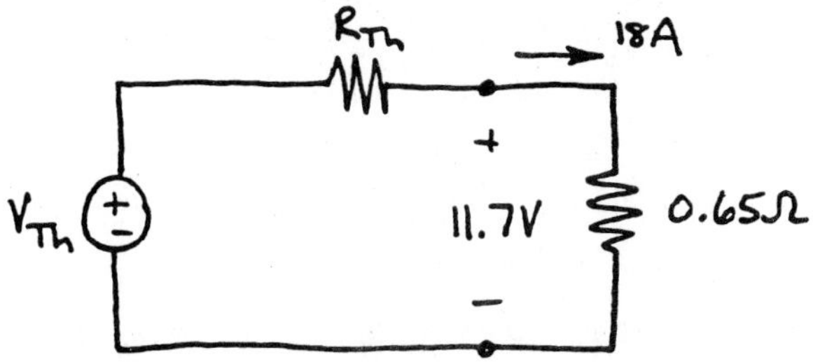

$$11.7 = V_{Th} - 18R_{Th}$$

Solving (1) and (2) for V_{Th} and R_{Th} yields

$$v_{\mathrm{Th}} = 12.6v, \qquad R_{\mathrm{Th}} = 50\ \mathrm{m}\Omega$$

$$\therefore\ I_N = 252\ \mathrm{A}, \qquad R_N = 50\ \mathrm{m}\Omega$$

P 4.56

$$v_{\mathrm{Th}} = \frac{60}{50}(40) = 48\ \mathrm{V}$$

$$R_{\mathrm{Th}} = 8 + \frac{(40)(10)}{50} = 16\,\Omega$$

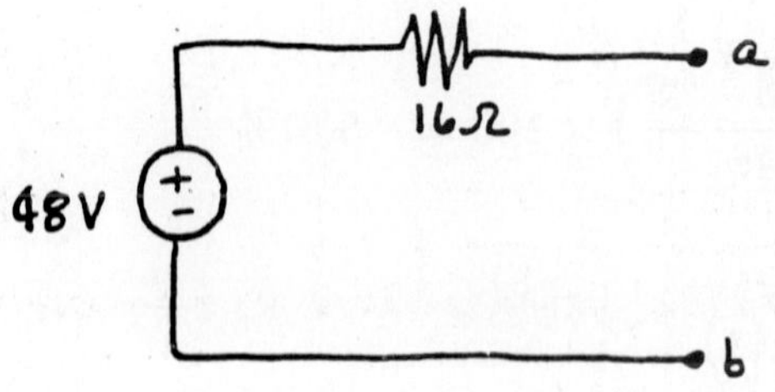

P 4.57 [a] First, find the Thévenin equivalent with respect to a,b using a succession of source transformations.

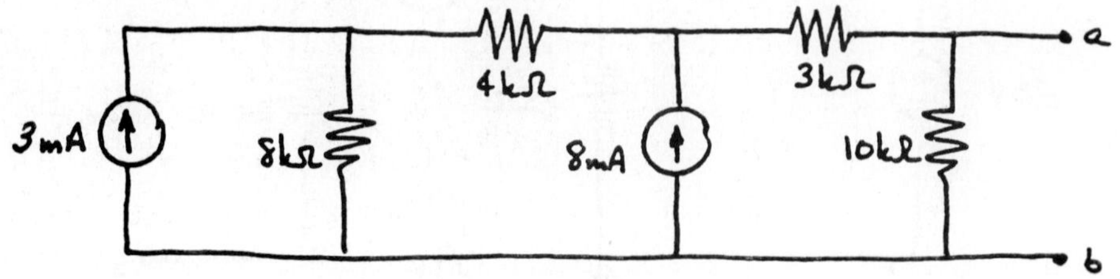

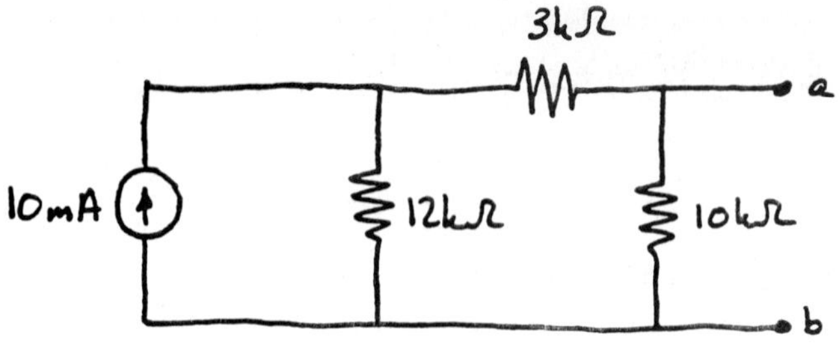

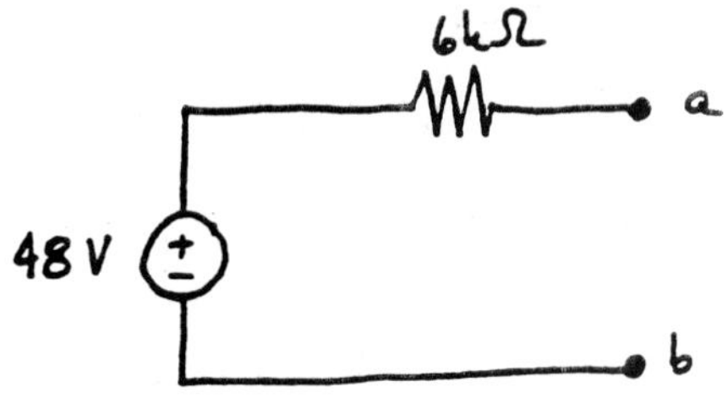

$$\therefore\ v_{\mathrm{Th}} = 48\ \mathrm{V} \qquad R_{\mathrm{Th}} = 6\ \mathrm{k}\Omega$$

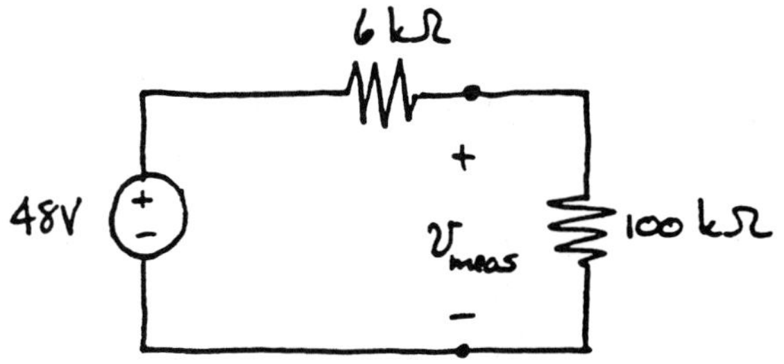

$$v_{\text{meas}} = \frac{100}{106}(48) = 45.28 \text{ V}$$

[b] $$\%\text{error} = \left(\frac{45.28 - 48}{48}\right) \times 100 = -5.67\%$$

P 4.58 [a] Open circuit:

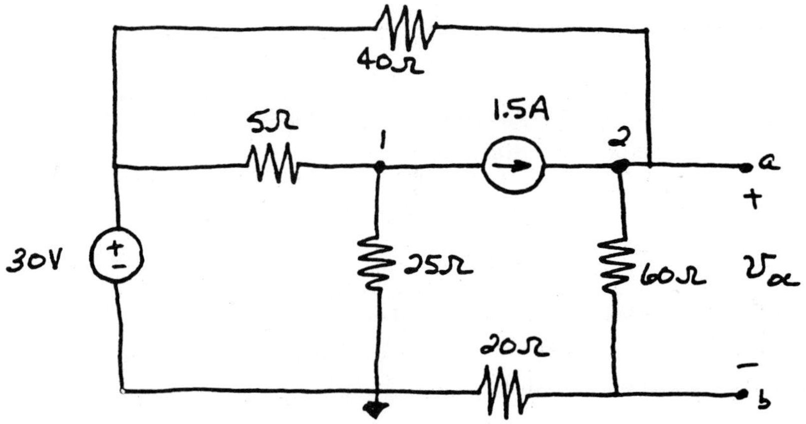

$$\frac{v_2}{80} + \frac{v_2 - 30}{40} - 1.5 = 0$$

$$\therefore \quad v_2 = 60 \text{ V}$$

$$v_{oc} = \frac{60}{80}v_2 = 45 \text{ V} = v_{\text{Th}}$$

Short circuit:

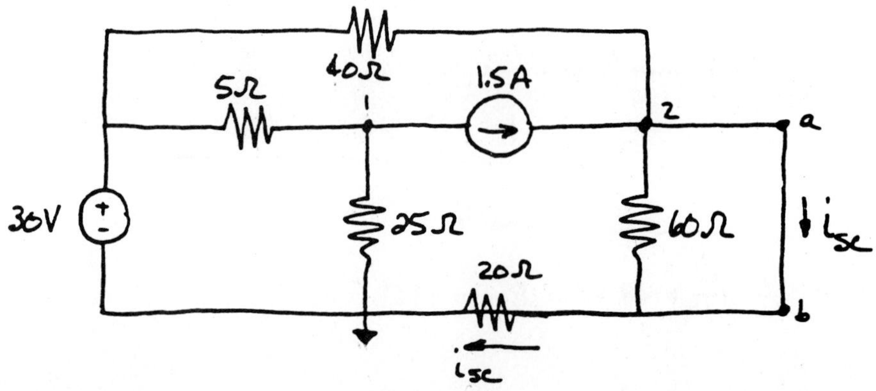

$$\frac{v_2 - 30}{40} - 1.5 + \frac{v_2}{20} = 0$$

$$\therefore \quad v_2 = 30 \text{ V}$$

$$i_{sc} = \frac{v_2}{20} = 1.5 \text{ A}$$

Therefore, $R_{Th} = 45/1.5 = 30\,\Omega$

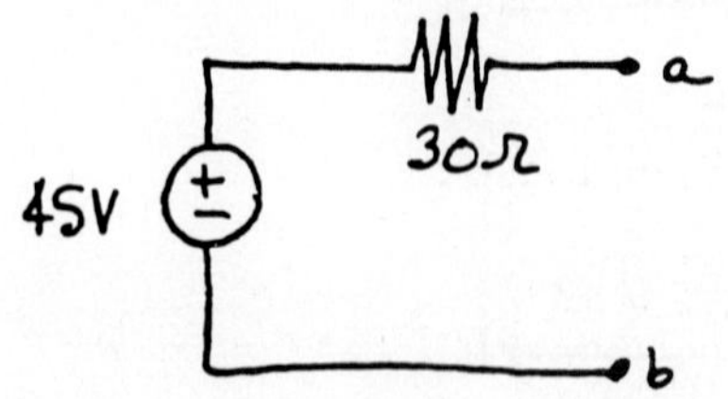

[b]

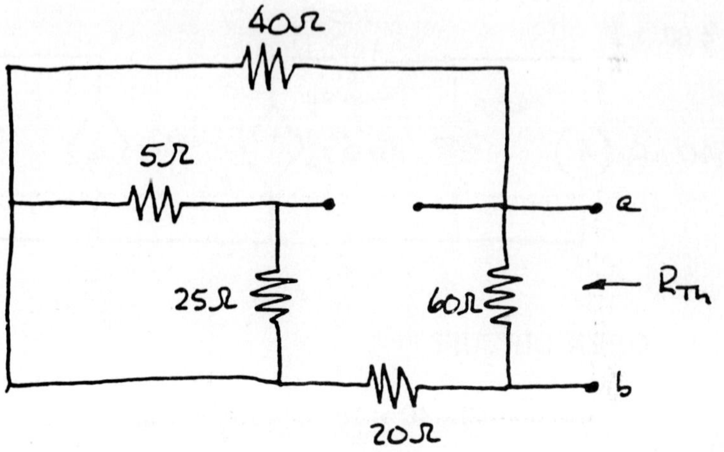

$$R_{Th} = 60\|(40+20) = 30\,\Omega \text{ (CHECKS)}$$

P 4.59

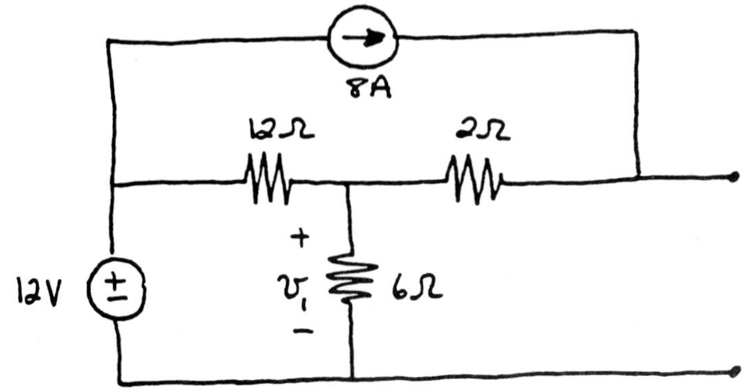

$$\frac{v_1 - 12}{12} + \frac{v_1}{6} - 8 = 0$$

$$v_1 = 36 \text{ V}$$

$$v_{\text{Th}} = v_1 + (2)(8) = 52 \text{ V}$$

$$R_{\text{Th}} = 2 + \frac{(12)(6)}{18} = 6\,\Omega$$

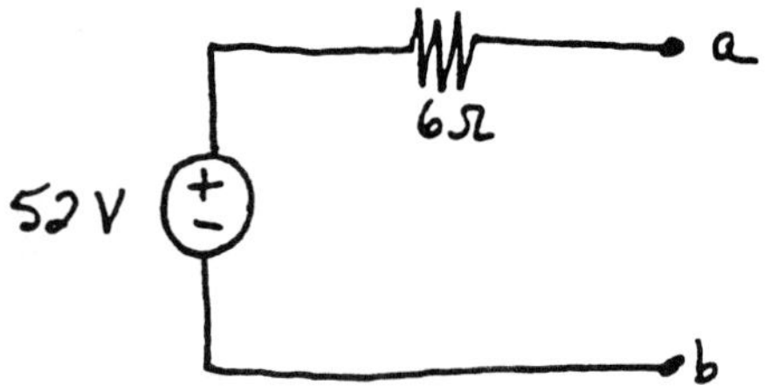

P 4.60

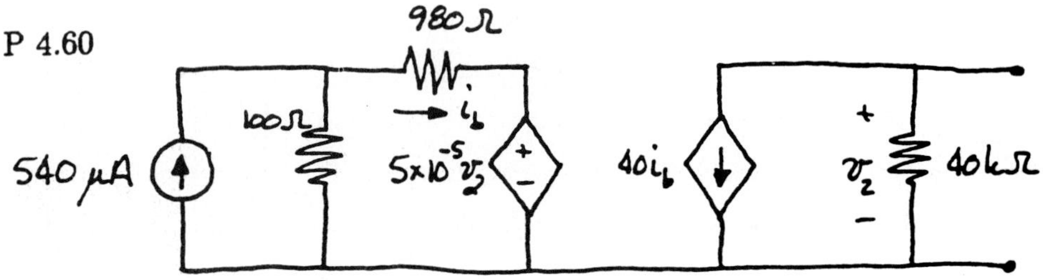

OPEN CIRCUIT

$$v_2 = -40i_b\, 40 \times 10^3 = -16 \times 10^5 i_b$$

$$5 \times 10^{-5} v_2 = -80i_b$$

$$980i_b + 5 \times 10^{-5} v_2 = 900i_b$$

$$100(540 \times 10^{-6} = 54 \text{ mV}$$

$$\therefore \quad i_b = \frac{54 \times 10^{-3}}{1000} = 54\,\mu\text{A}$$

$$v_{\text{Th}} = -16 \times 10^5 (54 \times 10^{-6}) = -86.40 \text{ V}$$

SHORT CIRCUIT

$$v_2 = 0; \qquad i_{sc} = -40i_b$$

$$i_{b_{sc}} = \frac{54 \times 10^{-3}}{1080} = \frac{54}{1.08} \times 10^{-6} = 50\,\mu\text{A}$$

$$i_{sc} = -40(50) = -2000\,\mu\text{A} = -2\text{ mA}$$

$$R_{Th} = \frac{-86.4}{-2} \times 10^3 = 43.2\text{ k}\Omega$$

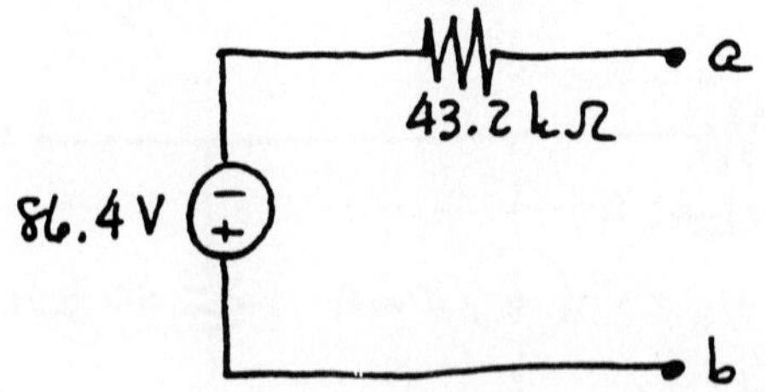

P 4.61 After making a source transformation the circuit becomes

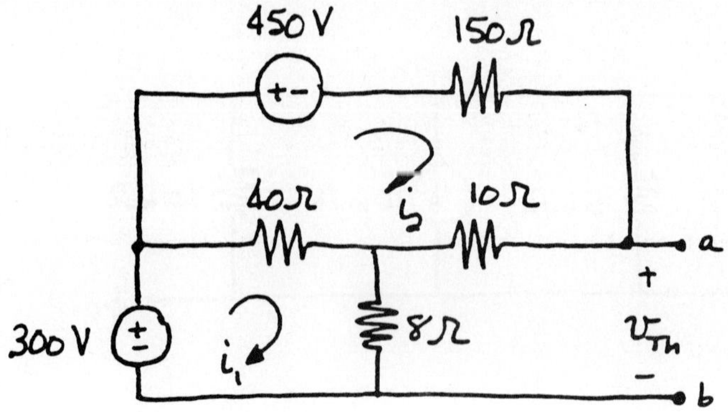

$$300 = 48i_1 - 40i_2$$

$$-450 = -40i_1 + 200i_2$$

$$\therefore\quad i_1 = 5.25\text{ A and } i_2 = -1.2\text{ A}$$

$$v_{Th} = 8i_1 + 10i_2 = 30\text{ V}$$

$$R_{Th} = (40\|8 + 10)\|50 = 15\,\Omega$$

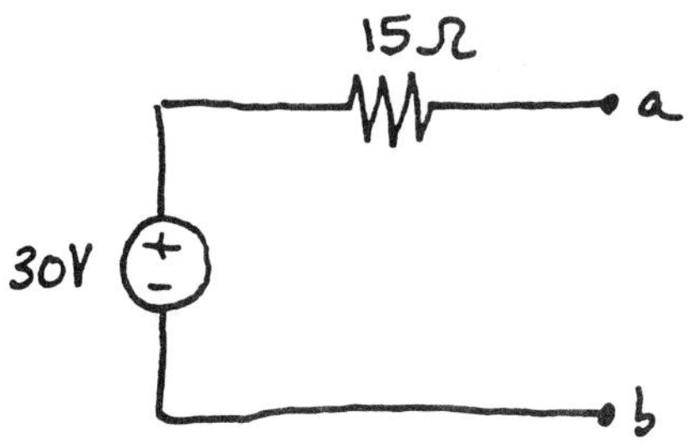

P 4.62 First we make the observation that the 8-mA current source and the 20 kΩ resistor will have no influence on the behavior of the circuit with respect to the terminals a,b. This follows because they are in parallel with an ideal voltage source. Hence our circuit can be simplified to

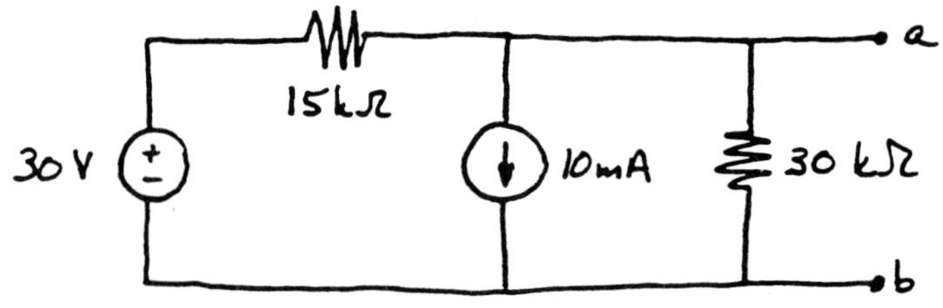

or

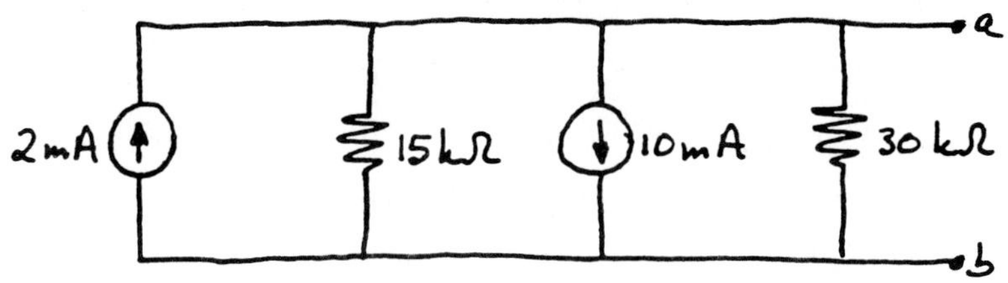

Therefore the Norton equivalent is

P 4.63 First, find the Thévenin equivalent with respect to R_o.

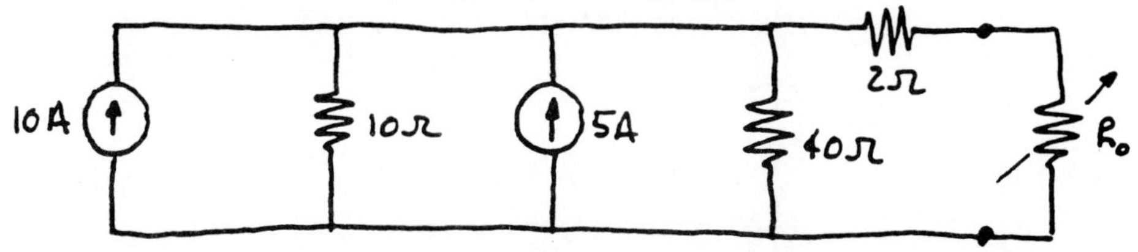

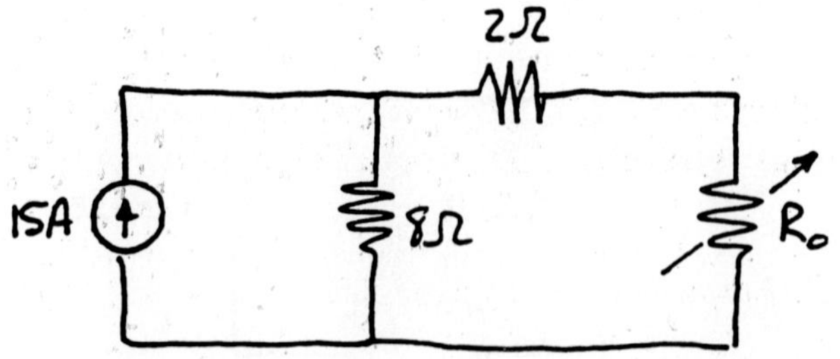

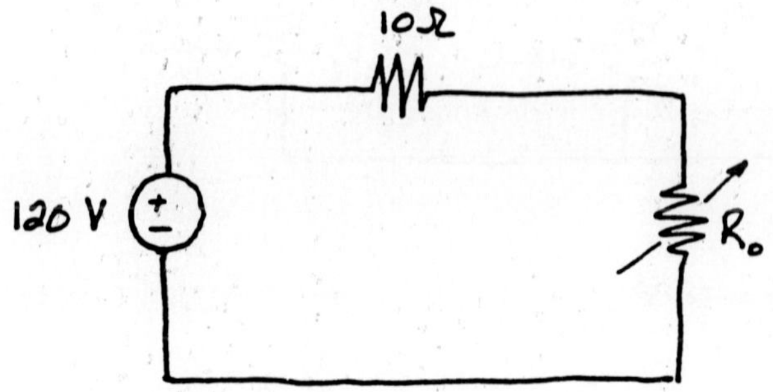

R_o	i_o	v_o	R_o	i_o	v_o
0	12	0	20	4	80
2	10	20	30	3	90
6	7.5	45	40	2.4	96
10	6	60	50	2	100
15	4.8	72	70	1.5	105

P 4.64

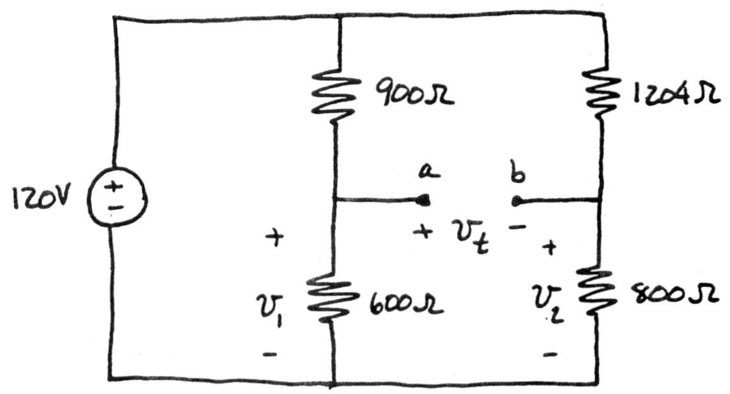

$$v_1 = \frac{600}{1500}(120) = 48\ \text{V}$$

$$v_2 = \frac{800}{2004}(120) = 47.9042\ \text{V}$$

$$v_{\text{Th}} = v_1 - v_2 = 48 - 47.9042 = 95.8\ \text{mV}$$

$$R_{\text{Th}} = \frac{(900)(600)}{1500} + \frac{(1204)(800)}{2004} = \frac{2,105,800}{2505} = 840.64\,\Omega$$

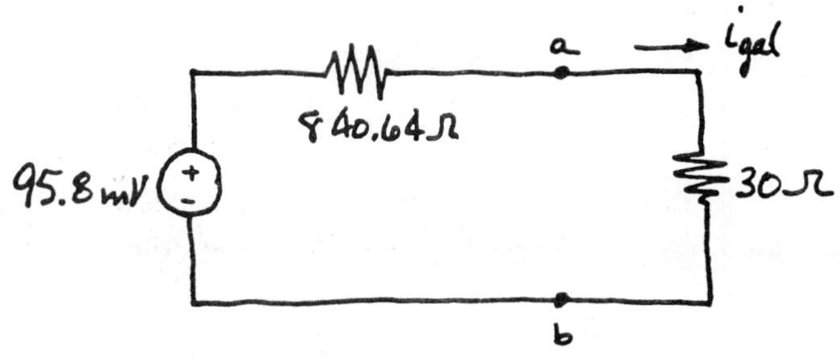

$$i_{\text{gal}} = \frac{95.8 \times 10^{-3}}{0.87064 \times 10^{3}} = 110.03\,\mu\text{A}$$

P 4.65 [a] Use source transformations to simplify the left side of the circuit.

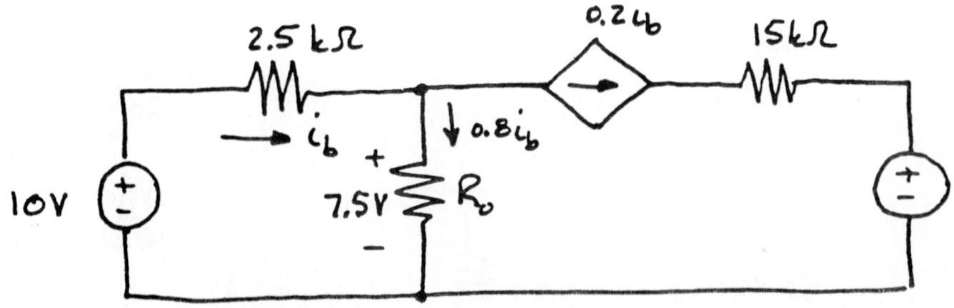

$$i_b = \frac{10 - 7.5}{2.5} = 1 \text{ mA}$$

Let $\quad R_o = R_{\text{meter}} \| 10 \text{ k}\Omega = 7.5/0.8 = 9.375 \text{ k}\Omega$

$$\therefore \quad \frac{(R_{\text{meter}})(10)}{R_{\text{metere}} + 10} = 9.375; \qquad R_{\text{meter}} = \frac{(9.375)(10)}{0.625} = 150 \text{ k}\Omega$$

[b] Actual value of v_e:

$$i_b = \frac{10}{2.5 + (0.8)(10)} = 0.9524 \text{ mA}$$

$$v_e = 0.8i_b(10) = 7.62 \text{ V}$$

$$\% \text{ error } = \left(\frac{7.5 - 7.62}{7.62}\right) \times 100 = -1.57\%$$

P 4.66 Open circuit voltage:

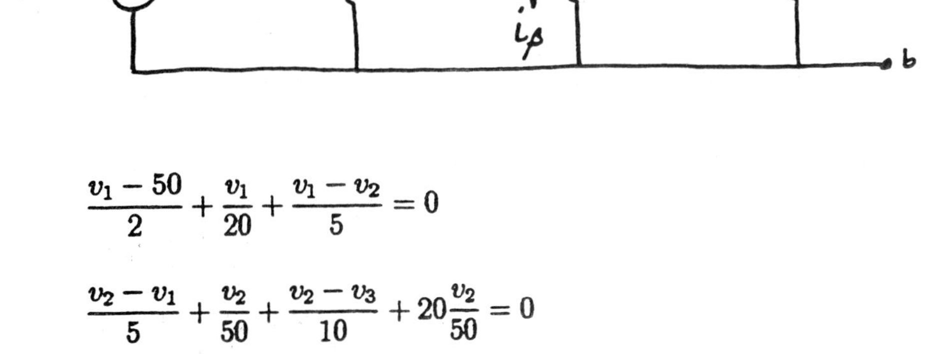

$$\frac{v_1 - 50}{2} + \frac{v_1}{20} + \frac{v_1 - v_2}{5} = 0$$

$$\frac{v_2 - v_1}{5} + \frac{v_2}{50} + \frac{v_2 - v_3}{10} + 20\frac{v_2}{50} = 0$$

$$\frac{v_3}{40} + \frac{v_3 - v_2}{10} - 20\frac{v_2}{50} = 0$$

Solving, $v_3 = 100$ V $= v_{\text{Th}}$
Short circuit current:

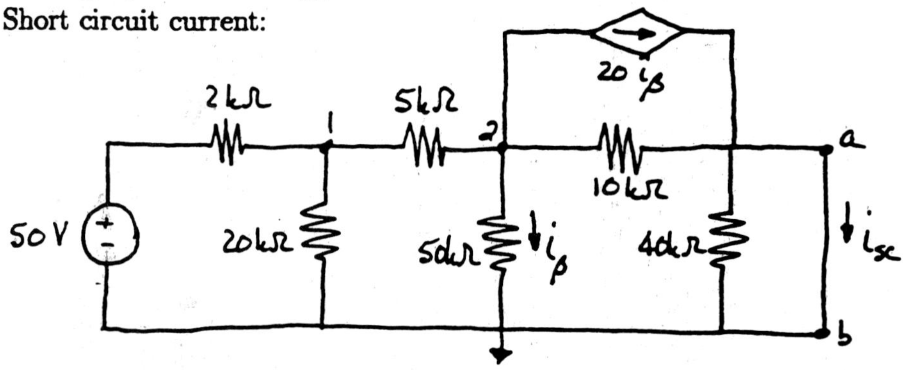

$$\frac{v_1}{20} + \frac{v_1 - 50}{2} + \frac{v_1 - v_2}{5} = 0$$

$$\frac{v_2 - v_1}{5} + \frac{v_2}{50} + \frac{v_2}{10} + 20\frac{v_2}{50} = 0$$

Solving, $v_2 = 10$ V

$$i_{sc} = \frac{20(10)}{50} + \frac{10}{10} = 4 + 1 = 5 \text{ mA}$$

$$\therefore\ R_{\text{Th}} = \frac{v_{\text{Th}}}{i_{sc}} = 100/5 = 20 \text{ k}\Omega$$

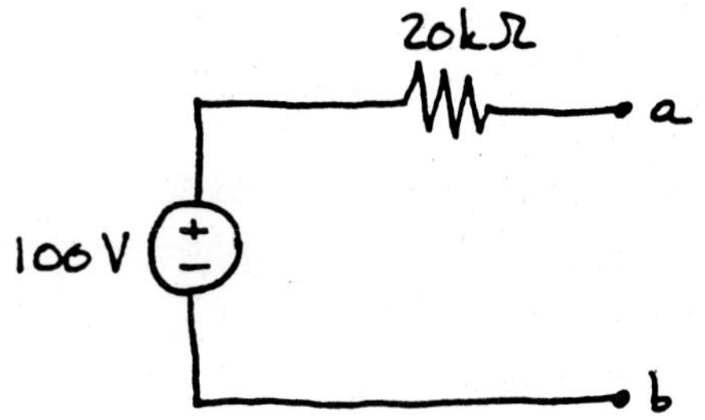

P 4.67

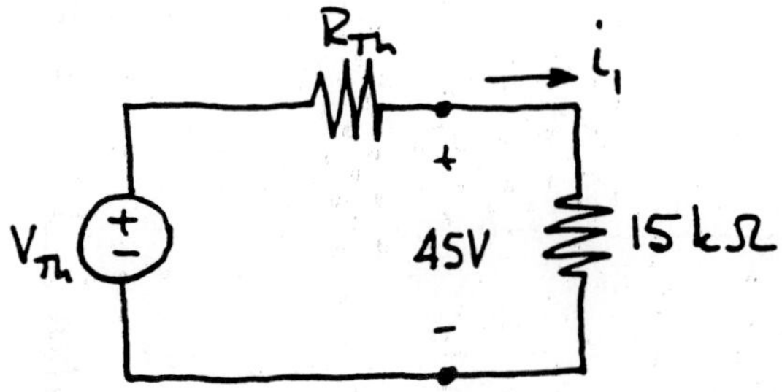

$i_1 = 45/15 = 3$ mA

$45 = v_{Th} - 3R_{Th}, \qquad v_{Th} = 45 + 3R_{Th}$

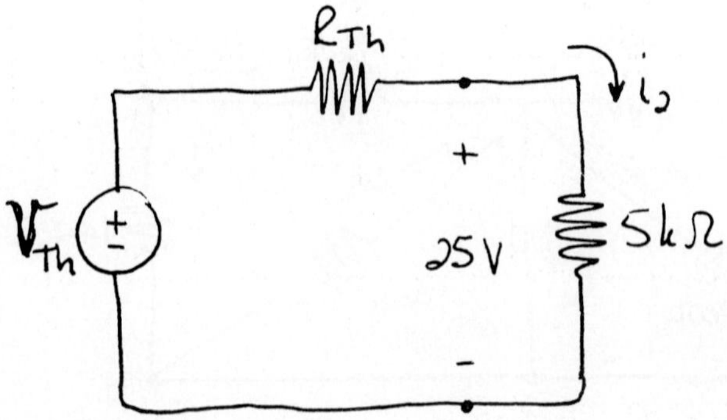

$i_2 = 25/5 = 5$ mA

$25 = v_{Th} - 5R_{Th}, \qquad v_{Th} = 25 + 5R_{Th}$

$\therefore \quad 45 + 3R_{Th} = 25 + 5R_{Th} \qquad \text{so} \qquad R_{Th} = 10\ \text{k}\Omega$

$v_{Th} = 45 + 30 = 75$ V

P 4.68 [a] Find the Thévenin equivalent with respect to the terminals of the ammeter. This is most easily done by first finding the Thévenin with respect to the terminals of the 50 Ω resistor.
Thévenin voltage: note i_ϕ is zero.

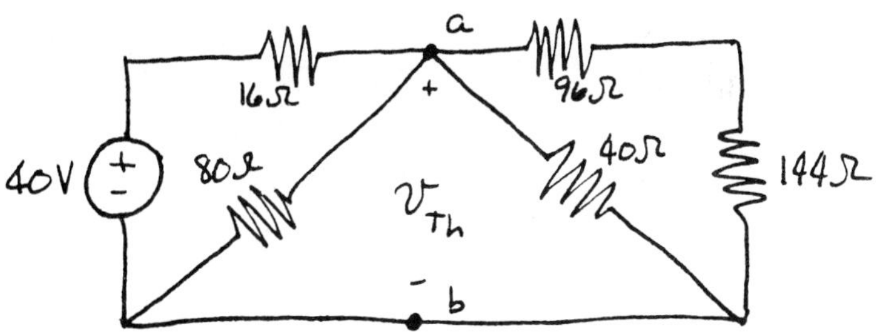

$$\frac{v_{Th}}{80} + \frac{v_{Th}}{40} + \frac{v_{Th}}{240} + \frac{v_{Th} - 40}{16} = 0$$

Solving, $v_{\mathrm{Th}} = 24$ V Short-circuit current:

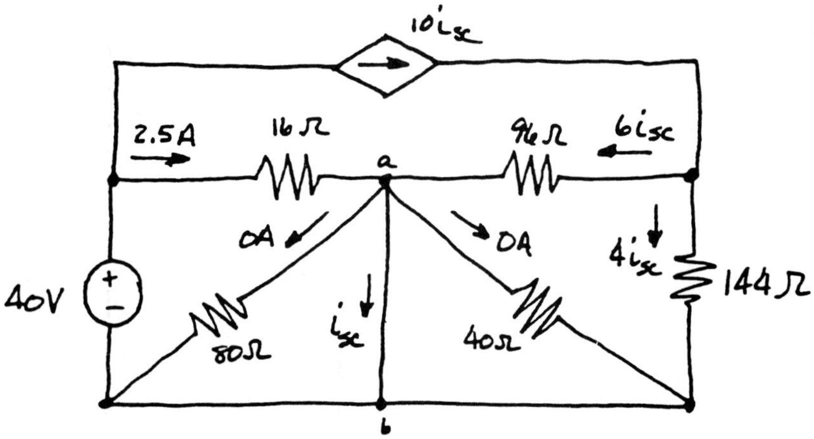

$$i_{sc} = 2.5 + 6i_{sc}, \qquad \therefore\ i_{sc} = -0.5 \text{ A}$$

$$R_{\mathrm{Th}} = \frac{24}{-0.5} = -48\,\Omega$$

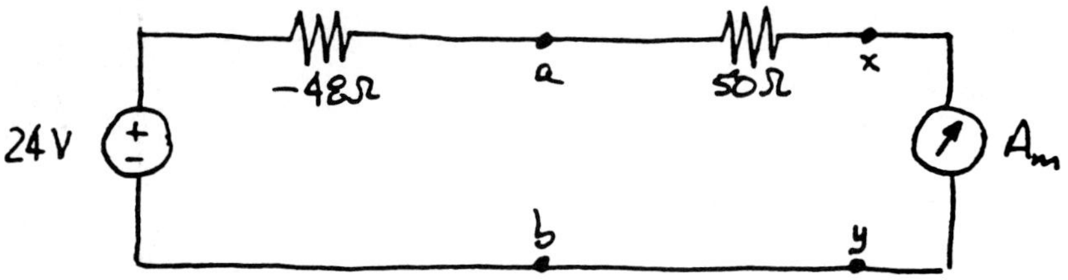

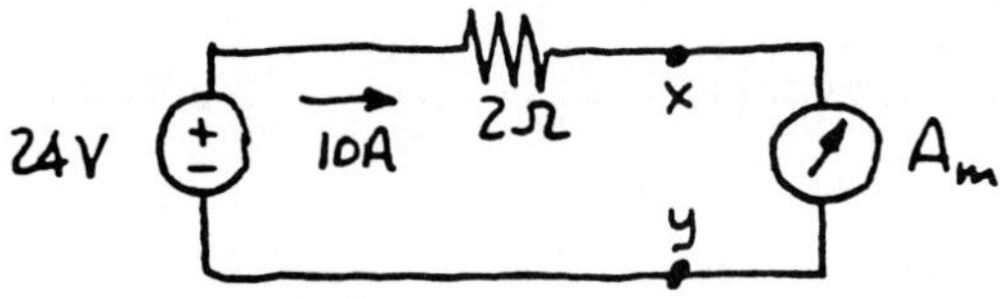

$$R_{\mathrm{total}} = \frac{24}{10} = 2.4\,\Omega$$

$$R_{\mathrm{meter}} = 2.4 - 2 = 0.40\,\Omega$$

[b] Actual current:

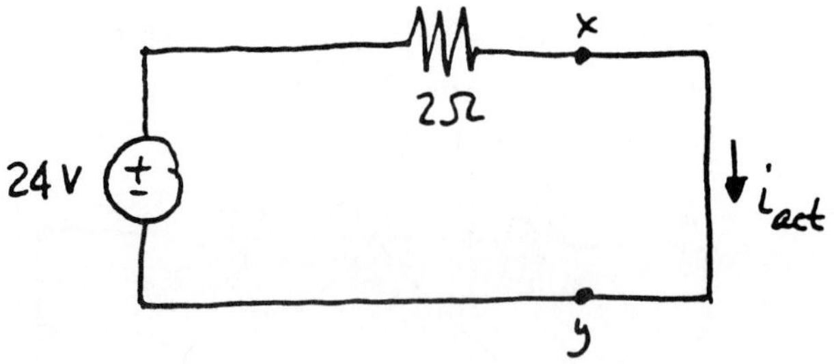

$$i_{\text{actual}} = \frac{24}{2} = 12 \text{ A}$$

$$\% \text{ error} = \frac{10-12}{12} \times 100 = -16.67\%$$

P 4.69 $V_{\text{Th}} = 0$, since circuit contains no independent sources.

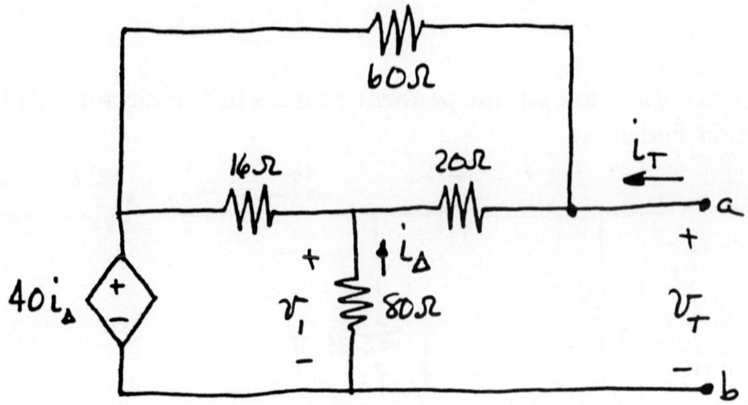

$$i_T = \frac{v_T - v_1}{20} + \frac{v_T - 40i_\Delta}{60}$$

$$\frac{v_1 - 40i_\Delta}{16} + \frac{v_1}{80} + \frac{v_1 - v_T}{20} = 0$$

$$\therefore \quad 10v_1 - 200i_\Delta = 4v_T \qquad i_\Delta = \frac{-v_1}{80}, \qquad 200i_\Delta = -2.5v_1$$

$$\therefore \quad 12.5v_1 = 4v_T; \qquad v_1 = 0.32v_T$$

$$i_\Delta = \frac{-v_1}{80} = \frac{-0.32v_T}{80}$$

$$\therefore \quad 40i_\Delta = -0.16v_T$$

$$\begin{aligned} \therefore \quad i_T &= \frac{v_T - 0.32v_T}{20} = \frac{v_T + 0.16v_T}{60} \\ &= \frac{(0.68v_T)(3) + 1.16v_T}{60} \\ &= \frac{(2.04 + 1.16)v_T}{60} = \frac{3.20}{60}v_T \end{aligned}$$

$$\therefore \quad \frac{v_T}{i_T} = \frac{60}{3.2} = 18.75\,\Omega$$

$$R_{\text{Th}} = 18.75\,\Omega$$

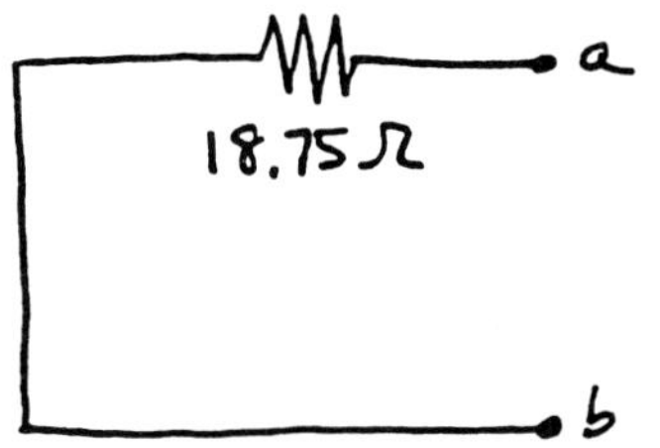

P 4.70 $V_{Th} = 0$ since there are no independent sources in the circuit. To find R_{Th} we first find $R_{a'b'}$.

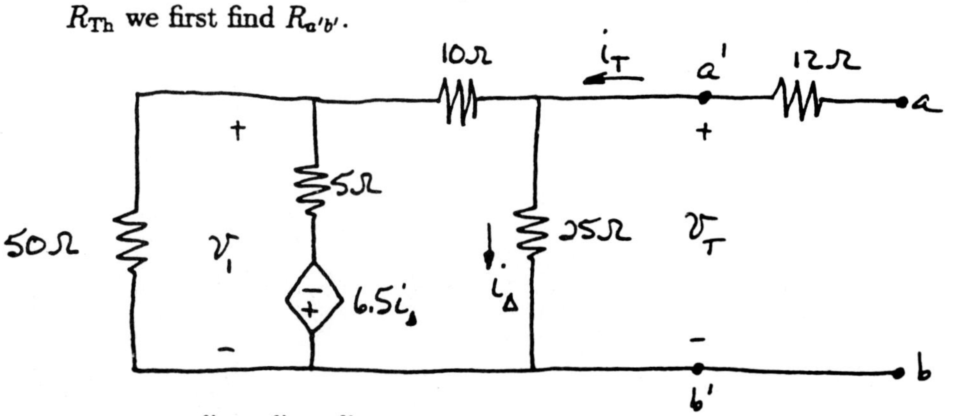

$$i_T = \frac{v_T}{25} + \frac{v_T - v_1}{10}$$

$$\frac{v_1}{50} + \frac{v_1 + 6.5i_\Delta}{5} + \frac{v_1 - v_T}{10} = 0 \text{ so } 16v_1 + 65i_\Delta = 5v_T$$

$$i_\Delta = \frac{v_T}{25}, \qquad 65i_\Delta = 2.6v_T$$

$$16v_1 + 2.6v_T = 5v_T$$

$$\therefore \quad v_1 = 0.15v_T$$

$$i_T = \frac{v_T}{25} + \frac{v_T - 0.15v_T}{10} = \frac{6.25}{50}v_T$$

$$\frac{v_T}{i_T} = 50/6.25 = 8\,\Omega = R_{a'b'}$$

$$\therefore \quad R_{Th} = 12 + 8 = 20\,\Omega$$

P 4.71 [a] Since $0 \leq R_o \leq \infty$ maximum power will be delivered to the 6 Ω resistor when $R_o = 0$.

[b]
$$P = \frac{30^2}{6} = 150 \text{ W}$$

P 4.72 [a] From the solution of Problem 4.66 we have $R_{\text{Th}} = 20$ kΩ and $v_{\text{Th}} = 100$ V. Therefore

$$R_o = R_{\text{Th}} = 20 \text{ k}\Omega$$

[b]
$$p = \frac{(50)^2}{20} = 125 \text{ mW}$$

[c]

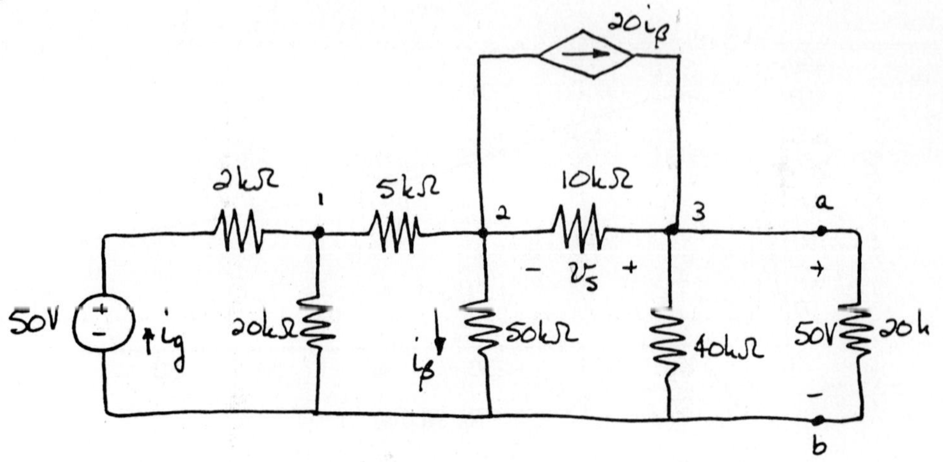

$$\frac{v_1}{20} + \frac{v_1 - 50}{2} + \frac{v_1 - v_2}{5} = 0$$

$$\frac{v_2}{50} + \frac{v_2 - v_1}{5} + \frac{v_2 - 50}{10} + 20\left(\frac{v_2}{50}\right) = 0$$

Solving, $v_1 = 38$ V; $v_2 = 17.5$ V

$$i_g = \frac{50 - 38}{2} = 6 \text{ mA}$$

$$p_{50\text{V}} \text{ (delivered)} = (50)(6) = 300 \text{ mW}$$

$$v_2 + v_s = 50 \text{ V}$$

$$v_s = 50 - (17.5) = 32.5 \text{ V}$$

$$i_\beta = \frac{v_2}{50} = 0.35 \text{ mA}$$

$$20i_\beta = 7 \text{ mA}$$

$$p_{20i_\beta} \text{ (delivered)} = (32.5)(7) = 227.5 \text{ mW}$$

$$\sum p_{\text{dev}} = 300 + 227.5 = 527.5 \text{ mW}$$

$$\% \text{ delivered} = \frac{125}{527.5} \times 100 = 23.7\%$$

P 4.73 [a] From the solution to Problem 4.63 we have

$R_o(\Omega)$	$P_o(\text{W})$	$R_o(\Omega)$	$P_o(\text{W})$
0	0	20	320.00
2	200.00	30	270.00
6	337.50	40	230.40
10	360.00	50	200.00
15	345.60	70	157.50

[b]

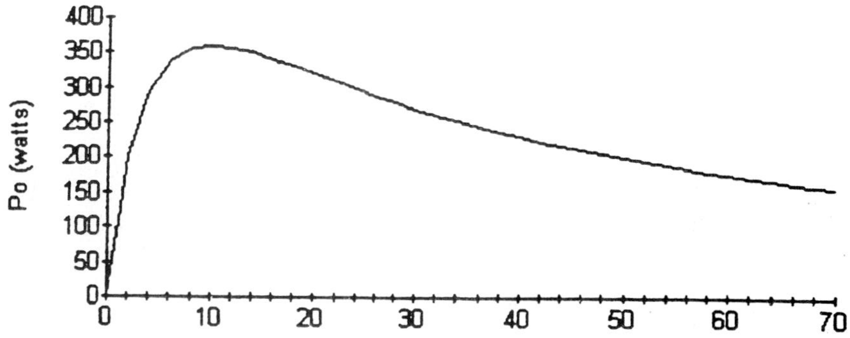

[c] $R_o = 10\,\Omega$, $P_o\ (\text{max}) = 360$ W

P 4.74 We begin by finding the Thévenin equivalent with respect to R_o. After making a couple of source transformations the circuit simplifies to

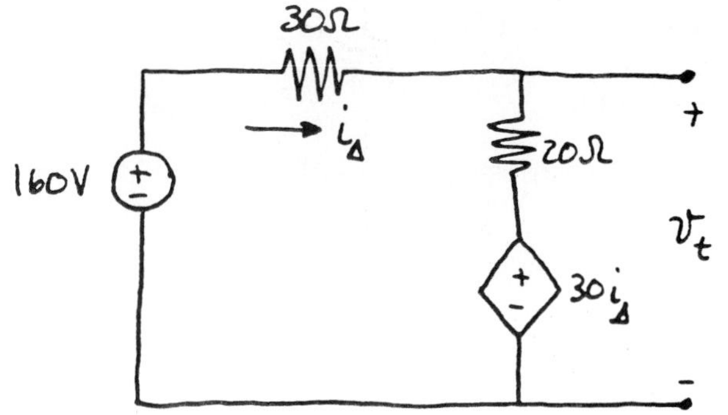

$$i_\Delta = \frac{160 - 30i_\Delta}{50}; \qquad i_\Delta = 2\ \text{A}$$

$$v_{\text{Th}} = 20i_\Delta + 30i_\Delta = 50i_\Delta = 100\ \text{V}$$

Using the test-source method to find the Thévenin resistance gives

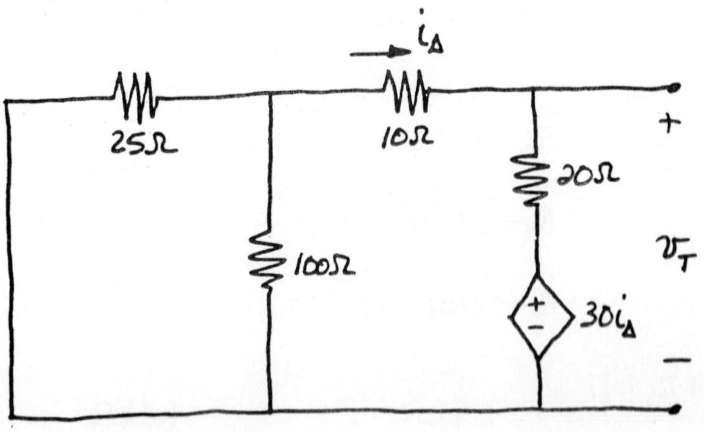

$$i_T = \frac{v_T}{30} + \frac{v_T - 30(-v_T/30)}{20}$$

$$\frac{i_T}{v_T} = \frac{1}{30} + \frac{1}{10} = \frac{4}{30} = \frac{2}{15}$$

$$R_{Th} = \frac{v_T}{i_T} = \frac{15}{2} = 7.5\,\Omega$$

Thus our problem is reduced to analyzing the circuit shown below.

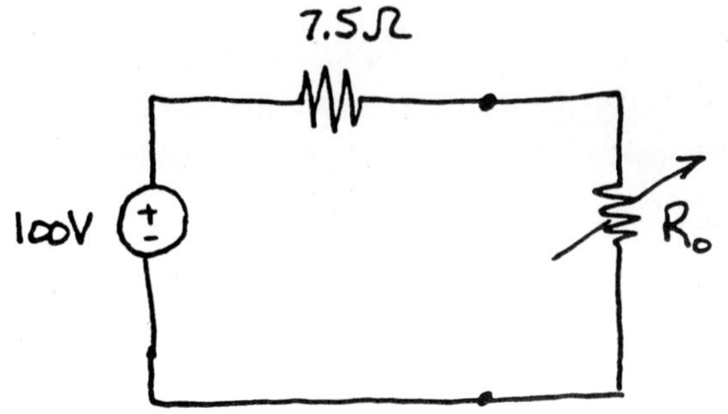

$$p = \left(\frac{100}{7.5 + R_o}\right)^2 R_o = 250$$

$$\frac{10^4}{R_o^2 + 15R_o + 56.25} R_o = 250$$

$$\frac{10^4 R_o}{250} = R_o^2 + 15R_o + 56.25$$

$$40R_o = R_o^2 + 15R_o + 56.25$$

$$R_o^2 - 25R_o + 56.25 = 0$$

$$R_o = 12.5 \pm \sqrt{156.25 - 56.25} = 12.5 \pm 10$$

$$R_o = 22.5\,\Omega$$

$$R_o = 2.5\,\Omega$$

P 4.75 [a]

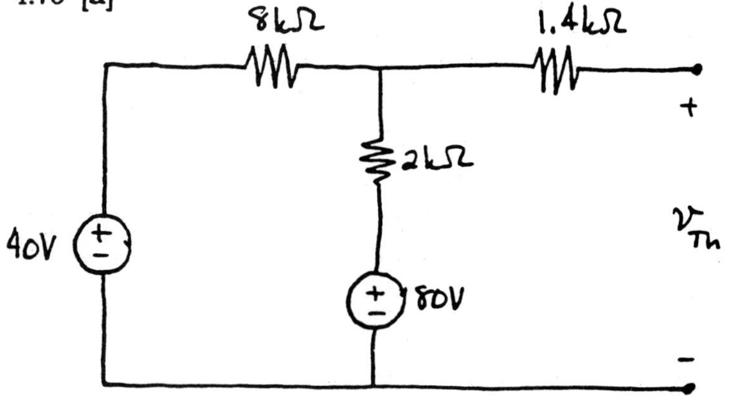

$$\frac{v_{Th} - 40}{8} + \frac{v_{Th} - 80}{2} = 0$$

$$\therefore\ v_{Th} = 72\text{ V}$$

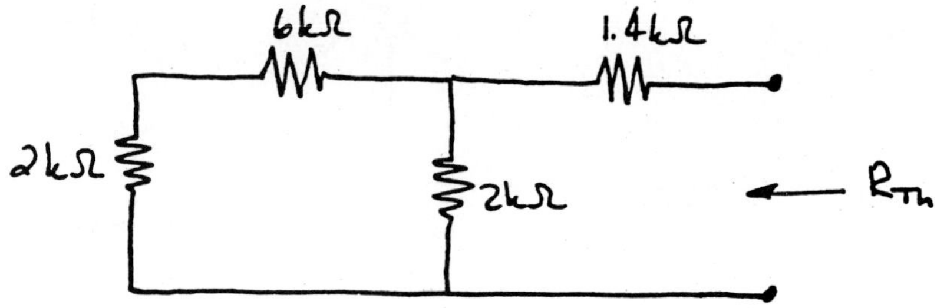

$$R_{Th} = 1.4 + (2)(8)/10 = 3\text{ k}\Omega$$

$$R_o = R_{Th} = 3\text{ k}\Omega$$

[b]

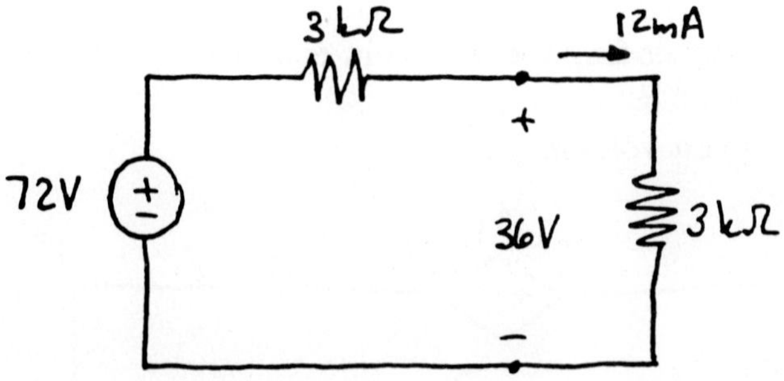

$$p_{\text{max}} = \frac{(36)^2}{3} \times 10^{-3} = 432 \text{ mW}$$

P 4.76

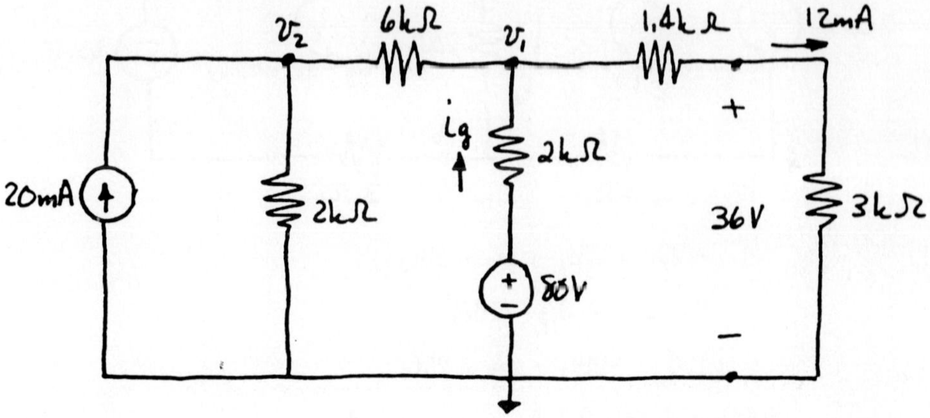

$$v_1 = (12 \times 10^{-3})(1.4 + 3) \times 10^3 = 12(4.4) = 52.8 \text{ V}$$

$$i_g = \frac{80 - 52.8}{2} = 13.6 \text{ mA}$$

$$p_{80V} \text{ (dev)} = (80)(13.6) = 1088 \text{ mW}$$

$$-20 + \frac{v_2}{2} + \frac{v_2 - 52.8}{6} = 0$$

$$\therefore \quad v_2 = 43.2 \text{ V}$$

$$p_{20mA} \text{ (dev)} = (20)(43.2) = 864 \text{ mW}$$

$$\sum p_{\text{dev}} = 1088 + 864 = 1952 \text{ mW}$$

$$\% \text{ delivered to } R_o = \frac{432}{1952} \times 100 = 22.13\%$$

P 4.77 [a] We begin by finding the Thévenin equivalent with respect to the terminals of R_o.
Open circuit voltage

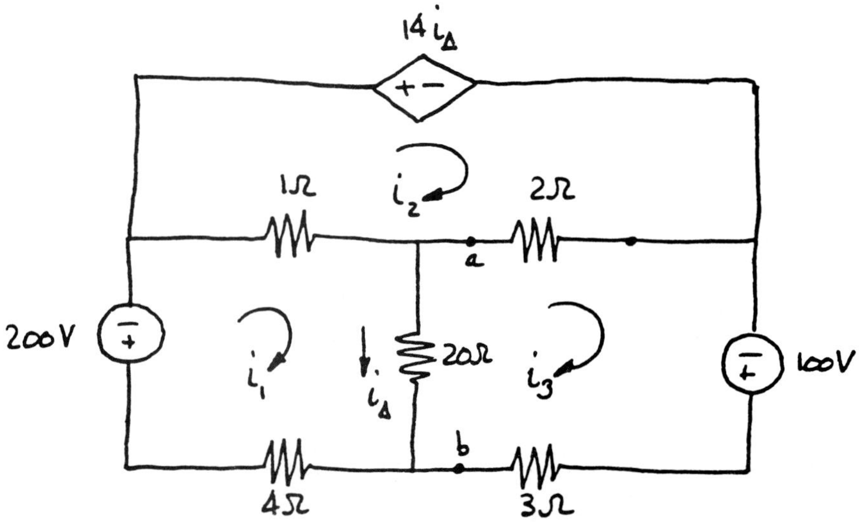

$$-200 = 25i_1 - 1i_2 - 20i_3$$

$$0 = 13i_1 + 3i_2 - 16i_3$$

$$100 = -20i_1 - 2i_2 + 25i_3$$

Solving, $i_1 = -2.5$ A; $i_3 = 5$ A

$$v_{Th} = 20(i_1 - i_3) = 20(-7.5) = -150 \text{ V}$$

Now find the short-circuit current.

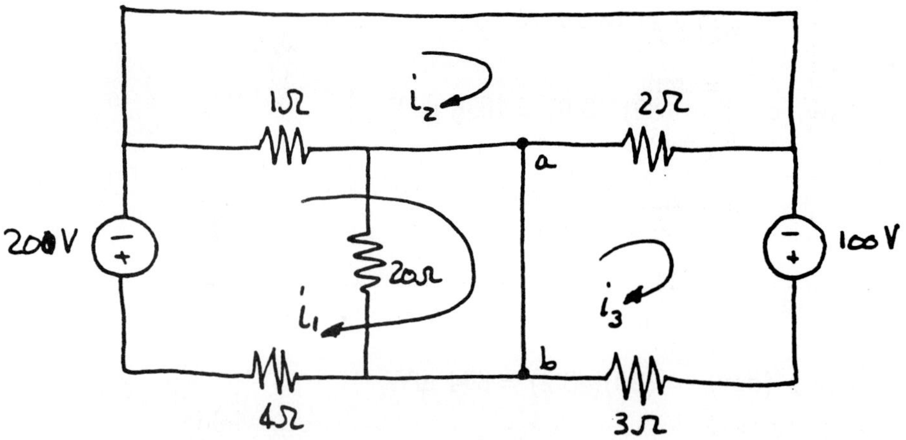

Note with the short circuit from a to b that i_Δ is zero, hence $14i_\Delta$ is also zero.

$$-200 = 5i_1 - 1i_2 + 0i_3$$

$$0 = -1i_1 + 3i_2 - 2i_3$$

$$100 = 0i_1 - 2i_2 + 5i_3$$

Solving, $i_1 = -40$ A; $\quad i_3 = 20$ A

$$i_{sc} = i_1 - i_3 = -60 \text{ A}$$

$$R_{Th} = (-150)/(-60) = 2.5\,\Omega$$

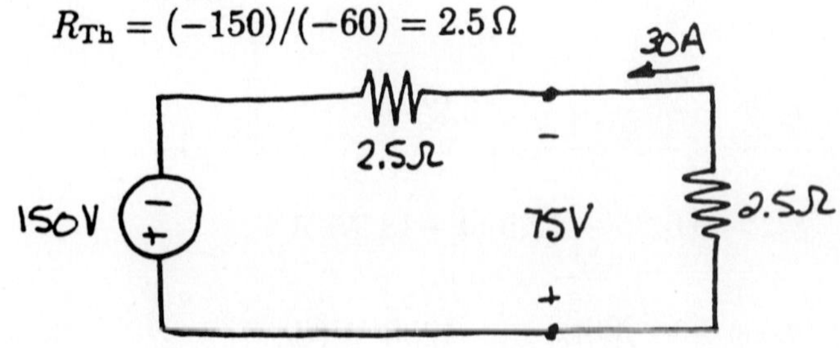

For maximum power transfer $\quad R_o = R_{Th} = 2.5\,\Omega$

[b] $\quad p_{max} = \dfrac{75^2}{2.5} = 2250$ W

P 4.78 From the solution of Problem 4.77 we know that when R_o is 2.5 Ω, the voltage across R_o is 75 V, positive at the lower terminal. Therefore our problem reduces to the analysis of the following circuit. In constructing the circuit we have used the fact that i_Δ is -3.75 A, and hence $14i_\Delta$ is -52.5 V.

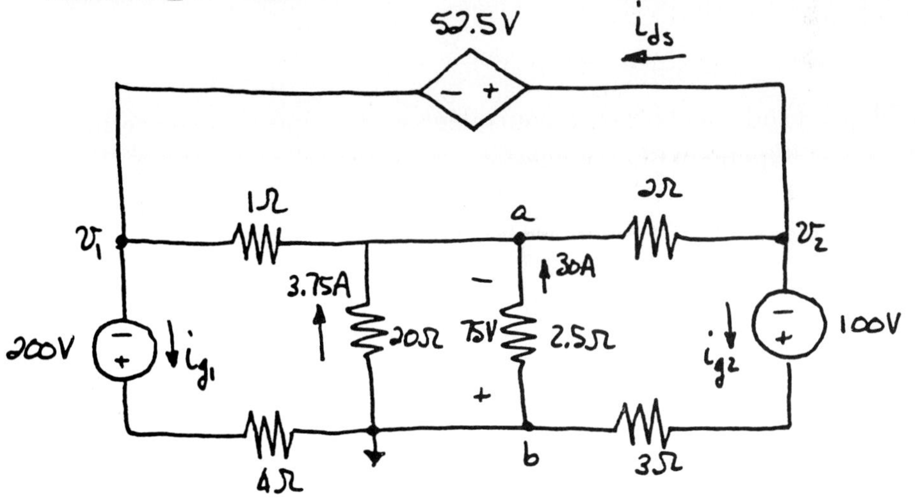

Using the node Voltage method to find v_1 and v_2 yields

$$-33.75 + \frac{-75 - v_1}{1} + \frac{-75 - v_2}{2} = 0$$

$$v_1 + 52.5 = v_2$$

Solving, $v_1 = -115$ V; $v_2 = -62.5$ V.It follows that

$$i_{g_1} = \frac{-155 + 200}{4} = 21.25 \text{ A}$$

$$i_{g_2} = \frac{-62.5 + 100}{3} = 12.5 \text{ A}$$

$$i_2 = \frac{-62.5 + 75}{2} = 6.25 \text{ A}$$

$$i_{\text{ds}} = -6.25 - 12.5 = -18.75 \text{ A}$$

$$p_{200\text{V}} = -200 i_{g_1} = -4250 \text{ W(dev)}$$

$$p_{100\text{V}} = -100 i_{g_2} = -1250 \text{ W(dev)}$$

$$p_{\text{ds}} = 52.5 i_{\text{ds}} = -984.375 \text{ W(dev)}$$

$$\therefore \sum p_{\text{dev}} = 4250 + 1250 + 984.375 = 6484.375 \text{ W}$$

$$\therefore \text{ \% delivered } = \frac{2250}{6484.375}(100) = 34.7\%$$

$\therefore$ 34.7% of developed power is delivered to load

P 4.79 [a] Find the Thévenin equivalent with respect to the terminals of R_L.
Open circuit voltage:

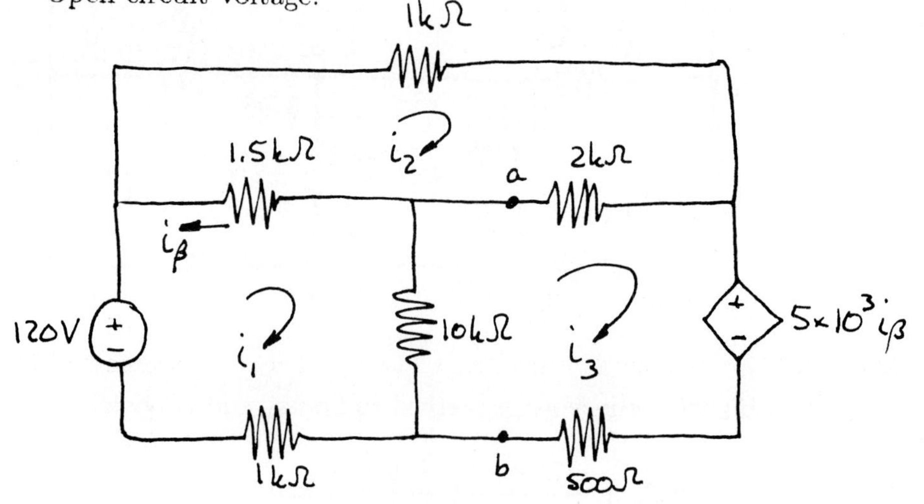

$$120 = 12.5 i_1 - 1.5 i_2 - 10 i_3$$

$$0 = -1.5 i_1 + 4.5 i_2 - 2 i_3$$

$$0 = -15 i_1 + 3 i_2 + 12.5 i_3$$

Solving, $i_1 = 99.6$ mA; $\quad i_3 = 100.8$ mA

$$v_{Th} = v_{ab} = 10 \times 10^3(i_1 - i_3) = -12 \text{ V}$$

Short-circuit current:

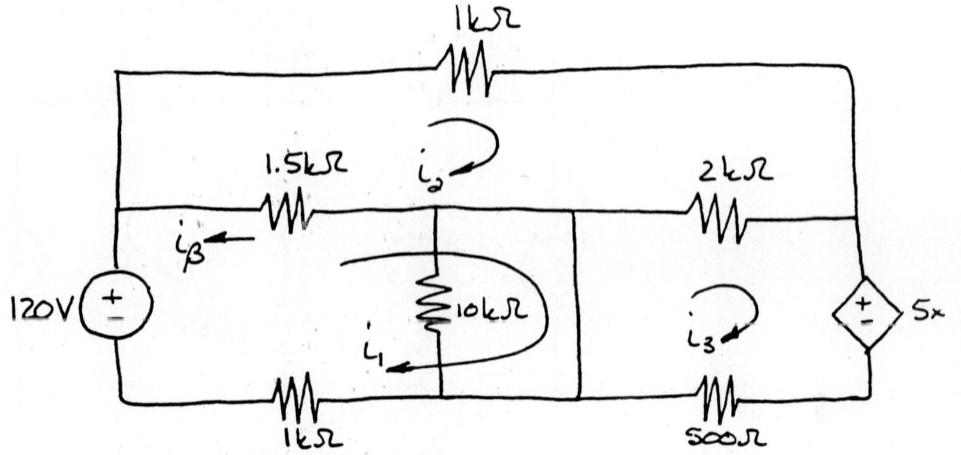

$$120 = 2.5i_1 - 1.5i_2 + 0i_3$$

$$0 = -1.5i_1 + 4.5i_2 - 2i_3$$

$$0 = -5i_1 + 3i_2 + 2.5i_3$$

Solving, $i_1 = 92$ mA; $\quad i_3 = 96$ mA

$$i_{sc} = i_1 - i_3 = -4 \text{ mA}; \qquad R_{Th} = \frac{v_{Th}}{i_{sc}} = \frac{-12}{-4 \times 10^{-3}} = 3 \text{ k}\Omega$$

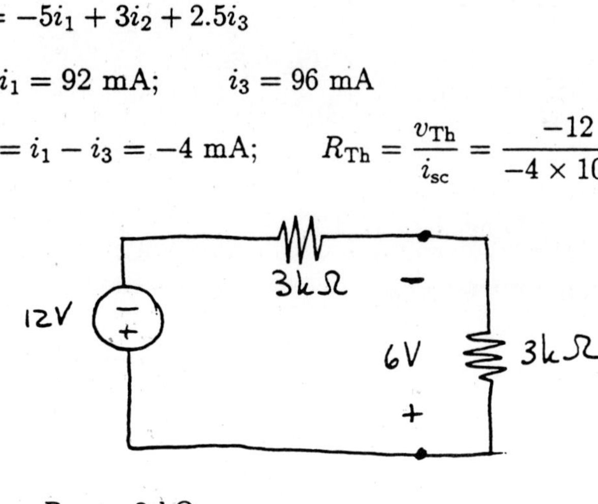

$$R_L = R_{Th} = 3 \text{ k}\Omega$$

[b] $$p_{max} = \frac{6^2}{3 \times 10^3} = 12 \text{ mW}$$

P 4.80 Find the Thévenin equivalent with respect to the terminals of R_o.
Open circuit voltage:

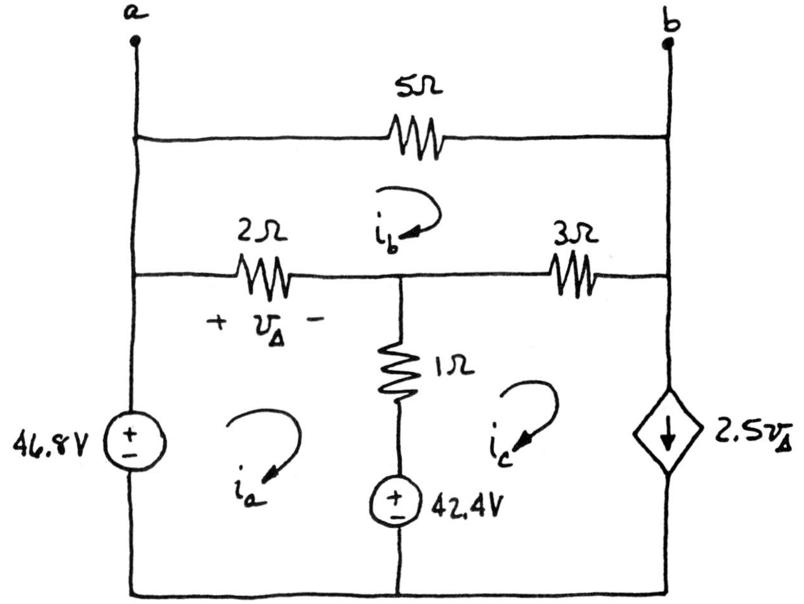

$$(46.8 - 42.4) = 3i_a - 2i_b - i_c$$

$$0 = -2i_a + 10i_b - 3i_c$$

$$i_c = 2.5v_\Delta; \qquad v_\Delta = 2(i_a - i_b)$$

Solving, $i_b = 74.8$ A

$$\therefore \quad v_{\text{Th}} = 5i_b = 374 \text{ V}$$

Short circuit current:

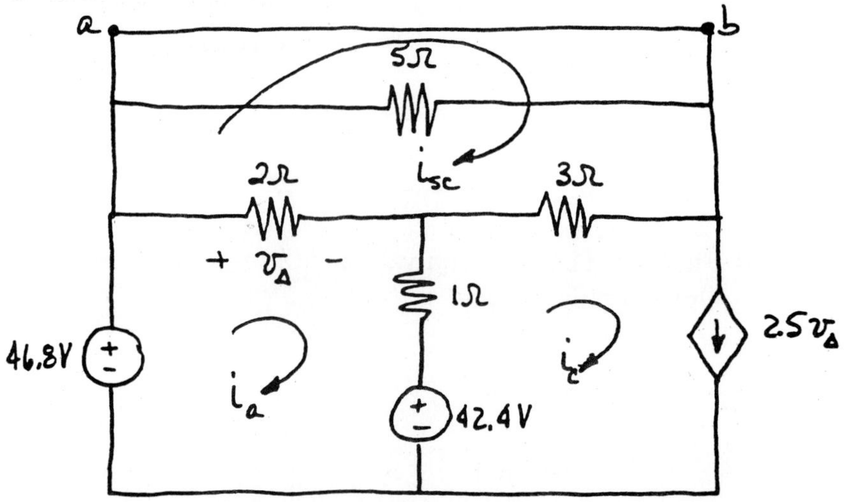

$$46.8 - 42.4 = 3i_a - 2i_{sc} - i_c$$

$$0 = -2i_a + 5i_{sc} - 3i_c$$

$$i_c = 2.5v_\Delta; \qquad v_\Delta = 2(i_a - i_{sc})$$

Solving, $i_{sc} = 6.8$ A

$$R_{\text{Th}} = v_{\text{Th}}/i_{sc} = 374/6.8 = 55\,\Omega$$

$$R_o = 55\,\Omega$$

with R_o equal to 55 Ω the circuit becomes

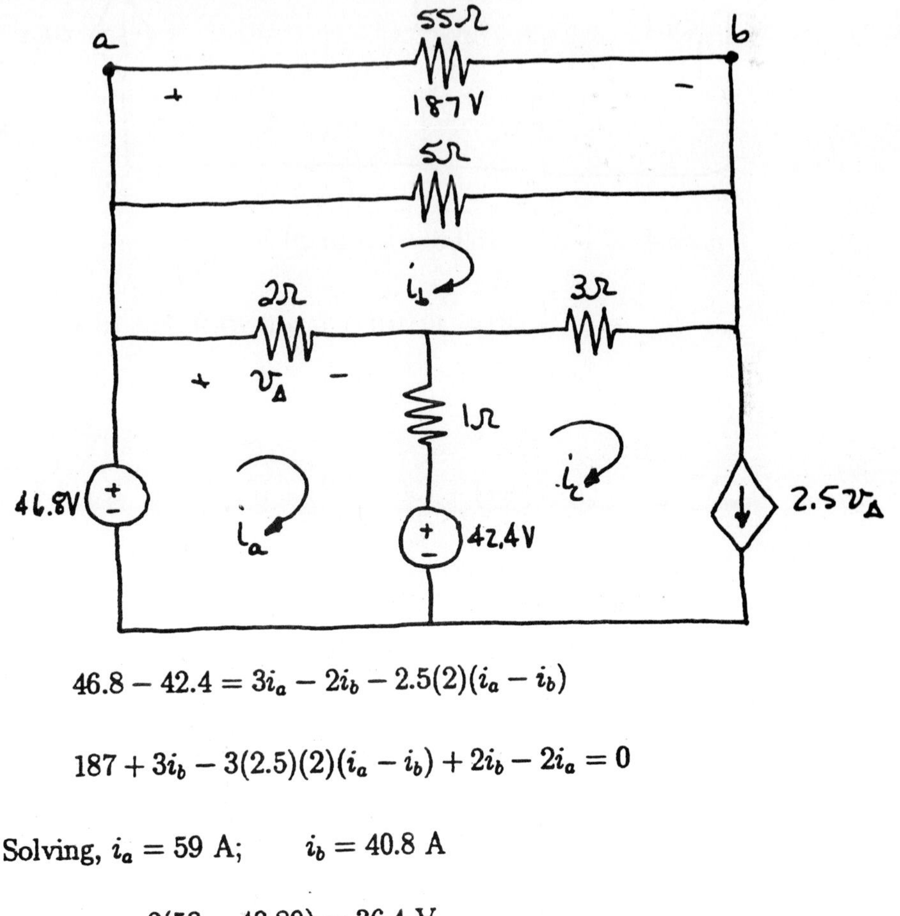

$$46.8 - 42.4 = 3i_a - 2i_b - 2.5(2)(i_a - i_b)$$

$$187 + 3i_b - 3(2.5)(2)(i_a - i_b) + 2i_b - 2i_a = 0$$

Solving, $i_a = 59$ A; $\qquad i_b = 40.8$ A

$$v_\Delta = 2(59 - 40.80) = 36.4 \text{ V}$$

$$i_c = 91 \text{ A}$$

Thus we have

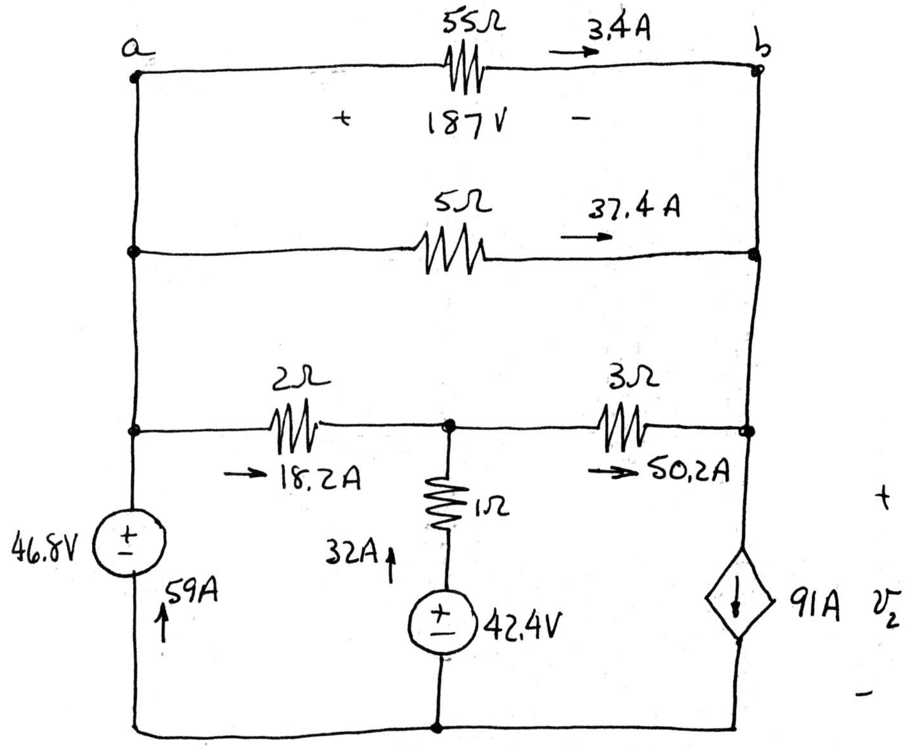

$$v_c = 42.4 - 32 - 150.6 = -140.20 \text{ V}$$

$$\sum P_{\text{dev}} = 46.8(59) + 42.4(32) + 140.20(91) = 16{,}876.20 \text{ W}$$

CHECK:

$$\sum P_{\text{dis}} = (18.2)^2(2) + (50.2)^2(3) + (32)^2(1) + 187(3.4) + 187(37.4) = 16{,}876.20$$

$$\% \text{ delivered} = \frac{(55)(3.4)(100)}{16{,}876.2} = 3.77\%$$

P 4.81 [a] Open circuit voltage

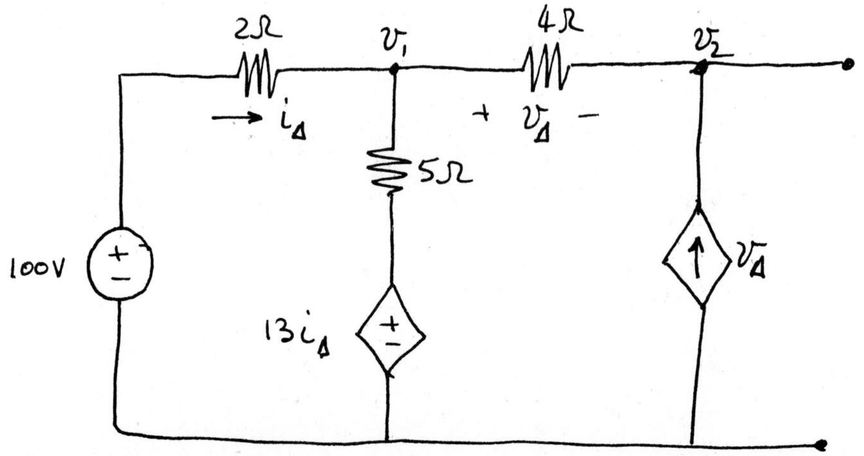

Node voltage equation:

$$\frac{v_1 - 100}{2} + \frac{v_1 - 13i_\Delta}{5} + \frac{v_1 - v_2}{4} = 0$$

Constraint equations:

$$i_\Delta = \frac{100 - v_1}{2}; \qquad \frac{v_2 - v_1}{4} - v_\Delta = 0; \qquad v_\Delta = v_1 - v_2$$

Solving, $v_2 = 90\text{ V} = v_{\text{Th}}$

Short circuit current:

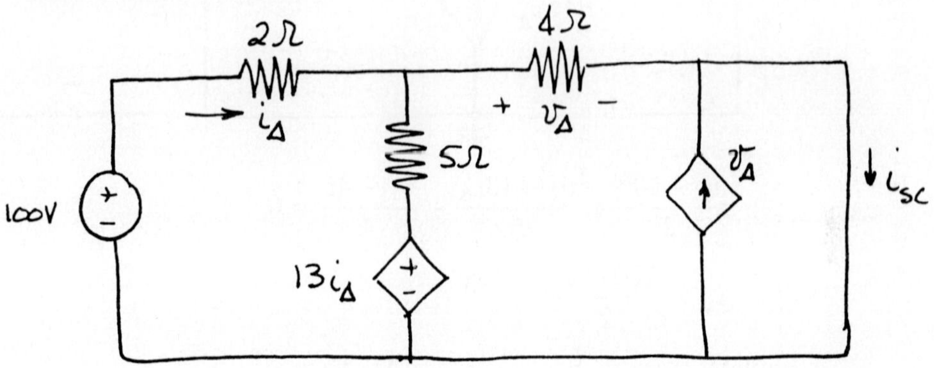

$$\frac{v_1 - 100}{2} + \frac{v_1 - 13i_\Delta}{5} + \frac{v_1}{4} = 0$$

$$i_\Delta = \frac{100 - v_1}{2}$$

Solving, $v_1 = 80\text{ V} = v_\Delta$

$$i_{\text{sc}} = \frac{v_1}{4} + v_\Delta = 20 + 80 = 100\text{ A}$$

$$R_{\text{Th}} = \frac{v_{\text{Th}}}{i_{\text{sc}}} = \frac{90}{100} = 0.9\,\Omega$$

$$\therefore \quad R_o = R_{\text{Th}} = 0.9\,\Omega$$

[b]

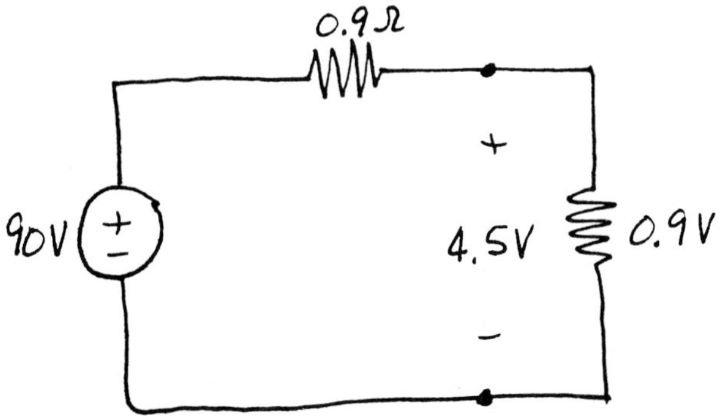

$$p_{\text{max}} = \frac{(45)^2}{0.9} = 2250\text{ W}$$

[c]

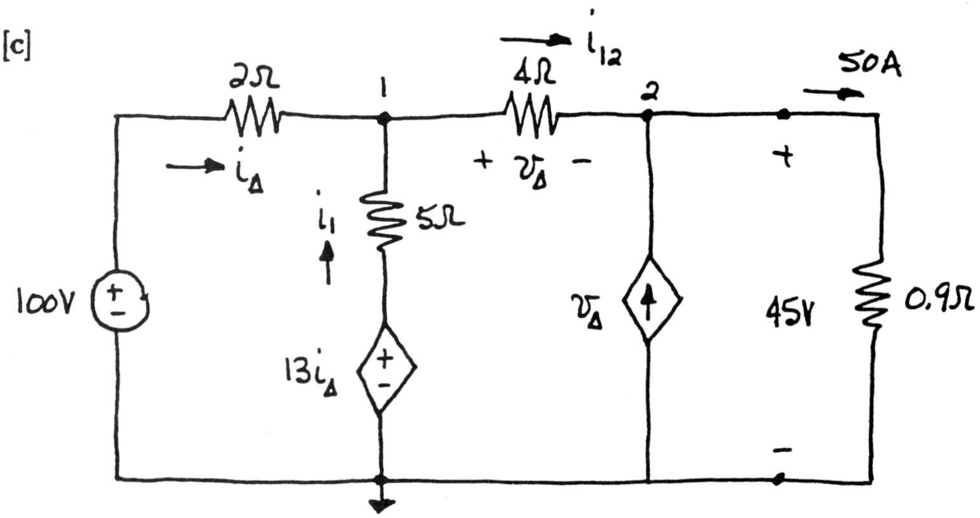

$$\frac{v_1 - 100}{2} + \frac{v_1 - 13i_\Delta}{5} + \frac{v_1 - 45}{4} = 0$$

$$i_\Delta = \frac{100 - v_1}{2}$$

Solving, $v_1 = 85$ V; $i_\Delta = 7.5$ A;
$v_\Delta = v_1 - v_2 = 85 - 45 = 40$ V

$$i_{100V} = i_\Delta = 7.5 \text{ A}$$

$$p_{100V}\ (\text{dev}) = 100(7.5) = 750 \text{ W}$$

$$i_{12} = v_\Delta/4 = 40/4 = 10 \text{ A}$$

$$i_1 = i_{12} - i_\Delta - 10 - 7.5 = 2.5 \text{ A}$$

$$p_{13i_\Delta}\ (\text{dev}) = (97.5)(2.5) = 243.75 \text{ W}$$

$$p_{v_\Delta}\ (\text{dev}) = (45)(40) = 1800 \text{ W}$$

$$\sum p_{\text{dev}} = 750 + 243.75 + 1800 = 2793.75 \text{ W}$$

$$\% \text{ delivered} = \frac{2250}{2793.75} \times 100 = 80.54\%$$

P 4.82 [a] First find the Thévenin equivalent with respect to R_o.
Open circuit voltage: $i_\phi = 0$; $50i_\phi = 0$

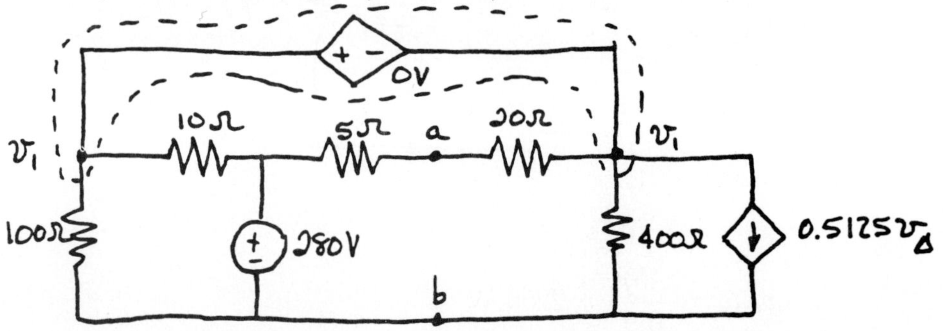

$$\frac{v_1}{100} + \frac{v_1 - 280}{10} + \frac{v_1 - 280}{25} + \frac{v_1}{400} + 0.5125v_\Delta = 0$$

$$61v_1 + 205v_\Delta = 15{,}680$$

$$v_\Delta = \frac{(280 - v_1)}{25}5 = 56 - 0.2v_1$$

$$205v_\Delta = 11{,}480 - 41v_1$$

$$20v_1 = 4200$$

$$v_1 = 210 \text{ V}$$

$$v_{\text{Th}} = 280 - v_\Delta = 280 - 56 + 0.2(210) = 266 \text{ V}$$

Short circuit current

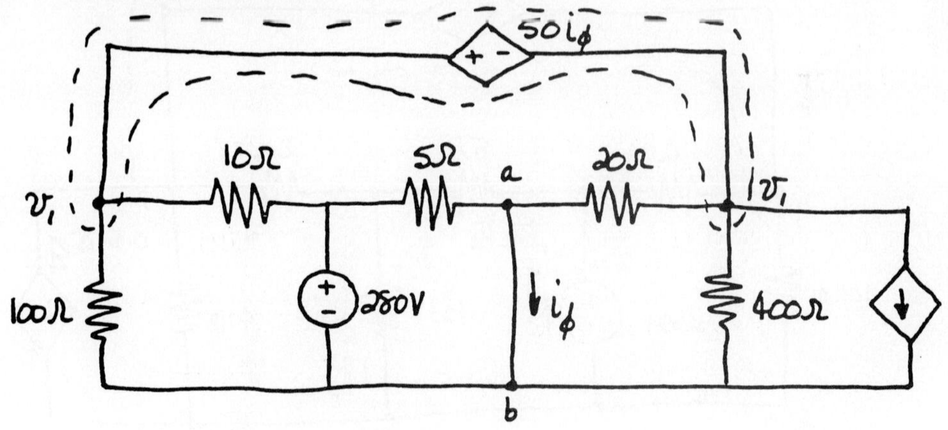

$$\frac{v_1}{100} + \frac{v_1 - 280}{10} + \frac{v_2}{20} + \frac{v_2}{400} + 0.5125(280) = 0$$

$$44v_1 + 21v_2 = -46{,}200$$

$$v_2 + 50i_\phi = v_1$$

$$i_\phi = \frac{280}{5} + \frac{v_2}{20} = 56 + 0.05v_2$$

$$50i_\phi = 2800 + 2.5v_2$$

$$\therefore \quad v_1 = 3.5v_2 + 2800$$

$$\therefore \quad 44v_1 = 154v_2 + 123{,}200$$

$$154v_2 + 123{,}000 + 21v_2 = -46{,}200$$

$$v_2 = -968 \text{ V}$$

$$i_\phi = i_{sc} = 56 + 0.05(-968) = 7.6 \text{ A}$$

$$R_{\text{Th}} = v_{\text{Th}}/i_{sc} = 266/7.6 = 35\,\Omega$$

$$\therefore \quad R_o = 35\,\Omega$$

[b]

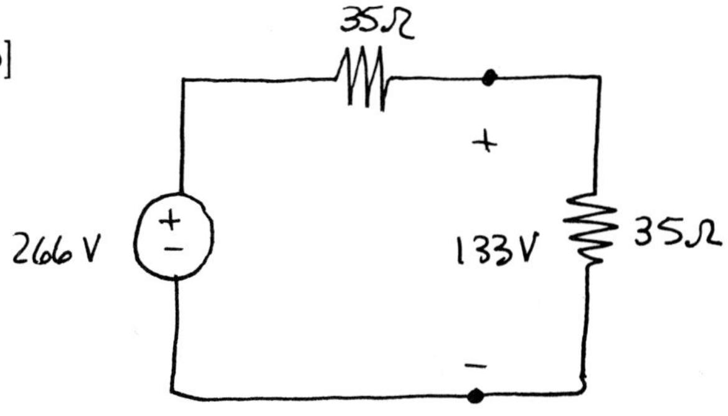

$$p_{\max} = (133)^2/35 = 505.4 \text{ W}$$

[c]

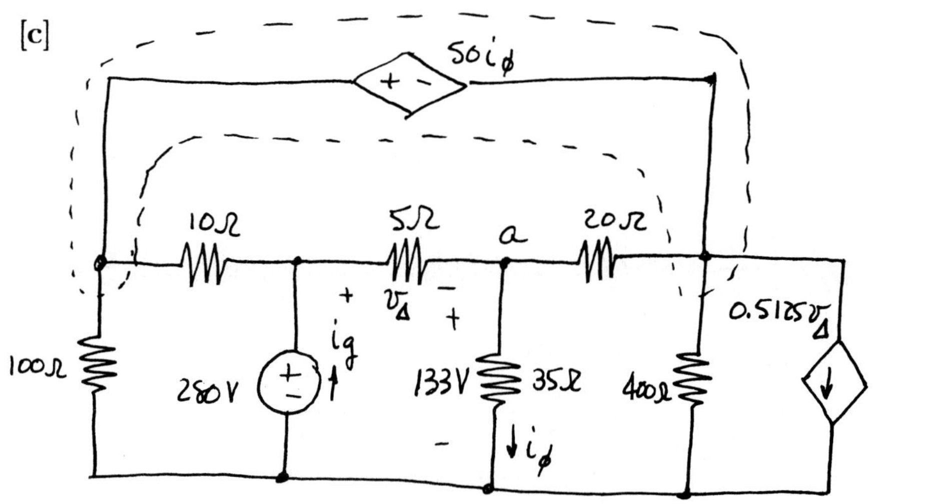

$$\frac{v_1}{100} + \frac{v_1 - 280}{10} + \frac{v_2 - 133}{20} + \frac{v_2}{400} + 0.5125(280 - 133) = 0$$

$$44v_1 + 21v_2 = -16{,}275$$

$$v_2 + 50i_\phi = v_1; \qquad i_\phi = 133/35 = 3.8 \text{ A}$$

$$\therefore \quad v_2 + 190 = v_1, \qquad v_2 = v_1 - 190$$

$$21v_2 = 21v_1 - 3390$$

$$\therefore \quad 65v_1 = -12{,}285$$

Therefore, $v_1 = -189$ V and thus,

$$i_g = \frac{280 - 133}{5} + \frac{280 + 189}{10} = 76.30 \text{ A}$$

$$p_{280\text{V}} \text{ (dev)} = (280)(76.3) = 21{,}364 \text{ W}$$

P 4.83 50 V source acting alone:

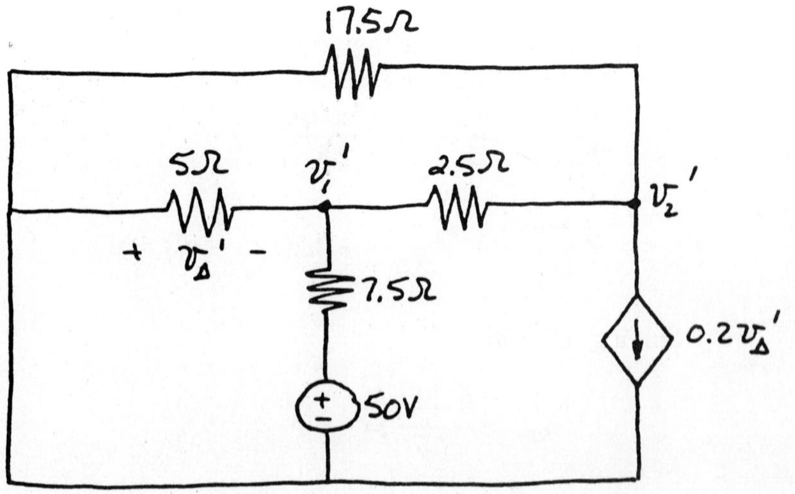

$$\frac{v_1'}{5} + \frac{v_1' - 50}{7.5} + \frac{v_1' - v_2'}{2.5} = 0$$

$$\frac{v_2'}{17.5} + \frac{v_2' - v_1'}{2.5} + 0.2(-v_1') = 0$$

Solving, $v_1' = 32$ V

$$\therefore \quad i_{50\text{V}}' = \frac{50 - 32}{7.5} = 2.4 \text{ A}$$

125 V source acting alone:

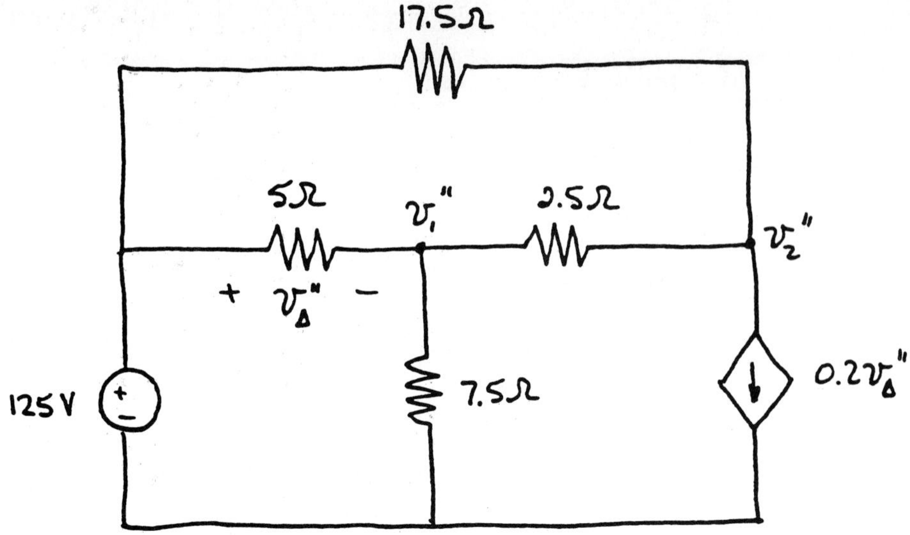

In writing the node voltage equations, use the fact that $v''_\Delta = 125 - v''_1$

$$\frac{v''_1}{7.5} + \frac{v''_1 - 125}{5} + \frac{v''_1 - v''_2}{2.5} = 0$$

$$\frac{v''_2 - 125}{17.5} + \frac{v''_2 - v''_1}{2.5} + 0.2(125 - v''_1) = 0$$

Solving, $v''_1 = 45$ V

$$\therefore \quad i''_{50V} = \frac{0 - 45}{7.5} = -6 \text{ A}$$

Thus, $i_{50V} = 2.4 - 6.0 = -3.6$ A

P 4.84 15 V source acting alone:

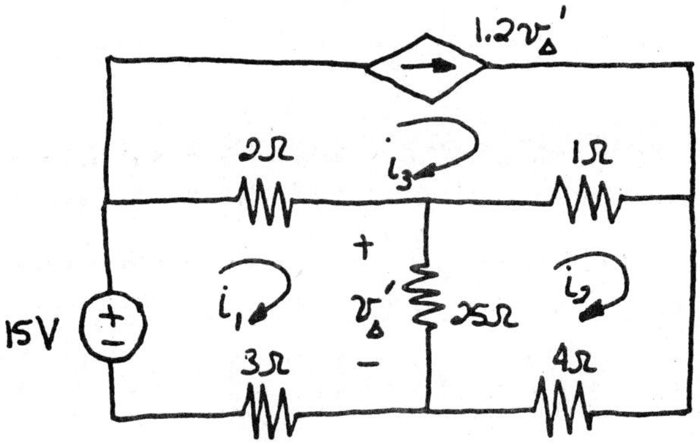

$$15 = 30i_1 - 25i_2 - 2i_3$$

$$0 = -25i_1 + 30i_2 - 1i_3$$

$$i_3 = 1.2v'_\Delta; \qquad v'_\Delta = 25(i_1 - i_2)$$

Solving, $i_1 = 7.2$ A; $\qquad i_2 = 6.6$ A; $\qquad v'_\Delta = 15$ V
10 V source acting alone:

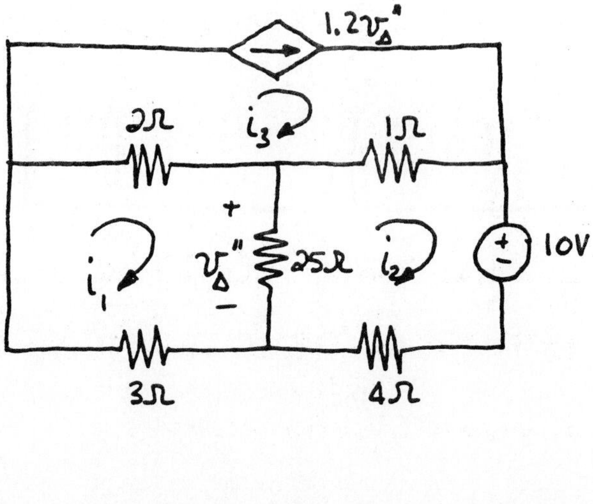

$$0 = 30i_1 - 25i_2 - 2i_3$$

$$-10 = -25i_1 + 30i_2 - 1i_3$$

$$i_3 = 1.2v''_\Delta; \qquad v''_\Delta = 25(i_1 - i_2)$$

Solving, $i_1 = 2.8$ A; $\quad i_2 = 2.4$ A; $\quad v''_\Delta = 10$ V

$$\therefore \quad v_\Delta = v'_\Delta + v''_\Delta = 15 + 10 = 25 \text{ V}$$

P 4.85 125 V left source acting alone:

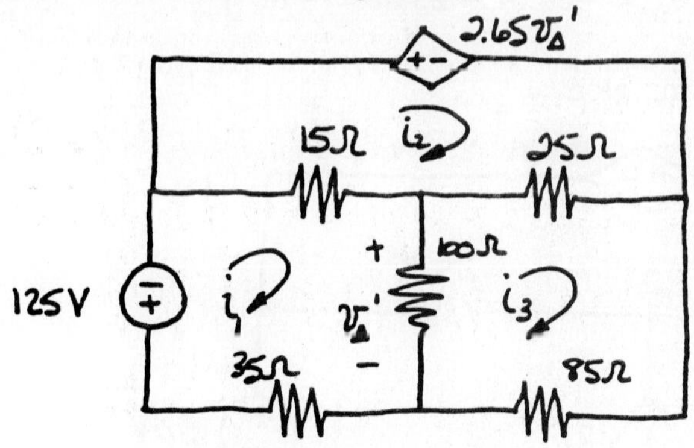

$$-125 = 150i_1 - 15i_2 - 100i_3$$

$$0 = 2.65v'_\Delta + 40i_2 - 15i_1 - 25i_3$$

$$0 = -100i_1 - 25i_2 + 210i_3$$

$$v'_\Delta = 100(i_1 - i_3)$$

Solving, $i_1 = -0.192$ A; $\quad i_3 = 0.375$ A; $\quad v'_\Delta = -56.67$ V
125 V (right) source acting alone:

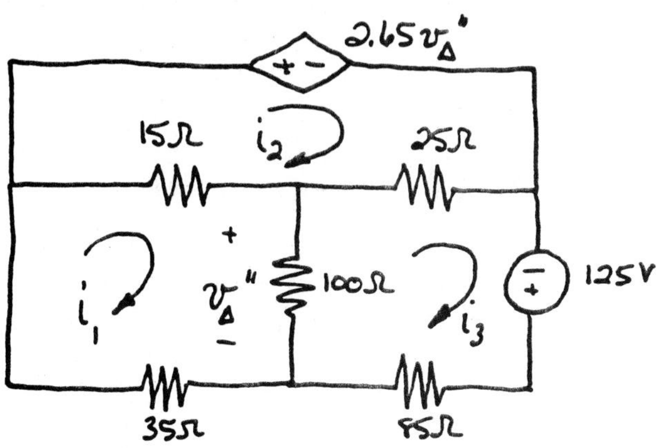

$$0 = 150i_1 - 15i_2 - 100i_3$$

$$0 = 2.65v''_{\Delta} + 40i_2 - 15i_1 - 25i_3$$

$$125 = -100i_1 - 25i_2 + 210i_3$$

$$v''_{\Delta} = 100(i_1 - i_3)$$

Solving, $i_1 = 1.39167$ A; $i_3 = 1.625$ A; $v''_{\Delta} = -23.33$ V

$$v_{\Delta} = v'_{\Delta} + v''_{\Delta} = -56.67 - 23.33 = -80 \text{ V}$$

P 4.86 150 V source acting alone:

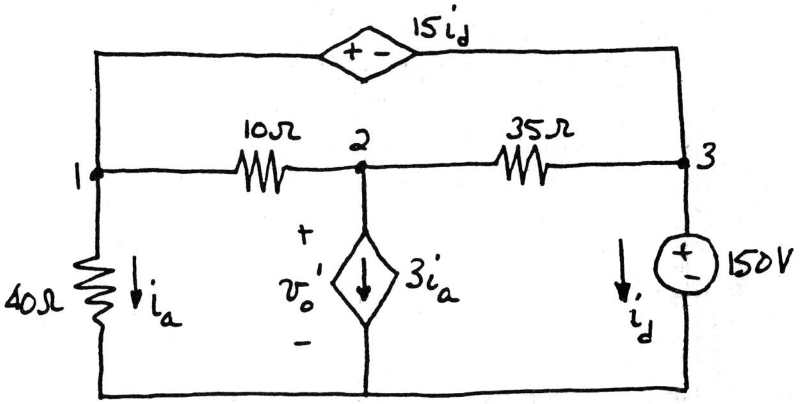

$$3i_a + \frac{v_2 - 150}{35} + \frac{v_2 - v_1}{10} = 0$$

$$v_1 = 150 + 15i_d$$

$$i_a = \frac{v_1}{40}$$

$$i_a + 3i_a + i_d = 0$$

Solving, $v_1 = 60$ V; $v_2 = 45$V

$$\therefore \; v'_o = v_2 = 45 \text{ V}$$

30 A source acting alone:

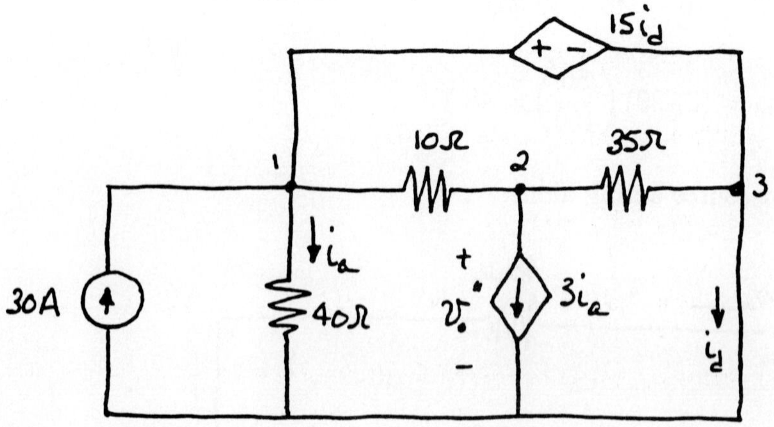

$$3i_a + \frac{v_2}{35} + \frac{v_2 - v_1}{10} = 0$$

$$v_1 = 15i_d$$

$$i_a = \frac{v_1}{40}$$

$$i_a + 3i_a + i_d = 30$$

Solving, $v_1 = 180$ V; $\qquad v_2 = 35$V

$$\therefore \quad v_o'' = v_2 = 35 \text{ V}$$

Thus, $v_o = v_o' + v_o'' = 45 + 35 = 80$ V

P 4.87 Voltage source acting alone:

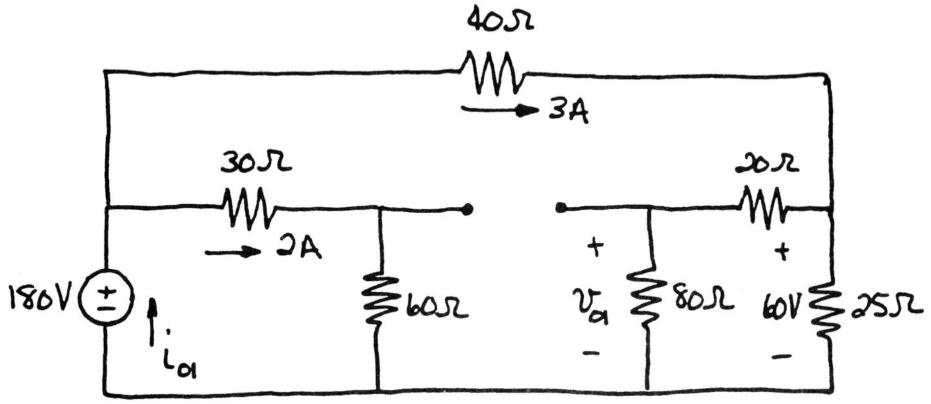

$$i_{o1} = \frac{180}{90} + \frac{180}{40 + 100\|25} = 2 + 3 = 5 \text{ A}$$

$$v_{o1} = (3)(20)\left(\frac{80}{100}\right) = 48 \text{ V}$$

Current source acting alone:

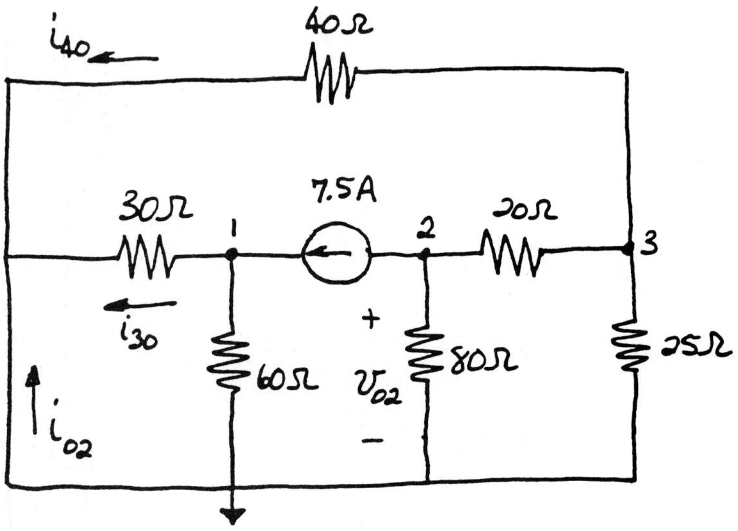

$$\frac{v_2}{80} + 7.5 + \frac{v_2 - v_3}{20} = 0$$

$$\frac{v_3}{25} + \frac{v_3 - v_2}{20} + \frac{v_3}{40} = 0$$

Solving, $v_2 = -184 \text{ V} = v_{o2}$; $v_3 = -80 \text{ V}$

$$i_{40} = \frac{v_3}{40} = -2 \text{ A}$$

$$i_{30} = \frac{7.5(60)}{90} = 5 \text{ A}$$

$$i_{o2} = -i_{30} - i_{40} = -5 + 2 = -3 \text{ A}$$

$$\therefore \quad v_o = v_{o1} + v_{o2} = 48 - 184 = -136 \text{ V}$$

$$i_o = i_{o1} + i_{o2} = 5 - 3 = 2 \text{ A}$$

P 4.88 45 V source acting alone:

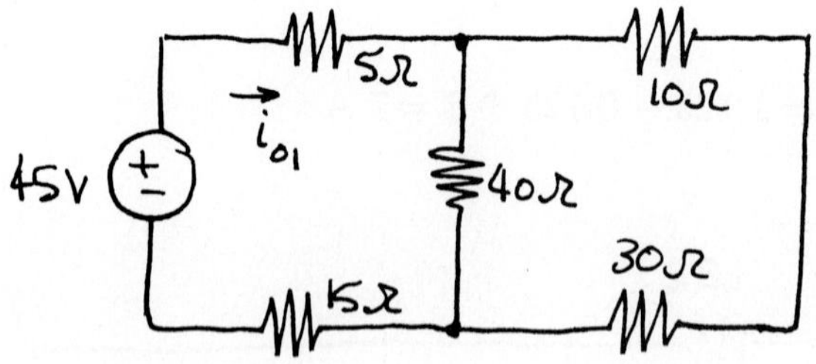

$$i_{o1} = 45/40 = 1.125 \text{ A}$$

10 V source acting alone:

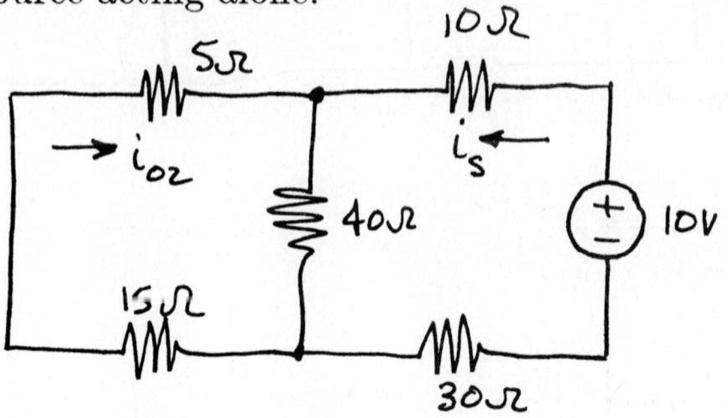

$$i_s = \frac{10}{40 + 40/3} = \frac{30}{160} \text{ A}$$

$$i_{o2} = -\frac{30}{160} \cdot \frac{40}{60} = -0.125 \text{ A}$$

8 A current source acting alone:

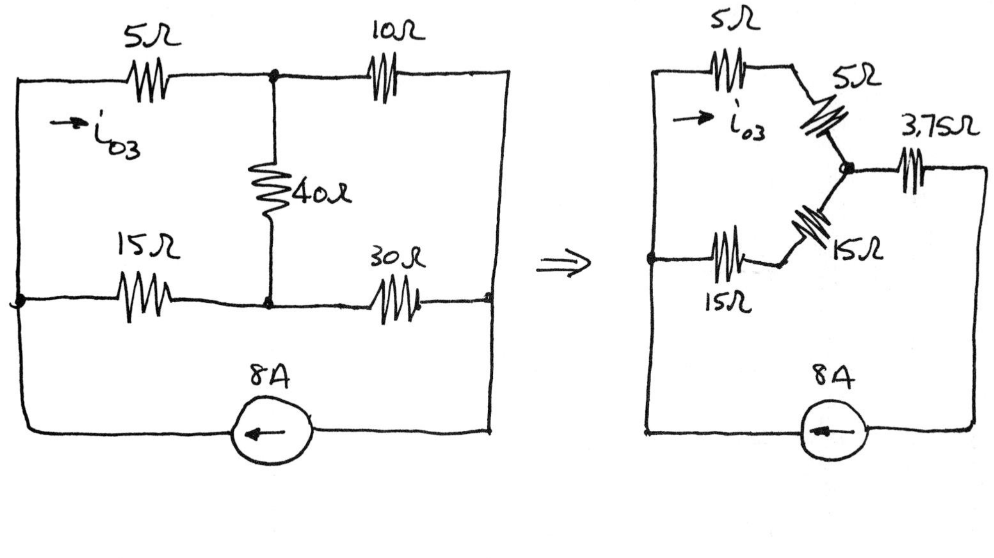

$$i_{o3} = \frac{(8)(30)}{40} = 6 \text{ A}$$

$$i_o = i_{o1} + i_{o2} + i_{o3} = 1.125 - 0.125 + 6 = 7 \text{ A}$$

P 4.89 4.5 A source:

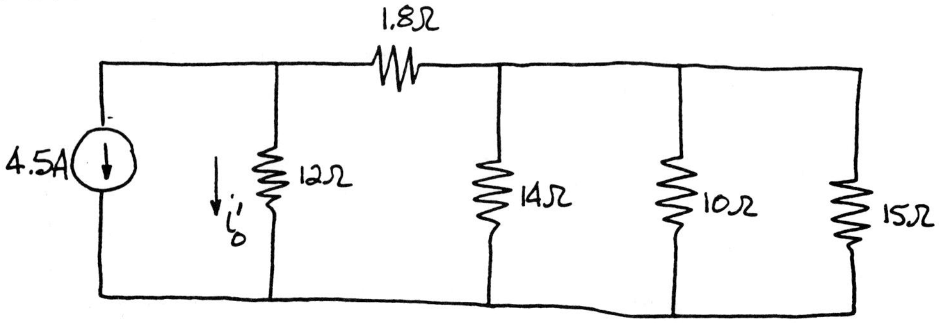

$$14\,\Omega \| 10\,\Omega \| 15\,\Omega = 4.2\,\Omega$$

$$\therefore \quad i_o' = \frac{-4.5(6)}{18} = -1.5 \text{ A}$$

20 A source:

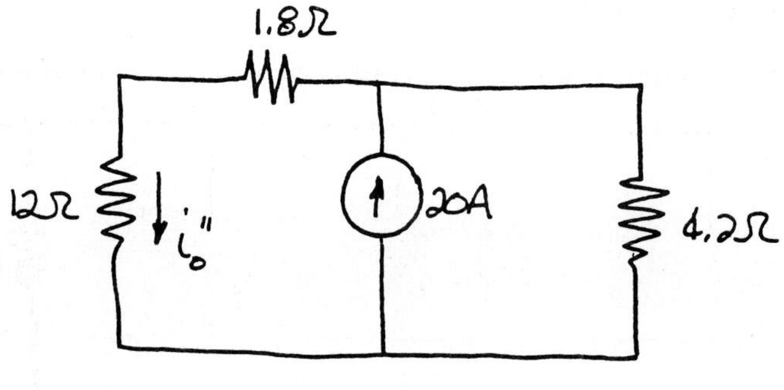

$$i_o'' = \frac{4.2(20)}{18} = 4.67 \text{ A}$$

50 V source:

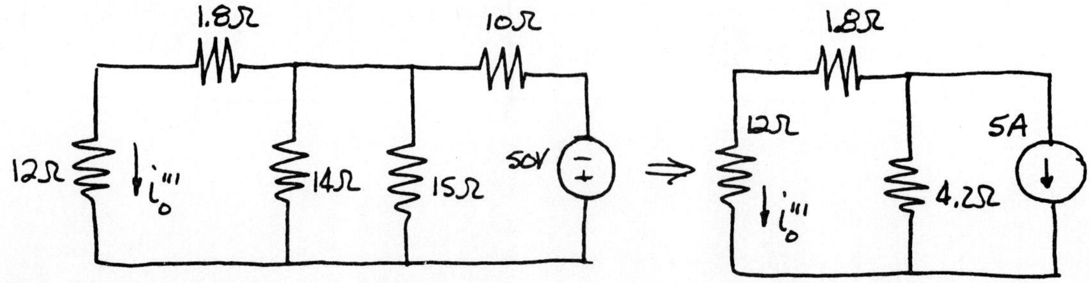

$$i_o''' = \frac{4.2(-5)}{18} = -1.167 \text{ A}$$

$$i_o = i_o' + i_o'' + i_o''' = -1.5 + 4.67 - 1.167 = 2 \text{ A}$$

P 4.90 [a] 500 V source:

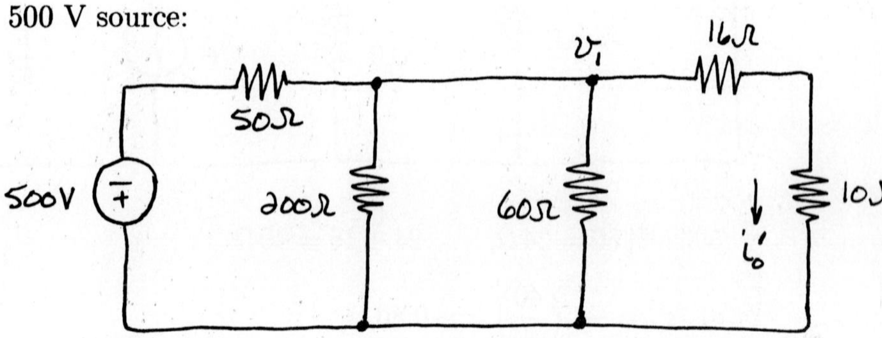

$$\frac{v_1 + 500}{50} + \frac{v_1}{200} + \frac{v_1}{60} + \frac{v_1}{26} = 0$$

So, $v_1 = -124.8$ V

$$i_o' = \frac{v_1}{26} = \frac{-124.8}{26} = -4.80 \text{ A}$$

20 A source:

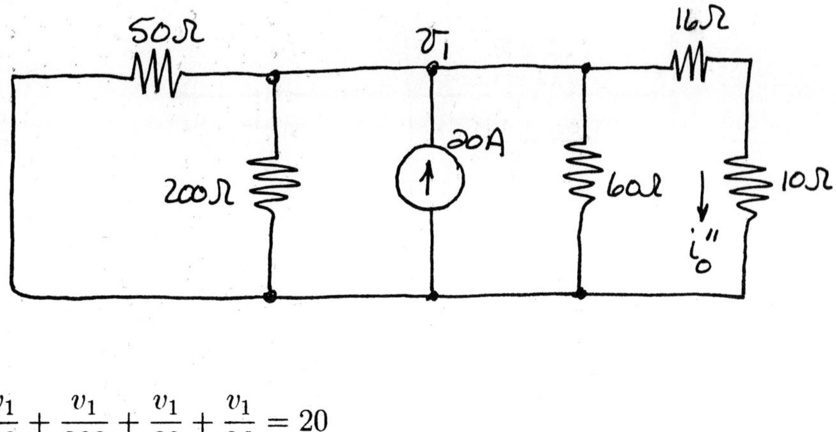

$$\frac{v_1}{50} + \frac{v_1}{200} + \frac{v_1}{60} + \frac{v_1}{26} = 20$$

$v_1 = 249.60$ V

$i_o'' = 249.60/26 = 9.6$ A

1 A source:

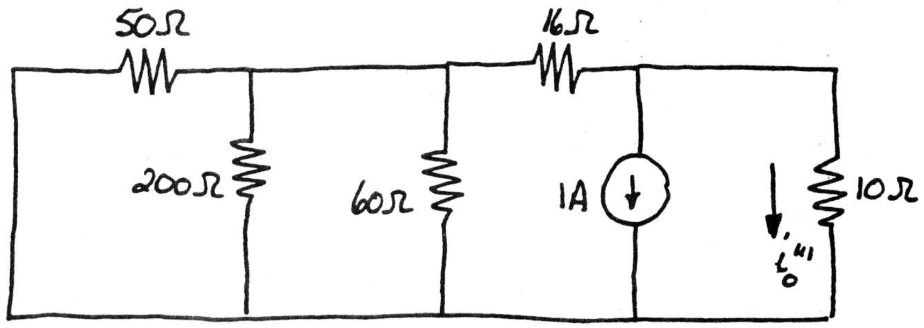

$50\|200\|60 = 24\,\Omega;\qquad 24 + 16 = 40\,\Omega$

$$\therefore\quad i_o'''' = -1\left(\frac{40}{50}\right) = -0.80\text{ A}$$

$$i_o = i_o' + i_o'' + i_o''' = -4.8 + 9.6 - 0.8 = 4\text{ A}$$

[b] $\quad p = i_o^2 10 = 16 \times 10 = 160$ W

P 4.91 Voltage source acting alone:

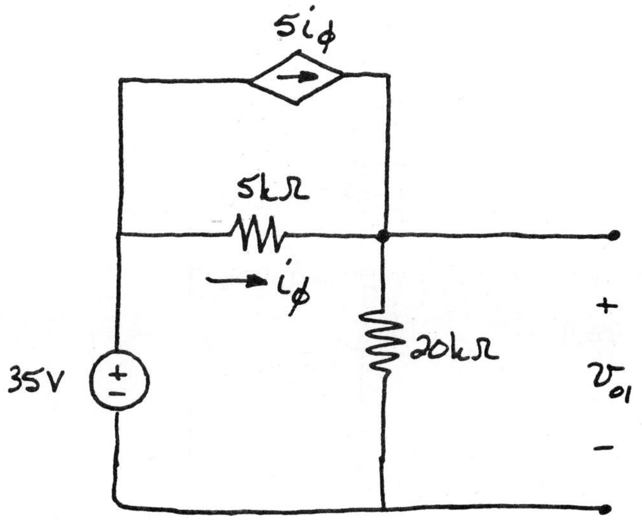

$$\frac{v_{o1}}{20} + \frac{v_{o1} - 35}{5} - 5\left(\frac{35 - v_{o1}}{5}\right) = 0$$

$$\therefore\quad v_{o1} = 33.6\text{ V}$$

Current source acting alone:

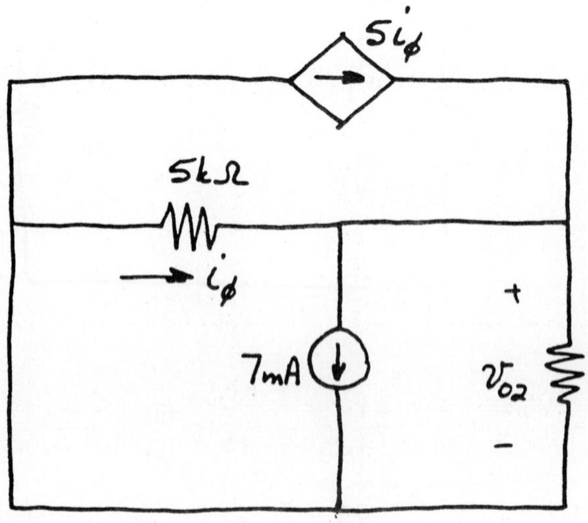

$$\frac{v_{o2}}{20} + 7 + \frac{v_{o2}}{5} - 5\left(\frac{-v_{o2}}{5}\right) = 0$$

$\therefore\quad v_{o2} = -5.6$ V

$v_o = v_{o1} + v_{o2} = 33.6 - 5.6 = 28$ V

P 4.92 [a] By hypothesis $i_o' + i_o'' = 1.5$ mA.

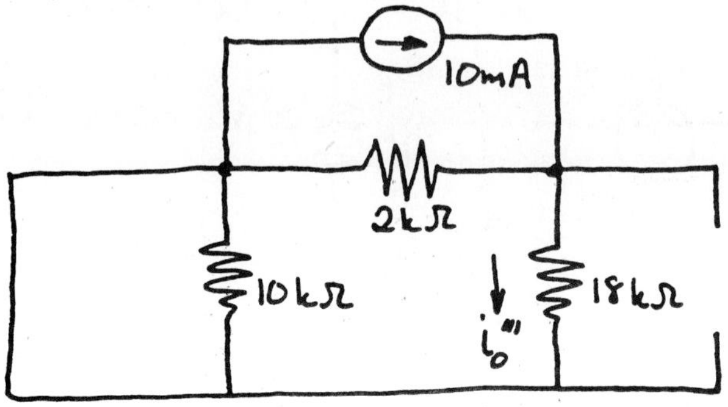

$$i_o''' = 10\frac{(2)}{(20)} = 1 \text{ mA}; \qquad \therefore\quad i_o = 1.5 + 1 = 2.5 \text{ mA}$$

[b] With all three sources in the circuit write a single node voltage equation.

$$\frac{v_b}{18} + \frac{v_b - 20}{2} - 5 - 10 = 0$$

$\therefore\quad v_b = 45$ V

$$i_o = \frac{v_b}{18} = 2.5 \text{ mA}$$

P 4.93 [a]

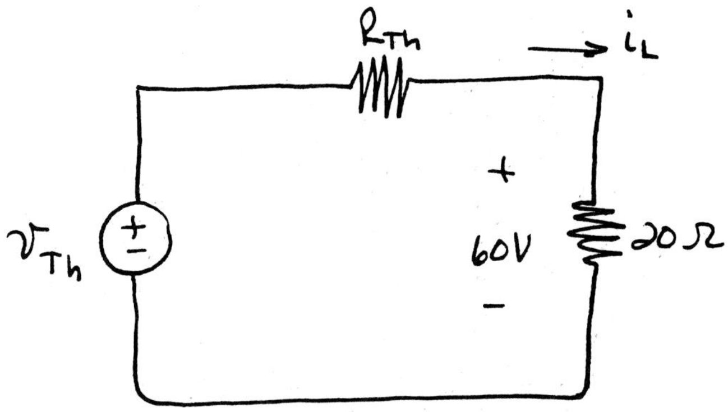

$$v_{oc} = V_{Th} = 75\text{ V}; \qquad i_L = \frac{60}{20} = 3\text{ A}; \qquad i_L = \frac{75-60}{R_{Th}} = \frac{15}{R_{Th}}$$

Therefore $R_{Th} = \dfrac{15}{3} = 5\,\Omega$

[b] $$i_L = \frac{v_o}{R_L} = \frac{V_{Th} - v_o}{R_{Th}}$$

Therefore $R_{Th} = \dfrac{V_{Th} - v_o}{v_o/R_L} = \left(\dfrac{V_{Th}}{v_o} - 1\right) R_L$

P 4.94 [a]

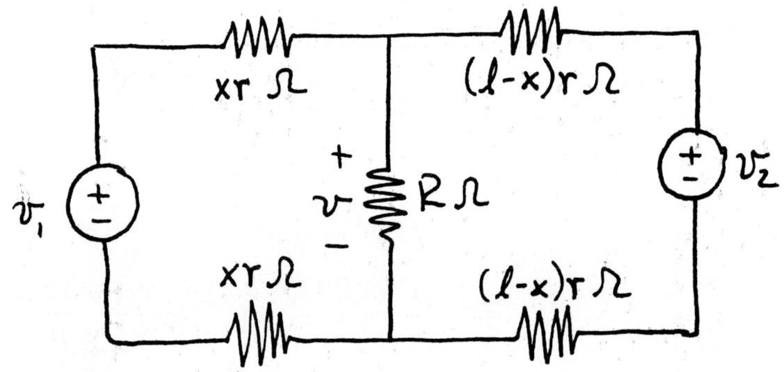

$$\frac{v - V_1}{2xr} + \frac{v}{R} + \frac{v - V_2}{2r(\ell - x)} = 0$$

$$v\left[\frac{1}{2xr} + \frac{1}{R} + \frac{1}{2r(\ell - x)}\right] = \frac{V_1}{2xr} + \frac{V_2}{2r(\ell - x)}$$

$$v = \frac{V_1 R\ell + xR(V_2 - V_1)}{R\ell + 2r\ell x - 2rx^2}$$

[b] Let $D = R\ell + 2r\ell x - 2rx^2$

$$\frac{dv}{dx} = \frac{(R\ell + 2r\ell x - 2rx^2)R(V_2 - V_1) - [V_1 R\ell + xR(v_2 - -v_1)]2r(\ell - 2x)}{D^2}$$

$$\frac{dv}{dx} = 0 \quad \text{when numerator is zero.}$$

The numerator simplifies to

$$x^2 + \frac{2\ell - V_1}{(V_2 - V_1)}x + \frac{R\ell(V_2 - V_1) - 2rV_1\ell^2}{2r(V_2 - V_1)} = 0$$

Solving for the roots of the quadratic yields

$$x = \frac{\ell}{V_2 - V_1}\left\{-V_1 \pm \sqrt{V_1V_2 - \frac{R}{2r\ell}(V_2 - V_1)^2}\right\}$$

[c] $$x = \frac{\ell}{V_2 - V_1}\left\{-V_1 \pm \sqrt{V_1V_2 - \frac{R}{2r\ell}(V_1 - V_2)^2}\right\}$$

$$V_2 = 1200 \text{ V}, \qquad V_1 = 1000 \text{ V}, \qquad \ell = 16 \text{ km}$$

$$r = 5 \times 10^{-5}\,\Omega/m; \qquad R = 3.9\,\Omega$$

$$\frac{\ell}{V_2 - V_1} = \frac{16{,}000}{1200 - 1000} = 80; \qquad V_1V_2 = 1.2 \times 10^6$$

$$\frac{R}{2r\ell}(V_1 - V_2)^2 = \frac{3.9(-200)^2}{(10 \times 10^{-5})(16 \times 10^3)} = 0.975 \times 10^5$$

$$x = 80\{-1000 \pm \sqrt{1.2 \times 10^6 - 0.0975 \times 10^6}\}$$

$$= 80\{-1000 \pm 1050\} = 80(50) = 4000 \text{ m}$$

[d]

$$\begin{aligned} v_{\min} &= \frac{V_1R\ell + R(v_2 - -v_1)x}{R\ell + 2r\ell x - 2rx^2} \\ &= \frac{(1000)(3.9)(16 \times 10^3) + 3.9(200)(4000)}{(3.9)(16{,}000) + 10 \times 10^{-5}(16{,}000)(4000) - 10 \times 10^{-5}(16 \times 10^6)} \\ &= 975 \text{ V} \end{aligned}$$

P 4.95 [a] In studying the circuit in Fig. P4.95 we note it contains six meshes and six essential nodes. Further study shows that by replacing the parallel resistors with their equivalent values the circuit reduces to four meshes and four essential nodes as shown in the following diagram.

The node Voltage approach will require solving three node Voltage equations along with equations involving v_Δ and i_β.

The mesh-current approach will require writing one supermesh equation plus three constraint equations involving the three current sources. Thus at the outset we know the supermesh equation can be reduced to a single unknown current. Since we are interested in the power developed by the 1 V source, we will retain the mesh current i_b and eliminate the mesh currents i_a, i_c And i_d.

The supermesh is denoted by the dashed line in the following figure.

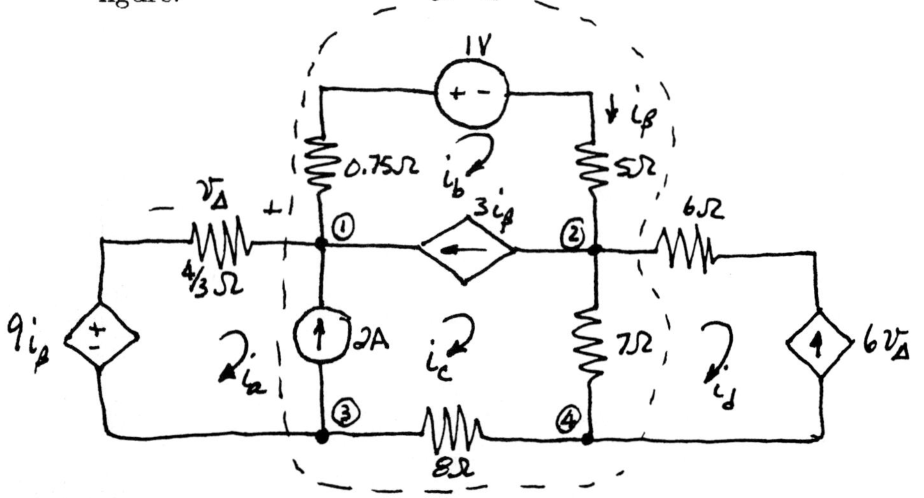

[b] Summing the voltages around the supermesh yields

$$-9i_\beta + \frac{4}{3}i_a + 0.75i_b + 1 + 5i_b + 7(i_c - i_d) + 8i_c = 0$$

Note that $i_\beta = i_b$ And multiply the equation by 12:

$$-108i_b + 16i_a + 9i_b + 12 + 60i_b + 84(i_c - i_d) + 96i_c = 0$$

or

$$16i_a - 39i_b + 180i_c - 84i_d = -12$$

Now note:

$$i_b - i_c = 3i_\beta = 3i_b; \qquad \therefore \quad i_c = -2i_b$$

whence

$$16i_a - 39i_b - 360i_b - 84i_d = -12$$

Now use the constraint that

$$i_a - i_c = -2$$

$$i_a = -2 + i_c = -2 - 2i_b$$

Therefore

$$-32 - 32i_b - 399i_b - 84i_d = -12$$

$$-431i_b - 84i_d = 20$$

Now use the constraint

$$i_d = -6v_\Delta = -6\left(\frac{-4}{3}i_a\right) = 8i_a = -16 - 16i_b$$

Therefore

$$-431i_b - 84(-16 - 16i_b) = 20$$

or

$$913i_b = -1324$$

$$\therefore\ i_b \approx -1.45\text{ A}$$

$$p_{1V} = 1i_b \cong -1.45\text{ W}; \qquad \therefore\ p_{1V}\text{ (developed)} \cong 1.45\text{ W}$$

P 4.96

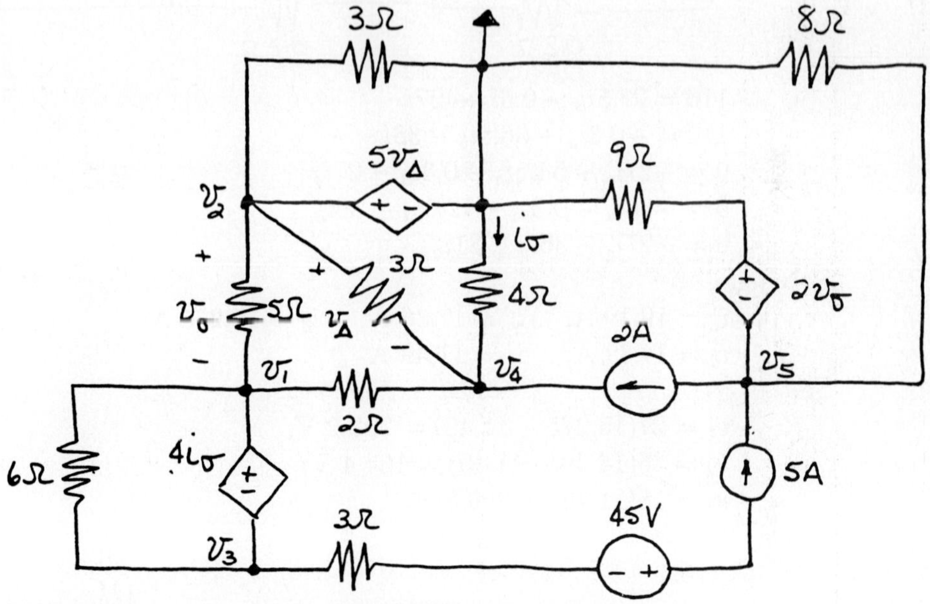

$$\text{At } v_1: \quad \frac{v_1 - v_2}{5} + \frac{v_1 - v_4}{2} + 5 = 0$$

$$\text{At } v_4: \quad \frac{v_4 - v_1}{2} + \frac{v_4 - v_2}{3} + \frac{v_4}{4} - 2 = 0$$

Also, $v_2 = 5v_\Delta = 5(v_2 - v_4)$
Solving, $v_1 = -20$ V; $\quad v_2 = -15$ V; $\quad v_4 = -12$ V

$$\text{At } v_5: \quad 2 - 5 + \frac{v_5}{8} + \frac{v_5 + 2v_\sigma}{9} = 0$$

Also, $v_\sigma = v_2 - v_1 = 5$ V Solving, $v_5 = 8$ V

$$\therefore\ p_{2A} = 2(v_5 - v_4) = 40\text{ W}$$

P 4.97

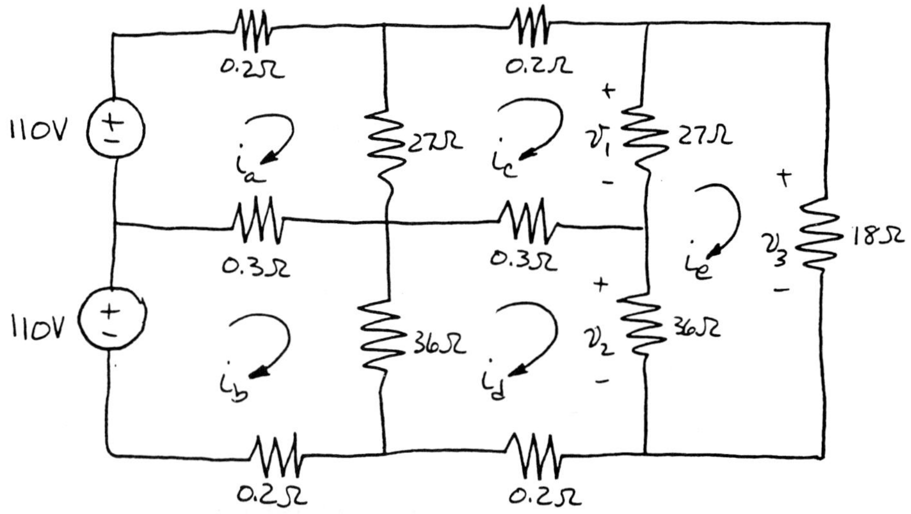

$$110 = 27.5i_a - 0.3i_b - 27i_c$$
$$110 = -0.3i_a + 36.5i_b - 36i_d$$
$$0 = -27i_a + 54.5i_c - 0.3i_d - 27i_e$$
$$0 = -36i_b - 0.3i_c + 72.5i_d - 36i_e$$
$$0 = -27i_c - 36i_d + 81i_e$$

Solving,

$i_a = 19.19$ A; $i_b = 17.36$ A; $i_c = 15.275$ A;
$i_d = 14.39$ A; $i_e = 11.49$ A

So,

$v_1 = 27(15.275 - 11.49) = 102.2$ V;
$v_2 = 36(14.49 - 11.49) = 104.4$ V;
$v_3 = 18(11.49) = 206.8$ V.

P 4.98

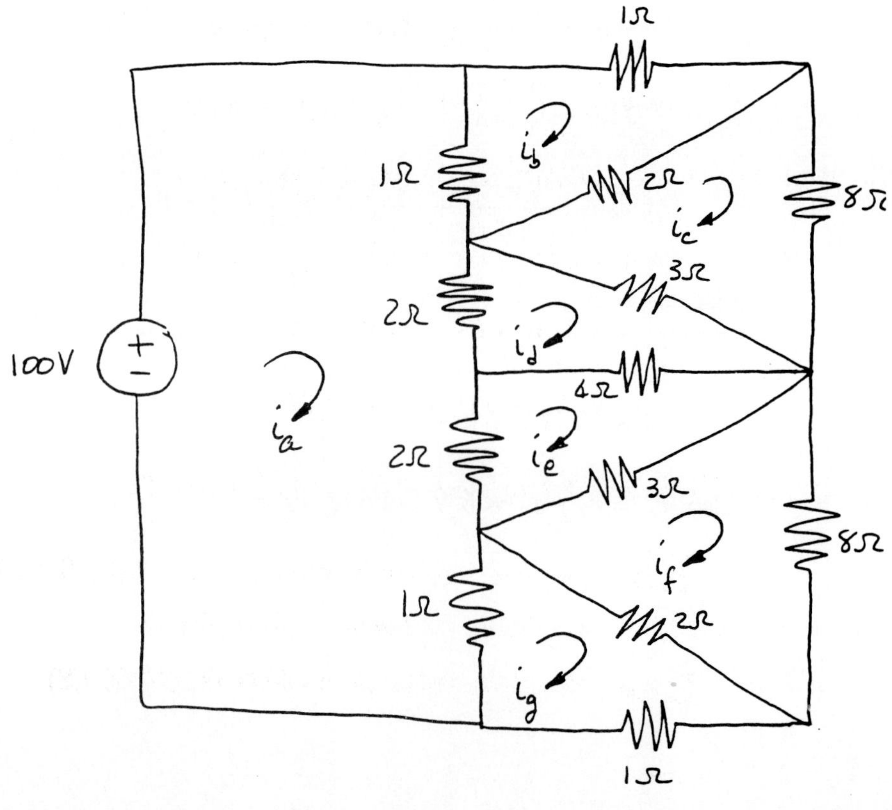

$$100 = 6i_a - 1i_b + 0i_c - 2i_d - 2i_e + 0i_f - 1i_g$$

$$0 = -1i_a + 4i_b - 2i_c + 0i_d + 0i_e + 0i_f + 0i_g$$

$$0 = 0i_a - 2i_b + 13i_c - 3i_d + 0i_e + 0i_f + 0i_g$$

$$0 = -2i_a + 0i_b - 3i_c + 9i_d - 4i_e + 0i_f + 0i_g$$

$$0 = -2i_a + 0i_b + 0i_c - 4i_d + 9i_e - 3i_f + 0i_g$$

$$0 = 0i_a + 0i_b + 0i_c + 0i_d - 3i_e + 13i_f - 2i_g$$

$$0 = -1i_a + 0i_b + 0i_c + 0i_d + 0i_e - 2i_f + 4i_g$$

A computer solution yields

$i_a = 30$ A; $\quad i_e = 15$ A;

$i_b = 10$ A; $\quad i_f = 5$ A;

$i_c = 5$ A; $\quad i_g = 10$ A;

$i_d = 15$ A

$$\therefore \quad i = i_d - i_e = 0 \text{ A}$$

CHECK:

$$p_{1T} = p_{1B} = (i_b)^2 = (i_g)^2 = 100 \text{ W}$$

$$p_{1L} = (i_a - i_b)^2 = (i_a - i_g)^2 = 400 \text{ W}$$

$$p_{2C} = 2(i_b - i_c)^2 = (i_g - i_f)^2 = 50 \text{ W}$$

$$p3 = 3(i_c - i_d)^2 = 3(i_e - i_f)^2 = 300 \text{ W}$$

$$p4 = 4(i_d - i_e)^2 = 0 \text{ W}$$

$$p8 = 8(i_c)^2 = 8(i_f)^2 = 200 \text{ W}$$

$$p2L = 2(i_a - i_d)^2 = 2(i_a - i_e)^2 = 450 \text{ W}$$

$$\sum p_{\text{abs}} = 100 + 400 + 50 + 200 + 300 + 450 + 0 + 450 + 300 + 200 + 50 + 400 + 100 = 3000 \text{ W}$$

$$\sum p_{\text{gen}} = 100i_a = 100(30) = 3000 \text{ W (CHECKS)}$$

P 4.99
$$\frac{dv_1}{dI_{g1}} = \frac{-R_1[R_2(R_3+R_4)+R_3R_4]}{(R_1+R_2)(R_3+R_4)+R_3R_4}$$

$$\frac{dv_1}{dI_{g2}} = \frac{R_1R_3R_4}{(R_1+R_2)(R_3+R_4)+R_3R_4}$$

$$\frac{dv_2}{dI_{g1}} + \frac{-R_1R_3R_4}{(R_1+R_2)(R_3+R_4)+R_3R_4}$$

$$\frac{dv_2}{dI_{g2}} = \frac{R_3R_4(R_1+R_2)}{(R_1+R_2)(R_3+R_4)+R_3R_4}$$

P 4.100 From the solution to Problem 4.99 we have

$$\frac{dv_1}{dI_{g1}} = \frac{-25[5(125)+3750]}{30(125)+3750} = -\frac{175}{12}\ \text{V/A}$$

and

$$\frac{dv_2}{dI_{g1}} = \frac{-(25)(50)(75)}{30(125)+3750} = -12.5\ \text{V/A}$$

By hypothesis, $\Delta I_{g1} = 11 - 12 = -1$ A

$$\therefore\ \Delta v_1 = (-\frac{175}{12})(-1) = \frac{175}{12} = 14.58\ \text{V}$$

Thus, $v_1 = 25 + 14.58 = 39.58$ V
Also,

$$\Delta v_2 = (-12.5)(-1) = 12.5\ \text{V}$$

Thus, $v_2 = 90 + 12.5 = 102.5$ V
The PSpice solution is

$$v_1 = 39.5830\ \text{V}$$

and

$$v_2 = 102.5000\ \text{V}$$

These values are in agreement with our predicted values.

P 4.101 From the solution to Problem 4.99 we have

$$\frac{dv_1}{dI_{g2}} = \frac{(25)(50)(75)}{30(125) + 3750} = 12.5 \text{ V/A}$$

and

$$\frac{dv_2}{dI_{g2}} = \frac{(50)(75)(30)}{30(125) + 3750} = 15 \text{ V/A}$$

By hypothesis, $\Delta I_{g2} = 17 - 16 = 1$ A

$$\therefore \quad \Delta v_1 = (12.5)(1) = 12.5 \text{ V}$$

Thus, $v_1 = 25 + 12.5 = 37.5$ V
Also,

$$\Delta v_2 = (15)(1) = 15 \text{ V}$$

Thus, $v_2 = 90 + 15 = 105$ V
The PSpice solution is

$$v_1 = 37.5 \text{ V}$$

and

$$v_2 = 105 \text{ V}$$

These values are in agreement with our predicted values.

P 4.102 From the solutions to Problems 4.99 — 4.101 we have

$$\frac{dv_1}{dI_{g1}} = -\frac{175}{12} \text{ V/A}; \qquad \frac{dv_1}{dI_{g2}} = 12.5 \text{ V/A}$$

$$\frac{dv_2}{dI_{g1}} = -12.5 \text{ V/A}; \qquad \frac{dv_2}{dI_{g2}} = 15 \text{ V/A}$$

By hypothesis,

$$\Delta I_{g1} = 11 - 12 = -1 \text{ A}$$

$$\Delta I_{g2} = 17 - 16 = 1 \text{ A}$$

Therefore,

$$\Delta v_1 = \frac{175}{12} + 12.5 = 27.0833 \text{ V}$$

$$\Delta v_2 = 12.5 + 15 = 27.5 \text{ V}$$

Hence

$$v_1 = 25 + 27.0833 = 52.0833 \text{ V}$$

$$v_2 = 90 + 27.5 = 117.5 \text{ V}$$

The PSpice solution is

$$v_1 = 52.0830 \text{ V}$$

and

$$v_2 = 117.5 \text{ V}$$

These values are in agreement with our predicted values.

P 4.103 By hypothesis,

$$\Delta R_1 = 27.5 - 25 = 2.5\,\Omega$$

$$\Delta R_2 = 4.5 - 5 = -0.5\,\Omega$$

$$\Delta R_3 = 55 - 50 = 5\,\Omega$$

$$\Delta R_4 = 67.5 - 75 = -7.5\,\Omega$$

So

$$\Delta v_1 = 0.5833(2.5) - 5.417(-0.5) + 0.45(5) + 0.2(-7.5) = 4.9168 \text{ V}$$

$$\therefore \quad v_1 = 25 + 4.9168 = 29.9168 \text{ V}$$

$$\Delta v_2 = 0.5(2.5) + 6.5(-0.5) + 0.54(5) + 0.24(-7.5) = -1.1 \text{ V}$$

$$\therefore \quad v_2 = 90 - 1.1 = 88.9 \text{ V}$$

The PSpice solution is

$$v_1 = 29.6710 \text{ V}$$

and

$$v_2 = 88.5260 \text{ V}$$

Note our predicted values are within a fraction of a volt of the actual values.

5

The Operational Amplifier

Drill Exercises

DE 5.1 [a] $v_o = (-80/16)v_s, \qquad v_o = -5v_s$

v_s(V)	0.4	2.0	3.5	−0.6	−1.6	−2.4
v_o(V)	−2.0	−10.0	−15.0	3.0	8.0	10.0

[b] $-15 = -5v_s, \quad v_s = 3$ V; $\quad 10 = -5v_s, \quad v_s = -2$ V

Therefore $-2 \le v_s \le 3$ V

DE 5.2 $v_o = (-R_x/16)v_s = (0.64R_x/16) = 10$ V

Therefore $R_x = \dfrac{160}{0.64} = 250\,\text{k}\Omega, \qquad 0 \le R_x \le 250\,\text{k}\Omega$

DE 5.3 [a] $v_o = -\dfrac{250}{5}v_a - \dfrac{250}{25}v_b = -50(0.1) - 10(0.25) = -5 - 2.5 = -7.5$ V

[b] $v_o = -50v_a - 2.5 = -10$ V; $\quad$ therefore $50v_a = 7.5, \quad v_a = 0.15$ V

[c] $v_o = -5 - 10v_b = -10$ V; $\quad 10v_b = 5, \quad v_b = 0.5$ V

[d] $v_o = -50v_a + 10v_b = -5 + 2.5 = -2.5$ V

$v_o = -50v_a + 2.5 = -10$ V;

$50v_a = 12.5, \quad v_a = 0.25$ V

$-50v_a + 2.5 = 15, \quad 50v_a = -12.5, \quad v_a = -0.25$ V

$v_o = -5 + 10v_b = -10$ V; $\quad 10v_b = -5; \quad v_b = -0.5$ V

$-5 + 10v_b = 15; \quad 10v_b = 20; \quad v_b = 2.0$ V

DE 5.4 [a] $\frac{v_n}{4.5} + \frac{v_n - v_o}{63} = 0,$ therefore $v_o = 15v_n, \quad v_n = v_p$

Thus $v_o = 15v_p, \quad v_p = \frac{0.4R_x}{15 + R_x}$

So when $R_x = 60\,\text{k}\Omega, \quad v_p = 0.32\ \text{V}, \quad v_o = 4.8\ \text{V}$

[b] $\frac{15(0.4R_x)}{15 + R_x} = 5, \quad R_x = 75\,\text{k}\Omega$

DE 5.5 [a] Assume v_a is acting along. Replacing v_b with a short circuit yields $v_2 = 0$, therefore $v_1 = 0$ and we have

$$\frac{0 - v_a}{R_a} + \frac{0 - v_o'}{R_b} + i_n = 0, \qquad i_n = 0$$

Therefore

$$\frac{v_o'}{R_b} = -\frac{v_a}{R_a}, \qquad v_o' = \frac{R_b}{R_a}v_a$$

Assume v_b is acting alone. Replace v_a with a short circuit. Now

$$v_p = v_n = \frac{v_b R_d}{R_c + R_d}$$

$$\frac{v_n}{R_a} + \frac{v_n - v_o''}{R_b} + i_n = 0, \qquad i_n = 0$$

$$\left(\frac{1}{R_a} + \frac{1}{R_b}\right)\left(\frac{R_d}{R_c + R_d}\right)v_b - \frac{v_o''}{R_b} = 0$$

$$v_o'' = \left(\frac{R_b}{R_a} + 1\right)\left(\frac{R_d}{R_c + R_d}\right)v_b = \frac{R_d}{R_a}\left(\frac{R_a + R_b}{R_c + R_d}\right)v_b$$

$$v_o = v_o' + v_o'' = \frac{R_d}{R_a}\left(\frac{R_a + R_b}{R_c + R_d}\right)v_b - \frac{R_b}{R_a}v_a$$

[b] $\frac{R_d}{R_a}\left(\frac{R_a + R_b}{R_c + R_d}\right) = \frac{R_b}{R_a},$ therefore $R_d(R_a + R_b) = R_b(R_c + R_d)$

$R_d R_a = R_b R_c,$ therefore $\frac{R_a}{R_b} = \frac{R_c}{R_d}$

When $\frac{R_d}{R_a}\left(\frac{R_a + R_b}{R_c + R_d}\right) = \frac{R_b}{R_a}$

Eq. (6.21) reduces to $v_o = \frac{R_b}{R_a}v_b - \frac{R_b}{R_a}v_a = \frac{R_b}{R_a}(v_b - v_a).$

DE 5.6 [a]
$$v_o = \frac{20(60)}{10(24)}v_b - \frac{50}{10}v_a = 5(v_b - v_a) = 20 - 5v_a$$

$$20 - 5v_a = \pm 10 \text{ V}$$

$$5v_a = 20 \mp 10, \qquad v_a = 2 \text{ V}, \qquad v_a = 6 \text{ V}$$

$$\text{Therefore} \quad 2 \leq v_a \leq 6 \text{ V}$$

[b]
$$v_o = \frac{8(60)}{10(12)}v_b - 5v_a = 4v_b - 5v_a$$

$$4v_b - 5v_a = 16 - 5v_a = \pm 10 \text{ V}$$

$$16 \mp 10 = 5v_a, \qquad v_a = 1.2 \text{ V}, \qquad v_a = 5.2 \text{ V}$$

$$\text{Therefore} \quad 1.2 \leq v_a \leq 5.2 \text{ V}$$

DE 5.7 [a]
$$A_{\mathrm{dm}} = \frac{(24)(26) + (25)(25)}{(2)(1)(25)} = 24.98$$

[b]
$$A_{\mathrm{cm}} = \frac{(1)(24) - 25(1)}{1(25)} = -0.04$$

[c]
$$\text{CMRR} = \left|\frac{24.98}{0.04}\right| = 624.50$$

DE 5.8
$$A_{\mathrm{cm}} = \frac{(20)(50) - (50)R_x}{20(50 + R_x)}$$

$$A_{\mathrm{dm}} = \frac{50(20 + 50) + 50(50 + R_x)}{2(20)(50 + R_x)}$$

$$\frac{A_{\mathrm{dm}}}{A_{\mathrm{cm}}} = \frac{R_x + 120}{2(20 - R_x)}$$

$$\therefore \quad \frac{R_x + 120}{2(20 - R_x)} = \pm 1000$$

If we use +1000 $R_x = 19.93\,\text{k}\Omega$

If we use −1000 $R_x = 20.07\,\text{k}\Omega$

Problems

P 5.1 Since the current into the inverting input terminal of an ideal op-amp is zero, the voltage across the 3.3 MΩ resistor is (2.5)(3.3) or 8.25 V. Therefore the voltmeter reads 8.25 V.

P 5.2
$$v_p = \frac{18}{24}(12) = 9 \text{ V} = v_n$$

$$\frac{v_n - 24}{30} + \frac{v_n - v_o}{20} = 0$$

$$2v_n - 48 + 3v_n - 3v_o = 0$$

$$3v_o = 5v_n - 48$$

$$v_o = (45 - 48)/3 = -1.0 \text{ V}$$

$$i_L = \frac{v_o}{5} \times 10^{-3} = -\frac{1}{5} \times 10^{-3} = -200 \times 10^{-6}$$

$$i_L = -200\,\mu\text{A}$$

P 5.3
$$\frac{v_b - v_a}{20} + \frac{v_b - v_o}{160} = 0, \qquad \text{therefore} \quad v_o = 9v_b - 8v_a$$

[a] $v_a = 1.5$ V, $v_b = 0$ V, $v_o = -12$ V

[b] $v_a = 3.0$ V, $v_b = 0$ V, $v_o = -18$ V (sat)

[c] $v_a = 1.0$ V, $v_b = 2$ V, $v_o = 10$ V

[d] $v_a = 4.0$ V, $v_b = 2$ V, $v_o = -14$ V

[e] $v_a = 6.0$ V, $v_b = 8$ V, $v_o = 18$ V (sat)

[f] If $v_b = 4.5$ V, $v_o = 40.5 - 8v_a = \pm 18$

$$\therefore\ 2.8125 \leq v_a \leq 7.3125 \text{ V}$$

P 5.4 [a]
$$i_a = \frac{120}{6} \times 10^{-6} = 20\,\mu\text{A}$$

$$v_a = -20 \times 10^3 i_a = -400\,\text{mV}$$

[b]
$$\frac{v_a}{60} + \frac{v_a}{20} + \frac{v_a - v_o}{240} = 0$$

$$\therefore\ v_o = 17v_a = -6.8 \text{ V}$$

[c] $i_a = 20\,\mu\text{A}$

[d] $i_o + \dfrac{v_o}{80{,}000} = i_b; \qquad i_b = \dfrac{v_a - v_o}{240{,}000} = 26.67\,\mu\text{A}$

$$i_o = 26.67 - (-85) = 111.67\,\mu\text{A}$$

P 5.5 $\dfrac{0-3}{15} + \dfrac{0-v_o}{70} = 0; \qquad v_o = -14\text{ V}$

This is impossible, so the output saturates at $v_o = -5$ V. This also means that the voltage at v_- is not 0, since the op amp is no longer operating in its linear region. So v_- can be found by writing a KCL equation at the inverting terminal:

$$\frac{3 - v_-}{15{,}000} = \frac{v_- - (-5)}{70{,}000} \qquad \therefore \quad v_- = 1.588\text{ V}$$

P 5.6 $v_o = (1)(9) = 9\text{ V}; \qquad i_{15k\Omega} = \dfrac{9}{15} = 0.6\,\text{mA};$

$$i_{6k\Omega} = \frac{9}{6} = 1.5\,\text{mA}; \qquad i_{9k\Omega} = \frac{9}{9} = 1\,\text{mA}$$

$$\therefore \quad i_o = -0.6 - 1.5 - 1 = -3.1\,\text{mA}$$

P 5.7 [a] First, note that $v_n = v_p = 2.5$ V

Let v_{o1} equal the voltage output of the op-amp. Then

$$\frac{2.5 - v_g}{5} + \frac{2.5 - v_{o1}}{10} = 0, \qquad \therefore \quad v_{o1} = 7.5 - 2v_g$$

Also note that $v_{o1} - 2.5 = v_o, \qquad \therefore \quad v_o = 7.5 - 2.5v_g$

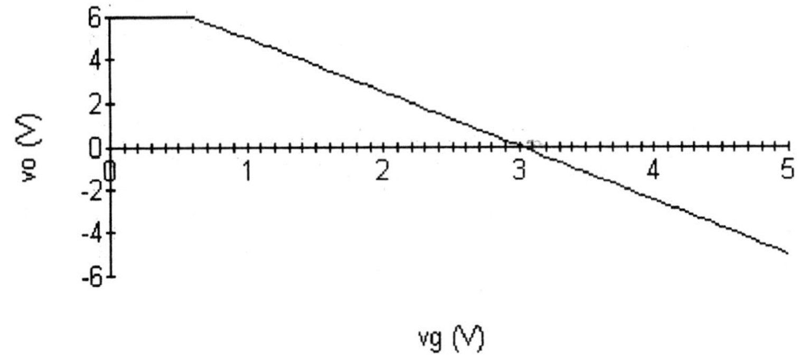

[b] No, the output voltage is bipolar for a different range of input values, i.e., $-5\text{ V} \le v_o \le 6\text{ V}$ while the input voltage is unipolar in the range $0.6 \le v_g \le 5$ V. The output saturates at -6 V for $0 \le v_g \le 0.6$ V.

P 5.8 [a] Replace the combination of v_g, 3.2 kΩ, and the 4.8 kΩ resistors with its Thévenin equivalent.

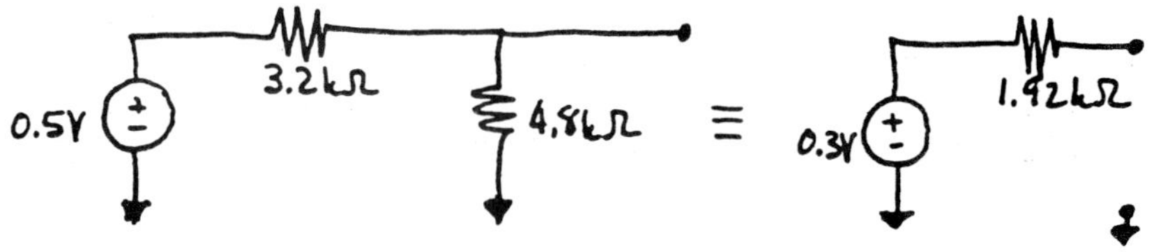

Then $v_o = \frac{-[30+\sigma 170]}{1.92}(0.30)$

At saturation $v_o = -10$ V; therefore

$$-\left(\frac{30+\sigma 170}{1.92}\right)(0.3) = -10, \quad \text{or} \quad \sigma = 0.2$$

Thus for $0 \leq \sigma < 0.20$ the operational amplifier will not saturate.

[b] When $\sigma = 0.12$, $v_o = \frac{-(30+20.4)}{1.92}(0.30) = -7.875$ V

Also $\frac{v_o}{180} + \frac{v_o}{50.4} + i_o = 0$

$$\therefore \; i_o = -\frac{v_o}{180} - \frac{v_o}{50.4} = \frac{7.875}{180} + \frac{7.875}{50.4}\,\text{mA} = 200\,\mu\text{A}$$

P 5.9 [a] Let v_Δ be the voltage from the potentiometer contact to ground. Then

$$\frac{0-v_g}{5} + \frac{0-v_\Delta}{15} = 0$$

$$-3v_g - v_\Delta = 0, \qquad \therefore \; v_\Delta = -150\,\text{mV}$$

$$\frac{v_\Delta}{\alpha R_\Delta} + \frac{v_\Delta - 0}{15} + \frac{v_\Delta - v_o}{(1-\alpha)R_\Delta} = 0$$

$$\frac{v_\Delta}{\alpha} + 10v_\Delta + \frac{v_\Delta - v_o}{1-\alpha} = 0$$

$$v_\Delta\left(\frac{1}{\alpha} + 10 + \frac{1}{1-\alpha}\right) = \frac{v_o}{1-\alpha}$$

$$\therefore \; v_o = -0.15\left[1 + 10(1-\alpha) + \frac{(1-\alpha)}{\alpha}\right]$$

When $\alpha = 0.3$, $v_o = -0.15(1+7+7/3) = -1.55$ V

When $\alpha = 0.70$, $v_o = -0.15(1+2.5+1/3) = -0.575$ V

$\therefore \; -1.55\text{ V} \leq v_o \leq -0.575$ V

[b] $$-0.15\left[1+10(1-\alpha)+\frac{(1-\alpha)}{\alpha}\right]=-6$$

$$\alpha+10\alpha(1-\alpha)+(1-\alpha)=40\alpha$$

$$\alpha+10\alpha-10\alpha^2+1-\alpha=40\alpha$$

$$\therefore\quad 10\alpha^2+30\alpha-1=0\quad\text{so}\quad\alpha\cong 0.033$$

P 5.10 [a] $$\frac{v_\text{d}-v_\text{a}}{72}+\frac{v_\text{d}-v_\text{b}}{120}+\frac{v_\text{d}-v_\text{c}}{450}+\frac{v_\text{d}}{600}+\frac{v_\text{d}-v_o}{180}=0$$

$$v_o=180\left(-\frac{10}{72}+\frac{2}{120}+\frac{23}{450}+\frac{8}{600}+\frac{8}{180}\right)=-2.4\text{ V}$$

[b] $$v_o=-8.4-0.4v_\text{c}$$

$$-8.4-0.4v_\text{c}=-16;\qquad v_\text{c}=19\text{ V}$$

$$-8.4-0.4v_\text{c}=16;\qquad v_\text{c}=-61\text{ V}$$

$$-61\text{ V}\le v_\text{c}\le 19\text{ V}$$

P 5.11 [a] $$\frac{v_\text{d}-v_\text{a}}{72}+\frac{v_\text{d}-v_\text{b}}{120}+\frac{v_\text{d}-v_\text{c}}{450}+\frac{v_\text{d}}{600}+\frac{v_\text{d}-v_o}{R_\text{f}}=0$$

$$(25/3)v_\text{d}-(25/3)v_\text{a}+5v_\text{d}-5v_\text{b}+(4/3)v_\text{d}-(4/3)v_\text{c}+v_\text{d}+$$

$$\frac{600}{R_\text{f}}v_\text{d}=\frac{600}{R_\text{f}}v_o$$

$$(47/3)v_\text{d}+\frac{600}{R_\text{f}}v_\text{d}-(25/3)v_\text{a}-5v_\text{b}-(4/3)v_\text{c}=\frac{600}{R_\text{f}}v_o$$

$$(376/3)+\frac{4800}{R_\text{f}}-150-30+20=\frac{600}{R_\text{f}}v_o$$

$$14400-104R_\text{f}=1800v_o\quad\text{or}\quad 104R_\text{f}=14400-1800v_o$$

$$v_o=\pm16\text{ V},\qquad\text{but}\quad R_\text{f}>0$$

$$\therefore\quad 104R_\text{f}=14400-1800(-16)\quad\text{or}\quad R_\text{f}=415.38\,\text{k}\Omega$$

[b] $$i_\text{f}=\frac{8-(-16)}{415.38\times10^3}=57.78\,\mu\text{A}$$

$$i_{27\text{k}\Omega}=\frac{v_o}{0.027\times10^6}=-592.59\,\mu\text{A}$$

$$i_o-i_\text{f}+i_{27\text{k}\Omega}=0$$

$$i_o=57.78-(-592.59)=650.37\,\mu\text{A}$$

P 5.12 [a] $$v_o = -\frac{220}{33}v_a - \frac{220}{22}v_b - \frac{220}{80}v_c = -8 + 15 - 11 = -4 \text{ V}$$

[b] $$v_o = -19 - 10v_b = \pm 6$$

$$\therefore \quad v_b = -1.3 \text{ V} \quad \text{when} \quad v_o = -6 \text{ V};$$

$$v_b = -2.5 \text{ V} \quad \text{when} \quad v_o = 6 \text{ V}$$

$$\therefore \quad -2.5 \text{ V} \leq v_b \leq -1.3 \text{ V}$$

P 5.13 $$v_o = -\left[\frac{R_f}{3}(0.15) + \frac{R_f}{5}(0.1) + \frac{R_f}{25}(0.25)\right]$$

$$-6 = -0.08R_f; \qquad R_f = 75\,\text{k}\Omega; \qquad \therefore \quad 0 \leq R_f \leq 75\,\text{k}\Omega$$

P 5.14

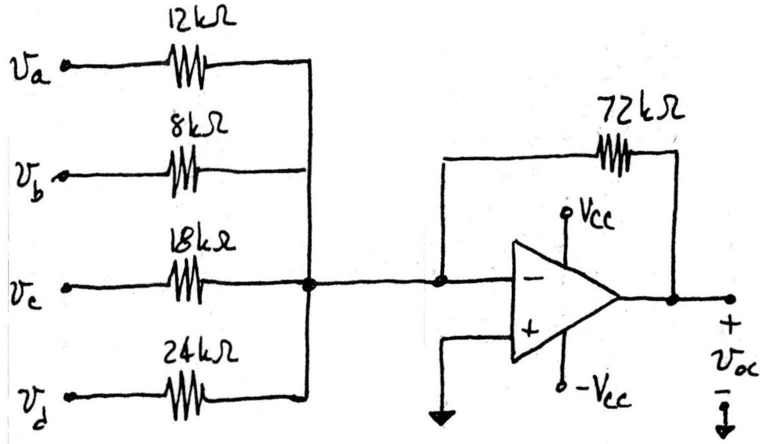

$$v_o = -\left[\frac{72}{R_a}v_a + \frac{72}{R_b}v_b + \frac{72}{R_c}v_c + \frac{72}{R_d}v_d\right]$$

$$\therefore \quad R_a = 72/6 = 12\,\text{k}\Omega \qquad R_c = 72/4 = 18\,\text{k}\Omega$$

$$R_b = 72/9 = 8\,\text{k}\Omega \qquad R_d = 72/3 = 24\,\text{k}\Omega$$

P 5.15 [a]

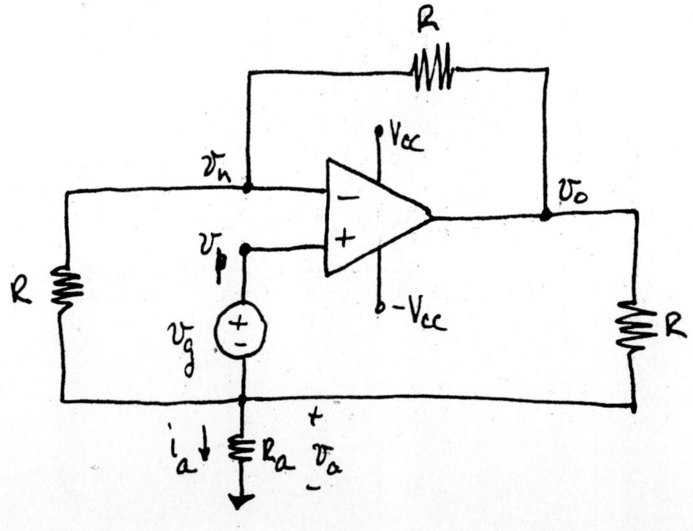

$$\frac{v_n - v_a}{R} + \frac{v_n - v_o}{R} = 0$$

$$2v_n - v_a = v_o$$

$$\frac{v_a}{R_a} + \frac{v_a - v_n}{R} + \frac{v_a - v_o}{R} = 0$$

$$v_a\left[\frac{1}{R_a} + \frac{2}{R}\right] - \frac{v_n}{R} = \frac{v_o}{R}$$

$$v_a\left(2 + \frac{R}{R_a}\right) - v_n = v_o$$

$$v_n = v_p = v_a + v_g$$

$$\therefore\quad 2v_n - v_a = 2v_a + 2v_g - v_a = v_a + 2v_g$$

$$\therefore\quad v_a - v_o = -2v_g \qquad (1)$$

$$2v_a + v_a\left(\frac{R}{R_a}\right) - v_a - v_g = v_o$$

$$\therefore\quad v_a\left(1 + \frac{R}{R_a}\right) - v_o = v_g \qquad (2)$$

Now combining equations (1) and (2) yields

$$-v_a\frac{R}{R_a} = -3v_g$$

$$\text{or}\quad v_a = 3v_g\frac{R_a}{R}$$

$$\text{Hence}\quad i_a = \frac{v_a}{R_a} = \frac{3v_g}{R} \qquad \text{Q.E.D.}$$

[b] At saturation $V_o = \pm V_{cc}$

$$\therefore\quad v_a = \pm V_{cc} - 2v_g \qquad (3)$$

and

$$\therefore\quad v_a\left(1 + \frac{R}{R_a}\right) = \pm V_{cc} + v_g \qquad (4)$$

Dividing Eq (4) by Eq (3) gives

$$1 + \frac{R}{R_a} = \frac{\pm V_{cc} + v_g}{\pm V_{cc} - 2v_g}$$

$$\therefore\quad \frac{R}{R_a} = \frac{\pm V_{cc} + v_g}{\pm V_{cc} - 2v_g} - 1 = \frac{3v_g}{\pm V_{cc} - 2v_g}$$

$$\text{or}\quad R_a = \frac{(\pm V_{cc} - 2v_g)}{3v_g}R \qquad \text{Q.E.D.}$$

P 5.16 [a] Assume the op-amp is operating within its linear range, then

$$i_L = \frac{3}{1.5} = 2\,\text{mA}$$

For $R_L = 2.5\,\text{k}\Omega$ $\qquad v_o = (2.5 + 1.5)(2) = 8\ \text{V}$

Now since $v_o < 9$ V our assumption of linear operation is correct, therefore

$$i_L = 2\,\text{mA}$$

[b] $\quad 9 = 2(1.5 + R_L); \qquad R_L = 3\,\text{k}\Omega$

[c] As long as the op-amp is operating in its linear region i_L is independent of R_L. From (b) we found the op-amp is operating in its linear region as long as $R_L \leq 3\,\text{k}\Omega$. Therefore when $R_L = 6.5\,\text{k}\Omega$ the op-amp is saturated. We can estimate the value of i_L by assuming $i_p = i_n \ll i_L$. Then $i_L = 9/(1.5 + 6.5) = 1.125\,\text{mA}$. To justify neglecting the current into the op-amp assume the drop across the 47 kΩ resistor is negligible, and the input resistance to the op-amp is at least 500 kΩ. Then $i_p = i_n = (3 - 1.5)/500 \times 10^{-3} = 3\,\mu\text{A}$. But $3\,\mu\text{A} \ll 1.125\,\text{mA}$, hence our assumption is reasonable.

[d]

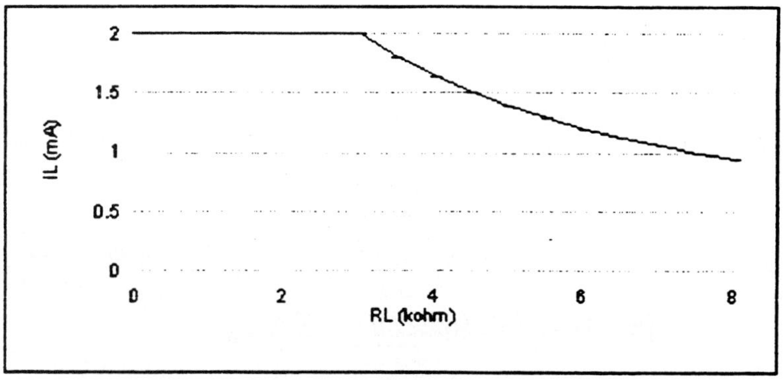

P 5.17 [a] The output voltage of the first op-amp is
$v_{o1} = -(80/20)v_g = -4v_g$
The output voltage of the second op-amp is
$v_{o2} = -1.6v_{o1} = 6.4v_g$
When v_g has its largest value, i.e., 1.2 V,

$$v_{o1} = -4.8\ \text{V} \quad \text{and} \quad v_{o2} = 7.68\ \text{V}$$

Therefore neither op-amp saturates. The expression for i_g is

$$i_g = \frac{v_g}{20} + \frac{v_g - 6.4v_g}{R_o} = v_g\left[\frac{1}{20} - \frac{5.4}{R_o}\right]$$

$$i_g = 0 \quad \text{when} \quad \left(\frac{1}{20} - \frac{5.4}{R_o}\right) = 0, \quad \text{or} \quad R_o = 108\,\text{k}\Omega$$

[b] $$i_{R_o} = \frac{6.4v_g - v_g}{R_o} = \frac{5.4v_g}{R_o} = 50v_g\,\mu\text{A} = 50\,\mu\text{A}$$

$$p_{R_o} = (50 \times 10^{-6})^2(108 \times 10^3) = 270\,\mu\text{W}$$

P 5.18 Let v_{o1} be the output voltage of the first operational amplifier and v_{o2} the output voltage of the second operational amplifier. Then

$$\frac{0-1}{12} + \frac{0-v_{o1}}{48} + \frac{0-v_{o2}}{100} = 0$$

$$-50 - 12.5v_{o1} - 6v_{o2} = 0$$

$$\frac{v_{o1}}{30} + \frac{v_{o1}-v_{o2}}{6} = 0$$

$$\therefore\quad 6v_{o1} = 5v_{o2}$$

$$\therefore\quad -50 - 12.5[(5/6)v_{o2}] - 6v_{o2} = 0 \quad \text{so} \quad v_{o2} = -3.05\ \text{V}$$

$$i_a = \frac{v_{o2}}{36} = -0.0846\,\text{mA}$$

$$i_a = -84.6\,\mu\text{A}$$

P 5.19 [a] Let v_{o1} = output voltage of the amplifier on the left. Let v_{o2} = output voltage of the amplifier on the right. Then

$$v_{o1} = \frac{-47}{10}(1) = -4.7\ \text{V}; \qquad v_{o2} = \frac{-220}{33}(-0.15) = 1.0\ \text{V}$$

$$i_a = \frac{v_{o2} - v_{o1}}{1000} = 5.7\,\text{mA}$$

[b] $i_a = 0$ when $v_{o1} = v_{02}$ so from (a) $v_{o2} = 1$ V

Thus

$$\frac{-47}{10}(v_L) = 1$$

$$v_L = -\frac{10}{47} = -212.77\,\text{mV}$$

P 5.20 [a] $$p_{16\,\text{k}\Omega} = \frac{(320 \times 10^{-3})^2}{(16 \times 10^3)} = 6.4\,\mu\text{W}$$

[b] $$v_{16\,\text{k}\Omega} = \left(\frac{16}{64}\right)(320) = 80\,\text{mV}$$

$$p_{16\,\text{k}\Omega} = \frac{(80 \times 10^{-3})^2}{(16 \times 10^3)} = 0.4\,\mu\text{W}$$

[c] $$\frac{p_a}{p_b} = \frac{6.4}{0.4} = 16$$

[d] Yes, the operational amplifier serves several useful purposes:

- First, it enables the source to control 16 times as much power delivered to the load resistor. When a small amount of power controls a larger amount of power, we refer to it as *power amplification.*
- Second, it allows the full source voltage to appear across the load resistor, no matter what the source resistance. This is the *voltage follower* function of the operational amplifier.
- Third, it allows the load resistor voltage (and thus its current) to be set without drawing any current from the input voltage source. This is the *current amplification* function of the circuit.

P 5.21 [a] $$v_p = v_s, \qquad v_n = \frac{R_1 v_o}{R_1 + R_2}, \qquad v_n = v_p$$

Therefore $$v_o = \left(\frac{R_1 + R_2}{R_1}\right) v_s = \left(1 + \frac{R_2}{R_1}\right) v_s$$

[b] $v_o = v_s$

[c] Because $v_o = v_s$, thus the output voltage follows the signal voltage.

P 5.22 [a] $$v_p = v_n = \frac{45}{75} v_g = 0.6 v_g$$

$$\therefore \quad \frac{0.6v_g}{15} + \frac{0.6v_g - v_o}{48} = 0; \qquad \therefore \quad v_o = 2.52v_g = 2.52(3), \qquad v_o = 7$$

[b] $$v_o = 2.52v_g = \pm 10$$

$$v_g = \pm 3.97 \text{ V}, \qquad -3.97 \leq v_g \leq 3.97 \text{ V}$$

[c] $$\frac{0.6v_g}{15} + \frac{0.6v_g - v_o}{R_f} = 0$$

$$\left(\frac{0.6R_f}{15} + 0.6\right) v_g = v_o = \pm 10$$

$$\therefore \quad 3R_f + 45 = \pm 150; \qquad 3R_f = 150 - 45; \qquad R_f = 35\,\text{k}\Omega$$

P 5.23 [a] $$\frac{v_p - v_a}{R_a} + \frac{v_p - v_b}{R_b} + \frac{v_p - v_c}{R_c} + \frac{v_p}{R_g} = 0$$

$$\therefore \quad v_p = \frac{R_b R_c R_g}{D} v_a + \frac{R_a R_c R_g}{D} v_b + \frac{R_a R_b R_g}{D} v_c$$

where $D = R_b R_c R_g + R_a R_c R_g + R_a R_b R_g + R_a R_b R_c$

$$\frac{v_n}{R_s} + \frac{v_n - v_o}{R_f} = 0$$

$$v_n\left(\frac{1}{R_s} + \frac{1}{R_f}\right) = \frac{v_o}{R_f}$$

$$\therefore \quad v_o = \left(1 + \frac{R_f}{R_s}\right) v_n = k v_n$$

$$\text{where} \quad k = \left(1 + \frac{R_f}{R_s}\right)$$

$$v_p = v_n$$

$$\therefore \quad v_o = k v_p$$

or

$$v_o = \frac{kR_gR_bR_c}{D}v_a + \frac{kR_gR_aR_c}{D}v_b + \frac{kR_gR_aR_b}{D}v_c$$

$$\frac{kR_gR_bR_c}{D} = 3 \qquad \therefore \quad \frac{R_b}{R_a} = 1.5$$

$$\frac{kR_gR_aR_c}{D} = 2 \qquad \therefore \quad \frac{R_c}{R_b} = 2$$

$$\frac{kR_gR_aR_b}{D} = 1 \qquad \therefore \quad \frac{R_c}{R_a} = 3$$

Since $R_a = 2\,\text{k}\Omega \qquad R_b = 3\,\text{k}\Omega \qquad R_c = 6\,\text{k}\Omega$

$$\therefore \quad D = (3)(6)(4) + (2)(6)(4) + (2)(3)(4) + (2)(3)(6) = 180$$

$$\frac{k(4)(3)(6)}{180} = 3$$

$$k = \frac{540}{72} = 7.5$$

$$\therefore \quad 7.5 = 1 + \frac{R_f}{R_s}$$

$$\frac{R_f}{R_s} = 6.5$$

$$R_f = (6.5)(12) = 78\,\text{k}\Omega$$

[b] $$v_o = 3(0.8) + 2(1.5) + 2.10 = 7.5 \text{ V}$$

$$v_n = v_p = \frac{7.5}{7.5} = 1.0 \text{ V}$$

$$i_a = \frac{0.8 - 1}{2} = \frac{-0.2}{2} = -0.1\,\text{mA} = -100\,\mu\text{A}$$

$$i_b = \frac{1.5 - 1.0}{3} = \frac{0.5}{3}\,\text{mA} = 166.67\,\mu\text{A}$$

$$i_c = \frac{2.10 - 1.0}{6} = \frac{1.1}{6}\,\text{mA} = 183.33\,\mu\text{A}$$

$$i_g = \frac{1}{4} = 0.25\,\text{mA} = 250\,\mu\text{A}$$

$$i_s = \frac{v_n}{12} = \frac{1}{12}\,\text{mA} = 83.33\,\mu\text{A}$$

P 5.24 [a]

$$\frac{v_p - v_a}{80 \times 10^3} + \frac{v_p - v_b}{64 \times 10^3} = 0$$

$$\therefore \quad 9v_p = 4v_a + 5v_b$$

$$\frac{v_n}{18} + \frac{v_n - v_o}{72} = 0$$

$$\therefore \quad v_o = 5v_n = 5v_p = (20/9)v_a + (25/9)v_b = 4.44 \text{ V}$$

[b]

$$v_p = v_n = \frac{v_o}{5} = 0.889 \text{ V}$$

$$i_a = \frac{v_a - v_p}{80 \times 10^3} = -4.86\,\mu\text{A}$$

$$i_b = \frac{v_b - v_p}{64 \times 10^3} = 4.866\,\mu\text{A}$$

[c] (20/9) for v_a

(25/9) for v_b

P 5.25 [a]

$$\frac{v_p - v_a}{R_a} + \frac{v_p - v_b}{R_b} + \frac{v_p - v_c}{R_c} = 0$$

$$\therefore \quad v_p = \frac{R_b R_c}{D} v_a + \frac{R_a R_c}{D} v_b + \frac{R_a R_b}{D} v_c$$

where $D = R_b R_c + R_a R_c + R_a R_b$

$$\frac{v_n}{10} + \frac{v_n - v_o}{R_f} = 0$$

$$\left(\frac{R_f}{10} + 1\right) v_n = v_o$$

Let $\dfrac{R_f}{10} + 1 = k$

$$v_o = k v_n = k v_p$$

$$\therefore \quad v_o = \frac{kR_bR_c}{D}v_a + \frac{kR_aR_c}{D}v_b + \frac{kR_aR_b}{D}v_c$$

$$\therefore \quad \frac{kR_bR_c}{D} = 5 \qquad \therefore \quad \frac{R_c}{R_a} = 5$$

$$\frac{kR_aR_c}{D} = 4$$

$$\frac{kR_aR_b}{D} = 1 \qquad \therefore \quad \frac{R_c}{R_b} = 4$$

$$\therefore \quad R_c = 5R_a = 5\,\text{k}\Omega$$

$$R_b = R_c/4 = 1.25\,\text{k}\Omega$$

$$\therefore \quad D = (1.25)(5) + (1)(5) + (1.25)(1) = 12.5 \times 10^6$$

$$\therefore \quad k = \frac{5D}{R_bR_c} = \frac{(5)(12.5) \times 10^6}{(1.25)(5) \times 10^6} = 10$$

$$\therefore \quad \frac{R_f}{10} + 1 = 10, \qquad R_f = 90\,\text{k}\Omega$$

[b] $$v_o = 5(0.5) + 4(1) + 1.5 = 8 \text{ V}$$

$$v_n = v_o/10 = 0.8 \text{ V} = v_p$$

$$i_a = \frac{v_a - v_p}{1} = \frac{0.5 - 0.8}{1} = -300\,\mu\text{A}$$

$$i_b = \frac{v_b - v_p}{1.25} = \frac{1 - 0.8}{1.25} = 160\,\mu\text{A}$$

$$i_c = \frac{v_c - v_p}{5} = \frac{1.5 - 0.8}{5} = 140\,\mu\text{A}$$

P 5.26 [a] $$v_o = \frac{R_d(R_a + R_b)}{R_a(R_c + R_d)}v_b - \frac{R_b}{R_a}v_a = \frac{33(100)}{20(80)}(0.90) - 4(0.45)$$

$$v_o = 1.8563 - 1.8 = 56.3\text{ mV}$$

[b] $$v_n = v_p = \frac{(900)(33)}{80} = 371.25\,\text{mV}$$

$$i_a = \frac{(450 - 371.25)10^{-3}}{20 \times 10^3} = 3.9375\,\mu\text{A}$$

$$R_a = \frac{v_a}{i_a} = \frac{450 \times 10^{-3}}{3.9375 \times 10^{-6}} = 114.3\,\text{k}\Omega$$

[c] $R_{\text{in b}} = R_c + R_d = 80\,\text{k}\Omega$

P 5.27 [a]

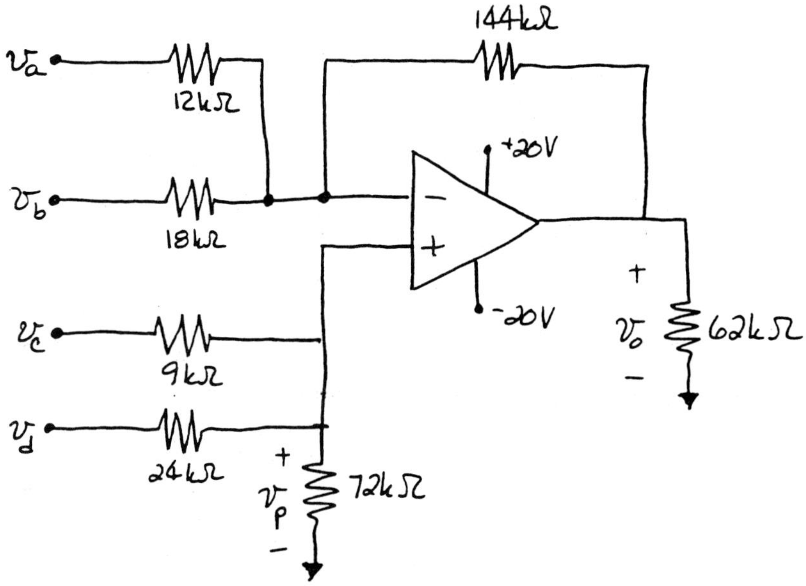

$$\frac{v_p}{72} + \frac{v_p - v_c}{9} + \frac{v_p - v_d}{24} = 0$$

$$\therefore \quad v_p = (2/3)v_c + 0.25v_d = v_n$$

$$\frac{v_n - v_a}{12} + \frac{v_n - v_b}{18} + \frac{v_n - v_o}{144} = 0$$

$$\begin{aligned}\therefore \quad v_o &= 21v_n - 12v_a - 8v_b \\ &= 21[(2/3)v_c + 0.25v_d] - 12v_a - 8v_b \\ &= 21(0.4 + 0.2) - 12(0.5) - 8(0.3) = 4.2 \text{ V}\end{aligned}$$

[b] $v_o = 14v_c + 4.2 - 6 - 2.4$

$$\pm 15 = 14v_c - 4.2$$

$$\therefore \quad 14v_c = \pm 15 + 4.2$$

$$\therefore \quad v_c = 1.371 \text{ V} \qquad \text{and} \qquad v_c = -0.771 \text{ V}$$

$$\therefore \quad -771 \le v_c \le 1371\,\text{mV}$$

P 5.28 [a]

$$v_n = v_p = \alpha v_g$$

$$\frac{v_n - v_g}{R_1} + \frac{v_n - v_o}{R_f} = 0$$

$$(v_n - v_g)\frac{R_f}{R_1} + v_n - v_o = 0$$

$$\begin{aligned} v_o &= (\alpha v_g - v_g)4 + \alpha v_g \\ &= [(\alpha - 1)4 + \alpha]v_g \\ &= (5\alpha - 4)v_g \\ &= (5\alpha - 4)(2) = 10\alpha - 8\end{aligned}$$

α	v_o	α	v_o	α	v_o
0.0	-8 V	0.4	-4 V	0.8	0 V
0.1	-7 V	0.5	-3 V	0.9	1 V
0.2	-6 V	0.6	-2 V	1.0	2 V
0.3	-5 V	0.7	-1 V		

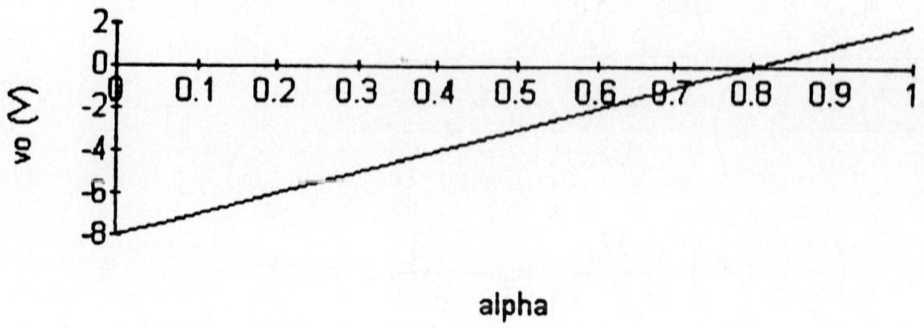

[b] Rearranging the equation for v_o from (a) gives

$$v_o = \left(\frac{R_f}{R_1} + 1\right) v_g \alpha + -\left(\frac{R_f}{R_1}\right) v_g$$

Therefore,

$$\text{slope} = \left(\frac{R_f}{R_1} + 1\right) v_g; \qquad \text{intercept} = -\left(\frac{R_f}{R_1}\right) v_g$$

[c] Using the equations from (b),

$$-6 = \left(\frac{R_f}{R_1} + 1\right) v_g; \qquad 4 = -\left(\frac{R_f}{R_1}\right) v_g$$

Solving,

$$v_g = -2 \text{ V}; \qquad \frac{R_f}{R_1} = 2$$

P 5.29 $v_p = v_n = R_b i_b$

$$\frac{R_b i_b - 3000 i_a}{3000} + \frac{R_b i_b - v_o}{R_f} = 0$$

$$\left(\frac{R_b}{3000} + \frac{R_b}{R_f}\right) i_b - i_a = \frac{v_o}{R_f}$$

$$v_o = \left[\frac{R_b R_f}{3000} + R_b\right] i_b - R_f i_a$$

$$\therefore \quad R_f = 2000\,\Omega$$

$$(2/3)R_b + R_b = 2000$$

$$\therefore \quad R_b = 1200\,\Omega$$

P 5.30 $$v_p = \frac{v_b R_b}{R_a + R_b} = v_n$$

$$\frac{v_n - v_a}{4.7} + \frac{v_n - v_o}{R_f} = 0$$

$$v_n\left(\frac{R_f}{4.7} + 1\right) - \frac{v_a R_f}{4.7} = v_o$$

$$\therefore \quad \left(\frac{R_f}{4.7} + 1\right)\frac{R_b}{R_a + R_b}v_b - \frac{R_f}{4.7}v_a = v_o$$

$$\therefore \quad \frac{R_f}{4.7} = 10; \qquad R_f = 47\,\text{k}\Omega$$

$$\therefore \quad \frac{R_f}{4.7} + 1 = 11$$

$$\therefore \quad 11\left(\frac{R_b}{R_a + R_b}\right) = 10$$

$$11R_b = 10R_b + 10R_a \qquad R_b = 10R_a$$

$$R_a + R_b = 220\,\text{k}\Omega$$

$$11R_a = 220\,\text{k}\Omega$$

$$R_a = 20\,\text{k}\Omega$$

$$R_b = 220 - 20 = 200\,\text{k}\Omega$$

P 5.31 $$v_o = \frac{R_d(R_a + R_b)}{R_a(R_c + R_d)}v_b - \frac{R_b}{R_a}v_a$$

By hypothesis: $R_b/R_a = 5$; $R_c + R_d = 600\,\text{k}\Omega$; $\frac{R_d(R_a + R_b)}{R_a(R_c + R_d)} = 2$

$$\therefore \quad \frac{R_d}{R_a}\frac{(R_a + 5R_a)}{600} = 2 \quad \text{so} \quad R_d = 200\,\text{k}\Omega; \quad R_c = 400\,\text{k}\Omega$$

Also, when $v_o = 0$ we have

$$\frac{v_n - v_a}{R_a} + \frac{v_n}{R_b} = 0$$

$$\therefore \quad v_n\left(1 + \frac{R_a}{R_b}\right) = v_a; \qquad v_n = (5/6)v_a$$

$$i_a = \frac{v_a - (5/6)v_a}{R_a} = \frac{1}{6}\frac{v_a}{R_a}; \qquad R_{in} = \frac{v_a}{i_a} = 6R_a = 18\,\text{k}\Omega$$

$$\therefore \quad R_a = 3\,\text{k}\Omega; \qquad R_b = 15\,\text{k}\Omega$$

P 5.32 Let the top op-amp be No. 1 and the lower op-amp be No. 2. Then

$$i_a = \frac{1.98}{3.3} = 0.6\,\text{mA} = 600\,\mu\text{A}$$

$$v_{o2} = (3.3 + 4.7)i_a = 4.8 \text{ V}$$

$$i_{30\,\text{k}\Omega} = \frac{v_{o2}}{30\,\text{k}\Omega} = \frac{4.8}{30\,\text{k}\Omega} = 0.16\,\text{mA} = 160\,\mu\text{A}$$

$$v_x = -20(0.16) = -3.2 \text{ V}$$

$$i_a + i_o + i_{30\,\text{k}\Omega} = 0$$

$$i_o = -600 - 160 = -760\,\mu\text{A}$$

P 5.33

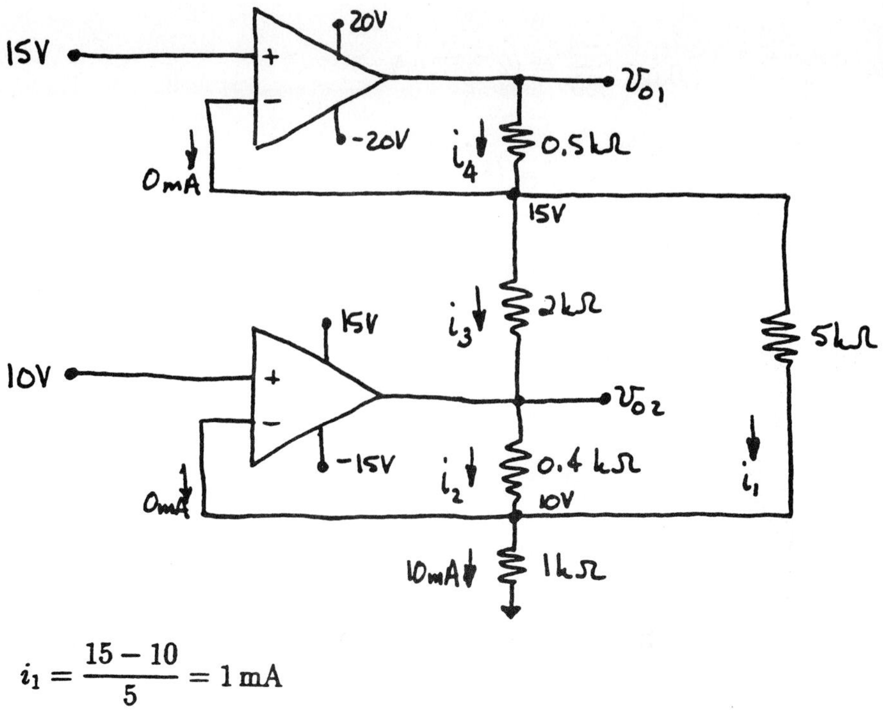

$$i_1 = \frac{15 - 10}{5} = 1\,\text{mA}$$

$$i_2 + i_1 + 0 = 10; \qquad i_2 = 9\,\text{mA}$$

$$v_{o2} = 13.6 \text{ V}$$

$$i_3 = \frac{15 - 13.6}{2} = 0.7\,\text{mA}$$

$$i_4 = i_3 + i_1 = 1.7\,\text{mA}$$

$$v_{o1} = 15 + 1.7(0.5) = 15.85 \text{ V}$$

P 5.34 Let v_{o1} be the output voltage of the first op-amp. Then

$$\frac{0 - 1.1}{3} + \frac{0 - v_{o1}}{18} + \frac{0 - v_o}{24} = 0$$

$$-26.4 - 4v_{o1} - 3v_o = 0$$

$$\text{But} \quad v_{o1} = \frac{v_o}{30}(27) = 0.9v_o$$

$$\therefore \quad -3.6v_o - 3v_o = 26.4 \quad \text{or} \quad v_o = -4 \text{ V}$$

$$i_{24\,\text{k}\Omega} = \frac{0 - (-4)}{24} = (1/6)\,\text{mA}$$

$$i_{3\,\text{k}\Omega} = \frac{-4}{30} = (2/15)\,\text{mA}$$

$$i_{4.5\,\text{k}\Omega} = \frac{-4}{4.5} = (8/9)\,\text{mA}$$

$$(1/6) = i_o - (2/15) - (8/9); \qquad i_o = 1.1889\,\text{mA}$$

P 5.35 [a] The circuit of Fig. P5.35 is redrawn with intermediate voltages defined to facilitate the analysis.

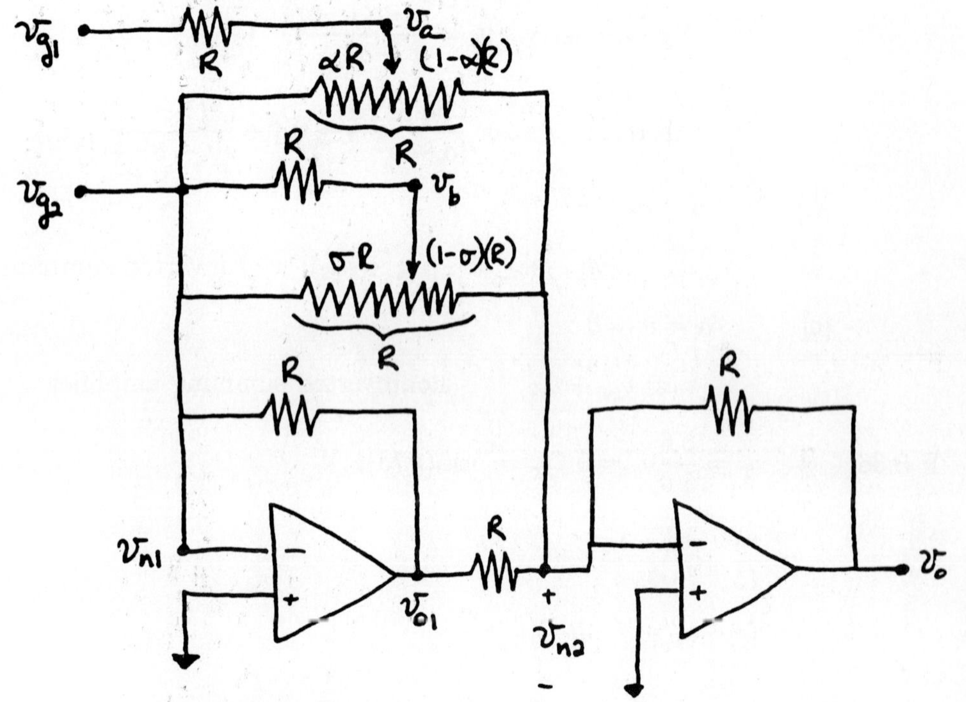

$$v_{n1} = v_{n2} = 0$$

$$\frac{0 - v_{o1}}{R} + \frac{0 - v_b}{\sigma R} + \frac{0 - v_a}{\alpha R} = 0$$

therefore $\quad v_{o1} = -\frac{v_a}{\alpha} - \frac{v_b}{\sigma}$

$$\frac{0 - v_b}{(1-\sigma)R} + \frac{0 - v_a}{(1-\alpha)R} + \frac{0 - v_{o1}}{R} + \frac{0 - v_o}{R} = 0$$

therefore $\quad v_o = -v_{o1} - \frac{v_a}{1-\alpha} - \frac{v_b}{1-\sigma}$

$$v_o = \frac{v_a}{\alpha} + \frac{v_b}{\sigma} - \frac{v_a}{1-\alpha} - \frac{v_b}{1-\sigma} = \frac{v_a(1-2\alpha)}{\alpha(1-\alpha)} + v_b\frac{(1-2\sigma)}{\sigma(1-\sigma)}$$

$$\frac{v_a - v_{g1}}{R} + \frac{v_a - 0}{\alpha R} + \frac{v_a - 0}{(1-\alpha)R} = 0$$

$$v_a + \frac{v_a}{\alpha} + \frac{v_a}{1-\alpha} = v_{g1}$$

$$v_a\left(\frac{\alpha(1-\alpha) + (1-\alpha) + \alpha}{\alpha(1-\alpha)}\right) = v_{g1}$$

$$v_a = \frac{v_{g1}\alpha(1-\alpha)}{(\alpha-\alpha^2+1)}$$

By symmetry $v_b = \dfrac{v_{g2}\sigma(1-\sigma)}{\sigma-\sigma^2+1)}$

therefore $v_o = \dfrac{(1-2\alpha)}{(\alpha-\alpha^2+1)}v_{g1} + \dfrac{(1-2\sigma)}{(\sigma-\sigma^2+1)}v_{g2}$

[b] $\alpha = \sigma = 1:$

$v_o = -v_{g1} - v_{g2} = -(v_{g1} + v_{g2});$ inverted summing amplifier

[c] $\alpha = \sigma = 0:$

$v_o = v_{g1} + v_{g2};$ noninverted summing amplifier

P 5.36 $v_p = \dfrac{5.6}{8.0}v_g = 0.7v_g = 7\sin(\pi/3)t$ V

$$\frac{v_n}{15} + \frac{v_n - v_o}{75} = 0$$

$6v_n = v_o;$ $v_n = v_p$

$\therefore$ $v_o = 42\sin(\pi/3)t$ V $0 \le t \le \infty$

$v_o = 0$ $t \le 0$

At saturation

$42\sin\left(\dfrac{\pi}{3}\right)t = \pm 21;$ $\sin\dfrac{\pi}{3}t = \pm 0.5$

$\therefore$ $\dfrac{\pi}{3}t = \dfrac{\pi}{6}, \dfrac{5\pi}{6}, \dfrac{7\pi}{6}, \dfrac{11\pi}{6},$ etc.

$t = 0.50$ s, 2.50 s, 3.50 s, etc.

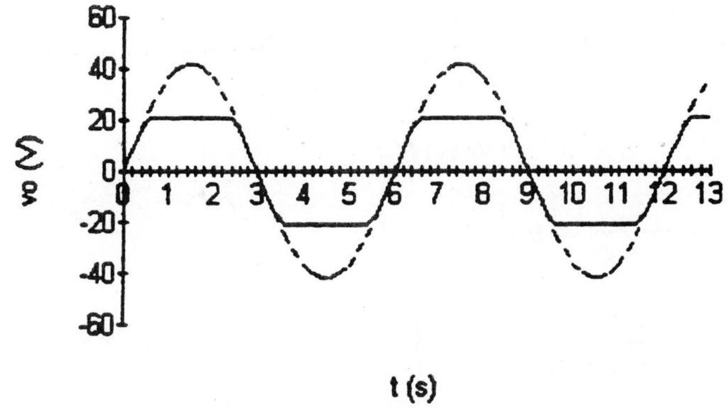

P 5.37 It follows directly from the circuit that $v_o = -16v_g$

From the plot of v_g we have $v_g = 0, \quad t < 0$

$$v_g = (1/4)t \qquad 0 \leq t \leq 2$$

$$v_g = -(1/4)t + 1 \qquad 2 \leq t \leq 6$$

$$v_g = (1/4)t - 2 \qquad 6 \leq t \leq 10$$

$$v_g = -(1/4)t + 3 \qquad 10 \leq t \leq 14$$

$$v_g = (1/4)t - 4 \qquad 14 \leq t \leq 18, \quad \text{etc.}$$

Therefore

$$v_o = -4t \qquad 0 \leq t \leq 2$$

$$v_o = 4t - 16 \qquad 2 \leq t \leq 6$$

$$v_o = -4t + 32 \qquad 6 \leq t \leq 10$$

$$v_o = 4t - 48 \qquad 10 \leq t \leq 14$$

$$v_o = -4t + 64 \qquad 14 \leq t \leq 18, \quad \text{etc.}$$

These expressions for v_o are valid as long as the op amp is not saturated. Since the peak values of v_o are ± 6, the output is clipped at ± 6. The plot is shown below.

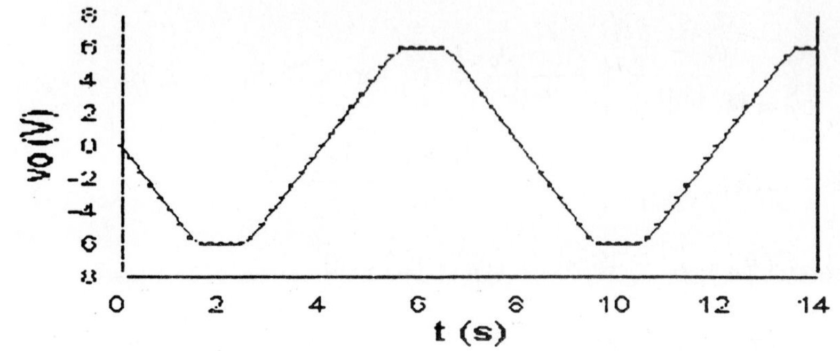

P 5.38 [a]

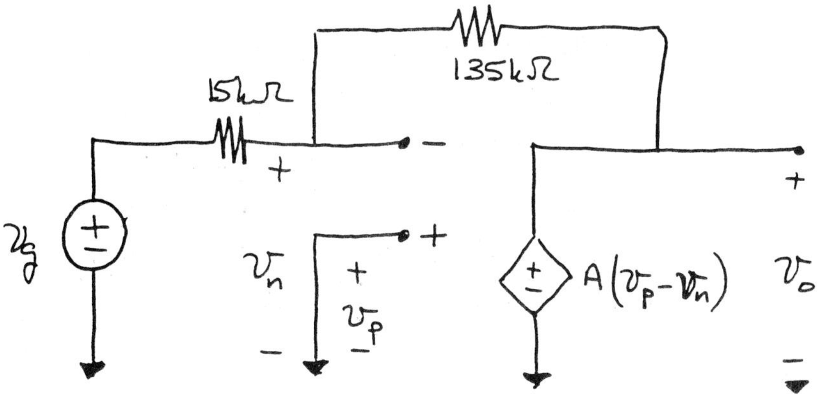

$$\frac{v_n - v_g}{15} + \frac{v_n - v_o}{135} = 0$$

$$\therefore \quad v_o = 10v_n - 9v_g$$

Also $\quad v_o = A(v_p - v_n) = -Av_n$

$$\therefore \quad v_n = \frac{-v_o}{A}$$

$$\therefore \quad v_o\left(1 + \frac{10}{A}\right) = -9v_g$$

$$v_o = \frac{-9A}{(10 + A)}v_g$$

[b] $$v_o = \frac{-9(90)(0.4)}{(10 + 90)} = -3.24 \text{ V}$$

[c] $$v_o = -9(0.4) = -3.60 \text{ V}$$

[d] $$-3.42 = \frac{-9(0.4)A}{10 + A}$$

$$\therefore \quad A = 190$$

P 5.39 [a] $$\frac{v_n}{8} + \frac{v_n - v_g}{600} + \frac{v_n - v_o}{240} = 0 \quad \text{or} \quad 78.5v_1 - 2.5v_o = v_g$$

$$\frac{v_o}{30} + \frac{v_o - v_n}{240} + \frac{v_o - 100{,}000(v_p - v_n)}{5} = 0$$

$$57v_o - v_n - 48 \times 10^5(v_p - v_n) = 0$$

$$v_p = v_g + \frac{(v_n - v_g)(160)}{600} = (11/15)v_g + (4/15)v_n$$

$$57v_o - v_n - 48 \times 10^5[(11/15)v_g - (11/15)v_n] = 0$$

$$57v_o + 3{,}520{,}000v_n = 3{,}520{,}000v_g$$

$$\Delta = \begin{vmatrix} 78.5 & -2.5 \\ 3.52 \times 10^6 & 57 \end{vmatrix} = 8{,}804{,}474.5$$

$$N_o = \begin{vmatrix} 78.5 & v_g \\ 3.52 \times 10^6 & 3.52 \times 10^6 v_g \end{vmatrix} = 272.8 \times 10^6 v_g$$

$$v_o = \frac{N_o}{\Delta} = 30.98v_g; \qquad \frac{v_o}{v_g} = 30.98$$

[b]
$$N_1 = \begin{vmatrix} v_g & -2.5 \\ 3.52 \times 10^6 v_g & 57 \end{vmatrix} = 8{,}800{,}057 v_g$$

$$v_n = \frac{N_1}{\Delta} = 0.9995 v_g; \qquad v_n = 999.5\,\text{mV}$$

$$v_p = (11/15)(1000) + (4/15)(999.5) = 999.87\,\text{mV}$$

[c] $v_p - v_n = 367.94\,\mu$ V

[d]
$$i_g = \frac{(1000 - 999.87)10^{-3}}{160 \times 10^3} = 836.22\,\text{pA}$$

[e]
$$\frac{v_g}{8} + \frac{v_g - v_o}{240} = 0, \qquad \text{since } v_n = v_p = v_g$$

$$\therefore \; v_o = 31 v_g, \qquad \frac{v_o}{v_g} = 31$$

$$v_n = v_p = 1 \text{ V}; \qquad v_p - v_n = 0 \text{ V}; \qquad i_g = 0 \text{ A}$$

P 5.40 [a]

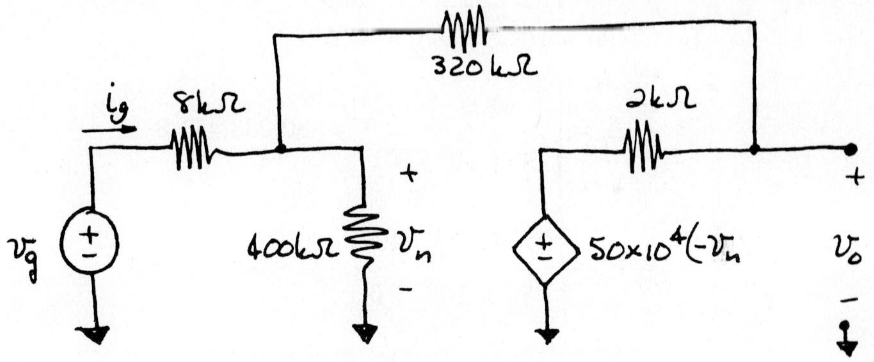

$$\frac{v_n}{400} + \frac{v_n - v_g}{8} + \frac{v_n - v_o}{320} = 0$$

$$\therefore \; 41.8 v_n - v_o = 40 v_g$$

$$\frac{v_o - 500{,}000(-v_n)}{2} + \frac{v_o - v_n}{320} = 0$$

$$\therefore \; 80 \times 10^6 v_n + 161 v_o = 0$$

$$\Delta = \begin{vmatrix} 41.8 & -1 \\ 80 \times 10^6 & 161 \end{vmatrix} = 80{,}006{,}729.8$$

$$N_o = \begin{vmatrix} 41.8 & 40 v_g \\ 80 \times 10^6 & 0 \end{vmatrix} = -32 \times 10^8 v_g$$

$$v_o = \frac{N_o}{\Delta} = -39.997 v_g; \qquad \text{so } \frac{v_o}{v_g} = -39.997$$

[b] $$N_1 = \begin{vmatrix} 40v_g & -1 \\ 0 & 161 \end{vmatrix} = 6440v_g$$

$$v_n = \frac{N_1}{\Delta} = 8.05 \times 10^{-5}v_g$$

$$v_g = 50\,\text{mV}, \qquad v_n = 4.02\,\mu\text{ V}$$

[c] $$i_g = \frac{v_g - v_n}{8} = \frac{v_g - 8.05 \times 10^{-5}v_g}{8}$$

$$R_g = \frac{v_g}{i_g} = \frac{v_g}{v_g - 8.05 \times 10^{-5}v_g} \cdot (8000) = 8000.644\Omega$$

[d] $$\frac{v_o}{v_g} = -40; \qquad v_n = 0\text{ V}; \qquad R_g = 8000\,\Omega$$

P 5.41 [a] From the solution of Problem 5.40 we have $41.8v_n - v_o = 40v_g$
At the output we now have

$$\frac{v_o + 50 \times 10^4 v_n}{2} + \frac{v_o - v_n}{320} + \frac{v_o}{0.5} = 0$$

or $$80 \times 10^6 v_n + 801v_o = 0$$

$$\Delta = \begin{vmatrix} 41.8 & -1 \\ 80 \times 10^6 & 801 \end{vmatrix} = 80{,}033{,}481.8$$

$$N_o = \begin{vmatrix} 41.8 & 40v_g \\ 80 \times 10^6 & 0 \end{vmatrix} = -32 \times 10^8 v_g$$

$$v_o = \frac{N_o}{\Delta} = -39.98v_g; \qquad \frac{v_o}{v_g} = -39.98$$

[b] $$N_1 = \begin{vmatrix} 40v_g & -1 \\ 0 & 801 \end{vmatrix} = 32{,}040v_g; \qquad v_n = \frac{N_1}{\Delta} = 4.003 \times 10^{-4}v_g$$

When $v_g = 50\,\text{mV}, \qquad v_n = 20.017\,\mu\text{ V}$

[c] $$R_g = \frac{v_g}{i_g}, \qquad i_g = \frac{v_g - v_n}{8000} = \frac{v_g - 4.003 \times 10^{-4}v_g}{8000} = 8003.2\,\Omega$$

[d] $$\frac{v_o}{v_g} = -40; \qquad v_n = 0\text{ V}; \qquad R_g = 8000\,\Omega$$

P 5.42 $$v_p = \frac{-3(50)}{200} = -0.75\text{ V} = v_n$$

$$\frac{-0.75 + 3}{5} + \frac{-0.75 - v_o}{R_f} = 0$$

$$\therefore \quad v_o = 0.45R_f - 0.75$$

$$v_o = 10 \text{ V}; \qquad R_f = 23.89\,\text{k}\Omega$$

$$v_o = -20 \text{ V}; \qquad R_f = -42.78\,\text{k}\Omega$$

But $R_f \geq 0, \quad \therefore \; R_f = 23.89\,\text{k}\Omega$

P 5.43 [a]

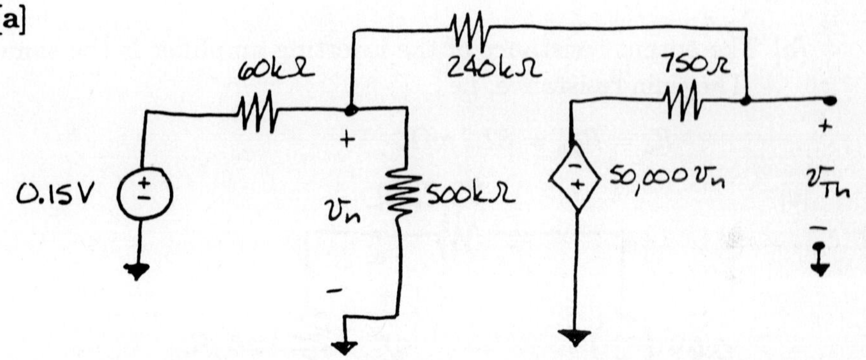

$$\frac{v_n - 0.15}{60} + \frac{v_n}{500} + \frac{v_n - v_{\text{Th}}}{240} = 0$$

$$\frac{v_{\text{Th}} + 5 \times 10^4 v_n}{0.75} + \frac{v_{\text{Th}} - v_n}{240} = 0$$

Solving, $v_{\text{Th}} = -0.6$ V

Short-circuit current calculation:

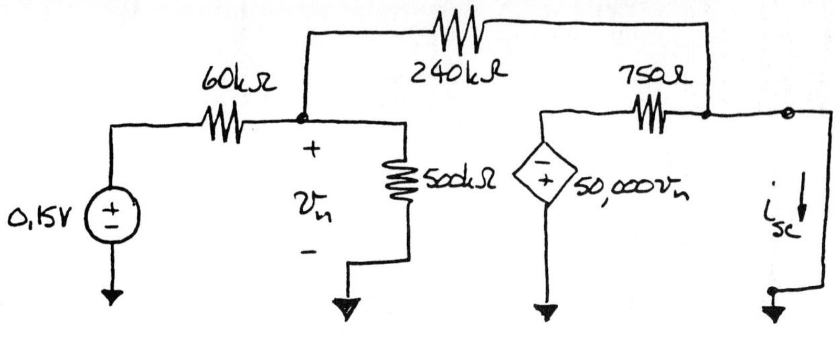

$$\frac{v_n}{500} + \frac{v_n - 0.15}{60} + \frac{v_n - 0}{240} = 0$$

$$\therefore \quad v_n = 0.1095 \text{ V}$$

$$i_{sc} = \frac{v_n}{240{,}000} - \frac{5 \times 10^4}{750} v_n = -7.3 \text{ A}$$

$$R_{\text{Th}} = \frac{v_{\text{Th}}}{i_{sc}} = 82.2\,\text{m}\Omega$$

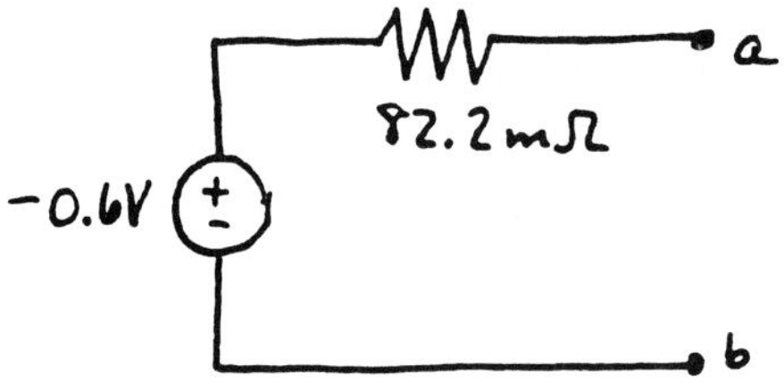

[b] The output resistance of the inverting amplifier is the same as the Thévenin resistance, i.e.,

$$R_o = R_{\text{Th}} = 82.2\,\text{m}\Omega$$

[c]

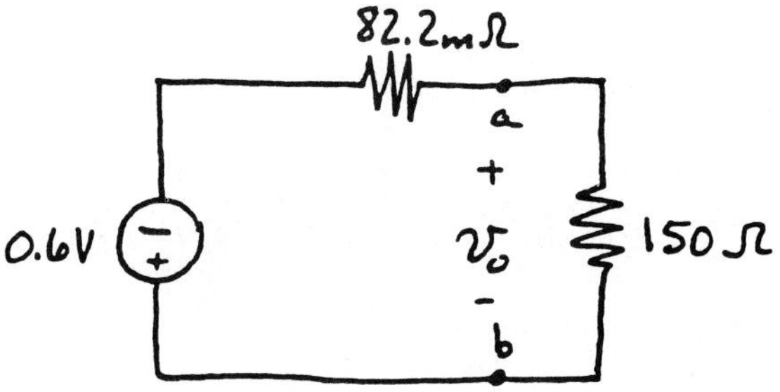

$$v_o = \left(\frac{150}{150.082}\right)(-0.6) = -0.5997\ \text{V}$$

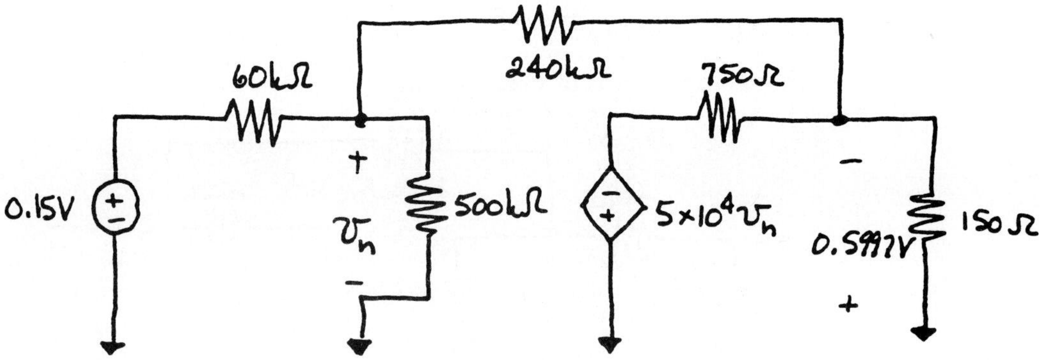

$$\frac{v_n - 0.15}{60} + \frac{v_n}{500} + \frac{v_n + 0.5997}{240} = 0$$

$$\therefore\ v_n = 54.7445\,\mu\text{V}$$

$$i_g = \frac{0.15 - 54.7445 \times 10^{-6}}{60{,}000} = 2.4991\,\mu\text{A}$$

$$R_g = \frac{0.15}{i_g} = 60{,}021.6\,\Omega$$

P 5.44 [a] $$v_{\rm Th} = \frac{-240}{60}(0.15) = -0.6 \text{ V}$$

$R_{\rm Th} = 0$, since op-amp is ideal

[b] $R_o = R_{\rm Th} = 0\,\Omega$

[c] $R_g = 60\,\text{k}\Omega$ since $v_n = 0$

P 5.45 From Eq. 5.57,

$$\frac{v_{\rm ref}}{R+\Delta R} = v_n\left(\frac{1}{R+\Delta R} + \frac{1}{R-\Delta R} + \frac{1}{R_f}\right) - \frac{v_o}{R_f}$$

Substituting Eq. 5.59 for $v_p = v_n$:

$$\frac{v_{\rm ref}}{R+\Delta R} = \frac{v_{\rm ref}\left(\frac{1}{R+\Delta R} + \frac{1}{R-\Delta R} + \frac{1}{R_f}\right)}{(R-\Delta R)\left(\frac{1}{R+\Delta R} + \frac{1}{R-\Delta R} + \frac{1}{R_f}\right)} - \frac{v_o}{R_f}$$

Rearranging,

$$\frac{v_o}{R_f} = v_{\rm ref}\left(\frac{1}{R-\Delta R} - \frac{1}{R+\Delta R}\right)$$

Thus,

$$v_o = v_{\rm ref}\left(\frac{2\Delta R}{R^2 + \Delta R^2}\right) R_f$$

P 5.46 [a]

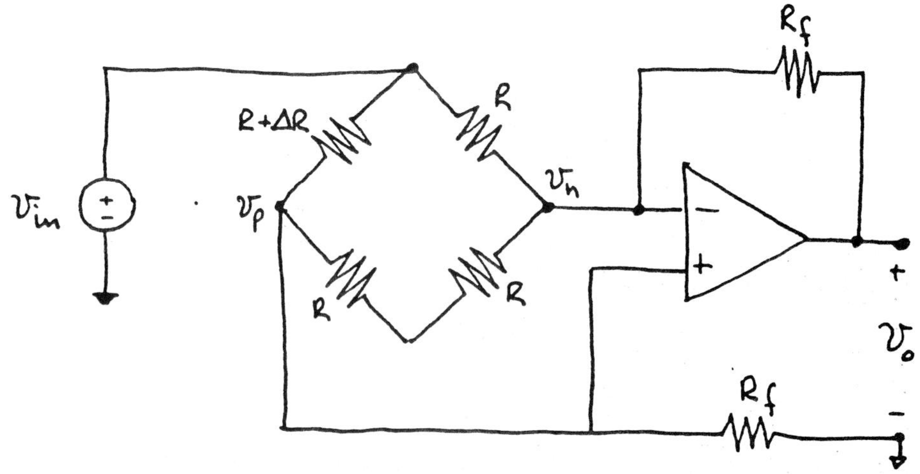

Let $R_1 = R + \Delta R$

$$\frac{v_p}{R_f} + \frac{v_p}{R} + \frac{v_p - v_{\text{in}}}{R_1} = 0$$

$$\therefore \quad v_p\left[\frac{1}{R_f} + \frac{1}{R} + \frac{1}{R_1}\right] = \frac{v_{\text{in}}}{R_1}$$

$$\therefore \quad v_p = \frac{RR_f v_{\text{in}}}{RR_1 + R_fR_1 + R_fR} = v_n$$

$$\frac{v_n}{R} + \frac{v_n - v_{\text{in}}}{R} + \frac{v_n - v_o}{R_f} = 0$$

$$v_n\left[\frac{1}{R} + \frac{1}{R} + \frac{1}{R_f}\right] - \frac{v_o}{R_f} = \frac{v_{\text{in}}}{R}$$

$$\therefore \quad v_n\left[\frac{R + 2R_f}{RR_f}\right] - \frac{v_{\text{in}}}{R} = \frac{v_o}{R_f}$$

$$\therefore \quad \frac{v_o}{R_f} = \left[\frac{R + 2R_f}{RR_f}\right]\frac{RR_f v_{\text{in}}}{[RR_1 + R_fR_1 + R_fR]} - \frac{v_{\text{in}}}{R}$$

$$\therefore \quad \frac{v_o}{R_f} = \left[\frac{R + 2R_f}{RR_1 + R_fR_1 + R_fR} - \frac{1}{R}\right]v_{\text{in}}$$

$$\therefore \quad v_o = \frac{[R^2 + 2RR_f - R_1(R + R_f) - RR_f]R_f}{R[R_1(R + R_f) + RR_f]}v_{\text{in}}$$

Now substitute $R_1 = R + \Delta R$ and get

$$v_o = \frac{-\Delta R(R + R_f)R_f v_{\text{in}}}{R[(R + \Delta R)(R + R_f) + RR_f]}$$

If $\Delta R \ll R$

$$v_o = \frac{(R+R_f)R_f(-\Delta R)v_{\text{in}}}{R^2(R+2R_f)}$$

[b] $$v_o \approx \frac{47 \times 10^4(48 \times 10^4)(-95)15}{10^8(95 \times 10^4)} \approx -3.384 \text{ V}$$

[c] $$v_o = \frac{-95(48 \times 10^4)(47 \times 10^4)15}{10^4[(1.0095)10^4(48 \times 10^4) + 47 \times 10^8]} = -3.368 \text{ V}$$

P 5.47 [a] $$v_o \approx \frac{(R+R_f)R_f(-\Delta R)v_{\text{in}}}{R^2(R+2R_f)}$$

$$v_o = \frac{(R+R_f)(-\Delta R)R_f v_{\text{in}}}{R[(R+\Delta R)(R+R_f)+RR_f]}$$

$$\therefore \frac{\text{approx value}}{\text{true value}} = \frac{R[(R+\Delta R)(R+R_f)+RR_f]}{R^2(R+2R_f)}$$

$$\therefore \text{ Error } = \frac{R[(R+\Delta R)(R+R_f)+RR_f] - R^2(R+2R_f)}{R^2(R+2R_f)}$$

$$= \frac{\Delta R}{R}\frac{(R+R_f)}{(R+2R_f)}$$

$$\therefore \text{ \% error } = \frac{\Delta R(R+R_f)}{R(R+2R_f)} \times 100$$

[b] $$\text{\% error} = \frac{95(48 \times 10^4) \times 100}{10^4(95 \times 10^4)} = 0.48\%$$

P 5.48 $$1 = \frac{\Delta R(48 \times 10^4)}{10^4(95 \times 10^4)} \times 100$$

$$\therefore \Delta R = \frac{9500}{48} = 197.91667\,\Omega$$

$$\therefore \text{ \% change in } R = \frac{197.19667}{10^4} \times 100 \approx 1.98\%$$

P 5.49 [a] It follows directly from the solution to Problem 5.45 that

$$v_o = \frac{[R^2 + 2RR_f - R_1(R+R_f) - RR_f]R_f v_{\text{in}}}{R[R_1(R+R_f)+RR_f]}$$

Now $R - 1 = R - \Delta R$. Substituting into the expression gives

$$v_o = \frac{(R+R_f)R_f(\Delta R)v_{\text{in}}}{R[(R-\Delta R)(R+R_f)+RR_f]}$$

Now let $\Delta R \ll R$ and get

$$v_o = \frac{(R+R_f)R_f\Delta R v_{\text{in}}}{R^2(R+2R_f)}$$

[b] It follows directly from the solution to Problem 5.46 that

$$\therefore \quad \frac{\text{approx value}}{\text{true value}} = \frac{R[(R-\Delta R)(R+R_f)+RR_f]}{R^2(R+2R_f)}$$

$$\therefore \quad \text{Error} = \frac{(R-\Delta R)(R+R_f)+RR_f-R(R+2R_f)}{R(R+2R_f)}$$

$$= \frac{-\Delta R(R+R_f)}{R(R+2R_f)}$$

$$\therefore \quad \%\ \text{error} = \frac{-\Delta R(R+R_f)}{R(R+2R_f)} \times 100$$

[c] $R-\Delta R = 9810\,\Omega \qquad \therefore \quad \Delta R = 10{,}000 - 9810 = 190\,\Omega$

$$\therefore \quad v_o \approx \frac{(48\times 10^4)(47\times 10^4)(190)(15)}{10^8(95\times 10^4)} \approx 6.768 \text{ V}$$

[d] $$\%\ \text{error} = \frac{-190(48\times 10^4)(100)}{10^4(95\times 10^4)} = -0.96\%$$

6

Inductance, Capacitance, and Mutual Inductance

Drill Exercises

DE 6.1 [a] $i_g = 8e^{-300t} - 8e^{-1200t}\,\text{A}$

$$v = L\frac{di_g}{dt} = -9.6e^{-300t} + 38.4e^{-1200t}, \qquad t > 0^+$$

$$v(0^+) = -9.6 + 38.4 = 28.8\,\text{V}$$

[b] $v = 0$ when $38.4e^{-1200t} = 9.6e^{-300t}$ or $t = (\ln 4)/900 = 1.54\,\text{ms}$

[c] $p = vi = 384e^{-1500t} - 76.8e^{-600t} - 307.2e^{-2400t}\,\text{W}$

[d] $\dfrac{dp}{dt} = 0$ when $e^{1800t} - 12.5e^{900t} + 16 = 0$

Let $x = e^{900t}$ and solve the quadratic $x^2 - 12.5x + 16 = 0$

$$x = 1.45, \quad x = 11.15, \quad t = \frac{\ln 1.45}{900} = 411.05\,\mu\text{s}, \quad t = \frac{\ln 11.15}{900} = 2.67\,\text{ms}$$

p is maximum at $t = 411.05\,\mu\text{s}$

[e] $p_{\text{max}} = 384e^{-1.5(0.41105)} - 76.8e^{-0.6(0.41105)} - 307.2e^{-2.4(0.41105)} = 32.72\,\text{W}$

[f] $i_{\text{max}} = 8[e^{-0.3(1.54)} - e^{-1.2(1.54)}] = 3.78\,\text{A}$

$$w_{\text{max}} = (1/2)(4 \times 10^{-3})(3.78)^2 = 28.6\,\text{mJ}$$

[g] W is max when i is max, i is max when di/dt is zero.

When $di/dt = 0$, $v = 0$, therefore $t = 1.54\,\text{ms}$.

DE 6.2 [a] $i = C\dfrac{dv}{dt} = 24 \times 10^{-6}\dfrac{d}{dt}[e^{-15{,}000t}\sin 30{,}000t]$

$$= [0.72\cos 30{,}000t - 0.36\sin 30{,}000t]e^{-15{,}000t}\,\text{A}, \qquad i(0^+) = 0.72\,\text{A}$$

[b] $$i\left(\frac{\pi}{80}\,\text{ms}\right) = -31.66\,\text{mA}, \quad v\left(\frac{\pi}{80}\,\text{ms}\right) = 20.505\,\text{V},$$

$$p = vi = -649.23\,\text{mW}$$

[c] $$w = \left(\frac{1}{2}\right) Cv^2 = 126.13\,\mu\text{J}$$

DE 6.3 [a] $$v = \left(\frac{1}{C}\right)\int_{0^-}^{t} i\,dx + v(0^-)$$

$$= \frac{1}{0.6\times 10^{-6}}\int_{0^-}^{t} 3\cos 50{,}000x\,dx = 100\sin 50{,}000t\ \text{V}$$

[b] $$p(t) = vi = [300\cos 50{,}000t]\sin 50{,}000t$$

$$= 150\sin 100{,}000t\ \text{W}, \qquad p_{(\text{max})} = 150\ \text{W}$$

[c] $$w_{(\text{max})} = \left(\frac{1}{2}\right) Cv_{\text{max}}^2 = 0.30(100)^2 = 3000\,\mu\text{J} = 3\,\text{mJ}$$

DE 6.4 [a] $$L_{\text{eq}} = \frac{60(240)}{300} = 48\,\text{mH}$$

[b] $$i(0^+) = 3 + -5 = 2\,\text{A}, \quad \text{up}$$

[c] $$i = \frac{125}{6}\int_{0^+}^{t}(-0.03e^{-5x})\,dx - 2 = 0.125e^{-5t} - 2.125\,\text{A}$$

[d] $$i_1 = \frac{50}{3}\int_{0^+}^{t}(-0.03e^{-5x})\,dx + 3 = 0.1e^{-5t} + 2.9\,\text{A}$$

$$i_2 = \frac{25}{6}\int_{0^+}^{t}(-0.03e^{-5x})\,dx - 5 = 0.025e^{-5t} - 5.025\,\text{A}$$

$$i_1 + i_2 = i$$

DE 6.5 $$v_1 = 0.5\times 10^6\int_{0^+}^{t} 240\times 10^{-6}e^{-10x}\,dx - 10 = -12e^{-10t} + 2\,\text{V}$$

$$v_2 = 0.125\times 10^6\int_{0^+}^{t} 240\times 10^{-6}e^{-10x}\,dx - 5 = -3e^{-10t} - 2\,\text{V}$$

$$v_1(\infty) = 2\,\text{V}, \qquad v_2(\infty) = -2\,\text{V}, \qquad W = \frac{1}{2}(2)(4) + \frac{1}{2}(8)(4) = 20\,\mu\text{J}$$

DE 6.6 [a] Rearrange by organizing the equations by di_1/dt, i_1, di_2/dt, i_2 and transfer the i_g terms to the right hand side of the equations. We get

$$4\frac{di_1}{dt} + 25i_1 - 8\frac{di_2}{dt} - 20i_2 = 5i_g - 8\frac{di_g}{dt}$$

$$-8\frac{di_1}{dt} - 20i_1 + 16\frac{di_2}{dt} + 80i_2 = 16\frac{di_g}{dt}$$

$$16\frac{di_g}{dt} = 1280e^{-5t}$$

$$2560e^{-5t} - 2176e^{-4t} - 80 - 1280e^{-5t} + 1360e^{-4t} + 4160e^{-5t} - 3264e^{-4t}$$

$$+80 - 4160e^{-5t} + 4080e^{-4t} \stackrel{?}{=} 1280e^{-5t}$$

$$(-80 + 80) + (2560 - 1280 + 4160 - 4160)e^{-5t}$$

$$+(1360 - 2176 - 3264 + 4080)e^{-4t} \stackrel{?}{=} 1280e^{-5t}$$

$$0 + 1280e^{-5t} + 0e^{-4t} = 1280e^{-5t} \quad \text{(OK)}$$

DE 6.7 [a] Summing the voltages around mesh 1 yields

$$4\frac{di_1}{dt} + 8\frac{d(i_2 + i_g)}{dt} + 20(i_1 - i_2) + 5(i_1 + i_g) = 0$$

or

$$4\frac{di_1}{dt} + 25i_1 + 8\frac{di_2}{dt} - 20i_2 = -\left(5i_g + 8\frac{di_g}{dt}\right)$$

Summing the voltages around mesh 2 yields

$$16\frac{d(i_2 + i_g)}{dt} + 8\frac{di_1}{dt} + 20(i_2 - i_1) + 780i_2 = 0$$

or

$$8\frac{di_1}{dt} - 20i_1 + 16\frac{di_2}{dt} + 800i_2 = -16\frac{di_g}{dt}$$

[b] From the solutions given in part (b)

$$i_1(0) = -0.4 - 11.6 + 12 = 0; \qquad i_2(0) = -0.01 - 0.99 + 1 = 0$$

These values agree with zero initial energy in the circuit. At infinity,

$$i_1(\infty) = -0.4\text{A}; \qquad i_2(\infty) = -0.01\text{A}$$

When $t = \infty$ the circuit reduces to

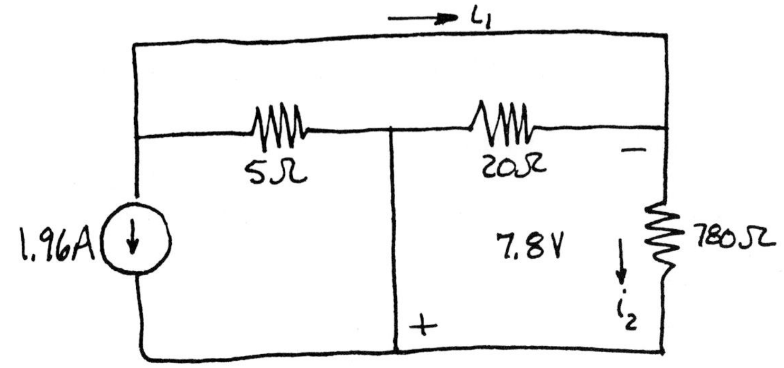

$$\therefore\ i_1(\infty) = -\left(\frac{7.8}{20} + \frac{7.8}{780}\right) = -0.4\text{A}; \quad i_2(\infty) = -\frac{7.8}{780} = -0.01\text{A}$$

$$16\frac{di_g}{dt} = 125.44e^{-4t}$$

Test:

$$371.20e^{-4t} - 480e^{-5t} + 8 + 232e^{-4t} - 240e^{-5t} + 63.36e^{-4t} - 80e^{-5t}$$

$$-8 - 792e^{-4t} + 800e^{-5t} \stackrel{?}{=} -125.44e^{-4t}$$

$$(8-8) + (800 - 480 - 240 - 80)e^{-5t}$$

$$+(371.20 + 232 + 63.36 - 792)e^{-4t} \stackrel{?}{=} -125.44e^{-4t}$$

$$(800 - 800)e^{-5t} + (666.56 - 792)e^{-4t} \stackrel{?}{=} -125.44e^{-4t}$$

$$-125.44e^{-4t} = -125.44e^{-4t} \quad \text{(OK)}$$

DE 6.8 [a]

$$L_2 = \left(\frac{M^2}{k^2 L_1}\right) = \frac{(0.09)^2}{(0.75)^2(0.288)} = 50\,\text{mH}$$

$$\frac{N_1}{N_2} = \sqrt{\frac{L_1}{L_2}} = \sqrt{\frac{288}{50}} = 2.4$$

[b]

$$\mathcal{P}_1 = \frac{L_1}{N_1^2} = \frac{0.288}{(1200)^2} = 0.2 \times 10^{-6}\ \text{Wb/A}$$

$$\mathcal{P}_2 = \frac{L_2}{N_2^2} = \frac{0.05}{(500)^2} = 0.2 \times 10^{-6}\ \text{Wb/A}$$

DE 6.9

$$\mathcal{P}_1 = \frac{L_1}{N_1^2} = 2\ \text{nWb/A}; \qquad \mathcal{P}_2 = \frac{L_2}{N_2^2} = 2\ \text{nWb/A}$$

$$\mathcal{P}_{12} = \mathcal{P}_{21} = \frac{M}{N_1 N_2} = 1.2\ \text{nWb/A}$$

$$\mathcal{P}_{11} = \mathcal{P}_1 - \mathcal{P}_{21} = 0.8\ \text{nWb/A}$$

DE 6.10 [a]

$$W = (0.5)L_1 i_1^2 + (0.5)L_2 i_2^2 + M i_1 i_2$$

$$M = 0.85\sqrt{(18)(32)} = 20.4\,\text{mH}$$

$$W = [9(36) + 16(81) + 20.4(54)] = 2721.6\,\text{mJ}$$

[b] $W = [324 + 1296 + 1101.6] = 2721.6\,\text{mJ}$

[c] $W = [324 + 1296 - 1101.6] = 518.4\,\text{mJ}$

[d] $W = [324 + 1296 - 1101.6] = 518.4\,\text{mJ}$

[b] From the given solutions we have

$$\frac{di_1}{dt} = -320e^{-5t} + 272e^{-4t}$$

$$\frac{di_2}{dt} = 260e^{-5t} - 204e^{-4t}$$

Thus,

$$4\frac{di_1}{dt} = -1280e^{-5t} + 1088e^{-4t}$$

$$25i_1 = 100 + 1600e^{-5t} - 1700e^{-4t}$$

$$8\frac{di_2}{dt} = 2080e^{-5t} - 1632e^{-4t}$$

$$20i_2 = 20 - 1040e^{-5t} + 1020e^{-4t}$$

$$5i_g = 80 - 80e^{-5t}$$

$$8\frac{di_g}{dt} = 640e^{5t}$$

Thus,

$$-1280e^{-5t} + 1088e^{-4t} + 100 + 1600e^{-5t} - 1700e^{-4t} - 2080e^{-5t}$$
$$+1632e^{-4t} - 20 + 1040e^{-5t} - 1020e^{-4t} \stackrel{?}{=} 80 - 80e^{-5t} - 640e^{-5t}$$

$$80 + (1088 - 1700 + 1632 - 1020)e^{-4t}$$
$$+(1600 - 1280 - 2080 + 1040)e^{-5t} \stackrel{?}{=} 80 - 720e^{-5t}$$

$$80 + (2720 - 2720)e^{-4t} + (2640 - 3360)e^{-5t} = 80 - 720e^{-5t} \quad \text{(OK)}$$

$$8\frac{di_1}{dt} = -2560e^{-5t} + 2176e^{-4t}$$

$$20i_1 = 80 + 1280e^{-5t} - 1360e^{-4t}$$

$$16\frac{di_2}{dt} = 4160e^{-5t} - 3264e^{-4t}$$

$$80i_2 = 80 - 4160e^{-5t} + 4080e^{-4t}$$

From the solutions for i_1 and i_2 we have

$$\frac{di_1}{dt} = 46.40e^{-4t} - 60e^{-5t}$$

$$\frac{di_2}{dt} = 3.96e^{-4t} - 5e^{-5t}$$

Also, $$\frac{di_g}{dt} = 7.84e^{-4t}$$

Thus

$$4\frac{di_1}{dt} = 185.60e^{-4t} - 240e^{-5t}$$

$$25i_1 = -10 - 290e^{-4t} + 300e^{-5t}$$

$$8\frac{di_2}{dt} = 31.68e^{-4t} - 40e^{-5t}$$

$$20i_2 = -0.20 - 19.80e^{-4t} + 20e^{-5t}$$

$$5i_g = 9.8 - 9.8e^{-4t}$$

$$8\frac{di_g}{dt} = 62.72e^{-4t}$$

Test:

$$185.60e^{-4t} - 240e^{-5t} - 10 - 290e^{-4t} + 300e^{-5t} + 31.68e^{-4t} - 40e^{-5t}$$

$$+0.20 + 19.80e^{-4t} - 20e^{-5t} \stackrel{?}{=} -[9.8 - 9.8e^{-4t} + 62.72e^{-4t}]$$

$$-9.8 + (300 - 240 - 40 - 20)e^{-5t}$$

$$+(185.60 - 290 + 31.68 + 19.80)e^{-4t} \stackrel{?}{=} -(9.8 + 52.92e^{-4t})$$

$$-9.8 + 0e^{-5t} + (237.08 - 290)e^{-4t} \stackrel{?}{=} -9.8 - 52.92e^{-4t}$$

$$-9.8 - 52.92e^{-4t} = -9.8 - 52.92e^{-4t} \quad \text{(OK)}$$

Also,

$$8\frac{di_1}{dt} = 371.20e^{-4t} - 480e^{-5t}$$

$$20i_1 = -8 - 232e^{-4t} + 240e^{-5t}$$

$$16\frac{di_2}{dt} = 63.36e^{-4t} - 80e^{-5t}$$

$$800i_2 = -8 - 792e^{-4t} + 800e^{-5t}$$

DE 6.11 [a] $M = 1.0\sqrt{(18)(32)} = 24\,\text{mH}, \qquad i_1 = 6\,\text{A}$

Therefore $16i_2^2 + 144i_2 + 324 = 0, \qquad i_2^2 + 9i_2 + 20.25 = 0$

Therefore $i_2 = -\left(\frac{9}{2}\right) \pm \sqrt{\left(\frac{9}{2}\right)^2 - 20.25} = -4.5 \pm \sqrt{0}$

Therefore $i_2 = -4.5\,\text{A}$

[b] No, setting W equal to a negative value will make the quantity under the square root sign negative.

Problems

P 6.1 $$p = vi = 40t[e^{-10t} - 10te^{-20t} - e^{-20t}]$$

$$\mathrm{W} = \int_0^{\infty} p\,dx = \int_0^{\infty} 40x[e^{-10x} - 10xe^{-20x} - e^{-20x}]\,dx = 0.2\,\mathrm{J}$$

This is energy stored in the inductor at $t = \infty$.

P 6.2 $0 \le t \le \infty$

$$i_L = \frac{10^3}{4}\int_0^t 30 \times 10^{-3} e^{-3x}\,dx + 2.5 = 7.5\frac{e^{-3x}}{-3}\Bigg|_0^t + 2.5$$

$$= 5 - 2.5e^{-3t}\,\mathrm{A}, \qquad 0 < t < \infty$$

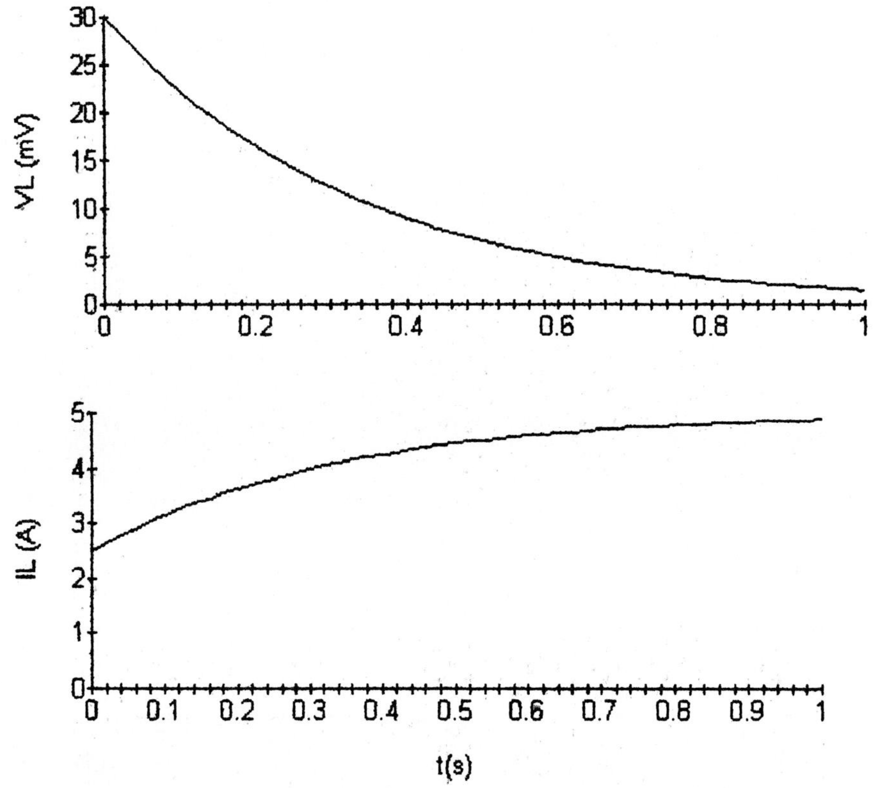

P 6.3 [a] $$v = L\frac{di}{dt}$$

$$\frac{di}{dt} = 50[t(-10e^{-10t}) + e^{-10t}] = 50e^{-10t}(1 - 10t)$$

$$v = (2 \times 10^{-3})(50)e^{-10t}(1 - 10t) = 100e^{-10t}(1 - 10t)\,\mathrm{mV}$$

[b] $$p = vi$$

$$v(200\,\text{ms}) = 100e^{-2}(1-2) = -13.53\,\text{mV}$$

$$i(200\,\text{ms}) = 50(0.2)e^{-2} = 1.35\,\text{A}$$

$$p(200\,\text{ms}) = -13.53(1.35) = -18.32\,\text{mW}$$

[c] delivering

[d] $$w = \frac{1}{2}Li^2 = \frac{1}{2}(2\times10^{-3})(1.35)^2 = 1.83\,\text{mJ}$$

[e] $$\frac{di}{dt} = 0 \quad \text{when} \quad t = \frac{1}{10}\,\text{s} = 100\,\text{ms}$$

$$i_{\max} = 50(0.1)e^{-1} = 1.84\,\text{A}$$

$$w_{\max} = \frac{1}{2}(2\times10^{-3})(1.84)^2 = 3.38\,\text{mJ}$$

P 6.4 [a] $0 \le t \le 1\,\text{ms}$:

$$i = \frac{1}{L}\int_0^t v_s\,dx + i(0) = \frac{10^6}{300}\int_0^t 6\times10^{-3}\,dx + 0$$

$$= 20x\Big|_0^t = 20t\,\text{mA}$$

$1\,\text{ms} \le t \le 2\,\text{ms}$:

$$i = \frac{10^6}{300}\int_{10^{-3}}^t (12\times10^{-3} - 6x)\,dx + 20\times10^{-3}$$

$$\therefore\; i = 40t - 10{,}000t^2 - 10\times10^{-3}\,\text{mA}$$

$2\,\text{ms} \le t \le \infty$:

$$i = \frac{10^6}{300}\int_{2\times10^{-3}}^t (0)\,dx + 30\times10^{-3} = 30\,\text{mA}$$

[b]

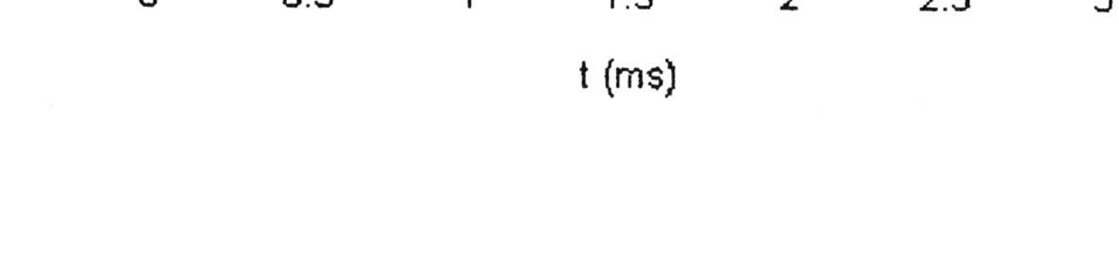

P 6.5 [a]
$$\begin{aligned} i &= 0 && t < 0 \\ i &= 16t\,\text{A} && 0 \leq t \leq 25\,\text{ms} \\ i &= 0.8 - 16t\,\text{A} && 25 \leq t \leq 50\,\text{ms} \\ i &= 0 && 50\,\text{ms} < t \end{aligned}$$

[b]
$$v = L\frac{di}{dt} = 375 \times 10^{-3}(16) = 6\,\text{V} \qquad 0 \leq t \leq 25\,\text{ms}$$
$$v = 375 \times 10^{-3}(-16) = -6\,\text{V} \qquad 25 \leq t \leq 50\,\text{ms}$$

$$\begin{aligned} v &= 0 && t < 0 \\ v &= 6\,\text{V} && 0 \leq t \leq 25\,\text{ms} \\ v &= -6\,\text{V} && 25 \leq t \leq 50\,\text{ms} \\ v &= 0 && 50\,\text{ms} < t \end{aligned}$$

$$p = vi$$

$$\begin{aligned} p &= 0 && t < 0 \\ p &= (16t)(6) = 96t\,\text{W} && 0 \leq t \leq 25\,\text{ms} \\ p &= (0.8 - 16t)(-6) = 96t - 4.8\,\text{W} && 25 \leq t \leq 50\,\text{ms} \\ p &= 0 && 50\,\text{ms} < t \end{aligned}$$

$$\begin{aligned} w &= 0 && t < 0 \\ w &= \int_0^t (16x)6\,dx = 96\frac{x^2}{2}\Big|_0^t = 48t^2\,\text{J} && 0 \leq t \leq 25\,\text{ms} \\ w &= \int_{0.025}^t (96x - 4.8)\,dx + 0.03 \\ &= \int_{0.025}^t 96x\,dx - \int_{0.025}^t 4.8\,dx + 0.03 \\ &= 96\frac{x^2}{2}\Big|_{0.025}^t - 4.8x\Big|_{0.025}^t + 0.03 \\ &= 48t^2 - 4.8t + 0.12\,\text{J} && 25 \leq t \leq 50\,\text{ms} \\ w &= 0 && 50\,\text{ms} < t \end{aligned}$$

P 6.6 [a] $0 \leq t \leq 1\,\text{s}$:

$$v = -100t$$
$$i = \frac{1}{5}\int_0^t -100x\,dx + 0 = -20\frac{x^2}{2}\Big|_0^t$$

$i = -10t^2$ [A]

$1\,\mathrm{s} \leq t \leq 3\,\mathrm{s}:$

$v = -200 + 100t$

$i(1) = -10\,\mathrm{A}$

$$\therefore\ i = \frac{1}{5}\int_1^t (100x - 200)\,dx - 10$$

$$= 20\int_1^t x\,dx - 40\int_1^t dx - 10$$

$$= 10(t^2 - 1) - 40(t - 1) - 10$$

$3\,\mathrm{s} \leq t \leq 5\,\mathrm{s}:$

$v = 100$

$i(3) = 10(9) - 120 + 20 = -10\,\mathrm{A}$

$$i = \frac{1}{5}\int_3^t 100\,dx - 10$$

$$= 20t - 60 - 10 = 20t - 70\ [\mathrm{A}]$$

$5\,\mathrm{s} \leq t \leq 6\,\mathrm{s}:$

$v = -100t + 600$

$i(5) = 100 - 70 = 30$

$$i = \frac{1}{5}\int_5^t (-100x + 600)\,dx + 30$$

$$= -20\int_5^t x\,dx + 120\int_5^t dx + 30$$

$$= -10(t^2 - 25) + 120(t - 5) + 30$$

$$= -10t^2 + 120t - 320\,\mathrm{A}$$

[b] $i(6) = -10(36) + 120(6) - 320 = 720 - 680 = 40\,\mathrm{A}, \qquad 6 \leq t \leq \infty$

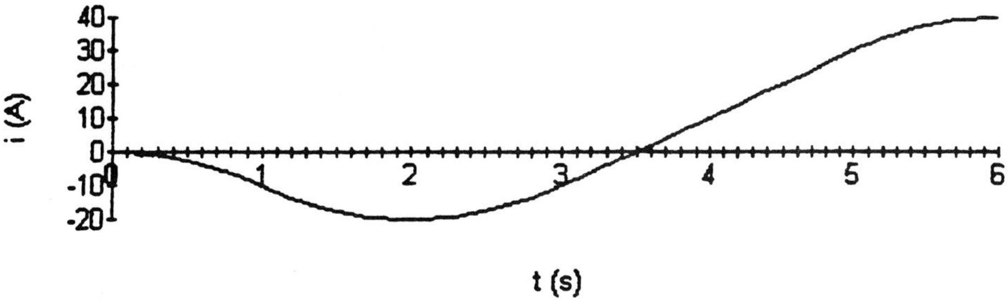

P 6.7 [a]

$$i(0) = A_1 + A_2 = 0.05$$

$$\frac{di}{dt} = -2500A_1e^{-2500t} - 7500A_2e^{-7500t}$$

$$v = -50A_1e^{-2500t} - 150A_2e^{-7500t} \text{ V}$$

$$v(0) = -50A_1 - 150A_2 = 10$$

$$\therefore \quad -5A_1 - 15A_2 = 1$$

But from the equation for $i(0)$, $5A_1 + 5A_2 = 0.25$

Solving, $A_1 = 0.175\,\text{A}$ and $A_2 = -0.125\,\text{A}$

Thus,

$$i_1 = 0.175e^{-2500t} - 0.125e^{-7500t} \text{ A}, \qquad t \geq 0$$

$$v = -8.75e^{-2500t} + 18.75e^{-7500t} \text{ V}, \qquad t \geq 0$$

[b]

$$p = vi = 4.375e^{-10,000t} - 1.53125e^{-5000t} - 2.34375e^{-15,000t}\text{W}$$

$$p = 0 \quad \text{when } 4.375e^{-10,000t} - 1.53125e^{-5000t} - 2.34375e^{-15,000t} = 0$$

Let $x = e^{5000t}$, then

$$4.375x - 1.53125x^2 - 2.34375 = 0$$

Solving,

$$x = 0.7143, \quad x = 2.143$$

If $x < 1$, t must be negative hence the solution for $t > 0$ must be $x = 2.143$

$$e^{5000t} = 2.143 \quad \text{so} \quad t = 152.43\,\mu\text{s}$$

P 6.8 [a] From Prob. 6.7 we have

$$i = A_1e^{-2500t} + A_2e^{-7500t} \text{ A}$$

$$v = -50A_1e^{-2500t} - 150A_2e^{-7500t} \text{ V}$$

$$i(0) = A_1 + A_2 = 0.05$$

$$v(0) = -50A_1 - 150A_2 = -100$$

$$\therefore \quad A_1 + A_2 = 0.05 \quad \text{and} \quad A_1 + 3A_2 = 2$$

$$\therefore \quad A_2 = 0.975\text{A}, \qquad A_1 = -0.925\text{A}$$

Thus,

$$i = -0.925e^{-2500t} + 0.975e^{-7500t} \text{ A} \qquad t \geq 0$$

$$v = 46.25e^{-2500t} - 146.25e^{-7500t} \text{ V} \qquad t \geq 0$$

[b] $i = 0$ when $0.975e^{-7500t} = 0.925e^{-2500t}$

$$\therefore \quad e^{5000t} = 1.0541$$

$$t = (\ln 1.054)/5000 = 10.53\,\mu\text{s}$$

$v = 0$ when $46.25e^{-2500t} = 146.25e^{-7500t}$

$$\therefore \quad t = \ln 3.1622/5000 = 230.25\,\mu\text{s}$$

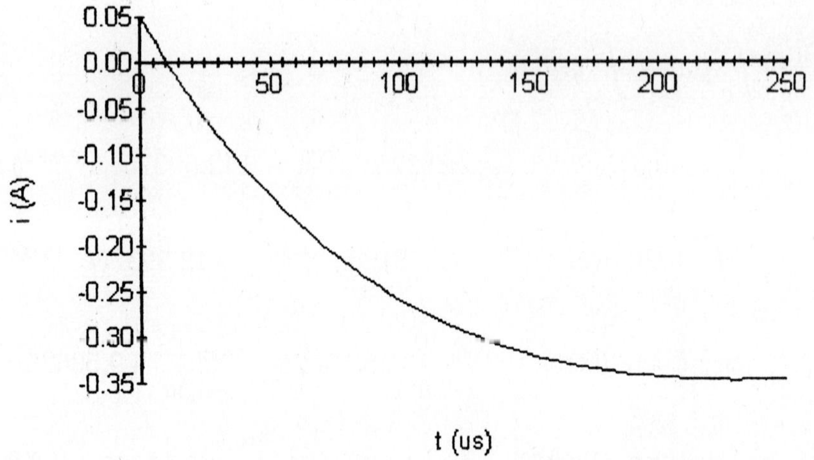

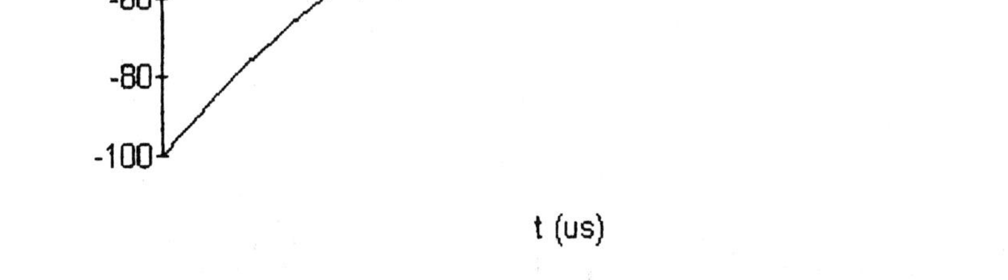

∴ Energy is being stored between 10.53 μs and 230.25 μs; energy is being extracted between 0 and 10.53 μs and between 230.25 μs and infinity.

[c] $$p = vi = 180.375e^{-10{,}000t} - 42.78125e^{-5000t} - 142.59375e^{-15{,}000t}\ \text{W}$$

$$\therefore \quad \text{W}_{\text{stored}} = \int_{t_1}^{t_2} p\,dt + w(0)$$

$$W_{\text{stored}} = 10^{-3}\left\{-18.0375e^{-10{,}000t}\Big|_{t_1}^{t_2} + 8.55625e^{-5000t}\Big|_{t_1}^{t_2} + 9.50625e^{-15{,}000t}\Big|_{t_1}^{t_2}\right\} + 25\times10^{-6}$$

$$= 8.55625e^{-5000t_2} + 9.50625e^{-15{,}000t_2} - 18.0375e^{-10{,}000t_2} - 8.55625e^{-5000t_1} - 9.50625e^{-15{,}000t_1} + 18.0375e^{-10{,}000t_1} + 0.025\,\text{mW}$$

where $t_1 = 10.52\,\mu\text{s}, \quad t_2 = 230.11\,\mu\text{s}$

$W_{\text{stored}} = 1.23\,\text{mJ}.$

$$W_{\text{extracted}} = \int_0^{t_1} p\,dt + \int_{t_2}^{\infty} p\,dt$$

$$= \int_0^{t_1}(180.375e^{-10^4t} - 42.78125e^{-5000t} - 142.59375e^{-15{,}000t})\,dt$$

$$+\int_{t_2}^{\infty}(180.375e^{-10^4t} - 42.78125e^{-5000t} - 142.59375e^{-15{,}000t})\,dt$$

$$= 10^{-3}\left\{-18.0375e^{-10{,}000t}\Big|_0^{t_1} + 8.55625e^{-5000t}\Big|_0^{t_1} + 9.50625e^{-15{,}000t}\Big|_0^{t_1} - 18.0375e^{-10{,}000t}\Big|_{t_2}^{\infty} + 8.55625e^{-5000t}\Big|_{t_2}^{\infty} + 9.50625e^{-15{,}000t}\Big|_{t_2}^{\infty}\right\}$$

$$= \{18.0375e^{-10{,}000t_2} - 8.55625e^{-5000t_2} - 9.50625e^{-15{,}000t_2} + 8.55625e^{-5000t_1} + 9.50625e^{-15{,}000t_1} - 18.0375e^{-10{,}000t_1} - 0.025\}\,\text{mJ}$$

$W_{\text{ext.}} = -1.23\,\text{mJ} \qquad \therefore\; W_{\text{stored}} = W_{\text{extracted}}$

P 6.9 [a] $v_L = L\dfrac{di}{dt} = [125\sin 400t]e^{-200t}\ \text{V}$

$\therefore\; \dfrac{dv_L}{dt} = 25{,}000(2\cos 400t - \sin 400t)e^{-200t}\ \text{V/s}$

$\dfrac{dv_L}{dt} = 0$ when $\tan 400t = 2$

$\therefore\; t = 2.77\,\text{ms}$

Also $400t = 1.107 + \pi$ etc.

Because of the decaying exponential v_L will be maximum the first time the derivative is zero.

[b] $v_L(\text{max}) = [125\sin 1.107]e^{-0.554} = 64.27\ \text{V}$

$v_L\ \text{max} = 64.27\ \text{V}$

Note: When $t = (1.107+\pi)/400$; $\quad v_L = -13.36\ \text{V}$

P 6.10 [a]

$$\begin{aligned}
i &= \frac{1000}{50}\int_0^t 250\sin 1000x\,dx - 5 \\
&= 5000\int_0^t \sin 1000x\,dx - 5 \\
&= 5000\left[\frac{-\cos 1000x}{1000}\right|_0^t - 5 \\
&= 5(1-\cos 1000t) - 5 \\
i &= -5\cos 1000t \text{ A}
\end{aligned}$$

[b]

$$\begin{aligned}
p &= vi = (250\sin 1000t)(-5\cos 1000t) \\
&= -1250\sin 1000t\cos 1000t \\
p &= -625\sin 2000t \text{ W} \\
w &= \frac{1}{2}Li^2 \\
&= \frac{1}{2}(50\times 10^{-3})25\cos^2 1000t \\
&= 625\cos^2 1000t \text{ mJ} \\
w &= [312.5 + 312.5\cos 2000t] \text{ mJ.}
\end{aligned}$$

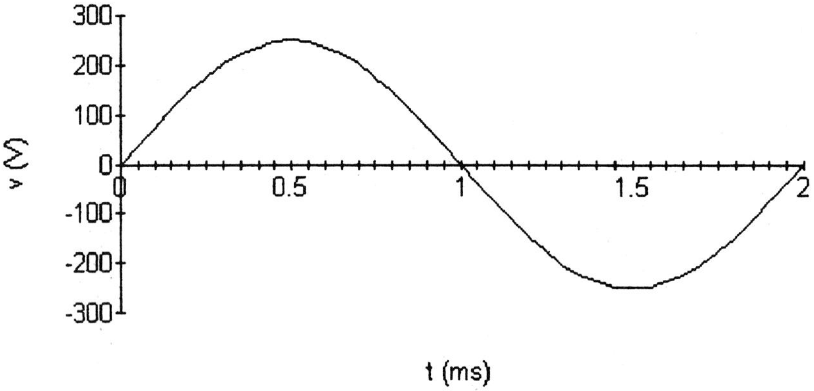
300
200
100
0
-100
-200
-300
v (V)
0
0.5
1
1.5
2
t (ms)

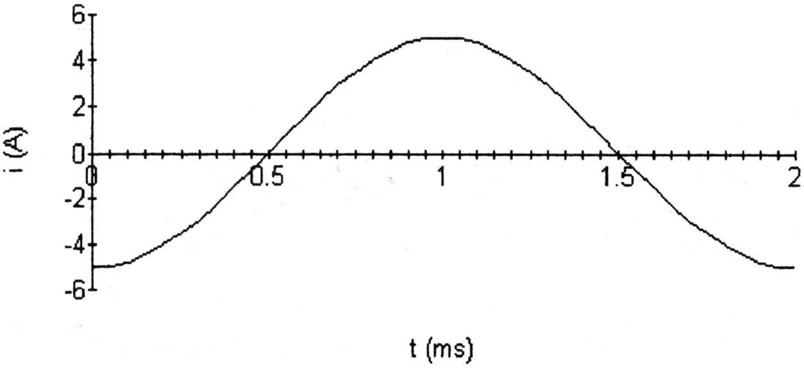
6
4
2
0
-2
-4
-6
i (A)
0
0.5
1
1.5
2
t (ms)

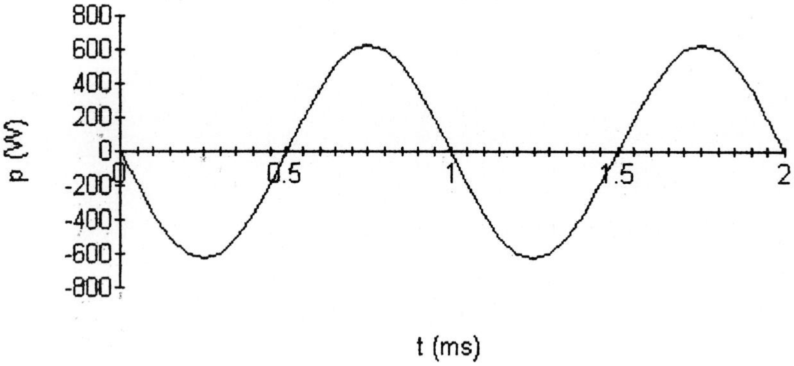
800
600
400
200
0
-200
-400
-600
-800
p (W)
0
0.5
1
1.5
2
t (ms)

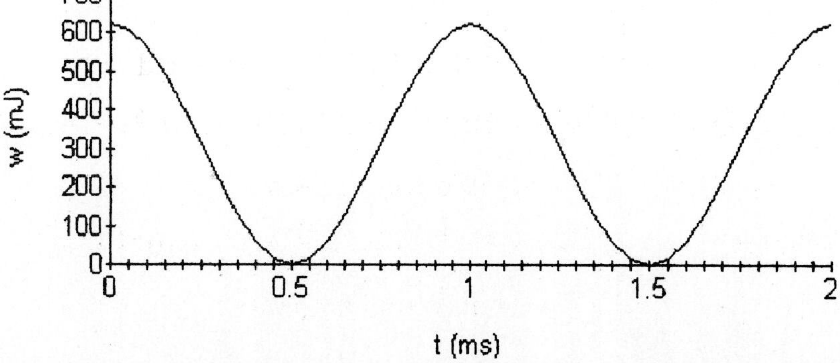
700
600
500
400
300
200
100
0
w (mJ)
0
0.5
1
1.5
2
t (ms)

[c] Absorbing power: Delivering power:

Absorbing power:	Delivering power:
$0.5\pi \leq t \leq \pi$ ms	$0 \leq t \leq 0.5\pi$ ms
$1.5\pi \leq t \leq 2\pi$ ms	$\pi \leq t \leq 1.5\pi$ ms

P 6.11 $$I_o = \frac{1}{25}\int_0^1 20 \times 10^{-3}\,dt = 0.8t\Big|_0^1 = 0.8\,\text{mA}$$

$$R_m = (50)(1000) = 50\,\text{k}\Omega$$

$$V_m = (0.8)(50) = 40\,\text{V}$$

P 6.12 $$i = (B_1 \cos 5t + B_2 \sin 5t)e^{-t}$$

$$i(0) = B_1 = 25\,\text{A}$$

$$\frac{di}{dt} = (B_1 \cos 5t + B_2 \sin 5t)(-e^{-t}) + e^{-t}(-5B_1 \sin 5t + 5B_2 \cos 5t)$$

$$= [(5B_2 - B_1)\cos 5t - (5B_1 + B_2)\sin 5t]e^{-t}$$

$$v = 2\frac{di}{dt} = [(10B_2 - 2B_1)\cos 5t - (10B_1 + 2B_2)\sin 5t]e^{-t}$$

$$v(0) = 100 = 10B_2 - 2B_1 = 10B_2 - 50 \quad \therefore \quad B_2 = 150/10 = 15\,\text{A}$$

Thus,

$$i = (25 \cos 5t + 15 \sin 5t)e^{-t}\,\text{A}, \qquad t \geq 0$$

$$v = (100 \cos 5t - 280 \sin 5t)e^{-t}\,\text{V}, \qquad t \geq 0$$

$$i(0.5) = -6.70\,\text{A}; \qquad v(0.5) = -150.23\,\text{V}$$

$$p(0.5) = (-6.70)(-150.23) = 1007.00\,\text{W absorbing}$$

P 6.13 [a]

$$\begin{aligned}
v(20\,\mu\text{s}) &= 12.5 \times 10^9(20 \times 10^{-6})^2 = 5\,\text{V} \quad \text{(end of first interval)}\\
v(20\,\mu\text{s}) &= 10^6(20 \times 10^{-6}) - (12.5)(400) \times 10^{-3} - 10\\
&= 5\,\text{V (start of second interval)}\\
v(40\,\mu\text{s}) &= 10^6(40 \times 10^{-6}) - (12.5)(1600) \times 10^{-3} - 10\\
&= 10\,\text{V (end of second interval)}
\end{aligned}$$

[b] $p(10\mu s) = 62.5 \times 10^{12}(10^{-5})^3 = 62.5\,\text{mW}, \qquad v(10\,\mu s) = 1.25\,\text{V},$

$i(10\mu s) = 50\,\text{mA}, \qquad p(10\,\mu s) = vi = 62.5\,\text{mW},$

$p(30\,\mu s) = 437.50\,\text{mW}, \qquad v(30\,\mu s) = 8.75\,\text{V}, \qquad i(30\,\mu s) = 0.05\,A$

[c] $w(10\,\mu s) = 15.625 \times 10^{12}(10 \times 10^{-6})^4 = 0.15625\,\mu\text{J}$

$w = 0.5Cv^2 = 0.5(0.2 \times 10^{-6})(1.25)^2 = 0.15625\,\mu\text{J}$

$w(30\,\mu s) = 7.65625\,\mu\text{J}$

$w(30\,\mu s) = 0.5(0.2 \times 10^{-6})(8.75)^2 = 7.65625\,\mu\text{J}$

P 6.14 [a] $0 \le t \le 50\,\mu s$

$C = 0.5\,\mu\text{F} \qquad \frac{1}{C} = 2 \times 10^6$

$$v = 2 \times 10^6 \int_0^t 20 \times 10^{-3}\,dx + 20$$

$v = 40 \times 10^3 t + 20\,\text{V} \qquad 0 \le t \le 50\,\mu s$

$v(50\,\mu s) = 2 + 20 = 22\,\text{V}$

[b] $50\,\mu s \le t \le 200\,\mu s$

$$v = 2 \times 10^6 \int_{50\times 10^{-6}}^t -40 \times 10^{-3}\,dx + 22 = -8 \times 10^4 t + 4 + 22$$

$v = -8 \times 10^4 t + 26\text{V} \qquad 50 \le t \le 200\,\mu s$

$v(200\,\mu s) = -8 \times 10^4(200 \times 10^{-6}) + 26 = 10\,\text{V}$

[c] $200 \le t \le \infty$

$$v = 2 \times 10^6 \int_{200\times 10^{-6}}^t 0\,dx + 10$$

$v = 10\,\text{V} \qquad 200\,\mu s \le t \le \infty$

[d]

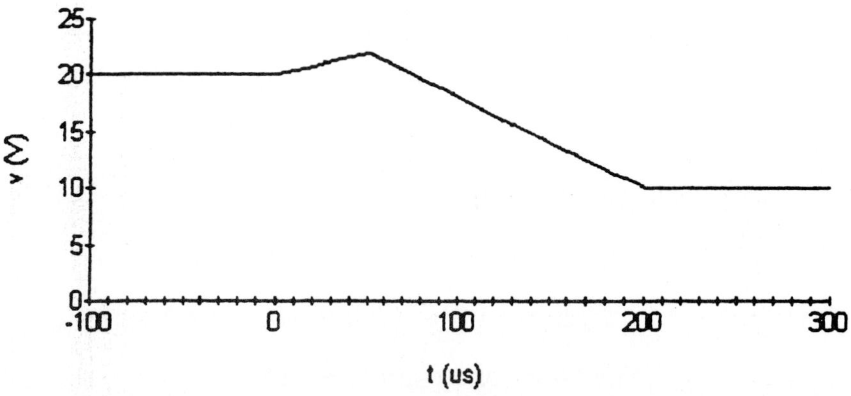

P 6.15 $$i_C = C\frac{dv}{dt}$$

$0 < t < 1$:

$$i_C = 0.8 \times 10^{-6}(60)t^2 = 48t^2\ \mu\text{A}$$

$1 < t < 3$:

$$i_C = 0.8 \times 10^{-6}(7.5)(3-t)^2(-1)$$

$$i_C = -6(3-t)^2\ \mu\text{A}$$

P 6.16 [a]

$$v = 5 \times 10^6 \int_0^{250\times 10^{-6}} 100 \times 10^{-3} e^{-1000t}\,dt - 60.6$$

$$= 500 \times 10^3 \frac{e^{-1000t}}{-1000}\Big|_0^{250\times10^{-6}} - 60.6$$

$$= 500(1 - e^{-0.25}) - 60.6 = 50\ \text{V}$$

$$w = \tfrac{1}{2}Cv^2 = 0.1 \times 10^{-6}(2500) = 250\ \mu\text{J}$$

[b] $$v = 500 - 60.6 = 439.40\ \text{V}$$

$$w = \frac{1}{2}(0.2) \times 10^{-6}(439.40)^2 = 19.31\ \text{mJ}$$

P 6.17 [a] $$w(0) = \frac{1}{2}C[v(0)]^2 = \frac{1}{2}(0.40) \times 10^{-6}(25)^2 = 125\ \mu\text{J}$$

[b] $$v = (A_1 t + A_2)e^{-15,00t}$$

$$v(0) = A_2 = 25\ \text{V}$$

$$\frac{dv}{dt} = -1500e^{-1500t}(A_1 t + A_2) + e^{-1500t}(A_1)$$

$$= (-1500A_1 t - 1500A_2 + A_1)e^{-1500t}$$

$$\frac{dv}{dt}(0) = A_1 - 1500A_2$$

$$i = C\frac{dv}{dt}, \qquad i(0) = C\frac{dv(0)}{dt}$$

$$\therefore \quad \frac{dv(0)}{dt} = \frac{i(0)}{C} = \frac{90 \times 10^{-3}}{0.40 \times 10^{-6}} = 225 \times 10^3$$

$$\therefore \quad 225 \times 10^3 = A_1 - 1500(25)$$

Thus, $A_1 = 2.25 \times 10^5 + 3.75 \times 10^4 = 262{,}500\ \frac{\text{V}}{\text{s}}$

[c] $$v = (262{,}500t + 25)e^{-1500t}$$

$$i = C\frac{dv}{dt} = 0.40 \times 10^{-6}\frac{d}{dt}(262{,}500t + 25)e^{-1500t}$$

$$i = \frac{d}{dt}[(0.105t + 10 \times 10^{-6})e^{-1500t}]$$

$$= (0.105t + 10 \times 10^{-6})(-1500)e^{-1500t} + e^{-1500t}(0.105)$$

$$= (-157.5t - 15 \times 10^{-3} + 0.105)e^{-1500t}$$

$$= (0.09 - 157.5t)e^{-1500t}\,\text{A}, \qquad t \geq 0$$

$$= (90 - 157{,}500t)e^{-1500t}\,\text{mA}, \qquad t \geq 0$$

P 6.18 [a] $$i = \frac{50 \times 10^{-3}}{10 \times 10^{-6}}t = 5 \times 10^3 t \qquad 0 \leq t \leq 10\,\mu\text{s}$$

$$i = 50 \times 10^{-3} \qquad 10 \leq t \leq 30\,\mu\text{s}$$

$$q = \int_0^{10\times10^{-6}} 5 \times 10^3 t\,dt + \int_{10\times10^{-6}}^{30\times10^{-6}} 50 \times 10^{-3}\,dt$$

$$= 5 \times 10^3 \frac{t^2}{2}\Big|_0^{10\times10^{-6}} + 50 \times 10^{-3}(20 \times 10^{-6})$$

$$= 5 \times 10^3(\tfrac{1}{2})(100 \times 10^{-12}) + 1000 \times 10^{-3} \times 10^{-6}$$

$$= 1.25\,\mu\text{C}$$

[b] $$i = 200 \times 10^{-3} - 5 \times 10^{-3}t \qquad 30\,\mu\text{s} \leq t \leq 50\,\mu\text{s}$$

$$q = 1.25 \times 10^{-6} + \int_{30\times10^{-6}}^{50\times10^{-6}} [200 \times 10^{-3} - 5 \times 10^3 t]\,dt$$

$$= 1.25 \times 10^{-6} + 200 \times 10^{-3}(20 \times 10^{-6}) - 5 \times 10^3 \frac{t^2}{2}\Big|_{30\times10^{-6}}^{50\times10^{-6}}$$

$$= 1.25 \times 10^{-6} + 4000 \times 10^{-9} - 5 \times 10^3 \left[\frac{2500 - 900}{2}\right] 10^{-12}$$

$$= 1.25\,\mu\text{C}$$

Since $q = vC$, $\quad\therefore\; v = 1.25/0.25 = 5\,\text{V}$.

[c] $$i = -300 \times 10^{-3} + 5 \times 10^{-3}t \qquad 50\,\mu\text{s} \leq t \leq 60\,\mu\text{s}$$

$$q = 1.25 \times 10^{-6} + \int_{50\times10^{-6}}^{60\times10^{-6}} [-300 \times 10^{-3} + 5 \times 10^{3}t]\,dt$$

$$= 1.25 \times 10^{-6} - 300 \times 10^{-3}(10 \times 10^{-6}) + 5 \times 10^{3}\left[\frac{3600 - 2500}{2}\right]10^{-12}$$

$$= 1\,\mu\text{C}$$

$$v = \frac{1 \times 10^{-6}}{0.25 \times 10^{-6}} = 4\,\text{V}$$

$$w = \frac{C}{2}v^2 = \frac{1}{2}(0.25)(16) = 2\,\mu\text{J}$$

P 6.19 $v = -60\,\text{V}, \quad t \le 0; \qquad C = 0.4\,\mu\text{F}$

$$v = 15 - 15e^{-500t}(5\cos 2000t + \sin 2000t)\text{V}, \quad t \ge 0$$

[a] $i = 0, \quad t < 0$

[b]

$$\frac{dv}{dt} = -15[(5\cos 2000t + \sin 2000t)(-500e^{-500t}) + (e^{-500t})(-10{,}000\sin 2000t + 2000\cos 2000t)]$$

$$= 15e^{-500t}(500\cos 2000t + 10{,}500\sin 2000t)$$

$$i = C\frac{dv}{dt} = 0.4 \times 10^{-6}(7500)e^{-500t}(\cos 2000t + 21\sin 2000t)$$

$$= 3e^{-500t}(\cos 2000t + 21\sin 2000t)\,\text{mA}, \quad t > 0$$

[c] no

[d] yes, from 0 to 3 mA

[e] $v(\infty) = 15\,\text{V}$

$$w = \frac{1}{2}Cv^2 = \frac{1}{2}(0.4)225 \times 10^{-6} = 45\,\mu\text{J}$$

P 6.20 $10\|(15 + 25) = 8\,\text{H}$

$8\|12 = 4.8\,\text{H}$

$44\|(1.2 + 4.8) = 5.28\,\text{H}$

$21\|4 = 3.36\,\text{H}$

$5.28 + 3.36 = 8.64\,\text{H}$

P 6.21 $6\|14 = 4.2\,\text{H}$

$15.8 + 4.2 = 20\,\text{H}$

$20\|60 = 15\,\text{H}$

$15 + 5 = 20\,\text{H}$

$20\|80 = 16\,\text{H}$

$16 + 24 = 40\,\text{H}$

$40\|10 = 8\,\text{H}$

$L_{\text{ab}} = 12 + 8 = 20\,\text{H}$

P 6.22 From Figure 6.17(a) we have

$$v = \frac{1}{C_1}\int_0^t i + v_1(0) + \frac{1}{C_2}\int_0^t i\,dx + v_2(0) + \cdots$$

$$v = \left[\frac{1}{C_1} + \frac{1}{C_2} + \cdots\right]\int_0^t i\,dx + v_1(0) + v_2(0) + \cdots$$

Therefore $\frac{1}{C_{\text{eq}}} = \left[\frac{1}{C_1} + \frac{1}{C_2} + \cdots\right], \qquad v_{\text{eq}}(0) = v_1(0) + v_2(0) + \cdots$

P 6.23 From Fig. 6.18(a)

$$i = C_1\frac{dv}{dt} + C_2\frac{dv}{dt} + \cdots = [C_1 + C_2 + \cdots]\frac{dv}{dt}$$

Therefore $C_{\text{eq}} = C_1 + C_2 + \cdots$. Because the capacitors are in parallel, the initial voltage on every capacitor must be the same. This initial voltage would appear on C_{eq}.

P 6.24 $\frac{1}{4} + \frac{1}{6} = \frac{5}{12} \quad \therefore \; C_{\text{eq}} = 2.4\,\mu\text{F}$

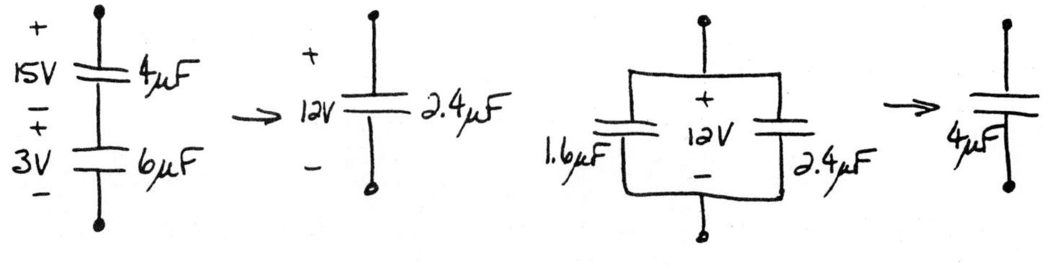

$\frac{1}{4} + \frac{1}{12} = \frac{4}{12} \quad \therefore \; C_{\text{eq}} = 3\,\mu\text{F}$

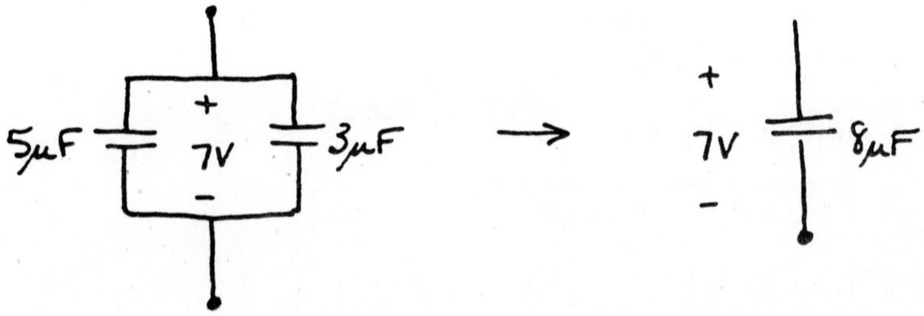

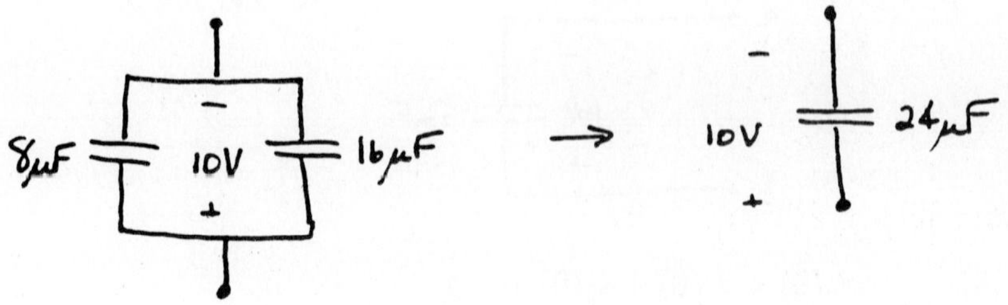

$$\frac{1}{24} + \frac{1}{8} = \frac{4}{24} \quad \therefore \; C_{eq} = 6\,\mu\text{F}$$

$\therefore \; C_{eq} = 6\,\mu\text{F}$

P 6.25 $$\frac{1}{C_1} = \frac{1}{8} + \frac{1}{32} = \frac{5}{32}; \qquad C_1 = 6.4\,\text{nF}$$

$$C_2 = 5.6 + 6.4 = 12\,\text{nF}$$

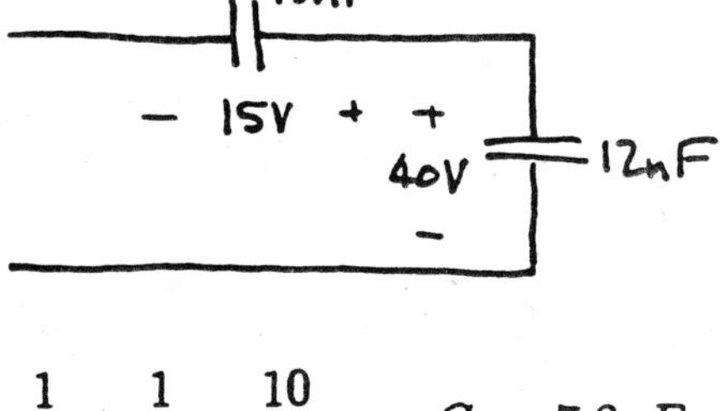

$$\frac{1}{C_3} = \frac{1}{18} + \frac{1}{12} = \frac{10}{72}; \qquad C_3 = 7.2\,\text{nF}$$

$$C_4 = 12.8 + 7.2 = 20\,\text{nF}$$

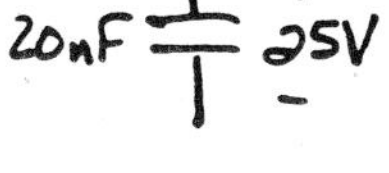

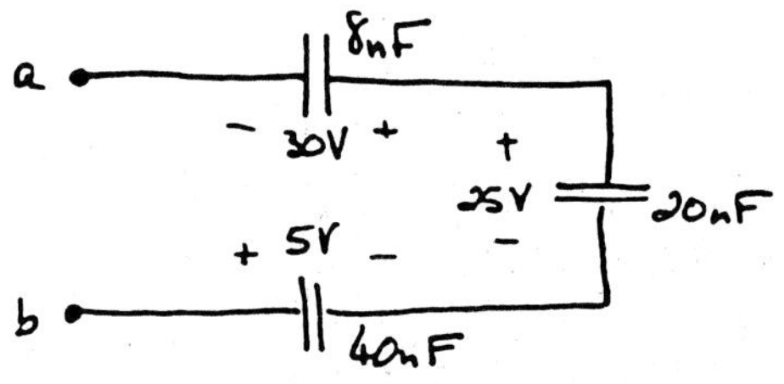

$$\frac{1}{C_5} = \frac{1}{8} + \frac{1}{20} + \frac{1}{40} = \frac{1}{5}; \qquad C_5 = 5\,\text{nF}$$

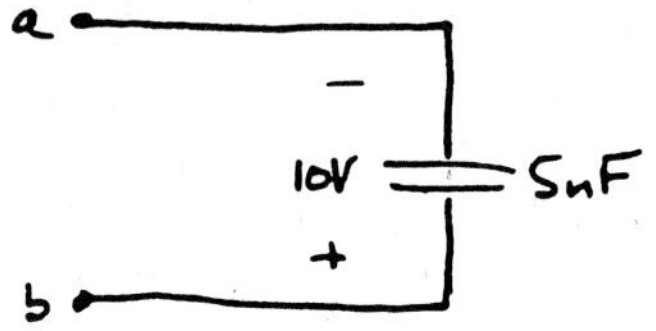

P 6.26 [a] $i_o(0) = i_1(0) + i_2(0) = 5\,\text{A}$

[b]

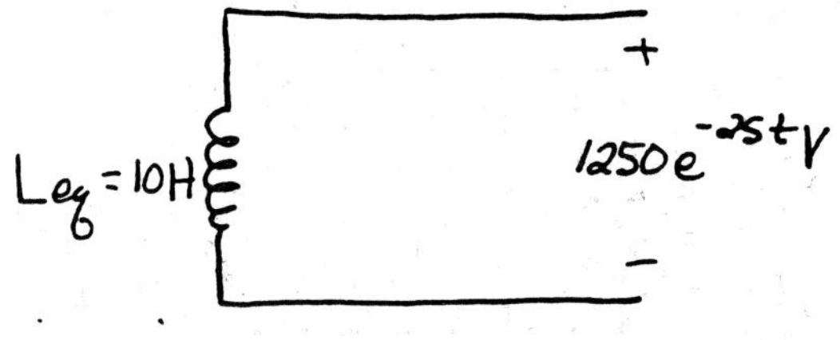

$$\begin{aligned} i_o &= -\frac{1}{10}\int_0^t 1250e^{-25x}\,dx + 5 = -125\left[\frac{e^{-25x}}{-25}\right]_0^t + 5 \\ &= 5(e^{-25t} - 1) + 5 = 5e^{-25t}\,\text{A}, \qquad t \geq 0 \end{aligned}$$

[c]

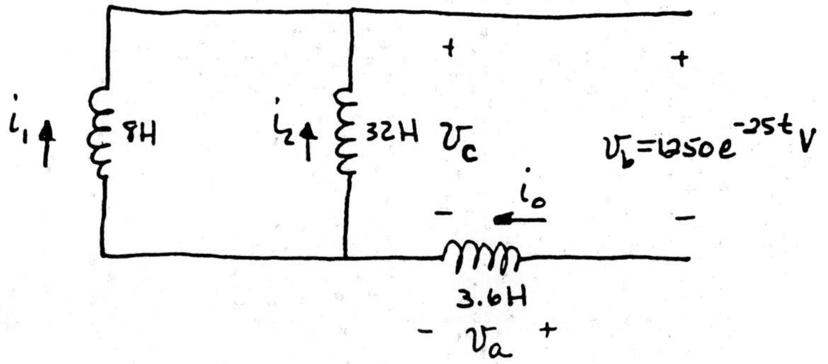

$$v_a = 3.6\frac{d}{dt}(5e^{-25t}) = -450e^{-25t}\text{ V}$$

$$v_c = v_a + v_b = -450e^{-25t} + 1250e^{-25t}$$

$$= 800e^{-25t}\text{ V}$$

$$i_1 = -\frac{1}{8}\int_0^t 800e^{-25x}\,dx + 10$$

$$= 4e^{-25t} - 4 + 10$$

$$i_1 = 4e^{-25t} + 6\text{ A} \qquad t \geq 0$$

[d] $$i_2 = \frac{1}{32}\int_0^t 800e^{-25x}\,dx - 5$$

$$= e^{-25t} - 1 - 5$$

$$i_2 = e^{-25t} - 6\text{ A}, \qquad t \geq 0$$

[e] $$w(0) = \frac{1}{2}(8)(100) + \frac{1}{2}(32)(25) + \frac{1}{2}(3.6)(25) = 845\text{ J}$$

[f] $$w_{\text{del}} = \frac{1}{2}(10)(25) = 125\text{ J}$$

[g] $$w_{\text{trapped}} = 845 - 125 = 720\text{ J}$$

P 6.27 $$v_b = 1250e^{-25t}\text{ V}$$

$$i_o = 5e^{-25t}\text{ A}$$

$$p = 6250e^{-50t}\text{ W}$$

$$w = \int_0^t 6250e^{-50x}\,dx = 6250\frac{e^{-50x}}{-50}\Big|_0^t = 125(1 - e^{-50t})\text{ W}$$

$$w_{\text{total}} = 125\text{ J}$$

$$80\%w_{\text{total}} = 100\text{ J}$$

Thus,

$$125 - 125e^{-50t} = 100; \qquad e^{50t} = 5; \qquad \therefore\ t = 32.19\text{ ms}$$

P 6.28 [a]

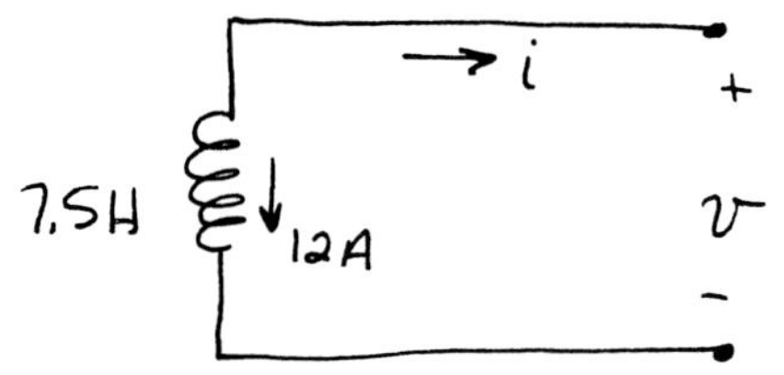

$$i(t) = -\frac{1}{7.5}\int_0^t -1800e^{-20x}\,dx - 12$$

$$= 240\frac{e^{-20x}}{-20}\Big|_0^t -12$$

$$= -12(e^{-20t} - 1) - 12$$

$$i(t) = -12e^{-20t}\text{ A}$$

[b] $$i_1(t) = -\frac{1}{10}\int_0^t -1800e^{-20x}\,dx + 4$$

$$= 180\frac{e^{-20x}}{-20}\Big|_0^t +4$$

$$= -9(e^{-20t} - 1) + 4$$

$$i_1(t) = -9e^{-20t} + 13\text{ A}$$

[c] $$i_2(t) = -\frac{1}{30}\int_0^t -1800e^{-20x}\,dx - 16$$

$$= 60\frac{e^{-20x}}{-20}\Big|_0^t -16$$

$$= -3(e^{-20t} - 1) - 16$$

$$i_2(t) = -3e^{-20t} - 13\text{ A}$$

[d] $$p = vi = (-1800e^{-20t})(-12e^{-20t}) = 21{,}600e^{-40t}\text{ W}$$

$$w = \int_0^\infty p\,dt = \int_0^\infty 21{,}600e^{\;40t}\,dt$$

$$= 21{,}600\frac{e^{-40t}}{-40}\Big|_0^\infty$$

$$= 540\text{ J}$$

[e] $$w = \frac{1}{2}(10)(16) + \frac{1}{2}(30)(256) = 3920\text{ J}$$

[f] $$w_{\text{trapped}} = \frac{1}{2}(10)(13)^2 + \frac{1}{2}(30)(13)^2 = 3380\text{ J}$$

$$w_{\text{trapped}} = 3920 - 540 = 3380\text{ J} \qquad \text{checks}$$

[g] Yes, they agree.

P 6.29 [a]

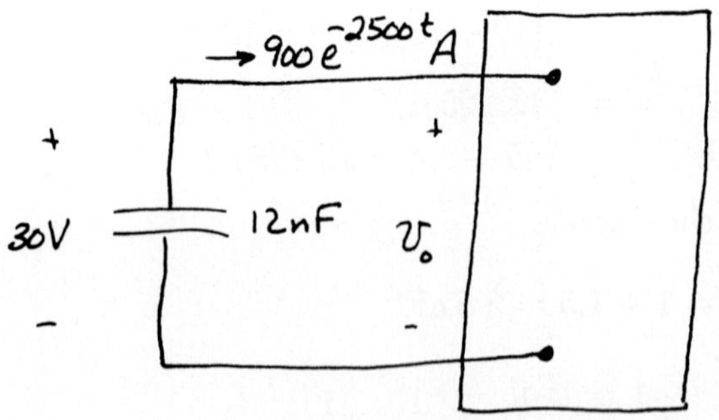

$$v_o = -\frac{10^9}{12}\int_0^t 900 \times 10^{-6} e^{-2500x}\,dx + 30$$

$$= -75{,}000\frac{e^{-2500x}}{-2500}\Big|_0^t + 30$$

$$= 30e^{-2500t}\ \text{V}, \qquad t \geq 0$$

[b] $$v_1 = -\frac{10^9}{20}(900 \times 10^{-6})\frac{e^{-2500x}}{-2500}\Big|_0^t + 45$$

$$= 18e^{-2500t} + 27\ \text{V}, \qquad t \geq 0$$

[c] $$v_2 = -\frac{10^9}{30}(900 \times 10^{-6})\frac{e^{-2500x}}{-2500}\Big|_0^t - 15$$

$$= 12e^{-2500t} - 27\ \text{V}, \qquad t \geq 0$$

[d] $$p = vi = (30e^{-2500t})(900 \times 10^{-6})e^{-2500t}$$

$$= 27 \times 10^{-3} e^{-5000t}$$

$$w = \int_0^\infty 27 \times 10^{-3} e^{-5000t}\,dt$$

$$= 27 \times 10^{-3}\frac{e^{-5000t}}{-5000}\Big|_0^\infty$$

$$= -5.4 \times 10^{-6}(0 - 1) = 5.4\,\mu\text{J}$$

[e] $$w = \tfrac{1}{2}(20 \times 10^{-9})(45)^2 + \tfrac{1}{2}(30 \times 10^{-9})(15)^2$$

$$= 20.25 \times 10^{-6} + 3.375 \times 10^{-6}$$

$$= 23.625\,\mu\text{J}$$

[f] $$w_{\text{trapped}} = \tfrac{1}{2}(20 \times 10^{-9})(27)^2 + \tfrac{1}{2}(30 \times 10^{-9})(27)^2$$
$$= (10 + 15)(27)^2 \times 10^{-9}$$
$$= 18.225\,\mu\text{J}$$

CHECK: $18.225 + 5.4 = 23.625\,\mu\text{J}$

[g] Yes, they agree.

P 6.30 $C_1 = 1 + 1.5 = 2.5\,\text{nF}$

$$\frac{1}{C_2} = \frac{1}{2.5} + \frac{1}{12.5} + \frac{1}{50} = \frac{1}{2}$$

$\therefore\ C_2 = 2\,\text{nF}$

$$v_d(0) + v_a(0) - v_c(0) = 40 + 15 + 45 = 100\,\text{V}$$

[a]

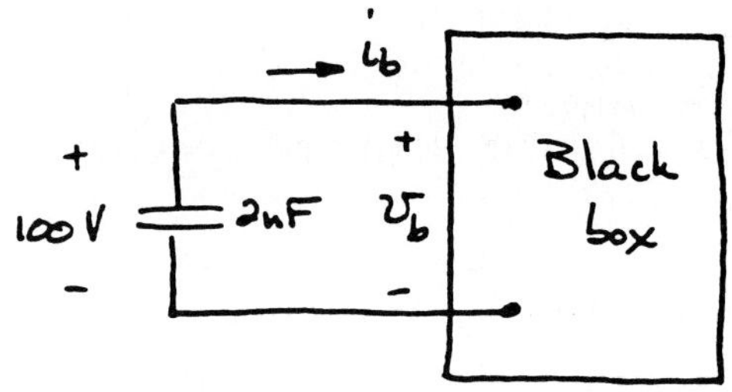

$$v_b = -\frac{10^9}{2}\int_0^t 50 \times 10^{-6} e^{-250x}\,dx + 100$$
$$= -25{,}000 \frac{e^{-250x}}{-250}\Big|_0^t + 100$$
$$= 100(e^{-250t} - 1) + 100$$
$$= 100e^{-250t}\ \text{V}$$

[b]
$$\begin{aligned} v_a &= -\frac{10^9}{12.5}\int_0^t 50\times 10^{-6}e^{-250x}\,dx + 15 \\ &= -4000\frac{e^{-250x}}{-250}\Big|_0^t + 15 \\ &= 16(e^{-250t}-1)+15 \\ &= 16e^{-250t} - 1\text{ V} \end{aligned}$$

[c]
$$\begin{aligned} v_c &= \frac{10^9}{50}\int_0^t 50\times 10^{-6}e^{-250x}\,dx - 45 \\ &= 1000\frac{e^{-250x}}{-250}\Big|_0^t - 45 \\ &= -4(e^{-250t}-1)-45 \\ &= -4e^{-250t} - 41\text{ V} \end{aligned}$$

[d]
$$\begin{aligned} v_d &= -\frac{10^9}{2.5}\int_0^t 50\times 10^{-6}e^{-250x}\,dx + 40 \\ &= -20{,}000\frac{e^{-250x}}{-250}\Big|_0^t + 40 \\ &= 80(e^{-250t}-1)+40 \\ &= 80e^{-250t} - 40\text{ V} \end{aligned}$$

$$\begin{aligned} \text{CHECK: } v_b &= v_d + v_a - v_c \\ &= 80e^{-250t} - 40 + 16e^{-250t} - 1 + 4e^{-250t} + 41 \\ &= 100e^{-250t}\text{ V} \quad \text{(checks)} \end{aligned}$$

[e]
$$\begin{aligned} i_1 &= -10^{-9}\frac{d}{dt}[80e^{-250t} - 40] \\ &= -10^{-9}(-20{,}000e^{-250t}) \\ &= 20e^{-250t}\ \mu\text{A} \end{aligned}$$

[f]
$$\begin{aligned} i_2 &= -1.5\times 10^{-9}\frac{d}{dt}[80e^{-250t} - 40] \\ &= -1.5\times 10^{-9}(-20{,}000e^{-250t}) \\ &= 30e^{-250t}\ \mu\text{A} \end{aligned}$$

CHECK: $i_1 + i_2 = 50e^{-250t}\ \mu\text{A} = i_b$

P 6.31 [a]
$$w(0) = [\tfrac{1}{2}(2.5)(40)^2 + \tfrac{1}{2}(12.5)(15)^2 + \tfrac{1}{2}(50)(45)^2] \times 10^{-9} = 54{,}031.25\,\text{nJ}$$

[b]
$$v_{\text{a}}(\infty) = -1\,\text{V}$$
$$v_{\text{c}}(\infty) = -41\,\text{V}$$
$$v_{\text{d}}(\infty) = -40\,\text{V}$$
$$w(\infty) = [\tfrac{1}{2}(2.5)(40)^2 + \tfrac{1}{2}(12.5)(1)^2 + \tfrac{1}{2}(50)(41)^2] \times 10^{-9} = 44{,}031.25\,\text{nJ}$$

[c]
$$w = \int_0^{\infty}(100e^{-250t})(50e^{-250t}) \times 10^{-6}\,dt = 10{,}000\,\text{nJ}$$

CHECK: $54{,}031.25 - 44{,}031.25 = 10{,}000$

[d]
$$\%\ \text{delivered} = \frac{10{,}000}{54{,}031.25} \times 100 = 18.51\%$$

[e]
$$w = 5 \times 10^{-3}\int_0^t e^{-500x}\,dx = 10^4(1 - e^{-500t})\,\text{nJ}$$

$$\therefore\ 10^4(1 - e^{-500t}) = 5000; \qquad e^{-500t} = 0.5$$

Thus, $t = 2\ln 2 = 1.39\,\text{ms}$.

P 6.32

$$v_2(t) = 20 \times 10^{-3}\frac{di_o}{dt}$$
$$= (20 \times 10^{-3})(50 \times 10^{-3})\{e^{-8000t}[-6000\sin 6000t + 12{,}000\cos 6000t] + (-8000e^{-8000t})[\cos 6000t + 2\sin 6000t]\}$$
$$= e^{-8000t}\{4\cos 6000t - 22\sin 6000t\}\ \text{V}$$

$$\therefore\ v_2(0) = 4\,\text{V}$$

$$i_0(0) = 50\,\text{mA}$$

$$v_R(0) = 320(50 \times 10^{-3}) = 16\,\text{V}$$

$$v_1(0) = 16 + 4 = 20\,\text{V}$$

P 6.33
$$v_c = \frac{-10^6}{20}\int_0^t e^{-80x}\sin 60x\,dx - 300$$
$$= 5e^{-80t}[80\sin 60t + 60\cos 60t] + 300 - 300$$
$$= 400e^{-80t}\sin 60t + 300e^{-80t}\cos 60t \text{ V}$$
$$v_L = 5\frac{di_o}{dt}$$
$$= 5[-80e^{-80t}\sin 60t + 60e^{-80t}\cos 60t]$$
$$= -400e^{-80t}\sin 60t + 300e^{-80t}\cos 60t \text{ V}$$
$$v_o = v_c - v_L$$
$$= (300e^{-80t}\cos 60t - 300e^{-80t}\cos 60t + 400e^{-80t}\sin 60t +$$
$$400e^{-80t}\sin 60t)$$
$$= 800e^{-80t}\sin 60t \text{ V}$$

P 6.34 [a] Yes, $v_o = 20(i_2 - i_1) + 60i_2$

[b]
$$v_o = 20(1 - 52e^{-5t} + 51e^{-4t} - 4 - 64e^{-5t} + 68e^{-4t}) +$$
$$60(1 - 52e^{-5t} + 51e^{-4t})$$
$$= 20(-3 - 116e^{-5t} + 119e^{-4t}) + 60 - 3160e^{-5t} + 3060e^{-4t}$$
$$v_o = -5440e^{-5t} + 5440e^{-4t} \text{ V}$$

[c]
$$v_o = L_2\frac{d}{dt}(i_g - i_2) + M\frac{di_1}{dt}$$
$$= 16\frac{d}{dt}(15 + 36e^{-5t} - 51e^{-4t}) + 8\frac{d}{dt}(4 + 64e^{-5t} - 68e^{-4t})$$
$$= -2880e^{-5t} + 3264e^{-4t} - 2560e^{-5t} + 2176e^{-4t}$$
$$v_o = -5440e^{-5t} + 5440e^{-4t} \text{ V}$$

P 6.35 [a]
$$v_g = 5(i_g - i_1) + 20(i_2 - i_1) + 60i_2$$
$$= 5(16 - 16e^{-5t} - 4 - 64e^{-5t} + 68e^{-4t}) +$$
$$20(1 - 52e^{-5t} + 51e^{-4t} - 4 - 64e^{-5t} + 68e^{-4t}) +$$
$$60(1 - 52e^{-5t} + 51e^{-4t})$$
$$= 60 + 5780e^{-4t} - 5840e^{-5t} \text{ V}$$

[b] $v_g(0) = 60 + 5780 - 5840 = 0$ V

[c] $$p_{\text{dev}} = v_g i_g$$
$$= 960 + 92{,}480e^{-4t} - 94{,}400e^{-5t} - 92{,}480e^{-9t} + 93{,}440e^{-10t}\,\text{W}$$

[d] $p_{\text{dev}}(\infty) = 960$ W

[e] $i_1(\infty) = 4$ A; $\quad i_2(\infty) = 1$ A; $\quad i_g(\infty) = 16$ A;

$$p_{5\Omega} = (16 - 4)^2(5) = 720\ \text{W}$$

$$p_{20\Omega} = 3^2(20) = 180\ \text{W}$$

$$p_{60\Omega} = 1^2(60) = 60\ \text{W}$$

$$\sum p_{\text{abs}} = 720 + 180 + 60 = 960\ \text{W}$$

$$\therefore\ \sum p_{\text{dev}} = \sum p_{\text{abs}} = 960\ \text{W}$$

P 6.36 [a]
$$-2\frac{di_g}{dt} + 16\frac{di_2}{dt} + 32i_2 = 0$$

$$16\frac{di_2}{dt} + 32i_2 = 2\frac{di_g}{dt}$$

[b]
$$i_2 = e^{-t} - e^{-2t}\ \text{A}$$

$$\frac{di_2}{dt} = -e^{-t} + 2e^{-2t}\ \text{A/s}$$

$$i_g = 8 - 8e^{-t}\ \text{A}$$

$$\frac{di_g}{dt} = 8e^{-t}\ \text{A/s}$$

$$\therefore\ -16e^{-t} + 32e^{-2t} + 32e^{-t} - 32e^{-2t} = 16e^{-t}$$

[c]
$$v_1 = 4\frac{di_g}{dt} - 2\frac{di_2}{dt}$$
$$= 4(8e^{-t}) - 2(-e^{-t} + 2e^{-2t})$$
$$= 34e^{-t} - 4e^{-2t}\ \text{V}, \qquad t \geq 0$$

[d] $v_1(0) = 34 - 4 = 30$ V; $\qquad$ Also
$$v_1(0) = 4\frac{di_g}{dt}(0) - 2\frac{di_2}{dt}(0)$$
$$= 4(8) - 2(-1 + 2) = 32 - 2 = 30\ \text{V}$$

Yes, the initial value of v_1 is consistent with known circuit behavior.

[e]

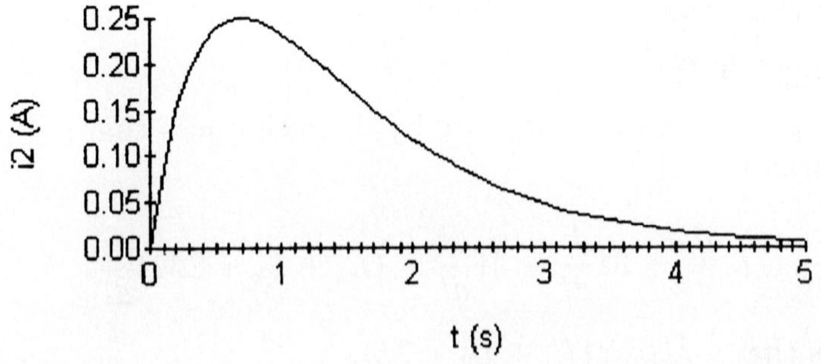

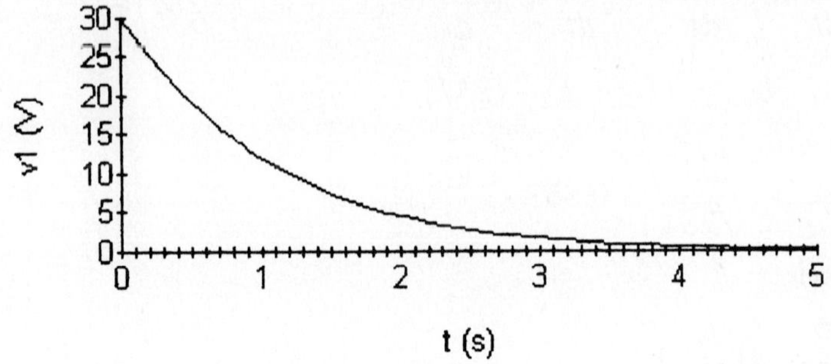

P 6.37 [a] $$\frac{1}{k^2} = \left(1 + \frac{\mathcal{P}_{11}}{\mathcal{P}_{12}}\right)\left(1 + \frac{\mathcal{P}_{22}}{\mathcal{P}_{12}}\right) = \left(1 + \frac{\mathcal{P}_{11}}{\mathcal{P}_{21}}\right)\left(1 + \frac{\mathcal{P}_{22}}{\mathcal{P}_{12}}\right)$$

Therefore

$$k^2 = \frac{\mathcal{P}_{12}\mathcal{P}_{21}}{(\mathcal{P}_{21} + \mathcal{P}_{11})(\mathcal{P}_{12} + \mathcal{P}_{22})}$$

Now note that

$$\phi_1 = \phi_{11} + \phi_{21} = \mathcal{P}_{11}N_1i_1 + \mathcal{P}_{21}N_1i_1 = N_1i_1(\mathcal{P}_{11} + \mathcal{P}_{21})$$

and similarly

$$\phi_2 = N_2i_2(\mathcal{P}_{22} + \mathcal{P}_{12})$$

It follows that

$$(\mathcal{P}_{11} + \mathcal{P}_{21}) = \frac{\phi_1}{N_1i_1}$$

and

$$(\mathcal{P}_{22} + \mathcal{P}_{12}) = \left(\frac{\phi_2}{N_2i_2}\right)$$

Therefore

$$k^2 = \frac{(\phi_{12}/N_2i_2)(\phi_{21}/N_1i_1)}{(\phi_1/N_1i_1)(\phi_2/N_2i_2)} = \frac{\phi_{12}\phi_{21}}{\phi_1\phi_2}$$

or

$$k = \sqrt{\left(\frac{\phi_{21}}{\phi_1}\right)\left(\frac{\phi_{12}}{\phi_2}\right)}$$

[b] The fractions (ϕ_{21}/ϕ_1) and (ϕ_{12}/ϕ_2) are by definition less than 1.0, therefore $k < 1$.

P 6.38 [a]

$$v_{ab} = L_1\frac{di}{dt} + L_2\frac{di}{dt} + M\frac{di}{dt} + M\frac{di}{dt} = (L_1 + L_2 + 2M)\frac{di}{dt}$$

It follows that $L_{ab} = (L_1 + L_2 + 2M)$

[b]

$$v_{ab} = L_1\frac{di}{dt} - M\frac{di}{dt} + L_2\frac{di}{dt} - M\frac{di}{dt} = (L_1 + L_2 - 2M)\frac{di}{dt}$$

Therefore $L_{ab} = (L_1 + L_2 - 2M)$

P 6.39 [a]

$$k = \frac{M}{\sqrt{L_1L_2}} = \frac{23.8}{\sqrt{784}} = 0.85$$

[b] $M = 28\,\text{mH}$

[c]

$$\frac{L_1}{L_2} = \frac{N_1^2\mathcal{P}_1}{N_2^2\mathcal{P}_2} = \left(\frac{N_1}{N_2}\right)^2$$

$$\therefore \left(\frac{N_1}{N_2}\right)^2 = \frac{196}{4} = 49$$

$$\frac{N_1}{N_2} = 7$$

P 6.40 [a]

$$M = k\sqrt{L_1L_2} = 0.4\sqrt{9 \times 10^4} = 120\,\text{mH}$$

$$\mathcal{P}_1 = \frac{L_1}{N_1^2} = \frac{400 \times 10^{-3}}{4 \times 10^6} = 100\ \text{nWb/A}$$

$$\frac{d\phi_{11}}{d\phi_{21}} = \frac{\mathcal{P}_{11}}{\mathcal{P}_{21}} = 0.25; \qquad \mathcal{P}_{21} = 4\mathcal{P}_{11}$$

$$\mathcal{P}_1 = \mathcal{P}_{11} + \mathcal{P}_{21} = 5\mathcal{P}_{11}$$

$$\mathcal{P}_{11} = \frac{1}{5}\mathcal{P}_1 = 20\ \text{nWb/A}$$

$$\mathcal{P}_{21} = 4\mathcal{P}_{11} = 80\ \text{nWb/A}$$

$$N_2 = \frac{M}{N_1\mathcal{P}_{21}} = \frac{120 \times 10^{-3}}{(2000)(80 \times 10^{-9})} = 750\ \text{turns}$$

[b]

$$\mathcal{P}_2 = \frac{L_2}{N_2^2} = \frac{225 \times 10^{-3}}{(0.75)^2 \times 10^6} = 400\ \text{nWb/A}$$

[c] $\mathcal{P}_{11} = 20$ nWb/A [see part (a)]

[d] $$\frac{\phi_{22}}{\phi_{12}} = \frac{\mathcal{P}_2}{\mathcal{P}_{12}} - 1 = \frac{400}{80} - 1 = 4$$

P 6.41 [a] Dot terminal 1; the flux is up in coil 1-2, and down in coil 3-4. Assign the current into terminal 3; the flux is down in coil 3-4. Therefore, dot terminal 3. Hence, 1 and 3 or 2 and 4.

[b] Dot terminal 2; the flux is up in coil 1-2, and right-to-left in coil 3-4. Assign the current into terminal 4; the flux is right-to-left in coil 3-4. Therefore, dot terminal 4. Hence, 2 and 4 or 1 and 3.

[c] Dot terminal 2; the flux is up in coil 1-2, and right-to-left in coil 3-4. Assign the current into terminal 4; the flux is right-to-left in coil 3-4. Therefore, dot terminal 4. Hence, 2 and 4 or 1 and 3.

[d] Dot terminal 1; the flux is down in coil 1-2, and down in coil 3-4. Assign the current into terminal 4; the flux is down in coil 3-4. Therefore, dot terminal 4. Hence, 1 and 4 or 2 and 3.

P 6.42 When the switch is opened the induced voltage is negative at the dotted terminal. Since the voltmeter kicks upscale, the induced voltage across the voltmeter must be positive at its positive terminal. Therefore, the voltage is negative at the negative terminal of the voltmeter.

Thus, the lower terminal of the unmarked coil has the same instantaneous polarity as the dotted terminal. Therefore, place a dot on the lower terminal of the unmarked coil.

P 6.43 [a] $$v_{ab} = L_1\frac{d(i_1 - i_2)}{dt} + M\frac{di_2}{dt}$$

$$0 = L_1\frac{d(i_2 - i_1)}{dt} - M\frac{di_2}{dt} + M\frac{d(i_1 - i_2)}{dt} + L_2\frac{di_2}{dt}$$

Collecting coefficients of $[di_1/dt]$ and $[di_2/dt]$, the two mesh-current equations become

$$v_{ab} = L_1\frac{di_1}{dt} + (M - L_1)\frac{di_2}{dt}$$

and

$$0 = (M - L_1)\frac{di_1}{dt} + (L_1 + L_2 - 2M)\frac{di_2}{dt}$$

Solving for $[di_1/dt]$ gives

$$\frac{di_1}{dt} = \frac{L_1 + L_2 - 2M}{L_1L_2 - M^2}v_{ab}$$

from which we have

$$v_{\rm ab} = \left(\frac{L_1L_2 - M^2}{L_1 + L_2 - 2M}\right)\left(\frac{di_1}{dt}\right)$$

$$\therefore\ L_{\rm ab} = \frac{L_1L_2 - M^2}{L_1 + L_2 - 2M}$$

[b] If the magnetic polarity of coil 2 is reversed, the sign of M reverses, therefore

$$L_{\rm ab} = \frac{L_1L_2 - M^2}{L_1 + L_2 + 2M}$$

P 6.44 When the button is not pressed we have

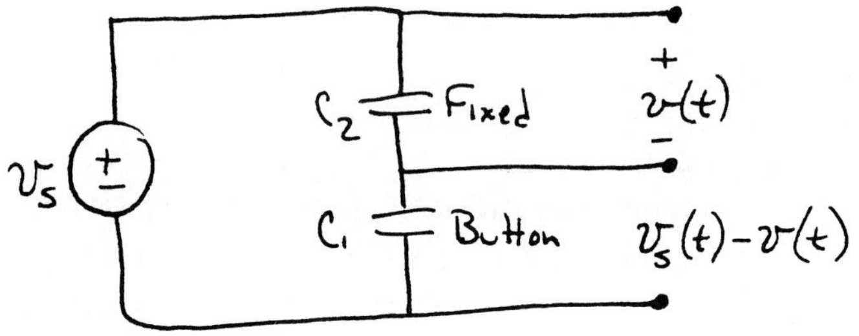

$$C_2\frac{dv}{dt} = C_1\frac{d}{dt}(v_s - v)$$

or

$$(C_1 + C_2)\frac{dv}{dt} = C_1\frac{dv_s}{dt}$$

$$\frac{dv}{dt} = \frac{C_1}{(C_1 + C_2)}\frac{dv_s}{dt}$$

Assuming $C_1 = C_2 = C$

$$\frac{dv}{dt} = 0.5\frac{dv_s}{dt}$$

or

$$v = 0.5v_s(t) + v(0)$$

When the button is pressed we have

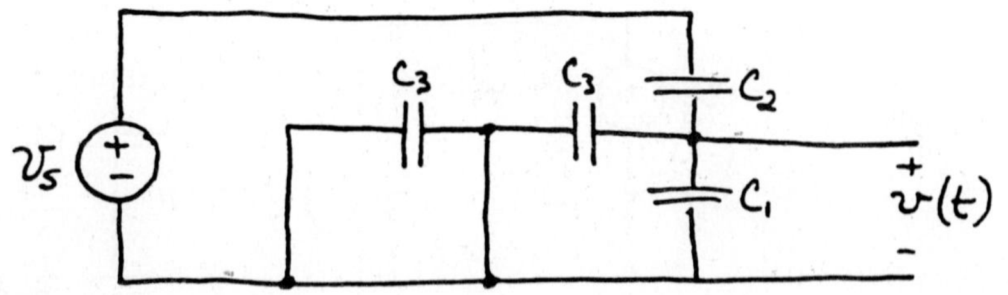

$$C_1\frac{dv}{dt} + C_3\frac{dv}{dt} + C_2\frac{d(v - v_s)}{dt} = 0$$

$$\therefore \quad \frac{dv}{dt} = \frac{C_2}{C_1 + C_2 + C_3}\frac{dv_s}{dt}$$

Assuming $C_1 = C_2 = C_3 = C$

$$\frac{dv}{dt} = \frac{1}{3}\frac{dv_s}{dt}$$

$$v = \frac{1}{3}v_s(t) + v(0)$$

Therefore interchanging the fixed capacitor and the button has no effect on the change in $v(t)$.

P 6.45 With no finger touching and equal 10 pF capacitors

$$v(t) = \frac{10}{20}(v_s(t)) + 0 = 0.5v_s(t)$$

With a finger touching

Let C_e = equivalent capacitance of person touching lamp

$$C_e = \frac{(10)(100)}{110} = 9.091 \text{ pF}$$

Then $\quad C_2 + C_e = 10 + 9.091 = 19.091$ pF

$$\therefore \quad v(t) = \frac{10}{29.091}v_s = 0.344v_s$$

$$\therefore \quad \Delta v(t) = (0.5 - 0.344)v_s = 0.156v_s$$

P 6.46 With no finger on the button the circuit is

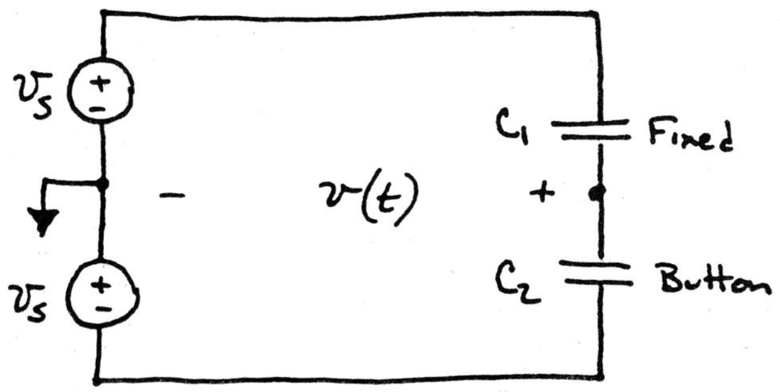

$$C_1\frac{dv}{dt}(v - v_s) + C_2\frac{d}{dt}(v + v_s) = 0$$

when $\quad C_1 = C_2 = C \qquad (2C)\frac{dv}{dt} = 0$

With a finger on the button

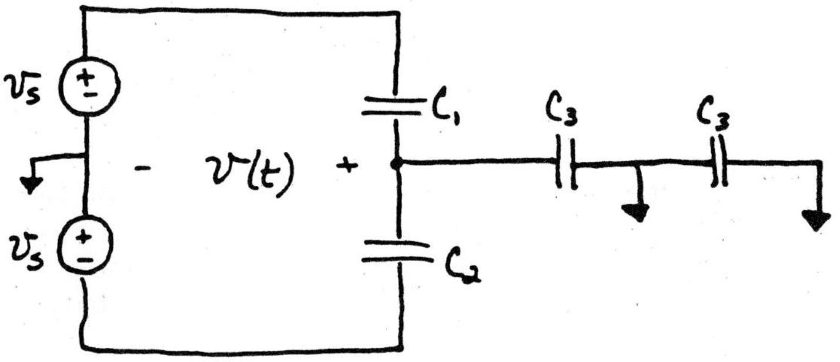

$$C_1\frac{d(v - v_s)}{dt} + C_2\frac{d(v + v_s)}{dt} + C_3\frac{dv}{dt} = 0$$

$$(C_1 + C_2 + C_3)\frac{dv}{dt} + C_2\frac{dv_s}{dt} - C_1\frac{dv_s}{dt} = 0$$

when $\quad C_1 = C_2 = C_3 = C \qquad (3C)\frac{dv}{dt} = 0$

$\therefore$ there is no change in the output voltage of this circuit.

7 Response of First-Order RL and RC Circuits

Drill Exercises

DE 7.1 [a] $i = \left(\frac{120}{3+5}\right)\left(\frac{-30}{36}\right) = -12.5\,\text{A}$

[b] $w = 0.5(8 \times 10^{-3})(12.5)^2 = 625\,\text{mJ}$

[c] $\tau = \frac{L}{R} = \frac{8 \times 10^{-3}}{2} = 4\,\text{ms}$

[d] $i = -12.5e^{-250t}\,\text{A}, \qquad t \geq 0$

[e] $i(5\,\text{ms}) = -3.58\,\text{A}, \qquad w\,(5\,\text{ms}) = (0.5)(8)(3.58)^2 = 51.3\,\text{mJ}$

$$w\,(\text{dis}) = 625 - 51.3 = 573.7\,\text{mJ}$$

$$\%\ \text{dissipated} = \left(\frac{573.7}{625}\right)100 = 91.8\%$$

DE 7.2 [a] $i_L(0^-) = 6.4\left(\frac{10}{16}\right) = 4\,\text{A} = i_L(0^+), \qquad t > 0$

$$R_{\text{eq}} = \frac{(4)(16)}{20} = 3.2\,\Omega, \qquad \tau = \frac{0.32}{3.2} = 0.1\,\text{s}$$

$$\text{Therefore}\quad \frac{1}{\tau} = 10, \qquad i_L = 4e^{-10t}\,\text{A}$$

Let i_1 equal the current in the $10\,\Omega$ resistor. Let the reference direction for i_1 be up. Then

$$i_1 = \left(\frac{4}{20}\right) i_L = 0.8e^{-10t}\,\text{A}, \qquad v_o = -10i_1 = -8e^{-10t}\,\text{V}, \qquad t \geq 0$$

[b] $v_{4\Omega} = L\frac{di_L}{dt} = 0.32(-40)e^{-10t} = -12.8e^{-10t}\,\text{V}, \qquad t \geq 0$

$$p_{4\Omega} = \frac{v_{4\Omega}^2}{4} = 40.96e^{-20t}\,\text{W}, \qquad t \geq 0$$

$$w_{4\Omega} = \int_0^\infty 40.96e^{-20t}dt = 2.048\,\text{J}$$

$$w_i = \frac{1}{2}Li^2 = \frac{1}{2}(0.32)(16) = 2.56\,\text{J}$$

$$\%\ \text{dissipated} = \left(\frac{2.048}{2.56}\right)100 = 80\%$$

DE 7.3 [a] $v(0) = \left[\frac{7.5(80)}{150}\right]50 = 200\,\text{V}$

[b] $\tau = RC = (50 \times 10^3)(0.4 \times 10^{-6}) = 20\,\text{ms}$

[c] $v = 200e^{-50t}\,\text{V}$

[d] $w(0) = 0.5(0.4 \times 10^{-6})(200)^2 = 8\,\text{mJ}$

[e] $w(t) = 0.5(0.4 \times 10^{-6})(4 \times 10^4)e^{-100t} = 8e^{-100t}\,\text{mJ}$

$8e^{-100t} = 2, \qquad t = (\ln 4)/100 = 13.86\,\text{ms}$

DE 7.4 [a] For $t < 0$:

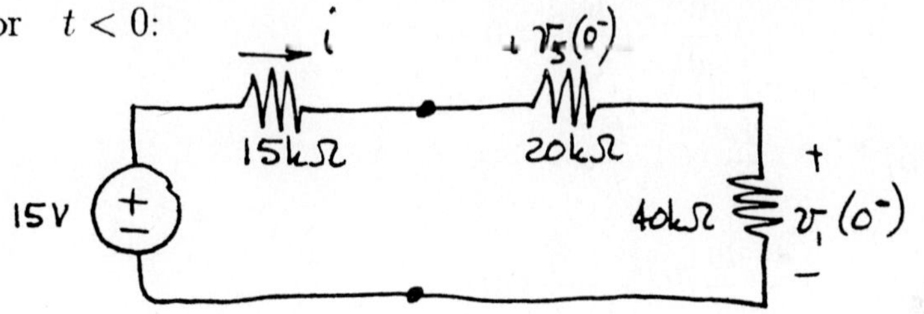

$i = \frac{15}{75} = \frac{1}{5}\,\text{mA}, \qquad v_5(0^-) = 4\,\text{V}, \qquad v_1(0^-) = 8\,\text{V}$

$\tau_5 = (20 \times 10^3)(5 \times 10^{-6}) = 100\,\text{ms}, \qquad 1/\tau_5 = 10$

$\tau_1 = (40 \times 10^3)(1 \times 10^{-6}) = 40\,\text{ms}, \qquad 1/\tau_1 = 25$

Therefore $v_5 = 4e^{-10t}\,\text{V}, \quad t \geq 0; \qquad v_1 = 8e^{-25t}\,\text{V}, \quad t \geq 0;$

$v_o = v_1 + v_5 = [8e^{-25t} + 4e^{-10t}]\,\text{V}, \qquad t \geq 0$

[b] $v_1(60\,\text{ms}) \cong 1.79\,\text{V}, \qquad v_5(60\,\text{ms}) \cong 2.20\,\text{V}$

$w_1(60\,\text{ms}) = (1/2)(1)(1.79)^2 \cong 1.59\,\mu\text{J}$

$w_5(60\,\text{ms}) = (1/2)(5)(2.20)^2 \cong 12.05\,\mu\text{J}$

$w_1(0) = (1/2)(1)(64) + (1/2)(5)(16) = 72\,\mu\text{J}$

$w_{\text{diss}} = 72 - 13.64 = 58.36\,\mu\text{J}$

$\%\ \text{dissipated} = (58.36/72)(100) = 81.05\,\%$

DE 7.5 [a] $i(0^+) = 24/2 = 12\,\text{A}$

[b] $v(0^+) = -10(8 + 12) = -200$ V

[c] $\tau = L/R = (200/10) \times 10^{-3} = 20$ ms

[d] $i = -8 + [12 - (-8)]e^{-50t} = [-8 + 20e^{-50t}]$ A, $\quad t \geq 0^+$

[e] $v = 0 + [-200 - 0]e^{-50t}$ V $= -200e^{-50t}$ V, $\quad t \geq 0^+$

DE 7.6 [a]

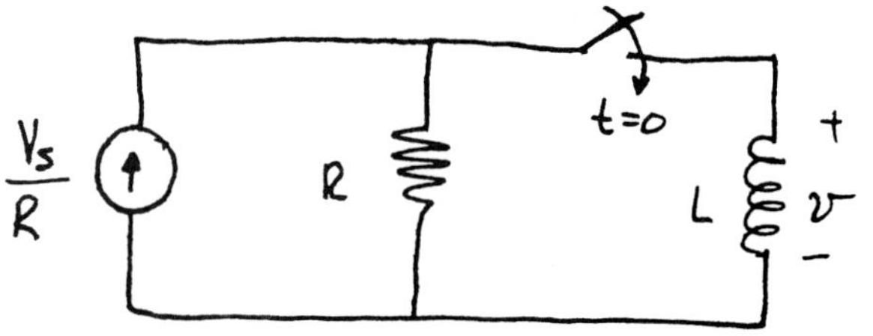

$$\frac{v}{R} + \frac{1}{L}\int_0^t v\,dx = \frac{V_s}{R}$$

$$\frac{1}{R}\frac{dv}{dt} + \frac{v}{L} = 0$$

$$\frac{dv}{dt} + \frac{R}{L}v = 0$$

[b]
$$\frac{dv}{dt} = -\frac{R}{L}v$$

$$\frac{dv}{dt}dt = -\frac{R}{L}v\,dt$$

$$\therefore \quad \frac{dv}{v} = -\frac{R}{L}dt$$

$$\int_{v(0^+)}^{v(t)} \frac{dy}{y} = -\frac{R}{L}\int_{0^+}^t dx$$

$$\ln y \Big|_{v(0^+)}^{v(t)} = -\left(\frac{R}{L}\right)t$$

$$\ln\left[\frac{v(t)}{v(0^+)}\right] = -\left(\frac{R}{L}\right)t$$

$$v(t) = v(0^+)e^{-(R/L)t}; \qquad v(0^+) = \left(\frac{V_s}{R} - I_o\right)R = V_s - I_oR$$

$$\therefore \quad v(t) = (V_s - I_oR)e^{-(R/L)t}$$

DE 7.7 [a]

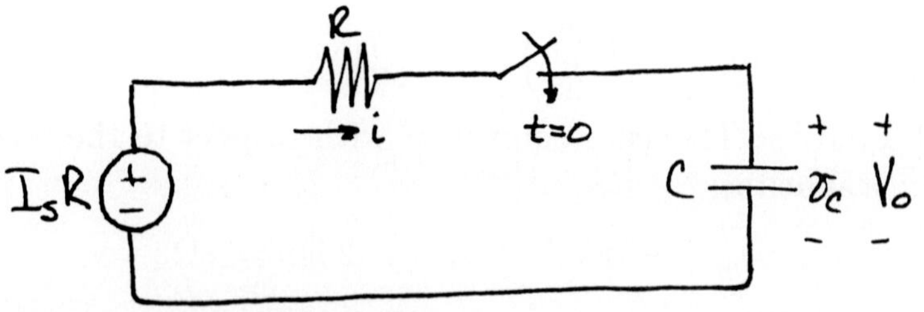

$$I_sR = Ri + \frac{1}{C}\int_{0^+}^{t} i\,dx + V_o$$

$$0 = R\frac{di}{dt} + \frac{i}{C} + 0$$

$$\therefore \quad \frac{di}{dt} + \frac{i}{RC} = 0$$

[b] $$\frac{di}{dt} = -\frac{i}{RC}; \qquad \frac{di}{i} = -\frac{dt}{RC}$$

$$\int_{i(0^+)}^{i(t)} \frac{dy}{y} = -\frac{1}{RC}\int_{0^+}^{t} dx$$

$$\ln\frac{i(t)}{i(0^+)} = \frac{-t}{RC}$$

$$i(t) = i(0^+)e^{-t/RC}; \qquad i(0^+) = \frac{I_sR - V_o}{R} = \left(I_s - \frac{V_o}{R}\right)$$

$$\therefore \quad i(t) = \left(I_s - \frac{V_o}{R}\right)e^{-t/RC}$$

DE 7.8 [a]

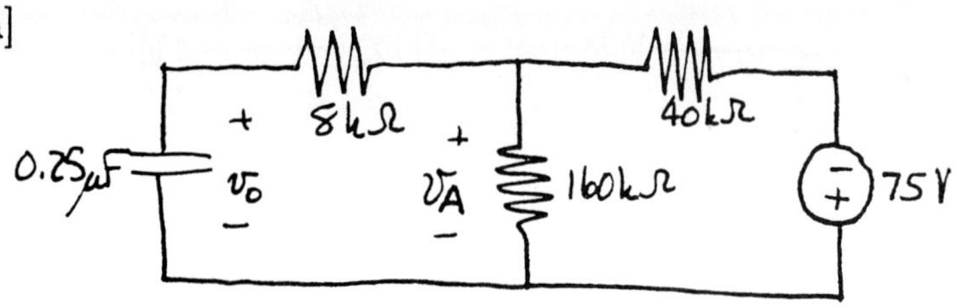

$$\frac{v_A - v_o}{8} + \frac{v_A}{160} + \frac{v_A + 75}{40} = 0$$

$$20v_A - 20v_o + v_A + 4v_A + 300 = 0$$

$$25v_A = 20v_o - 300$$

$$v_A = 0.8v_o - 12$$

$$v_A = -48 + 72e^{-100t} - 12 = -60 + 72e^{-100t}\ \text{V}, \qquad t \geq 0^+$$

[b] $t \geq 0^+$

DE 7.9 [a] $$v_c(0^+) = 50\ \text{V}$$

[b] $$v_c(\infty) = \left(-\frac{30}{25}\right)20 = -24\,\text{V}$$

[c] Find the Thévenin equivalent with respect to the terminals of the capacitor:

$$v_{\text{Th}} = -24\,\text{V}, \qquad R_{\text{Th}} = 20\|5 = 4\,\Omega,$$

Therefore $\tau = 4(0.025) = 0.1\,\mu\text{s}$

[d] $$i(0^+) = -\frac{50+24}{4} = -18.5\,\text{A}$$

[e] $$v_c = -24 + [50-(-24)]e^{-t/\tau} = -24 + 74e^{-10^7 t}\,\text{V}, \qquad t \geq 0^+$$

[f] $$i = -18.5e^{-t/\tau} = -18.5e^{-10^7 t}\,\text{A}, \qquad t \geq 0$$

DE 7.10 [a] $$v_c(0^+) = (9/12)(120) = 90\,\text{V}$$

[b] $$v_c(\infty) = -1.5(40) = -60\,\text{V}$$

[c] Find the Thévenin equivalent with respect to the terminals of the capacitor:

$$v_{\text{Th}} = -60\,\text{V}, \qquad R_{\text{Th}} = 50\,\text{k}\Omega$$

$$\tau = R_{\text{Th}}C = 1\,\text{ms}$$

[d] $$v_c = -60 + (90+60)e^{-1000t} = -60 + 150e^{-1000t}$$

Therefore $$t = \frac{\ln(150/60)}{1000} = 916.3\,\mu\text{s}$$

DE 7.11 [a] For $t < 0$, calculate the Thévenin equivalent for the circuit to the left and right of the 400-mH inductor. We get

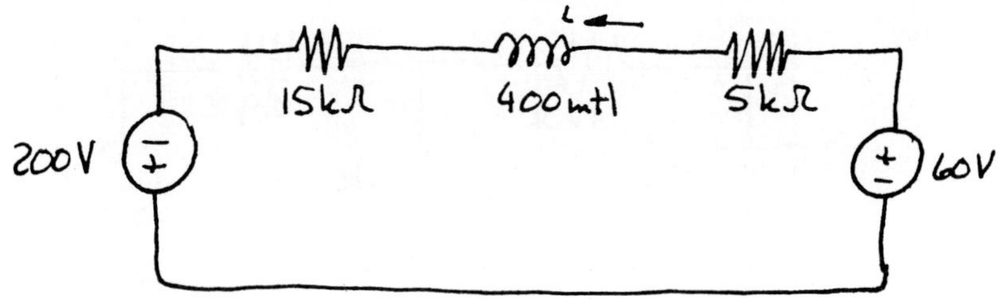

$$i(0^-) = 260/20 = 13\,\text{mA}$$

$$i(0^-) = i(0^+) = 13\,\text{mA}$$

[b] For $t > 0$, the circuit reduces to

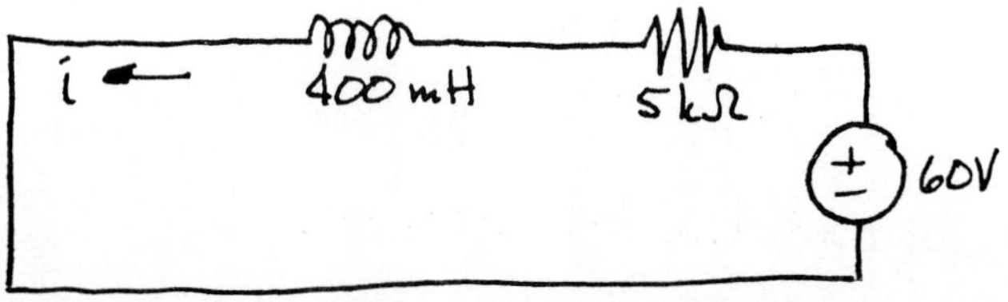

Therefore $i(\infty) = 60/5 = 12\,\text{mA}$

[c] $\tau = (400/5) \times 10^{-6} = 80\,\mu\text{s}$

[d] $i(t) = 12 + [13 - 12]e^{-12{,}500t} = 12 + e^{-12{,}500t}\ \text{mA}, \qquad t \geq 0$

DE 7.12 [a] $$L_{\text{eq}} = \frac{L_1L_2 - M^2}{L_1 + L_2 - 2M} = \frac{36 - 16}{20 - 8} = \frac{5}{3}\ \text{H}$$

$$\tau = \frac{L_{\text{eq}}}{R} = \frac{(5/3)}{(50/3)} = \frac{1}{10}$$

$$i_o = \frac{100}{(50/3)} - \frac{100}{(50/3)}e^{-10t} = 6 - 6e^{-10t}\ \text{A} \quad t \geq 0$$

[b] $$v_o = 100 - \frac{50}{3}(6 - 6e^{-10t}) = 100e^{-10t}\ \text{V} \quad t \geq 0^+$$

[c] $$v_o = 2\frac{di_1}{dt} + 4\frac{di_2}{dt}$$

$$i_o = i_1 + i_2$$

$$\frac{di_o}{dt} = \frac{di_1}{dt} + \frac{di_2}{dt}$$

$$\frac{di_2}{dt} = \frac{di_o}{dt} - \frac{di_1}{dt} = 60e^{-10t} - \frac{di_1}{dt}$$

$$\therefore\ 100e^{-10t} = 2\frac{di_1}{dt} + 4\left(60e^{-10t} - \frac{di_1}{dt}\right)$$

$$\therefore\ \frac{di_1}{dt} = 70e^{-10t}$$

$$di_1 = 70e^{-10t}\,dt$$

$$\int_0^{i_1} dx = 70\int_0^t e^{-10y}\,dy$$

$$\therefore\ i_1 = 70\frac{e^{-10y}}{-10}\Big|_0^t = 7 - 7e^{-10t}\ \text{A}$$

[d] $$\begin{aligned} i_2 &= i_o - i_1 \\ &= 6 - 6e^{-10t} - 7 + 7e^{-10t} \\ &= -1 + e^{-10t}\ \text{A} \end{aligned}$$

[e] $$\begin{aligned} v_o &= L_2\frac{di_2}{dt} + M\frac{di_1}{dt} \\ &= 18(-10e^{-10t}) + 4(70e^{-10t}) \\ &= 100e^{-10t}\ \text{V}, \quad t \geq 0 \qquad \text{(checks)} \end{aligned}$$

Also,

$$v_o = L_1\frac{di_1}{dt} + M\frac{di_2}{dt}$$

$$= 2(70e^{-10t}) + 4(-10e^{-10t})$$

$$= 100e^{-10t}\,\text{V}, \quad t \geq 0 \text{ CHECKS}$$

$i_1(0) = 7 - 7 = 0$; agrees with initial conditions;
$i_2(0) = -1 + 1 = 0$; agrees with initial conditions;
The final values of i_o, i_1, and i_2 can be checked via the conservation of Wb-turns:

$$i_o(\infty)L_{eq} = 6 \times (5/3) = 10 \text{ Wb-turns}$$

$$i_1(\infty)L_1 + i_2(\infty)M = 7(2) - 1(4) = 10 \text{ Wb-turns}$$

$$i_2(\infty)L_2 + i_1(\infty)M = -1(18) + 7(4) = 10 \text{ Wb-turns}$$

Thus our solutions make sense in terms of known circuit behavior.

DE 7.13 [a] For $t < 0$:

$$i = \left(\frac{40}{125}\right)10 = 3.2\,\text{mA}$$

$$v_c(0^-) = (3.2)(25) = 80\,\text{V}$$

$$v_c(0^+) = 80\,\text{V}$$

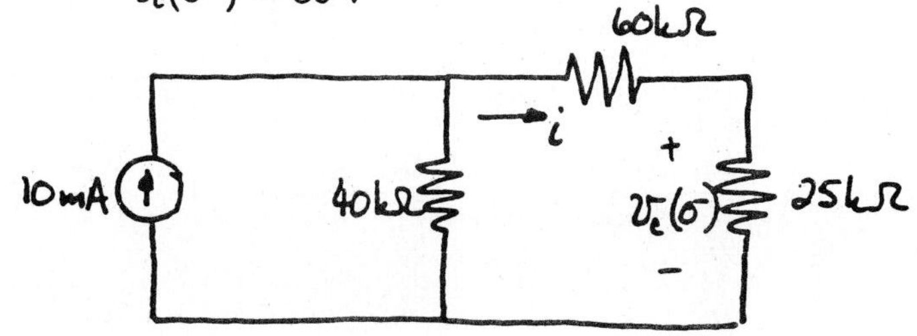

For $0 \leq t \leq 100\,\text{ms}$:

$$\tau = (25)(1)10^{-3} = 25\,\text{ms}; \qquad 1/\tau = 40$$

$$v_c = 80e^{-40t}\,\text{V}$$

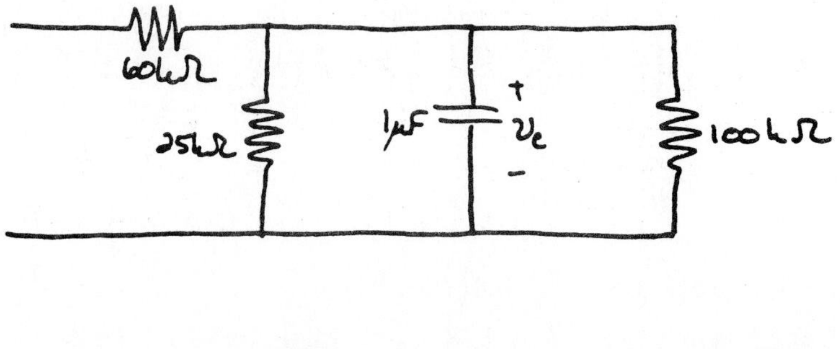

[b] $v_c(0.01) = 80e^{-0.4} = 53.63\text{ V}$

For $t \geq 10\text{ ms}$:

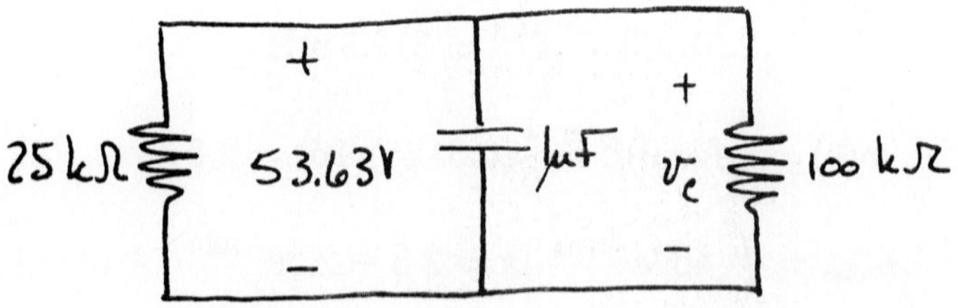

$$R_{eq} = \frac{25(100)}{125} = 20\text{ k}\Omega$$

$$\tau = (20)(1)10^{-3} = 0.02\text{ s}; \qquad \frac{1}{\tau} = 50$$

Therefore $v_c = 53.63e^{-50(t-0.01)}\text{ V}, \qquad t \geq 0.01\text{ s}$

[c] $$w_{25\text{k}} = \int_0^{0.01} \frac{[80e^{-40t}]^2}{25{,}000}dt + \int_{0.01}^{\infty} \frac{[53.63e^{-50(t-0.01)}]^2}{25{,}000}dt = 2.91\text{ mJ}$$

[d] $$w_{100\text{k}\Omega} = \int_{0.01}^{\infty} \frac{[53.63e^{-50(t-0.01)}]^2}{100{,}000}dt = 0.29\text{ mJ}$$

Check: $w_{\text{stored}} = (1/2)(1 \times 10^{-6})(80)^2 = 3.2\text{ mJ}$

$$w_{\text{diss}} = 2.91 + 0.29 = 3.2\text{ mJ}$$

DE 7.14 [a] At the instant A is closed, $i(0^+) = 0$. For $0 \leq t \leq 1\text{ s}$, the Thévenin equivalent with respect to the terminals of the 2 H inductor is $v_{\text{Th}} = 3\text{ V}, R_{\text{Th}} = 1\,\Omega$; therefore in this interval $i(0^+) = 0$ and $i(\infty) = 3\text{ A}$, also $\tau = 2/1 = 2\text{ s}$. Thus $i = 3 - 3e^{-0.5t}\text{ A}$, $0^+ \leq t \leq 1$, and $i(1) = 3 - 3e^{-0.5} = 1.18\text{ A}$.

[b] When $t > 1\text{ s}$, the Thévenin equivalent with respect to the 2 H inductor is $v_{\text{Th}} = -12\text{ V}$, $R_{\text{Th}} = 2.5\,\Omega$. Therefore $i(\infty) = -12/2.5 = -4.8\text{ A}$ and $\tau = 2/2.5 = 0.8$, thus
$i = -4.8 + (1.18 + 4.8)e^{-1.25(t-1)}$
$= -4.8 + 5.98e^{-1.25(t-1)}\text{ A}, \quad 1 \leq t \leq \infty.$

Problems

P 7.1 [a] $$\frac{v}{i} = R = \frac{100e^{-80t}}{4e^{-80t}} = 25\,\Omega$$

[b] $$\tau = \frac{1}{80} = 12.5\,\text{ms}$$

[c] $$\tau = \frac{L}{R} = 12.5 \times 10^{-3}$$

$$L = (12.5)(25) \times 10^{-3} = 312.5\,\text{mH}$$

[d] $$w(0) = \frac{1}{2}L[i(0)]^2 = \frac{1}{2}(0.3125)(16) = 2.5\,\text{J}$$

[e] $$w_{\text{diss}} = \int_0^t 400e^{-160x}\,dx = 2.5 - 2.5e^{-160t}$$

$$0.8w(0) = (0.8)(2.5) = 2\,\text{J}$$

$$2.5 - 2.5e^{-160t} = 2 \qquad \therefore \quad e^{160t} = 5$$

Solving, $t = 10.06$ ms.

P 7.2 [a] $t < 0$:

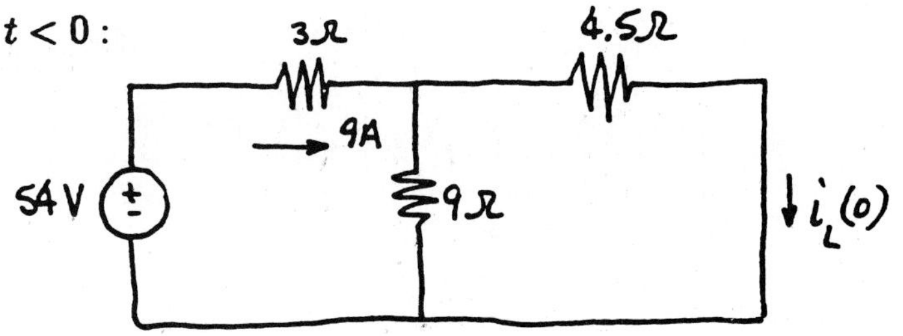

$$\frac{(9)(4.5)}{13.5} = 3\,\Omega; \qquad i_L(0) = 9\frac{9}{13.5} = 6\,\text{A}$$

$t > 0$:

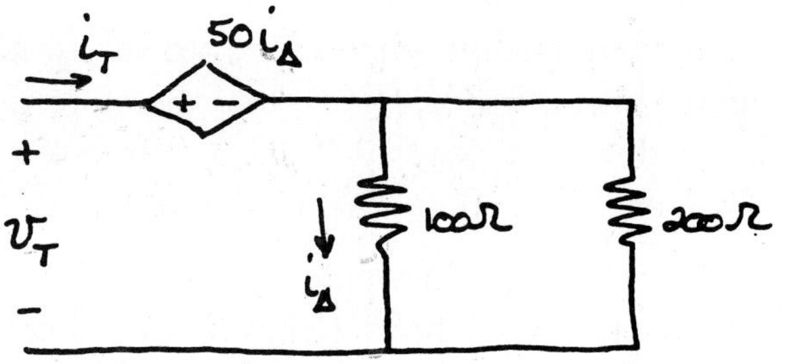

$$i_\Delta = \frac{i_T(200)}{300} = \frac{2}{3}i_T$$

$$v_T = 50i_\Delta + i_T\frac{(100)(200)}{300} = 50i_T\frac{2}{3} + \frac{200}{3}i_T$$

$$\frac{v_T}{i_T} = R_{\text{Th}} = \frac{100}{3} + \frac{200}{3} = 100\,\Omega$$

$$\tau = \frac{L}{R} = \frac{200}{100} \times 10^{-3} \qquad \frac{1}{\tau} = 500$$

$$i_L = 6e^{-500t}\,\text{A}, \qquad t \geq 0$$

[b] $$v_L = 200 \times 10^{-3}(-3000e^{-500t}) = -600e^{-500t}\,\text{V}, \quad t \geq 0^+$$

[c]

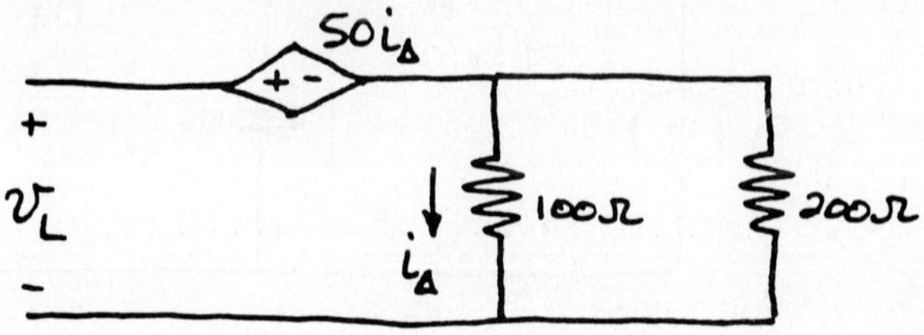

$$v_L = 50i_\Delta + 100i_\Delta = 150i_\Delta$$

$$i_\Delta = \frac{v_L}{150} = -4e^{-500t}\,\text{A} \qquad t \geq 0^+$$

P 7.3 $$w(0) = \frac{1}{2}(200 \times 10^{-3})(36) = 3.6\,\text{J}$$

$$p_{50i_\Delta} = -50i_\Delta i_L = -50(-4e^{-500t})(6e^{-500t}) = 1200e^{-1000t}$$

$$w_{50i_\Delta} = \int_0^\infty 1200e^{-1000t}\,dt = 1200\frac{e^{-1000t}}{-1000}\Big|_0^\infty = 1.2\,\text{J}$$

$$\%\ \text{dissipated} = \frac{1.2}{3.6}(100) = 33.33\%$$

P 7.4 [a] $$i(0) = 125/25 = 5\,\text{A}$$

[b] $$\tau = \frac{L}{R} = \frac{4}{100} = 40\,\text{ms}$$

[c] $$i = 5e^{-25t}\,\text{A}, \qquad t \geq 0$$

$$v_1 = L\frac{di_1}{dt} = 4(-125e^{-25t}) = -500e^{-25t}\,\text{V} \qquad t \geq 0^+$$

$$v_2 = -80i = -400e^{-25t}\,\text{V} \qquad t \geq 0$$

[d] $$p_{\text{diss}} = i^2(20) = 25e^{-50t}(20) = 500e^{-50t}\,\text{W}$$

$$w_{\text{diss}} = \int_0^t 500e^{-50x}\,dx = 500\frac{e^{-50x}}{-50}\Big|_0^t = 10 - 10e^{-50t}\,\text{J}$$

$$w_{\text{diss}}(12\,\text{ms}) = 10 - 10e^{-0.6} = 4.51\,\text{J}$$

$$w(0) = \frac{1}{2}(4)(25) = 50\,\text{J}$$

$$\%\ \text{dissipated} = \frac{4.51}{50}(100) = 9.02\%$$

P 7.5 [a] $t < 0$

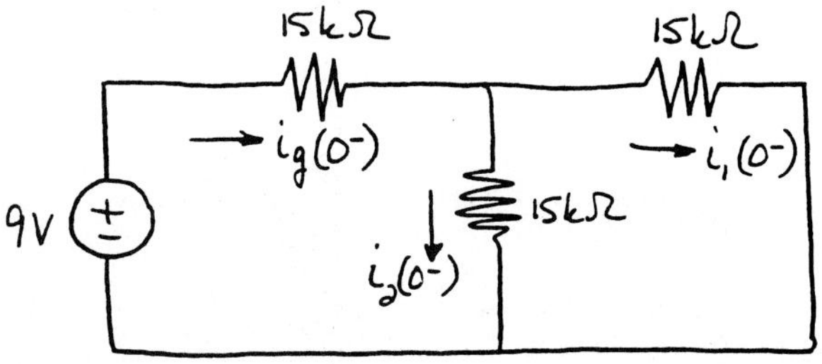

$$15\,\text{k}\Omega \| 15\,\text{k}\Omega = 7.5k\Omega$$

$$i_g(0^-) = \frac{9}{(15 + 7.5)} = 0.4\,\text{mA}$$

$$i_1(0^-) = i_2(0^-) = (0.4)\frac{(15)}{(30)} = 0.2\,\text{mA}$$

[b] $$i_1(0^+) = i_1(0^-) = 0.2\,\text{mA}$$

$$i_2(0^+) = -i_1(0^+) = -0.2\,\text{mA} \qquad \text{(when switch is open)}$$

[c] $$\tau = \frac{L}{R} = \frac{30 \times 10^{-3}}{30 \times 10^3} = 10^{-6}; \qquad \frac{1}{\tau} = 10^6$$

$$i_1(t) = i_1(0^+)e^{-t/\tau}$$

$$i_1(t) = 0.2e^{-10^6 t}\,\text{mA}, \qquad t \geq 0$$

[d] $$i_2(t) = -i_1(t) \qquad \text{when} \quad t \geq 0^+$$

$$\therefore\ i_2(t) = -0.2e^{-10^6 t}\,\text{mA}, \qquad t \geq 0^+$$

[e] The current in a resistor can change instantaneously. The switching operation forces $i_2(0^-)$ to equal 0.2 mA and $i_2(0^+) = -0.2$ mA.

P 7.6 [a] For $t < 0$

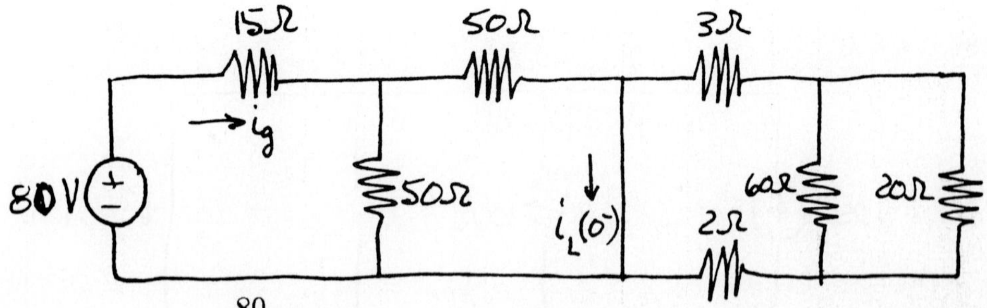

$$i_g = \frac{80}{40} = 2\,\text{A}$$

$$i_L(0^-) = \frac{2(50)}{(100)} = 1\,\text{A} = i_L(0^+)$$

For $t > 0$

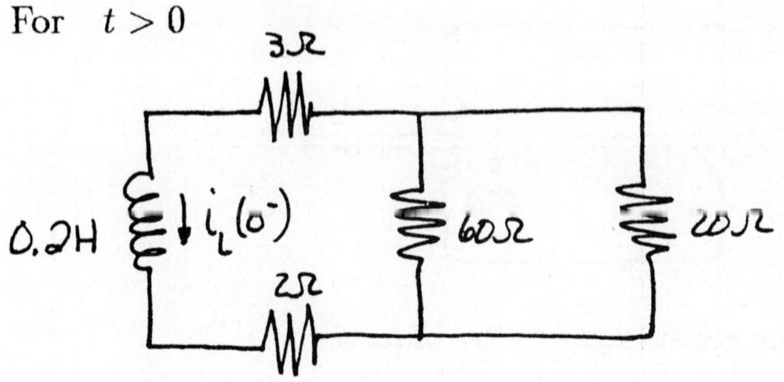

$$i_L(t) = i_L(0^+)e^{-t/\tau}\,\text{A}, \qquad t \geq 0$$

$$\tau = \frac{L}{R} = \frac{0.20}{5+15} = \frac{1}{100} = 0.01\,\text{s}$$

$$i_L(0^+) = 1\,\text{A}$$

$$i_L(t) = e^{-100t}\,\text{A}, \qquad t \geq 0$$

$$v_o(t) = -15i_L(t)$$

$$v_o(t) = -15e^{-100t}\,\text{V}, \qquad t \geq 0^+$$

P 7.7

$$P_{20\Omega} = \frac{v_o^2}{20} = 11.25e^{-200t}\text{W}$$

$$\begin{aligned} w_{\text{diss}} &= \int_0^{0.01} 11.25e^{-200t}\,dt \\ &= \frac{11.25}{-200}e^{-200t}\Big|_0^{0.01} \\ &= 56.25(1 - e^{-2}) = 48.64\,\text{mJ} \end{aligned}$$

$$w_{\text{stored}} = \frac{1}{2}(0.2)(1)^2 = 100\,\text{mJ}.$$

$$\% \text{ diss} = \frac{48.64}{100} \times 100 = 48.64\%$$

P 7.8 $t < 0$

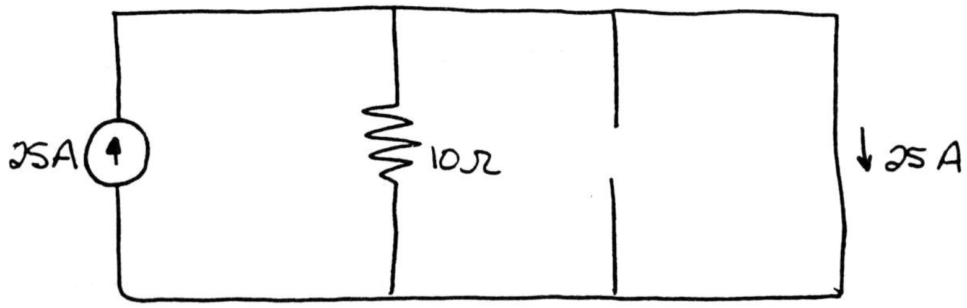

$i_L(0^-) = i_L(0^+) = 25\,\text{A}$

$t > 0$

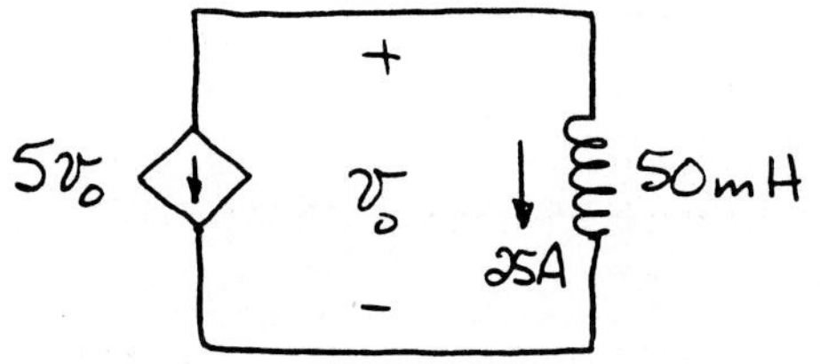

Find Thévenin resistance seen by inductor

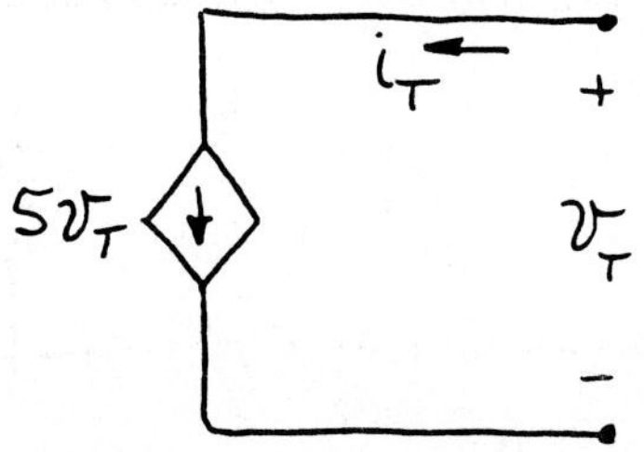

$i_T = 5v_T$; $\quad \frac{v_T}{i_T} = R_{\text{Th}} = \frac{1}{5} = 0.2\,\Omega$

$$\tau = \frac{L}{R} = \frac{50 \times 10^{-3}}{0.2} = 250\,\text{ms}; \qquad 1/\tau = 4$$

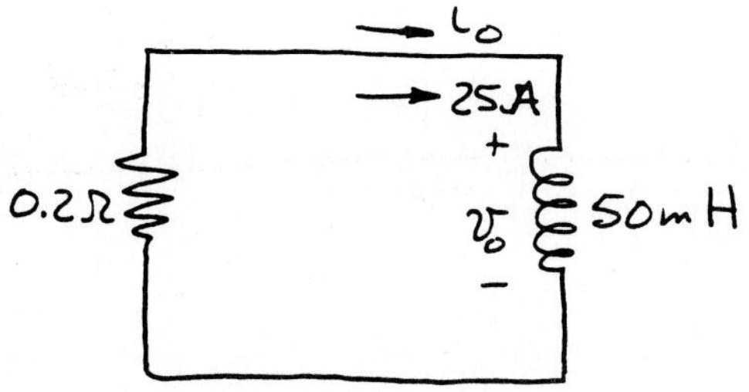

$i_o = 25e^{-4t}\,\text{A}, \qquad t \geq 0$

$$v_o = L\frac{di_o}{dt} = (50 \times 10^{-3})(-100e^{-4t}) = -5e^{-4t}\,\text{V}, \quad t \geq 0^+$$

P 7.9 [a] $t < 0$:

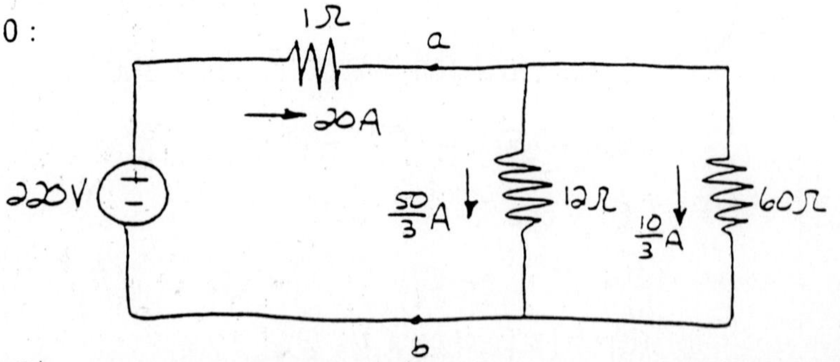

$t = 0^+$:

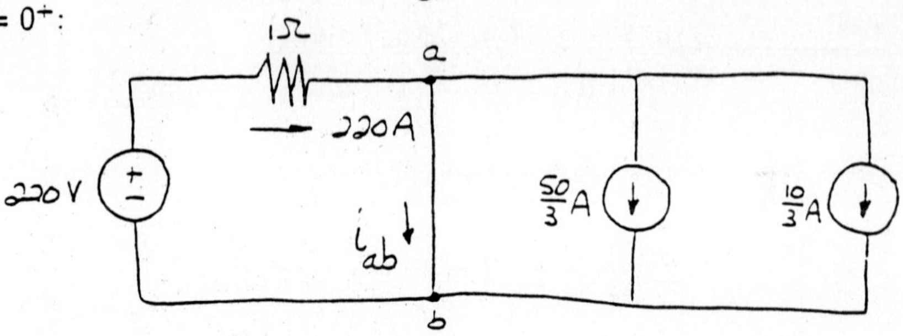

$$220 = i_{ab} + (50/3) + (10/3), \qquad i_{ab} = 200\text{ A}, \quad t = 0^+$$

[b] At $t = \infty$:

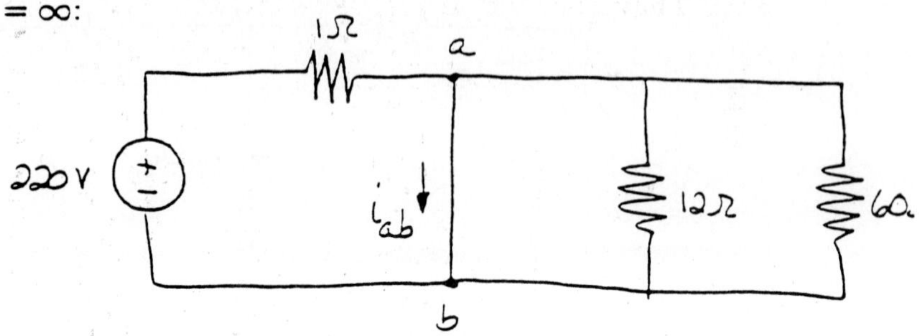

$$i_{ab} = 220/1 = 220\text{ A}, \quad t = \infty$$

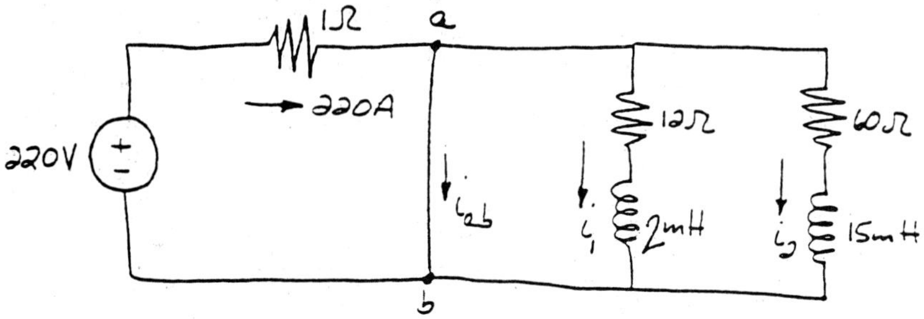

[c] $i_1(0) = 50/3, \qquad \tau_1 = \frac{2}{12} \times 10^{-3} = .167\,\text{ms}$

$i_2(0) = 10/3, \qquad \tau_2 = \frac{15}{60} \times 10^{-3} = 0.25\,\text{ms}$

$i_1(t) = (50/3)e^{-6000t}$ A, $t \geq 0$

$i_2(t) = (10/3)e^{-4000t}$ A, $t \geq 0$

$i_{ab} = 220 - (50/3)e^{-6000t} - (10/3)e^{-4000t}$ A, $t \geq 0$

$220 - (50/3)e^{-6000t} - (10/3)e^{-4000t} = 210$

$30 = 50e^{-6000t} + 10e^{-4000t}$

$5e^{-6000t} + e^{-4000t} = 3$

By trial and error

$t = 123.1$ μs

P 7.10 [a] $i_o(0^-) = 0$ since the switch is open for $t < 0$.

[b] For $t = 0^-$ the circuit is:

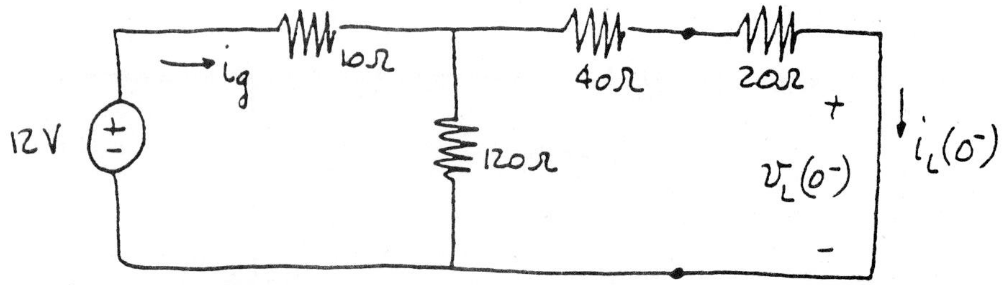

$120\,\Omega // 60\,\Omega = 40\,\Omega$

$\therefore\quad i_g = \frac{12}{10 + 40} = 0.24\text{ A} = 240\text{ mA}$

$i_L(0^-) = \left(\frac{120}{180}\right) i_g = 160\text{ mA}$

[c] For $t = 0^+$ the circuit is:

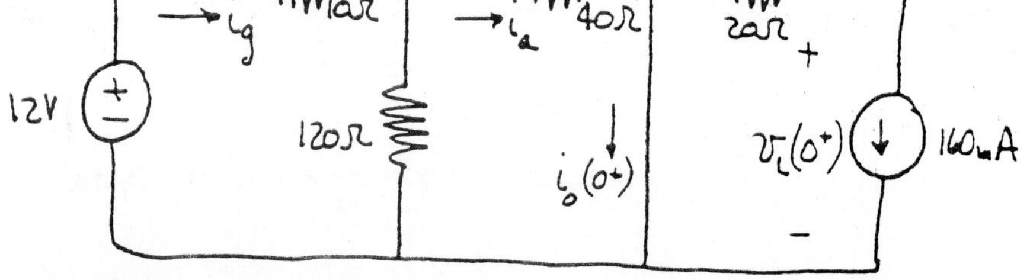

$120\,\Omega // 40\,\Omega = 30\,\Omega$

$$\therefore \quad i_g = \frac{12}{10+30} = 0.30\,\text{A} = 300\,\text{mA}$$

$$i_a = \left(\frac{120}{160}\right) 300 = 225\,\text{mA}$$

$$\therefore \quad i_o(0^+) = 225 - 160 = 65\,\text{mA}$$

[d] $i_L(0^+) = i_L(0^-) = 160\,\text{mA}$

[e] $i_o(\infty) = i_a = 225\,\text{mA}$

[f] $i_L(\infty) = 0,$ since the switch short circuits the branch containing the 20 Ω resistor and the 100 mH inductor.

[g] $$\tau = \frac{L}{R} = \frac{100 \times 10^{-3}}{20} = 5\,\text{ms}; \qquad \frac{1}{\tau} = 200$$

$$\therefore \quad i_L = 0 + (160 - 0)e^{-200t} = 160e^{-200t}\,\text{mA}, \qquad t \geq 0$$

[h] $v_L(0^-) = 0$ since for $t < 0$ the current in the inductor is constant

[i] Refer to the circuit at $t = 0^+$ and note:

$$20(0.16) + v_L(0^+) = 0; \qquad \therefore \quad v_L(0^+) = -3.2\,\text{V}$$

[j] $v_L(\infty) = 0,$ since the current in the inductor is a constant at $t = \infty$.

[k] $$v_L(t) = 0 + (-3.2 - 0)e^{-200t} = -3.2e^{-200t}\,\text{V}, \qquad t \geq 0^+$$

[l] $$i_o = i_a - i_L = 225 - 160e^{-200t}\,\text{mA}, \qquad t \geq 0^+$$

P 7.11 [a] $t < 0$:

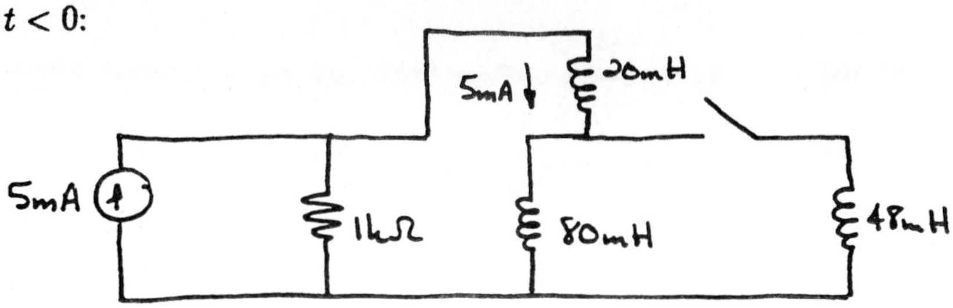

$t = 0^+$:

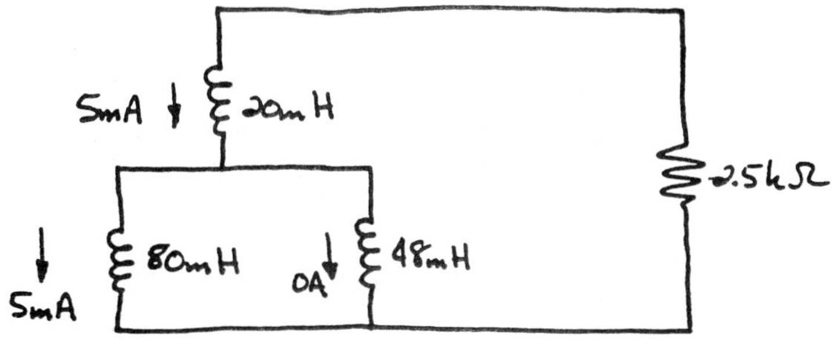

$t > 0$:

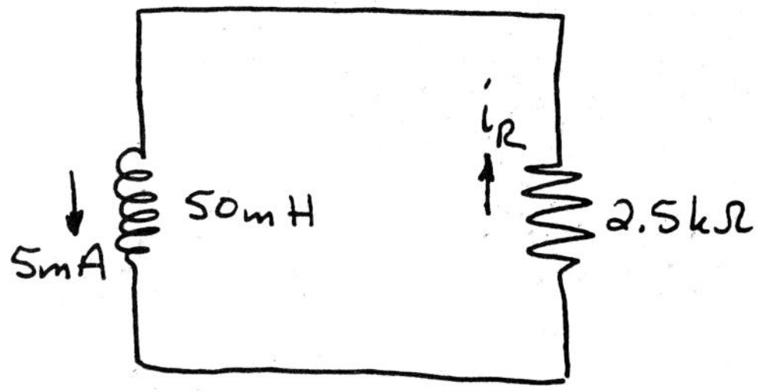

$$i_R = 5e^{t/\tau}\,\text{mA}; \qquad \tau = \frac{L}{R} = 20 \times 10^{-6}$$

$$i_R = 5e^{-50{,}000t}\,\text{mA}$$

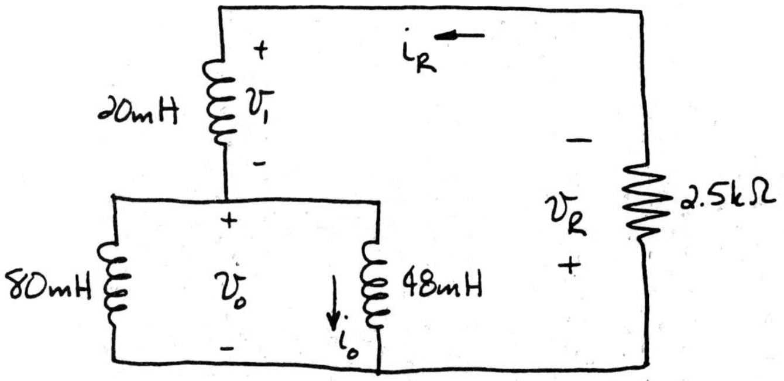

$$v_R = (2.5 \times 10^3)(5 \times 10^{-3})e^{-50{,}000t} = 12.5e^{-50{,}000t}\,\text{V}$$

$$v_1 = 20 \times 10^{-3}[5 \times 10^{-3}(-50{,}000)e^{-50{,}000t}] = -5e^{-50{,}000t}\,\text{V}$$

$$v_o = -v_1 - v_R = -7.5e^{-50{,}000t}\,\text{V}$$

[b] $$i_o = \frac{10^3}{48}\int_0^t -7.5e^{-50{,}000x}\,dx + 0 = 3.125e^{-50{,}000t} - 3.125\,\text{mA}$$

P 7.12 [a] From the solution to Problem 7.11,

$$i_R = 5 \times 10^{-3}e^{-50{,}000t}\,\text{A}$$

$$p_R = (25 \times 10^{-6}e^{-100{,}000t})(2.5 \times 10^3) = 62.5 \times 10^{-3}e^{-100{,}000t}\,\text{W}$$

$$w_{\text{diss}} = \int_0^\infty 62.5 \times 10^{-3}e^{-100{,}000t}\,dt$$

$$= 62.5 \times 10^{-3}\frac{e^{-100{,}000t}}{-10^5}\Bigg|_0^\infty = 625\,\text{nJ}$$

[b] $$w_{\text{trapped}} = \frac{1}{2}L_{\text{eq}}i_R^2(0) = \frac{1}{2}(50 \times 10^{-3})(5 \times 10^{-3})^2 = 625\,\text{nJ}$$

CHECK:

$$w(0) = \tfrac{1}{2}(20)(25\times10^{-6})\times10^{-3} + \tfrac{1}{2}(80)(25\times10^{-6})\times10^{-3} = 1250\,\text{nJ}$$

$$\therefore\; w(0) = w_{\text{diss}} + w_{\text{trapped}}$$

P 7.13 [a] $$i_L(0) = \frac{80}{40} = 2\,\text{A}$$

$$i_o(0^+) = \frac{80}{20} - 2 = 4 - 2 = 2\,\text{A}$$

$$i_o(\infty) = \frac{80}{20} = 4\,\text{A}$$

[b] $$i_L = 2e^{-t/\tau}; \qquad \tau = \frac{L}{R} = \frac{20}{20} \times 10^{-3} = 1\,\text{ms}$$

$$i_L = 2e^{-1000t}\,\text{A}$$

$$i_o = 4 - i_L = 4 - 2e^{-1000t}\,\text{A}, \qquad t \geq 0^+$$

[c] $$4 - 2e^{-1000t} = 3.8$$

$$0.2 = 2e^{-1000t}$$

$$e^{1000t} = 10 \qquad \therefore\; t = 2.30\,\text{ms}$$

P 7.14 [a] $t < 0$

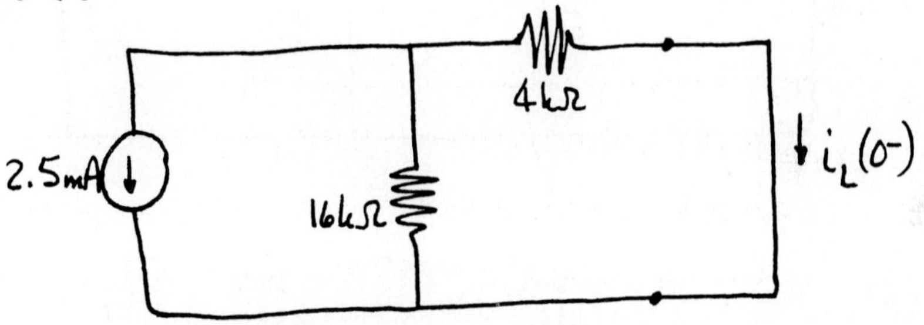

$$i_L(0^-) = \frac{-2.5(16)}{(20)} = -2\,\text{mA}$$

$t \geq 0$

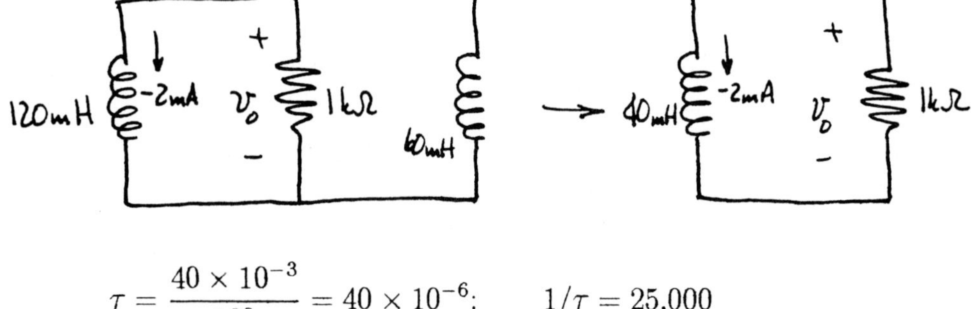

$$\tau = \frac{40 \times 10^{-3}}{10^3} = 40 \times 10^{-6}; \qquad 1/\tau = 25{,}000$$

$$v_o = -1000(-2 \times 10^{-3})e^{-25{,}000t} = 2e^{-25{,}000t}\,\text{V}, \qquad t \geq 0^+$$

[b] $$w_{\text{del}} = \frac{1}{2}(40 \times 10^{-3})(4 \times 10^{-6}) = 80\,\text{nJ}$$

[c] $0.95w_{\text{del}} = 76\,\text{nJ}$

$$\therefore\quad 76\times10^{-9} = \int_0^{t_o}\frac{4e^{-50{,}000t}}{1000}\,dt$$

$$\therefore\quad 76\times10^{-9} = 80\times10^{-9}e^{-500{,}000t}\Big|_0^{t_o} = 80\times10^{-9}(1-e^{-50{,}000t_o})$$

$$\therefore\quad e^{-50{,}000t_o} = 0.05$$

$$50{,}000t_o = \ln 20 \quad \text{so} \quad t_o = 59.9\,\mu\text{s}$$

$$\tau = \frac{L_e}{R} = \frac{40\times10^{-3}}{10^3} = 40\,\mu\text{s}$$

$$\therefore\quad \frac{t_o}{\tau} = \frac{59.9}{40} = 1.498 \quad \text{so} \quad t_o \approx 1.5\tau$$

P 7.15 $t < 0$:

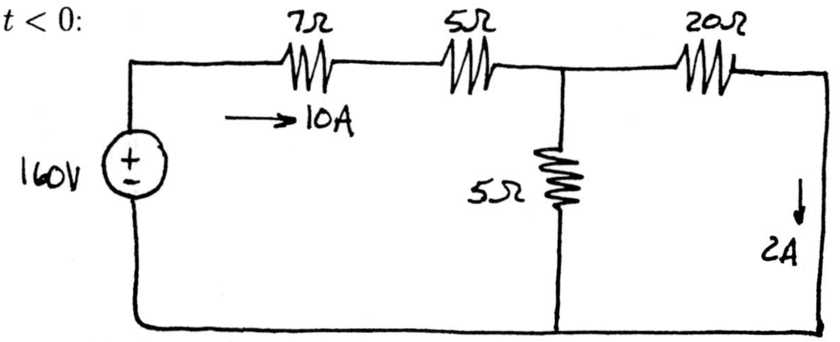

$$i_L(0^+) = 2\,\text{A}$$

$t > 0$:

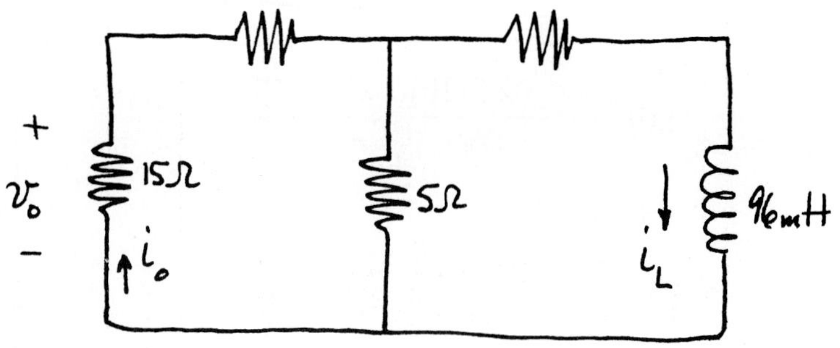

$$R_e = \frac{(20)(5)}{25} + 20 = 24\,\Omega$$

$$\tau = \frac{L}{R_e} = \frac{96}{24}\times10^{-3} = 4\,\text{ms}; \qquad \frac{1}{\tau} = 250$$

$$\therefore\quad i_L = 2e^{-250t}\,\text{A}$$

$$\therefore\quad i_o = \frac{5}{25}i_L = 0.4e^{-250t}\,\text{A}$$

$$v_o = -15i_o = -6e^{-250t}\,\text{V}$$

P 7.16 $$p_{20\Omega} = 20i_L^2 = 20(4)(e^{-250t})^2 = 80e^{-500t}\,\text{W}$$

$$w_{20\Omega} = \int_0^\infty 80e^{-500t}\,dt = 80\frac{e^{-500t}}{-500}\Big|_0^\infty = 160\,\text{mJ}$$

$$w(0) = \frac{1}{2}(96)(10^{-3})(4) = 192\,\text{mJ}$$

$$\%\ \text{diss} = \frac{160}{192}(100) = 83.33\%$$

P 7.17 $$w(0) = \frac{1}{2}(20\times 10^{-3})(10^2) = 1\,\text{J}$$

$$0.5w(0) = 0.5\,\text{J}$$

$$i_R = 10e^{-t/\tau}$$

$$p_{\text{diss}} = i_R^2 R = 100Re^{-2t/\tau}$$

$$w_{\text{diss}} = \int_0^t R(100)e^{-2x/\tau}\,dx$$

$$w_{\text{diss}} = 100R\frac{e^{-2x/\tau}}{-2/\tau}\Big|_0^{t_o} = -50\tau R(e^{-2t_o/\tau} - 1) = 50L(1 - e^{-2t_o/\tau})$$

$$50L = (50)(20)\times 10^{-3} = 1; \qquad t_o = 10\,\mu\text{s}$$

$$1 - e^{-2t_o/\tau} = 0.5$$

$$e^{2t_o/\tau} = 2; \qquad \frac{2t_o}{\tau} = \frac{2t_oR}{L} = \ln 2$$

$$R = \frac{L\ln 2}{2t_o} = \frac{20\times 10^{-3}\ln 2}{20\times 10^{-6}} = 693.15\,\Omega$$

P 7.18 [a] $$w(0) = \frac{1}{2}LI_g^2$$

$$\begin{aligned} w_{\text{diss}} &= \int_0^{t_o} I_g^2Re^{-2t/\tau}\,dt = I_g^2R\frac{e^{-2t/\tau}}{(-2/\tau)}\Big|_0^{t_o} \\ &= \frac{1}{2}I_g^2R\tau(1 - e^{-2t_o/\tau}) = \frac{1}{2}I_g^2L(1 - e^{-2t_o/\tau}) \end{aligned}$$

$$w_{\text{diss}} = \sigma w(0)$$

$$\therefore\quad \frac{1}{2}LI_g^2(1 - e^{-2t_o/\tau}) = \tau\left(\frac{1}{2}LI_g^2\right)$$

$$1 - e^{-2t_o/\tau} = \sigma; \qquad e^{2t_o/\tau} = \frac{1}{(1-\sigma)}$$

$$\frac{2t_o}{\tau} = \ln\left[\frac{1}{(1-\sigma)}\right]; \qquad \frac{R(2t_o)}{L} = \ln[1/(1-\sigma)]$$

$$R = \frac{L\ln[1/(1-\sigma)]}{2t_o}$$

[b] $$R = \frac{(20\times 10^{-3})\ln[1/0.5]}{20\times 10^{-6}}$$

$$R = 693.15\,\Omega$$

P 7.19 [a] $$v_o(t) = v_o(0^+)e^{-t/\tau}$$

$$\therefore\quad v_o(0^+)e^{-5\times10^{-3}/\tau} = 0.25v_o(0^+)$$

$$\therefore\quad e^{5\times10^{-3}/\tau} = 4$$

$$\therefore\quad \tau = \frac{L}{R} = \frac{5\times 10^{-3}}{\ln 4}$$

$$\therefore\quad L = \frac{250\times 10^{-3}}{\ln 4} = 180.34\,\text{mH}$$

[b] $$i_L(0^-) = 60\left(\frac{1}{6}\right) = 10\,\text{mA} = i_L(0^+)$$

$$w_{\text{stored}} = \frac{1}{2}Li_L(0^+)^2 = \frac{1}{2}(R\tau)(100\times 10^{-6}) = 2500\tau\,\mu\text{J}.$$

$$i_L(t) = 10e^{-t/\tau}\,\text{mA}$$

$$p_{50\Omega} = i_L^2(50) = 5000\times 10^{-6}e^{-2t/\tau}$$

$$\begin{aligned} w_{\text{diss}} &= \int_0^{5\times10^{-3}} 5000\times 10^{-6}e^{-2t/\tau}\,dt \\ &= 5000\times 10^{-6}\frac{e^{-2t/\tau}}{(-2/\tau)}\Bigg|_0^{5\times10^{-3}} \\ &= 2500\times 10^{-6}\tau\left[1 - e^{\frac{-10\times10^{-3}}{\tau}}\right] \end{aligned}$$

$$e^{\frac{-10\times10^{-3}}{\tau}} = e^{-2\ln 4} = 0.0625$$

$$w_{\text{diss}} = 2500\times 10^{-6}\tau(0.9375)$$

$$\%\ \text{diss} = \frac{2500\times 10^{-6}\tau(0.9375)}{2500\times 10^{-6}\tau}\times 100$$

$$w_{\text{diss}} = 93.75\%$$

P 7.20 [a] $t < 0$

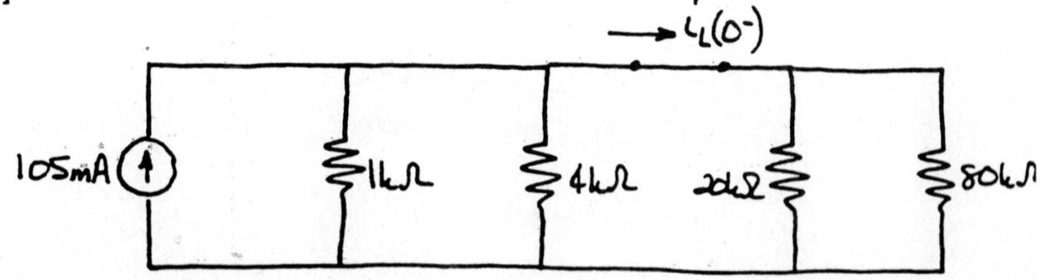

$$1\,\text{k}\Omega \| 4\,\text{k}\Omega = 0.8\,\text{k}\Omega$$

$$20\,\text{k}\Omega \| 80\,\text{k}\Omega = 16\,\text{k}\Omega$$

$$(105)(0.8) = 84\,\text{V}$$

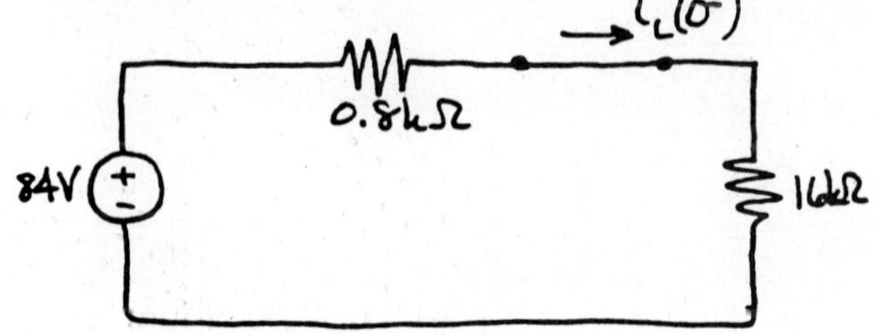

$$i_L(0^-) = \frac{84}{16.8} = 5\,\text{mA}$$

$t > 0$

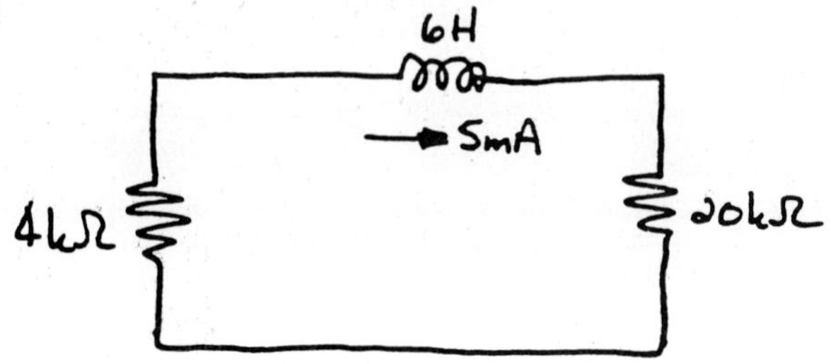

$$\tau = \frac{L}{R} = \frac{6}{24} \times 10^{-3} = 250\,\mu\text{s}; \qquad \frac{1}{\tau} = 4000$$

$$i_L(t) = 5e^{-4000t}\,\text{mA}, \qquad t \geq 0$$

$$p_{4k} = 25 \times 10^{-6} e^{-8000t}(4000) = 0.10e^{-8000t}\,\text{W}$$

$$w_{\text{diss}} = \int_0^t 0.10e^{-8000x}\,dx = 12.5 \times 10^{-6}[1 - e^{8000t}]\,\text{J}$$

$$w(0) = \frac{1}{2}(6)(25 \times 10^{-6}) = 75\,\mu\text{J}$$

$$0.10w(0) = 7.5\,\mu\text{J}$$

$12.5(1 - e^{-8000t}) = 7.5; \qquad \therefore\ e^{8000t} = 2.5$

$t = 125\ \ln 2.5 = 114.54\,\mu\text{s}$

[b] $w_{\text{diss}}(\text{total}) = 75(1 - e^{-8000t})\,\mu\text{J}$

$w_{\text{diss}}(114.54\,\mu\text{s}) = 45\,\mu\text{J}$

$\% = (45/75)(100) = 60\%$

P 7.21 [a] $R = \dfrac{v}{i} = 20\,\text{k}\Omega$

[b] $\dfrac{1}{\tau} = \dfrac{1}{RC} = 1000; \qquad C = \dfrac{1}{(10^3)(20\times 10^3)} = 0.05\,\mu\text{F}$

[c] $\tau = \dfrac{1}{1000} = 1\,\text{ms}$

[d] $w(0) = \dfrac{1}{2}(0.05\times 10^{-6})(10^4) = 250\,\mu\text{J}$

[e]

$$W_{\text{diss}} = \int_0^{t_o} \frac{v^2}{R}dt = \int_0^{t_o} \frac{(10^4)e^{-2000t}}{(20\times 10^3)}dt$$
$$= 0.5\frac{e^{-2000t}}{-2000}\Big|_0^{t_o} = 250(1 - e^{-2000t_o})\,\mu\text{J}$$

$200 = 250(1 - e^{-2000t_o})$

$\therefore\ e^{-2000t_o} = 0.2; \qquad e^{2000t_o} = 5$

$t_o = \dfrac{1}{2000}\ln 5; \qquad t_o \cong 804.72\,\mu\text{s}$

P 7.22 [a] $v_1(0^-) = v_1(0^+) = 75\,\text{V} \qquad v_2(0^+) = 0$

$C_{\text{eq}} = 2\times 8/10 = 1.6\,\mu\text{F}$

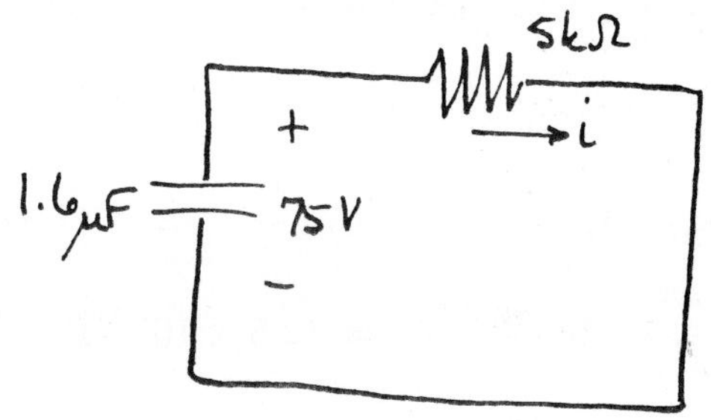

$\tau = (5)(1.6)\times 10^{-3} = 8\text{ms}; \qquad \dfrac{1}{\tau} = 125$

$i = \dfrac{75}{5}\times 10^{-3}e^{-125t} = 15e^{-125t}\,\text{mA}, \qquad t \geq 0^+$

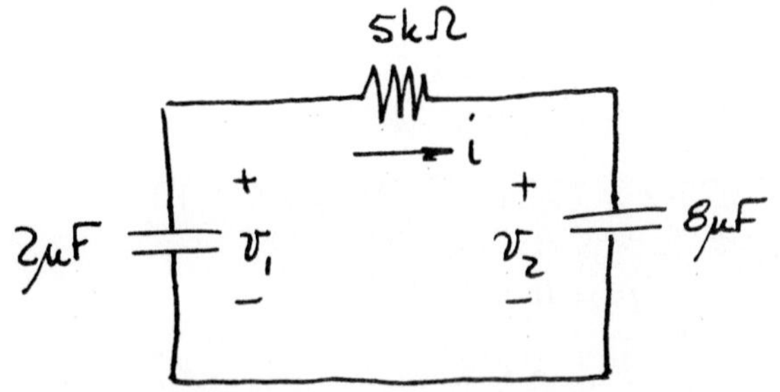

$$v_1 = \frac{-10^6}{2}\int_0^t 15\times 10^{-3}e^{-125x}\,dx + 75 = 60e^{-125t} + 15\,\text{V}, \qquad t\ge 0$$

$$v_2 = \frac{10^6}{8}\int_0^t 15\times 10^{-3}e^{-125x}\,dx + 0 = -15e^{-125t} + 15\,\text{V}, \qquad t\ge 0$$

[b] $w(0) = \frac{1}{2}(2\times 10^{-6})(5625) = 5625\,\mu\text{J}$

[c] $w_{\text{trapped}} = \frac{1}{2}(2\times 10^{-6})(225) + \frac{1}{2}(8\times 10^{-6})225 = 1125\,\mu\text{J}.$

$$w_{\text{diss}} = \frac{1}{2}(1.6\times 10^{-6})(5625) = 4500\,\mu\text{J}.$$

Check:

$w_{\text{trapped}} + w_{\text{diss}} = 1125 + 4500 = 5625\,\mu\text{J};\qquad w(0) = 5625\,\mu\text{J}.$

P 7.23 [a] The equivalent circuit for $t > 0$:

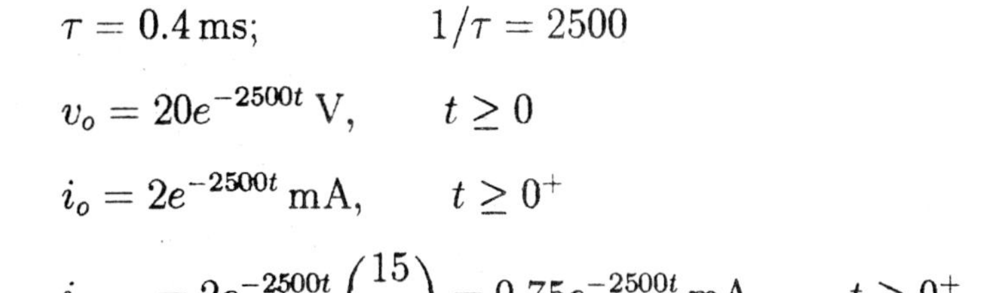

$\tau = 0.4\,\text{ms};\qquad 1/\tau = 2500$

$v_o = 20e^{-2500t}\,\text{V},\qquad t\ge 0$

$i_o = 2e^{-2500t}\,\text{mA},\qquad t\ge 0^+$

$$i_{25k\Omega} = 2e^{-2500t}\left(\frac{15}{40}\right) = 0.75e^{-2500t}\,\text{mA},\qquad t\ge 0^+$$

$$p_{25k\Omega} = (0.5625\times 10^{-6}e^{-5000t})(25{,}000) = 14{,}062.5\times 10^{-6}e^{-5000t}\,\text{W}$$

$$w_{25k\Omega} = \int_0^\infty 14{,}062.5\times 10^{-6}e^{-5000t}\,dt = -2.8125\times 10^{-6}(0-1) = 2.8125\,\mu\text{J}$$

$$w(0) = \frac{1}{2}(0.2\times 10^{-6})(100) + \frac{1}{2}(0.05\times 10^{-6})(900) = 32.5\,\mu\text{J}$$

$$\% \text{ diss}\,(25\,\text{k}\Omega) = \frac{2.8125}{32.5} \times 100 = 8.65\%$$

[b] $$p_{625\Omega} = 625(2 \times 10^{-3}e^{-2500t})^2 = 2.5 \times 10^{-3}e^{-5000t}$$

$$w_{625\Omega} = \int_0^\infty p_{625}\,dt = 0.50\,\mu\text{J}$$

$$\% \text{ diss}\,(625\Omega) = \frac{0.5}{32.5} \times 100 = 1.54\%$$

$$i_{15k\Omega} = 2e^{-2500t}\left(\frac{25}{40}\right) = 1.25e^{-2500t}\,\text{mA}, \quad t \geq 0^+$$

$$p_{15k\Omega} = (1.25 \times 10^{-3}e^{-2500t})^2(15{,}000) = 23.4375 \times 10^{-3}e^{-5000t}\,\text{W}$$

$$w_{15k\Omega} = \int_0^\infty 23.4375 \times 10^{-3}e^{-5000t}\,dt = 4.6875\,\mu\text{J}$$

$$\% \text{ diss}\,(15\text{k}\Omega) = 14.42\%$$

[c] $$\sum w_{\text{diss}} = 2.8125 + 0.50 + 4.6875 = 8\,\mu\text{J}$$

$$w_{\text{trapped}} = w(0) - \sum w_{\text{diss}} = 32.5 - 8 = 24.5\,\mu\text{J}$$

$$\% \text{ trapped} = \frac{24.5}{32.5} \times 100 = 75.38\%$$

Check: $8.65 + 1.54 + 14.42 + 75.38 = 99.99 \approx 100\%$

P 7.24 [a] $$\frac{1}{C_e} = 1 + \frac{1}{4} = 1.25$$

$$\therefore \quad C_e = 0.8\,\mu\text{F}; \qquad v_o(0) = 60 - 10 = 50\,\text{V}$$

$$\tau = (0.8)(25) \times 10^{-3} = 20\,\text{ms}; \qquad \frac{1}{\tau} = 50$$

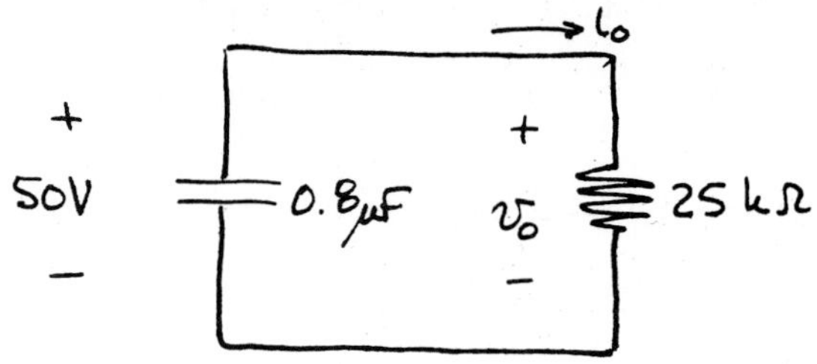

$$v_o = 50e^{-50t}\,\text{V}, \qquad t > 0^+$$

[b] $$w_o = \frac{1}{2}(1 \times 10^{-6})(3600) + \frac{1}{2}(4 \times 10^{-6})(100) = 2\,\text{mJ}$$

$$w_{\text{diss}} = \frac{1}{2}(0.8 \times 10^{-6})(2500) = 1\,\text{mJ}$$

$$\% \text{ diss} = \frac{1}{2} \times 100 = 50\%$$

[c] $$i_o = \frac{v_o}{25} \times 10^{-3} - 2e^{-50t}\ \text{mA}$$

$$v_1 = -\frac{10^6}{4}\int_0^t 2 \times 10^{-3} e^{-50x}\,dx - 10 = -500\int_0^t e^{-50x}\,dx - 10$$

$$= -500\frac{e^{-50x}}{-50}\bigg|_0^t - 10 = 10e^{-50t} - 20\ \text{V} \qquad t \geq 0$$

[d] $$v_1 + v_2 = v_o$$

$$v_2 = v_o - v_1 = 50e^{-50t} - 10e^{-50t} + 20 = 40e^{-50t} + 20\ \text{V} \quad t \geq 0$$

[e] $$w_{\text{trapped}} = \frac{1}{2}(4 \times 10^{-6})(400) + \frac{1}{2}(1 \times 10^{-6})(400) = 1\ \text{mJ}$$

$$w_{\text{diss}} + w_{\text{trapped}} = 2\ \text{mJ} \qquad \text{(check)}$$

P 7.25 [a] $$\tau = RC = R_{\text{Th}}(0.2) \times 10^{-6} = 10^{-3}; \qquad \therefore\ R_{\text{Th}} = \frac{1000}{0.2} = 5\,\text{k}\Omega$$

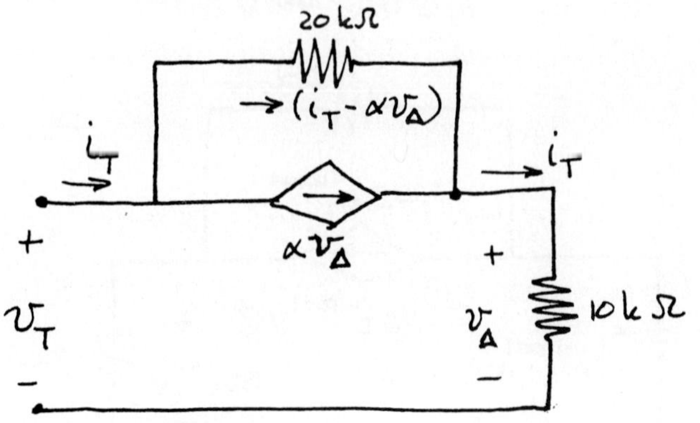

$$v_T = 20 \times 10^3(i_T - \alpha v_\Delta) + 10 \times 10^3 i_T$$

$$v_\Delta = 10 \times 10^3 i_T$$

$$v_T = 30 \times 10^3 i_T - 20 \times 10^3 \alpha 10 \times 10^3 i_T$$

$$\frac{v_T}{i_T} = 30 \times 10^3 - 200 \times 10^6 \alpha = 5 \times 10^3$$

$$\therefore\ 30 - 200{,}000\alpha = 5; \qquad \alpha = 125 \times 10^{-6}\ \text{A/V}$$

[b] $$v_o(0) = (18)(5) = 90\ \text{V} \qquad t < 0$$

$t > 0$:

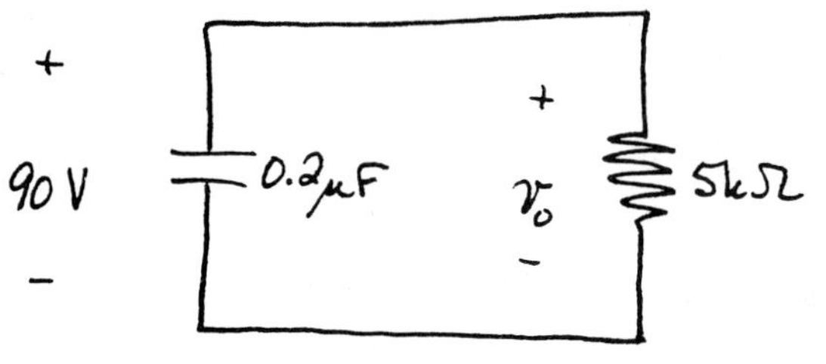

$$v_o = 90e^{-1000t}\ \text{V}$$

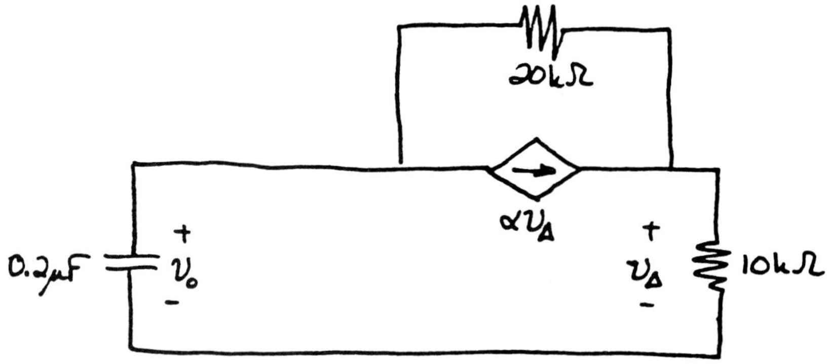

$$\frac{v_\Delta}{10\times 10^3}+\frac{v_\Delta - v_o}{20{,}000} - 125\times 10^{-6}v_\Delta = 0$$

$$2v_\Delta + v_\Delta - v_o - 2500\times 10^{-3}v_\Delta = 0$$

$$\therefore\ \ v_\Delta = 2v_o = 180e^{-1000t}\text{ V}$$

P 7.26 [a]

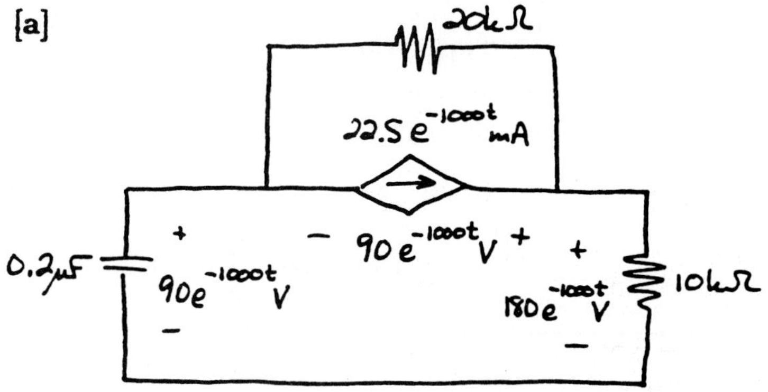

$$p_{ds} = (-90e^{-1000t})(22.5\times 10^{-3}e^{-1000t}) = -2025\times 10^{-3}e^{-2000t}\text{ W}$$

$$w_{ds} = \int_0^\infty p_{ds}\,dt = -1012.5\,\mu\text{J}.$$

$\therefore$ dependent source is delivering 1012.5 μJ

[b]

$$p_{10k} = \frac{(180)^2e^{-2000t}}{10\times 10^3}$$

$$w_{10k} = \int_0^\infty p_{10k}\,dt = 1620\,\mu\text{J}$$

$$p_{20k} = \frac{(90)^2e^{-2000t}}{20\times 10^3}$$

$$w_{20k} = \int_0^\infty p_{20k}\,dt = 202.5\,\mu\text{J}$$

$$w_c(0) = \frac{1}{2}(0.2) \times 10^{-6}(90)^2 = 810\,\mu\text{J}$$

$$\sum w_{\text{dev}} = 810 + 1012.5 = 1822.5\,\mu\text{J}$$

$$\sum w_{\text{diss}} = 202.5 + 1620 = 1822.5\,\mu\text{J}.$$

P 7.27 [a] $t < 0$:

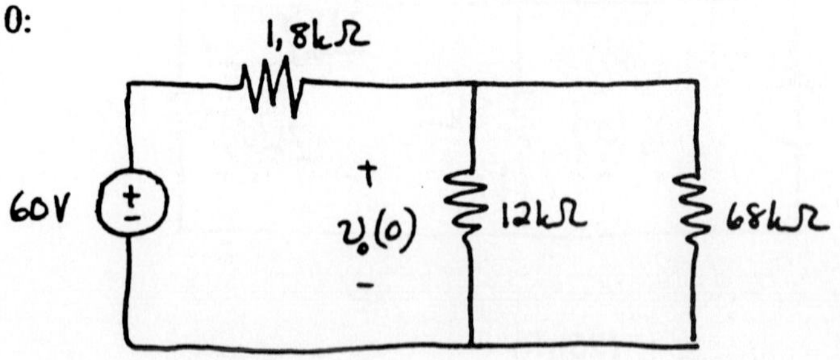

$$v_o(0) = \frac{(60)(10.2)}{12} = 51\text{ V}$$

$t > 0$:

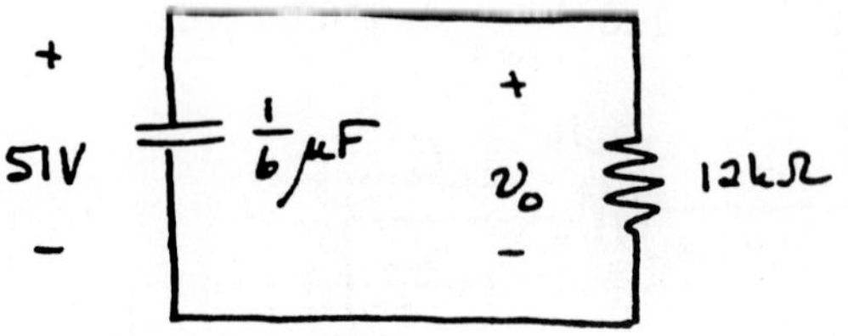

$$\tau = \frac{1}{6}(12) \times 10^{-3} = 2\text{ ms}; \qquad \frac{1}{\tau} = 500$$

$$v_o = 51e^{-500t}\text{ V}$$

$$p = \frac{v_o^2}{12} \times 10^{-3} = 216.75 \times 10^{-3}e^{-1000t}\text{ W}$$

$$\begin{aligned} w_{\text{diss}} &= \int_0^{2\times10^{-3}} 216.75 \times 10^{-3}e^{-1000t}\,dt = 216.75 \times 10^{-6}(1 - e^- \\ &= 187.42\,\mu\text{J} \end{aligned}$$

[b] $$w(0) = \left(\frac{1}{2}\right)\left(\frac{1}{6}\right)(51)^2 \times 10^{-6} = 216.75\,\mu\text{J}$$

$$0.95w(0) = 205.9125\,\mu\text{J}$$

$$\int_0^{t_o} 216.75 \times 10^{-3}e^{-1000x}\,dx = 205.9125 \times 10^{-6}$$

$$\int_0^{t_o} e^{-1000x}\,dx - 0.95 \times 10^{-3}$$

$$\therefore \quad 1 - e^{-1000t_o} = 0.95; \qquad e^{1000t_o} = 20; \quad \text{so} \quad t_o = 3\,ms$$

P 7.28 [a] $t < 0$:

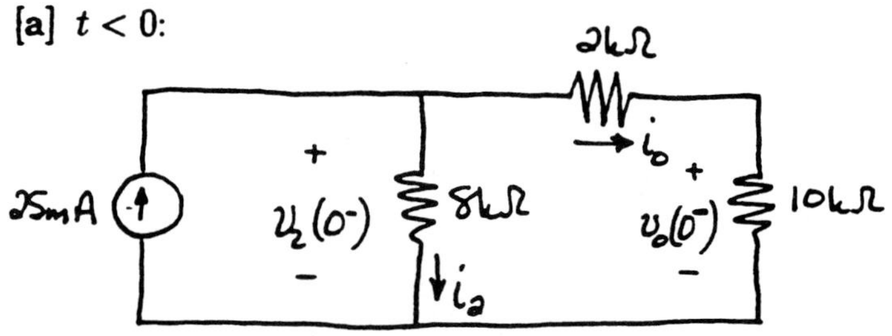

$$i_o(0^-) = \frac{(25)(8)}{(20)} = 10\,\text{mA}$$

$$v_o(0^-) = (10)(10) = 100\,\text{V}$$

$$i_2(0^-) = 25 - 10 = 15\,\text{mA}$$

$$v_2(0^-) = 15(8) = 120\,\text{V}$$

$t > 0$

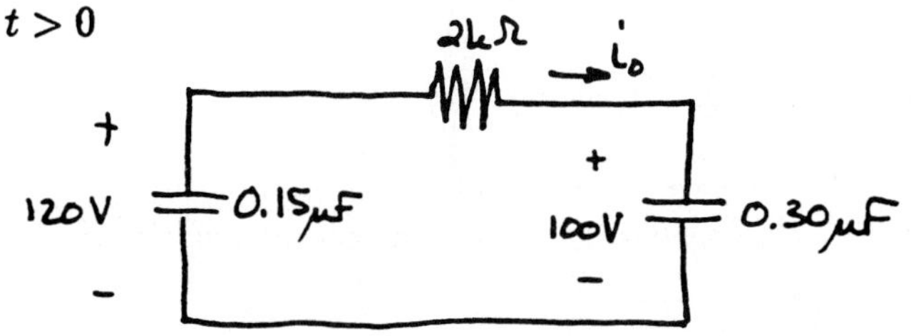

$$\tau = RC = 0.2\,\text{ms} = 200\,\mu\text{s}; \qquad \frac{1}{\tau} = 5000$$

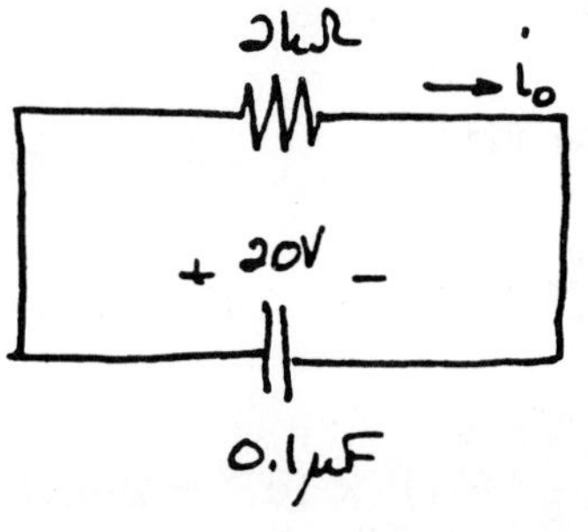

$$i_o(t) = \frac{20}{2 \times 10^3} e^{-t/\tau} = 10e^{-5000t}\,\text{mA}, \qquad t \geq 0^+$$

[b]

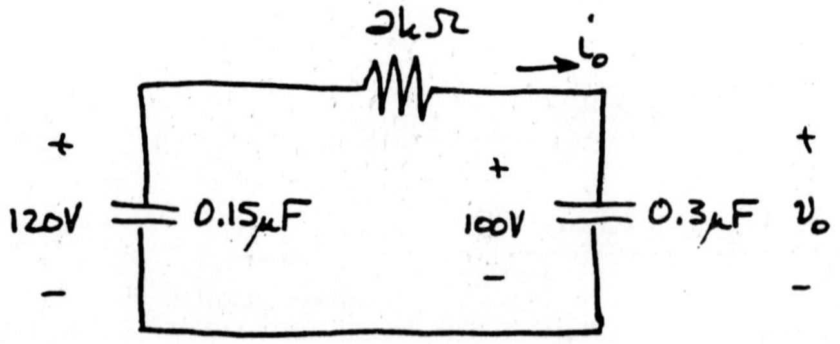

$$\begin{aligned} v_o &= \frac{10^6}{0.3}\int_0^t 10 \times 10^{-3}e^{-5000x}\,dx + 100 \\ &= \frac{10^5}{3}\frac{e^{-5000x}}{-5000}\Big|_0^t + 100 \\ &= -(20/3)e^{-5000t} + (20/3) + 100 \\ v_o &= [-(20/3)e^{-5000t} + (320/3)]\,\text{V}, \qquad t \geq 0 \end{aligned}$$

[c] $w_{\text{trapped}} = (1/2)(0.15) \times 10^{-6}(320/3)^2 + (1/2)(0.3) \times 10^{-6}(320/3)^2$

$w_{\text{trapped}} = 2560\,\mu\text{J}.$

Check:

$$w_{\text{diss}} = \frac{1}{2}(0.1 \times 10^{-6})(20)^2 = 20\,\mu\text{J}$$

$$w(0) = \frac{1}{2}(0.15) \times 10^{-6}(120)^2 + \frac{1}{2}(0.3 \times 10^{-6})(100)^2 = 2580\,\mu\text{J}.$$

$$w_{\text{trapped}} + w_{\text{diss}} = w(0)$$

$2560 + 20 = 2580$ OK.

P 7.29 [a] $v(0) = \dfrac{(8)(27)(33)}{60} = 118.80\,\text{V}$

$$R_e = \frac{(3)(6)}{9} = 2\,\text{k}\Omega$$

$$\tau = R_eC = (2000)(0.25) \times 10^{-6} = 500\,\mu\text{s}; \qquad \frac{1}{\tau} = 2000$$

$$v = 118.80e^{-2000t}\,\text{V} \qquad t \geq 0$$

$$i_o = \frac{v}{3000} = 39.6e^{-2000t}\,\text{mA}$$

[b] $$w(0) = \frac{1}{2}(0.25)(118.80)^2 = 1764.18\,\mu\text{J}$$

$$i_{4k} = \frac{118.80e^{-2000t}}{6} = 19.8e^{-2000t}\,\text{mA}$$

$$p_{4k} = [(19.8)e^{-2000t}]^2(4000) \times 10^{-6} = 1568.16 \times 10^{-3}e^{-4000t}$$

$$w_{4k} = 1568.16 \times 10^{-3}\frac{e^{-4000x}}{-4000}\Big|_0^{250\times10^{-6}} = 392.04(1 - e^{-1})\,\mu\text{J}$$

$$\% = \frac{392.04}{1764.18}(1 - e^{-1}) \times 100 = 14.05\%$$

P 7.30 [a] At $t = 0^-$ the voltage on each capacitor will be 5 V($25 \times 10^{-3} \times 200$), positive at the upper terminal. Hence at $t \geq 0^+$ we have

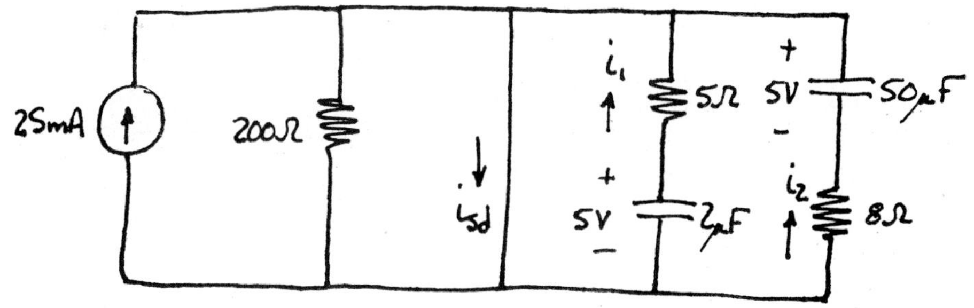

$$\therefore\ i_{sd}(0^+) = 0.025 + \frac{5}{5} + \frac{5}{8} = 1.65\,\text{A}$$

At $t = \infty$, both capacitors will have completely discharged.

$$\therefore\ i_{sd}(\infty) = 25\,\text{mA}$$

[b] $$i_{sd}(t) = 0.025 + i_1(t) + i_2(t)$$

$$\tau_1 = (5)(2) \times 10^{-6} = 10\,\mu\text{s}$$

$$\tau_2 = (8)(50 \times 10^{-6}) = 400\,\mu\text{s}$$

$$\therefore\ i_1(t) = e^{-10^5 t}\,\text{A}, \qquad t \geq 0^+$$

$$i_2(t) = 0.625e^{-2500t}\,\text{A}, \qquad t \geq 0$$

$$\therefore\ i_{sd} = 25 + 1000e^{-100{,}000t} + 625e^{-2500t}\,\text{mA}, \qquad t \geq 0^+$$

P 7.31 $t < 0$

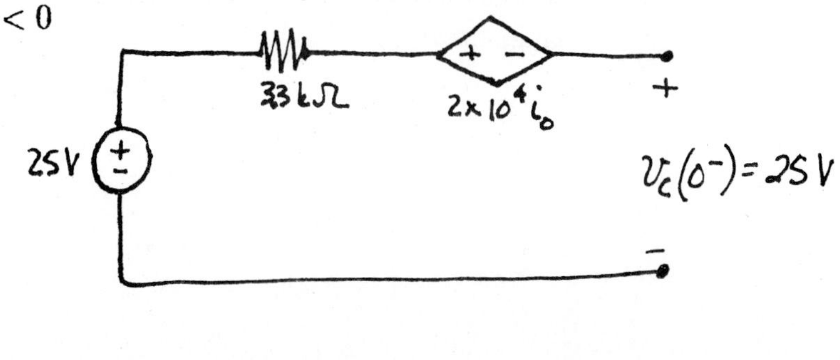

$t > 0$

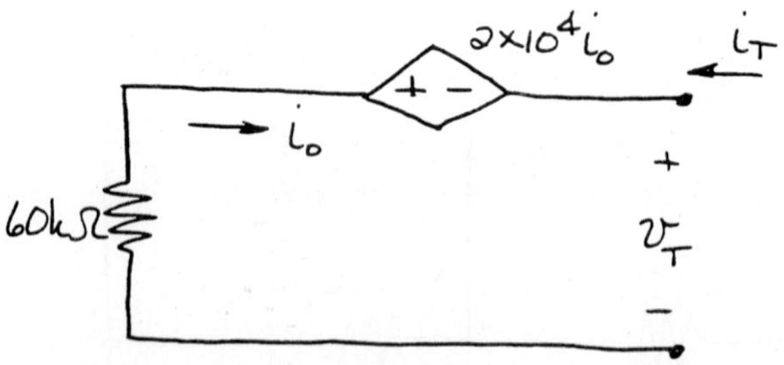

$$v_T = -2 \times 10^4 i_o + 60{,}000 i_T$$
$$= -20{,}000(-i_T) + 60{,}000 i_T = 80{,}000 i_T$$

$$\therefore \quad \frac{v_T}{i_T} = R_{\text{Th}} = 80\,\text{k}\Omega$$

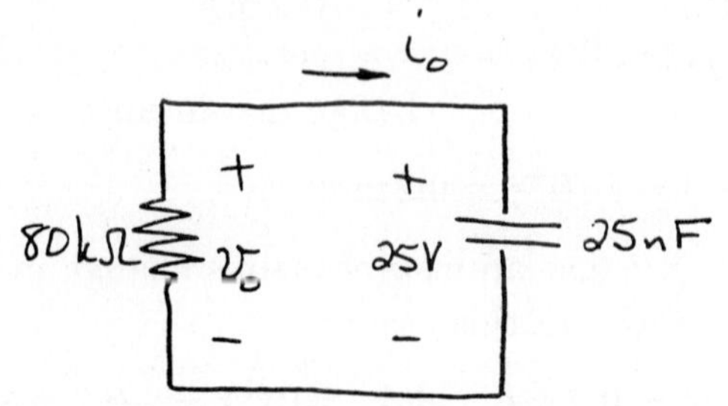

$$\tau = RC = 2\,\text{ms}; \qquad \frac{1}{\tau} = 500$$

$$v_o = 25e^{-500t}\,\text{V}, \qquad t \geq 0$$

$$i_o = 25 \times 10^{-9}\frac{d}{dt}[25e^{-500t}] = -312.5e^{-500t}\,\mu\text{A}, \qquad t \geq 0^+$$

P 7.32 [a] $t < 0$:

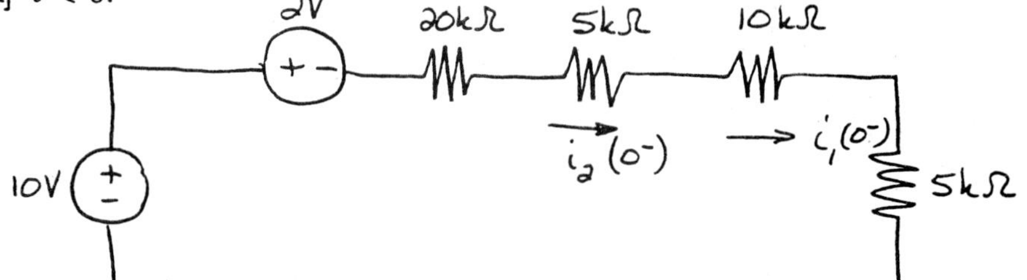

$$i_1(0^-) = i_2(0^-) = \left(\frac{8}{40} \times 10^{-3}\right) = 0.2\,\text{mA}$$

[b] $t > 0$:

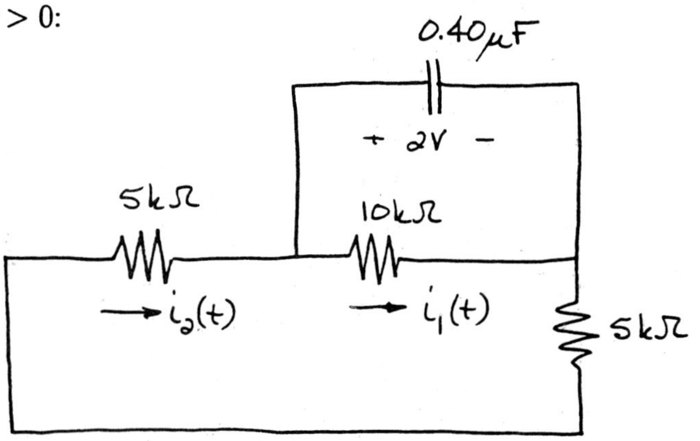

$$i_1(0^+) = \frac{2}{10} \times 10^{-3} = 0.2\,\text{mA}$$

$$i_2(0^+) = \frac{-2}{10} \times 10^{-3} = -0.2\,\text{mA}$$

[c] Capacitor voltage cannot change instantaneously, therefore,

$$i_1(0^-) = i_1(0^+) = 0.2\,\text{mA}$$

[d] Switching can cause an instantaneous change in the current in a resistive branch. In this circuit

$$i_2(0^-) = 0.2\,\text{mA} \quad \text{and} \quad i_2(0^+) = -0.2\,\text{mA}$$

[e] $$v_c = 2e^{-t/\tau}\,\text{V}, \qquad t \geq 0$$

$$\tau = R_eC = 5000(0.4) \times 10^{-6} = 2 \times 10^{-3}$$

$$v_c = 2e^{-500t}\,\text{V}, \qquad t \geq 0$$

$$i_1 = \frac{v_c}{10{,}000} = 0.2e^{-500t}\,\text{mA}, \qquad t \geq 0$$

[f] $$i_2 = \frac{-v_c}{10{,}000} = -0.2e^{-500t}\,\text{mA}, \qquad t \geq 0^+$$

P 7.33 After making a Thévenin equivalent we have

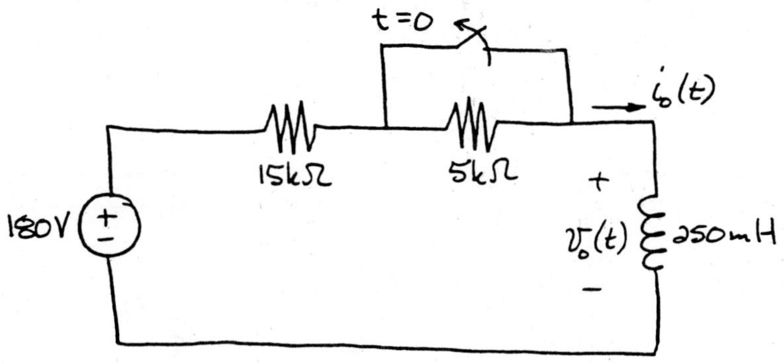

$$I_o = 180/15 = 12\,\text{mA}$$

$$\tau = (0.25/20) \times 10^{-3} = 0.125 \times 10^{-4}; \qquad \frac{1}{\tau} = 80{,}000$$

$$\frac{V_s}{R} = \frac{180}{20} = 9\,\text{mA}$$

$$i_o = 9 + (12 - 9)e^{-80{,}000t} = 9 + 3e^{-80{,}000t}\ \text{mA}$$

$$v = [180 - 12(20)]e^{-80{,}000t} = -60e^{-80{,}000t}\ \text{V}$$

P 7.34 [a] $v_o(0^+) = -I_g R_2; \qquad \tau = \dfrac{L}{R_1 + R_2}$

$$v_o(\infty) = 0$$

$$v_o(t) = -I_g R_2 e^{-[(R_1+R_2)/L]t}\ \text{V}, \qquad t \geq 0$$

[b] $v_o = -(12 \times 10^{-3})(5 \times 10^3)e^{-[\frac{15{,}000+5000}{0.25}]t} = -60e^{-80{,}000t}\ \text{V}, \qquad t \geq 0$

[c] $v_o(0^+) \to \infty$, and the duration of $v_o(t) \to$ zero

[d] $v_{sw} = R_2 i_o; \qquad \tau = \dfrac{L}{R_1 + R_2}$

$$i_o(0^+) = I_g; \qquad i_o(\infty) = I_g \frac{R_1}{R_1 + R_2}$$

Therefore $\quad i_o(t) = \dfrac{I_g R_1}{R_1+R_2} + \left[I_g - \dfrac{I_g R_1}{R_1+R_2}\right] e^{-[(R_1+R_2)/L]t}$

$$i_o(t) = \frac{R_1 I_g}{(R_1+R_2)} + \frac{R_2 I_g}{(R_1+R_2)} e^{-[(R_1+R_2)/L]t}$$

Therefore $\quad v_{sw} = \dfrac{R_1 I_g}{(1+R_1/R_2)} + \dfrac{R_2 I_g}{(1+R_1/R_2)} e^{-[(R_1+R_2)/L]t}, \qquad t \geq 0$

[e] $|v_{sw}(0^+)| \to \infty; \qquad$ duration $\to 0$

P 7.35 Opening the inductive circuit causes a very large voltage to be induced across the inductor L. This voltage also appears across the switch (part [e] of Problem 7.34) causing the switch to arc over. At the same time, the large voltage across L damages the meter movement.

P 7.36 $t > 0$

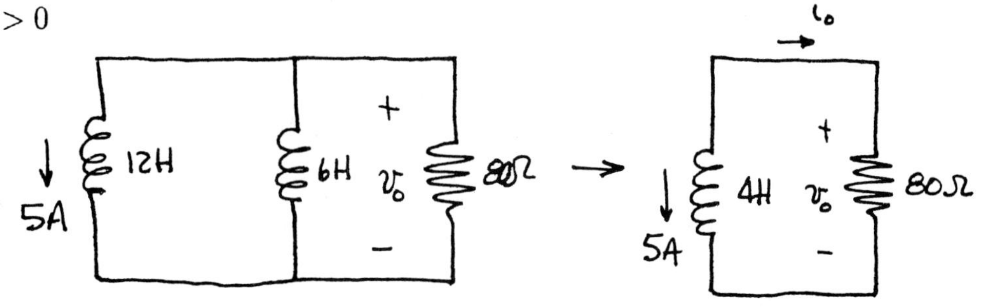

$$\tau = \frac{4}{80} = \frac{1}{20}$$

$$i_o = -5e^{-20t}\,\text{A}, \qquad t \geq 0$$

$$v_o = 80i_o = -400e^{-20t}\,\text{V}, \qquad t > 0^+$$

$$-400e^{-20t} = -80; \qquad e^{20t} = 5$$

$$\therefore\ t = \frac{1}{20}\ln 5 = 80.47\,\text{ms}$$

P 7.37 [a] $w_{\text{diss}} = \frac{1}{2}L_e i^2(0) = \frac{1}{2}(4)(25) = 50\,\text{J}$

[b]

$$\begin{aligned} i_{12H} &= \frac{1}{12}\int_0^t (-400)e^{-20x}\,dx + 5 \\ &= \frac{-100}{3}\frac{e^{-20x}}{-20}\Big|_0^t + 5 = \frac{5}{3}e^{-20t} + \frac{10}{3}\,\text{A} \\ i_{6H} &= \frac{1}{6}\int_0^t (-400)e^{-20x}\,dx + 0 \\ &= \frac{-200}{3}\frac{e^{-20x}}{-20}\Big|_0^t \frac{10}{3}e^{-20t} - \frac{10}{3}\,\text{A} \end{aligned}$$

$$w_{\text{trapped}} = \frac{1}{2}(18)(100/9) = 100\,\text{J}$$

[c] $w(0) = \frac{1}{2}(12)(25) = 150\,\text{J}$

P 7.38 [a] $t > 0$

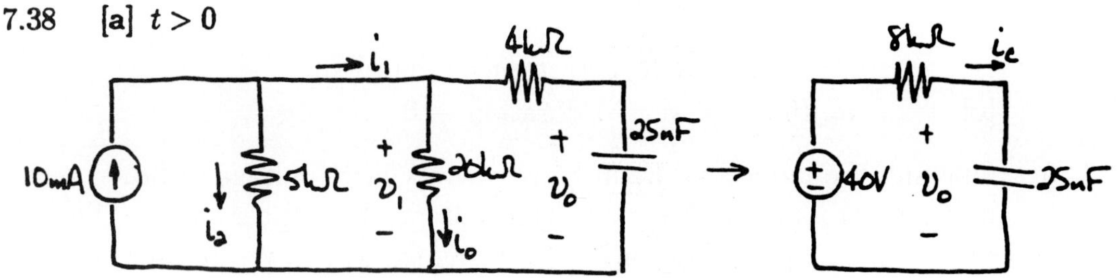

$$v_o(0^-) = v_o(0^+) = 0\,\text{V}$$

$$v_o(\infty) = 40\,\text{V}$$

$$\tau = (8 \times 10^3)(25) \times 10^{-9} = 0.2\,\text{ms} \qquad 1/\tau = 5000$$

$$v_o = (40 - 40e^{-5000t})\,\text{V}, \qquad t \geq 0$$

[b] $$i_c = 25 \times 10^{-9}\frac{dv_o}{dt}$$

$$i_c = 25 \times 10^{-9}(200{,}000e^{-5000t}) = 5e^{-5000t}\text{ mA}$$

$$v_1 = 4(5e^{-5000t}) + 40 - 40e^{-5000t} = 40 - 20e^{-5000t}$$

$$i_o = \frac{v_1}{20 \times 10^3} = 2 - e^{-5000t}\text{ mA}$$

[c] $$i_1(t) = i_o + i_c = 2 + 4e^{-5000t}\text{ mA}$$

[d] $$i_2(t) = \frac{v_1}{5 \times 10^3} = 8 - 4e^{-5000t}\text{ mA}$$

[e] $$i_1(0^+) = 2 + 4 = 6\text{ mA}$$

Checks: $i_1 + i_2 = 10\text{ mA}$

$$i_c(0^+) = \frac{10\left(\frac{1}{4}\right)}{\left(\frac{1}{5} + \frac{1}{20} + \frac{1}{4}\right)} = 5\text{ mA}$$

$$i_o(0^+) = \frac{10\left(\frac{1}{20}\right)}{\left(\frac{1}{5} + \frac{1}{20} + \frac{1}{4}\right)} = 1\text{ mA}$$

$$i_1(0^+) = 5 + 1 = 6\text{ mA}$$

P 7.39 [a] From Eqs. (7.35) and (7.42)

$$i = \frac{V_s}{R} + \left(I_o - \frac{V_s}{r}\right)e^{-(R/L)t}$$

$$v = (V_s - I_oR)e^{-(R/L)t}$$

$$\therefore \quad \frac{V_s}{R} = 4; \qquad I_o - \frac{V_s}{R} = 4$$

$$V_s - I_oR = -80; \qquad \frac{R}{L} = 40$$

$$\therefore \quad I_o = 4 + \frac{V_s}{R} = 8\text{ A}$$

Now since $V_s = 4R$ we have

$$4R - 8R = -80; \qquad R = 20\,\Omega$$

$$V_s = 80\text{ V}; \qquad L = \frac{R}{40} = 0.5\text{ H}$$

[b] $$i = 4 + 4e^{-40t}; \qquad i^2 = 16 + 32e^{-40t} + 16e^{-80t}$$

$$w = \frac{1}{2}Li^2 = \frac{1}{2}(0.5)[16 + 32e^{-40t} + 16e^{-80t}] = 4 + 8e^{-40t} + 4e^{-80t}$$

$$\therefore \; 4 + 8e^{-40t} + 4e^{-80t} = 9 \quad \text{or} \quad e^{-80t} + 2e^{-40t} - 1.25 = 0$$

Let $x = e^{-40t}$:

$$x^2 + 2x - 1.25 = 0; \quad \text{Solving,} \quad x = 0.5; \quad x = -2.25$$

But $x \geq 0$ for all t. Thus,

$$e^{-40t} = 0.5; \qquad e^{40t} = 2; \qquad t = 25 \ln 2 = 17.33\,\text{ms}$$

P 7.40 [a] For $t > 0$:

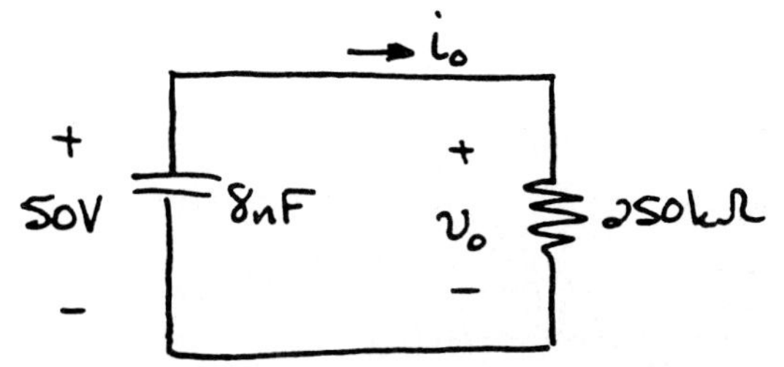

$$\tau = RC = 250 \times 10^3 \times 8 \times 10^{-9} = 2\,\text{ms}; \qquad \frac{1}{\tau} = 500$$

$$v_o = 50e^{-500t}\,\text{V}, \qquad t \geq 0^+$$

[b] $$i_o = \frac{v_o}{250} \times 10^{-3} = \frac{50e^{-500t}}{250} \times 10^{-3} = 200e^{-500t}\,\mu\text{A}$$

$$v_1 = \frac{-10^9}{40} \times 200 \times 10^{-6} \int_0^t e^{-500x}\,dx + 50 = 10e^{-500t} + 40\,\text{V}, \quad t \geq$$

P 7.41 [a] $$w = \frac{1}{2}C_e v_e^2 = \frac{1}{2}(8 \times 10^{-9})(2500) = 10\,\mu\text{J}$$

[b] $$w_{\text{trapped}} = \frac{1}{2}(40)^2(50) \times 10^{-9} = 40\,\mu\text{J}$$

[c] $$w(0) = \frac{1}{2}(40 \times 10^{-9})(2500) = 50\,\mu\text{J}$$

P 7.42 For $t < 0$

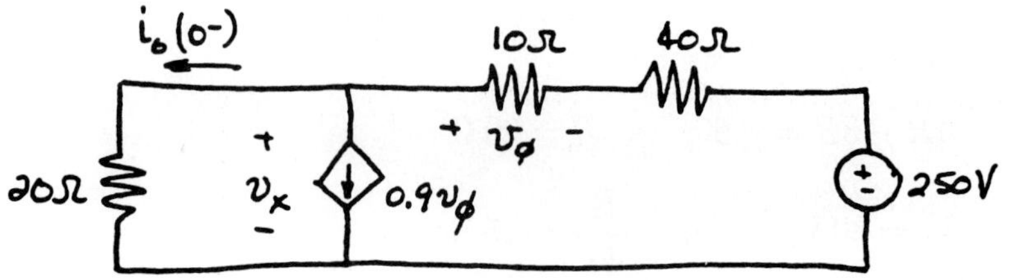

$$\frac{v_x}{20} + 9\left[\frac{v_x - 250}{50}\right] + \left[\frac{v_x - 250}{50}\right] = 0$$

$$\frac{v_x}{20} + 10\frac{(v_x - 250)}{50} = 0$$

$$5v_x - 5000 + 20v_x = 0; \qquad v_x = 200\text{ V}$$

$$i_o(0^-) = 200/20 = 10\text{ A}$$

$t > 0$

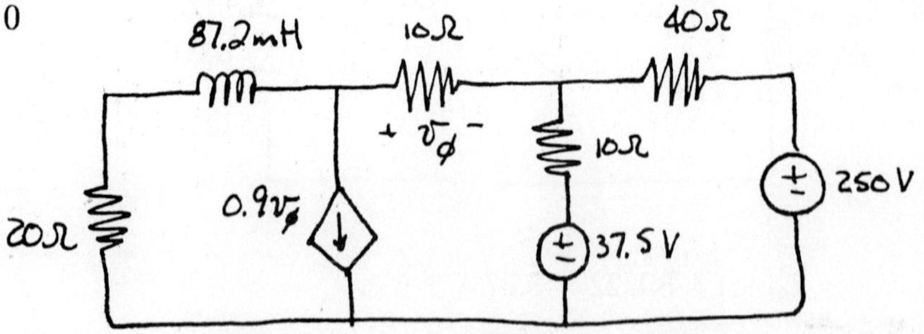

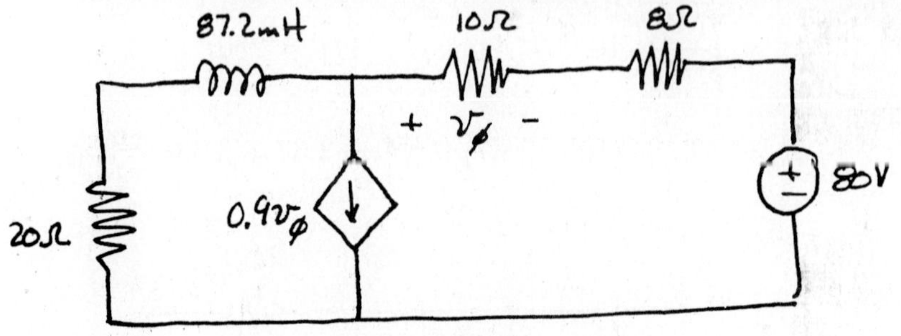

Find Thévenin equivalent with respect to a, b

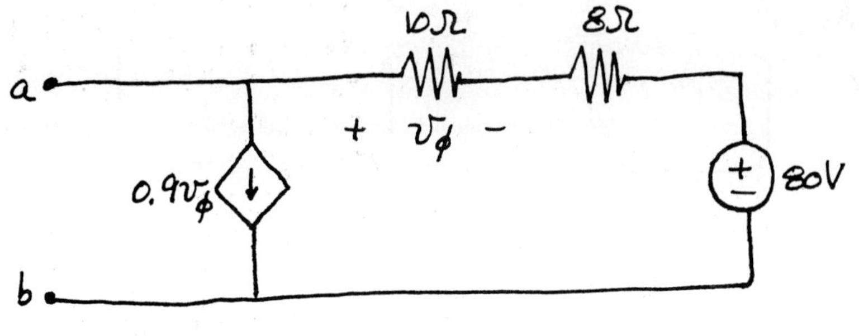

$$\frac{V_{\text{Th}} - 80}{18} + 9\frac{(V_{\text{Th}} - 80)}{18} = 0 \qquad V_{\text{Th}} = 80\text{ V}$$

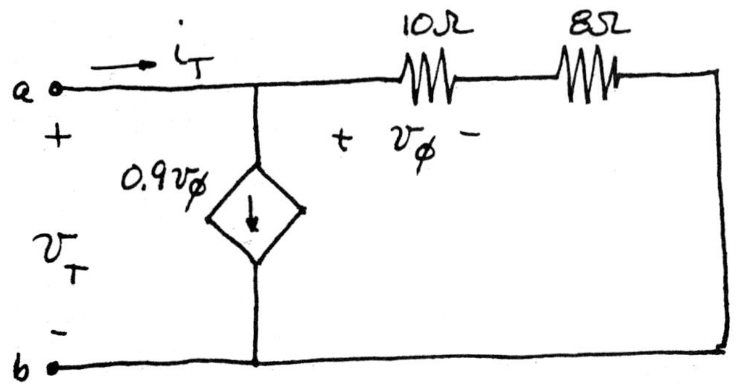

$$v_T = (i_T - 0.9v_\phi)18 = \left[i_T - 0.9\left(\frac{10v_T}{18}\right)\right]18$$

$$v_T = 18t_T - 9v_T \qquad \therefore \quad 10v_T = 18i_T$$

$$\frac{v_T}{i_T} = R_{\text{Th}} = 1.8\,\Omega$$

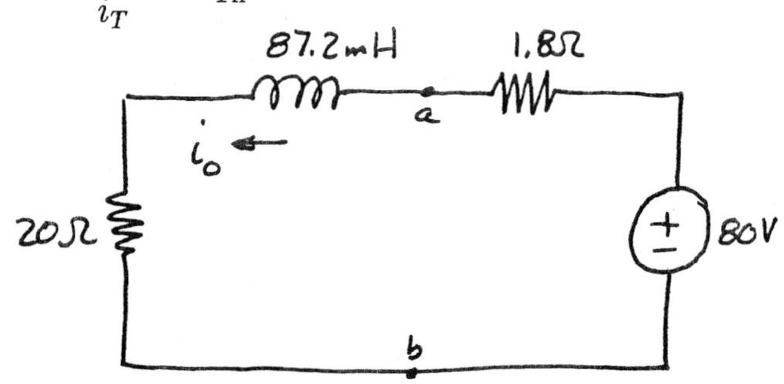

$$i_o(\infty) = 80/22 = 3.67\text{ A}$$

$$\tau = \frac{87.2}{21.8} \times 10^{-3} = 4\text{ ms}; \qquad 1/\tau = 250$$

$$i_o = 3.67 + (10 - 3.67)e^{-250t} = 3.67 + 6.33e^{-250t}\text{ A}, \qquad t \geq 0$$

P 7.43 [a] $t < 0$

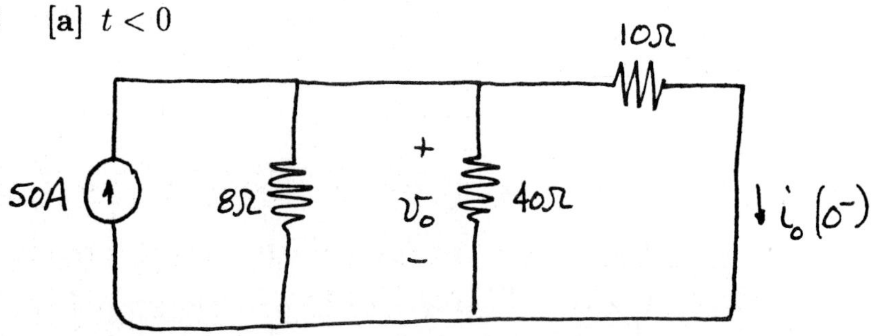

$$50 = \frac{v_o}{8} + \frac{v_o}{40} + \frac{v_o}{10}$$

$$2000 = (5 + 1 + 4)v_o; \qquad v_o = 200\text{ V}$$

$$\therefore \quad i_o(0^-) = 200/10 = 20\text{ A}$$

$t > 0$

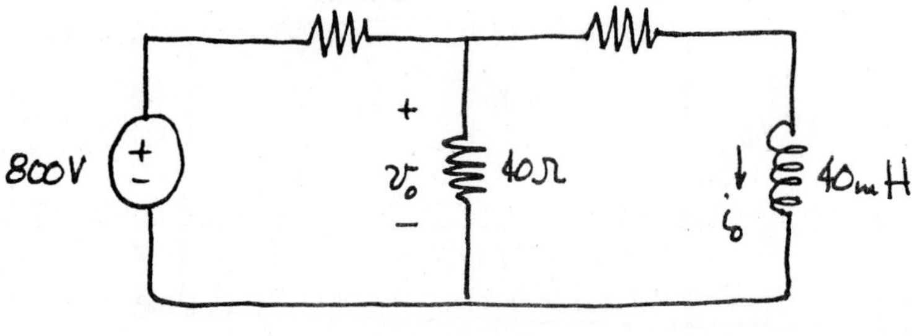

$$V_{\text{Th}} = \frac{800}{160}(40) = 200\text{ V}$$

$$R_{\text{Th}} = 10 + \frac{(40)(120)}{160} = 40\,\Omega$$

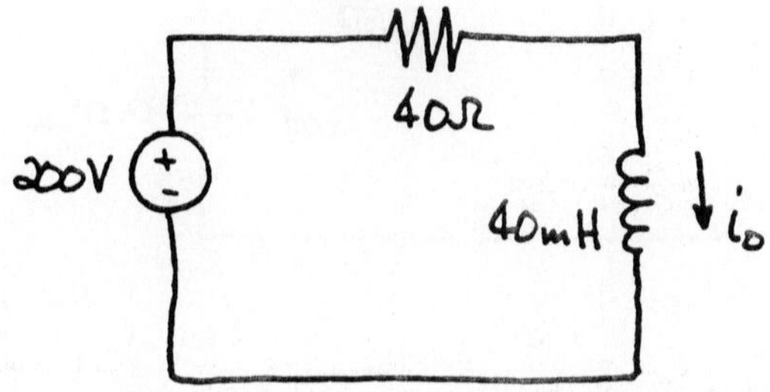

$$\tau = \frac{40}{40} \times 10^{-3} = 1\text{ ms}; \qquad \frac{1}{\tau} = 1000$$

$$i_o(\infty) = \frac{200}{40} = 5\text{ A}$$

$$\therefore\ i_o = 5 + (20 - 5)e^{-1000t} = 5 + 15e^{-1000t}\text{ A}, \qquad t \geq 0$$

[b]
$$\begin{aligned} v_o &= 10i_o + 0.04\tfrac{di_o}{dt} \\ &= 50 + 150e^{\ 1000t} - 0.04(15{,}000)e^{\ 1000t} \\ &= 50 + 150e^{-1000t} - 600e^{-1000t} \\ v_o &= 50 - 450e^{-1000t}\text{ V}, \qquad t \geq 0^+ \end{aligned}$$

P 7.44 For $t < 0$

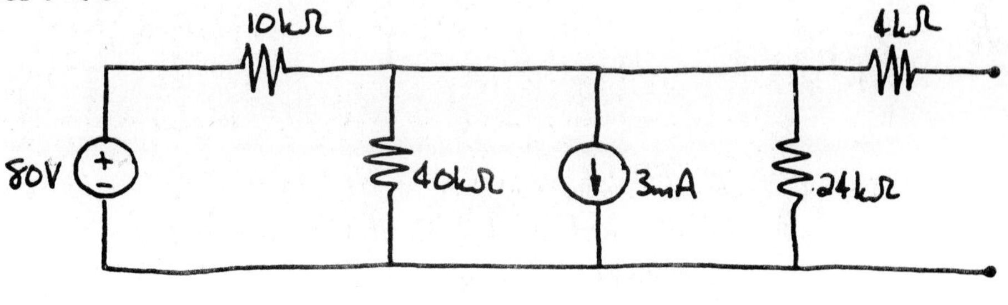

$80/10 = 8\text{ mA}, \qquad 10\text{ k}\Omega \| 40\text{ k}\Omega \| 24\text{ k}\Omega = 6\text{ k}\Omega$

$8\text{ mA} - 3\text{ mA} = 5\text{ mA}$

$5\text{ mA} \times 6\text{ k}\Omega = 30\text{ V}$

$t < 0$

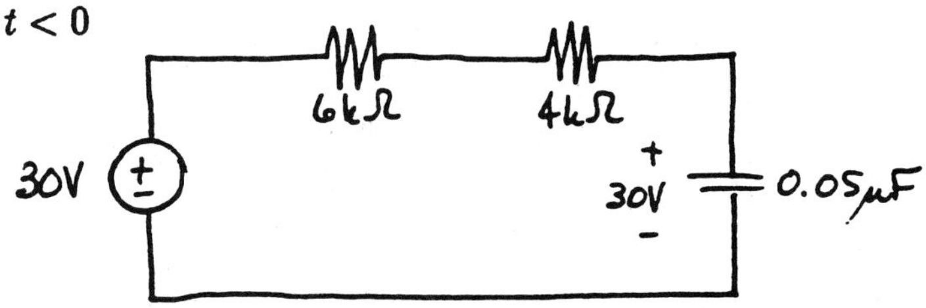

$$\therefore \quad v_o(0^-) = v_o(0^+) = 30 \text{ V}$$

$t > 0$

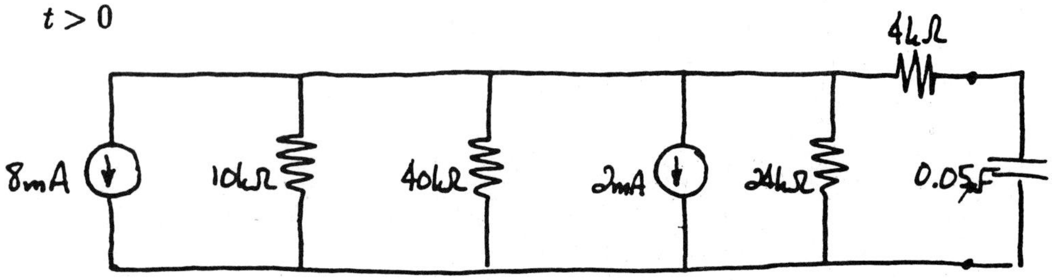

$$v_o(\infty) = -10 \times 10^{-3}(6 \times 10^3) = -60 \text{ V}$$

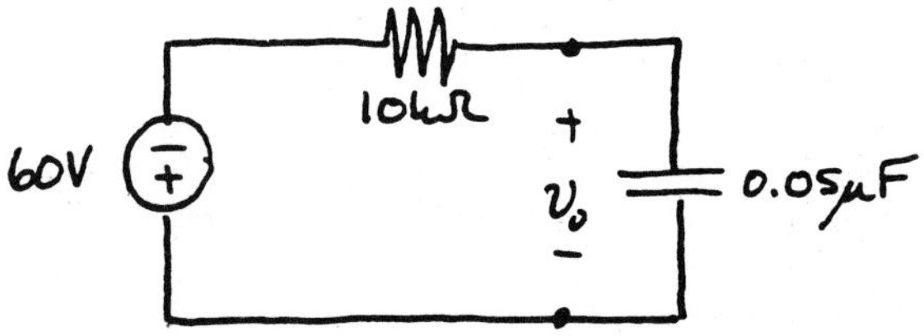

$$\tau = 0.5 \text{ ms}; \qquad \frac{1}{\tau} = 2000$$

$$v_o = -60 + (30 - (-60))e^{-2000t}$$

$$v_o = -60 + 90e^{-2000t} \text{ V} \qquad t \geq 0$$

P 7.45 $\quad t > 0;$ $\quad$ calculate $v_o(0^+)$

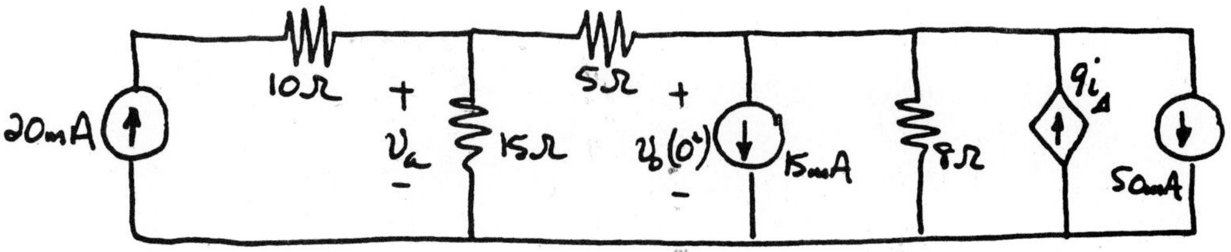

$$\frac{v_a}{15} + \frac{v_a - v_o(0^+)}{5} = 20 \times 10^{-3}$$

$$\therefore\quad v_a = 0.75v_o(0^+) + 75 \times 10^{-3}$$

$$15 \times 10^{-3} + \frac{v_o(0^+) - v_a}{5} + \frac{v_o(0^+)}{8} - 9i_\Delta + 50 \times 10^{-3} = 0$$

$$13v_o(0^+) - 8v_a - 360i_\Delta = -2600 \times 10^{-3}$$

$$i_\Delta = \frac{v_o(0^+)}{8} - 9i_\Delta + 50 \times 10^{-3}$$

$$\therefore\quad i_\Delta = \frac{v_o(0^+)}{80} + 5 \times 10^{-3}$$

$$\therefore\quad 360i_\Delta = 4.5v_o(0^+) + 1800 \times 10^{-3}$$

$$8v_a = 6v_o(0^+) + 600 \times 10^{-3}$$

$$\therefore\quad 13v_o(0^+) - 6v_o(0^+) - 600 \times 10^{-3} - 4.5v_o(0^+) -$$

$$1800 \times 10^{-3} = -2600 \times 10^{-3}$$

$$2.5v_o(0^+) = -200 \times 10^{-3}; \qquad v_o(0^+) = -80\,\text{mV}$$

$$v_o(\infty) = 0$$

Find the Thévenin resistance seen by the 4 mH inductor:

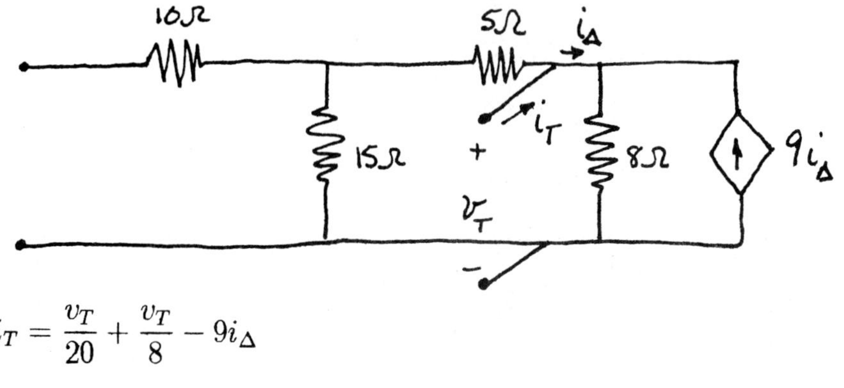

$$i_T = \frac{v_T}{20} + \frac{v_T}{8} - 9i_\Delta$$

$$i_\Delta = \frac{v_T}{8} - 9i_\Delta \qquad \therefore\quad 10i_\Delta = \frac{v_T}{8}; \qquad i_\Delta = \frac{v_T}{80}$$

$$i_T = \frac{v_T}{20} + \frac{10v_T}{80} - \frac{9v_T}{80}$$

$$\frac{i_T}{v_T} = \frac{1}{20} + \frac{1}{80} = \frac{5}{80} = \frac{1}{16}\,\mho$$

$$\therefore \quad R_{\rm Th} = 16\Omega$$

$$\tau = \frac{4 \times 10^{-3}}{16} = 0.25\,\text{ms}; \qquad 1/\tau = 4000$$

$$v_o(\infty) = 0$$

$$\therefore \quad v_o = 0 + (-80 - 0)e^{-4000t} = -80e^{-4000t}\,\text{mV}, \qquad t \geq 0^+$$

P 7.46 $t < 0$

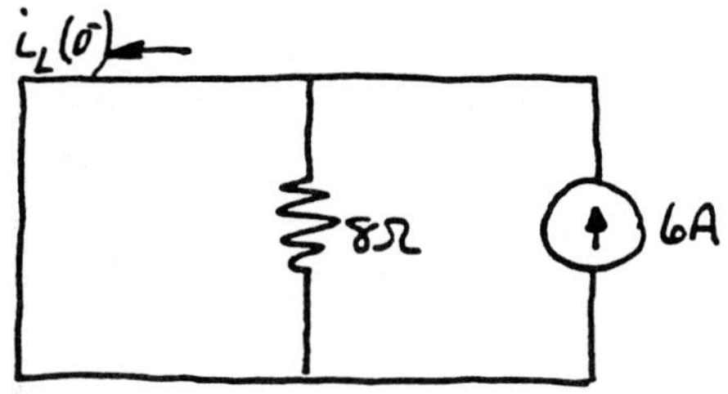

$$i_L(0^-) = 6\,\text{A}$$

$t > 0$

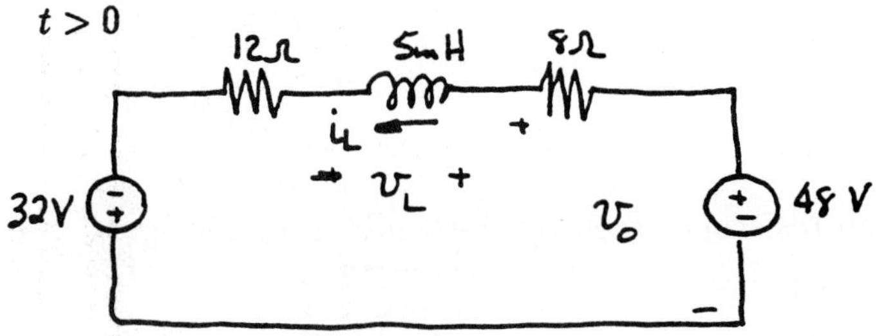

$$i_L(\infty) = \frac{32 + 48}{20} = 4\,\text{A}$$

$$\tau = \frac{L}{R} = \frac{5 \times 10^{-3}}{20} = 250\,\mu\text{s}; \qquad \frac{1}{\tau} = 4000$$

$$i_L = 4 + (6 - 4)e^{-4000t} = 4 + 2e^{-4000t}\,\text{A}, \qquad t \geq 0$$

$$v_o = -8i_L + 48 = -8(4 + 2e^{-4000t}) + 48 = 16 - 16e^{-4000t}\,\text{V}, \qquad t \geq 0^+$$

[b] $$v_L = 5 \times 10^{-3}\frac{di_L}{dt} = 5 \times 10^{-3}[-8000e^{-4000t}] = -40e^{-4000t}\text{ V}, \qquad t \geq 0^+$$

$$v_L(0^+) = -40\text{ V}$$

$$v_o(0^+) = 0\text{ V}$$

Check: at $t = 0^+$ the circuit is:

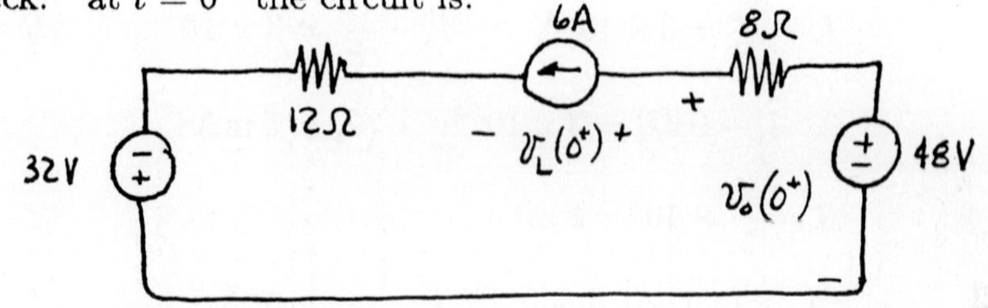

$$v_L(0^+) = 32 - 72 + 0 = -40\text{ V}, \qquad v_o(0^+) = 48 - 48 = 0\text{ V}$$

P 7.47 [a] $t < 0$

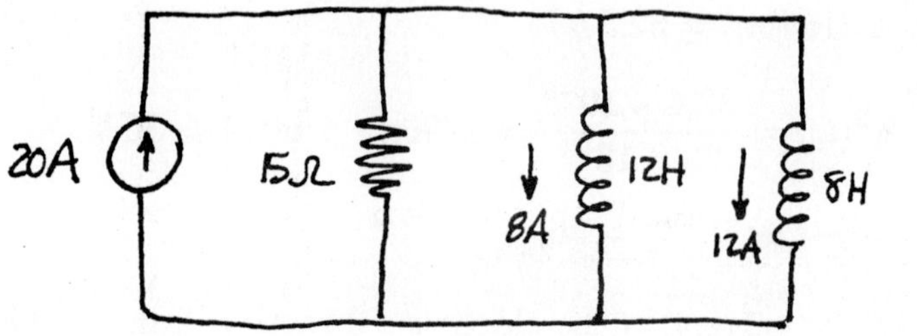

$t > 0$

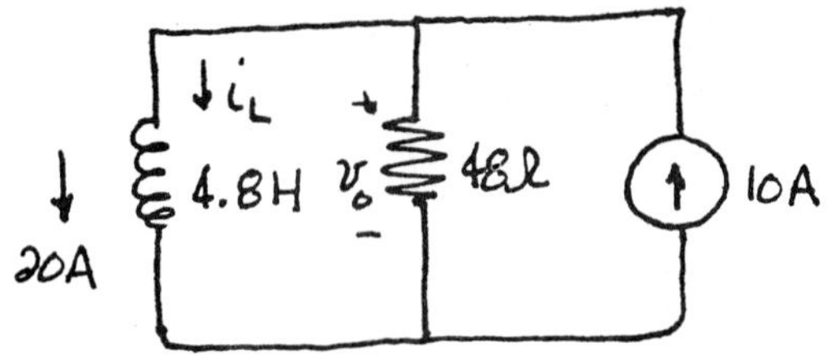

$$i_L(0^-) = i_L(0^+) = 20\text{ A}; \qquad \tau = \frac{4.8}{48} = 0.1\text{ s}; \qquad \frac{1}{\tau} = 10$$

$$i_L(\infty) = 10\text{ A}$$

$$i_L = 10 + [20 - 10]e^{-10t} = 10 + 10e^{-10t}\text{ A}, \qquad t \geq 0$$

$$v_o = 4.8[-100e^{-10t}] = -480e^{-10t}\text{ V}, \qquad t \geq 0^+$$

[b] $$i_1 = \frac{1}{12}\int_0^t -480e^{-10x}\,dx + 8 = 4e^{-10t} + 4\text{ A}, \qquad t \geq 0$$

[c] $$i_2 = \frac{1}{8}\int_0^t -480e^{-10x}\,dx + 12 = 6e^{-10t} + 6\,\text{A}, \qquad t \geq 0$$

P 7.48 [a] $$v = I_sR + (V_o - I_sR)e^{-t/RC} \qquad i = \left(I_s - \frac{V_o}{R}\right)e^{-t/RC}$$

$$\therefore\ I_sR = 40, \qquad V_o - I_sR = -24$$

$$\therefore\ V_o = 16\,\text{V}$$

$$I_s - \frac{V_o}{R} = 3\times10^{-3}; \qquad I_s - \frac{16}{R} = 3\times10^{-3}; \qquad R = \frac{40}{I_s}$$

$$\therefore\ I_s - 0.4I_s = 3\times10^{-3}; \qquad I_s = 5\,\text{mA}$$

$$R = \frac{40}{5}\times10^3 = 8\,\text{k}\Omega$$

$$\frac{1}{RC} = 2500; \qquad C = \frac{1}{2500R} = \frac{10^{-3}}{20\times10^3} = 50\,\text{nF}$$

[b] $$v(\infty) = 40\,\text{V}$$

$$w(\infty) = \frac{1}{2}(50)\times10^{-9}(1600) = 40\,\mu\text{J}$$

$$0.81w(\infty) = 32.5\,\mu\text{J}$$

$$v^2(t_o) = \frac{32.4\times10^{-6}}{25\times10^{-9}} = 1296; \qquad v(t_o) = 36\,\text{V}$$

$$40 - 24e^{-2500t_o} = 36; \qquad e^{2500t_o} = 6; \qquad \therefore\ t_o = 716.70\,\mu\text{s}$$

P 7.49 [a] Let i be the current in the clockwise direction around the circuit. Then

$$\begin{aligned} V_g &= iR_g + \frac{1}{C_1}\int_0^t i\,dx + \frac{1}{C_2}\int_0^t i\,dx \\ &= iR_g + \left(\frac{1}{C_1} + \frac{1}{C_2}\right)\int_0^t i\,dx = iR_g + \frac{1}{C_e}\int_0^t i\,dx \end{aligned}$$

Now differentiate the equation

$$0 = R_g\frac{di}{dt} + \frac{i}{C_e} \quad \text{or} \quad \frac{di}{dt} + \frac{1}{R_gC_e}i = 0$$

Therefore $$i = \frac{V_g}{R_g}e^{-t/R_gC_e} = \frac{V_g}{R_g}e^{-t/\tau}; \qquad \tau = R_gC_e$$

$$v_1(t) = \frac{1}{C_1}\int_0^t \frac{V_g}{R_g}e^{-x/\tau}\,dx = \frac{V_g}{R_gC_1}\,\frac{e^{-x/\tau}}{-1/\tau}\Big|_0^t = -\frac{V_gC_e}{C_1}(e^{-t/\tau} - 1)$$

$$v_1(t) = \frac{V_gC_2}{C_1 + C_2}(1 - e^{-t/\tau}); \qquad \tau = R_gC_e$$

$$v_2(t) = \frac{V_g C_1}{C_1 + C_2}(1 - e^{-t/\tau}); \qquad \tau = R_g C_e$$

[b] $$v_1(\infty) = \frac{C_2}{C_1 + C_2}V_g; \qquad v_2(\infty) = \frac{C_1}{C_1 + C_2}V_g$$

P 7.50 [a] Let v be the voltage drop across the parallel branches, positive at the top node, then

$$-I_g + \frac{v}{R_g} + \frac{1}{L_1}\int_0^t v\,dx + \frac{1}{L_2}\int_0^t v\,dx = 0$$

$$\frac{v}{R_g} + \left(\frac{1}{L_1} + \frac{1}{L_2}\right)\int_0^t v\,dx = I_g$$

$$\frac{v}{R_g} + \frac{1}{L_e}\int_0^t v\,dx = I_g$$

$$\frac{1}{R_g}\frac{dv}{dt} + \frac{v}{L_e} = 0$$

$$\frac{dv}{dt} + \frac{R_g}{L_e}v = 0$$

Therefore $v = I_g R_g e^{-t/\tau}; \qquad \tau = L_e/R_g$

Thus

$$i_1 = \frac{1}{L_1}\int_0^t I_g R_g e^{-x/\tau}\,dx = \frac{I_g R_g}{L_1}\frac{e^{-x/\tau}}{(-1/\tau)}\Bigg|_0^t = \frac{I_g L_e}{L_1}(1 - e^{-t/\tau})$$

$$i_1 = \frac{I_g L_2}{L_1 + L_2}(1 - e^{-t/\tau}) \quad \text{and} \quad i_2 = \frac{I_g L_1}{L_1 + L_2}(1 - e^{-t/\tau})$$

[b] $$i_1(\infty) = \frac{L_2}{L_1 + L_2}I_g; \qquad i_2(\infty) = \frac{L_1}{L_1 + L_2}I_g$$

P 7.51 For $t < 0$, $\quad i_{40\text{mH}}(0) = 75/5 = 15\,\text{A}$

For $t > 0$, after making a Thévenin equivalent we have

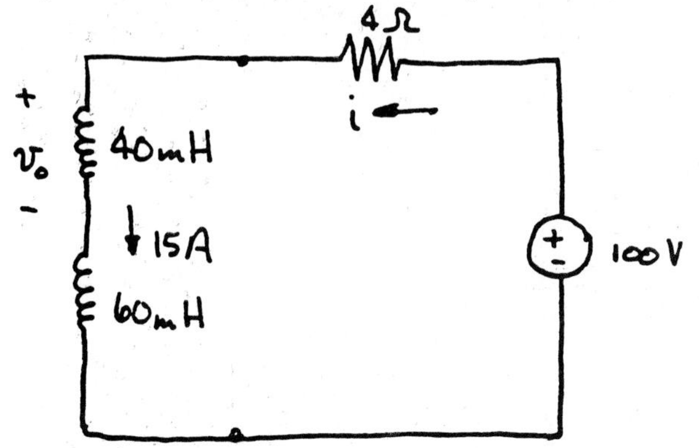

$$i = \frac{V_s}{R} + \left(I_o - \frac{V_s}{R}\right)e^{-t/\tau}$$

$$\frac{1}{\tau} = \frac{R}{L} = \frac{4}{100} \times 10^3 = 40$$

$$I_o = 15\text{ A}; \qquad \frac{V_s}{R} = \frac{100}{4} = 25\text{ A}$$

$$i = 25 + (15 - 25)e^{-40t} = 25 - 10e^{-40t}\text{ A}, \qquad t \geq 0$$

$$v_o = 0.04\frac{di}{dt} = 0.04(400e^{-40t}) = 16e^{-40t}\text{ V}, \qquad t > 0^+$$

P 7.52 [a]

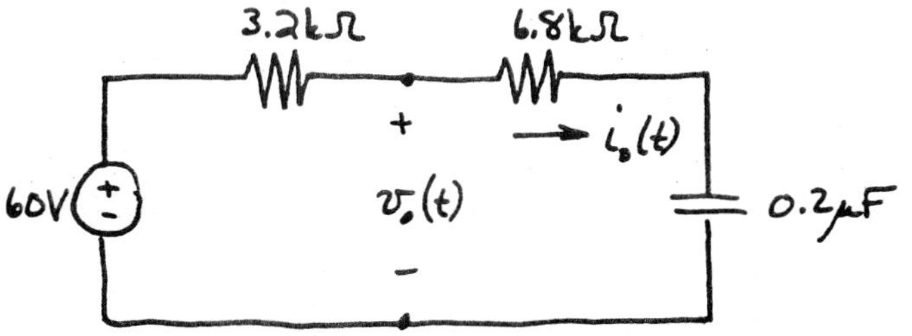

$$i_o(0^+) = \frac{60}{10} \times 10^{-3} = 6\text{ mA}$$

[b] $i_o(\infty) = 0$

[c] $\tau = RC = (10 \times 10^3)(0.2 \times 10^{-6}) = 2\text{ ms}$

[d] $i_o = 0 + (6 - 0)e^{-500t} = 6e^{-500t}\text{ mA}, \qquad t \geq 0^+$

[e] $v_o = 60 - 3.2 \times 10^3 i_o = 60 - 19.2e^{-500t}\text{ V}, \qquad t \geq 0^+$

P 7.53 For $t < 0$, $\quad v_o(0) = 80\text{ V}$

$t > 0$:

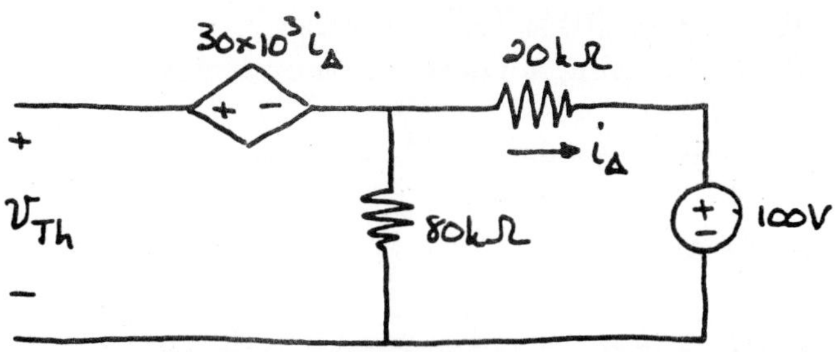

$$v_{\text{Th}} = 30 \times 10^3 i_\Delta + 0.8(100) = 30 \times 10^3\left(\frac{-100}{100 \times 10^3}\right) + 80 = 50\text{ V}$$

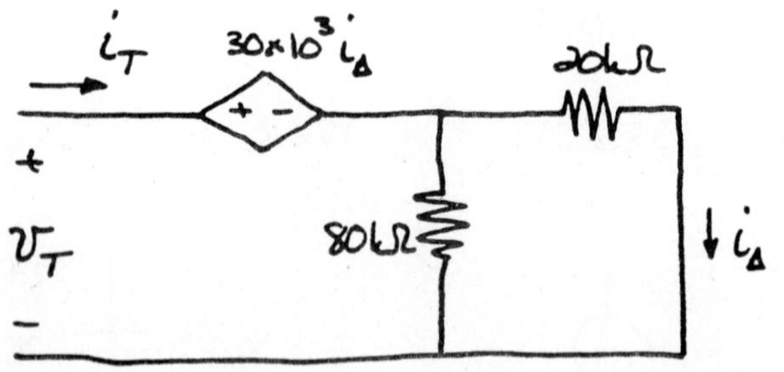

$$v_T = 30 \times 10^3 i_\Delta + 16 \times 10^3 i_T = 30 \times 10^3(0.8)i_T + 16 \times 10^3 i_T = 40 \times 1$$

$$R_{\text{Th}} = \frac{v_T}{i_T} = 40\,\text{k}\Omega$$

$t > 0$

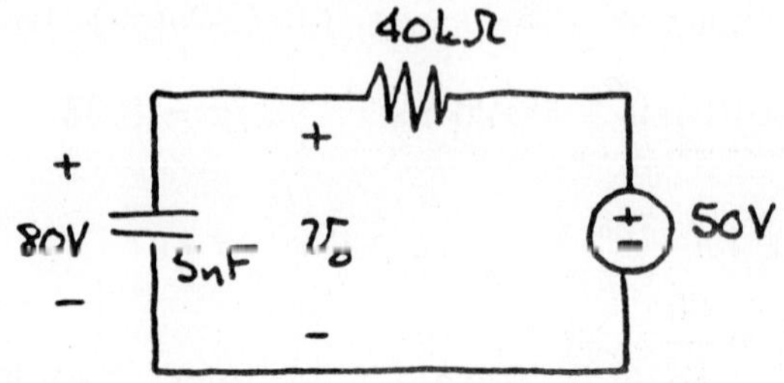

$$v_o = 50 + (80 - 50)e^{-t/\tau}$$

$$\tau = RC = (40 \times 10^3)(5 \times 10^{-9}) = 200 \times 10^{-6}; \qquad \frac{1}{\tau} = 5000$$

$$v_o = 50 + 30e^{-5000t}\ \text{V}$$

P 7.54 $\quad v_o(0) = 50\,\text{V}; \qquad v_o(\infty) = 80\,\text{V}$

$$R_{\text{Th}} = 16\,\text{k}\Omega$$

$$\tau = (16)(5 \times 10^{-6}) = 80 \times 10^{-6}; \qquad \frac{1}{\tau} = 12{,}500$$

$$v = 80 + (50 - 80)e^{-12{,}500t} = 80 - 30e^{-12{,}000t}\ \text{V}$$

P 7.55 $\quad$ For $t > 0$

$$V_{\text{Th}} = (-15)(30)i_b = -450 \times 10^3 i_b$$

$$i_b = \frac{400(12)}{48} = 100\,\mu\text{A}$$

$$V_{\rm Th} = -450 \times 10^3(100 \times 10^{-6}) = -45\,\rm V$$

$$R_{\rm Th} = 15\,\rm k\Omega$$

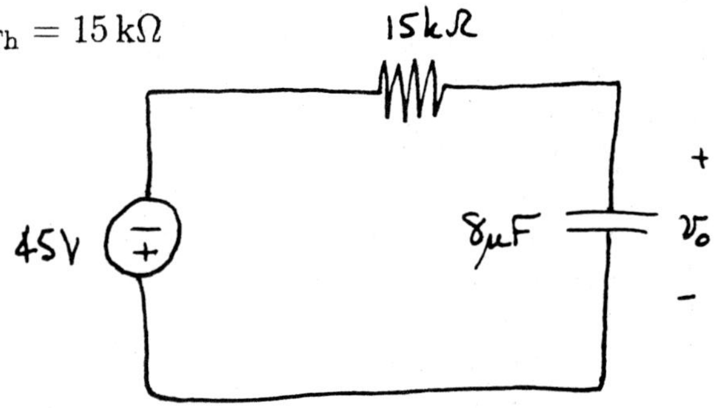

$$v_o(\infty) = -45\,\rm V; \qquad v_o(0^+) = 0$$

$$\tau = (15,000)(8)10^{-6} = 120\,\rm ms; \qquad 1/\tau = 8.33$$

$$v_o = -45 + 45e^{-8.33t}\,\rm V, \qquad t \geq 0$$

$$w(t) = \frac{1}{2}(8 \times 10^{-6})v_o^2 = 8100(1 - 2e^{-8.33t} + e^{-16.67t})\,\mu\rm J$$

$$w(\infty) = 8100\,\mu\rm J$$

$$\therefore\ \ 8100(1 - 2e^{-8.33t_o} + e^{-16.67t_o}) = 0.90(8100)$$

$$\therefore\ \ 1 - 2x + x^2 = 0.90; \qquad x = e^{-8.33t_o}$$

$$\therefore\ \ x^2 - 2x + 0.10 = 0$$

$$x_{1,2} = 1.9487, \qquad 0.0513$$

$$e^{-(25/3)t_o} = 0.0513; \qquad (25/3)t_o = \ln 19.4868; \qquad t_o = 356.4\,\rm ms$$

P 7.56 $t < 0$;

$$i_o(0^-) = (15)\frac{20}{50} = 6\,\rm mA; \qquad v_o(0^-) = (6)(10) = 60\,\rm V$$

$t = \infty$:

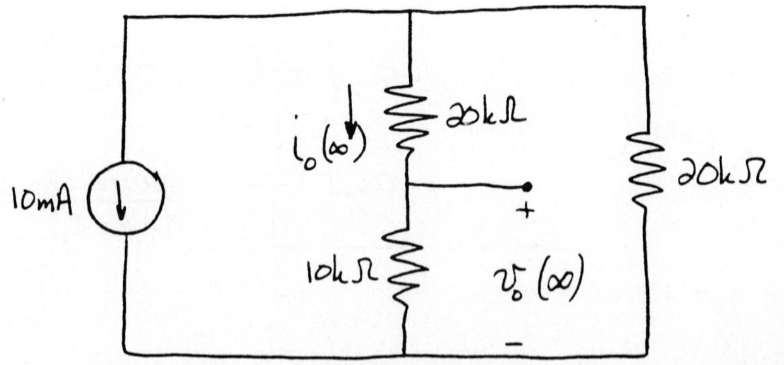

$$i_o(\infty) = -10\left(\frac{20}{50}\right) = -4\,\text{mA}; \qquad v_o(\infty) = i_o(\infty)(10) = -40\,\text{V}$$

$$R_{\text{Th}} = 10\,\text{k}\Omega\|40\,\text{k}\Omega = 8\,\text{k}\Omega; \qquad C = 125\,\text{nF}$$

$$\tau = (8)(0.125) = 1\,\text{ms}; \qquad \frac{1}{\tau} = 1000$$

$$\therefore \quad v_o(t) = -40 + 100e^{-1000t}\,\text{V}, \qquad t \geq 0^+$$

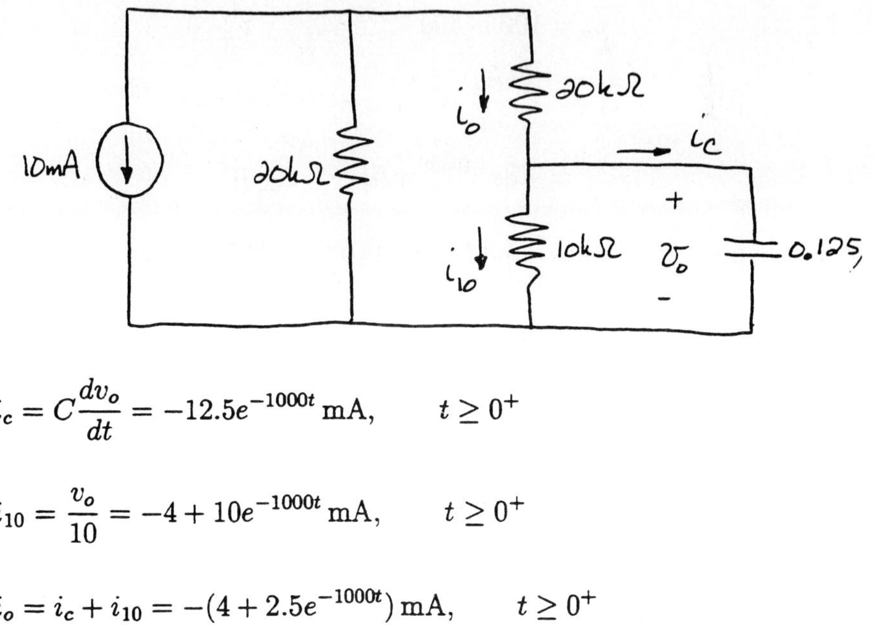

$$i_c = C\frac{dv_o}{dt} = -12.5e^{-1000t}\,\text{mA}, \qquad t \geq 0^+$$

$$i_{10} = \frac{v_o}{10} = -4 + 10e^{-1000t}\,\text{mA}, \qquad t \geq 0^+$$

$$i_o = i_c + i_{10} = -(4 + 2.5e^{-1000t})\,\text{mA}, \qquad t \geq 0^+$$

P 7.57 [a] $t < 0$

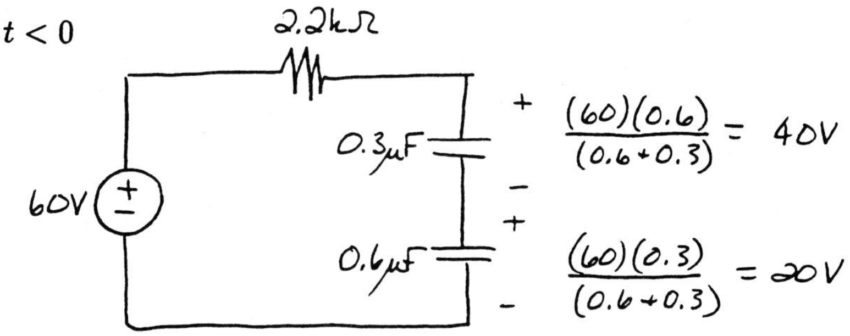

$t > 0$

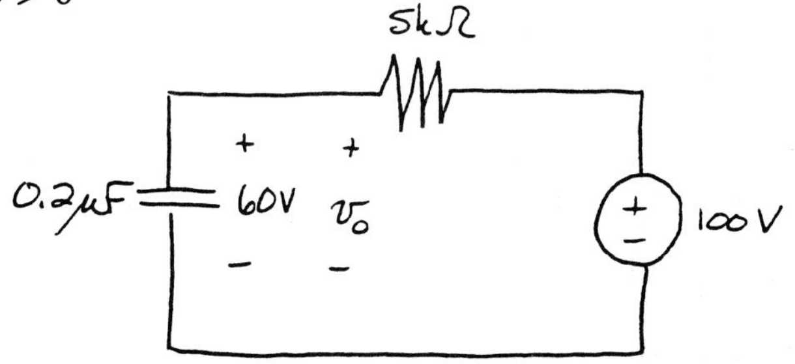

$$v_o(0^-) = v_o(0^+) = 60\,\text{V}$$

$$v_o(\infty) = 100\,\text{V}$$

$$\tau = (0.2)(5) \times 10^{-3} = 1\,\text{ms}; \qquad 1/\tau = 1000$$

$$v_o = 100 - 40e^{-1000t}\,\text{V}, \qquad t \geq 0$$

[b] $$i_o = -C\frac{dv_o}{dt} = -0.2 \times 10^{-6}[40{,}000e^{-1000t}]$$

$$= -8e^{-1000t}\,\text{mA}; \qquad t \geq 0^+$$

[c] $$v_1 = \frac{-10^6}{0.3}\int_0^t -8 \times 10^{-3}e^{-1000x}\,dx + 40$$

$$= 66.67 - 26.67e^{-1000t}\,\text{V}, \qquad t \geq 0$$

[d] $$v_2 = \frac{-10^6}{0.6}\int_0^t -8 \times 10^{-3}e^{-1000x}\,dx + 20$$

$$= 33.33 - 13.33e^{-1000t}\,\text{V}, \qquad t \geq 0$$

[e] $$w_{\text{trapped}} = \frac{1}{2}(0.3)10^{-6}(66.67)^2 + \frac{1}{2}(0.6)10^{-6}(33.33)^2$$

$$= 666.67 + 333.33 = 1000\,\mu\text{J}.$$

P 7.58 [a] $v_o(0^-) = v_o(0^+) = 48\,\text{V}$

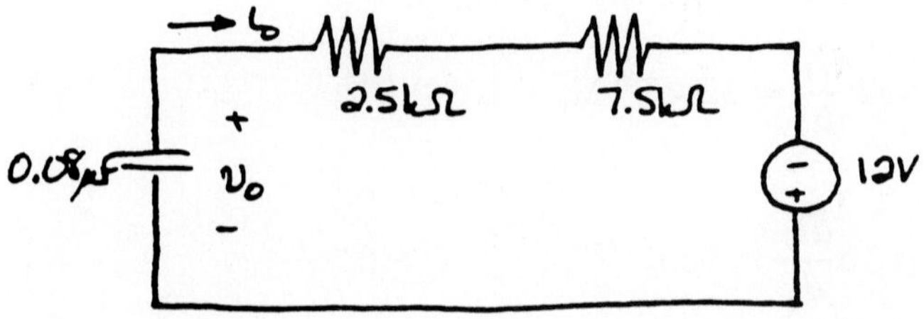

$$v_o(\infty) = 12\,\text{V}; \qquad \tau = 0.8\,\text{ms}; \qquad \frac{1}{\tau} = 1250$$

$$v_o = -12 + (48 - (-12))e^{-1250t}$$

$$v_o = -12 + 60e^{-1250t}\,\text{V}, \qquad t \geq 0$$

[b] $$i_o = -0.08 \times 10^{-6}[-75{,}000e^{-1250t}]$$

$$i_o = 6e^{-1250t}\,\text{mA}, \qquad t \geq 0^+$$

[c] $$v_g = v_o - 2.5 \times 10^3 i_o$$

$$v_g = -12 + 45e^{-1250t}\,\text{V}$$

[d] $$v_g(0^+) = -12 + 45 = 33\,\text{V}$$

Checks:

$$v_g(0^+) = i_o(0^+)7.5 \times 10^3 - 12 = 45 - 12 = 33\,\text{V}$$

$$i_{10\text{k}} = \frac{v_g}{10\text{k}} = -1.2 + 4.5e^{-1250t}\,\text{mA}$$

$$i_{30\text{k}} = \frac{v_g}{30\text{k}} = -0.4 + 1.5e^{-1250t}\,\text{mA}$$

$$-i_o + i_{10} + i_{30} + 1.6 = 0 \qquad \text{(ok)}$$

P 7.59 [a] $$L_{eq} = \frac{(3)(15)}{3 + 15} = 2.5\,\text{H}$$

$$\tau = \frac{L_{eq}}{R} = \frac{2.5}{7.5} = \frac{1}{3}\,\text{s}$$

$$i_o(0) = 0; \qquad i_o(\infty) = \frac{120}{7.5} = 16\,\text{A}$$

$$\therefore \; i_o = 16 - 16e^{-3t}\,\text{A}, \qquad t \geq 0$$

$$v_o = 120 - 7.5i_o = 120e^{-3t}\,\text{V}, \qquad t \geq 0^+$$

$$i_1 = \frac{1}{3}\int_0^t 120e^{-3x}\,dx = \frac{40}{3} - \frac{40}{3}e^{-3t}\,\text{A}, \qquad t \geq 0$$

$$i_2 = i_o - i_1 = \frac{8}{3} - \frac{8}{3}e^{-3t}\,\text{A}, \qquad t \geq 0$$

[b] $i_o(0) = i_1(0) = i_2(0) = 0$, consistent with initial conditions.
$v_o(0^+) = 120$ V, consistent with $i_o(0) = 0$.

$$v_o = 3\frac{di_1}{dt} = 120e^{-3t}\text{ V}, \qquad t \geq 0^+$$

or

$$v_o = 15\frac{di_2}{dt} = 120e^{-3t}\text{ V}, \qquad t \geq 0^+$$

The voltage solution is consistent with the current solutions.

$$\lambda_1 = 3i_1 = 40 - 40e^{-3t}\text{ Wb-turns}$$

$$\lambda_2 = 15i_2 = 40 - 40e^{-3t}\text{ Wb-turns}$$

$\therefore\ \lambda_1 = \lambda_2$ as it must, since

$$v_o = \frac{d\lambda_1}{dt} = \frac{d\lambda_2}{dt}$$

$$\lambda_1(\infty) = \lambda_2(\infty) = 40\text{ Wb-turns}$$

$$\lambda_1(\infty) = 3i_1(\infty) = 3(40/3) = 40\text{ Wb-turns}$$

$$\lambda_2(\infty) = 15i_2(\infty) = 15(8/3) = 40\text{ Wb-turns}$$

$\therefore\ i_1(\infty)$ and $i_2(\infty)$ are consistent with $\lambda_1(\infty)$ and $\lambda_2(\infty)$.

P 7.60 [a]

$$L_{eq} = \frac{L_1L_2 - M^2}{L_1 + L_2 + 2M} = \frac{50 - 25}{15 + 10} = 1\text{ H}$$

$$\tau = \frac{L}{R} = \frac{1}{20}; \qquad \frac{1}{\tau} = 20$$

$$\therefore\ i_o(t) = 4 - 4e^{-20t}\text{ A}, \qquad t \geq 0$$

[b]

$$v_o = 80 - 20i_o = 80 - 80 + 80e^{-20t} = 80e^{-20t}\text{ V}, \qquad t \geq 0^+$$

[c]

$$v_o = 5\frac{di_1}{dt} - 5\frac{di_2}{dt} = 80e^{-20t}\text{ V}$$

$$i_o = i_1 + i_2$$

$$\frac{di_o}{dt} = \frac{di_1}{dt} + \frac{di_2}{dt} = 80e^{-20t}\text{ A/s}$$

$$\therefore\ \frac{di_2}{dt} = 80e^{-20t} - \frac{di_1}{dt}$$

$$\therefore\ 80e^{-20t} = 5\frac{di_1}{dt} - 400e^{-20t} + 5\frac{di_1}{dt}$$

$$\therefore\ 10\frac{di_1}{dt} = 480e^{-20t}; \qquad di_1 = 48e^{-20t}\,dt$$

$$\int_0^{t_1} dx = \int_0^t 48e^{-20y}\,dy$$

$$i_1 = \frac{48}{-20}e^{-20y}\Big|_0^t = 2.4 - 2.4e^{-20t}\ \text{A}, \qquad t \geq 0$$

[d] $$i_2 = i_o - i_1 = 4 - 4e^{-20t} - 2.4 + 2.4e^{-20t}$$

$$= 1.6 - 1.6e^{-20t}\ \text{A}, \qquad t \geq 0$$

[e] $i_o(0) = i_1(0) = i_2(0) = 0$, consistent with zero initial stored energy.

$$v_o = L_{\text{eq}}\frac{di_o}{dt} = 1(80)e^{-20t} = 80e^{-20t}\ \text{V}, \qquad t \geq 0^+ \text{ (checks)}$$

Also,

$$v_o = 5\frac{di_1}{dt} - 5\frac{di_2}{dt} = 80e^{-20t}\ \text{V}, \qquad t \geq 0^+ \text{ (checks)}$$

$$v_o = 10\frac{di_2}{dt} - 5\frac{di_1}{dt} = 80e^{-20t}\ \text{V}, \qquad t \geq 0^+ \text{ (checks)}$$

$v_o(0^+) = 80\ \text{V}$, wich agrees with $i_o(0^+) = 0\ \text{A}$

$i_o(\infty) = 4\ \text{A}; \qquad i_o(\infty)L_{\text{eq}} = (4)(1) = 4$ Wb-turns

$i_1(\infty)L_1 + i_2(\infty)M = (2.4)(5) + (1.6)(-5) = 4$ Wb-turns (ok)

$i_2(\infty)L_2 + i_1(\infty)M = (1.6)(10) + (2.4)(-5) = 4$ Wb-turns (ok)

Therefore, the final values of i_o, i_1, and i_2 are consistent with conservation of flux linkage. Hence, the answers make sense in terms of known circuit behavior.

P 7.61 **[a]** $$L_{\text{eq}} = 5 + 10 - 2.5(2) = 10\ \text{H}$$

$$\tau = \frac{L}{R} = \frac{10}{40} = \frac{1}{4}; \qquad \frac{1}{\tau} = 4$$

$$i = 2 - 2e^{-4t}\ \text{A}$$

[b] $$v_1(t) = 5\frac{di_1}{dt} - 2.5\frac{di}{dt} = 2.5\frac{di}{dt} = 2.5(8e^{-4t}) = 20e^{-4t}\ \text{V}$$

[c] $$v_2(t) = 10\frac{di_1}{dt} - 2.5\frac{di}{dt} = 7.5\frac{di}{dt} = 7.5(8e^{-4t}) = 60e^{-4t}\ \text{V}$$

[d] $i(0) = 2 - 2 = 0$, which agrees with initial conditions.

$$80 = 40i_1 + v_1 + v_2 = 40(2 - 2e^{-4t}) + 20e^{-4t} + 60e^{-4t} = 80\ \text{V}$$

Therefore, Kirchhoff's voltage law is satisfied for all values of $t \geq 0$. Thus, the answers make sense in terms of known circuit behavior.

P 7.62 [a] $L_{eq} = 5 + 10 + 2.5(2) = 20\,\text{H}$

$$\tau = \frac{L}{R} = \frac{20}{40} = \frac{1}{2}; \qquad \frac{1}{\tau} = 2$$

$$i = 2 - 2e^{-2t}\ \text{A}$$

[b] $v_1(t) = 5\frac{di_1}{dt} + 2.5\frac{di}{dt} = 7.5\frac{di}{dt} = 7.5(4e^{-2t}) = 30e^{-2t}\ \text{V}$

[c] $v_2(t) = 10\frac{di_1}{dt} + 2.5\frac{di}{dt} = 12.5\frac{di}{dt} = 12.5(4e^{-2t}) = 50e^{-2t}\ \text{V}$

[d] $i(0) = 0$, which agrees with initial conditions.

$$80 = 40i_1 + v_1 + v_2 = 40(2 - 2e^{-2t}) + 30e^{-2t} + 50e^{-2t} = 80\ \text{V}$$

Therefore, Kirchhoff's voltage law is satisfied for all values of $t \geq 0$. Thus, the answers make sense in terms of known circuit behavior.

P 7.63 Note that for $t > 0$, $v_o = (35/40)v_c$, where v_c is the voltage across the 50 nF capacitor. Thus we will find v_c first.

$t < 0$

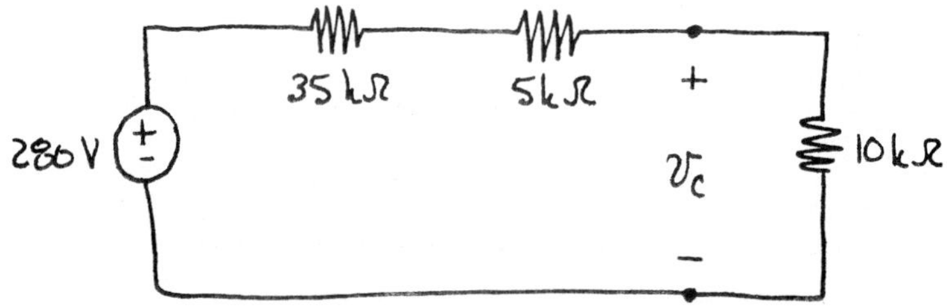

$$v_c(0) = \frac{280}{50}(10) = 56\ \text{V}$$

$0 \leq t \leq 400\,\mu\text{s}$:

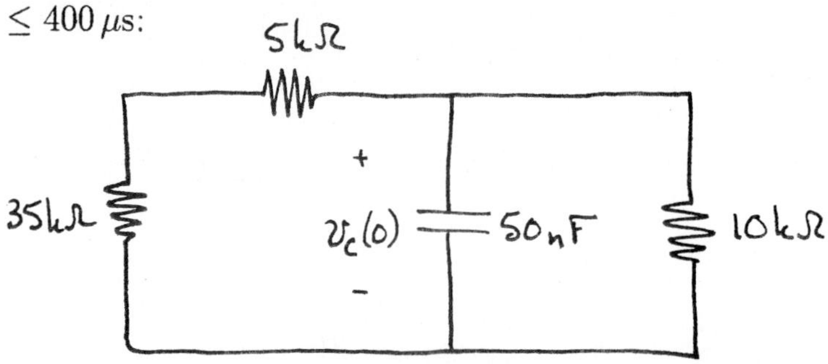

$$\tau = R_eC, \qquad R_e = \frac{(10)(40)}{50} = 8\,\text{k}\Omega$$

$$\tau = (8 \times 10^3)(50 \times 10^{-9}) = 400\,\mu\text{s}, \qquad \frac{1}{\tau} = 2500$$

$$v_c = 56e^{-2500t}\ \text{V}, \qquad t \geq 0$$

$$v_c(400\,\mu\text{s}) = 56e^{-1} = 20.60\ \text{V}$$

$400\,\mu s \le t \le 1.4\,ms$:

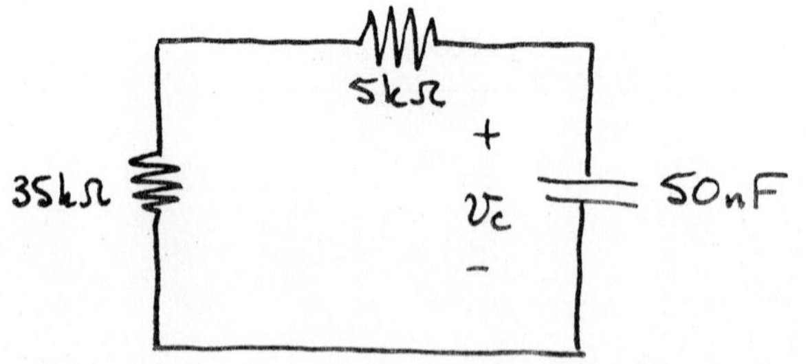

$$\tau = (40 \times 10^3)(50 \times 10^{-9}) = 2\,\text{ms}, \qquad \frac{1}{\tau} = 500$$

$$v_c = 20.60e^{-500(t-400\times 10^{-6})}\ \text{V}$$

$1.4\,ms \le t \le \infty$:

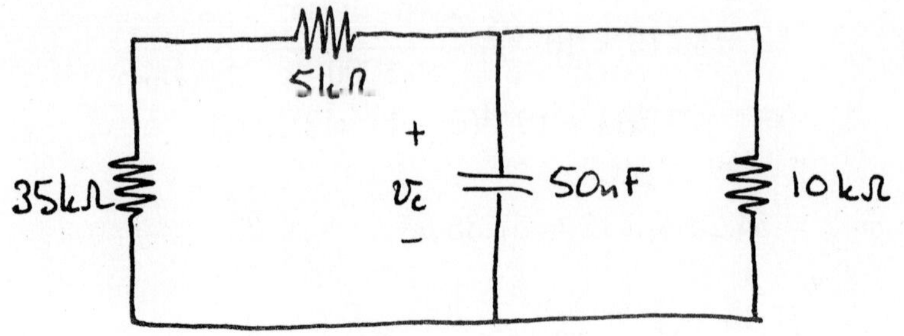

$$\tau = 400\,\mu s, \qquad \frac{1}{\tau} = 2500$$

$$v_c(1.4\text{ms}) = 20.60e^{-500(1400-400)10^{-6}} = 20.60e^{-0.5} = 12.50\ \text{V}$$

$$v_c = 12.50e^{-2500(t-1.4\times 10^{-3})}\ \text{V}$$

$$v_c(1.6\text{ms}) = 12.50e^{-2500(1.6-1.4)10^{-3}} = 12.50e^{-0.5} = 7.58\ \text{V}$$

$$v_o = (35/40)(7.58) = 6.63\ \text{V}$$

P 7.64 $$w(0) = \frac{1}{2}(50 \times 10^{-9})(56)^2 = 78.4\,\mu\text{J}$$

$0 \le t \le 400\,\mu s$:

$$v_c = 56e^{-2500t}: \qquad v_c^2 = 3136e^{-5000t}$$

$$p_{10k} = 3136 \times 10^{-4}e^{-5000t}$$

$$\begin{aligned} w_{10k} &= \int_0^{400\times10^{-6}} 3136 \times 10^{-4} e^{-5000t}\,dt \\ &= 3136 \times 10^{-4} \frac{e^{-5000t}}{-5000}\Bigg|_0^{400\times10^{-6}} \\ &= -6272 \times 10^{-8}(e^{-2} - 1) = 54.23\,\mu\text{J} \end{aligned}$$

$1.4\,\text{ms} \le t \le \infty$:

$$v_c = 12.50e^{-2500(t-1.4\times10^{-3})}\ \text{V}; \qquad v_c^2 = 156.13e^{-5000(t-1.4\times10^{-3})}$$

$$p_{10k} = 156.13 \times 10^{-4} e^{-5000(t-1.4\times10^{-3})}$$

$$\begin{aligned} w_{10k} &= \int_{1.4\times10^{-3}}^{\infty} 156.13 \times 10^{-4} e^{-5000(t-1.4\times10^{-3})}\,dt \\ &= 156.13 \times 10^{-4} \frac{e^{-5000(t-1.4\times10^{-3})}}{-5000}\Bigg|_{1.4\times10^{-3}}^{\infty} \\ &= -311.83 \times 10^{-8}(0 - 1) = 3.12\,\mu\text{J} \end{aligned}$$

$$w_{10k} = 54.23 + 3.12 = 57.35\,\mu\text{J}$$

$$\% = \frac{57.35}{78.4}(100) = 73.15\%$$

To check, find the energy dissipated in the 40 kΩ resistance:
$0 \le t \le 400\,\mu\text{s}$:

$$v_c = 56e^{-2500t}; \qquad v_c^2 = 3136e^{-5000t}$$

$$p_{40k} = \frac{3136}{40} \times 10^{-3} e^{-5000t}$$

$$\begin{aligned} w_{40k} &= 784 \times 10^{-4} \frac{e^{-5000t}}{-5000}\Bigg|_0^{400\times10^{-6}} \\ &= -156.8(10^{-7})(e^{-2} - 1) = 13.56\,\text{mJ} \end{aligned}$$

$400\,\mu\text{s} \le t \le 1\,\text{ms}$:

$$v_c = 20.60e^{-500(t-400\times10^{-6})}; \qquad v_c^2 = 424.41e^{-1000(t-400\times10^{-6})}$$

$$w_{40k} = 106.10 \times 10^{-4} \int_{400\times10^{-6}}^{10^{-3}}$$

$$= 106.10 \times 10^{-4} \frac{e^{-1000(t-400\times10^{-6})}}{-1000}\Bigg|_{400\times10^{-6}}^{10^{-3}}$$

$$= -106.10(10^{-7})(e^{-0.6} - 1) = 4.79\,\text{mJ}$$

$1.4\,\text{ms} \leq t \leq \infty$:

$$v_c = 12.49e^{-2500(t-1.4\times10^{-3})}; \qquad v_c^2 = 156.13e^{-5000(t-1.4\times10^{-3})}$$

Note in this interval the energy dissipated in the 40k resistor will be 1/4th that dissipated in the 10k resistor.

$$w_{40k} = \frac{1}{4}(3.12) = 0.78\,\mu\text{J}$$

$$w_{40k} = 13.56 + 6.71 + 0.78 = 21.05\,\mu\text{J}$$

$$w_{40k} + w_{10k} = 57.35 + 21.05 = 78.40\,\mu\text{J}$$

P 7.65

$$v_o(0) = \frac{120}{120}(80) = 80\ \text{V}$$

$$v_o(\infty) = -6(25) = -150\ \text{V}$$

$$\tau = (25 \times 10^3)(40 \times 10^{-9}) = 10^{-3}\,\text{s}; \qquad \frac{1}{\tau} = 1000$$

$$v_o = -150 + (80 + 150)e^{-1000t} = -150 + 230e^{-1000t}\ \text{V}, \qquad t \geq 0$$

P 7.66 [a] $t < 0$:

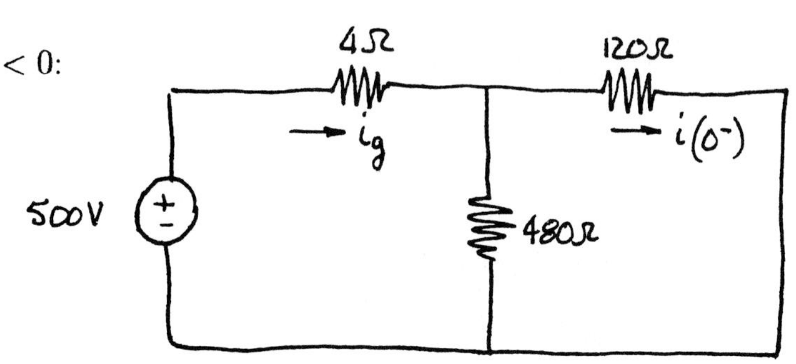

$$i_g = \frac{500}{4 + 96} = 5\ \text{A}$$

$$i(0^-) = \frac{5(480)}{600} = 4\ \text{A} = i(0^+)$$

[b] $0 \leq t \leq 100\,\mu$s:

$$i = 4e^{-t/\tau}$$

$$\frac{1}{\tau} = \frac{R}{L} = \frac{120 + 96\|480}{20 \times 10^{-3}} = 10{,}000$$

$$i = 4e^{-10{,}000t}$$

$$i(25\mu\text{s}) = 4e^{-10^4(25)\times 10^{-6}} = 4e^{-0.25} = 3.12\,\text{A}$$

[c] $$i(100\mu\text{s}) = 4e^{-1} = 1.47\,\text{A}$$

$100\,\mu\text{s} \leq t \leq \infty$:

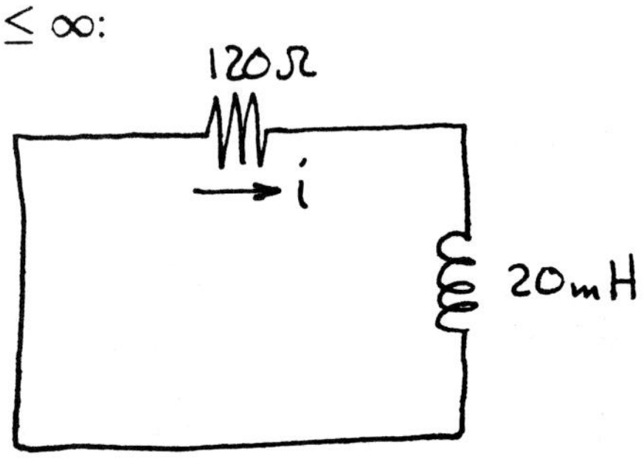

$$\frac{1}{\tau} = \frac{R}{L} = \frac{120}{20} \times 10^3 = 6000$$

$$i = 1.47e^{-6000(t-100\times 10^{-6})}\,\text{A}$$

$$i(200\mu\text{s}) = 1.47e^{-6000(100)\times 10^{-6}} = 1.47e^{-0.6} = 807.59\,\text{mA}$$

[d] $0 \leq t \leq 100\,\mu$s:

$$i = 4e^{-10{,}000t}$$

$$v = L\frac{di}{dt} = (20 \times 10^{-3})(4)(-10^4)e^{-10^4t} = -800e^{-10^4t}\,\text{V}$$

$$v(100^-\mu\text{s}) = -800e^{-10^4(100\times 10^{-6})} = -800e^{-1} = -294.30\,\text{V}$$

[e] $100\,\mu\text{s} \leq t \leq \infty$:

$$i = 1.47e^{-6000(t-100\times 10^{-6})}$$

$$v = (20 \times 10^{-3})(1.47)(-6000)e^{-6000(t-100\times 10^{-6})}$$

$$= -176.58e^{-6000(t-100\times 10^{-6})}\,\text{V}$$

$$v(100^+\mu\text{s}) = -176.58\,\text{V}$$

P 7.67 $0 \le t \le 100\,\mu s$;

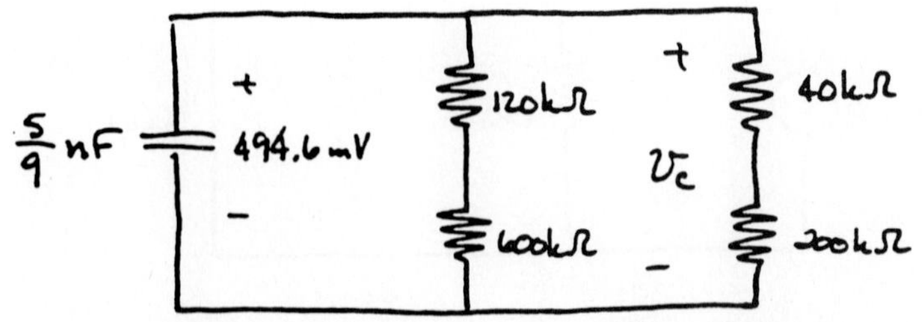

$$R_e = 720\|240 = 180\,\text{k}\Omega; \qquad \tau = \left(\frac{5}{9}\right)(180) = 100\,\mu\text{s}$$

$$v_c = 494.6e^{-10{,}000t}\ \text{mV}$$

$$v_c(50\,\mu\text{s}) = 494.6e^{-0.5} = 300\,\text{mV}$$

$50\,\mu s \le t \le \infty$:

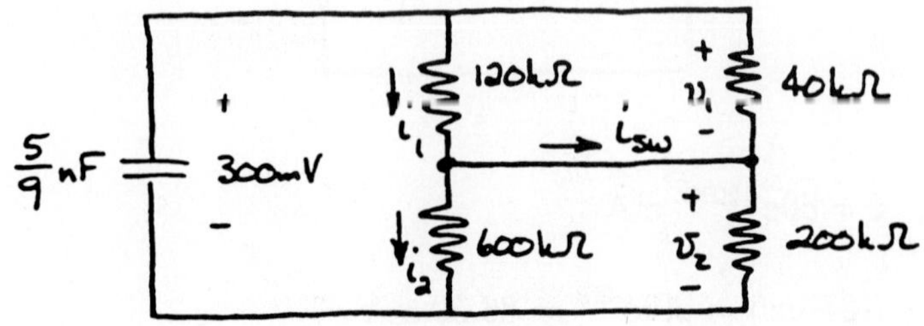

$$R_e = 120\|400 + 600\|200 = 30 + 150 = 180\,\text{k}\Omega$$

$$\tau = \left(\frac{5}{9}\right)(180) = 100\,\mu\text{s}; \qquad \frac{1}{\tau} = 10{,}000$$

$$v_c = 300e^{-10{,}000(t-50\,\mu s)}\ \text{mV}$$

$$v_1 = \frac{30}{180}v_c = 50e^{-10{,}000(t-50\,\mu s)}\ \text{mV}$$

$$v_2 = \frac{150}{180}v_c = 250e^{-10{,}000(t-50\,\mu s)}\ \text{mV}$$

$$i_1 = \frac{v_1}{120\times 10^3} = 4166.67e^{-10{,}000(t-50\,\mu s)}\ \text{nA}$$

$$i_2 = \frac{v_2}{600\times 10^3} = 4166.67e^{-10{,}000(t-50\,\mu s)}\ \text{nA}$$

$$i_{sw} = i_1 - i_2 = 0\,\text{A}$$

$$i_{sw}(100\,\mu\text{s}) = 0\,\text{A}$$

P 7.68 For $t < 0$:

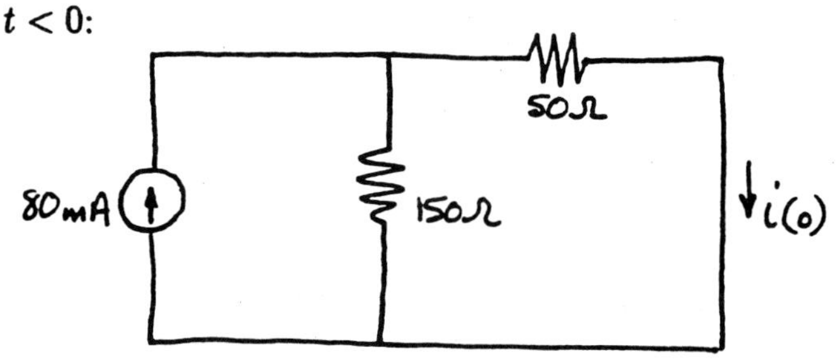

$$i(0) = \frac{80(150)}{200} = 60\,\text{mA}$$

$0 \leq t \leq 250\,\mu\text{s}$:

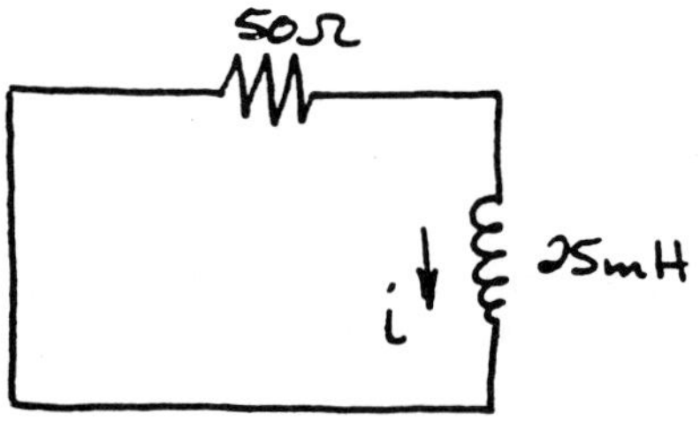

$$i = 60e^{-2000t}\ \text{mA}$$

$$i(250\mu\text{s}) = 60e^{-0.5} = 36.39\,\text{mA}$$

$250\,\mu\text{s} \leq t \leq 650\,\mu\text{s}$:

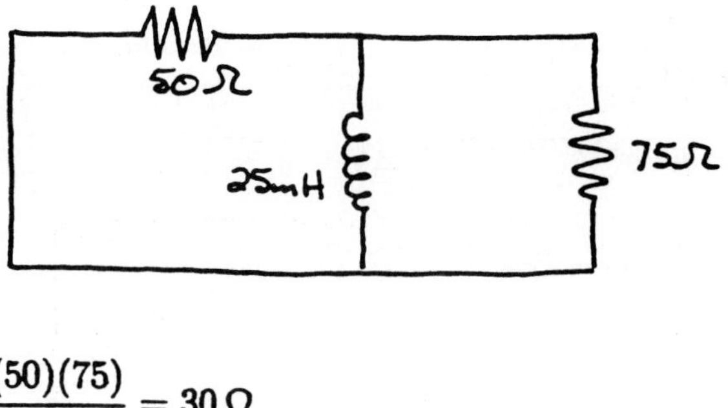

$$R_{eq} = \frac{(50)(75)}{125} = 30\,\Omega$$

$$\frac{1}{\tau} = \frac{R}{L} = \frac{30}{25} \times 10^3 = 1200$$

$$i = 36.39e^{-1200(t-250\times10^{-3})}\ \text{mA}$$

$650\,\mu\text{s} \leq t \leq \infty$:

$$i(650\mu\text{s}) = 36.39e^{-0.48} = 22.52\,\text{mA}$$

$$i = 22.52e^{-2000(t-650\times10^{-6})}\ \text{mA}$$

$$v = L\frac{di}{dt}; \qquad L = 25\ \text{mH}$$

$$\frac{di}{dt} = 22.52(-2000)\times10^{-3}e^{-2000(t-650\times10^{-6})} = -45.04e^{-2000(t-650\times10^{-6})}$$

$$v = (25\times10^{-3})(-45.04)e^{-2000(t-650\times10^{-6})}$$

$$= -1.13e^{-2000(t-650\times10^{-6})}\ \text{V}, \qquad t > 650^{+}\ \mu\text{s}$$

$$v(1\text{ms}) = -1.13e^{-2000(350)\times10^{-6}} = -559.12\ \text{mV}$$

P 7.69 From the solution to Problem 7.68, the initial energy is

$$w(0) = \frac{1}{2}(25\ \text{mH})(60\ \text{mA})^2 = 45\ \mu\text{J}$$

For $650\ \mu\text{s} \le t \le \infty$:

$$w(t) = \frac{1}{2}(25\ \text{mH})(22.52e^{-2000(t-650\times10^{-3})}\ \text{mA})^2 = (0.04)(45\ \mu\text{J})$$

Solving,

$$t = 964.72\ \mu\text{s}$$

P 7.70 $0 \le t \le 3\ \mu\text{s}$:

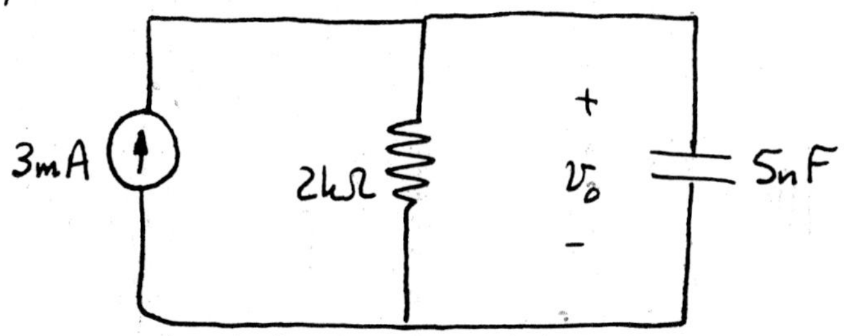

$$\tau = RC = (2\times10^3)(5\times10^{-9}) = 10\ \mu\text{s}; \qquad 1/\tau = 100{,}000$$

$$v_o(0) = 0\ \text{V}; \qquad v_o(\infty) = 6\ \text{V}$$

$$v_o = 6 - 6e^{-100{,}000t}\ \text{V} \qquad 0 \le t \le 3\ \mu\text{s}$$

$3\,\mu s \leq t \leq \infty$:

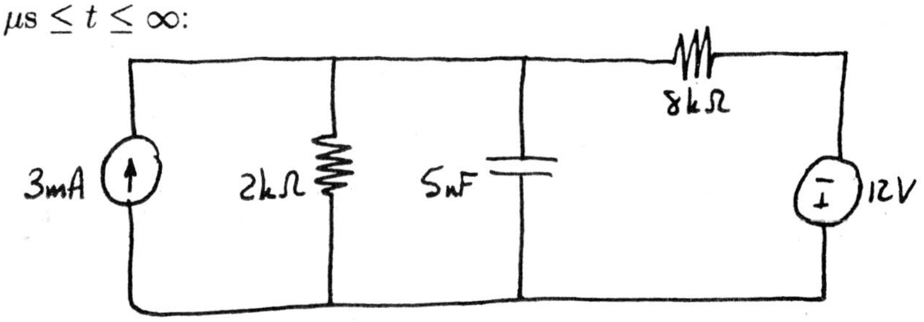

$t = \infty$:

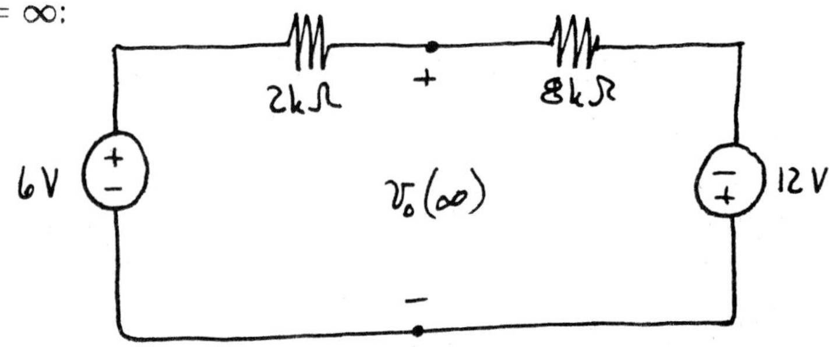

$$i = \frac{6 - (-12)}{10} = 1.8\,\text{mA}$$

$$v_o(\infty) = 6 - 2i = 2.4\,\text{V}$$

$$v_o(3\,\mu s) = 6 - 6^{-0.3} = 1.555\,\text{V}$$

$$v_o = 2.4 + (1.555 - 2.4)e^{-(t\,-\,3\,\mu s)/\tau}$$

$$R_{\text{Th}} = 2\,\text{k}\Omega \| 8\,\text{k}\Omega = 1.6\,\text{k}\Omega$$

$$\tau = (1.6)(5) = 8\,\mu s; \qquad 1/\tau = 125{,}000$$

$$v_o = 2.4 - 0.845e^{-125{,}000(t\,-\,3\,\mu s)} \qquad 3\,\mu s \leq t \leq \infty$$

P 7.71 $t < 0$:

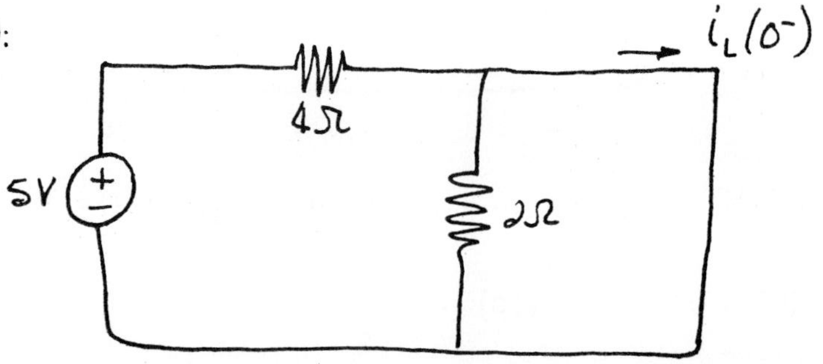

$$i_L(0^-) = 5/4 = 1.25\,\text{A} = i_L(0^+)$$

$0 \le t \le 1$:

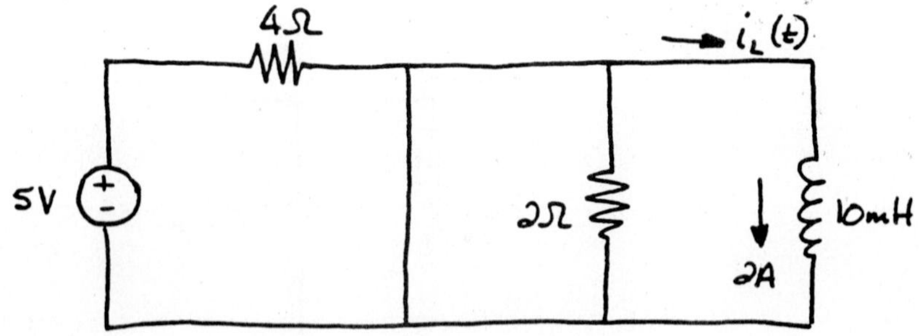

$\tau = 5/0 = \infty$

$i_L(t) = 1.25e^{-t/\infty} = 1.25e^{-0} = 1.25$

$i_L(t) = 1.25\text{ A}$

$1 \le t \le \infty$:

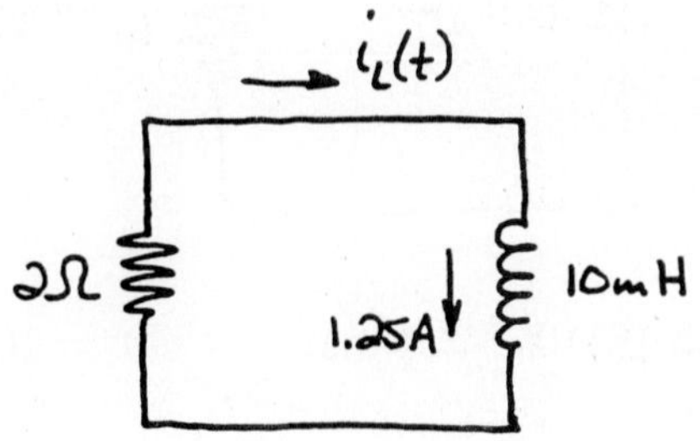

$$\tau = \frac{10 \times 10^{-3}}{2} = 5\text{ ms}; \qquad 1/\tau = 200$$

$i_L(t) = 1.25e^{-200(t-1)}\text{ A}$

P 7.72 $t < 0$:

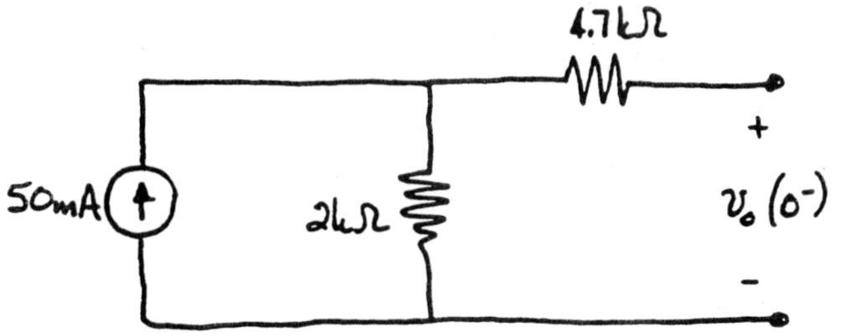

$v_c(0^-) = (50)(2000) \times 10^{-3} = 100\text{ V} = v_c(0^+)$

$0 \leq t \leq 250$ ms:

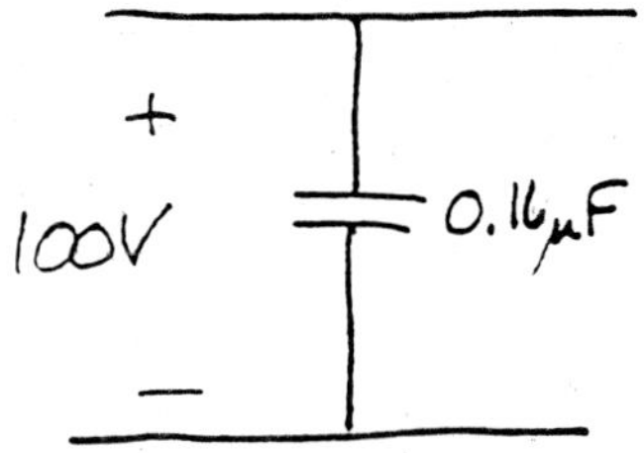

$$\tau = \infty; \qquad 1/\tau = 0; \qquad v_o = 100e^{-0} = 100 \text{ V}$$

250 ms $\leq t \leq \infty$:

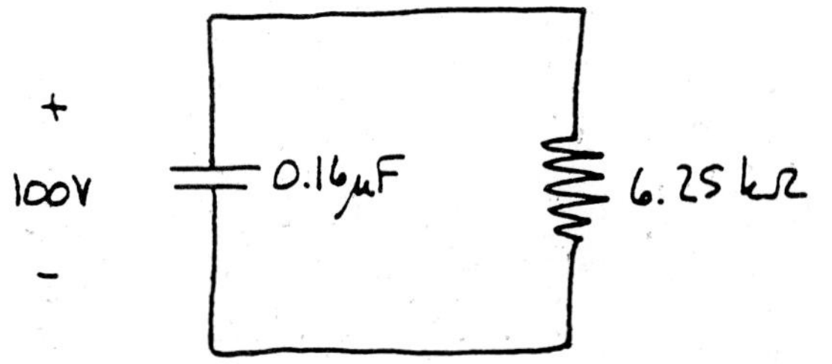

$$\tau = (6.25)(0.16)10^{-3} = 1 \text{ ms}; \qquad 1/\tau = 1000; \qquad v_o = 100e^{-1000(t-0.25)} \text{ V}$$

Summary:

$$v_o = 100 \text{ V}, \qquad 0 \leq t \leq 250 \text{ ms}$$

$$v_o = 100e^{-1000(t-0.25)} \text{ V}, \qquad 250 \text{ ms} \leq t \leq \infty$$

P 7.73 [a] $\tau = RC = (8000)(100) \times 10^{-9} = 800\,\mu\text{s}; \qquad 1/\tau = 1250$

$$i_o = v_o = 0 \qquad t < 0$$

$$i_o(0^+) = 20\left(\frac{6}{8}\right) = 15 \text{ mA}, \qquad i_o(\infty) = 0$$

$$\therefore \; i_o = 15e^{-1250t} \text{ mA} \qquad 0^+ \leq t \leq 0.5^- \text{ ms}$$

$$i_{6k\Omega} = 20 - 15e^{-1250t} \text{ mA}$$

$$\therefore \; v_o = 120 - 90e^{-1250t} \text{ V} \qquad 0^+ \leq t \leq 05^- \text{ ms}$$

$$v_c = v_o - 2 \times 10^3 i_o = 120 - 120e^{-1250t} \text{ V} \qquad 0 \leq t \leq 0.5 \text{ ms}$$

$$v_c(0.5 \text{ ms}) = 120 - 120e^{-0.625} = 55.77 \text{ V}$$

$$\therefore \; i_o(0.5^+ \text{ ms}) = \frac{-55.77}{8} = -6.97 \text{ mA}$$

$$i_o(\infty) = 0$$

$$i_o = -6.97e^{-1250(t-500\mu s)}\,\text{mA}, \qquad 0.5^+\ \text{ms} \le t \le \infty$$

$$v_o = -6000i_o = 41.83e^{-1250(t-500\mu s)}\,\text{V} \qquad 0.5^+\ \text{ms} \le t \le \infty$$

Summary part (a)

$$i_o = 0 \qquad t < 0$$

$$i_o = 15e^{-1250t}\,\text{mA} \qquad (0^+ \le t \le 0.5^-\ \text{ms})$$

$$i_o = -6.97e^{-1250(t-500\mu s)}\,\text{mA} \qquad 0.5^+\ \text{ms} \le t \le \infty$$

$$v_o = 0 \qquad t < 0$$

$$v_o = 120 - 90e^{-1250t}\,\text{V}, \qquad 0 \le t \le 0.5^-\ \text{ms}$$

$$v_o = 41.83e^{-1250(t-500\mu s)}\,\text{V}, \qquad 0.5^+\ \text{ms} \le t \le \infty$$

[b] $i_o(0^-) = 0$

$$i_o(0^+) = 15\,\text{mA}$$

$$i_o(0.5^-\ \text{ms}) = 15e^{-0.625} = 8.03\,\text{mA}$$

$$i_o(0.5^+\ \text{ms}) = -6.97\,\text{mA}$$

[c] $v_o(0^-) = 0$

$$v_o(0^+) = 30\,\text{V}$$

$$v_o(0.5^-\ \text{ms}) = 120 - 90e^{-0.625} = 71.83\,\text{V}$$

$$v_o(0.5^+\ \text{ms}) = 41.83$$

[d]

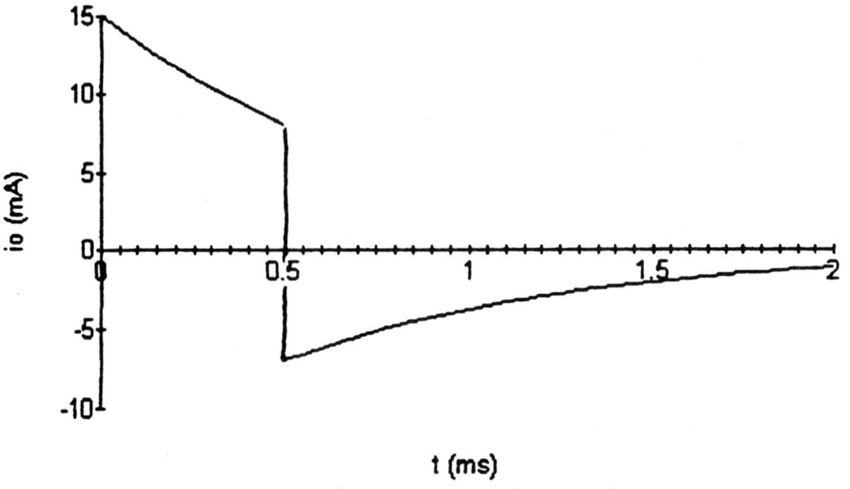

[e]

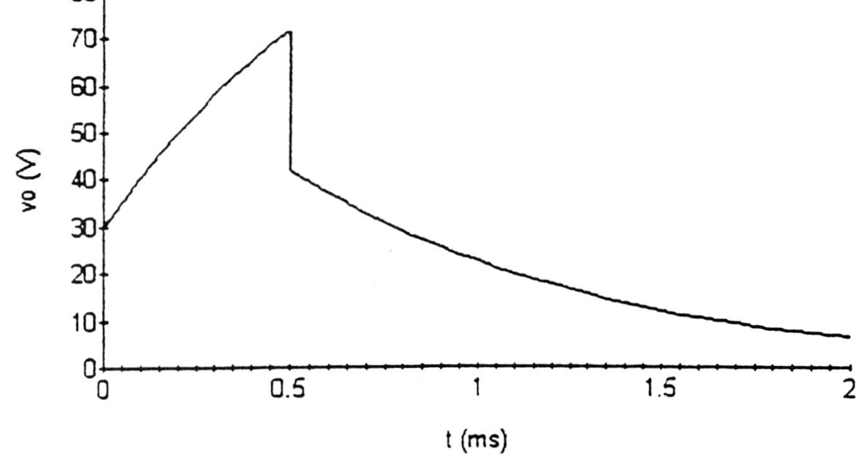

P 7.74 [a] $0 \leq t \leq 1$ ms:

$$v_c(0^+) = 0; \qquad v_c(\infty) = 50\,\text{V};$$

$$RC = 400 \times 10^3(0.01 \times 10^{-6}) = 4\,\text{ms}; \qquad 1/RC = 250$$

$$v_c = 50 - 50e^{-250t}$$

$$v_o = 50 - 50 + 50e^{-250t} = 50e^{-250t}\,\text{V}, \qquad 0 \leq t \leq 1\,\text{ms}$$

$1\,\text{ms} \leq t \leq \infty$:

$$v_c(1\,\text{ms}) = 50 - 50^{-0.25} = 11.06\,\text{V}$$

$$v_c(\infty) = 0\,\text{V}$$

$$\tau = 4\,\text{ms}; \qquad 1/\tau = 250$$

$$v_c = 11.06e^{-250(t-0.001)}\,\text{V}$$

$$v_o = -v_c = -11.06e^{-250(t-0.001)}\,\text{V}, \qquad 1\,\text{ms} \leq t \leq \infty$$

[b]

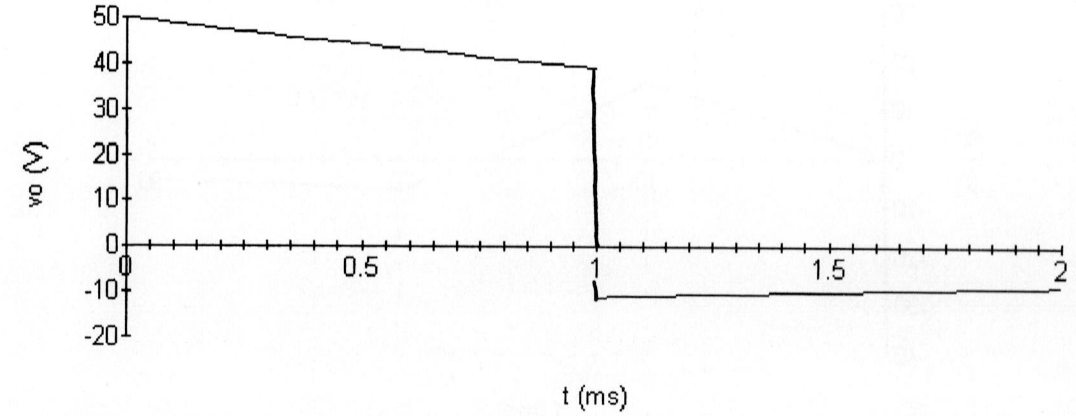

P 7.75 [a] $t < 0; \qquad v_o = 0$

$0 \le t \le 10\,\text{ms}$:

$$\tau = (50)(0.4) \times 10^{-3} = 20\,\text{ms}; \qquad 1/\tau = 50$$

$$v_o = 40 - 40e^{-50t}\ \text{V}, \qquad 0 \le t \le 10\,\text{ms}$$

$$v_o(10\,\text{ms}) = 40(1 - e^{-0.5}) = 15.74\,\text{V}$$

$10\,\text{ms} \le t \le 20\,\text{ms}$:

$$v_o = -40 + 55.74e^{-50(t-0.01)}\ \text{V}$$

$$v_o(20\,\text{ms}) = -40 + 55.74e^{-0.5} = -6.19\,\text{V}$$

$20\,\text{ms} \le t \le \infty$:

$$v_o = -6.19e^{-50(t-0.02)}\ \text{V}$$

[b]

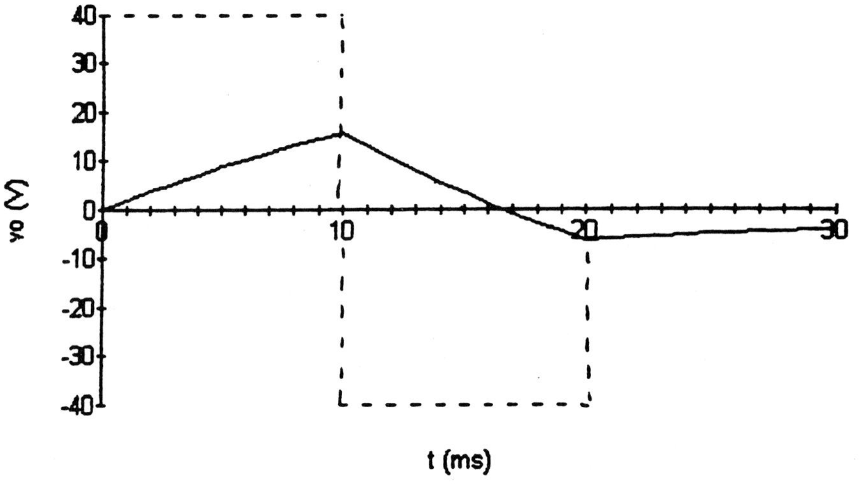

[c] $t \leq 0: \qquad v_o = 0$

$0 \leq t \leq 10\,\text{ms}$:

$$v_o = 40 - 40e^{-250t}\,\text{V}, \qquad 0 \leq t \leq 10\,\text{ms}$$

$$v_o(10\,\text{ms}) = 40 - 40e^{-2.5} = 36.72\,\text{V}$$

$10\,\text{ms} \leq t \leq 20\,\text{ms}$:

$$v_o = -40 + 76.72e^{-250(t-0.01)}\,\text{V}, \qquad 10\,\text{ms} \leq t \leq 20\,\text{ms}$$

$$v_o(20\,\text{ms}) = -40 + 76.72e^{-2.5} = -33.7\,\text{V}$$

$20\,\text{ms} \leq t \leq \infty$:

$$v_o = -33.7e^{-250(t-0.02)}\,\text{V}, \qquad 20\,\text{ms} \leq t \leq \infty$$

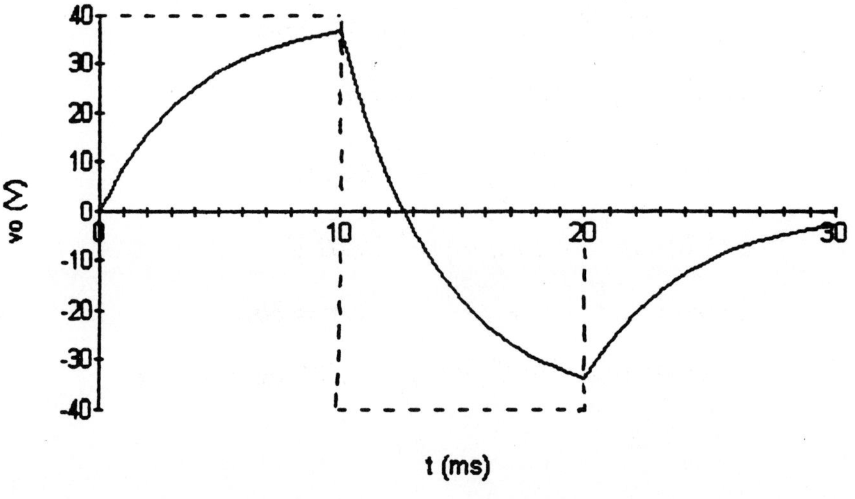

P 7.76 [a] $i_o(0) = 0; \qquad i_o(\infty) = 25\,\text{mA}$

$$\frac{1}{\tau} = \frac{R}{L} = \frac{8000}{250} \times 10^3 = 32{,}000$$

$$i_o = (25 - 25e^{-32{,}000t})\,\text{mA}, \qquad 0 \le t \le 50\,\mu s$$

$$v_o = 0.25\frac{di_o}{dt} = 200e^{-32{,}000t}\,\text{V}, \qquad 0 \le t \le 50\,\mu s$$

$50\,\mu s \le t \le \infty$:

$$i_o(50\mu s) = 25 - 25e^{-1.6} = 19.95\,\text{mA}; \qquad i_o(\infty) = 0$$

$$i_o = 19.95e^{-32{,}000(t-50\times10^{-6})}\,\text{mA}$$

$$v_o = (0.25)\frac{di_o}{dt} = -159.62e^{-32{,}000(t-50\mu s)}$$

$$\therefore\ t < 0: \quad v_o = 0$$

$$0 \le t \le 50\,\mu s: \quad v_o = 200e^{-32{,}000t}\,\text{V}$$

$$50\,\mu s \le t \le \infty: \quad v_o = -159.62e^{-32{,}000(t-50\mu s)}$$

[b] $v_o(50^-\,\mu s) = 200e^{-1.6} = 40.38\,\text{V}$

$$v_o(50^+\mu s) = -159.62\,\text{V}$$

[c] $i_o(50^-\,\mu s) = i_o(50^+\mu s) = 19.95\,\text{mA}$

P 7.77 [a] $0 \le t \le 2.5\,\text{ms}$

$$v_o(0^+) = 80\,\text{V}; \qquad v_o(\infty) = 0$$

$$\tau = \frac{L}{R} = 2\,\text{ms}; \qquad 1/\tau = 500$$

$$v_o(t) = 80e^{-500t}\,\text{V}, \qquad 0^+ \le t \le 2.5\,\text{ms}$$

$$v_o(2.5^-\ \text{ms}) = 80e^{-1.25} = 22.92\,\text{V}$$

$$i_o(2.5^-\ \text{ms}) = \frac{(80 - 22.92)}{20} = 2.85\,\text{A}$$

$$v_o(2.5^+\ \text{ms}) = -20(2.85) = -57.08\,\text{V}$$

$$v_o(\infty) = 0; \qquad \tau = 2\,\text{ms}; \qquad 1/\tau = 500$$

$$v_o = -57.08e^{-500(t-0.0025)}\,\text{V} \qquad 2.5^+\ \text{ms} \le t \le \infty$$

[b]

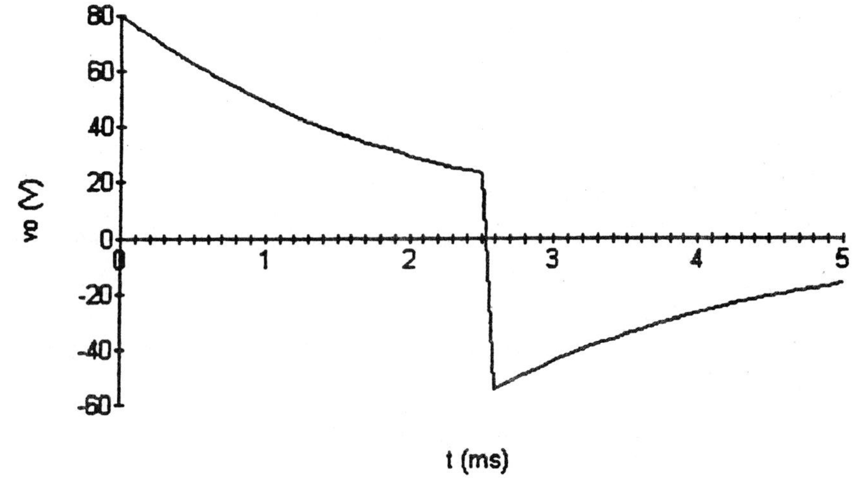

[c] $v_o(5\,\text{ms}) = -16.35\,\text{V}$

$$i_o = \frac{+18.60}{20} = 817.68\,\text{mA}$$

P 7.78 $t > 0$:

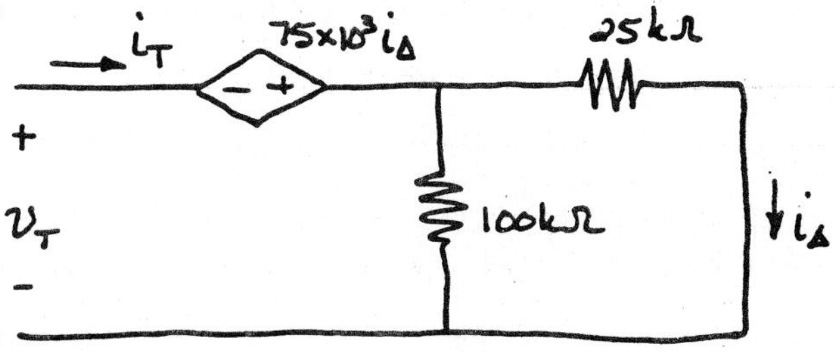

$$v_T = -75 \times 10^3 i_\Delta + 20 \times 10^3 i_T$$

$$i_\Delta = \frac{100}{125} i_T = 0.8 i_T$$

$$\therefore \quad v_T = -60 \times 10^3 i_T + 20 \times 10^3 i_T$$

$$R_{\text{Th}} = \frac{v_T}{i_T} = -40\,\text{k}\Omega$$

$$\tau = RC = -40 \times 10^3 (0.025) \times 10^{-6} = -10^{-3}$$

$$v_c = 25e^{1000t}\,\text{V}; \qquad 25e^{1000t} = 50{,}000$$

$$1000t = \ln 2000 \quad \therefore \quad t = 7.6\,\text{ms}$$

P 7.79 Find the Thévenin equivalent with respect to the terminals of the capacitor.

R_{Th} calculation:

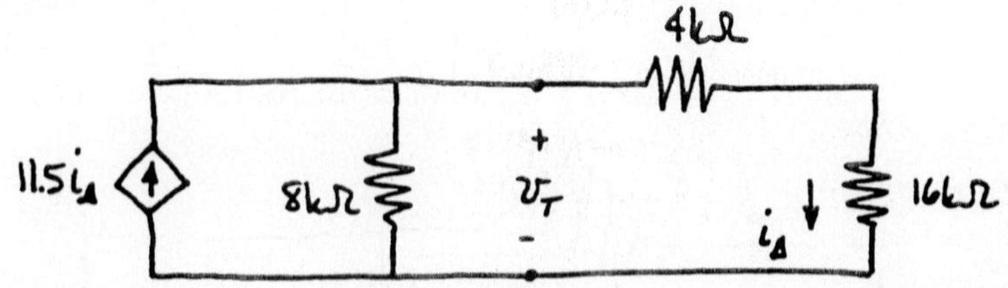

$$i_T = \frac{v_T}{8000} + \frac{v_T}{20{,}000} - 11.5\frac{v_T}{20{,}000}$$

$$\frac{i_T}{v_T} = \frac{2.5 + 1 - 11.5}{20{,}000} = \frac{-8}{20{,}000}$$

$$\therefore \quad \frac{v_T}{i_T} = \frac{-20{,}000}{8} = -2500\,\Omega$$

Open circuit voltage calculation:

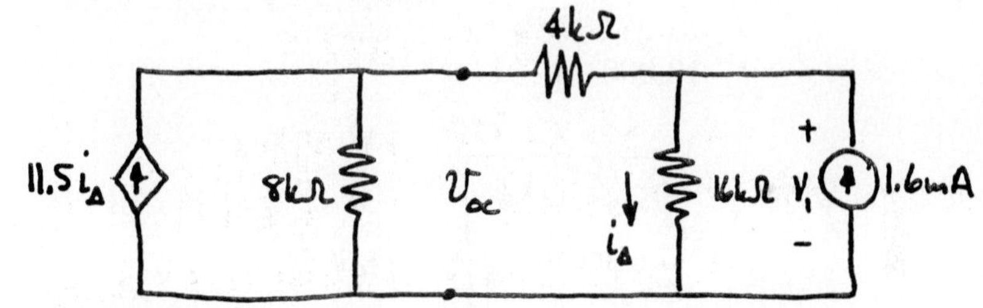

$$\frac{v_{oc}}{8000} + \frac{v_{oc} - v_1}{4000} - 11.5i_\Delta = 0$$

$$\frac{v_1 - v_{oc}}{4000} + \frac{v_1}{16{,}000} - 1.6 \times 10^{-3} = 0$$

$$i_\Delta = \frac{v_1}{16{,}000}$$

Solving, $v_{oc} = -12.4\text{ V}$

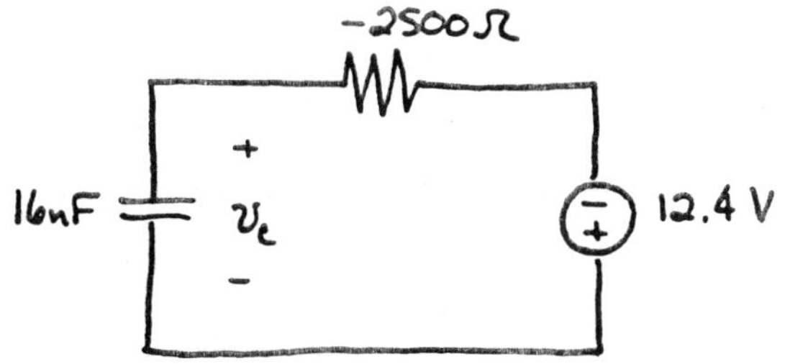

$v_c(0) = 0; \qquad v_c(\infty) = -12.4\text{ V}$

$$\tau = RC = (-2500)(16 \times 10^{-9}) = -40 \times 10^{-6}; \qquad \frac{1}{\tau} = -25{,}000$$

$$v_c = -12.4 + 12.4e^{25{,}000t} = 930$$

$$e^{25{,}000t} = 76; \qquad 25{,}000t = \ln 76; \qquad t = 173.23\,\mu\text{s}$$

P 7.80

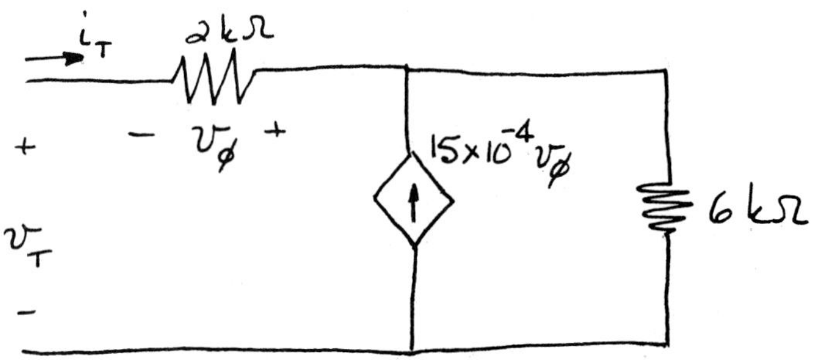

$$v_T = 2000i_T + 6000(i_T + 15 \times 10^{-4}v_\phi) = 8000i_T + 9v_\phi$$

$$= 8000i_T + 9(-2000i_T)$$

$$\frac{v_T}{i_T} = -10{,}000$$

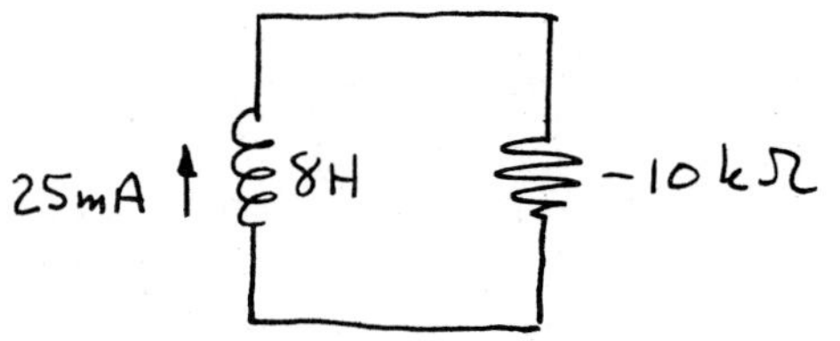

$$\tau = \frac{8}{-10} \times 10^{-3} = -0.8\,\text{ms}; \qquad 1/\tau = -1250$$

$$i = 25e^{1250t}\ \text{mA}$$

$$\therefore \quad 25e^{1250t} \times 10^{-3} = 12; \qquad t = \frac{\ln 480}{1250} = 4.94\,\text{ms}$$

P 7.81 [a]

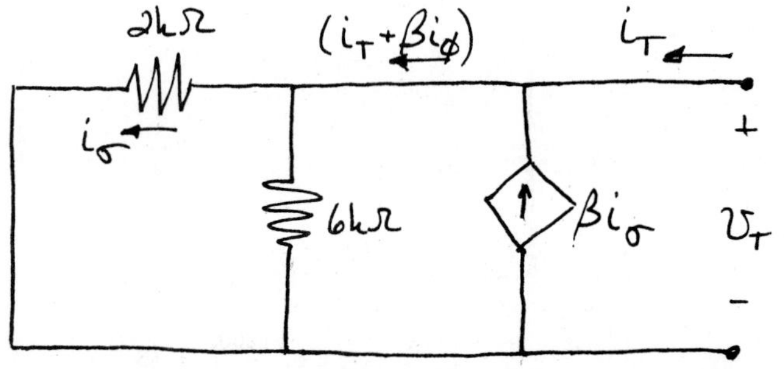

$$v_T = 2000i_\sigma$$

$$i_\sigma = \frac{6}{8}(i_T + \beta i_\sigma) = 0.75 i_T + 0.75\beta i_\sigma$$

$$i_\sigma(1 - 0.75\beta) = 0.75 i_T$$

$$i_\sigma = \frac{0.75 i_T}{1 - 0.75\beta}; \qquad 2000 i_\sigma = \frac{1500 i_T}{(1 - 0.75\beta)}$$

$$R_{\text{Th}} = \frac{v_T}{i_T} = \frac{1500}{1 - 0.75\beta} = -3000$$

$$1 - 0.75\beta = -0.5 \qquad \therefore\ \beta = 2$$

[b] Find V_{Th};

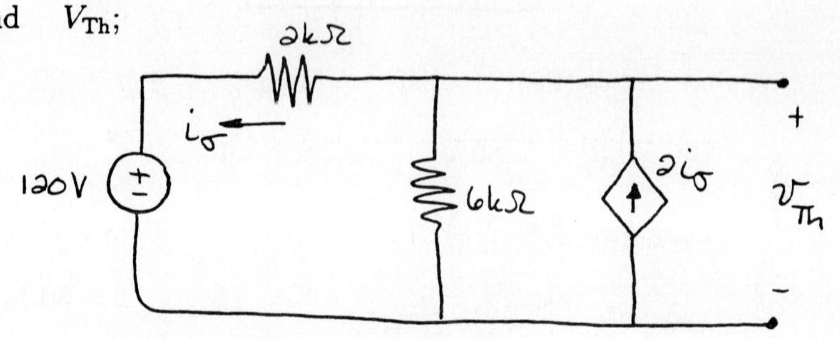

$$\frac{V_{\text{Th}} - 120}{2000} + \frac{V_{\text{Th}}}{6000} - 2\frac{(V_{\text{Th}} - 120)}{2000} = 0$$

$V_{\text{Th}} = 180$ V

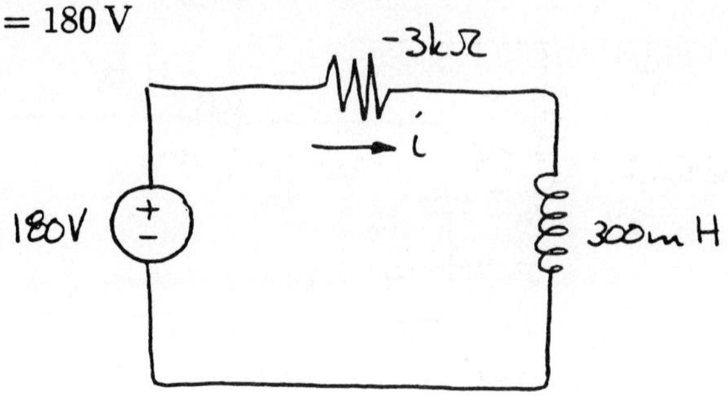

$$180 = -3000i + 0.3\frac{di}{dt}$$

$$\frac{di}{dt} = 600 + 10{,}000i = 10{,}000(i + 0.06)$$

$$\frac{di}{i + 0.06} = 10{,}000\,dt$$

$$\int_0^i \frac{dx}{x + 0.06} = \int_0^t 10{,}000\,dx$$

$$\therefore\ i = -60 + 60e^{10{,}000t}\ \text{mA}$$

$$\frac{di}{dt} = (60 \times 10^{-3})(10{,}000)e^{10{,}000t} = 600e^{10{,}000t}$$

$$v = 0.3\frac{di}{dt} = 180e^{10{,}000t} = 36{,}000; \qquad e^{10{,}000t} = 200$$

$$\therefore \quad t = \frac{\ln 200}{10{,}000} = 529.83\,\mu\text{s}$$

P 7.82 [a]

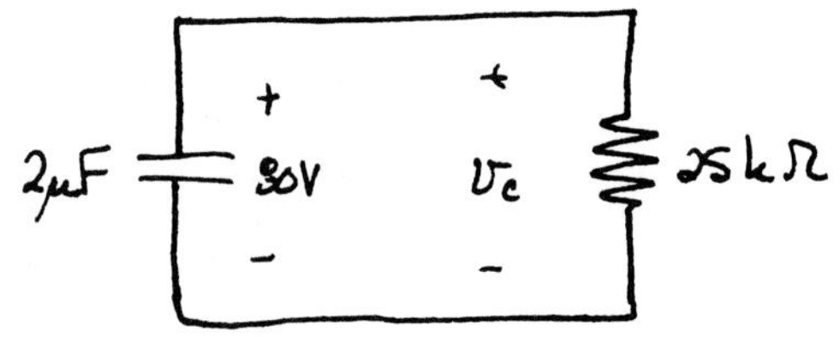

$$\tau = (25)(2) \times 10^{-3} = 50\,\text{ms}; \qquad 1/\tau = 20$$

$$v_c(0^+) = 80\,\text{V}; \qquad v_c(\infty) = 0$$

$$v_c = 80e^{-20t}\,\text{V}$$

$$\therefore \quad 80e^{-20t} = 5; \qquad e^{20t} = 16; \qquad t = 50\,\ln 16\,\text{ms} = 138.63\,\text{ms}$$

[b] $0^+ < t < 138.63$ ms:

$$i = (2 \times 10^{-6})(-1600e^{-20t}) = -3.2e^{-20t}\,\text{mA}$$

138.63^+ ms $< t \leq \infty$:

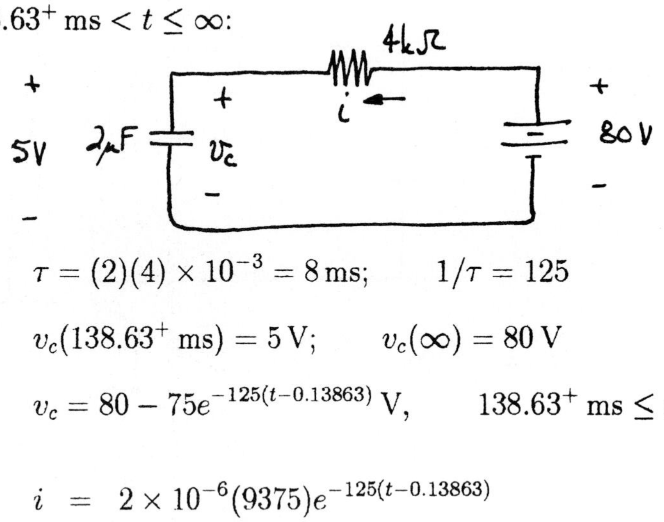

$$\tau = (2)(4) \times 10^{-3} = 8\,\text{ms}; \qquad 1/\tau = 125$$

$$v_c(138.63^+\,\text{ms}) = 5\,\text{V}; \qquad v_c(\infty) = 80\,\text{V}$$

$$v_c = 80 - 75e^{-125(t-0.13863)}\,\text{V}, \qquad 138.63^+\,\text{ms} \leq t \leq \infty$$

$$\begin{aligned} i &= 2 \times 10^{-6}(9375)e^{-125(t-0.13863)} \\ &= 18.75e^{-125(t-0.13863)}\,\text{mA}, \qquad 138.63^+\,\text{ms} \leq t \leq \infty \end{aligned}$$

[c] $$80 - 75e^{-125\Delta t} = 0.85(80) = 68$$

$$80 - 68 = 75e^{-125\Delta t} = 12$$

$$e^{125\Delta t} = 6.25; \qquad \Delta t = 8\,\ln 6.25\,\text{ms} \cong 14.66\,\text{ms}$$

P 7.83 $0 \leq t \leq 20\,\text{ms}$:

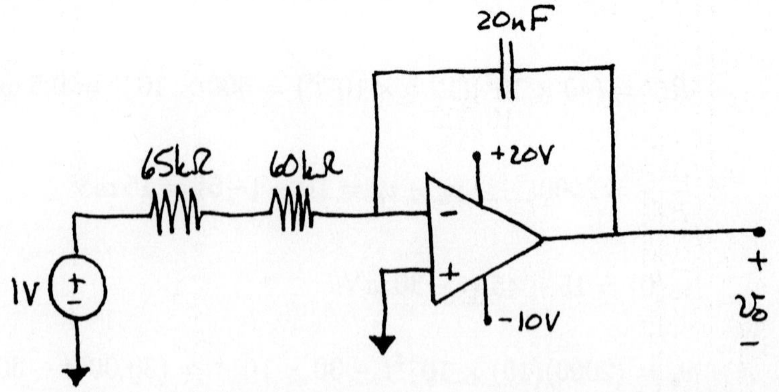

$$v_o = -\frac{1}{RC_f}\int_0^{20\times 10^{-3}} 1\,dt + 0$$

$$RC_f = (125 \times 10^3)(20 \times 10^{-9}) = 2500 \times 10^{-6}$$

$$\frac{1}{RC_f} = \frac{1{,}000{,}000}{2500} = 400$$

$$v_o = -400(20 \times 10^{-3} - 0) = -8\,\text{V}$$

$20 \leq t \leq \infty$:

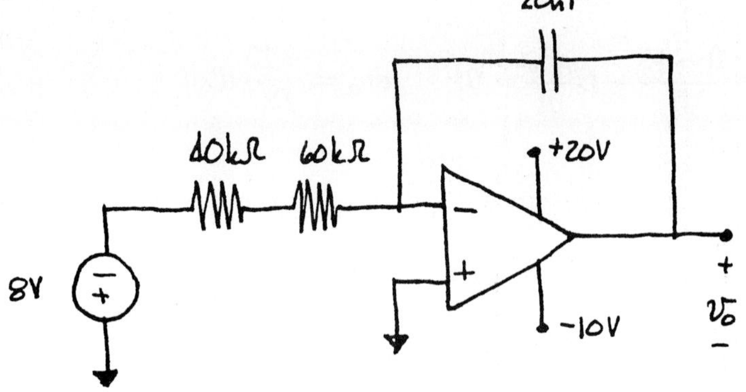

$$v_o = -\frac{1}{RC_f}\int_{20\times 10^{-3}}^{t} -8\,dy - 8$$

$$RC_f = (100 \times 10^3)(20 \times 10^{-9}) = 2 \times 10^{-3}$$

$$v_o = -500(-8)(t - 20 \times 10^{-3}) + (-8) = 4000t - 88$$

$$4000t - 88 = 20; \qquad \therefore \quad t = 27\,\text{ms}$$

P 7.84

$$v_o = \frac{1}{RC}\int_0^t (v_b - v_a)\,dy + v_o(0)$$

$$RC = (40\times10^3)(12.5\times10^{-9}) = 500\times10^{-6} = 0.5\,\text{ms}$$

$$\frac{1}{RC} = 2000; \qquad v_b - v_a = 10 - (-5) = 15\,\text{mV}$$

$$v_o(0) = 15 - 45 = -30\,\text{mV}$$

$$v_o = (2000)(15)\times10^{-3}t - 30\times10^{-3} = (30{,}000t - 30)\,\text{mV}$$

$$v_p = 10 + (15-10)e^{-2000t}\,\text{mV} = [10 + 5e^{-2000t}]\,\text{mV}$$

$$v_f = v_o - v_p = (30{,}000t - 40 - 5e^{-2000t})\,\text{mV}$$

P 7.85

$$\frac{0-15}{R} - 60\times10^{-9}\frac{dv_o}{dt} = 0$$

$$\therefore\quad v_o = \frac{-250\times10^6 t}{R}$$

$$\therefore\quad R = \frac{(-250\times10^6)(3\times10^{-3})}{-15} = 50\times10^3 = 50\,\text{k}\Omega$$

P 7.86

$$\frac{0-15}{R} - C\frac{dv_o}{dt} = 0; \qquad dv_o = \frac{-15}{RC}\,dt$$

$$v_o - v_o(0) = \frac{-15}{RC}t$$

$$v_o = \frac{-15}{RC}t + v_o(0) = \frac{-250\times10^6 t}{R} + 5 = -15$$

$$\therefore\quad R = \frac{250\times10^6(8\times10^{-3})}{20} = 100\,\text{k}\Omega$$

P 7.87

$$v_2 = \frac{15(20)}{(50)} = 6\,\text{V}$$

$$\frac{6+4}{50{,}000} + C\frac{d}{dt}(6 - v_o) = 0$$

$$\therefore \quad \frac{dv_o}{dt} = \frac{10 \times 10^6}{50{,}000(0.5)} = 400$$

$$dv_o = 400\,dt; \qquad v_o = 400t + v_o(0)$$

$$v_o(0) = 6 - 16 = -10\,\text{V}$$

$$\therefore \quad v_o = 400t - 10\,\text{V}$$

$$0 = 400t_o - 10$$

$$t_o = \frac{10}{400} = 25\,\text{ms}$$

P 7.88 [a] $v_p = 3 + (0 - 3)e^{-t/\tau}$

$$\tau = (125 \times 10^3)(8 \times 10^{-9}) = 10^{-3}; \qquad 1/\tau = 1000$$

$$v_p = 3 - 3e^{-1000t}\,\text{V}; \qquad v_n = v_p$$

$$\frac{v_n}{5} + \frac{v_n - v_o}{20} = 0$$

$$\therefore \quad v_o = 5v_n = 5v_p = 15 - 15e^{-1000t}\,\text{V}$$

$$15 - 15e^{-1000t} = 10; \qquad e^{1000t} = 3$$

$$\therefore \quad t = \ln 3 = 1.10\,\text{ms}$$

[b] $v_p = 3 + (-2 - 3)e^{-1000t} = 3 - 5e^{-1000t}$

$$v_o = 5v_p = 15 - 25e^{-1000t}\,\text{V}$$

$$15 - 25e^{-1000t} = 10; \qquad e^{1000t} = 5$$

$$\therefore \quad t = \ln 5 = 1.61\,\text{ms}$$

P 7.89 [a] $\dfrac{Cdv_p}{dt} + \dfrac{v_p - v_b}{R} = 0;$ therefore $\dfrac{dv_p}{dt} + \dfrac{1}{RC}v_p = \dfrac{v_b}{RC}$

$$\frac{v_n - v_a}{R} + C\frac{d(v_n - v_o)}{dt} = 0;$$

therefore $\dfrac{dv_o}{dt} = \dfrac{dv_n}{dt} + \dfrac{v_n}{RC} - \dfrac{v_a}{RC}$

But $v_n = v_p$

Therefore $\dfrac{dv_n}{dt} + \dfrac{v_n}{RC} = \dfrac{dv_p}{dt} + \dfrac{v_p}{RC} = \dfrac{v_b}{RC}$

Therefore $\dfrac{dv_o}{dt} = \dfrac{1}{RC}(v_b - v_a); \qquad v_o = \dfrac{1}{RC}\displaystyle\int_0^t (v_b - v_a)\,dy$

[b] The output is the integral of the difference between v_b and v_a and then scaled by a factor of $1/RC$.

[c] $$v_o = \frac{1}{RC}\int_0^t (v_b - v_a)\,dx$$

$$RC = (40)\times 10^3(25)\times 10^{-9} = 1\,\text{ms}$$

$$v_b - v_a = 50\,\text{mV}$$

$$v_o = 50\int_0^t dx = 50t; \qquad 50t_{sat} = 12; \qquad t_{sat} = 240\,\text{ms}$$

P 7.90 [a] $$RC = (200\times 10^3)(25\times 10^{-9}) = 5\times 10^{-3}; \qquad \frac{1}{RC} = 200$$

$0 \le t \le 5\,\mu s$:

$$\begin{aligned} v_g &= 0.6\times 10^6 t \\ v_o &= -200\int_0^t 0.6\times 10^6 x\,dx + 0 \\ &= -12\times 10^7\frac{x^2}{2}\Big|_0^t = -6\times 10^7 t^2 \end{aligned}$$

$$v_o(5\,\mu s) = -6\times 10^7(5\times 10^{-6})^2 = -1.5\times 10^{-3}\,\text{V}$$

$5\,\mu s \le t \le 15\,\mu s$:

$$\begin{aligned} v_g &= 6 - 0.6\times 10^6 t \\ v_o &= 200\int_{5\times 10^{-6}}^t (6 - 0.6\times 10^6 x)\,dx - 1.5\times 10^{-3} \\ &= -200\left[1200x\Big|_{5\times 10^{-6}}^t + 12\times 10^7\frac{x^2}{2}\Big|_{5\times 10^{-6}}^t\right] - 1.5\times 10^{-3} \\ &= -1200t + 6\times 10^{-3} + 6\times 10^7 t^2 - 1.5\times 10^{-3} - 1.5\times 10^{-3} \\ &= 6\times 10^7 t^2 - 1200t + 3\times 10^{-3} \end{aligned}$$

$$v_o(15\,\mu s) = 6\times 10^7(15\times 10^{-6})^2 - 1200(15\times 10^{-6}) + 3\times 10^{-3}$$

$$= -1.5\times 10^{-3}$$

$15\,\mu s \le t \le 20\,\mu s$:

$$\begin{aligned} v_g &= -12 + 0.6\times 10^6 t \\ v_o &= -200\int_{15\times 10^{-6}}^t (-12 + 0.6\times 10^6 x)\,dx - 1.5\times 10^{-3} \\ &= -200\left[2400x\Big|_{15\times 10^{-6}}^t - 12\times 10^7\frac{x^2}{2}\Big|_{15\times 10^{-6}}^t\right] - 1.5\times 10^{-3} \\ &= 2400t - 36\times 10^{-3} - 6\times 10^7 t^2 + 13.5\times 10^{-3} - 1.5\times 10^{-3} \\ &= -6\times 10^7 t^2 + 2400t - 24\times 10^{-3} \end{aligned}$$

$$v_o(20\,\mu s) = -6\times 10^7(20\times 10^{-6})^2 + 2400(20\times 10^{-6}) - 24\times 10^{-3} = 0$$

[b]

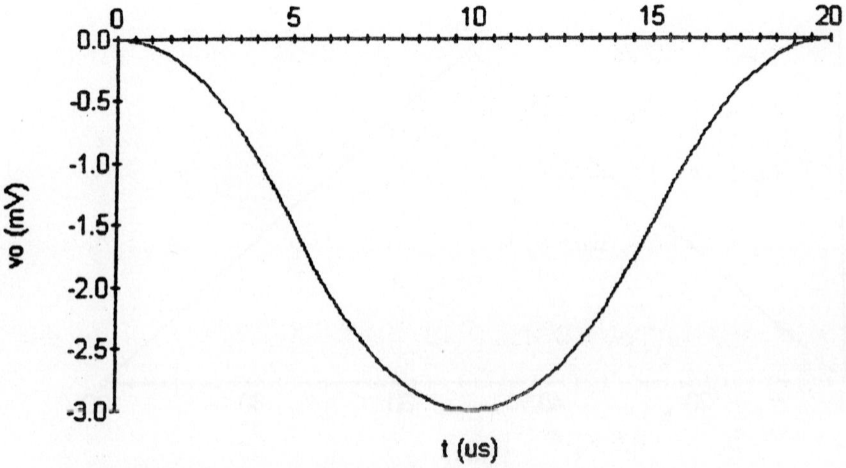

[c] The output voltage will also repeat. This follows from the observation that at $t = 20\,\mu s$ the output voltage is zero, hence there is no energy stored in the capacitor. This means the circuit is in the same state at $t = 20\,\mu s$ as it was at $t = 0$, thus as v_g repeats itself, so will v_o.

P 7.91 [a] $RC = 40(50) \times 10^{-6} = 2\,\text{ms}; \qquad \frac{1}{RC} = 500; \qquad v_o = 0, \quad t < 0$

[b] $0 \leq t \leq 50\,\text{ms}:$

$$v_o = -500\int_0^t -0.50\,dx = 250t\ \text{V}$$

[c] $50\,\text{ms} \leq t \leq 100\,\text{ms};$

$$v_o(0.05) = 250(0.05) = 12.5\ \text{V}$$

$$v_o(t) = -500\int_{0.05}^t 0.50\,dx + 12.5 = -250(t - 0.05) + 12.5 = -250t$$

[d] $100\,\text{ms} \leq t \leq \infty:$

$$v_o(0.1) = -25 + 25 = 0\ \text{V}$$

$$v_o(t) = 0\ \text{V}$$

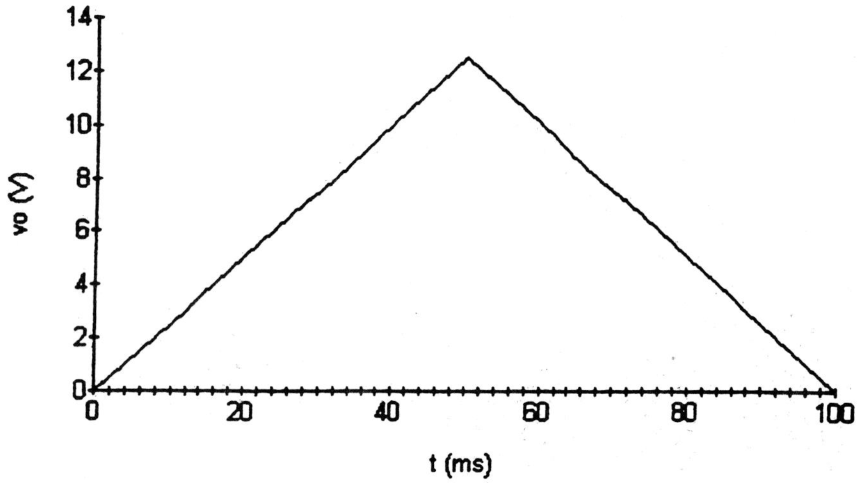

P 7.92 [a] $v_o = 0, \qquad t < 0$

[b] $R_fC_f = (4 \times 10^6)(50 \times 10^{-9}) = 0.2; \qquad \dfrac{1}{R_fC_f} = 5$

$$v_o = \frac{-4 \times 10^6}{40 \times 10^3}(-0.5)[1 - e^{-5t}] = 50(1 - e^{-5t})\text{ V}, \qquad 0 \le t \le 50\text{ ms}$$

[c] $v_o(0.05) = 50(1 - e^{-0.25}) \cong 11.06\text{ V}$

$$\begin{aligned} v_o &= \frac{-V_mR_f}{R_s} + \frac{V_mR_f}{R_s}(2 - e^{-0.25})e^{-5(t-0.05)} \\ &= -50 + 50(2 - e^{-0.25})e^{-5(t-0.05)} \\ &= -50 + 61.06e^{-5(t-0.05)}\text{ V}, \qquad 50\text{ ms} \le t \le 100\text{ ms} \end{aligned}$$

[d] $v_o(0.10) = -50 + 61.06e^{-0.25} \cong -2.45\text{ V}$

$$v_o = -2.45e^{-5(t-0.1)}\text{ V}, \qquad 100\text{ ms} \le t \le \infty$$

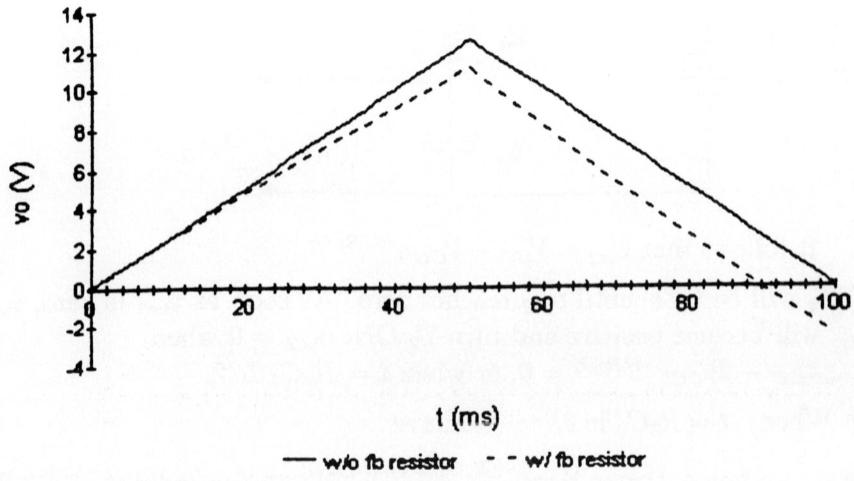

P 7.93 [a] While T_2 has been ON, C_2 is charged to V_{CC}, positive on the left terminal. At the instant T_1 turns ON the capacitor C_2 is connected across $b_2 - e_2$, thus $v_{be2} = -V_{CC}$. This negative voltage snaps T_2 OFF. Now the polarity of the voltage on C_2 starts to reverse, that is, the right-hand terminal of C_2 starts to charge toward $+V_{CC}$. At the same time, C_1 is charging toward V_{CC}, positive on the right. At the instant the charge on C_2 reaches zero, v_{be2} is zero, T_2 turns ON. This makes $v_{be1} = -V_{CC}$ and T_1 snaps OFF. Now the capacitors C_1 and C_2 start to charge with the polarities to turn T_1 ON and T_2 OFF. This switching action repeats itself over and over as long as the circuit is energized. At the instant T_1 turns ON, the voltage controlling the state of T_2 is governed by the following circuit:

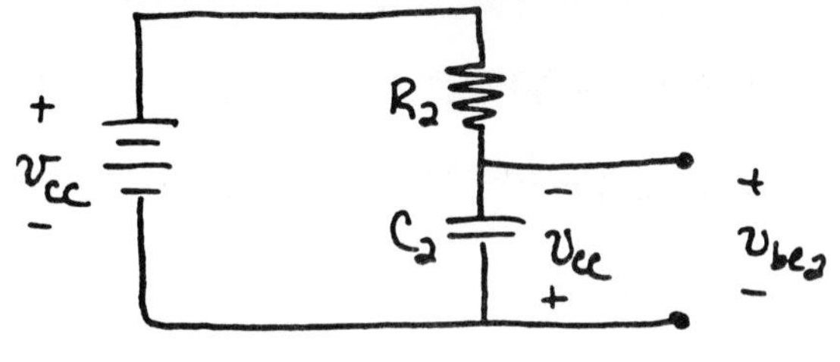

It follows that $v_{be2} = V_{CC} - 2V_{CC}e^{-t/R_2C_2}$.

[b] While T_2 is OFF and T_1 is ON, the output voltage v_{ce2} is the same as the voltage across C_1, thus

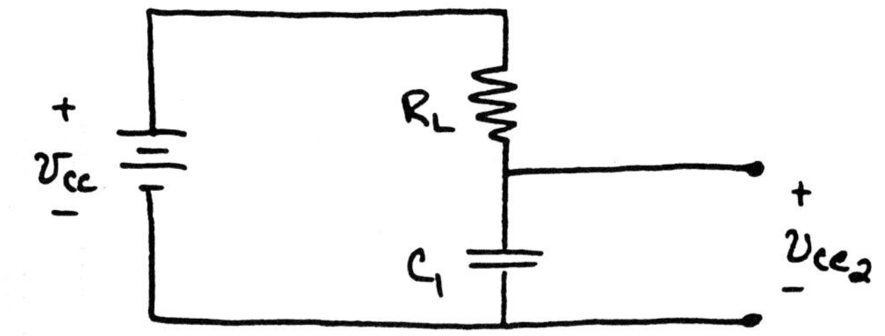

It follows that $v_{ce2} = V_{CC} - V_{CC}e^{-t/R_LC_1}$.

[c] T_2 will be OFF until v_{be2} reaches zero. As soon as v_{be2} is zero, i_{b2} will become positive and turn T_2 ON. $v_{be2} = 0$ when $V_{CC} - 2V_{CC}e^{-t/R_2C_2} = 0$, or when $t = R_2C_2 \ln 2$.

[d] When $t = R_2C_2 \ln 2$, we have

$$v_{ce2} = V_{CC} - V_{CC}e^{-[(R_2C_2 \ln 2)/(R_LC_1)]} = V_{CC} - V_{CC}e^{-10 \ln 2} \cong V_{CC}$$

[e] Before T_1 turns ON, i_{b1} is zero. At the instant T_1 turns ON, we have

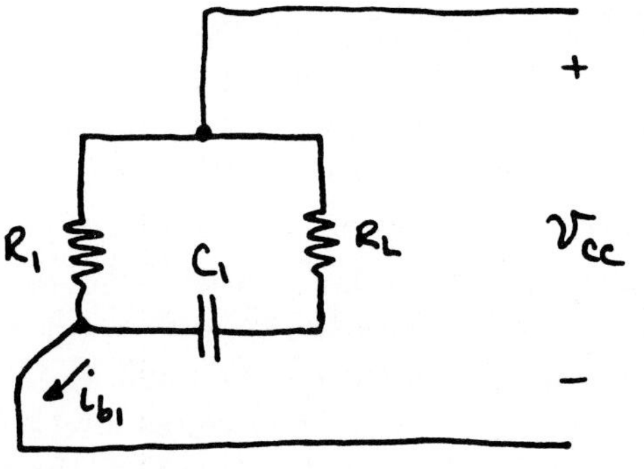

$$i_{b1} = \frac{V_{CC}}{R_1} + \frac{V_{CC}}{R_L}e^{-t/R_LC_1}$$

[f] At the instant T_2 turns back ON, $t = R_2C_2 \ln 2$; therefore

$$i_{b1} = \frac{V_{CC}}{R_1} + \frac{V_{CC}}{R_L}e^{-10 \ln 2} \cong \frac{V_{CC}}{R_1}$$

When T_2 turns OFF, i_{b1} drops to zero instantaneously.

[g]

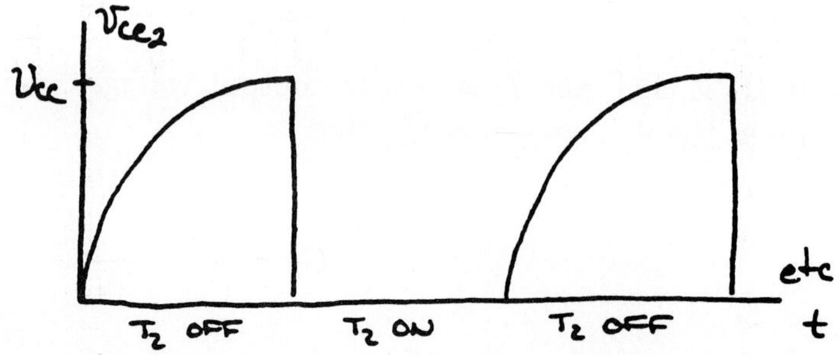

[h]

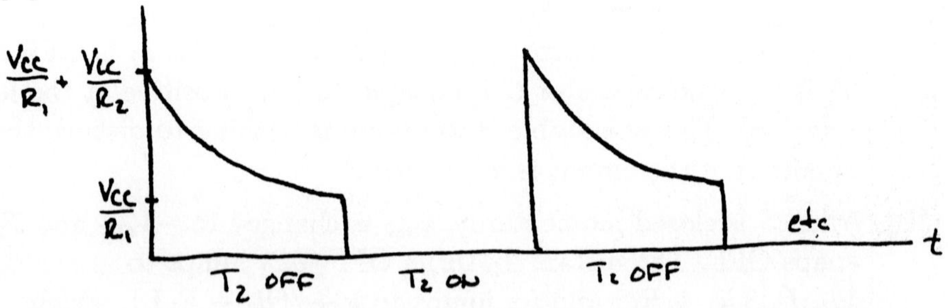

P 7.94 [a] $t_{OFF2} = R_2C_2 \ln 2 = 18 \times 10^3(2 \times 10^{-9}) \ln 2 \cong 25\,\mu s$

[b] $t_{ON2} = R_1C_1 \ln 2 \cong 25\,\mu s$

[c] $t_{OFF1} = R_1C_1 \ln 2 \cong 25\,\mu s$

[d] $t_{ON1} = R_2C_2 \ln 2 \cong 25\,\mu s$

[e] $i_{b1} = \frac{9}{3} + \frac{9}{18} = 3.5\,\text{mA}$

[f] $i_{b1} = \frac{9}{18} + \frac{9}{3}e^{-25/6} \cong 0.5465\,\text{mA}$

[g] $v_{ce2} = 9 - 9e^{-25/6} \cong 8.86\,\text{V}$

P 7.95 [a] $t_{OFF2} = R_2C_2 \ln 2 = (18 \times 10^3)(2.8 \times 10^{-9}) \ln 2 \cong 35\,\mu s$

[b] $t_{ON2} = R_1C_1 \ln 2 \cong 37.4\,\mu s$

[c] $t_{OFF1} = R_1C_1 \ln 2 \cong 37.4\,\mu s$

[d] $t_{ON1} = R_2C_2 \ln 2 = 35\,\mu s$

[e] $i_{b1} = 3.5\,\text{mA}$

[f] $i_{b1} = \frac{9}{18} + 3e^{-35/6} \cong 0.509\,\text{mA}$

[g] $v_{ce2} = 9 - 9e^{-35/6} \cong 9\,\text{V}$

Note in this circuit T_2 is OFF 35 μs and ON 37.4 μs of every cycle, whereas T_1 is ON 35 μs and OFF 37.4 μs every cycle.

P 7.96 If $R_1 = R_2 = 50R_L = 100\,\text{k}\Omega$, then

$$C_1 = \frac{48 \times 10^{-6}}{100 \times 10^3 \ln 2} = 692.49\,\text{pF}; \qquad C_2 = \frac{36 \times 10^{-6}}{100 \times 10^3 \ln 2} = 519.37\,\text{pF}$$

If $R_1 = R_2 = 6R_L = 12\,\text{k}\Omega$, then

$$C_1 = \frac{48 \times 10^{-6}}{12 \times 10^3 \ln 2} = 5.77\,\text{nF}; \qquad C_2 = \frac{36 \times 10^{-6}}{12 \times 10^3 \ln 2} = 4.33\,\text{nF}$$

Therefore $692.49\,\text{pF} \leq C_1 \leq 5.77\,\text{nF}$ and $519.37\,\text{pF} \leq C_2 \leq 4.33\,\text{nF}$

P 7.97 [a] T_2 is normally ON since its base current i_{b2} is greater than zero, i.e., $i_{b2} = V_{CC}/R$ when T_2 is ON. When T_2 is ON, $v_{ce2} = 0$, therefore $i_{b1} = 0$. When $i_{b1} = 0$, T_1 is OFF. When T_1 is OFF and T_2 is ON, the capacitor C is charged to V_{CC}, positive at the left terminal. This is a stable state; there is nothing to disturb this condition if the circuit is left to itself.

[b] When S is closed momentarily, v_{be2} is changed to $-V_{CC}$ and T_2 snaps OFF. The instant T_2 turns OFF, v_{ce2} jumps to $V_{CC}R_1/(R_1 + R_L)$ and i_{b1} jumps to $V_{CC}/(R_1 + R_L L)$, which turns T_1 ON.

[c] As soon as T_1 turns ON, the charge on C starts to reverse polarity. Since v_{be2} is the same as the voltage across C, it starts to increase from $-V_{CC}$ toward $+V_{CC}$. However, T_2 turns ON as soon as $v_{be2} = 0$. The equation for v_{be2} is $v_{be2} = V_{CC} - 2V_{CC}e^{-t/RC}$. $v_{be2} = 0$ when $t = RC\ln 2$, therefore T_2 stays OFF for $RC \ln 2$ seconds.

P 7.98 [a] For $t < 0$, $v_{ce2} = 0$. When the switch is momentarily closed, v_{ce2} jumps to

$$v_{ce2} = \left(\frac{V_{CC}}{R_1 + R_L}\right) R_1 = \frac{6(5)}{25} = 1.2\,\text{V}$$

T_2 remains open for $(23{,}083)(250) \times 10^{-12} \ln 2 \cong 4\,\mu\text{s}$.

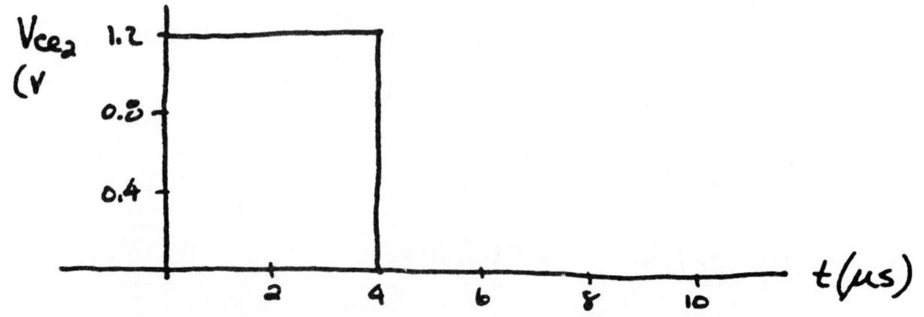

[b] $$i_{rb2} = \frac{V_{CC}}{R} = 259.93\,\mu\text{A}, \qquad -5 \le t \le 0\,\mu\text{s}$$

$$i_{rb2} = 0, \qquad 0 < t < RC\ln 2$$

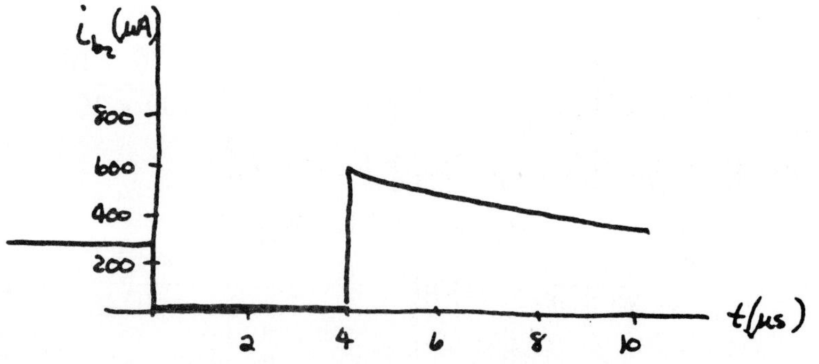

$$i_{rb2} = \frac{V_{CC}}{R} + \frac{V_{CC}}{R_L} e^{-(t-RC\ln 2)/R_L C}$$

$$= 259.93 + 300e^{-0.2\times10^6(t-4\times10^{-6})}\ \mu A, \qquad RC\ln 2 < t$$

P 7.99 [a] Replace the circuit attached to the capacitor with its Thévenin equivalent, where the equivalent resistance is the parallel combination of the two resistors, and the open-circuit voltage is obtained by voltage division across the lamp resistance. The resulting circuit is

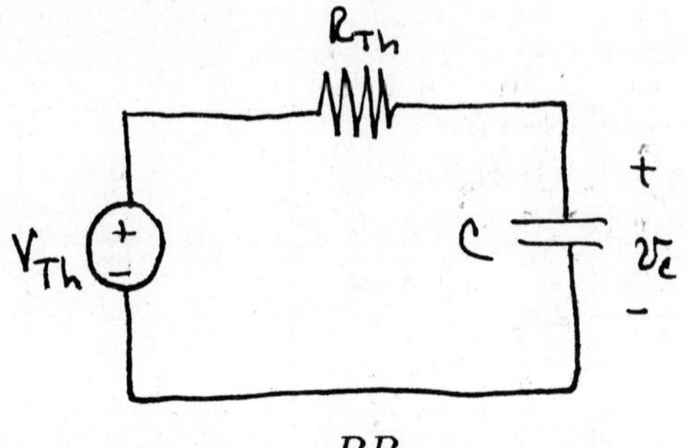

$$R_{Th} = R\|R_L = \frac{RR_L}{R+R_L}; \qquad V_{Th} = \frac{R_L}{R+R_L}V_s$$

From this circuit,

$$v_C(\infty) = V_{Th}; \qquad v_C(0) = V_{max}; \qquad \tau = R_{Th}C$$

Thus,

$$v_C(t) = V_{Th} + (V_{max} - V_{Th})e^{-(t-t_o)/\tau}$$

where

$$\tau = \frac{RR_LC}{R+R_L}$$

[b] Now, set $v_C(t) = V_{min}$ and solve for $(t - t_o)$:

$$V_{Th} + (V_{max} - V_{Th})e^{-(t-t_o)/\tau} = V_{min}$$

$$e^{-(t-t_o)/\tau} = \frac{V_{min} - V_{Th}}{V_{max} - V_{Th}}$$

$$\frac{-(t-t_o)}{\tau} = \ln\frac{V_{min} - V_{Th}}{V_{max} - V_{Th}}$$

$$(t - t_o) = -\frac{RR_LC}{R + R_L}\left(\frac{V_{min} - V_{Th}}{V_{max} - V_{Th}}\right)$$

P 7.100 [a] At $t = 0$ we have

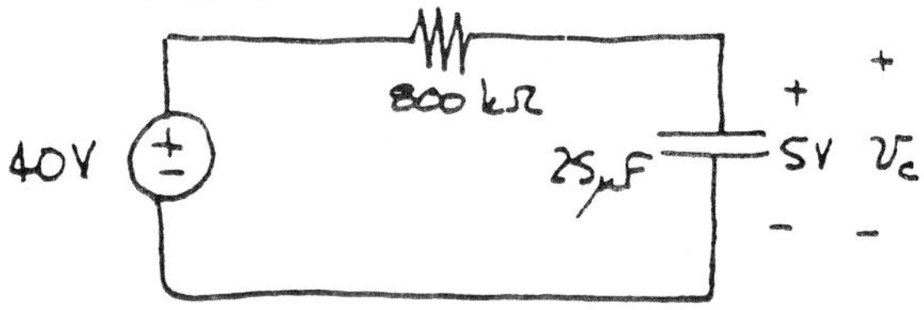

$$\tau = (800)(25) \times 10^{-3} = 20 \text{ sec}; \qquad 1/\tau = 0.05$$

$$v_c(\infty) = 40\text{ V}; \qquad v_c(0) = 5\text{ V}$$

$$v_c = 40 - 35e^{-0.05t}\text{ V}, \qquad 0 \leq t \leq t_o$$

$$40 - 35e^{-0.05t_o} = 15; \qquad \therefore \quad e^{0.05t_o} = 1.4$$

$$t_o = 20 \ln 1.4\,\text{s} = 6.73\,\text{s}$$

At $t = t_o$ we have

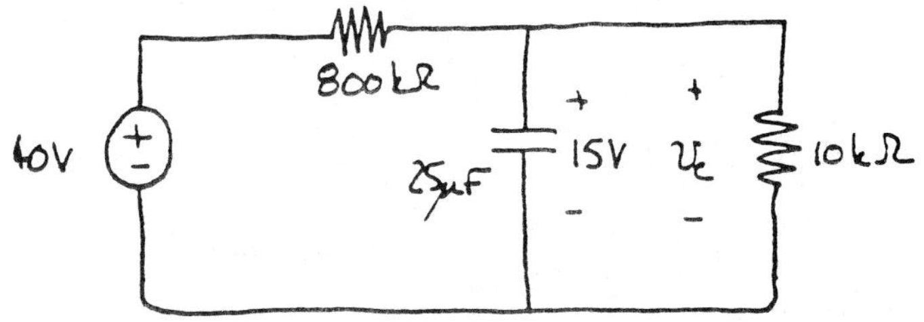

The Thévenin equivalent with respect to the capacitor is

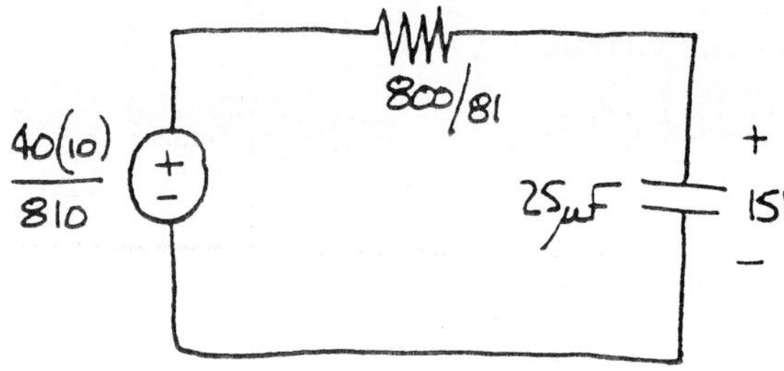

$$\tau = \left(\frac{800}{81}\right)(25) \times 10^{-3} = \frac{20}{81}\text{ s}; \qquad \frac{1}{\tau} = \frac{81}{20} = 4.05$$

$$v_c(t_o) = 15\text{ V}; \qquad v_c(\infty) = \frac{40}{81}\text{ V}$$

$$v_c(t) = \frac{40}{81} + \left(15 - \frac{40}{81}\right)e^{-4.05(t-t_o)}\text{ V} = \frac{40}{81} + \frac{1175}{81}e^{-4.05(t-t_o)}$$

$$\therefore \quad \frac{40}{81} + \frac{1175}{81}e^{-4.05(t-t_o)} = 5$$

$$\frac{1175}{81}e^{-4.05(t-t_o)} = \frac{365}{81}$$

$$e^{4.05(t-t_o)} = \frac{1175}{365} = 3.22$$

$$t - t_o = \frac{1}{4.05}\ln 3.22 \cong 0.29\,\text{s}$$

One cycle = 7.02 seconds.

$$N = 60/7.02 = 8.55 \quad \text{flashes per minute}$$

[b] At $t = 0$ we have

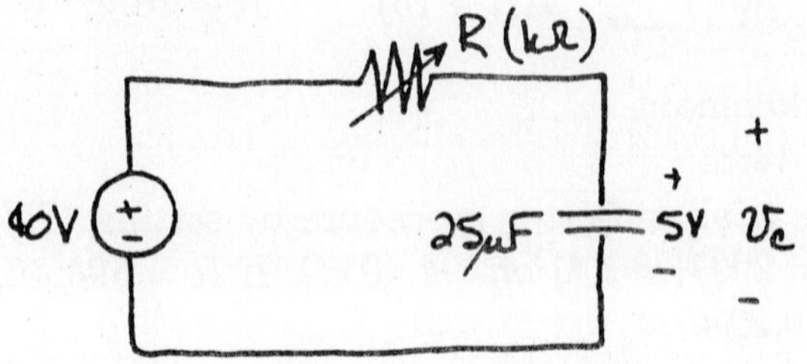

$$\tau = 25R \times 10^{-3}; \qquad 1/\tau = 40/R$$

$$v_c = 40 - 35e^{-(40/R)t}$$

$$40 - 35e^{-(40/R)t_o} = 15$$

$$\therefore \quad t_o = \frac{R}{40}\ln 1.4, \qquad R \;\text{ in }\; \text{k}\Omega$$

At $t = t_o$:

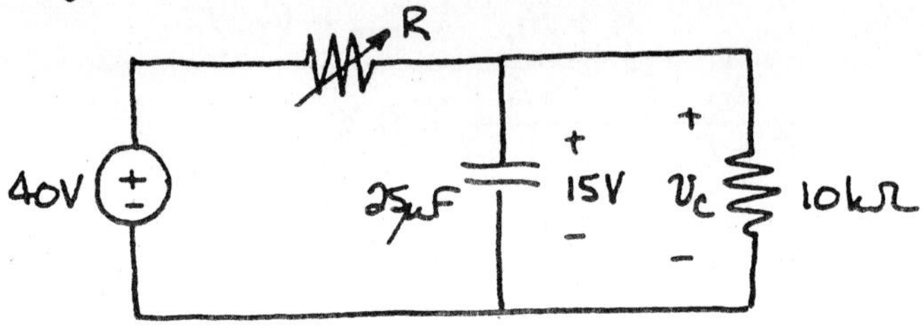

$$v_{\text{Th}} = \frac{10}{R+10}(40) = \frac{400}{R+10}; \qquad R_{\text{Th}} = \frac{10R}{R+10}\,\text{k}\Omega$$

$$\tau = \frac{(25)(10R)\times 10^{-3}}{R+10} = \frac{0.25R}{R+10}; \qquad \frac{1}{\tau} = \frac{4(R+10)}{R}$$

$$v_c = \frac{400}{R+10} + \left(15 - \frac{400}{R+10}\right)e^{-\frac{4(R+10)}{R}(t-t_o)}$$

$$\therefore \quad \frac{400}{R+10} + \left[\frac{15R-250}{R+10}\right]e^{-\frac{4(R+10)}{R}(t-t_o)} = 5$$

$$\text{or}\quad \left(\frac{15R-250}{R+10}\right)e^{-\frac{4(R+10)}{R}(t-t_o)} = \frac{5R-350}{(R+10)}$$

$$\therefore\quad e^{\frac{4(R+10)}{R}(t-t_o)} = \frac{3R-50}{R-70}$$

$$\therefore\quad t-t_o = \frac{R}{4(R+10)}\ln\left(\frac{3R-50}{R-70}\right)$$

At 12 flashes per minute $t_o + (t-t_o) = 5\,\text{s}$

$$\therefore\quad \underbrace{\frac{R}{40}\ln 1.4}_{\text{dominant term}} + \frac{R}{4(R+10)}\ln\left(\frac{3R-50}{R-70}\right) = 5$$

Start the trial-and-error procedure by setting $(R/40)\ln 1.4 = 5$, then $R = 200/(\ln 1.4)$ or $594.40\,\text{k}\Omega$. If $R = 594.40\,\text{k}\Omega$ then $t - t_o \cong 0.29\,\text{s}$.
Second trial set $(R/40)\ln 1.4 = 4.7\,\text{s}$ or $R = 558.74\,\text{k}\Omega$.

With $R = 558.74\,\text{k}\Omega,\quad t - t_o \cong 0.30\,\text{s}$

$$\therefore\quad R = 558.74\,\text{k}\Omega$$

P 7.101 [a]

$$t_o = RC\ln\left(\frac{V_{\text{min}}-V_s}{V_{\text{max}}-V_s}\right) = (3700)(250\times10^{-6})\ln\left(\frac{-700}{-100}\right)$$

$$= 1.80\,\text{s}$$

$$t_c - t_o = \frac{RCR_{\text{L}}}{R+R_{\text{L}}}\ln\left(\frac{V_{\text{max}}-V_{\text{Th}}}{V_{\text{min}}-V_{\text{Th}}}\right)$$

$$\frac{R_{\text{L}}}{R+R_{\text{L}}} = \frac{1.3}{1.3+3.7} = 0.26$$

$$V_{\text{Th}} = \frac{1000(1.3)}{1.3+3.7} = 260\,\text{V}$$

$$\therefore\quad t_c - t_o = (0.925)(0.26)\ln(640/40) = 0.67\,\text{s}$$

$$\therefore\quad t_c = 1.8 + 0.67 = 2.47\,\text{s}$$

$$\text{flashes/min} = \frac{60}{2.47} = 24.32$$

[b] $0 \le t \le t_o$:

$$v_L = 1000 - 700e^{-t/\tau_1}$$

$$\tau_1 = RC = 0.925\,\text{s}$$

$t_o \le t \le t_c$:

$$v_L = 260 + 640e^{-(t-t_o)/\tau_2}$$

$$\tau_2 = R_{\text{Th}}C = 962(250) \times 10^{-6} = 0.2405\,\text{s}$$

$$0 \le t \le t_o: \qquad i = \frac{1000 - v_L}{3700} = \frac{7}{37}e^{-t/0.925}\,\text{A}$$

$$t_o \le t \le t_c: \qquad i = \frac{1000 - v_L}{3700} = \frac{74}{370} - \frac{64}{370}e^{-(t-t_o)/0.2405}$$

Graphically, i versus t is

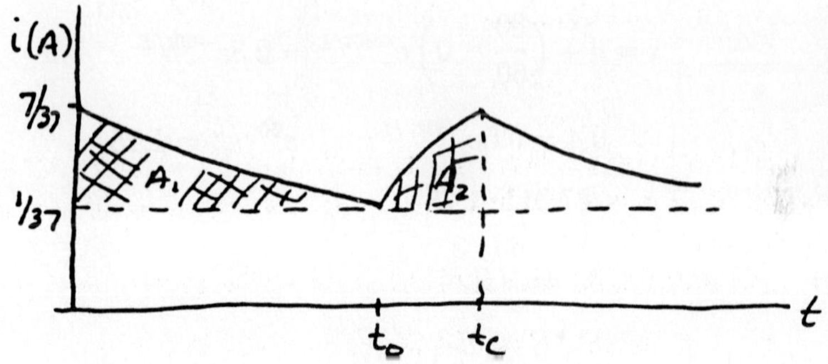

The average value of i will equal the areas $(A_1 + A_2)$ divided by t_c.

$$\therefore \quad i_{\text{avg}} = \frac{A_1 + A_2}{t_c}$$

$$\begin{aligned}
A_1 &= \frac{7}{37}\int_0^{t_o} e^{-t/0.925}\,dt \\
&= \frac{6.475}{37}(1 - e^{-\ln 7}) = 0.15\ \text{A–s} \\
A_2 &= \int_{t_o}^{t_c} \frac{74 - 64e^{-(t-t_o)/0.2405}}{370}\,dt \\
&= \frac{74}{370}(t_c - t_o) + \frac{15.392}{370}(e^{-\ln 16} - 1) \\
&= \frac{17.797}{370}\ln 16 - \frac{15.392}{370}(1 - e^{-\ln 16}) \\
&= 0.09436\ \text{A–s}
\end{aligned}$$

$$i_{\text{avg}} = \frac{(0.15 + 0.09436)}{0.925\ln 7 + 0.2405\ln 16}(1000) = 99.06\,\text{mA}$$

[c] $$P_{\text{avg}} = (1000)(99.06 \times 10^{-3}) = 99.06\,\text{W}$$

$$\text{No. of kw hrs/yr} = \frac{(99.06)(24)(365)}{1000} = 867.77$$

$$\text{Cost/year} = (867.77)(0.05) = 43.39\ \text{dollars/year}$$

P 7.102 [a] $0 \leq t \leq 0.5$:

$$i = \frac{21}{60} + \left(\frac{30}{60} - \frac{21}{60}\right)e^{-t/\tau} \qquad \text{where } \tau = L/R.$$

$$i = 0.35 + 0.15e^{-60t/L}$$

$$i(0.5) = 0.35 + 0.15e^{-30/L} = 0.40$$

$$\therefore \quad e^{30/L} = 3; \qquad L = \frac{30}{\ln 3} = 27.31\text{ H}$$

[b] $0 \leq t \leq t_r$, where t_r is the time the relay releases:

$$i = 0 + \left(\frac{30}{60} - 0\right)e^{-60t/L} = 0.5e^{-60t/L}$$

$$\therefore \quad 0.4 = 0.5e^{-60t_r/L}; \qquad e^{60t_r/L} = 1.25$$

$$t_r = \frac{27.31 \ln 1.25}{60} \cong 0.10\text{ s}$$

8

Natural and Step Responses of *RLC* Circuits

Drill Exercises

DE 8.1 [a] $$\frac{1}{(2RC)^2} = \frac{1}{LC}, \qquad \text{therefore} \quad C = 500\,\text{nF}$$

[b] $$\alpha = 5000 = \frac{1}{2RC}, \qquad \text{therefore} \quad C = 1\,\mu\text{F}$$

$$s_{1,2} = -5000 \pm \sqrt{25 \times 10^6 - \frac{(10^3)(10^6)}{20}} = (-5000 \pm j5000)\ \text{rad/s}$$

[c] $$\frac{1}{\sqrt{LC}} = 20{,}000, \qquad \text{therefore} \quad C = 125\,\text{nF}$$

$$s_{1,2} = \left[-40 \pm \sqrt{(40)^2 - 20^2}\right] 10^3,$$

$$s_1 = -5.36\,\text{krad/s}, \qquad s_2 = -74.64\,\text{krad/s}$$

DE 8.2

$$\begin{aligned}
i_L &= \frac{1000}{50}\int_0^t [-14e^{-5000x} + 26e^{-20{,}000x}]\,dx + 30 \times 10^{-3} \\
&= 20\left\{\frac{-14e^{-5000x}}{-5000}\Big|_0^t + \frac{26e^{-20{,}000t}}{-20{,}000}\Big|_0^t\right\} + 30 \times 10^{-3} \\
&= 56 \times 10^{-3}(e^{-5000t} - 1) - 26 \times 10^{-3}(e^{-20{,}000t} - 1) + 30 \times 10^{-3} \\
&= [56e^{-5000t} - 56 - 26e^{-20{,}000t} + 26 + 30]\ \text{mA} \\
&= 56e^{-5000t} - 26e^{-20{,}000t}\ \text{mA}, \qquad t \geq 0
\end{aligned}$$

DE 8.3 From the given values of R, L, and C, $s_1 = -10\,\text{krad/s}$ and $s_2 = -40$ krad/s.

[a] $v(0^-) = v(0^+) = 0, \qquad \text{therefore} \quad i_R(0^+) = 0$

[b] $i_C(0^+) = 4\,\text{A}$

[c] $C\dfrac{dv_c(0^+)}{dt} = 4, \qquad \text{therefore} \quad \dfrac{dv_c(0^+)}{dt} = 4 \times 10^8\,\text{V/s}$

[d] $v = [A_1e^{-10{,}000t} + A_2e^{-40{,}000t}]\,\text{V}, \qquad t \geq 0^+$

$$v(0^+) = A_1 + A_2, \qquad \frac{dv(0^+)}{dt} = -10{,}000A_1 - 40{,}000A_2$$

Therefore $A_1 + A_2 = 0, \qquad -A_1 - 4A_2 = 40{,}000, \qquad A_1 = 40{,}000/3$

[e] $A_2 = -40{,}000/3$

[f] $v = [40{,}000/3][e^{-10{,}000t} - e^{-40{,}000t}]\,\text{V}, \qquad t \geq 0^+$

DE 8.4 [a] $\dfrac{1}{2RC} = 8000, \qquad \text{therefore} \quad R = 62.5\,\Omega$

[b] $i_R(0^+) = \dfrac{10}{62.5} = 160\,\text{mA}$

$$i_C(0^+) = -80 - 160 = -240\,\text{mA}, \qquad i_C(0^+) = C\frac{dv(0^+)}{dt}$$

Therefore $\dfrac{dv(0^+)}{dt} = -240\,\text{kV/s}$

[c] $B_1 = v(0^+) = 10\,\text{V}, \qquad \dfrac{dv_c(0^+)}{dt} = \omega_d B_2 - \alpha B_1$

Therefore $6000B_2 - 8000B_1 = -240{,}000, \qquad B_2 = (-80/3)\,\text{V}$

[d] $i_L = -(i_R + i_C); \qquad i_R = v/R; \qquad i_C = C\dfrac{dv}{dt}$

$$v = e^{-8000t}[10\cos 6000t - \frac{80}{3}\sin 6000t]\,\text{V}$$

Therefore $i_R = e^{-8000t}[160\cos 6000t - \dfrac{1280}{3}\sin 6000t]\,\text{mA}$

$$i_C = e^{-8000t}[-240\cos 6000t + \frac{460}{3}\sin 6000t]\,\text{mA}$$

$$i_L = 10e^{-8000t}[8\cos 6000t + \frac{82}{3}\sin 6000t]\,\text{mA}, \qquad t \geq 0^+$$

DE 8.5 [a] $\left(\dfrac{1}{2RC}\right)^2 = \dfrac{1}{LC} = \dfrac{10^6}{4}, \qquad \text{therefore} \quad \dfrac{1}{2RC} = 500, \quad R = 100\,\Omega$

[b] $0.5CV_0^2 = 12.5 \times 10^{-3}, \qquad \text{therefore} \quad V_0 = 50\,\text{V}$

[c] $0.5LI_0^2 = 12.5 \times 10^{-3}, \qquad I_0 = 250\,\text{mA}$

[d] $D_2 = v(0^+) = 50, \qquad \frac{dv(0^+)}{dt} = D_1 - \alpha D_2$

$$i_R(0^+) = \frac{50}{100} = 500\,\text{mA}$$

Therefore $i_C(0^+) = -(500 + 250) = -750\,\text{mA}$

Therefore $\frac{dv(0^+)}{dt} = -750 \times \frac{10^{-3}}{C} = -75{,}000\,\text{V/s}$

Therefore $D_1 - \alpha D_2 = -75{,}000; \qquad \alpha = \frac{1}{2RC} = 500, \quad D_1 = -50{,}000$

[e] $v = [50e^{-500t} - 50{,}000te^{-500t}]\,\text{V}$

$$i_R = \frac{v}{R} = [0.5e^{-500t} - 500te^{-500t}]\,\text{A}, \qquad t \geq 0^+$$

DE 8.6 [a] $i_R(0^+) = \frac{V_0}{R} = \frac{40}{500} = 0.08\,\text{A}$

[b] $i_C(0^+) = I - i_R(0^+) - i_L(0^+) = -1 - 0.08 - 0.5 = -1.58\,\text{A}$

[c] $\frac{di_L(0^+)}{dt} = \frac{40}{0.64} = 62.5\,\text{A/s}$

[d] $\alpha = \frac{1}{2RC} = 1000; \qquad \frac{1}{LC} = 1{,}562{,}500; \qquad s_{1,2} = -1000 \pm j750$

[e] $i_L = i_f + B_1'e^{-\alpha t}\cos\omega_d t + B_2'e^{-\alpha t}\sin\omega_d t, \qquad i_f = -1\,\text{A}$

$i_L(0^+) = 0.5 = i_f + B_1', \qquad$ therefore $B_1' = 1.5\,\text{A}$

$\frac{di_L(0^+)}{dt} = 62.5 = -\alpha B_1' + \omega_d B_2', \qquad$ therefore $B_2' = (25/12)\,\text{A}$

Therefore $i_L(t) = -1 + e^{-1000t}[1.5\cos 750t + (25/12)\sin 750t]\,\text{A}, \qquad t \geq 0^+$

[f] $v(t) = \frac{Ldi_L}{dt} = 40e^{-1000t}[\cos 750t - (154/3)\sin 750t]V \qquad t \geq 0$

DE 8.7 [a] $i(0^+) = 0$

[b] $v_c(0^+) = v_C(0^-) = \left(\frac{80}{24}\right)(15) = 50\,\text{V}$

[c] $50 + L\frac{di(0^+)}{dt} = 100, \qquad \frac{di(0^+)}{dt} = 10{,}000\,\text{A/s}$

[d] $\alpha = 8000; \qquad \frac{1}{LC} = 100 \times 10^6; \qquad s_{1,2} = -8000 \pm j6000$

[e] $i = i_f + e^{-\alpha t}[B_1'\cos\omega_d t + B_2'\sin\omega_d t]; \qquad i_f = 0, \quad i(0^+) = 0$

Therefore $B_1' = 0; \qquad \frac{di(0^+)}{dt} = 10{,}000 = -\alpha B_1' + \omega_d B_2'$

Therefore $B_2' = 1.67\,\text{A}; \qquad i = 1.67e^{-8000t}\sin 6000t\,\text{A}, \qquad t \geq 0^+$

DE 8.8 $$v_c(t) = v_f + e^{-\alpha t}[B_1' \cos\omega_d t + B_2' \sin\omega_d t], \qquad v_f = 100\text{ V}$$

$$v_c(0^+) = 50\text{ V}; \qquad \frac{dv_c(0^+)}{dt} = 0; \qquad \text{therefore} \quad 50 = 100 + B_1'$$

$$B_1' = -50\text{ V}; \qquad 0 = -\alpha B_1' + \omega_d B_2'$$

$$\text{Therefore} \quad B_2' = \frac{\alpha}{\omega_d} B_1' = \left(\frac{8000}{6000}\right)(-50) = -66.67\text{ V}$$

$$\text{Therefore} \quad v_c(t) = 100 - e^{-8000t}[50\cos 6000t + 66.67\sin 6000t]\text{ V}, \qquad t \geq 0^+$$

DE 8.9 At $t = 0$ the voltage across each capacitor is zero. It follows that since the operational amplifiers are ideal, the current in the 500 kΩ is zero. Therefore there cannot be an instantaneous change in the current in the 1 μF capacitor. Since the capacitor current equals $C(dv_o/dt)$, the derivative must be zero.

DE 8.10 [a] From Example 8.13 $$\frac{d^2v_o}{dt^2} = 2$$

$$\text{therefore} \quad \frac{dg(t)}{dt} = 2, \quad g(t) = \frac{dv_o}{dt}$$

$$g(t) - g(0) = 2t; \qquad g(t) = 2t + g(0); \qquad g(0) = \frac{dv_o(0)}{dt}$$

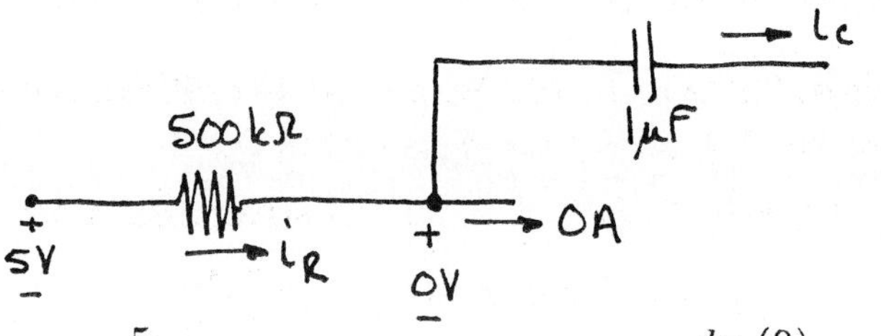

$$i_R = \frac{5}{500} \times 10^{-3} = 1\,\mu\text{A} = i_C = -C\frac{dv_o(0)}{dt}$$

$$\frac{dv_o(0)}{dt} = \frac{-1 \times 10^{-6}}{1 \times 10^{-6}} = -1 = g(0)$$

$$\frac{dv_o}{dt} = 2t - 1$$

$$dv_o = 2t\,dt - dt$$

$$v_o - v_o(0) = t^2 - t; \qquad v_o(0) = 8\text{ V}$$

$$v_o = t^2 - t + 8, \qquad 0 \leq t \leq (2 + \sqrt{5})\text{ s}$$

[b] $$t^2 - t + 8 = 9$$

$$t^2 - t - 1 = 0$$

$$t = (1/2) \pm (\sqrt{5}/2) \cong 2.12\,\text{s}$$

(Negative value has no physical significance.)

DE 8.11 [a] $R_a = 100\,\text{k}\Omega;\quad C_1 = 0.1\,\mu\text{F};\quad R_b = 25\,\text{k}\Omega;\quad C_2 = 1\,\mu\text{F}$

$$\frac{d^2 v_o}{dt^2} = \left(\frac{1}{R_a C_1}\right)\left(\frac{1}{R_b C_2}\right) v_g; \qquad \frac{1}{R_a C_1} = 100 \quad \frac{1}{R_b C_2} = 40$$

$$v_g = 250 \times 10^{-3}; \qquad \text{therefore} \quad \frac{d^2 v_o}{dt^2} = 1000$$

[b] Since $v_o(0) = 0 = \dfrac{dv_o(0)}{dt}$, our solution is $v_o = 500t^2$

The second op-amp will saturate when

$$v_o = 6\,\text{V}, \quad \text{or} \quad t_{sat} = \sqrt{6/500} \cong 0.1095\,\text{s}$$

[c] $$\frac{dv_{o1}}{dt} = -\frac{1}{R_a C_1} v_g = -25$$

[d] Since $v_{o1}(0) = 0$, $v_{o1} = -25t$ V

At $t = 0.1095\,\text{s}$, $v_{o1} \cong -2.74$ V

Therefore the second amplifier saturates before the first amplifier saturates. Our expressions are valid for $0 \le t \le 0.1095\,\text{s}$. Once the second op-amp saturates, our linear model is no longer valid.

DE 8.12 [a] Initial conditions will not change the differential equation; hence the equation is the same as Example 8.14.

[b] $v_o = 5 + A_1' e^{-10t} + A_2' e^{-20t}$ (from Example 8.14)

$$v_o(0) = 4 = 5 + A_1' + A_2'$$

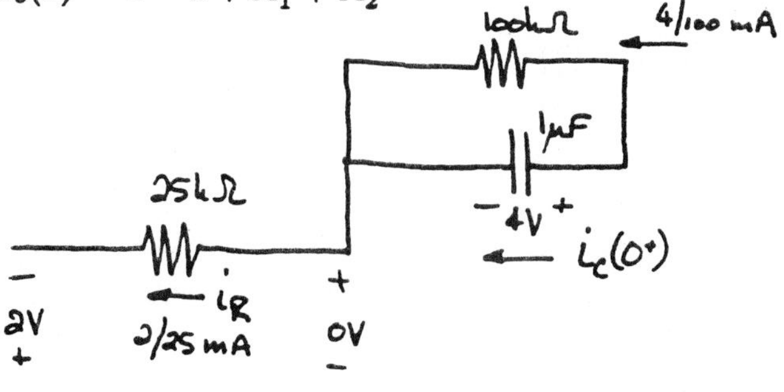

$$\frac{4}{100} + i_C(0^+) - \frac{2}{25} = 0$$

$$i_C(0^+) = \frac{4}{100}\,\text{mA} = C\frac{dv_o(0^+)}{dt}$$

$$\frac{dv_o(0^+)}{dt} = \frac{0.04 \times 10^{-3}}{10^{-6}} = 40\,\text{V/s}$$

$$\frac{dv_o}{dt} = -10A_1'e^{-10t} - 20A_2'e^{-20t}$$

$$\frac{dv_o}{dt}(0^+) = -10A_1' - 20A_2' = 40$$

Therefore $-A_1' - 2A_2' = 4$ and $A_1' + A_2' = -1$
Thus, $A_1' = 2$ and $A_2' = -3$

$$v_o = 5 + 2e^{-10t} - 3e^{-20t}\,\text{V}$$

[c] Same as Example 8.14:

$$\frac{dv_{o1}}{dt} + 20v_{o1} = -25$$

[d] From Example 8.14:

$$v_{o1}(\infty) = -1.25\,\text{V}; \qquad v_1(0) = -2\,\text{V} \quad \text{(given)}$$

Therefore

$$v_{o1} = -1.25 + (-2 + 1.25)e^{-20t} = -1.25 - 0.75e^{-20t}\,\text{V}$$

Problems

P 8.1 [a]

$$\alpha = \frac{1}{2RC} = 1$$

$$\omega_o^2 = \frac{1}{LC} = 10$$

$$\omega_d = \sqrt{10 - 1} = 3\,\text{rad/s}$$

$$\therefore \quad v = B_1e^{-t}\cos 3t + B_2e^{-t}\sin t$$

$$v(0) = B_1 = 0; \qquad v = B_2e^{-t}\sin 3t$$

$$\frac{dv}{dt} = B_2\left[e^{-t}(3\cos 3t) - e^{-t}\sin 3t\right] = B_2e^{-t}[3\cos 3t - \sin 3t]$$

$$C\frac{dv}{dt}(0) = 0.25B_2(3) = 0.75B_2$$

$$\therefore \quad 0.75B_2 = -(-3) = 3; \qquad B_2 = 4$$

$$\therefore \quad v = 4e^{-t}\sin 3t \text{ V}, \qquad t \geq 0$$

[b] $$\frac{dv}{dt} = 4e^{-t}(3\cos 3t - \sin 3t)$$

$$\frac{dv}{dt} = 0 \quad \text{when} \quad 3\cos 3t = \sin 3t \quad \text{or} \quad \tan 3t = 3$$

$$\therefore \quad 3t_1 = 1.25, \qquad t_1 = 416.35 \text{ ms}$$

$$3t_2 = 1.25 + \pi, \qquad t_2 = 1463.55 \text{ ms}$$

$$3t_3 = 1.25 + 2\pi, \qquad t_3 = 2510.74 \text{ ms}$$

[c] $$t_3 - t_1 = 2094.40 \text{ ms}; \qquad T_d = \frac{2\pi}{\omega_d} = \frac{2\pi}{3} = 2094.40 \text{ ms}$$

[d] $$t_2 - t_1 = 1047.20 \text{ ms}; \qquad \frac{T_d}{2} = \frac{2094.40}{2} = 1047.20 \text{ ms}$$

[e] $$v(t_1) = 4e^{-(0.41635)}\sin 3(0.41635) = 2.50 \text{ V}$$

$$v(t_2) = 4e^{-(1.46355)}\sin 3(1.46355) = -0.88 \text{ V}$$

$$v(t_3) = 4e^{-(2.51074)}\sin 3(2.51074) = 0.31 \text{ V}$$

[f]

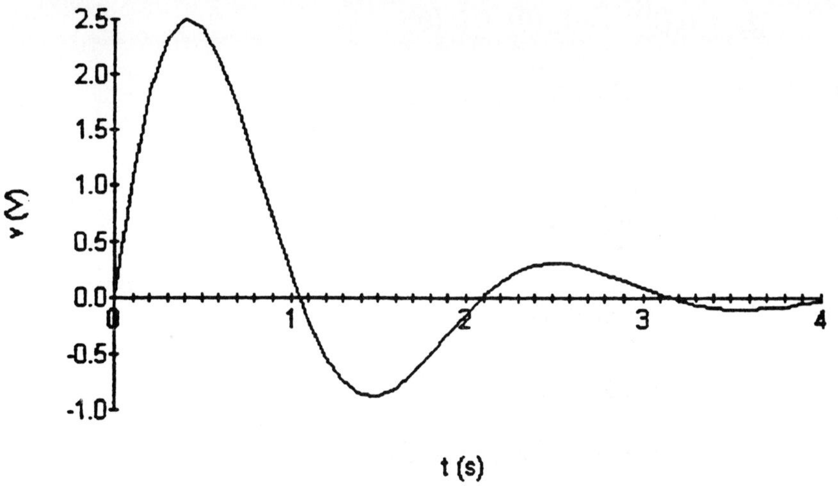

P 8.2 [a] $$\alpha = 0; \qquad \omega_d = \omega_o = \sqrt{10} = 3.16 \text{ rad/s}$$

$$v = B_1\cos\omega_o t + B_2\sin\omega_o t; \qquad v(0) = B_1 = 0; \qquad v = B_2\sin\omega_o t$$

$$\frac{dv}{dt} = \omega_o B_2 \cos\omega_o t; \qquad C\frac{dv}{dt}(0) = \omega_o C B_2 = -i_L(0) = 3$$

$$\therefore\ B_2 = \frac{3}{0.25\sqrt{10}} = 3.79$$

$$v = 3.79\sin 3.16t\ \text{V}, \qquad t \geq 0$$

[b] $2\pi f = 3.16; \qquad f = \frac{3.16}{2\pi} \cong 0.50\,\text{Hz}$

[c] 3.79 V

P 8.3 [a] $\alpha = 4000; \qquad \omega_d = 3000$

$$\omega_d = \sqrt{\omega_o^2 - \alpha^2}$$

$$\therefore\ \omega_o^2 = \omega_d^2 + \alpha^2 = 9\times10^6 + 16\times10^6 = 25\times10^6$$

$$\frac{1}{LC} = 25\times10^6$$

$$L = \frac{1}{(25\times10^6)(50\times10^{-9})} = 0.8\,\text{H} = 800\,\text{mH}$$

[b] $\alpha = \frac{1}{2RC}$

$$\therefore\ R = \frac{1}{2\alpha C} = \frac{10^9}{(8000)(50)} = 2500\,\Omega$$

[c] $V_o = v(0) = 125\,\text{V}$

[d] $I_o = i_L(0) = -i_R(0) - i_C(0)$

$$i_R(0) = \frac{V_o}{R} = \frac{125}{2.5}\times10^{-3} = 50\,\text{mA}$$

$$i_C(0) = C\frac{dv}{dt}(0)$$

$$\frac{dv}{dt} = 125\{e^{-4000t}[-3000\sin 3000t - 6000\cos 3000t] -$$

$$4000e^{-4000t}[\cos 3000t - 2\sin 3000t]$$

$$\frac{dv}{dt}(0) = 125\{1(-6000) - 4000\} = -125\times10^4$$

$$C\frac{dv}{dt}(0) = -125\times10^4(40\times10^{-9}) = -6250\times10^{-5} = -62.5\,\text{mA}$$

$$\therefore\ I_o = -50 + 62.5 = 12.5\,\text{mA}$$

[e]
$$\frac{dv}{dt} = 125e^{-4000t}[5000\sin 3000t - 10{,}000\cos 3000t]$$

$$= 625\times 10^{3}e^{-4000t}[\sin 3000t - 2\cos 3000t]$$

$$C\frac{dv}{dt} = 31{,}250\times 10^{-6}e^{-4000t}(\sin 3000t - 2\cos 3000t)$$

$$i_{\rm C}(t) = 31.25e^{-4000t}(\sin 3000t - 2\cos 3000t)\,\text{mA}$$

$$i_{\rm R}(t) = 50e^{-4000t}(\cos 3000t - 2\sin 3000t)\,\text{mA}$$

$$i_{\rm L}(t) = -i_{\rm R}(t) - i_{\rm C}(t)$$

$$= e^{-4000t}(12.5\cos 3000t + 68.75\sin 3000t)\,\text{mA}$$

CHECK:

$$\frac{di_{\rm L}}{dt} = \{-4000e^{-4000t}[12.5\cos 3000t + 68.75\sin 3000t]$$

$$+e^{-4000t}[-37.5\times 10^{3}\sin 3000t$$

$$+206.25\times 10^{3}\cos 3000t]\times 10^{-3}$$

$$= e^{-4000t}[156.25\cos 3000t - 312.5\sin 3000t]$$

$$L\frac{di_{\rm L}}{dt} = e^{-4000t}[125\cos 3000t - 250\sin 3000t]$$

$$= 125e^{-4000t}[\cos 3000t - 2\sin 3000t]\,\text{V}$$

P 8.4 [a]
$$\left(\frac{1}{2RC}\right)^2 = \frac{1}{LC} = (4000)^2$$

$$\therefore\ C = \frac{1}{(16\times 10^{6})(5)} = 12.5\,\text{nF}$$

$$\frac{1}{2RC} = 4000$$

$$\therefore\ R = \frac{10^{9}}{(8000)(12.5)} = 10\,\text{k}\Omega$$

$$v(0) = D_2 = 25\,\text{V}$$

$$i_{\rm R}(0) = \frac{25}{10} = 2.5\text{mA}$$

$$i_{\rm C}(0) = -2.5 - 5 = -7.5\,\text{mA}$$

$$\frac{dv}{dt}(0) = D_1 - 4000D_2 = \frac{-7.5\times 10^{-3}}{12.5\times 10^{-9}} = -6\times 10^{5}$$

$$\therefore\ D_1 = -6\times 10^{5} + 4000(25) = -5\times 10^{5}$$

[b] $$v = -5 \times 10^5 te^{-4000t} + 25e^{-4000t}$$

$$\frac{dv}{dt} = [20 \times 10^8 t - 6 \times 10^5]e^{-4000t}$$

$$i_C = C\frac{dv}{dt} = 12.5 \times 10^{-9}[20 \times 10^8 t - 6 \times 10^5]e^{-4000t}$$

$$= (25{,}000t - 7.5)e^{-4000t}\,\text{mA}, \qquad t > 0$$

P 8.5 $$-\alpha + \sqrt{\alpha^2 - \omega_o^2} = -5000$$

$$-\alpha - \sqrt{\alpha^2 - \omega_o^2} = -20{,}000$$

$$\therefore \quad -2\alpha = -25{,}000$$

$$\alpha = 12{,}500\,\text{nepers}$$

$$\frac{1}{2RC} = \frac{10^6}{2R(0.05)} = 12{,}500$$

$$R = 800\,\Omega$$

$$2\sqrt{\alpha^2 - \omega_o^2} = 15{,}000$$

$$4(\alpha^2 - \omega_o^2) = 225 \times 10^6$$

$$\therefore \quad \omega_o = 10{,}000\,\text{rad/s}$$

$$\omega_o^2 = 10^8 = \frac{1}{LC}$$

$$\therefore \quad L = \frac{1}{10^8 C} = 200\,\text{mH}$$

$$i_R = \frac{v(t)}{R} = -6.25e^{-5000t} + 25e^{-20{,}000t}\,\text{mA}, \qquad t \geq 0^+$$

$$i_C = C\frac{dv(t)}{dt} = 1.25e^{-5000t} - 20e^{-20{,}000t}\,\text{mA}, \qquad t \geq 0^+$$

$$i_L = -(i_R + i_C) = 5e^{-5000t} - 5e^{-20{,}000t}\,\text{mA}, \qquad t \geq 0^+$$

P 8.6 [a] $$\omega_o^2 = \frac{1}{LC} = \frac{10^9}{40} = 25 \times 10^6$$

$$\omega_o = 5000 \text{ rad/s}$$

$$\frac{1}{2RC} = 5000; \qquad R = \frac{1}{10{,}000C}$$

$$R = \frac{10^9}{8 \times 10^4} = 12.5\,\text{k}\Omega$$

[b] $$v(t) = D_1te^{-5000t} + D_2e^{-5000t}$$

$$v(0) = -25 = D_2$$

$$\frac{dv}{dt} = (D_1t - 25)(-5000e^{-5000t}) + D_1e^{-5000t}$$

$$\frac{dv}{dt}(0) = 125 \times 10^3 + D_1 = \frac{i_C(0)}{C}$$

$$i_C(0) = -i_R(0) - i_L(0)$$

$$i_R(0) = \frac{-25}{12.5} = -2\,\text{mA}$$

$$\therefore \quad i_C(0) = 2 - (-1) = 3\,\text{mA}$$

$$\therefore \quad \frac{dv}{dt}(0) = \frac{3 \times 10^{-3}}{8 \times 10^{-9}} = 0.375 \times 10^6 = 3.75 \times 10^5$$

$$\therefore \quad 1.25 \times 10^5 + D_1 = 3.75 \times 10^5$$

$$D_1 = 2.5 \times 10^5 = 25 \times 10^4$$

$$\therefore \quad v(t) = (25 \times 10^4t - 25)e^{-5000t}\,\text{V}, \qquad t \geq 0$$

[c] $$i_C(t) = 0 \text{ when } \frac{dv}{dt}(t) = 0$$

$$\frac{dv}{dt} = (25 \times 10^4t - 25)(-5000)e^{-5000t} + e^{-5000t}(25 \times 10^4)$$

$$= (375{,}000 - 125 \times 10^7t)e^{-5000t}$$

$$\frac{dv}{dt} = 0 \text{ when } 125 \times 10^7t = 375{,}000; \qquad \therefore \quad t = 300\,\mu\text{s}$$

$$v(300\mu\text{s}) = 50e^{-1.5} = 11.16\,\text{V}$$

[d] $$i_L(300\mu s) = -i_R(300\mu s) = \frac{11.16}{12.5} = 0.89\,\text{mA}$$

$$w_C(300\mu s) = 4 \times 10^{-9}(11.16)^2 = 497.87\,\text{nJ}$$

$$w_L(300\mu s) = (2.5)(0.89)^2 \times 10^{-6} = 1991.48\,\text{nJ}$$

$$w(300\mu s) = w_C + w_L = 2489.35\,\text{nJ}$$

$$w(0) = 4 \times 10^{-9}(625) + 2.5(10^{-6}) = 5000\,\text{nJ}$$

$$\%\text{ remaining} = \frac{2489.35}{5000}(100) = 49.79\%$$

P 8.7 [a] $$i_R(0) = \frac{90}{2000} = 45\text{mA}$$

$$i_L(0) = -30\text{mA}$$

$$i_C(0) = -i_L(0) - i_R(0) = 30 - 45 = -15\,\text{mA}$$

[b] $$\alpha = \frac{1}{2RC} = \frac{10^9}{(4000)(10)} = 25{,}000$$

$$\omega_o^2 = \frac{1}{LC} = \frac{(10^3)(10^9)}{(250)(10)} = 4 \times 10^8$$

$$s_{1,2} = -25{,}000 \pm \sqrt{6.25 \times 10^8 - 10^8(4)} = -25{,}000 \pm 15{,}000$$

$$s_1 = -10{,}000 \text{ rad/s}; \qquad s_2 = -40{,}000 \text{ rad/s}$$

$$v = A_1e^{-10{,}000t} + A_2e^{-40{,}000t}$$

$$v(0) = A_1 + A_2 = 90$$

$$\frac{dv}{dt}(0) = -10^4A_1 - 4A_2 \times 10^4 = \frac{-15 \times 10^{-3}}{10 \times 10^{-9}}$$

$$-A_1 - 4A_2 = -150$$

$$\therefore \quad -3A_2 = -60; \qquad A_2 = 20; \qquad A_1 = 70$$

$$v = 70e^{-10{,}000t} + 20e^{-40{,}000t}\,\text{V}, \qquad t \geq 0$$

[c] $$i_C = C\frac{dv}{dt}$$

$$= 10 \times 10^{-9}[-70 \times 10^4e^{-10{,}000t} - 80 \times 10^4e^{-40{,}000t}]$$

$$= -7e^{-10{,}000t} - 8e^{-40{,}000t}\,\text{mA}$$

$$i_R = 35e^{-10{,}000t} + 10e^{-40{,}000t}\,\text{mA}$$

$$i_L = -i_C - i_R = -28e^{-10{,}000t} - 2e^{-40{,}000t}\,\text{mA}$$

P 8.8
$$\frac{1}{2RC} = \frac{3 \times 10^9}{(25{,}000)(10)} = 12{,}000$$

$$\frac{1}{LC} = 4 \times 10^8$$

$$s_{1,2} = -12{,}000 \pm j16{,}000\,\text{rad/s}$$

$\therefore$ response is underdamped

$$v(t) = B_1 e^{-16{,}000t} \cos 12{,}000t + B_2 e^{-16{,}000t} \sin 12{,}000t$$

$$v(0^+) = 90\,\text{V} = B_1; \qquad i_{\text{R}}(0^+) = \frac{90}{(12{,}500/3)} = 21.6\,\text{mA}$$

$$i_{\text{C}}(0^+) = [-i_{\text{L}}(0^+) + i_{\text{R}}(0^+)] = -[-30 + 21.6] = 8.4\,\text{mA}$$

$$\frac{dv(0^+)}{dt} = \frac{8.4 \times 10^{-3}}{10 \times 10^{-9}} = 840{,}000\,\text{V/s}$$

$$\frac{dv(0)}{dt} = -16{,}000B_1 + 12{,}000B_2 = 840{,}000$$

or $-4B_1 + 3B_2 = 210; \qquad \therefore \; B_2 = 190\,\text{V}$

$$v(t) = 90e^{-16{,}000t} \cos 12{,}000t + 190e^{-16{,}000t} \sin 12{,}000t\,\text{V}, \qquad t \geq 0$$

P 8.9
$$\alpha = \frac{1}{2RC} = \frac{10^9}{(5000)(10)} = 2 \times 10^4$$

$$\alpha^2 = 4 \times 10^8; \qquad \therefore \; \alpha^2 = \omega_o^2$$

Critical damping:

$$v = D_1 t e^{-\alpha t} + D_2 e^{-\alpha t}$$

$$v(0) = D_2 = 90$$

$$\frac{dv}{dt} = D_1[t(-\alpha e^{-\alpha t}) + e^{-\alpha t}] - \alpha D_2 e^{-\alpha t}$$

$$\frac{dv}{dt}(0) = D_1 - \alpha D_2 = \frac{i_{\text{C}}(0)}{C} = \frac{-6 \times 10^{-3}}{10 \times 10^{-9}} = -6 \times 10^5$$

$$D_1 = \alpha D_2 - 6 \times 10^5 = (2 \times 10^4)(90) - 6 \times 10^5 = 120 \times 10^4$$

$$v = (120 \times 10^4 t + 90)e^{-20{,}000t}\,\text{V}, \qquad t \geq 0$$

P 8.10 [a]

$$\alpha = \frac{1}{2RC} = \frac{10^9}{(10{,}000)(8)} = 12{,}500$$

$$\omega_o^2 = \frac{1}{LC} = \frac{10^9}{(1.25)(8)} = 10^8$$

$$s_{1,2} = -12{,}500 \pm \sqrt{(1.5625 - 1)10^8} = -12{,}500 \pm 7500$$

$$s_1 = -5000 \text{ rad/s}$$

$$s_2 = -20{,}000 \text{ rad/s}$$

[b] overdamped

[c]

$$\omega_d = \sqrt{\omega_o^2 - \alpha^2}$$

$$\therefore \quad \alpha^2 = \omega_o^2 - \omega_d^2 = 10^8 - 36 \times 10^6 = 0.64 \times 10^8$$

$$\alpha = 0.8 \times 10^4 = 8000$$

$$\frac{1}{2RC} = 8000; \qquad \therefore \quad R = \frac{10^9}{(16{,}000)(8)} = 7812.5\,\Omega$$

[d]

$$s_1 = -8000 + j; \qquad s_2 = -8000 - j6000 \text{ rad/s}$$

[e]

$$\alpha = 10^4 = \frac{1}{2RC}; \qquad \therefore \quad R = \frac{1}{2C(10^4)} = 6250\,\Omega$$

P 8.11

$$\alpha = 2000/2 = 1000$$

$$R = \frac{1}{2\alpha C} = \frac{10^6}{(2000)(18)} = 27.78\,\Omega$$

$$v(0^+) = -24\,\text{V}$$

$$i_{\text{R}}(0^+) = \frac{-24}{27.78} = -864\,\text{mA}$$

$$\frac{dv}{dt} = 2400e^{-200t} + 21{,}600e^{-1800t}$$

$$\frac{dv(0^+)}{dt} = 2400 + 21{,}600 = 24{,}000\,\text{V/s}$$

$$i_{\text{C}}(0^+) = 18 \times 10^{-6}(24{,}000) = -432\,\text{mA}$$

$$i_{\text{L}}(0^+) = -[i_{\text{R}}(0^+) + i_{\text{C}}(0^+)] = -[-864 - 432] = 432\,\text{mA}$$

P 8.12 [a] $2\alpha = 200; \qquad \alpha = 100\,\text{nepers}$

$$2\sqrt{\alpha^2 - \omega_o^2} = 120; \qquad \omega_o = 80\,\text{rad/s}$$

$$C = \frac{1}{2\alpha R} = \frac{1}{200(200)} = 25\,\mu F$$

$$L = \frac{1}{\omega_o^2 C} = \frac{10^6}{(80)^2(25)} = 6.25\,\text{H}$$

$$i_C(0^+) = A_1 + A_2 = 15\,\text{mA}$$

$$\frac{di_C}{dt} + \frac{di_L}{dt} + \frac{di_R}{dt} = 0$$

$$\frac{di_C(0)}{dt} = -\frac{di_L(0)}{dt} - \frac{di_R(0)}{dt}$$

$$\frac{di_L(0)}{dt} = \frac{0}{6.25} = 0\,\text{A/s}$$

$$\frac{di_R(0)}{dt} = \frac{1}{R}\frac{dv(0)}{dt} = \frac{1}{R}\frac{i_C(0)}{C} = \frac{15 \times 10^{-3}}{(200)(25 \times 10^{-6})} = 3\,\text{A/s}$$

$$\therefore \quad \frac{di_C(0)}{dt} = -3\,\text{A/s}$$

$$\therefore \quad 160A_1 + 40A_2 = 3$$

$$4A_1 + A_2 = 75 \times 10^{-3}; \qquad \therefore \quad A_1 = 20\,\text{mA}; \qquad A_2 = -5\,\text{mA}$$

$$\therefore \quad i_C = 20e^{-160t} - 5e^{-40t}\,\text{mA}, \qquad t \geq 0$$

[b] By hypothesis

$$v = A_3 e^{-160t} + A_4 e^{-40t}, \qquad t \geq 0$$

$$v(0) = A_3 + A_4 = 0$$

$$\frac{dv(0)}{dt} = \frac{15 \times 10^{-3}}{25 \times 10^{-6}} = 600\,\text{V/s}$$

$$-160A_3 - 40A_4 = 600; \qquad \therefore \quad A_3 = -5\,\text{V}; \qquad A_4 = 5\,\text{V}$$

$$v = -5e^{-160t} + 5e^{-40t}\,\text{V}, \qquad t \geq 0$$

[c] $$i_R(t) = \frac{v}{200} = -25e^{-160t} + 25e^{-40t}\,\text{mA}, \qquad t \geq 0^+$$

[d] $$i_L = -i_R - i_C = 25e^{-160t} - 25e^{-40t} - 20e^{-160t} + 5e^{-40t}$$

$$i_L = 5e^{-160t} - 20e^{-40t}\,\text{mA}, \qquad t \geq 0$$

P 8.13 From the form of the solution we have

$$v(0) = A_1 + A_2$$

$$\frac{dv(0^+)}{dt} = -\alpha(A_1 + A_2) + j\omega_d(A_1 - A_2)$$

We know both $v(0)$ and $dv(0^+)/dt$ will be real numbers. To facilitate the algebra we let these numbers be K_1 and K_2, respectively. Then our two simultaneous equations are

$$K_1 = A_1 + A_2$$

$$K_2 = (-\alpha + j\omega_d)A_1 + (-\alpha - j\omega_d)A_2$$

The characteristic determinate is

$$\Delta = \begin{vmatrix} 1 & 1 \\ (-\alpha + j\omega_d) & (-\alpha - j\omega_d) \end{vmatrix} = -j2\omega_d$$

The numerator determinates are

$$N_1 = \begin{vmatrix} K_1 & 1 \\ K_2 & (-\alpha - j\omega_d) \end{vmatrix} = -(\alpha + j\omega_d)K_1 - K_2$$

and $N_2 = \begin{vmatrix} 1 & K_1 \\ (-\alpha + j\omega_d) & K_2 \end{vmatrix} = K_2 + (\alpha - j\omega_d)K_1$

It follows that $A_1 = \frac{N_1}{\Delta} = \frac{\omega_d K_1 - j(\alpha K_1 + K_2)}{2\omega_d}$

and $A_2 = \frac{N_2}{\Delta} = \frac{\omega_d K_1 + j(\alpha K_1 + K_2)}{2\omega_d}$

We see from these expressions that $A_1 = A_2^*$

P 8.14 By definition, $B_1 = A_1 + A_2$. From the solution to Problem 8.13 we have

$$A_1 + A_2 = \frac{2\omega_d K_1}{2\omega_d} = K_1$$

But K_1 is $v(0)$, therefore, $B_1 = v(0)$, which is identical to Eq. (8.27). By definition, $B_2 = j(A_1 - A_2)$. From Problem 8.13 we have

$$B_2 = j(A_1 - A_2) = \frac{j[-2j(\alpha K_1 + K_2)]}{2\omega_d} = \frac{\alpha K_1 + K_2}{\omega_d}$$

It follows that

$$K_2 = -\alpha K_1 + \omega_d B_2, \quad \text{but} \quad K_2 = \frac{dv(0^+)}{dt} \quad \text{and} \quad K_1 = B_1$$

Thus we have

$$\frac{dv}{dt}(0^+) = -\alpha B_1 + \omega_d B_2,$$

which is identical to Eq. (8.28).

P 8.15

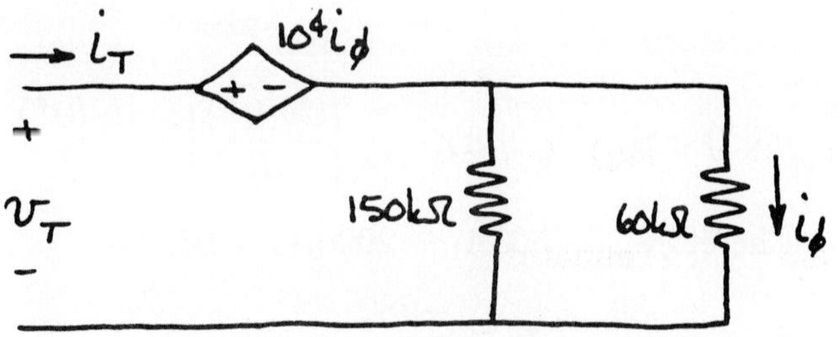

$$v_T = 10^4 \frac{i_T(150 \times 10^3)}{210 \times 10^3} + \frac{(150)(60)10^6}{210 \times 10^3} i_T$$

$$\frac{v_T}{i_T} = \frac{1500 \times 10^3}{210} + \frac{9000 \times 10^3}{210} = \frac{10{,}500}{210} \times 10^3 = 50\,\text{k}\Omega$$

$$V_o = \frac{75}{10}(6) = 45\,\text{V}; \qquad I_o = 0$$

$$i_C(0) = -i_R(0) - i_L(0) = -\frac{45}{50} = -0.9\,\text{mA}$$

$$\frac{i_C(0)}{C} = \frac{-0.9}{1.25} \times 10^6 = -720 \times 10^3$$

$$\omega_o^2 = \frac{1}{LC} = \frac{10^9}{(8)(1.25)} = 10^8; \qquad \omega_o = 10^4\ \text{rad/s}$$

$$\alpha = \frac{1}{2RC} = \frac{10^9}{(2)(50)(1.25) \times 10^3} = 8000\ \text{nepers}$$

$$\omega_d = \sqrt{(100 - 64) \times 10^6} = 6000 \text{ rad/s}$$

$$v_o = B_1 e^{-8000t} \cos 6000t + B_2 e^{-8000t} \sin 6000t$$

$$v_o(0) = B_1 = 45 \text{ V}$$

$$\frac{dv_o}{dt}(0) = 6000B_2 - 8000B_1 = -720 \times 10^3$$

$$\therefore\ 6000B_2 = 8000(45) - 720 \times 10^3; \qquad \therefore\ B_2 = -60 \text{ V}$$

$$v_o = 45e^{-8000t} \cos 6000t - 60e^{-8000t} \sin 6000t \text{ V}, \qquad t > 0$$

P 8.16 [a] $\alpha = \dfrac{1}{2RC} = 1250, \qquad \omega_o = 10^3,$ therefore overdamped

$s_1 = -500, \qquad s_2 = -2000$

therefore $v = A_1 e^{-500t} + A_2 e^{-2000t}$

$$v(0^+) = 0 = A_1 + A_2; \qquad \left[\frac{dv(0^+)}{dt}\right] = \frac{i_C(0^+)}{C} = 98{,}000 \text{ V/s}$$

Therefore $-500A_1 - 2000A_2 = 98{,}000$

$$A_1 = \frac{+980}{15}, \quad A_2 = \frac{-980}{15}$$

$$v(t) = \left[\frac{980}{15}\right][e^{-500t} - e^{-2000t}] \text{ V}, \qquad t \geq 0^+$$

[b]

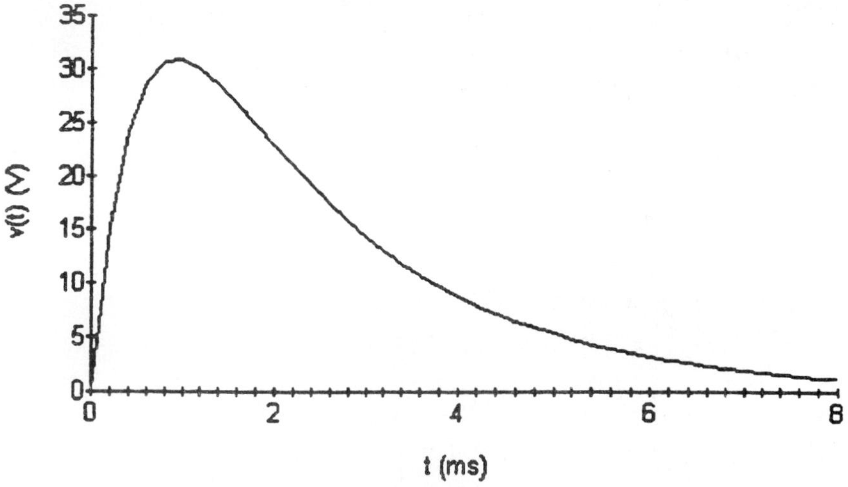

Example 8.4: $v_{max} \cong 74$ V at 1.4 ms

Example 8.5: $v_{max} \cong 36\,\text{V}$ at 1.0 ms

Problem 8.16: $v_{max} \cong 30.8$ at 0.92 ms

P 8.17 [a] $$v = L\left(\frac{di_L}{dt}\right) = 16[e^{-20{,}000t} - e^{-80{,}000t}]\,\text{V}, \qquad t \geq 0^+$$

[b] $$i_R = \frac{v}{R} = 40[e^{-20{,}000t} - e^{-80{,}000t}]\,\text{mA}, \qquad t \geq 0^+$$

[c] $$i_C = I - i_L - i_R = [-8e^{-20{,}000t} + 32e^{-80{,}000t}]\,\text{mA}, \qquad t \geq 0^+$$

P 8.18 [a] $$v = L\left(\frac{di_L}{dt}\right) = 40e^{-32{,}000t}\sin 24{,}000t\,\text{V}, \qquad t \geq 0^+$$

[b] $$i_C(t) = I - i_R - i_L = 24 \times 10^{-3} - \frac{v}{625} - i_L$$

$$= [24e^{-32{,}000t}\cos 24{,}000t - 32e^{-32{,}000t}\sin 24{,}000t]\,\text{mA}, \qquad t \geq 0^+$$

P 8.19 $$v = L\left(\frac{di_L}{dt}\right) = 960{,}000te^{-40{,}000t}\,\text{V}, \qquad t \geq 0^+$$

P 8.20 $t < 0$: $V_o = 60\,\text{V}$, $I_o = 45\,\text{mA}$

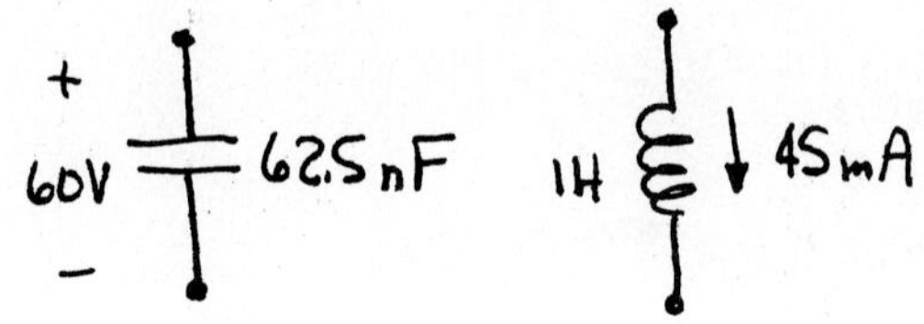

$t > 0$:

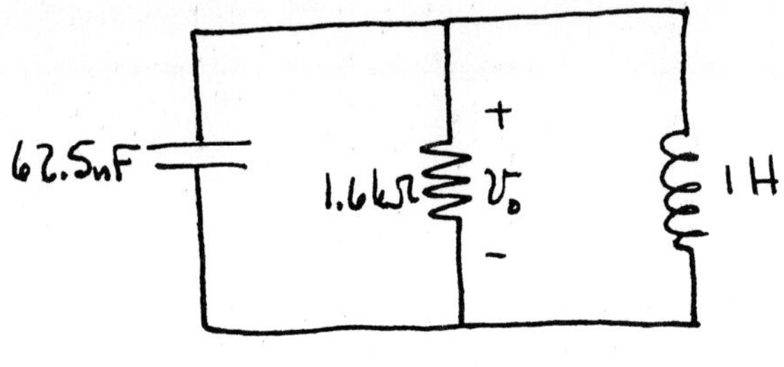

$$i_R(0) = \frac{60}{1.6} = 37.5\,\text{mA}; \qquad i_L(0) = 45\,\text{mA}$$

$$i_C(0) = -37.5 - 45 = -82.5\,\text{mA}$$

$$\alpha = \frac{1}{2RC} = \frac{10^9}{3200(62.5)} = 5000\ \text{rad/s}$$

$$\omega_o^2 = \frac{1}{LC} = \frac{10^9}{62.5} = 16 \times 10^6$$

$$s_1 = -2000 \text{ rad/s}; \qquad s_2 = -8000 \text{ rad/s}$$

$$\therefore \quad v_o = A_1 e^{-2000t} + A_2 e^{-8000t}$$

$$A_1 + A_2 = v_o(0) = 60$$

$$\frac{dv_o}{dt}(0) = -2000A_1 - 8000A_2 = \frac{-82.5 \times 10^{-3}}{62.5 \times 10^{-9}} = -1320 \times 10^3$$

Solving, $\quad A_1 = -140\,\text{V}, \qquad A_2 = 200\,\text{V}$

$$\therefore \quad v_o = -140e^{-2000t} + 200e^{-8000t}\,\text{V}, \qquad t \geq 0$$

P 8.21 $$\omega_o^2 = \frac{1}{LC} = \frac{16 \times 10^6}{0.64} = 25 \times 10^6$$

$$\alpha = \frac{1}{2RC} = \frac{16 \times 10^6}{4000} = 4000 \text{ nepers}; \qquad \alpha^2 = 16 \times 10^3$$

$$\omega_d = \sqrt{(25 - 16) \times 10^6} = 3000 \text{ rad/s}$$

$$s_{1,2} = -4000 \pm j3000 \text{rad/s}$$

$$v_o(t) = B_1 e^{-4000t} \cos 3000t + B_2 e^{-4000t} \sin 3000t$$

$$v_o(0) = B_1 = 60$$

$$i_R(0) = \frac{60}{2} = 30\,\text{mA}$$

$$i_L(0) = 45\,\text{mA}$$

$$i_C(0) = -i_R(0) - i_L(0) = -75\,\text{mA}$$

$$\frac{i_C(0)}{C} = (-75 \times 10^{-3})(16 \times 10^6) = -12 \times 10^5$$

$$\frac{dv_o}{dt}(0) = -4000B_1 + 3000B_2 = -12 \times 10^5$$

$$\therefore \quad 3B_2 = 4B_1 - 1200 = 240 - 1200 = -960; \quad \therefore \quad B_2 = -320$$

$$v_o(t) = 60e^{-4000t} \cos 3000t - 320e^{-4000t} \sin 3000t\,\text{V}, \qquad t > 0$$

P 8.22

$$\omega_o^2 = \frac{1}{LC} = \frac{16 \times 10^6}{0.16} = 10^8; \qquad \omega_o = 10^4$$

$$\alpha = \frac{1}{2RC} = \frac{16 \times 10^6}{1600} = 10^4$$

$$\therefore \quad \alpha^2 = \omega_o^2 \text{ (critical damping)}$$

$$v_o(t) = D_1 te^{-10{,}000t} + D_2 e^{-10{,}000t}$$

$$v_o(0) = D_2 = 60$$

$$i_R(0) = \frac{60}{0.8} = 75\,\text{mA}$$

$$i_L(0) = 45\,\text{mA}$$

$$i_C(0) = -120\,\text{mA}$$

$$\frac{dv_o}{dt}(0) = -10{,}000D_2 + D_1$$

$$\frac{i_C(0)}{C} = (-120 \times 10^{-3})(16 \times 10^6) = -1920 \times 10^3$$

$$D_1 - 10{,}000D_2 = -1920 \times 10^3; \qquad D_1 = -1320 \times 10^3\,\text{V/s}$$

$$v_o(t) = (60 - 132 \times 10^4 t)e^{-10{,}000t}\,\text{V}, \qquad t > 0$$

P 8.23 [a]

$$2\alpha = 5000; \quad \alpha = 2500\,\text{nepers}$$

$$\sqrt{\alpha^2 - \omega_o^2} = 1500; \qquad \omega_o^2 = 4 \times 10^6; \qquad \omega_o = 2000\,\text{rad/s}$$

$$\alpha = \frac{R}{2L} = 2500; \qquad R = 5000L$$

$$\omega_o^2 = \frac{1}{LC} = 4 \times 10^6; \qquad L = \frac{10^9}{4 \times 10^6(50)} = 5\text{H}$$

$$R = 25{,}000\,\Omega$$

[b]

$$i(0) = 0$$

$$L\frac{di(0)}{dt} = v_c(0); \qquad \frac{1}{2}(50) \times 10^{-9} v_c^2(0) = 90 \times 10^{-6}$$

$$\therefore \quad v_c^2(0) = 3600; \qquad v_c(0) = 60\,\text{V}$$

$$\frac{di(0)}{dt} = \frac{60}{5} = 12\,\text{A/s}$$

[c] $$i(t) = A_1 e^{-1000t} + A_2 e^{-4000t}$$

$$i(0) = A_1 + A_2 = 0$$

$$\frac{di(0)}{dt} = -1000A_1 - 4000A_2 = 12$$

$$\therefore \quad A_1 + 4A_2 = -12 \times 10^{-3}$$

$$\therefore \quad A_2 = -4\,\text{mA}; \qquad A_1 = +4\,\text{mA}$$

$$i(t) = +4e^{-1000t} - 4e^{-4000t}\,\text{mA} \qquad t \geq 0$$

[d] $$\frac{di(t)}{dt} = -4e^{-1000t} + 16e^{-4000t}$$

$$\frac{di}{dt} = 0 \text{ when } 16e^{-4000t} = 4e^{-1000t}$$

$$\text{or } e^{3000t} = 4$$

$$\therefore \quad t = \frac{\ln 4}{0.003}\mu\text{s} = 462.10\,\mu\text{s}$$

[e] $$i_{\text{max}} = 4e^{-0.4621} - 4e^{-1.8484} = 1.89\,\text{mA}$$

[f] $$v_i(t) = 5\frac{di}{dt} = [-20e^{-1000t} + 80e^{-4000t}]\,\text{V}, \quad t \geq 0$$

P 8.24 $$i_L(0^-) = i_L(0^+) = 37.5\,\text{mA}$$

For $t > 0$

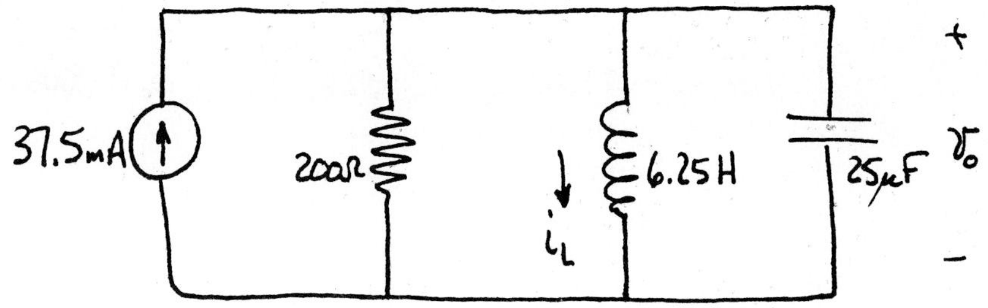

$$i_L(0^-) = i_L(0^+) = 37.5\,\text{mA}$$

$$\alpha = \frac{1}{2RC} = 100\,\text{nepers}; \qquad \omega_o^2 = \frac{1}{LC} = 6400$$

$$s_1 = -40\,\text{rad/s} \qquad s_2 = -160\,\text{rad/s}$$

$$v_o(\infty) = 0 = V_f$$

$$v_o = A_1' e^{-40t} + A_2' e^{-160t}$$

$$i_C(0^+) = -37.5 + 37.5 + 0 = 0$$

$$\therefore \quad \frac{dv_o}{dt} = 0$$

$$\frac{dv_o(0)}{dt} - 40A_1' - 160A_2' = 0$$

$$\therefore \quad A_1' + 40A_2' = 0; \qquad A_1' + A_2' = 0$$

$$\therefore \quad A_1' = 0; \qquad A_2' = 0$$

$$\therefore \quad v_o = 0 \text{ for } t \geq 0$$

Note: $\quad v_o(0) = 0; \qquad v_o(\infty) = 0; \qquad \dfrac{dv_o(0)}{dt} = 0$

Hence the 37.5 mA current circulates between the current source and the ideal inductor in the equivalent circuit. In the original circuit the 30 V source sustains a current of 37.5 mA in the inductor. This is an example of a circuit going directly into steady state when the switch is closed. There is no transient period, or interval.

P 8.25 $\quad i_C(0) = 0; \qquad v_c(0) = 200\text{ V}$

$$\alpha = \frac{R}{2L} = \frac{2}{0.04} = 50 \text{ nepers}$$

$$\omega_o^2 = \frac{1}{LC} = \frac{10^3}{0.4} = 2500$$

$$\therefore \quad \alpha^2 = \omega_o^2; \qquad \text{critical damping}$$

$$v_c(t) = V_f + D_1'te^{-50t} + D_2'e^{-50t}$$

$$V_f = 100\text{ V}$$

$$v_c(0) = 100 + D_2' = 200; \qquad D_2' = 100$$

$$\frac{dv_c}{dt}(0) = -50D_2' + D_1' = 0$$

$$D_1' = 50D_2' = 5000$$

$$v_c = 100 + 5000te^{-50t} + 100e^{-50t}\text{ V}, \quad t \geq 0$$

P 8.26 $\alpha = 800\,\text{nepers}; \qquad \omega_d = 600\,\text{rad/s}$

$$\omega_o^2 - \alpha^2 = 36 \times 10^4; \qquad \omega_o^2 = 100 \times 10^4; \quad w_o = 1000\,\text{rad/s}$$

$$\alpha = \frac{R}{2L} = 800; \qquad R = 1600L$$

$$\frac{1}{LC} = 100 \times 10^4; \qquad L = \frac{10^6}{(100 \times 10^4)(500)} = 2\,\text{mH}$$

$$\therefore \quad R = 3.2\,\Omega$$

$$i(0^+) = B_1 = 0\,\text{A}; \qquad \text{at } t = 0^+$$

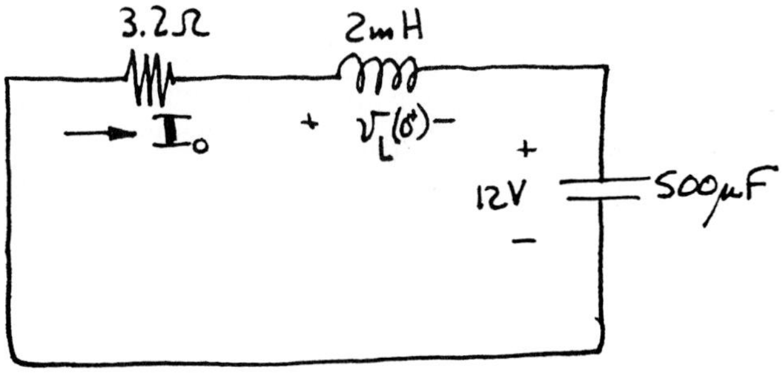

$$-12 + 0 + v_L(0^+) = 0; \qquad v_L(0^+) = 12\,\text{V}$$

$$\frac{di(0^+)}{dt} = \frac{-12}{0.002} = -6000\,\text{A/s}$$

$$\therefore \quad \frac{di(0^+)}{dt} = 600B_2 - 800B_1 = -6000$$

$$\therefore \quad 600B_2 = 800B_1 - 6000; \qquad \therefore \quad B_2 = -10\,\text{A}$$

$$\therefore \quad i = -10e^{-800t} \sin 600t\,\text{A}, \quad t \geq 0$$

P 8.27 From Prob. 8.26 we know v_c will be of the form

$$v_c = B_3 e^{-800t} \cos 600t + B_4 e^{-800t} \sin 600t$$

From Prob. 8.26 we have

$$v_c(0) = -12\,\text{V} = B_3$$

and

$$\frac{dv_c(0)}{dt} = \frac{i_C(0)}{C} = 0$$

$$\frac{dv_c(0)}{dt} = 600B_4 - 800B_3$$

$$\therefore \quad 600B_4 = 800B_3 + 0; \qquad B_4 = 16$$

$$v_c(t) = 12e^{-800t}\cos 600t + 16e^{-800t}\sin 600t \text{ V} \qquad t \geq 0$$

P 8.28 $$v_C(0^+) = \frac{1}{2}(240) = 120 \text{ V}$$

$$i_L(0^+) = 60\,\text{mA}; \qquad i_L(\infty) = \frac{240}{5} \times 10^{-3} = 48\,\text{mA}$$

$$\alpha = \frac{1}{2RC} = \frac{10^6}{2(2500)(5)} = 40$$

$$\omega_o^2 = \frac{1}{LC} = \frac{10^6}{400} = 2500$$

$$\alpha^2 = 1600; \qquad \alpha^2 < \omega_o^2; \qquad \therefore \quad \text{underdamped}$$

$$s_{1,2} = -40 \pm j\sqrt{2500 - 1600} = -40 \pm j30 \text{ rad/s}$$

$$\begin{aligned} i_L &= I_f + B_1'e^{-\alpha t}\cos\omega_d t + B_2'e^{-\alpha t}\sin\omega_d t \\ &= 48 + B_1'e^{-40t}\cos 30t + B_2'e^{-40t}\sin 30t \end{aligned}$$

$$i_L(0) = 48 + B_1'; \qquad B_1' = 60 - 48 = 12\,\text{mA}$$

$$\frac{di_L}{dt}(0) = 30B_2' - 40B_1' = \frac{120}{80} = 1.5 = 1500 \times 10^{-3}$$

$$\therefore \quad 30B_2 = 40(12) \times 10^{-3} + 1500 \times 10^{-3}; \qquad B_2' = 66 \times 10^{-3}$$

$$\therefore \quad i_L = 48 + 12e^{-40t}\cos 30t + 66e^{-40t}\sin 30t \,\text{mA}, \qquad t \geq 0^+$$

P 8.29 $$\alpha = \frac{R}{2L} = 5000 \text{ nepers}$$

$$\omega_o^2 = \frac{1}{LC} = \frac{10^9}{200} = 50 \times 10^6$$

$$s_{1,2} = -5000 \pm \sqrt{25 \times 10^6 - 50 \times 10^6} = -5000 \pm j5000 \text{ rad/s}$$

$$v_o = V_f + B_1' e^{-5000t} \cos 5000t + B_2' e^{-5000t} \sin 5000t$$

$$v_o(0) = 0 = V_f + B_1'$$

$$v_o(\infty) = 40 \text{ V}; \qquad \therefore \quad B_1' = -40 \text{ V}$$

$$\frac{dv_o(0)}{dt} = 0 = 5000B_2' - 5000B_1'$$

$$\therefore \quad B_2' = B_1' = -40 \text{ V}$$

$$v_o = 40 - 40e^{-5000t} \cos 5000t - 40e^{-5000t} \sin 5000t \text{ V}, \quad t \geq 0$$

P 8.30 $$\alpha = \frac{1}{2RC} = \frac{10^6}{(1600)(6.25)} = 100; \qquad \alpha^2 = 10^4$$

$$\omega_o^2 = \frac{1}{LC} = \frac{10^6}{(25)(6.25)} = 6400$$

$$s_{1,2} = -200 \pm \sqrt{10^4 - 6400} = -100 \pm 60$$

$$s_1 = -40 \text{ rad/s}; \qquad s_2 = -160 \text{ rad/s}$$

$$v_o(\infty) = 0 = V_f$$

$$\therefore \quad v_o = A_1' e^{-40t} + A_2' e^{-160t}$$

$$v_o(0) = 30 = A_1' + A_2'$$

Note: $i_C(0^+) = 0$

$$\therefore \quad \frac{dv_o}{dt}(0) = 0 = -40A_1' - 160A_2'$$

Solving, $A_1' = 40$ V, $A_2' = -10$ V

$$v_o(t) = 40e^{-40t} - 10e^{-160t} \text{ V}, \qquad t > 0^+$$

P 8.31 [a] $$i_o = I_f + A_1' e^{-40t} + A_2' e^{-160t}$$

$$I_f = \frac{30}{800} = 37.5\text{mA}; \qquad i_o(0) = 0$$

$$0 = 37.5 \times 10^{-3} + A_1' + A_2', \qquad \therefore \quad A_1' + A_2' = -37.5 \times 10^{-3}$$

$$\frac{di_o}{dt}(0) = \frac{30}{25} = -40A_1' - 160A_2'$$

Solving, $\quad A_1' = -40\,\text{mA}; \qquad A_2' = 2.5\,\text{mA}$

$$i_o = 37.5 - 40e^{-40t} + 2.5e^{-160t}\ \text{mA}$$

[b] $$\frac{di_o}{dt} = [1600e^{-40t} - 400e^{-160t}] \times 10^{-3}$$

$$L\frac{di_o}{dt} = 25(1.6)e^{-40t} - 25(0.4)e^{-160t}$$

$$\therefore \quad v_o = 40e^{-40t} - 10e^{-160t}\ \text{V}$$

This agrees with the solution to Problem 8.27.

P 8.32 For $t > 0$

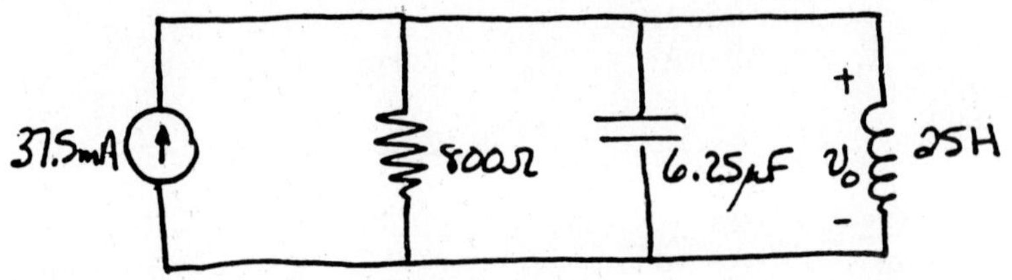

$$\alpha = \frac{1}{2RC} = 100; \qquad \frac{1}{LC} = 6400$$

$$s_{1,2} = -100 \pm 60$$

$$s_1 = -40\,\text{rad/s}; \qquad s_2 = -160\,\text{rad/s}$$

$$v_o = V_f + A_1' e^{-40t} + A_2' e^{-160t}$$

$$V_f = 0; \qquad v_o(0^+) = 0; \qquad i_C(0^+) = 37.5\,\text{mA}$$

$$\therefore \quad A_1' + A_2' = 0$$

$$\frac{dv_o(0^+)}{dt} = \frac{i_C(0^+)}{6.25 \times 10^{-6}} = 6000\,\text{V/s}$$

$$\frac{dv_o(0^+)}{dt} = -40A_1' - 160A_2'$$

$$-40A_1' - 160A_2' = 6000$$

$$A_1' + 4A_2' = -150$$

$$-A_1' + A_2' = 0$$

$$\therefore \quad A_1' = 50\,\text{V}; \qquad A_2' = -50\,\text{V}$$

$$v_o = 50e^{-40t} - 50e^{-160t}\,\text{V}, \qquad t \geq 0$$

P 8.33 [a] From the solution to Prob. 8.32 $s_1 = -40\,\text{rad/s}$ and $s_2 = -160\,\text{rad/s}$, therefore

$$i_o = I_f + A_1'e^{-40t} + A_2'e^{-160t}$$

$$I_f = 37.5\,\text{mA}; \qquad i_o(0^+) = 0; \qquad \frac{di_o(0^+)}{dt} = 0$$

$$\therefore \quad 0 = 37.5 + A_1' + A_2'; \qquad -40A_1' - 160A_2' = 0$$

It follows that

$$A_1' = -50\,\text{mA}; \qquad A_2' = 12.5\,\text{mA}$$

$$\therefore \quad i_o = 37.5 - 50e^{-40t} + 12.5e^{-160t}\,\text{mA}, \qquad t \geq 0$$

[b]

$$\frac{di_o}{dt} = 2e^{-40t} - 2e^{-160t}$$

$$v_o = L\frac{di_o}{dt} = 25[2e^{-40t} - 2e^{-160t}]$$

$$v_o = 50e^{-40t} - 50e^{-160t}\,\text{V}, \qquad t \geq 0$$

This agrees with the solution to Problem 8.32

P 8.34 $t < 0$: $\quad i_L = 3/150 = 20\,\text{mA}$

$t > 0$:

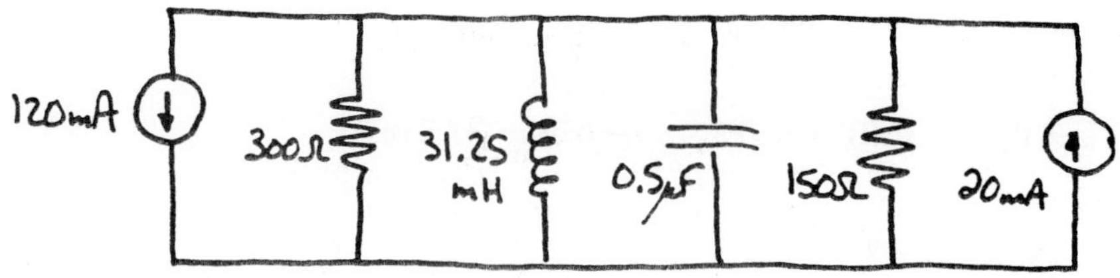

$$300\|150 = 100\,\Omega$$

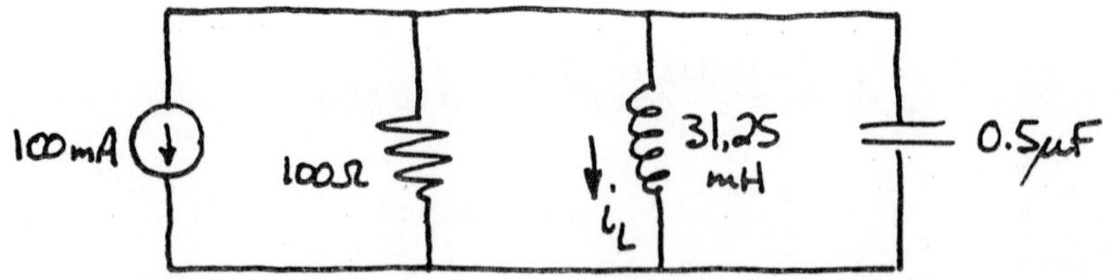

$i_L(0) = 20\,\text{mA}, \qquad i_L(\infty) = -100\,\text{mA}$

$$\omega_o^2 = \frac{1}{LC} = \frac{10^9}{(31.25)(0.5)} = 64 \times 10^6; \qquad \omega_o = 8000 \text{ rad/s}$$

$$\alpha = \frac{1}{2RC} = \frac{10^6}{(200)(0.5)} = 10^4; \qquad \alpha^2 = 100 \times 10^6$$

$$\alpha^2 - \omega_o^2 = (100 - 64)10^6 = 36 \times 10^6$$

$$s_{1,2} = -10{,}000 \pm 6000$$

$$s_1 = -4000 \text{ rad/s}; \qquad s_2 = -16{,}000 \text{ rad/s}$$

$$i_L = I_f + A_1' e^{-4000t} + A_2' e^{-16{,}000t}$$

$$i_L(\infty) = I_f = -100\text{mA}$$

$$i_L(0) = A_1' + A_2' + I_f = 20\,\text{mA}$$

$$\therefore \;\; A_1' + A_2' - 100 = 20 \;\; \text{so} \;\; A_1' + A_2' = 120\,\text{mA}$$

$$\frac{di_L}{dt}(0) = 0 = -4000A_1 - 16{,}000A_2'$$

Solving, $\quad A_1' = 160\,\text{mA}, \qquad A_2' = -40\,\text{mA}$

$$i_L = -100 + 160e^{-4000t} - 40e^{-16{,}000t}\,\text{mA}, \qquad t \geq 0$$

P 8.35

$$\omega_o^2 = \frac{1}{LC} = \frac{10^6}{200} = 5000$$

$$\alpha = \frac{R}{2L} = \frac{400}{40} = 10; \qquad \alpha^2 = 100$$

$$\alpha^2 < \omega_o^2 \quad \therefore \quad \text{underdamped}$$

$$s_{1,2} = -10 \pm j\sqrt{4900} = -10 \pm j70 \text{ rad/s}$$

$$i = B_1 e^{-10t}\cos 70t + B_2 e^{-10t}\sin 70t$$

$$i(0) = 0 = B_1$$

$$\frac{di}{dt}(0) = \frac{84}{20} = 4.2 \text{ A/s} = 70B_2 - 10B_1$$

$$\therefore \quad B_2 = 60\,\text{mA}$$

$$i = 60e^{-10t}\sin 70t\,\text{mA}, \qquad t \geq 0^+$$

P 8.36 [a] $t < 0$:

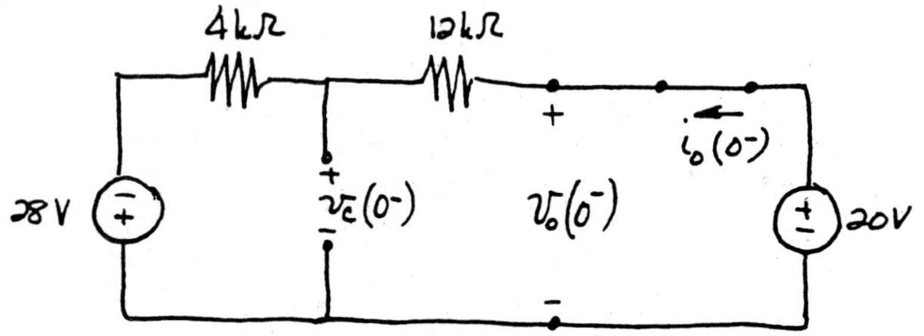

$$i_o(0^-) = \frac{48}{16} = 3\,\text{mA}$$

$$v_C(0^-) = 20 - 12(3) = -16\text{ V}$$

$t = 0^+$:

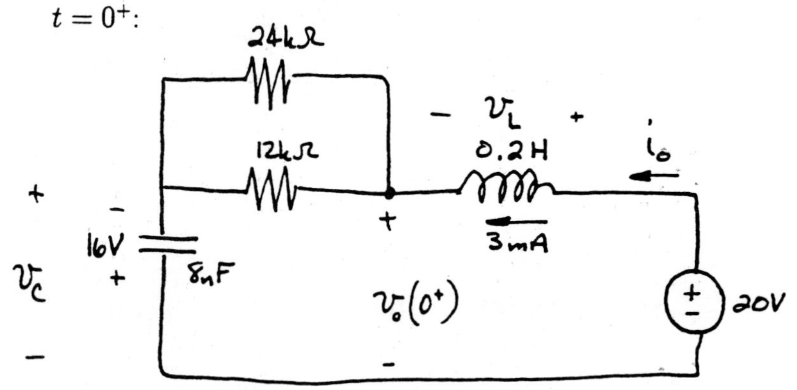

$$12\|24 = 8\,\text{k}\Omega$$

$$\therefore \quad v_o(0^+) = (3)(8) - 16 = 24 - 16 = 8\text{ V}$$

[b] $v_o(t) = 8000i_o + v_C$

$$\frac{dv_o}{dt}(t) = 8000\frac{di_o}{dt} + \frac{dv_C}{dt}$$

$$\frac{dv_o}{dt}(0^+) = 8000\frac{di_o}{dt}(0^+) + \frac{dv_C}{dt}(0^+)$$

$$20 = L\frac{di_o}{dt} + 8000i_o + v_C$$

$$20 = 0.2\frac{di_o}{dt}(0^+) + 24 - 16$$

$$\therefore \quad 0.2\frac{di_o}{dt}(0^+) = 20 - 8 = 12$$

$$\frac{di_o}{dt}(0^+) = \frac{12}{0.2} = 60 \text{ A/s}$$

$$C\frac{dv_c}{dt}(0^+) = i_o(0^+)$$

$$\therefore \quad \frac{dv_c}{dt}(0^+) = \frac{3 \times 10^{-3}}{8 \times 10^{-9}} = 375{,}000$$

$$\therefore \quad \frac{dv_o}{dt}(0^+) = 8000(60) + 375{,}000 = 855{,}000 \text{ V/s}$$

[c] $\omega_o^2 = \dfrac{1}{LC} = \dfrac{10^9}{1.6} = 625 \times 10^6; \qquad \omega_o = 25{,}000 \text{ rad/s}$

$$\alpha = \frac{R}{2L} = \frac{8000}{0.4} = 20{,}000 \text{ nepers}; \qquad \alpha^2 = 400 \times 10^6$$

$\alpha^2 < \omega_o^2$ underdamped

$$s_{1,2} = -20{,}000 \pm j15{,}000 \text{ rad/s}$$

$$v_o(t) = V_f + B_1'e^{-20{,}000t}\cos 15{,}000t + B_2'e^{-20{,}000t}\sin 15{,}000t$$

$$V_f = v_o(\infty) = 20 \text{ V}$$

$$8 = 20 + B_1'; \qquad B_1' = -12 \text{ V}$$

$$-20{,}000B_1' + 15{,}000B_2' = 855{,}000$$

Solving, $B_2' = 41$ V

$$\therefore \quad v_o(t) = 20 - 12e^{-20{,}000t}\cos 15{,}000t + 41e^{-20{,}000t}\sin 15{,}000t \text{ V},$$

P 8.37 $t < 0$:

$$i_o(t) = \frac{120}{8} = 15\,\text{mA}; \qquad v_o(t) = (5)(15) = 75\,\text{V}$$

$t > 0$:

$$\alpha = \frac{R}{2L} = \frac{5000}{2(1)} = 2500 \text{ nepers}$$

$$\omega_o^2 = \frac{1}{LC} = \frac{10^9}{(1)(250)} = 4 \times 10^6 = 400 \times 10^4$$

$$\alpha^2 - \omega_o^2 = 625 \times 10^4 - 400 \times 10^4 = 225 \times 10^4$$

$$\therefore \quad s_{1,2} = -2500 \pm 1500$$

$$s_1 = -1000 \text{ rad/s} \qquad s_2 = -4000 \text{ rad/s}$$

$$\therefore \quad i_o(t) = A_1 e^{-1000t} + A_2 e^{-4000t}$$

$$i_o(0) = A_1 + A_2 = 15 \times 10^{-3}$$

$$\frac{di_o}{dt}(0) = -1000A_1 - 4000A_2 = 0$$

Solving, $\quad A_1 = 20\,\text{mA}; \quad A_2 = -5\,\text{mA}$

$$i_o(t) = 20e^{-1000t} - 5e^{-4000t}\,\text{mA}, \qquad t \geq 0^+$$

$$v_o(t) = A_1 e^{-1000t} + A_2 e^{-4000t}$$

$$v_o(0) = A_1 + A_2 = 75$$

$$\frac{dv_o}{dt}(0) = -1000A_1 - 4000A_2 = \frac{-15 \times 10^{-3}}{250 \times 10^{-9}}$$

Solving, $\quad A_1 = 80\,\text{V}; \quad A_2 = -5\,\text{V}$

$$v_o(t) = 80e^{-1000t} - 5e^{-4000t}\,\text{V}, \qquad t \geq 0^+$$

Check:

$$5000i_o + 1\frac{di_o}{dt} = v_o$$

$$5000i_o = 100e^{-1000t} - 25e^{-4000t}$$

$$\frac{di_o}{dt} = -20e^{-1000t} + 20e^{-4000t}$$

$$\therefore \quad 5000i_o + \frac{di_o}{dt} = 80e^{-1000t} - 5e^{-4000t}\,\text{V} \qquad \text{(checks)}$$

P 8.38 $$\omega_o^2 = \frac{1}{LC} = \frac{10^6}{(20)(5)} = 10^4; \qquad \omega_o = 100 \text{ rad/s}$$

$$\alpha = \frac{1}{2RC} = \frac{10^6}{(1600)(5)} = \frac{10^4}{80} = 125 \text{ nepers}$$

$$s_{1,2} = -125 \pm \sqrt{(125)^2 - 10^4} = -125 \pm 75$$

$$s_1 = -50 \text{ rad/s}; \qquad s_2 = -200 \text{ rad/s}$$

$$I_f = 15\,\text{mA}$$

$$i_L = 15 + A_1' e^{-50t} + A_2' e^{-200t}$$

$$\therefore \quad -30 = 15 + A_1' + A_2'; \qquad A_1' + A_2' = -45 \times 10^{-3}$$

$$\frac{di_L}{dt} = -50A_1' - 200A_2' = \frac{60}{20} = 3$$

Solving, $A_1' = -40\,\text{mA}; \qquad A_2' = -5\,\text{mA}$

$$i_L = 15 - 40e^{-50t} - 5e^{-200t}\,\text{mA}$$

P 8.39 $$\alpha = \frac{1}{2RC} = \frac{10^6}{(2500)(5)} = 80; \qquad \alpha^2 = 6400$$

$$\omega_o^2 = 10^4$$

$$s_{1,2} = -80 \pm j\sqrt{10^4 - 6400} = -80 \pm j60 \text{ rad/s}$$

$$i_L = 15 + B_1' e^{-80t} \cos 60t + B_2' e^{-80t} \sin 60t$$

$$-30 = 15 + B_1' \qquad \therefore \quad B_1' = -45\,\text{mA}$$

$$\frac{di_L}{dt}(0) = -80B_1' + 60B_2' = 3$$

$$\therefore \quad B_2' = -10\,\text{mA}$$

$$i_L = 15 - 45e^{-80t} \cos 60t - 10e^{-80t} \sin 60t\,\text{mA}$$

P 8.40 $$\alpha = \frac{1}{2RC} = \frac{10^6}{(2000)(5)} = 100$$

$$\alpha^2 = 10^4 = \omega_o^2 \qquad \text{critical damping}$$

$$i_L = I_f + D_1' te^{-100t} + D_2' e^{-100t} = 15 + D_1' te^{-100t} + D_2' e^{-100t}$$

$$i_L(0) = -30 = 15 + D_2'; \qquad \therefore\ D_2' = -45\,\text{mA}$$

$$\frac{di_L}{dt}(0) = -100D_2' + D_1' = 3000 \times 10^{-3}$$

$$\therefore\ D_1' = 3000 \times 10^{-3} + 100(-45 \times 10^{-3}) = -1500 \times 10^{-3}$$

$$i_L = 15 - 1500te^{-100t} - 45e^{-100t}\ \text{mA}$$

P 8.41 $t < 0$:

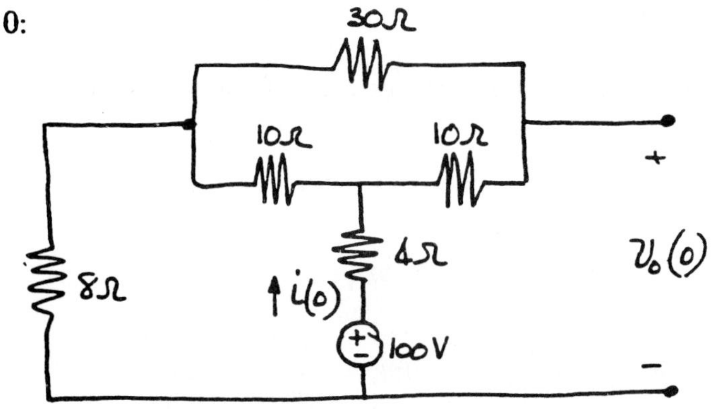

$$i(0) = \frac{100}{4+8+8} = \frac{100}{20} = 5\ \text{A}$$

$$v_o(0) = 100 - 5(4) - 10(5)\left(\frac{10}{50}\right) = 70\ \text{V}$$

$t > 0$:

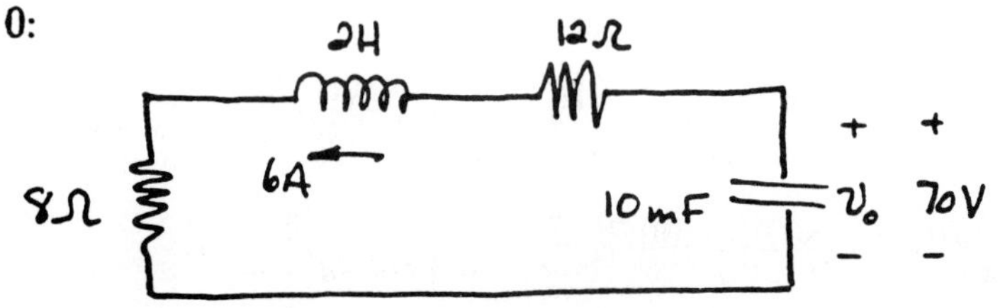

$$\alpha = \frac{R}{2L} = \frac{20}{4} = 5, \qquad \alpha^2 = 25$$

$$\omega_o^2 = \frac{1}{LC} = \frac{100}{2} = 50$$

$\omega_o^2 > \alpha^2$ underdamped

$$v_o = B_1 e^{-\alpha t}\cos\omega_d\, t + B_2 e^{-\alpha t}\sin\omega_d\, t; \qquad \omega_d = \sqrt{50-25} = 5$$

$$v_o = B_1 e^{-5t}\cos 5t + B_2 e^{-5t}\sin 5t$$

$$v_o(0) = B_1 = 70\text{ V}$$

$$C\frac{dv_o}{dt}(0) = -5, \qquad \frac{dv_o}{dt} = \frac{-5}{10}\times 10^3 = -500\text{ V/s}$$

$$\frac{dv_o}{dt}(0) = -5B_1 + 5B_2 = -500$$

$$5B_2 = -500 + 5B_1 = -500 + 350; \qquad B_2 = -150/5 = -30\text{ V}$$

$$\therefore\ v_o = 70e^{-5t}\cos 5t - 30e^{-5t}\sin 5t\text{ V}, \qquad t \geq 0$$

P 8.42 [a] Let i be the current in the direction of the voltage drop $v_o(t)$. Then by hypothesis

$$i = i_f + B_1' e^{-\alpha t}\cos\omega_d t + B_2' e^{-\alpha t}\sin\omega_d t$$

$$i_f = i(\infty) = 0, \qquad i(0) = \frac{V_g}{R} = B_1'$$

Therefore $i = B_1' e^{-\alpha t}\cos\omega_d t + B_2' e^{-\alpha t}\sin\omega_d t$

$$L\frac{di(0)}{dt} = 0, \qquad \text{therefore}\quad \frac{di(0)}{dt} = 0$$

$$\frac{di}{dt} = [(\omega_d B_2' - \alpha B_1')\cos\omega_d t - (\alpha B_2' + \omega_d B_1')\sin\omega_d t]\, e^{-\alpha t}$$

Therefore $\omega_d B_2' - \alpha B_1' = 0; \qquad B_2' = \dfrac{\alpha}{\omega_d}B_1' = \dfrac{\alpha}{\omega_d}\dfrac{V_g}{R}$

Therefore

$$\begin{aligned}
v_L &= L\frac{di}{dt} = -\left\{L\left(\frac{\alpha^2 V_g}{\omega_d R} + \frac{\omega_d V_g}{R}\right)\sin\omega_d t\right\}e^{-\alpha t} \\
&= -\left\{\frac{LV_g}{R}\left(\frac{\alpha^2}{\omega_d} + \omega_d\right)\sin\omega_d t\right\}e^{-\alpha t} \\
&= -\frac{V_g L}{R}\left(\frac{\alpha^2+\omega_d^2}{\omega_d}\right)e^{-\alpha t}\sin\omega_d t \\
v_L &= -\frac{V_g}{RC\omega_d}e^{-\alpha t}\sin\omega_d t
\end{aligned}$$

[b] $$\frac{dv_L}{dt} = -\frac{V_g}{\omega_d RC}\{\omega_d \cos\omega_d t - \alpha \sin\omega_d t\}e^{-\alpha t}$$

$$\frac{dv_L}{dt} = 0 \quad \text{when} \quad \tan\omega_d t = \frac{\omega_d}{\alpha}$$

Therefore $\omega_d t = \tan^{-1}(\omega_d/\alpha)$ (smallest t)

$$t = \frac{1}{\omega_d}\tan^{-1}\left(\frac{\omega_d}{\alpha}\right)$$

P 8.43 [a] From Problem 8.42 we have

$$v_o = \frac{-V_g}{RC\omega_d}e^{-\alpha t}\sin\omega_d t$$

$$\alpha = \frac{R}{2L} = \frac{120}{0.01} = 12{,}000\,\text{nepers}$$

$$\omega_o^2 = \frac{1}{LC} = \frac{10^{12}}{2500} = 400 \times 10^6$$

$$\omega_d = \sqrt{\omega_o^2 - \alpha^2} = 16\,\text{krad/s}$$

$$\frac{-V_g}{RC\omega_d} = \frac{-(-600)10^9}{(120)(500)(16) \times 10^3} = 625$$

$$\therefore \quad v_o = 625e^{-12{,}000t}\sin 16{,}000t\ \text{V}$$

[b] From Problem 8.42

$$t_d = \frac{1}{\omega_d}\tan^{-1}\left(\frac{\omega_d}{\alpha}\right) = \frac{1}{16{,}000}\tan^{-1}\left(\frac{16{,}000}{12{,}000}\right)$$

$$t_d = 57.96\,\mu\text{s}$$

[c] $$v_{\text{max}} = 625e^{-0.012(57.96)}\sin[(0.016)(57.96)] = 249.42\,\text{V}$$

[d] $R = 12\,\Omega$; $\alpha = 1200\,\text{nepers}$

$$\omega_d = 19{,}963.97\,\text{rad/s}$$

$$v_o = 5009.02e^{-1200t}\sin 19{,}963.97t\ \text{V}$$

$$t_d = 75.67\,\mu\text{s}$$

$$v_{\text{max}} = 4565.96\,\text{V}$$

P 8.44 $t < 0$:

$$v_o(0^-) = v_o(0^+) = \frac{1000}{1250}(25) = 20\,\text{V}$$

$$i_L(0^-) = i_L(0^+) = 0$$

$t > 0$

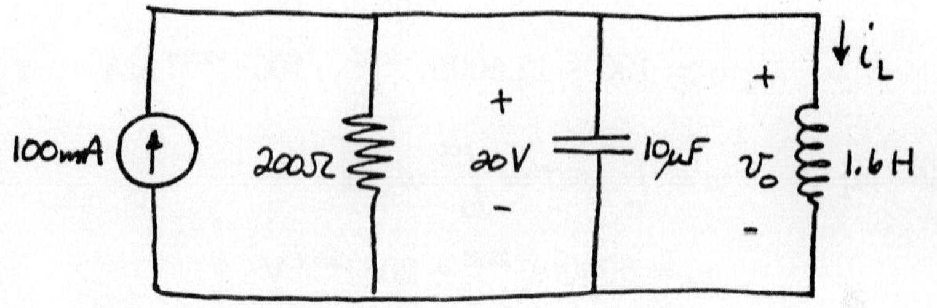

$$-100 + \frac{20}{0.2} + i_C(0^+) + 0 = 0; \qquad \therefore\ i_C(0^+) = 0$$

$$\frac{1}{2RC} = \frac{10^6}{(400)(10)} = 250\,\text{nepers}$$

$$\omega_o^2 = \frac{1}{LC} = \frac{10^9}{10(1.6)} = 62{,}500$$

$$\therefore\ \alpha^2 = \omega_o^2 \quad \text{critically damped}$$

$$v_o = V_f + D_1' te^{-250t} + D_2' e^{-250t}$$

$$V_f = 0$$

$$\frac{dv_o(0)}{dt} = -250D_2' + D_1' = 0$$

$$v_o(0^+) = 20 = D_2'$$

$$D_1' = 250D_2' = 5000\,\text{V/s}$$

$$\therefore\ v_o = 5000te^{-250t} + 20e^{-250t}\,\text{V}, \quad t \geq 0^+$$

[b] $$i_L = I_f + D_3' te^{-250t} + D_4' e^{-250t}$$

$$i_L(0^+) = 0; \qquad I_f = 100\,\text{mA}; \qquad \frac{di_L(0^+)}{dt} = \frac{20}{1.6} = 12.5\ \text{A/s}$$

$$\therefore\ 0 = 100 + D_4'; \qquad D_4' = -100\,\text{mA};$$

$$-250D_4' + D_3' = 12.5; \qquad D_3' = -12.5\,\text{A/s}$$

$$\therefore\ i_L = 100 - 12{,}500te^{-250t} - 100e^{-250t}\ \text{mA} \qquad t \geq 0$$

P 8.45 [a] $$w = \int_0^\infty p\,dt = \int_0^\infty v i_L\,dt$$

$$v_o = 5000te^{-250t} + 20e^{-250t}\ \text{V}$$

$$i_L = 0.1 - 12.5te^{-250t} - 0.1e^{-250t}\ \text{A}$$

$$p = 2e^{-250t} + 500te^{-250t} - 750te^{-500t} - 62{,}000t^2e^{-500t} - 2e^{-500t}\ \text{W}$$

$$\frac{w_L}{2} = \int_0^\infty e^{-250t}\,dt + 250\int_0^\infty te^{-250t}\,dt - 375\int_0^\infty te^{-500t} - 31{,}250\int_0^\infty t^2e^{-500t}\,dt - \int_0^\infty e^{-500t}\,dt$$

$$= \left.\frac{e^{-250t}}{-250}\right|_0^\infty + \left.\frac{250}{(250)^2}e^{-250t}(-250t-1)\right|_0^\infty - \left.\frac{375}{(500)^2}e^{-500t}(-500t-1)\right|_0^\infty - \left.\frac{31{,}250}{(-500)^3}e^{-500t}(500^2t^2 + 1000t + 2)\right|_0^\infty - \left.\frac{e^{-500t}}{(-500)}\right|_0^\infty$$

All the upper limits evaluate to zero hence

$$\frac{w_L}{2} = \frac{1}{250} + \frac{250}{62{,}500} - \frac{375}{250\times10^4} - \frac{(31{,}250)(2)}{(5)^3 10^6} - \frac{1}{500}$$

$$w_L = 8 + 8 - 3 - 1 - 4 = 8\,\text{mJ}$$

Note this value corresponds to the final energy stored in the inductor, i.e.

$$w_L(\infty) = \frac{1}{2}(1.6)(0.1)^2 = 8\,\text{mJ}.$$

[b]
$$v = 5000te^{-250t} + 20e^{-250t}\ \text{V}$$
$$i_R = \frac{v}{200} = 25te^{-250t} + 0.1e^{-250t}\ \text{A}$$
$$p_R = vi_R = 2e^{-500t}[62{,}500t^2 + 500t + 1]$$
$$w_R = \int_0^\infty p_R\, dt$$
$$\frac{w_R}{2} = 62{,}500\int_0^\infty t^2e^{-500t}\,dt + 500\int_0^\infty te^{-500t}\,dt + \int_0^\infty e^{-500t}\,dt$$
$$= \frac{62{,}500e^{-500t}}{-125\times 10^6}[25\times 10^4t^2 + 1000t + 2]\Big|_0^\infty +$$
$$\frac{500e^{-500t}}{25\times 10^4}(-500t - 1)\Big|_0^\infty + \frac{e^{-500t}}{(500)}\Big|_0^\infty$$

Since all the upper limits evaluate to zero we have
$$\frac{w_R}{2} = \frac{62{,}500(2)}{125\times 10^6} + \frac{500}{25\times 10^4} + \frac{1}{500}$$
$$w_R = 2 + 4 + 4 = 10\,\text{mJ}$$

[c]
$$100 = i_R + i_C + i_L \quad (\text{mA})$$
$$i_R + i_L = 25{,}000te^{-250t} + 100e^{-250t} + 100 - 12{,}500te^{-250t} - 100e^{-250t}\ \text{mA}$$
$$= 100 + 12{,}500te^{-250t}\ \text{mA}$$
$$\therefore\ i_C = 100 - (i_R + i_L) = -12{,}500te^{-250t}\ \text{mA} = -12.5te^{-250t}\ \text{A}$$
$$p_C = vi_C = [5000te^{-250t} + 20e^{-250t}][-12.5te^{-250t}]$$
$$= -250[250t^2e^{-500t} + te^{-500t}]$$
$$\frac{w_C}{-250} = 250\int_0^\infty t^2e^{-500t}\,dt + \int_0^\infty te^{-500t}\,dt$$
$$\frac{w_C}{-250} = \frac{250e^{-500t}}{-125\times 10^6}[25\times 10^4t^2 + 1000t + 2]\Big|_0^\infty + \frac{e^{-500t}}{25\times 10^4}(-500t - 1)\Big|_0^\infty$$

Since all upper limits evaluate to zero we have
$$w_C = \frac{-250(250)(2)}{125\times 10^6} - \frac{250(1)}{25\times 10^4} = -1000\times 10^{-6} - 10\times 10^{-4} = -2\,\text{mJ}$$

Note this 2 mJ corresponds to the initial energy stored in the capacitor, i.e.,
$$w_C(0) = \frac{1}{2}(10\times 10^{-6})(20)^2 = 2\,\text{mJ}.$$

Thus $w_C(\infty) = 0\,\text{mJ}$ which agrees with the final value of $v = 0$.

[d] $i_s = 100\,\text{mA}$

$$\begin{aligned} p_s(\text{del}) &= 100v\,\text{mW} \\ &= 0.1[5000te^{-250t} + 20e^{-250t}] \\ &= 2e^{-250t} + 500te^{-250t}\,\text{W} \\ \frac{w_s}{2} &= \int_0^\infty e^{-250t}\,dt + \int_0^\infty 250te^{-250t}\,dt \\ &= \frac{e^{-250t}}{-250}\Big|_0^\infty + \frac{250e^{-250t}}{62{,}500}(-250t - 1)\Big|_0^\infty \\ &= \frac{1}{250} + \frac{1}{250} \\ w_s &= \frac{2(2)}{250} = \frac{4}{250} = 16\,\text{mJ} \end{aligned}$$

[e] $w_L = 8\,\text{mJ}$ (absorbed)

$w_R = 10\,\text{mJ}$ (absorbed)

$w_C = 2\,\text{mJ}$ (delivered)

$w_S = 16\,\text{mJ}$ (delivered)

$\sum w_{\text{del}} = w_{\text{abs}} = 18\,\text{mJ}.$

P 8.46 [a] $\omega_o^2 = \dfrac{1}{LC} = \dfrac{10^9}{(0.25)(160)} = \dfrac{10^8}{4} = 25 \times 10^6$

$\alpha = \dfrac{R}{2L} = \omega_o = 5000$

$\therefore\ R = (5000)(2)L = 2500\,\Omega$

[b] $i(0) = i_L(0) = 24\,\text{mA}$

$v_L(0) = 90 - 24(2.5) = 30\,\text{V}$

$\dfrac{di}{dt}(0) = \dfrac{30}{0.25} = 120\ \text{A/s}$

$v_C = D_1te^{-5000t} + D_2e^{-5000t}$

$v_C(0) = D_2 = 90\,\text{V}$

$\dfrac{dv_C}{dt}(0) = D_1 - 5000D_2 = \dfrac{i_C(0)}{C} = \dfrac{-i_L(0)}{C}$

$D_1 - 450{,}000 = -\dfrac{24 \times 10^{-3}}{160 \times 10^{-9}} = -150{,}000$

$\therefore \quad D_1 = 300{,}000\ \text{V/s}$

$v_C = 300{,}000te^{-5000t} + 90e^{-5000t}\ \text{V}, \qquad t \geq 0^+$

P 8.47 $t < 0$:

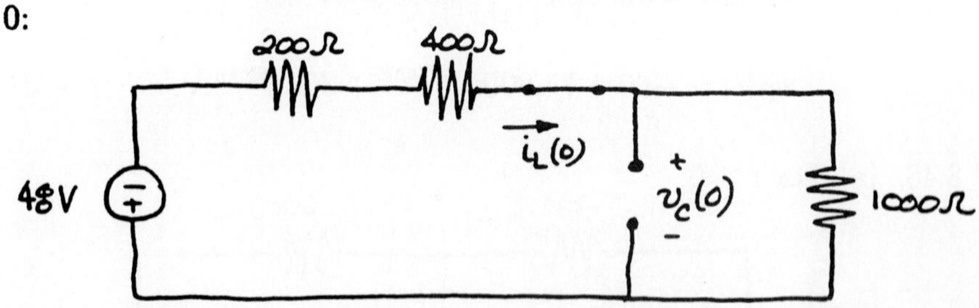

$$i_L(0) = \frac{-48}{1600} = -30\ \text{mA}$$

$$v_C(0) = 1000 i_L(0) = -30\ \text{V}$$

$t > 0$:

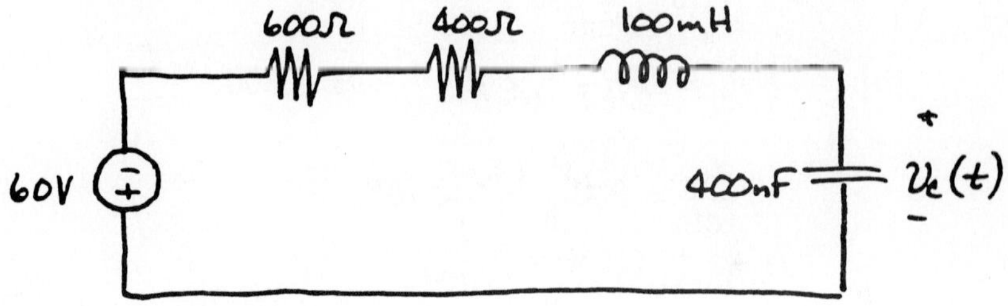

$$\alpha = \frac{R}{2L} = \frac{1000}{200} \times 10^3 = 5000 \text{ nepers}$$

$$\omega_o^2 = \frac{1}{LC} = \frac{(10^9)(10^3)}{(100)(400)} = \frac{10^8}{4} = 25 \times 10^6$$

$\omega_o = 5000$ rad/s $\qquad \therefore$ critical damping

$$v_C(t) = V_f + D_1' te^{-5000t} + D_2' e^{-5000t}$$

$v_C(0) = -30\ \text{V}; \qquad V_f = -60\ \text{V}$

$\therefore \quad -30 = -60 + D_2'; \qquad D_2' = 30\ \text{V}$

$$C\frac{dv_C}{dt}(0) = i_L(0) = -30 \times 10^{-3}$$

$$\frac{dv_C}{dt}(0) = \frac{-30 \times 10^{-3}}{400 \times 10^{-9}} = -75{,}000 \text{ V/s}$$

$$\therefore \quad D_1' = 5000(30) - 75{,}000 = 75{,}000$$

$$v_C(t) = -60 + 75{,}000te^{-5000t} + 30e^{-5000t} \text{ V}, \qquad t \geq 0^+$$

P 8.48 [a] For $t > 0$:

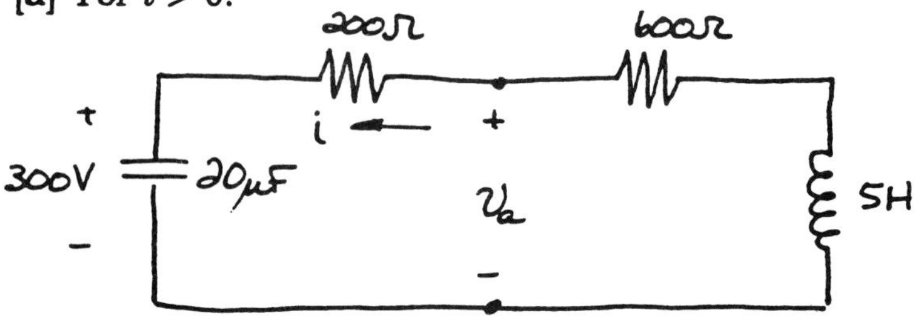

Since $i(0^-) = i(0^+) = 0$

$$v_a(0^+) = 300 \text{ V}$$

[b]

$$v_a = 200i + 5 \times 10^4 \int_0^t i\,dx + 300$$

$$\frac{dv_a}{dt} = 200\frac{di}{dt} + 5 \times 10^4 i$$

$$\frac{dv_a(0^+)}{dt} = 200\frac{di(0^+)}{dt} + 5 \times 10^4 i(0^+) = 200\frac{di(0^+)}{dt}$$

$$-L\frac{di(0^+)}{dt} = 300$$

$$\frac{di(0^+)}{dt} = -0.2(300) = -60 \text{ A/s}$$

$$\therefore \quad \frac{dv_a(0^+)}{dt} = -12{,}000 \text{ V/s}$$

[c]

$$\alpha = \frac{R}{2L} = \frac{800}{10} = 80 \text{ nepers}$$

$$\omega_o^2 = \frac{1}{LC} = \frac{10^6}{(5)(20)} = 10^4$$

$$s_{1,2} = -80 \pm \sqrt{6400 - 10^4} = -80 \pm j60$$

Underdamped:

$$v_a = B_1e^{-80t}\cos 60t + B_2e^{-80t}\sin 60t$$

$$v_a(0) = B_1 = 300$$

$$\frac{dv_a(0)}{dt} = -80B_1 - 60B_2 = -12{,}000; \qquad \therefore\ B_2 = -200$$

$$v_a = 300e^{-80t}\cos 60t - 200e^{-80t}\sin 60t\,\text{V}, \quad t \geq 0^+$$

P 8.49 [a] $v_c = V_f + [A_1' \cos\omega_d t + A_2' \sin\omega_d t]\,e^{-\alpha t}$

$$\frac{dv_c}{dt} = [(\omega_d A_2' - \alpha A_1')\cos\omega_d t - (\alpha A_2' + \omega_d A_1')\sin\omega_d t]e^{-\alpha t}$$

Since the initial stored energy is zero,

$$v_c(0^+) = 0 \quad \text{and} \quad \frac{dv_c(0^+)}{dt} = 0$$

It follows that $A_1' = -V_f$ and $A_2' = \dfrac{\alpha A_1'}{\omega_d}$

When these values are substituted into the expression for $[dv_c/dt]$, we get

$$\frac{dv_c}{dt} = \left(\frac{\alpha^2}{\omega_d} + \omega_d\right)V_f e^{-\alpha t}\sin\omega_d t$$

But $V_f = V$ and $\dfrac{\alpha^2}{\omega_d} + \omega_d = \dfrac{\alpha^2 + \omega_d^2}{\omega_d} = \dfrac{\omega_o^2}{\omega_d}$

Therefore $\dfrac{dv_c}{dt} = \left(\dfrac{\omega_o^2}{\omega_d}\right)Ve^{-\alpha t}\sin\omega_d t$

[b] $\dfrac{dv_c}{dt} = 0$ when $\sin\omega_d t = 0$, or $\omega_d t = n\pi$

where $n = 1, 2, 3, \ldots$

Therefore $t = \dfrac{n\pi}{\omega_d}$

[c] When $t_n = \dfrac{n\pi}{\omega_d}$, $\cos\omega_d t_n = \cos n\pi = (-1)^n$

and $\sin\omega_d t = \sin n\pi = 0$

Therefore $v_c(t_n) = V[1 - (-1)^n e^{-\alpha n\pi/\omega_d}]$

[d] It follows from [c] that

$$v(t_1) = V + Ve^{-(\alpha\pi/\omega_d)} \quad \text{and} \quad v_c(t_3) = V + Ve^{-(3\alpha\pi/\omega_d)}$$

Therefore $\dfrac{v_c(t_1) - V}{v_c(t_3) - V} = \dfrac{e^{-(\alpha\pi/\omega_d)}}{e^{-(3\alpha\pi/\omega_d)}} = e^{(2\alpha\pi/\omega_d)}$

But $\dfrac{2\pi}{\omega_d} = t_3 - t_1 = T_d$, thus $\alpha = \dfrac{1}{T_d}\ln\dfrac{[v_c(t_1) - V]}{[v_c(t_3) - V]}$

P 8.50

$$\frac{1}{T_d}\ln\left\{\frac{v_c(t_1)-V}{v_c(t_3)-V}\right\}; \qquad T_d = t_3 - t_1 = \frac{3\pi}{12} - \frac{\pi}{12} = \frac{2\pi}{12}\,\text{ms}$$

$$\alpha = \frac{12{,}000}{2\pi}\ln\left[\frac{13.505}{0.985}\right] = 5000; \qquad \omega_d = \frac{2\pi}{T_d} = 12{,}000\,\text{rad/s}$$

$$\omega_o^2 = \omega_d^2 + \alpha^2 = 144\times10^6 + 25\times10^6 = 169\times10^6$$

$$L = \frac{1}{(169)(0.2)} = 29.6\,\text{mH}; \qquad R = 2\alpha L = 295.86\,\Omega$$

P 8.51 [a]

$$\frac{d^2v_o}{dt^2} = \frac{1}{R_1C_1R_2C_2}v_g$$

$$\frac{1}{R_1C_1R_2C_2} = \frac{10^{-6}}{(50)(20)(2)(4)\times10^{-6}\times10^{-6}} = 125$$

$$\therefore\ \frac{d^2v_o}{dt^2} = 125v_g$$

$0 \le t \le 0.2^-$:

$$v_g = 400\,\text{mV}$$

$$\frac{d^2v_o}{dt^2} = 50$$

Let $g(t) = \dfrac{dv_o}{dt}$, then $\dfrac{dg}{dt} = 50$ or $dg = 50\,dt$

$$\int_{g(0)}^{g(t)} dx = 50\int_0^t dy$$

$$g(t) - g(0) = 50t, \quad g(0) = \frac{dv_o}{dt}(0) = 0$$

$$g(t) = \frac{dv_o}{dt} = 50t$$

$$dv_o = 50t\,dt$$

$$\int_{v_o(0)}^{v_o(t)} dx = 50\int_0^t x\,dx; \qquad v_o(t) - v_o(0) = 25t^2, \quad v_o(0) = 0$$

$$v_o(t) = 25t^2\,\text{V}, \quad 0 \le t \le 0.2^-$$

$$\frac{dv_{o1}}{dt} = -\frac{1}{R_1C_1}v_g = -10v_g = -4$$

$$dv_{o1} = -4\,dt$$

$$\int_{v_{o1}(0)}^{v_{o1}(t)} dx = -4\int_0^t dy$$

$$v_{o1}(t) - v_{o1}(0) = -4t, \qquad v_{o1}(0) = 0$$

$$v_{o1}(t) = -4t\,\text{V}, \qquad 0 \le t \le 0.2^-$$

$0.2^+ \le t \le t_{sat}$:

$$\frac{d^2v_o}{dt^2} = -12.5, \qquad \text{let } g(t) = \frac{dv_o}{dt}$$

$$\frac{dg(t)}{dt} = -12.5; \qquad dg(t) = -12.5\,dt$$

$$\int_{g(0.2^+)}^{g(t)} dx = -12.5\int_{0.2}^t dy$$

$$g(t) - g(0.2^+) = -12.5(t - 0.2) = -12.5t + 2.5$$

$$g(0.2^+) = \frac{dv_o(0.2^+)}{dt}$$

$$C\frac{dv_o}{dt}(0.2^+) = \frac{0 - v_{o1}(0.2^+)}{20\times 10^3}$$

$$v_{o1}(0.2^+) = v_o(0.2^-) = -4(0.2) = -0.80\,\text{V}$$

$$\therefore\quad C\frac{dv_{o1}(0.2^+)}{dt} = \frac{0.80}{20\times 10^3} = 40\,\mu\text{A}$$

$$\frac{dv_{o1}}{dt}(0.2^+) = \frac{40\times 10^{-6}}{4\times 10^{-6}} = 10\,\text{V/s}$$

$$\therefore\quad g(t) = -12.5t + 2.5 + 10 = -12.5t + 12.5 = \frac{dv_o}{dt}$$

$$\therefore\quad dv_o = -12.5t\,dt + 12.5\,dt$$

$$\int_{v_o(0.2^+)}^{v_o(t)} dx = \int_{0.2^+}^t -12.5y\,dy + \int_{0.2^+}^t 12.5\,dy$$

$$v_o(t) - v_o(0.2^+) = -6.25y^2\Big|_{0.2}^t + 12.5y\Big|_{0.2}^t$$

$$v_o(t) = v_o(0.2^+) - 6.25t^2 + 0.25 + 12.5t - 2.5$$

$$v_o(0.2^+) = v_o(0.2^-) = 1\,\text{V}$$

$$\therefore\quad v_o(t) = -6.25t^2 + 12.5t - 1.25\,\text{V}, \qquad 0.2^+ \le t \le t_{sat}$$

$$\frac{dv_{o1}}{dt} = -10(0.1) = 1, \qquad 0.2^+ \le t \le t_{sat}$$

$$dv_{o1} = dt; \qquad \int_{v_{o1}(0.2^+)}^{v_{o1}(t)} dx = \int_{0.2^+}^{t} dy$$

$$v_{o1}(t) - v_{o1}(0.2^+) = t - 0.2; \qquad v_{o1}(0.2^+) = v_{o1}(0.2^-) = -0.8\,\text{V}$$

$$\therefore \quad v_{o1}(t) = t - 1\,\text{V}, \qquad 0.2^+ \leq t \leq t_{\text{sat}}$$

Summary:

$$0 \leq t \leq 0.2^-\text{s}: \qquad v_{o1} = -4t\,\text{V}, \quad v_o = 25t^2\,\text{V}$$

$$0.2^+\text{s} \leq t \leq t_{\text{sat}}: \qquad v_{o1} = t - 1\,\text{V}, \quad v_o = -6.25t^2 + 12.5t - 1.25\,\text{V}$$

[b] $$-10 = -6.25t_{\text{sat}}^2 + 12.5t_{\text{sat}} - 1.25$$

$$\therefore \quad 6.25t_{\text{sat}}^2 - 12.5t_{\text{sat}} - 8.75 = 0$$

$$t_{\text{sat}}^2 - 2t_{\text{sat}} - 1.4 = 0$$

$$t_{\text{sat}} = 1 \pm \sqrt{1 + 1.4} = 1 \pm 1.55$$

$$\therefore \quad t_{\text{sat}} = 2.55\,\text{sec}$$

$$v_{o1}(t_{\text{sat}}) = 2.55 - 1 = 1.55\,\text{V}$$

P 8.52 $$\tau_1 = (0.25 \times 10^6)(2 \times 10^{-6}) = 0.50\,\text{s}$$

$$\frac{1}{\tau_1} = 2; \qquad \tau_2 = (0.25 \times 10^6)(4 \times 10^{-6}) = 1\,\text{s}; \qquad \therefore \quad \frac{1}{\tau_2} = 1$$

$$\therefore \quad \frac{d^2v_o}{dt^2} + 3\frac{dv_o}{dt} + 2v_o = 50$$

$$s^2 + 3s + 2 = 0$$

$$(s + 1)(s + 2) = 0; \qquad s_1 = -1, \quad s_2 = -2$$

$$v_o = V_f + A_1'e^{-t} + A_2'e^{-2t}; \qquad V_f = \frac{50}{2} = 25\,\text{V}$$

$$v_o = 25 + A_1'e^{-t} + A_2'e^{-2t}$$

$$v_o(0) = 0 = 25 + A_1' + A_2'; \qquad \frac{dv_o}{dt}(0) = 0 = -A_1' - 2A_2'$$

$$\therefore \quad A_1' = -50, \qquad A_2' = 25\,\text{V}$$

$$v_o(t) = 25 - 50e^{-t} + 25e^{-2t}\,\text{V}, \qquad 0 \leq t \leq 0.2\,\text{s}$$

$$\frac{dv_{o1}}{dt} + 2v_{o1} = -4; \qquad \therefore \;\; v_{o1} = -2 + 2e^{-2t}\,\text{V}, \quad 0 \le t \le 0.2\,\text{s}$$

$$v_o(0.2) = 25 - 50e^{-0.2} + 25e^{-0.4} = 0.8215\,\text{V}$$

$$v_{o1}(0.2) = -2 + 2e^{-0.4} = -0.6594\,\text{V}$$

At $t = 0.2\,\text{s}$

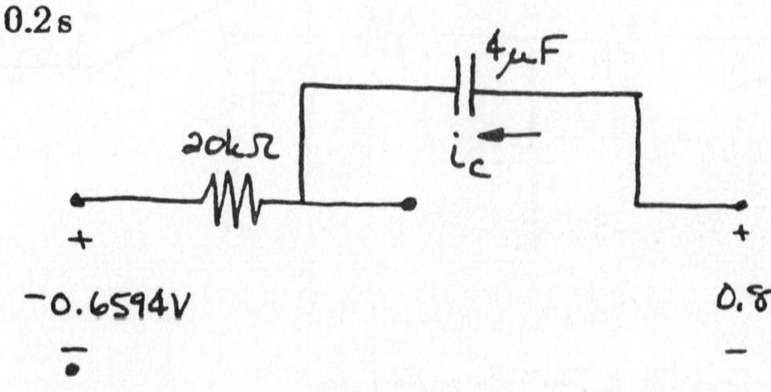

$$i_C = \frac{0 + 0.6594}{20 \times 10^3} = 32.97\,\mu\text{A}$$

$$C\frac{dv_o}{dt} = 32.97\,\mu\text{A}; \qquad \frac{dv_o}{dt} = \frac{32.97}{4} = 8.24\,\text{V/s}$$

$0.2\,\text{s} \le t \le \infty$:

$$\frac{d^2v_o}{dt^2} + 3\frac{dv_o}{dt} + 2 = -12.5$$

$$v_o(\infty) = -6.25$$

$$\therefore \;\; v_o = -6.25 + A_1'e^{-(t-0.2)} + A_2'e^{-2(t-0.2)}$$

$$0.8215 = -6.25 + A_1' + A_2'$$

$$\frac{dv_o}{dt}(0.2) = 8.24 = -A_1' - 2A_2'$$

$$\therefore \;\; A_1' + A_2' = 7.07; \qquad -A_1' - 2A_2' = 8.24$$

$$A_1' = 22.38; \qquad A_2' = -15.31$$

$$\therefore \;\; v_o = -6.25 + 22.38e^{-(t-0.2)} - 15.31e^{-2(t-0.2)}\,\text{V}, \qquad 0.2 \le t \le \infty$$

$$\frac{dv_{o1}}{dt} + 2v_{o1} = 1$$

$$\therefore \;\; v_{o1} = 1 + (-0.6594 - 1)e^{-2(t-0.2)} = 1 - 1.66e^{-2(t-0.2)}\,\text{V}, \qquad 0.2 \le t$$

P 8.53 [a]

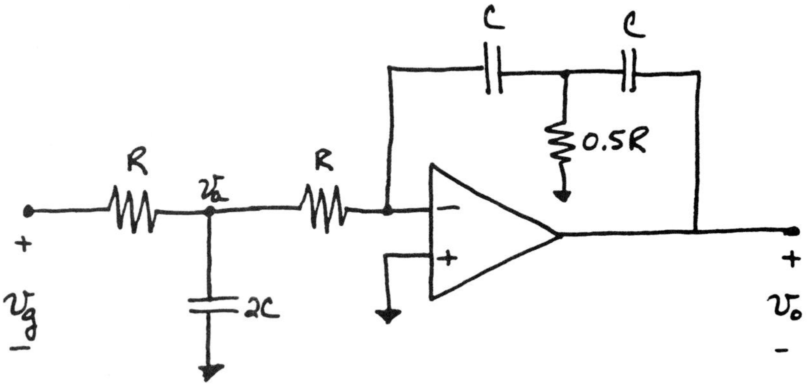

$$2C\frac{dv_a}{dt} + \frac{v_a - v_g}{R} + \frac{v_a}{R} = 0$$

(1) Therefore $\quad \frac{dv_a}{dt} + \frac{v_a}{RC} = \frac{v_g}{2RC}; \qquad \frac{0 - v_a}{R} + C\frac{d(0 - v_b)}{dt} = 0$

(2) Therefore $\quad \frac{dv_b}{dt} + \frac{v_a}{RC} = 0, \quad v_a = -RC\frac{dv_b}{dt}$

$$\frac{2v_b}{R} + C\frac{dv_b}{dt} + C\frac{d(v_b - v_o)}{dt} = 0$$

(3) Therefore $\quad \frac{dv_b}{dt} + \frac{v_b}{RC} = \frac{1}{2}\frac{dv_o}{dt}$

From (2) we have $\quad \frac{dv_a}{dt} = -RC\frac{d^2v_b}{dt^2} \quad$ and $\quad v_a = -RC\frac{dv_b}{dt}$

When these are substituted into (1) we get

(4) $\quad -RC\frac{d^2v_b}{dt^2} - \frac{dv_b}{dt} = \frac{v_g}{2RC}$

Now differentiate (3) to get

(5) $\quad \frac{d^2v_b}{dt^2} + \frac{1}{RC}\frac{dv_b}{dt} = \frac{1}{2}\frac{d^2v_o}{dt^2}$

But from (4) we have

(6) $\quad \frac{d^2v_b}{dt^2} + \frac{1}{RC}\frac{dv_b}{dt} = -\frac{v_g}{2R^2C^2}$

Now substitute (6) into (5)

$$\frac{d^2v_o}{dt^2} = -\frac{v_g}{R^2C^2}$$

[b] When $R_1C_1 = R_2C_2 = RC$: $\frac{d^2v_o}{dt^2} = \frac{v_g}{R^2C^2}$

The two equations are the same except for a reversal in algebraic sign.

[c] Two integrations of the input signal with one operational amplifier.

P 8.54 [a] $f(t) =$ inertial force + frictional force + spring force

$$= M[d^2x/dt^2] + D[dx/dt] + Kx$$

[b] $$\frac{d^2x}{dt^2} = \frac{f}{M} - \left(\frac{D}{M}\right)\left(\frac{dx}{dt}\right) - \left(\frac{K}{M}\right)x$$

Given $v_A = \frac{d^2x}{dt^2}$, then

$$v_B = -\frac{1}{R_1C_1}\int_0^t \left(\frac{d^2x}{dy^2}\right) dy = -\frac{1}{R_1C_1}\frac{dx}{dt}$$

$$v_C = -\frac{1}{R_2C_2}\int_0^t v_B\,dy = \frac{1}{R_1R_2C_1C_2}x$$

$$v_D = -\frac{R_3}{R_4}\cdot v_B = \frac{R_3}{R_4R_1C_1}\frac{dx}{dt}$$

$$v_E = \left[\frac{R_5+R_6}{R_6}\right]v_C = \left[\frac{R_5+R_6}{R_6}\right]\cdot\frac{1}{R_1R_2C_1C_2}\cdot x$$

$$v_F = \left[\frac{-R_8}{R_7}\right]f(t), \qquad v_A = -(v_D + v_E + v_F)$$

Therefore $$\frac{d^2x}{dt^2} = \left[\frac{R_8}{R_7}\right]f(t) - \left[\frac{R_3}{R_4R_1C_1}\right]\frac{dx}{dt} - \left[\frac{R_5+R_6}{R_6R_1R_2C_1C_2}\right]x$$

Therefore $M = \frac{R_7}{R_8}$, $\quad D = \frac{R_3R_7}{R_8R_4R_1C_1}\quad$ and $\quad K = \frac{R_7(R_5+R_6)}{R_8R_6R_1R_2C_1C_2}$

Box Number	Function
1	inverting and scaling
2	inverting and scaling
3	integrating and scaling
4	integrating and scaling
5	inverting and scaling
6	noninverting and scaling

P 8.55 [a] Given that the current response is underdamped we know i will be of the form

$$i = I_f + [B_1' \cos\omega_d t + B_2' \sin\omega_d t]e^{-\alpha t}$$

where $$\alpha = \frac{R}{2L}$$

and $$\omega_d = \sqrt{\omega_o^2 - \alpha^2} = \sqrt{\frac{1}{LC} - \alpha^2}$$

The capacitor will force the final value of i to be zero, therefore $I_f = 0$.
By hypothesis $i(0^+) = V_{dc}/R$ therefore $B_1' = V_{dc}/R$.
At $t = 0^+$ the voltage across the primary winding is zero hence $di(0^+)/dt = 0$.
From our equation for i we have

$$\frac{di}{dt} = [(\omega_d B_2' - \alpha B_1') \cos\omega_d t - (\omega_d B_1' + \alpha B_2') \sin\omega_d t]e^{-\alpha t}$$

Hence

$$\frac{di(0^+)}{dt} = \omega_d B_2' - \alpha B_1' = 0$$

Thus

$$B_2' = \frac{\alpha}{\omega_d} B_1' = \frac{\alpha V_{dc}}{\omega_d R}$$

It follows directly that

$$i = \frac{V_{dc}}{R}\left[\cos\omega_d t + \frac{\alpha}{\omega_d} \sin\omega_d t\right] e^{-\alpha t}$$

[b] Since $\omega_d B_1' - \alpha B_1' = 0$ it follows that

$$\frac{di}{dt} = -(\omega_d B_1' + \alpha B_2')e^{-\alpha t} \sin\omega_d t$$

But $\alpha B_2' = \dfrac{\alpha^2 V_{dc}}{\omega_d R}$ and $\omega_d B_1' = \dfrac{\omega_d V_{dc}}{R}$

Therefore

$$\omega_d B_1' + \alpha B_2' = \frac{\omega_d V_{dc}}{R} + \frac{\alpha^2 V_{dc}}{\omega_d R} = \frac{V_{dc}}{R}\left[\frac{\omega_d^2 + \alpha^2}{\omega_d}\right]$$

But $\omega_d^2 + \alpha^2 = \omega_o^2 = \dfrac{1}{LC}$

Hence

$$\omega_d B_1' + \alpha B_2' = \frac{V_{dc}}{\omega_d RLC}$$

Now since $v_1 = L\frac{di}{dt}$ we get

$$v_1 = -L\frac{V_{dc}}{\omega_d RLC}e^{-\alpha t}\sin\omega_d t = -\frac{V_{dc}}{\omega_d RC}e^{-\alpha t}\sin\omega_d t$$

[c] $$v_c = V_{dc} - iR - L\frac{di}{dt}$$

$$iR = V_{dc}\left(\cos\omega_d t + \frac{\alpha}{\omega_d}\sin\omega_d t\right)e^{-\alpha t}$$

$$\begin{aligned} v_c &= V_{dc} - V_{dc}\left(\cos\omega_d t + \frac{\alpha}{\omega_d}\sin\omega_d t\right)e^{-\alpha t} + \frac{V_{dc}}{\omega_d RC}e^{-\alpha t}\sin\omega_d t \\ &= V_{dc} - V_{dc}e^{-\alpha t}\cos\omega_d t + \left(\frac{V_{dc}}{\omega_d RC} - \frac{\alpha V_{dc}}{\omega_d}\right)e^{-\alpha t}\sin\omega_d t \\ &= V_{dc}\left[1 - e^{-\alpha t}\cos\omega_d t + \frac{1}{\omega_d}\left(\frac{1}{RC} - \alpha\right)e^{-\alpha t}\sin\omega_d t\right] \\ &= V_{dc}\left[1 - e^{-\alpha t}\cos\omega_d t + Ke^{-\alpha t}\sin\omega_d t\right] \end{aligned}$$

P 8.56 $$v_{sp} = V_{dc}\left[1 - \frac{a}{\omega_d RC}e^{-\alpha t}\sin\omega_d t\right]$$

$$\begin{aligned} \frac{dv_{sp}}{dt} &= \frac{-aV_{dc}}{\omega_d RC}\frac{d}{dt}[e^{-\alpha t}\sin\omega_d t] \\ &= \frac{-aV_{dc}}{\omega_d RC}[-\alpha e^{-\alpha t}\sin\omega_d t + \omega_d\cos\omega_d t e^{-\alpha t}] \\ &= \frac{aV_{dc}e^{-\alpha t}}{\omega_d RC}[\alpha\sin\omega_d t - \omega_d\cos\omega_d t] \end{aligned}$$

$\frac{dv_{sp}}{dt} = 0$ when $\alpha\sin\omega_d t = \omega_d\cos\omega_d t$

or $\tan\omega_d t = \frac{\omega_d}{\alpha}$; $\omega_d t = \tan^{-1}\left(\frac{\omega_d}{\alpha}\right)$

$$\therefore\ t_{max} = \frac{1}{\omega_d}\tan^{-1}\left(\frac{\omega_d}{\alpha}\right)$$

Note that because $\tan\theta$ is periodic, i.e., $\tan\theta = \tan(\theta \pm n\pi)$, where n is an integer, there are an infinite number of solutions for t where $dv_{sp}/dt = 0$, that is

$$t = \frac{\tan^{-1}(\omega_d/\alpha) \pm n\pi}{\omega_d}$$

Because of $e^{-\alpha t}$ in the expression for v_{sp} and knowing $t \geq 0$ we know v_{sp} will be maximum when t has its smallest positive value. Hence

$$t_{\max} = \frac{\tan^{-1}(\omega_d/\alpha)}{\omega_d}.$$

P 8.57 [a] $$v_c = V_{dc}[1 - e^{-\alpha t}\cos\omega_d t + Ke^{-\alpha t}\sin\omega_d t]$$

$$\begin{aligned}\frac{dv_c}{dt} &= V_{dc}\frac{d}{dt}[1 + e^{-\alpha t}(K\sin\omega_d t - \cos\omega_d t)] \\ &= V_{dc}\{(-\alpha e^{-\alpha t})(K\sin\omega_d t - \cos\omega_d t) + \\ &\quad e^{-\alpha t}[\omega_d K\cos\omega_d t + \omega_d\sin\omega_d t]\} \\ &= V_{dc}e^{-\alpha t}[(\omega_d - \alpha K)\sin\omega_d t + (\alpha + \omega_d K)\cos\omega_d t]\end{aligned}$$

$$\frac{dv_c}{dt} = 0 \quad \text{when} \quad (\omega_d - \alpha K)\sin\omega_d t = -(\alpha + \omega_d K)\cos\omega_d t$$

$$\text{or} \quad \tan\omega_d t = \left[\frac{\alpha + \omega_d K}{\alpha K - \omega_d}\right]$$

$$\therefore \quad \omega_d t \pm n\pi = \tan^{-1}\left[\frac{\alpha + \omega_d K}{\alpha K - \omega_d}\right]$$

$$t_c = \frac{1}{\omega_d}\left\{tan^{-1}\left(\frac{\alpha + \omega_d K}{\alpha K - \omega_d}\right) \pm n\pi\right\}$$

$$\alpha = \frac{R}{2L} = \frac{4 \times 10^3}{6} = 666.67 \text{ nepers}$$

$$\omega_d = \sqrt{\frac{10^9}{1.2} - (666.67)^2} = 28{,}859.81 \text{ rad/s}$$

$$K = \frac{1}{\omega_d}\left(\frac{1}{RC} - \alpha\right) = 21.63$$

$$t_c = \frac{1}{\omega_d}\left\{\tan^{-1}(-43.29) + n\pi\right\} = \frac{1}{\omega_d}\{-1.55 + n\pi\}$$

The smallest positive value of t occurs when $n = 1$, therefore

$$t_{c\max} = 55.23\ \mu s$$

[b] $$v_c(t_{c\max}) = 12[1 - e^{-\alpha t_{c\max}}\cos\omega_d t_{c\max} + Ke^{-\alpha t_{c\max}}\sin\omega_d t_{c\max}]$$

$$= 262.42 \text{ V}$$

[c] From the text example the voltage across the spark plug reaches its maximum value in 53.63 μs. If the spark plug does not fire the capacitor voltage peaks in 55.23 μs. When v_{sp} is maximum the voltage across the capacitor is 262.15 V. If the spark plug does not fire the capacitor voltage reaches 262.42 V.

P 8.58 [a]
$$w = \frac{1}{2}L[i(0^+)]^2 = \frac{1}{2}(5)(16) \times 10^{-3} = 40\,\text{mJ}$$

[b]
$$\alpha = \frac{R}{2L} = \frac{3 \times 10^3}{10} = 300 \text{ rad/s}$$

$$\omega_d = \sqrt{\frac{10^9}{1.25} - (300)^2} = 28{,}282.68 \text{ rad/s}$$

$$\frac{1}{Rc} = \frac{10^6}{0.75} = \frac{4 \times 10^6}{3}$$

$$t_{\text{max}} = \frac{1}{\omega_d} \tan^{-1}\left(\frac{\omega_d}{\alpha}\right) = 55.16\,\mu\text{s}$$

$$v_{sp}\,(t_{\text{max}}) = 12 - \frac{12(50)(4 \times 10^6)}{3(28{,}282.68)} e^{-\alpha t_{\text{max}}} \sin \omega_d t_{\text{max}} = -27{,}808.04$$

[c]
$$v_c\,(t_{\text{max}}) = 12[1 - e^{-\alpha t_{\text{max}}} \cos \omega_d t_{\text{max}} + Ke^{-\alpha t_{\text{max}}} \sin \omega_d t_{\text{max}}]$$

$$K = \frac{1}{\omega_d}\left[\frac{1}{RC} - \alpha\right] = 47.13$$

$$v_c\,(t_{\text{max}}) = 568.15\,\text{V}$$

9

Sinusoidal Steady State Analysis

Drill Exercises

DE 9.1 [a] $\omega = 2\pi f = 3769.91\,\text{rad/s}, \qquad f = 600\,\text{Hz}$

[b] $T = 1/f = 1.67\,\text{ms}$

[c] $V_m = 10\,\text{V}$

[d] $v(0) = 10(0.6) = 6\,\text{V}$

[e] $\phi = -53.13^\circ; \qquad \phi = \dfrac{-53.13^\circ(2\pi)}{360^\circ} = -0.9273\,\text{rad}$

[f] $3769.91t = 143.13/57.3 = 2.498\,\text{rad}, \qquad t = 662.62\,\mu\text{s}$

[g] $(dv/dt) = (-10)3769.91\sin(3769.91t - 53.13^\circ)$

$$(dv/dt) = 0 \quad \text{when} \quad 3769.91t - 53.13^\circ = 0^\circ$$

$$\text{or} \qquad 3769.91t = 0.9273\,\text{rad}$$

$$\text{Therefore} \quad t = 245.97\,\mu\text{s}$$

DE 9.2 $V_{\text{rms}} = \sqrt{\dfrac{1}{T}\displaystyle\int_0^{T/2} V_m^2 \sin^2 \frac{2\pi}{T} t\, dt}$

$$\int_0^{T/2} V_m^2 \sin^2\left(\frac{2\pi}{T}\right) t\, dt = \frac{V_m^2}{2}\int_0^{T/2}\left(1 - \cos\frac{4\pi}{T}t\right) dt = \frac{V_m^2 T}{4}$$

$$\text{Therefore} \quad V_{\text{rms}} = \sqrt{\frac{1}{T}\frac{V_m^2 T}{4}} = \frac{V_m}{2}$$

DE 9.3 [a] The numerical values of the terms in Eq. 9.8 are

$$V_m = 20, \qquad R/L = 1066.67, \qquad \omega L = 60$$

$$\sqrt{R^2 + \omega^2 L^2} = 100$$

$$\phi = 25^\circ, \qquad \theta = \tan^{-1} 60/80, \qquad \theta = 36.87^\circ$$

$$i = \left[-195.72e^{-1066.67t} + 200\cos(800t - 11.87^\circ)\right] \text{ mA}, \qquad t \geq 0^+$$

[b] Transient component $= -195.72e^{-1066.67t}$
Steady-state component $= 200\cos(800t - 11.87^\circ)$

[c] By direct substitution into Eq 9.9, $i(1.875\text{ ms}) = 28.39\text{ mA}$

[d] 0.2 A, 800 rad/s, −11.87°

[e] The current lags the voltage by 36.87°.

DE 9.4 [a] $\mathbf{V} = 170\underline{/-40^\circ}$

[b] $\mathbf{I} = 10\underline{/-70^\circ}$

[c]
$$\begin{aligned}\mathbf{I} &= 5\underline{/36.87^\circ} + 10\underline{/-53.13^\circ}\\ &= 4 + j3 + 6 - j8 = 10 - j5 = 11.18\underline{/-26.6^\circ}\end{aligned}$$

[d]
$$\begin{aligned}\mathbf{V} &= 300\underline{/45^\circ} - 100\underline{/-60^\circ} = 212.13 + j212.13 - (50 - j86.60)\\ &= 162.13 + j298.73 = 339.90\underline{/61.51^\circ}\text{ mV}\end{aligned}$$

DE 9.5 [a] $v = 18.6\cos(\omega t - 54^\circ)$ V

[b]
$$\begin{aligned}\mathbf{I} &= 20\underline{/45^\circ} - 50\underline{/-30^\circ} = 14.14 + j14.14 - 43.3 + j25\\ &= -29.16 + j39.14 = 48.81\underline{/126.68^\circ}\end{aligned}$$

Therefore $i = 48.81\cos(\omega t + 126.68^\circ)$ mA

[c]
$$\begin{aligned}\mathbf{V} &= 20 + j80 - 30\underline{/15^\circ} = 20 + j80 - 28.98 - j7.76\\ &= -8.98 + j72.24 = 72.79\underline{/97.08^\circ}\end{aligned}$$

$$v = 72.79\cos(\omega t + 97.08^\circ)\text{ V}$$

DE 9.6 [a] $\omega L = (10^4)(20 \times 10^{-3}) = 200\,\Omega$

[b] $Z_L = j200\,\Omega$

[c] $\mathbf{V}_L = \mathbf{I}Z_L = (10\underline{/30^\circ})(200\underline{/90^\circ}) \times 10^{-3} = 2\underline{/120^\circ}$ V

[d] $v_L = 2\cos(10{,}000t + 120^\circ)$ V

DE 9.7 [a]
$$X_C = \frac{-1}{\omega C} = -\frac{10^6}{4000(5)} = -50\,\Omega$$

[b] $Z_C = jX_C = -j50\,\Omega$

[c] $\mathbf{I} = \dfrac{30\underline{/25^\circ}}{50\underline{/-90^\circ}} = 0.6\underline{/115^\circ}\text{ A}$

[d] $i = 0.6\cos(4000t + 115^\circ)\text{ A}$

DE 9.8 $\mathbf{I}_1 = 100\underline{/25^\circ} = 90.63 + j42.26$

$\mathbf{I}_2 = 100\underline{/145^\circ} = -81.92 + j57.36$

$\mathbf{I}_3 = 100\underline{/-95^\circ} = -8.71 - j99.62$

$\mathbf{I}_4 = -(\mathbf{I}_1 + \mathbf{I}_2 + \mathbf{I}_3) = (0 + j0)\text{ A},$ therefore $i_4 = 0\text{ A}$

DE 9.9 [a] $\mathbf{I} = \dfrac{125\underline{/-60^\circ}}{|Z|\underline{/\theta_z}} = \dfrac{125}{|Z|}\underline{/(-60 - \theta_Z)^\circ}$

But $-60 - \theta_Z = -105^\circ$ $\quad\therefore\ \theta_Z = 45^\circ$

$Z = 90 + j160 + jX_C$

$\therefore\ X_C = -70\,\Omega;\qquad -\dfrac{1}{\omega C} = -70$

$\therefore\ C = \dfrac{1}{(70)(5000)} = 2.86\,\mu\text{F}$

[b] $\mathbf{I} = \dfrac{125\underline{/-60^\circ}}{(90 + j90)} = 0.982\underline{/-105^\circ}A;\qquad \therefore\ |\mathbf{I}| = 0.982\text{ A}$

DE 9.10 [a]

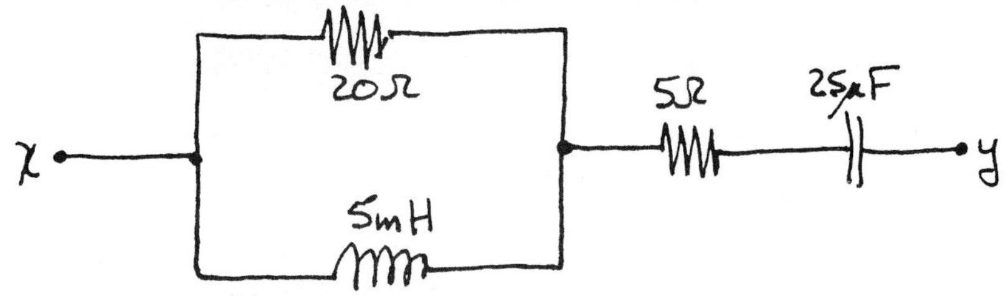

$\omega = 2000\text{ rad/s}$

$\omega L = 10\,\Omega,\qquad \dfrac{-1}{\omega C} = -20\,\Omega$

$Z_{xy} = \dfrac{20(j10)}{(20 + j10)} + 5 - j20 = 4 + j8 + 5 - j20 = (9 - j12)\,\Omega$

[b] $$\omega L = 40\,\Omega, \qquad \frac{-1}{\omega C} = -5\,\Omega$$

$$Z_{xy} = 5 - j5 + \left[\frac{(20)(j40)}{20 + j40}\right] = 5 - j5 + 16 + j8 = (21 + j3)\,\Omega$$

[c] $$Z_{xy} = \left[\frac{20(j\omega L)}{20 + j\omega L}\right] + \left(5 - \frac{j10^6}{25\omega}\right)$$

$$= \frac{20\omega^2 L^2}{400 + \omega^2 L^2} + \frac{j400\omega L}{400 + \omega^2 L^2} + 5 - \frac{j10^6}{25\omega}$$

The impedance will be purely resistive when the j terms cancel, i.e.,

$$\frac{400\omega L}{400 + \omega^2 L^2} = \frac{10^6}{25\omega}$$

Solving for ω yields $\omega = 4000\,\text{rad/s}$.

[d] $$Z_{xy} = \frac{20\omega^2 L^2}{400 + \omega^2 L^2} + 5 = 10 + 5 = 15\,\Omega$$

DE 9.11

$$\mathbf{V} = 150\angle 0^\circ, \qquad \mathbf{I}_s = \frac{150\angle 0^\circ}{15} = 10\angle 0^\circ\text{ A}$$

$$\mathbf{I}_L = \frac{10(20)}{20 + j20} = 5 - j5 = 7.07\angle -45^\circ\text{ A}$$

$$i_L = 7.07\cos(4000t - 45^\circ)\text{ A}, \qquad I_m = 7.07\text{ A}$$

DE 9.12 [a]

$$Y = \frac{1}{3 + j4} + \frac{1}{16 - j12} + \frac{1}{-j4}$$

$$= 0.12 - j0.16 + 0.04 + j0.03 + j0.25$$

$$= 0.16 + j0.12 = 0.2\angle 36.87^\circ\ \mho$$

[b] $G = 0.16\ \mho$

[c] $B = 0.12\ \mho$

[d] $$\mathbf{I} = 8\angle 0^\circ\text{ A}, \qquad \mathbf{V} = \frac{\mathbf{I}}{Y} = \frac{8}{0.2\angle 36.87^\circ} = 40\angle -36.87^\circ\text{ V}$$

$$\mathbf{I}_C = \frac{\mathbf{V}}{Z_C} = \frac{40\angle -36.87^\circ}{4\angle -90^\circ} = 10\angle 53.13^\circ\text{ A}$$

$$i_C = 10\cos(\omega t + 53.13^\circ)\text{ A}, \qquad I_m = 10\text{ A}$$

DE 9.13 Construct the phasor domain equivalent circuit:

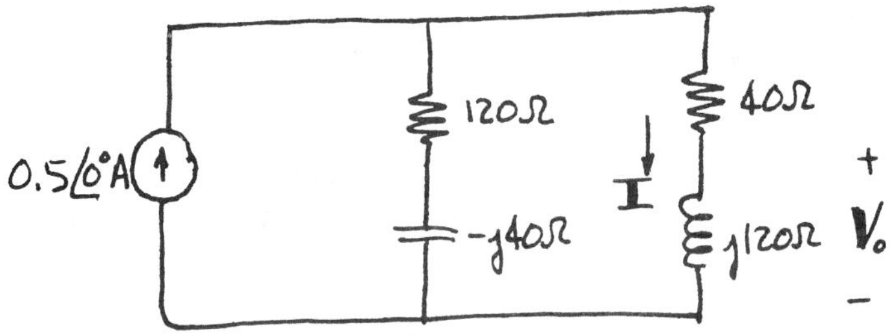

$$\mathbf{I} = \frac{0.5(120 - j40)}{160 + j80} = 0.25 - j0.25\text{ A}$$

$$\mathbf{V}_o = j120\mathbf{I} = 30 + j30 = 42.43\underline{/45^\circ}$$

$$v_o = 42.43\cos(2000t + 45^\circ)\text{ V}$$

DE 9.14 After replacing the delta made up of the 50 Ω, 40 Ω, and 10 Ω resistors with its equivalent wye, the circuit becomes

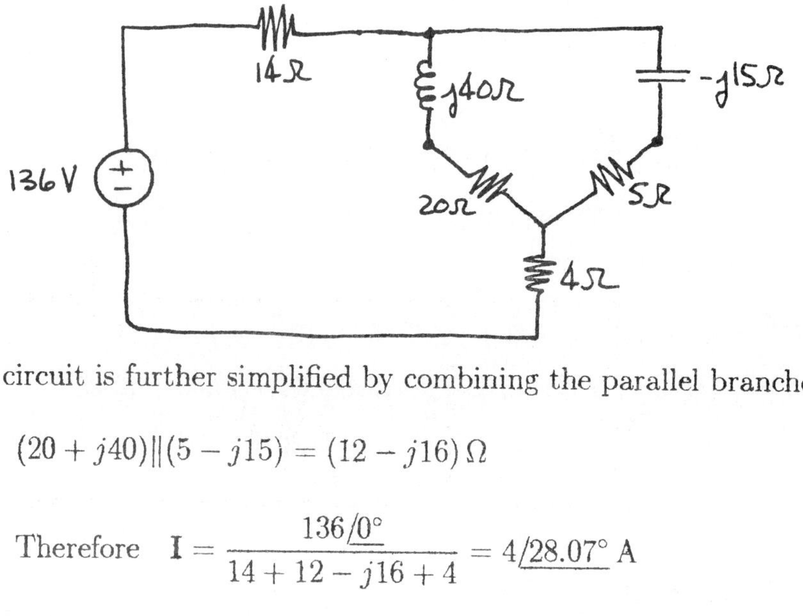

The circuit is further simplified by combining the parallel branches,

$$(20 + j40)\|(5 - j15) = (12 - j16)\,\Omega$$

Therefore $\mathbf{I} = \dfrac{136\underline{/0^\circ}}{14 + 12 - j16 + 4} = 4\underline{/28.07^\circ}\text{ A}$

DE 9.15 Use the lower node as the reference node. Let $\mathbf{V}_1$ = node voltage across the 20 Ω resistor and $\mathbf{V}_{\text{Th}}$ = node voltage across the capacitor. Writing the node voltage equations gives us

$$\frac{\mathbf{V}_1}{20} - 2\underline{/45^\circ} + \frac{\mathbf{V}_1 - 10\mathbf{I}_x}{j10} = 0 \quad \text{and} \quad \mathbf{V}_{\text{Th}} = \frac{-j10}{10 - j10}(10\mathbf{I}_x)$$

We also have

$$\mathbf{I}_x = \frac{\mathbf{V}_1}{20}$$

Solving these equations for $\mathbf{V}_{\mathrm{Th}}$ gives $\mathbf{V}_{\mathrm{Th}} = 10\underline{/45°}V$. To find the Thévenin impedance, we remove the independent current source and apply a test voltage source at the terminals a, b. Thus

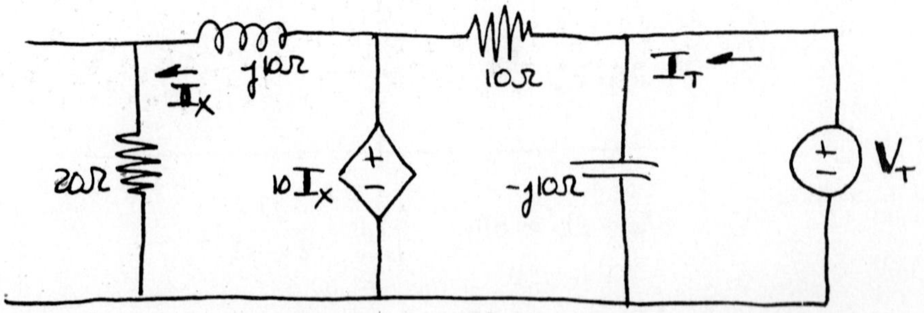

It follows from the circuit that

$$10\mathbf{I}_x = (20 + j10)\mathbf{I}_x$$

Therefore

$$\mathbf{I}_x = 0 \quad \text{and} \quad \mathbf{I}_T = \frac{\mathbf{V}_T}{-j10} + \frac{\mathbf{V}_T}{10}$$

$$Z_{\mathrm{Th}} = \frac{\mathbf{V}_T}{\mathbf{I}_T}, \quad \text{therefore} \quad Z_{\mathrm{Th}} = (5 - j5)\ \Omega$$

DE 9.16 Short circuit current

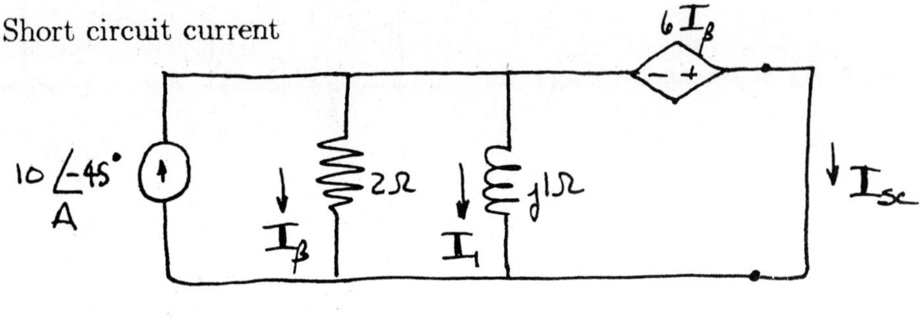

With the short circuit

$$\mathbf{I}_\beta = \frac{-6\mathbf{I}_\beta}{2}$$

$$2\mathbf{I}_\beta = -6\mathbf{I}_\beta; \qquad \therefore\ \mathbf{I}_\beta = 0$$

$$\mathbf{I}_1 = 0; \qquad \therefore\ \mathbf{I}_{sc} = 10\underline{/-45°}\ \mathrm{A} = \mathbf{I}_N$$

The Norton impedance is the same as the Thévenin impedance. Thus

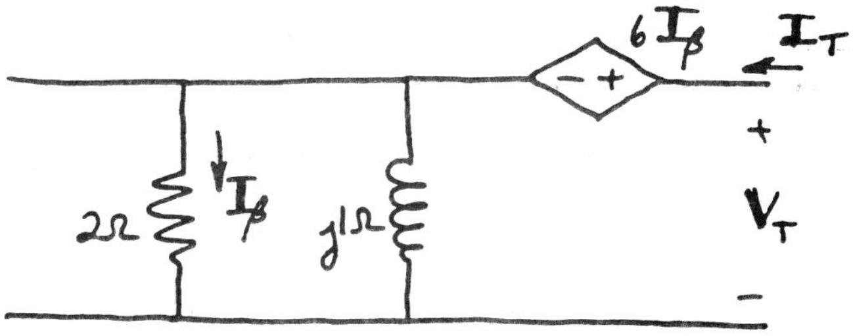

$$V_T = 6I_\beta + 2I_\beta = 8I_\beta, \qquad I_\beta = \frac{j1}{2+j1} I_T$$

$$Z_{Th} = \frac{V_T}{I_T} = \frac{8I_\beta}{[(2+j1)/j1]I_\beta} = \frac{j8}{2+j1} = 1.6 + j3.2\,\Omega$$

DE 9.17 The phasor domain circuit is as shown in the following diagram. The node voltage equation is

$$-10 + \frac{V}{5} + \frac{9V}{-j20} + \frac{V}{j5} + \frac{V - 100\angle{-90^\circ}}{20} = 0$$

Therefore $V = 10 - j30 = 31.62\angle{-71.57^\circ}$

Therefore $v = 31.62\cos(50{,}000t - 71.57^\circ)$ V

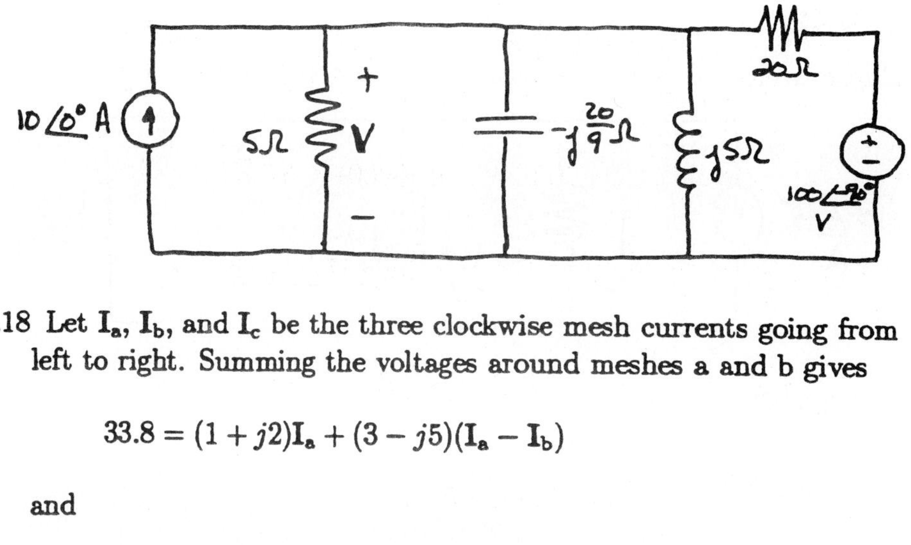

DE 9.18 Let I_a, I_b, and I_c be the three clockwise mesh currents going from left to right. Summing the voltages around meshes a and b gives

$$33.8 = (1 + j2)I_a + (3 - j5)(I_a - I_b)$$

and

$$0 = (3 - j5)(I_b - I_a) + 2(I_b - I_c).$$

But

$$V_x = -j5(I_a - I_b),$$

therefore

$$\mathbf{I}_c = -0.75[-j5(\mathbf{I}_a - \mathbf{I}_b)].$$

Solving for $\mathbf{I} = \mathbf{I}_a = 29 + j2 = 29.07\underline{/3.95^\circ}$ A.

DE 9.19 [a]

$$M = 0.4\sqrt{0.0625} = 0.1\,\text{H}, \qquad \omega M = 80\,\Omega$$

$$Z_{22} = 40 + j800(0.125) + 360 + j800(0.25) = (400 + j300)\,\Omega$$

Therefore $|Z_{22}| = 500\,\Omega$, $\quad Z_{22}^* = (400 - j300)\,\Omega$

$$Z_r = \left(\frac{80}{500}\right)^2 (400 - j300) = (10.24 - j7.68)\,\Omega$$

[b]

$$\mathbf{I}_1 = \frac{245.20}{184 + 100 + j400 + Z_r} = 0.50\underline{/-53.13^\circ}\text{ A}$$

$$i_1 = 0.5\cos(800t - 53.13^\circ)\text{ A}$$

[c]

$$\mathbf{I}_2 = \left(\frac{j\omega M}{Z_{22}}\right)\mathbf{I}_1 = \frac{j80}{500\underline{/36.87^\circ}}(0.5\underline{/-53.13^\circ}) = 0.08\underline{/0^\circ}\text{ A}$$

$$i_2 = 80\cos 800t\text{ mA}$$

[d]

$$P = \left(\frac{0.50}{\sqrt{2}}\right)^2 (110.24) = 13.78\text{ W}$$

DE 9.20

$$\mathbf{I}_1 = \frac{25\times 10^3\underline{/0^\circ}}{1500 + j6000 + (25)^2(4 - j14.4)} = 4 + j3 = 5\underline{/36.87^\circ}\text{ A}$$

$$\mathbf{V}_1 = 25{,}000\underline{/0^\circ} - (4 + j3)(1500 + j6000) = 37{,}000 - j28{,}500$$

$$\mathbf{V}_2 = -\frac{1}{25}\mathbf{V}_1 = -1480 + j1140 = 1868.15\underline{/142.39^\circ}\text{ V}$$

$$\mathbf{I}_2 = \frac{1868.15\underline{/142.39^\circ}}{4 - j14.4} = 125\underline{/216.87^\circ}\text{ A}$$

DE 9.21 [a]

$$\mathbf{I} = \frac{240}{24} + \frac{240}{j32} = (10 - j7.5)\text{ A}$$

$$\mathbf{V}_s = 240\underline{/0^\circ} + (0.1 + j0.8)(10 - j7.5) = 247 + j7.25 = 247.11\underline{/1.68^\circ}\text{ V}$$

[b] Use the capacitor to eliminate the j component of $\mathbf{I}$, therefore

$$\mathbf{I}_c = j7.5\text{ A}, \qquad Z_c = \frac{240}{j7.5} = -j32\,\Omega$$

$$\mathbf{V}_s = 240 + (0.1 + j0.8)10 = 241 + j8 = 241.13\underline{/1.90^\circ}\text{ V}$$

[c] Let $\mathbf{I}_c$ denote the magnitude of the current in the capacitor branch. Then

$$\mathbf{I} = (10 - j7.5 + j\mathbf{I}_c) = 10 + j(\mathbf{I}_c - 7.5)\text{ A}$$

$$\begin{aligned}\mathbf{V}_s &= 240\underline{/\alpha} = 240 + (0.1 + j0.8)[10 + j(\mathbf{I}_c + 7.5)] \\ &= (247 - 0.8\mathbf{I}_c) + j(7.25 + 0.1\mathbf{I}_c)\end{aligned}$$

It follows that

$$240\cos\alpha = (247 - 0.8\mathbf{I}_c) \quad \text{and} \quad 240\sin\alpha = (7.25 + 0.1\mathbf{I}_c)$$

Now square each term and then add to generate the quadratic equation

$$\mathbf{I}_c^2 - 605.77\mathbf{I}_c + 5325.48 = 0; \qquad \mathbf{I}_c = 302.88 \pm 293.96$$

Therefore

$$\mathbf{I}_c = 8.92\text{ A (smallest value) and } Z_c = 240/j8.92 = -j26.90\,\Omega.$$

Problems

P 9.1 [a] By hypothesis

$$i = 10\cos(\omega t + \theta)$$

$$\frac{di}{dt} = -10\omega\sin(\omega t + \theta)$$

$$\therefore\ 10\omega = 20{,}000\pi; \qquad \omega = 2000\pi\text{ rad/s}$$

[b]
$$f = \frac{\omega}{2\pi} = 1000\text{ Hz}; \qquad T = \frac{1}{f} = 1\text{ ms} = 1000\,\mu\text{s}$$

$$\frac{150}{1000} = \frac{3}{20}, \qquad \therefore\ \theta = \frac{3}{20}(360) = 54^\circ$$

$$\therefore\ i = 10\cos(2000\pi t + 54^\circ)\text{ A}$$

P 9.2

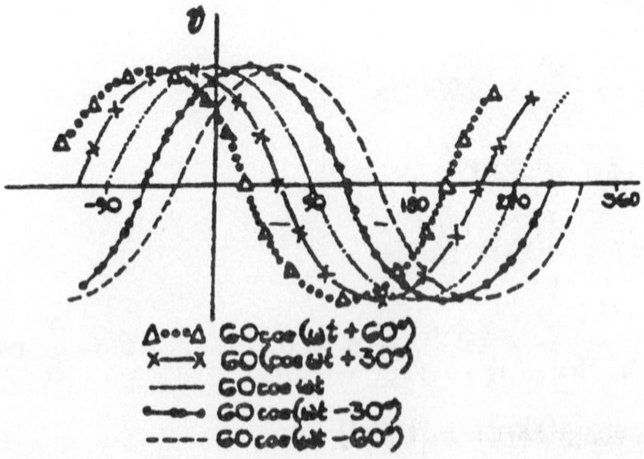

[a] Left as ϕ becomes more positive

[b] Right

P 9.3 [a] 170 V

[b] $2\pi f = 120\pi; \qquad f = 60\text{Hz}$

[c] $\omega = 120\pi = 376.99 \text{ rad/s}$

[d] $\theta(\text{rad}) = \frac{-\pi}{180}(60) = \frac{-\pi}{3} = -1.05 \text{ rad}$

[e] $\theta = -60^\circ$

[f] $T = \frac{1}{f} = \frac{1}{60} = 16.67 \text{ ms}$

[g] $120\pi t - \frac{\pi}{3} = 0; \qquad \therefore \; t = \frac{1}{360} = 2.78 \text{ ms}$

[h]
$$
\begin{aligned}
v &= 170\cos\left[120\pi\left(t + \frac{0.125}{18}\right) - \frac{\pi}{3}\right] \\
&= 170\cos[120\pi t + (15\pi/18) - (\pi/3)] \\
&= 170\cos[120\pi t + (\pi/2)] \\
&= -170\sin 120\pi t \text{ V}
\end{aligned}
$$

[i] $120\pi(t - t_o) - (\pi/3) = 120\pi t - (\pi/2)$

$$\therefore \; 120\pi t_o = \frac{\pi}{6}; \qquad t_o = \frac{25}{18} \text{ ms}$$

[j] $120\pi(t - t_o) - (\pi/3) = 120\pi t$

$$\therefore \; 120\pi t_o = \frac{\pi}{3}; \qquad t_o = \frac{25}{9} \text{ ms}$$

P 9.4 [a] $$\frac{T}{2} = \frac{1250}{6} + \frac{250}{6} = 250\,\mu\text{s}; \qquad T = 500\,\mu\text{s}$$

$$f = \frac{1}{T} = \frac{10^6}{500} = 2000\text{Hz}$$

[b] $$v = V_m \sin(\omega t + \theta)$$

$$\omega = 2\pi f = 4000\pi \text{ rad/s}$$

$$4000\pi\left(\frac{-250}{6} \times 10^{-6}\right) + \theta = 0; \qquad \therefore\ \theta = \frac{\pi}{6} \text{ rad}$$

$$v = V_m \sin[4000\pi t + (\pi/6)]$$

$$75 = V_m \sin(\pi/6); \qquad V_m = 150$$

$$v = 150 \sin[4000\pi t + (\pi/6)] = 150 \cos[4000\pi t - (\pi/3)] \text{ V}$$

P 9.5 [a] From Eq. 9.9 we have

$$L\frac{di}{dt} = \frac{V_m R \cos(\phi - \theta)}{\sqrt{R^2 + \omega^2 L^2}} e^{-(R/L)t} - \frac{\omega L V_m \sin(\omega t + \phi - \theta)}{\sqrt{R^2 + \omega^2 L^2}}$$

$$Ri = \frac{-V_m R \cos(\phi - \theta) e^{-(R/L)t}}{\sqrt{R^2 + \omega^2 L^2}} + \frac{V_m R \cos(\omega t + \phi - \theta)}{\sqrt{R^2 + \omega^2 L^2}}$$

$$L\frac{di}{dt} + Ri = V_m \left[\frac{R\cos(\omega t + \phi - \theta) - \omega L \sin(\omega t + \phi - \theta)}{\sqrt{R^2 + \omega^2 L^2}}\right]$$

But

$$\frac{R}{\sqrt{R^2 + \omega^2 L^2}} = \cos\theta \quad \text{and} \quad \frac{\omega L}{\sqrt{R^2 + \omega^2 L^2}} = \sin\theta$$

Therefore the right-hand side reduces to

$$V_m \cos(\omega t + \phi)$$

At $t = 0$, Eq. 9.9 reduces to

$$i(0) = \frac{-V_m \cos(\phi - \theta)}{\sqrt{R^2 - \omega^2 L^2}} + \frac{V_m \cos(\phi - \theta)}{\sqrt{R^2 + \omega^2 L^2}} = 0$$

[b] $$i_{ss} = \frac{V_m}{\sqrt{R^2 + \omega^2 L^2}} \cos(\omega t + \phi - \theta)$$

Therefore

$$L\frac{di_{ss}}{dt} = \frac{-\omega L V_m}{\sqrt{R^2 + \omega^2 L^2}} \sin(\omega t + \phi - \theta)$$

and

$$Ri_{ss} = \frac{V_m R}{\sqrt{R^2 + \omega^2 L^2}} \cos(\omega t + \phi - \theta)$$

$$\begin{aligned} L\frac{di_{ss}}{dt} + Ri_{ss} &= V_m\left[\frac{R\cos(\omega t + \phi - \theta) - \omega L\sin(\omega t + \phi - \theta)}{\sqrt{R^2 + \omega^2 L^2}}\right] \\ &= V_m\cos(\omega t + \phi) \end{aligned}$$

P 9.6 [a] $\mathbf{Y} = 100\underline{/45^\circ} + 500\underline{/-60^\circ} = 483.86\underline{/-48.48^\circ}$

$y = 483.86\cos(300t - 48.48^\circ)$

[b] $\mathbf{Y} = 250\underline{/30^\circ} - 150\underline{/50^\circ} = 120.51\underline{/4.8^\circ}$

$y = 120.51\cos(377t + 4.8^\circ)$

[c] $\mathbf{Y} = 60\underline{/60^\circ} - 120\underline{/-215^\circ} + 100\underline{/90^\circ} = 152.88\underline{/32.94^\circ}$

$y = 152.88\cos(100t + 32.94^\circ)$

[d] $\mathbf{Y} = 100\underline{/40^\circ} + 100\underline{/160^\circ} + 100\underline{/-80^\circ} = 0$

$y = 0$

P 9.7

$$\begin{aligned} u &= \int_{t_o}^{t_o+T} V_m^2\cos^2(\omega t + \phi)\,dt \\ &= V_m^2\int_{t_o}^{t_o+T}\frac{1}{2} + \frac{1}{2}\cos(2\omega t + 2\phi)\,dt \\ &= \frac{V_m^2}{2}\left\{\int_{t_o}^{t_o+T}dt + \int_{t_o}^{t_o+T}\cos(2\omega t + 2\phi)\,dt\right\} \\ &= \frac{V_m^2}{2}\left\{T + \frac{1}{2\omega}\left[\sin(2\omega t + 2\phi)\,\Big|_{t_o}^{t_o+T}\right]\right\} \\ &= \frac{V_m^2}{2}\left\{T + \frac{1}{2\omega}\left[\sin(2\omega t_o + 4\pi + 2\phi) - \sin(2\omega t_o + 2\phi)\right]\right\} \\ &= V_m^2\left(\frac{T}{2}\right) + \frac{1}{2\omega}(0) = V_m^2\left(\frac{T}{2}\right) \end{aligned}$$

P 9.8 $V_m = \sqrt{2}V_{\text{rms}} = \sqrt{2}(120) = 169.71$ V

P 9.9 [a] $j\omega L = j(5\times 10^4)(40\times 10^{-6}) = j2\,\Omega$

$\frac{1}{j\omega C} = -j\frac{10^6}{5\times 10^4} = -j20\,\Omega;\qquad \mathbf{I}_g = 20\underline{/-20^\circ}$ A

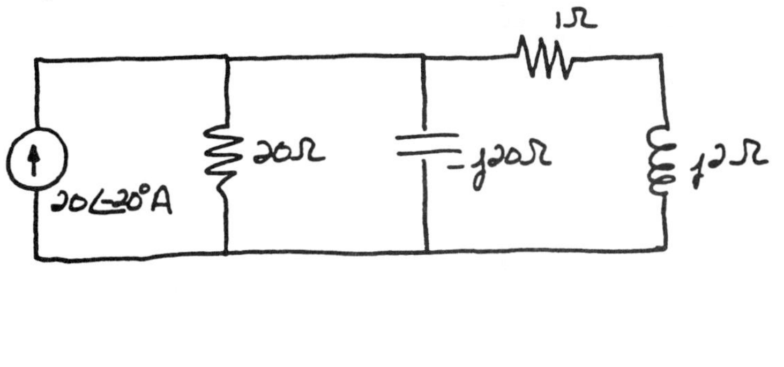

[b] $\mathbf{V}_o = 20\underline{/-20^\circ} Z_e$

$$Z_e = \frac{1}{Y_e}; \qquad Y_e = \frac{1}{20} + j\frac{1}{20} + \frac{1}{1+j2}$$

$$Y_e = 0.05 + j0.05 + 0.20 - j0.40 = 0.25 - j0.35\,\mho$$

$$Z_e = \frac{1}{0.25 - j0.35} = 2.32\underline{/54.46^\circ}\,\Omega$$

$$\mathbf{V}_o = (20\underline{/-20^\circ})(2.32\underline{/54.46^\circ}) = 46.4\underline{/34.46^\circ}\text{ V}$$

[c] $v_o = 46.4\cos(5\times10^4 t + 34.46^\circ)$ V

P 9.10 [a]

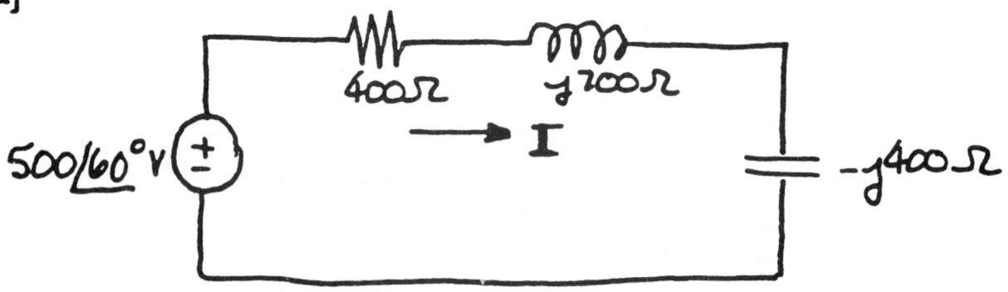

[b] $$\mathbf{I} = \frac{500\underline{/60^\circ}}{400 + j700 - j400} = 1\underline{/23.13^\circ}\text{ A}$$

[c] $i = 1\cos(8000t + 23.13^\circ)$ A

P 9.11 [a] 50Hz

[b] $\theta_v = 0^\circ$

[c] $$\mathbf{I} = \frac{340\underline{/0^\circ}}{j\omega L} = \frac{340}{\omega L}\underline{/-90^\circ} = 8.5\underline{/-90^\circ}; \qquad \theta_i = -90^\circ$$

[d] $$\frac{340}{\omega L} = 8.5; \qquad \omega L = 40\,\Omega$$

[e] $$L = \frac{40}{100\pi} = \frac{400}{\pi}\text{ mH} = 127.32\text{ mH}$$

[f] $Z_L = j\omega L = j40\,\Omega$

P 9.12 [a] $\omega = 2\pi f = 80\pi \times 10^3 = 251.33$ krad/s $= 251{,}327.41$ rad/s

[b] $$\mathbf{I} = \frac{2.5\times10^{-3}\underline{/0^\circ}}{1/j\omega C} = j\omega C(2.5\times10^{-3})\underline{/0^\circ} = 2.5\times10^{-3}\omega C\underline{/90^\circ}$$

$$\therefore\ \theta_i = 90^\circ$$

[c] $$125.66\times10^{-6} = 2.5\times10^{-3}\omega C$$

$$\therefore\ \frac{1}{\omega C} = \frac{2.5\times10^{-3}}{125.66\times10^{-6}} = 19.89\,\Omega$$

[d] $$C = \frac{1}{19.89(\omega)} = \frac{1}{(19.89)(80\pi \times 10^3)}$$

$$C = 0.2 \times 10^{-6} = 0.2\,\mu\text{F}$$

[e] $$Z_c = -j\left(\frac{1}{\omega C}\right) = -j19.89\,\Omega$$

P 9.13 $$\frac{1}{j\omega C} = \frac{10^9}{(31.25)(8000)} = -j4000\,\Omega$$

$$j\omega L = j8000(500)10^{-3} = j4000\,\Omega$$

$$\mathbf{V}_g = 64\underline{/0^\circ}\text{ V}$$

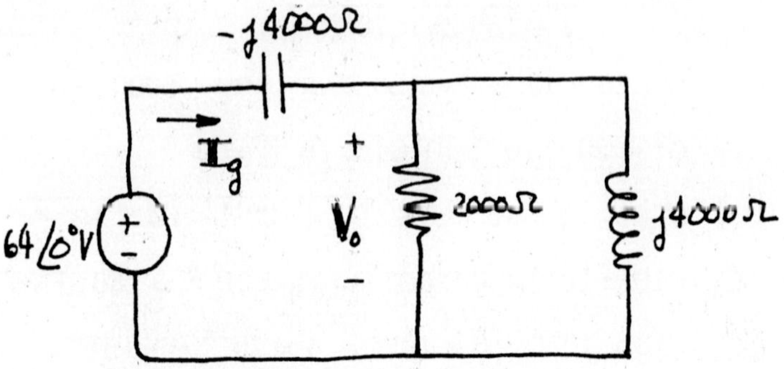

$$Z_e = \frac{(2000)(j4000)}{2000 + j4000} = 1600 + j800\,\Omega$$

$$Z_T = 1600 + j800 - j4000 = 1600 - j3200\,\Omega$$

$$\mathbf{I}_g = \frac{64\underline{/0^\circ}}{1600 - j3200} = 8 + j16\text{ mA}$$

$$\mathbf{V}_o = Z_e\mathbf{I}_g = (1600 + j800)(0.008 + j0.016) = j32 = 32\underline{/90^\circ}$$

$$v_o = 32\cos(8000t + 90^\circ)\text{ V}$$

P 9.14 $$Z = 400 + j(5)(40) - j\frac{1000}{(5)(0.4)} = 500\underline{/-36.87^\circ}\,\Omega$$

$$\mathbf{I}_o = \frac{750\underline{/0^\circ} \times 10^{-3}}{500\underline{/-36.87^\circ}} = 1.5\underline{/36.87^\circ}\text{ mA}$$

$$i_o(t) = 1.5\cos(5000t + 36.87^\circ)\text{ mA}$$

P 9.15 [a]

$$Z_p = \frac{\frac{R}{j\omega C}}{R + j(1/j\omega C)} = \frac{R}{1 + j\omega RC}$$

$$= \frac{12{,}500}{1 + j(1000)(12{,}500)C} = \frac{12{,}500}{1 + j12.5 \times 10^6 C}$$

$$= \frac{12{,}500(1 - j12.5 \times 10^6 C)}{1 + 156.25 \times 10^{12} C^2}$$

$$= \frac{12{,}500}{1 + 156.25 \times 10^{12} C^2} - j\frac{156.25 \times 10^9 C}{1 + 156.25 \times 10^{12} C^2}$$

$j\omega L = j1000(5) = j5000$

$$\therefore \quad 5000 = \frac{156.25 \times 10^9 C}{1 + 156.25 \times 10^{12} C^2}$$

$$\therefore \quad 781.25 \times 10^{15} C^2 - 156.25 \times 10^9 C + 5000 = 0$$

$$\therefore \quad C^2 - 20 \times 10^{-8} C + 64 \times 10^{-16} = 0$$

$$\therefore \quad C_{1,2} = 10 \times 10^{-8} \pm \sqrt{100 \times 10^{-16} - 64 \times 10^{-16}}$$

$$C_1 = 10 \times 10^{-8} + 6 \times 10^{-8} = 16 \times 10^{-8} = 160\,\text{nF}$$

$$C_2 = 10 \times 10^{-8} - 6 \times 10^{-8} = 4 \times 10^{-8} = 40\,\text{nF}$$

[b]

$$R_e = \frac{12{,}500}{1 + 156.25 \times 10^{12} C^2}$$

When $C = 160\,\text{nF}$ $\quad R_e = 2500\,\Omega$;

$$\mathbf{I}_g = \frac{250/\underline{0^\circ}}{2500} = 0.1/\underline{0^\circ}\text{ A}; \qquad i_g = 100\cos 1000t \text{ mA}$$

When $C = 40\,\text{nF}$ $\quad R_e = 10{,}000\,\Omega$;

$$\mathbf{I}_g = \frac{250/\underline{0^\circ}}{10{,}000} = 0.025/\underline{0^\circ}\text{ A}; \qquad i_g = 25\cos 1000t \text{ mA}$$

P 9.16 [a]

$$Y_p = \frac{1}{10 + j2\omega} + j4 \times 10^{-3}\omega$$

$$= \frac{10 - j2\omega}{100 + 4\omega^2} + j4 \times 10^{-3}\omega$$

$$= \frac{10}{100 + 4\omega^2} - \frac{j2\omega}{100 + 4\omega^2} + j4 \times 10^{-3}\omega$$

Y_p is real when

$$4 \times 10^{-3}\omega = \frac{2\omega}{100 + 4\omega^2}$$

or $\quad \omega^2 = 100; \qquad \omega = 10 \text{ rad/s}; \qquad f = 5/\pi = 1.59\text{Hz}$

[b]
$$Y_p(10\,\text{rad/s}) = \frac{10}{500} = 20\,\text{m℧}$$

$$Z_p(10\,\text{rad/s}) = \frac{10^3}{20} = 50\,\Omega$$

$$Z(10\,\text{rad/s}) = 50 + 150 = 200\,\Omega$$

$$\mathbf{I}_o = \frac{\mathbf{V}_g}{200}\,\text{A} = \frac{10\angle 0^\circ}{200} = 50\angle 0^\circ\,\text{mA}$$

$$i_o = 50\cos 10t\,\text{mA}$$

P 9.17
$$\mathbf{V}_g = 50\angle -45^\circ\,\text{V}; \qquad \mathbf{I}_g = 100\angle -8.13^\circ\,\text{mA}$$

$$Z = \frac{\mathbf{V}_g}{\mathbf{I}_g} = 500\angle -36.87^\circ\,\Omega = 400 - j300\,\Omega$$

$$Z = 400 + j\left(0.04\omega - \frac{2.5\times 10^6}{\omega}\right)$$

$$\therefore\ 0.04\omega - \frac{2.5\times 10^6}{\omega} = -300$$

$$\therefore\ \omega^2 + 7500\omega - 62.5\times 10^6 = 0$$

$$\therefore\ \omega = -3750 \pm \sqrt{(3750)^2 + 62.5\times 10^6} = -3750 \pm 8750$$

$$\omega > 0, \qquad \therefore\ \omega = 5000\,\text{rad/s}$$

P 9.18
$$j\omega L = j1.6\times 10^6(25\times 10^{-6}) = j40\,\Omega$$

$$\frac{1}{j\omega C} = \frac{10^{-6}\times 10^9}{j1.6(25)} = -j25\,\Omega$$

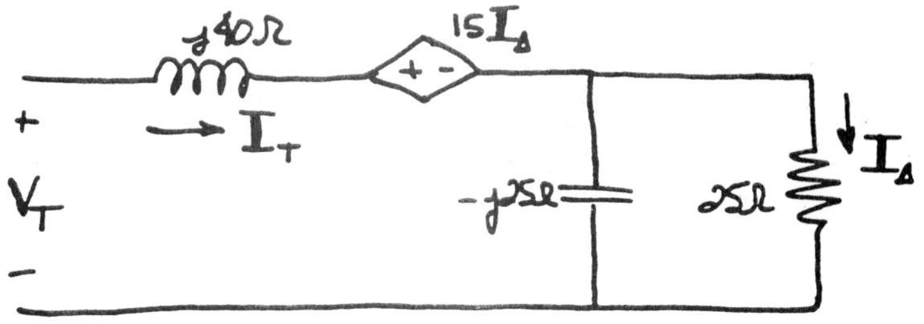

$$\mathbf{V}_T = j40\mathbf{I}_T + 15\mathbf{I}_\Delta + 25\mathbf{I}_\Delta$$

$$\mathbf{I}_\Delta = \frac{\mathbf{I}_T(-j25)}{25 - j25} = \frac{-j\mathbf{I}_T}{1 - j1}$$

$$\mathbf{V}_T = j40\mathbf{I}_T + 40\frac{(-j\mathbf{I}_T)}{1 - j1}$$

$$\frac{\mathbf{V}_T}{\mathbf{I}_T} = Z_{ab} = j40 + 20(-j)(1 + j) = 20 + j20\,\Omega = 28.28\underline{/45^\circ}\,\Omega$$

P 9.19 First find the admittance of the parallel branches

$$Y_p = \frac{1}{6 - j2} + \frac{1}{4 + j12} + \frac{1}{5} + \frac{1}{j10} = 0.375 - j0.125\,\mho$$

$$Z_p = \frac{1}{Y_p} = \frac{1}{0.375 - j0.125} = 2.4 + j0.8\,\Omega$$

$$Z_{ab} = -j12.8 + 2.4 + j0.8 + 13.6 = 16 - j12\,\Omega$$

$$Y_{ab} = \frac{1}{Z_{ab}} = \frac{1}{16 - j12} = 0.04 + j0.03\,\mho$$

$$= 40 + j30\,\text{m}\mho = 50\underline{/36.87^\circ}\,\text{m}\mho$$

P 9.20 [a]

$$Z_g = 4000 - j\frac{10^9}{25\omega} + \frac{10^4(j2\omega)}{10^4 + j2\omega}$$

$$= 4000 - j\frac{10^9}{25\omega} + \frac{2 \times 10^4 j\omega(10^4 - j2\omega)}{10^8 + 4\omega^2}$$

$$= 4000 - j\frac{10^9}{25\omega} + \frac{4 \times 10^4\omega^2}{10^8 + 4\omega^2} + j\frac{2 \times 10^8\omega}{10^8 + 4\omega^2}$$

$$\therefore \quad \frac{10^9}{25\omega} = \frac{0.2 \times 10^9\omega}{10^8 + 4\omega^2}$$

$$10^8 + 4\omega^2 = 5\omega^2$$

$$\omega^2 = 10^8; \qquad \omega = 10{,}000\,\text{rad/s}$$

[b] When $\omega = 10{,}000\,\text{rad/s}$

$$Z_g = 4000 + \frac{4 \times 10^4(10^4)^2}{10^8 + 4(10^4)^2} = 12{,}000\,\Omega$$

$$\therefore \quad \mathbf{I}_g = \frac{45\underline{/0^\circ}}{9000} = 3.75\underline{/0^\circ}\,\text{mA}$$

$$\mathbf{V}_o = \mathbf{V}_g - \mathbf{I}_g Z_1$$

$$Z_1 = 4000 - j\frac{10^9}{25 \times 10^4} = 4000 - j4000\,\Omega$$

$$\mathbf{V}_o = 45\underline{/0^\circ} - (5 \times 10^{-3})(4000 - j4000) = 45 - (20 - j20)$$

$$= 25 + j20 = 32.02\underline{/38.65^\circ}\text{ V}$$

$$v_o = 32.02\cos(10{,}000t + 38.65^\circ)\text{ V}$$

P 9.21 [a]

$$Z_1 = 1600 - j\frac{10^9}{10^4(62.5)} = 1600 - j1600\,\Omega$$

$$Z_2 = \frac{4000(j10^4L)}{4000 + j10^4L} = \frac{4 \times 10^5L^2 + j16 \times 10^4L}{16 + 100L^2}$$

$$Z_T = Z_1 + Z_2 = 1600 + \frac{4 \times 10^5L^2}{16 + 100L^2} - j1600 + j\frac{16 \times 10^4L}{16 + 100L^2}$$

Z_T is resistive when

$$\frac{16 \times 10^4L}{16 + 100L^2} = 1600 \qquad \text{or}$$

$$1600L^2 - L - 0.16 = 0$$

Solving, $L_1 = 0.8$ H and $L_2 = 0.2$ H.

[b] When $L = 0.8$ H:

$$Z_T = 1600 + \frac{4 \times 10^5(0.64)}{16 + 64} = 4800\,\Omega$$

$$\mathbf{I}_g = \frac{96\underline{/0^\circ}}{4.8} \times 10^{-3} = 20\underline{/0^\circ}\text{ mA}$$

$$i_g = 20\cos 10{,}000t\text{ mA}$$

When $L = 0.2$ H:

$$Z_T = 1600 + \frac{4 \times 10^5(0.04)}{16 + 4} = 2400\,\Omega$$

$$i_g = 40\cos 10{,}000t\text{ mA}$$

P 9.22 [a]

$$Z_{ab} = j5\omega + \frac{(4000)(10^9/j\omega 625)}{4000 + (10^9/j625\omega)}$$

$$= j5\omega + \frac{4 \times 10^{12}}{2500 \times 10^3 j\omega + 10^9}$$

$$= j5\omega + \frac{4 \times 10^7}{10^4 + j25\omega}$$

$$= j5\omega + \frac{4 \times 10^{11}}{10^8 + 625\omega^2} - j\frac{100 \times 10^7\omega}{10^8 + 625\omega^2}$$

$$\therefore \quad 5 = \frac{10^9}{10^8 + 625\omega^2}$$

$$5 \times 10^8 + 3125\omega^2 = 10^9$$

$$\omega = 4 \times 10^2 = 400\,\text{rad/s}$$

[b]

$$Z_{ab}(400) = j2000 + \frac{(4000)(-j4000)}{4000 - j4000} = 2\,\text{k}\Omega$$

P 9.23

$$Z_1 = 10 - j40\,\Omega$$

$$Z_2 = \frac{(5 - j10)(10 + j30)}{15 + j20} = 10 - j10\,\Omega$$

$$Z_3 = \frac{20(j20)}{20 + j20} = 10 + j10\,\Omega$$

$$\therefore \quad Z_{ab} = Z_1 + Z_2 + Z_3 = 30 - j40\,\Omega = 50\underline{/-53.15^\circ}\,\Omega$$

P 9.24 [a]

$$Y_1 = \frac{1}{5000} = 0.2 \times 10^{-3}\,\mho$$

$$Y_2 = \frac{1}{1200 + j0.2\omega}$$

$$= \frac{1200}{1.44 \times 10^6 + 0.04\omega^2} - j\frac{0.2\omega}{1.44 \times 10^6 + 0.04\omega^2}$$

$$Y_3 = j\omega 50 \times 10^{-9}$$

$$Y_T = Y_1 + Y_2 + Y_3$$

For i_g and v_o to be in phase the j component of Y_T must be zero; thus,

$$\omega 50 \times 10^{-9} = \frac{0.2\omega}{1.44 \times 10^6 + 0.04\omega^2}$$

or

$$0.04\omega^2 + 1.44 \times 10^6 = \frac{0.2 \times 10^9}{50} = 4 \times 10^6$$

$$\therefore \quad 0.04\omega^2 = 2.56 \times 10^6 \qquad \therefore \quad \omega = 8000\,\text{rad/s} = 8\,\text{krad/s}$$

[b] $$Y_T = 0.2 \times 10^{-3} + \frac{1200}{1.44 \times 10^6 + 0.04(64) \times 10^6} = 0.5 \times 10^{-3}\,\mho$$

$$\therefore \quad Z_T = 2000\,\Omega$$

$$\mathbf{V}_o = (2.5 \times 10^{-3}\underline{/0^\circ})(2000) = 5\underline{/0^\circ}$$

$$v_o = 5\cos 8000t\,\text{V}$$

P 9.25 [a] $$Z_1 = R_1 + j\omega L_1$$

$$Z_2 = \frac{R_2(j\omega L_2)}{R_2 + j\omega L_2} = \frac{\omega^2 L_2^2 R_2 + j\omega L_2 R_2^2}{R^2 + \omega^2 L_2^2}$$

$$Z_1 = Z_2 \quad \text{when} \quad R_1 = \frac{\omega^2 L_2^2 R_2}{R_2^2 + \omega^2 L_2^2} \quad \text{and} \quad L_1 = \frac{R_2^2 L_2}{R_2^2 + \omega^2 L_2^2}$$

[b] $$R_1 = \frac{(4 \times 10^8)(6.25)(5 \times 10^4)}{25 \times 10^8 + (4 \times 10^8)(6.25)} = 2.5 \times 10^4$$

$$\therefore \quad R_1 = 25\,\text{k}\Omega$$

$$L_1 = \frac{(25 \times 10^8)2.5}{50 \times 10^8} = 1.25\,\text{H}$$

P 9.26 [a] $$Y_2 = \frac{1}{R_2} - \frac{j}{\omega L_2}$$

$$Y_1 = \frac{1}{R_1 + j\omega L_1} = \frac{R_1 - j\omega L_1}{R_1^2 + \omega^2 L_1^2}$$

Therefore $Y_2 = Y_1$ when

$$R_2 = \frac{R_1^2 + \omega^2 L_1^2}{R_1} \quad \text{and} \quad L_2 = \frac{R_1^2 + \omega^2 L_1^2}{\omega^2 L_1}$$

[b] $$R_2 = \frac{25 \times 10^6 + 10^8(0.25)}{5 \times 10^3} = 10 \times 10^3$$

$$\therefore \quad R_2 = 10\,\text{k}\Omega$$

$$L_2 = \frac{50 \times 10^6}{10^8(0.5)} = 1\,\text{H}$$

P 9.27 [a]

$$Z_1 = R_1 - j\frac{1}{\omega C_1}$$

$$Z_2 = \frac{R_2/j\omega C_2}{R_2 + (1/j\omega C_2)} = \frac{R_2}{1 + j\omega R_2 C_2} = \frac{R_2 - j\omega R_2^2 C_2}{1 + \omega^2 R_2^2 C_2^2}$$

$$Z_1 = Z_2 \quad \text{when} \quad R_1 = \frac{R_2}{1 + \omega^2 R_2^2 C_2^2} \quad \text{and}$$

$$\frac{1}{\omega C_1} = \frac{\omega R_2^2 C_2^2}{1 + \omega^2 R_2^2 C_2^2} \quad \text{or} \quad C_1 = \frac{1 + \omega^2 R_2^2 C_2^2}{\omega^2 R_2^2 C_2}$$

[b]

$$R_1 = \frac{500}{1 + (64 \times 10^8)(25 \times 10^4)(625 \times 10^{-18})} = 250\,\Omega$$

$$C_1 = \frac{2}{(64 \times 10^8)(25 \times 10^4)(25 \times 10^{-9})} = 50\,\text{nF}$$

P 9.28 [a]

$$Y_2 = \frac{1}{R_2} + j\omega C_2$$

$$Y_1 = \frac{1}{R_1 + (1/j\omega C_1)} = \frac{j\omega C_1}{1 + j\omega R_1 C_1} = \frac{\omega^2 R_1 C_1^2 + j\omega C_1}{1 + \omega^2 R_1^2 C_1^2}$$

Therefore $Y_1 = Y_2$ when

$$R_2 = \frac{1 + \omega^2 R_1^2 C_1^2}{\omega^2 R_1 C_1^2} \quad \text{and} \quad C_2 = \frac{C_1}{1 + \omega^2 R_1^2 C_1^2}$$

[b]

$$R_2 = \frac{1 + (4 \times 10^8)(4 \times 10^6)(2500 \times 10^{-18})}{(4 \times 10^8)(2 \times 10^3)(2500 \times 10^{-18})} = 2500 = 2.5\text{k}\Omega$$

$$C_2 = \frac{50 \times 10^{-9}}{5} = 10\,\text{nF}$$

P 9.29 [a]

$$\mathbf{V}_g = 150\angle 20^\circ; \qquad \mathbf{I}_g = 30\angle -52^\circ$$

$$\therefore \quad Z = \frac{\mathbf{V}_g}{\mathbf{I}_g} = 5\angle 72^\circ\,\Omega$$

[b] i_g lags v_g by 72°:

$$2\pi f = 8000\pi; \qquad f = 4000\,\text{Hz}; \qquad T = 1/f = 250\,\mu\text{s}$$

$$\therefore \quad i_g \text{ lags } v_g \text{ by } \frac{72}{360}(250) = 50\,\mu\text{s}$$

P 9.30 $\frac{1}{j\omega C} = -j\frac{10^6}{10^4} = -j100\,\Omega$

$j\omega L = j(500)(1) = j500\,\Omega$

Let $Z_1 = 50 - j100\,\Omega$; $\qquad Z_2 = 250 + j500\,\Omega$

$\mathbf{I}_g = 125\underline{/0^\circ}\,\text{mA}$

$$\mathbf{I}_o = \frac{\mathbf{I}_g Z_1}{Z_1 + Z_2} = \frac{125\underline{/0^\circ}(50 + j100)}{(300 + j400)}$$

$$= -12.5 - j25\,\text{mA} = 27.95\underline{/-116.57^\circ}\,\text{mA}$$

$i_o = 27.95\cos(500t - 116.57^\circ)\,\text{mA}$

P 9.31 $Z_o = 600 - j\frac{10^6}{(5000)(0.25)} = 600 - j800\,\Omega$

$Z_T = 300 + j2000 + 600 - j800 = 900 + j1200\,\Omega = 1500\underline{/53.13^\circ}\,\Omega$

$$\mathbf{V}_o = \mathbf{V}_g\frac{Z_o}{Z_T} = \frac{(75\underline{/0^\circ})(1000\underline{/-53.13^\circ})}{1500\underline{/53.13^\circ}} = 50\underline{/-106.26^\circ}\,\text{V}$$

$v_o = 50\cos(5000t - 106.26^\circ)\,\text{V}$

P 9.32 $\mathbf{V}_1 = 240\underline{/53.13^\circ} = 144 + j192\,\text{V}$

$\mathbf{V}_2 = 96\underline{/-90^\circ} = -j96\,\text{V}$

$j\omega L = j(4000)(15 \times 10^{-3}) = j60\,\Omega$

$\frac{1}{j\omega C} = -j\frac{6 \times 10^6}{(4000)(25)} = -j60\,\Omega$

$\frac{\mathbf{V}_1}{j60} = \frac{144 + j192}{j60} = 3.2 - j2.4\,\text{A}$

$\frac{\mathbf{V}_2}{20} = -j\frac{96}{20} = -j4.8\,\text{A}$

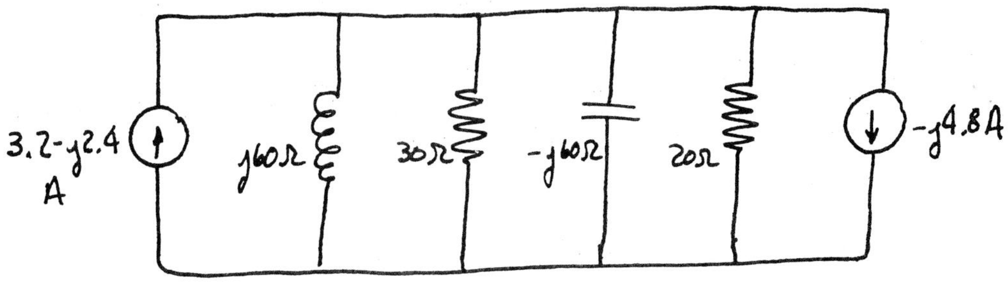

$$Y = \frac{1}{j60} + \frac{1}{30} + \frac{1}{-j60} + \frac{1}{20} = \frac{j5}{j60} = \frac{1}{12}$$

$$Z = \frac{1}{Y} = 12\,\Omega$$

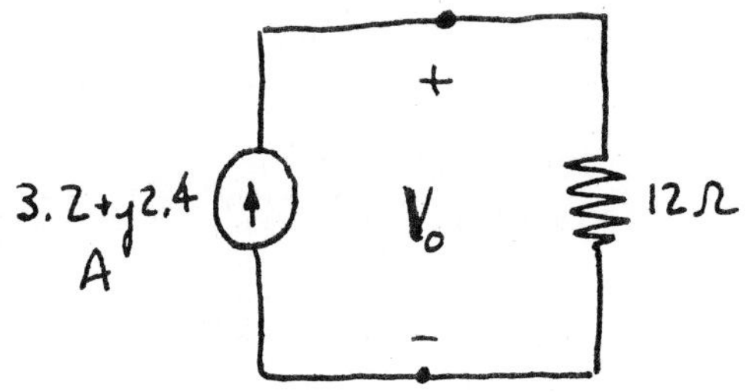

$$\mathbf{V}_o = 12(3.2 + j0.6) = 38.4 + j7.2\,\text{V} = 39.07\underline{/10.61^\circ}\,\text{V}$$

$$v_o = 39.07\cos(4000t + 10.61^\circ)\,\text{V}$$

P 9.33 [a]

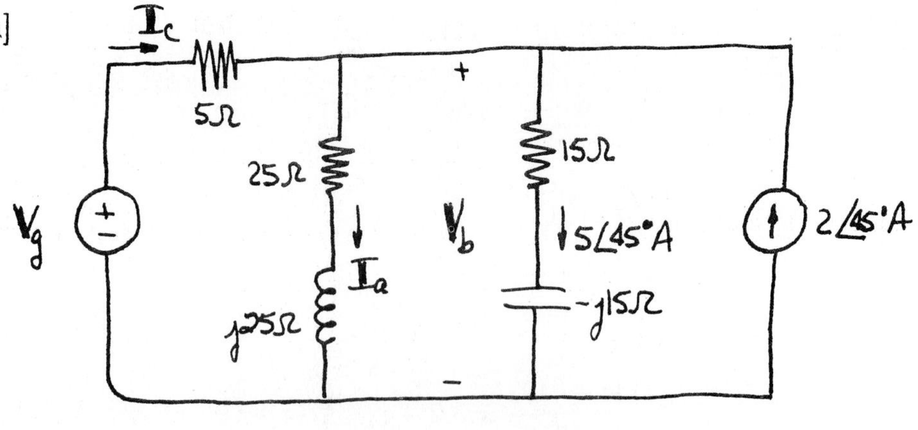

$$\mathbf{V}_b = (15 - j15)5\underline{/45^\circ} = 75\sqrt{2}\underline{/0^\circ}\,\text{V}$$

$$\mathbf{I}_a = \frac{75\sqrt{2}}{25 + j25} = 3\underline{/-45^\circ}\,\text{A}$$

$$\mathbf{I}_c = \mathbf{I}_a + 5\underline{/45^\circ} - 2\underline{/45^\circ} = 3\sqrt{2}\,\text{A}$$

$$\mathbf{V}_g = 5\mathbf{I}_c + \mathbf{V}_b = 15\sqrt{2} + 75\sqrt{2} = 90\sqrt{2}\,\text{V} = 127.27\underline{/0^\circ}\,\text{V}$$

[b] $i_a = 3\cos(800t - 45^\circ)$ A

$i_c = 4.24\cos 800t$ A

$v_g = 127.27\cos 800t$ V

P 9.34 $\mathbf{I}_s = 15\underline{/0^\circ}$ mA

$$\frac{1}{j\omega C} = \frac{10^6}{j0.05(8000)} = -j2500\,\Omega$$

$$j\omega L = j8000(1.25) = j10{,}000\,\Omega$$

After two source transformations we have

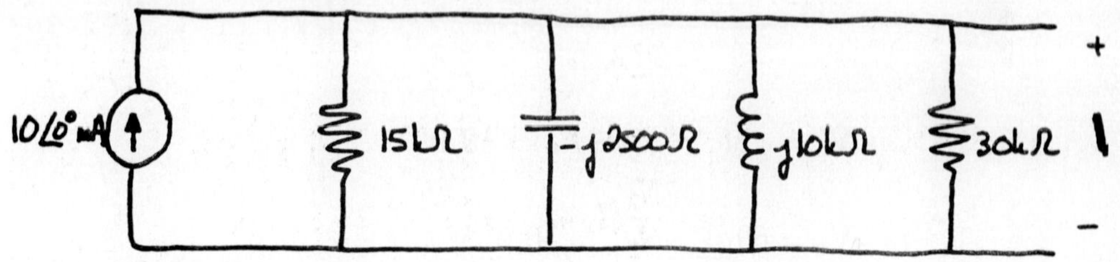

$15\,\text{k}\Omega \| 30\,\text{k}\Omega = 10\,\text{k}\Omega$

$$Y_o = \frac{10^{-3}}{10} + \frac{1}{-j2500} + \frac{1}{j10^4} = 10^{-4}(1 + j3)$$

$$Z_o = \frac{10^4}{1 + j3} = (1 - j3)\,\text{k}\Omega$$

$$\mathbf{V}_o = \mathbf{I}_g Z_o = (1)(1 - j3) = 10 - j30 = 31.62\underline{/-71.57^\circ}$$

$$v_o = 31.62\cos(8000t - 71.57^\circ)\text{ V}$$

P 9.35

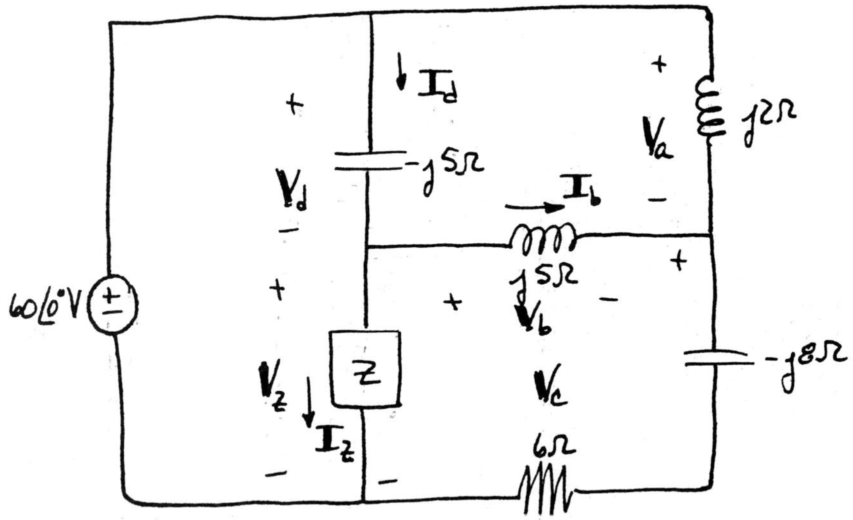

$$\mathbf{V}_a = j2\mathbf{I}_a = j2(-j5) = 10\underline{/0^\circ}\ \mathrm{V}$$

$$\mathbf{V}_c = 60\underline{/0^\circ} - \mathbf{V}_a = 50\underline{/0^\circ}\ \mathrm{V}$$

$$\mathbf{I}_c = \frac{\mathbf{V}_c}{6 - j8} = \frac{50\underline{/0^\circ}}{10\underline{/-53.13^\circ}} = 5\underline{/53.13^\circ} = 3 + j4\ \mathrm{A}$$

$$\mathbf{I}_b = \mathbf{I}_c - \mathbf{I}_a = 3 + j4 - (-j5) = 3 + j9\ \mathrm{A} = 9.49\underline{/71.57^\circ}\ \mathrm{A}$$

$$\mathbf{V}_b = \mathbf{I}_b(j5) = (3 + j9)(j5) = -45 + j15\ \mathrm{V}$$

$$\mathbf{V}_z = \mathbf{V}_b + \mathbf{V}_c = -45 + j15 + 50 + j0 = 5 + j15\ \mathrm{V}$$

$$\mathbf{V}_d + \mathbf{V}_z = 60\underline{/0^\circ}; \qquad \therefore\ \mathbf{V}_d = 60 - 5 - j15 = 55 - j15\ \mathrm{V}$$

$$\mathbf{I}_d = \frac{\mathbf{V}_d}{-j5} = 3 + j11\ \mathrm{A}$$

$$\mathbf{I}_z = \mathbf{I}_d - \mathbf{I}_b = 3 + j11 - 3 - j9 = j2\ \mathrm{A}$$

$$Z = \frac{\mathbf{V}_z}{\mathbf{I}_z} = \frac{5 + j15}{j2} = 7.5 - j2.5\,\Omega$$

P 9.36
$$\frac{1}{\omega C_1} = \frac{(10^{-3})(10^9)}{25(10/3)} = 12\,\text{k}\Omega$$

$$\frac{1}{\omega C_2} = \frac{(10^{-3})(10^9)}{25(5/3)} = 24\,\text{k}\Omega$$

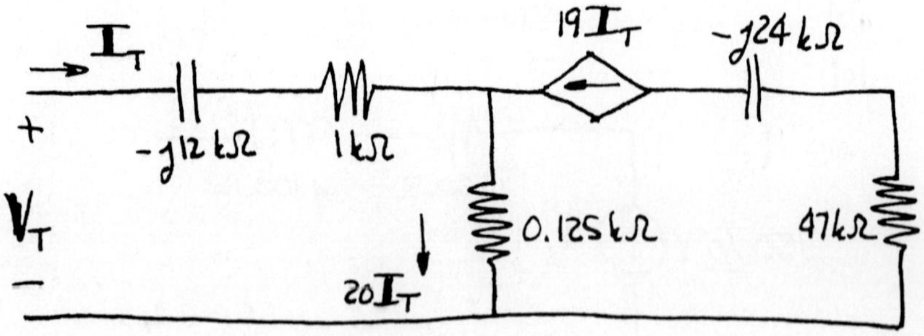

$$\mathbf{V}_T = (1 - j12)\mathbf{I}_T + 20\mathbf{I}_T(0.125)$$

$$Z_{\text{Th}} = \frac{\mathbf{V}_T}{\mathbf{I}_T} = 3.5 - j12\,\text{k}\Omega$$

P 9.37 [a]
$$j\omega L = j(1000)(100) \times 10^{-3} = j100\,\Omega$$

$$\frac{1}{j\omega C} = -j\frac{10^6}{(1000)(10)} = -j100\,\Omega$$

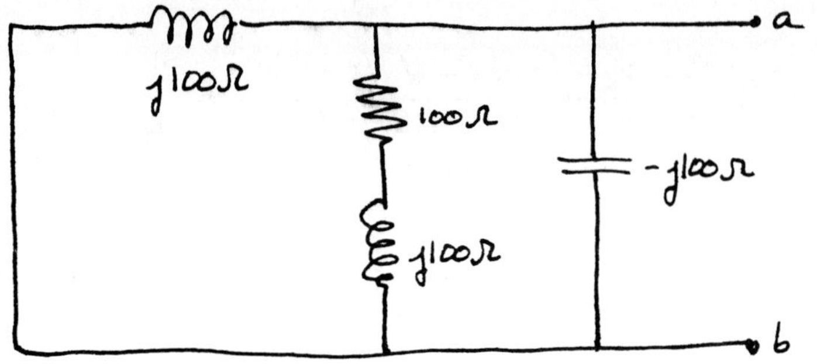

$$Y_{\text{ab}} = \frac{1}{j100} + \frac{1}{100 + j100} + \frac{1}{-j100}$$

$$= \frac{1}{100}\left[\frac{1}{j} + \frac{1}{1 + j1} + \frac{j}{1}\right]$$

$$Y_{\text{ab}} = \frac{1}{100}\left[-j + \frac{1 - j1}{2} + j\right]$$

$$= \frac{1 - j1}{200}; \qquad Z_{\text{ab}} = \frac{200}{1 - j1} = 100(1 + j1)$$

$$\therefore\ \mathbf{V}_{ab} = 100(1+j1)\left[\frac{247.49\underline{/45^\circ}}{j100}\right]$$

$$= \sqrt{2}\underline{/45^\circ}\cdot 1\underline{/-90^\circ}\cdot 247.49\underline{/45^\circ}$$

$$\mathbf{V}_{Th} = 350\underline{/0^\circ}\text{ V}$$

[b] $Z_{Th} = Z_{ab} = 100 + j100\,\Omega$

[c]

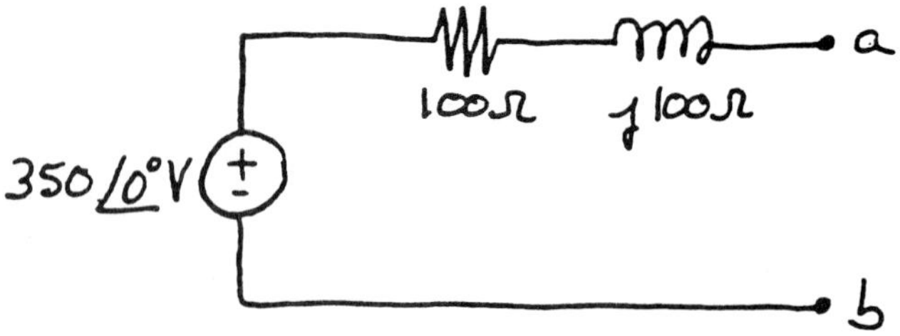

P 9.38

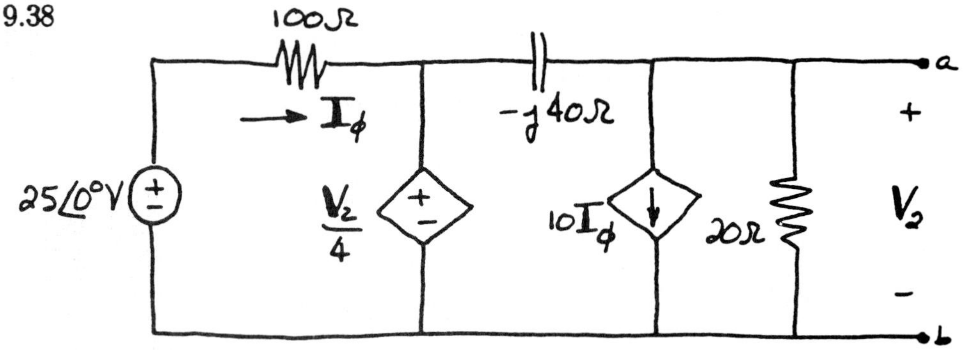

$$\frac{\mathbf{V}_2}{20} + \frac{25 - \mathbf{V}_2/4}{10} + \frac{\mathbf{V}_2 - \mathbf{V}_2/4}{-j40} = 0$$

Solving,

$$\mathbf{V}_2 = -64 + j48\text{ V} = 80\underline{/143.13^\circ}\text{ V}$$

$$\mathbf{I}_{sc} = -10\mathbf{I}_\phi = \frac{-25\underline{/0^\circ}}{10} = -2.5\underline{/0^\circ}$$

$$Z_{Th} = \frac{80\underline{/143.13^\circ}}{-2.5\underline{/0^\circ}} = 32\underline{/-36.87^\circ}\,\Omega$$

$$\mathbf{I}_N = \frac{\mathbf{V}_{Th}}{Z_{Th}} = \frac{80\underline{/143.13^\circ}}{32\underline{/-36.87^\circ}} = 2.5\underline{/180^\circ} = -2.5\text{ A}$$

$$Z_N = Z_{\rm Th} = 32\underline{/-36.87^\circ} = 25.6 - j19.2\,\Omega$$

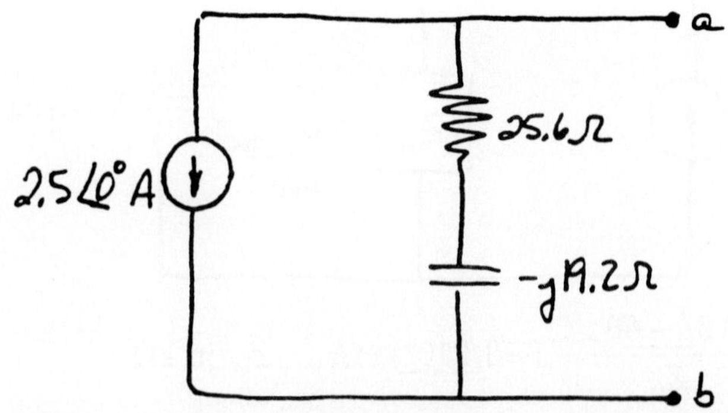

P 9.39 $$\mathbf{I}_N = \mathbf{I}_{sc} = \frac{(16/0^\circ)(25)}{25+15+j30} = 6.4 - j4.8\,\mathrm{A}$$

$$Z_N = \frac{(-j50)(40+j30)}{40+j30-j50} = 50 - j25\,\Omega$$

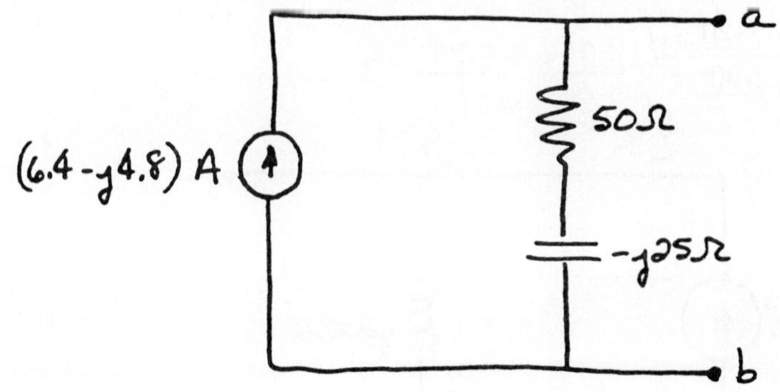

P 9.40

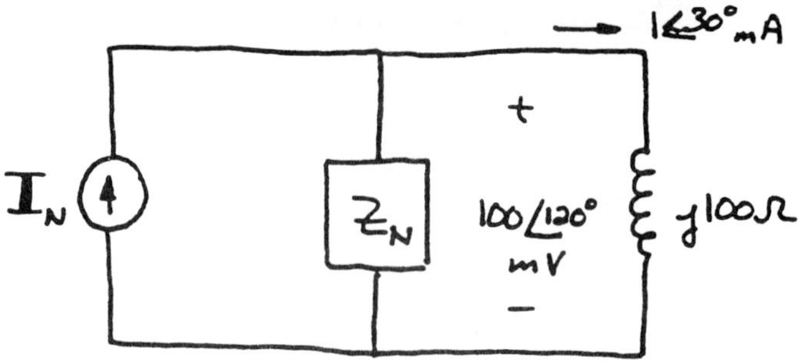

$$\mathbf{I}_N = \frac{0.1/120^\circ}{Z_N} + 1\underline{/30^\circ}\,\mathrm{mA}, \quad Z_N \text{ in k}\Omega$$

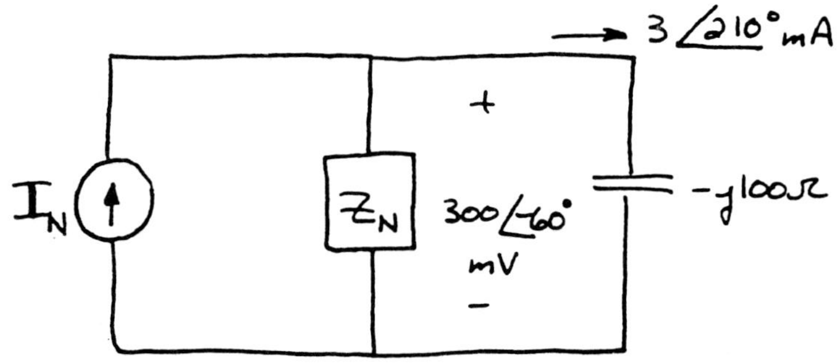

$$\mathbf{I}_N = \frac{0.3\angle -60^\circ}{Z_N} + (-3\angle 210^\circ)\text{ mA}, \quad Z_N \text{ in k}\Omega$$

$$\frac{0.1\angle 120^\circ}{Z_N} + 1\angle 30^\circ = \frac{0.3\angle -60^\circ}{Z_N} + (-3\angle 210^\circ)$$

$$\frac{0.3\angle -60^\circ - 0.1\angle 120^\circ}{Z_N} = 1\angle 30^\circ + 3\angle 210^\circ$$

$$Z_N = \frac{0.3\angle -60^\circ - 0.1\angle 120^\circ}{1\angle 30^\circ + 3\angle 210^\circ} = 0.2\angle 90^\circ = j0.2\,\text{k}\Omega$$

$$\mathbf{I}_N = \frac{0.1\angle 120^\circ}{0.2\angle 90^\circ} + 1\angle 30^\circ = 1.5\angle 30^\circ\,\text{mA}$$

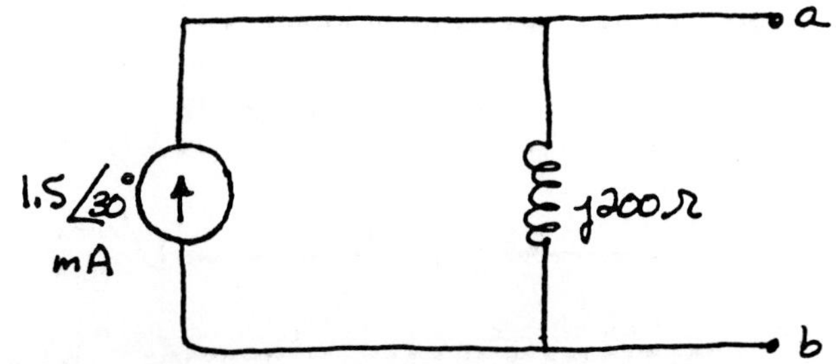

P 9.41 $$\mathbf{V}_{\text{Th}} = \frac{75(24)}{24 + j18} = 60\angle -36.87^\circ\text{ V}$$

$$Z_{\text{Th}} = \frac{(24)(j18)}{24 + j18} = 8.64 + j11.52\,\Omega$$

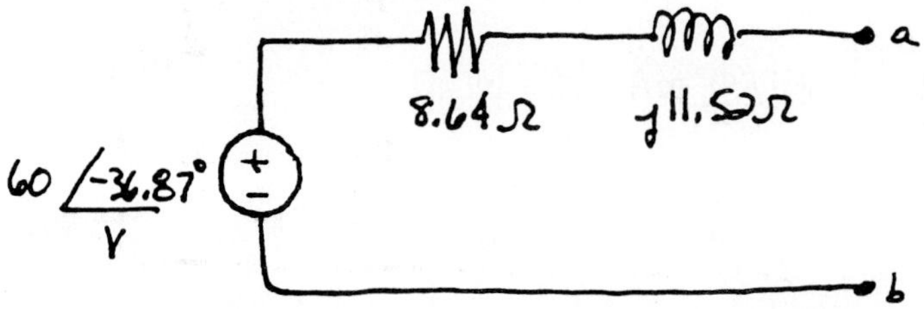

P 9.42

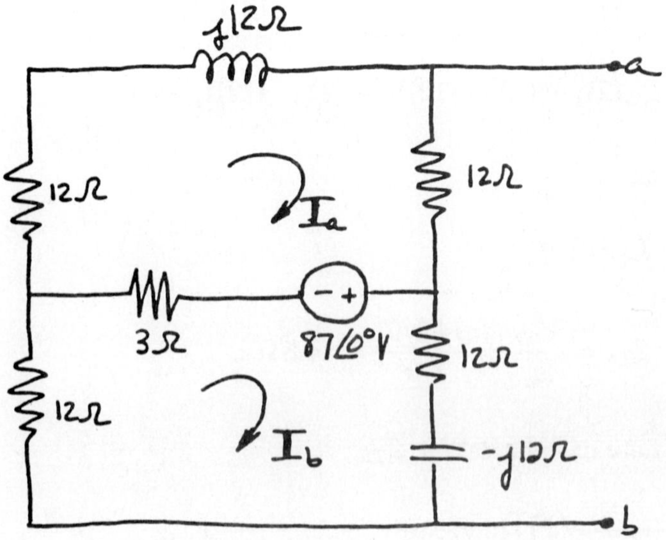

$$(27 + j12)\mathbf{I}_a - 3\mathbf{I}_b = -87\underline{/0^\circ}$$

$$-3\mathbf{I}_a + (27 - j12)\mathbf{I}_b = 87\underline{/0^\circ}$$

Solving,

$$\mathbf{I}_a = -2.4167 + j1.21; \qquad \mathbf{I}_b = 2.4167 + j1.21$$

$$\mathbf{V}_{\text{Th}} = 12\mathbf{I}_a + (12 - j12)\mathbf{I}_b = 14.5\underline{/0^\circ}\text{ V}$$

Short Circuit Test:

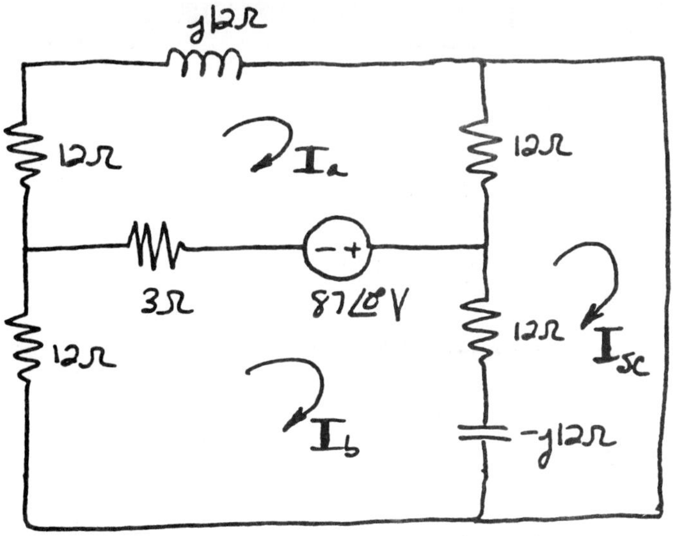

$$(27 + j12)\mathbf{I}_a - 3\mathbf{I}_b - 12\mathbf{I}_{sc} = -87$$

$$-3\mathbf{I}_a + (27 - j12)\mathbf{I}_b - (12 - j12)\mathbf{I}_{sc} = 87$$

$$-12\mathbf{I}_a - (12 - j12)\mathbf{I}_b + (24 - j12)\mathbf{I}_{sc} = 0$$

Solving,

$$\mathbf{I}_{sc} = 1\underline{/0^\circ}$$

$$Z_{Th} = \frac{\mathbf{V}_{Th}}{\mathbf{I}_{sc}} = \frac{14.5\underline{/0^\circ}}{1\underline{/0^\circ}} = 14.5\,\Omega$$

Alternate calculation for Z_{Th}:

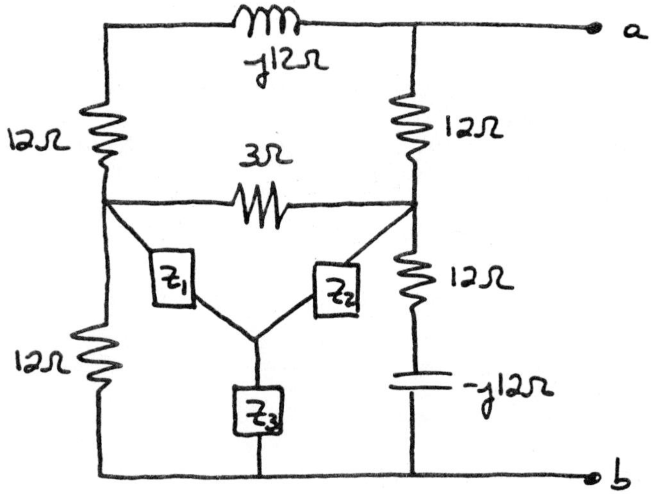

$$\sum Z = 12 + 3 + 12 - j12 = 27 - j12$$

$$Z_1 = \frac{36}{27 - j12} = \frac{12}{9 - j4}$$

$$Z_2 = \frac{36 - j36}{27 - j12} = \frac{12 - j12}{9 - j4}$$

$$Z_3 = \frac{12(12 - j12)}{27 - j12} = \frac{48 - j48}{9 - j4}$$

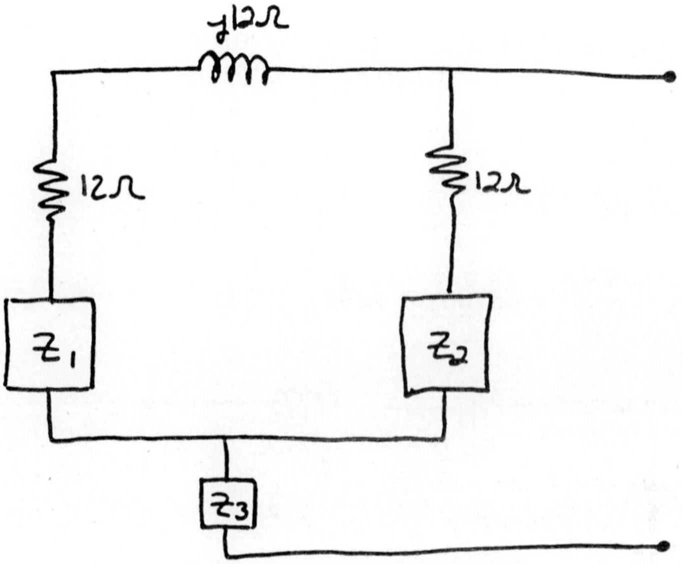

$$Z_a = 12 + j12 + \frac{12}{9-j4} = \frac{12(14+j5)}{9-j4}$$

$$Z_b = 12 + \frac{12-j12}{9-j4} = \frac{12(10-j5)}{9-j4}$$

$$Z_a \| Z_b = \frac{165-j20}{18-j8}$$

$$Z_3 + Z_a\|Z_b = \frac{48-j48}{9-j4} + \frac{165-j20}{18-j8} = 14.5\,\Omega$$

P 9.43

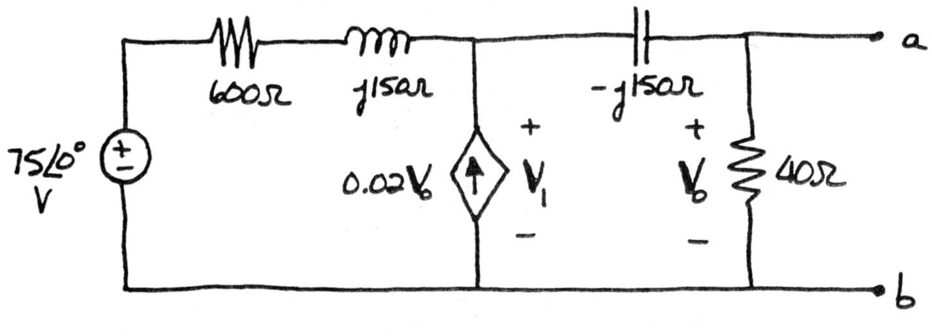

$$\frac{\mathbf{V}_1 - 75}{150(4+j1)} - \frac{0.02\mathbf{V}_1(40)}{40-j150} + \frac{\mathbf{V}_1}{40-j150} = 0$$

$$\therefore\ \mathbf{V}_1 = \frac{75(4-j15)}{16-j12}$$

$$\mathbf{V}_{\text{Th}} = \frac{40\mathbf{V}_1}{40 - j150} = \frac{4}{4 - j15} \cdot \frac{75(4 - j15)}{16 - j12}$$

$$= \frac{75}{4 - j3} = 15\underline{/36.87^\circ}\ \text{V}$$

$$\mathbf{I}_{sc} = \frac{75}{600} = \frac{1}{8}\ \text{A}$$

$$Z_{\text{Th}} = \frac{\mathbf{V}_{\text{Th}}}{\mathbf{I}_{sc}} = 120\underline{/36.87^\circ} = 96 + j72\,\Omega$$

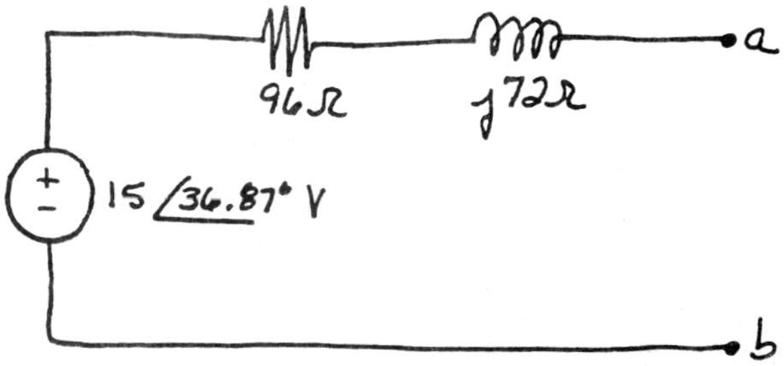

P 9.44 [a]

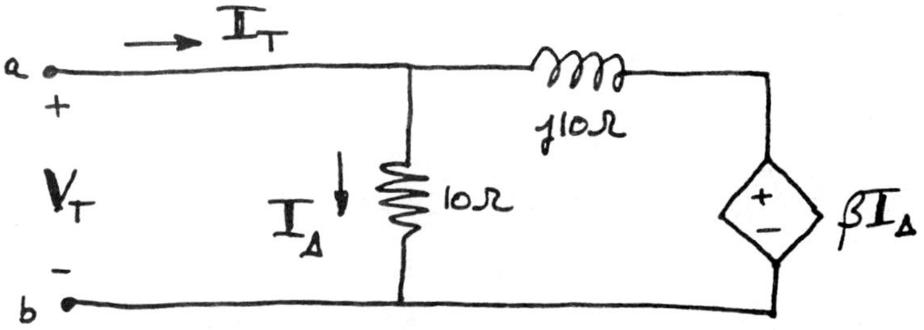

$$\mathbf{I}_T = \frac{\mathbf{V}_T}{10} + \frac{\mathbf{V}_T - \beta\mathbf{V}_T/10}{j10}$$

$$\frac{\mathbf{I}_T}{\mathbf{V}_T} = \frac{1}{10} + \frac{(1 - \beta/10)}{j10} = \frac{(10 - \beta) + j10}{j100}$$

$$\therefore\ Z_{\text{Th}} = \frac{\mathbf{V}_T}{\mathbf{I}_T} = \frac{1000 + j100(10 - \beta)}{(10 - \beta)^2 + 100}$$

Z_{Th} is real when $\beta = 10$.

[b] $$Z_{\text{Th}} = \frac{1000}{100} = 10\,\Omega$$

[c] $$Z_{\text{Th}} = 5 + j5$$

$$\frac{1000}{(10 - \beta)^2 + 100} = 5; \qquad (10 - \beta)^2 = 100$$

$$\therefore\ 10 - \beta = \pm 10; \qquad \beta = 10 \mp 10$$

$\beta = 0; \qquad \beta = 20$

But the j term can only equal the real term with $\beta = 0$. Thus, $\beta = 0$.

[d] $Z_{\rm Th}$ will be capacitive when $\beta > 10$:

$\therefore \quad 10 < \beta \leq 50$

P 9.45

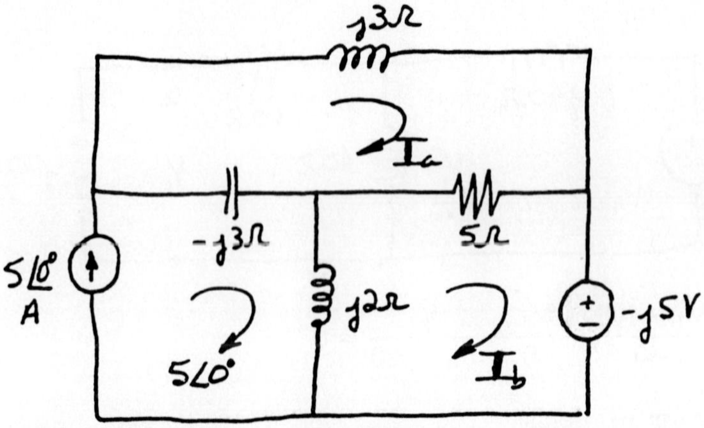

$j3\mathbf{I}_a + 5(\mathbf{I}_a - \mathbf{I}_b) - j3(\mathbf{I}_a - 5) = 0$

$j2(\mathbf{I}_b - 5) + 5(\mathbf{I}_b - \mathbf{I}_a) - j5 = 0$

Solving,

$\mathbf{I}_a = -j3; \qquad \mathbf{I}_g = -j3 = 3\angle -90^\circ\ \mathrm{A}$

P 9.46

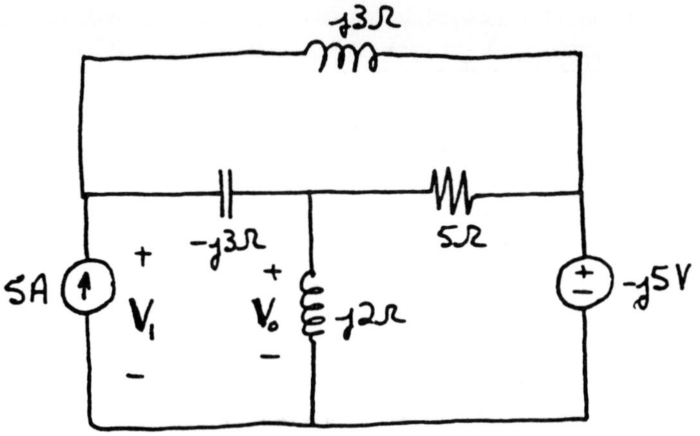

$$\frac{\mathbf{V}_o}{j2} + \frac{\mathbf{V}_o + j5}{5} + \frac{\mathbf{V}_o - \mathbf{V}_1}{-j3} = 0$$

$(5 + j6)\mathbf{V}_o + 10\mathbf{V}_1 = 30$

$$-5 + \frac{\mathbf{V}_1 - \mathbf{V}_o}{-j3} + \frac{\mathbf{V}_1 + j5}{j3} = 0$$

$$\mathbf{V}_o = j10; \qquad \mathbf{V}_1 = 9 + j5$$

$$\mathbf{V}_c = \mathbf{V}_1 - \mathbf{V}_o = 9 + j5 - j10 = 9 - j5 = 10.3\underline{/-29.05^\circ}$$

P 9.47

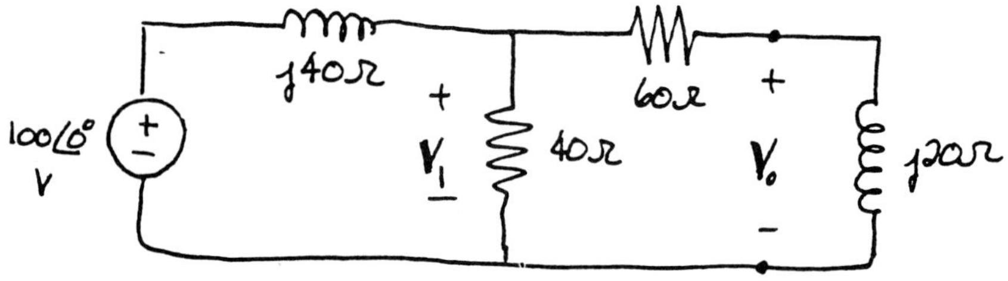

$$\frac{\mathbf{V}_1 - 100}{j40} + \frac{\mathbf{V}_1}{40} + \frac{\mathbf{V}_1}{60 + j20} = 0$$

Solving for $\mathbf{V}_1$ yields

$$\mathbf{V}_1 = 30 - j40\,\text{V}$$

$$\mathbf{V}_o = \frac{\mathbf{V}_1}{60 + j20}(j20) = \left(\frac{j}{3 + j}\right)\mathbf{V}_1$$

$$\mathbf{V}_o = 15 + j5\,\text{V} = 15.81\underline{/18.43^\circ}\,\text{V}$$

P 9.48 $j\omega L = j5000(14 \times 10^{-3}) = j70\,\Omega$

$$\frac{1}{j\omega C} = \frac{-j}{(5000)(0.5 \times 10^{-6})} = -j400\,\Omega$$

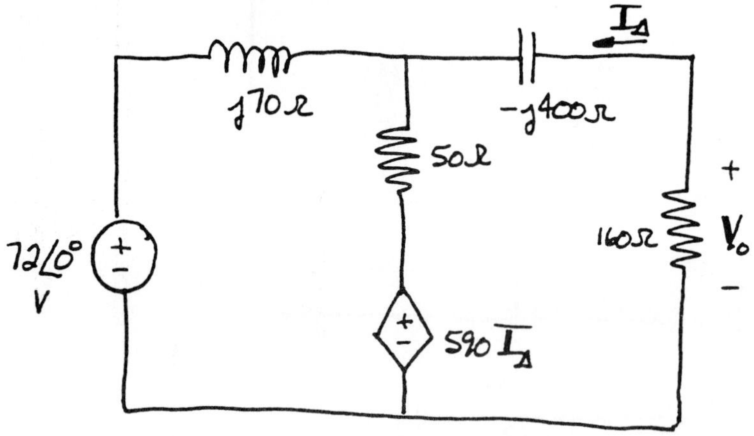

$$72\underline{/0^\circ} = (50 + j70)\mathbf{I}_a - 50\mathbf{I}_b + 590(-\mathbf{I}_b)$$

$$0 = -50\mathbf{I}_a - 590(-\mathbf{I}_b) + (210 - j400)\mathbf{I}_b$$

Solving,

$$\mathbf{I}_b = (50 - j50)\text{ mA}$$

$$\mathbf{V}_o = 160\mathbf{I}_b = 8 - j8 = 11.31\underline{/-45^\circ}$$

$$v_o = 11.31\cos(5000t - 45^\circ)\text{ V}$$

P 9.49 $j\omega L = j(5000)(0.4\times10^{-3}) = j2\,\Omega$

$$\frac{1}{j\omega C} = -j\frac{10^6}{(5000)(50)} = -j4\,\Omega$$

$$\mathbf{V}_{g1} = 10\underline{/53.13^\circ} = 6 + j8\text{ V}$$

$$\mathbf{V}_{g2} = 8\underline{/-90^\circ} = -j8\text{ V}$$

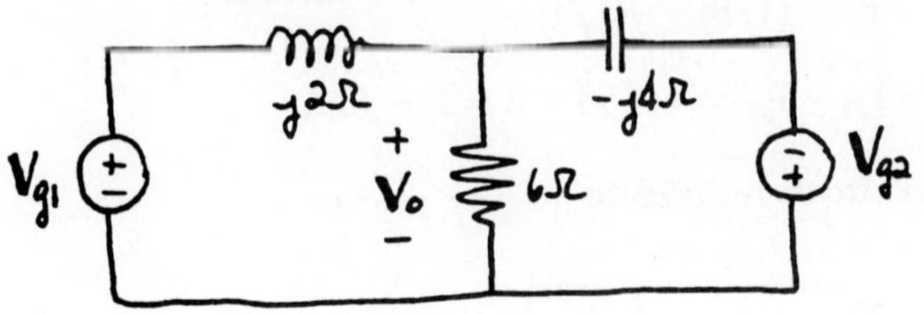

$$\frac{\mathbf{V}_o - 6 - j8}{j2} + \frac{\mathbf{V}_o}{6} + \frac{\mathbf{V}_o + (-j8)}{-j4} = 0$$

Solving,

$$\mathbf{V}_o = 12\underline{/0^\circ}$$

$$v_o(t) = 12\cos 5000t\text{ V}$$

P 9.50 From the solution to Problem 9.49 the phasor-domain circuit is

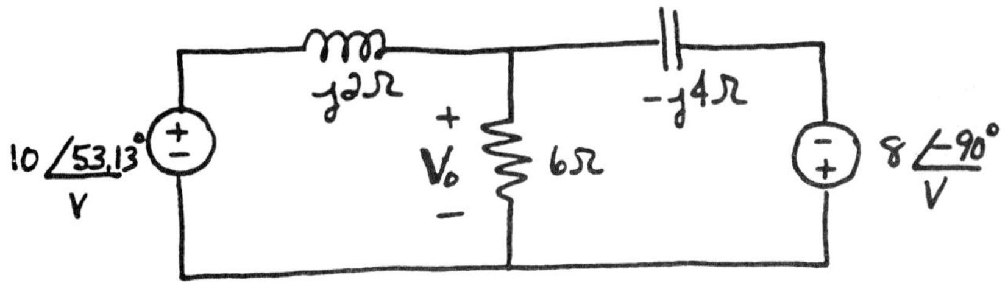

Making two source transformations yields

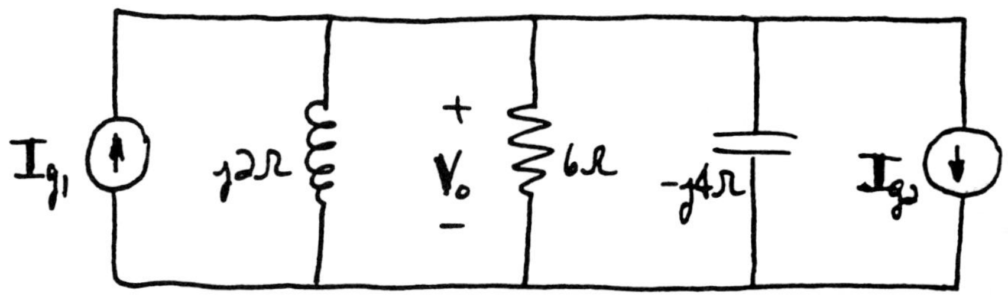

$$I_{g1} = \frac{10\angle 53.13^\circ}{j2} = 5\angle -36.87^\circ = 4 - j3\,\text{A}$$

$$I_{g2} = \frac{8\angle -90^\circ}{-j4} = 2\angle 0^\circ = 2\,\text{A}$$

$$Y = \frac{1}{j2} + \frac{1}{6} - j\frac{1}{4}\,\mho$$

$$Z = \frac{1}{Y} = \frac{1}{(1/6) - j(1/4)} = 1.85 + j2.77\,\Omega$$

$$I_e = I_{g1} - I_{g2} = 4 - j3 - 2 = 2 - j3\,\text{A}$$

Hence the circuit reduces to

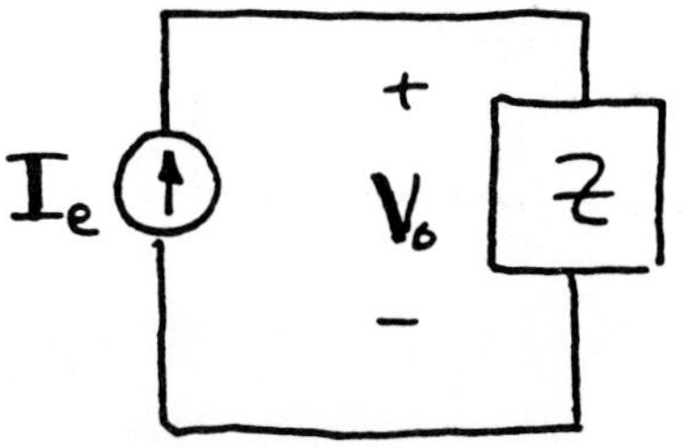

$$V_o = ZI_e = (1.85 + j2.77)(2 - j3) = 12\angle 0^\circ$$

$$\therefore \quad v_o(t) = 12\cos 5000t\ \text{V}$$

P 9.51 From the solution to Problem 9.49 the phasor-domain circuit is

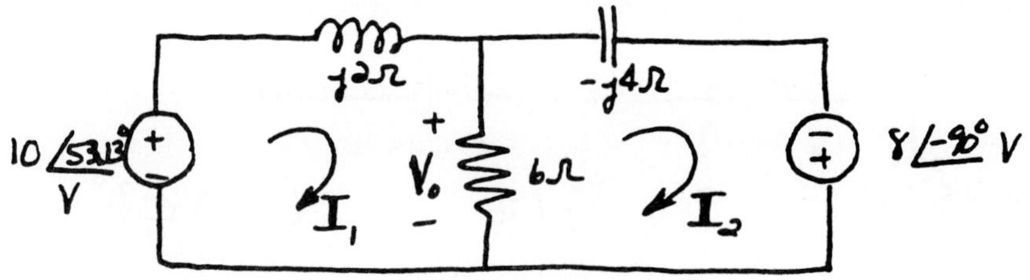

$$10\angle 53.13^\circ = (6 + j2)I_1 - 6I_2$$

$8\underline{/-90^\circ} = -6\mathbf{I}_1 + (6 - j4)\mathbf{I}_2$

$\mathbf{V}_o = (\mathbf{I}_1 - \mathbf{I}_2)6$

Solving,

$\mathbf{V}_o = 12\underline{/0^\circ}\text{ V}$

$v_o(t) = 12\cos 5000t\text{ V}$

P 9.52

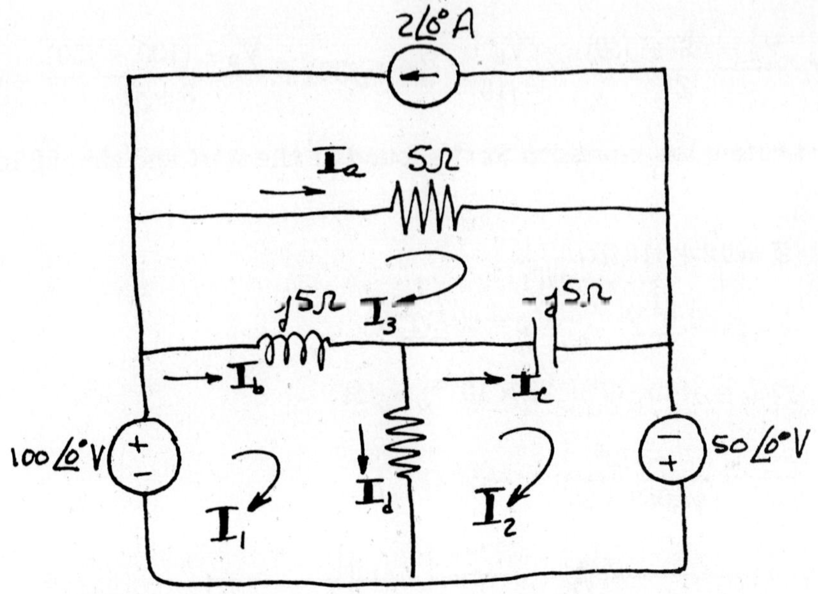

$10\underline{/0^\circ} = (1 + j)\mathbf{I}_1 - j\mathbf{I}_2 - \mathbf{I}_3$

$1\underline{/0^\circ} = -j\mathbf{I}_1 + \mathbf{I}_2 + j\mathbf{I}_3$

$-5\underline{/0^\circ} = -\mathbf{I}_1 + j\mathbf{I}_2 + (1 - j)\mathbf{I}_3$

Solving,

$\mathbf{I}_1 = 11 - j10\text{ A}; \qquad \mathbf{I}_2 = 6\text{ A}; \qquad \mathbf{I}_3 = 11 - j5\text{ A}$

$\mathbf{I}_a = \mathbf{I}_2 - 1 = 5\text{ A}$

$\mathbf{I}_b = \mathbf{I}_1 - \mathbf{I}_2 = 11 - j10 - 6 = 5 - j10\text{ A}$

$\mathbf{I}_c = \mathbf{I}_3 - \mathbf{I}_2 = 11 - j5 - 6 = 5 - j5\text{ A}$

$\mathbf{I}_d = \mathbf{I}_1 - \mathbf{I}_3 = 11 - j10 - 11 + j5 = -j5\text{ A}$

P 9.53 $\mathbf{V}_2$ is the voltage across the $-j10\,\Omega$ impedance.

$$\frac{\mathbf{V}_1 - \mathbf{V}_g}{20} + \frac{\mathbf{V}_1}{j5} + \frac{\mathbf{V}_1 - \mathbf{V}_2}{Z} = 0$$

$$\frac{(40 + j30) - (100 - j50)}{20} + \frac{40 + j30}{j5} + \frac{(40 + j30) - \mathbf{V}_2}{Z} = 0$$

$$\therefore \quad \mathbf{V}_2 = 40 + j30 + (3 - j4)Z$$

$$\frac{\mathbf{V}_2 - \mathbf{V}_1}{Z} + \frac{\mathbf{V}_L}{-j10} - \mathbf{I}_g + \frac{\mathbf{V}_2 - \mathbf{V}_g}{3 + j1} = 0$$

$$\frac{\mathbf{V}_2 - (40 + j30)}{Z} + \frac{\mathbf{V}_2}{-j10} - (20 + j30) + \frac{\mathbf{V}_2 - (100 - j50)}{3 + j1} = 0$$

Substituting the expression for $\mathbf{V}_2$ found at the start and simplifying yields

$$Z = 12 + j16\,\Omega$$

P 9.54 $\mathbf{V}_a = 60\underline{/0^\circ}\text{ V}; \qquad \mathbf{V}_b = 90\underline{/90^\circ}\text{ V}$

$$j\omega L = j(4 \times 10^4)(125 \times 10^{-6}) = j5\Omega$$

$$\frac{-j}{\omega C} = \frac{-j10^6}{40{,}000(1.25)} = -j20\,\Omega$$

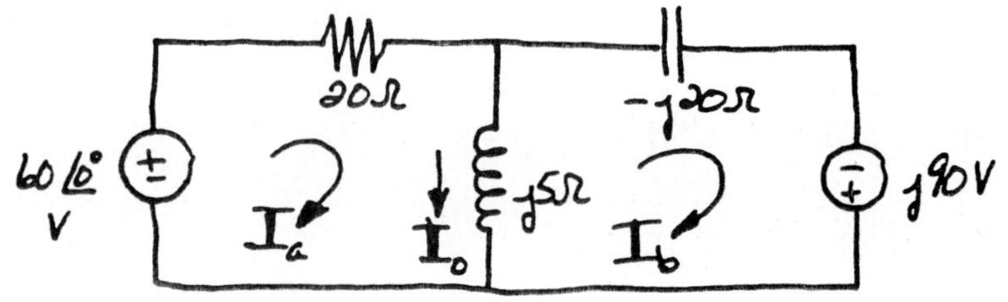

$$60 = (20 + j5)\mathbf{I}_a - j5\mathbf{I}_b$$

$$j90 = -j5\mathbf{I}_a - j15\mathbf{I}_b$$

Solving,

$$\mathbf{I}_a = 2.25 - j2.25\text{ A}; \qquad \mathbf{I}_b = -6.75 + j0.75\text{ A}$$

$$\mathbf{I}_o = \mathbf{I}_a - \mathbf{I}_b = 9 - j3 = 9.49\underline{/-18.43^\circ}\text{ A}$$

$$i_o(t) = 9.49\cos(40{,}000t - 18.43^\circ)\text{ A}$$

P 9.55 [a] $$\frac{1}{j\omega C} = \frac{10^9}{j8 \times 10^5(125)} = -j10\,\Omega$$

$$j\omega L = j8 \times 10^5(25 \times 10^{-6}) = j20\,\Omega$$

$$Z_e = \frac{(-j10)(20)}{20 - j10} = 4 - j8\,\Omega$$

$$\mathbf{I}_g = 5\underline{/0^\circ}$$

$$\mathbf{V}_g = \mathbf{I}_g Z_e = 5(4 - j8) = 20 - j40\text{ V}$$

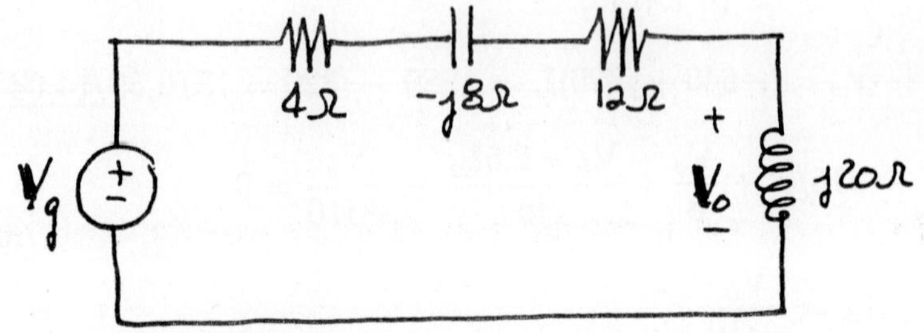

$$\mathbf{V}_o = \frac{(20 - j40)(j20)}{(16 + j12)} = 44 - j8 = 44.72\underline{/-10.30^\circ}\text{ V}$$

$$v_o = 44.72\cos(8 \times 10^5 t - 10.30^\circ)\text{ V}$$

[b] $$\omega = 2\pi f = 8 \times 10^5; \qquad f = \frac{4 \times 10^5}{\pi}$$

$$T = \frac{1}{f} = \frac{\pi}{4 \times 10^5} = 2.5\pi\ \mu\text{s}$$

$$\therefore\quad \frac{10.30}{360}(2.5\pi) = 224.71\text{ ns}$$

$\therefore\quad v_o$ lags i_g by 224.71 ns

P 9.56

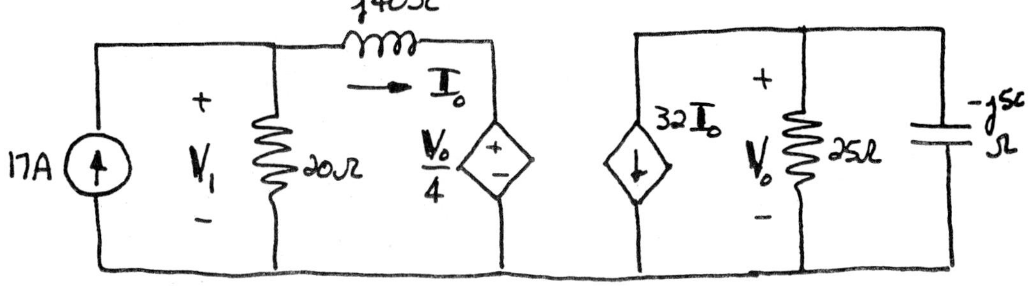

$$\frac{\mathbf{V}_o}{25} + \frac{\mathbf{V}_o}{-j50} + 32\mathbf{I}_o = 0$$

$$(2 + j)\mathbf{V}_o = -1600\mathbf{I}_o$$

$$\mathbf{V}_o = (-640 + j320)\mathbf{I}_o$$

$$\mathbf{I}_o = \frac{\mathbf{V}_1 - (\mathbf{V}_o/4)}{j40}$$

$$\therefore \quad \mathbf{V}_1 = (-160 + j120)\mathbf{I}_o$$

$$17 = \frac{\mathbf{V}_1}{20} + \mathbf{I}_o = (-8 + j6)\mathbf{I}_o + \mathbf{I}_o = (-7 + j6)\mathbf{I}_o$$

$$\therefore \quad \mathbf{I}_o = \frac{17}{(-7 + j6)} = -1.4 - j1.2\,\text{A}$$

$$\mathbf{V}_o = (-640 + j320)\mathbf{I}_o = 1280 + j320 = 1319.39\underline{/14.04^\circ}\,\text{V}$$

P 9.57

$$-15\underline{/0^\circ} + \frac{\mathbf{V}_o}{8} + \frac{\mathbf{V}_o - 2.5\mathbf{I}_\Delta}{j5} + \frac{\mathbf{V}_o}{-j10} = 0$$

$$\mathbf{I}_\Delta = \frac{\mathbf{V}_o}{-j10}$$

Solving,

$$\mathbf{V}_o = 72 + j96 = 120\underline{/53.13^\circ}\,\text{V}$$

P 9.58

$$j\omega L = j10^4(1.2 \times 10^{-3}) = j12\,\Omega$$

$$\frac{1}{j\omega C} = \frac{-j10^6}{5 \times 10^4} = -j20\,\Omega$$

$$\mathbf{V}_a = 100\underline{/-90^\circ} = -j100\,\text{V}$$

$$\mathbf{V}_b = 500\underline{/0^\circ} = 500\,\text{V}$$

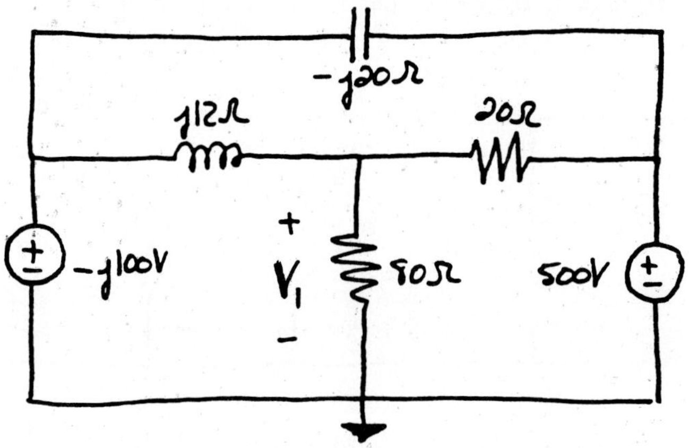

$$\frac{\mathbf{V}_1}{80} + \frac{\mathbf{V}_1 - 500}{20} + \frac{\mathbf{V}_1 + j100}{j12} = 0$$

Solving,

$$\mathbf{V}_1 = 160\underline{/53.13^\circ}\text{ V} = 96 + j128\text{ V}$$

$$\mathbf{I}_\text{a} = \frac{-j100 - 96 - j128}{j12} + \frac{-j100 - 500}{-j20}$$

$$= 24 - j17 = 29.41\underline{/-35.31^\circ}\text{ A}$$

$$i_\text{a} = 29.41\cos(10{,}000t - 35.31^\circ)\text{ A}$$

$$\mathbf{I}_\text{b} = \frac{500 - 96 - j128}{20} + \frac{500 + j100}{-j20}$$

$$= 15.2 - j39 = 41.86\underline{/-68.71^\circ}\text{ A}$$

$$i_\text{b} = 41.86\cos(10{,}000t - 68.71^\circ)\text{ A}$$

P 9.59 From the solution to Problem 9.49 the phasor-domain circuit with the right-hand source removed is

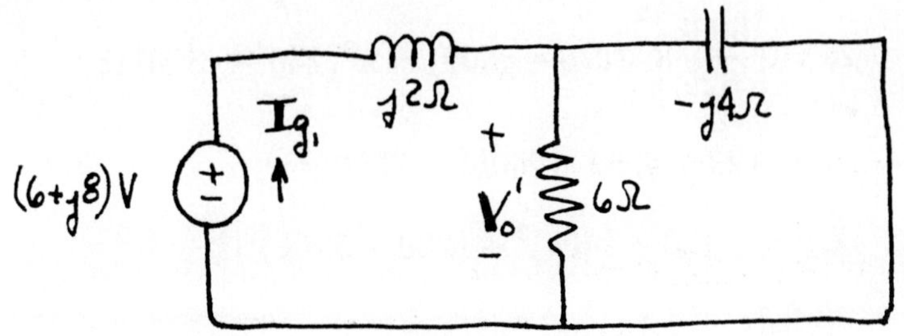

$$Z_{e1} = \frac{6(-j4)}{(6 - j4)} = \frac{-j24}{6 - j4}\ \Omega$$

$$\mathbf{V}_o' = \frac{Z_{e1}}{Z_{e1} + j2}(6 + j8) = \frac{192 - j144}{8 - j12}\text{ V}$$

With the left hand source removed

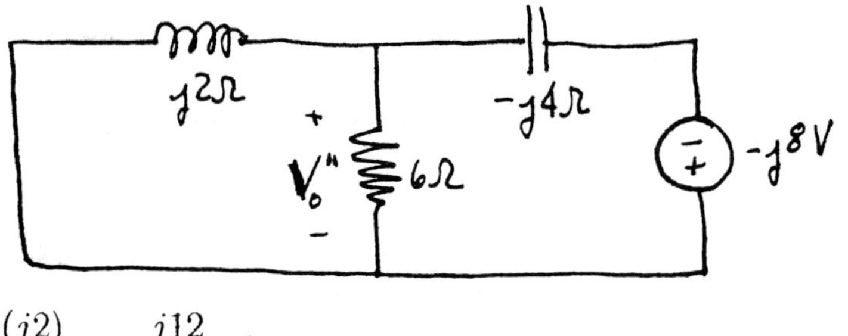

$$Z_{e2} = \frac{6(j2)}{6 + j2} = \frac{j12}{6 + j2}\ \Omega$$

$$\mathbf{V}_o'' = \frac{Z_{e2}}{-j4 + Z_{e2}}(j8) = \frac{-96}{8 - j12}\,\text{V}$$

$$\mathbf{V}_o = \mathbf{V}_o' + \mathbf{V}_o'' = \frac{192 - j144 - 96}{8 - j12} = 12 + j0\,\text{V}$$

$$v_o(t) = 12\cos 5000t\,\text{V}$$

P 9.60 [a]

$$j\omega L_1 = j(50)(5) = j250\,\Omega$$

$$j\omega L_2 = j(50)(20) = j1000\,\Omega$$

$$\frac{1}{j\omega C} = \frac{10^9}{j(50\times 10^3)(40)} = -j500\,\Omega$$

$$\therefore\quad Z_{22} = 75 + 300 + j1000 - j500 = 375 + j500\,\Omega$$

$$\therefore\quad Z_{22}^* = 375 - j500\,\Omega$$

$$M = k\sqrt{L_1L_2} = 10k \times 10^{-3}$$

$$\omega M = (50)(10k) = 500k$$

$$Z_r = \left[\frac{500k}{625}\right]^2 (375 - j500) = k^2(240 - j320)\,\Omega$$

$$Z_{\text{in}} = 120 + j250 + 240k^2 - j320k^2$$

$$|Z_{\text{in}}| = [(120 + 240k)^2 + (250 - 320k)^2]^{\frac{1}{2}}$$

$$\frac{d|Z_{\text{in}}|}{dk} = \frac{1}{2}[(120 + 240k)^2 + (250 - 320k)^2]^{-\frac{1}{2}} \times$$

$$[2(120 + 240k^2)480k + 2(250 - 320k^2)(-640k)]$$

$$\frac{d|Z_{\text{in}}|}{dk} = 0 \text{ when}$$

$$960k(120 + 240k^2) - 1280k(250 - 320k^2) = 0$$

$$\therefore\quad k^2 = 0.32; \qquad \therefore\quad k = \sqrt{0.32} = 0.5657$$

[b]

$$Z_{\text{in}}\,(\text{min}) = 120 + 240(0.32) + j[250 - 0.32(320)]$$

$$= 196.8 + j147.6 = 246\underline{/36.87^\circ}\,\Omega$$

$$\mathbf{I}_1\,(\text{max}) = \frac{369\underline{/0^\circ}}{246\underline{/36.87^\circ}} = 1.5\underline{/-36.87^\circ}\,\text{A}$$

$$\therefore \quad i_1 \text{ (peak)} = 1.5\,\text{A}$$

Note — You can test that the k value obtained from setting $d|Z_{\text{in}}|/dt = 0$ leads to a minimum by noting $0 \le k \le 1$. If $k = 1$,

$$Z_{\text{in}} = 360 - j70 = 366.74\underline{/-11^\circ}\,\Omega$$

Thus,

$$|Z_{\text{in}}|_{k=1} > |Z_{\text{in}}|_{k=\sqrt{0.32}}$$

If $k = 0$,

$$Z_{\text{in}} = 120 + j250 = 277.31\underline{/64.36^\circ}\,\Omega$$

Thus,

$$|Z_{\text{in}}|_{k=0} > |Z_{\text{in}}|_{k=\sqrt{0.32}}$$

P 9.61 [a]

$$j\omega L_1 = j(5000)(2 \times 10^{-3}) = j10\,\Omega$$

$$j\omega L_2 = j(5000)(8 \times 10^{-3}) = j40\,\Omega$$

$$j\omega M = j10\,\Omega$$

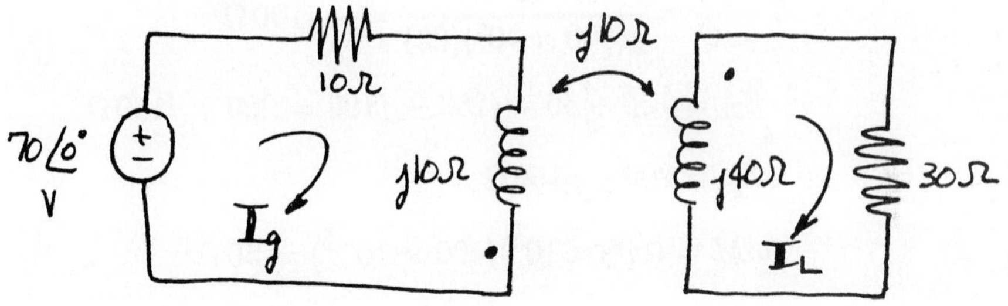

$$70 = (10 + j10)\mathbf{I}_g + j10\mathbf{I}_L$$

$$0 = j10\mathbf{I}_g + (30 + j40)\mathbf{I}_L$$

Solving,

$$\mathbf{I}_g = 4 - j3\,\text{A}; \qquad \mathbf{I}_L = -1\,\text{A}$$

$$i_g = 5\cos(5000t - 36.87^\circ)\,\text{A}$$

$$i_L = 1\cos(5000t - 180^\circ)\,\text{A}$$

[b]

$$k = \frac{M}{\sqrt{L_1 L_2}} = \frac{2}{\sqrt{16}} = 0.5$$

[c] When $t = 100\pi\ \mu s$,

$$5000t = (5000)(100\pi) \times 10^{-6} = 0.5\pi = \pi/2\,\text{rad} = 90^\circ$$

$$i_g(100\pi\mu s) = 5\cos(53.13^\circ) = 3\,\text{A}$$

$$i_L(100\pi\mu s) = 1\cos(-90^\circ) = 0\,\text{A}$$

$$w = \frac{1}{2}L_1 i_1^2 + \frac{1}{2}L_2 i_2^2 + M i_1 i_2 = \frac{1}{2}(2 \times 10^{-3})(9) + 0 + 0 = 9\,\text{mJ}$$

When $t = 200\pi\ \mu s$,

$$5000t = \pi\,\text{rad} = 180^\circ$$

$$i_g(200\pi\mu s) = 5\cos(180 - 53.13) = -4\,\text{A}$$

$$i_L(200\pi\mu s) = 1\cos(180 - 180) = 1\,\text{A}$$

$$w = \frac{1}{2}(2 \times 10^{-3})(16) + \frac{1}{2}(8 \times 10^{-3})(1) + 2 \times 10^{-3}(-4)(1) = 12\,\text{mJ}$$

P 9.62 [a] $j\omega L_2 = j(500)10^3(500)10^{-6} = j250\,\Omega$

$$\frac{1}{j\omega C} = \frac{10^9}{j(500 \times 10^3)(20)} = -j100\,\Omega$$

$$Z_{22} = 150 + 50 + j250 - j100 = 200 + j150\,\Omega$$

$$Z_{22}^* = 200 - j150\,\Omega$$

$$\omega M = (500 \times 10^3)(100 \times 10^{-6}) = 50\,\Omega$$

$$Z_r = \left(\frac{50}{250}\right)^2 [200 - j150] = 8 - j6\,\Omega$$

[b] $Z_{ab} = R_1 + j\omega L_1 + 8 - j6$

$$j\omega L_1 = j(500 \times 10^3)(80 \times 10^{-6}) = j40\,\Omega$$

$$Z_{ab} = 20 + j34\,\Omega$$

P 9.63 $j\omega L_1 = j(25 \times 10^3)(3.2 \times 10^{-3}) = j80\,\Omega$

$$j\omega L_2 = j(25 \times 10^3)(12.8 \times 10^{-3}) = j320\,\Omega$$

$$\frac{1}{j\omega C} = \frac{10^9}{j(25 \times 10^3)(250)} = -j160\,\Omega$$

$$j\omega M = j(25 \times 10^3)k\sqrt{(3.2)(12.8)} \times 10^{-3} = j160k\,\Omega$$

$$Z_{22} = 40 + j320 - j160 = 40 + j160\,\Omega$$

$$Z_{22}^{*} = 40 - j160\,\Omega$$

$$Z_r = \left[\frac{160k}{|40 + j160|}\right]^2 (40 - j160) = 37.647k^2 - j150.588k^2$$

$$Z_{ab} = 10 + j80 + 37.647k^2 - j150.588k^2 = (10 + 37.647k^2) + j(80 - 150.588k^2)$$

Z_{ab} is resistive when

$$80 - 150.588k^2 = 0 \quad \text{or} \quad k^2 = 0.53125$$

$$\therefore \quad Z_{ab} = 10 + (37.647)(0.53125) = 30\,\Omega$$

P 9.64 $$Z_{Th} = 30 + j200 + (50/25)^2(15 - j20) = 90 + j120\,\Omega$$

$$\mathbf{V}_{Th} = \frac{225/\underline{0^\circ}}{15 + j20}(j50) = 450/\underline{36.87^\circ}\text{ V}$$

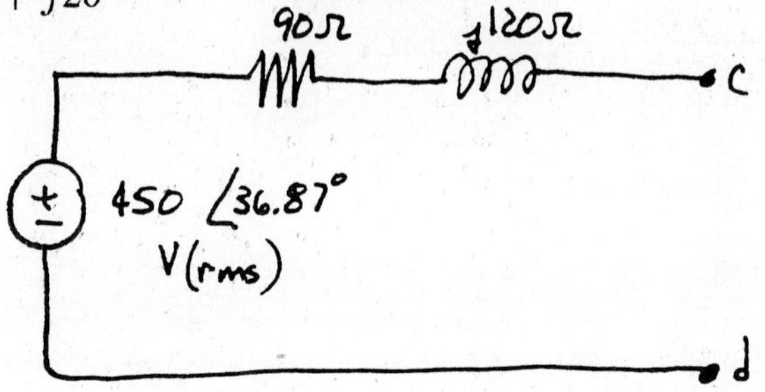

P 9.65 [a]

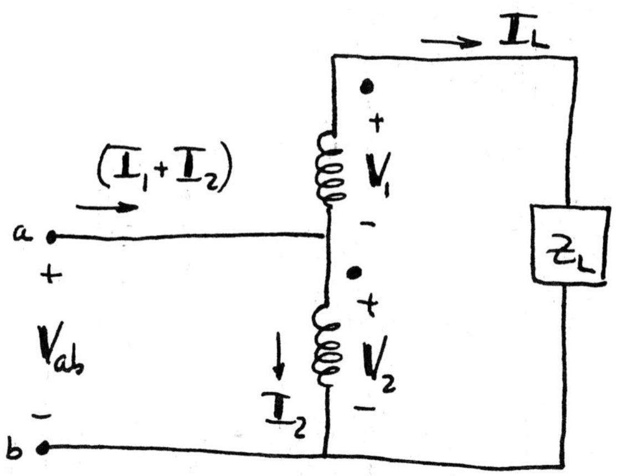

$$Z_{ab} = \frac{\mathbf{V}_{ab}}{\mathbf{I}_1 + \mathbf{I}_2} = \frac{\mathbf{V}_2}{\mathbf{I}_1 + \mathbf{I}_2} = \frac{\mathbf{V}_2}{(1 + N_1/N_2)\mathbf{I}_1}$$

$$N_1\mathbf{I}_1 = N_2\mathbf{I}_2, \qquad \mathbf{I}_2 = \frac{N_1}{N_2}\mathbf{I}_1$$

$$\frac{\mathbf{V}_1}{\mathbf{V}_2} = \frac{N_1}{N_2}, \qquad \mathbf{V}_1 = \frac{N_1}{N_2}\mathbf{V}_2$$

$$\mathbf{V}_1 + \mathbf{V}_2 = Z_L\mathbf{I}_1 = \left(\frac{N_1}{N_2} + 1\right)\mathbf{V}_2$$

$$Z_{ab} = \frac{\mathbf{I}_1 Z_L}{(N_1/N_2 + 1)(1 + N_1/N_2)\mathbf{I}_1}$$

$$\therefore \; Z_{ab} = \frac{Z_L}{[1 + (N_1/N_2)]^2} \quad \text{Q.E.D.}$$

[b] Assume dot on the N_2 coil is moved to the lower terminal. Then

$$\mathbf{V}_1 = -\frac{N_1}{N_2}\mathbf{V}_2 \quad \text{and} \quad \mathbf{I}_2 = -\frac{N_1}{N_2}\mathbf{I}_1$$

As before

$$Z_{ab} = \frac{\mathbf{V}_2}{\mathbf{I}_1 + \mathbf{I}_2} \quad \text{and} \quad \mathbf{V}_1 + \mathbf{V}_2 = Z_L\mathbf{I}_1$$

$$\therefore \; Z_{ab} = \frac{\mathbf{V}_2}{(1 - N_1/N_2)\mathbf{I}_1} = \frac{Z_L\mathbf{I}_1}{[1 - (N_1/N_2)]^2\mathbf{I}_1}$$

$$Z_{ab} = \frac{Z_L}{[1 - (N_1/N_2)]^2} \quad \text{Q.E.D.}$$

P 9.66 [a]

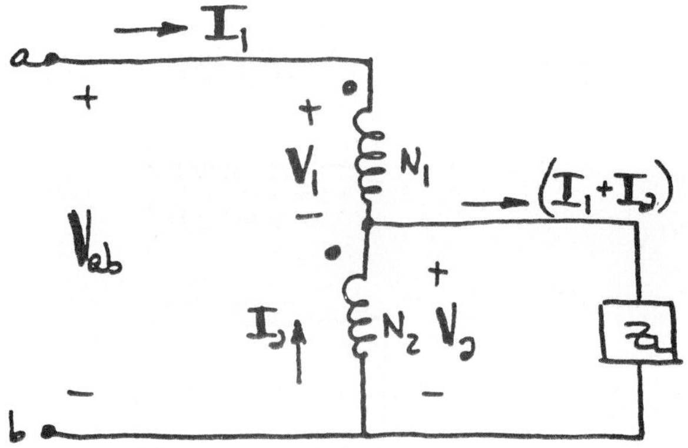

$$Z_{ab} = \frac{\mathbf{V}_{ab}}{\mathbf{I}_1} = \frac{\mathbf{V}_1 + \mathbf{V}_2}{\mathbf{I}_1}$$

$$\frac{\mathbf{V}_1}{N_1} = \frac{\mathbf{V}_2}{N_2}, \qquad \mathbf{V}_2 = \frac{N_2}{N_1}\mathbf{V}_1$$

$$N_1\mathbf{I}_1 = N_2\mathbf{I}_2, \qquad \mathbf{I}_2 = \frac{N_1}{N_2}\mathbf{I}_1$$

$$\mathbf{V}_2 = (\mathbf{I}_1 + \mathbf{I}_2)Z_L = \mathbf{I}_1\left(1 + \frac{N_1}{N_2}\right)Z_L$$

$$\mathbf{V}_1 + \mathbf{V}_2 = \left(\frac{N_1}{N_2} + 1\right)\mathbf{V}_2 = \left(1 + \frac{N_1}{N_2}\right)^2 Z_L\mathbf{I}_1$$

$$\therefore \quad Z_{ab} = \frac{(1 + N_1/N_2)^2 Z_L \mathbf{I}_1}{\mathbf{I}_1}$$

$$Z_{ab} = \left(1 + \frac{N_1}{N_2}\right)^2 Z_L \quad \text{Q.E.D.}$$

[b] Assume dot on N_2 is moved to the lower terminal, then

$$\frac{\mathbf{V}_1}{N_1} = \frac{-\mathbf{V}_2}{N_2}, \qquad \mathbf{V}_1 = \frac{-N_1}{N_2}\mathbf{V}_2$$

$$N_1\mathbf{I}_1 = -N_2\mathbf{I}_2, \qquad \mathbf{I}_2 = \frac{-N_1}{N_2}\mathbf{I}_1$$

As in part [a]

$$\mathbf{V}_2 = (\mathbf{I}_2 + \mathbf{I}_1)Z_L \quad \text{and} \quad Z_{ab} = \frac{\mathbf{V}_1 + \mathbf{V}_2}{\mathbf{I}_1}$$

$$Z_{ab} = \frac{(1 - N_1/N_2)\mathbf{V}_2}{\mathbf{I}_1} = \frac{(1 - N_1/N_2)(1 - N_1/N_2)Z_L\mathbf{I}_1}{\mathbf{I}_1}$$

$$Z_{ab} = [1 - (N_1/N_2)]^2 Z_L \quad \text{Q.E.D.}$$

P 9.67 In Eq. 9.69 replace $\omega^2 M^2$ with $k^2\omega^2 L_1 L_2$ and then write X_{ab} as

$$\begin{aligned} X_{ab} &= \omega L_1 - \frac{k^2\omega^2 L_1 L_2(\omega L_2 + \omega L_L)}{R_{22}^2 + (\omega L_2 + \omega L_L)^2} \\ &= \omega L_1 \left\{1 - \frac{k^2\omega L_2(\omega L_2 + \omega L_L)}{R_{22}^2 + (\omega L_2 + \omega L_L)^2}\right\} \end{aligned}$$

For X_{ab} to be negative requires

$$R_{22}^2 + (\omega L_2 + \omega L_L)^2 < k^2\omega L_2(\omega L_2 + \omega L_L)$$

or

$$R_{22}^2 + (\omega L_2 + \omega L_L)^2 - k^2\omega L_2(\omega L_2 + \omega L_L) < 0$$

which reduces to

$$R_{22}^2 + \omega^2 L_2^2(1 - k^2) + \omega L_2 \omega L_L(2 - k^2) + \omega^2 L_L^2 < 0$$

But $k \leq 1$ hence it is impossible to satisfy the inequality. Therefore X_{ab} can never be negative if X_L is an inductive reactance.

P 9.68 $Z_{ab} = (50)^2(1/25)^2 Z_L = 4Z_L$

$$\therefore \; Z_{ab} = 800 + j600\,\Omega$$

P 9.69 The phasor domain equivalent circuit is

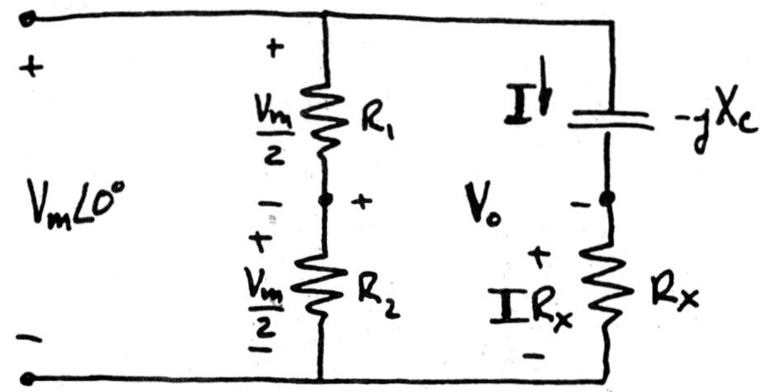

$$V_o = \frac{V_m}{2} - IR_x; \qquad \mathbf{I} = \frac{V_m}{R_x - jX_C}$$

As R_x varies from 0 to ∞, the amplitude of v_o remains constant and its phase angle increases from 0° to −180°.

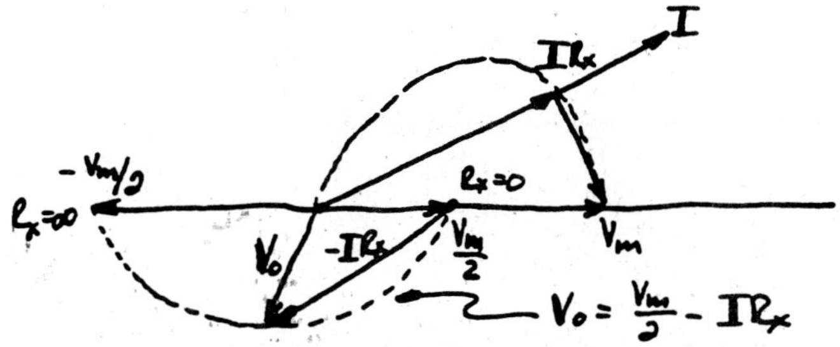

P 9.70 [a]

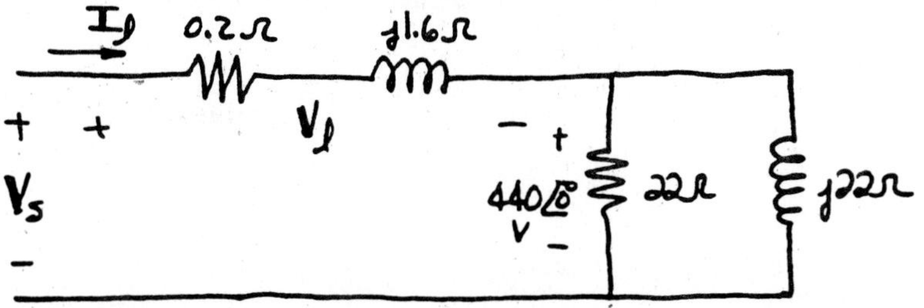

$$\mathbf{I}_\ell = \frac{440}{22} + \frac{440}{j22} = 20 - j20\ \text{A}$$

$$\mathbf{V}_\ell = (0.2 + j1.6)(20 - j20) = 36 + j28 = 45.61\angle 37.87^\circ\ \text{V(rms)}$$

$$\mathbf{V}_s = 440\angle 0^\circ + \mathbf{V}_\ell = 476 + j28 = 476.82\angle 3.37^\circ\ \text{V}$$

[b]

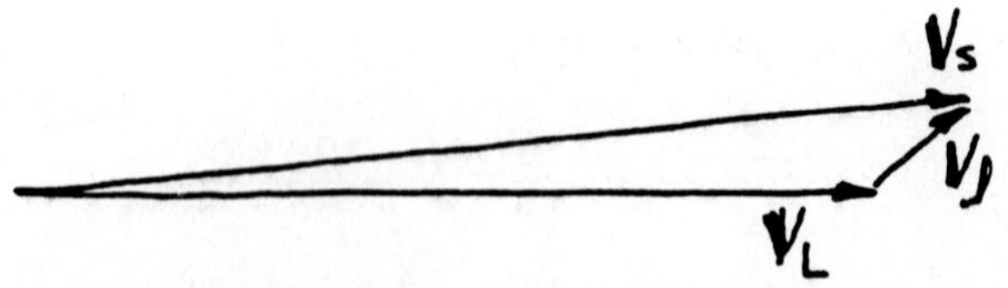

[c] $$\mathbf{I}_\ell = \frac{440}{22} + \frac{440}{j22} + \frac{440}{-j22} = 20 + j0\,\text{A}$$

$$\mathbf{V}_\ell = (0.2 + j1.6)(20 + j0) = 4 + j32 = 32.25\underline{/82.87^\circ}$$

$$\mathbf{V}_s = 440 + \mathbf{V}_\ell = 444 + j32 = 445.15\underline{/4.12^\circ}$$

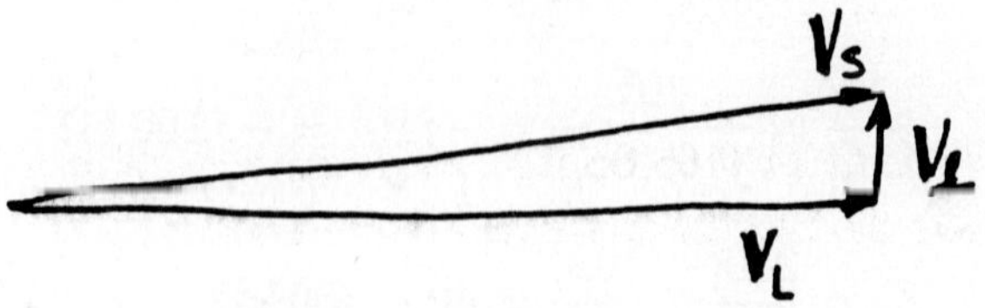

P 9.71 [a] $$\frac{1}{j\omega C} = \frac{-j10^9}{(2 \times 10^5)(12.5)} = -j400\,\Omega$$

$$\frac{\mathbf{V}_n}{200} + \frac{\mathbf{V}_n - \mathbf{V}_o}{-j400} = 0$$

$$\frac{\mathbf{V}_o}{-j400} = \frac{\mathbf{V}_n}{200} + \frac{\mathbf{V}_n}{-j400}$$

$$\mathbf{V}_o = \mathbf{V}_n - j2\mathbf{V}_n = (1 - j2)\mathbf{V}_n$$

$$\mathbf{V}_p = \frac{\mathbf{V}_g(1/j\omega C_o)}{500 + (1/j\omega C_o)} = \frac{\mathbf{V}_g}{1 + j(500)(2 \times 10^5)C_o}$$

$$\mathbf{V}_g = 10\underline{/0^\circ}\,\text{V}$$

$$\mathbf{V}_p = \frac{10\underline{/0^\circ}}{1 + j10^8 C_o} = \mathbf{V}_n$$

$$\therefore\quad \mathbf{V}_o = \frac{(1 - j2)10\underline{/0^\circ}}{1 + j10^8 C_o}$$

$$|\mathbf{V}_o| = \frac{\sqrt{5}(10)}{\sqrt{1 + 10^{16} C_o^2}} = 10$$

Solving,

$$C_o = 20\,\text{nF}$$

[b] $$\mathbf{V}_o = \frac{10(1-j2)}{1+j2} = 10\underline{/-126.87^\circ}$$

$$v_o = 10\cos(2\times10^5t - 126.87^\circ)\text{ V}$$

P 9.72 [a] $$\mathbf{V}_g = 2\underline{/0^\circ}\text{ V}$$

$$\mathbf{V}_\text{p} = \frac{80}{100}\mathbf{V}_g = 1.6\underline{/0^\circ}; \qquad \mathbf{V}_\text{n} = \mathbf{V}_\text{p} = 1.6\underline{/0^\circ}\text{ V}$$

$$\frac{1.6}{160} + \frac{1.6 - \mathbf{V}_o}{Z_\text{p}} = 0$$

$$Z_\text{p} = \frac{(200)(1/j\omega C)}{200 + (1/j\omega C)}$$

$$\frac{1}{j\omega C} = \frac{10^9}{j10^5(0.1)} = -j10^5 = -j100\,\text{k}\Omega$$

$$Z_\text{p} = \frac{200(-j100)}{200 - j100} = 40 - j80\,\text{k}\Omega$$

$$\mathbf{V}_o = 1.6 + \frac{Z_\text{p}}{100} = 2 - j0.8 = 2.15\underline{/-21.80^\circ}$$

$$v_o = 2.15\cos(10^5t - 21.80^\circ)\text{ V}$$

[b] $$\mathbf{V}_\text{p} = 0.8V_m\underline{/0^\circ}; \qquad \mathbf{V}_\text{n} = \mathbf{V}_\text{p} = 0.8V_m\underline{/0^\circ}$$

$$\frac{0.8V_m}{160} + \frac{0.8V_m - \mathbf{V}_o}{40 - j80} = 0$$

$$\therefore\ \mathbf{V}_o = 0.8V_m + \frac{40 - j80}{160}V_m(0.8) = 0.8V_m(1.25 - j0.5)$$

$$\therefore\ |0.8V_m(1.25 - j0.5)| \leq 5$$

$$\therefore\ V_m \leq 4.64\text{ V}$$

P 9.73 $$\mathbf{V}_g = 1.2\underline{/0^\circ}\text{ V}; \qquad \frac{1}{j\omega C} = \frac{10^6}{j100} = -j10\,\text{k}\Omega$$

Let $\mathbf{V}_\text{a}$ = voltage across 1 μF capacitor, positive at upper terminal
Then:

$$\frac{\mathbf{V}_\text{a} - 1.2\underline{/0^\circ}}{10} + \frac{\mathbf{V}_\text{a}}{-j10} + \frac{\mathbf{V}_\text{a}}{10} = 0; \qquad \therefore\ \mathbf{V}_\text{a} = (0.48 - j0.24)\text{ V}$$

$$\frac{0-\mathbf{V}_a}{10}+\frac{0-\mathbf{V}_o}{200}=0; \qquad \mathbf{V}_o=-20\mathbf{V}_a$$

$$\therefore \quad \mathbf{V}_o=-9.6+j4.8=10.73\underline{/153.43^\circ}\text{ V}$$

$$v_o=10.73\cos(100t+153.43^\circ)\text{ V}$$

P 9.74 [a]

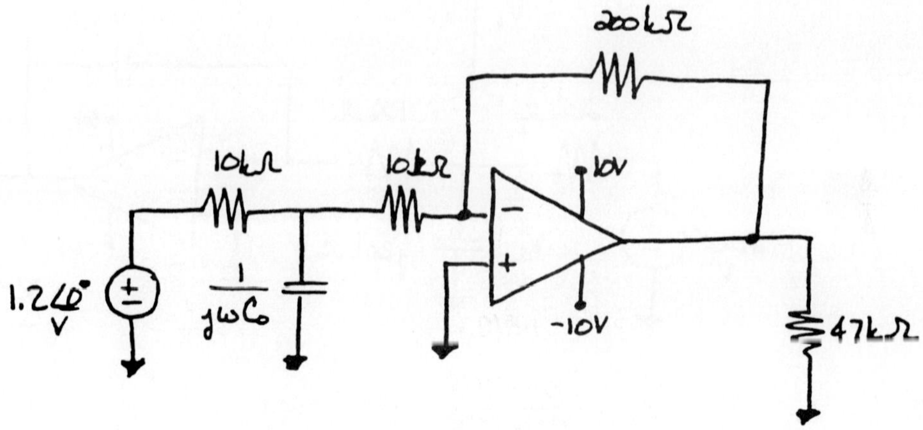

$$\frac{\mathbf{V}_a-1.2\underline{/0^\circ}}{10{,}000}+j\omega C_o\mathbf{V}_a+\frac{\mathbf{V}_a}{10{,}000}=0$$

$$\mathbf{V}_a=\frac{1.2}{2+j10^4\omega C_o}$$

$\mathbf{V}_o=-20\mathbf{V}_a$ (see solution to Prob. 9.73)

$$\mathbf{V}_o=\frac{-24}{2+j10^6C_o}=\frac{24\underline{/180^\circ}}{2+j10^6C_o}$$

$\therefore$ denominator angle $=60^\circ$

$$\tan 60^\circ=\sqrt{3}$$

$$\frac{10^6C_o}{2}=\sqrt{3}$$

$$\text{or } C_o=\frac{2\sqrt{3}}{10^6}=2\sqrt{3}\,\mu\text{F}=3.46\,\mu\text{F}$$

[b]

$$\mathbf{V}_o=\frac{24\underline{/180^\circ}}{2+j2\sqrt{3}}=6\underline{/120^\circ}\text{ V}$$

$$v_o=6\cos(100t+120^\circ)\text{ V}$$

P 9.75

$$\frac{1}{j\omega C_1} = \frac{10^{12}}{j10^6(100)} = -j10\,\text{k}\Omega$$

$$\frac{1}{j\omega C_2} = \frac{10^{12}}{j(10^6)(50)} = -j20\,\text{k}\Omega$$

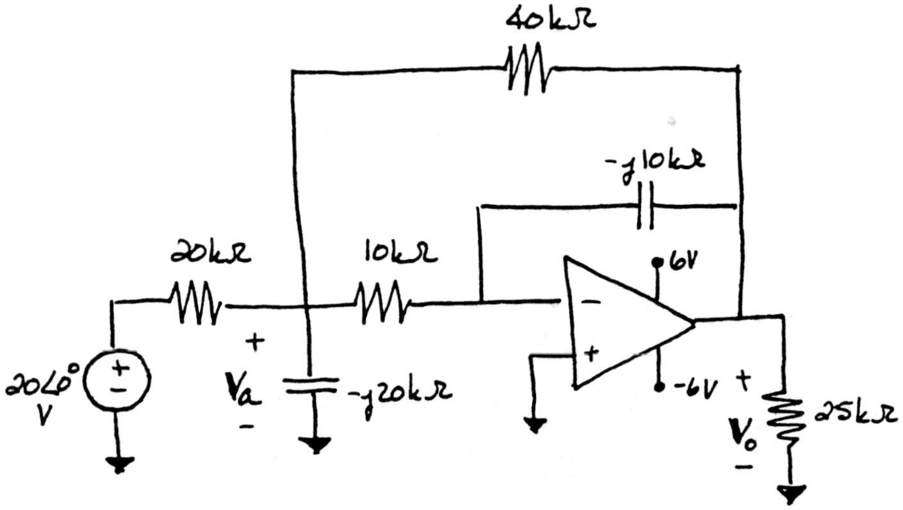

$$\frac{\mathbf{V_a}}{-j20} + \frac{\mathbf{V_a} - 20}{20} + \frac{\mathbf{V_a} - \mathbf{V_o}}{40} + \frac{\mathbf{V_a}}{10} = 0$$

$$\therefore \quad (7 + j2)\mathbf{V_a} - \mathbf{V_o} = 40$$

$$\frac{0 - \mathbf{V_a}}{10} + \frac{0 - \mathbf{V_o}}{-j10} = 0; \qquad \therefore \quad \mathbf{V_a} = -j\mathbf{V_o}$$

$$\therefore \quad (1 - j7)\mathbf{V_o} = 40$$

$$\mathbf{V_o} = \frac{40}{1 - j7} = 0.8 + j5.6 = 5.66\underline{/81.87^\circ}\ \text{V}$$

$$v_o(t) = 5.66\cos(10^6t + 81.87^\circ)\ \text{V}$$

P 9.76 [a]

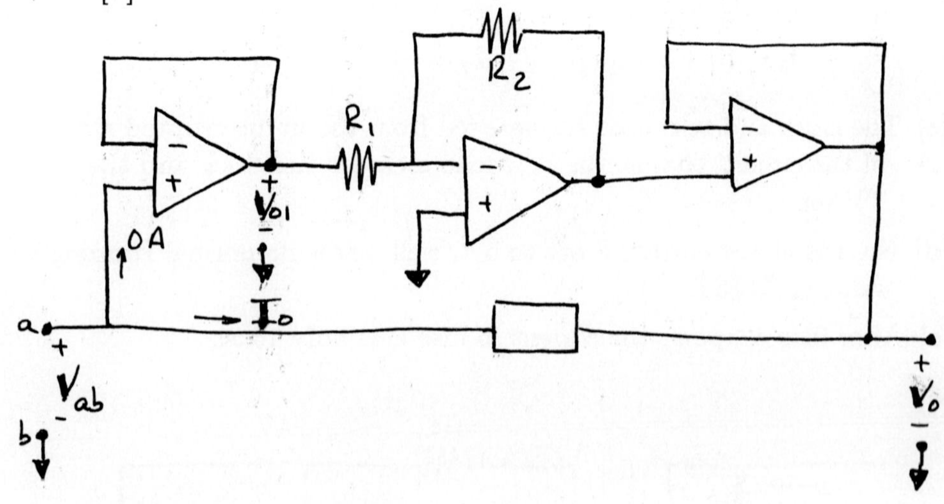

Because the op-amps are ideal $\mathbf{I}_{\text{in}} = \mathbf{I}_o$, thus

$$Z_{\text{ab}} = \frac{\mathbf{V}_{\text{ab}}}{\mathbf{I}_{\text{in}}} = \frac{\mathbf{V}_{\text{ab}}}{\mathbf{I}_o}; \qquad \mathbf{I}_o = \frac{\mathbf{V}_{\text{ab}} - \mathbf{V}_o}{Z}$$

$$\mathbf{V}_{o1} = \mathbf{V}_{\text{ab}}; \qquad \mathbf{V}_{o2} = -\left(\frac{R_2}{R_1}\right)\mathbf{V}_{o1} = -K\mathbf{V}_{o1} = -K\mathbf{V}_{\text{ab}}$$

$$\mathbf{V}_o = \mathbf{V}_{o2} = -K\mathbf{V}_{\text{ab}}$$

$$\therefore \ \mathbf{I}_o = \frac{\mathbf{V}_{\text{ab}} - (-K\mathbf{V}_{\text{ab}})}{Z} = \frac{(1+K)\mathbf{V}_{\text{ab}}}{Z}$$

$$\therefore \ Z_{\text{ab}} = \frac{\mathbf{V}_{\text{ab}}}{(1+K)\mathbf{V}_{\text{ab}}}Z = \frac{Z}{(1+K)}$$

[b] $$Z = \frac{1}{j\omega C}; \qquad Z_{\text{ab}} = \frac{1}{j\omega C(1+K)}; \qquad \therefore \ C_{\text{ab}} = C(1+K)$$

P 9.77 [a] $$\mathbf{I}_1 = \frac{120}{24} + \frac{240}{8.4 + j6} = 23.29 - j13.71 = 27.02\underline{/-30.5^\circ}\text{ A}$$

$$\mathbf{I}_2 = \frac{120}{12} - \frac{120}{24} = 5\underline{/0^\circ}\text{ A}$$

$$\mathbf{I}_3 = \frac{120}{12} + \frac{240}{8.4 + j6} = 28.29 - j13.71 = 31.44\underline{/-25.87^\circ}\text{ A}$$

$$\mathbf{I}_4 = \frac{120}{24} = 5\underline{/0^\circ}\text{ A}; \qquad \mathbf{I}_5 = \frac{120}{12} = 10\underline{/0^\circ}\text{ A}$$

$$\mathbf{I}_6 = \frac{240}{8.4 + j6.3} = 18.29 - j13.71 = 22.86\underline{/-36.87^\circ}\text{ A}$$

$$\mathbf{I}_1 = 0 \qquad \mathbf{I}_3 = 15\,\text{A} \qquad \mathbf{I}_5 = 10\,\text{A}$$

$$\mathbf{I}_2 = 10 + 5 = 15\,\text{A} \qquad \mathbf{I}_4 = -5\,\text{A} \qquad \mathbf{I}_6 = 5\,\text{A}$$

[c] The clock and television set were fed from the uninterrupted side of the circuit, that is, the 12 Ω load includes the clock and the TV set.

[d] No, the motor current drops to 5 A, well below its normal running value of 22.86 A.

[e] After fuse A opens, the current in fuse B is only 15 A.

P 9.78 [a]

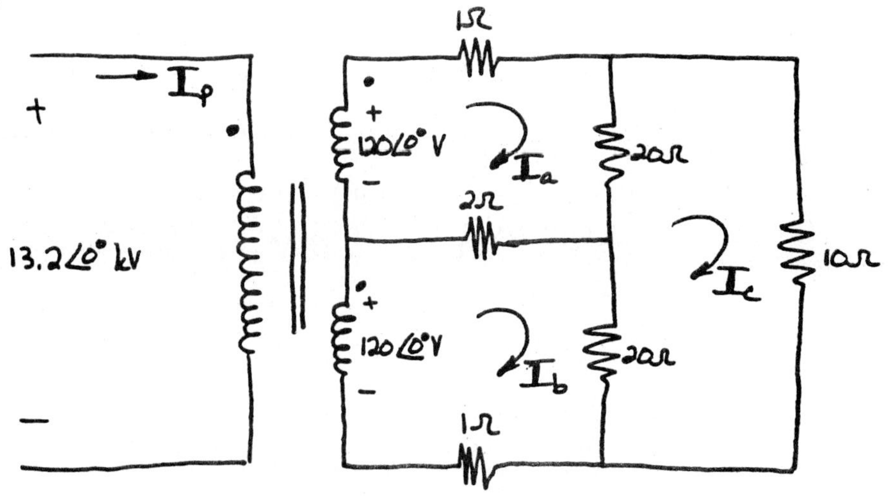

The three mesh current equations are

$$120\underline{/0^\circ} = 23\mathbf{I}_a - 2\mathbf{I}_b - 20\mathbf{I}_c$$

$$120\underline{/0^\circ} = -2\mathbf{I}_a + 23\mathbf{I}_b - 20\mathbf{I}_c$$

$$0 = -20\mathbf{I}_a - 20\mathbf{I}_b + 50\mathbf{I}_c$$

Solving,

$$\mathbf{I}_a = 24\underline{/0^\circ}\,\text{A}; \qquad \mathbf{I}_c = 24\underline{/0^\circ}\,\text{A}; \qquad \mathbf{I}_c = 19.2\underline{/0^\circ}\,\text{A}$$

$$\therefore \quad \mathbf{I}_2 = \mathbf{I}_a - \mathbf{I}_b = 0\,\text{A}$$

[b]

$$\mathbf{I}_p = \frac{N_2}{N_1}(\mathbf{I}_1 + \mathbf{I}_3) = \frac{N_2}{N_1}(\mathbf{I}_a + \mathbf{I}_b$$

$$= \frac{1}{110}(24 + 24) = 0.436\,\text{A}$$

[c] When the two loads are equal, more current is drawn from the primary.

P 9.79 [a]

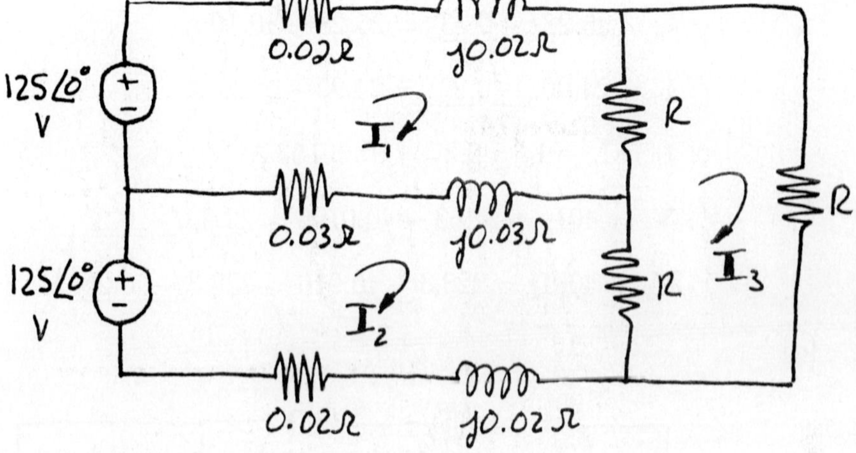

$$125 = (R + 0.05 + j0.05)\mathbf{I}_1 - (0.03 + j0.03)\mathbf{I}_2 - R\mathbf{I}_3$$

$$125 = -(0.03 + j0.03)\mathbf{I}_1 + (R + 0.05 + j0.05)\mathbf{I}_2 - R\mathbf{I}_3$$

Subtracting the above two equations gives

$$0 = (R + 0.08 + j0.08)\mathbf{I}_1 - R(0.08 + j0.08)\mathbf{I}_2$$

$$\therefore \quad \mathbf{I}_1 = \mathbf{I}_2 \quad \text{so} \quad \mathbf{I}_n = \mathbf{I}_1 - \mathbf{I}_2 = 0\text{ A}$$

[b] $\mathbf{V}_1 = R(\mathbf{I}_1 - \mathbf{I}_3);\qquad \mathbf{V}_2 = R(\mathbf{I}_2 - \mathbf{I}_3)$

Since $\mathbf{I}_1 = \mathbf{I}_2$ (from part [a]) $\mathbf{V}_1 = \mathbf{V}_2$

[c]

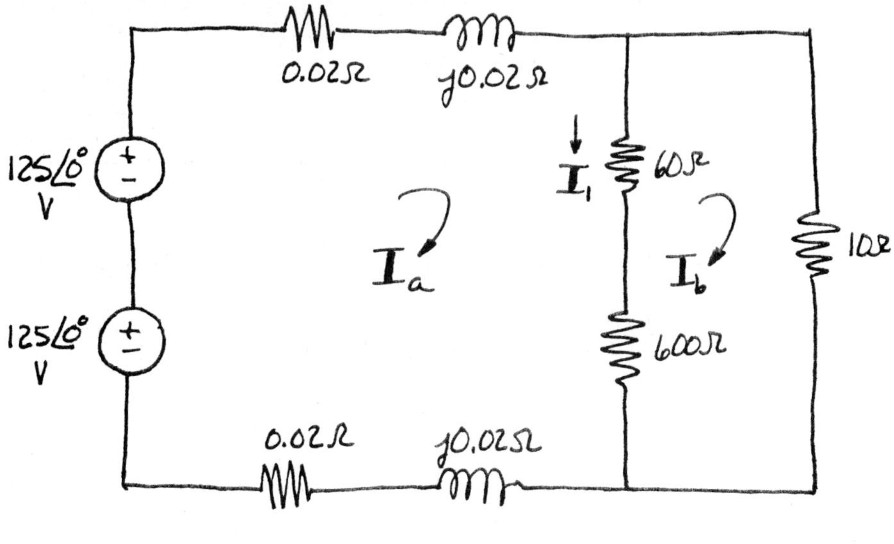

$$250 = (660.04 + j0.04)\mathbf{I}_a - 660\mathbf{I}_b$$

$$0 = -660\mathbf{I}_a + 668\mathbf{I}_b$$

Solving,

$$\mathbf{I}_a = 25.28\underline{/-0.23^\circ} = 25.28 - j0.10 \text{ A}$$

$$\mathbf{I}_b = 24.90\underline{/-0.23^\circ} = 24.90 - j0.10 \text{ A}$$

$$\mathbf{I}_1 = \mathbf{I}_a - \mathbf{I}_b = 0.37 - j0.00153 \text{ A}$$

$$\mathbf{V}_1 = 40\mathbf{I}_1 = 22.63 - j0.0196 = 22.63\underline{/-0.23^\circ} \text{ V}$$

$$\mathbf{V}_2 = 400\mathbf{I}_1 = 226.3 - j0.916 = 226.3\underline{/-0.23^\circ} \text{ V}$$

[d]

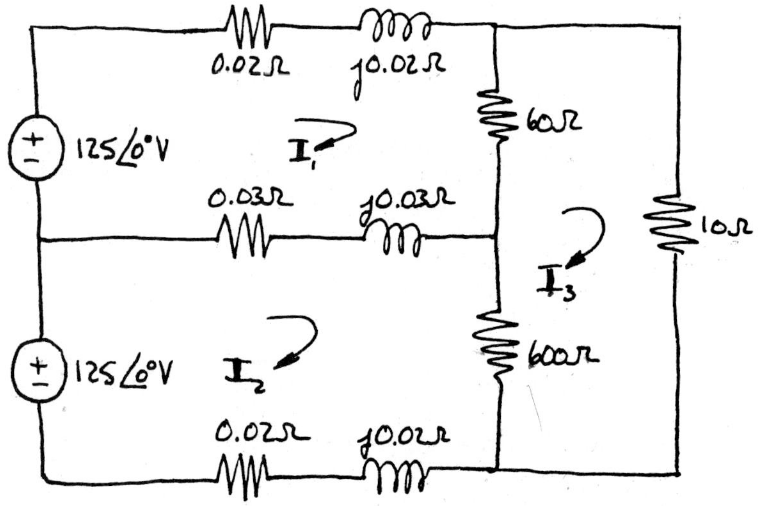

$$125 = (60.05 + j0.05)\mathbf{I}_1 - (0.03 + j0.03)\mathbf{I}_2 - 60\mathbf{I}_3$$

$$125 = -(0.03 + j0.03)\mathbf{I}_1 + (400.05 + j0.05)\mathbf{I}_2 - 600\mathbf{I}_3$$

$$0 = -60\mathbf{I}_1 - 600\mathbf{I}_2 + 668\mathbf{I}_3$$

Solving,

$$\mathbf{I}_1 = 26.97\underline{/-0.24^\circ} = 26.97 - j0.113 \text{ A}$$

$$\mathbf{I}_2 = 25.10\underline{/-0.24^\circ} = 25,10 - j0.104 \text{ A}$$

$$\mathbf{I}_3 = 24.90\underline{/-0.24^\circ} = 24.90 - j0.104 \text{ A}$$

$$\mathbf{V}_1 = 40(\mathbf{I}_1 - \mathbf{I}_3) = 124.4\underline{/-0.27^\circ} \text{ V}$$

$$\mathbf{V}_2 = 400(\mathbf{I}_2 - \mathbf{I}_3) = 124.6\underline{/-0.20^\circ} \text{ V}$$

[e] Because an open neutral can result in severely unbalanced voltages across the 125 V loads.

P 9.80 [a] Let N_1 = primary winding turns and $2N_2$ = secondary winding turns. Then

$$\frac{14{,}000}{N_1} = \frac{250}{2N_2}; \qquad \therefore \quad \frac{N_2}{N_1} = \frac{1}{112} = a$$

In part c),

$$\mathbf{I}_p = 2a\mathbf{I}_a$$

$$\therefore \; \mathbf{I}_p = \frac{2N_2\mathbf{I}_a}{N_1} = \tfrac{1}{56}\mathbf{I}_a$$

$$= \frac{1}{56}(25.28 - j0.10)$$

$$\mathbf{I}_p = 451.4 - j1.8\,\text{mA}$$

In part d),

$$\mathbf{I}_p N_1 = \mathbf{I}_1 N_2 + \mathbf{I}_2 N_2$$

$$\therefore \; \mathbf{I}_p = \frac{N_2}{N_1}(\mathbf{I}_1 + \mathbf{I}_2)$$

$$= \frac{1}{112}(26.97 - j0.11 + 25.10 - j0.10)$$

$$= \frac{1}{112}(52.07 - j0.22)$$

$$\mathbf{I}_p = 464.9 - j1.9\,\text{mA}$$

[b] Yes, because the neutral consudtor carries non-zero current whenever the load is not balanced.

10

Sinusoidal Steady State Power Calculations

Drill Exercises

DE 10.1 [a] $\mathbf{V} = 100\underline{/-45^\circ}$ V, $\quad \mathbf{I} = 20\underline{/15^\circ}$ A

Therefore

$$P = \frac{1}{2}(100)(20)\cos[-45 - (15)] = 500\,\text{W}, \qquad \text{A} \rightarrow \text{B}$$

$$Q = 1000\sin -60^\circ = -866.03\ \text{VAR}, \qquad \text{B} \rightarrow \text{A}$$

[b] $\mathbf{V} = 100\underline{/-45^\circ}$, $\quad \mathbf{I} = 20\underline{/165^\circ}$

$$P = 1000\cos(-210^\circ) = -866.03\,\text{W}, \qquad \text{B} \rightarrow \text{A}$$

$$Q = 1000\sin(-210^\circ) = 500\ \text{VAR}, \qquad \text{A} \rightarrow \text{B}$$

[c] $\mathbf{V} = 106\underline{/-45^\circ}$, $\quad \mathbf{I} = 20\underline{/-105^\circ}$

$$P = 1000\cos(60^\circ) = 500\,\text{W}, \qquad \text{A} \rightarrow \text{B}$$

$$Q = 1000\sin(60^\circ) = 866.03\ \text{VAR}, \qquad \text{A} \rightarrow \text{B}$$

[d] $P = 1000\cos(-120^\circ) = -500\,\text{W}, \qquad \text{B} \rightarrow \text{A}$

$$Q = 1000\sin(-120^\circ) = -866.03\ \text{VAR}, \qquad \text{B} \rightarrow \text{A}$$

DE 10.2 $p_f = \cos(\theta_v - \theta_i) = \cos[15 - (75)] = \cos -60^\circ = 0.5$ lagging

$$r_f = \sin(\theta_v - \theta_i) = \sin -60^\circ = -0.866$$

DE 10.3 [a] hair dryer = 600 W vacuum = 630 W

sun lamp = 279 W air conditioner = 800 W

television = 240 W $\sum P = 2549$ W

Therefore $I_{\text{eff}} = \frac{2549}{120} = 21.24$ A

Yes, the breaker will trip.

[b] $\sum P = 2549 - 909 = 1640$ W; $I_{\text{eff}} = \frac{1640}{120} = 13.67$ A

Yes, the breaker will not trip if the current is reduced to 13.67 A.

DE 10.4 [a] $I_{\text{eff}} = 40/115 \cong 0.35$ A; [b] $I_{\text{eff}} = 130/115 \cong 1.13$ A

DE 10.5 From Ex. 9.4 $I_{\text{eff}} = \frac{I_\rho}{\sqrt{3}} = \frac{0.18}{\sqrt{3}}$ A

$$P = I_{\text{eff}}^2 R = \left(\frac{0.0324}{3}\right)(5000) = 54\text{ W}$$

DE 10.6 [a] $Z = (39 + j26)\|(-j52) = 48 - j20 = 52\underline{/-22.62^\circ}\ \Omega$

Therefore $\mathbf{I}_\ell = \frac{250\underline{/0^\circ}}{48 - j20 + 1 + j4} = 4.85\underline{/18.08^\circ}$ A(rms)

$$\mathbf{V}_L = Z\mathbf{I}_\ell = (52\underline{/-22.62^\circ})(4.85\underline{/18.08^\circ}) = 252.20\underline{/-4.54^\circ}\text{ V(rms)}$$

$$\mathbf{I}_L = \frac{\mathbf{V}_L}{39 + j26} = 5.38\underline{/-38.23^\circ}\text{ A(rms)}$$

[b] $S_L = (252.20\underline{/-4.54^\circ})(5.38\underline{/+38.23^\circ}) = 1357\underline{/33.69^\circ}$

$= (1129.09 - j752.73)$ VA

$P_L = 1129.09$ W; $Q_L = 752.73$ VAR

[c] $P_\ell = |\mathbf{I}_\ell|^2 1 = (4.85)^2 \cdot 1 = 23.52$ W; $Q_\ell = |\mathbf{I}_\ell|^2 4 = 94.09$ VAR

[d] $S_g(\text{delivering}) = 250\mathbf{I}_\ell^* = (1152.62 - j376.36)$ VA

Therefore the source is delivering 1152.62 W and absorbing 376.36 magnetizing VAR.

[e] $Q_{\text{cap}} = \frac{|\mathbf{V}_L|^2}{-52} = \frac{(252.20)^2}{-52} = -1223.18$ VAR

Therefore the capacitor is delivering 1223.18 magnetizing VAR.

Check: $94.09 + 752.73 + 376.36 = 1223.18$ VAR and

$1129.09 + 23.52 = 1152.62$ W

DE 10.7 Series circuit derivation:

$250\mathbf{I}^* = (40{,}000 - j30{,}000)$

Therefore $\mathbf{I}^* = 160 - j120 = 200\underline{/-36.87^\circ}$ A(rms)

$\mathbf{I} = 200\underline{/36.87^\circ}$ A(rms)

$$Z = \frac{250}{200\underline{/36.87^\circ}} = 1.25\underline{/-36.87^\circ} = (1 - j0.75)\,\Omega$$

Therefore $R = 1\,\Omega$, $X_L = 0.75\,\Omega$

Parallel circuit derivation:

$$P = \frac{(250)^2}{R}; \qquad \text{therefore} \quad R = \frac{(250)^2}{40{,}000} = 1.5625\,\Omega$$

$$Q = \frac{(250)^2}{X_L}; \qquad \text{therefore} \quad X_L = \frac{(250)^2}{-30{,}000} = -2.083\,\Omega$$

DE 10.8 $S_1 = 15{,}000(0.6) + j15{,}000(0.8) = 9000 + j12{,}000$ VA

$S_2 = 6000(0.8) + j6000(0.6) = 4800 - j3600$ VA

$S_T = S_1 + S_2 = 13{,}800 + j8400$ VA

$S_T = 200\mathbf{I}^*$; therefore $\mathbf{I}^* = 69 + j42$ $\quad \mathbf{I} = 69 - j42$ A

$\mathbf{V}_s = 200 + j\mathbf{I} = 200 + j69 + 42 = 242 + j69 = 251.64\underline{/15.91^\circ}$ V(rms)

DE 10.9 [a] The phasor domain equivalent circuit and the Thévenin equivalent are shown below:
Phasor domain equivalent circuit:

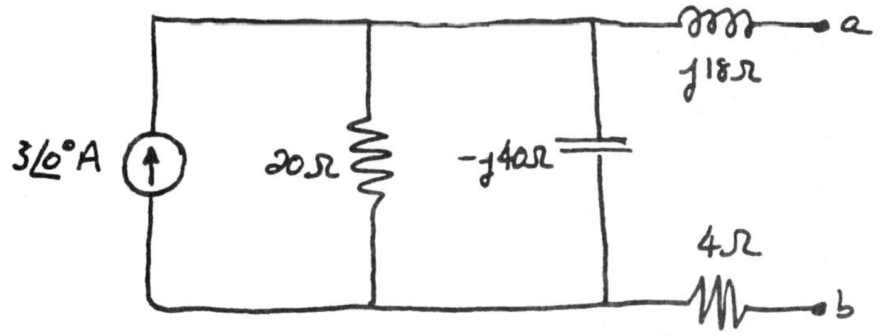

Thévenin equivalent:

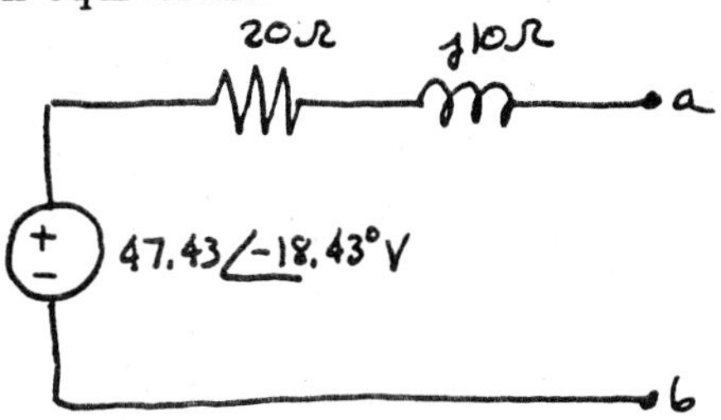

$$\mathbf{V}_{\text{Th}} = 3\frac{-j800}{20 - j40} = 48 - j24 = 53.67\underline{/-26.57^\circ}\text{ V}$$

$$Z_{\text{Th}} = 4 + j18 + \frac{-j800}{20 - j40} = 20 + j10 = 22.36\underline{/26.57^\circ}\,\Omega$$

For maximum power transfer, $Z_{\text{L}} = (20 - j10)\,\Omega$

[b] $\mathbf{I} = \dfrac{53.67\underline{/-26.57^\circ}}{40} = 1.34\underline{/-26.57^\circ}\text{ A}$

Therefore $P = \left(\dfrac{1.34}{\sqrt{2}}\right)^2 20 = 17.96\text{ W}$

[c] $R_{\text{L}} = |Z_{\text{Th}}| = 22.36\,\Omega$

[d] $\mathbf{I} = \dfrac{53.67\underline{/-26.57^\circ}}{42.36 + j10} = 1.23\underline{/-39.85^\circ}\text{ A}$

Therefore $P = \left(\dfrac{1.23}{\sqrt{2}}\right)^2 (22.36) = 16.91\text{ W}$

DE 10.10 [a] $V_{\text{Th}} = 210\text{ V}$; $\quad \mathbf{V}_2 = \dfrac{1}{4}\mathbf{V}_1$; $\quad \mathbf{I}_1 = \dfrac{1}{4}\mathbf{I}_2$

Short circuit equations:

$840 = 80\mathbf{I}_1 - 20\mathbf{I}_2 + \mathbf{V}_1$

$0 = 20(\mathbf{I}_2 - \mathbf{I}_1) - \mathbf{V}_2$

$\therefore\ \mathbf{I}_2 = 14\text{ A}$; $\quad R_{\text{Th}} = \dfrac{210}{14} = 15\,\Omega$

[b] $P_{\text{max}} = \left(\dfrac{210}{30}\right)^2 15 = 735\text{ W}$

DE 10.11 [a] $\mathbf{V}_{\text{Th}} = -4(146\underline{/0^\circ}) = -584\underline{/0^\circ}\text{ V(rms)}$

$\mathbf{V}_2 = 4\mathbf{V}_1$; $\quad \mathbf{I}_1 = -4\mathbf{I}_2$

Short circuit equations:

$146\underline{/0^\circ} = 80\mathbf{I}_1 - 20\mathbf{I}_2 + \mathbf{V}_1$

$$0 = 20(\mathbf{I}_2 - \mathbf{I}_1) - \mathbf{V}_2$$

$$\therefore \quad \mathbf{I}_2 = -146/365 = -0.40\text{ A}; \qquad R_{\text{Th}} = \frac{-584}{-0.4} = 1460\,\Omega$$

[b] $P = \left(\frac{-584}{2920}\right)^2 1460 = 58.40\text{ W}$

DE 10.12 [a]

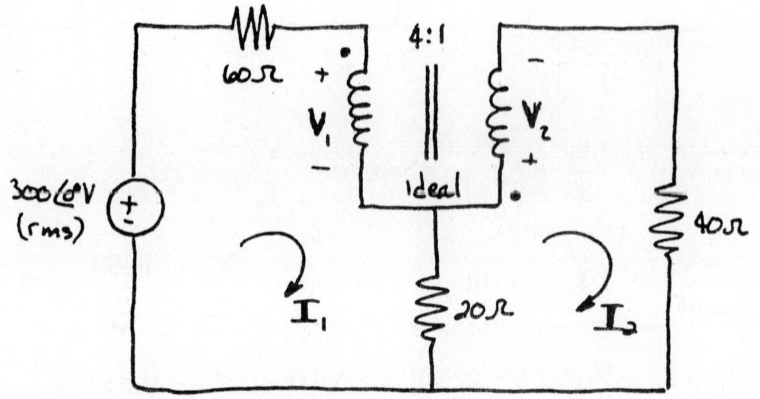

$$300 = 60\mathbf{I}_1 + \mathbf{V}_1 + 20(\mathbf{I}_1 - \mathbf{I}_2)$$

$$0 = 20(\mathbf{I}_2 - \mathbf{I}_1) + \mathbf{V}_2 + 40\mathbf{I}_2$$

$$\mathbf{V}_2 = \frac{1}{4}\mathbf{V}_1; \qquad \mathbf{I}_2 = -4\mathbf{I}_1$$

Solving,

$$\mathbf{V}_1 = 260\text{ V(rms)}; \qquad \mathbf{V}_2 = 65\text{ V(rms)}$$

$$\mathbf{I}_1 = 0.25\text{ A(rms)}; \qquad \mathbf{I}_2 = -1.0\text{ A(rms)}$$

$$\mathbf{V}_{5\text{A}} = \mathbf{V}_1 + 20(\mathbf{I}_1 - \mathbf{I}_2) = 285\text{ V(rms)}$$

$$\therefore \quad P = -(285)(5) = -1425\text{ W}$$

Thus 1425 W is delivered by the current source to the circuit.

[b] $\mathbf{I}_{20\Omega} = \mathbf{I}_1 - \mathbf{I}_2 = 1.25\text{ A(rms)}$

$$\therefore \quad P_{20\Omega} = (1.25)^2(20) = 31.25\text{ W}$$

DE 10.13

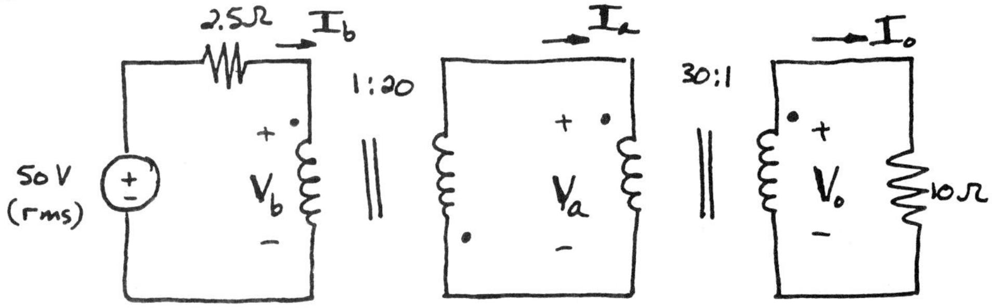

$$30\mathbf{V}_o = \mathbf{V}_a; \qquad \frac{\mathbf{I}_o}{30} = \mathbf{I}_a; \qquad \text{therefore} \quad \frac{\mathbf{V}_a}{\mathbf{I}_a} = 9\,\text{k}\Omega$$

$$\frac{\mathbf{V}_b}{1} = \frac{-\mathbf{V}_a}{20}; \qquad \mathbf{I}_b = -20\mathbf{I}_a; \qquad \text{therefore} \quad \frac{\mathbf{V}_b}{\mathbf{I}_b} = \frac{9000}{400} = 22.5\,\Omega$$

Therefore $\mathbf{I}_b = [50/(2.5 + 22.5)] = 2\,\text{A}$ (rms); since the ideal transformers are lossless, $P_{10\Omega} = P_{22.5\Omega}$, and the power delivered to the 22.5 Ω resistor is $2^2(22.5)$ or 90 W.

DE 10.14 [a] $\dfrac{\mathbf{V}_b}{\mathbf{I}_b} = \dfrac{a^2 10}{400} = 2.5\,\Omega;$ therefore $a^2 = 100,$ $a = 10$

[b] $\mathbf{I}_b = \dfrac{50}{5} = 10\,\text{A};$ $P = (100)(2.5) = 250\,\text{W}$

DE 10.15 From Drill Exercise 9.20,

$$V_g = 25\underline{/0^\circ}\,\text{kV(rms)}; \qquad \mathbf{I}_1 = 4 + j3 = 5\underline{/36.87^\circ}\,\text{A(rms)}$$

and $\mathbf{I}_2 = 125\underline{/216.87^\circ}\,\text{A(rms)}$

$$\therefore \quad S_g = -\mathbf{V}_g\mathbf{I}_1^* = -100{,}000 + j75{,}000\,\text{VA}$$

Therefore $\mathbf{V}_g$ is delivering 100 kW and absorbing 75 kVAR.
Primary circuit:

$$P_{1.5k\Omega} = (5)^2(1500) = 37.5\,\text{kW absorbing}$$

$$Q_{6k\Omega} = (5)^2(6000) = 150\,\text{kVAR absorbing}$$

Secondary circuit:

$$P_{4\Omega} = (125)^2(4) = 62.5\,\text{kW absorbing}$$

$$Q_{-14.4} = (125)^2(-14.4) = -225\,\text{kVAR delivering}$$

Therefore,

$$\sum P = 37.5 + 62.5 = 100\,\text{W absorbing}$$

$$\sum Q = 150 - 225 = -75\,\text{kVAR delivering}$$

Thus, $\mathbf{V}_g$ is delivering 100 kW and absorbing 75 kVAR of magnetizing VAR. The transformer is absorbing 100 kW and delivering 75 kVAR.

Problems

P 10.1 [a] $P = \frac{1}{2}(340)(20)\cos(60 - 15) = 2400\cos 45^\circ = 2404.16\,\text{W} \quad \text{(abs)}$

$Q = 2400\sin 45^\circ = 2404.16\,\text{VAR} \quad \text{(abs)}$

[b] $P = \frac{1}{2}(16)(75)\cos(-15 - 60) = 600\cos(-75^\circ) = 155.29\,\text{W} \quad \text{(abs)}$

$Q = 600\sin(-75^\circ) = -579.56\,\text{VAR} \quad \text{(del)}$

[c] $P = \frac{1}{2}(625)(4)\cos(40 - 150) = 1250\cos(-110^\circ) = -427.53\,\text{W} \quad \text{(del)}$

$Q = 1250\sin(-110^\circ) = -1174.62\,\text{VAR} \quad \text{(del)}$

[d] $P = \frac{1}{2}(180)(10)\cos(130 - 20) = 900\cos(110^\circ) = -307.82\,\text{W} \quad \text{(del)}$

$Q = 900\sin(110^\circ) = 845.72\,\text{VAR} \quad \text{(abs)}$

P 10.2 $p = P + P\cos 2\omega t - Q\sin 2\omega t; \qquad \frac{dp}{dt} = -2\omega P\sin 2\omega t - 2\omega Q\cos 2\omega t$

$$\frac{dp}{dt} = 0 \quad \text{when} \quad -2\omega P\sin 2\omega t = 2\omega Q\cos 2\omega t \quad \text{or} \quad \tan 2\omega t = -\frac{Q}{P}$$

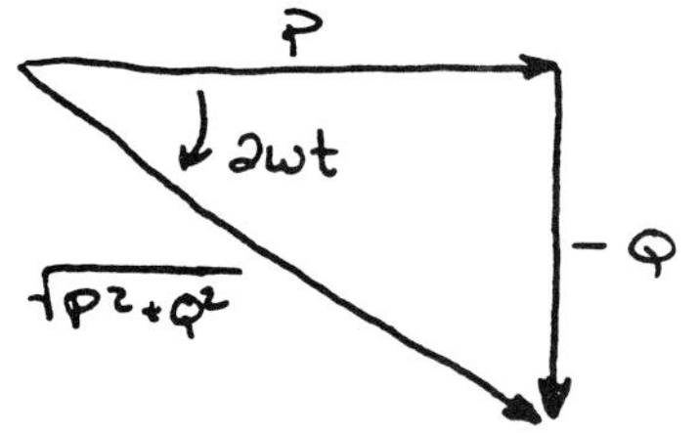

$$\cos 2\omega t = \frac{P}{\sqrt{P^2+Q^2}}; \qquad \sin 2\omega t = -\frac{Q}{\sqrt{P^2+Q^2}}$$

Let $\theta = \tan^{-1}(-Q/P)$, then p is maximum when $2\omega t = \theta$ and p is minimum when $2\omega t = (\theta + \pi)$.

Therefore $p_{\text{max}} = P + P \cdot \dfrac{P}{\sqrt{P^2+Q^2}} - \dfrac{Q(-Q)}{\sqrt{P^2+Q^2}} = P + \sqrt{P^2+Q^2}$

and $p_{\text{min}} = P - P \cdot \dfrac{P}{\sqrt{P^2+Q^2}} - Q \cdot \dfrac{Q}{\sqrt{P^2+Q^2}} = P - \sqrt{P^2+Q^2}$

P 10.3 $W_{\text{dc}} = \dfrac{V_{\text{dc}}^2}{R}T; \qquad W_s = \displaystyle\int_{t_o}^{t_o+T} \frac{v_s^2}{R}\,dt$

$$\therefore \quad \frac{V_{\text{dc}}^2}{R}T = \int_{t_o}^{t_o+T} \frac{v_s^2}{R}\,dt$$

$$V_{\text{dc}}^2 = \frac{1}{T}\int_{t_o}^{t_o+T} v_s^2\,dt$$

$$V_{\text{dc}} = \sqrt{\frac{1}{T}\int_{t_o}^{t_o+T} v_s^2\,dt} = V_{\text{rms}} = V_{\text{eff}}$$

P 10.4 [a] Area under on cycle of v_g^2:

$$A = (400)(4)(20 \times 10^{-6}) + 10{,}000(2)(20 \times 10^{-6})$$
$$= 21{,}600(20 \times 10^{-6})$$

Mean value of v_g^2:

$$\text{M.V.} = \frac{A}{120 \times 10^{-6}} = \frac{21{,}600(20 \times 10^{-6})}{120 \times 10^{-6}} = 3600$$

$$\therefore \quad V_{\text{rms}} = \sqrt{3600} = 60\,\text{V(rms)}$$

[b] $P = \frac{V_{\text{rms}}^2}{R} = \frac{3600}{12} = 300\,\text{W}$

P 10.5 $i(t) = \frac{30}{40} \times 10^3 t = 750t \qquad 0 \le t \le 40\,\text{ms}$

$$i(t) = M - \frac{30}{10} \times 10^3 t \qquad 40\,\text{ms} \le t \le 50\,\text{ms}$$

$$i(t) = 0 \text{ when } t = 50\,\text{ms}$$

$$\therefore \quad M = 3000(50 \times 10^{-3}) = 150$$

$$i(t) = 150 - 3000t \qquad 40\,\text{ms} \le t \le 50\,\text{ms}$$

$$\therefore \quad I_{\text{rms}} = \sqrt{\frac{1000}{50}\left\{\int_0^{0.04} (750)^2 t^2\,dt + \int_{0.04}^{0.05} (150 - 3000t)^2\,dt\right\}}$$

$$\int_0^{0.04} (750)^2 t^2\,dt = (750)^2 \frac{t^3}{3}\Big|_0^{0.04} = 12$$

$$(150 - 3000t)^2 = 22{,}500 - 9 \times 10^5 t + 9 \times 10^6 t^2$$

$$\int_{0.04}^{0.05} 22{,}500\,dt = 225$$

$$\int_{0.04}^{0.05} 9 \times 10^5 t\,dt = 45 \times 10^4 t^2 \Big|_{0.04}^{0.05} = 405$$

$$9 \times 10^6 \int_{0.04}^{0.05} t^2\,dt = 3 \times 10^6 t^3 \Big|_{0.04}^{0.05} = 183$$

$$\therefore \quad I_{\text{rms}} = \sqrt{20\{12 + (225 - 405 + 183)\}} = \sqrt{300} = 17.32\,\text{A}$$

P 10.6 $P = I_{\text{rms}}^2 R \qquad \therefore \quad R = \frac{24 \times 10^3}{300} = 80\,\Omega$

P 10.7 $\frac{1}{\omega C} = \frac{10^9}{(5000)(80)} = 2500\,\Omega$

$$Z_f = \frac{-j2500(7500)}{7500 - j2500} = 750 - j2250\,\Omega$$

$$Z_i = 1500\,\Omega$$

$$\therefore \quad \frac{Z_f}{Z_i} = \frac{750 - j2250}{1500} = 0.5 - j1.5$$

$$\mathbf{V}_o = -\frac{Z_f}{Z_i}\mathbf{V}_g; \qquad \mathbf{V}_g = 4\underline{/0^\circ}\,\text{V}$$

$$\mathbf{V}_o = (-0.5 + j1.5)(4) = -2 + j6 = 6.32\underline{/108.43^\circ}\,\text{V}$$

$$P = \frac{1}{2}\frac{V_m^2}{R} = \frac{1}{2}\frac{(4)(10)}{1000} = 20 \times 10^{-3} = 20\,\text{mW}$$

P 10.8 $\mathbf{I}_g = 30\underline{/0^\circ}\,\text{mA}$

$$j\omega L = j(100)(10) = j1000\,\Omega; \qquad \frac{1}{j\omega C} = \frac{10^6}{j(100)(2)} = -j5000\,\Omega$$

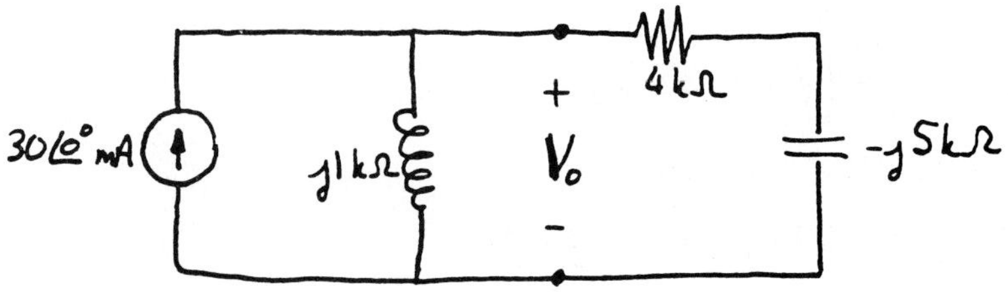

$$\mathbf{I}_o = \frac{30\underline{/0^\circ}(j1000)}{4000 - j4000} = 3.75\sqrt{2}\underline{/135^\circ}\,\text{mA}$$

$$P = |\mathbf{I}_o|^2_{\text{rms}}(4000) = (3.75)^2(4000) = 56.25\,\text{mW}$$

$$Q = |\mathbf{I}_o|^2_{\text{rms}}(-5000) = -70.3125\,\text{mVAR}$$

$$S = P + jQ = 56.25 - j70.3125\,\text{mVA}$$

$$|S| = 90.044\,\text{mVA}$$

P 10.9 $j\omega L = j10{,}000(10^{-3}) = j10\,\Omega; \qquad \frac{1}{j\omega C} = \frac{10^6}{j10{,}000(2.5)} = -j40\,\Omega$

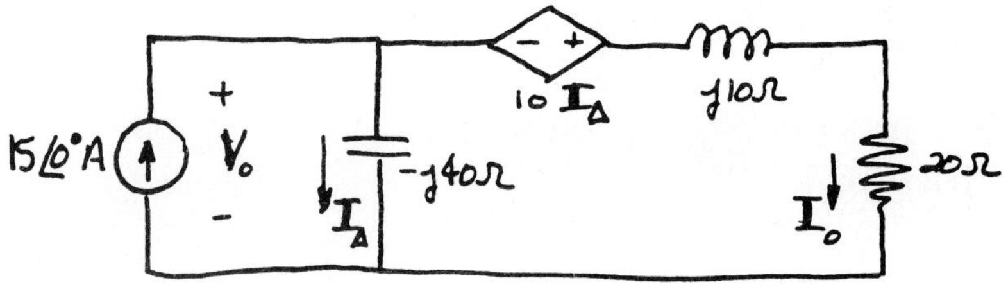

$$-15 + \frac{\mathbf{V}_o}{-j40} + \frac{\mathbf{V}_o - 10(\mathbf{V}_o/-j40)}{20 + j10} = 0$$

$$\therefore \quad \mathbf{V}_o \left[\frac{1}{-j40} + \frac{1 + j0.25}{20 + j10}\right] = 15$$

$$\therefore \quad \mathbf{V}_o = 300 - j100\,\text{V}$$

$$\therefore \quad \mathbf{I}_\Delta = \frac{\mathbf{V}_o}{-j40} = 2.5 + j7.5\,\text{A}$$

$$\mathbf{I}_o = 15\underline{/0^\circ} - \mathbf{I}_\Delta = 15 - 2.5 - j7.5 = 12.5 - j7.5 = 14.58\underline{/-30.9^\circ}\,\text{A}$$

$$P_{20\Omega} = \frac{1}{2}|\mathbf{I}_o|^2 20 = 2125\,\text{W}$$

P 10.10 [a] $Z_1 = 240 + j70 = 250\underline{/16.26^\circ}\,\Omega$

$$\text{pf} = \cos(16.26^\circ) = 0.96 \text{ lagging}$$

$$\text{rf} = \sin(16.26^\circ) = 0.28$$

$$Z_2 = 160 - j120 = 200\underline{/-36.87^\circ}\,\Omega$$

$$\text{pf} = \cos(-36.87^\circ) = 0.80 \text{ leading}$$

$$\text{rf} = \sin(-36.87^\circ) = -0.60$$

$$Z_3 = 30 - j40 = 50\underline{/-53.13^\circ}\,\Omega$$

$$\text{pf} = \cos(-53.13^\circ) = 0.6 \text{ leading}$$

$$\text{rf} = \sin(-53.13^\circ) = -0.8$$

[b] $Y = Y_1 + Y_2 + Y_3$

$$Y_1 = \frac{1}{250\underline{/16.26^\circ}}; \qquad Y_2 = \frac{1}{200\underline{/-36.87^\circ}}; \qquad Y_3 = \frac{1}{50\underline{/-53.13^\circ}}$$

$$Y = 19.84 + j17.88\,\text{m}\mho$$

$$Z = \frac{1}{Y} = 37.44\underline{/-42.03^\circ}\,\text{m}\Omega$$

$$\text{pf} = \cos(-42.03^\circ) = 0.74 \text{ leading}$$

$$\text{rf} = \sin(-42.03^\circ) = -0.67$$

P 10.11 [a]

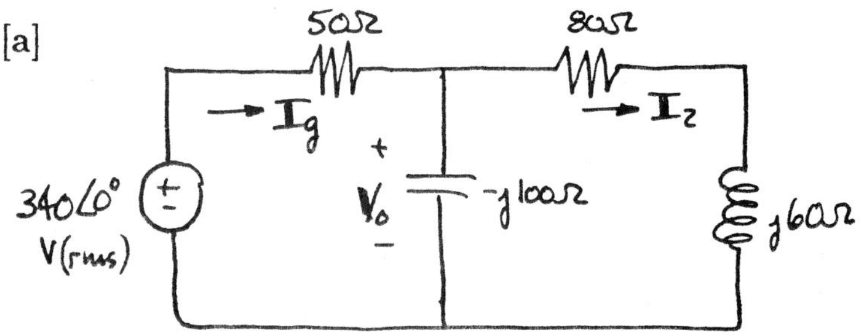

$$\frac{\mathbf{V}_o}{-j100} + \frac{\mathbf{V}_o - 340}{50} + \frac{\mathbf{V}_o}{80 + j60} = 0$$

$$\therefore \quad \mathbf{V}_o = 238 - j34\,\text{V}$$

$$\mathbf{I}_g = \frac{340 - 238 + j34}{50} = 2.04 + j0.68\,\text{A}$$

$$S_g = \mathbf{V}_g\mathbf{I}_g^* = (340)(2.04 - j0.68)$$

$$= 693.6 - j231.2\,\text{VA}$$

[b] Source is delivering 693.6 W.

[c] Source is absorbing 231.2 magnetizing VAR.

[d] $\mathbf{I}_1 = \dfrac{\mathbf{V}_o}{-j100} = 0.34 + j2.38\,\text{A}$

$$S_1 = \mathbf{V}_o\mathbf{I}_1^* = (238 - j34)(0.34 - j2.38)$$

$$= 0 - j578\,\text{VA}$$

$$\mathbf{I}_2 = \frac{\mathbf{V}_o}{80 + j60} = \frac{238 - j34}{80 + j60} = 1.7 - j1.7\,\text{A}$$

$$S_2 = \mathbf{V}_o\mathbf{I}_2^* = (238 - j34)(1.7 + j1.7)$$

$$= 462.4 + j346.8\,\text{VA}$$

$$S_{50\Omega} = |\mathbf{I}_g|^2(50) + j0 = (2.15)^2(50) = 231.2\,\text{W}$$

[e] $\sum P_{\text{del}} = 693.6\,\text{W}$

$$\sum P_{\text{diss}} = 462.4 + 231.2 = 693.6\,\text{W}$$

$$\therefore \quad \sum P_{\text{del}} = \sum P_{\text{diss}} = 693.6\,\text{W}$$

[f] $\sum Q_{\text{abs}} = 231.2 + 346.8 = 578\,\text{VAR}$

$$\sum Q_{\text{dev}} = 578\,\text{VAR}$$

$$\therefore \quad \sum \text{mag VAR dev} = \sum \text{mag VAR abs} = 578$$

P 10.12 $\mathbf{I}_g = 30\underline{/0^\circ}$ mA; $\quad \dfrac{1}{j\omega C} = \dfrac{10^6}{j(25\times 10^3)(40)} = -j1\,\Omega$

$$j\omega L = j(25\times 10^3)(40)\times 10^{-6} = j1\,\Omega$$

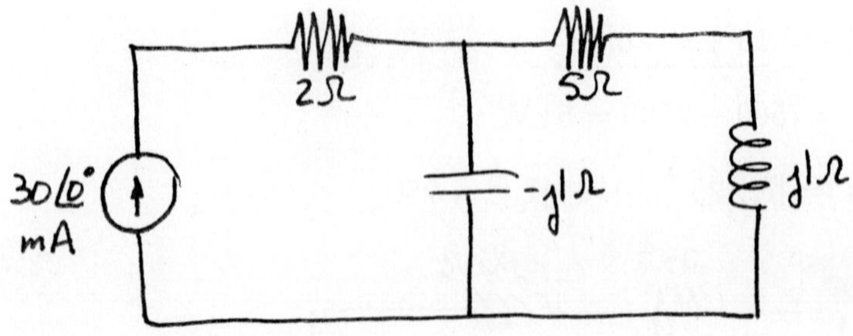

$$Z_1 = j1\|(5+j1) = 0.2 - j1\,\Omega$$

$$Z_{eq} = 2 + Z_1 = 2.2 - j1\,\Omega$$

$$P_g = |I_{rms}|^2\text{Re}\{Z_{eq}\} = \left(\frac{30}{\sqrt{2}}\times 10^{-3}\right)^2 (2.2) = 990\,\mu\text{W}$$

P 10.13 [a] $P = \dfrac{1}{2}\dfrac{(240)^2}{480} = 60$ W

$$-\frac{1}{\omega C} = \frac{-9\times 10^6}{(5000)(5)} = -360\,\Omega$$

$$Q = \frac{1}{2}\frac{(240)^2}{(-360)} = -80\text{ VAR}$$

$$p_{max} = P + \sqrt{P^2 + Q^2} = 60 + \sqrt{(60)^2 + (80)^2} = 160\text{ W(del)}$$

[b] $p_{min} = 60 - 100 = -40$ W(abs)

[c] $P = 60$ W

[d] $Q = -80$ VAR

[e] generate

[f] pf $= \cos(\theta_v - \theta_i)$

$$\mathbf{I} = \frac{240}{480} + \frac{240}{-j360} = 0.5 + j0.67 = 0.83\underline{/53.13^\circ}\text{ A}$$

$$\therefore\ \text{pf} = \cos(0 - 53.13^\circ) = 0.6\text{ leading}$$

[g] rf $= \sin(-53.13^\circ) = -0.8$

[f] pf $= \cos(\theta_v - \theta_i)$

$$\mathbf{I} = \frac{240}{480} + \frac{240}{-j360} = 0.5 + j0.67 = 0.83\underline{/53.13^\circ}\text{ A}$$

$\therefore$ pf $= \cos(0 - 53.13^\circ) = 0.6$ leading

[g] rf $= \sin(-53.13^\circ) = -0.8$

P 10.14 [a] line loss $= 7500 - 2500 = 5\,\text{kW}$

line loss $= |\mathbf{I}_g|^2 20 \quad \therefore \; |\mathbf{I}_g|^2 = 250$

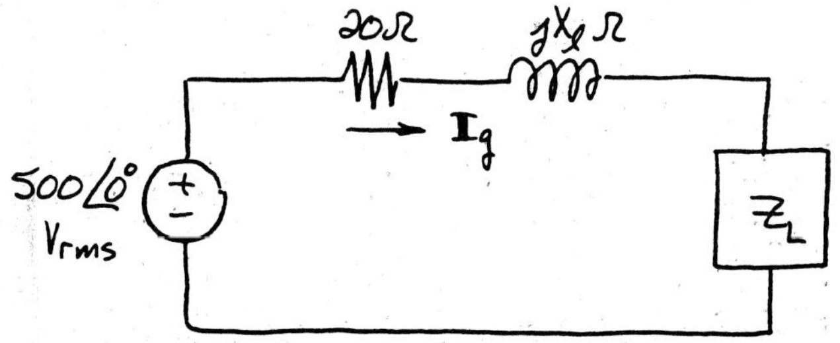

$|\mathbf{I}_g| = \sqrt{250}$ A

$|\mathbf{I}_g|^2 R_L = 2500 \quad \therefore \; R_L = 10\,\Omega$

$|\mathbf{I}_g|^2 X_L = -5000 \quad \therefore \; X_L = -20\,\Omega$

Thus,

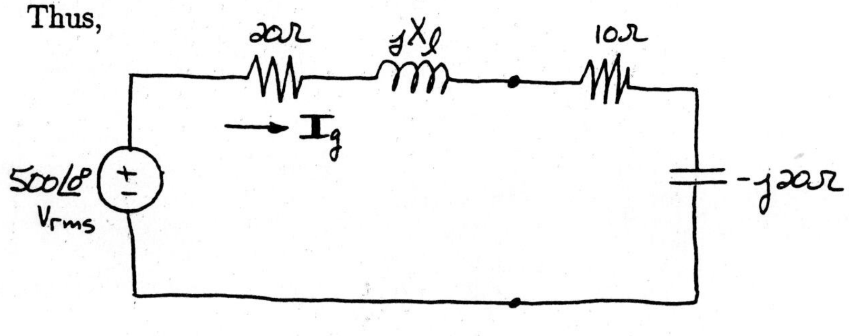

$|Z| = \sqrt{(30)^2 + (X_\ell - 20)^2} \qquad |\mathbf{I}_g| = \dfrac{500}{\sqrt{900 + (X_\ell - 20)^2}}$

$$\therefore \; 900 + (X_\ell - 20)^2 = \frac{25 \times 10^4}{250} = 1000$$

Solving, $(X_\ell - 20) = \pm 10.$

Thus, $X_\ell = 10\,\Omega$ or $X_\ell = 30\,\Omega$

[b] If $X_\ell = 30\,\Omega$:

$$\mathbf{I}_g = \frac{500}{30 + j10} = 15 - j5\,\text{A}$$

$$S_g = -500\mathbf{I}_g^* = -7500 - j2500\,\text{VA}$$

Thus, the voltage source is delivering 7500 W and 2500 magnetizing vars.

$$Q_{j30} = |\mathbf{I}_g|^2 X_\ell = 250(30) = 7500\,\text{VAR}$$

Therefore the line reactance is absorbing 7500 magnetizing vars.

$$Q_{-j20} = |\mathbf{I}_g|^2 X_\text{L} = 250(-20) = -5000\,\text{VAR}$$

Therefore the load reactance is generating 5000 magnetizing vars.

$$\sum Q_\text{gen} = 7500\,\text{VAR} = \sum Q_\text{abs}$$

If $X_\ell = 10\,\Omega$:

$$\mathbf{I}_g = \frac{500}{30 - j10} = 15 + j5\,\text{A}$$

$$S_g = -500\mathbf{I}_g^* = -7500 + j2500\,\text{VA}$$

Thus, the voltage source is delivering 7500 W and absorbing 2500 magnetizing vars.

$$Q_{j10} = |\mathbf{I}_g|^2(10) = 250(10) = 2500\,\text{VAR}$$

Therefore the line reactance is absorbing 2500 magnetizing vars. The load continues to generate 5000 magnetizing vars.

$$\sum Q_\text{gen} = 5000\,\text{VAR} = \sum Q_\text{abs}$$

P 10.15 **[a]** $\dfrac{1}{j\omega C} = \dfrac{10^6}{j10^5} = -j10\,\Omega$

$$j\omega L = j10^5(50 \times 10^{-6}) = j5\,\Omega$$

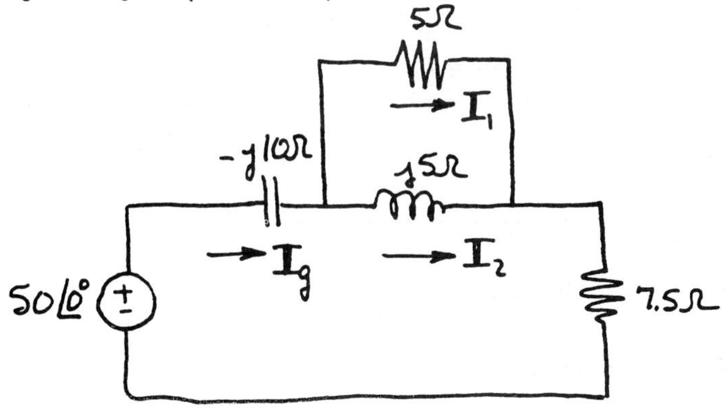

$$Z = -j10 + \frac{(5)(j5)}{5 + j5} + 7.5 = 10 - j7.5\,\Omega$$

$$\mathbf{I}_g = \frac{50\underline{/0^\circ}}{10 - j7.5} = 3.2 + j2.4\,\text{A}$$

$$S_g = \frac{1}{2}\mathbf{V}_g\mathbf{I}_g^* = 25(3.2 - j2.4) = 80 - j60\,\text{VA}$$

$$P = 80\,\text{W(del)}; \qquad Q = 60\,\text{VAR(abs)}$$

$$|S| = |S_g| = 100\,\text{VA}$$

[b] $$\mathbf{I}_1 = \frac{\mathbf{I}_g(j5)}{5 + j5} = \frac{1}{2}(3.2 + j2.4)(1 + j1) = 0.4 + j2.8\,\text{A}$$

$$P_{5\Omega} = \frac{1}{2}|\mathbf{I}_1|^2(5) = 20\,\text{W}$$

$$P_{7.5\Omega} = \frac{1}{2}|\mathbf{I}_g|^2(7.5) = 60\,\text{W}$$

$$\sum P_{\text{diss}} = 20 + 60 = 80\,\text{W} = \sum P_{\text{dev}}$$

[c] $$\mathbf{I}_{j5} = \frac{\mathbf{I}_g 5}{5 + j5} = \frac{1}{2}(3.2 + j2.4)(1 - j1) = 2.8 - j0.4\,\text{A}$$

$$Q_{j5\Omega} = \frac{1}{2}|\mathbf{I}_{j5}|^2(5) = 20\,\text{VAR(abs)}$$

$$Q_{-j10\Omega} = \frac{1}{2}|\mathbf{I}_g|^2(-10) = -80\,\text{VAR(dev)}$$

$$\sum Q_{\text{abs}} = 20 + 60 = 80\,\text{VAR} = \sum Q_{\text{dev}}$$

P 10.16 [a] $S_1 = 24{,}960 + j47{,}040\,\text{VA}$

$$S_2 = \frac{|\mathbf{V}_\text{L}|^2}{Z_2^*} = \frac{(480)^2}{5 + j5} = 23{,}040 - j23{,}040\,\text{VA}$$

$$S_1 + S_2 = 48{,}000 + j24{,}000\,\text{VA}$$

$$480\mathbf{I}_\text{L}^* = 48{,}000 + j24{,}000; \qquad \therefore\ \mathbf{I}_\text{L} = 100 - j50\,\text{A(rms)}$$

$$\mathbf{V}_g = \mathbf{V}_\text{L} + \mathbf{I}_\text{L}(0.02 + j0.20) = 480 + (100 - j50)(0.02 + j0.20)$$
$$= 492 + j19 = 492.37\underline{/2.21^\circ}\,\text{Vrms}$$

$$|\mathbf{V}_g| = 492.37\,\text{Vrms}$$

[b] $$T = \frac{1}{f} = \frac{1}{60} = 16.67\,\text{ms}$$

$$\frac{2.21^\circ}{360^\circ} = \frac{t}{16.67\,\text{ms}}; \qquad \therefore\ t = 102.31\,\mu\text{s}$$

[c] $\mathbf{V}_L$ lags $\mathbf{V}_g$ by 2.21° or 102.31 μs

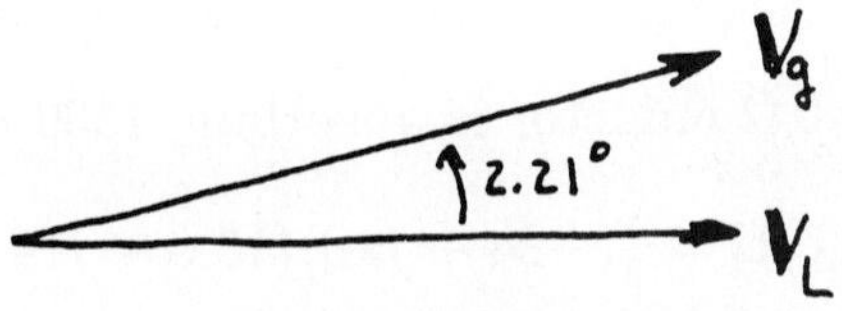

P 10.17 [a] From the solution to Problem 9.57 we have:

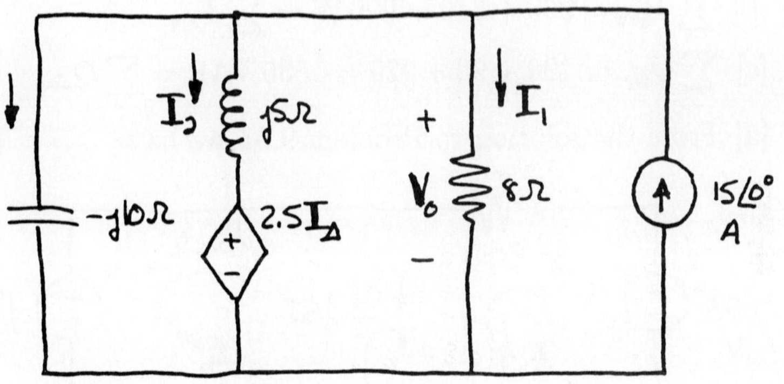

$\mathbf{V}_o = 72 + j96 = 120\underline{/53.13^\circ}$ V

$$S_g = -\frac{1}{2}\mathbf{V}_o\mathbf{I}_g^* = -\frac{1}{2}(72 + j96)(15) = -540 - j720\,\text{VA}$$

Therefore, the independent current source is delivering 540 W and 720 magnetizing vars.

$$\mathbf{I}_1 = \frac{\mathbf{V}_o}{8} = 15\underline{/53.13^\circ}\,\text{A}$$

$$P_{8\Omega} = \frac{1}{2}(15)^2(8) = 900\,\text{W}$$

Therefore, the 8 Ω resistor is absorbing 900 W.

$$\mathbf{I}_\Delta = \frac{\mathbf{V}_o}{-j10} = -9.6 + j7.2 = 12\underline{/143.13^\circ}\,\text{A}$$

$$Q_{cap} = \frac{1}{2}(12)^2(-10) = -720\,\text{VAR}$$

Therefore, the $-j10\,\Omega$ capacitor is developing 720 magnetizing vars.

$$2.5\mathbf{I}_\Delta = -24 + j18\,\text{V}$$

$$\mathbf{I}_2 = \frac{\mathbf{V}_o - 2.5\mathbf{I}_\Delta}{j5} = \frac{72 + j96 + 24 - j18}{j5}$$

$$= 15.6 - j19.2\,\text{A} = 24.72\underline{/-50.91^\circ}\,\text{A}$$

$$Q_{j5} = \frac{1}{2}|\mathbf{I}_2|^2(5) = 1530\,\text{VAR}$$

Therefore, the $j5\,\Omega$ inductor is absorbing 1530 magnetizing vars.

$$S_{2.5\mathbf{I}_\Delta} = \tfrac{1}{2}(2.5\mathbf{I}_\Delta)\mathbf{I}_2^* = \tfrac{1}{2}(-24 + j18)(15.6 + j19.2)$$
$$= -360 - j90\,\text{VA}$$

Thus the dependent source is delivering 360 W and 90 magnetizing vars.

[b] $\sum P_{gen} = 360 + 540 = 900\,\text{W} = \sum P_{abs}$

[c] $\sum Q_{gen} = 720 + 90 + 720 = 1530\,\text{VAR} = \sum Q_{abs}$

P 10.18 [a] From the solution to Problem 9.54 we have

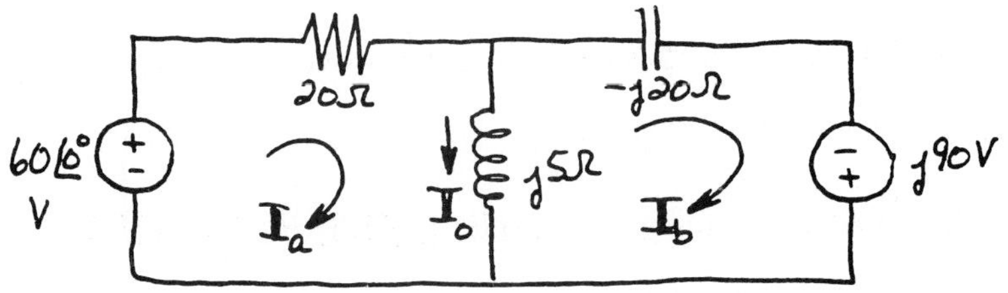

$\mathbf{I}_a = 2.25 - j2.25\,\text{A}$; $\mathbf{I}_b = -6.75 + j0.75\,\text{A}$; $\mathbf{I}_o = 9 - j3\,\text{A}$

$$S_{60V} = -\frac{1}{2}(60)\mathbf{I}_a^* = -30(2.25 + j2.25) = -67.5 - j67.5\,\text{VA}$$

Thus, the 60 V source is developing 67.5 W and 67.5 magnetizing vars.

$$S_{90V} = -\tfrac{1}{2}(j90)\mathbf{I}_b^* = -j45(-6.75 - j0.75)$$
$$= -33.75 + j303.75\,\text{VA}$$

Thus, the 90 V source is developing 33.75 W and absorbing 303.75 magnetizing vars.

$$P_{20\Omega} = \frac{1}{2}|\mathbf{I}_a|^2(20) = 101.25\,\text{W}$$

Thus the $20\,\Omega$ resistor is absorbing 101.25 W.

$$Q_{-j20\Omega} = \frac{1}{2}|\mathbf{I}_b|^2(-20) = -461.25\,\text{VAR}$$

Thus the $-j20\,\Omega$ capacitor is developing 461.25 magnetizing vars.

$$Q_{j5\Omega} = \frac{1}{2}|\mathbf{I}_o|^2(5) = 225\,\text{VAR}$$

Thus the $j5\,\Omega$ inductor is absorbing 225 magnetizing vars.

[b] $\sum P_{\text{dev}} = 67.5 + 33.75 = 101.25\,\text{W} = \sum P_{\text{abs}}$

[c] $\sum Q_{\text{dev}} = 67.5 + 461.25 = 528.75\,\text{VAR}$

$$\sum Q_{\text{abs}} = 225 + 303.75 = 528.75\,\text{VAR} = \sum Q_{\text{dev}}$$

P 10.19 [a] $S_1 = 18 + j24\,\text{kVA};\qquad S_2 = 36 - j48\,\text{kVA};\qquad S_3 = 18 + j0\,\text{kVA}$

$$S_T = S_1 + S_2 + S_3 = 72 - j24\,\text{kVA}$$

$$2400\mathbf{I}^* = (72 - j24) \times 10^3;\qquad \therefore\ \mathbf{I} = 30 + j10\,\text{A}$$

$$Z = \frac{2400}{30 + j10} = 72 - j24\,\Omega = 75.89\underline{/-18.43^\circ}\,\Omega$$

[b] pf $= \cos(-18.43^\circ) = 0.9487$ leading

P 10.20 [a] From the solution to Problem 10.19 we have

$$\mathbf{I}_L = 30 + j10\,\text{A(rms)}$$

$$\therefore\ \mathbf{V}_s = 2400\underline{/0^\circ} + (30 + j10)(0.2 + j1.6) = 2390 + j50$$

$$= 2390.52\underline{/1.20^\circ}\,\text{V(rms)}$$

[b] $|\mathbf{I}_L| = \sqrt{1000}$

$$P_\ell = (1000)(0.2) = 200\,\text{W}\qquad Q_\ell = (1000)(1.6) = 1600\,\text{VAR}$$

[c] $P_s = 72{,}000 + 200 = 72.2\,\text{kW}\qquad Q_s = -24{,}000 + 1600 = -22.4\,\text{kVAR}$

[d] $\eta = \dfrac{72}{72.2}(100) = 99.72\%$

P 10.21

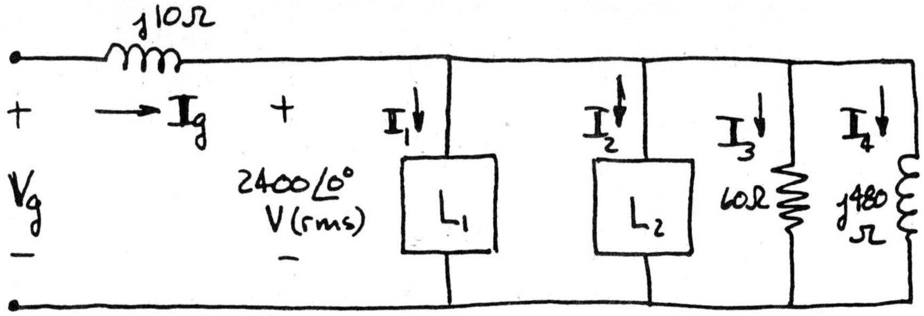

$$2400\mathbf{I}_1^* = 24{,}000 + j18{,}000$$

$$\mathbf{I}_1^* = 10 + j7.5;\qquad \therefore\ \mathbf{I}_1 = 10 - j7.5\,\text{A(rms)}$$

$$2400\mathbf{I}_2^* = 48{,}000 - j30{,}000$$

$$\mathbf{I}_2^* = 20 - j12.5;\qquad \therefore\ \mathbf{I}_2 = 20 + j12.5\,\text{A(rms)}$$

$$\mathbf{I}_3 = \frac{2400/0^\circ}{60} = 40 + j0\,\text{A}; \qquad \mathbf{I}_4 = \frac{2400/0^\circ}{j480} = 0 - j5\,\text{A}$$

$$\mathbf{I}_g = \mathbf{I}_1 + \mathbf{I}_2 + \mathbf{I}_3 + \mathbf{I}_4 = 70\,\text{A}$$

$$\mathbf{V}_g = 2400 + (70)(j10) = 2400 + j70 = 2500/16.26^\circ\,\text{V(rms)}$$

P 10.22 $S_\text{T} = 52{,}800 - j\dfrac{52{,}800}{0.8}(0.6) = 52{,}800 - j39{,}600\,\text{VA}$

$$S_1 = 40{,}000(0.96 + j0.28) = 38{,}400 + j11{,}200\,\text{VA}$$

$$S_2 = S_\text{T} - S_1 = 14{,}400 - j50{,}800 = 52{,}801.52/-74.17^\circ\,\text{VA}$$

$$\text{rf} = \sin(-74.17^\circ) = -0.9621$$

$$\text{pf} = \cos(-74.17^\circ) = 0.2727 \text{ leading}$$

P 10.23 [a] Let $\mathbf{V}_\text{L} = V_m/0^\circ$:

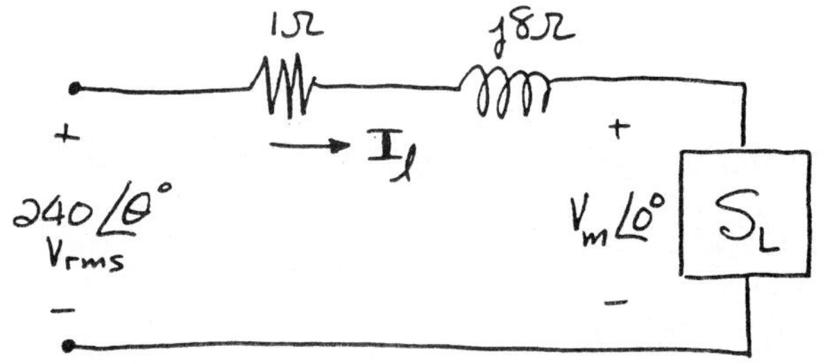

$$S_\text{L} = 250(0.6 + j0.8) = 150 + j200\,\text{VA}$$

$$\mathbf{I}_\ell^* = \frac{150}{V_m} + j\frac{200}{V_m}; \qquad \mathbf{I}_\ell = \frac{150}{V_m} - j\frac{200}{V_m}$$

$$240/\theta = V_m + \left(\frac{150}{V_m} - j\frac{200}{V_m}\right)(1 + j8)$$

$$240V_m/\theta = V_m^2 + (150 - j200)(1 + j8) = V_m^2 + 1750 + j1000$$

$$240V_m\cos\theta = V_m^2 + 1750; \qquad 240V_m\sin\theta = 1000$$

$$(240)^2V_m^2 = (V_m^2 + 1750)^2 + 1000^2$$

$$57{,}600V_m^2 = V_m^4 + 3500V_m^2 + (3.0625 + 1)\times 10^6$$

or

$$V_m^4 - 54{,}100V_m^2 + 4{,}062{,}500 = 0$$

Solving,

$V_m^2 = 27{,}050 \pm 26{,}974.8;$ $\qquad V_m = 232.43$ V and $V_m = 8.67$ V

If $V_m = 232.43$ V:

$$\sin\theta = \frac{1000}{(232.43)(240)} = 0.0179; \qquad \therefore\ \theta = 1.03^\circ$$

If $V_m = 8.67$ V:

$$\sin\theta = \frac{1000}{(8.67)(240)} = 0.4805; \qquad \therefore\ \theta = 28.72^\circ$$

[b]

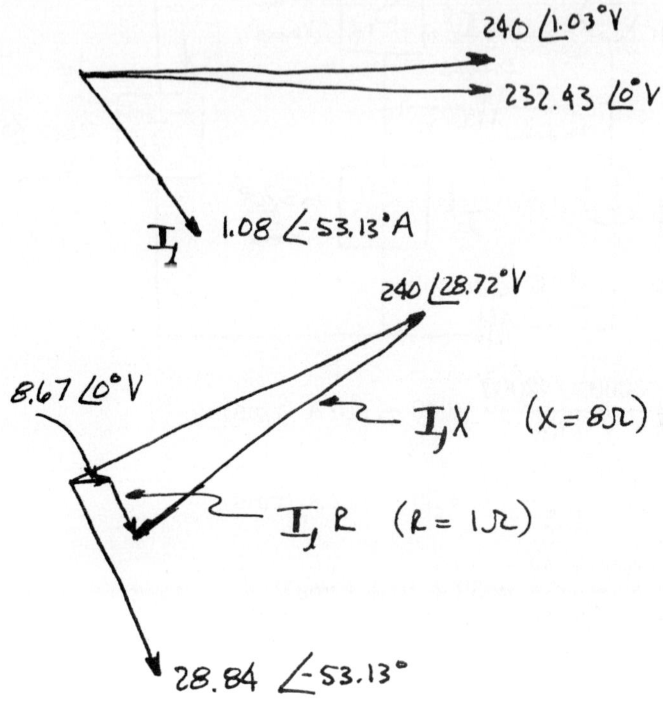

P 10.24 [a] $\mathbf{I} = \dfrac{7200\underline{/0^\circ}}{140 + j480} = 14.4\underline{/-73.74^\circ}\ \text{A(rms)}$

$$P = (14.4)^2(2) = 414.72\,\text{W}$$

[b] $Y_L = \dfrac{1}{138 + j460} = \dfrac{138 - j460}{230{,}644}$

$$\therefore\ -j\omega C = -j\frac{460}{230{,}644} \qquad \therefore\ X_C = \frac{-230{,}644}{460} = -501.40\,\Omega$$

[c] $Z_L = \dfrac{230{,}644}{138} = 1671.33\,\Omega$

[d] $\mathbf{I} = \dfrac{7200}{1673.33 + j20} = 4.30\underline{/-0.68^\circ}\ \text{A}$

$P = (4.30)^2(2) = 37.02\ \text{W}$

[e] $\% = \dfrac{37.02}{414.72}(100) = 8.93\%$

Thus the power loss after the capacitor is added is 8.93% of the power loss before the capacitor is added.

P 10.25 [a]

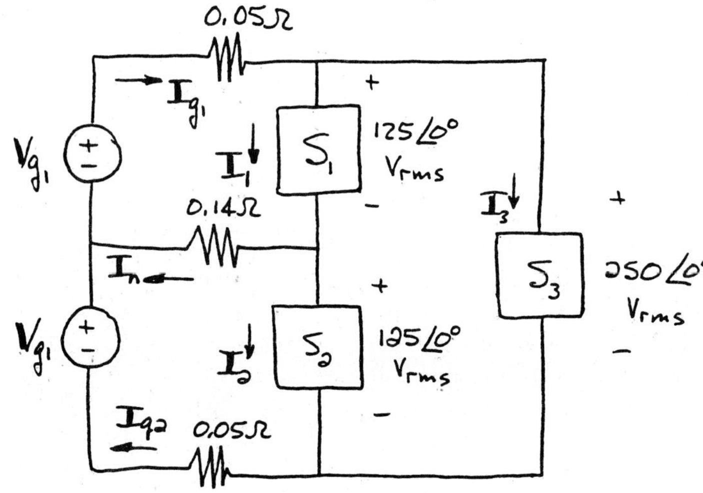

$\mathbf{I}_1 = \dfrac{5000 - j2000}{125} = 40 - j16\ \text{A (rms)}$

$\mathbf{I}_2 = \dfrac{3750 - j1500}{125} = 30 - j12\ \text{A (rms)}$

$\mathbf{I}_3 = \dfrac{8000 + j0}{250} = 32 + j0\ \text{A (rms)}$

$\therefore\ \mathbf{I}_{g1} = 72 - j16\ \text{A (rms)}$

$\mathbf{I}_n = \mathbf{I}_1 - \mathbf{I}_2 = 10 - j4\ \text{A (rms)}$

$\mathbf{I}_{g2} = 62 - j12\ \text{A}$

$\mathbf{V}_{g1} = 0.05\mathbf{I}_{g1} + 125 + j0 + 0.14\mathbf{I}_n = 130 + j1.36\ \text{V(rms)}$

$\mathbf{V}_{g2} = -0.14\mathbf{I}_n + 125 + j0 + 0.05\mathbf{I}_{g2} = 126.7 - j0.04\ \text{V(rms)}$

$S_{g1} = -[(130 - j1.36)(72 - j16)] = -[9381.76 + j1982.08]\ \text{VA}$

$S_{g2} = -[(126.7 - j0.04)(62 + j12)] = -[7855.88 + j1517.92]\ \text{VA}$

Note: Both sources are delivering average power and magnetizing VAR to the circuit.

[b] $P_{0.05} = |\mathbf{I}_{g1}|^2(0.05) = 272\,\text{W}$

$P_{0.15} = |\mathbf{I}_n|^2(0.14) = 16.24\,\text{W}$

$P_{0.05} = |\mathbf{I}_{g2}|^2(0.05) = 199.4\,\text{W}$

$\sum P_{\text{dis}} = 272 + 16.24 + 199.4 + 5000 + 3750 + 8000 = 17{,}237.64\,\text{W}$

$\sum P_{\text{dev}} = 9381.76 + 7855.88 = 17{,}237.64\,\text{W} = \sum P_{\text{dis}}$

$\sum Q_{\text{abs}} = 2000 + 1500 = 2500\,\text{VAR}$

$\sum Q_{\text{del}} = 1982.08 + 1517.92 = 3500\,\text{VAR} = \sum Q_{\text{abs}}$

P 10.26 [a]

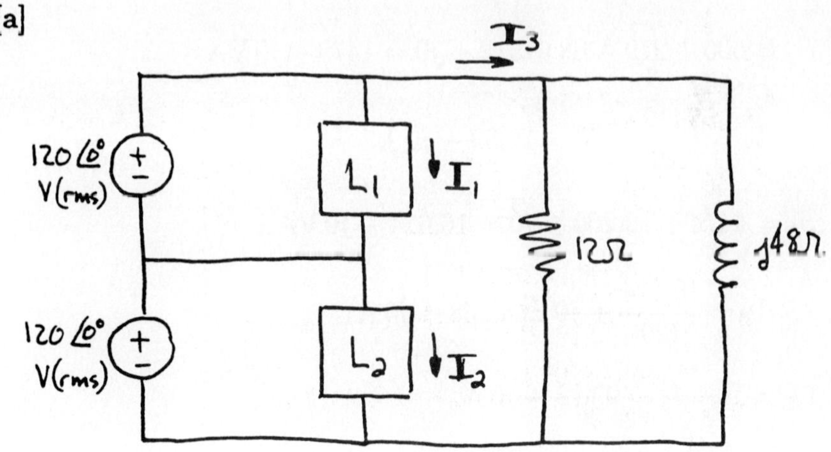

$120\mathbf{I}_1^* = 1800 + j600; \qquad \therefore\ \mathbf{I}_1 = 15 - j5\,\text{A(rms)}$

$120\mathbf{I}_2^* = 1200 - j900; \qquad \therefore\ \mathbf{I}_2 = 10 + j7.5\,\text{A(rms)}$

$$\mathbf{I}_3 = \frac{240}{12} + \frac{240}{j48} = 20 - j5\,\text{A(rms)}$$

$\mathbf{I}_{g1} = \mathbf{I}_1 + \mathbf{I}_3 = 35 - j10\,\text{A}$

$S_{g1} = -120(35 + j10) = -4200 - j1200\,\text{VA}$

Thus the $\mathbf{V}_{g1}$ source is delivering 4200 W and 1200 magnetizing vars.

$\mathbf{I}_{g2} = \mathbf{I}_2 + \mathbf{I}_3 = 30 + j2.5\,\text{A(rms)}$

$S_{g2} = -120(30 - j2.5) = -3600 + j300\,\text{VA}$

Thus the $\mathbf{V}_{g2}$ source is delivering 3600 W and absorbing 300 magnetizing vars.

[b] $\sum P_{\text{gen}} = 4200 + 3600 = 7800\,\text{W}$

$$\sum P_{\text{abs}} = 1800 + 1200 + \frac{(240)^2}{12} = 7800\,\text{W} = \sum P_{\text{gen}}$$

$$\sum Q_{\text{del}} = 1200 + 900 = 2100\,\text{VAR}$$

$$\sum Q_{\text{abs}} = 300 + 600 + \frac{(240)^2}{48} = 2100\,\text{VAR} = \sum Q_{\text{del}}$$

P 10.27 $S_1 = 1200 + 1196 + 516 + j0 = 2912 + j0\,\text{VA}$

$$\therefore\ \mathbf{I}_1 = \frac{2912}{120} + j0 = 24.27 + j0\,\text{A}$$

$$S_2 = 600 + 279 + 88 + 512 + j0 = 1479 + j0\,\text{VA}$$

$$\therefore\ \mathbf{I}_2 = \frac{1479}{120} + j0 = 12.33 + j0\,\text{A}$$

$$S_3 = 4474 + 12{,}200 + j0 = 16{,}674 + j0\,\text{VA}$$

$$\therefore\ \mathbf{I}_3 = \frac{16{,}674}{120} + j0 = 69.48 + j0\,\text{A}$$

$$\mathbf{I}_{g1} = \mathbf{I}_1 + \mathbf{I}_3 = 93.75 + j0\,\text{A}$$

$$\mathbf{I}_{g2} = \mathbf{I}_2 + \mathbf{I}_3 = 81.81 + j0\,\text{A}$$

Breakers will not trip since both feeder currents are less than 100 A.

P 10.28 [a] $S_{\text{L}} = 24 + j7\,\text{kVA}$

$$125\mathbf{I}_{\text{L}}^{*} = (24 + j7) \times 10^3; \quad \mathbf{I}_{\text{L}}^{*} = 192 - j56\,\text{A(rms)}$$

$$\therefore\ \mathbf{I}_{\text{L}} = 192 - j56\,\text{A(rms)}$$

$$\mathbf{V}_s = 125 + (192 - j56)(0.006 + j0.048) = 128.84 + j8.88$$

$$= 129.15\angle 3.94^\circ\,\text{V(rms)}$$

$$|\mathbf{V}_s| = 129.15\,\text{V(rms)}$$

[b] $P_\ell = |\mathbf{I}_\ell|^2(0.006) = (200)^2(0.006) = 240\,\text{W}$

[c] $\dfrac{(125)^2}{X_{\text{C}}} = -7000; \qquad X_{\text{C}} = -2.23\,\Omega$

$$-\frac{1}{\omega C} = -2.23; \qquad C = \frac{1}{(2.23)(120\pi)} = 1188.36\,\mu\text{F}$$

[d] $\mathbf{I}_\ell = 192 + j0\ \text{A(rms)}$

$$\mathbf{V}_s = 125 + 192(0.006 + j0.048) = 126.152 + j9.216$$
$$= 126.44\underline{/4.18^\circ}\ \text{V(rms)}$$

$$|\mathbf{V}_s| = 126.49\ \text{V(rms)}$$

[e] $P_\ell = (192)^2(0.006) = 221.184\ \text{W}$

P 10.29

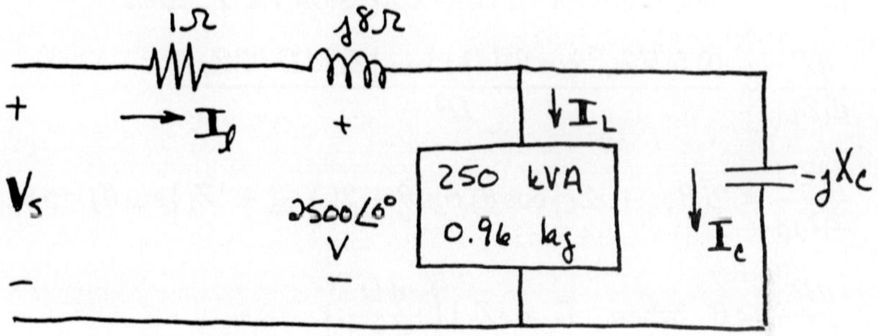

$$\mathbf{I}_L = \frac{240{,}000 - j70{,}000}{2500} = 96 - j28\ \text{A(rms)}$$

$$\mathbf{I}_C = \frac{2500}{-jX_C} = j\frac{2500}{X_C} = jI_C$$

$$\mathbf{I}_\ell = 96 - j28 + jI_C = 96 + j(I_C - 28)$$

$$\mathbf{V}_s = 2500 + (1 + j8)[96 + j(I_C - 28)]$$
$$= (2820 - 8I_C) + j(740 + I_C)$$

$$|\mathbf{V}_s|^2 = (2820 - 8I_C)^2 + (740 + I_C)^2 = (2500)^2$$

$$\therefore\quad 65I_C^2 - 43{,}640I_C + 2{,}250{,}000 = 0$$

$$I_C = \frac{43{,}640 \pm \sqrt{(43{,}640)^2 - 4(65)(2{,}250{,}000)}}{2(65)}$$
$$= 335.69 \pm 279.42 = 56.27\ \text{A(rms)}^*$$

*Select the smaller value of I_C to minimize the magnitude of I_ℓ.

$$\therefore\quad X_C = -\frac{2500}{56.27} = -44.43$$

$$\therefore\quad C = \frac{1}{(44.43)(120\pi)} = 59.7\ \mu\text{F}$$

P 10.30 $Z_L = |Z_L|\angle\theta^\circ = |Z_L|\cos\theta^\circ + j|Z_L|\sin\theta^\circ$

Thus $|\mathbf{I}| = \dfrac{|\mathbf{V}_{Th}|}{\sqrt{(R_{Th} + |Z_L|\cos\theta)^2 + (X_{Th} + |Z_L|\sin\theta)^2}}$

Therefore $P = \dfrac{0.5|\mathbf{V}_{Th}|^2|Z_L|\cos\theta}{(R_{Th} + |Z_L|\cos\theta)^2 + (X_{Th} + |Z_L|\sin\theta)^2}$

Let D = demoninator in the expression for P, then

$$\frac{dP}{d|Z_L|} = \frac{(0.5|\mathbf{V}_{Th}|^2\cos\theta)(D\cdot 1 - |Z_L|dD/d|Z_L|)}{D^2}$$

$$\frac{dD}{d|Z_L|} = 2(R_{Th} + |Z_L|\cos\theta)\cos\theta + 2(X_{Th} + |Z_L|\sin\theta)\sin\theta$$

$$\frac{dP}{d|Z_L|} = 0 \quad \text{when} \quad D = |Z_L|\left(\frac{dD}{d|Z_L|}\right)$$

Substituting the expressions for D and $(dD/d|Z_L|)$ into this equation gives us the relationship $R_{Th}^2 + X_{Th}^2 = |Z_L|^2$ or $|Z_{Th}| = |Z_L|$.

P 10.31 [a] First find the Thévenin equivalent:

$$\frac{1}{j\omega C} = \frac{10^6}{j10^4} = -j100\,\Omega$$

$$Z_{Th} = \frac{300(-j100)}{300 - j100} = 30 - j90\,\Omega$$

$$\mathbf{V}_{Th} = \frac{150(-j100)}{300 - j100} = 15 - j45\ \text{V(rms)}$$

$$j\omega L = j10^4(6\times 10^{-3}) = j60\,\Omega$$

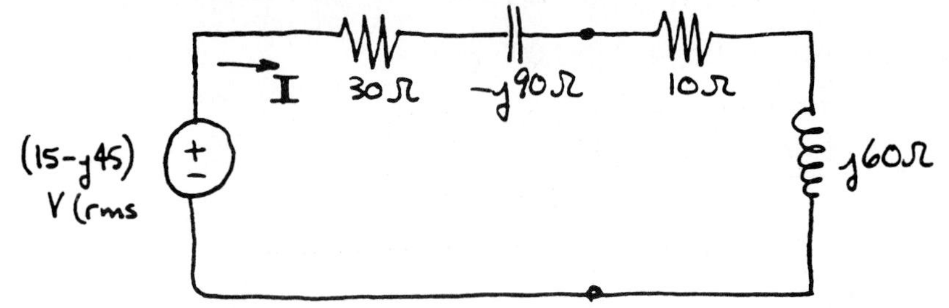

$$\mathbf{I} = \frac{15 - j45}{40 - j30} = \frac{1.5}{25}(13 - j9)\ \text{A(rms)}$$

$$|\mathbf{I}| = \frac{1.5}{25}\sqrt{250}\ \text{A(rms)}$$

$$P = \frac{2.25}{625}(250)(10) = 9\ \text{W}$$

[b] Set $L_o = 8\,\text{mH}$; Set R_o as close as possible to

$$R_o = \sqrt{(30)^2 + (10)^2} = \sqrt{1000} = 31.62\,\Omega$$

$$\therefore \quad R_o = 20\,\Omega$$

[c] $$\mathbf{I} = \frac{15 - j45}{50 - j10} = \frac{3 - j9}{10 - j2}\ \text{A(rms)}$$

$$\therefore \quad |\mathbf{I}| = \frac{\sqrt{90}}{104}$$

$$P = |\mathbf{I}|^2(20) = \frac{(90)(20)}{104} = 17.31\,\text{W}$$

Yes; 17.31 W > 9 W

[d] $$\mathbf{I} = \frac{15 - j45}{60} = \frac{1 - j3}{4}\ \text{A(rms)}$$

$$P = \left(\frac{\sqrt{10}}{4}\right)^2 30 = 18.75\,\text{W}$$

[e] $R_o = 30\,\Omega$; $L_o = 9\,\text{mH}$

[f] Yes; 18.75 W > 17.31 W

P 10.32 [a] $L_o = 8\,\text{mH}$; $R_o = \sqrt{30^2 + 10^2} = 31.62\,\Omega$

$$\mathbf{I} = \frac{15(1 - j3)}{61.62 - j10} = \frac{15\sqrt{10}}{62.43}\underline{/-62.35^\circ}\ \text{A(rms)}$$

$$P = \left(\frac{15\sqrt{10}}{62.43}\right)^2 (31.62) = 18.26\,\text{W}$$

[b] Yes; 18.26 W > 17.31 W

[c] Yes; 18.26 W < 18.75 W

P 10.33 [a]

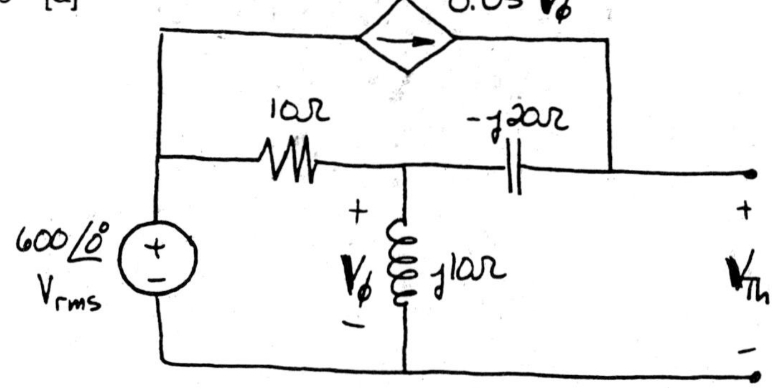

$$\frac{\mathbf{V}_\phi - 600}{10} + \frac{\mathbf{V}_\phi}{j10} - 0.05\mathbf{V}_\phi = 0$$

$\therefore \quad \mathbf{V}_\phi = 240 + j480\,\text{V(rms)}$

$\mathbf{V}_{\text{Th}} = \mathbf{V}_\phi + 0.05\mathbf{V}_\phi(-j20) = \mathbf{V}_\phi(1 - j1) = 720 + j240\,\text{V(rms)}$

Short circuit current:

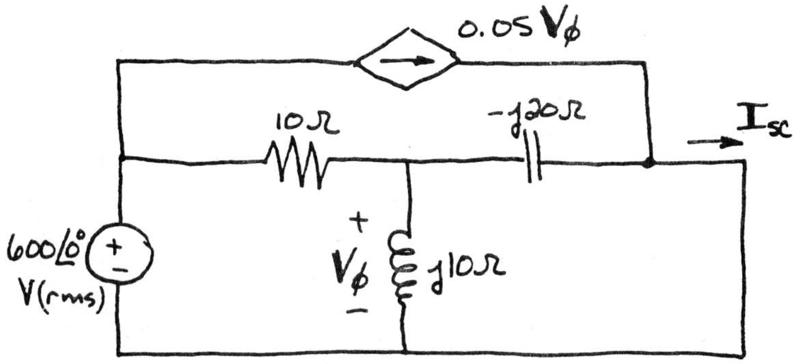

$$\mathbf{I}_{sc} = 0.05\mathbf{V}_\phi + \frac{\mathbf{V}_\phi}{-j20} = (0.05 + j0.05)\mathbf{V}_\phi$$

$$\frac{\mathbf{V}_\phi - 600}{10} + \frac{\mathbf{V}_\phi}{j10} + \frac{\mathbf{V}_\phi}{-j20} = 0$$

$\therefore \quad \mathbf{V}_\phi = 480 + j240\,\text{V(rms)}$

$\mathbf{I}_{sc} = (0.05 + j0.05)(480 + j240) = 12 + j36\,\text{A(rms)}$

$$Z_{\text{Th}} = \frac{\mathbf{V}_{\text{Th}}}{\mathbf{I}_{sc}} = \frac{720 + j240}{12 + j36} = 12 - j16 = 20\underline{/-53.13^\circ}\,\Omega$$

$\therefore \quad R_o = 20\,\Omega$

[b]

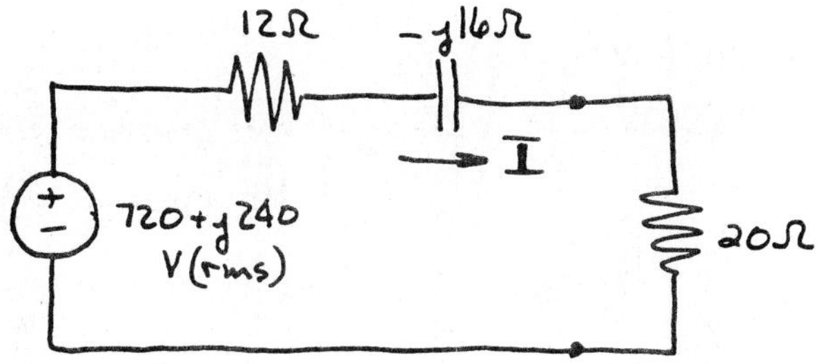

$$\mathbf{I} = \frac{720 + j240}{32 - j16} = 15 + j15 = 15\sqrt{2}\underline{/45^\circ}\,\text{A(rms)}$$

$P = (15\sqrt{2})^2(20) = 9000\,\text{W} = 9\,\text{kW}$

[c]

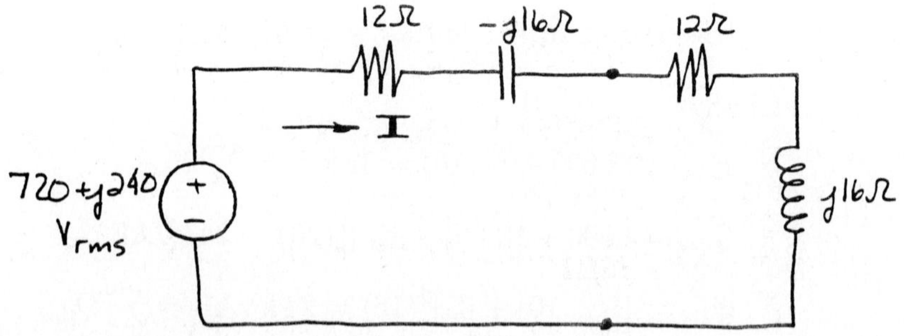

$$\mathbf{I} = \frac{720 + j240}{24} = 30 + j10\,\text{A(rms)}$$

$$P = (\sqrt{1000})^2(12) = 12\,\text{kW}$$

[d]

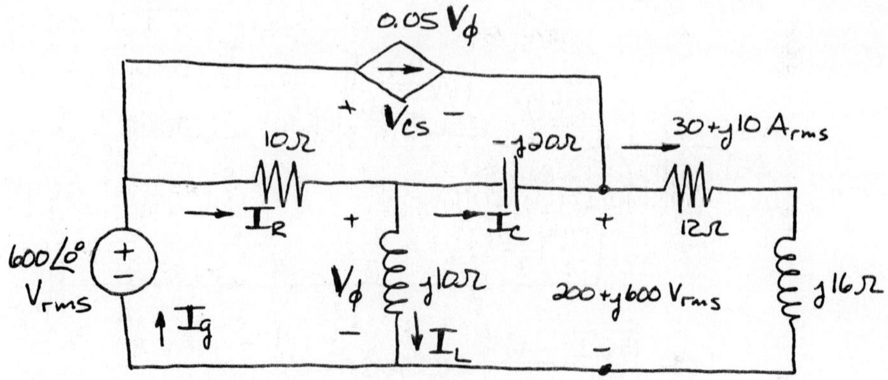

$$\frac{\mathbf{V}_\phi - 600}{10} + \frac{\mathbf{V}_\phi}{j10} + \frac{\mathbf{V}_\phi - 200 - j600}{-j20} = 0$$

$$\therefore \quad \mathbf{V}_\phi = 200 + j200\,\text{V}$$

$$0.05\mathbf{V}_\phi = 10 + j10\,\text{A}$$

$$10 + j10 + \mathbf{I}_\text{C} = 30 + j10; \qquad \therefore \quad \mathbf{I}_\text{C} = 20 + j0\,\text{A}$$

$$\mathbf{I}_\text{L} = \frac{\mathbf{V}_\phi}{j10} = 20 - j20\,\text{A}$$

$$\mathbf{I}_\text{R} = \mathbf{I}_\text{C} + \mathbf{I}_\text{L} = 40 - j20\,\text{A}$$

$$\mathbf{I}_g = \mathbf{I}_\text{R} + 0.05\mathbf{V}_\phi = 50 - j10\,\text{A(rms)}$$

$$S_g = -600\mathbf{I}_g^* = -30{,}000 - j6000\,\text{VA}$$

$$600 = \mathbf{V}_\text{cs} + 200 + j600; \qquad \mathbf{V}_\text{cs} = 400 - j600\,\text{V}$$

$$S_\text{cs} = (400 - j600)(10 - j10) = -2000 - j10{,}000\,\text{VA}$$

$$\sum P_\text{dev} = 30{,}000 + 2000 = 32{,}000\,\text{W} = 32\,\text{kW}$$

$$\% \text{ delivered to } R_o = \frac{12}{32}(100) = 37.50\%$$

Check:

$$\sum P_{\text{abs}} = 12{,}000 + \mathbf{I}_R^2(10) = 32\,\text{kW} = \sum P_{\text{dev}}$$

$$\sum Q_{\text{dev}} = 6000 + 10{,}000 + |\mathbf{I}_C|^2(20) = 24\,\text{kVAR}$$

$$\sum Q_{\text{abs}} = |\mathbf{I}_L|^2(10) + |\mathbf{I}_o|^2(16) = 24\,\text{kVAR} = \sum Q_{\text{dev}}$$

P 10.34 [a] $Z_{\text{Th}} = \frac{1}{j\omega C} + \frac{(60)(j60)}{60 + j60} = -j40 + 30 + j30 = 30 - j10\,\text{k}\Omega$

$\therefore \quad Z_L = Z_{\text{Th}}^* = 30 + j10\,\text{k}\Omega$

[b] $\mathbf{V}_{\text{Th}} = \frac{90\underline{/0^\circ}(60)}{60 + j60} = 45(1 - j1) = 45\sqrt{2}\underline{/-45^\circ}\,\text{V}$

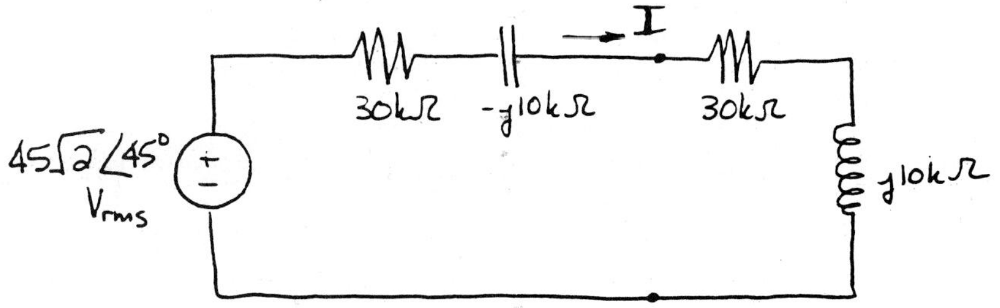

$$\mathbf{I} = \frac{45\sqrt{2}\underline{/-45^\circ}}{60 \times 10^3} = 0.75\sqrt{2}\underline{/-45^\circ}\,\text{mA}$$

$$|\mathbf{I}_{\text{rms}}| = 0.75\,\text{mA}$$

$$P_{\text{load}} = (0.75)^2 \times 10^{-6}(30 \times 10^3) = 16.875\,\text{W}$$

P 10.35 [a] $Z_{\text{Th}} = 8 + j15 + \frac{(-j24)(18 + j6)}{18 - j18} = 24 + j7 = 25\underline{/8.13^\circ}\,\Omega$

$\therefore \quad R = |Z_{\text{Th}}| = 25\,\Omega$

[b] $\mathbf{V}_{\text{Th}} = \frac{-j24}{18 + j6 - j24}(630\underline{/0^\circ}) = 420 - j420 = 420\sqrt{2}\underline{/-45^\circ}\,\text{V(rms)}$

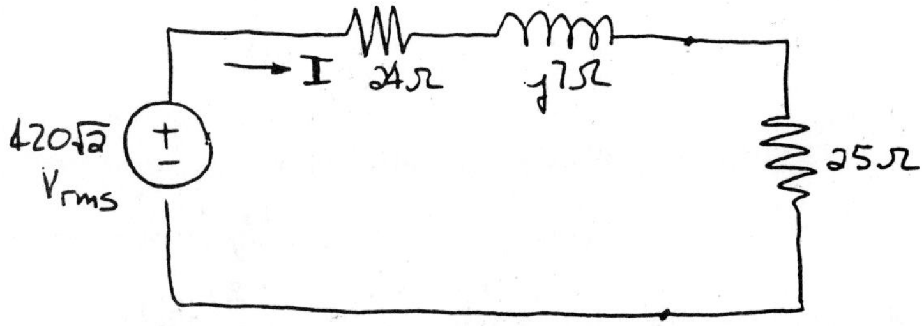

$$\mathbf{I} = \frac{420\sqrt{2}\underline{/0^\circ}}{49 + j7}; \qquad |\mathbf{I}| = \frac{60\sqrt{2}}{\sqrt{50}}$$

$$P = \frac{(3600)(2)}{50}(25) = 3600\,\text{W} = 3.6\,\text{kW}$$

P 10.36 [a] $$\frac{240 - j80 - 480}{Z_{\text{Th}}} + \frac{240 - j80}{100} = 0$$

$$\therefore \quad Z_{\text{Th}} = \frac{-100(240 + j80)}{-(240 - j80)} = 80 + j60\,\Omega$$

$$\therefore \quad Z_{\text{L}} = 80 - j60\,\Omega$$

[b] $$\mathbf{I} = \frac{480\angle 0^\circ}{160\angle 0^\circ} = 3\angle 0^\circ\ \text{A(rms)}$$

$$P = (9)(80) = 720\,\text{W}$$

P 10.37 [a]

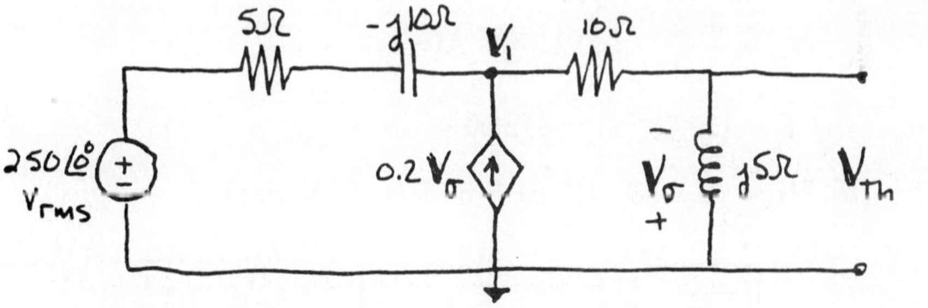

$$\frac{\mathbf{V}_1 - 250}{5 - j10} - 0.2\mathbf{V}_\sigma + \frac{\mathbf{V}_1}{10 + j5} = 0$$

$$\mathbf{V}_\sigma = \frac{-j5\mathbf{V}_1}{10 + j5} = \frac{-j\mathbf{V}_1}{2 + j1}$$

$$-0.2\mathbf{V}_\sigma = \frac{j0.2\mathbf{V}_1}{2 + j1}$$

$$\therefore \quad \mathbf{V}_1\left[\frac{1}{5 - j10} + \frac{j0.2}{2 + j1} + \frac{1}{10 + j5}\right] = \frac{250}{5 - j10}$$

Thus, $\mathbf{V}_1 = 10(10 + j5)$

$$\mathbf{V}_{\text{Th}} = \frac{j5}{10 + j5}\mathbf{V}_1 = j50 = 50\angle 90^\circ\ \text{V(rms)}$$

Short circuit current:

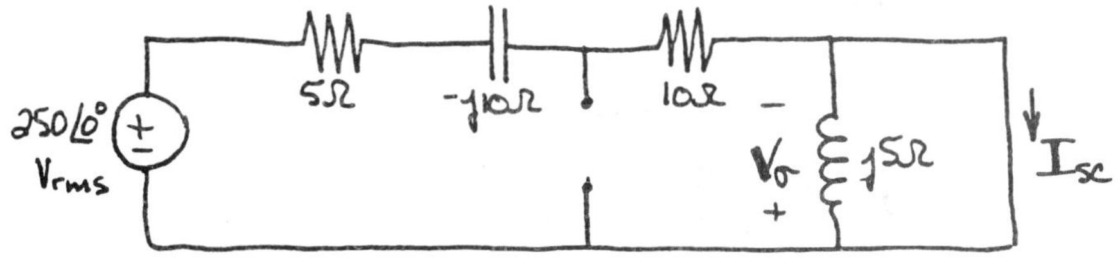

$$\mathbf{I}_{sc} = \frac{250\underline{/0^\circ}}{15 - j10} = \frac{50}{3 - j2}\,\text{A(rms)}$$

$$Z_{\text{Th}} = \frac{\mathbf{V}_{\text{Th}}}{\mathbf{I}_{sc}} = \frac{j50}{50}(3 - j2) = 2 + j3\,\Omega$$

$$\therefore\quad Z_{\text{L}} = 2 - j3\,\Omega$$

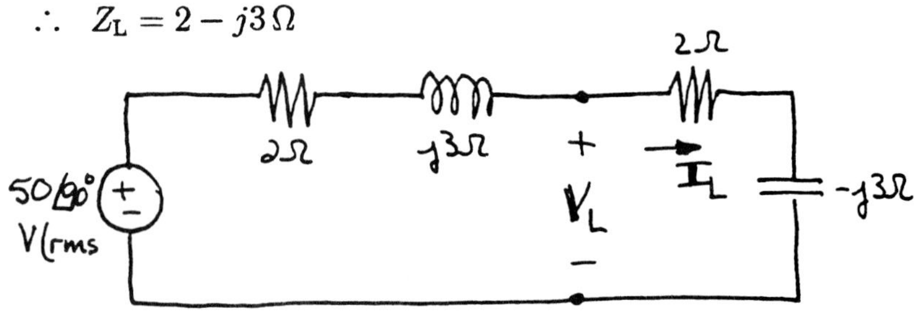

$$\mathbf{I}_{\text{L}} = \frac{50\underline{/90^\circ}}{4} = 12.5\underline{/90^\circ}\,\text{A(rms)}$$

$$P = (12.5)^2(2) = 312.50\,\text{W}$$

[b] $\mathbf{V}_{\text{L}} = (2 - j3)(j12.5) = 37.5 + j25\,\text{V(rms)}$

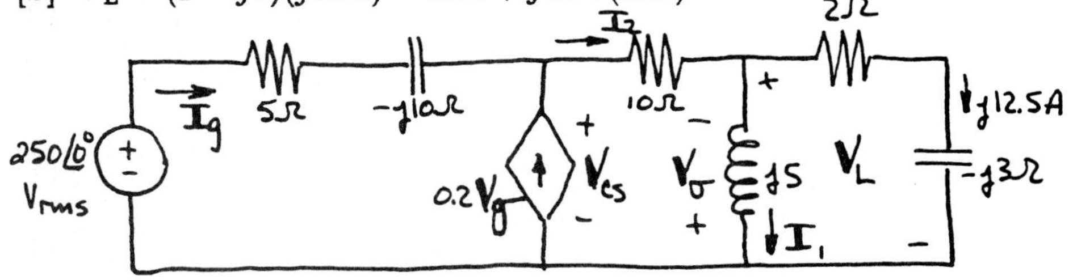

$$\mathbf{I}_1 = \frac{\mathbf{V}_{\text{L}}}{j5} = \frac{37.5 + j25}{j5} = 5 - j7.5\,\text{A(rms)}$$

$$\mathbf{I}_2 = \mathbf{I}_1 + \mathbf{I}_{\text{L}} = 5 - j7.5 + j12.5 = 5 + j5\,\text{A(rms)}$$

$$\mathbf{V}_{cs} = \mathbf{V}_{\text{L}} + 10\mathbf{I}_2 = 37.5 + j25 + 50 + j50 = 87.5 + j75\,\text{V(rms)}$$

$$\mathbf{V}_\sigma = -\mathbf{V}_{\text{L}} = -37.5 - j25$$

$$0.2\mathbf{V}_\sigma = -7.5 - j5$$

$$S_{cs} = -\mathbf{V}_{cs}\mathbf{I}_{cs}^* = -(87.5 + j75)(-7.5 + j5) = 1031.25 + j125\,\text{VA}$$

Therefore, the dependent source is absorbing 1031.25 W and 125 magnetizing vars. Only the independent voltage source is developing power.

$$\mathbf{I}_g = -0.2\mathbf{V}_\sigma + \mathbf{I}_2 = 7.5 + j5 + 5 + j5 = 12.5 + j10\,\text{A}$$

$$S_g = -250\mathbf{I}_g^* = -3125 + j2500\,\text{VA}$$

$\therefore \quad P_{\text{dev}} = 3125\,\text{W}$

$$\%\ \text{delivered} \;=\; \frac{312.5}{3125}(100) = 10\%$$

Thus, 10% of the developed power is delivered to the load.
Checks:

$$P_{10\Omega} = (5\sqrt{2})^2 10 = 500\,\text{W}$$

$$P_{2\Omega} = 312.5\,\text{W}$$

$$P_{5\Omega} = (\sqrt{256.25})^2 5 = 1281.25\,\text{W}$$

$$\therefore \quad \sum P_{\text{dev}} = \sum P_{\text{abs}} = 500 + 312.5 + 1281.25 + 1031.25 = 3125\,\text{W}$$

VAR Check:
The 250 V source is absorbing 2500 vars; the dependent current source is absorbing 125 vars; the $j5\,\Omega$ inductor is absorbing $|37.5 + j25|^2/5 = 406.25$ vars. Thus,

$$\sum Q_{\text{abs}} = 2625 + 406.25 = 3031.25\,\text{VAR}$$

$$\sum Q_{\text{dev}} = (12.5)^2(3) + 256.25(10) = 3031.25\,\text{VAR} = \sum Q_{\text{abs}}$$

P 10.38 [a] $\dfrac{1}{\omega C} = 240\,\Omega; \qquad C = \dfrac{1}{(240)(120\pi)} = 11.05\,\mu\text{F}$

[b] $\mathbf{I}_{\text{wo}} = \dfrac{4800}{160} + \dfrac{4800}{j240} = 30 - j20\,\text{A(rms)}$

$$\mathbf{V}_{\text{swo}} = 4800 + (30 - j20)(1 + j8) = 4990 + j220$$
$$= 4994.85\underline{/2.52^\circ}\,\text{V(rms)}$$

$$\mathbf{I}_{\text{w}} = \frac{4800}{160} + \frac{4800}{j240} + \frac{4800}{-j240} = 30 + j0\,\text{A(rms)}$$

$$\mathbf{V}_{\text{sw}} = 4800 + 30(1 + j8) = 4830 + j240 = 4835.96\underline{/2.84^\circ}\,\text{V(rms)}$$

$$\%\ \text{increase} \;=\; \left(\frac{4994.85}{4835.96} - 1\right)(100) = 3.29\%$$

[c] $P_{\ell\text{wo}} = |30 - j20|^2 1 = 1300\,\text{W}$

$$P_{\ell\text{w}} = 30^2(1) = 900\,\text{W}$$

$$\%\ \text{increase} \;=\; \left(\frac{1300}{900} - 1\right)(100) = 44.44\%$$

P 10.39 [a] $S_o = \text{ original load } = 1800 + j\frac{1800}{0.6}(0.8) = 1800 + j2400\,\text{kVA}$

$$S_f = \text{ final load } = 2400 + j\frac{2400}{0.96}(0.28) = 2400 + j700\,\text{kVA}$$

$$\therefore \quad Q_{\text{added}} = 700 - 2400 = -1700\,\text{kVAR}$$

[b] deliver

[c] $S_a = \text{ added load } = 600 - j1700 = 1802.78\underline{/-79.56^\circ}\,\text{kVA}$

$$\text{pf } = \cos(-70.56) = 0.3328 \text{ leading}$$

[d] $\mathbf{I}_L^* = \frac{(1800 + j2400) \times 10^3}{4800} = 375 + j500\,\text{A}$

$$\mathbf{I}_L = 375 - j500 = 625\underline{/53.13^\circ}\,\text{A(rms)}$$

$$|\mathbf{I}_L| = 625\,\text{A(rms)}$$

[e] $\mathbf{I}_L^* = \frac{(2400 + j700) \times 10^3}{4800} = 500 + j145.83$

$$\mathbf{I}_L = 500 - j145.83 = 520.83\underline{/-16.26^\circ}\,\text{A(rms)}$$

$$|\mathbf{I}_L| = 520.83\,\text{A(rms)}$$

P 10.40 [a] $P_{\text{before}} = (625)^2(0.02) = 7812.50\,\text{W}$

$$P_{\text{after}} = (520.83)^2(0.02) = 5425.35\,\text{W}$$

[b] $\mathbf{V}_s(\text{before}) = 4800 + (375 - j500)(0.02 + j0.16) = 4887.5 + j50$

$$= 4887.5\underline{/0.59^\circ}\,\text{V(rms)}$$

$$|\mathbf{V}_s(\text{before})| = 4887.76\,\text{V(rms)}$$

$$\mathbf{V}_s(\text{after}) = 4800 + (500 - j145.83)(0.02 + j0.16)$$

$$= 4833.33 + j77.08 = 4833.95\underline{/0.91^\circ}\,\text{V(rms)}$$

$$|\mathbf{V}_s(\text{after})| = 4833.95\,\text{V(rms)}$$

P 10.41 [a] From Problem 9.64, $Z_{\text{Th}} = 90 + j120\,\Omega$ and $\mathbf{V}_{\text{Th}} = 450\underline{/36.87^\circ}$ V. Thus, for maximum power transfer, $Z_{\text{L}} = Z_{\text{Th}}^* = 90 - j120\,\Omega$:

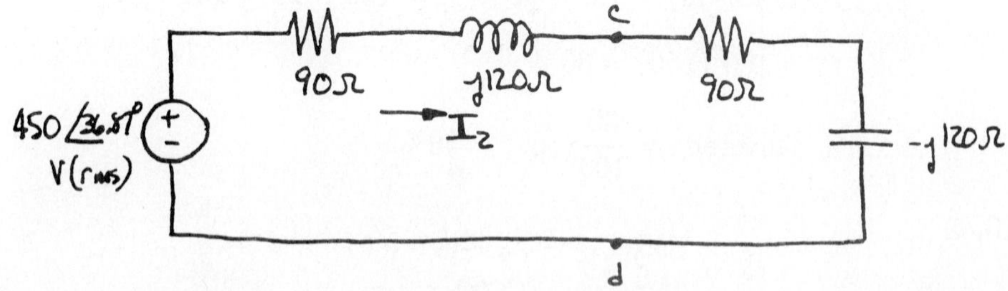

$$\mathbf{I}_2 = \frac{450\underline{/36.87^\circ}}{180} = 2.5\underline{/36.87^\circ} = 2 + j1.5\text{ A}$$

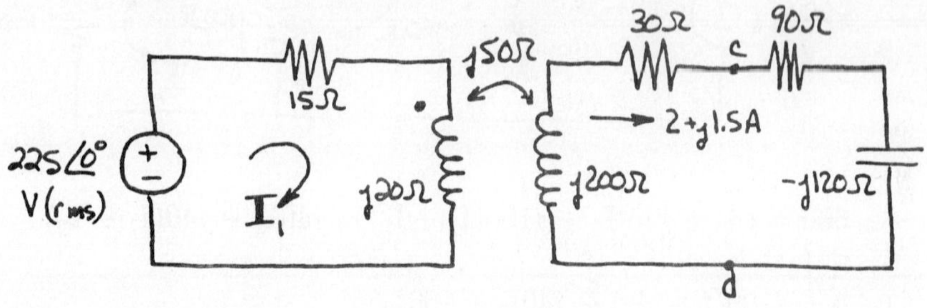

$$225\underline{/0^\circ} = (15 + j20)\mathbf{I}_1 = j50(2 + j1.5)$$

$$\therefore\ \ \mathbf{I}_1 = \frac{150 + j100}{15 + j20} = 6.8 - j2.4\text{ A}$$

$$S_g(\text{del}) = 225(6.8 + j2.4) = 1530 + j540\text{ VA}$$

$$P_g = 1530\text{ W}$$

[b] $P_{\text{loss}} = |\mathbf{I}_1|^2(15) + |\mathbf{I}_2|^2(30) = 780 + 187.5 = 967.5\text{ W}$

$$\%\text{ loss} = \frac{967.50}{1530}(100) = 63.24\%$$

P 10.42 [a] $\mathbf{I}_1 = \dfrac{125\underline{/0^\circ}}{20 + j34 + 5 + j16} = \dfrac{125}{25 + j50} = 1 - j2\text{ A}$

$$\mathbf{I}_2 = \frac{j\omega M}{Z_{22}}\mathbf{I}_1 = \frac{j50}{20 + j150}(1 - j2)$$

$$= 0.44 - j0.08 = 0.45\underline{/-10.30^\circ}\text{ A}$$

$$\mathbf{V}_{\text{L}} = (150 - j100)(0.44 - j0.08) = 58 - j56$$

$$= 80.62\underline{/-43.99^\circ}\text{ V}$$

$$|\mathbf{V}_{\text{L}}| = 80.62\text{ V}$$

[b] $P_g(\text{ideal}) = 125(1) = 125\,\text{W}$

$$P_g(\text{practical}) = 125 - |\mathbf{I}_1|^2(5) = 125 - 25 = 100\,\text{W}$$

$$P_L = |\mathbf{I}_2|^2(150) = 30\,\text{W}$$

$$\%\text{ delivered } = \frac{30}{100}(100) = 30\%$$

P 10.43

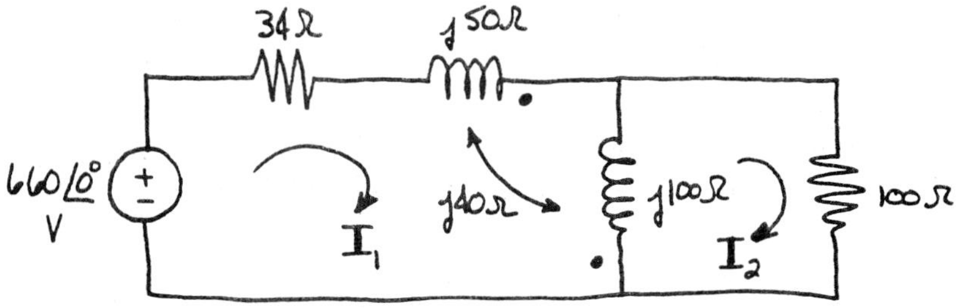

$$660 = (34 + j50)\mathbf{I}_1 + j100(\mathbf{I}_1 - \mathbf{I}_2) + j40\mathbf{I}_1 + j40(\mathbf{I}_1 - \mathbf{I}_2)$$

$$0 = j100(\mathbf{I}_2 - \mathbf{I}_1) - j40\mathbf{I}_1 + 100\mathbf{I}_2$$

Solving,

$$\mathbf{I}_2 = 3.5\underline{/0^\circ}\,\text{A}; \qquad \therefore\ P = \frac{1}{2}(3.5)^2(100) = 612.50\,\text{W}$$

P 10.44 [a] $\mathbf{V}_{\text{Th}} = \dfrac{760\underline{/0^\circ}}{28 + j96}(j50) = 380\underline{/16.26^\circ}\,\text{V}$

$$Z_{\text{Th}} = 31 + j100 + \left(\frac{50}{100}\right)^2(28 - j96) = 38 + j76\,\Omega$$

$$\therefore\ Z_L = 38 - j76\,\Omega$$

$$\mathbf{I}_L = \frac{380\underline{/16.26^\circ}}{76} = 4.8 + j1.4 = 5\underline{/16.26^\circ}\,\text{A(rms)}$$

$$P_L = |\mathbf{I}_L|^2(38) = 950\,\text{W}$$

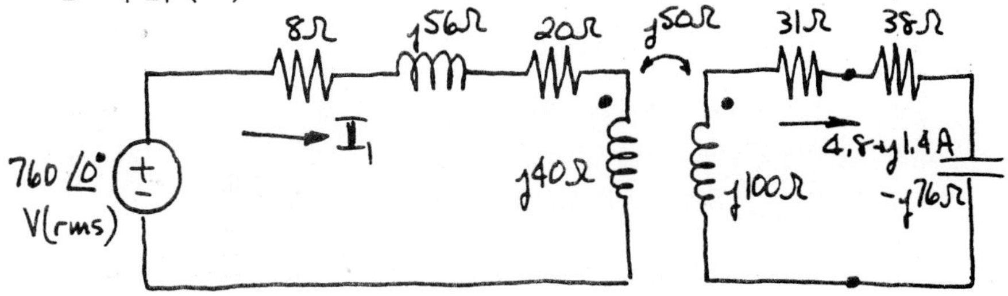

$$760\underline{/0^\circ} = \mathbf{I}_1(28 + j96) - j50(4.8 + j1.4)$$

$$\therefore \quad \mathbf{I}_1 = \frac{690 + j240}{100/\underline{73.74^\circ}} = 7.31/\underline{-54.56^\circ} = 4.24 - j5.95\ \text{A}$$

$$S_g(\text{delivered}) = 760(4.24 + j5.95) = 3219.36 + j4523.52\ \text{VA}$$

$$P_{\text{loss}} = |\mathbf{I}_1|^2(8) = 426.96\ \text{W}$$

$$P_{\text{in}}(\text{transformer}) = 3219.36 - 426.96 = 2792.40\ \text{W}$$

$$\%\ \text{delivered to}\ Z_L = \frac{950}{2792.4}(100) = 34.02\%$$

P 10.45 [a]

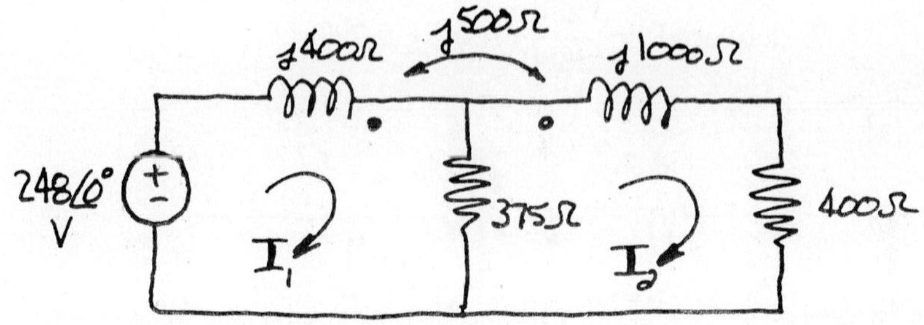

$$248 = j400\mathbf{I}_1 - j500\mathbf{I}_2 + 375(\mathbf{I}_1 - \mathbf{I}_2)$$

$$0 = 375(\mathbf{I}_2 - \mathbf{I}_1) + j1000\mathbf{I}_2 - j500\mathbf{I}_1 + 400\mathbf{I}_2$$

Solving,

$\mathbf{I}_1 = 0.80 - j0.62\ \text{A}$; $\quad \mathbf{I}_2 = 0.4 - j0.3 = 0.5/\underline{-36.87^\circ}$

$$\therefore \quad P = \frac{1}{2}(0.25)(400) = 50\ \text{W}$$

[b] $\mathbf{I}_1 - \mathbf{I}_2 = 0.4 - j0.32\ \text{A}$

$$P_{375} = \frac{1}{2}|\mathbf{I}_1 - \mathbf{I}_2|^2(375) = 49.20\ \text{W}$$

[c] $P_g = \frac{1}{2}(248)(0.8) = 99.20\ \text{W}$

$$\sum P_{\text{abs}} = 50 + 49.2 = 99.20\ \text{W} \quad \text{(checks)}$$

P 10.46 [a]

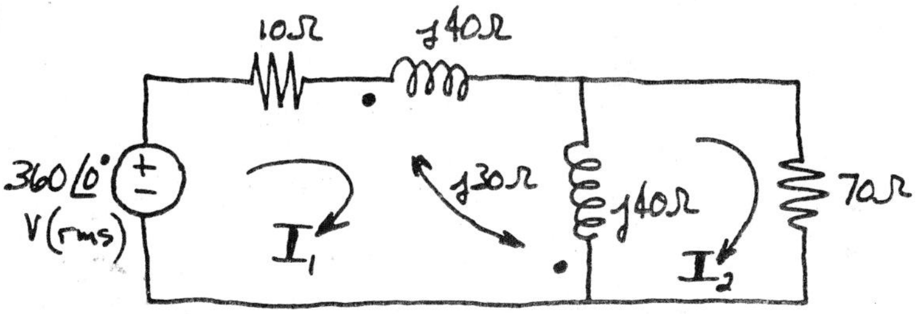

$$360/\underline{0^\circ} = 10\mathbf{I}_1 + j40\mathbf{I}_1 + 30(\mathbf{I}_2 - \mathbf{I}_1) - j30\mathbf{I}_1 + j40(\mathbf{I}_1 - \mathbf{I}_2)$$

$0 = j40(\mathbf{I}_2 - \mathbf{I}_1) + j30\mathbf{I}_1 + 70\mathbf{I}_2$

Solving,

$\mathbf{I}_2 = 2\angle 0^\circ$ A(rms); $\quad \therefore \quad \mathbf{V}_o = (2\angle 0^\circ)(70) = 140\angle 0^\circ$ V(rms)

[b] $P = 70|\mathbf{I}_2|^2 = 70(4) = 280$ W

[c] $360\angle 0^\circ = (10 + j20)\mathbf{I}_1 - j10(2 + j0); \quad \therefore \quad \mathbf{I}_1 = 8 - j14$ A

$P_g = (360)(8) = 2880$ W

$$\% \text{ delivered} = \frac{280}{2880}(100) = 9.72\%$$

P 10.47 [a]

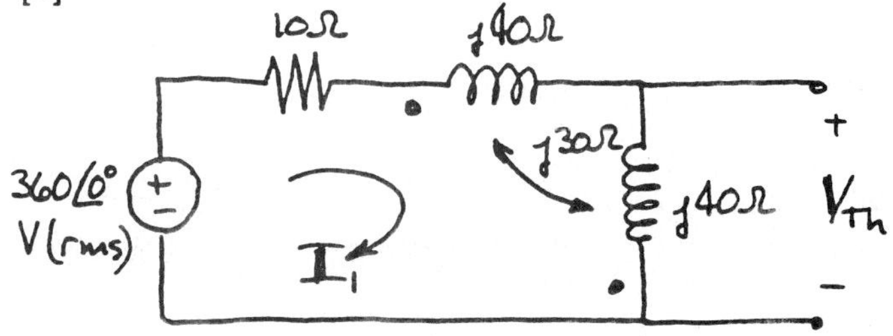

$360 = 10\mathbf{I}_1 + j40\mathbf{I}_1 - j30\mathbf{I}_1 + j40\mathbf{I}_1 - j30\mathbf{I}_1$

$\therefore \quad \mathbf{I}_1 = 7.2 - j14.4$ A(rms)

$\mathbf{V}_{Th} = j40\mathbf{I}_1 - j30\mathbf{I}_1 = j10\mathbf{I}_1 = 144 + j72$ V

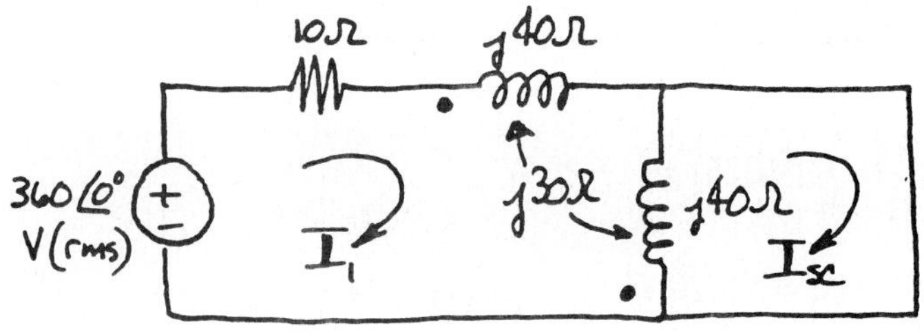

$360 = (10 + j20)\mathbf{I}_1 - j10\mathbf{I}_{sc}$

$0 = -j10\mathbf{I}_1 + j40\mathbf{I}_{sc}$

Solving,

$\mathbf{I}_{sc} = 2.215 - j3.877$ A

$$Z_{Th} = \frac{\mathbf{V}_{Th}}{\mathbf{I}_{sc}} = \frac{144 + j72}{2.215 - j3.877} = 2 + j36\,\Omega$$

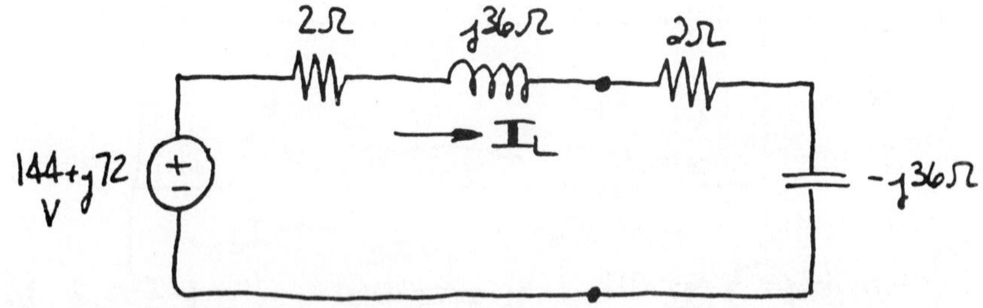

$$\mathbf{I}_L = \frac{144 + j72}{4} = 36 + j18\,\text{A}; \qquad \therefore \quad |\mathbf{I}_L| = 18\sqrt{5}\,\text{A}$$

$$P_L = (18)^2(5)(2) = 3240\,\text{W}$$

[b] $360 = (10 + j20)\mathbf{I}_1 - j10(36 + j18); \qquad \therefore \quad \mathbf{I}_1 = 18\underline{/0^\circ}\,\text{A}$

$$\therefore \quad P_g = (360)(18) = 6480\,\text{W}$$

P 10.48 [a]

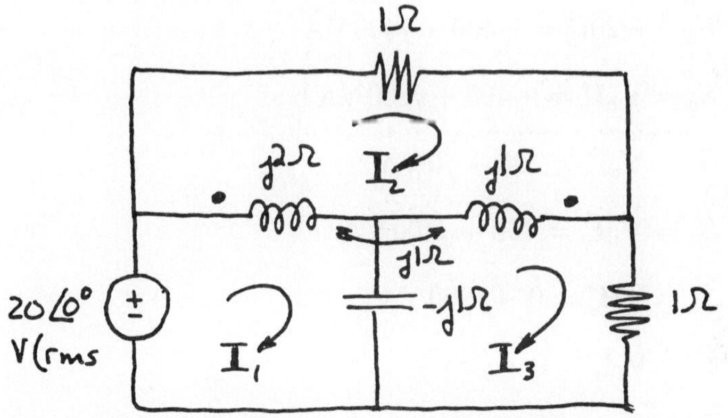

$$20 = j2(\mathbf{I}_1 - \mathbf{I}_2) + j1(\mathbf{I}_2 - \mathbf{I}_3) - j1(\mathbf{I}_1 - \mathbf{I}_3)$$

$$0 = 1\mathbf{I}_2 + j1(\mathbf{I}_2 - \mathbf{I}_3) + j1(\mathbf{I}_1 - \mathbf{I}_2) + j2(\mathbf{I}_2 - \mathbf{I}_1) - j1(\mathbf{I}_2 - \mathbf{I}_3)$$

$$0 = -j1(\mathbf{I}_3 - \mathbf{I}_1) + j1(\mathbf{I}_3 - \mathbf{I}_2) - j1(\mathbf{I}_1 - \mathbf{I}_2) + 1\mathbf{I}_3$$

Solving,

$\mathbf{I}_1 = 20 - j20\,\text{A(rms)}; \quad \mathbf{I}_2 = 20 + j0\,\text{A(rms)}; \quad \mathbf{I}_3 = 0\,\text{A(rms)}$

$\mathbf{I}_a = \mathbf{I}_1 = 20 - j20\,\text{A} \qquad \mathbf{I}_b = \mathbf{I}_1 - \mathbf{I}_2 = -j20\,\text{A}$

$\mathbf{I}_c = \mathbf{I}_2 = 20\,\text{A} \qquad \mathbf{I}_d = \mathbf{I}_3 - \mathbf{I}_2 = -20\,\text{A}$

$\mathbf{I}_e = \mathbf{I}_1 - \mathbf{I}_3 = 20 - j20\,\text{A} \qquad \mathbf{I}_f = \mathbf{I}_3 = 0\,\text{A}$

[b]

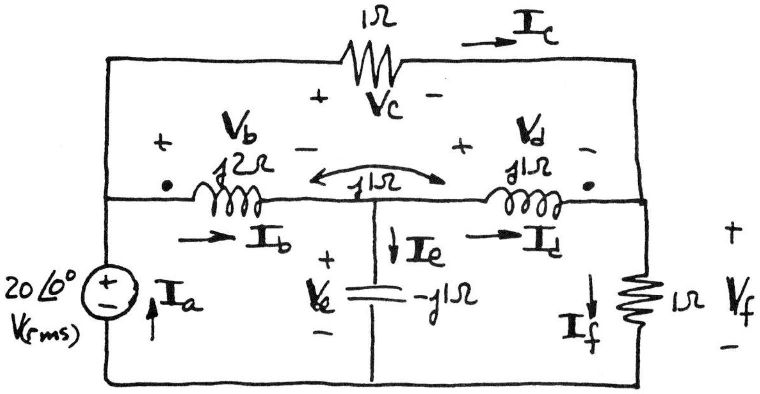

$\mathbf{V}_a = 20 + j0$ V

$\mathbf{V}_c = 1\mathbf{I}_c = 20 + j0$ V

$\mathbf{V}_e = -j1\mathbf{I}_e = -20 - j20$ V

$\mathbf{V}_b = j2\mathbf{I}_b - j1\mathbf{I}_d = 40 + j20$ V

$\mathbf{V}_d = j1\mathbf{I}_d - j1\mathbf{I}_b = -20 - j20$ V

$\mathbf{V}_f = 1\mathbf{I}_f = 0$ V

$S_a = -20\mathbf{I}_a^* = -400 - j400$ VA

$S_b = \mathbf{V}_b\mathbf{I}_b^* = -400 + j800$ VA

$S_c = \mathbf{V}_c\mathbf{I}_c^* = 400 + j0$ VA

$S_d = \mathbf{V}_d\mathbf{I}_d^* = 400 + j400$ VA

$S_e = \mathbf{V}_e\mathbf{I}_e^* = 0 - j800$ VA

$S_f = \mathbf{V}_f\mathbf{I}_f^* = 0 + j0$ VA

[c] $\sum P_{dev} = 400$ W

$\sum P_{abs} = -400 + 400 + 400 = 400$ W

Note that the total power absorbed by the coupled coils is zero:
$-400 + 400 = 0 = P_b + P_d$

[d] $\sum Q_{dev} = 400 + 800 = 1200$ VAR

Both the source and the capacitor are developing magnetizing vars.

$\sum Q_{abs} = 400 + 800 = 1200$ VAR

$\sum Q$ absorbed by the coupled coils is $Q_b + Q_d$

P 10.49 [a]

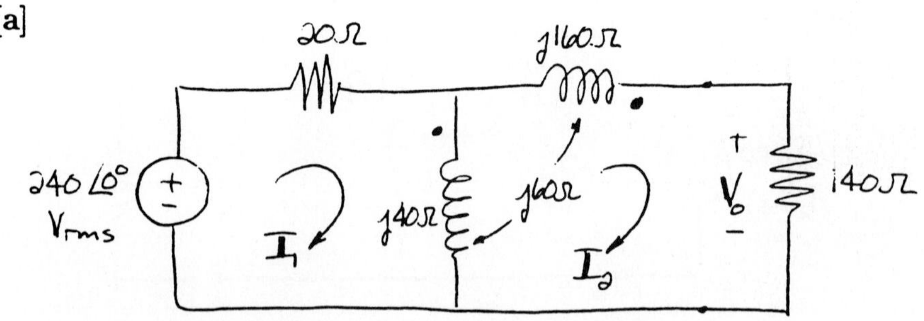

$$240 = 20\mathbf{I}_1 + j40(\mathbf{I}_1 - \mathbf{I}_2) - j60\mathbf{I}_2$$

$$0 = j40(\mathbf{I}_2 - \mathbf{I}_1) + j60\mathbf{I}_2 + j160\mathbf{I}_2 + j60(\mathbf{I}_2 - \mathbf{I}_1) + 140\mathbf{I}_2$$

Solving,

$\mathbf{I}_1 = 6.4 - j2.8\,\text{A(rms)}$; $\quad \mathbf{I}_2 = 2\underline{/0^\circ}\,\text{A(rms)}$

$\mathbf{V}_o = 140\mathbf{I}_2 = 280\underline{/0^\circ}\,\text{V(rms)}$

[b] $P = |\mathbf{I}_2|^2(140) = 560\,\text{W}$

[c] $P_g = (240)(6.4) = 1536\,\text{W}$

$$\%\ \text{delivered} = \frac{560}{1536}(100) = 36.46\%$$

P 10.50 [a] $\mathbf{V}_{\text{Th}} = \dfrac{240\underline{/0^\circ}}{20 + j40}(j40) + \dfrac{240\underline{/0^\circ}}{20 + j40}(j60) = 480 + j240\,\text{V(rms)}$

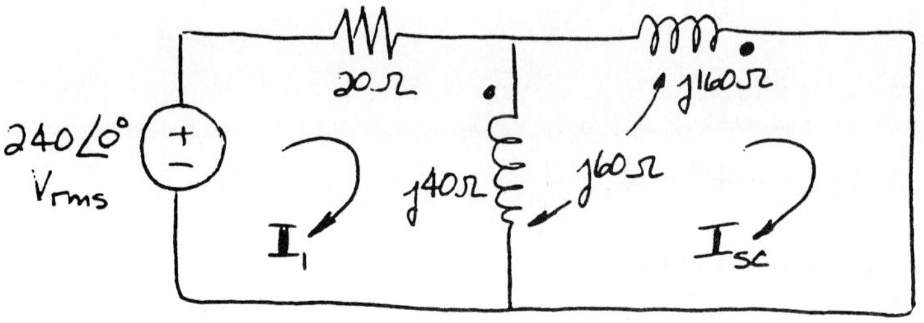

From the solution to Problem 10.49 we can write

$$240 = (20 + j40)\mathbf{I}_1 - j100\mathbf{I}_{sc}$$

$$0 = -j100\mathbf{I}_1 + j320\mathbf{I}_{sc}$$

Solving,

$$\mathbf{I}_{sc} = 3.15 - j1.377$$

$$Z_{\text{Th}} = \frac{\mathbf{V}_{\text{Th}}}{\mathbf{I}_{sc}} = \frac{480 + j240}{3.15 - j1.377} = 100 + j120 = 156.20\underline{/50.19^\circ}\,\Omega$$

$$\therefore\ R_L = 156.20\,\Omega$$

[b]

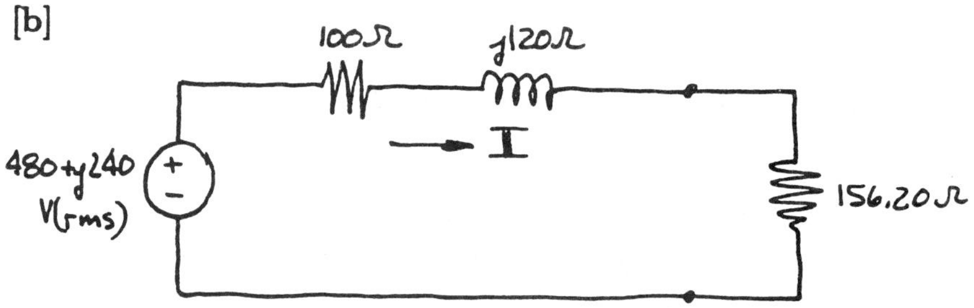

$$\mathbf{I} = \frac{536.66\underline{/26.57^\circ}}{282.92\underline{/25.10^\circ}} = 1.90\underline{/1.47^\circ}$$

$$P = |\mathbf{I}|^2(156.20) = 562.05\,\text{W}$$

P 10.51 [a]

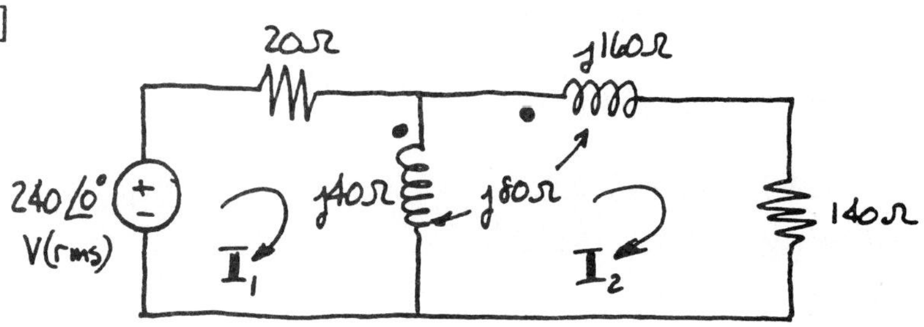

$$240 = 20\mathbf{I}_1 + j40(\mathbf{I}_1 - \mathbf{I}_2) + j80k\mathbf{I}_2$$

$$0 = j40(\mathbf{I}_2 - \mathbf{I}_1) - j80k\mathbf{I}_2 + j160\mathbf{I}_2 + j80k(\mathbf{I}_1 - \mathbf{I}_2) + 140\mathbf{I}_2$$

or

$$12 = (1 + j2)\mathbf{I}_1 + j(4k - 2)\mathbf{I}_2$$

$$0 = j(4k - 2)\mathbf{I}_1 + [7 + j(10 - 8k)]\mathbf{I}_2$$

$N_2 = -j(4k - 2)(12);$ $\quad\mathbf{I}_2 = 0$ when $N_2 = 0$

$\mathbf{V}_o = 0$ when $\mathbf{I}_2 = 0$

$\therefore\ k = 0.5$

[b] When $\mathbf{I}_2 = 0$

$$\mathbf{I}_1 = \frac{12}{1 + j2} = 2.4 - j4.8\,\text{A(rms)}$$

$$P_g = (240)(2.4) = 576\,\text{W}$$

Check:

$$P_{\text{loss}} = |\mathbf{I}_1|^2(20) = 576\,\text{W}$$

P 10.52 [a] $j\omega L_1 = j(5000)(2 \times 10^{-3}) = j10\,\Omega$

$j\omega L_2 = j(5000)(8 \times 10^{-3}) = j40\,\Omega$

$j\omega M = j10\,\Omega$

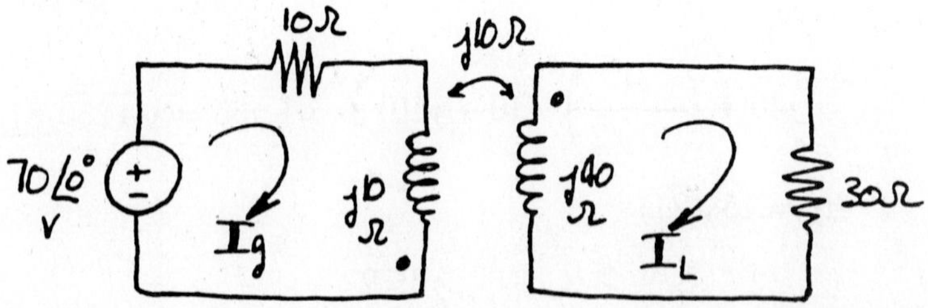

$70 = (10 + j10)\mathbf{I}_g + j10\mathbf{I}_L$

$0 = j10\mathbf{I}_g + (30 + j40)\mathbf{I}_L$

Solving,

$\mathbf{I}_g = 4 - j3\,\text{A}; \qquad \mathbf{I}_L = -1\,\text{A}$

Thus,

$i_g = 5\cos(5000t - 36.87^\circ)\,\text{A}$

$i_L = 1\cos(5000t - 180^\circ)\,\text{A}$

[b] $k = \dfrac{M}{\sqrt{L_1 L_2}} = \dfrac{2}{\sqrt{16}} = 0.5$

[c] When $t = 100\pi\ \mu$s:

$5000t = (5000)(100\pi) \times 10^{-6} = 0.5\pi \text{ rad } = 90^\circ$

$i_g(100\pi\ \mu\text{s}) = 5\cos(53.15^\circ) = 3\,\text{A}$

$i_L(100\pi\ \mu\text{s}) = 1\cos(-90^\circ) = 0\,\text{A}$

$w = \frac{1}{2}L_1 i_1^2 + \frac{1}{2}L_2 i_2^2 + M i_1 i_2 = \frac{1}{2}(2 \times 10^{-3})(9) + 0 + 0 = 9\,\text{mJ}$

When $t = 200\pi\ \mu$s:

$5000t = \pi \text{ rad } = 180^\circ$

$i_g(200\pi\ \mu\text{s}) = 5\cos(180 - 36.87^\circ) = -4\,\text{A}$

$i_L(200\pi\ \mu\text{s}) = 1\cos(180 - 180^\circ) = 1\,\text{A}$

$w = \frac{1}{2}(2 \times 10^{-3})(16) + \frac{1}{2}(8 \times 10^{-3})(1) + 2 \times 10^{-3}(-4)(1) = 12\,\text{mJ}$

[d] From (a), $I_m = 1$ A,

$$\therefore \quad P = \frac{1}{2}(1)^2(30) = 15\,\text{W}$$

[e] $$\mathbf{V}_{\text{Th}} = \frac{70}{10 + j10}(j10) = 25\sqrt{2}\underline{/45^\circ}\ \text{V}$$

$$Z_{\text{Th}} = j40 + \left(\frac{10}{10\sqrt{2}}\right)^2 (10 - j10) = 5 + j35 = \sqrt{1250}\underline{/81.78^\circ}\ \Omega$$

$$\therefore \quad R_{\text{L}} = 25\sqrt{2}\,\Omega$$

[f]

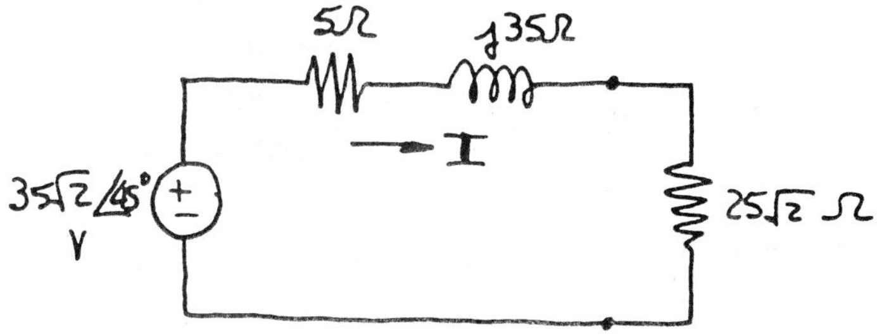

$$\mathbf{I} = \frac{35\sqrt{2}\underline{/45^\circ}}{(5 + 25\sqrt{2}) + j35} = 0.93\underline{/4.07^\circ}\ \text{A}$$

$$P = \frac{1}{2}(0.93)^2(25\sqrt{2}) = 15.18\,\text{W}$$

[g] $Z_{\text{L}} = Z_{\text{Th}}^* = 5 - j35\,\Omega$

[h] $$\mathbf{I} = \frac{35\sqrt{2}\underline{/45^\circ}}{10} = 3.5\sqrt{2}\underline{/45^\circ}$$

$$P = \frac{1}{2}(35\sqrt{2})^2(5) = 61.25\,\text{W}$$

P 10.53 [a]

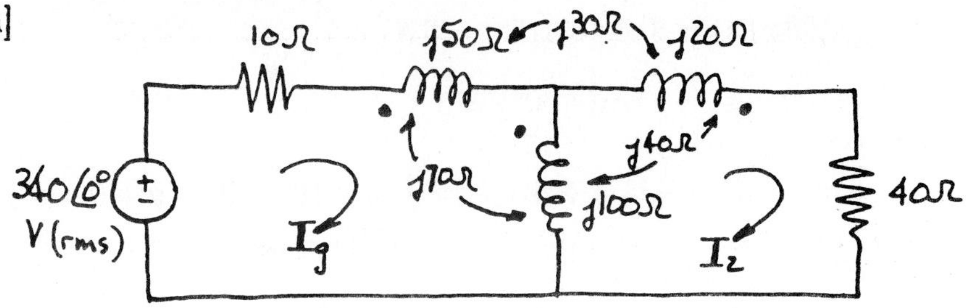

$$340\underline{/0^\circ} = 10\mathbf{I}_g + j50\mathbf{I}_g + j70(\mathbf{I}_g - \mathbf{I}_2) - j30\mathbf{I}_2$$
$$+ j70\mathbf{I}_g - j40\mathbf{I}_2 + j100(\mathbf{I}_g - \mathbf{I}_2)$$
$$0 = j100(\mathbf{I}_2 - \mathbf{I}_g) - j70\mathbf{I}_g + j40\mathbf{I}_2 + j20\mathbf{I}_2$$
$$+ j40(\mathbf{I}_2 - \mathbf{I}_g) - j30\mathbf{I}_g + 40\mathbf{I}_2$$

Solving,

$I_g = 5 - j1\ \text{A(rms)}; \qquad \mathbf{I}_2 = 6\underline{/0^\circ}\ \text{A(rms)}$

$P_{40\Omega} = (6)^2(40) = 1440\ \text{W}$

[b] $P_g(\text{developed}) = (340)(5) = 1700\ \text{W}$

[c] $Z_{ab} = \dfrac{\mathbf{V}_g}{\mathbf{I}_g} - 10 = \dfrac{340}{5-j} - 10 = 55.38 + j13.08 = 56.91\underline{/13.28^\circ}\ \Omega$

[d] $P_{10\Omega} = |I_g|^2(10) = 260\ \text{W}$

$\sum P_{\text{diss}} = 1440 + 260 = 1700\ \text{W} = \sum P_{\text{dev}}$

P 10.54

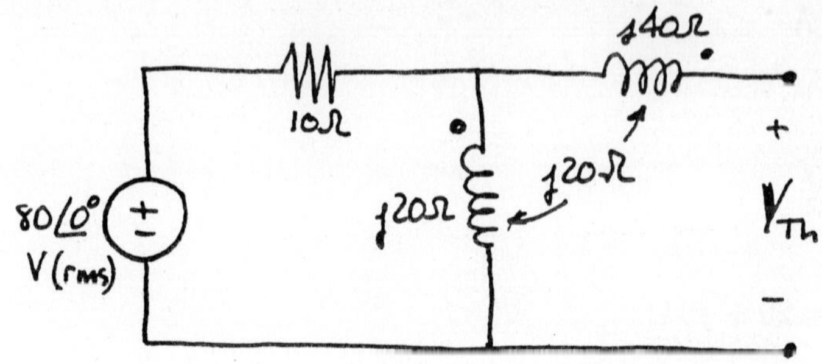

$$\mathbf{V}_{\text{Th}} = \frac{80}{10 + j20}(j20) + \frac{80}{10 + j20}(j20) = 128 + j64\ \text{V(rms)}$$

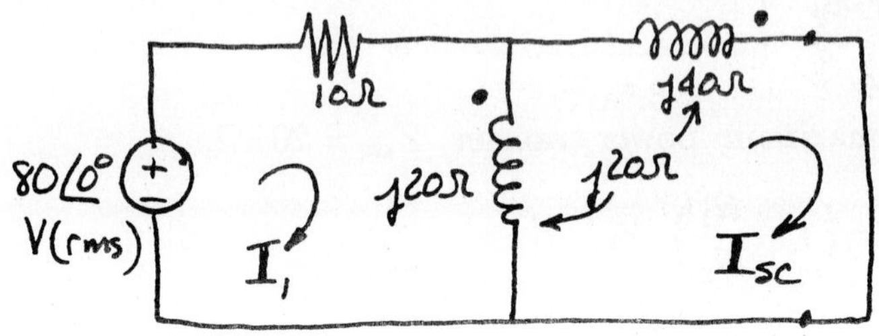

$$80 = 10\mathbf{I}_1 + j20(\mathbf{I}_1 - \mathbf{I}_{sc}) - j20\mathbf{I}_{sc}$$

$$0 = j20(\mathbf{I}_{sc} - \mathbf{I}_1) + j20\mathbf{I}_{sc} + j40\mathbf{I}_{sc} - j20(\mathbf{I}_1 - \mathbf{I}_{sc})$$

Solving,

$$\mathbf{I}_{sc} = 2.76 - j1.10\ \text{A}; \qquad Z_{\text{Th}} = \frac{128 + j64}{2.76 - j1.10} = 32 + j36\ \Omega$$

$$\therefore\ \mathbf{I}_{\text{L}} = \frac{128 + j64}{64} = 2 + j1\ \text{A}$$

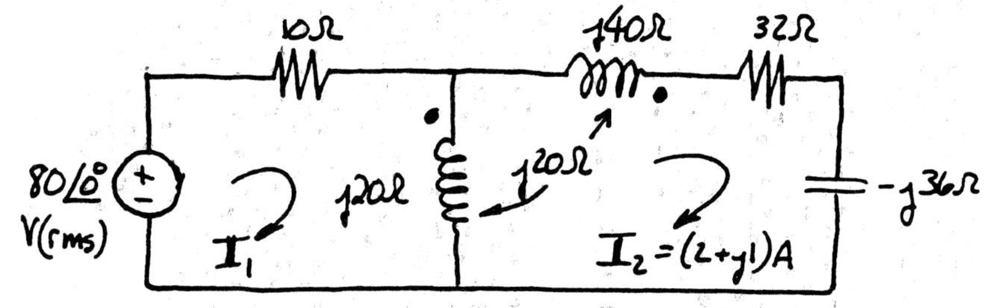

$$80 = 10\mathbf{I}_1 + j20(\mathbf{I}_1 - \mathbf{I}_2) - j20\mathbf{I}_2$$

$$\mathbf{I}_2 = 2 + j1\,\text{A}$$

Solving,

$$I_1 = 4\underline{/0^\circ}\,\text{A}$$

$$Z_g = 80/4 = 20 + j0\,\Omega$$

P 10.55 [a]

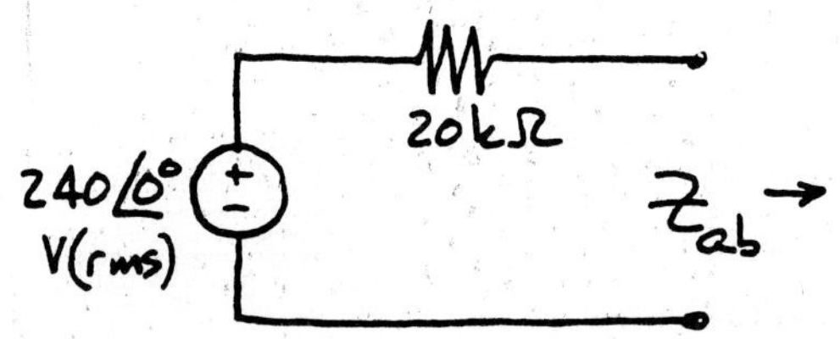

For maximum power transfer, $Z_{ab} = 20\,\text{k}\Omega$

$$Z_{ab} = \left(1 - \frac{N_1}{N_2}\right)^2 Z_L$$

$$\therefore \left(1 - \frac{N_1}{N_2}\right)^2 = \frac{20{,}000}{50} = 400$$

$$1 - \frac{N_1}{N_2} = \pm 20; \qquad \frac{N_1}{N_2} = 1 \mp 20$$

$$\frac{N_1}{N_2} > 0 \qquad \therefore \frac{N_1}{N_2} = 21$$

$$N_2 = \frac{N_1}{21} = \frac{2520}{21} = 120 \text{ turns}$$

[b]

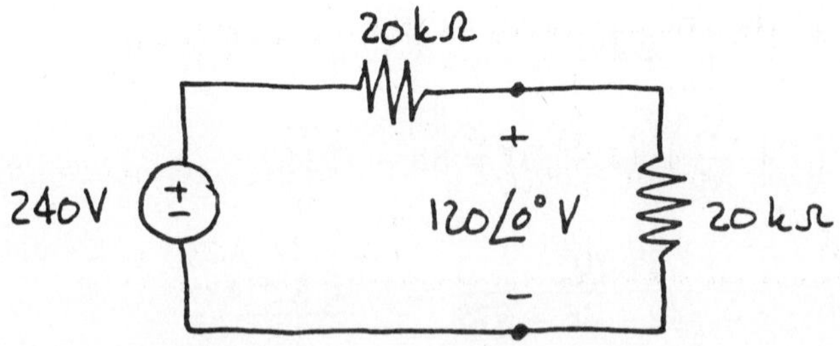

$$P_{50\Omega} = P_{20k\Omega} = \frac{(120)^2}{20} \times 10^{-3} = 720\,\text{mW}$$

[c]

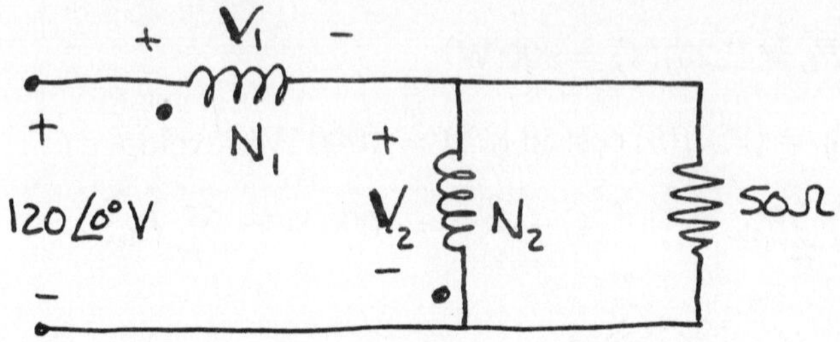

$$\mathbf{V}_1 + \mathbf{V}_2 = 120; \qquad \frac{\mathbf{V}_1}{N_1} = -\frac{\mathbf{V}_2}{N_2}$$

$$\mathbf{V}_2 = -\frac{N_2}{N_1}\mathbf{V}_1 = -\frac{\mathbf{V}_1}{21}$$

$$\mathbf{V}_1 - \frac{\mathbf{V}_1}{21} = 120; \qquad \therefore\ \mathbf{V}_1 = 126\,\text{V}$$

$$\therefore\ \mathbf{V}_2 = -6\,\text{V}$$

Check the power calculation:

$$P_{50\Omega} = \frac{36}{60} = 0.72\,\text{W} = 720\,\text{mW}$$

[d]

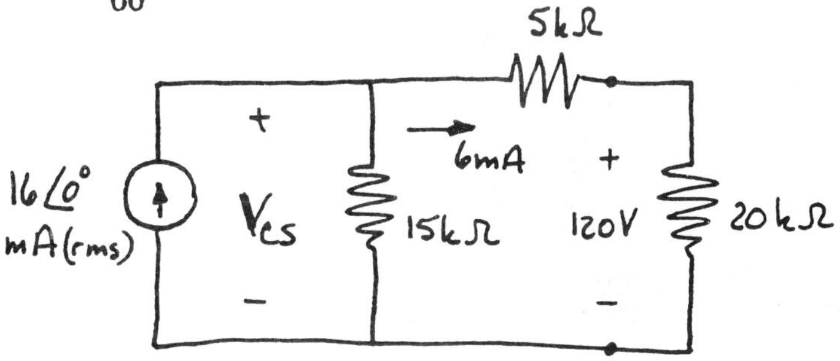

$$\mathbf{V}_{cs} = 120 + (6)(5) = 150\,\text{V}$$

$$P_{cs}(\text{del}) = (150)(16) = 2400\,\text{mW}$$

$$\% \text{ delivered} = \frac{720}{2400}(100) = 30\%$$

P 10.56 [a] $Z_{ab} = \left(1 + \frac{N_1}{N_2}\right)^2 (4 - j8) = 36 - j72\,\Omega$

$$\therefore \quad \mathbf{I}_1 = \frac{250\underline{/0^\circ}}{4 + j42 + 36 - j72} = 5\underline{/36.87^\circ}\text{ A}$$

$$\mathbf{I}_2 = \frac{N_1}{N_2}\mathbf{I}_1 = 10\underline{/36.87^\circ}\text{ A}$$

$$\therefore \quad \mathbf{I}_L = 15\underline{/36.87^\circ}\text{ A(rms)}$$

$$P_L = (225)(4) = 900\text{ W}$$

[b] $P_g = (250)(5)\cos(36.87^\circ) = 1000\text{ W(developed)}$

$$\sum P_{abs} = (5)^2(4) + 900 = 1000\text{ W} = \sum P_{dev}$$

P 10.57 [a]

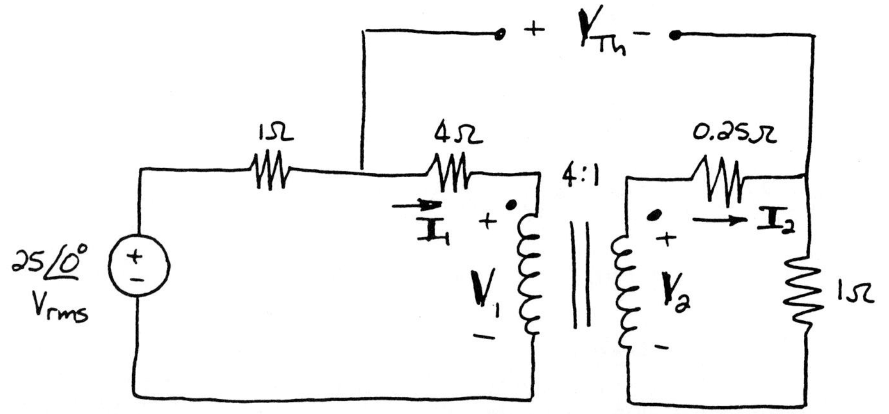

$$\mathbf{V}_2 = \frac{1}{4}\mathbf{V}_1; \qquad \mathbf{I}_2 = 4\mathbf{I}_1$$

$$25 = 5\mathbf{I}_1 + \mathbf{V}_1$$

$$0 = -\mathbf{V}_2 + 1.25\mathbf{I}_2$$

$$\therefore \quad \mathbf{I}_1 = 1\text{ A}; \qquad \mathbf{I}_2 = 4\text{ A}$$

$$25 = (1)\mathbf{I}_1 + \mathbf{V}_{Th} + (1)\mathbf{I}_2; \qquad \therefore \quad \mathbf{V}_{Th} = 20\text{ V}$$

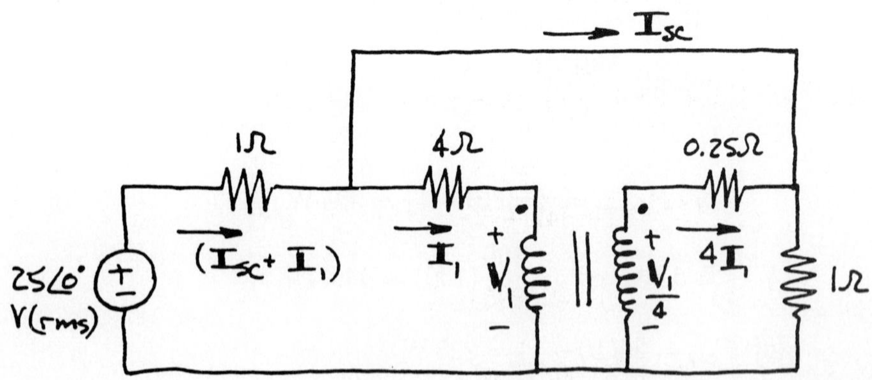

$$25 = (\mathbf{I}_{sc} + \mathbf{I}_1)(1) + (\mathbf{I}_{sc} + 4\mathbf{I}_1)(1)$$

$$\frac{\mathbf{V}_1}{4} = 4\mathbf{I}_1(0.25) + (\mathbf{I}_{sc} + 4\mathbf{I}_1)(1)$$

Solving,

$$\mathbf{I}_{sc} = 20\text{ A}$$

$$R_{\text{Th}} = \frac{\mathbf{V}_{\text{Th}}}{\mathbf{I}_{sc}} = \frac{20}{20} = 1\,\Omega$$

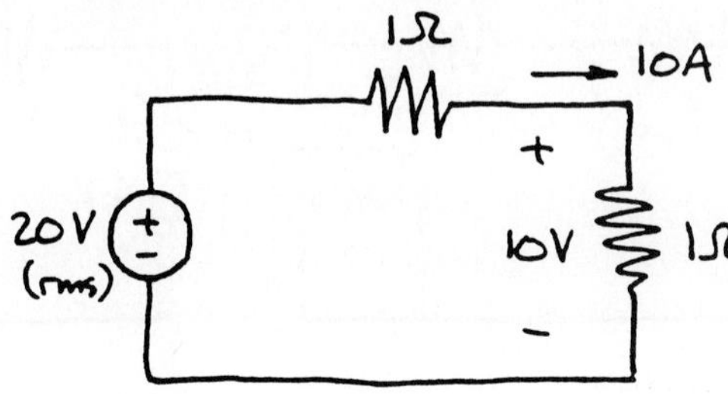

$$P = (10)^2(1) = 100\text{ W}$$

[b]

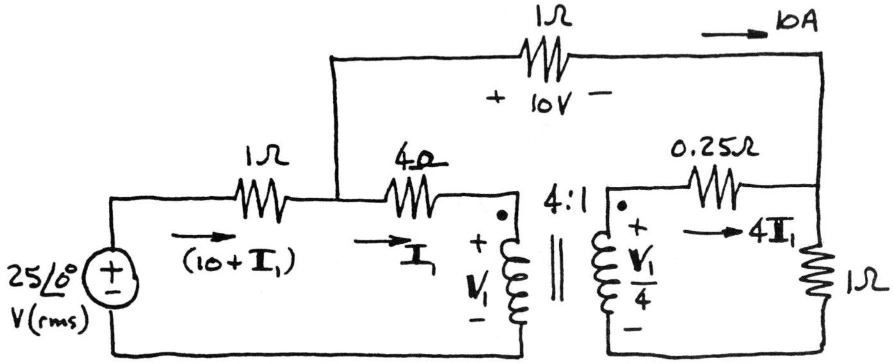

$$25 = (10 + \mathbf{I}_1)(1) + 4\mathbf{I}_1 + \mathbf{V}_1$$

$$\frac{\mathbf{V}_1}{4} = 4\mathbf{I}_1(0.25) + (4\mathbf{I}_1 + 10)(1)$$

Solving,

$$\mathbf{I}_1 = -1\,\text{A}$$

$$\therefore \quad P_{\text{source}} = (25)(10-1) = 225\,\text{W}$$

$$\%\ \text{delivered} = \frac{100}{225}(100) = 44.44\%$$

[c] $P_{\text{dev}} = 25(10-1) = 225\,\text{W}$

$$P_{1\Omega} = (9)^2(1) = 81\,\text{W}; \quad P_{4\Omega} = (-1)^2(4) = 4\,\text{W}$$

$$P_{1\Omega} = (10)^2(1) = 100\,\text{W}; \quad P_{0.25\Omega} = (-4)^2(0.25) = 4\,\text{W}$$

$$P_{1\Omega} = (10-4)^2(1) = 36\,\text{W}$$

$$\sum P_{\text{abs}} = 81 + 4 + 100 + 4 + 36 = 225\,\text{W} = \sum P_{\text{dev}}$$

P 10.58 [a]

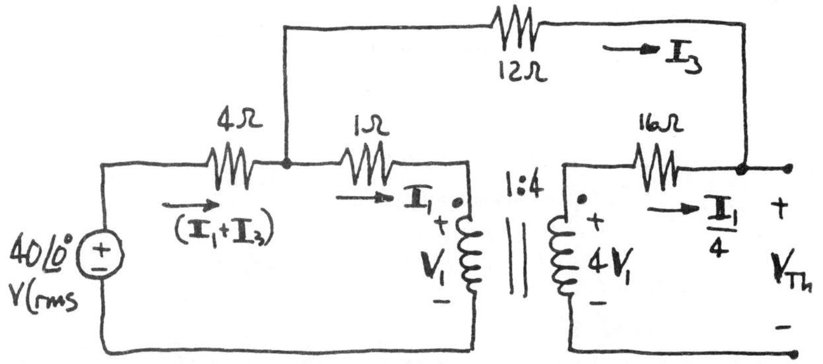

$$40\underline{/0^\circ} = 4(\mathbf{I}_1 + \mathbf{I}_3) + 12\mathbf{I}_3 + \mathbf{V}_{\text{Th}}$$

$$\frac{\mathbf{I}_1}{4} = -\mathbf{I}_3; \qquad \mathbf{I}_1 = -4\mathbf{I}_3$$

Solving,

$$\mathbf{V}_{\text{Th}} = 40\underline{/0^\circ}\,\text{V}$$

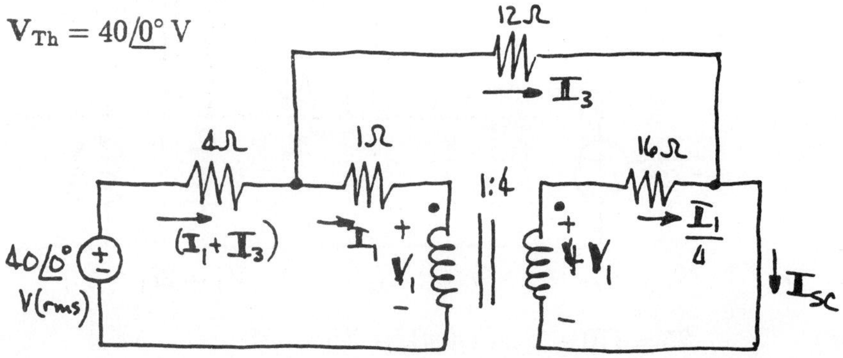

$40\underline{/0^\circ} = 4\mathbf{I}_1 + 4\mathbf{I}_3 + \mathbf{I}_1 + \mathbf{V}_1$

$4\mathbf{V}_1 = 16(\mathbf{I}_1/4) = 4\mathbf{I}_1; \qquad \therefore\ \mathbf{V}_1 = \mathbf{I}_1$

$\therefore\ 40\underline{/0^\circ} = 6\mathbf{I}_1 + 4\mathbf{I}_3$

Also,

$40\underline{/0^\circ} = 4(\mathbf{I}_1 + \mathbf{I}_3) + 12\mathbf{I}_3$

Solving,

$\mathbf{I}_1 = 6\text{ A}; \qquad \mathbf{I}_3 = 1\text{ A}; \qquad \mathbf{I}_{sc} = \mathbf{I}_1/4 + \mathbf{I}_3 = 2.5\text{ A}$

$$R_{Th} = \frac{\mathbf{V}_{Th}}{\mathbf{I}_{sc}} = \frac{40}{2.5} = 16\,\Omega$$

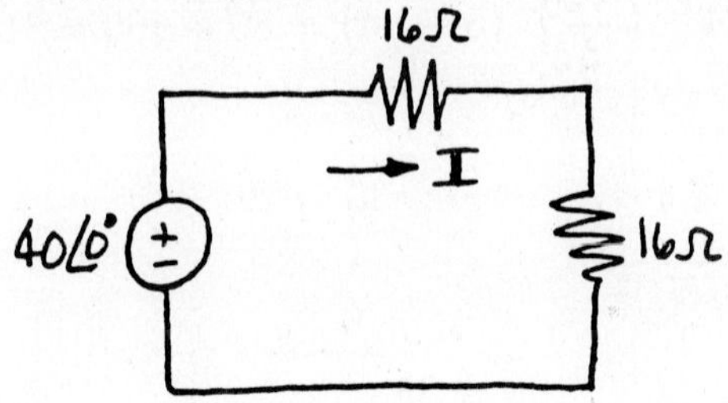

$$\mathbf{I} = \frac{40\underline{/0^\circ}}{32} = 1.25\underline{/0^\circ}\text{ A(rms)}$$

$P = (1.25)^2(16) = 25\text{ W}$

[b]

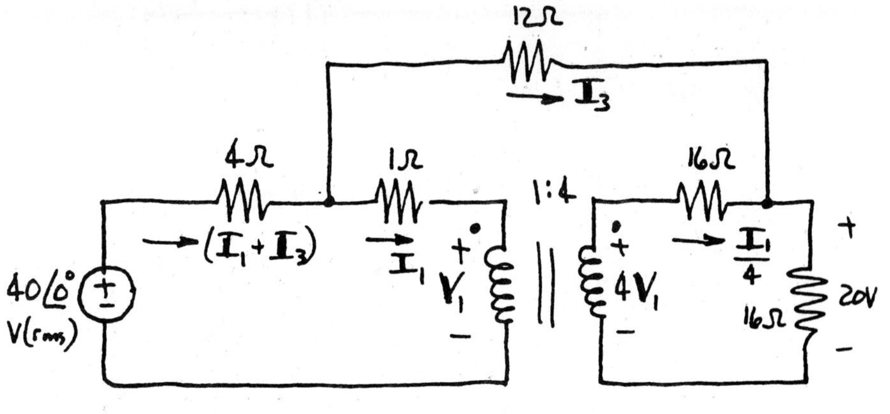

$40 = 4(\mathbf{I}_1 + \mathbf{I}_3) + 12\mathbf{I}_3 + 20$

$4\mathbf{V}_1 = 4\mathbf{I}_1 + 16(\mathbf{I}_1/4 + \mathbf{I}_3); \qquad \therefore\ \mathbf{V}_1 = 2\mathbf{I}_1 + 4\mathbf{I}_3$

$40 = 4\mathbf{I}_1 + 4\mathbf{I}_3 + \mathbf{I}_1 + \mathbf{V}_1$

$$\therefore \quad \mathbf{I}_1 = 6\,\text{A}; \qquad \mathbf{I}_3 = -0.25\,\text{A}; \qquad \mathbf{I}_1 + \mathbf{I}_3 = 5.75\underline{/0^\circ}\,\text{A}$$

$$P_{40V}\,(\text{developed}) = 40(5.75) = 230\,\text{W}$$

$$\therefore \quad \%\ \text{delivered} = \frac{25}{230}(100) = 10.87\%$$

[c] $P_{R_L} = 25\,\text{W}; \qquad P_{16\Omega} = (1.5)^2(16) = 36\,\text{W}$

$$P_{4\Omega} = (5.75)^2(4) = 132.25\,\text{W}; \qquad P_{1\Omega} = (6)^2(1) = 36\,\text{W}$$

$$P_{12\Omega} = (-0.25)^2(12) = 0.75\,\text{W}$$

$$\sum P_{\text{abs}} = 25 + 36 + 132.25 + 36 + 0.75 = 230\,\text{W} = \sum P_{\text{dev}}$$

P 10.59 [a] $Z_{\text{Th}} = 32 + j124 + \left(\frac{20}{5}\right)^2 (3 - j4) = 80 + j60 = 100\underline{/36.87^\circ}\,\Omega$

$$\therefore \quad Z_{\text{ab}} = 100\,\Omega$$

$$Z_{\text{ab}} = \frac{Z_L}{(1 + N_1/N_2)^2}$$

$$(1 + N_1/N_2)^2 = 3600/100 = 36$$

$$\therefore \quad N_1/N_2 = 5 \quad \text{or} \quad N_2 = N_1/5$$

$$\therefore \quad N_2 = 300\ \text{turns}$$

[b] $\mathbf{V}_{\text{Th}} = \frac{240\underline{/0^\circ}}{3 + j4}(j20) = 960\underline{/36.87^\circ}\,\text{V}$

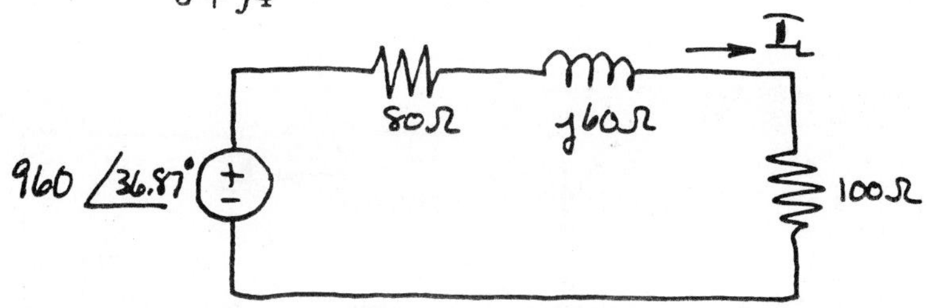

$$\mathbf{I} = \frac{960\underline{/36.87^\circ}}{180 + j60} = 1.6\sqrt{10}\underline{/18.43^\circ}\,\text{A(rms)}$$

$$|\mathbf{I}| = 1.6\sqrt{10}\,\text{A(rms)}$$

$$P = |\mathbf{I}|^2(100) = 2560\,\text{W}$$

[c]

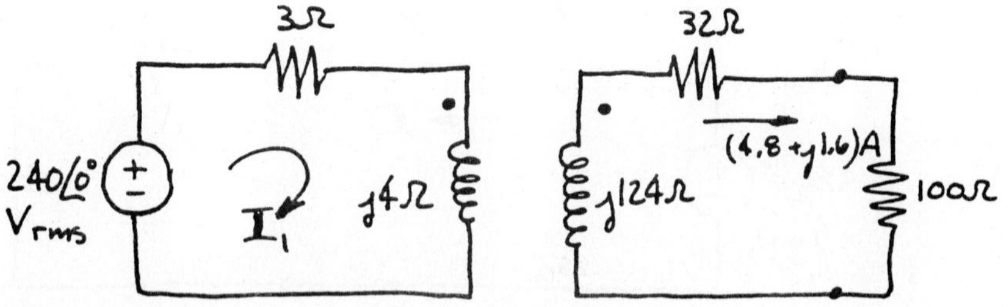

$$240\underline{/0^\circ} = (3 + j4)\mathbf{I}_1 - j20(4.8 - j1.6)$$

$$\therefore \quad \mathbf{I}_1 = 40.32 - j21.76\,\text{A(rms)}$$

[d] $P_{\text{gen}} = (240)(40.32) = 9676.80\,\text{W}$

$$P_{\text{trans}} = 9676.80 - 2560 = 7116.80\,\text{W}$$

$$\%\ \text{transmitted} = \frac{7116.80}{9676.80}(100) = 73.54\%$$

P 10.60 [a] $\mathbf{I}^2a_2^2(80) = 16\mathbf{I}^2a_1^2(320)$

$$\therefore \quad \left(\frac{a_2}{a_1}\right)^2 = 64; \qquad a_2 = 8a_1$$

$$a_1^2(320) + a_2^2(80) = 136{,}000$$

$$a_1^2(320) + 64a_1^2(80) = 136{,}000$$

$$\therefore \quad a_1^2 = 25; \qquad a_1 = 5; \qquad a_2 = 40$$

[b] $\mathbf{I} = \dfrac{680\underline{/0^\circ}}{(136 + 136)10^3} = 2.5\underline{/0^\circ}\,\text{mA(rms)}$

$$P_{80\Omega} = (2.5)^2 \times 10^{-6}(1600)(80) = 800\,\text{mW}$$

[c] $\mathbf{V}_{320} = \dfrac{1}{5}(2.5 \times 10^{-3})(25)(320) = 4\,\text{V(rms)}$

P 10.61 [a] $Z_{\text{ab}} = 30{,}000 - j10{,}000 = \left(1 - \dfrac{N_1}{N_2}\right)^2 Z_{\text{L}}$

$$\therefore \quad Z_{\text{L}} = \frac{1}{4}(30{,}000 - j10{,}000) = 7500 - j2500\,\Omega$$

[b]

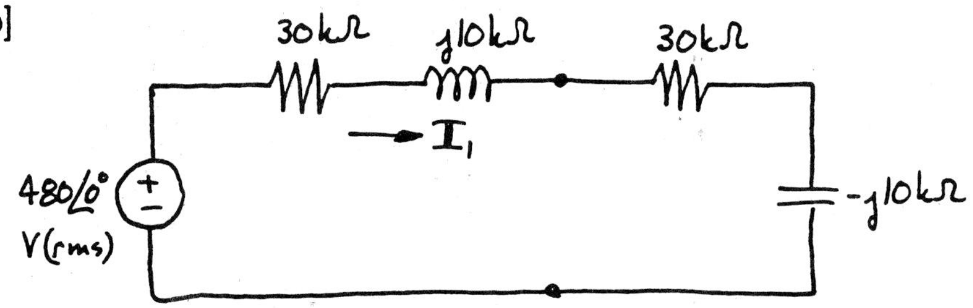

$$\mathbf{I}_1 = \frac{480}{60} \times 10^{-3} = 8\underline{/0^\circ}\,\text{mA}$$

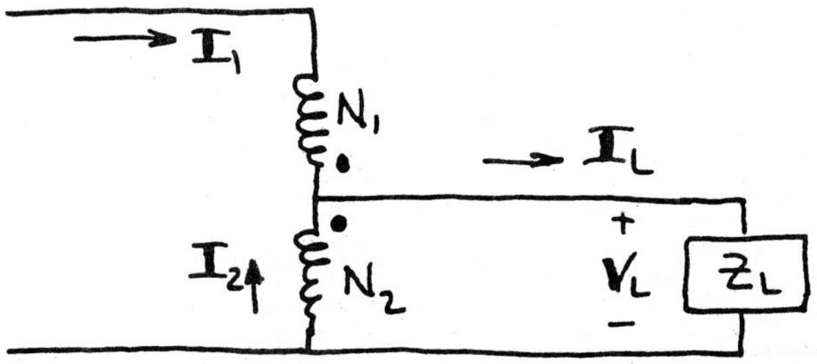

$$N_1\mathbf{I}_1 = -N_2\mathbf{I}_2$$

$$\mathbf{I}_2 = -3\mathbf{I}_1 = -24\underline{/0^\circ}\,\text{mA}$$

$$\mathbf{I}_\text{L} = \mathbf{I}_1 + \mathbf{I}_2 = -16\underline{/0^\circ}\,\text{mA}$$

$$\mathbf{V}_\text{L} = (7500 - j2500)\mathbf{I}_\text{L} = -120 + j40 = 126.49\underline{/161.57^\circ}\,\text{V(rms)}$$

P 10.62 [a] Replace the circuit to the left of the primary winding with a Thévenin equivalent:

$$\mathbf{V}_\text{Th} = \frac{250\underline{/0^\circ}}{25 + j50}(j50) = 200 + j100\,\text{mV}$$

$$Z_\text{Th} = 20\frac{(25)(j50)}{25 + j50} = 40 + j10\,\Omega$$

Transfer the secondary impedance to the primary side:

$$Z_p = \frac{1}{16}(160 - jX_\text{C}) = 10 - j\frac{X_\text{C}}{16}\,\Omega$$

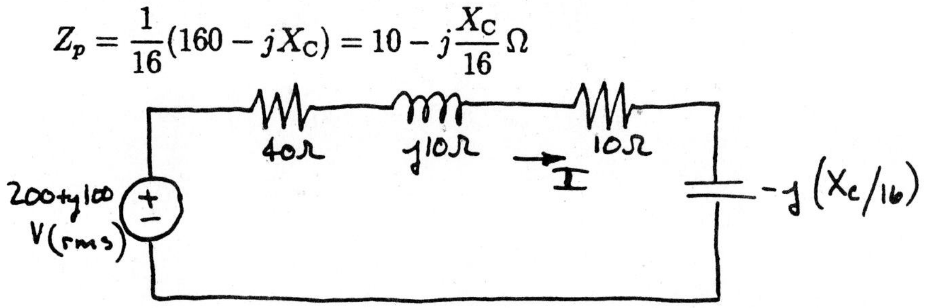

Now maximize **I** by setting $(X_C/16) = 10\,\Omega$:

$$\therefore \quad C = \frac{10^{-3}}{(160)(50)} = 125\,\text{nF}$$

[b] $$\mathbf{I} = \frac{200 + j100}{50} = 4 + j2\,\text{mA}$$

$$|\mathbf{I}| = \sqrt{20}\,\text{mA}$$

$$P = (20 \times 10^{-6})(10) = 200\,\mu\text{W}$$

[c] $$\frac{R_o}{16} = 40\,\Omega; \qquad \therefore \quad R_o = 640\,\Omega$$

[d] $$\mathbf{I} = \frac{200 + j100}{80} = 2.5 + j1.25\,\text{mA}$$

$$P = |\mathbf{I}|^2(40) = 312.50\,\mu\text{W}$$

P 10.63 [a] $$P_L = \frac{V_2}{R_1 + R_2}; \qquad R_1 + R_2 = \frac{V_2}{P_L}$$

$$P_M = \frac{V^2}{R_2}; \qquad R_2 = \frac{V^2}{P_M}$$

$$P_H = \frac{V^2(R_1 + R_2)}{R_1 R_2}$$

$$R_1 + R_2 = \frac{V^2}{P_L}; \qquad R_1 = \frac{V^2}{P_L} - \frac{V^2}{P_M}$$

$$P_H = \frac{V^2 V^2/P_L}{\left(\frac{V^2}{P_L} - \frac{V^2}{P_M}\right)\left(\frac{V^2}{P_M}\right)} = \frac{P_M P_L P_M}{P_L(P_M - P_L)}$$

$$P_H = \frac{P_M^2}{P_M - P_L}$$

[b] $$P_H = \frac{(750)^2}{(750 - 250)} = 1125\,\text{W}$$

P 10.64 First solve the expression derived in P10.63 for P_M as a function of P_L and P_H. Thus

$$P_M - P_L = \frac{P_M^2}{P_H} \quad \text{or} \quad \frac{P_M^2}{P_H} - P_M + P_L = 0$$

$$P_M^2 - P_M P_H + P_L P_H = 0$$

$$\therefore \quad P_M = \frac{P_H}{2} \pm \sqrt{\left(\frac{P_H}{2}\right)^2 - P_L P_H}$$

$$= \frac{P_H}{2} \pm P_H\sqrt{\frac{1}{4} - \left(\frac{P_L}{P_H}\right)}$$

For the specified values of P_L and P_H

$$P_M = 500 \pm 1000\sqrt{0.25 - 0.24} = 500 \pm 100$$

$$\therefore \quad P_{M1} = 600\,\text{W}; \qquad P_{M2} = 400\,\text{W}$$

Note in this case we design for two medium power ratings
If $P_{M1} = 600$ W

$$R_2 = \frac{(120)^2}{600} = 24\,\Omega$$

$$R_1 + R_2 = \frac{(120)^2}{240} = 60\,\Omega$$

$$R_1 = 60 - 24 = 36\,\Omega$$

$$\text{CHECK: } P_H = \frac{(120)^2(60)}{(36)(24)} = 1000\,\text{W}$$

If $P_{M2} = 400$ W

$$R_2 = \frac{(120)^2}{400} = 36\,\Omega$$

$$R_1 + R_2 = 60\,\Omega \quad \text{(as before)}$$

$$R_1 = 24\,\Omega$$

CHECK: $P_H = 1000$ W

P 10.65 $R_1 + R_2 + R_3 = \dfrac{(120)^2}{600} = 24\,\Omega$

$$R_2 + R_3 = \frac{(120)^2}{900} = 16\,\Omega$$

$$\therefore \quad R_1 = 24 - 16 = 8\,\Omega$$

$$R_3 + R_1 \| R_2 = \frac{(120)^2}{1200} = 12\,\Omega$$

$$\therefore \quad 16 - R_2 + \frac{8R_2}{8 + R_2} = 12$$

$$R_2 - \frac{8R_2}{8 + R_2} = 4$$

$$8R_2 + R_2^2 - 8R_2 = 32 + 4R_2$$

$$R_2^2 - 4R_2 - 32 = 0$$

$$R_2 = 2 \pm \sqrt{4 + 32} = 2 \pm 6$$

$$\therefore \quad R_2 = 8\,\Omega; \qquad \therefore \quad R_3 = 8\,\Omega$$

P 10.66 $R_2 = \frac{(220)^2}{500} = 96.8\,\Omega$

$$R_1 + R_2 = \frac{(220)^2}{250} = 193.6\,\Omega$$

$$\therefore \quad R_1 = 96.8\,\Omega$$

CHECK: $R_1 \| R_2 = 48.4\,\Omega$

$$P_{\text{H}} = \frac{(220)^2}{48.4} = 1000\,\text{W}$$

11

Balanced Three-Phase Circuits

Drill Exercises

DE 11.1 [a] $\mathbf{V}_a = 208\angle 27^\circ$; $\mathbf{V}_b = 208\angle -147^\circ$; $\mathbf{V}_c = 208\angle -93^\circ$

Therefore acb

[b] $\mathbf{V}_a = 4160\angle -18^\circ$; $\mathbf{V}_b = 4160\angle -138^\circ$; $\mathbf{V}_c = 4160\angle +102^\circ$

Therefore abc

DE 11.2 $\mathbf{V}_{BC} = \sqrt{3}\angle 30^\circ \cdot \mathbf{V}_{BN} = \sqrt{3}\angle 30^\circ \cdot 240\angle -150^\circ = 415.69\angle -120^\circ$ V

DE 11.3 $\mathbf{V}_{AB} = \sqrt{3}\angle -30^\circ \cdot \mathbf{V}_{AN} = \sqrt{3}\angle -30^\circ \cdot 450\angle 95^\circ = 779.42\angle 65^\circ$ V

DE 11.4 [a]

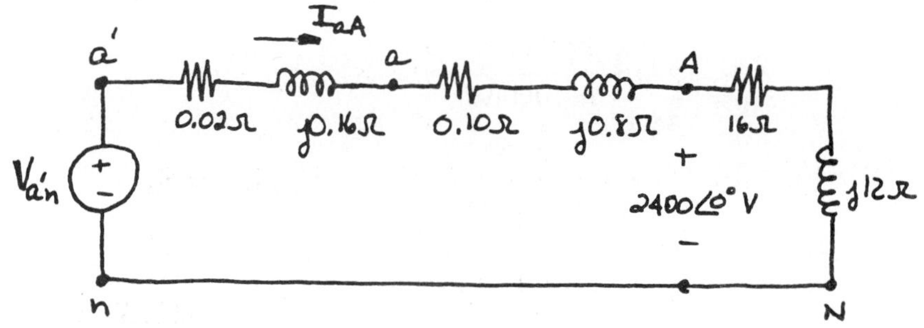

$$\mathbf{I}_{aA} = \frac{2400}{16 + j12} = 120\angle -36.87^\circ \text{ A}$$

Therefore $\mathbf{I}_{bB} = 120\angle 83.13^\circ$ A; $\mathbf{I}_{cC} = 120\angle -156.87^\circ$ A

[b] $\mathbf{V}_{an} = (120\angle -36.87^\circ)(16.1 + j12.8) = 2468.18\angle 1.62^\circ$ V

$\therefore$ $\mathbf{V}_{ab} = (\sqrt{3}\angle -30^\circ)(2468.18\angle 1.62^\circ) = 4275.02\angle -28.38^\circ$ V

$\mathbf{V}_{bc} = 4275.02\angle 91.62^\circ$ V and $\mathbf{V}_{ca} = 4275.02\angle -148.38^\circ$ V

[c] $\mathbf{V}_{a'n} = (120\angle -36.87^\circ)(16.12 + j12.96) = 2482.05\angle 1.93^\circ$ V

$\mathbf{V}_{b'n} = 2482.05\angle 121.93^\circ$ V; $\quad \mathbf{V}_{c'n} = 2482.05\angle -118.07^\circ$ V

DE 11.5 $\mathbf{I}_{cC} = (\sqrt{3}\angle -30^\circ)\mathbf{I}_{CA} = (\sqrt{3}\angle -30^\circ) \cdot 8\angle -15^\circ = 13.86\angle -45^\circ$ A

DE 11.6 $\mathbf{I}_{AB} = \left[\left(\frac{1}{\sqrt{3}}\right)\angle -30^\circ\right]\mathbf{I}_{aA} = \left(\frac{\angle -30^\circ}{\sqrt{3}}\right) \cdot 12\angle -55^\circ$

$= 6.93\angle -85^\circ$ A

DE 11.7 [a] $\mathbf{I}_{AB} = \left[\left(\frac{1}{\sqrt{3}}\right)\angle 30^\circ\right][69.28\angle -10^\circ] = 40\angle 20^\circ$ A

Therefore $\quad Z_\phi = \frac{4160\angle 0^\circ}{40\angle 20^\circ} = 104\angle -20^\circ\,\Omega$

[b] $\mathbf{I}_{AB} = \left[\left(\frac{1}{\sqrt{3}}\right)\angle -30^\circ\right][69.28\angle -10^\circ] = 40\angle -40^\circ$ A

Therefore $\quad Z_\phi = 104\angle 40^\circ\,\Omega$

DE 11.8 $\mathbf{I}_\phi = \frac{110}{3.667} + \frac{110}{j2.75} = 30 - j40 = 50\angle -53.13^\circ$ A

Therefore $\quad |\mathbf{I}_{aA}| = \sqrt{3}(50) = 86.60$ A

DE 11.9 [a] $|S| = \sqrt{3}(208)(73.8) = 26{,}587.67$ VA

$Q = \sqrt{(26{,}587.67)^2 - (22{,}659)^2} = 13{,}909.50$ VAR

[b] $\text{pf} = \frac{22{,}659}{26{,}587.67} = 0.8522$ lagging

DE 11.10 [a] $\mathbf{V}_{AN} = \left(\frac{2450}{\sqrt{3}}\right)\angle 0^\circ$ V; $\quad \mathbf{V}_{AN}\mathbf{I}^*_{aA} = S_\phi$

Therefore

$$\mathbf{I}^*_{aA} = \frac{(144 + j192)1000}{2450/\sqrt{3}} = (101.8 + j135.7)\text{ A}$$

$\mathbf{I}_{aA} = 101.8 - j135.7 = 169.67\angle -53.13^\circ$ A

$|\mathbf{I}_{aA}| = 169.67$ A

[b] $P = \frac{(2450)^2}{R}$; $\quad$ therefore $R = \frac{(2450)^2}{144{,}000} = 41.68\,\Omega$

$Q = \frac{(2450)^2}{X}$; $\quad$ therefore $X = \frac{(2450)^2}{192{,}000} = 31.26\,\Omega$

[c] $Z_\phi = \dfrac{\mathbf{V}_{\rm AN}}{\mathbf{I}_{\rm aA}} = \dfrac{2450/\sqrt{3}}{169.67\angle -53.13^\circ} = 8.34\angle 53.13^\circ = (5 + j6.67)\,\Omega$

$\therefore\quad R = 5\,\Omega, \qquad X = 6.67\,\Omega$

DE 11.11

$W_{m1} = (199.58)(2.4)\cos(65.68^\circ) = 197.29\,W$

$W_{m2} = (199.58)(2.4)\cos(5.68^\circ) = 476.63\,W$

CHECK: $W_1 + W_2 = 673.92 = (2.4)^2(39)(3) = 673.92\,W$

DE 11.12 [a] $W_2 - W_1 = V_L I_L[\cos(\theta - 30^\circ) - \cos(\theta + 30^\circ)]$

$= V_L I_L[\cos\theta\cos 30^\circ + \sin\theta\sin 30^\circ$

$- \cos\theta\cos 30^\circ + \sin\theta\sin 30^\circ]$

$= 2V_L I_L\sin\theta\sin 30^\circ = V_L I_L\sin\theta,$

therefore $\sqrt{3}(W_2 - W_1) = \sqrt{3}V_L I_L\sin\theta = Q_T$

[b] $Z_\phi = (8 + j6)\,\Omega$

$Q_T = \sqrt{3}[2476.25 - 979.75] = 2592$ VAR,

$Q_T = 3(12)^2(6) = 2592$ VAR;

$Z_\phi = (8 - j6)\,\Omega$

$Q_T = \sqrt{3}[979.75 - 2476.25] = -2592$ VAR,

$Q_T = 3(12)^2(-6) = -2592$ VAR;

$Z_\phi = 5(1 + j\sqrt{3})\,\Omega$

$Q_T = \sqrt{3}[2160 - 0] = 3741.23$ VAR,

$Q_T = 3(12)^2(5\sqrt{3}) = 3741.23$ VAR;

$Z_\phi = 10\angle 75^\circ\,\Omega$

$Q_T = \sqrt{3}[-645.53 - 1763.63] = -4172.79$ VAR,

$Q_T = 3(12)^2[-10\sin 75^\circ] = -4172.79$ VAR

Problems

P 11.1 [a] $\mathbf{V}_a = 339\angle 0^\circ$ V

$\mathbf{V}_b = 339\angle -120^\circ$ V

$\mathbf{V}_c = 339\angle 120^\circ$ V

Balanced, positive phase sequence

[b] $\mathbf{V}_a = 622\angle 0^\circ$ V

$\mathbf{V}_b = 622\angle -240^\circ \text{ V} = 622\angle 120^\circ$ V

$\mathbf{V}_c = 622\angle 240^\circ \text{ V} = 622\angle -120^\circ$ V

Balanced, negative phase sequence

[c] $\mathbf{V}_a = 933\angle -90^\circ$ V

$\mathbf{V}_b = 933\angle 150^\circ$ V

$\mathbf{V}_c = 933\angle 30^\circ$ V

Balanced, positive phase sequence

[d] $\mathbf{V}_a = 170\angle -30^\circ$ V

$\mathbf{V}_b = 170\angle 90^\circ$ V

$\mathbf{V}_c = 170\angle -150^\circ$ V

Balanced, negative phase sequence

[e] Unbalanced, due to unequal amplitudes

[f] Unbalanced, due to unequal phase angle separation

P 11.2 $\mathbf{V}_a = V_m\angle 0^\circ = V_m + j0$

$$\mathbf{V}_b = V_m\angle -120^\circ = -V_m(0.5 + j0.866)$$

$$\mathbf{V}_c = V_m\angle 120^\circ = V_m(-0.5 + j0.866)$$

$$\mathbf{V}_a + \mathbf{V}_b + \mathbf{V}_c = (V_m)(1 + j0 - 0.5 - j0.866 - 0.5 + j0.866)$$
$$= V_m(0) = 0$$

P 11.3 [a] $\mathbf{I}_{aA} = \dfrac{240\angle 0^\circ}{80 + j60} = 2.4\angle -36.87^\circ$ A

$$\mathbf{I}_{bB} = \frac{240\angle 120^\circ}{80 + j60} = 2.4\angle 83.13^\circ \text{ A}$$

$$\mathbf{I}_{\text{cC}} = \frac{240\underline{/-120^\circ}}{80 + j60} = 2.4\underline{/-156.87^\circ}\text{ A}$$

$$\mathbf{I}_o = \mathbf{I}_{\text{aA}} + \mathbf{I}_{\text{bB}} + \mathbf{I}_{\text{cC}} = 0$$

[b] $\mathbf{V}_{\text{BN}} = (79 + j52)\mathbf{I}_{\text{bB}} = 226.99\underline{/116.48^\circ}\text{ V}$

[c] $\mathbf{V}_{\text{BC}} = \mathbf{V}_{\text{BN}} - \mathbf{V}_{\text{CN}}$

$$\mathbf{V}_{\text{CN}} = (78 + j50)\mathbf{I}_{\text{cC}} = 222.36\underline{/-124.21^\circ}\text{ V}$$

$$\begin{aligned}\mathbf{V}_{\text{BC}} &= -101.22 + j203.17 - (-125.01 - j183.89)\\ &= 23.79 + j387.06 = 387.79\underline{/86.48^\circ}\text{ V}\end{aligned}$$

[d] Unbalanced

P 11.4 [a]

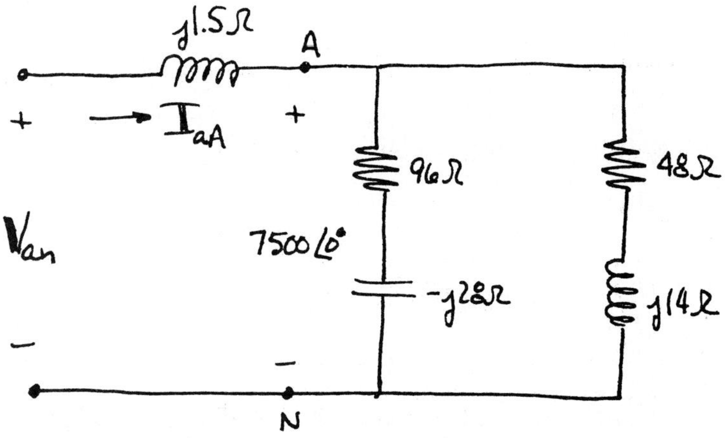

$$\mathbf{I}_{\text{aA}} = \frac{7500}{96 - j28} + \frac{7500}{48 + j14} = 217.02\underline{/-5.55^\circ}\text{ A}$$

$$|\mathbf{I}_{\text{aA}}| = 217.02\text{ A}$$

[b] $\mathbf{I}_{\text{AB}} = \dfrac{7500\sqrt{3}\underline{/30^\circ}}{144 + j42} = 86.60\underline{/13.74^\circ}\text{ A}$

$$|\mathbf{I}_{\text{AB}}| = 86.60\text{ A}$$

[c] $\mathbf{I}_{\text{AN}} = \dfrac{7500\underline{/0^\circ}}{96 - j28} = 75\underline{/16.26^\circ}\text{ A}$

$$|\mathbf{I}_{\text{AN}}| = 75\text{ A}$$

[d] $\mathbf{V}_{\text{an}} = (216 - j21)(j1.5) + 7500\underline{/0^\circ} = 7538.47\underline{/2.46^\circ}\text{ V}$

$$|\mathbf{V}_{\text{ab}}| = \sqrt{3}(7538.47) = 13{,}057.01\text{ V}$$

P 11.5 $\mathbf{I} = \dfrac{\mathbf{V}_{\text{a}} + \mathbf{V}_{\text{b}} + \mathbf{V}_{\text{c}}}{3(R_{\text{W}} + jX_{\text{W}})} = 0$

P 11.6 [a]

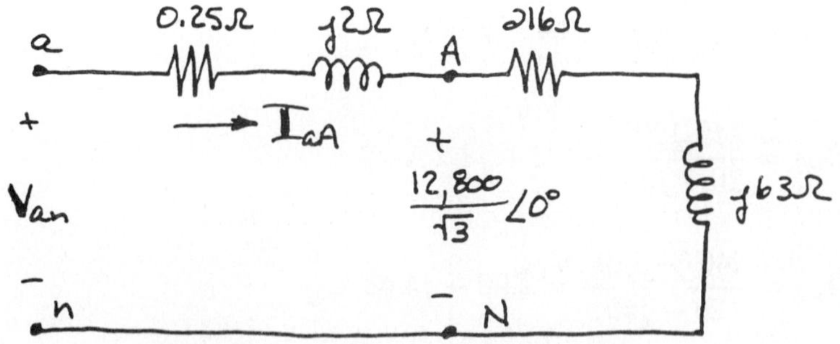

$$\mathbf{I}_{aA} = \frac{12{,}800}{\sqrt{3}(216 + j63)} = 32.84\underline{/-16.26°}\,\text{A(rms)}$$

$$|\mathbf{I}_{aA}| = |\mathbf{I}_L| = 32.84\,\text{A(rms)}$$

[b] $$\mathbf{V}_{an} = \frac{12{,}800}{\sqrt{3}} + (32.84\underline{/-16.26°})(0.25 + j2) = 7416.61\underline{/0.47°}$$

$$|\mathbf{V}_{AB}| = \sqrt{3}(7416.61) = 12{,}845.94\,\text{V(rms)}$$

P 11.7 [a] $$\mathbf{I}_{aA} = \frac{4800\underline{/0°}}{192 + j56} = 24\underline{/-16.26°}\,\text{A}$$

$$\mathbf{I}_{bB} = 24\underline{/120 - 16.26°} = 24\underline{/103.74°}\,\text{A}$$

$$\mathbf{I}_{cC} = 24\underline{/-136.26°}\,\text{A}$$

[b] $$\mathbf{V}_{AN} = 4800\underline{/0°}\,\text{V}$$

$$\mathbf{V}_{BN} = 4800\underline{/120°}\,\text{V}$$

$$\mathbf{V}_{CN} = 4800\underline{/-120°}\,\text{V}$$

$$\mathbf{V}_{AB} = \sqrt{3}\underline{/-30°}\mathbf{V}_{AN} = 8313.84\underline{/-30°}\,\text{V}$$

$$\mathbf{V}_{BC} = 8313.84\underline{/90°}\,\text{V}$$

$$\mathbf{V}_{CA} = 8313.84\underline{/-150°}\,\text{V}$$

[c] $$\mathbf{V}_{an} = (24\underline{/-16.26°})(190 + j40) = 4659.96\underline{/-4.37°}\,\text{V}$$

$$\mathbf{V}_{bn} = 4659.96\underline{/115.63°}\,\text{V}$$

$$\mathbf{V}_{cn} = 4659.96\underline{/-124.37°}\,\text{V}$$

[d] $$\mathbf{V}_{ab} = \sqrt{3}\underline{/-30°}\mathbf{V}_{an} = 8071.28\underline{/-34.37°}\,\text{V}$$

$$\mathbf{V}_{bc} = 8071.28\underline{/85.63°}\,\text{V}$$

$$\mathbf{V}_{ca} = 8071.28\underline{/-154.37°}\,\text{V}$$

P 11.8 $\mathbf{I}_{\text{aA}} = \dfrac{240\underline{/0^\circ}}{10 + j30} = 2.4 - j7.2\,\text{A}$

$$\mathbf{I}_{\text{bB}} = \frac{240\underline{/120^\circ}}{20 + j20} = 2.2 + j8.2\,\text{A}$$

$$\mathbf{I}_{\text{cC}} = \frac{240\underline{/-120^\circ}}{20 - j40} = 2.96 - j4.48\,\text{A}$$

$$\mathbf{I}_o = \mathbf{I}_{\text{aA}} + \mathbf{I}_{\text{bB}} + \mathbf{I}_{\text{cC}} = 7.55 - j3.48 = 8.32\underline{/-24.75^\circ}\,\text{A}$$

P 11.9 $\mathbf{V}_{\text{AN}} = 7967\underline{/0^\circ}\,\text{V}$

$$\mathbf{V}_{\text{BN}} = 7967\underline{/+120^\circ}\,\text{V}$$

$$\mathbf{V}_{\text{CN}} = 7967\underline{/-120^\circ}\,\text{V}$$

$$\mathbf{V}_{\text{AB}} = \mathbf{V}_{\text{AN}} - \mathbf{V}_{\text{BN}} = 13{,}799.25\underline{/-30^\circ}\,\text{V}$$

$$\mathbf{V}_{\text{BC}} = \mathbf{V}_{\text{BN}} - \mathbf{V}_{\text{CN}} = 13{,}799.25\underline{/90^\circ}\,\text{V}$$

$$\mathbf{V}_{\text{CA}} = \mathbf{V}_{\text{CN}} - \mathbf{V}_{\text{AN}} = 13{,}799.25\underline{/-150^\circ}\,\text{V}$$

$$v_{\text{AB}} = 13{,}799.25\cos(\omega t - 30^\circ)\,\text{V}$$

$$v_{\text{BC}} = 13{,}799.25\cos(\omega t + 90^\circ)\,\text{V}$$

$$v_{\text{CA}} = 13{,}799.25\cos(\omega t - 150^\circ)\,\text{V}$$

P 11.10 $Z_{ga} + Z_{la} + Z_{La} = 80 + j60\,\Omega$

$$Z_{gb} + Z_{lb} + Z_{Lb} = 40 + j30\Omega$$

$$Z_{gc} + Z_{lc} + Z_{Lc} = 160 + j120\Omega$$

$$\frac{\mathbf{V}_N - 480}{80 + j60} + \frac{\mathbf{V}_N - 480\underline{/-120^\circ}}{40 + j30} + \frac{\mathbf{V}_N - 480\underline{/120^\circ}}{160 + j120} + \frac{\mathbf{V}_N}{20} = 0$$

Solving for $\mathbf{V}_N$ yields

$$\mathbf{V}_N = 78.61\underline{/-122.69^\circ}\,\text{V}$$

$$\mathbf{I}_o = \frac{\mathbf{V}_N}{20} = 3.93\underline{/-122.69^\circ}\,\text{A}$$

P 11.11 [a] $\mathbf{I}_{AB} = \dfrac{33{,}000}{360 + j105} = 88\underline{/-16.26^\circ}$ A

$\mathbf{I}_{BC} = 88\underline{/-136.26^\circ}$ A

$\mathbf{I}_{CA} = 88\underline{/103.74^\circ}$ A

[b] $\mathbf{I}_{aA} = \sqrt{3}\underline{/-30^\circ}\mathbf{I}_{AB} = 152.42\underline{/-46.26^\circ}$ A

$\mathbf{I}_{bB} = 152.42\underline{/-166.26^\circ}$ A

$\mathbf{I}_{cC} = 152.42\underline{/73.74^\circ}$ A

[c]

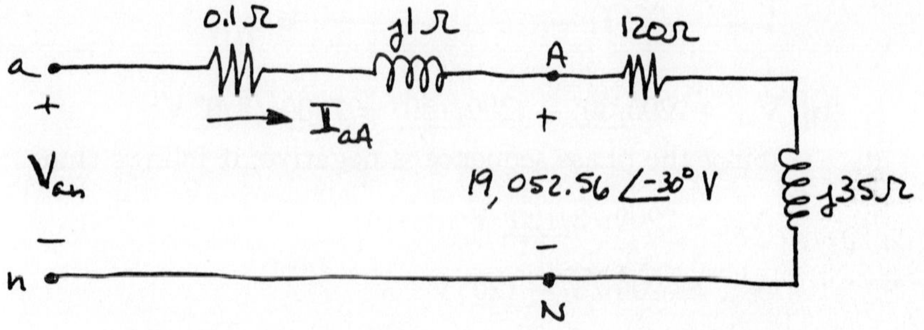

$\mathbf{V}_{an} = 19{,}052.56\underline{/-30^\circ} + (0.1 + j1.0)(152.42\underline{/-46.26^\circ})$

$= 19{,}110.40\underline{/-29.57^\circ}$ V

$\mathbf{V}_{ab} = \sqrt{3}\underline{/30^\circ}\mathbf{V}_{an} = 33{,}100.18\underline{/0.43^\circ}$ V

$\mathbf{V}_{bc} = 33{,}100.18\underline{/-119.57^\circ}$ V

$\mathbf{V}_{ca} = 33{,}100.18\underline{/120.43^\circ}$ V

P 11.12 [a] Since the phase sequence is acb (negative) we have:

$\mathbf{V}_{an} = 7200\underline{/30^\circ}$ V

$\mathbf{V}_{bn} = 7200\underline{/150^\circ}$ V

$\mathbf{V}_{cn} = 7200\underline{/-90^\circ}$ V

$Z_Y = \frac{1}{3}Z_\Delta = 1.8 + j9.0\,\Omega/\phi$

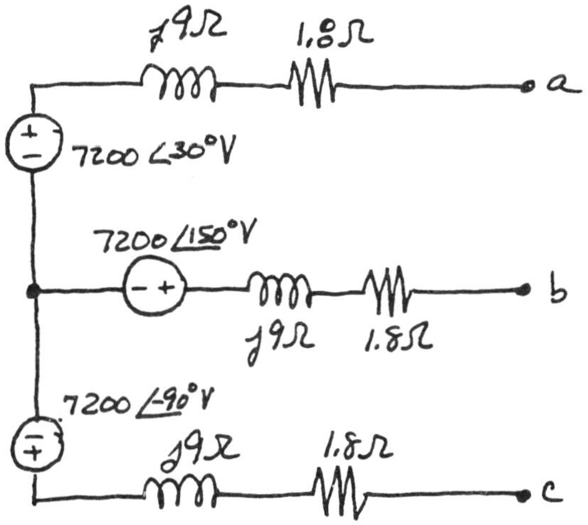

[b] $\mathbf{V}_{ab} = 7200\underline{/30^\circ} - 7200\underline{/150^\circ} = 7200\sqrt{3}\underline{/0^\circ}$ V

Since the phase sequence is negative, it follows that

$\mathbf{V}_{bc} = 7200\sqrt{3}\underline{/120^\circ}$ V

$\mathbf{V}_{ca} = 7200\sqrt{3}\underline{/-120^\circ}$ V

[c]

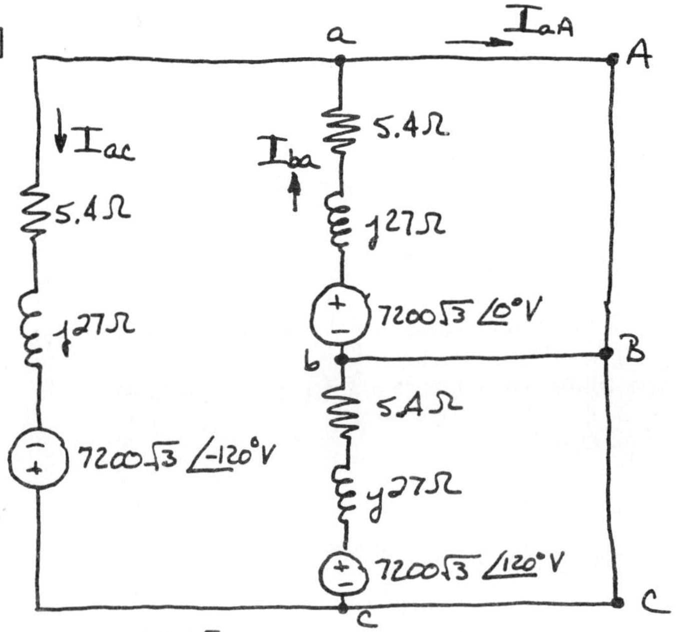

$$\mathbf{I}_{ba} = \frac{7200\sqrt{3}}{5.4 + j27} = 452.91\underline{/-78.69^\circ}\text{ A}$$

$$\mathbf{I}_{ac} = \frac{7200\sqrt{3}\underline{/-120^\circ}}{5.4 + j27} = 452.91\underline{/-198.69^\circ}\text{ A}$$

$\mathbf{I}_{aA} = \mathbf{I}_{ba} - \mathbf{I}_{ac} = 784.46\underline{/-48.69^\circ}$ A

Since we have a balanced three-phase circuit and a negative phase sequence we have:

$\mathbf{I}_{bB} = 784.46\underline{/71.31^\circ}$ A

$\mathbf{I}_{cC} = 784.46\underline{/-168.69^\circ}$ A

[d]

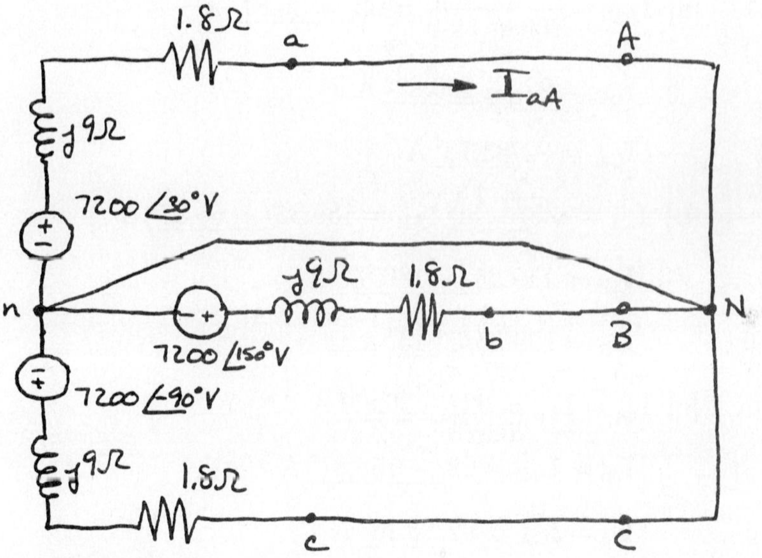

$$\mathbf{I}_{aA} = \frac{7200\underline{/30^\circ}}{1.8 + j9} = 784.46\underline{/-48.69^\circ}\text{ A}$$

P 11.13 [a]

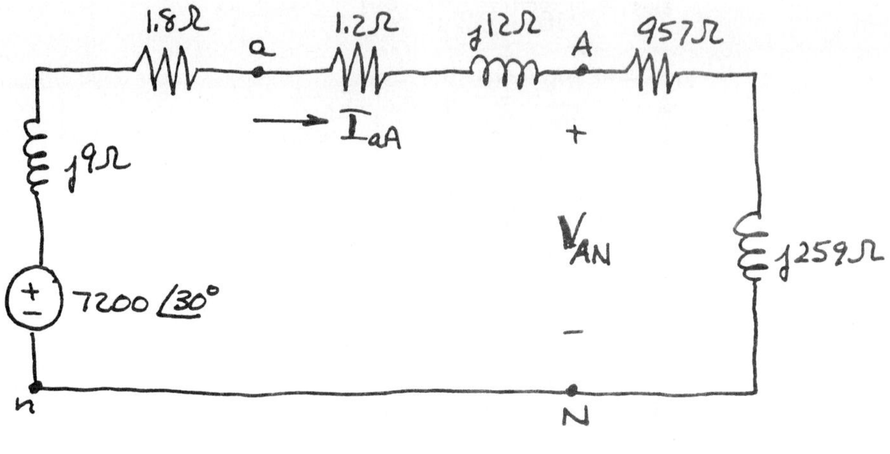

[b] $$\mathbf{I}_{aA} = \frac{7200\underline{/30^\circ}}{960 + j280} = 7.2\underline{/13.74^\circ}\text{ A}$$

$\mathbf{V}_{AN} = (957 + j259)(7.2\underline{/13.74^\circ}) = 7138.28\underline{/28.88^\circ}$ V

$|\mathbf{V}_{AB}| = \sqrt{3}(7138.28) = 12{,}363.87$ V

[c] $|\mathbf{I}_{ba}| = \dfrac{7.2}{\sqrt{3}} = 4.16\,\text{A}$

[d] $\mathbf{V}_{an} = (958.2 + j271)(7.20\underline{/13.74^\circ}) = 7169.65\underline{/29.54^\circ}\,\text{V}$

$|\mathbf{V}_{ab}| = \sqrt{3}(7169.65) = 12{,}418.20\,\text{V}$

P 11.14 [a] $\mathbf{I}_{AB} = \dfrac{69{,}000\underline{/0^\circ}}{600 + j450} = 92\underline{/-36.87^\circ}\,\text{A}$

$\mathbf{I}_{BC} = 92\underline{/-156.87^\circ}\,\text{A}$

$\mathbf{I}_{CA} = 92\underline{/83.13^\circ}\,\text{A}$

[b] $\mathbf{I}_{aA} = \sqrt{3}\underline{/-30^\circ}\mathbf{I}_{AB} = 159.35\underline{/-66.87^\circ}\,\text{A}$

$\mathbf{I}_{bB} = 159.35\underline{/-186.87^\circ}\,\text{A}$

$\mathbf{I}_{cC} = 159.35\underline{/53.13^\circ}\,\text{A}$

[c] $\mathbf{I}_{ba} = \mathbf{I}_{AB} = 92\underline{/-36.87^\circ}\,\text{A}$

$\mathbf{I}_{cb} = \mathbf{I}_{BC} = 92\underline{/-156.87^\circ}\,\text{A}$

$\mathbf{I}_{ac} = \mathbf{I}_{CA} = 92\underline{/83.13^\circ}\,\text{A}$

P 11.15 [a] $\mathbf{I}_{AB} = \dfrac{720\underline{/0^\circ}}{4.8 + j1.4} = 144\underline{/-16.26^\circ}\,\text{A}$

$\mathbf{I}_{BC} = \dfrac{720\underline{/-120^\circ}}{16 - j12} = 36\underline{/-83.13^\circ}\,\text{A}$

$\mathbf{I}_{CA} = \dfrac{720\underline{/120^\circ}}{25 + j25} = 20.36\underline{/75^\circ}\,\text{A}$

[b] $\mathbf{I}_{aA} = \mathbf{I}_{AB} - \mathbf{I}_{CA}$

$= 138.24 - j40.32 - 5.27 - j19.67$

$= 132.97 - j59.99 = 145.88\underline{/-24.28^\circ}\,\text{A}$

$\mathbf{I}_{bB} = \mathbf{I}_{BC} - \mathbf{I}_{AB}$

$= 4.31 - j35.74 - 138.24 + j40.32$

$= -133.93 + j4.58 = 134.01\underline{/178.04^\circ}\,\text{A}$

$\mathbf{I}_{cC} = \mathbf{I}_{CA} - \mathbf{I}_{BC}$

$= 5.27 + j19.67 - 4.31 + j35.74$

$= 0.96 + j55.41 = 55.42\underline{/89.01^\circ}\,\text{A}$

[c] By constructing three loop currents

$$\mathbf{I}_{ba} = \mathbf{I}_{AB} = 144\underline{/-16.26^\circ}\text{ A}$$

$$\mathbf{I}_{cb} = \mathbf{I}_{BC} = 36\underline{/-83.13^\circ}\text{ A}$$

$$\mathbf{I}_{ac} = \mathbf{I}_{CA} = 20.36\underline{/75^\circ}\text{ A}$$

P 11.16 From the solution to Problem 11.15 we have:

$$S_{AB} = (720\underline{/0^\circ})(144\underline{/16.26^\circ}) = 99{,}532.9 + j29{,}030.04\text{ VA}$$

$$S_{BC} = (720\underline{/-120^\circ})(36\underline{/83.13^\circ}) = 20{,}735.97 - j15{,}552.04\text{ VA}$$

$$S_{CA} = (720\underline{/120^\circ})(20.36\underline{/-75^\circ}) = 10{,}365.62 + j10{,}365.62\text{ VA}$$

P 11.17 [a]

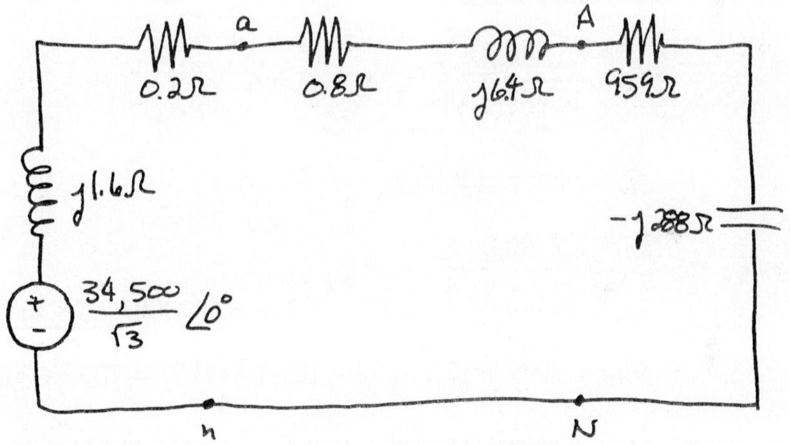

[b] $\mathbf{I}_{aA} = \dfrac{34{,}500}{\sqrt{3}(960 - j280)} = 19.92\underline{/16.26^\circ}\text{ A}$

$$|\mathbf{I}_{aA}| = 19.92\text{ A}$$

[c] $\mathbf{V}_{AN} = (959 - j288)(19.92\underline{/16.26^\circ}) = 19{,}944.71\underline{/-0.46^\circ}\text{ V}$

$$|\mathbf{V}_{AB}| = \sqrt{3}|\mathbf{V}_{AN}| = 34{,}545.25\text{ V}$$

[d] $\mathbf{V}_{an} = (959.8 - j281.6)(19.92\underline{/16.26^\circ}) = 19{,}923.71\underline{/-0.09^\circ}\text{ V}$

$$|\mathbf{V}_{ab}| = \sqrt{3}|\mathbf{V}_{an}| = 34{,}508.88\text{ V}$$

[e] $|\mathbf{I}_{AB}| = \dfrac{|\mathbf{I}_{aA}|}{\sqrt{3}} = 11.50\text{ A}$

[f] $|\mathbf{I}_{ba}| = |\mathbf{I}_{AB}| = 11.50\text{ A}$

P 11.18 [a]

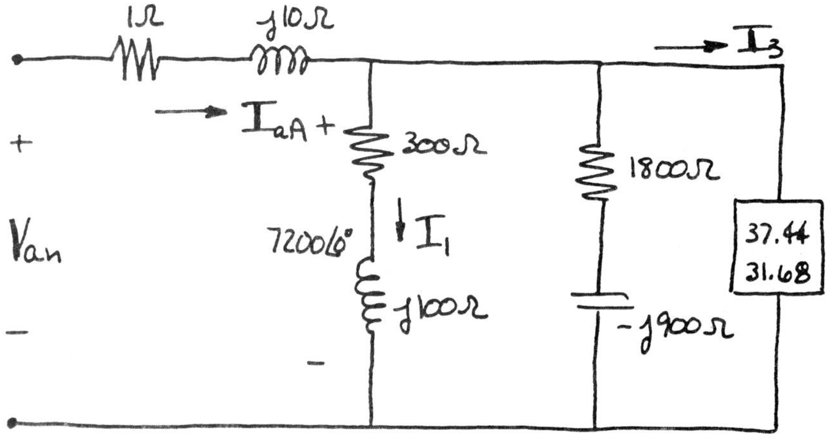

$$\mathbf{I}_1 = \frac{7200/0^\circ}{300 + j100} = 21.6 - j7.2\,\text{A}$$

$$\mathbf{I}_2 = \frac{7200/0^\circ}{1800 - j900} = 3.2 + j1.6\,\text{A}$$

$$\mathbf{I}_3^* = \frac{37{,}440 + j31{,}680}{7200} = 5.2 + j4.4$$

$$\mathbf{I}_3 = 5.2 - j4.4\,\text{A}$$

$$\mathbf{I}_{\text{aA}} = \mathbf{I}_1 + \mathbf{I}_2 + \mathbf{I}_3 = 30 - j10\,\text{A} = \sqrt{1000}/-18.43^\circ\,\text{A}$$

$$\mathbf{V}_{\text{an}} = 7200 + j0 + (30 - j10)(1 + j10) = 7330 + j290\,\text{V}$$

$$S_\phi = \mathbf{V}_{\text{an}}\mathbf{I}_{\text{aA}}^* = (7330 + j290)(30 + j10) = 217{,}000 + j82{,}000\,\text{VA}$$

$$S_T = 3S_\phi = 651 + j246\,\text{kVA}$$

[b] $S_{1/\phi} = 7200(21.6 + j7.2) = 155.52 + j51.84\,\text{kVA}$

$$S_{2\phi} = 7200(3.2 - j1.6) = 23.04 - j11.52\,\text{kVA}$$

$$S_{3\phi} = 37.44 + j31.68\,\text{kVA}$$

$$S_\phi(\text{load}) = 216 + j72\,\text{kVA}$$

$$\%\ \text{delivered} = \left(\frac{216}{217}\right)(100) = 99.54\%$$

P 11.19 [a]

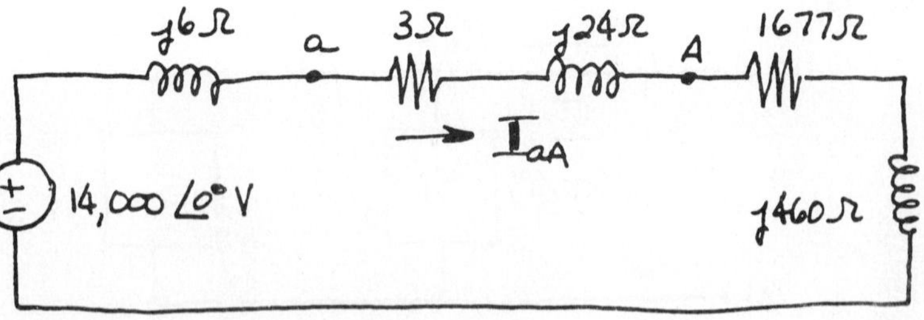

$$\mathbf{I}_{aA} = \frac{14{,}000\angle 0^\circ}{1680 + j490} = 8\angle -16.26^\circ \text{ A}$$

$$\mathbf{I}_{CA} = \frac{\mathbf{I}_{aA}}{\sqrt{3}}\angle 150^\circ = 4.62\angle 133.74^\circ \text{ A}$$

[b] $S_{g/\phi} = -14{,}000\mathbf{I}^*_{aA} = -107{,}520 - j31{,}360 \text{ VA}$

$$\therefore \quad P_{\text{developed/phase}} = 107.52 \text{ kW}$$

$$P_{\text{absorbed/phase}} = |\mathbf{I}_{aA}|^2 1677 = 107.328 \text{ kW}$$

$$\% \text{ delivered} = \frac{107.328}{107.52}(100) = 99.82\%$$

P 11.20 [a] $S_1 = (4.864 + j3.775) \text{ kVA}$

$$S_2 = 17.636(0.96) + j17.636(0.28) = (16.931 + j4.938) \text{ kVA}$$

$$\sqrt{3}V_L I_L \sin\theta_3 = 13{,}853; \qquad \sin\theta_3 = \frac{13{,}853}{\sqrt{3}(208)(73.8)} = 0.521$$

Therefore $\cos\theta_3 = 0.854$

Therefore

$$P_3 = \frac{13{,}853}{0.521} \times 0.854 = 22{,}693.584 \text{ W}$$

$$S_3 = 22.694 + j13.853 \text{ kVA}$$

$$S_T = S_1 + S_2 + S_3 = 44.49 + j22.57 \text{ kVA}$$

$$S_{T/\phi} = \frac{1}{3}S_T = 14.83 + j7.52 \text{ kVA}$$

$$\frac{208}{\sqrt{3}}\mathbf{I}^*_{aA} = (14.83 + j7.52)10^3; \qquad \mathbf{I}^*_{aA} = 123.49 + j62.64 \text{ A}$$

$$\mathbf{I}_{aA} = 123.49 - j62.64 = 138.46\angle 26.90^\circ \text{ A} \quad \text{(rms)}$$

[b] pf $= \cos 26.90^\circ = 0.892$ lag

P 11.21 [a]

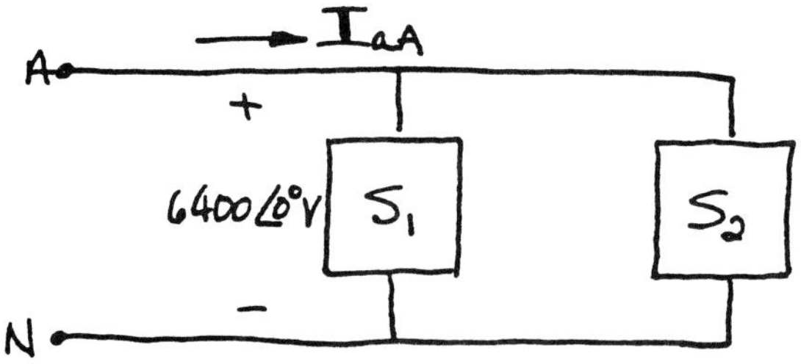

$$S_1 = \frac{1}{3}(1800)(0.96 - j0.28) = 576 - j168\,\text{kVA}$$

$$S_2 = \frac{1}{3}(192 + j1464) = 64 + j488\,\text{kVA}$$

$$S_1 + S_2 = 640 + j320\,\text{kVA}$$

$$\therefore\ \mathbf{I}^*_{aA} = \frac{(640 + j320)10^3}{6400} = 100 + j50$$

$$\mathbf{I}_{aA} = 100 - j50\,\text{A}$$

$$Z = \frac{6400}{100 - j50} = 25.6 + j12.8\,\Omega$$

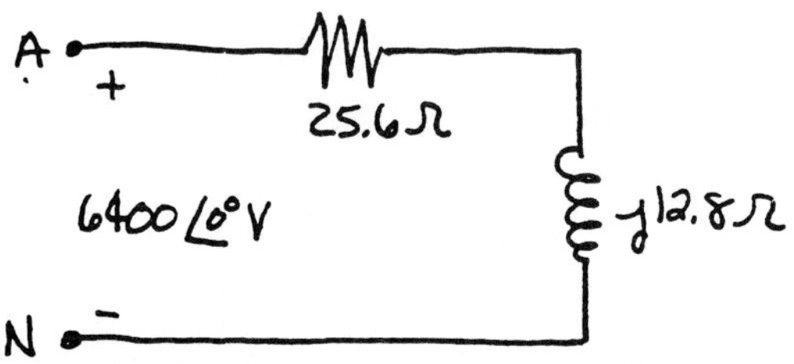

[b] $R = \dfrac{(6400)^2}{640 \times 10^3} = 64\,\Omega$

$$X_L = \frac{(6400)^2}{320 \times 10^3} = 128\,\Omega$$

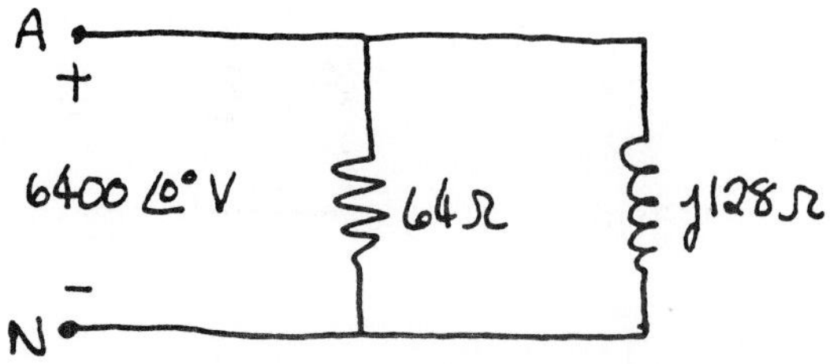

P 11.22

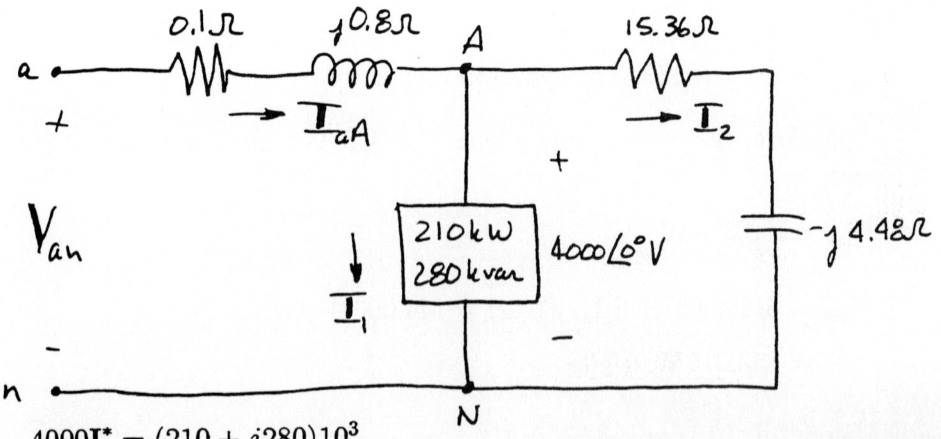

$$4000\mathbf{I}_1^* = (210 + j280)10^3$$

$$\mathbf{I}_1^* = \frac{210}{4} + j\frac{280}{4} = 52.5 + j70\text{ A}$$

$$\mathbf{I}_1 = 52.5 - j70\text{ A}$$

$$\mathbf{I}_2 = \frac{4000\underline{/0^\circ}}{15.36 - j4.48} = 240 + j70\text{ A}$$

$$\therefore\quad \mathbf{I}_{\mathbf{aA}} = \mathbf{I}_1 + \mathbf{I}_2 = 292.5 + j0\text{ A}$$

$$\mathbf{V}_{\mathbf{an}} = 4000 + j0 + 292.5(0.1 + j0.8) = 4136.04\underline{/3.32^\circ}\text{ V}$$

$$|\mathbf{V}_{\mathbf{ab}}| = \sqrt{3}|\mathbf{V}_{\mathbf{an}}| = 6990.62\text{ V}$$

P 11.23 $\mathbf{I}_{\mathbf{aA}}^* = \dfrac{(48 + j36)10^3}{480} = 100 + j75$

$$\mathbf{I}_{\mathbf{aA}} = 100 - j75\text{ A}$$

$$\mathbf{V}_{\mathbf{an}} = 480 + j0 + (100 - j75)(0.2 + j0.4) = 530 + j25\text{ V}$$

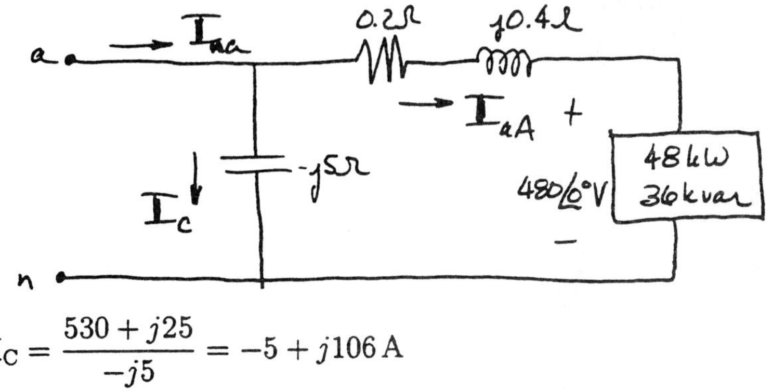

$$\mathbf{I}_{\mathrm{C}} = \frac{530 + j25}{-j5} = -5 + j106\text{ A}$$

$$\mathbf{I}_{\mathbf{na}} = \mathbf{I}_{\mathbf{aA}} + \mathbf{I}_{\mathrm{C}} = 95 + j31 = 99.93\underline{/18.07^\circ}\text{ A}$$

[b] $S_{g/\phi} = (530 + j25)(95 - j31) = 51{,}125 - j14{,}055\,\text{VA}$

$S_{gT} = 3S_{g/\phi} = 153{,}375 - j42{,}165\,\text{VA}$

Therefore, the source is delivering 153,375 W and absorbing 42,165 vars.

[c] $P_{\text{del}} = 153{,}375\,\text{W}$

$$P_{\text{abs}} = 3(48{,}000) + 3|\mathbf{I}_{\text{aA}}|^2(0.2) = 144{,}000 + 9375$$
$$= 153{,}375\,\text{W} = P_{\text{del}}$$

[d] $Q_{\text{del}} = 3|\mathbf{I}_{\text{C}}|^2(5) = 168{,}915\,\text{VAR}$

$$Q_{\text{abs}} = 3(36{,}000) + 42{,}165 + 3|\mathbf{I}_{\text{aA}}|^2(0.4)$$
$$= 168{,}915\,\text{VAR} = Q_{\text{del}}$$

P 11.24 [a] $P_{\text{OUT}} = 746 \times 200 = 149{,}200\,\text{W}$

$$P_{\text{IN}} = 149{,}200/(0.96) = 155{,}416.67\,\text{W}$$
$$\sqrt{3}V_L I_L \cos\theta = 155{,}416.67$$
$$I_L = \frac{155{,}416.67}{\sqrt{3}(208)(0.92)} = 468.91\,\text{A}$$

[b] $Q = \sqrt{3}V_L I_L \sin\phi = \sqrt{3}(208)(468.91)(0.39) = 66{,}207.79\,\text{VAR}$

P 11.25 $S_{g/\phi} = \frac{1}{3}(78)(0.8 - j0.6) \times 10^3 = 20{,}800 - j15{,}600\,\text{VA}$

$$\mathbf{I}^*_{\text{aA}} = \frac{20{,}800 - j15{,}600}{208} = 100 - j75\,\text{A}$$

$\mathbf{I}_{\text{aA}} = 100 + j75\,\text{A}$

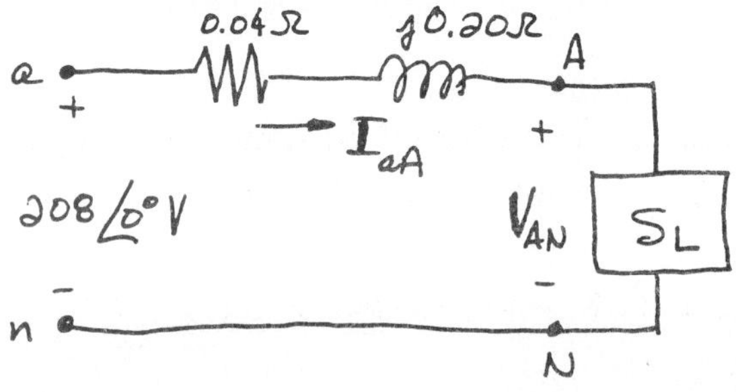

$$\mathbf{V}_{\text{AN}} = 208 - (100 + j75)(0.04 + j0.20)$$
$$= 219 - j23 = 220.20\angle{-6^\circ}\,\text{V}$$

$|\mathbf{V}_{\text{AB}}| = \sqrt{3}(220.20) = 381.41\,\text{V}$

[b] $S_{L/\phi} = (219 - j23)(100 - j75) = 20{,}175 - j18{,}725\,\text{VA}$

$$S_L = 3S_{L/\phi} = 60{,}525 - j56{,}175\,\text{VA}$$

Check:

$$S_g = 3(20{,}800 - j15{,}600) = 62{,}400 - j46{,}800\,\text{VA}$$

$$P_\ell = 3|\mathbf{I}_{aA}|^2(0.04) = 1875\,\text{W}$$

$$P_g = P_L + P_\ell = 60{,}525 + 1875 = 62{,}400\,\text{W} \quad \text{(checks)}$$

$$Q_\ell = 3|\mathbf{I}_{aA}|^2(0.20) = 9375\,\text{VAR}$$

$$Q_g = Q_L + Q_\ell = -56{,}175 + 9375 = -46{,}800\,\text{VAR} \quad \text{(checks)}$$

P 11.26 Let p_a, p_b, and p_c represent the instantaneous power of phases a, b, and c, respectively. Then assuming a positive phase sequence, we have

$$p_a = v_{an}i_{aA} = [V_m \cos\omega t][I_m \cos(\omega t - \theta_\phi)]$$

$$p_b = v_{bn}i_{bB} = [V_m \cos(\omega t - 120^\circ)][I_m \cos(\omega t - \theta_\phi - 120^\circ)]$$

$$p_c = v_{cn}i_{cC} = [V_m \cos(\omega t + 120^\circ)][I_m \cos(\omega t - \theta_\phi + 120^\circ)]$$

The total instantaneous power is $p_T = p_a + p_b + p_c$, so

$$p_T = V_m I_m[\cos\omega t \cos(\omega t - \theta_\phi) + \cos(\omega t + 120^\circ)\cos(\omega t - \theta_\phi - 120^\circ) + \cos(\omega t - 120^\circ)\cos(\omega t - \theta_\phi + 120^\circ)]$$

Now simplify using trigonometric identities. In simplifying, collect the coefficients of $\cos(\omega t - \theta_\phi)$ and $\sin(\omega t - \theta_\phi)$. We get

$$\begin{aligned}
p_T &= V_m I_m[\cos\omega t(1 + 2\cos^2 120^\circ)\cos(\omega t - \theta_\phi) \\
&\quad + 2\sin\omega t \sin^2 120^\circ \sin(\omega t - \theta_\phi)] \\
&= 1.5V_m I_m[\cos\omega t\cos(\omega t - \theta_\phi) + \sin\omega t \sin(\omega t - \theta_\phi)] \\
&= 1.5V_m I_m \cos\theta_\phi
\end{aligned}$$

P 11.27 [a] $S_1 = 72 - j21\,\text{kVA}$

$S_2 = 120 + j90\,\text{kVA}$

$S_3 = 168 + j36\,\text{kVA}$

$S_T = S_1 + S_2 + S_3 = 360 + j105\,\text{kVA}$

$S_T/\phi = 120 + j35\,\text{kVA}$

Single phase equivalent circuit

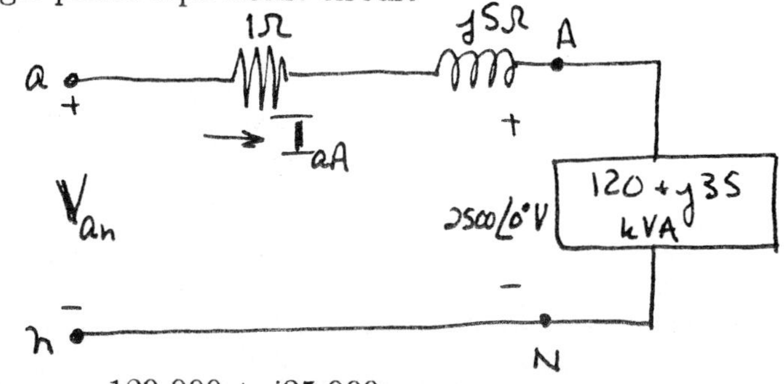

$$\therefore\quad \mathbf{I}_{aA}^{*} = \frac{120{,}000 + j35{,}000}{2500} = 48 + j14$$

$$\therefore\quad \mathbf{I}_{aA} = 48 - j14\,\text{A} = 50\underline{/-16.26^\circ}\,\text{A}$$

$$\mathbf{V}_{an} = 2500 + (1 + j5)(48 - j14) = 2618 + j226$$

$$= 2627.74\underline{/4.93^\circ}\,\text{V}$$

$$\therefore\quad |\mathbf{V}_{ab}| = \sqrt{3}(2627.74) = 4551.4\,\text{V}$$

[b] $P_L/\phi = 120\,\text{kW}$

$$P_S/\phi = 120{,}000 + |\mathbf{I}_{aA}|^2(1) = 122{,}500\,\text{W} = 122.5\,\text{kW}$$

$$\eta = \left(\frac{120}{122.5}\right)100 = 97.96\%$$

P 11.28 [a]

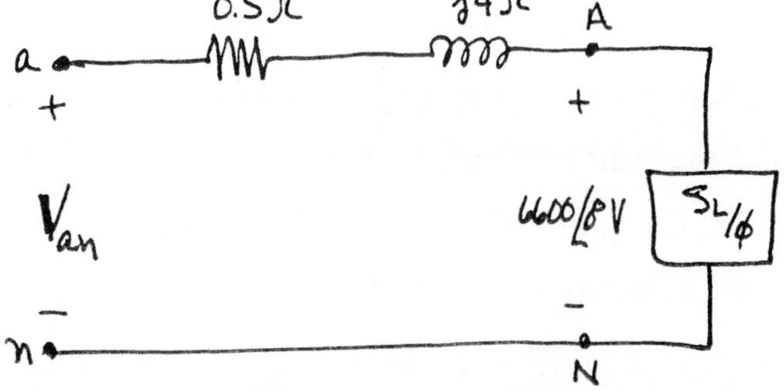

$$S_{L/\phi} = \frac{1}{3}\left[1188 + j\frac{1188}{0.6}(0.8)\right]10^3 = 396{,}000 + j528{,}000\,\text{VA}$$

$$\mathbf{I}^*_{aA} = \frac{396{,}000 + j528{,}000}{6600} = 60 + j80\text{ A}$$

$$\mathbf{I}_{aA} = 60 - j80\text{ A}$$

$$\mathbf{V}_{an} = 6600 + (60 - j80)(0.5 + j4)$$
$$= 6950 + j200 = 6952.88\angle 1.65^\circ\text{ V}$$

$$|\mathbf{V}_{ab}| = \sqrt{3}(6952.88) = 12{,}042.74\text{ V}$$

[b]

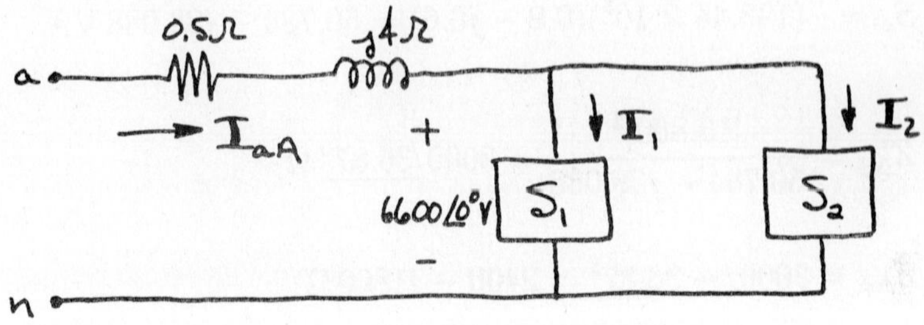

$$\mathbf{I}_1 = 60 - j80\text{ A} \qquad \text{(from part [a])}$$

$$S_2 = 0 - j\frac{1}{3}(1920) \times 10^3 = -j660{,}000\text{ VAR}$$

$$\mathbf{I}^*_2 = \frac{-j660{,}000}{6600} = -j100\text{ A}$$

$$\therefore\ \mathbf{I}_2 = j100\text{ A}$$

$$\mathbf{I}_{aA} = 60 - j80 + j100 = 60 + j20\text{ A}$$

$$\mathbf{V}_{an} = 6600 + (60 + j20)(0.5 + j4)$$
$$= 6550 + j250 = 6554.77\angle 2.19^\circ\text{ V}$$

$$|\mathbf{V}_{ab}| = \sqrt{3}(6554.77) = 11{,}353.19\text{ V}$$

[c] $\mathbf{I}_{aA} = 100\text{ A}$

$$P_{\text{loss}/\phi} = (100)^2(0.5) = 5000\text{ W}$$

$$P_{g/\phi} = 396{,}000 + 5000 = 401\text{ kW}$$

$$\%\eta = \frac{396}{401}(100) = 98.75\%$$

[d] $|\mathbf{I}_{aA}| = \sqrt{4000}\text{ A}$

$$P_{\ell/\phi} = (4000)(0.5) = 2000\text{ W}$$

$$\%\eta = \frac{396}{398}(100) = 99.50\%$$

[e] $Z_{cap/Y} = -j\frac{6600}{100} = -j66\,\Omega$

$$Z_{cap/\Delta} = 3Z_{cap/Y} = -j192\,\Omega$$

$$\therefore\quad \frac{1}{\omega C} = 192; \qquad C = \frac{1}{(192)(120\pi)} = 13.40\,\mu\text{F}$$

P 11.29 Assume a Δ-connect load (series):

$$S_\phi = \frac{1}{3}(190.44 \times 10^3)(0.8 - j0.6) = 50{,}784 - j38{,}088\text{ VA}$$

$$Z^*_{\Delta\phi} = \frac{|13{,}800|^2}{50{,}784 - j38{,}088} = 3000\underline{/36.87^\circ}\,\Omega$$

$$Z_{\Delta\phi} = 3000\underline{/-36.87^\circ} = 2400 - j1800\,\Omega$$

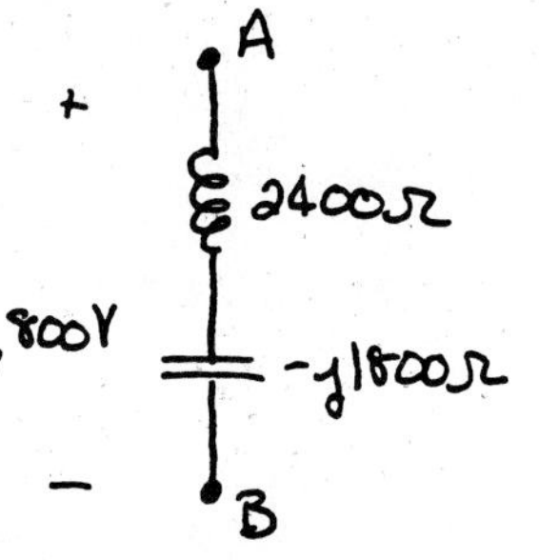

Now assume a Y-connected load (series):

$$Z_{Y\phi} = \frac{1}{3}Z_{\Delta\phi} = 800 - j600\,\Omega$$

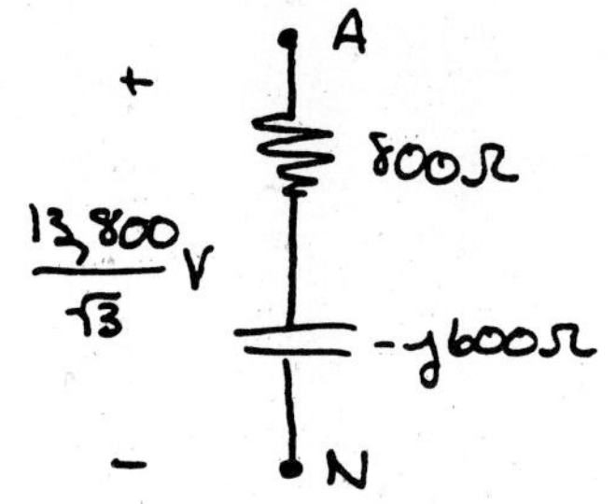

Now assume a Δ-connected load (parallel):

$$P_\phi = \frac{|13{,}800|^2}{R_\Delta}$$

$$R_{\Delta\phi} = \frac{|13{,}800|^2}{50{,}784} = 3750\,\Omega$$

$$Q_\phi = \frac{|13{,}800|^2}{X_\Delta}$$

$$X_\Delta\phi = \frac{|13{,}800|^2}{-38{,}088} = -5000\,\Omega$$

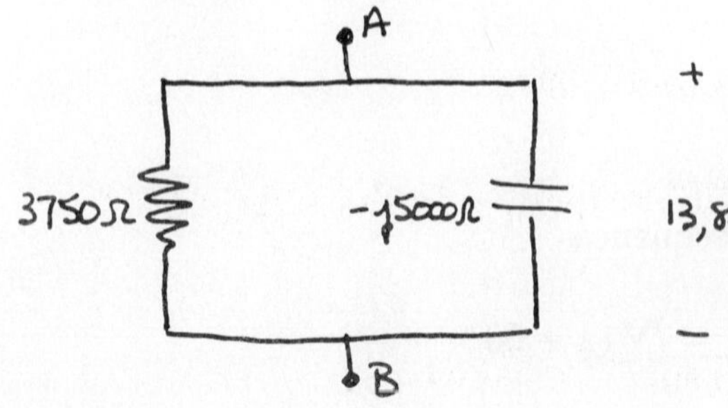

Now assume a Y-connected load (parallel):

$$R_{Y\phi} = \frac{1}{3}R_{\Delta\phi} = 1250\,\Omega$$

$$X_{Y\phi} = \frac{1}{3}X_{\Delta\phi} = -1666.67\,\Omega$$

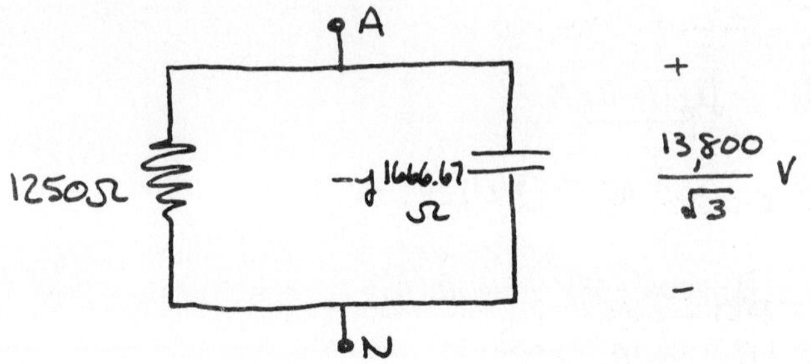

P 11.30 $Z_\phi = |Z|\underline{/\theta} = \dfrac{\mathbf{V_{AN}}}{\mathbf{I_{aA}}}$

$$\theta = \underline{/\mathbf{V_{AN}}} - \underline{/\mathbf{I_{aA}}}$$

$$\theta_1 = \underline{/\mathbf{V_{AB}}} - \underline{/\mathbf{I_{aA}}}$$

For a positive phase sequence,

$$\underline{/\mathbf{V_{AB}}} = \underline{/\mathbf{V_{AN}}} + 30^\circ$$

Thus,

$$\theta_1 = \underline{/\mathbf{V_{AN}}} + 30^\circ - \underline{/\mathbf{I_{aA}}} = \theta + 30^\circ$$

Similarly,

$$Z_\phi = |Z|\underline{/\theta} = \frac{\mathbf{V}_{\mathrm{CN}}}{\mathbf{I}_{\mathrm{cC}}}$$

$$\theta = \underline{/\mathbf{V}_{\mathrm{CN}}} - \underline{/\mathbf{I}_{\mathrm{cC}}}$$

$$\theta_2 = \underline{/\mathbf{V}_{\mathrm{CB}}} - \underline{/\mathbf{I}_{\mathrm{cC}}}$$

For a positive phase sequence,

$$\underline{/\mathbf{V}_{\mathrm{CB}}} = \underline{/\mathbf{V}_{\mathrm{BA}}} - 120^\circ = \underline{/\mathbf{V}_{\mathrm{AB}}} + 60^\circ$$

$$\underline{/\mathbf{I}_{\mathrm{cC}}} = \underline{/\mathbf{I}_{\mathrm{aA}}} + 120^\circ$$

Thus,

$$\theta_2 = \underline{/\mathbf{V}_{\mathrm{AB}}} + 60^\circ - \underline{/\mathbf{I}_{\mathrm{aA}}} + 120^\circ = \theta_1 - 60^\circ$$
$$= \theta + 30^\circ - 60^\circ = \theta - 30^\circ$$

P 11.31 $\mathbf{I}_{\mathrm{aA}} = (\mathbf{V}_{\mathrm{AN}} Z_\phi) = |\mathbf{I}_L|\underline{/-\theta_\phi}\,\mathrm{A},$

$$Z_\phi = |Z|\underline{/\theta_\phi}, \qquad \mathbf{V}_{\mathrm{BC}} = |\mathbf{V}_L|\underline{/90^\circ}\,\mathrm{V},$$

$$W_m = |\mathbf{V}_L|\,|\mathbf{I}_L|\cos[-90^\circ - (-\theta_\phi)]$$
$$= |\mathbf{V}_L|\,|\mathbf{I}_L|\cos(\theta_\phi - 90^\circ)$$
$$= |\mathbf{V}_L|\,|\mathbf{I}_L|\sin\theta_\phi,$$

therefore $\sqrt{3}W_m = \sqrt{3}|\mathbf{V}_L|\,|\mathbf{I}_L|\sin\theta_\phi = Q_{\mathrm{total}}$

P 11.32 [a] $Z = 96 + j72 = 120\underline{/36.87^\circ}\,\Omega$

$\mathbf{V}_{\mathrm{AN}} = 720\underline{/0^\circ}\,\mathrm{V}; \qquad \therefore\ \mathbf{I}_{\mathrm{aA}} = 6\underline{/-36.87^\circ}\,\mathrm{A}$

$\mathbf{V}_{\mathrm{BC}} = \mathbf{V}_{\mathrm{BN}} - \mathbf{V}_{\mathrm{CN}} = 720\sqrt{3}\underline{/-90^\circ}\,\mathrm{V}$

$W_m = (720\sqrt{3})(6)\cos(-90 + 36.87^\circ) = 4489.48\,\mathrm{W}$

$\sqrt{3}W_m = 7776\,\mathrm{VAR}$

[b] $Q_\phi = (36)(72) = 2592\,\mathrm{VAR}$

$Q_T = 3Q_\phi = 7776\,\mathrm{VAR} = \sqrt{3}W_m$

P 11.33 [a] $\mathbf{I}_{aA}^{*} = \frac{(192 + j56)10^3}{4800} = 41.67\underline{/16.26^\circ}\text{ A}$

$\mathbf{I}_{aA} = 41.67\underline{/-16.26^\circ}\text{ A}$

$\mathbf{I}_{bB} = 41.67\underline{/-136.26^\circ}\text{ A}$

$\mathbf{V}_{AB} = 4800\sqrt{3}\underline{/30^\circ}\text{ V}$

$\mathbf{V}_{BC} = 4800\sqrt{3}\underline{/-90^\circ}\text{ V}$

$W_1 = (4800\sqrt{3})(41.67)\cos 46.26^\circ = 239{,}502.58\text{ W}$

[b] Current coil in line aA, measure $\mathbf{I}_{aA}$.
Voltage coil across AC, measure $\mathbf{V}_{AC}$.

[c] $I_{aA} = 41.67\underline{/-16.76^\circ}\text{ A}$

$\mathbf{V}_{CA} = 4800\sqrt{3}\underline{/150^\circ}\text{ V}$

$\therefore\ \mathbf{V}_{AC} = 4800\sqrt{3}\underline{/-30^\circ}\text{ V}$

$W_2 = (4800\sqrt{3})(41.67)\cos 13.74^\circ = 336{,}497.42\text{ W}$

[d] $W_1 + W_2 = 576{,}000 = 576\text{kW}$

$P_T = 600(0.96) = 576\text{ kW} = W_1 + W_2$

P 11.34 [a] $Z_\phi = 600 + j450 = 750\underline{/36.87^\circ}\ \Omega$

$S_\phi = \frac{(69 \times 10^3)^2}{750\underline{/-36.87^\circ}} = 5{,}078{,}400 + j3{,}808{,}800\text{ VA}$

$S_T = 3S_\phi = 15{,}235{,}200 + j11{,}426{,}400\text{ VA}$

[b] $W_{m1} = (69{,}000)\sqrt{3}(92)\cos(0 + 66.87^\circ) = 4{,}318{,}082.44\text{ W}$

$W_{m2} = (69{,}000)\sqrt{3}(92)\cos(60 - 53.13^\circ) = 10{,}916{,}117.56\text{ W}$

Check: $P_T = 15{,}235{,}200\text{ W} = W_{m1} + W_{m2}.$

P 11.35 [a] $W_1 = |\mathbf{V}_{BA}||\mathbf{I}_{bB}|\cos\theta$
Positive phase sequence:

$\mathbf{V}_{BA} = 480\sqrt{3}\underline{/-150^\circ}\text{ V}$

$\mathbf{I}_{aA} = \frac{480\underline{/0^\circ}}{20\underline{/30^\circ}} = 24\underline{/-30^\circ}\text{ A}$

$\mathbf{I}_{bB} = 24\underline{/-150^\circ}\text{ A}$

$W_1 = (24)(480)\sqrt{3}\cos 0^\circ = 19{,}953.23\text{ W}$

$W_2 = |\mathbf{V}_{CA}||\mathbf{I}_{cC}|\cos\theta$

$\mathbf{V}_{CA} = 480\sqrt{3}\underline{/150^\circ}\text{ V}$

$\mathbf{I}_{cC} = 24\underline{/90^\circ}\text{ A}$

$W_2 = (24)(480)\sqrt{3}\cos 60^\circ = 9976.61\text{ W}$

[b] $P_\phi = (24)^2(20)\cos 30^\circ = 5760\sqrt{3}\text{ W}$

$P_T = 3P_\phi = 17{,}280\sqrt{3}\text{ W}$

$W_1 + W_2 = 11{,}520\sqrt{3} + 5760\sqrt{3} = 17{,}280\sqrt{3}\text{ W}$

$\therefore\; W_1 + W_2 = P_T \qquad \text{(checks)}$

P 11.36 [a] $Z = 276 - j207 = 345\underline{/-36.87^\circ}\,\Omega$

$$\mathbf{I}_{aA} = \frac{6900\underline{/0^\circ}}{345\underline{/-36.87^\circ}} = 20\underline{/36.87^\circ}\text{ A}$$

$\mathbf{I}_{bB} = 20\underline{/-83.13^\circ}\text{ A}$

$\mathbf{V}_{AC} = 6900\sqrt{3}\underline{/-30^\circ}\text{ V}$

$\mathbf{V}_{BC} = 6900\sqrt{3}\underline{/-90^\circ}\text{ V}$

$W_1 = (6900\sqrt{3})(20)\cos(-30 - 36.87^\circ) = 93{,}893.10\text{ W}$

$W_2 = (6900\sqrt{3})(20)\cos(-90 + 83.13^\circ) = 237{,}306.90\text{ W}$

[b] $W_1 + W_2 = 331{,}200\text{ W}$

$P_T = 3(20)^2(276) = 331{,}200\text{ W}$

[c] $\sqrt{3}(W_1 - W_2) = -248{,}400\text{ VAR}$

$Q_T = 3(20)^2(-207) = -248{,}400\text{ VAR}$

P 11.37 [a] Negative phase sequence:

$\mathbf{V}_{AB} = 480\sqrt{3}\underline{/-30^\circ}\text{ V}$

$\mathbf{V}_{BC} = 480\sqrt{3}\underline{/90^\circ}\text{ V}$

$\mathbf{V}_{CA} = 480\sqrt{3}\underline{/-150^\circ}\text{ V}$

$$\mathbf{I}_{AB} = \frac{480\sqrt{3}\underline{/-30^\circ}}{60\underline{/-30^\circ}} = 8\sqrt{3}\underline{/0^\circ}\text{ A}$$

$$\mathbf{I}_{BC} = \frac{480\sqrt{3}\underline{/90^\circ}}{24\underline{/30^\circ}} = 20\sqrt{3}\underline{/60^\circ}\text{ A}$$

$$\mathbf{I}_{CA} = \frac{480\sqrt{3}/\underline{-150^\circ}}{80/\underline{0^\circ}} = 6\sqrt{3}/\underline{-150^\circ}\text{ A}$$

$$\mathbf{I}_{aA} = \mathbf{I}_{AB} + \mathbf{I}_{AC}$$

$$= 8\sqrt{3}/\underline{0^\circ} + 6\sqrt{3}/\underline{30^\circ} = 23.44/\underline{12.81^\circ}\text{ A}$$

$$\mathbf{I}_{cC} = \mathbf{I}_{CB} + \mathbf{I}_{CA}$$

$$= 20\sqrt{3}/\underline{-120^\circ} + 6\sqrt{3}/\underline{-150^\circ} = 43.95/\underline{-126.79^\circ}\text{ A}$$

$$W_{m1} = 480\sqrt{3}(23.44)\cos(-30 - 12.81^\circ) = 14{,}296.61\text{ W}$$

$$W_{m2} = 480\sqrt{3}(43.95)\cos(-90 + 126.79^\circ) = 29{,}261.53\text{ W}$$

[b] $W_{m1} + W_{m2} = 43{,}558.14$ W

$$P_A = (8\sqrt{3})^2(60\cos 30^\circ) = 9976.61\text{ W}$$

$$P_B = (20\sqrt{3})^2(24\cos 30^\circ) = 24{,}941.53\text{ W}$$

$$P_C = (6\sqrt{3})^2(80) = 8640\text{ W}$$

$$P_A + P_B + P_C = 43{,}558.14 = W_{m1} + W_{m2}$$

P 11.38 $\tan\phi = \frac{\sqrt{3}(W_2 - W_1)}{W_1 + W_2} = \frac{873{,}290.66}{732{,}777.88} = 1.1918$

$\therefore\ \phi = 50^\circ$

$\therefore\ 7600\sqrt{3}|\mathbf{I}_L|\cos 80^\circ = 114{,}291.64$

$|\mathbf{I}_L| = 50$ A

$|Z| = \frac{7600}{50} = 152\,\Omega \qquad \therefore\ Z = 152/\underline{50^\circ}\,\Omega$

P 11.39 From the solution to Prob. 11.15 we have

$\mathbf{I}_{aA} = 145.88/\underline{-24.28^\circ}$ A and $\mathbf{I}_{bB} = 134.01/\underline{178.04^\circ}$ A

[a] $W_1 = |\mathbf{V}_{ac}|\,|\mathbf{I}_{aA}|\cos(\theta_{ac} - \theta_{aA})$

$$= 720(145.88)\cos(-60^\circ + 24.28^\circ) = 85{,}274.70\text{ W}$$

[b] $W_2 = |\mathbf{V}_{bc}|\,|\mathbf{I}_{bB}|\cos(\theta_{bc} - \theta_{bB})$

$$= 720(134.01)\cos(-120^\circ - 178.04^\circ) = 45{,}357.50\text{ W}$$

[c] $W_1 + W_2 = 130{,}632\,\text{W}$

$$P_{\text{AB}} = (144)^2(4.8) = 99{,}532.8\,\text{W}$$

$$P_{\text{BC}} = (36)^2(16) = 20{,}736\,\text{W}$$

$$P_{\text{CA}} = (20.36)^2(25) = 10{,}363.2\,\text{W}$$

$$P_{\text{AB}} + P_{\text{BC}} + P_{\text{CA}} = 130{,}632$$

therefore $W_1 + W_2 = P_{\text{total}}$

P 11.40 [a] From DE 11.10, $\mathbf{I}_{\text{aA}} = (101.8 - j135.7)\,\text{A}$

Therefore $\mathbf{I}_{\text{cap}} = j135.7\,\text{A}$

Therefore $$Z_{CY} = \frac{2450/\sqrt{3}}{j135.7} = -j10.42\,\Omega$$

Therefore $$C_Y = \frac{1}{(10.42)(2\pi)(60)} = 254.5\,\mu\text{F}$$

$$Z_{C\Delta} = (-j10.42)(3) = -j31.26\,\Omega$$

Therefore $$C_\Delta = \frac{254.5}{3} = 84.83\,\mu\text{F}$$

[b] $C_Y = 254.5\,\mu\text{F}$

[c] $|\mathbf{I}_{\text{aA}}| = 101.8\,\text{A}$

P 11.41 [a]

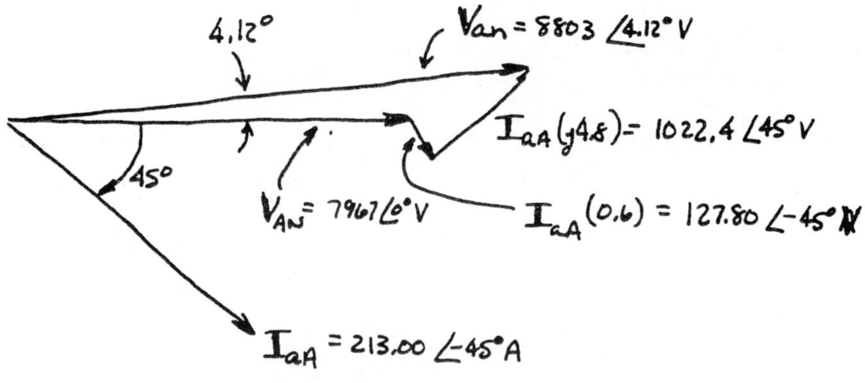

[b]

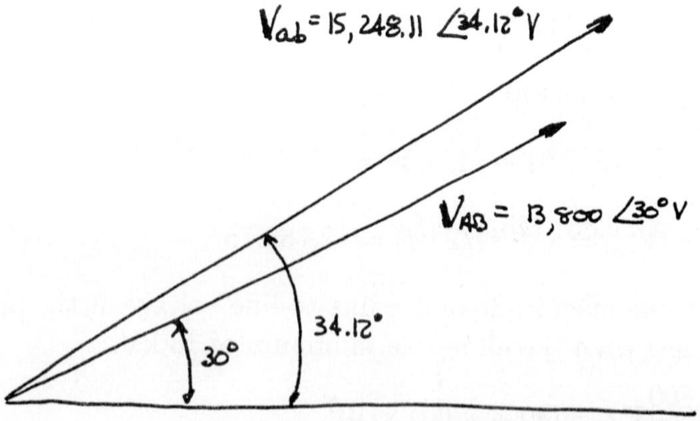

[c]

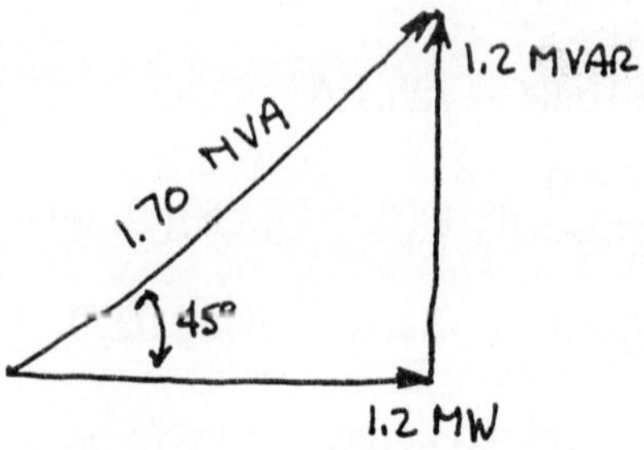

[d]

P 11.42 [a] $Q = \dfrac{|\mathbf{V}|^2}{X_C}$

$$\therefore \quad |X_C| = \frac{(13{,}800)^2}{1.2 \times 10^6} = 158.70\,\Omega$$

$$\therefore \quad \frac{1}{\omega C} = 158.70; \qquad C = \frac{1}{2\pi(60)(158.70)} = 16.71\,\mu\text{F}$$

[b] $|X_C| = \dfrac{(13{,}800/\sqrt{3})^2}{1.2 \times 10^6} = \dfrac{1}{3}(158.70)$

$$\therefore \quad C = 3(16.71) = 50.14\,\mu\text{F}$$

P 11.43 [a] $\dfrac{13{,}800}{\sqrt{3}}\mathbf{I}_{aA}^* = 80 \times 10^3 + j200 \times 10^3 - j1200 \times 10^3$

$$\mathbf{I}_{aA}^* = \frac{80\sqrt{3} - j100\sqrt{3}}{13.8} = 10.04 - j125.51\ \text{A}$$

$$\therefore\quad \mathbf{I}_{aA} = 10.04 + j125.51 \text{ A}$$

$$\mathbf{V}_{an} = \frac{13{,}800}{\sqrt{3}}\underline{/0^\circ} + (0.6 + j4.8)(10.04 + j125.51)$$
$$= 7371.01 + j123.50 = 7372.04\underline{/0.96^\circ} \text{ V}$$

$$\therefore\quad |\mathbf{V}_{ab}| = \sqrt{3}(7372.04) = 12{,}768.75 \text{ V}$$

[b] Yes, the magnitude of the line-to-line voltage at the power plant is less than the allowable minimum of 13 kV.

P 11.44 [a] $\frac{13{,}800}{\sqrt{3}}\mathbf{I}^*_{aA} = (80 + j200) \times 10^3$

$$\mathbf{I}^*_{aA} = \frac{80\sqrt{3} + j200\sqrt{3}}{13.8} = 10.04 + j25.1 \text{ A}$$

$$\therefore\quad \mathbf{I}_{aA} = 10.04 - j25.1 \text{ A}$$

$$\mathbf{V}_{an} = \frac{13{,}800}{\sqrt{3}}\underline{/0^\circ} + (0.6 + j4.8)(10.04 - j25.1)$$
$$= 8093.95 + j33.13 = 8094.02\underline{/0.23^\circ} \text{ V}$$

$$\therefore\quad |\mathbf{V}_{ab}| = \sqrt{3}(8094.02) = 14{,}019.25 \text{ V}$$

[b] Yes: $13\,\text{kV} < 14{,}019.25 < 14.6\,\text{kV}$

[c] $P_{loss} = 3|10.04 + j125.51|^2(0.6) = 28.54\,\text{kW}$

[d] $P_{loss} = 3|10.04 + j25.1|^2(0.6) = 1.32\,\text{kW}$

[e] Yes, the voltage at the generating plant is at an acceptable level and the line loss is greatly reduced.

12

Introduction to the Laplace Transform

Drill Exercises

DE 12.1 [a] $f(t) = 5t[u(t) - u(t-2)] + 10[u(t-2) - u(t-6)] +$
$(-5t + 40)[u(t-6) - u(t-8)]$

[b] $f(t) = 10\sin \pi t[u(t) - u(t-2)]$

[c] $f(t) = 4t[u(t) - u(t-5)]$

DE 12.2 [a] $A = \left(\frac{1}{2}\right) bh = \left(\frac{1}{2}\right)(2\varepsilon)\left(\frac{1}{\varepsilon}\right) = 1.0$

[b] 0; [c] ∞

DE 12.3 [a] $I = \int_{-1}^{3} (t^3 + 2)\delta(t)\, dt + \int_{-1}^{3} 4(t^3 + 2)\delta(t-1)\, dt = 2 + 8(1+2) = 26$

[b] $I = \int_{-2}^{2} t^2\delta(t)\, dt + \int_{-2}^{2} t^2\delta(t + 1.5)\, dt + 0 = 0 + (-1.5)^2 + 0 = 2.25$

DE 12.4 $f(t) = \frac{1}{2\pi}\int_{-\infty}^{\infty} \frac{(4 + j\omega)}{(9 + j\omega)} \cdot \pi\delta(\omega) \cdot e^{jt\omega}\, d\omega = \left(\frac{1}{2\pi}\right)\left(\frac{4\pi}{9}\right) = \frac{2}{9}$

DE 12.5 [a] $\mathcal{L}\{t\} = \int_{0^-}^{\infty} te^{-st}\, dt = \int_{0^+}^{\infty} te^{-st}\, dt = \frac{e^{-st}}{s^2}(-st - 1)\Big|_{0^+}^{\infty}$

$$= \left[\frac{e^{-st}}{s^2}\right](st + 1)\Big|_{\infty}^{0^+} = \left(\frac{1}{s^2}\right) - 0 = \frac{1}{s^2}$$

[b] $\sinh \beta t = \frac{e^{\beta t} - e^{-\beta t}}{2}$

Therefore,

$$\mathcal{L}\{\sinh \beta t\} = \frac{1}{2}\int_{0^-}^{\infty}\left[e^{-(s-\beta)t} - e^{-(s+\beta)t}\right] dt$$

$$= \frac{1}{2}\left[\frac{e^{-(s-\beta)t}}{-(s-\beta)}\right]_{0^-}^{\infty} - \frac{1}{2}\left[\frac{e^{-(s+\beta)t}}{-(s+\beta)}\right]_{0^-}^{\infty}$$

$$= \frac{1}{2}\left(\frac{1}{s-\beta} - \frac{1}{s+\beta}\right) = \frac{\beta}{(s^2-\beta^2)}$$

DE 12.6 [a] Since $\mathcal{L}\{t^2\} = \frac{2}{s^3}$, it follows that

$$\mathcal{L}\{t^2e^{-at}\} = \frac{2}{(s+a)^3}$$

[b] Let $f(t) = e^{-at}\sinh \beta t$, then

$$\mathcal{L}\{f(t)\} = F(s) = \frac{\beta}{(s+a)^2 - \beta^2}$$

$$\mathcal{L}\left\{\frac{df(t)}{dt}\right\} = sF(s) - f(0^-) = \frac{s(\beta)}{(s+a)^2-\beta^2} - 0 = \frac{\beta s}{(s+a)^2-\beta^2}$$

[c] Let $f(t) = \cos \omega t$. Then

$$F(s) = \frac{s}{(s^2+\omega^2)} \quad \text{and} \quad \frac{dF(s)}{ds} = \frac{-(s^2-\omega^2)}{(s^2+\omega^2)^2}$$

Therefore $\mathcal{L}\{t\cos\omega t\} = \dfrac{s^2-\omega^2}{(s^2+\omega^2)^2}$

DE 12.7 $I_g(s) = \dfrac{5s}{s^2+100}$; $\quad \dfrac{1}{RC} = 40$; $\quad \dfrac{1}{LC} = 64$; $\quad \dfrac{1}{C} = 40$

Therefore $V = \dfrac{(40)(5)s^2}{(s^2+40s+64)(s^2+100)} = \dfrac{200s^2}{(s^2+40s+64)(s^2+100)}$

DE 12.8 $F(s) = \dfrac{6s^2+26s+26}{(s+1)(s+2)(s+3)} = \dfrac{K_1}{s+1} + \dfrac{K_2}{s+2} + \dfrac{K_3}{s+3}$

$$K_1 = \frac{6-26+26}{(1)(2)} = 3; \qquad K_2 = \frac{24-52+26}{(-1)(1)} = 2$$

$$K_3 = \frac{54-72+26}{(-2)(-1)} = 4$$

Therefore $f(t) = [3e^{-t} + 2e^{-2t} + 4e^{-3t}]u(t)$

DE 12.9 $F(s) = \dfrac{7s^2 + 63s + 134}{(s+3)(s+4)(s+5)} = \dfrac{K_1}{s+3} + \dfrac{K_2}{s+4} + \dfrac{K_3}{s+5}$

$$K_1 = \frac{63 - 189 - 134}{1(2)} = 4; \qquad K_2 = \frac{112 - 252 + 134}{(-1)(1)} = 6$$

$$K_3 = \frac{175 - 315 + 134}{(-2)(-1)} = -3$$

$$f(t) = [4e^{-3t} + 6e^{-4t} - 3e^{-5t}]u(t)$$

DE 12.10 $F(s) = \dfrac{10(s^2 + 119)}{(s+5)(s^2 + 10s + 169)}$

$$s_{1,2} = -5 + \sqrt{25 - 169} = -5 + j12$$

$$F(s) = \frac{K_1}{s+5} + \frac{K_2}{s+5-j12} + \frac{K_2^*}{s+5+j12}$$

$$K_1 = \frac{10(25 + 119)}{25 - 50 + 169} = 10$$

$$K_2 = \frac{10[(-5+j12)^2 + 119]}{(j12)(j24)} = j4.17 = 4.17\underline{/90^\circ}$$

Therefore

$$\begin{aligned} f(t) &= [10e^{-5t} + 8.33e^{-5t}\cos(12t + 90^\circ)]\,u(t) \\ &= [10e^{-5t} - 8.33e^{-5t}\sin 12t]\,u(t) \end{aligned}$$

DE 12.11 $V(s) = \dfrac{200s^2}{(s^2 + 40s + 64)(s^2 + 100)}$

$$s^2 + 40s + 64 = (s+28)(s+52); \qquad s^2 + 100 = (s - j10)(s + j10)$$

Therefore

$$\begin{aligned} V(s) &= \frac{200s^2}{(s+28)(s+52)(s-j10)(s+j10)} \\ &= \frac{K_1}{s+28} + \frac{K_2}{s+52} + \frac{K_3}{s-j10} + \frac{K_3^*}{s+j10} \end{aligned}$$

$$K_1 = \frac{200s^2}{(s+52)(s^2+100)}\bigg|_{s=-28} = 7.39$$

$$K_2 = \frac{200s^2}{(s+28)(s^2+100)}\bigg|_{s=-52} = -8.03$$

$$K_3 = \frac{200s^2}{(s+28)(s+52)(s+j10)}\bigg|_{s=j10} = 0.64\underline{/59.46^\circ}$$

Therefore

$$v(t) = [1.28\cos(10t + 59.46^\circ) + 7.39e^{-28t} - 8.03e^{-52t}]u(t)$$

DE 12.12 $F(s) = \dfrac{4s^2+7s+1}{s(s+1)^2} = \dfrac{K_0}{s} + \dfrac{K_1}{(s+1)^2} + \dfrac{K_2}{s+1}$

$$K_0 = \frac{1}{(1)^2} = 1; \qquad K_1 = \frac{4-7+1}{-1} = 2$$

$$K_2 = \frac{d}{ds}\left[\frac{4s^2+7s+1}{s}\right]_{s=-1} = \frac{s(8s+7)-(4s^2+7s+1)}{s^2}\bigg|_{s=-1}$$

$$= \frac{1+2}{1} = 3$$

Therefore $f(t) = [1 + 2te^{-t} + 3e^{-t}]\,u(t)$

DE 12.13 $F(s) = \dfrac{40}{(s^2+4s+5)^2} = \dfrac{40}{(s+2-j1)^2(s+2+j1)^2}$

$$= \frac{K_1}{(s+2-j1)^2} + \frac{K_2}{(s+2-j1)} + \frac{K_1^*}{(s+2+j1)^2} + \frac{K_2^*}{(s+2+j1)}$$

$$K_1 = \frac{40}{(j2)^2} = -10 \quad \text{and} \quad K_1^* = -10$$

$$K_2 = \frac{d}{ds}\left[\frac{40}{(s+2+j1)^2}\right]_{s=-2+j1} = \frac{-80(j2)}{(j2)^4} = -j10$$

$$K_2^* = j10$$

Therefore

$$f(t) = [-20te^{-2t}\cos t + 20e^{-2t}\cos(t-90^\circ)]\,u(t)$$

$$= 20e^{-2t}[\sin t - t\cos t]\,u(t)$$

DE 12.14 $F(s) = \dfrac{5s^2 + 29s + 32}{(s+2)(s+4)} = \dfrac{5s^2 + 29s + 32}{s^2 + 6s + 8} = 5 - \dfrac{s+8}{(s+2)(s+4)}$

$$\frac{s+8}{(s+2)(s+4)} = \frac{K_1}{s+2} + \frac{K_2}{s+4}$$

$$K_1 = \frac{-2+8}{2} = 3; \qquad K_2 = \frac{-4+8}{-2} = -2$$

Therefore,

$$F(s) = 5 - \frac{3}{s+2} + \frac{2}{s+4}$$

$$f(t) = 5\delta(t) + [-3e^{-2t} + 2e^{-4t}]u(t)$$

DE 12.15 $F(s) = \dfrac{2s^3 + 8s^2 + 2s - 4}{s^2 + 5s + 4} = 2s - 2 + \dfrac{4(s+1)}{(s+1)(s+4)} = 2s - 2 + \dfrac{4}{s+4}$

$$f(t) = 2\frac{d\delta(t)}{dt} - 2\delta(t) + 4e^{-4t}\,u(t)$$

DE 12.16 $\lim_{s\to\infty} sF(s) = \lim_{s\to\infty}\left[\dfrac{7s^2[1 + (9/s) + (134/7s^2)]}{s^3[1 + (3/s)][1 + (4/s)][1 + (5/s)]}\right] = 7$

$$\therefore \quad f(0^+) = 7$$

$$\lim_{s\to 0} sF(s) = \lim_{s\to 0}\left[\frac{7s^3 + 63s^2 + 134s}{(s+3)(s+4)(s+5)}\right] = 0$$

$$\therefore \quad f(\infty) = 0$$

$$\lim_{s\to\infty} sF(s) = \lim_{s\to\infty}\left[\frac{s^2[4 + (7/s) + (1/s)^2]}{s^2[1 + (1/s)]^2}\right] = 4$$

$$\therefore \quad f(0^+) = 4$$

$$\lim_{s\to 0} sF(s) = \lim_{s\to 0}\left[\frac{4s^2 + 7s + 1}{(s+1)^2}\right] = 1$$

$$\therefore \quad f(\infty) = 1$$

$$\lim_{s\to\infty} sF(s) = \lim_{s\to\infty}\left[\frac{40s}{s^4[1+(4/s)+(5/s^2)]^2}\right] = 0$$

$$\therefore\ f(0^+) = 0$$

$$\lim_{s\to 0} sF(s) = \lim_{s\to 0}\left[\frac{40s}{(s^2+4s+5)^2}\right] = 0$$

$$\therefore\ f(\infty) = 0$$

DE 12.17 [a] $\lim_{s\to\infty} sV(s) = \lim_{s\to\infty}\left[\frac{1.92s^3}{s^4[1+(1.6/s)+(1/s^2)][1+(1/s^2)]}\right] = 0$

Therefore $v(0^+) = 0$

[b] No, V has a pair of poles on the imaginary axis.

Problems

P 12.1 [a] $f(t) = -50\sin\frac{\pi}{2}t[u(t) - u(t-4)]$

$= (-50\sin\frac{\pi}{2}t)u(t) + (50\sin\frac{\pi}{2}t)u(t-4)$

[b] $f(t) = 120 + 30t \qquad -4\,\text{s} \le t \le 0$

$f(t) = 120 - 30t \qquad 0 \le t \le 8\,\text{s}$

$f(t) = -360 + 30t \qquad 8\,\text{s} \le t \le 12\,\text{s}$

$f(t) = 0 \qquad$ elsewhere

$$f(t) = (120+30t)[(u(t+4) - u(t)] + (120-30t)[u(t) - u(t-8)]$$
$$+(-360+30t)[u(t-8) - u(t-12)]$$

P 12.2 [a]

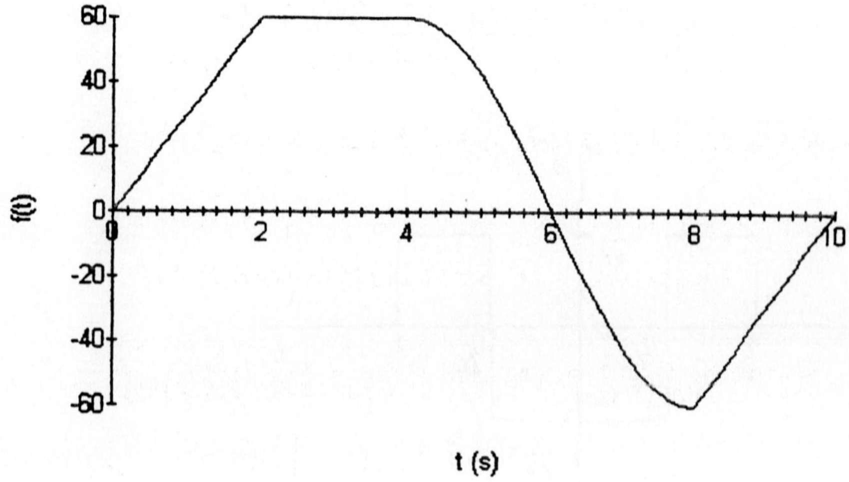

[b] $f(t) = 30t[u(t) - u(t-2)] + 60[u(t-2) - u(t-4)]$
$+60\cos(\frac{\pi}{4}t - \pi)[u(t-4) - u(t-8)]$
$+(30t - 300)[u(t-8) - u(t-10)]$

P 12.3

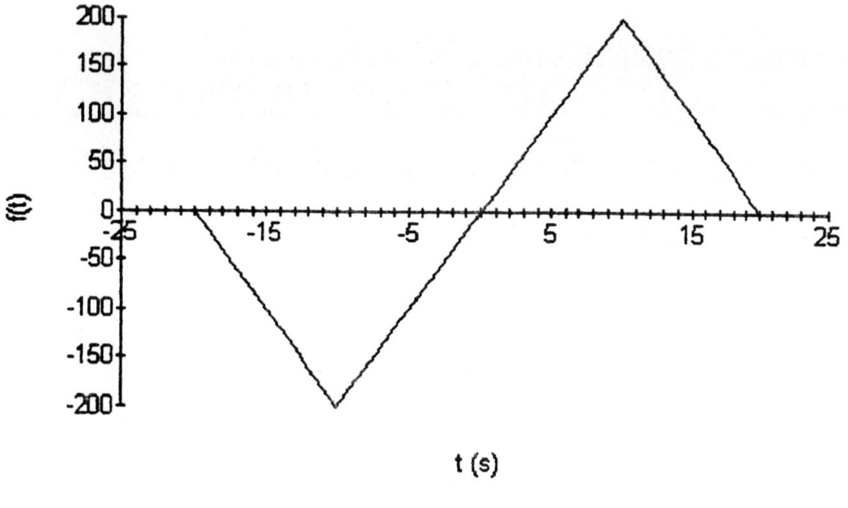

P 12.4 As $\varepsilon \to 0$ the amplitude $\to \infty$; the duration $\to 0$; and the area is independent of ε, i.e.,

$$A = \int_{-\infty}^{\infty} \frac{\varepsilon}{\pi} \frac{1}{\varepsilon^2 + t^2} dt = 1$$

P 12.5 $F(s) = \int_{-\varepsilon}^{\varepsilon} \frac{1}{2\varepsilon} e^{-st}\,dt = \frac{e^{s\varepsilon} - e^{-s\varepsilon}}{2\varepsilon s}$

$$\lim_{\varepsilon\to 0} F(s) = \frac{1}{2s} \lim_{\varepsilon\to\infty} \left[\frac{se^{s\varepsilon} + se^{-s\varepsilon}}{1}\right] = \frac{1}{2s} \cdot \frac{2s}{1} = 1$$

P 12.6

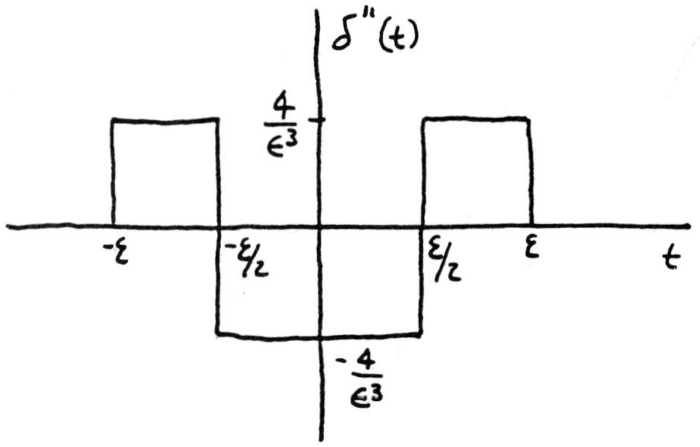

$$F(s) = \int_{-\varepsilon}^{-\varepsilon/2} \frac{4}{\varepsilon^3} e^{-st}\,dt + \int_{-\varepsilon/2}^{\varepsilon/2} \left(\frac{-4}{\varepsilon^3}\right) e^{-st}\,dt + \int_{\varepsilon/2}^{\varepsilon} \frac{4}{\varepsilon^3} e^{-st}\,dt$$

Therefore $F(s) = \frac{4}{s\varepsilon^3}[e^{s\varepsilon} - 2e^{-s\varepsilon/2} + 2e^{-s\varepsilon/2} - e^{-s\varepsilon}]$

$$\mathcal{L}\{\delta''(t)\} = \lim_{\varepsilon\to 0} F(s)$$

After applying L'Hopital's rule three times, we have

$$\lim_{\varepsilon\to\infty} \frac{2s}{3}\left[se^{s\varepsilon} - \frac{s}{4}e^{s\varepsilon/2} - \frac{s}{4}e^{+s\varepsilon/2} + se^{-s\varepsilon}\right] = \frac{2s}{3}\left(\frac{3s}{2}\right)$$

Therefore $\mathcal{L}\{\delta''(t)\} = s^2$

P 12.7 [a] Let $dv = \delta'(t-a)\,dt, \qquad v = \delta(t-a)$

$u = f(t), \qquad du = f'(t)\,dt$

Therefore

$$\int_{-\infty}^{\infty} f(t)\delta'(t-a)\,dt = f(t)\delta(t-a)\Big|_{-\infty}^{\infty} - \int_{-\infty}^{\infty} \delta(t-a)f'(t)\,dt$$

$$= 0 - f'(a)$$

[b] $\mathcal{L}\{\delta'(t)\} = \int_{0^-}^{\infty} \delta'(t)e^{-st}\,dt = -\left[\frac{d(e^{-st})}{dt}\right]_{t=0} = -\left[-se^{-st}\right]_{t=0} = s$

P 12.8 [a] $\mathcal{L}\{t\} = \frac{1}{s^2}$; therefore $\mathcal{L}\{te^{-at}\} = \frac{1}{(s+a)^2}$

[b] $\sin\omega t = \frac{e^{j\omega t} - e^{-j\omega t}}{j2}$

Therefore

$$\mathcal{L}\{\sin\omega t\} = \left(\frac{1}{j2}\right)\left(\frac{1}{s-j\omega} - \frac{1}{s+j\omega}\right) = \left(\frac{1}{j2}\right)\left(\frac{2j\omega}{s^2+\omega^2}\right)$$

$$= \frac{\omega}{s^2+\omega^2}$$

[c] $\sin(\omega t + \theta) = (\sin\omega t\cos\theta + \cos\omega t\sin\theta)$

Therefore

$$\mathcal{L}\{\sin(\omega t+\theta)\} = \cos\theta\mathcal{L}\{\sin\omega t\} + \sin\theta\mathcal{L}\{\cos\omega t\}$$

$$= \frac{\omega\cos\theta + s\sin\theta}{s^2+\omega^2}$$

[d] $\cosh t = \frac{1}{2}(e^t - e^{-t})$

Therefore

$$\mathcal{L}\{\cosh t\} = \frac{1}{2}\left(\frac{1}{s-1} + \frac{1}{s+1}\right) = \frac{s}{s^2-1}$$

[e] $f(t) = \cosh t\cosh\theta + \sinh t\sinh\theta$

From part [d]

$$\mathcal{L}\{\cosh t\} = \frac{s}{s^2-1}$$

From DE 12.5(b)

$$\mathcal{L}\{\sinh t\} = \frac{1}{s^2-1}$$

$$\therefore\ \mathcal{L}\{\cosh(t+\theta)\} = \cosh\theta\left[\frac{s}{(s^2-1)}\right] + \sinh\theta\left[\frac{1}{s^2-1}\right]$$

$$= \frac{\sinh\theta + s[\cosh\theta]}{(s^2-1)}$$

P 12.9 [a] $\mathcal{L}\{f'(t)\} = \int_{-\varepsilon}^{\varepsilon}\frac{e^{-st}}{2\varepsilon}dt + \int_{\varepsilon}^{\infty} - ae^{-a(t-\varepsilon)}e^{-st}\,dt$

$$= \frac{1}{2s\varepsilon}(e^{s\varepsilon} - e^{-s\varepsilon}) - \left(\frac{a}{s+a}\right)e^{-s\varepsilon} = F(s)$$

$$\lim_{\varepsilon\to 0} F(s) = 1 - \frac{a}{s+a} = \frac{s}{s+a}$$

[b] $\mathcal{L}\{e^{-at}\} = \dfrac{1}{s+a}$

Therefore $\mathcal{L}\{f'(t)\} = sF(s) - f(0^-) = \dfrac{s}{s+a} - 0 = \dfrac{s}{s+a}$

P 12.10 $\mathcal{L}\left\{\dfrac{d^n f(t)}{dt^n}\right\} = s^n F(s) - s^{n-1}f(0^-) - s^{n-2}f'(0^-) - \cdots,$

Therefore

$$\mathcal{L}\{\delta^n(t)\} = s^n(1) - s^{n-1}\delta(0^-) - s^{n-2}\delta'(0^-) - s^{n-3}\delta''(0^-) - \cdots = s^n$$

P 12.11 [a] $\mathcal{L}\{te^{-at}\} = \displaystyle\int_{0^-}^{\infty} te^{-(s+a)t}\,dt$

$$= \frac{e^{-(s+a)t}}{(s+a)^2}\Big[-(s+a)t - 1\Big]_{0^-}^{\infty}$$

$$= 0 + \frac{1}{(s+a)^2}$$

$$\therefore\ \mathcal{L}\{te^{-at}\} = \frac{1}{(s+a)^2}$$

[b] $\mathcal{L}\left\{\dfrac{d}{dt}(te^{-at})\right\} = \dfrac{s}{(s+a)^2} - 0$

$$\mathcal{L}\left\{\frac{d}{dt}(te^{-at})\right\} = \frac{s}{(s+a)^2}$$

[c] $\dfrac{d}{dt}(te^{-at}) = -ate^{-at} + e^{-at}$

$$\mathcal{L}\{-ate^{-at}\} = \frac{-a}{(s+a)^2} + \frac{1}{(s+a)} = \frac{-a}{(s+a)^2} + \frac{s+a}{(s+a)^2}$$

$$\therefore\ \mathcal{L}\left\{\frac{d}{dt}(te^{-at})\right\} = \frac{s}{(s+a)^2} \qquad \text{CHECKS}$$

P 12.12 [a] $\mathcal{L}\left\{\dfrac{d\sin\omega t}{dt}\right\} = \dfrac{s\omega}{s^2+\omega^2} - 0$

[b] $\mathcal{L}\left\{\dfrac{d\cos\omega t}{dt}\right\} = \dfrac{s^2}{s^2+\omega^2} - 0$

[c] $\mathcal{L}\left\{\dfrac{d^3(t^2)}{dt^3}\right\} = s^3\left(\dfrac{2}{s^3}\right) - s^2(0) - s(0) - 2(0) = 2$

[d] $\dfrac{d\sin\omega t}{dt} = (\cos\omega t)\cdot\omega, \qquad \mathcal{L}\{\omega\cos\omega t\} = \dfrac{\omega s}{s^2+\omega^2}$

$$\frac{d\cos\omega t}{dt} = -\omega\sin\omega t + \delta(t)$$

$$\mathcal{L}\{-\omega\sin\omega t + \delta(t)\} = -\frac{\omega^2}{s^2+\omega^2} + 1 = \frac{s^2}{s^2+\omega^2}$$

$$\frac{d^3(t)}{dt^3} = 2\delta(t); \qquad \mathcal{L}\{2\delta(t)\} = 2$$

P 12.13 [a] $\displaystyle\int_{0^-}^{t} x\,dx = \frac{t^2}{2}$

$$\mathcal{L}\left\{\frac{t^2}{2}\right\} = \frac{1}{2}\int_{0^-}^{\infty} t^2e^{-st}\,dt$$

$$= \frac{1}{2}\left[\frac{e^{-st}}{-s^3}(s^2t^2+2st+2)\Big|_{0^-}^{\infty}\right]$$

$$= \frac{1}{2s^3}(2) = \frac{1}{s^3}$$

$$\therefore\ \mathcal{L}\left\{\int_{0^-}^{t} x\,dx\right\} = \frac{1}{s^3}$$

[b] $\displaystyle\mathcal{L}\left\{\int_{0^-}^{t} x\,dx\right\} = \frac{\mathcal{L}\{t\}}{s} = \frac{1/s^2}{s} = \frac{1}{s^3}$

$$\therefore\ \mathcal{L}\left\{\int_{0^-}^{t} x\,dx\right\} = \frac{1}{s^3} \qquad \text{CHECKS}$$

P 12.14 [a] $\displaystyle\mathcal{L}\left\{\int_{0^-}^{t} e^{-ax}\,dx\right\} = \frac{F(s)}{s} = \frac{1}{s(s+a)}$

[b] $\displaystyle\mathcal{L}\left\{\int_{0^-}^{t} y\,dy\right\} = \frac{1}{s}\left(\frac{1}{s^2}\right) = \frac{1}{s^3}$

[c] $\displaystyle\int_{0^-}^{t} e^{-ax}\,dx = \frac{1}{a} - \frac{e^{-at}}{a}$

$$\mathcal{L}\left\{\frac{1}{a} - \frac{e^{-at}}{a}\right\} = \frac{1}{a}\left[\frac{1}{s} - \frac{1}{s+a}\right] = \frac{1}{s(s+a)}$$

$$\int_{0^-}^{t} y\,dy = \frac{t^2}{2}; \qquad \mathcal{L}\left\{\frac{t^2}{2}\right\} = \frac{1}{2}\cdot\frac{2}{s^3} = \frac{1}{s^3}$$

P 12.15 $\displaystyle\mathcal{L}\{e^{-at}f(t)\} = \int_{0^-}^{\infty}[e^{-at}f(t)]e^{-st}\,dt = \int_{0^-}^{\infty} f(t)e^{-(s+a)t}\,dt = F(s+a)$

P 12.16 [a] $\displaystyle\mathcal{L}\{-20e^{-5(t-2)}u(t-2)\} = \frac{-20e^{-2s}}{(s+5)}$

[b] First rewrite $f(t)$ as

$$\begin{aligned} f(t) &= (8t-8)u(t-1) + (24-8t-8t+8)u(t-2) \\ &\quad +(8t-40-24+8t)u(t-4) - (8t-40)u(t-5) \\ &= 8(t-1)u(t-1) - 16(t-2)u(t-2) \\ &\quad +16(t-4)u(t-4) - 8(t-5)u(t-5) \end{aligned}$$

$$\therefore \quad F(s) = \frac{8[e^{-s} - 2e^{-2s} + 2e^{-4s} - e^{-5s}]}{s^2}$$

P 12.17 [a] $f(t) = 4t[u(t) - u(t-4)]$

$$\begin{aligned} &\quad +(32-4t)[u(t-4) - u(t-12)] \\ &\quad +(4t-64)[u(t-12) - u(t-16)] \\ &= 4tu(t) - 8(t-4)u(t-4) \\ &\quad +8(t-12)u(t-12) - 4(t-16)u(t-16) \end{aligned}$$

$$\therefore \quad F(s) = \frac{4[1 - 2e^{-4s} + 2e^{-12s} - e^{-16s}]}{s^2}$$

[b]

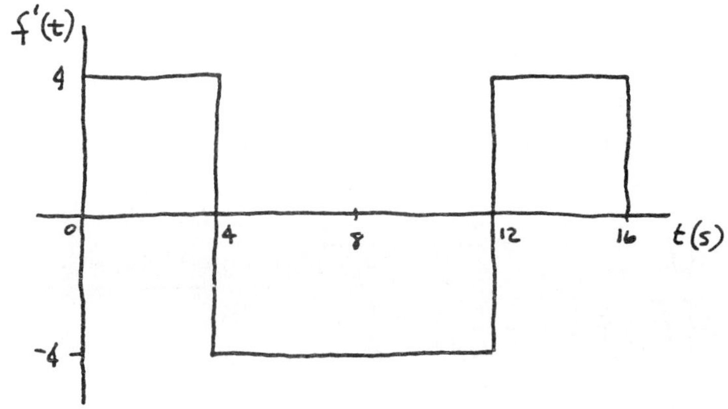

$$\begin{aligned} f'(t) &= 4[u(t) - u(t-4)] - 4[u(t-4) - u(t-12)] \\ &\quad +4[u(t-12) - u(t-16)] \\ &= 4u(t) - 8u(t-4) + 8u(t-12) - 4u(t-16) \end{aligned}$$

$$\mathcal{L}\{f'(t)\} = \frac{4[1 - 2e^{-4s} + 2e^{-12s} - e^{-16s}]}{s}$$

[c]

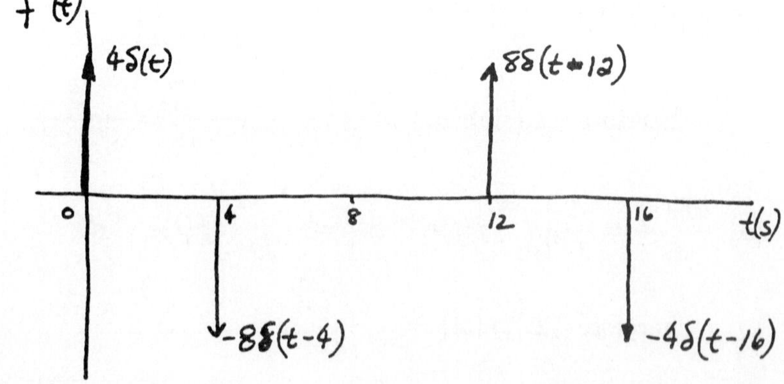

$$f''(t) = 4\delta(t) - 8\delta(t-4) + 8\delta(t-12) - 4\delta(t-16)$$

$$\mathcal{L}\{f''(t)\} = 4[1 - 2e^{-4s} + 2e^{-12s} - e^{-16s}]$$

P 12.18 [a] $f_1(t) = e^{-at}\sin\omega t; \qquad F_1(s) = \dfrac{\omega}{(s+a)^2+\omega^2}$

$$F(s) = sF_1(s) - f_1(0^-) = \frac{s\omega}{(s+a)^2+\omega^2} - 0$$

[b] $f_1(t) = e^{-at}\cos\omega t; \qquad F_1(s) = \dfrac{s+a}{(s+a)^2+\omega^2}$

$$F(s) = \frac{F_1(s)}{s} = \frac{s+a}{s[(s+a)^2+\omega^2]}$$

[c] $\dfrac{d}{dt}[e^{-at}\sin\omega t] = \omega e^{-at}\cos\omega t - ae^{-at}\sin\omega t$

Therefore $F(s) = \dfrac{\omega(s+a) - \omega a}{(s+a)^2+\omega^2} = \dfrac{\omega s}{(s+a)^2+\omega^2}$

$$\int_{0^-}^{t} e^{-ax}\cos\omega x\,dx = \frac{-ae^{-at}\cos\omega t + \omega e^{-at}\sin\omega t + a}{a^2+\omega^2}$$

Therefore

$$F(s) = \frac{1}{a^2+\omega^2}\left[\frac{-a(s+a)}{(s+a)^2+\omega^2} + \frac{\omega^2}{(s+a)^2+\omega^2} + \frac{a}{s}\right]$$

$$= \frac{s+a}{s[(s+a)^2+\omega^2]}$$

P 12.19 [a] $\mathcal{L}\{f(at)\} = \displaystyle\int_{0^-}^{\infty} f(at)e^{-st}\,dt$

Let $u = at, \quad du = a\,dt, \quad u = 0^-$ when $t = 0^-$

and $u = \infty$ when $t = \infty$

Therefore $\mathcal{L}\{f(at)\} = \displaystyle\int_{0^-}^{\infty} f(u)e^{-(u/a)s}\frac{du}{a} = \frac{1}{a}F(s/a)$

[b] $\mathcal{L}\{\sinh\beta t\} = \frac{1}{\beta}F(s/\beta); \qquad F(s) = \left[\frac{1}{s^2-1}\right]$

Therefore $\mathcal{L}\{\sinh\beta t\} = \frac{1}{\beta}\left[\frac{1}{(s/\beta)^2-1}\right] = \frac{\beta}{s^2-\beta^2}$

P 12.20 [a] $\frac{dF(s)}{ds} = \frac{d}{ds}\left[\int_{0^-}^{\infty} f(t)e^{-st}\,dt\right] = -\int_{0^-}^{\infty} tf(t)e^{-st}\,dt$

Therefore $\mathcal{L}\{tf(t)\} = -\frac{dF(s)}{ds}$

[b] $\frac{d^2F(s)}{ds^2} = \int_{0^-}^{\infty} t^2 f(t)e^{-st}\,dt; \qquad \frac{d^3F(s)}{ds^3} = \int_{0^-}^{\infty} -t^3 f(t)e^{-st}\,dt$

Therefore $\frac{d^nF(s)}{ds^n} = (-1)^n\int_{0^-}^{\infty} t^n f(t)e^{-st}\,dt = (-1)^n\mathcal{L}\{t^nf(t)\}$

[c] $\mathcal{L}\{t^5\} = \mathcal{L}\{t^4t\} = (-1)^4\frac{d^4}{ds^4}\left(\frac{1}{s^2}\right) = \frac{120}{s^6}$

$$\mathcal{L}\{t\sin\beta t\} = (-1)^1\frac{d}{ds}\left(\frac{\beta}{s^2+\beta^2}\right) = \frac{2\beta s}{(s^2+\beta^2)^2}$$

$\mathcal{L}\{te^{-t}\cosh t\}$:

First find $\mathcal{L}\{\cosh t\}$:

$$\mathcal{L}\{\cosh t\} = \int_{0+}^{\infty} e^{-st}\left[\frac{e^t+e^{-t}}{2}\right]dt$$

$$= \frac{1}{2}\int_0^{\infty} e^{-(s-1)t}\,dt + \frac{1}{2}\int_0^{\infty} e^{-(s+1)t}\,dt$$

$$= \frac{0.5}{s-1} + \frac{0.5}{s+1} = \frac{s}{s^2-1}$$

$$\frac{dF}{ds} = \frac{(s^2-1)1 - s(2s)}{(s^2-1)^2} = -\frac{s^2+1}{(s^2-1)^2}$$

Therefore $-\frac{dF}{ds} = \frac{s^2+1}{(s^2-1)^2}$

Thus

$$\mathcal{L}\{t\cosh t\} = \frac{s^2+1}{(s^2-1)^2}$$

$$\mathcal{L}\{e^{-t}t\cosh t\} = \frac{(s+1)^2+1}{[(s+1)^2-1]^2} = \frac{s^2+2s+2}{s^2(s+2)^2}$$

P 12.21 [a] $\int_s^\infty F(u)du = \int_s^\infty \left[\int_{0^-}^\infty f(t)e^{-ut}\,dt\right] du = \int_{0^-}^\infty \left[\int_s^\infty f(t)e^{-ut}\,du\right] dt$

$$= \int_{0^-}^\infty f(t)\int_s^\infty e^{-ut}\,du\,dt = \int_{0^-}^\infty f(t)\left[\frac{e^{-tu}}{-t}\Big|_s^\infty\right] dt$$

$$= \int_{0^-}^\infty f(t)\left[\frac{-e^{-st}}{-t}\right] dt = \mathcal{L}\left\{\frac{f(t)}{t}\right\}$$

[b] $\mathcal{L}\{t\sin\beta t\} = \dfrac{2\beta s}{(s^2+\beta^2)^2}$

therefore $\mathcal{L}\left\{\dfrac{t\sin\beta t}{t}\right\} = \int_s^\infty \left[\dfrac{2\beta u}{(u^2+\beta^2)^2}\right] du$

Let $\omega = u^2+\beta^2$, then $\omega = s^2+\beta^2$ when $u = s$, and $\omega = \infty$ when $u = \infty$; also $d\omega = 2u\,du$, thus

$$\mathcal{L}\left\{\frac{t\sin\beta t}{t}\right\} = \beta\int_{s^2+\beta^2}^\infty \left[\frac{d\omega}{\omega^2}\right] = \beta\left(\frac{-1}{\omega}\right)_{s^2+\beta^2}^\infty = \frac{\beta}{s^2+\beta^2}$$

P 12.22 [a] $I_{dc} = \dfrac{1}{L}\int_0^t v_o\,dt + \dfrac{v_o}{R} + C\dfrac{dv_o}{dt}$

[b] $\dfrac{I_{dc}}{s} = \dfrac{V_o(s)}{sL} + \dfrac{V_o(s)}{R} + sCV_o(s)$

$$\therefore\ V_o(s) = \frac{I_{dc}/C}{s^2 + (1/RC)s + (1/LC)}$$

[c] $i_o = C\dfrac{dv_o}{dt}$

$$\therefore\ I_o(s) = sCV_o(s) = \frac{sI_{dc}}{s^2 + (1/RC)s + (1/LC)}$$

P 12.23 [a] $\dfrac{1}{RC} = \dfrac{10^9}{(4\times 10^3)(25)} = 10^4$

$$\frac{1}{LC} = \frac{10^9}{(2.5)(25)} = 16\times 10^6$$

$$V_o(s) = \frac{40\times 10^6 I_{dc}}{s + 10{,}000s + 16\times 10^6}$$

$$= \frac{40\times 10^6 I_{dc}}{(s+2000)(s+8000)}$$

$$= \frac{120{,}000}{(s+2000)(s+8000)}$$

$$= \frac{K_1}{s+2000} + \frac{K_2}{s+8000}$$

$$K_1 = \frac{120{,}000}{6000} = 20; \qquad K_2 = \frac{120{,}000}{-6000} = -20$$

$$V_o(s) = \frac{20}{s+2000} - \frac{20}{s+8000}$$

$$v_o(t) = 20e^{-2000t} - 20e^{-8000t}\,\mathrm{V}, \quad t \geq 0$$

[b] $$I_o(s) = \frac{3\times10^{-3}s}{(s+2000)(s+8000)}$$

$$= \frac{K_1}{s+2000} + \frac{K_2}{s+8000}$$

$$K_1 = \frac{-(3\times10^{-3})(2000)}{6000} = -10^{-3}$$

$$K_2 = \frac{(3\times10^{-3})(-8000)}{-6000} = 4\times10^{-3}$$

$$I_o(s) = \frac{-10^{-3}}{s+2000} + \frac{4\times10^{-3}}{s+8000}$$

$$i_o(t) = (4e^{-8000t} - e^{-2000t})\,\mathrm{mA}, \quad t \geq 0$$

[c] $i_o(0) = 4 - 1 = 3\,\mathrm{mA}$

Yes. The initial inductor current is zero by hypothesis, the initial resistor current is zero because the initial capacitor voltage is zero by hypothesis. Thus at $t = 0$ the source current appears in the capacitor.

P 12.24 [a] $$C\frac{dv_o}{dt} + \frac{v_o}{R} + \frac{1}{L}\int_0^t (v_o - v_{dc})\,d\tau = 0$$

$$C\frac{dv_o}{dt} + \frac{v_o}{R} + \frac{1}{L}\int_0^t v_o\,d\tau = \frac{V_{dc}}{L}t$$

[b] $$sCV_o(s) + \frac{V_o(s)}{R} + \frac{V_o(s)}{sL} = \frac{V_{dc}}{s^2L}$$

$$V_o(s)[RLCs^2 + sL + R] = \frac{V_{dc}}{s}R$$

$$V_o(s) = \frac{V_{dc}/LC}{s[s^2 + (1/RC)s + (1/LC)]}$$

[c] $$i_o = \frac{v_o}{R} + C\frac{dv_o}{dt}$$

$$I_o(s) = \frac{V_o(s)}{R} + sCV_o(s)$$

$$= V_o(s)[(1/R) + sC]$$

$$= CV_o(s)[s + (1/RC)]$$

$$I_o(s) = \left(\frac{V_{dc}}{L}\right) \frac{[s + (1/RC)]}{s[s^2 + (1/RC)s + (1/LC)]}$$

P 12.25 [a] $\frac{1}{LC} = \frac{10^9}{(0.8)(100)} = 1250 \times 10^4$

$$\frac{1}{RC} = \frac{10^6}{(10)(100)} = 1000$$

$$V_o(s) = \frac{875 \times 10^6}{s(s^2 + 1000s + 1250 \times 10^4)}$$

$$s_{1,2} = -500 \pm \sqrt{25 \times 10^4 - 1250 \times 10^4} = -500 \pm j3500 \text{ rad/s}$$

$$V_o(s) = \frac{875 \times 10^6}{s(s + 500 - j3500)(s + 500 + j3500)}$$

$$= \frac{K_1}{s} + \frac{K_2}{s + 500 - j3500} + \frac{K_2^*}{s + 500 + j3500}$$

$$K_1 = \frac{875 \times 10^6}{125 \times 10^5} = 70$$

$$K_2 = \frac{875 \times 10^6}{(-500 + j3500)(j7000)} = 5\sqrt{50}\underline{/-171.87^\circ}$$

$$V_o(s) = \frac{70}{s} + \frac{5\sqrt{50}\underline{/-171.87^\circ}}{s + 500 - j3500} + \frac{5\sqrt{50}\underline{/171.87^\circ}}{s + 500 + j3500}$$

$$v_o(t) = 70 + 10\sqrt{50}e^{-500t}\cos(3500t - 171.87^\circ)\text{ V}, \quad t \geq 0$$

[b] $I_o(s) = \frac{87.5(s + 1000)}{s(s + 500 - j3500)(s + 500 + j3500)}$

$$= \frac{K_1}{s} + \frac{K_2}{s + 500 - j3500} + \frac{K_2^*}{s + 500 + j3500}$$

$$K_1 = \frac{87.5(1000)}{1250 \times 10^4} = 7\text{ mA}$$

$$K_2 = \frac{87.5(500 + j3500)}{(-500 + j3500)(j7000)} = 12.5\underline{/-106.26^\circ}\text{ mA}$$

$$i_o(t) = 7 + 25e^{-500t}\cos(3500t - 106.26^\circ)\text{ mA}. \quad t \geq 0$$

P 12.26 [a] $F(s) = \frac{K_1}{s+1} + \frac{K_2}{s+2} + \frac{K_3}{s+3}$

$$K_1 = \frac{18 - 66 + 54}{(1)(2)} = 3; \qquad K_2 = \frac{72 - 132 + 54}{(-1)(1)} = 6$$

$$K_3 = \frac{162 - 198 + 54}{(-2)(-1)} = 9$$

$$\therefore \quad f(t) = [3e^{-t} + 6e^{-2t} + 9e^{-3t}]u(t)$$

[b] $F(s) = \dfrac{K_1}{s} + \dfrac{K_2}{s+2} + \dfrac{K_3}{s+4}$

$$K_1 = \frac{40}{8} = 5; \qquad K_2 = \frac{100 - 172 + 40}{(-2)(2)} = 8$$

$$K_3 = \frac{400 - 344 + 40}{(-4)(2)} = 12$$

$$\therefore \quad f(t) = [5 + 8e^{-2t} + 12e^{-4t}]u(t)$$

[c] $s_{1,2} = -6 \pm \sqrt{36 - 100} = -6 \pm j8$

$$F(s) = \frac{11s^2 + 172s + 700}{(s+2)(s+6-j8)(s+6+j8)}$$

$$= \frac{K_1}{s+2} + \frac{K_2}{s+6-j8} + \frac{K_2^*}{s+6+j8}$$

$$K_1 = \frac{44 - 344 + 700}{4 - 24 + 100} = 5$$

$$K_2 = \frac{11(-6+j8)^2 + 172(-6+j8) + 700}{(-4+j8)j16}$$

$$= 3 - j4 = 5\underline{/-53.13^\circ}$$

$$\therefore \quad f(t) = [5e^{-2t} + 10e^{-6t}\cos(8t - 53.13^\circ)]u(t)$$

[d] $s_{1,2} = -7 \pm \sqrt{49 - 625} = -7 \pm j24$

$$F(s) = \frac{56s^2 + 112s + 5000}{s(s+7-j24)(s+7+j24)}$$

$$= \frac{K_1}{s} + \frac{K_2}{s+7-j24} + \frac{K_2^*}{s+7+j24}$$

$$K_1 = \frac{5000}{625} = 8$$

$$K_2 = \frac{56(-7+j24)^2 + 112(-7+j24) + 5000}{(-7+j24)j48}$$

$$= 24 + j7 = 25\underline{/16.26^\circ}$$

$$\therefore \quad f(t) = [8 + 50e^{-7t}\cos(24t + 16.26^\circ)]u(t)$$

P 12.27 [a] $F(s) = \frac{K_1}{s^2} + \frac{K_2}{s} + \frac{K_3}{s+10}$

$$K_1 = \frac{8(s^2 - 5s + 50)}{s+10}\bigg|_{s=0} = \frac{400}{10} = 40$$

$$K_2 = \frac{d}{ds}\left\{\frac{8(s^2 - 5s + 50)}{s+10}\right\}\bigg|_{s=0}$$

$$= \frac{8(s+10)(2s-5) - 8(s^2 - 5s + 50)(1)}{(s+10)^2}\bigg|_{s=0}$$

$$= \frac{10(-40) - 8(50)}{100} = -8$$

$$K_3 = \frac{8(s^2 - 5s + 50)}{s^2}\bigg|_{s=-10} = \frac{8(100 + 50 + 50)}{100} = 16$$

$$F(s) = \frac{40}{s^2} - \frac{8}{s} + \frac{16}{s+10}$$

$$f(t) = [40t - 8 + 16e^{-10t}]u(t)$$

[b] $F(s) = \frac{K_1}{s} + \frac{K_2}{(s+2)^2} + \frac{K_3}{s+2}$

$$K_1 = \frac{10(4)}{4} = 10; \qquad K_2 = \frac{10(12 - 8 + 4)}{-2} = -40$$

$$K_3 = \frac{d}{ds}\left\{\frac{10(3s^2 + 4s + 4)}{s}\right\}\bigg|_{s=-2}$$

$$= \frac{10[(s)(6s+4) - (3s^2 + 4s + 4)]}{s^2}\bigg|_{s=-2} = 20$$

$$F(s) = \frac{10}{s} - \frac{40}{(s+2)^2} + \frac{20}{s+2}$$

$$f(t) = [10 - 40te^{-2t} + 20e^{-2t}]u(t)$$

[c] $s_{1,2} = -2 \pm \sqrt{4-5} = -2 \pm j1$

$$F(s) = \frac{K_1}{s^2} + \frac{K_2}{s} + \frac{K_3}{s+2-j1} + \frac{K_3^*}{s+2+j1}$$

$$K_1 = \frac{50}{5} = 10$$

$$K_2 = \frac{d}{ds}\left\{\frac{s^3 - 6s^2 + 15s + 50}{s^2 + 4s + 5}\right\}\bigg|_{s=0}$$

$$= \frac{(s^2 + 4s + 5)(3s^2 - 12s + 15) - (s^3 - 6s^2 + 15s + 50)(2s + 4)}{(s^2 + 4s + 5)^2}\bigg|_{s=0}$$

$$= \frac{5(15) - 50(4)}{25} = -5$$

$$K_3 = \frac{s^3 - 6s^2 + 15s + 50}{s^2(s + 2 + j1)}\bigg|_{s=-2+j1}$$

$$(-2 + j1)^3 = -2 + j11; \qquad (-2 + j1)^2 = 3 - j4$$

$$K_3 = \frac{-2 + j11 - 6(3 - j4) + 15(-2 + j1) + 50}{(3 - j4)(j2)} = 3 + j4$$

$$F(s) = \frac{10}{s^2} - \frac{5}{s} + \frac{3 + j4}{s + 2 - j1} + \frac{3 - j4}{s + 2 + j1}$$

$$f(t) = [10t - 5 + 10e^{-2t}\cos(t + 53.13^\circ)]u(t)$$

[d] $F(s) = \frac{K_1}{(s+2)^3} + \frac{K_2}{(s+2)^2} + \frac{K_3}{s+2}$

$$K_1 = s^2 + 6s + 5\bigg|_{s=-2} = -3$$

$$K_2 = \frac{d}{ds}\{s^2 + 6s + 5\}\bigg|_{s=-2} = 2s + 6\bigg|_{s=-2} = 2$$

$$2K_3 = \frac{d}{ds}(2s + 6)\bigg|_{s=-2} = 2; \qquad K_3 = 1$$

$$F(s) = \frac{-3}{(s+2)^2} + \frac{2}{(s+2)^2} + \frac{1}{s+2}$$

$$f(t) = -\frac{3t^2e^{-2t}}{2} + 2te^{-2t} + e^{-2t} = [(2t - 1.5t^2 + 1)e^{-2t}]u(t)$$

[e] $s_{1,2} = -1 \pm \sqrt{1 - 5} = -1 + j2$

$$F(s) = \frac{K_1}{(s + 1 - j2)^2} + \frac{K_1^*}{(s + 1 + j2)^2} + \frac{K_2}{s + 1 - j2} + \frac{K_2^*}{(s + 1 + j2)}$$

$$K_1 = \frac{16s^3 + 72s^2 + 216s - 128}{(s + 1 + j2)^2}\bigg|_{s=-1+j2}$$

$$(-1 + j2)^3 = 11 - j2; \qquad (-1 + j2)^2 = -3 - j4$$

$$K_1 = \frac{176 - j32 - 216 - j288 - 216 + j432 - 128}{-16}$$

$$= 24 - j7 = 25\underline{/-16.26^\circ}$$

$$K_2 = \frac{d}{ds}\left\{\frac{16s^3 + 72s^2 + 216s - 128}{(s+1+j2)^2}\bigg|_{s=-1+j2}\right\}$$

$$= \frac{(s+1+j2)^2(48s^2 + 144s + 216)}{(s+1+j2)^4}\bigg|_{s=-1+j2}$$

$$- \frac{(16s^3 + 72s^2 + 216s - 128)2(s+1+j2)}{(s+1+j2)^4}\bigg|_{s=-1+j2}$$

$$= \frac{(j4)^2(-144 - j192 - 144 + j288 + 216) - (-384 + j112)(j8)}{(j4)^4}$$

$$= \frac{2048 + j1536}{256} = 8 + j6 = 10\underline{/36.87^\circ}$$

$$F(s) = \frac{25\underline{/-16.26^\circ}}{(s+1-j2)^2} + \frac{25\underline{/16.26^\circ}}{(s+1+j2)^2} + \frac{10\underline{/36.87^\circ}}{s+1-j2} + \frac{10\underline{/-36.87^\circ}}{s+1+j2}$$

$$f(t) = [50te^{-t}\cos(2t - 16.26^\circ) + 20e^{-t}\cos(2t + 36.87)]u(t)$$

P 12.28 [a]

$$F(s) = \begin{array}{r|l} & 10 \\ \hline s^2 + 6s + 5 & 10s^2 + 85s + 95 \\ & 10s^2 + 60s + 50 \\ \hline & 25s + 45 \end{array}$$

$$F(s) = 10 + \frac{25s + 45}{s^2 + 6s + 5} = 10 + \frac{K_1}{s+2} + \frac{K_2}{s+3}$$

$$K_1 = \frac{25s + 45}{s+3}\bigg|_{s=-2} = -5$$

$$K_2 = \frac{25s + 45}{s+2}\bigg|_{s=-3} = 30$$

$$F(s) = 10 - \frac{5}{s+2} + \frac{30}{s+3}$$

$$f(t) = 10\delta(t) + [-5e^{-2t} + 30e^{-3t}]u(t)$$

[b]

$$F(s) = \begin{array}{r|l} & 5 \\ \hline s^2+4s+5 & 5s^2+40s+25 \\ & 5s^2+20s+25 \\ \hline & 20s \end{array}$$

$$F(s) = 5 + \frac{20s}{s^2+4s+5} = 5 + \frac{K_1}{s+2-j} + \frac{K_1^*}{s+2+j}$$

$$K_1 = \left.\frac{20s}{s+2+j}\right|_{s=-2+j} = -1 + j2 = 2.23\underline{/116.57^\circ}$$

$$F(s) = 5 + \frac{2.23\underline{/116.57^\circ}}{s+2-j} + \frac{2.23\underline{/-116.57^\circ}}{s+2+j}$$

$$f(t) = 5\delta(t) + 4.46e^{-2t}\cos(t + 116.57^\circ)u(t)$$

[c]

$$F(s) = \begin{array}{r|l} & s+5 \\ \hline s+20 & s^2+25s+150 \\ & s^2+20s \\ \hline & 5s+150 \\ & 5s+100 \\ \hline & 50 \end{array}$$

$$F(s) = s + 5 + \frac{50}{(s+10)(s+15)} = s + 5 + \frac{K_1}{s+10} + \frac{K_2}{s+15}$$

$$K_1 = \left.\frac{50}{s+15}\right|_{s=-10} = 10$$

$$K_2 = \left.\frac{50}{s+10}\right|_{s=-15} = -10$$

$$F(s) = s + 5 + \frac{10}{s+10} - \frac{10}{s+15}$$

$$f(t) = \delta'(t) + 5\delta(t) + [10e^{-10t} - 10e^{-15t}]u(t)$$

P 12.29 [a] $F(s) = \dfrac{20s^2}{(s+1)^3} = \dfrac{K_1}{(s+1)^3} + \dfrac{K_2}{(s+1)^2} + \dfrac{K_3}{s+1}$

$$\therefore\ 20s^2 = K_1 + K_2(s+1) + K_3(s+1)^2$$

$$K_1 = \left.20s^2\right|_{s=-1} = 20$$

After differentiating each side

$$40s = 0 + K_2 + 2K_3(s+1); \qquad \therefore\ K_2 = 40s \Big|_{s=-1} = -40$$

After differentiating again

$$40 = 0 + 2K_3; \qquad \therefore\ K_3 = 20$$

$$\therefore\ \frac{20s^2}{(s+1)^3} = \frac{20}{(s+1)^3} - \frac{40}{(s+1)^2} + \frac{20}{s+1}$$

Test at $s = 0$:

$0 = 20 - 40 + 20 = 0$ OK

$$f(t) = \frac{20t^2e^{-t}}{2!} - 40te^{-t} + 20e^{-t} = (10t^2 - 40t + 20)e^{-t}u(t)$$

[b] $F(s) = \dfrac{5(s+2)^2}{s^4(s+1)} = \dfrac{K_1}{s+1} + \dfrac{K_2}{s^4} + \dfrac{K_3}{s^3} + \dfrac{K_4}{s^2} + \dfrac{K_5}{s}$

$$K_1 = \frac{5(s+2)^2}{s^4}\Big|_{s=-1} = 5; \qquad K_2 = \frac{5(s+2)^2}{s+1}\Big|_{s=0} 20$$

$$\frac{5(s+2)^2}{s+1} = \frac{K_1s^4}{s+1} + K_2 + K_3s + K_4s^2 + K_5s^3$$

Differentiating each side gives

$$5\left[\frac{(s+1)2(s+2) - (s+2)^2}{(s+1)^2}\right] = \frac{K_1[4s^3(s+1) - s^4]}{(s+1)^2}$$

$$+0 + K_3 + 2K_4s + 3K_5s^2$$

$$\frac{5s(s+2)}{(s+1)^2} = \frac{K_1s^3(3s+4)}{(s+1)^2} + K_3 + 2K_4s + 3K_5s^2$$

$$K_3 = \frac{5s(s+2)}{(s+1)^2}\Big|_{s=0} = 0$$

Note that two more derivatives of the term involving K_1 will drop out at $s = 0$. Hence,

$$2K_4 = 5\frac{d}{ds}\left[\frac{s(s+2)}{(s+1)^2}\right]_{s=0} - 6K_5s\Big|_{s=0}$$

$$2K_4 = 5\left\{\frac{(s+1)^2(2s+2) - s(s+2)2(s+1)}{(s+1)^4}\right\}\Big|_{s=0}$$

$$= 5(s+1)\frac{2(s+1)^2 - 2s(s+2)}{(s+1)^4}\Big|_{s=0}$$

$$= (5)\frac{2}{(s+1)^3}\Big|_{s=0} = 10$$

$\therefore\quad K_4 = 5$

Now differentiate once more to get

$$6K_5 = \frac{d}{ds}\left\{\frac{10}{(s+1)^3}\right\}\Big|_{s=0}$$

$$= \frac{-30(s+1)^2}{(s+1)^6}\Big|_{s=0}$$

$$= \frac{-30}{(s+1)^4}\Big|_{s=0} = -30$$

$\therefore\quad K_5 = -5$

$$\frac{5(s+2)^2}{s^4(s+1)} = \frac{5}{s+1} + \frac{20}{s^4} + \frac{0}{s^3} + \frac{5}{s^2} - \frac{5}{s}$$

$$= \frac{5}{s+1} + \frac{20}{s^4} + \frac{5}{s^2} - \frac{5}{s}$$

Test at $s = -2$:

$$0 = -5 + \frac{20}{16} + \frac{5}{4} + \frac{5}{2} = 0 \qquad \text{OK}$$

$$\therefore\quad F(s) = \frac{5}{s+1} + \frac{20}{s^4} + \frac{5}{s^2} - \frac{5}{s}$$

$$f(t) = 5e^{-t} + \frac{20t^3}{3!} + \frac{5t}{2!} - 5$$

$$= (5e^{-5t} + \tfrac{10}{3}t^3 + 2.5t - 5)u(t)$$

P 12.30 [a] For $t \geq 0^+$:

$$Ri_o + L\frac{di_o}{dt} + v_o = 0$$

$$i_o = C\frac{dv_o}{dt} \qquad \frac{di_o}{dt} = C\frac{d^2v_o}{dt^2}$$

$$\therefore\quad RC\frac{dv_o}{dt} + LC\frac{d^2v_o}{dt^2} + v_o = 0$$

or

$$\frac{d^2v_o}{dt^2} + \frac{R}{L}\frac{dv_o}{dt} + \frac{1}{LC}v_o = 0$$

[b] $s^2V_o(s) - sV_{dc} - 0 + \frac{R}{L}[sV_o(s) - V_{dc}] + \frac{1}{LC}V_o(s) = 0$

$$V_o(s)\left[s^2 + \frac{R}{L}s + \frac{1}{LC}\right] = V_{dc}(s + R/L)$$

$$V_o(s) = \frac{V_{dc}[s + (R/L)]}{[s^2 + (R/L)s + (1/LC)]}$$

P 12.31 $\frac{R}{L} = 5000; \qquad \frac{1}{LC} = 4 \times 10^6$

$$V_o(s) = \frac{15(s + 5000)}{s^2 + 5000s + 4 \times 10^6}$$

$$s_{1,2} = -2500 \pm \sqrt{6.25 \times 10^6 - 4 \times 10^6}$$

$$s_1 = -1000 \text{ rad/s}; \qquad s_2 = -4000 \text{ rad/s}$$

$$V_o(s) = \frac{15(s + 5000)}{(s + 1000)(s + 4000)} = \frac{K_1}{s + 1000} + \frac{K_2}{s + 4000}$$

$$K_1 = \frac{15(4000)}{3000} = 20 \text{ V}; \qquad K_2 = \frac{15(1000)}{-3000} = -5 \text{ V}$$

$$V_o(s) = \frac{20}{s + 1000} - \frac{5}{s + 4000}$$

$$v_o(t) = [20e^{-1000t} - 5e^{-4000t}]u(t) \text{ V}$$

P 12.32 **[a]** $C\frac{dv_1}{dt} + \frac{v_1 - v_2}{R} = i_g$

$$\frac{1}{L}\int_0^t v_2\, d\tau + \frac{v_2 - v_1}{R} = 0$$

or

$$C\frac{dv_1}{dt} + \frac{v_1}{R} - \frac{v_2}{R} = i_g$$

$$-\frac{v_1}{R} + \frac{v_2}{R} + \frac{1}{L}\int_0^t v_2\, d\tau = 0$$

[b] $CsV_1(s) + \frac{V_1(s)}{R} - \frac{V_2(s)}{R} = I_g(s)$

$$-\frac{V_1(s)}{R} + \frac{V_2(s)}{R} + \frac{V_2(s)}{sL} = 0$$

or

$$(RCs+1)V_1(s) - V_2(s) = RI_g(s)$$

$$-sLV_1(s) + (R+sL)V_2(s) = 0$$

Solving,

$$V_2(s) = \frac{sI_g(s)}{C[s^2 + (R/L)s + (1/LC)]}$$

P 12.33 $\frac{1}{C} = 5 \times 10^6; \qquad \frac{1}{LC} = 25 \times 10^6; \qquad \frac{R}{L} = 8000$

$$V_2(s) = \frac{(6 \times 10^{-3})(5 \times 10^6)}{s^2 + 8000s + 25 \times 10^6}$$

$$s_{1,2} = -4000 \pm j3000$$

$$V_2(s) = \frac{30{,}000}{(s+4000-j3000)(s+4000+j3000)}$$

$$= \frac{K_1}{s+4000-j3000} + \frac{K_1^*}{s+4000+j3000}$$

$$K_1 = \frac{30{,}000}{j6000} = -j5 = 5\underline{/-90^\circ}$$

$$v_2(t) = 10e^{-4000t}\cos(3000t - 90^\circ)$$

$$= [10e^{-4000t}\sin 3000t]u(t) \text{ V}$$

P 12.34 $f(t) = \mathcal{L}^{-1}\left\{\frac{K}{s+\alpha-j\beta} + \frac{K^*}{s+\alpha+j\beta}\right\}$

$$= Ke^{-\alpha t}e^{j\beta t} + K^*e^{-\alpha t}e^{-j\beta t}$$

$$= |K|e^{-\alpha t}[e^{-j\theta}e^{j\beta t} + e^{-j\theta}e^{-j\beta t}]$$

$$= |K|e^{-\alpha t}[e^{j(\beta t+\theta)} + e^{-j(\beta t+\theta)}]$$

$$= 2|K|e^{-\alpha t}\cos(\beta t + \theta)$$

P 12.35 [a] $\mathcal{L}\{t^n f(t)\} = (-1)^n \left[\frac{d^n F(s)}{ds^n}\right]$

Let $f(t) = 1$, then $F(s) = \frac{1}{s}$, thus $\frac{d^n F(s)}{ds^n} = \frac{(-1)^n n!}{s^{(n+1)}}$

Therefore $\mathcal{L}\{t^n\} = (-1)^n \left[\frac{(-1)^n n!}{s^{(n+1)}}\right] = \frac{n!}{s^{(n+1)}}$

It follows that $\mathcal{L}\{t^{(r-1)}\} = \frac{(r-1)!}{s^r}$

and $\mathcal{L}\{t^{(r-1)}e^{-at}\} = \frac{(r-1)!}{(s+a)^r}$

Therefore $\frac{K}{(r-1)!}\mathcal{L}\{t^{r-1}e^{-at}\} = \frac{K}{(s+a)^r} = \mathcal{L}\left\{\frac{Kt^{r-1}e^{-at}}{(r-1)!}\right\}$

[b] $f(t) = \mathcal{L}^{-1}\left\{\frac{K}{(s+\alpha-j\beta)^r} + \frac{K^*}{(s+\alpha+j\beta)^r}\right\}$

Therefore

$$f(t) = \frac{Kt^{r-1}}{(r-1)!}e^{-(\alpha-j\beta)t} + \frac{K^*t^{r-1}}{(r-1)!}e^{-(\alpha+j\beta)t}$$

$$= \frac{|K|t^{r-1}e^{-\alpha t}}{(r-1)!}\left[e^{j\theta}e^{j\beta t} + e^{-j\theta}e^{-j\beta t}\right]$$

$$= \left[\frac{2|K|t^{r-1}e^{-\alpha t}}{(r-1)!}\right]\cos(\beta t + \theta)$$

P 12.36 [a] $sF(s) = \frac{18s^3 + 66s^2 + 54s}{(s+1)(s+2)(s+3)}$

$\lim_{s\to 0} sF(s) = 0$, $\quad\therefore\ f(\infty) = 0$

$\lim_{s\to\infty} sF(s) = 18$, $\quad\therefore\ f(0^+) = 18$

[b] $sF(s) = \frac{25s^2 + 86s + 40}{(s+2)(s+4)}$

$\lim_{s\to 0} sF(s) = \frac{40}{8} = 5$; $\quad\therefore\ f(\infty) = 5$

$\lim_{s\to\infty} sF(s) = 25$, $\quad\therefore\ f(0^+) = 25$

[c] $sF(s) = \frac{11s^3 + 172s^2 + 700s}{(s+2)(s^2 + 12s + 100)}$

$\lim_{s\to 0} sF(s) = 0$, $\quad\therefore\ f(\infty) = 0$

$\lim_{s\to\infty} sF(s) = 11$, $\quad\therefore\ f(0^+) = 11$

[d] $sF(s) = \frac{56s^2 + 112s + 5000}{(s^2 + 14s + 625)}$

$$\lim_{s\to 0} sF(s) = \frac{5000}{625} = 8, \qquad \therefore\ f(\infty) = 8$$

$$\lim_{s\to\infty} sF(s) = 56, \qquad \therefore\ f(0^+) = 56$$

P 12.37 [a] $sF(s) = \frac{8(s^2 - 5s + 50)}{s(s+10)}$

$$\lim_{s\to 0} sF(s) = \infty, \qquad \therefore\ f(\infty) = \infty$$

$$\lim_{s\to\infty} sF(s) = 8, \qquad \therefore\ f(0^+) = 8$$

[b] $sF(s) = \frac{10(3s^2 + 4s + 4)}{(s+2)^2}$

$$\lim_{s\to 0} sF(s) = \frac{40}{4} = 10, \qquad \therefore\ f(\infty) = 10$$

$$\lim_{s\to\infty} sF(s) = 30, \qquad \therefore\ f(0^+) = 30$$

[c] $sF(s) = \frac{s^3 - 6s^2 + 15s + 50)}{s(s^2 + 4s + 5)}$

$$\lim_{s\to 0} sF(s) = \infty, \qquad \therefore\ f(\infty) = \infty$$

$$\lim_{s\to\infty} sF(s) = 1, \qquad \therefore\ f(0^+) = 1$$

[d] $sF(s) = \frac{s^3 + 6s^2 + 5s}{(s+2)^3}$

$$\lim_{s\to 0} sF(s) = 0, \qquad \therefore\ f(\infty) = 0$$

$$\lim_{s\to\infty} sF(s) = 1, \qquad \therefore\ f(0^+) = 1$$

[e] $sF(s) = \frac{16s^4 + 72s^3 + 216s^2 - 128s}{(s^2 + 2s + 5)^2}$

$$\lim_{s\to 0} sF(s) = 0, \qquad \therefore\ f(\infty) = 0$$

$$\lim_{s\to\infty} sF(s) = 16, \qquad \therefore\ f(0^+) = 16$$

P 12.38 All of the $F(s)$ functions referenced in this problem are improper rational functions, and thus the corresponding $f(t)$ functions contain impulses ($\delta(t)$). Thus, neither the initial value theorem nor the final value theorem may be applied to these $F(s)$ functions!

P 12.39 [a] $sF(s) = \frac{20s^3}{(s+1)^3}$

$$\lim_{s\to 0} sF(s) = 0, \qquad \therefore \ f(\infty) = 0$$

$$\lim_{s\to\infty} sF(s) = 20, \qquad \therefore \ f(0^+) = 20$$

[b] $sF(s) = \frac{5s(s+2)^2}{s^4(s+1)} = \frac{5(s+2)^2}{s^3(s+1)}$

$$\lim_{s\to\infty} sF(s) = 0, \qquad \therefore \ f(0^+) = 0$$

The final value theorem cannot be applied here, as $F(s)$ violates that requirement that all poles lie in the left-half plane, with the exception of a single pole at the origin. This $F(s)$ has four poles at the origin!

P 12.40 $sV_o(s) = \frac{(I_{dc}/C)s}{s^2 + (1/RC)s + (1/LC)}$

$$\lim_{s\to 0} sV_o(s) = 0, \qquad \therefore \ v_o(\infty) = 0$$

$$\lim_{s\to\infty} sV_o(s) = 0, \qquad \therefore \ v_o(0^+) = 0$$

$$sI_o(s) = \frac{s^2 I_{dc}}{s^2 + (1/RC)s + (1/LC)}$$

$$\lim_{s\to 0} sI_o(s) = 0, \qquad \therefore \ i_o(\infty) = 0$$

$$\lim_{s\to\infty} sI_o(s) = I_{dc}, \qquad \therefore \ v_o(0^+) = I_{dc}$$

P 12.41 $sV_o(s) = \frac{V_{dc}/LC}{s^2 + (1/RC)s + (1/LC)}$

$$\lim_{s\to 0} sV_o(s) = V_{dc}, \qquad \therefore \ v_o(\infty) = V_{dc}$$

$$\lim_{s\to\infty} sV_o(s) = 0, \qquad \therefore \ v_o(0^+) = 0$$

$$sI_o(s) = \left(\frac{V_{dc}}{L}\right) \frac{s + (1/RC)}{s^2 + (1/RC)s + (1/LC)}$$

$$\lim_{s\to 0} sI_o(s) = \left(\frac{V_{dc}}{L}\right) \frac{(1/RC)}{(1/LC)} = \frac{V_{dc}}{R}, \qquad \therefore \ i_o(\infty) = \frac{V_{dc}}{R}$$

$$\lim_{s\to\infty} sI_o(s) = 0, \qquad \therefore \ i_o(0^+) = 0$$

P 12.42 $$sV_o(s) = \frac{V_{dc}s[s+(R/L)]}{s^2+(1/RC)s+(1/LC)}$$

$$\lim_{s\to 0} sV_o(s) = 0, \qquad \therefore \quad v_o(\infty) = 0$$

$$\lim_{s\to\infty} sV_o(s) = V_{dc}, \qquad \therefore \quad v_o(0^+) = V_{dc}$$

P 12.43 [a] $$27 = 270i_1 + 25\frac{di_1}{dt} + 5\frac{d}{dt}(i_1 - i_2) + 10\frac{d}{dt}(i_1 - i_2) + 5\frac{di_1}{dt}$$

$$0 = 10\frac{d}{dt}(i_2 - i_1) - 5\frac{di_1}{dt} + 80i_2$$

Simplifying the above equations gives:

$$27 = 270i_1 + 45\frac{di_1}{dt} - 15\frac{di_2}{dt}$$

$$0 = 80i_2 - 15\frac{di_1}{dt} + 10\frac{di_2}{dt}$$

[b] $$\frac{27}{s} = (45s + 270)I_1(s) - 15sI_2(s)$$

$$0 = -15sI_1(s) + (10s + 80)I_2(s)$$

[c] Solving the equations in (b),

$$I_1(s) = \frac{1.2(s+8)}{s(s+4)(s+24)}$$

$$I_2(s) = \frac{1.8}{(s+4)(s+24)}$$

[d] $$I_1(s) = \frac{K_1}{s} + \frac{K_2}{s+4} + \frac{K_3}{s+24}$$

$$K_1 = \frac{(1.2)(8)}{(4)(24)} = 0.1; \qquad K_2 = \frac{(1.2)(4)}{(-4)(20)} = -0.06$$

$$K_3 = \frac{(1.2)(-16)}{(-24)(-20)} = -0.04$$

$$I_1(s) = \left(\frac{100}{s} - \frac{60}{s+4} - \frac{40}{s+24}\right) \times 10^{-3}$$

$$i_1(t) = (100 - 60e^{-4t} - 40e^{-24t})u(t)\,\text{mA}$$

$$I_2(s) = \frac{K_1}{s+4} + \frac{K_2}{s+24}$$

$$K_1 = \frac{1.8}{20} = 0.09; \qquad K_2 = \frac{1.8}{-20} = -0.09$$

$$I_2(s) = \left(\frac{90}{s+4} - \frac{90}{s+24}\right) \times 10^{-3}$$

$$i_2(t) = (90e^{-4t} - 90e^{-24t})u(t)\ \text{mA}$$

[e] $i_1(\infty) = 100\,\text{mA}; \qquad i_2(\infty) = 0\,\text{mA}$

[f] Yes, at $t = \infty$

$$i_1 = \frac{27}{270} = 0.1\ \text{A} = 100\,\text{mA}$$

Since i_1 is a dc current at $t = \infty$ there is no voltage induced in the 10 H inductor; hence, $i_2 = 0$. Also note that $i_1(0) = 0$ and $i_2(0) = 0$. Thus our solutions satisfy the condition of no initial energy stored in the circuit.

13

The Laplace Transform in Circuit Analysis

Drill Exercises

DE 13.1 [a] $Y = \frac{1}{R} + \frac{1}{sL} + sC = \frac{C[s^2 + (1/RC)s + (1/LC)]}{s}$

$$\frac{1}{RC} = \frac{10^6}{(500)(0.025)} = 80{,}000; \qquad \frac{1}{LC} = 25 \times 10^8$$

$$\text{Therefore} \quad Y = \frac{25 \times 10^{-9}(s^2 + 80{,}000s + 25 \times 10^8)}{s}$$

[b] $z_{1,2} = -40{,}000 \pm \sqrt{16 \times 10^8 - 25 \times 10^8} = -40{,}000 \pm j30{,}000$

$$-z_1 = -40{,}000 - j30{,}000$$

$$-z_2 = -40{,}000 + j30{,}000$$

$$p_1 = 0$$

DE 13.2 [a] NOTE — typo in problem statement; should add impedance of 2000Ω in series; then the following solution is correct:

$$Z = 2000 + \frac{1}{Y} = 2000 + \frac{4 \times 10^7 s}{s^2 + 80{,}000s + 25 \times 10^8}$$

$$= \frac{500(s^2 + 10^5 s + 25 \times 10^8)}{s^2 + 80{,}000s + 25 \times 10^8} = \frac{500(s + 50{,}000)^2}{s^2 + 80{,}000s + 25 \times 10^8}$$

[b] $z_1 = z_2 = 50{,}000$

$$-p_1 = -40{,}000 - j30{,}000$$

$$-p_2 = -40{,}000 + j30{,}000$$

DE 13.3 **[a]** At $t = 0^-$, $0.2v_1 = (0.8)v_2$; $v_1 = 4v_2$; $v_1 + v_2 = 100\,\text{V}$

Therefore $v_1(0^-) = 80V = v_1(0^+)$; $v_2(0^-) = 20V = v_2(0^+)$

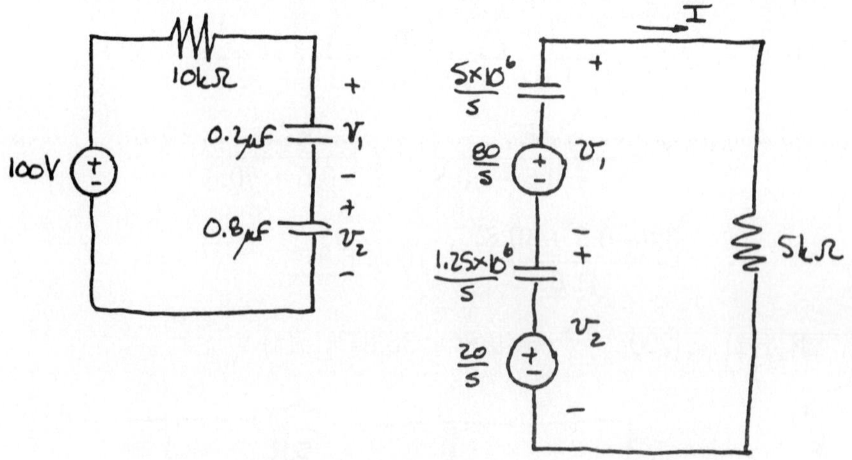

$$I = \frac{(80/s) + (20/s)}{5000 + [(5 \times 10^6)/s] + (1.25 \times 10^6/s)} = \frac{20 \times 10^{-3}}{s + 1250}$$

$$V_1 = \frac{80}{s} - \frac{5 \times 10^6}{s}\left(\frac{20 \times 10^{-3}}{s + 1250}\right) = \frac{80}{s + 1250}$$

$$V_2 = \frac{20}{s} - \frac{1.25 \times 10^6}{s}\left(\frac{20 \times 10^{-3}}{s + 1250}\right) = \frac{20}{s + 1250}$$

[b] $i = 20e^{-1250t}u(t)\,\text{mA}$; $v_1 = 80e^{-1250t}u(t)\,\text{V}$

$v_2 = 20e^{-1250t}u(t)\,\text{V}$

DE 13.4 **[a]**

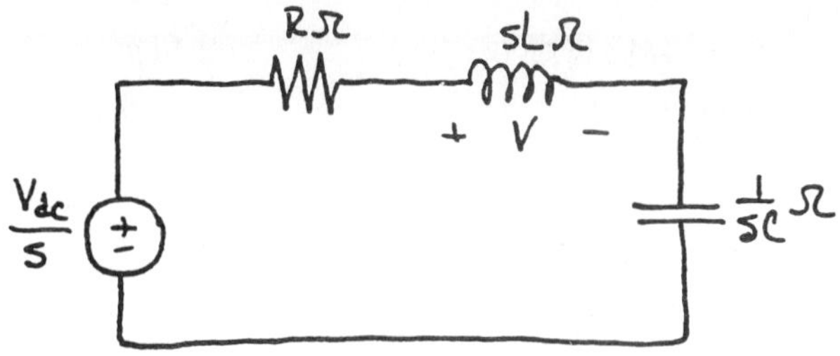

$$I = \frac{V_{\text{dc}}/s}{R + sL + (1/sC)} = \frac{V_{\text{dc}}/L}{s^2 + (R/L)s + (1/LC)}$$

$$\frac{V_{\text{dc}}}{L} = 40; \qquad \frac{R}{L} = 1.2; \qquad \frac{1}{LC} = 1.0$$

$$I = \frac{40}{(s + 0.6 - j0.8)(s + 0.6 + j0.8)} = \frac{K_1}{s + 0.6 - j0.8} + \frac{K_1^*}{s + 0.6 + j0.8}$$

$$K_1 = \frac{40}{j1.6} = -j25 = 25\underline{/-90^\circ}; \qquad K_1^* = 25\underline{/90^\circ}$$

[b] $i = 50e^{-0.6t}\cos(0.8t - 90^\circ) = [50e^{-0.6t}\sin 0.8t]u(t)$ A

[c] $V = sLI = \dfrac{160s}{(s + 0.6 - j0.8)(s + 0.6 + j0.8)}$

$$= \frac{K_1}{s + 0.6 - j0.8} + \frac{K_1^*}{s + 0.6 + j0.8}$$

$$K_1 = \frac{32(-0.6 + j0.8)}{j1.6} = 100\underline{/36.87^\circ}$$

[d] $v(t) = [200e^{-0.6t}\cos(0.8t + 36.87^\circ)]u(t)$ V

DE 13.5 [a]

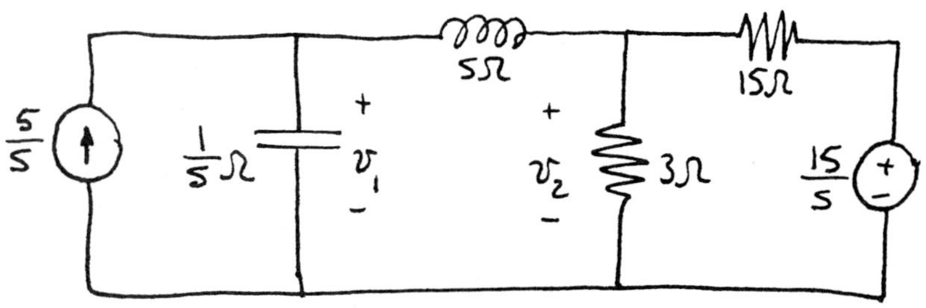

The two node voltage equations are

$$\frac{V_1 - V_2}{s} + V_1 s = \frac{5}{s} \quad \text{and} \quad \frac{V_2}{3} + \frac{V_2 - V_1}{s} + \frac{V_2 - (15/s)}{15} = 0$$

Solving for V_1 and V_2 yields

$$V_1 = \frac{5(s+3)}{s(s^2 + 2.5s + 1)}, \qquad V_2 = \frac{2.5(s^2 + 6)}{s(s^2 + 2.5s + 1)}$$

[b] The partial fraction expansions of V_1 and V_2 are

$$V_1 = \frac{15}{s} - \frac{50/3}{s + 0.5} + \frac{5/3}{s + 2} \quad \text{and} \quad V_2 = \frac{15}{s} - \frac{125/6}{s + 0.5} + \frac{25/3}{s + 2}$$

It follows that

$$v_1(t) = \left[15 - \frac{50}{3}e^{-0.5t} + \frac{5}{3}e^{-2t}\right]u(t) \text{ V} \quad \text{and}$$

$$v_2(t) = \left[15 - \frac{125}{6}e^{-0.5t} + \frac{25}{3}e^{-2t}\right]u(t) \text{ V}$$

[c] $v_1(0^+) = 15 - \dfrac{50}{3} + \dfrac{5}{3} = 0$

$$v_2(0^+) = 15 - \frac{125}{6} + \frac{25}{3} = 2.5 \text{ V}$$

[d] $v_1(\infty) = 15$ V; $\quad v_2(\infty) = 15$ V

DE 13.6 [a]

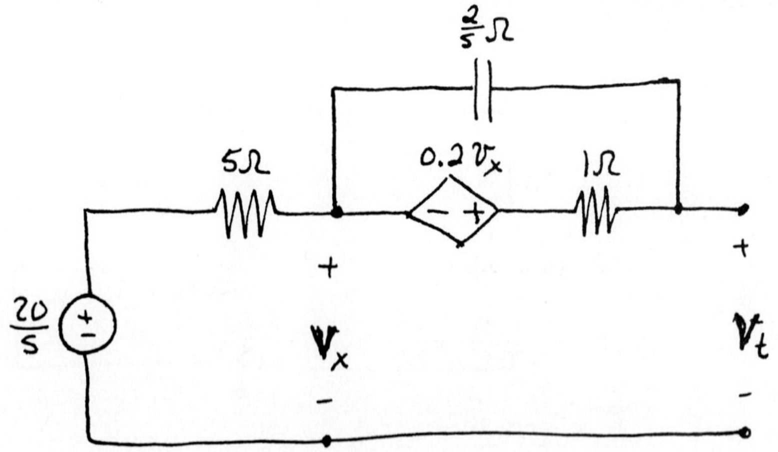

With no load across terminals $a-b$ $V_x = 20/s$:

$$\frac{1}{2}\left[\frac{20}{s} - V_t\right]s + \left[1.2\left(\frac{20}{s}\right) - V_t\right] = 0$$

therefore $V_t = \dfrac{20(s+2.4)}{s(s+2)}$

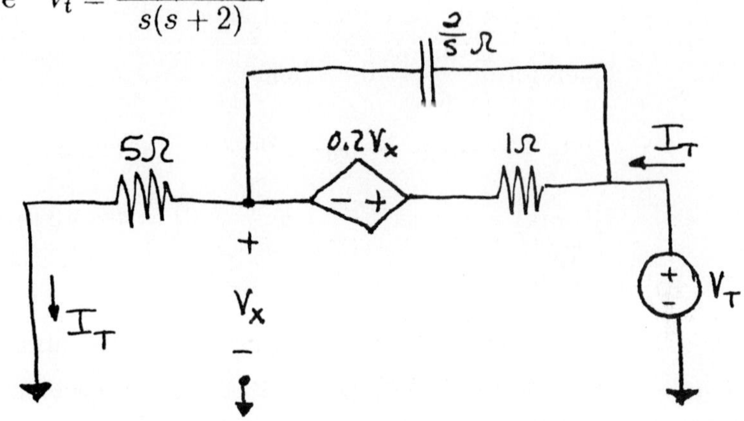

$V_x = 5I_T$ and $Z_t = \dfrac{V_T}{I_T}$

Solving for I_T gives

$$I_T = \frac{(V_T - 5I_T)s}{2} + V_T - 1.2I_T$$

Therefore

$$5(0.88+s)I_T = (s+2)V_T; \qquad \text{therefore} \quad Z_t = \frac{5(s+0.88)}{s+2}$$

[b]

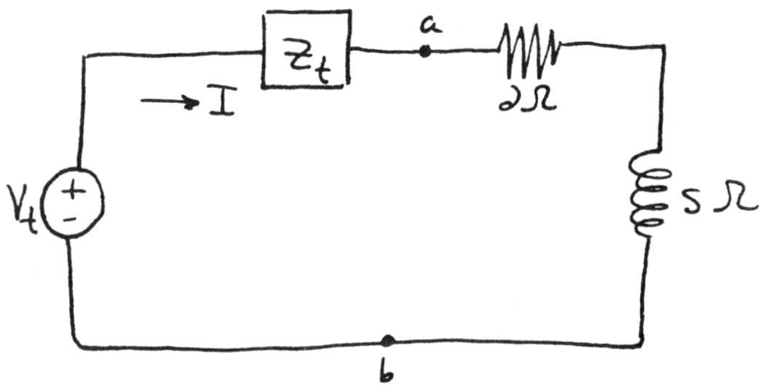

$$I = \frac{V_t}{Z_t + 2 + s} = \frac{20(s+2)}{s(s^2 + 9s + 8.4)}$$

DE 13.7 [a] $i_2 = 1.25e^{-t} - 1.25e^{-3t}$; therefore $\frac{di_2}{dt} = -1.25e^{-t} + 3.75e^{-3t}$

Therefore $\frac{di_2}{dt} = 0$ when

$1.25e^{-t} = 3.75e^{-3t}$ or $e^{2t} = 3$, $t = 0.5(\ln 3) = 549.31\,\text{ms}$

$i_2(\text{max}) = 1.25[e^{-0.549} - e^{-3(0.549)}] = 481.13\,\text{mA}$

[b] From Eqs. 13.68 and 13.69, we have

$\Delta = 12(s^2 + 4s + 3) = 12(s+1)(s+3)$ and $N_1 = 60(s+2)$

Therefore $I_1 = \frac{N_1}{\Delta} = \frac{5(s+2)}{(s+1)(s+3)}$

A partial fraction expansion leads to the expression

$$I_1 = \frac{2.5}{s+1} + \frac{2.5}{s+3}$$

Therefore we get

$i_1 = 2.5[e^{-t} + e^{-3t}]u(t)$ A

[c] $\frac{di_1}{dt} = -2.5[e^{-t} + 3e^{-3t}]$; $\frac{di_1(0.54931)}{dt} = -2.89\,\text{A/s}$

[d] When i_2 is at its peak value,

$$\frac{di_2}{dt} = 0$$

Therefore $L_2\left(\frac{di_2}{dt}\right) = 0$ and $i_2 = -\left(\frac{M}{12}\right)\left(\frac{di_1}{dt}\right)$

[e] $i_2(\text{max}) = \dfrac{-2(-2.89)}{12} = 481.13\,\text{mA}$ (checks)

DE 13.8 [a] The s-domain circuit with the voltage source acting alone is

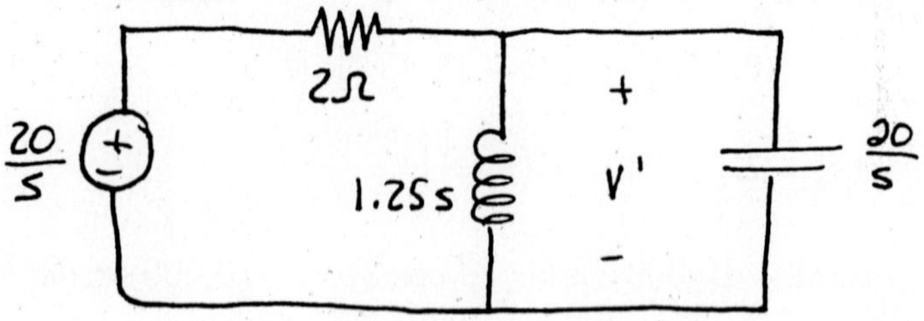

$$\frac{V' - (20/s)}{2} + \frac{V'}{1.25s} + \frac{V's}{20} = 0$$

$$V' = \frac{200}{(s+2)(s+8)} = \frac{100/3}{s+2} - \frac{100/3}{s+8}$$

$$v' = \frac{100}{3}[e^{-2t} - e^{-8t}]u(t)\text{ V}$$

[b] With the current source acting alone,

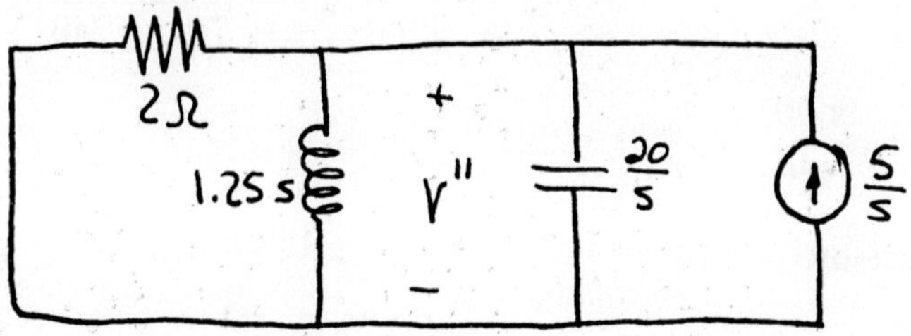

$$\frac{V''}{2} + \frac{V''}{1.25s} + \frac{V''s}{20} = \frac{5}{s}$$

$$V'' = \frac{100}{(s+2)(s+8)} = \frac{50/3}{s+2} - \frac{50/3}{s+8}$$

$$v'' = \frac{50}{3}[e^{-2t} - e^{-8t}]u(t)\text{ V}$$

[c] $v = v' + v'' = 50[e^{-2t} - e^{-8t}]u(t)$ V

DE 13.9 [a] $\dfrac{V_o}{s+2} + \dfrac{V_o s}{10} = I_G;$ therefore $\dfrac{V_o}{I_g} = H(s) = \dfrac{10(s+2)}{s^2 + 2s + 10}$

[b] $-z_1 = -2;$ $-p_1 = -1 + j3;$ $-p_2 = -1 - j3$

DE 13.10 [a] $V_o = \dfrac{10(s+2)}{s^2+2s+10} \cdot \dfrac{1}{s} = \dfrac{K_o}{s} + \dfrac{K_1}{s+1-j3} + \dfrac{K_1^*}{s+1+j3}$

$K_o = 2;$ $K_1 = 5/3\angle{-126.87^\circ};$ $K_1^* = 5/3\angle{126.87^\circ}$

$v_o = [2 + (10/3)e^{-t}\cos(3t - 126.87^\circ)]u(t)$ V

[b] $V_o = \dfrac{10(s+2)}{s^2+2s+10} \cdot 1 = \dfrac{K_2}{s+1-j3} + \dfrac{K_2^*}{s+1+j3}$

$K_2 = 5.27\underline{/-18.43^\circ}; \qquad K_2^* = 5.27\underline{/18.43^\circ}$

$v_o = [10.54e^{-t}\cos(3t - 18.43^\circ)]u(t)$ V

DE 13.11 [a] $H(s) = \mathcal{L}\{h(t)\} = \mathcal{L}\{v_o(t)\}$

$$v_o(t) = 10{,}000\cos\theta e^{-70t}\cos 240t - 10{,}000\sin\theta e^{-70t}\sin 240t$$
$$= 9600e^{-70t}\cos 240t - 2800e^{-70t}\sin 240t$$

Therefore $H(s) = \dfrac{9600(s+70)}{(s+70)^2+(240)^2} - \dfrac{2800(240)}{(s+70)^2+(240)^2}$

$$= \frac{9600s}{s^2+140s+62{,}500}$$

[b] $V_o(s) = H(s)\cdot\dfrac{1}{s} = \dfrac{9600}{s^2+140s+62{,}500}$

$$= \frac{K_1}{s+70-j240} + \frac{K_1^*}{s+70+j240}$$

$K_1 = \dfrac{9600}{j480} = -j20 = 20\underline{/-90^\circ}$

Therefore

$v_o(t) = [40e^{-70t}\cos(240t - 90^\circ)]u(t)$ V $= [40e^{-70t}\sin 240t]u(t)$ V

DE 13.12 $H(s) = \dfrac{V_o}{V_i} = \dfrac{1}{s+1}; \qquad h(t) = e^{-t}$

For $0 \le t \le 1$:

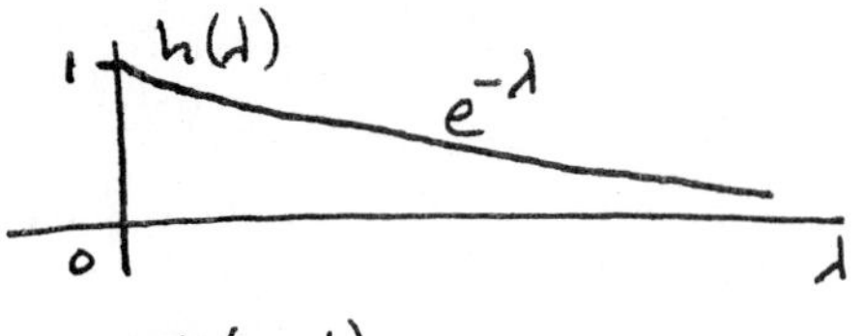

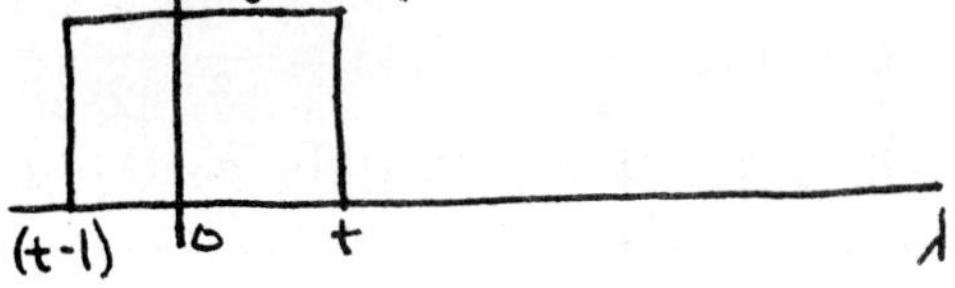

$$v_o = \int_0^t e^{-\lambda}\,d\lambda = (1 - e^{-t})\text{ V}$$

For $1 \leq t \leq \infty$:

$$v_o = \int_{t-1}^{t} e^{-\lambda}\,d\lambda = (e-1)e^{-t}\,\text{V}$$

DE 13.13 $H(s) = \frac{V_o}{V_i} = \frac{s}{s+1} = 1 - \frac{1}{s+1}; \qquad h(t) = \delta(t) - e^{-t}$

$$h(\lambda) = \delta(\lambda) - e^{-\lambda}$$

For $0 \leq t \leq 1$:

$$v_o = \int_0^t [\delta(\lambda) - e^{-\lambda}]\,d\lambda = [1 + e^{-\lambda}]\,\Big|_0^t = e^{-t}\text{V}$$

For $1 \leq t \leq \infty$:

$$v_o = \int_{t-1}^{t} (-e^{-\lambda})\,d\lambda = e^{-\lambda}\Big|_{t-1}^{t} = (1-e)e^{-t}\,\text{V}$$

DE 13.14 From DE 13.9:

$$H(s) = \frac{10(s+2)}{s^2+2s+10}$$

Therefore $H(j4) = \frac{10(2+j4)}{10-16+j8} = 4.47\underline{/-63.43^\circ}$

Thus,

$$v_o = (10)(4.47)\cos(4t - 63.43^\circ) = 44.7\cos(4t - 63.43^\circ)\,\text{V}$$

DE 13.15 [a] Let $R_1 = 10\,\text{k}\Omega, \quad R_2 = 50\,\text{k}\Omega$

then $V_1 = V_2 = \frac{V_g R_2}{R_2 + (1/sC)}$

Also $\frac{V_1 - V_g}{R_1} + \frac{V_1 - V_o}{R_1} = 0$

therefore $V_o = 2V_1 - V_g$

Now solving for V_o/V_g, we get $H(s) = \frac{R_2Cs - 1}{R_2Cs + 1}$

It follows that $H(j50{,}000) = \frac{j-1}{j+1} = j1 = 1\underline{/90^\circ}$

Therefore $v_o = 10\cos(50{,}000t + 90^\circ)\,\text{V}$

[b] Replacing R_2 by R_x gives us $H(s) = \dfrac{R_xCs - 1}{R_xCs + 1}$

Therefore

$$H(j50{,}000) = \frac{j20 \times 10^{-6}R_x - 1}{j20 \times 10^{-6}R_x + 1} = \frac{R_x + j50{,}000}{R_x - j50{,}000}$$

Thus,

$$\frac{50{,}000}{R_x} = \tan 60^\circ = 1.7321, \qquad R_x = 28{,}867.51\,\Omega$$

DE 13.16 [a] For $t < 0$, $0.5v_1 = 2v_2$; therefore $v_1 = 4v_2$

$v_1 + v_2 = 100$; therefore $v_1(0^-) = 80\,\text{V}$

[b] $v_2(0^-) = 20\,\text{V}$

[c] $v_3(0^-) = 0\,\text{V}$

[d] For $t > 0$:

$$I = \frac{100/s}{3.125/s} \times 10^{-6} = 32 \times 10^{-6}$$

$i(t) = 32\delta(t)\,\mu\text{A}$

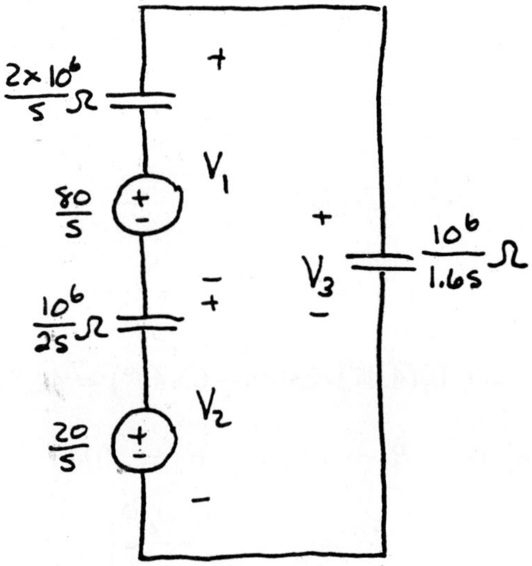

[e] $v_1(0^+) = -\dfrac{10^6}{0.5}\displaystyle\int_{0^-}^{0^+} 32 \times 10^{-6}\delta(t)\,dt + 80 = -64 + 80 = 16\,\text{V}$

[f] $v_2(0^+) = -\dfrac{10^6}{2}\displaystyle\int_{0^-}^{0^+} 32 \times 10^{-6}\delta(t)\,dt + 20 = -16 + 20 = 4\,\text{V}$

[g] $V_3 = \dfrac{0.625 \times 10^6}{s} \cdot 32 \times 10^{-6} = \dfrac{20}{s}$

$v_3(t) = 20u(t)\,\text{V}$; $v_3(0^+) = 20\,\text{V}$

DE 13.17 [a] For $t < 0$:

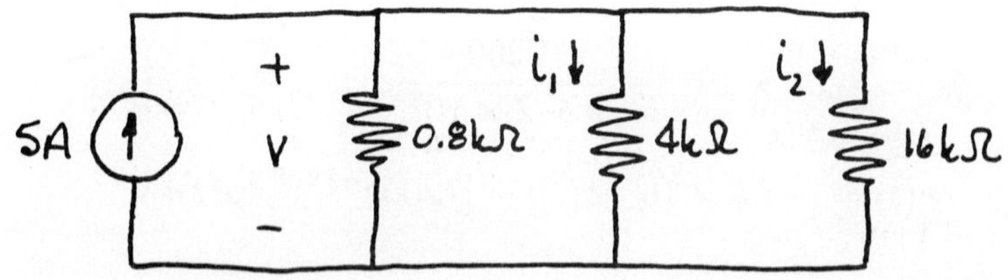

$R_{eq} = 0.8\|4\|16 = 0.64\,\text{k}\Omega; \qquad v = 5(640) = 3200\text{ V}$

$$i_1(0^-) = \frac{3200}{4000} = 0.8\text{ A}; \qquad i_2(0^-) = \frac{3200}{1600} = 0.2\text{ A}$$

[b] For $t > 0$:

$i_1 + i_2 = 0$

$8(\Delta i_1) = 2(\Delta i_2)$

$i_1(0^-) + \Delta i_1 + i_2(0^-) + \Delta i_2 = 0;$ therefore $\Delta i_1 = -0.2\text{ A}$

$\Delta i_2 = -0.8\text{ A}; \qquad i_1(0^+) = 0.8 - 0.2 = 0.6\text{ A}$

[c] $i_2(0^-) = 0.2\text{ A}$

[d] $i_2(0^+) = 0.2 - 0.8 = -0.6\text{ A}$

[e] The s-domain equivalent circuit for $t > 0$ is

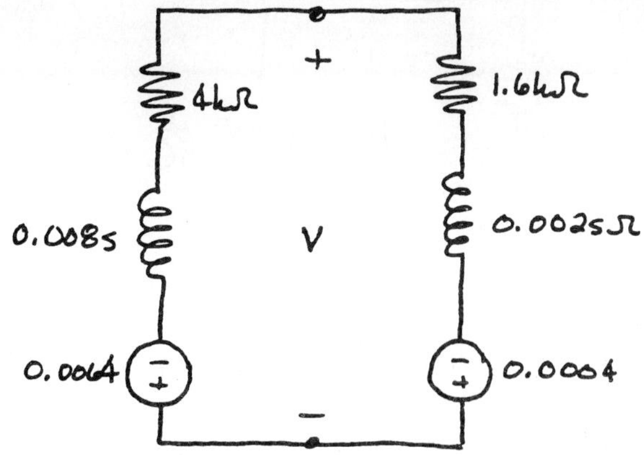

$$I_1 = \frac{0.006}{0.01s + 20{,}000} = \frac{0.6}{s + 2\times10^6}$$

$i_1(t) = 0.6e^{-2\times10^6 t}u(t)\text{ A}$

[f] $i_2(t) = -i_1(t) = -0.6e^{-2\times10^6 t}u(t)\text{ A}$

[g] $V = -0.0064 + (0.008s + 4000)I_1 = \dfrac{-0.0016(s + 6.5 \times 10^6)}{s + 2 \times 10^6}$

$$= -1.6 \times 10^{-3} - \frac{7200}{s + 2 \times 10^6}$$

$$v(t) = [-1.6 \times 10^{-3}\delta(t)] - [7200e^{-2\times10^6 t}u(t)]\ \mathrm{V}$$

Problems

P 13.1 $I_{sc_{ab}} = I_N = \dfrac{-LI_0}{sL} = \dfrac{-I_0}{s}; \qquad Z_N = sL$

Therefore, the Norton equivalent is the same as the circuit in Fig. 13.4.

P 13.2 $i = \dfrac{1}{L}\displaystyle\int_{0^-}^{t} v\,d\tau + I_0; \qquad$ therefore $I = \left(\dfrac{1}{L}\right)\left(\dfrac{V}{s}\right) + \dfrac{I_0}{s} = \dfrac{V}{sL} + \dfrac{I_0}{s}$

P 13.3 $V_{\mathrm{Th}} = V_{\mathrm{ab}} = CV_o\left(\dfrac{1}{sC}\right) = \dfrac{V_o}{s}; \qquad Z_{\mathrm{Th}} = \dfrac{1}{sC}$

P 13.4 [a]

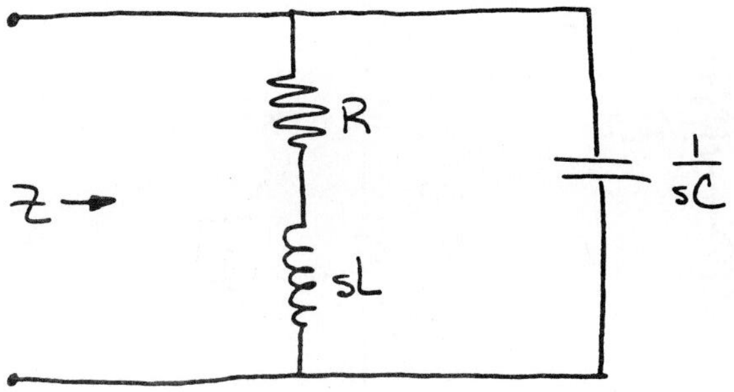

$$Z = \frac{(R + sL)(1/sC)}{R + sL + (1/sC)} = \frac{(1/C)(s + R/L)}{s^2 + (R/L)s + (1/LC)}$$

$$\frac{R}{L} = \frac{1000}{0.5} = 2000; \qquad \frac{1}{LC} = \frac{10^6}{0.2} = 5 \times 10^6$$

$$Z = \frac{2.5 \times 10^6(s + 2000)}{s^2 + 2000s + 5 \times 10^6}$$

[b] $s_{1,2} = -1000 \pm \sqrt{10^6 - 5 \times 10^6} = -1000 \pm j2000$

$$Z = \frac{2.5 \times 10^6(s + 2000)}{(s + 1000 - j2000)(s + 1000 + j2000)}$$

$-z_1 = -2000$ rad/s; $\quad -p_1 = -1000 + j2000$ rad/s

$-p_2 = -1000 - j2000$ rad/s

P 13.5 [a] $Z = R + sL + \dfrac{1}{sC} = \dfrac{L[s^2 + (R/L)s + (1/LC)]}{s}$

$$= \frac{5[s^2 + 2000s + 10^7]}{s}$$

[b] $s_{1,2} = -1000 \pm \sqrt{10^6 - 10^7} = -1000 \pm j3000$ rad/s
Zeros at $-1000 + j3000$ rad/s and $-1000 - j3000$ rad/s
Pole at 0.

P 13.6 [a] $Y = \dfrac{1}{R} + \dfrac{1}{sL} + sC = \dfrac{C[s^2 + (1/RC)s + (1/LC)]}{s}$

$$Z = \frac{1}{Y} = \frac{s/C}{s^2 + (1/RC)s + (1/LC)} = \frac{25 \times 10^6 s}{s^2 + 5000s + 4 \times 10^6}$$

[b] zero at $z_1 = 0$
poles at $-p_1 = -1000$ rad/s and $-p_2 = -4000$ rad/s

P 13.7 Transform the Y-connection of the two resistors and the inductor into the equivalent delta-connection:

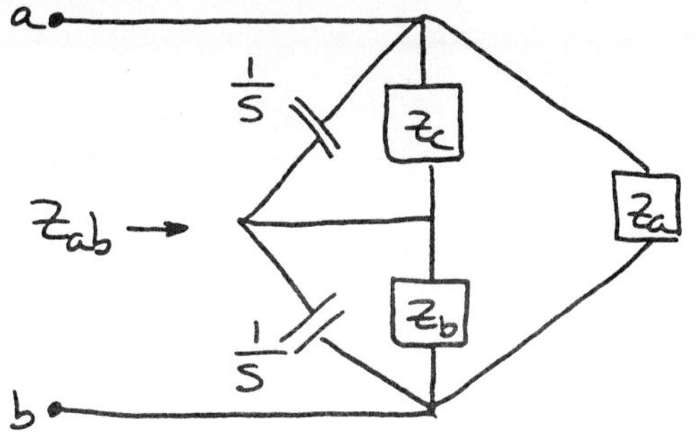

where

$$Z_a = \frac{(s)(1) + (1)(s) + (1)(1)}{s} = \frac{2s + 1}{s}$$

$$Z_b = Z_c = \frac{(s)(1) + (1)(s) + (1)(1)}{1} = 2s + 1$$

Then

$$Z_{ab} = Z_a \| [(1/s \| Z_c) + (1/s \| Z_b)] = Z_a \| 2(1/s \| Z_b)$$

$$1/s \| Z_b = \frac{\frac{1}{s}(2s+1)}{\frac{1}{s} + 2s + 1} = \frac{2s+1}{2s^2+s+1}$$

$$Z_{ab} = \left(\frac{2s+1}{s}\right) \| \frac{2(2s+1)}{2s^2+s+1}$$

$$= \frac{2(2s+1)^2}{(2s+1)(2s^2+s+1) + 2s(2s+1)} = \frac{2}{s+1}$$

No zeros; one pole at -1 rad/s.

P 13.8 $$Z_1 = 0.5s + \frac{2(50/s)}{(2+50/s)} = \frac{s^2+25s+100}{2s+50}$$

$$Y_{ab} = \frac{1}{25} + \frac{2s+50}{s^2+25s+100} = \frac{s^2+75s+1350}{25(s^2+25s+100}$$

$$Z_{ab} = \frac{25(s^2+25s+100)}{s^2+75s+1350} = \frac{25(s+5)(s+20)}{(s+30)(s+45)}$$

Zeros at -5 rad/s and -20 rad/s; poles at -30 rad/s and -45 rad/s.

P 13.9 [a] For $t < 0$:

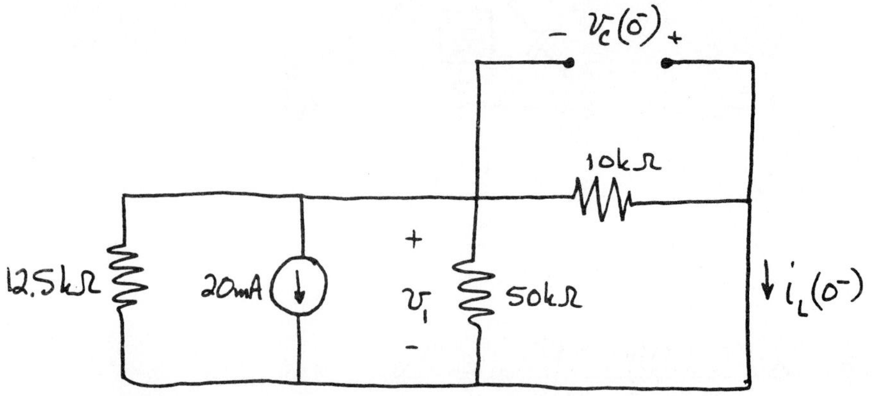

$$\frac{1}{R_e} = \frac{1}{12.5} + \frac{1}{50} + \frac{1}{10} = \frac{1}{5}; \qquad R_e = 5\,\text{k}\Omega$$

$$v_1 = -20(5) = -100\,\text{V}$$

$$i_L(0^-) = \frac{-100}{10} \times 10^{-3} = -10\,\text{mA}$$

$$v_C(0^-) = -10(-10) = 100\,\text{V}$$

For $t = 0^+$:

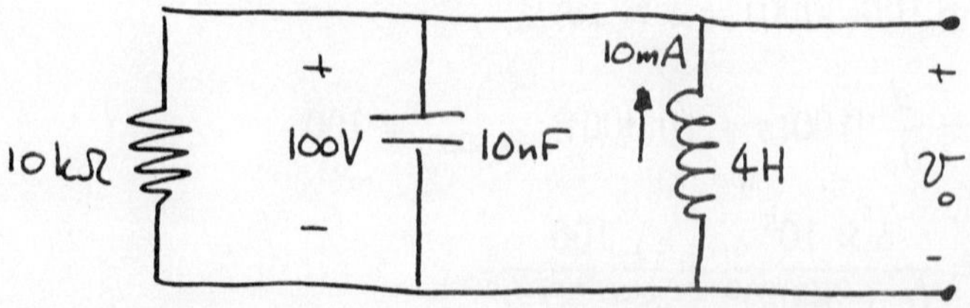

s-domain circuit:

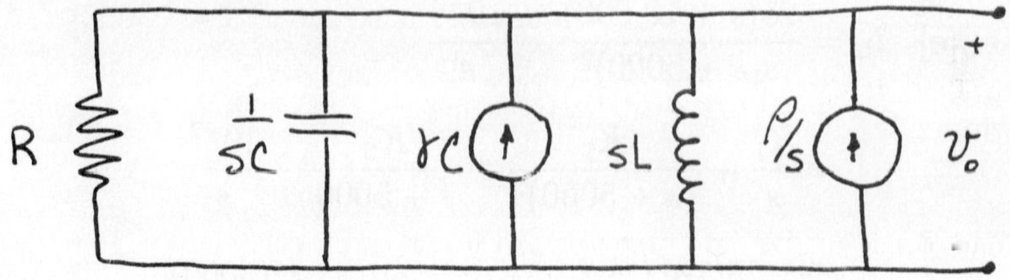

where

$R = 10\,\text{k}\Omega$; $C = 10\,\text{nF}$; $\gamma = 100\,\text{V}$;

$L = 4\,\text{H}$; and $\rho = 10\,\text{mA}$

[b] $$\frac{V_o}{R} + V_o sC - \gamma C + \frac{V_o}{sL} - \frac{\rho}{s} = 0$$

$$\therefore \quad V_o = \frac{\gamma[s + (\rho/\gamma C)]}{s^2 + (1/RC)s + (1/LC)}$$

$$\frac{\rho}{\gamma C} = \frac{10 \times 10^{-3}}{(100)(10)10^{-9}} = 10^4$$

$$\frac{1}{RC} = \frac{10^9}{10^5} = 10^4$$

$$\frac{1}{LC} = \frac{10^9}{40} = 25 \times 10^6$$

$$V_o = \frac{100(s + 10^4)}{s^2 + 10^4 s + 25 \times 10^6}$$

[c] $$I_L = \frac{V_o}{sL} - \frac{\rho}{s} = \frac{V_o}{4s} - \frac{10 \times 10^{-3}}{s}$$

$$I_L = \frac{25(s + 10^4)}{s(s^2 + 10^4 s + 25 \times 10^6)} - \frac{10^{-2}}{s}$$

[d] $V_o = \dfrac{100(s+10^4)}{s^2+10^4 s+25\times10^6}$

$= \dfrac{100(s+10^4)}{(s+5000)^2} = \dfrac{K_1}{(s+5000)^2} + \dfrac{K_2}{s+5000}$

$K_1 = 100(5000) = 5\times10^5$

$K_2 = \dfrac{d}{ds}[100(s+10{,}000)]_{s=-5000} = 100$

$V_o = \dfrac{5\times10^5}{(s+5000)^2} + \dfrac{100}{s+5000}$

$v_o = [5\times10^5 te^{-5000t} + 100e^{-5000t}]u(t)$ V

[e] $I_L = \dfrac{25(s+10{,}000)}{s(s+5000)^2} - \dfrac{10^{-2}}{s}$

$= \dfrac{K_1}{s} + \dfrac{K_2}{(s+5000)^2} + \dfrac{K_3}{s+5000} - \dfrac{10^{-2}}{s}$

$K_1 = \dfrac{25(10^4)}{25\times10^6} = 10^{-2}; \qquad K_2 = \dfrac{25(5000)}{-5000} = -25$

$K_3 = 25\dfrac{d}{ds}\left(\dfrac{s+10{,}000}{s}\right)\Big|_{s=-5000}$

$= 25\dfrac{-10{,}000}{s^2}\Big|_{s=-5000} = -10\times10^{-3}$

$I_L = \left[\dfrac{-25{,}000}{(s+5000)^2} - \dfrac{10}{s+5000}\right]\times10^{-3}$

$i_L = -[25{,}000t + 10]e^{-5000t}u(t)$ mA

P 13.10 [a] For $t>0$:

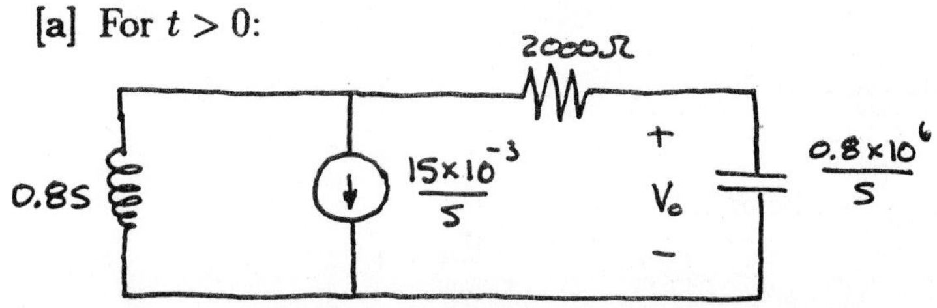

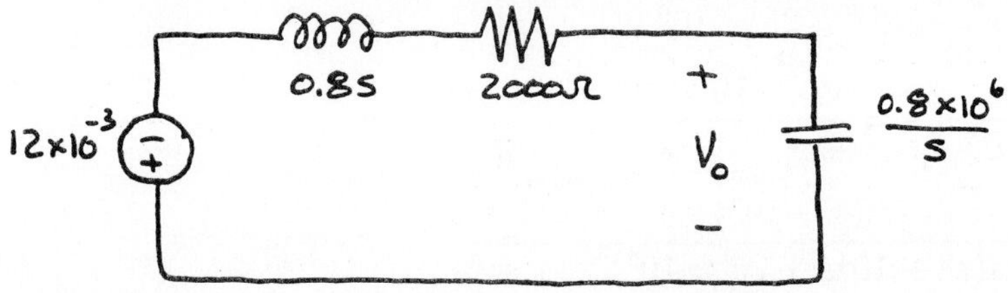

P 13.13 [a]

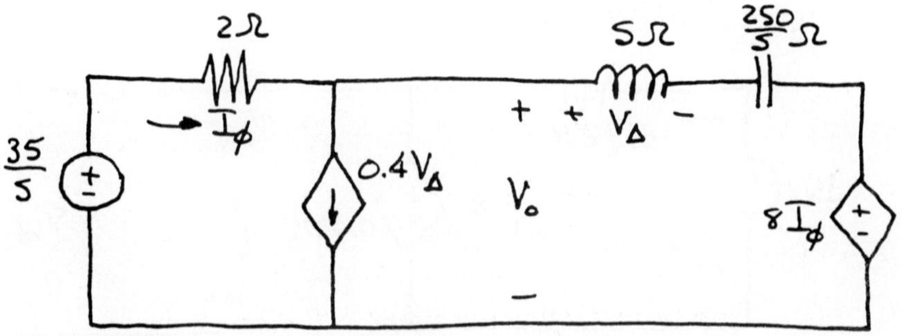

$$\frac{V_o - 35/s}{2} + 0.4V_\Delta + \frac{V_o - 8I_\phi}{s + (250/s)} = 0$$

$$V_\Delta = \left[\frac{V_o - 8I_\phi}{s + (250/s)}\right] s; \qquad I_\phi = \frac{(35/s) - V_o}{2}$$

Solving for V_o yields:

$$V_o = \frac{29.4s^2 + 56s + 1750}{s(s^2 + 2s + 50)} = \frac{29.4s^2 + 56s + 1750}{s(s + 1 - j7)(s + 1 + j7)}$$

$$V_o = \frac{K_1}{s} + \frac{K_2}{s + 1 - j7} + \frac{K_2^*}{s + 1 + j7}$$

$$K_1 = \left.\frac{29.4s^2 + 56s + 1750}{s^2 + 2s + 50}\right|_{s=0} = 35$$

$$K_2 = \left.\frac{29.4s^2 + 56s + 1750}{s(s + 1 + j7)}\right|_{s=-1+j7}$$

$$= -2.8 + j0.6 = 2.86\underline{/167.91^\circ}$$

$$\therefore \quad v_o(t) = [35 + 5.73e^{-t}\cos(7t + 167.91^\circ)]u(t)\text{ V}$$

[b] At $t = 0^+$ $\qquad v_o = 35 + 5.73\cos(167.91^\circ) = 29.4\text{ V}$

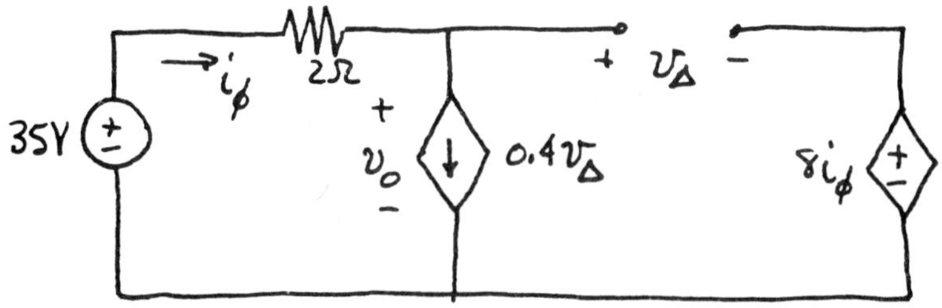

$$\frac{v_o - 35}{2} + 0.4v_\Delta = 0; \qquad v_o - 35 + 0.8v_\Delta = 0$$

$$v_o = v_\Delta + 8i_\phi = v_\Delta + 8(0.4v_\Delta) = 2.4\text{ V}$$

$$v_o + (0.8)\frac{v_o}{4.2} = 35; \qquad \therefore \quad v_o(0^+) = 29.4\text{(checks)}$$

At $t = \infty$, the circuit is

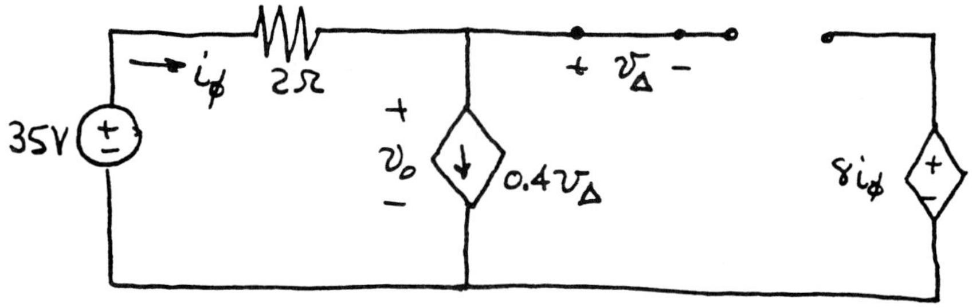

$$v_\Delta = 0, \quad i_\phi = 0 \qquad \therefore \; v_o = 35\,\text{V(checks)}$$

P 13.14 [a] For $t < 0$:

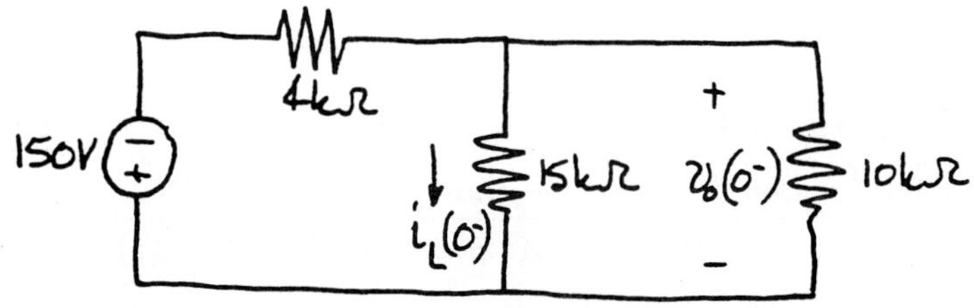

$$\frac{v_o(0^-) + 150}{4} + \frac{v_o(0^-)}{15} + \frac{v_o(0^-)}{10} = 0$$

$$\therefore \; v_o(0^-) = -90\,\text{V}; \qquad \therefore \; i_L(0^-) = -6\,\text{mA}$$

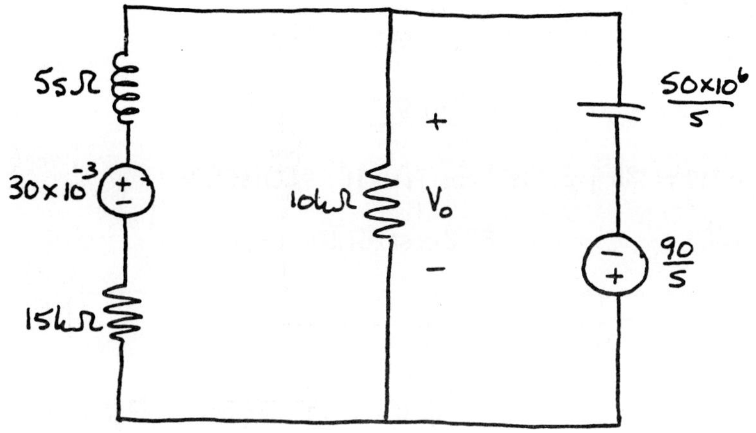

$$\frac{V_o - 30 \times 10^{-3}}{5s + 15{,}000} + \frac{V_o}{10^4} + \frac{(V_o + 90/s)s}{50 \times 10^6} = 0$$

$$V_o = \frac{30(1000 - 3s)}{s^2 + 8000s + 25 \times 10^6}$$

$$= \frac{30(1000 - 3s)}{(s + 4000 - j3000)(s + 4000 + j3000)}$$

$$K_1 = \frac{30(1000 + 12{,}000 - j9000)}{j6000} = 79.06\underline{/-124.70^\circ} \text{ V}$$

$$v_o(t) = 158.11e^{-4000t}\cos(3000t - 124.70^\circ)u(t)\ V$$

Check: $v_o(0) = 158.11\cos(-124.70^\circ) = -90\text{ V}$

P 13.15 [a] For $t < 0$:

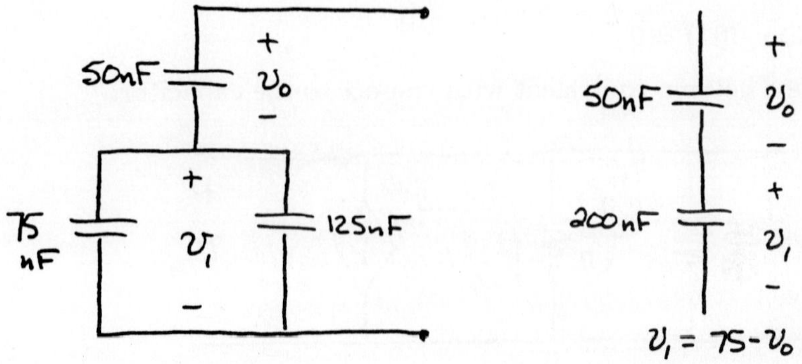

$50v_o = 200(75 - v_0)$; $\therefore\ v_o = 60\text{ V}$; $v_1 = 15\text{ V}$

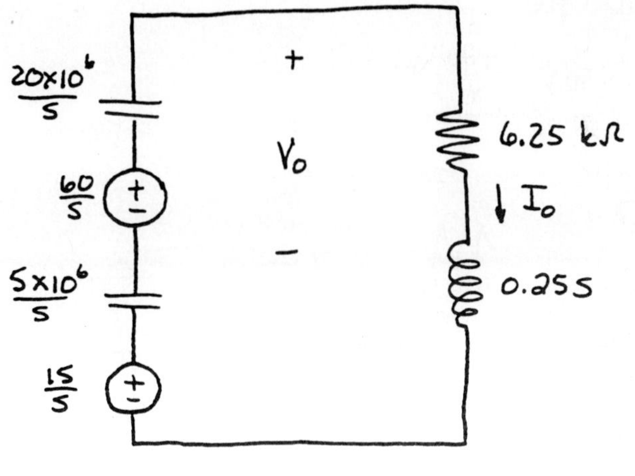

[b] $$I_o = \frac{75/s}{(25\times 10^6/s) + 6250 + 0.25s} = \frac{300}{s^2 + 25{,}000s + 10^8}$$

$$= \frac{300}{(s+5000)(s+20{,}000)} = \frac{20\times 10^{-3}}{s+5000} - \frac{20\times 10^{-3}}{s+20{,}000}$$

$$i_o(t) = (20e^{-5000t} - 20e^{-20{,}000t})u(t)\text{ mA}$$

[c] $V_o = \frac{60}{s} - \frac{20 \times 10^6}{s} \cdot \frac{300}{(s+5000)(s+20{,}000)}$

$$= \frac{60}{s} - \left[\frac{60}{s} - \frac{80}{s+5000} + \frac{20}{s+20{,}000}\right]$$

$$= \frac{80}{s+5000} - \frac{20}{s+20{,}000}$$

$$v_o(t) = (80e^{-5000t} - 20e^{-20{,}000t})u(t)\ \text{V}$$

P 13.16 $v_C(0^-) = v_C(0^+) = 0$

Find the Thévenin equivalent with respect to the capacitor:

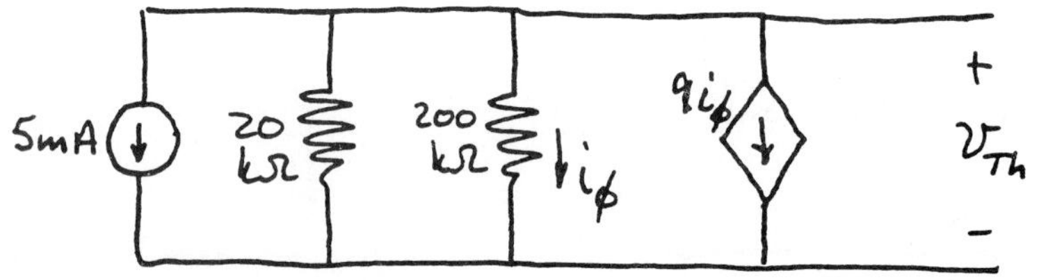

$$\frac{v_{\text{Th}}}{20} + \frac{v_{\text{Th}}}{200} + \frac{9v_{\text{Th}}}{200} = -5$$

$$\therefore\quad v_{\text{Th}} = -50\ \text{V}$$

$$i_{sc} = -5\ \text{mA}; \qquad \therefore\quad R_{\text{Th}} = 10\ \text{k}\Omega$$

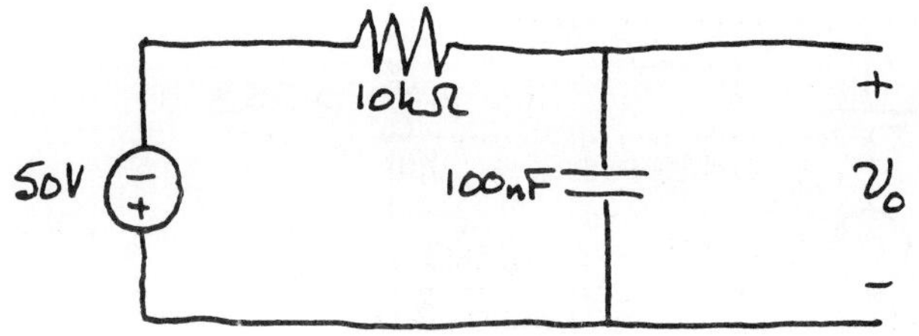

$$V_o = \frac{-50/s}{10{,}000 + (10^7/s)} \cdot \frac{10^7}{s}$$

$$= \frac{-50 \times 10^3}{s(s+1000)} = \frac{-50}{s} + \frac{50}{s+1000}$$

$$v_o(t) = [-50 + 50e^{-1000t}]u(t)\ \text{V}$$

P 13.17 [a]

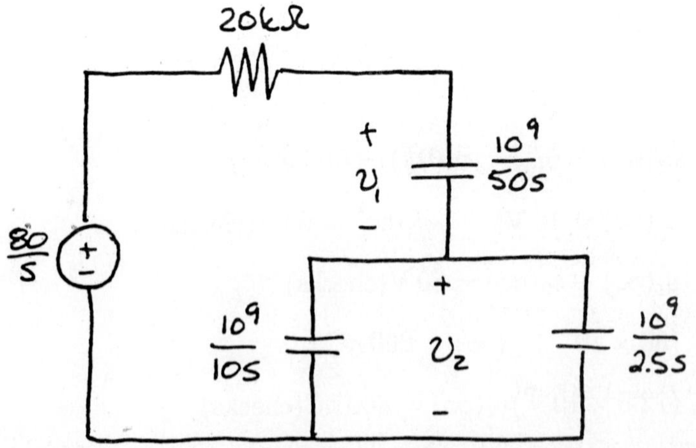

$$Y_e = \frac{10s}{10^9} + \frac{2.5s}{10^9} = \frac{12.5s}{10^9}$$

$$Z_e = \frac{10^9}{12.5s} = \frac{80 \times 10^6}{s}$$

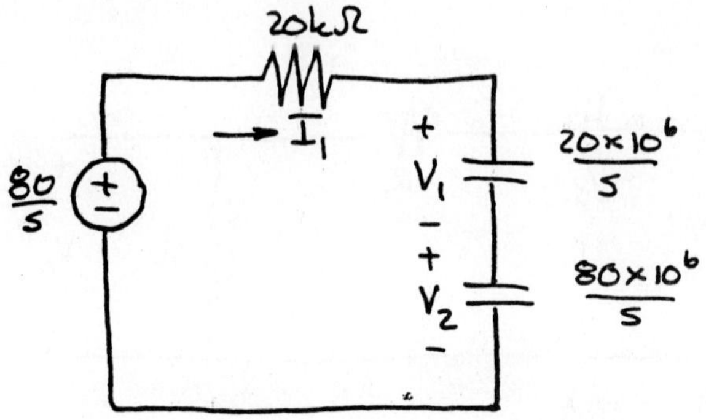

[b] $I_1 = \dfrac{80/s}{20{,}000 + (100 \times 10^6/s)} = \dfrac{4 \times 10^{-3}}{s + 5000}$

$$V_1 = \frac{4 \times 10^{-3}}{s + 5000} \cdot \frac{20 \times 10^6}{s} = \frac{80{,}000}{s(s + 5000)}$$

$$V_2 = \frac{4 \times 10^{-3}}{s + 5000} \cdot \frac{80 \times 10^6}{s} = \frac{320{,}000}{s(s + 5000)}$$

[c] $i_1(t) = 4e^{-5000t}u(t)\,\text{mA}$

$$V_1 = \frac{16}{s} - \frac{16}{s + 5000}; \qquad v_1(t) = (16 - 16e^{-5000t})u(t)\ \text{V}$$

$$V_2 = \frac{64}{s} - \frac{64}{s + 5000}; \qquad v_2(t) = (64 - 64e^{-5000t})u(t)\ \text{V}$$

[d] $i_1(0^+) = 4\,\text{mA}$

$$i_1(0^+) = \frac{80}{20} \times 10^{-3} = 4\,\text{mA}(\text{checks})$$

$$v_1(0^+) = 0; \qquad v_2(0^+) = 0(\text{checks})$$

$$v_1(\infty) = 16\text{ V}; \qquad v_2(\infty) = 64\text{ V}(\text{checks})$$

$$v_1(\infty) + v_2(\infty) = 80\text{ V}(\text{checks})$$

$$(50 \times 10^{-9})v_1(\infty) = 800\,\text{nC}$$

$$(12.5 \times 10^{-9})v_2(\infty) = 800\,\text{nC}(\text{checks})$$

P 13.18 [a]

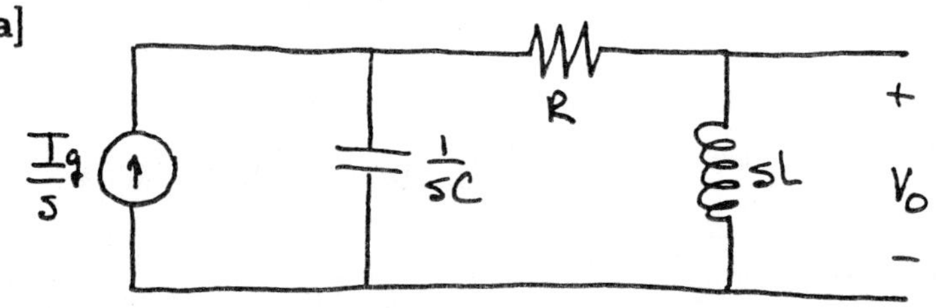

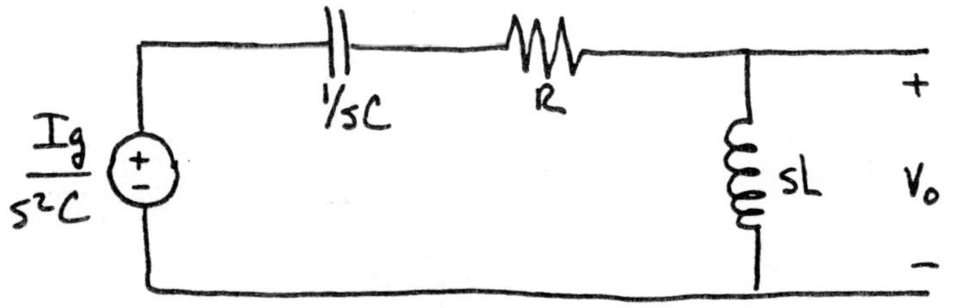

$$V_o = \frac{(I_g/s^2C)(sL)}{R + sL + (1/sC)} = \frac{I_g/C}{s^2 + (R/L)s + (1/LC)}$$

$$\frac{I_g}{C} = \frac{9.6 \times 10^{-3}}{3.2 \times 10^{-9}} = 3000 \times 10^3 = 3 \times 10^6$$

$$\frac{R}{L} = \frac{7000}{0.5} = 14{,}000; \qquad \frac{1}{LC} = \frac{2}{3.2} \times 10^9 = 625 \times 10^6$$

$$V_o = \frac{3 \times 10^6}{s^2 + 14{,}000s + 625 \times 10^6}$$

[b] $$sV_o = \frac{3 \times 10^6 s}{s^2 + 14{,}000s + 625 \times 10^6}$$

$$\lim_{s\to 0} sV_o = 0; \qquad \therefore\ v_o(\infty) = 0$$

$$\lim_{s\to \infty} sV_o = 0; \qquad \therefore\ v_o(0^+) = 0$$

[c] $s_{1,2} = -7000 \pm \sqrt{49 \times 10^6 - 625 \times 10^6} = -7000 \pm j24{,}000$ rad/s

$$V_o = \frac{3{,}000{,}000}{(s + 7000 - j24{,}000)(s + 7000 + j24{,}000)}$$

$$K_1 = \frac{3 \times 10^6}{j48{,}000} = -j62.5 = 62.5\underline{/-90^\circ}$$

$$v_o = 125e^{-7000t}\cos(24{,}000t - 90^\circ) = [125e^{-7000t}\sin 24{,}000t]u(t)\ \text{V}$$

P 13.19 $$I_C = \frac{I_g}{s} - \frac{V_o}{sL}$$

$$= \frac{9.6 \times 10^{-3}}{s} - \frac{2}{s}\left[\frac{3 \times 10^6}{(s + 7000 - j24{,}000)(s + 7000 + j24{,}000)}\right]$$

$$= \frac{9.6 \times 10^{-3}}{s} - \frac{6 \times 10^6}{s(s + 7000 - j24{,}000)(s + 7000 + j24{,}000)}$$

$$= \frac{9.6 \times 10^{-3}}{s} - \frac{K_1}{s} - \frac{K_2}{s + 7000 - j24{,}000} - \frac{K_2^*}{s + 7000 + j24{,}000}$$

$$K_1 = \frac{6 \times 10^6}{625 \times 10^6} = 9.6 \times 10^{-3}$$

$$K_2 = \frac{6 \times 10^6}{(-7000 + j24{,}000)(j48{,}000)}$$

$$= \frac{6}{(-7 + j24)(j48)} = 5 \times 10^{-3}\underline{/163.74^\circ}$$

$$\therefore\ I_C = \frac{9.6 \times 10^{-3}}{s} - \frac{9.6 \times 10^{-3}}{s} - [\text{congugate terms}]$$

$$= \left[\frac{-5\underline{/163.74^\circ}}{s + 7000 - j24{,}000} + \text{ congugate }\right] \times 10^{-3}$$

$$= \left[\frac{5\underline{/-16.26^\circ}}{s + 7000 - j24{,}000} + \text{ congugate }\right] \times 10^{-3}$$

$$i_C = 10e^{-7000t}\cos(24{,}000t - 16.26^\circ)u(t)\ \text{mA}$$

Check:

$$i_C(0^+) = 10\cos(-16.26^\circ) = 9.6\ \text{mA} \quad \text{(ok)}$$

$$i_C(\infty) = 0 \quad \text{(ok)}$$

P 13.20 [a] $V_g = \dfrac{50{,}000}{(s+30)^2}$

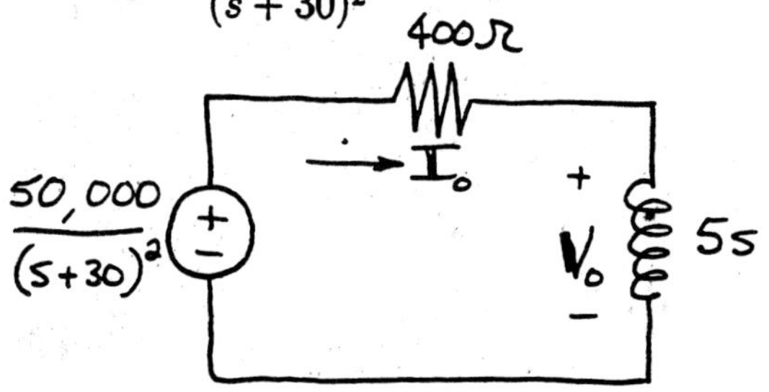

$$I_o = \frac{50{,}000}{(s+30)^2(5s+400)} = \frac{10{,}000}{(s+30)^2(s+80)}$$

$$V_o = 5sI_o = \frac{50{,}000s}{(s+30)^2(s+80)}$$

[b] $I_o = \dfrac{K_1}{(s+30)^2} + \dfrac{K_2}{s+30} + \dfrac{K_3}{s+80}$

$$K_1 = \frac{10{,}000}{50} = 200$$

$$K_2 = \frac{d}{ds}\left[\frac{10{,}000}{s+80}\right]_{s=-30} = -4$$

$$K_3 = \frac{10{,}000}{(-50)^2} = 4$$

$$I_o = \frac{200}{(s+30)^2} - \frac{4}{s+30} + \frac{4}{s+80}$$

$$i_o(t) = [200te^{-30t} - 4e^{-30t} + 4e^{-80t}]u(t)\text{ A}$$

$$V_o = \frac{K_1}{(s+30)^2} + \frac{K_2}{s+30} + \frac{K_3}{s+80}$$

$$K_1 = \frac{50{,}000(-30)}{50} = -30{,}000$$

$$K_2 = \frac{d}{ds}\left[\frac{50{,}000s}{s+80}\right]_{s=-30} = 1600$$

$$K_3 = \frac{50{,}000(-80)}{(-50)^2} = -1600$$

$$v_o(t) = [-30{,}000te^{-30t} + 1600e^{-30t} - 1600e^{-80t}]u(t)\text{ A}$$

P 13.21 [a] For $t < 0$:

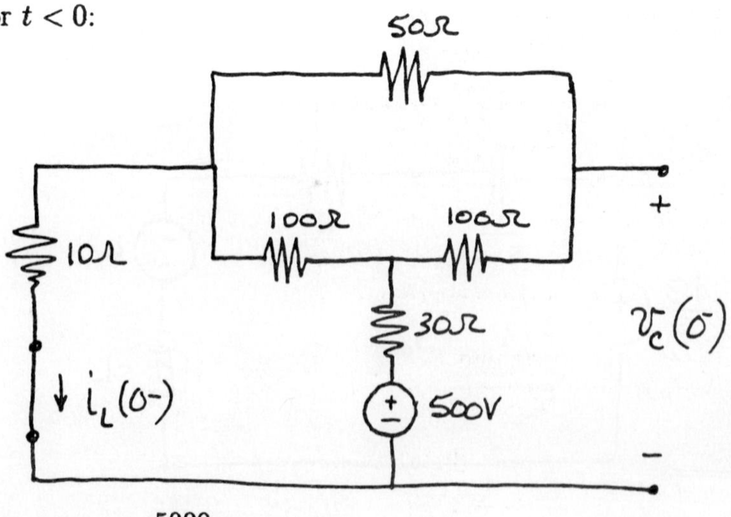

$$i_L(0^-) = \frac{5000}{30 + 60 + 10} = 5\text{ A}$$

$$i_1 = \frac{5(100)}{250} = 2\text{ A}$$

$$v_C(0^-) = 500 - 5(30) - 2(100) = 500 - 350 = 150\text{ V}$$

For $t > 0$:

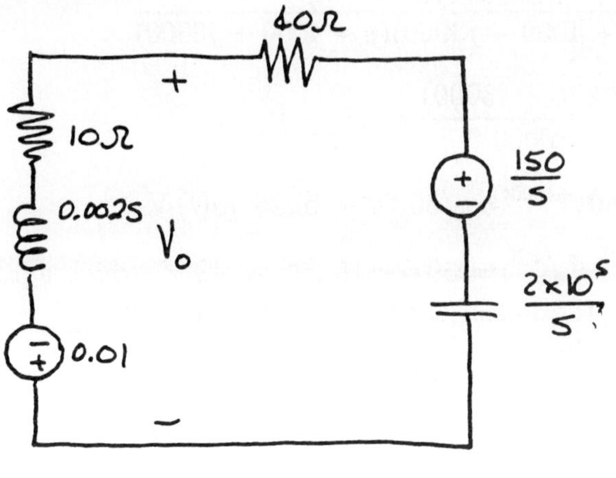

[b] $$\frac{V_o + 0.01}{10 + 0.02s} + \frac{V_o - 150/s}{40 + 2 \times 10^5/s} = 0$$

$$V_o\left[\frac{1}{10 + 0.002s} + \frac{s}{40s + 2 \times 10^5}\right] = \frac{150}{40s + 2 \times 10^5} - \frac{0.01}{10 + 0.002s}$$

$$V_o = \frac{-50(s + 5000)}{s^2 + 25{,}000s + 10^8} = \frac{-50(s + 5000)}{(s + 5000)(s + 20{,}000)}$$

$$V_o = \frac{-50}{s + 20{,}000}$$

[c] $v_o(t) = -50e^{-20,000t}u(t)$ V

P 13.22 [a] $i_o(0^-) = \frac{48}{4} \times 10^{-3} = 12\,\text{mA} = \rho$

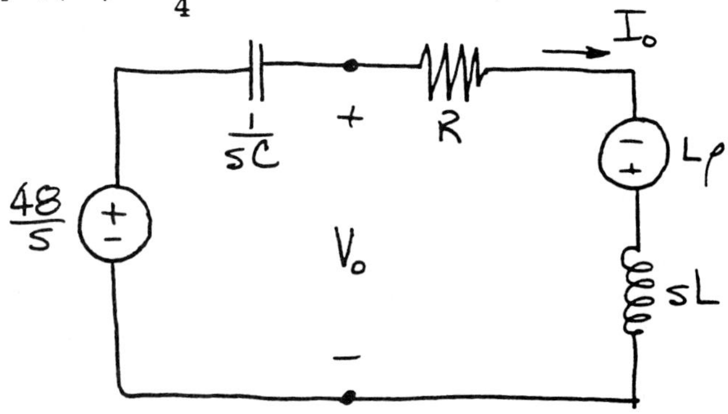

$$\frac{V_o - 48/s}{(1/sC)} + \frac{V_o + \rho L}{R + sL} = 0$$

$$\therefore \quad V_o = \frac{48(s + R/L) - \rho/C}{s^2 + (R/L)s + (1/LC)}$$

When the numerical values are substituted we get

$$V_o = \frac{48(s + 4875)}{(s + 4000 - j3000)(s + 4000 + j3000)}$$

$$K_1 = \frac{48(875 + j3000)}{j6000} = 25\underline{/-16.26^\circ}$$

$$v_o(t) = 50e^{-4000t}\cos(3000t - 16.26^\circ)u(t)\text{ V}$$

Check: $v_o(0^+) = 50\cos(16.26^\circ) = 48$ V, which agrees with the fact that the initial capacitor voltage is zero.

[b] $I_o = \dfrac{48/s + \rho L}{R + sL + (1/sC)} = \dfrac{\rho[s + (48/\rho L)]}{s^2 + (R/L)s + (1/LC)}$

$$I_o = \frac{12 \times 10^{-3}(s + 8000)}{(s + 4000 - j3000)(s + 4000 + j3000)}$$

$$K_1 = \frac{12 \times 10^{-3}(4000 + j3000)}{j6000} = 10 \times 10^{-3}\underline{/-53.13^\circ}$$

$$i_o(t) = 20e^{-4000t}\cos(3000t - 53.13^\circ)u(t)\text{ mA}$$

P 13.23 [a] $i_L(0^-) = i_L(0^+) = 5$ A, down

$v_C(0^-) = v_C(0^+) = 0$

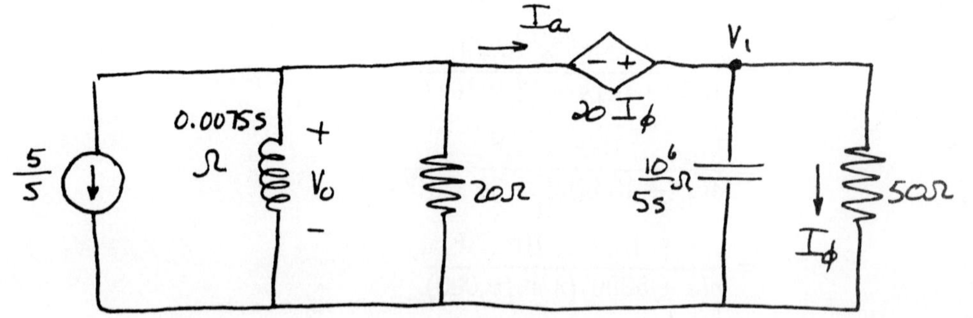

$$\frac{V_o}{20} + \frac{V_o}{0.0075s} + I_a = \frac{-5}{s}$$

$$I_a = \frac{V_1(5s)}{10^6} + \frac{V_1}{50} = \left(\frac{250s + 10^6}{50 \times 10^6}\right) V_1$$

$$V_o + 20I_\phi = V_1; \qquad V_o + 20\frac{V_1}{50} = V_1; \qquad \therefore\ 0.6V_1 = V_o$$

$$\therefore\ \frac{V_o}{20} + \frac{V_o}{0.0075s} + \frac{250s + 10^6}{30 \times 10^6} V_o = \frac{-5}{s}$$

$$\therefore\ (s^2 + 10{,}000s + 16 \times 10^6)V_o = -6 \times 10^5$$

$$V_o = \frac{-6 \times 10^5}{s^2 + 10{,}000s + 16 \times 10^6}$$

[b] $V_o = \dfrac{-6 \times 10^5}{(s + 2000)(s + 8000)}$

$$K_1 = \frac{-6 \times 10^5}{-6000} = 100$$

$$K_2 = \frac{-6 \times 10^5}{6000} = -100$$

$$v_o(t) = [100e^{-8000t} - 100e^{-2000t}]u(t)\ \text{V}$$

P 13.24

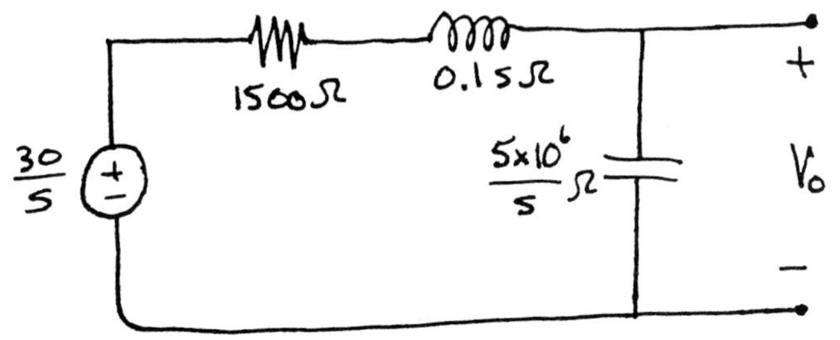

$$V_o = \frac{(30/s)(5 \times 10^6/s)}{1500 + 0.1s + (5 \times 10^6/s)}$$

$$= \frac{1500 \times 10^6}{s(s^2 + 15{,}000s + 50 \times 10^6)}$$

$$= \frac{1500 \times 10^6}{s(s + 5000)(s + 10{,}000)}$$

$$= \frac{K_1}{s} + \frac{K_2}{s + 5000} + \frac{K_3}{s + 10{,}000}$$

$$K_1 = \frac{1500 \times 10^6}{(5000)(10{,}000)} = 30$$

$$K_2 = \frac{1500 \times 10^6}{(-5000)(5000)} = -60$$

$$K_3 = \frac{1500 \times 10^6}{(-5000)(-10{,}000)} = 30$$

$$V_o = \frac{30}{s} - \frac{60}{s + 5000} + \frac{30}{s + 10{,}000}$$

$$v_o(t) = [30 - 60e^{-5000t} + 30e^{-10{,}000t}]u(t)\text{ V}$$

P 13.25 Since we already have the solution for $v_o(t)$ when the initial voltage is zero, we will use superposition to determine the contribution of the initial voltage of -20 V.

$V_{o1} =$ output when $\gamma = 0$

$V_{o2} =$ output when $\gamma = -20$ V

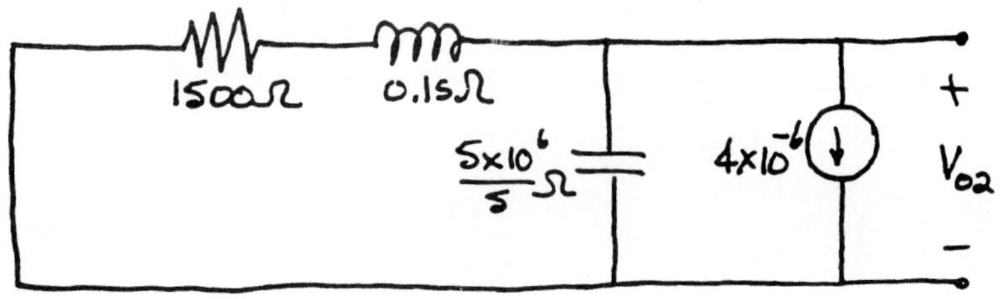

$$4 \times 10^{-6} + \frac{V_{o2}s}{5 \times 10^6} + \frac{V_{o2}}{1500 + 0.1s} = 0$$

$$\therefore \quad V_{o2} = \frac{-20(s+15{,}000)}{s^2+15{,}000s+50\times10^6}$$

$$= \frac{K_1}{s+5000} + \frac{K_2}{s+10{,}000}$$

$$K_1 = \frac{-20(10{,}000)}{5000} = -40$$

$$K_2 = \frac{-20(5000)}{-5000} = 20$$

$$V_{o2} = \frac{-40}{s+5000} + \frac{20}{s+10{,}000}$$

From the solution to Problem 13.24 we have

$$V_{o1} = \frac{30}{s} - \frac{60}{s+5000} + \frac{30}{s+10{,}000}$$

$$V_o - V_{o1} + V_{o2}$$

$$\therefore \quad V_o = \frac{30}{s} - \frac{100}{s+5000} + \frac{50}{s+10{,}000}$$

$$v_o(t) = [30 - 100e^{-5000t} + 50e^{-10{,}000t}]u(t)\ \text{V}$$

P 13.26 [a]

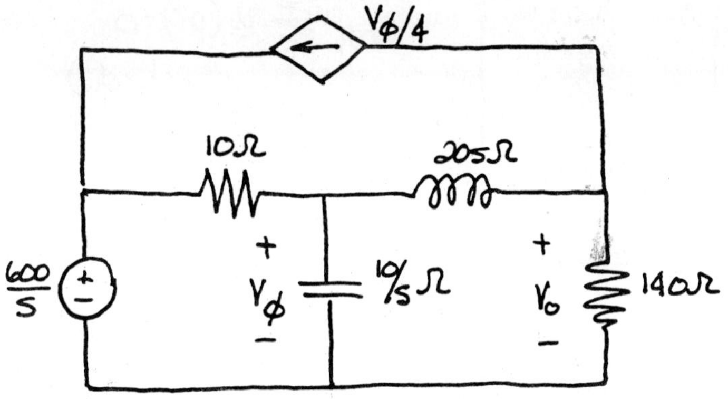

$$\frac{V_\phi}{10/s} + \frac{V_\phi - (600/s)}{10} + \frac{V_\phi - V_o}{20s} = 0$$

$$\frac{V_o}{140} + \frac{V_o - V_\phi}{20s} + \frac{V_\phi}{4} = 0$$

Simplfying,

$(2s^2 + 2s + 1)V_\phi - V_o = 1200$

$(35s - 7)V_\phi + (s + 7)V_o = 0$

$$\Delta = \begin{vmatrix} 2s^2 + 2s + 1 & -1 \\ 35s - 7 & s + 7 \end{vmatrix} = 2s(s^2 + 8s + 25)$$

$$N_2 = \begin{vmatrix} 2s^2 + 2s + 1 & 1200 \\ 35s - 7 & 0 \end{vmatrix} = -42{,}000s + 8400$$

$$V_o = \frac{N_2}{\Delta} = \frac{-21{,}000s + 4200}{s(s^2 + 8s + 25)}$$

[b] $v_o(0^+) = \lim_{s\to\infty} sV_o = 0$

$$v_o(\infty) = \lim_{s\to 0} sV_o = \frac{4200}{25} = 168$$

[c] At $t = 0^+$ the circuit is

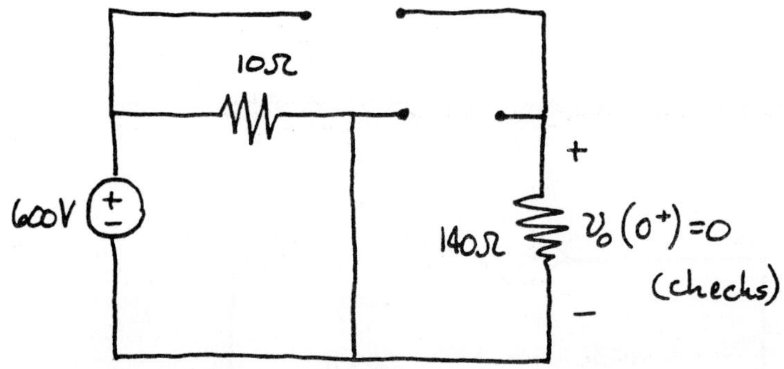

At $t = \infty$ the circuit is

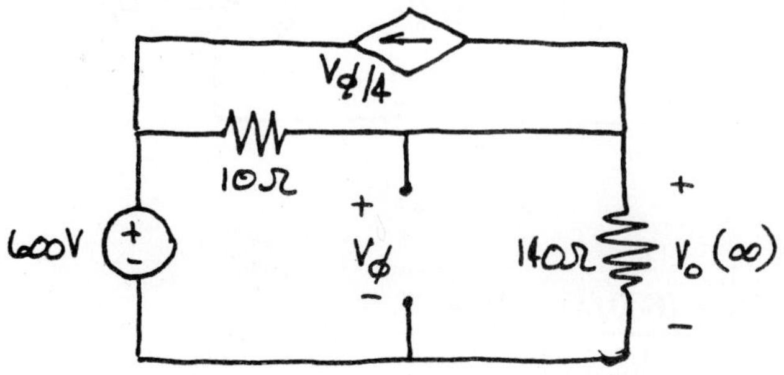

$$\frac{V_\phi - 600}{10} + \frac{V_\phi}{140} + \frac{V_\phi}{4} = 0$$

$\therefore \quad V_\phi = 168\,\text{V} = V_o(\infty) \qquad \text{(checks)}$

[d] $V_o = \dfrac{N_2}{\Delta} = \dfrac{-21{,}000s + 4200}{s(s^2 + 8s + 25)} = \dfrac{K_1}{s} + \dfrac{K_2}{s + 4 - j3} + \dfrac{K_2^*}{s + 4 + j3}$

$$K_1 = \frac{4200}{25} = 168$$

$$K_2 = \frac{-21{,}000(-4 + j3) + 4200}{(-4 + j3)(j6)} = -84 + j3612 = 3612.98\underline{/91.33^\circ}$$

$$v_o(t) = [168 + 7225.95e^{-4t}\cos(3t + 91.33^\circ)]u(t)\,\text{V}$$

Check: $\quad v_o(0^+) = 0\,\text{V}; \qquad v_o(\infty) = 168\,\text{V}$

P 13.27 [a]

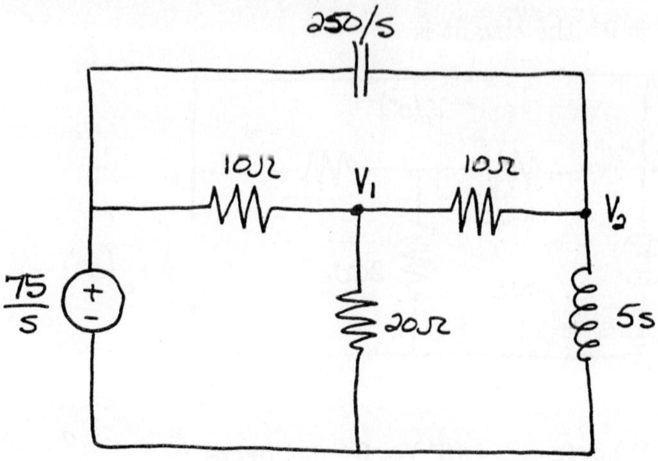

$$\frac{V_1 - 75/s}{10} + \frac{V_1}{20} + \frac{V_1 - V_2}{10} = 0$$

$$\frac{V_2}{5s} + \frac{V_2 - V_1}{10} + \frac{(V_2 - 75/s)s}{250} = 0$$

Thus,

$$5V_1 - 2V_2 = \frac{150}{s}$$

$$-25sV_1 + (s^2 + 25s + 50)V_2 = 75s$$

$$\Delta = \begin{vmatrix} 5 & -2 \\ -25s & s^2 + 25s + 50 \end{vmatrix} = 5(s + 5)(s + 10)$$

$$N_2 = \begin{vmatrix} 5 & 150/s \\ -25s & 75s \end{vmatrix} = 375(s+10)$$

$$V_2 = \frac{N_2}{\Delta} = \frac{375(s+10)}{5(s+5)(s+10)} = \frac{75}{s+5}$$

$$V_o = \frac{75}{s} - \frac{75}{s+5} = \frac{375}{s(s+5)}$$

$$I_o = \frac{V_2}{5s} = \frac{15}{s(s+5)} = \frac{3}{s} - \frac{3}{s+5}$$

[b] $v_o(t) = (75 - 75e^{-5t})u(t)$ V

$i_o(t) = (3 - 3e^{-5t})u(t)$ A

[c] At $t = 0^+$ the circuit is

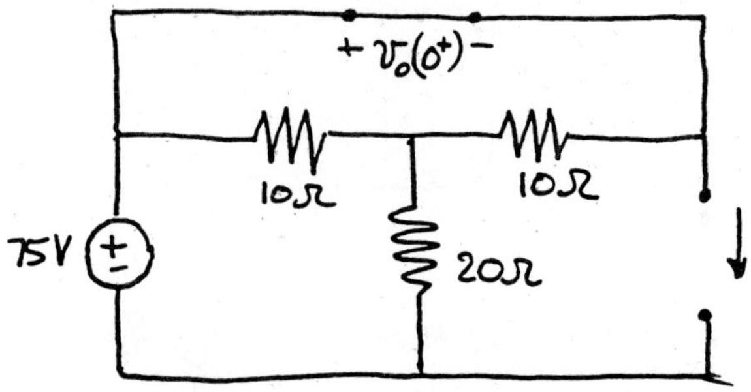

$v_o(0^+) = 0$; $i_o(0^+) = 0$ Checks

At $t = \infty$ the circuit is

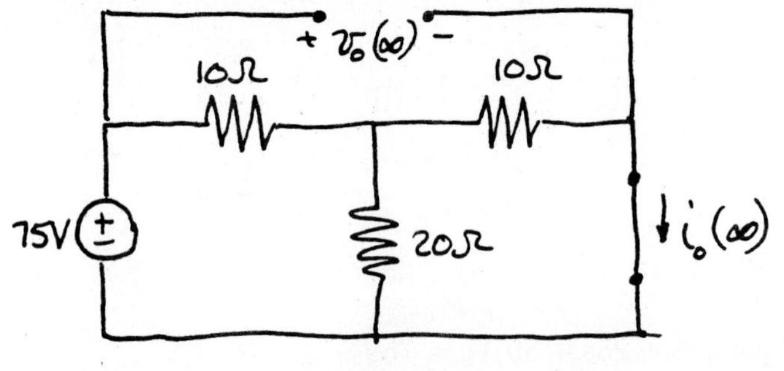

$v_o(\infty) = 75$ V; $i_o(\infty) = \dfrac{75}{10 + (200/30)} \cdot \dfrac{20}{30} = 3$ A Checks

P 13.28 [a]

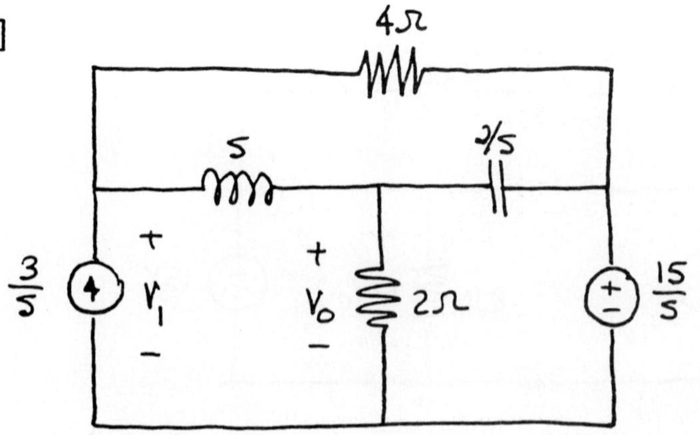

$$\frac{-3}{s} + \frac{V_1 - V_o}{s} + \frac{V_1 - (15/s)}{4} = 0$$

$$\frac{V_o}{2} + \frac{V_o - V_1}{s} + \frac{V_o - (15/s)}{2/s} = 0$$

Simplfying,

$$(s+4)V_1 - 4V_o = 27$$

$$(s^2 + s + 2)V_o - 2V_1 = 15s$$

$$\Delta = \begin{vmatrix} s+4 & -4 \\ -2 & s^2+s+2 \end{vmatrix} = s(s+2)(s+3)$$

$$N_2 = \begin{vmatrix} s+4 & 27 \\ -2 & 15s \end{vmatrix} = 15s^2 + 60s + 54$$

$$V_o = \frac{N_2}{\Delta} = \frac{15s^2 + 60s + 54}{s(s+2)(s+3)} = \frac{K_1}{s} + \frac{K_2}{s+2} + \frac{K_3}{s+3}$$

$$K_1 = \frac{54}{(2)(3)} = 9; \quad K_2 = \frac{60 - 120 + 54}{(-2)(1)} = 3$$

$$K_3 = \frac{135 - 180 + 54}{(-3)(-1)} = 3$$

$$\therefore \quad V_o = \frac{9}{s} + \frac{3}{s+2} + \frac{3}{s+3}$$

[b] $v_o(t) = (9 + 3e^{-2t} + 3e^{-3t})u(t)$ V

At $t = 0^+$:

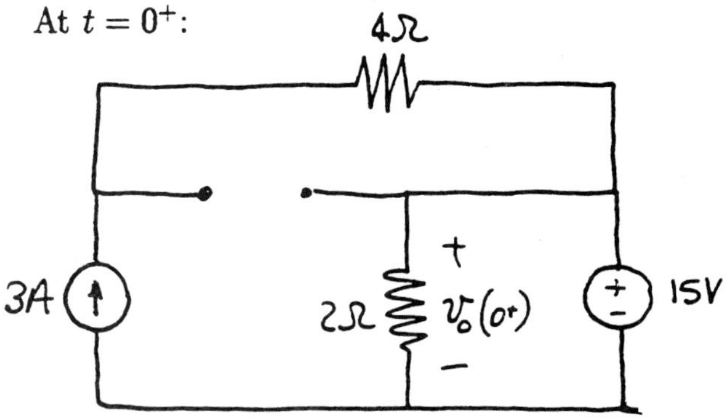

$v_o(0^+) = 15\,\text{V(checks)}$

At $t = \infty$:

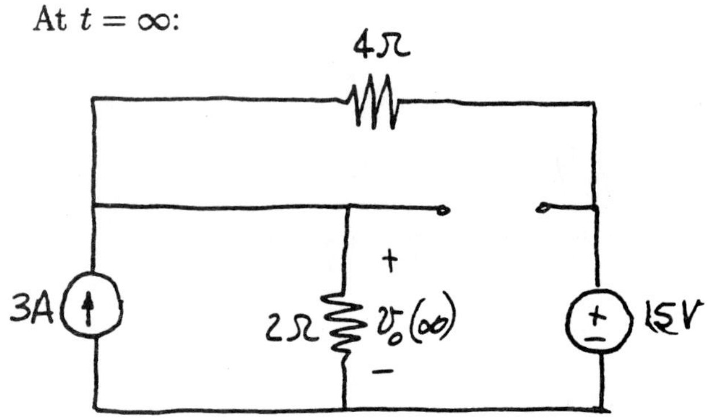

$$\frac{v_o(\infty)}{2} - 3 + \frac{v_o(\infty) - 15}{4} = 0$$

$\therefore\ 3v_o(\infty) = 27; \qquad \therefore\ v_o(\infty) = 9\,\text{V(checks)}$

P 13.29 [a]

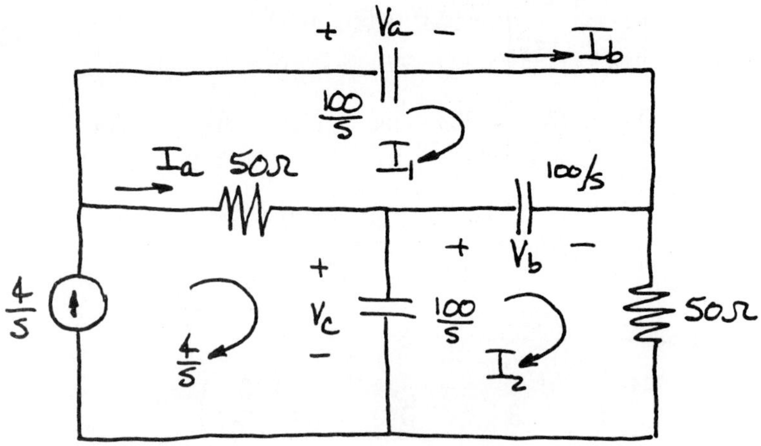

$$\frac{100}{s}I_1 + \frac{100}{s}(I_1 - I_2) + 50(I_1 - 4/s) = 0$$

$$\frac{100}{s}(I_2 - 4/s) + \frac{100}{s}(I_2 - I_1) + 50I_2 = 0$$

Simplifying,

$$(s+4)I_1 - 2I_2 = 4$$

$$-2I_1 + (s+4)I_2 = \frac{8}{s}$$

$$\Delta = \begin{vmatrix} (s+4) & -2 \\ -2 & (s+4) \end{vmatrix} = s^2 + 8s + 12 = (s+2)(s+6)$$

$$N_1 = \begin{vmatrix} 4 & -2 \\ 8/s & (s+4) \end{vmatrix} = \frac{4s^2 + 16s + 16}{s} = \frac{4(s+2)^2}{s}$$

$$I_1 = \frac{N_1}{\Delta} = \frac{4(s+2)^2}{s(s+2)(s+6)} = \frac{4(s+2)}{s(s+6)} = \frac{4/3}{s} + \frac{8/3}{s+6}$$

$$N_2 = \begin{vmatrix} (s+4) & 4 \\ -2 & 8/s \end{vmatrix} = \frac{16s + 32}{s} = \frac{16(s+2)}{s}$$

$$I_2 = \frac{N_2}{\Delta} = \frac{16(s+2)}{s(s+2)(s+6)} = \frac{16}{s(s+6)} = \frac{8/3}{s} - \frac{8/3}{s+6}$$

$$I_a = \frac{4}{s} - I_1 = \frac{8/3}{s} - \frac{8/3}{s+6}$$

$$I_b = I_1 = \frac{4/3}{s} + \frac{8/3}{s+6}$$

[b] $i_a(t) = (8/3)(1 - e^{-6t})u(t)$ A

$i_b(t) = (4/3)(1 + 2e^{-6t})u(t)$ A

[c] $$V_a = \frac{100}{s}I_b = \frac{100}{s}\left(\frac{4/3}{s} + \frac{8/3}{s+6}\right)$$

$$= \frac{400/3}{s^2} + \frac{800/3}{s(s+6)} = \frac{400/3}{s^2} + \frac{400/9}{s} - \frac{400/9}{s+6}$$

$$V_b = \frac{100}{s}(I_2 - I_1) = \frac{100}{s}\left(\frac{4/3}{s} - \frac{16/3}{s(s+6)}\right)$$

$$= \frac{400/3}{s^2} - \frac{1600/3}{s(s+6)} = \frac{400/3}{s^2} - \frac{800/9}{s} + \frac{800/9}{s+6}$$

$$V_c = \frac{100}{s}(4/s - I_2) = \frac{100}{s}\left(\frac{4/3}{s} + \frac{8/3}{s+6}\right)$$

$$= \frac{400/3}{s^2} + \frac{800/3}{s(s+6)} = \frac{400/3}{s^2} + \frac{400/9}{s} - \frac{400/9}{s+6}$$

[d] $v_a(t) = (400/9)(3t + 1 - e^{-6t})u(t)$ V

$v_b(t) = (400/9)(3t - 2 + 2e^{-6t})u(t)$ V

$v_c(t) = (400/9)(3t + 1 - e^{-6t})u(t)$ V

P 13.30 [a]

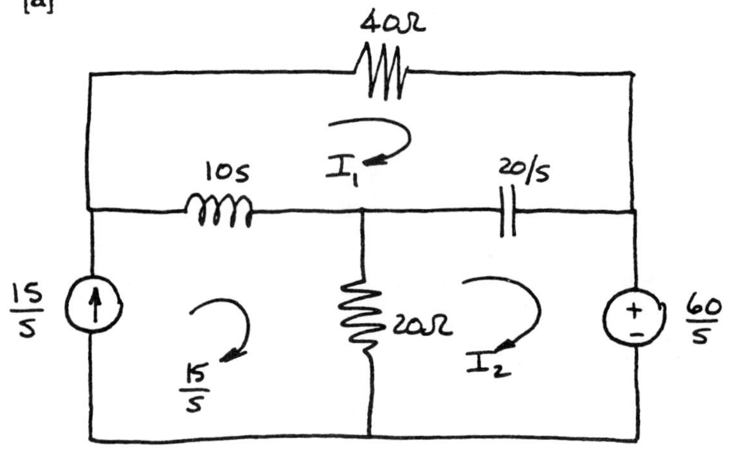

$$40I_1 + \frac{20}{s}(I_1 - I_2) + 10s(I_1 - 15/s) = 0$$

$$20(I_2 - 15/s) + \frac{20}{s}(I_2 - I_1) + \frac{60}{s} = 0$$

or

$$(s^2 + 4s + 2)I_1 - 2I_2 = 15s$$

$$-I_1 + (s+1)I_2 = 12$$

$$\Delta = \begin{vmatrix} (s^2+4s+2) & -2 \\ -1 & (s+1) \end{vmatrix} = 5(s+2)(s+3)$$

$$N_1 = \begin{vmatrix} 15s & -2 \\ 12 & (s+1) \end{vmatrix} = 15s^2 + 15s + 24$$

$$I_1 = \frac{N_1}{\Delta} = \frac{15s^2 + 15s + 24}{s(s+2)(s+3)}$$

$$N_2 = \begin{vmatrix} (s^2+4s+2) & 15s \\ -1 & 12 \end{vmatrix} = 12s^2 + 63s + 24$$

$$I_2 = \frac{N_2}{\Delta} = \frac{12s^2 + 63s + 24}{s(s+2)(s+3)}$$

[b] $sI_1 = \dfrac{15s^2 + 15s + 24}{(s+2)(s+3)}$

$$\lim_{s\to\infty} sI_1 = 15 \qquad \therefore \; i_1(0^+) = 15\,\text{A}$$

$$\lim_{s\to 0} sI_1 = 4 \qquad \therefore \; i_1(\infty) = 4\,\text{A}$$

$$sI_2 = \frac{12s^2 + 63s + 24}{(s+2)(s+3)}$$

$$\lim_{s\to\infty} sI_2 = 12 \qquad \therefore \; i_2(0^+) = 12\,\text{A}$$

$$\lim_{s\to 0} sI_2 = 4 \qquad \therefore \; i_2(\infty) = 4\,\text{A}$$

[c] $I_1 = \dfrac{4}{s} - \dfrac{27}{s+2} + \dfrac{38}{s+3}$

$$i_1(t) = (4 - 27e^{-2t} + 38e^{-3t})u(t)\,\text{A}$$

$$I_2 = \frac{4}{s} + \frac{27}{s+2} - \frac{19}{s+3}$$

$$i_2(t) = (4 + 27e^{-2t} - 19e^{-3t})u(t)\,\text{A}$$

P 13.31 [a]

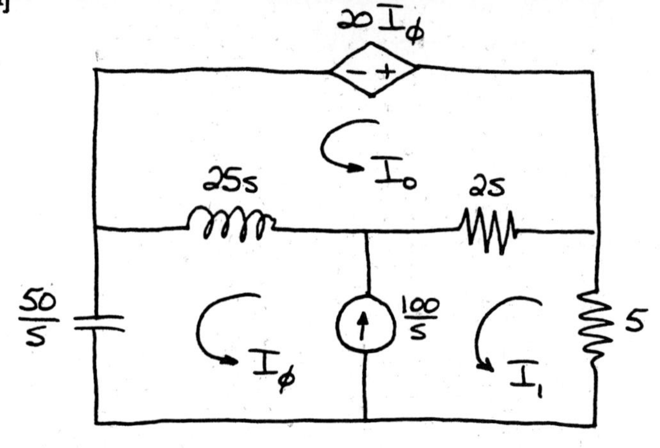

$$20I_\phi + 25s(I_o - I_\phi) + 25(I_o - I_1) = 0$$

$$25s(I_\phi - I_o) + \frac{50}{s}I_o + 5I_1 + 2s(I_1 - I_o) = 0$$

$$I_\phi - I_1 = \frac{100}{s}; \qquad \therefore \quad I_1 = I_\phi - \frac{100}{s}$$

Simplifying,

$$(-5s-1)I_\phi + (5s+5)I_o = -500/s$$

$$(5s^2+6s+10)I_\phi + (-5s^2-5s)I_o = 600$$

$$\Delta = \begin{vmatrix} -5s-1 & 5s+5 \\ 5s^2+6s+10 & -5s^2-5s \end{vmatrix} = -25(s^2+3s+2)$$

$$N_2 = \begin{vmatrix} -5s-1 & -500/s \\ 5s^2+6s+10 & 600 \end{vmatrix} = -\frac{500}{s}(s^2-4.8s-10)$$

$$I_o = \frac{N_2}{\Delta} = \frac{20s^2-96s-200}{s(s+1)(s+2)}$$

[b] $i_o(0^+) = \lim_{s\to\infty} sI_o = 20\,\text{A}$

$$i_o(\infty) = \lim_{s\to 0} sI_o = \frac{-200}{2} = -100\,\text{A}$$

[c] At $t = 0^+$ the circuit is

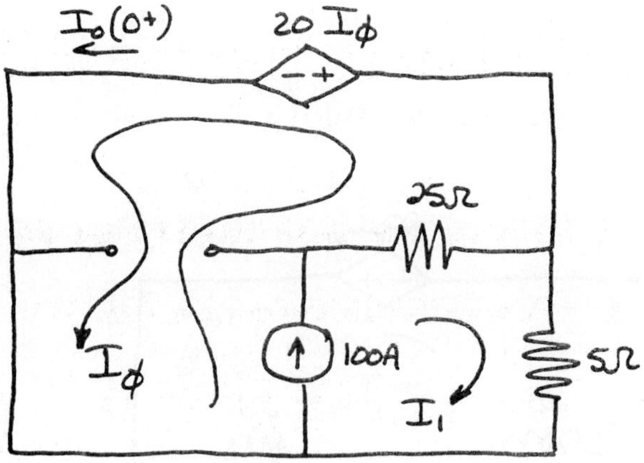

$$20I_\phi - 5I_1 = 0; \quad I_1 + I_\phi = 100$$

$$\therefore \quad 20I_\phi - 5(100 - I_\phi) = 0; \qquad 25I_\phi = 500$$

$$\therefore \quad I_\phi = I_o(0^+) = 20\,\text{A}(\text{checks})$$

At $t + \infty$ the circuit is

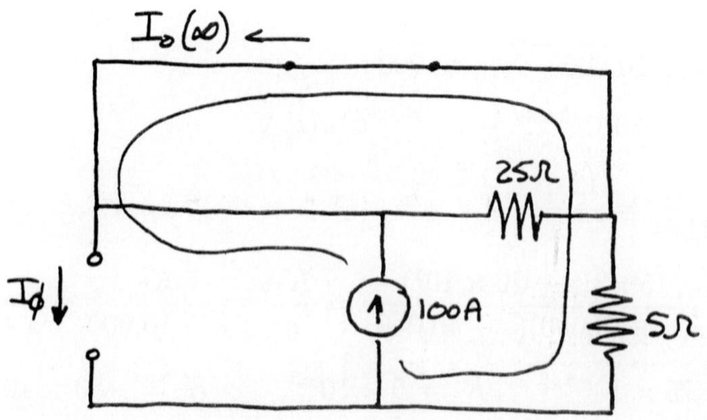

$$I_o(\infty) = -100\,\text{A(checks)}$$

[d] $$I_o = \frac{20s^2 - 96s - 200}{s(s+1)(s+2)} = \frac{K_1}{s} + \frac{K_2}{s+1} + \frac{K_3}{s+2}$$

$$K_1 = \frac{-200}{(1)(2)} = -100; \qquad K_2 - \frac{20 + 96 - 200}{(-1)(1)} = 84$$

$$K_3 = \frac{80 + 192 - 200}{(-2)(-1)} = 36$$

$$I_o = \frac{-100}{s} + \frac{84}{s+1} + \frac{36}{s+2}$$

$$i_o(t) = (-100 + 84e^{-t} + 36e^{-2t})u(t)\,\text{A}$$

$$i_o(\infty) = -100\,\text{A(checks)}$$

$$i_o(0^+) = -100 + 84 + 36 = 20\,\text{A(checks)}$$

P 13.32 [a]

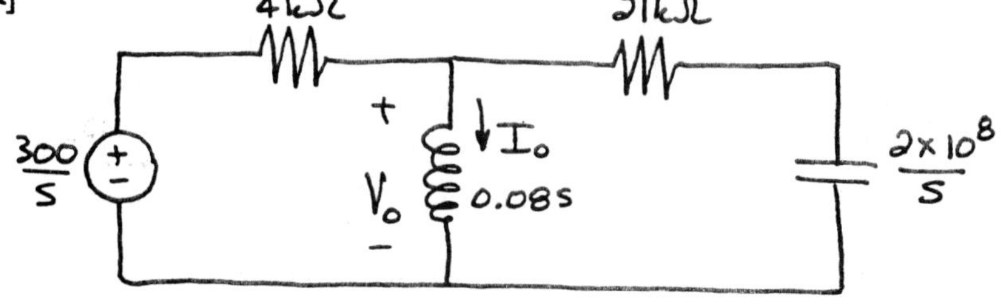

$$\frac{V_o - 300/s}{4000} + \frac{12.5V_o}{s} + \frac{V_o s}{21{,}000s + 2 \times 10^8} = 0$$

$$\therefore \quad V_o = \frac{12(21s + 20 \times 10^4)}{(s + 10{,}000)(s + 40{,}000)} = \frac{K_1}{s + 10{,}000} + \frac{K_2}{s + 40{,}000}$$

$K_1 = -4; \qquad K_2 = 256$

$$V_o = \frac{-4}{s + 10{,}000} + \frac{256}{s + 40{,}000}$$

$v_o(t) = (256e^{-40{,}000t} - 4e^{-10{,}000t})u(t)\ \text{V}$

[b] $I_o = \dfrac{V_o}{0.08s} = \dfrac{12.5V_o}{s}$

$$I_o = \frac{150(21s + 20 \times 10^4)}{s(s + 10{,}000)(s + 40{,}000)} = \frac{K_1}{s} + \frac{K_2}{s + 10{,}000} + \frac{K_3}{s + 40{,}000}$$

$K_1 = 75 \times 10^{-3}; \qquad K_2 = 5 \times 10^{-3}; \qquad K_3 = -80 \times 10^{-3}$

$i_o(t) = (75 + 5e^{-10{,}000t} - 80e^{-40{,}000t})u(t)\ \text{mA}$

[c] At $t = 0^+$ the circuit is

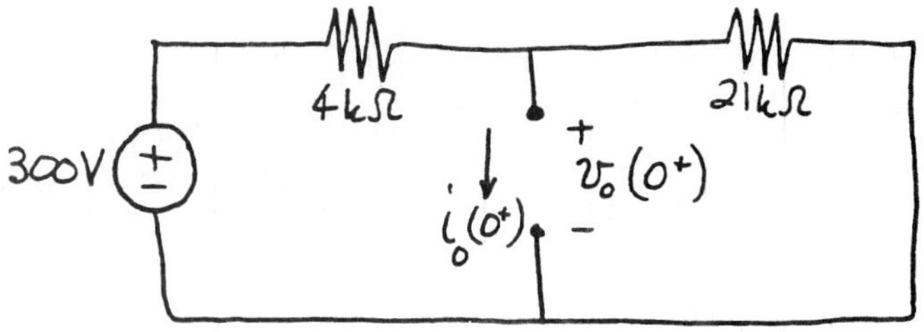

$\therefore \quad v_o(0^+) = \dfrac{300}{25}(21) = 252\ \text{V}; \qquad i_o(0^+) = 0$

Both values agree with our solutions for v_o and i_o.
At $t = \infty$ the circuit is

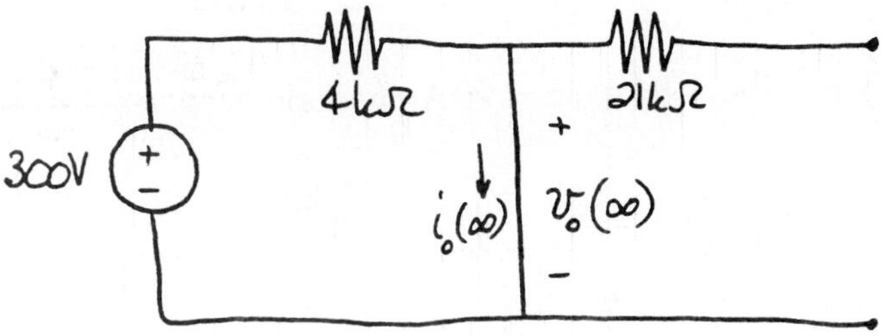

$\therefore \quad v_o(\infty) = 0; \qquad i_o(\infty) = 75\ \text{mA}$

Both values agree with our solutions for v_o and i_o.

P 13.33 $\quad v_C = 12 \times 10^5 te^{-5000t}\ \text{V}, \quad C = 5\ \mu\text{F}; \qquad$ therefore

$$i_C = C\left(\frac{dv_C}{dt}\right) = 6e^{-5000t}(1 - 5000t)\ \text{V}$$

$i_C > 0$ when $1 > 5000t$ or $i_C \geq 0$ when $0 \leq t \leq 200\ \mu\text{s}$

and $i_C < 0$ when $t > 200\,\mu s$

$i_C = 0$ when $1 - 5000t = 0$, or $t = 200\,\mu s$

$$\frac{dv_C}{dt} = 12 \times 10^5 e^{-5000t}[1 - 5000t]$$

$$\therefore\ i_C = 0 \text{ when } \frac{dv_C}{dt} = 0$$

P 13.34 [a] The s-domain equivalent circuit is

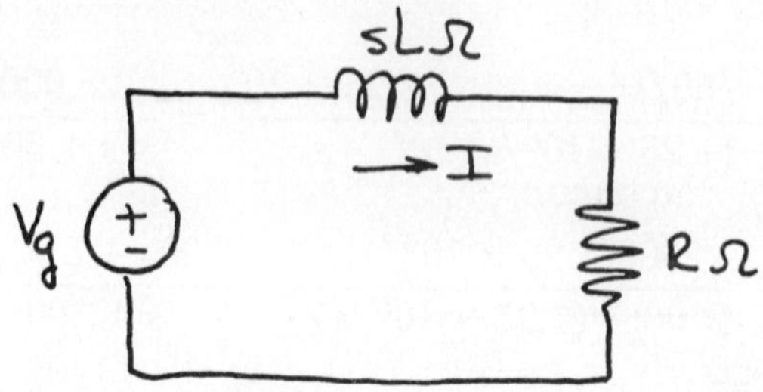

$$I = \frac{V_g}{R + sL} = \frac{V_g/L}{s + (R/L)}, \qquad V_g = \frac{V_m(\omega\cos\phi + s\sin\phi)}{s^2 + \omega^2}$$

$$I = \frac{K_0}{s + R/L} + \frac{K_1}{s - j\omega} + \frac{K_1^*}{s + j\omega}$$

$$K_0 = \frac{V_m(\omega L\cos\phi - R\sin\phi)}{R^2 + \omega^2 L^2}, \qquad K_1 = \frac{V_m\underline{/\phi - 90 - \theta(\omega)}}{2\sqrt{R^2 + \omega^2 L^2}}$$

where $\tan\theta(\omega) = \omega L/R$. Therefore, we have

$$i(t) = \frac{V_m(\omega L\cos\phi - R\sin\phi)}{R^2 + \omega^2 L^2}e^{-(R/L)t} + \frac{V_m\sin[\omega t + \phi - \theta(\omega)]}{\sqrt{R^2 + \omega^2 L^2}}$$

[b] $$i_{ss}(t) = \frac{V_m}{\sqrt{R^2 + \omega^2 L^2}}\sin[\omega t + \phi - \theta(\omega)]$$

[c] $$i_{tr} = \frac{V_m(\omega L\cos\phi - R\sin\phi)}{R^2 + \omega^2 L^2}e^{-(R/L)t}$$

[d] $$\mathbf{I} = \frac{\mathbf{V}_g}{R + j\omega L}, \qquad \mathbf{V}_g = V_m\underline{/\phi}$$

Therefore $$\mathbf{I} = \frac{V_m\underline{/\phi}}{\sqrt{R^2 + \omega^2 L^2}\underline{/\theta(\omega)}} = \frac{V_m}{\sqrt{R^2 + \omega^2 L^2}}\underline{/\phi - \theta(\omega)}$$

Therefore $$i_{ss} = \frac{V_m}{\sqrt{R^2 + \omega^2 L^2}}\sin[\omega t + \phi - \theta(\omega)]$$

[e] The transient component vanishes when

$$\omega L \cos\phi = R\sin\phi \quad \text{or} \quad \tan\phi = \frac{\omega L}{R} \quad \text{or} \quad \phi = \theta(\omega)$$

P 13.35

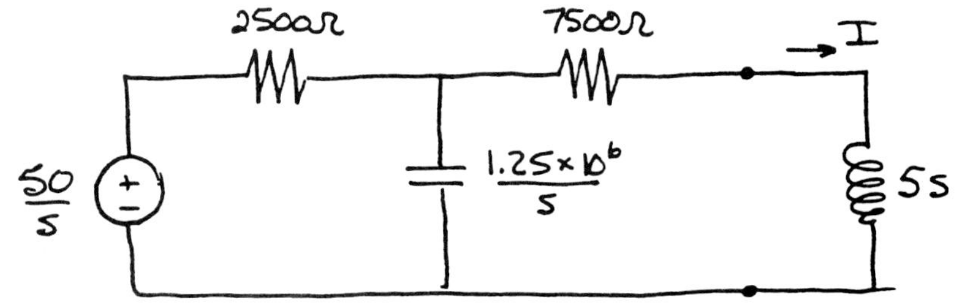

$$V_{\rm Th} = \frac{50/s}{2500 + (1.25 \times 10^6/s)} \cdot \frac{1.25 \times 10^6}{s} = \frac{25{,}000}{s(s+500)}$$

$$Z_{\rm Th} = 7500 + \frac{2500(1.25 \times 10^6/s)}{2500 + (1.25 \times 10^6/s)} = \frac{7500s + 5 \times 10^6}{s+500}$$

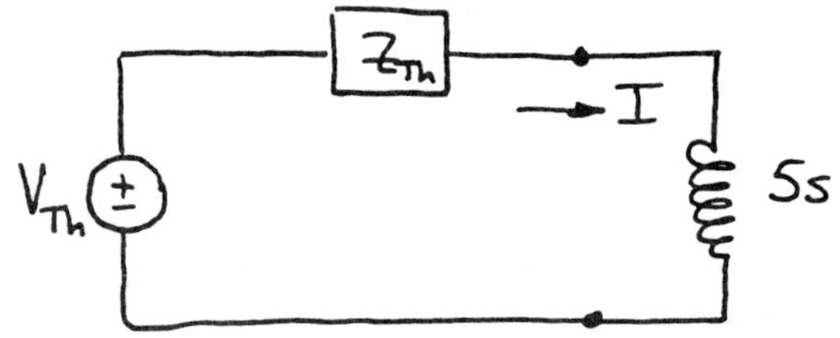

$$I = \frac{25{,}000/s(s+500)}{5s + \dfrac{7500s + 5 \times 10^6}{s+500}}$$

$$= \frac{5000}{s(s^2 + 2000s + 10^6)} = \frac{5000}{s(s+1000)^2}$$

$$= \frac{K_1}{s} + \frac{K_2}{(s+1000)^2} + \frac{K_3}{s+1000}$$

$$K_1 = \frac{5000}{10^6} = 5 \times 10^{-3}$$

$$K_2 = \frac{5000}{-1000} = -5000 \times 10^{-3}$$

$$K_3 = \frac{d}{ds}\left(\frac{5000}{s}\right)_{s=-1000} = -5 \times 10^{-3}$$

$$i(t) = [5 - 5000te^{-1000t} - 5e^{-1000t}]u(t)\,\text{mA}$$

P 13.36 For $t < 0$:

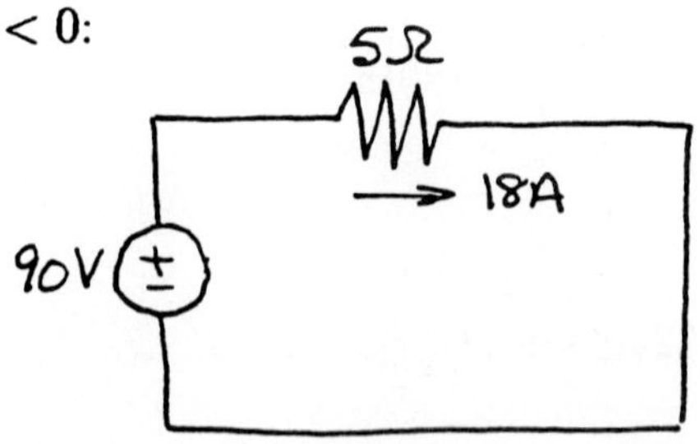

For $t > 0^+$:

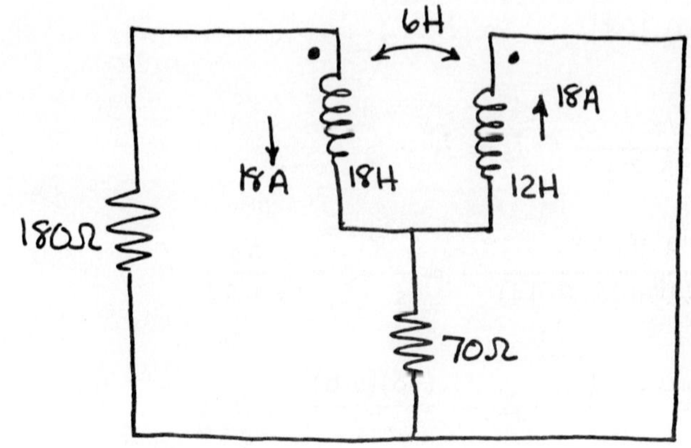

$L_1 - M = 18 - 6 = 12\,\text{H}; \qquad L_2 - M = 12 - 6 = 6\,\text{H}$

$18 \times 12 = 216; \qquad 18 \times 6 = 108$

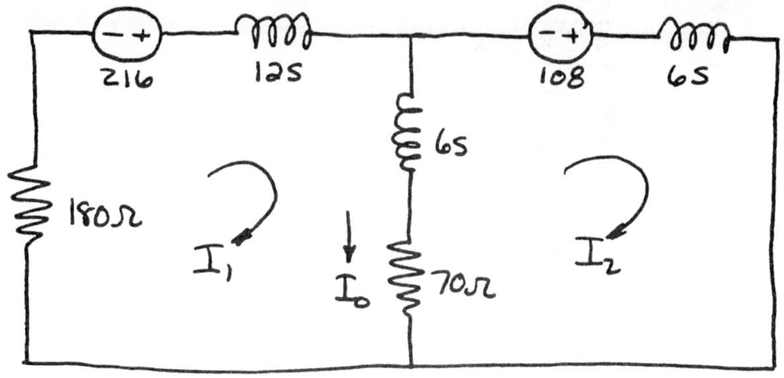

$$180I_1 - 216 + 12sI_1 + 6s(I_1 - I_2) + 70(I_1 - I_2) = 0$$

$$70(I_2 - I_1) + 6s(I_2 - I_1) - 108 + 6sI_2 = 0$$

$$\therefore\quad \Delta = \begin{vmatrix} (18s+250) & -(6s+70) \\ -(6s+70) & (12s+70) \end{vmatrix} = 180(s+5)(s+14)$$

$$N_1 = \begin{vmatrix} 216 & -(6s+70) \\ 108 & (12s+70) \end{vmatrix} = 3240(s+7)$$

$$N_2 = \begin{vmatrix} (18s+250) & 216 \\ -(6s+70) & 108 \end{vmatrix} = 3240(s+13)$$

$$I_1 = \frac{N_1}{\Delta}; \qquad I_2 = \frac{N_2}{\Delta}; \qquad I_o = I_1 - I_2$$

$$\therefore\quad I_o = \frac{3240[(s+7)-(s+13)]}{180(s+5)(s+14)} = \frac{K_1}{s+5} + \frac{K_2}{s+14}$$

$$K_1 = \frac{(18)(-6)}{9} = -12; \qquad K_2 = \frac{(18)(-6)}{-9} = 12$$

$$I_o = \frac{-12}{s+5} + \frac{12}{s+14}$$

$$i_o(t) = (12e^{-14t} - 12e^{-5t})u(t)\text{ A}$$

P 13.37 The s-domain equivalent circuit is

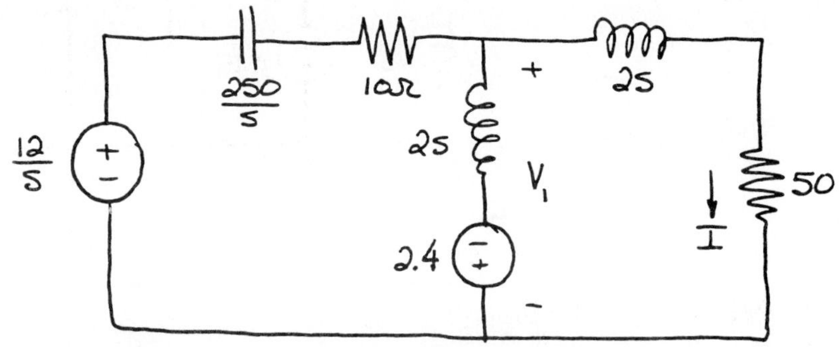

$$\frac{V_1 - 12/s}{10 + (250/s)} + \frac{V_1 + 2.4}{2s} + \frac{V_1}{2s+50} = 0$$

$$V_1 = \frac{-300(s+25)}{(s+25)(s^2+10s+125)} = \frac{-300}{s^2+10s+125}$$

$$I_o = \frac{-300}{(2s + 50)(s^2 + 10s + 125)}$$

$$= \frac{-150}{(s + 25)(s + 5 - j10)(s + 5 + j10)}$$

$$= \frac{K_1}{s + 25} + \frac{K_2}{s + 5 - j10} + \frac{K_2^*}{s + 5 + j10}$$

$$K_1 = \frac{-150}{625 - 250 + 125} = -300 \times 10^{-3}$$

$$K_2 = \frac{-150}{(-5 + j10 + 25)(j20)} = 150\sqrt{5} \times 10^{-3}\underline{/63.43^\circ}$$

$$i_o(t) = [-300e^{-25t} + 300\sqrt{5}e^{-5t}\cos(10t + 63.43^\circ)]u(t)\,\text{mA}$$

P 13.38 [a] $w = \frac{1}{2}L_1 i_1^2 + \frac{1}{2}L_2 i_2^2 + M i_1 i_2$

$$w = \left[\frac{1}{2}(40)(9) + \frac{1}{2}(90)(4) + 30(6)\right] \times 10^{-3} = 540\,\text{mJ}$$

[b] The s-domain circuit:

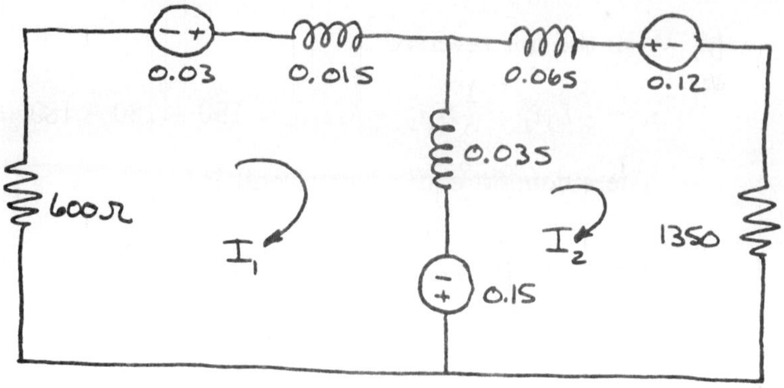

$$(600 + 0.04s)I_1 - 0.03sI_2 = 0.18$$

$$-0.03sI_1 + (0.09s + 1350)I_2 = -0.27$$

$$\Delta = \begin{vmatrix} 0.04(s + 15{,}000) & -0.03s \\ -0.03s & 0.09(s + 15{,}000) \end{vmatrix}$$

$$= 27 \times 10^{-4}(s + 10{,}000)(s + 30{,}000)$$

$$N_1 = \begin{vmatrix} 0.18 & -0.03s \\ -0.27 & 0.09(s+15{,}000) \end{vmatrix} = 81 \times 10^{-4}(s + 30{,}000)$$

$$I_1 = \frac{N_1}{\Delta} = \frac{3}{s + 10{,}000}$$

$$N_2 = \begin{vmatrix} 0.04(s+15{,}000) & 0.18 \\ -0.03s & -0.27 \end{vmatrix} = -54 \times 10^{-4}(s + 30{,}000)$$

$$I_2 = \frac{N_2}{\Delta} = \frac{-2}{s + 10{,}000}$$

[c] $i_1(t) = 3e^{-10{,}000t}u(t)$ A; $\quad i_2(t) = -2e^{-10{,}000t}u(t)$ A

[d] $p_{600\Omega} = (600)(9e^{-20{,}000t}) = 5400e^{-20{,}000t}$ W

$$p_{1350\Omega} = (1350)(4e^{-20{,}000t}) = 5400e^{-20{,}000t} \text{ W}$$

$$w_{600} = \frac{5400}{20} \times 10^{-3} = 270 \text{ mJ}$$

$$w_{1350} = \frac{5400}{20} \times 10^{-3} = 270 \text{ mJ}$$

$$w_T = 540 \text{ mJ}$$

[e] With the dot reversed,

$$w = \frac{1}{2}L_1 i_1^2 + \frac{1}{2}L_2 i_2^2 - M i_1 i_2 = 180 + 180 - 180 = 180 \text{ mJ}$$

The s-domain equivalent circuit is

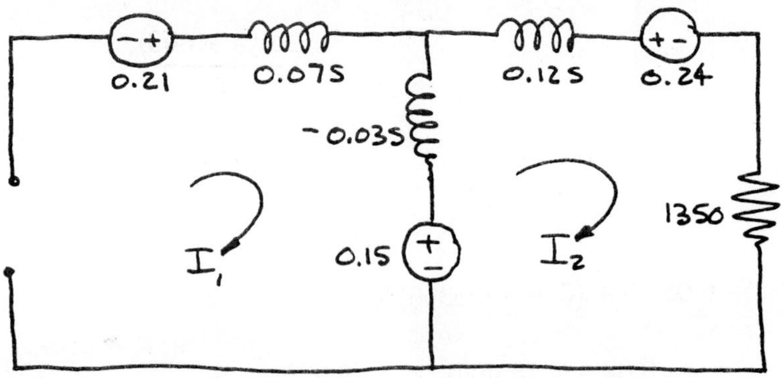

Solving for I_1 and I_2 yields

$$I_1 = \frac{3}{s + 30{,}000}; \qquad I_2 = \frac{-2}{s + 30{,}000}$$

$$\therefore \quad i_1(t) = 3e^{-20{,}000t}u(t)\text{ A}; \qquad i_2(t) = -2e^{-20{,}000t}u(t)\text{ A}$$

$$w_{600} = 5400\int_0^{\infty} e^{-60{,}000t}\,dt = 90\text{ mJ}$$

$$w_{1350} = 5400\int_0^{\infty} e^{-60{,}000t}\,dt = 90\text{ mJ}$$

$$w_T = 180\text{ mJ}$$

P 13.39 [a]

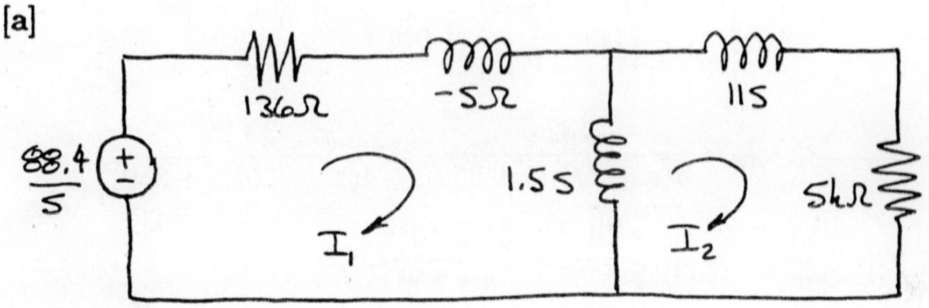

$$\frac{88.4}{s} = 136I_1 - sI_1 + 1.5s(I_1 - I_2)$$

$$0 = 1.5s(I_2 - I_1) + 11sI_2 + 5000I_2$$

Simplifying,

$$\frac{88.4}{s} = (0.5s + 136)I_1 - 1.5sI_2$$

$$0 = -1.5sI_1 + (12.5s + 5000)I_2$$

$$\Delta = \begin{vmatrix} 0.5s + 136 & -1.5s \\ -1.5s & 12.5s + 5000 \end{vmatrix} = 4(s + 200)(s + 850)$$

$$N_1 = \begin{vmatrix} 88.4/s & -1.5s \\ 0 & 12.5s + 5000 \end{vmatrix} = \frac{1105(s + 400)}{s}$$

$$I_1 = \frac{N_1}{\Delta} = \frac{276.25(s + 400)}{s(s + 200)(s + 850)}$$

[b] $$sI_1 = \frac{276.25(s + 400)}{(s + 200)(s + 850)}$$

$$\lim_{s\to 0} sI_1 = i_1(\infty) = 650\text{ mA}$$

$$\lim_{s\to\infty} sI_1 = i_1(0) = 0$$

[c] $I_1 = \dfrac{K_1}{s} + \dfrac{K_2}{s+200} + \dfrac{K_3}{s+850}$

$K_1 = 650 \times 10^{-3}; \qquad K_2 = -425 \times 10^{-3}; \qquad K_3 = -225 \times 10^{-3}$

$i_1(t) = (650 - 425e^{-200t} - 225e^{-850t})u(t)$ mA

P 13.40 [a] From the solution to Problem 13.39 we have

$$N_2 = \begin{vmatrix} 0.5s + 136 & 88.4/s \\ -1.5s & 0 \end{vmatrix} = 132.6$$

$$\therefore \quad I_2 = \frac{132.6}{4(s+200)(s+850)} = \frac{33.15}{4(s+200)(s+850)}$$

$$= \frac{51 \times 10^{-3}}{s+200} - \frac{51 \times 10^{-3}}{s+850}$$

$i_2(t) = (51e^{-200t} - 51e^{-850t})u(t)$ mA

[b] Reversing the dot on the 12.5 H coil will reverse the sign of M, thus the circuit becomes

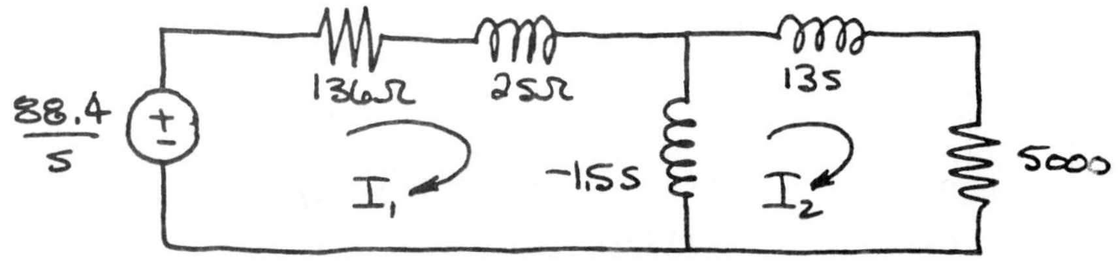

The two simulanteous equations are

$$\frac{88.4}{s} = (136 + 0.5s)I_1 + 1.5sI_2$$

$$0 = 1.5sI_1 + (12.5s + 5000)I_2$$

When these equations are compared to those derived in Problem 13.39 we see the only difference is the algebraic sign of the 1.5s term. Thus reversing the dot will have no effect on I_1 and will reverse the sign of I_2. Hence,

$i_2(t) = (-51e^{-200t} + 51e^{-850t})u(t)$ mA

P 13.41 [a] s-domain equivalent circuit is

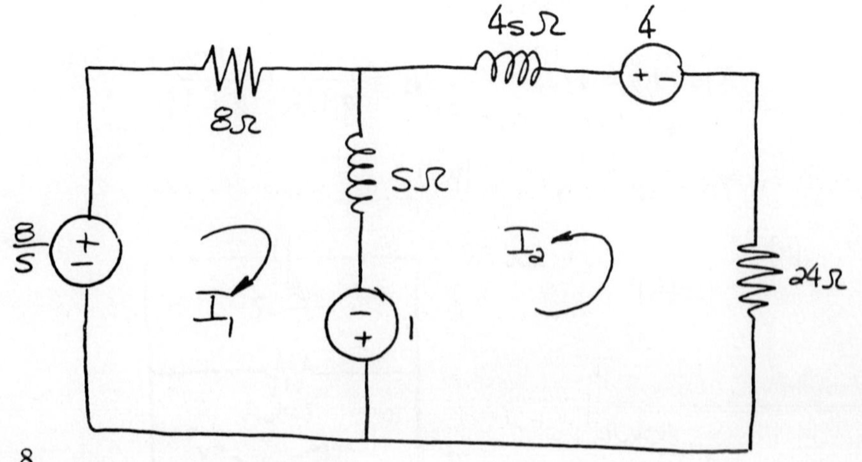

[b] $\frac{8}{s} = 8I_1 + s(I_1 - I_2) - 10$

$0 = -1 + s(I_2 - I_1) + 4sI_2 - 4 + 24I_2$

or

$\frac{8}{s} + 1 - (s + 8)I_1 + sI_2$

$5 = -sI_1 + (5s + 24)I_2$

$$\Delta = \begin{vmatrix} s+8 & s \\ s & 5s+24 \end{vmatrix} = 4(s + 4)(s + 12)$$

$$I_2 = \frac{N_2}{\Delta}$$

$$N_2 = \begin{vmatrix} s+8 & (8/s)+1 \\ s & 5 \end{vmatrix} = 4(s + 8)$$

$$\therefore \quad I_2 = \frac{s + 8}{(s + 4)(s + 12)}$$

[c] $sI_2 = \frac{s(s + 8)}{(s + 4)(s + 12)}$

$\lim_{s\to\infty} sI_2 = i_2(0^+) = 1\,\text{A}$

$\lim_{s\to 0} sI_2 = i_2(\infty) = 0$

[d] $I_2 = \frac{K_1}{s+4} + \frac{K_2}{s+12}$

$$K_1 = K_2 = 1/2; \qquad \therefore \quad I_2 = \frac{1/2}{s+4} + \frac{1/2}{s+12}$$

$$i_2(t) = \frac{1}{2}[e^{-4t} + e^{-12t}]u(t) \text{ A}$$

P 13.42 [a]

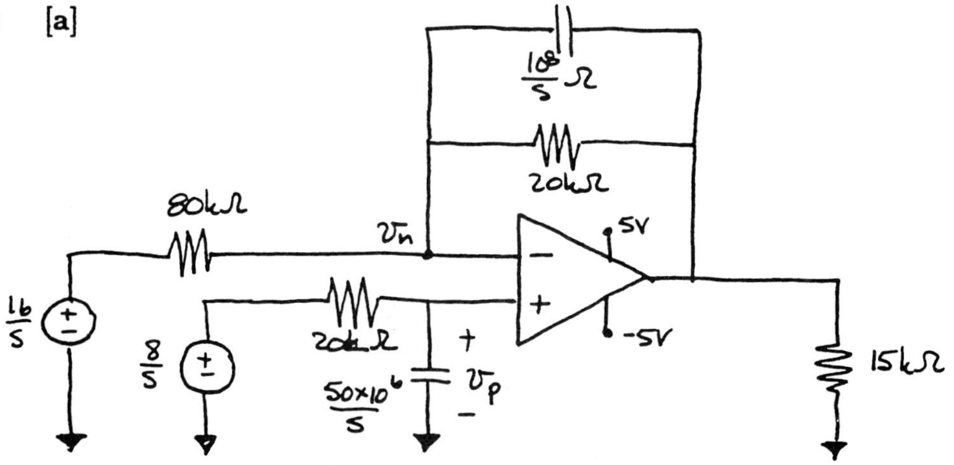

$$\frac{V_p s}{50 \times 10^6} + \frac{V_p - V_{g2}}{20{,}000} = 0; \qquad V_p = \frac{2500}{s + 2500} V_{g2}$$

$$\frac{V_p - V_{g1}}{80{,}000} + \frac{V_p - V_o}{20{,}000} + \frac{(V_p - V_o)s}{10^8} = 0$$

$$(s + 6250)V_p - (s + 5000)V_o = 1250V_{g1}$$

$$\therefore \quad (s + 5000)V_o = \frac{(s + 6250)(2500)}{(s + 2500)} V_{g2} - 1250V_{g1}$$

$$V_{g1} = \frac{16}{s}; \qquad V_{g2} = \frac{8}{s}$$

$$\therefore \quad V_o = \frac{7500 \times 10^4}{s(s + 2500)(s + 5000)}$$

$$= \frac{K_1}{s} + \frac{K_2}{s + 2500} + \frac{K_3}{s + 5000}$$

$$K_1 = \frac{7500 \times 10^4}{(2500)(5000)} = \frac{750}{125} = 6$$

$$K_2 = \frac{7500 \times 10^4}{(-2500)(2500)} = -12$$

$$K_3 = \frac{7500 \times 10^4}{(-5000)(-2500)} = 6$$

$$v_o = [6 - 12e^{-2500t} + 6e^{-5000t}]u(t)\ \text{V}$$

[b] $6 - 12e^{-2500t} + 6e^{-5000t} = 5$

$$6 - 12x + 6x^2 = 5$$

$$x^2 - 2x + \frac{1}{6} = 0$$

$$x = 1 - \sqrt{5/6} = 0.0871$$

$$\therefore \quad e^{-2500t} = 0.0871; \qquad t = 976.15\,\mu\text{s}$$

P 13.43 [a] $V_o = -\frac{Z_f}{Z_i}V_g$

$$Z_f = \frac{10^8}{s + \left[\frac{10^9}{(10)(2)\times 10^4}\right]} = \frac{10^8}{s + 5000}$$

$$Z_i = \frac{8000}{s}\left(s + \frac{10^9}{(50)(8000)}\right) = \frac{8000}{s}(s + 2500)$$

$$V_g = \frac{20{,}000}{s^2}$$

$$\therefore \quad V_o = \frac{-250 \times 10^6}{s(s + 2500)(s + 5000)}$$

[b] $V_o = \frac{K_1}{s} + \frac{K_2}{s + 2500} + \frac{K_3}{s + 5000}$

$$K_1 = \frac{-250 \times 10^6}{(5000)(2500)} = -20$$

$$K_2 = \frac{-250 \times 10^6}{(-2500)(2500)} = 40$$

$$K_3 = \frac{-250 \times 10^6}{(-5000)(-2500)} = -20$$

$$\therefore \quad v_o(t) = (-20 + 40e^{-2500t} - 20e^{-5000t})u(t)\ \text{V}$$

[c] $-20 + 40e^{-2500t_s} - 20e^{-5000t_s} = -5$

$$\therefore \quad 40e^{-2500t_s} - 20e^{-5000t_s} = 15$$

Let $x = e^{-2500t_s}$. Then

$$40x - 20x^2 = 15; \qquad \text{or } x^2 - 2x + 0.75 = 0$$

Solving,

$x = 1 \pm 0.5 \quad \text{so} \quad x = 0.5$

$$\therefore \quad e^{-2500t_s} = 0.5; \qquad \therefore \quad t_s = \frac{\ln 2}{0.0025} \times 10^{-6} = 277.26\,\mu\text{s}$$

[d] $v_g = \text{m}\,tu(t); \qquad V_g = \dfrac{\text{m}}{s^2}$

$$V_o = \frac{-10^8 s}{8000(s+2500)(s+5000)} \cdot \frac{\text{m}}{s^2}$$

$$= \frac{-12{,}000\text{m}}{s(s+2500)(s+5000)}$$

$$K_1 = \frac{-12{,}500\text{m}}{(2500)(5000)} = -\text{m} \times 10^{-3}$$

$$\therefore \quad -5 = -\text{m} \times 10^{-3} \qquad \therefore \quad \text{m} = 5000\,\text{V/s}$$

P 13.44

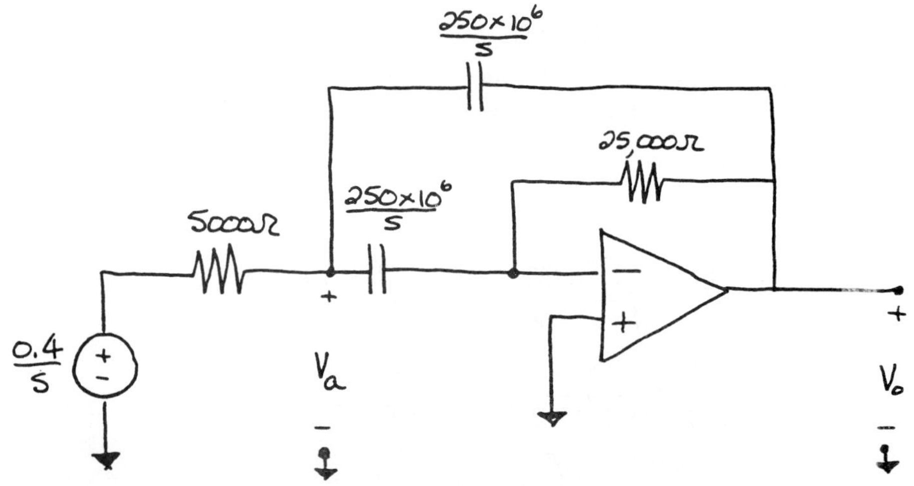

$$\frac{V_a - 0.4/s}{5000} + \frac{V_a s}{250 \times 10^6} + \frac{(V_a - V_o)s}{250 \times 10^6} = 0$$

$$\frac{(0 - V_a)s}{250 \times 10^6} + \frac{(0 - V_o)}{25{,}000} = 0$$

$$V_a = \frac{-10^4 V_o}{s}$$

$$\therefore \quad V_o(s^2 + 20{,}000s + 500 \times 10^6) = -20{,}000$$

$$V_o = \frac{-20{,}000}{(s + 10{,}000 - j20{,}000)(s + 10{,}000 + j20{,}000)}$$

$$K_1 = \frac{-20{,}000}{j40{,}000} = j0.5 = 0.5\underline{/90^\circ}$$

$$v_o(t) = e^{-10{,}000t}\cos(20{,}000t + 90^\circ) = -e^{-10{,}000t}\sin(20{,}000t)u(t)\text{ V}$$

P 13.45 $$Z_{i1} = 400{,}000 + \frac{(4\times10^5/s)(2\times10^5)}{2\times10^5 + (4\times10^5/s)} = \frac{4\times10^5(s+3)}{s+2}$$

$$Z_{f1} = 8\times10^5$$

$$V_{o1} = -\frac{Z_{f1}}{Z_{i1}}V_g = \frac{-8\times10^5(s+2)}{4\times10^5(s+3)}\frac{(0.18)}{s} = \frac{-0.36(s+2)}{s(s+3)}$$

The final value of v_{o1} is

$$v_{o1}(\infty) = \lim_{s\to0}\left(\frac{-0.36(s+2)}{s+3}\right) = -0.24\text{ V}$$

Thus, the first stage will not saturate.

$$V_o = -\frac{Z_{f2}}{Z_{i2}}V_{o1}$$

$$Z_{f2} = \frac{10^9}{250s} = \frac{4\times10^6}{s}; \qquad Z_{i2} = 50\times10^3$$

$$V_o = \frac{-0.36(s+2)}{s(s+3)}\left(\frac{-80}{s}\right) = \frac{28.8(s+2)}{s^2(s+3)}$$

$$= \frac{19.2}{s^2} + \frac{3.2}{s} - \frac{3.2}{s+3}$$

$$v_o(t) = (19.2t + 3.2 - 3.2e^{-3t})u(t)\text{ V}$$

The second stage saturates when v_o reaches 6.4 V. Thus

$$19.2t_s + 3.2 - 3.2e^{-3t_s} = 6.4; \qquad \therefore\ 6t_s - 1 = e^{-3t_s}$$

t_s must be greater than $\frac{1}{6}$ or 166.68 ms. Using trial and error we find

$$t_s = 246.28\text{ ms}$$

P 13.46 [a] Let V_a be the voltage across the 0.2 μF capacitor, positive at the upper terminal and let V_b be the voltage across the 200 kΩ resistor, positive at the upper terminal. Then

$$\frac{V_a s}{5\times 10^6} + \frac{V_a - V_g}{400{,}000} + \frac{V_a}{400{,}000} = 0; \qquad \therefore\ V_a = \frac{12.5}{s+25}V_g$$

$$\frac{-V_a}{400{,}000} - \frac{sV_b}{10^7} = 0; \qquad \therefore\ V_b = \frac{-25}{s}V_a = \frac{-312.5}{s(s+25)}V_g$$

$$\frac{V_b}{200{,}000} + \frac{sV_b}{10^7} + \frac{(V_b - V_o)s}{10^7} = 0$$

$$\therefore\ V_o = \frac{2(s+25)}{s}V_b = \left[\frac{2(s+25)}{s}\right]\left[\frac{-312.5}{s(s+25)}\right]\left(\frac{8}{s}\right) = \frac{-5000}{s^3}$$

[b] $v_o(t) = -2500t^2u(t)$ V

[c] The op amp will saturate when $v_o = -12.5$ V.

$$-12.5 = -2500t^2; \qquad t^2 = 0.005; \qquad \therefore\ t = 0.071 = 71\text{ ms}$$

P 13.47
$$\Delta = \begin{vmatrix} Y_{11} & Y_{12} \\ Y_{12} & Y_{22} \end{vmatrix} = Y_{11}Y_{22} - Y_{12}^2$$

$$N_2 = \begin{vmatrix} Y_{11} & [(V_g/R_1) + \gamma C - (\rho/s)] \\ Y_{12} & (I_g - \gamma C) \end{vmatrix}$$

$$V_2 = \frac{N_2}{\Delta}$$

Substitution and simplification lead directly to Eq. 13.90.

P 13.48 [a] Voltage source acting alone:

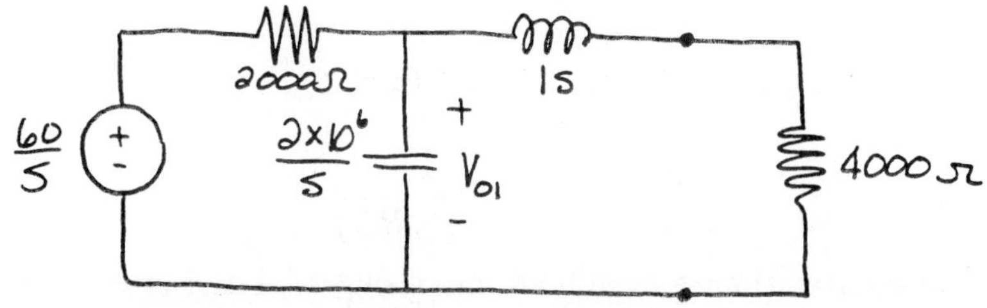

$$\frac{V_{o1} - 60/s}{2000} + \frac{V_{o1}s}{2\times 10^6} + \frac{V_{o1}}{s+4000} = 0$$

$$\therefore\ V_{o1} = \frac{60{,}000(s+4000)}{s(s+2000)(s+3000)}$$

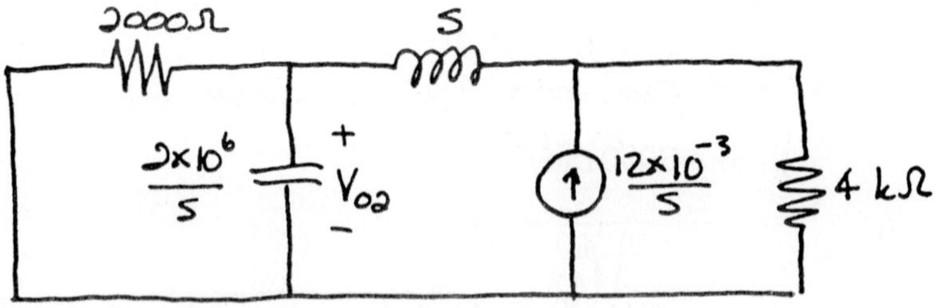

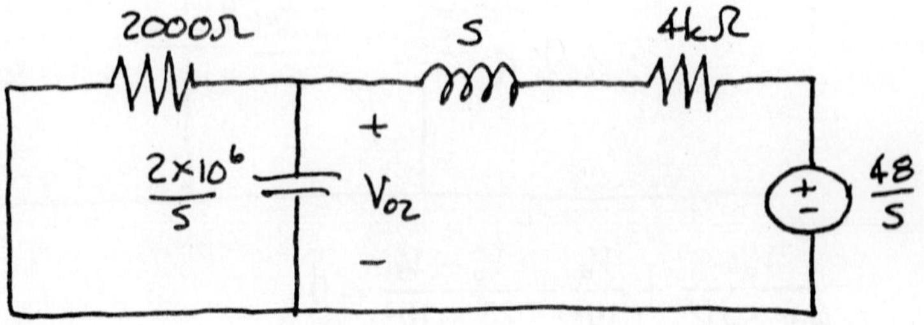

$$\frac{V_{o2}}{2000} + \frac{V_{02}s}{2\times10^6} + \frac{V_{02} - 48/s}{4000 + s} = 0$$

$$\therefore \quad V_{02} = \frac{96\times10^6}{s(s+2000)(s+3000)}$$

$$V_o = V_{o1} + V_{o2} = \frac{6\times10^4(s+4000) + 96\times10^6}{s(s+2000)(s+3000)}$$

[b] $V_o = \dfrac{K_1}{s} + \dfrac{K_2}{s+2000} + \dfrac{K_3}{s+3000}$

$$= \frac{56}{s} - \frac{108}{s+2000} + \frac{52}{s+3000}$$

$$v_o(t) = (56 - 108e^{-2000t} + 52e^{-3000t})u(t)\text{ V}$$

P 13.49 [a] $\dfrac{V_o}{V_i} = \dfrac{1/sC}{R + 1/sC} = \dfrac{1}{RCs + 1}$

$$H(s) = \frac{(1/RC)}{s + (1/RC)} = \frac{50}{s+50}; \qquad -p_1 = -50\,\text{rad/s}$$

[b] $\dfrac{V_o}{V_i} = \dfrac{R}{R + 1/sC} = \dfrac{RCs}{RCs + 1} = \dfrac{s}{s + (1/RC)}$

$$= \frac{s}{s+50}; \qquad z_1 = 0, \quad -p_1 = -50\,\text{rad/s}$$

[c] $\dfrac{V_o}{V_i} = \dfrac{sL}{R + sL} = \dfrac{s}{s + R/L} = \dfrac{s}{s + 3000}$

$$z_1 = 0; \qquad -p_1 = -3000\,\text{rad/s}$$

[d] $\dfrac{V_o}{V_i} = \dfrac{R}{R+sL} = \dfrac{R/L}{s+(R/L)} = \dfrac{3000}{s+3000}$

$-p_1 = -3000\,\text{rad/s}$

[e]

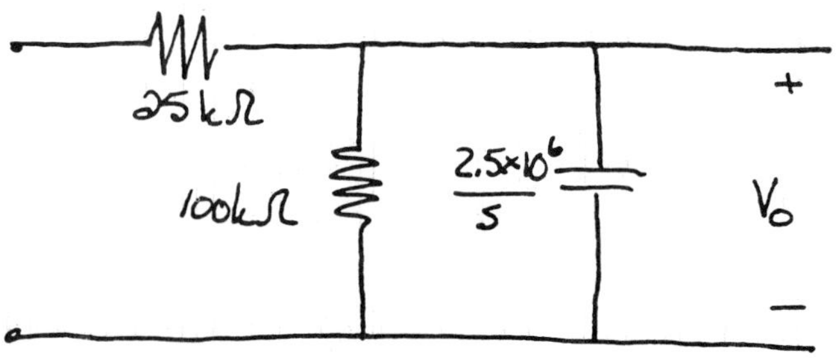

$$\frac{V_o s}{2.5\times10^6} + \frac{V_o}{10^5} + \frac{V_o - V_i}{25\times10^3} = 0$$

$$sV_o + 25V_o + 100V_o = 100V_i$$

$$H(s) = \frac{V_o}{V_i} = \frac{100}{s+125}$$

$$-p_1 = -125\,\text{rad/s}$$

P 13.50 [a] Let $R_1 = 250\,\text{k}\Omega$; $R_2 = 125\,\text{k}\Omega$; $C_2 = 1.6\,\text{nF}$; and $C_f = 0.4\,\text{nF}$. Then

$$Z_f = \frac{(R_2 + 1/sC_2)1/sC_f}{\left(R_2 + \frac{1}{sC_2} + \frac{1}{sC_f}\right)} = \frac{(s + 1/R_2C_2)}{C_f s\left(s + \frac{C_2+C_f}{C_2C_fR_2}\right)}$$

$$\frac{1}{C_f} = 2.5\times10^9$$

$$\frac{1}{R_2C_2} = \frac{62.5\times10^9}{125\times10^3} = 5000\,\text{rad/s}$$

$$\frac{C_2+C_f}{C_2C_fR_2} = \frac{2\times10^{-9}}{(0.64\times10^{-18})(125\times10^3)} = 25{,}000\,\text{rad/s}$$

$$\therefore\quad Z_f = \frac{2.5\times10^9(s+5000)}{s(s+25{,}000)}\Omega$$

$$Z_A = R_1 = 250\times10^3\,\Omega$$

$$H(s) = \frac{V_o}{V_g} = \frac{-Z_f}{Z_A} = \frac{-10^4(s+5000)}{s(s+25{,}000)}$$

[b] $-z_1 = -5000\,\text{rad/s}$

$p_1 = 0;\qquad -p_2 = -25{,}000\,\text{rad/s}$

P 13.51 [a]

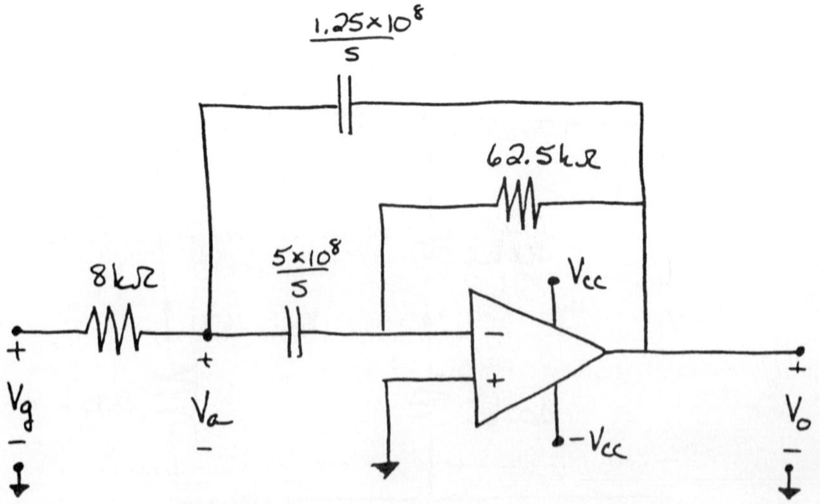

$$\frac{V_a - V_g}{8000} + \frac{V_a s}{5 \times 10^8} + \frac{(V_a - V_o)s}{1.25 \times 10^8} = 0$$

$$\frac{-V_a s}{5 \times 10^8} - \frac{V_o}{62{,}500} = 0$$

$$\therefore \quad \frac{-8000V_o}{s}(5s + 62{,}500) - 4sV_o = 62{,}500V_g$$

$$\therefore \quad H(s) = \frac{V_o}{V_g} = \frac{-15{,}625s}{s^2 + 10{,}000s + 125 \times 10^6}$$

$$s_{1,2} = -5000 \pm \sqrt{25 \times 10^6 - 125 \times 10^6} = -5000 \pm j10{,}000$$

$$H(s) = \frac{-15{,}625s}{(s + 5000 - j10{,}000)(s + 5000 + j10{,}000)}$$

[b] $-p_1 = -5000 + j10{,}000$ rad/s

$-p_2 = -5000 - j10{,}000$ rad/s

$z = 0$

P 13.52 [a] $Z_i = 10{,}000 + \dfrac{10^9}{20s} = \dfrac{10^4(s + 5000)}{s}$

$$Z_f = \frac{25{,}000}{(25{,}000)(4 \times 10^{-9})s + 1} = \frac{250 \times 10^6}{s + 10{,}000}$$

$$H(s) = -\frac{Z_f}{Z_i} = \frac{-25{,}000s}{(s + 5000)(s + 10{,}000)}$$

[b] Zero at $s = 0$
Poles at $-p_1 = -5000$ rad/s and $-p_2 = -10{,}000$ rad/s.

P 13.53 [a]

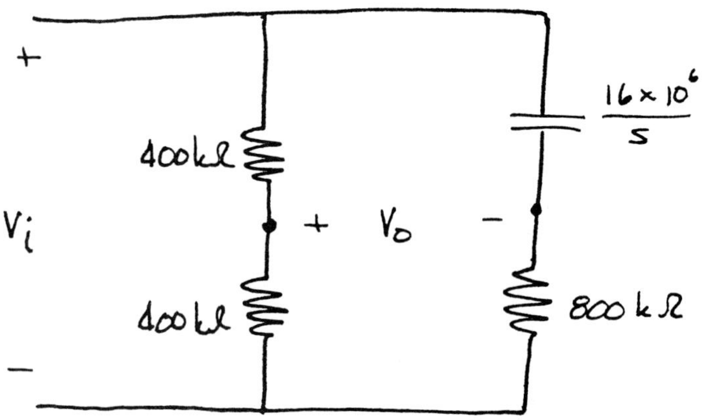

$$\frac{4}{8}V_i = V_o + \frac{800{,}000V_i}{800{,}000 + (16 \times 10^6/s)}$$

$$0.5V_i - \frac{sV_i}{s+20} = V_o$$

$$\therefore \quad \frac{V_o}{V_i} = H(s) = \frac{-0.5(s-20)}{(s+20)}$$

[b] $-z_1 = 20\,\text{rad/s}$

$-p_1 = -20\,\text{rad/s}$

P 13.54

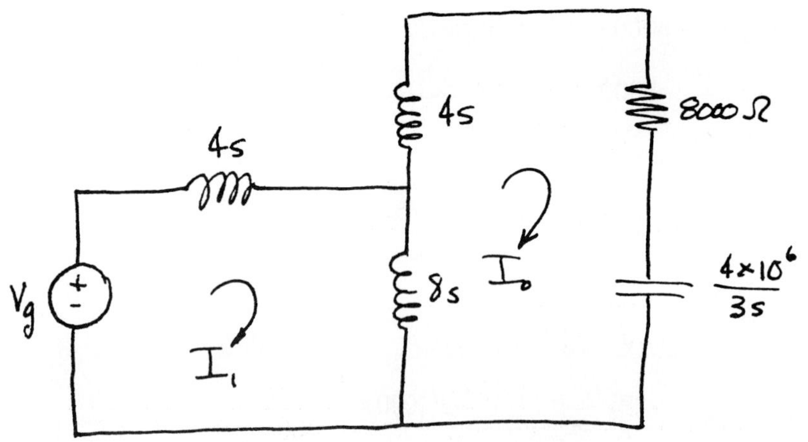

$$V_g = 12sI_1 - 8sI_o$$

$$0 = -8sI_1 + (12s + 8000 + 4 \times 10^6/3s)I_o$$

$$\Delta = \begin{vmatrix} 12s & -8s \\ -8s & 12s + 8000 + 4 \times 10^6/3s \end{vmatrix} = 80(s + 200)(s + 1000)$$

$$N_o = \begin{vmatrix} 12s & V_g \\ -8s & 0 \end{vmatrix} = 8sV_g$$

$$I_o = \frac{N_o}{\Delta} = \frac{8sV_g}{80(s + 200)(s + 1000)}$$

$$H(s) = \frac{I_o}{V_g} = \frac{0.1s}{(s + 200)(s + 1000)}$$

$$z_1 = 0; \qquad -p_1 = -200 \text{ rad/s}; \qquad -p_2 = -1000 \text{ rad/s}$$

P 13.55 [a]

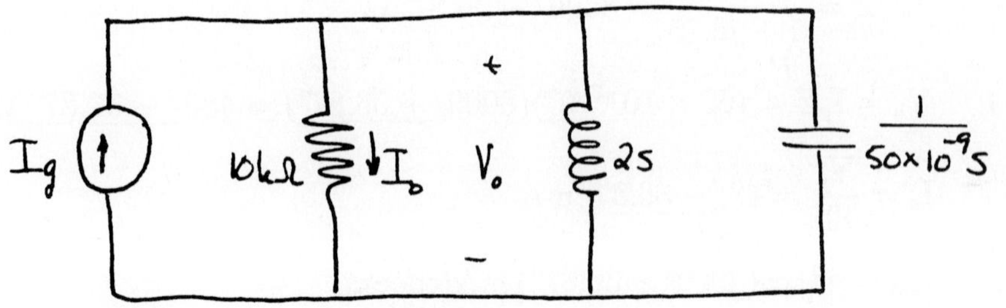

$$\frac{V_o}{10{,}000} + \frac{V_o}{2s} + V_o(50 \times 10^{-9})s = I_g$$

$$\therefore \quad V_o = \frac{20 \times 10^6 s}{s^2 + 2000s + 10 \times 10^6} \cdot I_g$$

$$I_g = \frac{60 \times 10^{-3}s}{s^2 + 16 \times 10^6}; \qquad I_o = \frac{V_o}{10^4}$$

$$\therefore \quad H(s) = \frac{2000s}{s^2 + 2000s + 10^7}$$

[b] $$I_o = \frac{(2000s)(60 \times 10^{-3}s)}{(s + 1000 - j3000)(s + 1000 + j3000)(s^2 + 16 \times 10^6)}$$

$$I_o = \frac{120s^2}{(s + 1000 - j3000)(s + 1000 + j3000)(s + j4000)(s - j4000)}$$

[c] Damped sinusoid of the form

$Me^{-1000t}\cos(3000t + \theta_1)$

[d] Steady-state sinusoid of the form

$N\cos(4000t + \theta_2)$

[e] $I_o = \frac{K_1}{s + 1000 - j3000} + \frac{K_1^*}{s + 1000 + j3000} + \frac{K_2}{s - j4000} + \frac{K_2^*}{s + j4000}$

$$K_1 = \frac{120(-1000 + j3000)^2}{(j6000)(-1000 - j1000)(-j1000 + j7000)} = 20 \times 10^{-3}\underline{/163.74^\circ}$$

$$K_2 = \frac{120(-16 \times 10^6)}{(j8000)(1000 + j1000)(j1000 + j7000)} = 24 \times 10^{-3}\underline{/-36.87^\circ}$$

$i_o(t) = [40e^{-1000t}\cos(3000t + 163.74^\circ) + 48\cos(4000t - 36.87^\circ)]$ mA

Test:

$i_o(0) = 40\cos(163.74^\circ) + 48\cos(-36.87^\circ) = -384 + 384 = 0$

$$Z = \frac{1}{Y}; \qquad Y = \frac{1}{10{,}000} + \frac{1}{j8000} + \frac{1}{-j5000} = \frac{1 + j0.75}{10{,}000}$$

$$\therefore \quad Z = \frac{10{,}000}{1 + j0.75} = 8000\underline{/-36.87^\circ}\,\Omega$$

$\mathbf{V}_o = \mathbf{I}_g Z = (60 \times 10^{-3}\underline{/0^\circ})(8000\underline{/-36.87^\circ}) = 480\underline{/-36.87^\circ}$ V

$$\mathbf{I}_o = \frac{\mathbf{V}_o}{10^4} = 48\underline{/-36.87^\circ}\text{ mA}$$

$i_{oss} = 48\cos(4000t - 36.87^\circ)$ mA(checks)

P 13.56 [a]

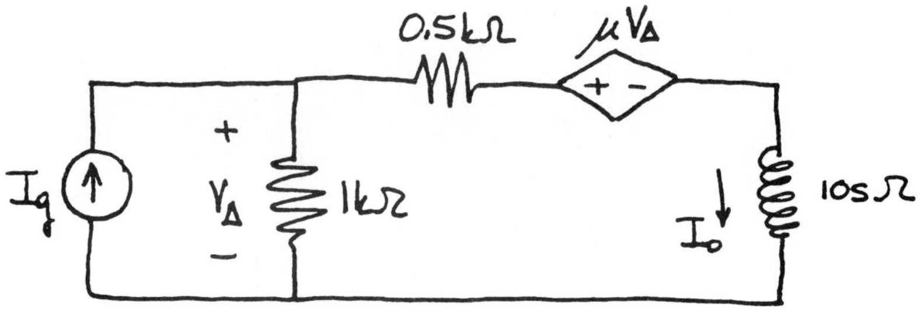

$1000(I_o - I_g) + 500I_o + \mu(I_g - I_o)(1000) + 10sI_o = 0$

$$\therefore \quad I_o = \frac{100(1 - \mu)}{s + 100(1.5 - \mu)}I_g$$

$$\therefore \quad H(s) = \frac{100(1 - \mu)}{s + 100(1.5 - \mu)}$$

[b] $\mu < 1.5$

[c]

μ	$H(s)$	I_o
-0.5	$150/(s+200)$	$1500/s(s+200)$
0	$100/(s+150)$	$1000/s(s+150)$
1.0	0	0
1.5	$-50/s$	$-50/s^2$
2.0	$-100/(s-50)$	$-100/s(s-50)$

$\mu = -0.5$:

$$I_o = \frac{7.5}{s} - \frac{7.5}{(s+200)}; \qquad i_o = [7.5 - 7.5e^{-200t}]u(t),\ \mathrm{A}$$

$\mu = 0$:

$$I_o = \frac{20/3}{s} - \frac{20/3}{s+150}; \qquad i_o = \frac{20}{3}[1 - e^{-150t}]u(t),\ \mathrm{A}$$

$\mu = 1$: $\quad i_o = 0\ \mathrm{A}$

$\mu = 1.5$:

$$I_o = \frac{-50}{s^2}; \qquad i_o = -50t\,u(t)\ \mathrm{A}$$

$\mu = 2$:

$$I_o = \frac{2}{s} - \frac{2}{s-50}; \qquad i_o = 2[1 - e^{50t}]u(t),\ \mathrm{A}$$

P 13.57 [a]

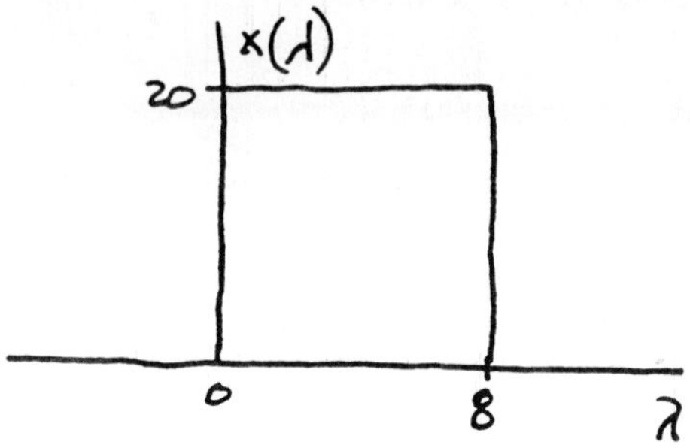

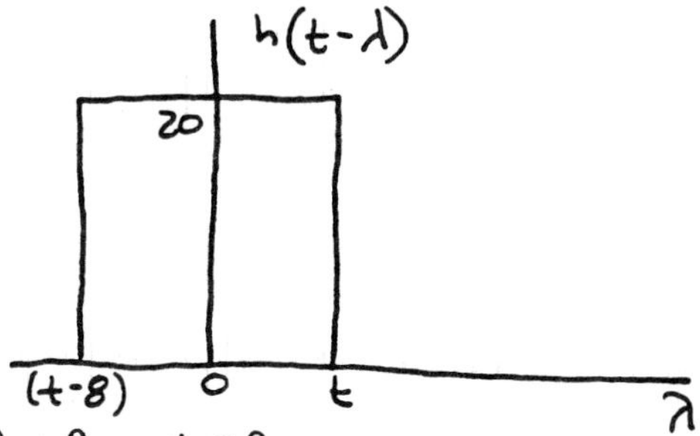

$y(t) = 0 \qquad t < 0$

$0 \leq t \leq 8: \qquad y(t) = \int_0^t 400\, d\lambda = 400t$

$8 \leq t \leq 16: \qquad y(t) = \int_{t-8}^{8} 400\, d\lambda = 400(8 - t + 8) = 400(16 - t)$

$16 \leq t < \infty: \qquad y(t) = 0$

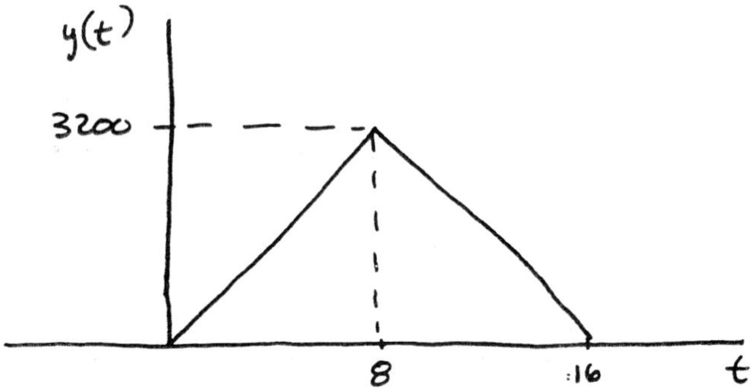

[b]

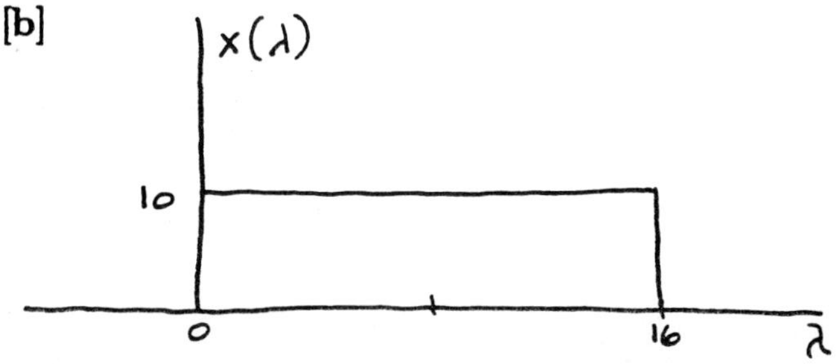

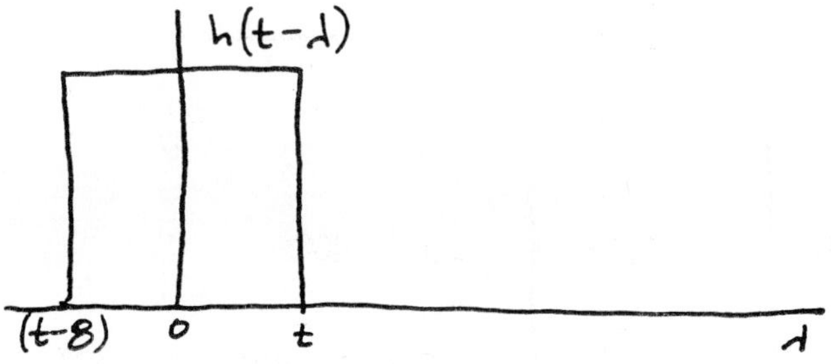

$y(t) = 0 \qquad t < 0$

$0 \leq t \leq 8: \qquad y(t) = \int_0^t 200\, d\lambda = 200t$

$8 \leq t \leq 16: \qquad y(t) = \int_{t-8}^{t} 200\, d\lambda = 200(t - t + 8) = 1600$

$16 \leq t \leq 24: \qquad y(t) = \int_{t-8}^{16} 200\, d\lambda = 200(24 - t)$

$24 \leq t < \infty: \qquad y(t) = 0$

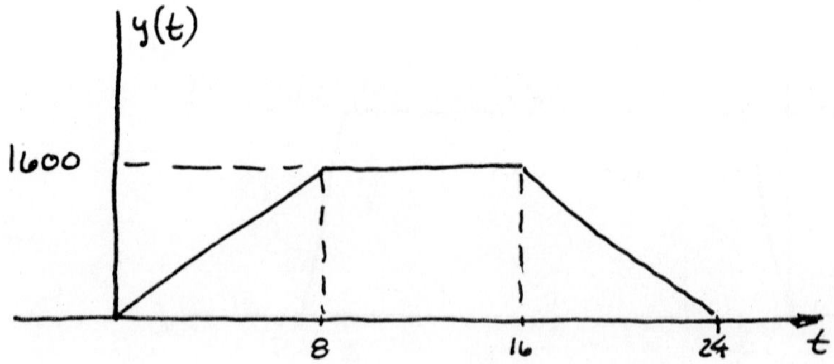

[c]

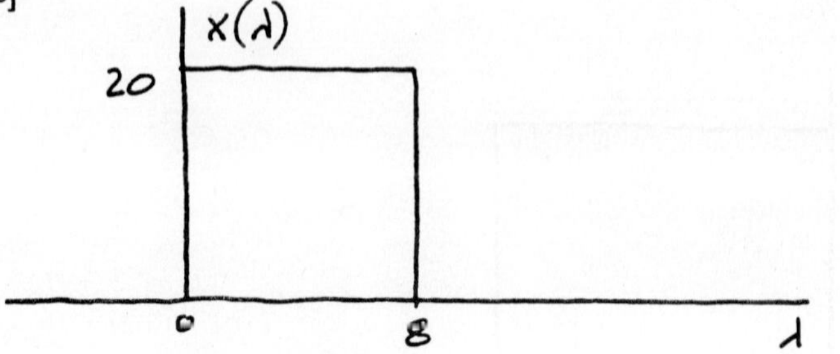

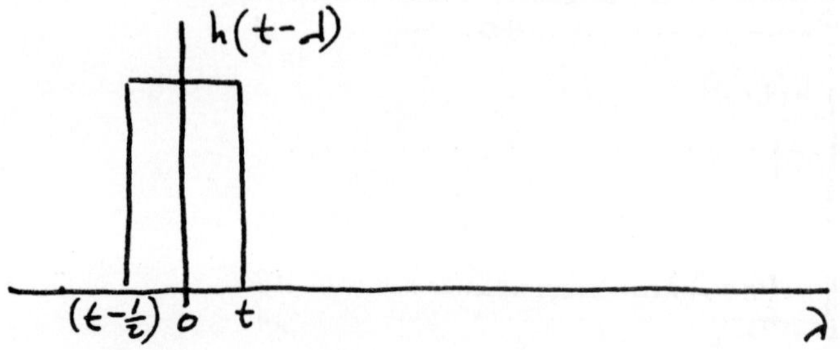

$y(t) = 0 \qquad t < 0$

$$0 \leq t \leq 0.5: \qquad y(t) = \int_0^t 400\,d\lambda = 400t$$

$$0.5 \leq t \leq 8: \qquad y(t) = \int_{t-0.5}^{t} 400\,d\lambda = 400(t - t + 0.5) = 200$$

$$8 \leq t \leq 8.5: \qquad y(t) = \int_{t-0.5}^{8} 400\,d\lambda = 400(8.5 - t)$$

$$8.5 \leq t < \infty: \qquad y(t) = 0$$

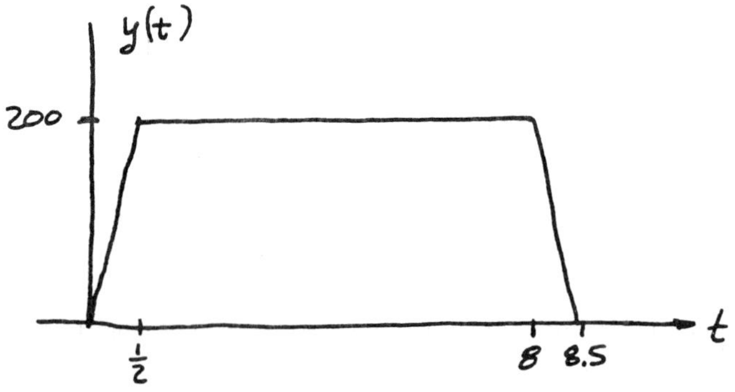

P 13.58 [a] $0 \le t \le 40$:

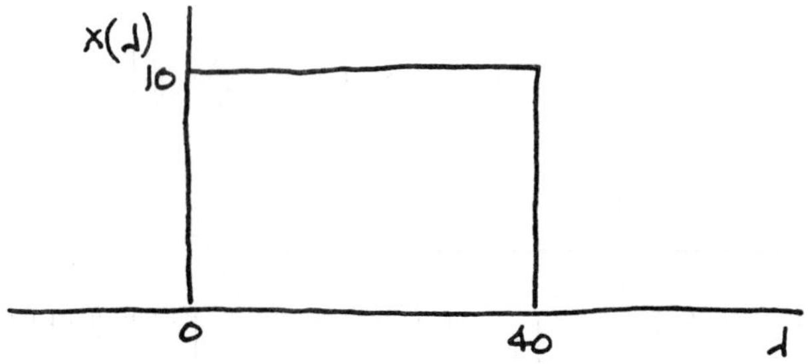

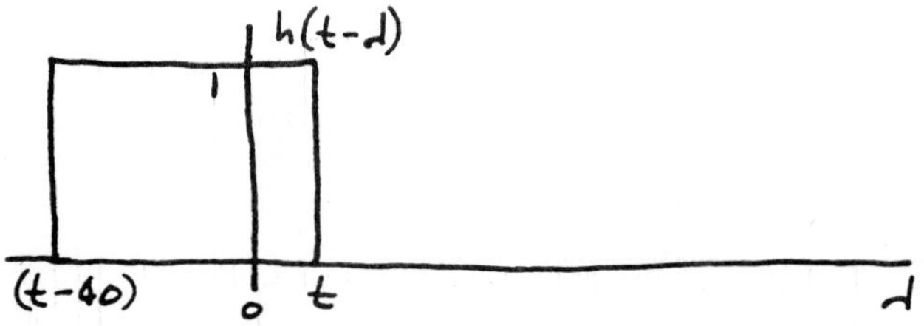

$$y(t) = \int_0^t (10)(1)(d\lambda) = 10\lambda \Big|_0^t = 10t$$

$40 \le t \le 80$:

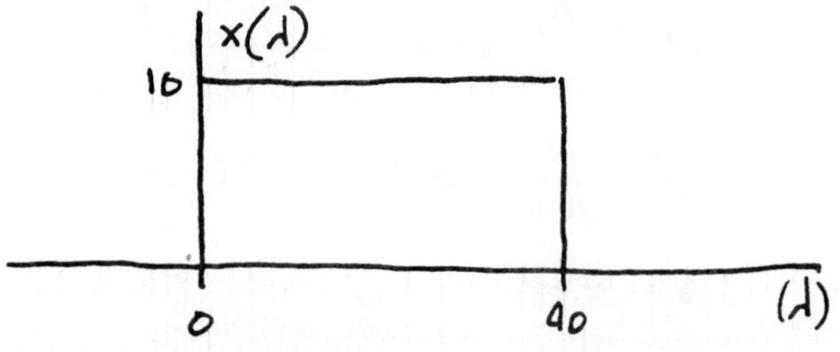

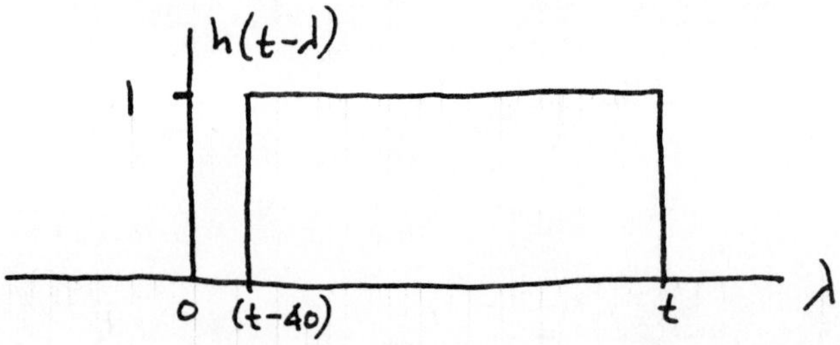

$$y(t) = \int_{t-40}^{40} (10)(1)(d\lambda) = 10\lambda \Big|_{t-40}^{40} = 10(80 - t)$$

$t \geq 80: \qquad y(t) = 0$

[b] $0 \leq t \leq 10$:

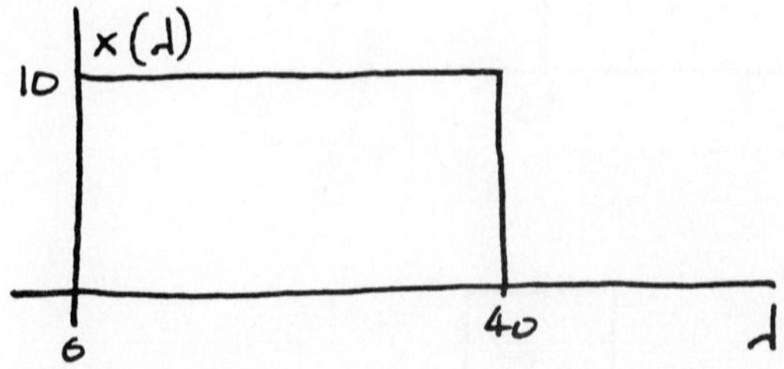

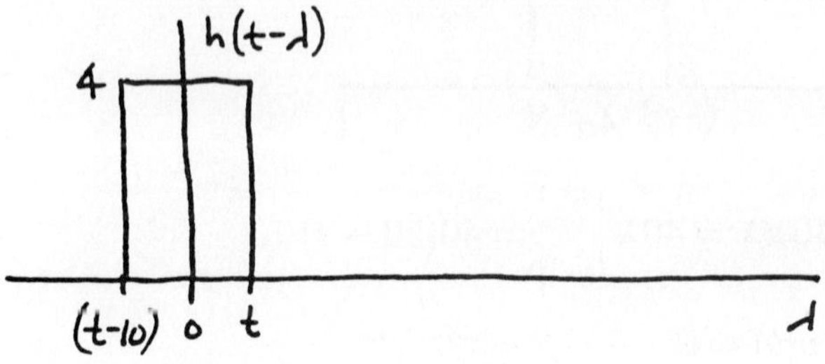

$$y(t) = \int_{0}^{t} 40\, d\lambda = 40\lambda \Big|_{0}^{t} = 40t$$

$10 \leq t \leq 40$:

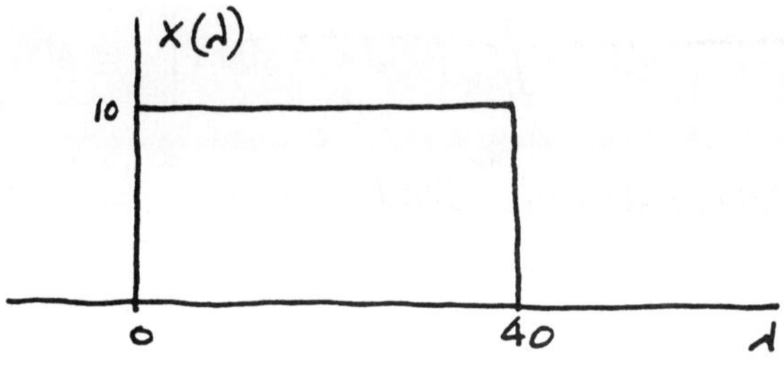

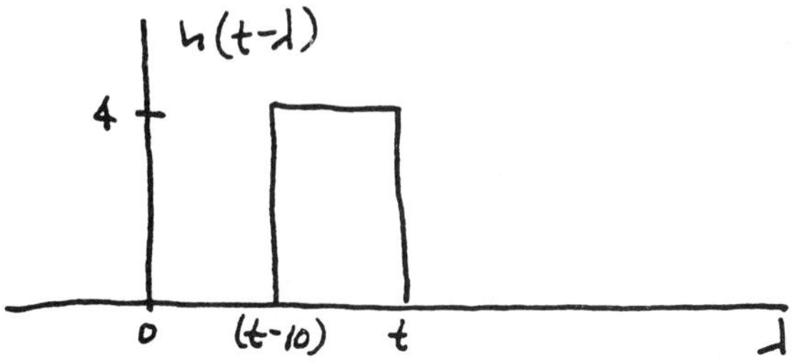

$$y(t) = \int_{t-10}^{t} 40\, d\lambda = 40\lambda \Big|_{t-10}^{t} = 400$$

$40 \le t \le 50$:

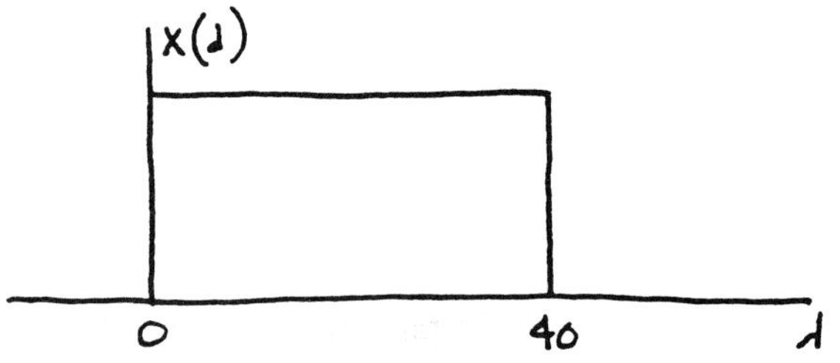

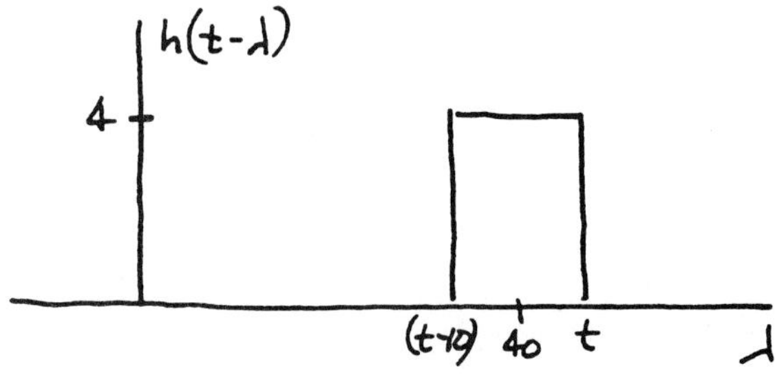

$$y(t) = \int_{t-10}^{40} 40\,d\lambda = 40\lambda \Big|_{t-10}^{40} = 40(50-t)$$

$t \ge 50: \qquad y(t) = 0$

The expresions are

$0 \le t \le 1.0: \qquad y(t) = \int_{0}^{t} 400\,d\lambda = 400\lambda \Big|_{0}^{t} = 400t$

$1.0 \le t \le 40: \qquad y(t) = \int_{t-1}^{t} 400\,d\lambda = 400\lambda \Big|_{t-1}^{t} = 400$

$40 \le t \le 41: \qquad y(t) = \int_{t-1}^{40} 400\,d\lambda = 400\lambda \Big|_{t-1}^{40} = 400(41-t)$

$41 \le t < \infty: \qquad y(t) = 0$

[d]

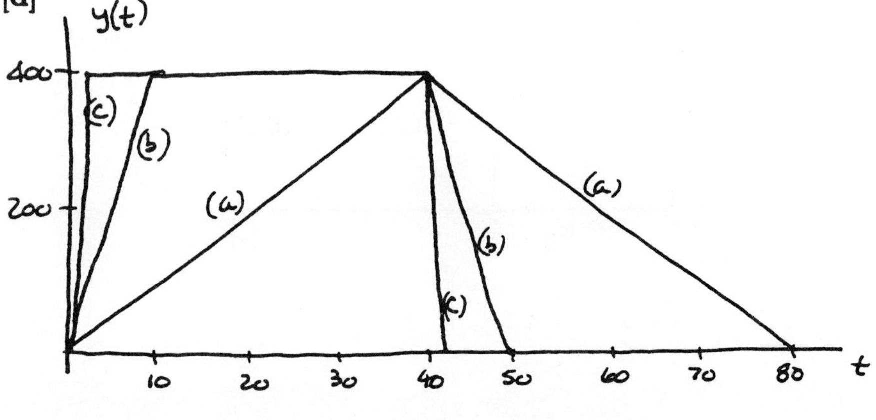

[e] Yes, note that $h(t)$ is approaching $40\delta(t)$, therefore $y(t)$ must approach $40x(t)$, i.e.

$$y(t) = \int_0^t h(t-\lambda)x(\lambda)\,d\lambda \to \int_0^t 40\delta(t-\lambda)x(\lambda)\,d\lambda$$

$$\to 40x(t)$$

This can be seen in the plot, e.g., in part (c), $y(t) \cong 40x(t)$.

P 13.59 [a] $-1 \le t \le 4$:

$$v_o = 20\int_0^{t+1} 3\lambda\,d\lambda = 30\lambda^2 \Big|_0^{t+1} = 30t^2 + 60t + 30$$

$4 \le t \le 7$:

$$v_o = 20\int_0^5 3\lambda\,d\lambda + 20\int_5^{t+1} (20-\lambda)\,d\lambda$$

$$= 30\lambda^2 \Big|_0^5 + 400\lambda \Big|_5^{t+1} - 10\lambda^2 \Big|_5^{t+1}$$

$$= -10t^2 + 380t - 610$$

$7 \le t \le 12$:

$$v_o = 20\int_{t-7}^5 3\lambda\,d\lambda + 20\int_5^{t+1} (20-\lambda)\,d\lambda$$

$$= 30\lambda^2 \Big|_{t-7}^5 + 400\lambda \Big|_5^{t+1} - 10\lambda^2 \Big|_5^{t+1}$$

$$= -40t^2 + 800t - 2080$$

$12 \le t \le 19$:

$$v_o = 20\int_{t-7}^{t+1} (20-\lambda)\,d\lambda = 400\lambda \Big|_{t-7}^{t+1} - 10\lambda^2 \Big|_{t-7}^{t+1}$$

$$= -160t + 3680$$

$19 \le t \le 27$:

$$v_o = 20\int_{t-7}^{20} (20-\lambda)\,d\lambda = 400\lambda \Big|_{t-7}^{20} - 10\lambda^2 \Big|_{t-7}^{20}$$

$$= 10t^2 - 540t + 7290$$

[b]

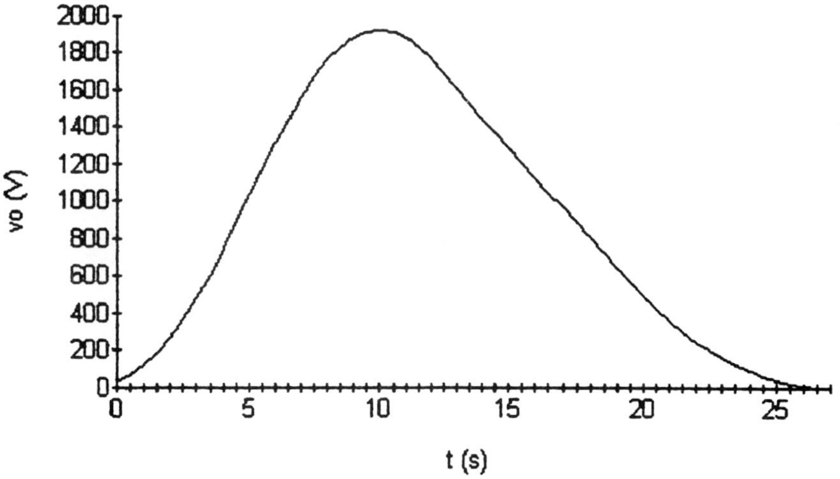

P 13.60 [a] $h(\lambda) = \frac{5}{10}\lambda \qquad 0 \le \lambda \le 10\,\text{s}$

$$h(\lambda) = 10 - \frac{5}{10}\lambda \qquad 10 \le \lambda \le 20\,\text{s}$$

$$h(\lambda) = 0 \qquad 20 \le \lambda \le \infty$$

$0 \le t \le 10\,\text{s}$:

$$v_o = \int_0^t (0.5\lambda)(4)\,d\lambda = 2\frac{\lambda^2}{2}\bigg|_0^t = t^2$$

$10 \le t \le 20\,\text{s}$:

$$v_o = \int_0^{10} 2\lambda\,d\lambda + \int_{10}^t 4(10 - 0.5\lambda)\,d\lambda$$

$$v_o = 100 + 40t - 400 - t^2 + 100 = 40t - 200 - t^2\ \text{V}$$

$20 \le t \le \infty$:

$$v_o = \int_0^{10} 2\lambda\,d\lambda + \int_0^{20} 4(10 - 0.5\lambda)\,d\lambda$$

$$v_o = 100 + 400 - (400 - 100) = 200\ \text{V}$$

[b]

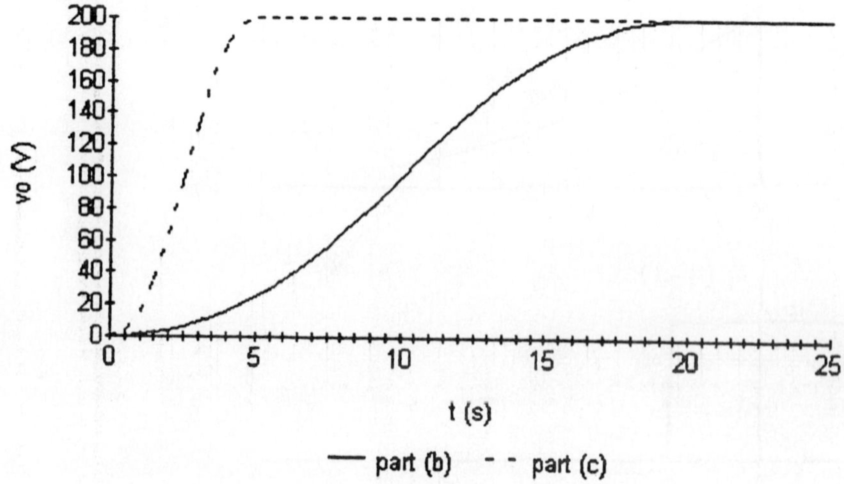

[c] $h(\lambda) = 8\lambda \quad 0 \le \lambda \le 2.5\,\text{s}$

$h(\lambda) = 40 - 8\lambda \quad 2.5 \le \lambda \le 5\,\text{s}$

$h(\lambda) = 0 \quad 5 \le \lambda \le \infty$

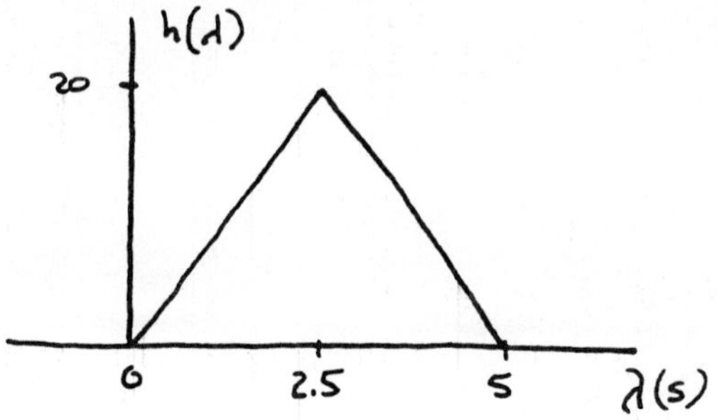

$0 \le t \le 2.5\,\text{s}$:

$$v_o = \int_0^t 32\lambda\,d\lambda = 16t^2\ \text{V}$$

$2.5 \le t \le 5\,\text{s}$:

$$v_o = \int_0^{2.5} 32\lambda\,d\lambda + \int_{2.5}^{t} 4(40 - 8\lambda)\,d\lambda = 160t - 200 - 16t^2\ \text{V}$$

$5 \le t \le \infty$:

$$v_o = \int_0^{2.5} 32\lambda\,d\lambda + \int_{2.5}^{5} 4(40 - 8\lambda)\,d\lambda = 200\ \text{V}$$

[d] The waveform in part (c) is closer to replicating the input waveform because in part (c) $h(\lambda)$ is closer to being an ideal impulse response. That is, the area was preserved as the base was shortened.

P 13.61 [a]

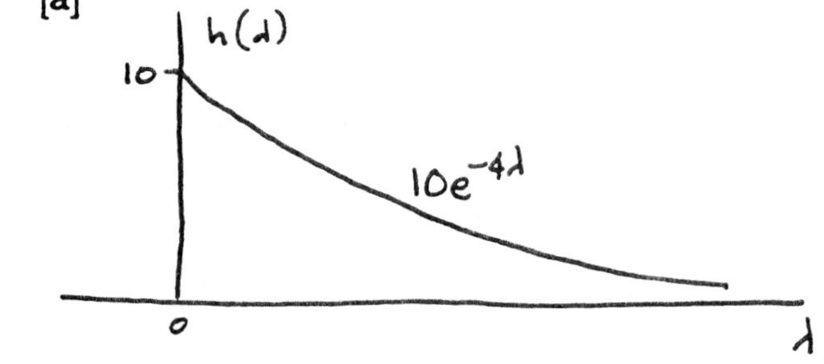

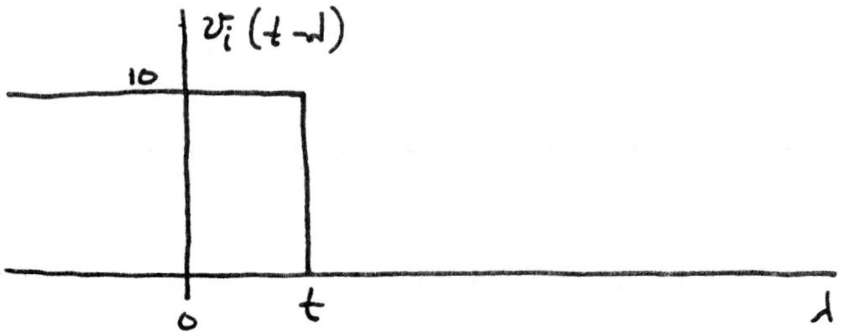

$$v_o = \int_0^t 10(10e^{-4\lambda})\,d\lambda$$

$$= 100\frac{e^{-4\lambda}}{-4}\Bigg|_0^t = -25[e^{-4t} - 1]$$

$$= 25(1 - e^{-4t})\text{ V}, \qquad 0 \le t \le \infty$$

[b]

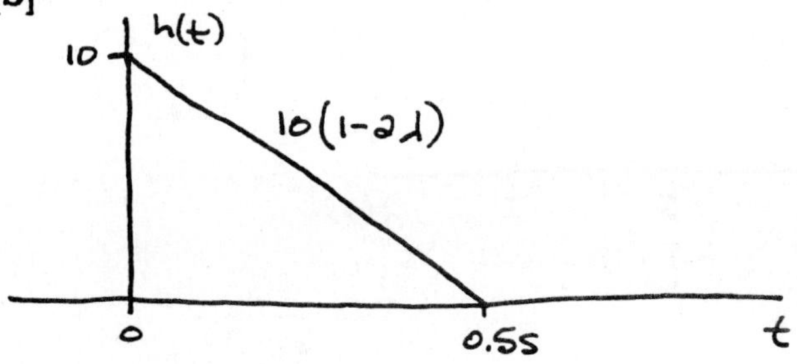

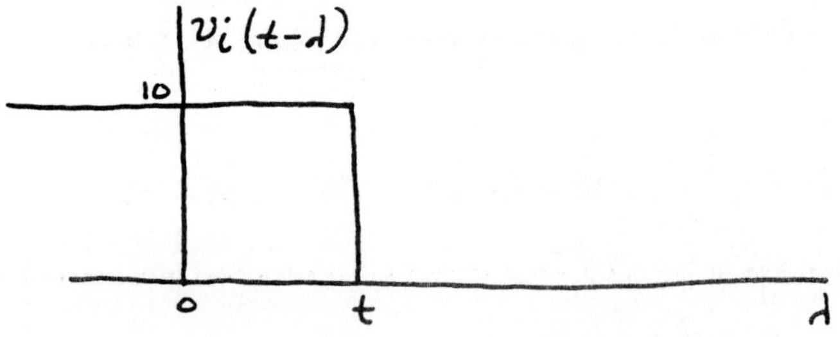

$0 \le t \le 0.5$:

$$v_o = \int_0^t 100(1 - 2\lambda)\,d\lambda = 100(\lambda - \lambda^2)\Bigg|_0^t = 100t(1 - t)$$

$0.5 \le t \le \infty$:

$$v_o = \int_0^{0.5} 100(1 - 2\lambda)\, d\lambda = 100(\lambda - \lambda^2)\Big|_0^{0.5} = 25$$

[c]

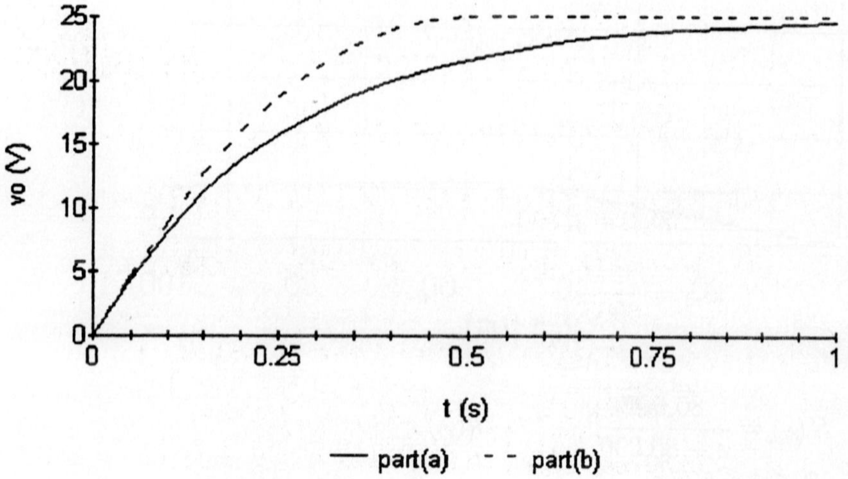

P 13.62 [a] From Problem 13.49(d)

$$H(s) = \frac{3000}{s + 3000}$$

$$h(\lambda) = 3000e^{-3000\lambda}$$

$0 \le t \le 50\,\mu$s:

$$v_o = \int_0^t 20(3000)e^{-3000\lambda}\, d\lambda = 20(1 - e^{-3000t})\text{ V}$$

$50\,\mu\text{s} \le t \le \infty$:

$$v_o = \int_{t-50\times 10^{-6}}^t 20(3000)e^{-3000\lambda}\, d\lambda = 20(e^{0.15} - 1)e^{-3000t}\text{ V}$$

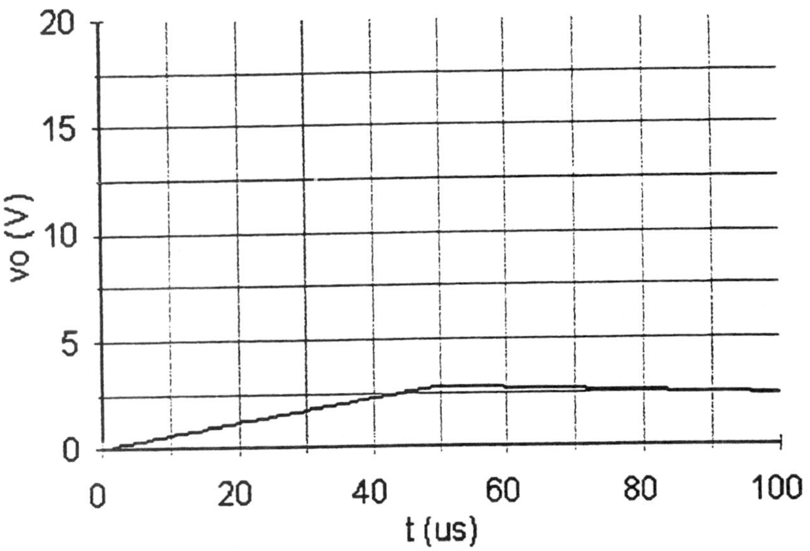

P 13.63 [a] $H(s) = \dfrac{80{,}000}{s + 80{,}000}$ $\quad\therefore\; h(\lambda) = 80{,}000e^{-80{,}000\lambda}$

$0 \le t \le 50\,\mu s$:

$$v_o = \int_0^t 20(80 \times 10^3)e^{-80{,}000\lambda}\,d\lambda = 20(1 - e^{-80{,}000t})\text{ V}$$

$50\,\mu s \le t \le \infty$:

$$v_o = \int_{t-50\times10^{-6}}^{t} 20(80 \times 10^3)e^{-80{,}000\lambda}\,d\lambda = 20(e^4 - 1)e^{-80{,}000t}\text{ V}$$

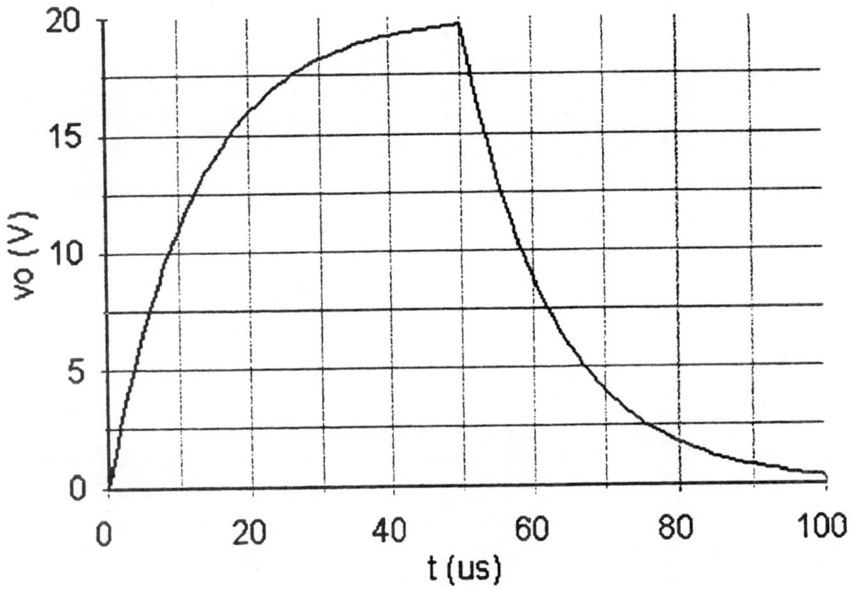

[b] decrease

[c] The circuit with $R = 400\,\Omega$.

P 13.64 [a] $I_o = \frac{20I_g}{25 + 0.025s} = \frac{800I_g}{s + 1000}$

$$\frac{I_o}{I_g} = H(s) = \frac{800}{s + 1000}$$

$$h(\lambda) = 800e^{-1000\lambda}u(\lambda)$$

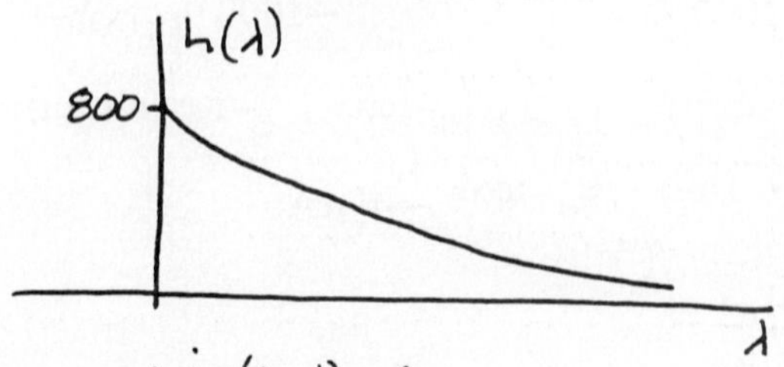

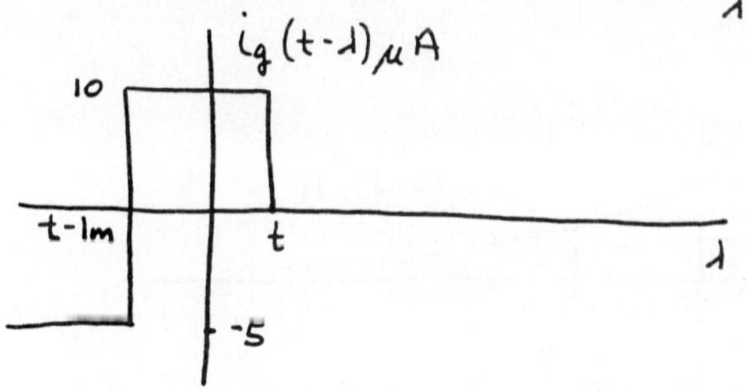

$0 \leq t \leq 1\,\text{ms}$:

$$i_o = \int_0^t (10 \times 10^{-6})(800)e^{-1000\lambda}\,d\lambda = 0.008\frac{e^{-1000\lambda}}{-1000}\Big|_0^t$$

$$= 8(1 - e^{-1000t})\,\mu\text{A}$$

$1\,\text{ms} \leq t \leq 4\,\text{ms}$:

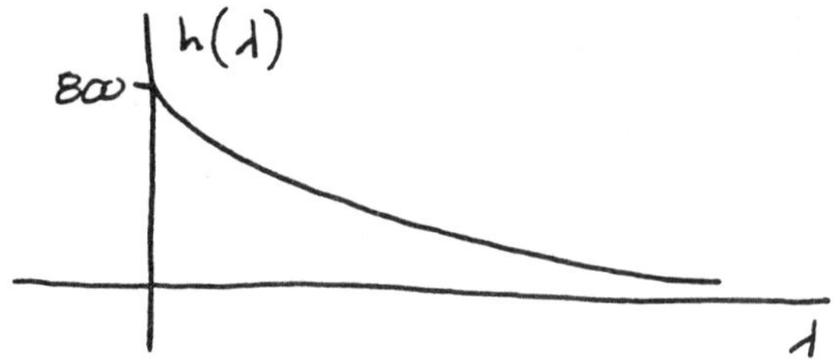

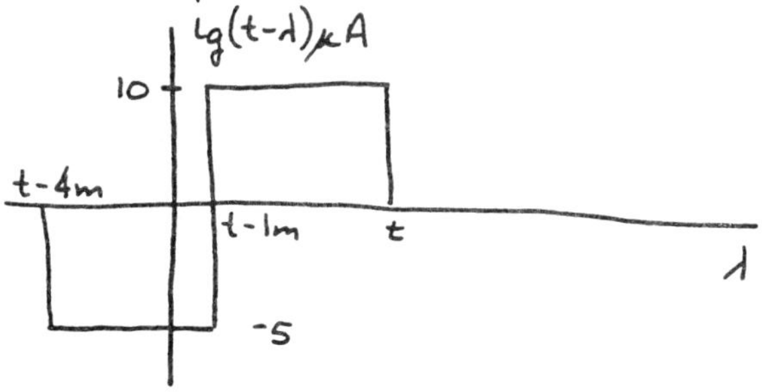

$$i_o = \int_0^{t-1\times10^{-3}} (-5\times10^{-6})(800e^{-1000\lambda}\,d\lambda)$$

$$+\int_{t-1\times10^{-3}}^{t} (10\times10^{-6})(800e^{-1000\lambda}\,d\lambda)$$

$$= -0.004\frac{e^{-1000\lambda}}{-1000}\Big|_0^{t-1\times10^{-3}} + 0.008\frac{e^{-1000\lambda}}{-1000}\Big|_{t-1\times10^{-3}}^{t}$$

$$= 4\left[e^{-1000(t-0.001)} - 1\right] - 8\left[e^{-1000t} - e^{-1000(t-0.001)}\right]$$

$$i_o = [12e^{-1000(t-0.001)} - 8e^{-1000t} - 4]\ \mu\text{A}$$

$4\,\text{ms} \le t \le \infty$:

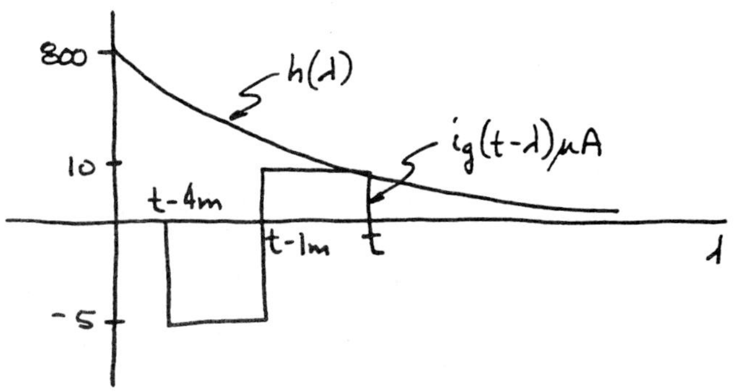

$$i_o(\mu\text{A}) = \int_{t-0.004}^{t-0.001} -4e^{-1000\lambda}\,d\lambda + \int_{t-0.001}^{t} 8e^{-1000\lambda}\,d\lambda$$

$$= 4e^{-1000\lambda}\Big|_{t-0.004}^{t-0.001} - 8e^{-1000\lambda}\Big|_{t-0.001}^{t}$$

$$i_o = [12e^{-1000(t-0.001)} - 4e^{-1000(t-0.004)} - 8e^{-1000t}]\ \mu\text{A}$$

[b] $V_o = 0.025sI_o = \dfrac{20sI_g}{s+1000}$

$$\frac{V_o}{I_g} = H(s) = \frac{20s}{s+1000} = 20 - \frac{20{,}000}{s+1000}$$

$$h(\lambda) = 20\delta(\lambda) - 20{,}000e^{-1000\lambda}$$

$0 < t < 0.001$ s:

$$v_o = \int_0^t (10\times10^{-6})[20\delta(\lambda) - 20{,}000e^{-1000\lambda}]\,d\lambda$$

$$= 200\times10^{-6} - 0.2\frac{e^{-1000\lambda}}{-1000}\Big|_0^t$$

$$= 200\times10^{-6} + 200\times10^{-6}[e^{-1000t} - 1] = 200e^{-1000t}\ \mu\text{V}$$

$0.001\,\text{s} < t < 0.004\,\text{s}$:

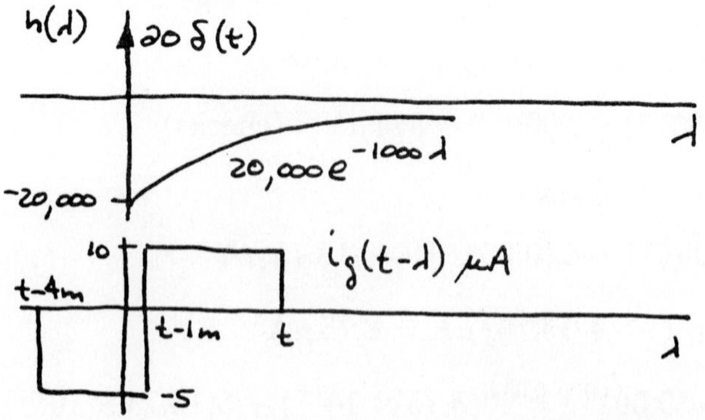

$$v_o = \int_0^{t-0.001} (-5\times10^{-6})[20\delta(\lambda) - 20{,}000e^{-1000\lambda}]\,d\lambda$$

$$+\int_{t-0.001}^{t} (10\times10^{-6})(-20{,}000e^{-1000\lambda})\,d\lambda$$

$$= -100\times10^{-6} + 0.1\frac{e^{-1000\lambda}}{-1000}\Bigg|_0^{t-0.001} - 0.2\frac{e^{-1000\lambda}}{-1000}\Bigg|_{t-0.001}^{t}$$

$$= -100\times10^{-6} - 0.1\times10^{-3}e^{-1000(t-0.001)} + 0.1\times10^{-3}$$

$$+0.2\times10^{-3}e^{-1000t} - 0.2\times10^{-3}e^{-1000(t-0.001)}$$

$$= 200e^{-1000t} - 300e^{-1000(t-0.001)}\,\mu\text{V}$$

$0.004\,\text{s} < t < \infty$:

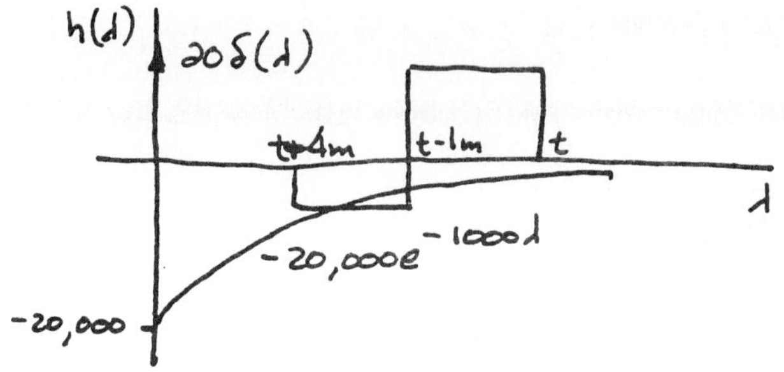

$$v_o = \int_{t-0.004}^{t-0.001} (-5\times10^{-6})(-20{,}000e^{-1000\lambda})\,d\lambda$$

$$+\int_{t-0.001}^{t} (10\times10^{-6})(-20{,}000e^{-1000\lambda})\,d\lambda$$

$$= 200e^{-1000t} - 300e^{-1000(t-0.001)} + 100e^{-1000(t-0.004)}\,\mu\text{V}$$

[c] At $t = 0.001^-$:

$$i_o = 8(1-e^{-1}) = -13.75\,\mu\text{A}; \qquad i_{20\Omega} = (10+13.75) = 23.75\,\mu\text{A}$$

$\therefore \quad v_o = 20(23.75 \times 10^{-6}) + 5(13.75 \times 10^{-6}) = 544\,\mu\text{V}$

From the solution for v_o we have

$v_o(0.001^-) = 200e^{-1} = 544\,\mu\text{V}$ (checks)

At $t = 0.001^+$:

$i_o(0.001^+) = i_o(0.001^-) = -13.75\,\mu\text{A}$

$i_{20\Omega} = (-5 + 13.75)\,\mu\text{A} = 8.75\,\mu\text{A}$

$\therefore \quad v_o(0.001^+) = 20(8.75 \times 10^{-6}) + 5(13.73 \times 10^{-6}) = 244\,\mu\text{V}$

From the solution for v_o we have

$v_o(0.001^+) = 200e^{-1} - 300 = 244\,\mu\text{V}$ (checks)

At $t = 0.004^-$:

$i_o = 12e^{-3} - 8e^{-4} - 4 = -3.55\,\mu\text{A}$

$i_{20\Omega} = (-5 + 3.55) = -1.45\,\mu\text{A}$

$v_o = 20(-1.45 \times 10^{-6}) + 5(3.55 \times 10^{-6}) = -11.25\,\mu\text{V}$

From the solution for v_o,

$v_o((0.004^-) = 200e^{-4} - 300e^{-3} = -11.25\,\mu\text{V}$ (checks)

At $t = 0.004^+$:

$i_o(0.004^+) = i_o(0.004^-) = -3.55\,\mu\text{A}; \qquad i_{20\Omega} = 3.55\,\mu\text{A}$

$i_o = 20(3.55 \times 10^{-6}) + 5(3.55 \times 10^{-6}) = 88.75\,\mu\text{V}$

From the solution for v_o,

$v_o(0.004^+) = 200e^{-4} - 300e^{-3} + 100 = 88.75\,\mu\text{V}$(checks)

P 13.65 $v_i = 10 \sin \lambda\,[u(\lambda) - u(\lambda - \pi)]$

$$H(s) = \frac{1}{s+1}$$

$$h(\lambda) = e^{-\lambda}$$

$$h(t - \lambda) = e^{-(t-\lambda)} = e^{-t}e^{\lambda}$$

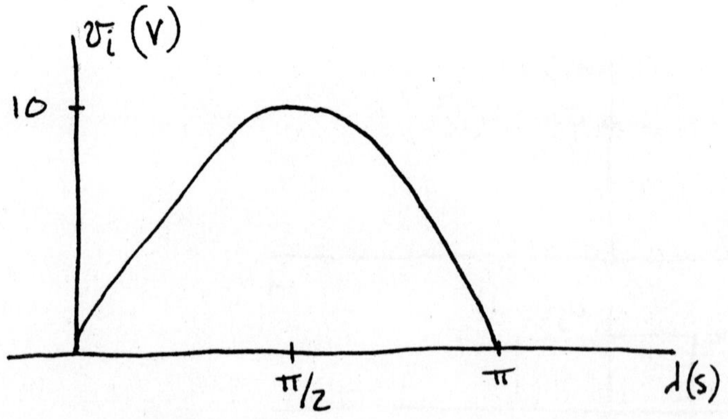

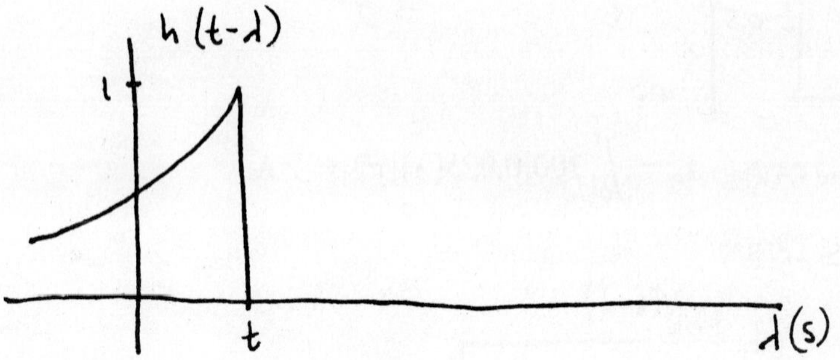

$$v_o = 10e^{-t}\int_0^t e^{\lambda}\sin\lambda\,d\lambda$$

$$= 10e^{-t}\left[\frac{e^{\lambda}}{2}(\sin\lambda - \cos\lambda\,\Big|_0^t\right]$$

$$= 5e^{-t}[e^t(\sin t - \cos t) + 1]$$

$$= 5(\sin t - \cos t + e^{-t})$$

$$v_o(2.2) = 7.539\,\text{mV}$$

P 13.66 **[a]** $I_o = \dfrac{60}{100}I_g; \qquad I_g = \dfrac{V_g}{30}$

$$\therefore\; I_o = \frac{V_g}{50}; \qquad H(s) = \frac{I_o}{V_g} = \frac{1}{50}$$

$$h(\lambda) = 0.02\delta(\lambda)$$

[b]

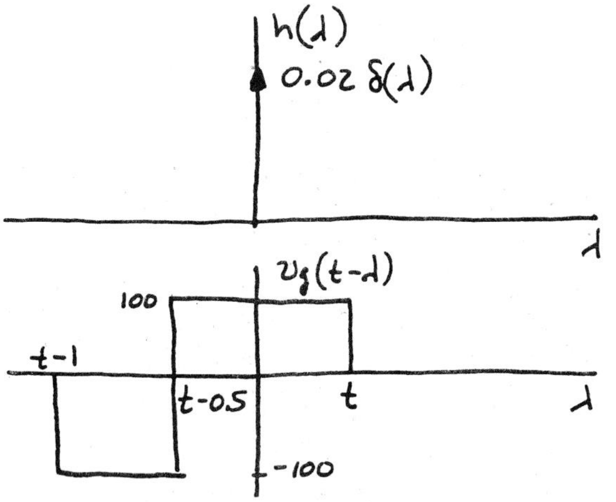

$0 < t < 0.5\,\mathrm{s}:$ $\qquad i_o = \int_0^t 100[0.02\delta(\lambda)]\,d\lambda = 2\,\mathrm{A}$

$0.5\,\mathrm{s} \leq t \leq 1.0\,\mathrm{s}:$

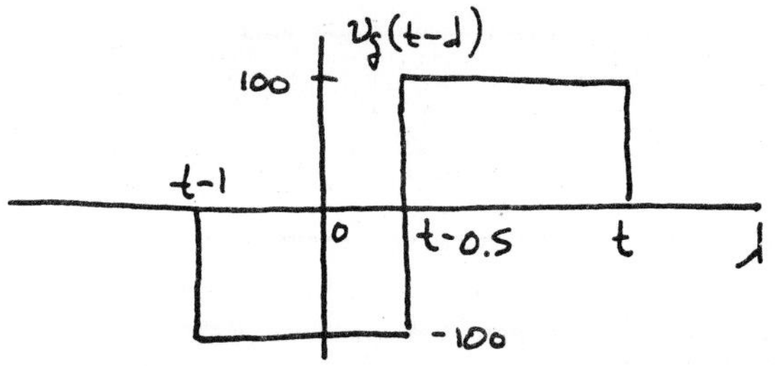

$$i_o = \int_0^{t-0.5} -100[0.02\delta(\lambda)]\,d\lambda = -2\,\mathrm{A}$$

$1\,\mathrm{s} < t < \infty:$ $\qquad v_o = 0$

[c]

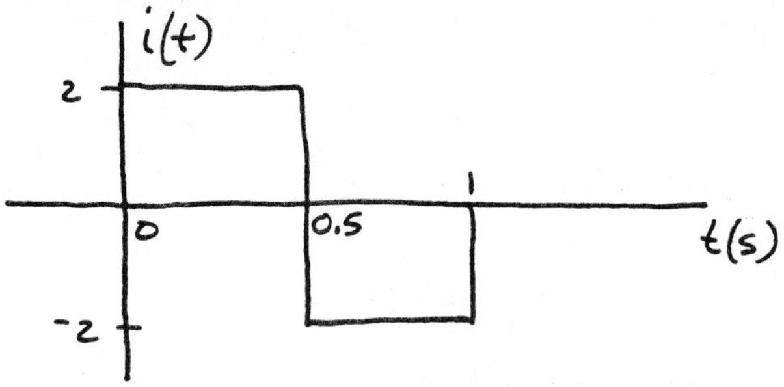

Yes, because the circuit has no memory.

P 13.67 [a]

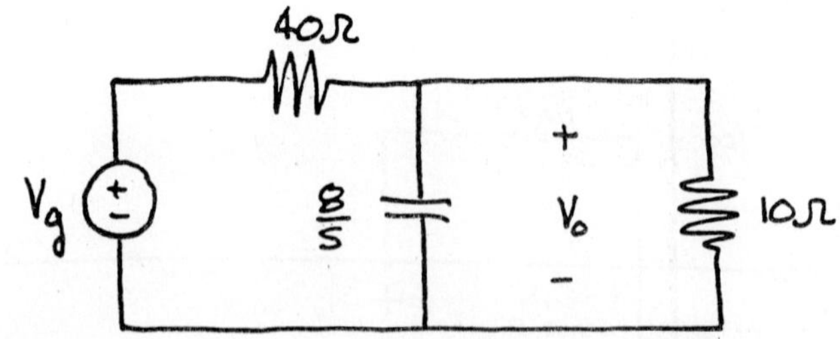

$$\frac{V_o - V_g}{40} + \frac{V_o s}{8} + \frac{V_o}{10} = 0$$

$$(5s + 5)V_o = V_g$$

$$H(s) = \frac{V_o}{V_g} = \frac{0.2}{s+1}; \qquad h(\lambda) = 0.2e^{-\lambda}u(\lambda)$$

[b]

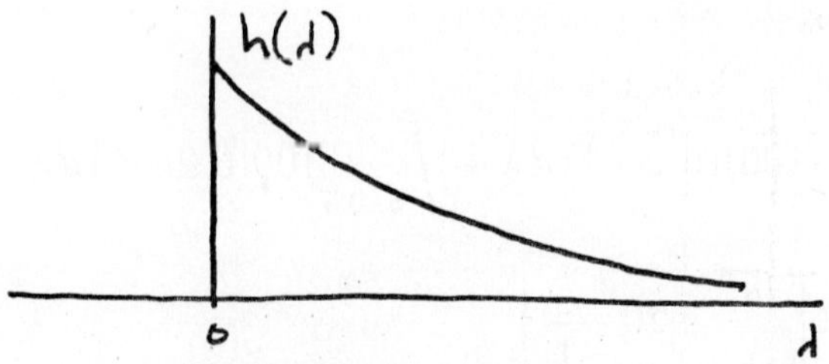

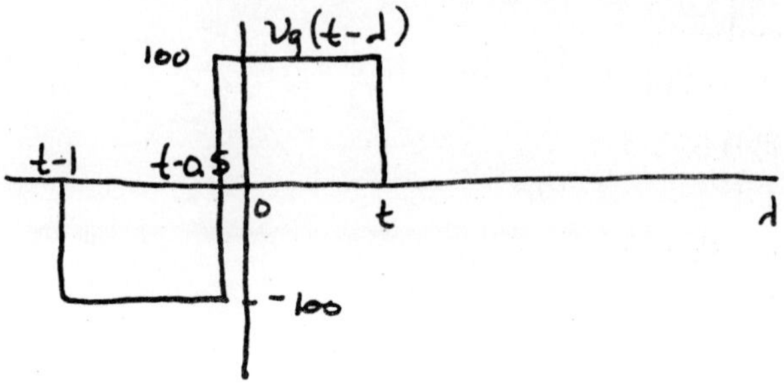

$0 \le t \le 0.5\,\text{s};$

$$v_o = \int_0^t 100(0.2e^{-\lambda})\,d\lambda = 20\frac{e^{-\lambda}}{-1}\bigg|_0^t$$

$$v_o = 20 - 20e^{-t}\,\text{V}, \qquad 0 \le t \le 0.5\,\text{s}$$

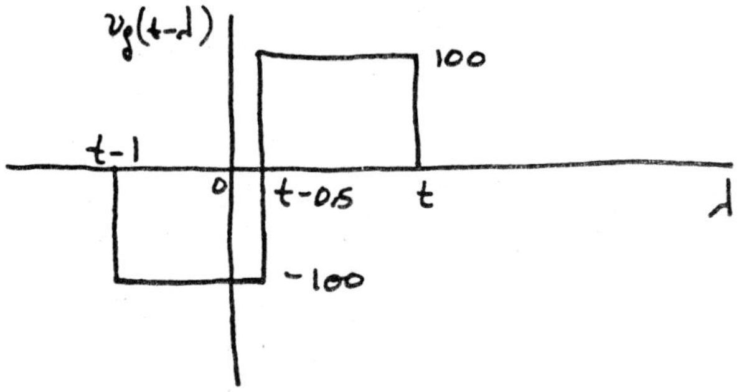

$0.5\,\mathrm{s} \leq t \leq 1\,\mathrm{s}$:

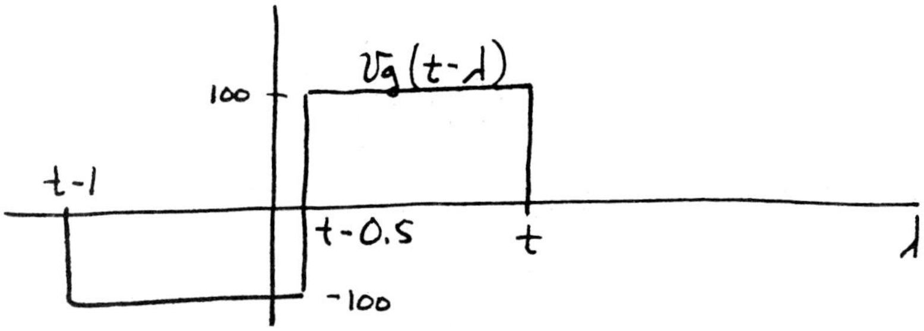

$$v_o = \int_0^{t-0.5} (-100)(0.2e^{-\lambda})\,d\lambda + \int_{t-0.5}^{t} 100(0.2e^{-\lambda})\,d\lambda$$

$$= -20\frac{e^{-\lambda}}{-1}\Bigg|_0^{t-0.5} + 20\frac{e^{-\lambda}}{-1}\Bigg|_{t-0.5}^{t}$$

$$= 40e^{-(t-0.5)} - 20e^{-t} - 20\,\mathrm{V}, \qquad 0.5\,\mathrm{s} \leq t \leq 1\,\mathrm{s}$$

$1\,\mathrm{s} \leq t \leq \infty$;

$$v_o = \int_{t-1}^{t-0.5} (-100)(0.2e^{-\lambda})\,d\lambda + \int_{t-0.5}^{t} 100(0.2e^{-\lambda})\,d\lambda$$

$$= -20\frac{e^{-\lambda}}{-1}\Bigg|_{t-1}^{t-0.5} + 20\frac{e^{-\lambda}}{-1}\Bigg|_{t-0.5}^{t}$$

$$= 40e^{-(t-0.5)} - 20e^{-(t-1)} - 20e^{-t}\,\mathrm{V}, \qquad 1\,\mathrm{s} \leq t \leq \infty$$

[c]

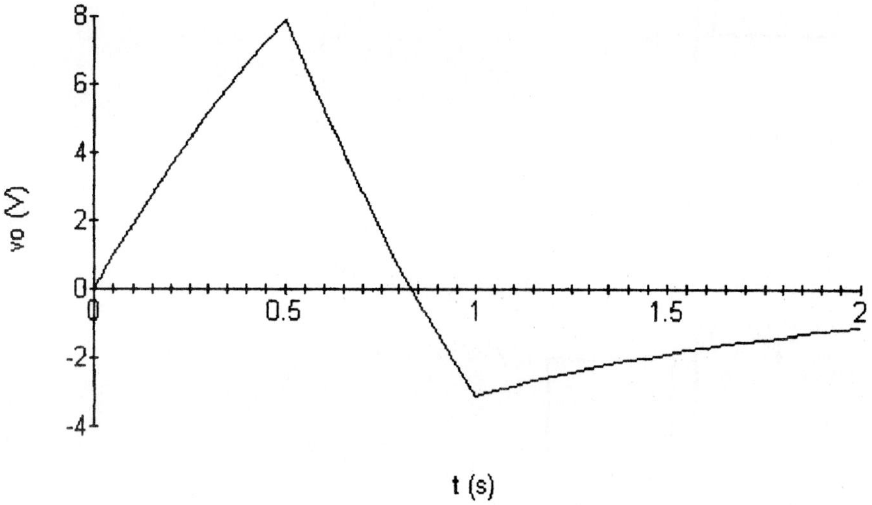

[d] No, the circuit has memory because of the capacitive storage element.

P 13.68

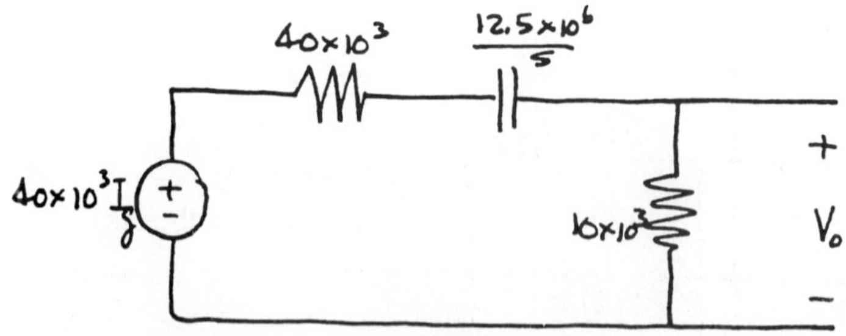

$$V_o = \frac{40 \times 10^3 I_g}{50 \times 10^3 + 12.5 \times 10^6/s}(10 \times 10^3)$$

$$\frac{V_o}{I_g} = H(s) = \frac{8000s}{s + 250}$$

$$H(s) = 8000\left[1 - \frac{250}{s + 250}\right] = 8000 - \frac{2 \times 10^6}{s + 250}$$

$$h(t) = 8000\delta(t) - 2 \times 10^6 e^{-250t}$$

$$v_o = \int_0^{5\times10^{-3}} (-10 \times 10^{-3})[8000\delta(\lambda) - 2 \times 10^6 e^{-250\lambda}]\,d\lambda$$

$$+\int_{5\times10^{-3}}^{7\times10^{-3}} (5 \times 10^{-3})[-2 \times 10^6 e^{-250\lambda}]\,d\lambda$$

$$= -80 + 20{,}000\int_0^{5\times10^{-3}} e^{-250\lambda}\,d\lambda - 10{,}000\int_{5\times10^{-3}}^{7\times10^{-3}} e^{-250\lambda}\,d\lambda$$

$$= -80 - 80(e^{-1.25} - 1) + 40(e^{-1.75} - e^{-1.25})$$

$$= -120e^{-1.25} + 40e^{-1.75} = -27.43\,\text{V}$$

Alternate:

$$I_g = \int_0^{2\times10^{-3}} (5 \times 10^{-3})e^{-st}\,dt + \int_{2\times10^{-3}}^{8\times10^{-3}} (-10 \times 10^{-3})e^{-st}\,dt$$

$$= \left[\frac{5}{s} - \frac{15}{s}e^{-2\times10^{-3}s} + \frac{10}{s}e^{-8\times10^{-3}s}\right] \times 10^{-3}$$

$$V_o = I_g H(s) = \frac{8}{s + 250}[5 - 15e^{-2\times10^{-3}s} + 10e^{-8\times10^{-3}s}]$$

$$= \frac{40}{s + 250} - \frac{120e^{-2\times10^{-3}s}}{s + 250} + \frac{80e^{-8\times10^{-3}s}}{s + 250}]$$

$$v_o(t) = 40e^{-250t} - 120e^{-250(t-2\times10^{-3})}u(t-2\times10^{-3})$$
$$+80e^{-250(t-8\times10^{-3})}u(t-8\times10^{-3})$$

$$v_o(7\times10^{-3}) = 40e^{-1.75} - 120e^{-1.25} + 0 = -27.43\text{ V} \quad \text{(checks)}$$

P 13.69 [a] $H(s) = \dfrac{V_o}{V_i} = \dfrac{1/LC}{s^2 + (R/L)s + (1/LC)}$

$$= \frac{25}{s^2 + 10s + 25} = \frac{25}{(s+5)^2}$$

$$h(\lambda) = 25\lambda e^{-5\lambda}u(\lambda)$$

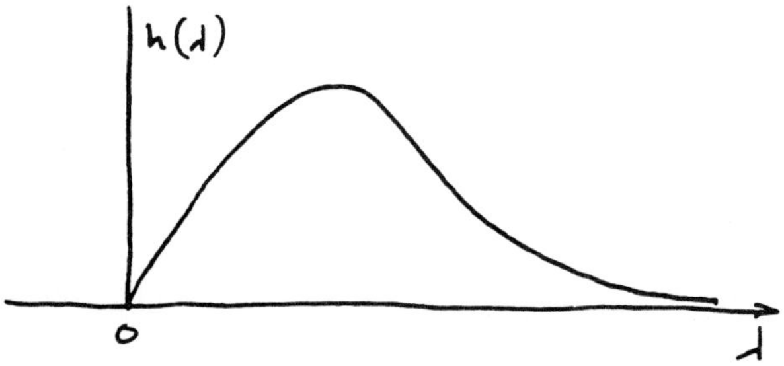

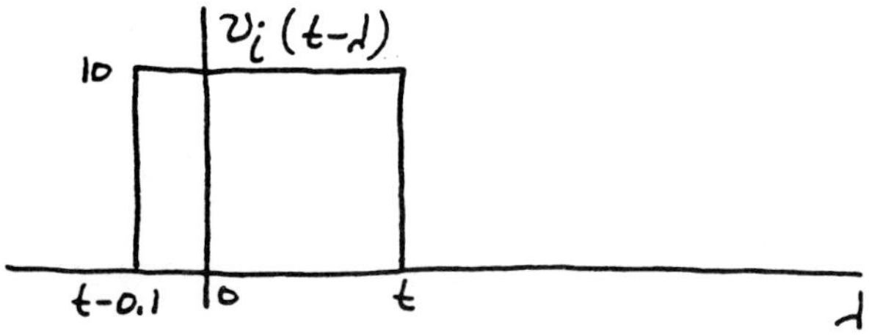

$0 \leq t \leq 0.10s$:

$$v_o = 250\int_0^t \lambda e^{-5\lambda}\,d\lambda$$

$$= 250\left\{\frac{e^{-5\lambda}}{25}(-5\lambda - 1)\Big|_0^t\right\}$$

$$= 10[1 - e^{-5t}(5t+1)]$$

$0.1 \leq t \leq \infty$:

$$v_o = 250\int_{t-0.1}^t \lambda e^{-5\lambda}\,d\lambda$$

$$= 250\left\{\frac{e^{-5\lambda}}{25}(-5\lambda - 1)\Big|_{t-0.1}^t\right\}$$

$$= -10e^{-5t}[(5t+1) - e^{0.5}(5t+0.5)]$$

[b]

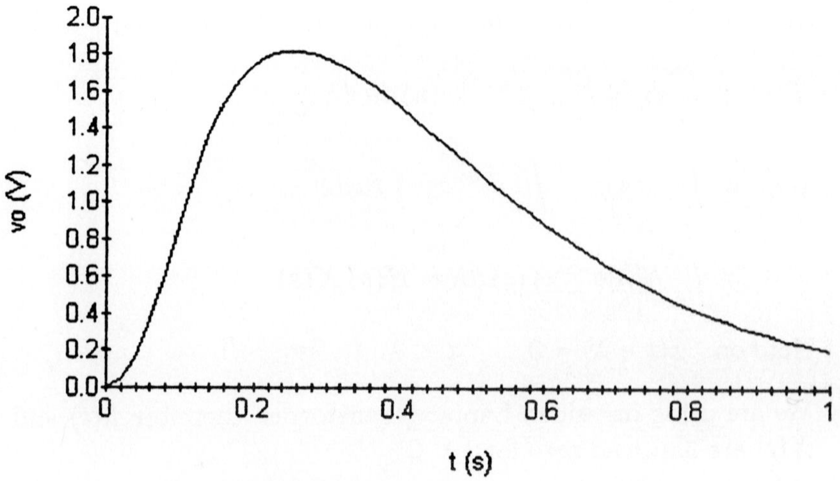

P 13.70 $H(s) = \frac{V_o}{V_i} = \frac{8s}{50+10s} = \frac{0.8s}{s+5}$

$$= 0.8\left[1 - \frac{5}{s+5}\right] = 0.8 - \frac{5}{s+5}$$

$$h(t) = 0.8\delta(t) - 4e^{-5t}$$

$$v_o = \int_0^t 75[0.8\delta(\lambda) - 4e^{-5\lambda}]\,d\lambda$$

$$= \int_0^t 60\delta(\lambda)\,d\lambda - 300\int_0^t e^{-5\lambda}\,d\lambda$$

$$= 60 - 300\frac{e^{-5\lambda}}{-5}\Big|_0^t$$

$$= 60 + 60[e^{-5t} - 1] = 60e^{-5t}\text{ V} \qquad 0 \le t \le \infty$$

P 13.71 [a] $Y(s) = \int_0^\infty y(t)e^{-st}\,dt$

$$Y(s) = \int_0^\infty e^{-st}\left[\int_0^\infty h(\lambda)x(t-\lambda)\,d\lambda\right]dt$$

$$= \int_0^\infty\int_0^\infty e^{-st}h(\lambda)x(t-\lambda)\,d\lambda\,dt$$

$$= \int_0^\infty h(\lambda)\int_0^\infty e^{-st}x(t-\lambda)\,dt\,d\lambda$$

But $x(t-\lambda) = 0$ when $t < \lambda$

Therefore $Y(s) = \int_0^\infty h(\lambda) \int_\lambda^\infty e^{-st} x(t-\lambda)\, dt\, d\lambda$

Let $u = t - \lambda$; $du = dt$; $u = 0$, $t = \lambda$; $u = \infty$, $t = \infty$

$$Y(s) = \int_0^\infty h(\lambda) \int_0^\infty e^{-s(u+\lambda)} x(u)\, du\, d\lambda$$

$$= \int_0^\infty h(\lambda) e^{-s\lambda} \int_0^\infty e^{-su} x(u)\, du\, d\lambda$$

$$= \int_0^\infty h(\lambda) e^{-s\lambda} X(s)\, d\lambda = H(s)\, X(s)$$

Note on $x(t-\lambda) = 0, \quad t < \lambda$

We are using one-sided Laplace transforms; therefore $h(t)$ and $X(t)$ are assumed zero for $t < 0$.

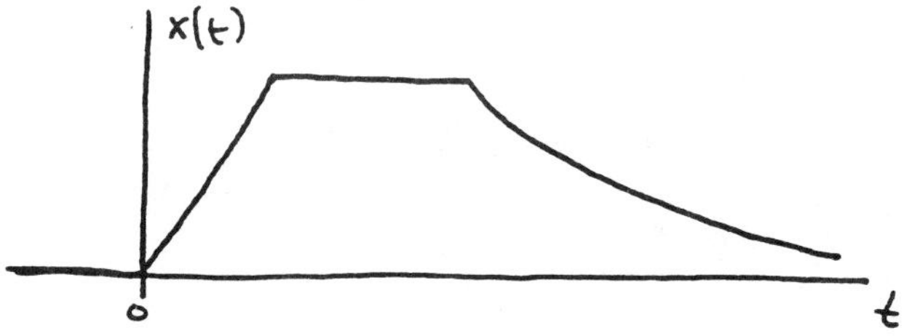

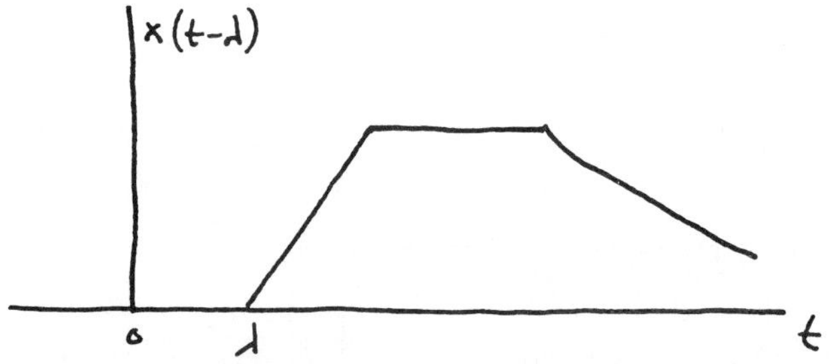

[b] $F(s) = \dfrac{a}{s(s+a)^2} = \dfrac{1}{s} \cdot \dfrac{a}{(s+a)^2} = H(s)X(s)$

$\therefore \quad h(t) = u(t), \qquad x(t) = at\, e^{-at} u(t)$

$$\therefore \quad f(t) = \int_0^t (1)a\lambda e^{-a\lambda}\,d\lambda = a\left[\frac{e^{-a\lambda}}{a^2}(-a\lambda - 1)\right]_0^t$$

$$= \frac{1}{a}[e^{-at}(-at - 1) - 1(-1)] = \frac{1}{a}[1 - e^{-at} - ate^{-at}]$$

$$= \left[\frac{1}{a} - \frac{1}{a}e^{-at} - te^{-at}\right]u(t)$$

Check:

$$F(s) = \frac{a}{s(s+a)^2} = \frac{K_0}{s} + \frac{K_1}{(s+a)^2} + \frac{K_2}{s+a}$$

$$K_0 = \frac{1}{a}; \qquad K_1 = -1; \qquad K_2 = \frac{d}{ds}\left(\frac{a}{s}\right)_{s=-a} = -\frac{1}{a}$$

$$f(t) = \left[\frac{1}{a} - te^{-at} - \frac{1}{a}e^{-at}\right]u(t)$$

P 13.72 $$H(j8000) = \frac{10^4(6000 + j8000)}{-64 \times 10^6 + j7 \times 10^6 + 88 \times 10^6}$$

$$= \frac{10^7(6 + j8)}{10^6(24 + j7)} = 4\underline{/36.87^\circ}$$

$$\therefore \quad v_o(t) = 50\cos(8000t + 36.87^\circ)\text{ V}$$

P 13.73 [a] The s-domain circuit is

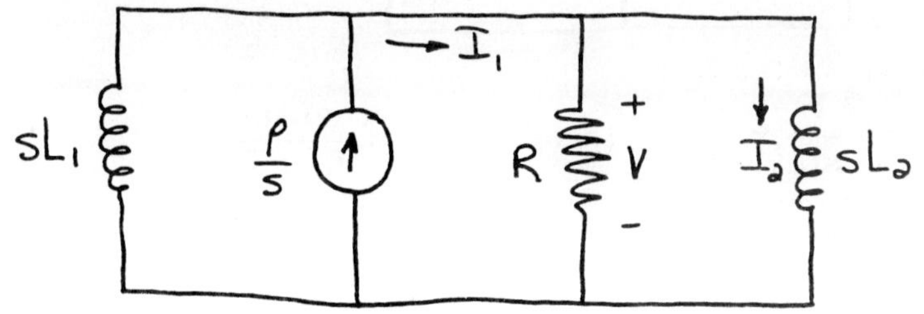

The node-voltage equation is $\dfrac{V}{sL_1} + \dfrac{V}{R} + \dfrac{V}{sL_2} = \dfrac{\rho}{s}$

Therefore $V = \dfrac{\rho R}{s + (R/L_e)}$ where $L_e = \dfrac{L_1L_2}{L_1 + L_2}$

Therefore $v = \rho R e^{-(R/L_e)t}u(t)$ V

[b] $$I_1 = \frac{V}{R} + \frac{V}{sL_2} = \frac{\rho[s + (R/L_2)]}{s[s + (R/L_e)]} = \frac{K_0}{s} + \frac{K_1}{s + (R/L_e)}$$

$$K_0 = \frac{\rho L_1}{L_1 + L_2}; \qquad K_1 = \frac{\rho L_2}{L_1 + L_2}$$

Thus we have $i_1 = \dfrac{\rho}{L_1 + L_2}[L_1 + L_2 e^{-(R/L_e)t}]u(t)$ A

[c] $I_2 = \dfrac{V}{sL_2} = \dfrac{(\rho R/L_2)}{s[s + (R/L_e)]} = \dfrac{K_2}{s} + \dfrac{K_3}{s + (R/L_e)}$

$$K_2 = \frac{\rho L_1}{L_1 + L_2}; \qquad K_3 = \frac{-\rho L_1}{L_1 + L_2}$$

Therefore $i_2 = \dfrac{\rho L_1}{L_1 + L_2}[1 - e^{-(R/L_e)t}]u(t)$

[d] $\lambda(t) = L_1 i_1 + L_2 i_2 = \rho L_1$

P 13.74 [a] As $R \to \infty$, $v(t) \to \rho L_e \delta(t)$ since the area under the impulse generating function is ρL_e.

$$i_1(t) \to \frac{\rho L_1}{L_1 + L_2} \quad \text{as} \quad R \to \infty$$

$$i_2(t) \to \frac{\rho L_1}{L_1 + L_2} \quad \text{as} \quad R \to \infty$$

[b] The s-domain circuit is

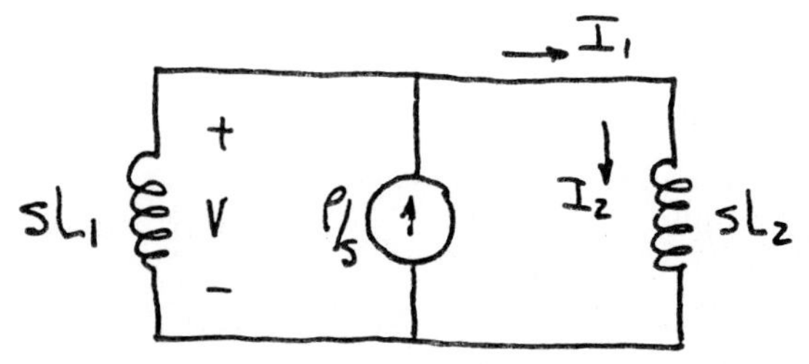

$$\frac{V}{sL_1} + \frac{V}{sL_2} = \frac{\rho}{s}; \qquad \text{therefore} \quad V = \frac{\rho L_1 L_2}{L_1 + L_2} = \rho L_e$$

Therefore $v(t) = \rho L_e \delta(t)$

$$I_1 = I_2 = \frac{V}{sL_2} = \left(\frac{\rho L_1}{L_1 + L_2}\right)\left(\frac{1}{s}\right)$$

Therefore $i_1 = i_2 = \dfrac{\rho L_1}{L_1 + L_2}u(t)$ A

P 13.75 [a]

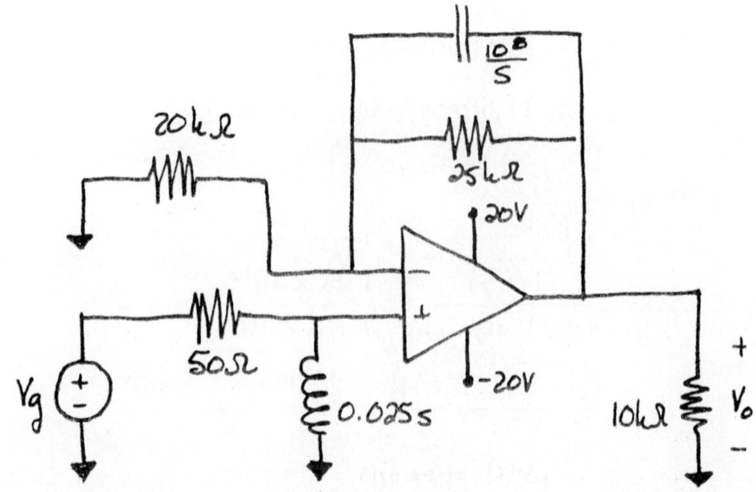

$$V_p = \frac{-0.025s}{50 + 0.025s}V_g = \frac{s}{s + 2000}V_g$$

$$V_n = V_p$$

$$\frac{V_p}{20{,}000} + \frac{V_p - V_o}{25{,}000} + \frac{(V_p - V_o)s}{10^8} = 0$$

$$\therefore \quad V_p = \frac{(s + 4000)}{(s + 9000)}V_o$$

$$\frac{sV_g}{s + 2000} = \frac{s + 4000}{s + 9000}V_o$$

$$\therefore \quad H(s) = \frac{V_o}{V_g} = \frac{s(s + 9000)}{(s + 2000)(s + 4000)}$$

[b] $v_g = u(t); \qquad V_g = \dfrac{1}{s}$

$$V_o = \frac{10(s + 9000)}{(s + 2000)(s + 4000)} = \frac{K_1}{s + 2000} + \frac{K_2}{s + 4000}$$

$$K_1 = \frac{7000}{2000} = 35; \qquad K_2 = \frac{50{,}000}{-2000} = -25$$

$$\therefore \quad v_o(t) = (35e^{-2000t} - 25e^{-4000t})u(t)\ \text{V}$$

[c] $\omega = 2000$ rad/s

$$H(j\omega) = \frac{j2000(9000 + j2000)}{(2000 + j2000)(4000 + j2000)}$$

$$= 1.25 + j0.75 = 1.46\underline{/30.96^\circ}$$

$$\therefore \quad V_{oss} = (8)(1.46)\cos(2000t + 30.96^\circ)$$

$$= 11.68\cos(2000t + 30.96^\circ)\text{ V}$$

P 13.76 [a] $H(s) = \dfrac{-Z_f}{Z_i}$

$$Z_f = \frac{(1/C_f)}{s + (1/R_fC_f)} = \frac{1.25\times10^{12}}{s + 5\times10^6}$$

$$Z_i = \frac{R_i[s + (1/R_iC_i)]}{s} = \frac{25{,}000(s + 8000)}{s}$$

$$H(s) = \frac{-50\times10^6 s}{(s + 8000)(s + 5\times10^6)}$$

$$H(j8000) = \frac{-50\times10^6(j8000)}{(8000 + j8000)(5\times10^6 + j8000)} = 10/\sqrt{2}\underline{/-135^\circ}$$

$$v_o(t) = (200\sqrt{10})\times10^{-3}(10/\sqrt{2})\cos(8000t - 135^\circ)$$

$$= 4.47\cos(8000t - 135^\circ)\text{ V}$$

P 13.77 $V_o = \dfrac{75}{s} - \dfrac{100}{s + 800} + \dfrac{25}{s + 3200} = \dfrac{192\times10^6}{s(s + 800)(s + 3200)}$

$$V_o = H(s)V_g = H(s)\left(\frac{240}{s}\right)$$

$$\therefore \quad H(s) = \frac{800{,}000}{(s + 800)(s + 3200)}$$

$$H(j1600) = \frac{8\times10^5}{(800 + j1600)(3200 + j1600)} = 0.125\underline{/-90^\circ}$$

$$\therefore \quad v_o(t) = (40)(0.125)\cos(1600t - 90^\circ)\text{ V} = 5\sin1600t\text{ V}$$

P 13.78 Original charge on C_1; $q_1 = V_0C_1$

The charge transferred to C_2; $q_2 = V_0C_e = \dfrac{V_0C_1C_2}{C_1 + C_2}$

The charge remaining on C_1; $q_1' = q_1 - q_2 = \dfrac{V_0C_1^2}{C_1 + C_2}$

Therefore $V_2 = \dfrac{q_2}{C_2} = \dfrac{V_0C_1}{C_1 + C_2}$ and $V_1 = \dfrac{q_1'}{C_1} = \dfrac{V_0C_1}{C_1 + C_2}$

P 13.79 [a] $Z_1 = \dfrac{1/C_1}{s + 1/R_1C_1} = \dfrac{20 \times 10^{10}}{s + 20 \times 10^4}\Omega$

$$Z_2 = \frac{1/C_2}{s + 1/R_2C_2} = \frac{5 \times 10^{10}}{s + 12{,}500}\Omega$$

$$\frac{V_0}{Z_2} + \frac{V_0 - 10/s}{Z_1} = 0$$

$$\frac{V_0(s + 12{,}500)}{5 \times 10^{10}} + \frac{V_0(s + 20 \times 10^4)}{20 \times 10^{10}} = \frac{10}{s}\,\frac{(s + 20 \times 10^4)}{20 \times 10^{10}}$$

$$V_0 = \frac{2(s + 200{,}000)}{s(s + 50{,}000)} = \frac{K_1}{s} + \frac{K_2}{s + 50{,}000}$$

$$K_1 = \frac{2(200{,}000)}{50{,}000} = 8$$

$$K_2 = \frac{2(150{,}000)}{-50{,}000} = -6$$

$$\therefore \quad v_o = [8 - 6e^{-50{,}000t}]u(t)\text{ V}$$

[b] $I_0 = \dfrac{V_0}{Z_2} = \dfrac{2(s + 200{,}000)(s + 12{,}500)}{s(s + 50{,}000)5 \times 10^{10}}$

$$= 40 \times 10^{-12}\left[1 + \frac{162{,}500s + 25 \times 10^8}{s(s + 50{,}000)}\right]$$

$$= 40 \times 10^{-12}\left[1 + \frac{K_1}{s} + \frac{K_2}{s + 50{,}000}\right]$$

$$K_1 = 50{,}000; \qquad K_2 = 112{,}500$$

$$i_o = 40\delta(t) + [2 \times 10^6 + 4.5 \times 10^6 e^{-50{,}000t}]u(t)\,pA$$

[c] When $C_1 = 80\,\text{pF}$

$$Z_1 = \frac{125 \times 10^8}{s + 12{,}500}\Omega$$

$$\frac{V_0(s + 12{,}500)}{500 \times 10^8} + \frac{V_0(s + 12{,}500)}{125 \times 10^8} = \frac{10}{s}\,\frac{(s + 12{,}500)}{125 \times 10^8}$$

$$\therefore \quad V_0 + 4V_0 = \frac{40}{s}$$

$$V_0 = \frac{8}{s}$$

$$v_o = 8u(t)\text{ V}$$

$$I_0 = \frac{V_0}{s} = \frac{8}{s}\frac{(s+12{,}500)}{5\times 10^{10}} = 160\times 10^{-12}\left[1+\frac{12{,}500}{s}\right]$$

$$i_o(t) = 160\delta(t) + 2\times 10^{-6}u(t)\,\text{pA}$$

P 13.80 Return to Problem 13.79[a] and make a partial fraction expansion of V_0 in terms of the circuit parameters. The result is

$$V_0 = \frac{10R_e/R_1}{s} + \frac{10[(C_1/C_e)-(R_e/R_1)]}{s+(1/R_eC_e)}$$

Now observe that the exponential term is eliminated when $C_1/C_e = R_e/R_1$, and this equality reduces to $R_1C_1 = R_2C_2$.

P 13.81

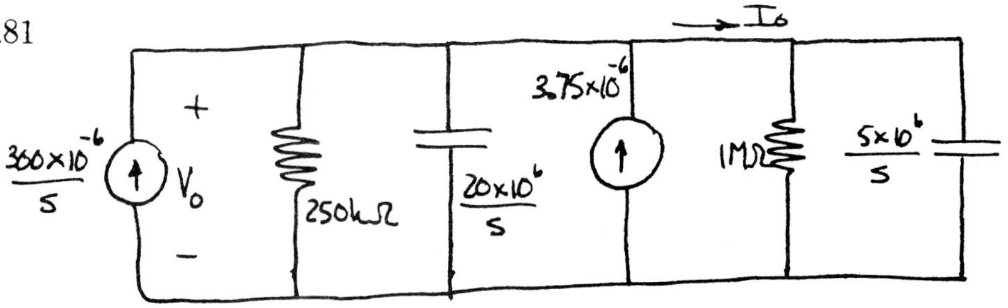

$$\frac{V_o}{0.25\times 10^6} + \frac{V_o s}{20\times 10^6} + \frac{V_o}{10^6} + \frac{V_o s}{5\times 10^6} = \left(\frac{300}{s}+3.75\right)10^{-6}$$

$$\therefore\ V_o = \frac{15(s+80)}{s(s+20)} = \frac{60}{s} - \frac{45}{s+20}$$

$$v_o(t) = (60 - 45e^{-20t})u(t)\,\text{V}$$

$$I_o = \frac{V_o}{10^6} + \frac{V_o s}{5\times 10^6} = 0.2\times 10^{-6}(s+5)V_o$$

$$= \frac{(3\times 10^{-6})(s+5)(s+80)}{s(s+20)}$$

$$= 3\times 10^{-6}\left[1+\frac{65s+400}{s(s+20)}\right]$$

$$= 3\times 10^{-6}\left[1+\frac{20}{s}+\frac{45}{s+20}\right]$$

$$= \left(3+\frac{60}{s}+\frac{135}{s+20}\right)10^{-6}$$

$$i_o(t) = 3\delta(t) + [60+135e^{-20t}]u(t)\,\mu\text{A}$$

[b] First consider the 0.05 μF capacitor:

$$v_{0.05}(0^-) = 75\text{ V}; \qquad v_{0.05}(0^+) = 15\text{ V}$$

$$\therefore \quad \frac{dv}{dt}(0) = (15 - 75)\delta(t) = -60\delta(t)$$

$$\therefore \quad i_{0.05\mu F}(0) = (0.05)(-60)\delta(t) \times 10^{-6} = -3\delta(t)\,\mu\text{A}$$

At the terminals of the 0.2 μF capacitor

$$v_{0.2}(0^-) = 0\text{ V}; \qquad v_{0.2}(0^+) = 15\text{ V}$$

$$\therefore \quad \frac{dv}{dt}(0) = (15 - 0)\delta(t) = 15\delta(t)$$

$$\therefore \quad i_{0.2\mu F}(0) = (0.2)(15)\delta(t) \times 10^{-6} = 3\delta(t)\,\mu\text{A(checks)}$$

At $t = 0^+$ our solution predicts

$$i_o - 60 + 135 - 195\,\mu\text{A}$$

$$\frac{dv_o}{dt}(0^+) = 900\text{ V/s}; \qquad v_o(0^+) = 15\text{ V}$$

$$i_{0.05\mu F} = (0.05)(900) = 45\,\mu\text{A}$$

$$i_{0.2\mu F} = (0.2)(900) = 180\,\mu\text{A}$$

$$i_{1M} = \frac{15}{1} = 15\,\mu\text{A}$$

$$i_{250k\Omega} = \left(\frac{75 - 15}{0.25}\right) = 240\,\mu\text{A}$$

Note: $240 - 45 = 195\,\mu$A and $180 + 15 = 195\,\mu$A. Therefore, $i_o(0^+)$ makes sense.
Also note

$$i_o(\infty) = 60\,\mu\text{A} \qquad \text{from solution}$$

$$i_o(\infty) = \frac{75}{1.25 \times 10^6} = 60\,\mu\text{A} \qquad \text{from circuit}$$

$$v_o(\infty) = 60\text{ V} \qquad \text{from solution}$$

$$v_o(\infty) = (60)(1) \times 10^{-6} \times 10^6 = 60\text{ V} \qquad \text{from circuit}$$

P 13.82 [a]

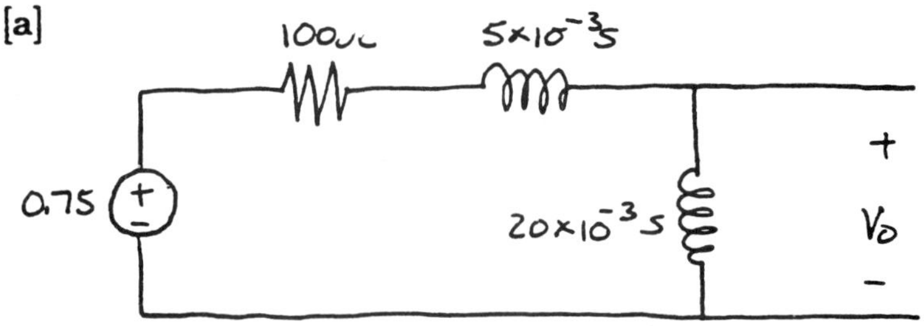

$$V_o = \frac{0.75}{100 + 25 \times 10^{-3}s} \cdot 20 \times 10^{-3}s$$

$$= \frac{0.6s}{s + 4000} = 0.6 - \frac{2400}{s + 4000}$$

$$v_o(t) = 0.6\delta(t) - 2400e^{-4000t}u(t)\text{ V}$$

[b] At $t = 0$ the voltage impulse establishes a current in the inductors; thus

$$i_L(0) = \frac{10^3}{25}\int_{0^-}^{0^+} 750 \times 10^{-3}\delta(t)\,dt = 30\text{ A}$$

It follows that since $i_L(0^-) = 0$ that

$$\frac{di_L}{dt}(0) = 30\delta(t)$$

$$\therefore \quad v_o(0) = (20 \times 10^{-3})(30\delta(t)) = 0.6\delta(t)$$

This agrees with our solution.
At $t = 0^+$ our circuit is

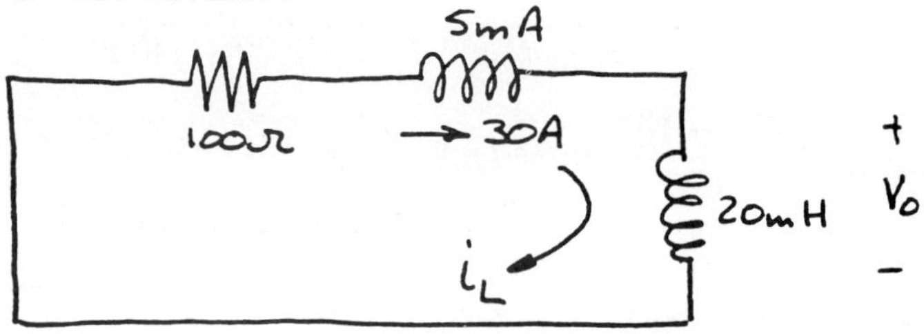

$$\therefore \quad i_L(t) = 30e^{-t/\tau}\text{ A}, \qquad t \geq 0^+$$

$$\tau = L/R = 0.25\text{ ms}$$

$$\therefore \quad i_L(t) = 30e^{-4000t}\text{ A}, \qquad t \geq 0^+$$

$$v_o(t) = 20 \times 10^{-3}\frac{di_L}{dt} = -2400e^{-4000t}\text{ V}, \qquad t \geq 0^+$$

which agrees with our solution.

P 13.83 [a] After making a source transformation, the circuit is as shown. The impulse current will pass through the capacitive branch since it appears as a short circuit to the impulsive current,

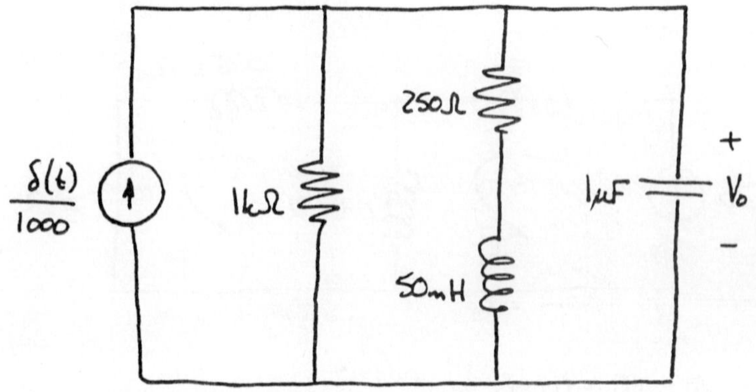

Therefore $v_o(0^+) = 10^6 \int_{0^-}^{0^+} \left[\frac{\delta(t)}{1000}\right] dt = 1000\,\text{V}$

Therefore $w_C = (0.5)Cv^2 = 0.5\,\text{J}$

[b] $i_L(0^+) = 0;$ therefore $w_L = 0\,\text{J}$

[c] $V_o(10^{-6})s + \frac{V_o}{250 + 0.05s} + \frac{V_o}{1000} = 10^{-3}$

Therefore

$$V_o = \frac{1000(s + 5000)}{s^2 + 6000s + 25 \times 10^6}$$

$$= \frac{K_1}{s + 3000 - j4000} + \frac{K_1^*}{s + 3000 + j4000}$$

$K_1 = 559.02\underline{/26.57^\circ};$ $K_1^* = 559.02\underline{/26.57^\circ}$

$v_o = [1118.03e^{-3000t}\cos(4000t - 26.57^\circ)]u(t)\,\text{V}$

[d] The s-domain circuit is

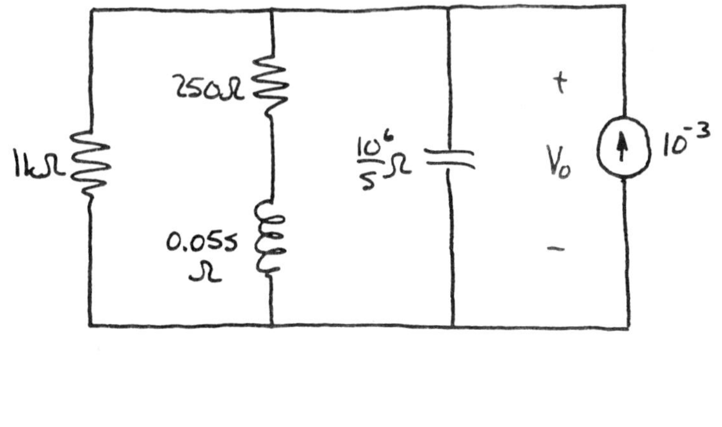

$$\frac{V_o s}{10^6} + \frac{V_o}{250 + 0.05s} + \frac{V_o}{1000} = 10^{-3}$$

Note that this equation is identical to that derived in part [c], therefore the solution for V_o will be the same.

P 13.84 [a]

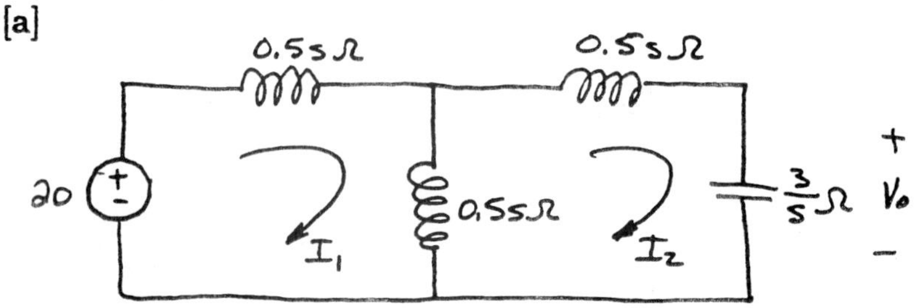

$$20 = sI_1 - 0.5sI_2$$

$$0 = -0.5sI_1 + \left(s + \frac{3}{s}\right) I_2$$

$$\Delta = \begin{vmatrix} s & -0.5s \\ -0.5s & (s + 3/s) \end{vmatrix} = s^2 + 3 - 0.25s^2 = 0.75(s^2 + 4)$$

$$N_1 = \begin{vmatrix} 20 & -0.5s \\ 0 & (s + 3/s) \end{vmatrix} = 20s + \frac{60}{s} = \frac{20s^2 + 60}{s} = \frac{20(s^2 + 3)}{s}$$

$$I_1 = \frac{N_1}{\Delta} = \frac{20(s^2 + 3)}{s(0.75)(s^2 + 4)} = \frac{80}{3} \cdot \frac{s^2 + 3}{s(s^2 + 4)}$$

$$= \frac{K_0}{s} + \frac{K_1}{s - j2} + \frac{K_1^*}{s + j2}$$

$$K_0 = \frac{80}{3}\left(\frac{3}{4}\right) = 20; \qquad K_1 = \frac{80}{3}\left[\frac{-4 + 3}{(j2)(j4)}\right] = \frac{10}{3}\underline{/0^\circ}$$

$$\therefore\ i_1 = \left[20 + \frac{20}{3}\cos 2t\right] u(t)\ \text{A}$$

[b] $$N_2 = \begin{vmatrix} s & 20 \\ -0.5s & 0 \end{vmatrix} = 10s$$

$$I_2 = \frac{N_2}{\Delta} = \frac{10s}{0.75(s^2 + 4)} = \frac{40}{3}\left(\frac{s}{s^2 + 4}\right) = \frac{K_1}{s - j2} + \frac{K_1^*}{s + j2}$$

$$K_1 = \frac{40}{3}\left(\frac{j2}{j4}\right) = \frac{20}{3}\underline{/0^\circ}$$

$$i_2 = \frac{40}{3}\cos 2tu(t) \text{ A}$$

[c] $V_0 = \frac{3}{s}I_2 = \left(\frac{3}{s}\right)\frac{40}{3}\left(\frac{s}{s^2+4}\right) = \frac{40}{s^2+4} = \frac{K_1}{s-j2} = \frac{K_1^*}{s+j2}$

$$K_1 = \frac{40}{j4} = -j10 = 10\underline{/90^\circ}$$

$$v_o = 20\cos(2t - 90^\circ) = 20\sin 2t$$

$$v_o = [20\sin 2t]u(t) \text{ V}$$

[d] Let us begin by noting i_1 jumps from 0 to (80/3) A between 0^- and 0^+ and in this same interval i_2 jumps from 0 to (40/3) A. Therefore in the derivatives of i_1 and i_2 there will be impulses of $(80/3)\delta(t)$ and $(40/3)\delta(t)$, respectively. Thus

$$\frac{di_1}{dt} = \frac{80}{3}\delta(t) - \frac{40}{3}\sin 2t \text{ A/s}$$

$$\frac{di_2}{dt} = \frac{40}{3}\delta(t) - \frac{80}{3}\sin 2t \text{ A/s}$$

From the circuit diagram we have

$$20\delta(t) = 1\frac{di_1}{dt} - 0.5\frac{di_2}{dt}$$

$$= \frac{80}{3}\delta(t) - \frac{40}{3}\sin 2t - \frac{20\delta(t)}{3} + \frac{40}{3}\sin 2t$$

$$= 20\delta(t)$$

Thus our solutions for i_1 and i_2 are in agreement with known circuit behavior.

Let us also note the impulsive voltage will impart energy into the circuit. Since there is no resistance in the circuit, the energy will not dissipate. Thus the fact that i_1, i_2, and v_o exist for all time is consistent with known circuit behavior.

Also note that although i_1 has a dc component, i_2 does not. This follows from known transformer behavior.

Finally we note the flux linkage prior to the appearance of the impulsive voltage is zero. Now since $v = d\lambda/dt$, the impulsive voltage source must be matched to an instantaneous change in flux linkage at $t = 0^+$ of 20.

For the given polarity dots and reference directions of i_1 and i_2 we have

$$\lambda(0^+) = L_1 i_1(0^+) + M i_1(0^+) - L_2 i_2(0^+) - M i_2(0^+)$$

$$\lambda(0^+) = 1\left(\frac{80}{3}\right) + 0.5\left(\frac{80}{3}\right) - 1\left(\frac{40}{3}\right) - 0.5\left(\frac{40}{3}\right)$$

$$= \frac{120}{3} - \frac{60}{3} = 20 \quad \text{(checks)}$$

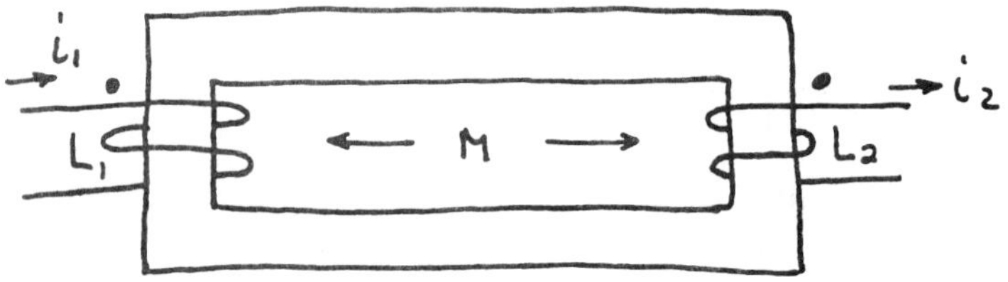

P 13.85 [a]

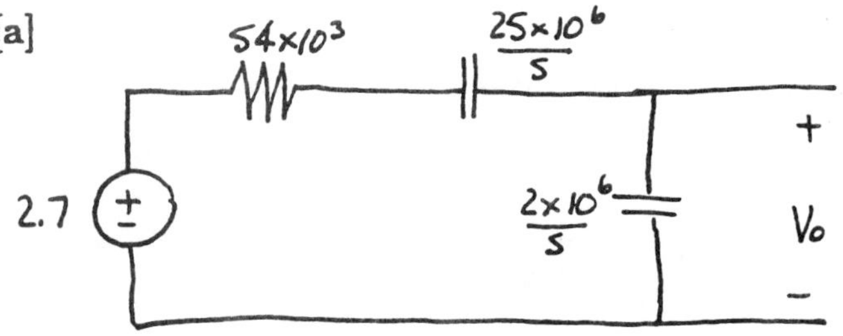

$$V_o = \frac{2.7}{54\times10^3 + 25\times10^6/s + 2\times10^6/s}\cdot\frac{2\times10^6}{s}$$

$$= \frac{5.4\times10^6}{54\times10^3 s + 27\times10^6} = \frac{100}{s+500}$$

$v_o(t) = 100e^{-500t}u(t)$ V

At $t = 0$ the impulsive current passes through the two capacitors. The voltage on the 0.04 μF capacitor at $t = 0^+$ is

$$v_{0.04} = 25\times10^6 \int_{0^-}^{0^+} 50\times10^{-6}\delta(t)\,dt = 1250\,\text{V}$$

The voltage on the 0.5 μF capacitor at $t = 0^+$ is

$$v_{0.5} = 2\times10^6 \int_{0^-}^{0^+} 50\times10^{-6}\delta(t)\,dt = 100\,\text{V}$$

Note this agrees with our solution.

At $t = 0^+$ the circuit is

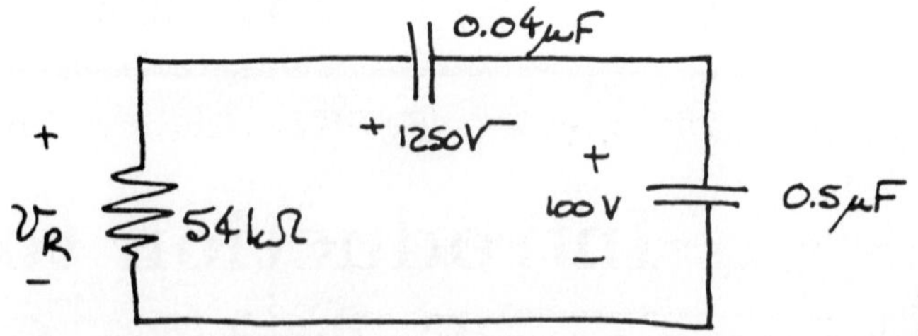

The equivalent capacitance is

$$C_e = \frac{(0.04)(0.5) \times 10^{-12}}{0.54 \times 10^{-6}} = \frac{1}{27}\,\mu\text{F}$$

Thus, the time constant is

$$\tau = 54 \times 10^3 C_e = 2\text{ ms}$$

Therefore, $1/\tau = 500$, which agrees with our solution. It follows that

$$v_R(t) = 1350e^{-500t}\text{ V}, \qquad t \geq 0^+$$

Therefore

$$v_o(t) = \frac{0.04}{0.54} v_R = 100e^{-500t}\text{ V}, \qquad t \geq 0^+$$

which also agrees with our solution.

14

Introduction to Frequency-Selective Circuits

Drill Exercises

DE 14.1 $f_c = 8\,\text{kHz}, \quad \omega_C = 16\pi\,\text{krad/s}$

$$\omega_c = \frac{1}{RC}; \qquad R = 10\,\text{k}\Omega;$$

$$\therefore \quad C = \frac{1}{\omega_c R} = \frac{1}{(16\pi \times 10^3)(10^4)} = 1.99\,\text{nF}$$

DE 14.2 [a] $\omega_c = 2\pi(2000) = 4\pi\,\text{krad/s}$

$$L = \frac{R}{\omega_c} = \frac{5000}{4000\pi} = 0.40\,\text{H}$$

[b] $$H(j\omega) = \frac{\omega_c}{\omega_c + j\omega} = \frac{4000\pi}{4000\pi + j\omega}$$

When $\omega = 100{,}000\pi$ rad/s

$$H(j\omega) = \frac{4000\pi}{4000\pi + j100{,}000\pi} = \frac{1}{1 + j25} = 0.04\underline{/87.71^\circ}$$

$$\therefore \quad |H(j\omega)| = 0.04$$

[c] $\therefore \quad \theta(\omega) = -87.71^\circ$

DE 14.3 $$\omega_c = \frac{R}{L} = \frac{5000}{3.5 \times 10^{-3}} = 1.43\,\text{Mrad/s}$$

DE 14.4 [a] $$\omega_c = \frac{1}{RC} = \frac{10^6}{R} = \frac{10^6}{100} = 10\,\text{krad/s}$$

[b] $\omega_c = \dfrac{10^6}{5000} = 200\,\text{rad/s}$

[c] $\omega_c = \dfrac{10^6}{3 \times 10^4} = 33.33\,\text{rad/s}$

DE 14.5 Let Z represent the parallel combination of $(1/SC)$ and R_L. Then

$$Z = \frac{R_L}{(R_L Cs + 1)}$$

Thus $$H(s) = \frac{Z}{R+Z} = \frac{R_L}{R(R_L Cs + 1) + R_L}$$
$$= \frac{(1/RC)}{s + \frac{R+R_L}{R_L}\left(\frac{1}{RC}\right)} = \frac{(1/RC)}{s + \frac{1}{K}\left(\frac{1}{RC}\right)}$$

where $$K = \frac{R_L}{R + R_L}$$

DE 14.6 $$L = \frac{1}{\omega_o^2 C} = \frac{10^6}{(24\pi \times 10^3)^2(0.1)} = 1.76\,\text{mH}$$

$$R = \frac{\omega_o L}{Q} = \frac{(24\pi \times 10^3)(1.76 \times 10^{-3})}{6} = 22.10\,\Omega$$

DE 14.7 $\omega_o = 2\pi(2000) = 4000\pi\,\text{rad/s};$

$\beta = 1000\pi\,\text{rad/s}; \qquad R = 250\,\Omega$

$$C = \frac{1}{\beta R} = \frac{1}{(1000\pi)(250)} = 1.27\,\mu\text{F}$$

$$L = \frac{1}{\omega_o^2 C} = \frac{10^6}{(4000\pi)^2(1.27)} = 4.97\,\text{mH}$$

DE 14.8 $$L = \frac{1}{\omega_o^2 C} = \frac{5 \times 10^6}{(10^4\pi)^2} = 5.07\,\text{mH}$$

$$R = \frac{1}{\beta C} = \frac{5 \times 10^6}{400\pi} = 3.98\,\text{k}\Omega$$

DE 14.9 $L = \dfrac{1}{\omega_o^2 C} = \dfrac{5 \times 10^6}{(400\pi)^2} = 31.66\,\text{mH}$

$$Q = \frac{5 \times 10^3}{200} = 25 = \omega_o RC$$

$$\therefore \quad R = \frac{25 \times 10^6}{(400\pi)(0.2)} = 9.95\,\text{k}\Omega$$

DE 14.10 $\omega_o = 8000\pi\,\text{rad/s}$

$$C = 500\,\text{nF}$$

$$L = \frac{1}{\omega_o^2 C} = 3.17\,\text{mH}$$

$$Q = \frac{\omega_o L}{R} = \frac{1}{\omega_o CR}$$

$$\therefore \quad R = \frac{1}{\omega_o CQ} = \frac{10^9}{(8000\pi)(500)(5)} = 15.92\,\Omega$$

DE 14.11 $\omega_o = 40\pi\,\text{krad/s}; \qquad R = 100\,\Omega; \qquad Q = 5$

$$C = \frac{1}{\omega_o RQ} = \frac{1}{(40\pi \times 10^3)(100)(5)} = 15.92\,\text{nF}$$

$$L = \frac{1}{\omega_o^2 C} = 3.98\,\text{mH}$$

DE 14.12 [a] $H(j\omega) = \dfrac{[1 + j(\omega/5)]}{[1 + j(\omega/100)][1 + j(\omega/5000)]}$

Straight-line approximation: 0 dB for $\omega < 5$ rad/s, +20 dB/decade between 5 and 100 rad/s, constant at 26 dB between 100 and 5000 rad/s, -20 dB/decade for $\omega > 5000$ rad/s. This segment crosses the 0 dB axis at 98 krad/s. Therefore maximum amplitude $\approx$ 26 dB, and

[b] $|H(j\omega)|$ is unity at 98 krad/s.

DE 14.13 [a] Straight-line approximation: angle increases from 0° at 0.5 rad/s, passing through 45° at 5 rad/s, to approximately 58° at 10 rad/s. The angle is constant at 58° until $\omega = 50$ rad/s, then drops off linearly to approximately 12.5° at 500 rad/s. Between 500 and 1000 rad/s, the angle decreases linearly from 12.5° to −15°. From 1000 rad/s to 50 krad/s, the angle decreases from −15° to −90°. The values read from the straight line plot are $\theta(30) = 58°$, $\theta(50) = 58°$, $\theta(100) = 45°$, and $\theta(5000) = -45°$.

[b] Using the expression for $H(j\omega)$, the calculated values are $\theta(30) = 63.49^\circ$, $\theta(50) = 57.15^\circ$, $\theta(100) = 40.99^\circ$, and $\theta(5000) = -43.91^\circ$.

DE 14.14 [a] $\omega_n^2 = 25 \times 10^8;$ therefore $\omega_n = 50\,\text{krad/s}$

[b] $2\zeta\omega_n = 20{,}000;$ therefore $\zeta = 0.2$

[c] $\omega = 0,$ and $\omega = \sqrt{2}\omega_n\sqrt{1-2\zeta^2} = 67.82\,\text{krad/s}$

[d] $A_{\text{dB}}(\text{peak}) = -10\log_{10}[4\zeta^2(1-\zeta^2)] = 8.136\,\text{dB}$

[e] $\omega_p = \omega_n\sqrt{1-2\zeta^2} = 47.96\,\text{krad/s}$

[f] $A_{\text{dB}_{C/2}} = -10\log_{10}(\zeta^2 + 0.5625) = -10\log_{10}(0.6025) = 2.20\,\text{dB}$

DE 14.15 [a] $H(j\omega) = 5/[1 - u^2 + j2\zeta u]$ where $u = \omega/800$ and $\zeta = 0.25$. Therefore, straight-line approximation is constant at $20\log_{10}5$, or 13.98 db, for $\omega \leq 800\,\text{rad/s}$, and then drops off at -40 db/decade for $\omega \geq 800\,\text{rad/s}$. The straight-line approximation crosses the 0–dB axis at 1800 rad/s.

[b] $u = \dfrac{1800}{800} = 2.25$

$$H(j1800) = \frac{5}{1 - 2.25^2 + j0.5(2.25)} = 1.1861\underline{/-164.52^\circ}$$

Therefore $A_{\text{dB}} = 20\log_{10}(1.1861) = 1.48\,\text{dB}$

[c] $A_{\text{dB}}(\text{peak}) = 13.98 + \left\{-10\log_{10}[4\zeta^2(1-\zeta^2)]\right\} = 20.28\,\text{dB}$

[d] $\omega_p = \omega_n\sqrt{1-2\zeta^2} = 748.33\,\text{rad/s}$

[e] $A_{\text{dB}}(\text{peak}) = 20.28;$ therefore $|H(j\omega_p)| = 10^{1.014} = 10.328$

Thus $V_m = 103.28\,\text{V}$

Problems

P 14.1 [a] $\omega_c = \dfrac{10^9}{80 \times 10^3} = 12{,}500\,\text{rad/s}$

$f_c = 1989.44\,\text{Hz}$

[b] $H(j\omega) = \dfrac{12{,}500}{12{,}500 + j\omega}$

$\therefore\quad H(j\omega_c) = 0.7071\underline{/-45^\circ}$

$$H(j0.2\omega_c) = \frac{12{,}500}{12{,}500 + j2500} = 0.9806\underline{/-11.31^\circ}$$

$$H(j8\omega_c) = \frac{12{,}500}{12{,}500 + j100{,}000} = 0.1240\underline{/-82.87^\circ}$$

[c] $v_o(\omega_c) = 339.41\cos(12{,}500t - 45^\circ)\,\text{mV}$

$v_o(0.2\omega_c) = 470.68\cos(2500t - 11.31^\circ)\,\text{mV}$

$v_o(8\omega_c) = 59.54\cos(100{,}000t - 82.87^\circ)\,\text{mV}$

P 14.2 [a] $\omega_c = \dfrac{R}{L} = \dfrac{1.5\times 10^3}{0.25} = 6000\ \text{rad/s}$

$\therefore\quad f_c = \dfrac{6000}{2\pi} = 954.93\,\text{Hz}$

[b] $H(s) = \dfrac{R/L}{s + R/L} = \dfrac{6000}{s + 6000}$

$$H(j\omega) = \frac{6000}{6000 + j\omega}$$

$$H(j\omega_c) = \frac{6000}{6000 + j6000} = 0.7071\underline{/-45^\circ}$$

$$H(j0.3\omega_c) = \frac{6000}{6000 + j1800} = 0.9578\underline{/-16.70^\circ}$$

$$H(j3\omega_c) = \frac{6000}{6000 + j18{,}000} = 0.3162\underline{/-71.57^\circ}$$

[c] $v_o(\omega_c) = 35.36\cos(6000t - 45^\circ)\,\text{V}$

$v_o(0.3\omega_c) = 47.89\cos(1800t - 16.70^\circ)\,\text{V}$

$v_o(3\omega_c) = 15.81\cos(18{,}000t - 71.57^\circ)\,\text{V}$

P 14.3 [a] Let $Z = \frac{R_L(1/SC)}{R_L + 1/SC} = \frac{R_L}{R_L Cs + 1}$

Then $H(s) = \frac{Z}{Z + R}$

$$= \frac{R_L}{RR_L Cs + R + R_L}$$

$$= \frac{(1/RC)}{s + \left(\frac{R + R_L}{RR_L C}\right)}$$

[b] $|H(j\omega)| = \frac{(1/RC)}{\sqrt{\omega^2 + [(R + R_L)/RR_L C]^2}}$

$|H(j\omega)|$ is maximum at $\omega = 0$

[c] $|H(j\omega)|_{\max} = \frac{R_L}{R + R_L}$

[d] $|H(j\omega_c)| = \frac{R_L}{\sqrt{2}(R + R_L)} = \frac{(1/RC)}{\sqrt{\omega_C^2 + [(R + R_L)/RR_L C]^2}}$

$\therefore\ \omega_c = \frac{R + R_L}{RR_L C} = \frac{1}{RC}(1 + (R/R_L))$

[e] $\omega_c = 12{,}500\left(1 + \frac{20}{300}\right) = 13{,}333.33$ rad/s

$$H(j0) = \frac{300}{320} = 0.9375$$

$$H(j\omega_c) = \frac{12{,}500}{13{,}333.33 + j13{,}333.33} = 0.6629\underline{/-45^\circ}$$

$$H(j0.2\omega_c) = \frac{12{,}500}{13{,}333.33 + j2666.67} = 0.9193\underline{/-11.31^\circ}$$

$$H(j8\omega_c) = \frac{12{,}500}{13{,}333.33 + j106{,}666.67} = 0.1163\underline{/-82.87^\circ}$$

P 14.4 [a] $H(s) = \frac{V_o}{V_i} = \frac{R}{sL + R + R_l} = \frac{(R/L)}{s + (R + R_l)/L}$

[b] $H(j\omega) = \frac{(R/L)}{\left(\frac{R+R_l}{L}\right) + j\omega}$

$$|H(j\omega)| = \frac{(R/L)}{\sqrt{\left(\frac{R+R_l}{L}\right)^2 + \omega^2}}$$

$|H(j\omega)|_{\max}$ occurs when $\omega = 0$

[c] $|H(j\omega)|_{\max} = \dfrac{R}{R+R_l}$

[d] $|H(j\omega_c)| = \dfrac{R}{\sqrt{2}(R+R_l)} = \dfrac{R/L}{\sqrt{\left(\frac{R+R_l}{L}\right)^2 + \omega_c^2}}$

$$\therefore\ \omega_c^2 = \left(\frac{R+R_l}{L}\right)^2; \qquad \therefore\ \omega_c = (R+R_l)/L$$

[e] $\omega_c = \dfrac{1575}{0.25} = 6300$ rad/s

$$H(j\omega) = \frac{6000}{6300 + j\omega}$$

$$H(j0) = 0.9524$$

$$H(j6300) = \frac{0.9524}{\sqrt{2}}\underline{/-45^\circ} = 0.6734\underline{/-45^\circ}$$

$$H(j1890) = \frac{6000}{6300 + j1890} = 0.9122\underline{/-16.70^\circ}$$

$$H(j18{,}900) = \frac{6000}{6300 + j18{,}900} = 0.3012\underline{/-71.57^\circ}$$

P 14.5 [a] $f_c = \dfrac{160}{2\pi} \times 10^3 = 25.46\,\text{kHz}$

[b] $\dfrac{1}{RC} = 160 \times 10^3$

$$R = \frac{1}{(160 \times 10^3)(25 \times 10^{-9})} = 250\,\Omega$$

[c] $\omega_c = \dfrac{1}{RC}\left(1 + \dfrac{R}{R_L}\right)$

$$\therefore\ \frac{R}{R_L} = 0.08 \qquad \therefore\ R_L = 12.5R = 3125\,\Omega$$

[d] $H(j0) = \dfrac{R_L}{R+R_L} = \dfrac{3125}{3375} = 0.9259$

$$H(j0) = 0.9259$$

P 14.6 [a] $\dfrac{R}{L} = 5000\pi$ rad/s

$$R = (0.025)(5000)(\pi) = 392.70\,\Omega$$

[b] $R_e = 392.70 \| 750 = 257.74\,\Omega$

$$\omega_{\text{loaded}} = \frac{R_e}{L} = 10{,}309.78 \text{ rad/s}$$

$$\therefore \quad f_{\text{loaded}} = 1640.85\,\text{Hz}$$

P 14.7 [a] $\frac{1}{RC} = \frac{10^9}{(40 \times 10^3)(2.5)} = 10\,\text{krad/s}$

$$f_c = \frac{5000}{\pi} = 1591.55\,\text{Hz}$$

[b] $H(j\omega) = \frac{j\omega}{10{,}000 + j\omega}$

$$H(j\omega_c) = \frac{j10{,}000}{10{,}000 + j10{,}000} = 0.7071\underline{/45^\circ}$$

$$H(j0.1\omega_c) = \frac{j1000}{10{,}000 + j1000} = 0.0995\underline{/84.29^\circ}$$

$$H(j10\omega_c) = \frac{j100{,}000}{10{,}000 + j100{,}000} = 0.9950\underline{/5.71^\circ}$$

[c] $v_o(\omega_c) = 565.69\cos(10{,}000t + 45^\circ)\,\text{mV}$

$$v_o(0.1\omega_c) = 79.60\cos(1000t + 84.29^\circ)\,\text{mV}$$

$$v_o(10\omega_c) = 796.03\cos(100{,}000t + 5.71^\circ)\,\text{mV}$$

P 14.8 [a] $H(s) = \frac{V_o}{V_i} = \frac{R}{R + R_c + (1/sC)}$

$$= \frac{R}{R + R_c} \cdot \frac{s}{[s + (1/(R + R_c)C)]}$$

[b] $H(j\omega) = \frac{R}{R + R_c} \cdot \frac{j\omega}{j\omega + (1/(R + R_c)C)}$

$$|H(j\omega)| = \frac{R}{R + R_c} \cdot \frac{\omega}{\sqrt{\omega^2 + \frac{1}{(R+R_c)^2C^2}}}$$

The magnitude will be maximum when $\omega = \infty$

[c] $|H(j\omega)|_{\text{max}} = \frac{R}{R + R_c}$

[d] $|H(j\omega_c)| = \dfrac{R\omega_c}{(R+R_c)\sqrt{\omega_c^2 + [1/(R+R_c)C]^2}}$

$\therefore \quad |H(j\omega)| = \dfrac{R}{\sqrt{2}(R+R_c)}$ when

$\therefore \quad \omega_c^2 = \dfrac{1}{(R+R_c)^2C^2}$

or $\omega_c = \dfrac{1}{(R+R_c)C}$

[e] $\omega_c = \dfrac{1}{(R+R_C)C} = \dfrac{10^9}{(50 \times 10^3)(2.5)} = 8000$ rad/s

$$H(j\omega_c) = \left(\frac{40}{50}\right)\frac{j8000}{8000 + j8000} = 0.5657\underline{/45^\circ}$$

$$H(j0.1\omega_c) = \frac{(0.8)j800}{8000 + j800} = 0.0796\underline{/84.29^\circ}$$

$$H(j10\omega_c) = \frac{(0.8)j80{,}000}{8000 + j80{,}000} = 0.7960\underline{/5.71^\circ}$$

P 14.9 [a] $R = \omega_c L = (160 \times 10^3)(25 \times 10^{-3}) = 4000\,\Omega = 4\,\text{k}\Omega$

[b] $\dfrac{R}{L} \cdot \dfrac{R_L}{R+R_L} = 150{,}000$

$\therefore \quad \dfrac{R_L}{R+R_L} = \dfrac{150{,}000}{160{,}000} = 0.9375$

$\therefore \quad 0.0625R_L = (0.9375)(4000); \qquad \therefore \quad R_L = 60\,\text{k}\Omega$

P 14.10 [a] $\dfrac{1}{RC} = 2\pi(800) = 1600\pi$ rad/s

$\therefore \quad R = \dfrac{10^9}{(1600\pi)(20)} = 9.95\,\text{k}\Omega$

[b] $R_e = 9.95\|68 = 8.68\,\text{k}\Omega$

$$\omega_c = \frac{10^9}{(8.68)(10^3)(20)} = 5761.84 \text{ rad/s}$$

$$f_c = \frac{5761.84}{2\pi} = 917.03\,\text{Hz}$$

P 14.11 By definition $Q = \omega_o/\beta$ therefore $\beta = \omega_o/Q$. Substituting this expression into Eqs. 14.34 and 14.35 yields

$$\omega_{c1} = -\frac{\omega_o}{2Q} + \sqrt{\left(\frac{\omega_o}{2Q}\right)^2 + \omega_o^2}$$

$$\omega_{c2} = \frac{\omega_o}{2Q} + \sqrt{\left(\frac{\omega_o}{2Q}\right)^2 + \omega_o^2}$$

Now factor ω_o out to get

$$\omega_{c1} = \omega_o\left[-\frac{1}{2Q} + \sqrt{1 + \left(\frac{1}{2Q}\right)^2}\right]$$

$$\omega_{c2} = \omega_o\left[\frac{1}{2Q} + \sqrt{1 + \left(\frac{1}{2Q}\right)^2}\right]$$

P 14.12 [a] $\omega_o^2 = \frac{1}{LC} = \frac{(10^6)(10^9)}{(40)(25)} = 10^{12}$

$\omega_o = 10^6\ \text{rad/s} = 1\,\text{Mrad/s}$

[b] $f_o = \frac{500}{\pi}\,\text{kHz} = 159.15\,\text{kHz}$

[c] $Q = \omega_o RC = (10^6)(300)(25 \times 10^{-9}) = 7.5$

[d] $\omega_{c1} = 10^6\left[-\frac{1}{15} + \sqrt{1 + \frac{1}{225}}\right] = 935.55\,\text{krad/s}$

[e] $\therefore\ f_{c1} = 148.90\,\text{kHz}$

[f] $\omega_{c2} = 10^6\left[\frac{1}{15} + \sqrt{1 + \frac{1}{225}}\right] = 1068.89\,\text{krad/s}$

[g] $\therefore\ f_{c2} = 170.12\,\text{kHz}$

[h] $\beta = \frac{\omega_o}{Q} = 133.33\,\text{krad/s or } 21.22\,\text{kHz}$

P 14.13 [a] $\omega_o^2 = \frac{1}{LC} = \frac{(10^3)(10^{12})}{(312.5)(1.25)} = 2.56 \times 10^{12}$

$\omega_o = 1.6 \times 10^6\ \text{rad/s}$

$f_o = \frac{800}{\pi} = 254.65\,\text{kHz}$

[b] $Q = \dfrac{\omega_o L}{R + R_i} = \dfrac{(1.6 \times 10^6)(312.5 \times 10^{-3})}{(50 + 12.5)10^3} = 8$

[c] $f_{c1} = \dfrac{800}{\pi}\left[-\dfrac{1}{16} + \sqrt{1 + \dfrac{1}{256}}\right] = 239.23\,\text{kHz}$

[d] $f_{c2} = \dfrac{800}{\pi}\left[\dfrac{1}{16} + \sqrt{1 + \dfrac{1}{256}}\right] = 271.06\,\text{kHz}$

[e] $\beta = f_{c2} - f_{c1} = 31.83\,\text{kHz}$

or

$$\beta = \frac{\omega_o}{Q} = 200\,\text{krad/s} = \frac{100}{\pi}\,\text{kHz} = 31.83\,\text{kHz}$$

P 14.14 [a] $H(s) = \dfrac{(R/L)s}{s^2 + \frac{(R+R_i)}{L}s + \frac{1}{LC}}$

For the numerical values in Problem 14.13 we have

$$H(s) = \frac{16 \times 10^4 s}{s^2 + 2 \times 10^5 s + 2.56 \times 10^{12}}$$

$$\therefore \quad H(j\omega) = \frac{j16 \times 10^4 \omega}{(2.56 \times 10^{12} - \omega^2) + j2 \times 10^5 \omega}$$

$$H(j\omega_o) = \frac{j16 \times 10^4(1.6 \times 10^6)}{j2 \times 10^5(1.6 \times 10^6)} = 0.8\underline{/0^\circ}$$

$$\therefore \quad v_o(1) = 640 \cos \omega t\,\text{mV}$$

[b] $\omega_{c1} = 1.6 \times 10^6\left[-\dfrac{1}{16} + \sqrt{1 + \dfrac{1}{256}}\right] = 1.5 \times 10^6\ \text{rad/s}$

$$H(j\omega_{c1}) = \frac{j16 \times 10^4(1.5 \times 10^6)}{2.56 \times 10^{12} - 1.5^2 \times 10^{12} + j2 \times 10^5(1.5 \times 10^6)}$$

$$= 0.57\underline{/45^\circ}$$

$$\therefore \quad v_o(t) = 452.55 \cos(1.5 \times 10^6 t + 45^\circ)\,\text{mV}$$

[c] $\omega_{c2} = 1.6 \times 10^6\left[\dfrac{1}{16} + \sqrt{1 + \dfrac{1}{256}}\right] = 1.7 \times 10^6\ \text{rad/s}$

$$H(j\omega_{c2}) = \frac{j16 \times 10^4(1.7 \times 10^6)}{2.56 \times 10^{12} - 1.7^2 \times 10^{12} + j2 \times 10^5(1.7 \times 10^6)}$$

$$= 0.57\underline{/45^\circ}$$

$$\therefore \quad v_o(t) = 452.55 \cos(1.7 \times 10^6 t - 45^\circ)\,\text{mV}$$

P 14.15 $\beta = \frac{\omega_o}{Q} = \frac{80}{8} = 10\,\text{krad/s} = \frac{5}{\pi} = 1.59\,\text{kHz}$

$$\omega_{c2} = 80\left[\frac{1}{16} + \sqrt{1 + \left(\frac{1}{16}\right)^2}\right] = 85.16\,\text{krad/s}$$

$$f_{c2} = \frac{85.16}{2\pi} = 13.55\,\text{kHz}$$

$$\omega_{c1} = 80\left[-\frac{1}{16} + \sqrt{1 + \left(\frac{1}{16}\right)^2}\right] = 75.16\,\text{krad/s}$$

$$f_{c1} = \frac{75.16}{2\pi} = 11.96\,\text{kHz}$$

P 14.16 $\omega_o = \sqrt{\omega_{c1}\omega_{c2}} = \sqrt{(180)(200)} = 189.74\,\text{krad/s}$

$$f_o = \frac{\omega_o}{2\pi} = 30.20\,\text{kHz}$$

$$\beta = 200 - 180 = 20\,\text{krad/s} = 3.18\,\text{kHz}$$

$$Q = \frac{\omega_o}{\beta} = \frac{189.74}{20} = 9.49 = \frac{30.20}{3.18}$$

P 14.17 [a] $\omega_o^2 = \frac{1}{LC} = \frac{(10^3)(10^{12})}{(10)(4)} = 25 \times 10^{12}$

$$\omega_o = 5\,\text{Mrad/s}$$

[b] $\beta = \frac{R + R_L}{R_L} \cdot \frac{1}{RC} = \left(\frac{6.25}{5.0}\right)\left(\frac{10^{12}}{5 \times 10^6}\right) = 250\,\text{krad/s}$

[c] $Q = \frac{\omega_o}{\beta} = \frac{5}{0.25} = 20$

[d] $H(j\omega_o) = \frac{R_L}{R + R_L} = 0.8\angle 0^\circ$

$$\therefore\ v_o(t) = 600\cos(5 \times 10^6 t)\,\text{mV}$$

[e] $\beta = \left(1 + \frac{R}{R_L}\right)\frac{1}{RC} = \left(1 + \frac{1.25}{R_L}\right)(200 \times 10^3)\ \text{rad/s}$

$$\omega_o = 5 \times 10^6\ \text{rad/s}$$

$$Q = \frac{\omega_o}{\beta} = \frac{25}{1 + (1.25/R_L)} \qquad \text{where } R_L \text{ is in megohms}$$

[f]

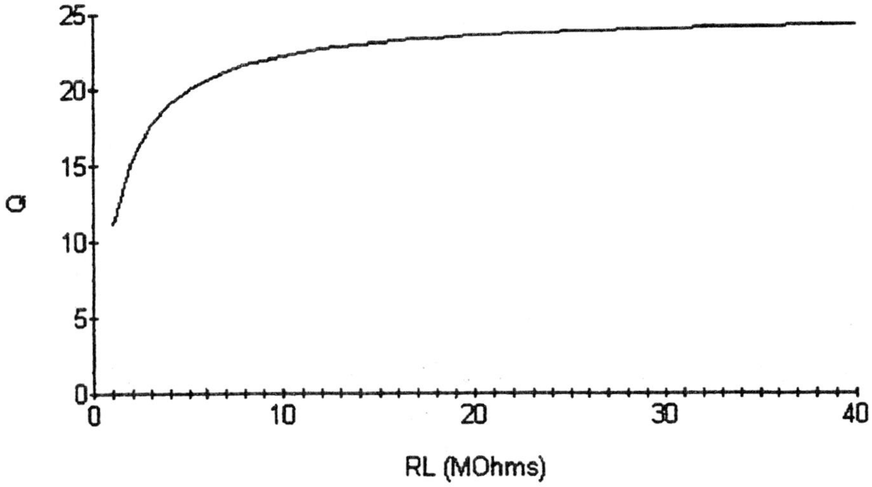

P 14.18 $\omega_o^2 = \frac{1}{LC} = \frac{(10^6)(10^{12})}{(400)(4)} = 625 \times 10^{12}$

$\omega_o = 25\,\text{Mrad/s}$

$Q_u = \omega_o RC = 25(10 \times 10^5)(4 \times 10^{-12}) = 10$

$\therefore \quad \left(\frac{R_L}{R + R_L}\right) 10 = 9; \qquad \therefore \quad R_L = 9R = 900\,\text{k}\Omega$

P 14.19 [a] $L = \frac{10^9}{20(1600\pi)^2 \times 10^6} = 3.17\,\text{mH}$

$R = \frac{\omega_o L}{Q} = \frac{40\pi \times 10^3(3.17 \times 10^{-3})}{5} = 79.58\,\Omega$

[b] $f_{c1} = 20\left[-\frac{1}{10} + \sqrt{1 + \frac{1}{100}}\right] = 18.10\,\text{kHz}$

[c] $f_{c2} = 20\left[\frac{1}{10} + \sqrt{1 + \frac{1}{100}}\right] = 22.10\,\text{kHz}$

[d] $\beta = f_{c2} - f_{c1} = 4\,\text{kHz}$

or

$\beta = \frac{f_o}{Q} = \frac{20}{5} = 4\,\text{kHz}$

P 14.20 [a] $\omega_o^2 = \frac{1}{LC} = \frac{10^9}{L(25)} = 25 \times 10^8$

$$\therefore \quad L = \frac{10^9}{625 \times 10^8} = 16\,\text{mH}; \qquad R = \frac{10 \times 10^9}{(50 \times 10^3)(25)} = 8\,\text{k}\Omega$$

[b] $\omega_{c2} = 50\left[\frac{1}{20} + \sqrt{1 + \frac{1}{400}}\right] = 52.56\,\text{krad/s}$

$\therefore \quad f_{c2} = 8.37\,\text{kHz}$

$$\omega_{c1} = 50\left[-\frac{1}{20} + \sqrt{1 + \frac{1}{400}}\right] = 47.56\,\text{krad/s}$$

$\therefore \quad f_{c1} = 7.57\,\text{kHz}$

[c] $\beta = \frac{\omega_o}{Q} = 5000\,\text{rad/s} = 795.77\,\text{Hz}$

Check: $\beta = f_{c2} - f_{c1} = 795.77\,\text{Hz}$

P 14.21 [a] $\frac{V_o}{V_i} = \frac{Z}{Z+R}$ where $Z = \frac{1}{Y}$

and $Y = sC + \frac{1}{sL} + \frac{1}{R_L} = \frac{LCR_Ls^2 + sL + R_L}{R_LLs}$

$$H(s) = \frac{R_LLs}{R_LRLCs^2 + (R+R_L)Ls + RR_L}$$

$$= \frac{(1/RC)s}{s^2 + \left[\left(\frac{R+R_L}{R_L}\right)\left(\frac{1}{RC}\right)\right]s + \frac{1}{LC}}$$

$$= \frac{\left(\frac{R_L}{R+R_L}\right)\left(\frac{R+R_L}{R_L}\right)\left(\frac{1}{RC}\right)s}{s^2 + \left[\left(\frac{R+R_L}{R_L}\right)\left(\frac{1}{RC}\right)\right]s + \frac{1}{LC}}$$

$$= \frac{K\beta s}{s^2 + \beta s + \omega_o^2}$$

[b] $\beta = \left(\frac{R+R_L}{R_L}\right)\frac{1}{RC}$

[c] $\beta_u = \frac{1}{RC}$

$$\therefore \quad \beta_L = \left(\frac{R+R_L}{R_L}\right)\beta_u = \left(1 + \frac{R}{R_L}\right)\beta u$$

[d] $Q = \frac{\omega_o}{\beta} = \frac{\omega_oRC}{\left(\frac{R+R_L}{R_L}\right)}$

[e] $Q_u = \omega_o RC$

$$\therefore \quad Q_L = \left(\frac{R_L}{R+R_L}\right) Q_u = \frac{1}{[1+(R/R_L)]} Q_u$$

[f] $H(j\omega) = \dfrac{Kj\omega\beta}{\omega_o^2 - \omega^2 + j\omega\beta}$

$$H(j\omega_o) = K$$

Let ω_c represent a corner frequency. Then

$$|H(j\omega_c)| = \frac{K}{\sqrt{2}} = \frac{K\omega_c\beta}{\sqrt{(\omega_o^2 - \omega_c^2)^2 + \omega_c^2\beta^2}}$$

$$\therefore \quad \frac{1}{\sqrt{2}} = \frac{\omega_c\beta}{\sqrt{(\omega_o^2 - \omega_c^2)^2 + \omega_c^2\beta^2}}$$

Squaring both sides leads to

$(\omega_o^2 - \omega_c^2)^2 = \omega_c^2\beta^2$ or $(\omega_o^2 - \omega_c^2) = \pm\omega_c\beta$

$$\therefore \quad \omega_c^2 \pm \omega_c\beta - \omega_o^2 = 0$$

or

$$\omega_c = \mp\frac{\beta}{2} \pm \sqrt{\frac{\beta^2}{4} + \omega_o^2}$$

The two positive roots are

$$\omega_{c1} = -\frac{\beta}{2} + \sqrt{\frac{\beta^2}{4} + \omega_o^2} \quad \text{and} \quad \omega_{c2} = \frac{\beta}{2} + \sqrt{\frac{\beta^2}{4} + \omega_o^2}$$

where

$$\beta = \left(1 + \frac{R}{R_L}\right)\frac{1}{RC} \text{ and } \omega_o^2 = \frac{1}{LC}$$

P 14.22 [a]

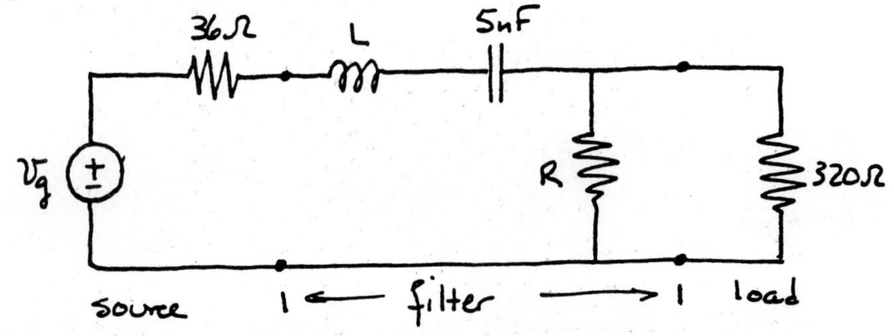

[b] $L = \dfrac{1}{\omega_o^2 C} = \dfrac{10^9}{(625 \times 10^8)5} = 3.2 \times 10^{-3} = 3.2\,\text{mH}$

$$R = \frac{\omega_o L}{Q} = \frac{800}{10} = 80\,\Omega$$

[c] $R_e = 80\|320 = 64\,\Omega$

$$R_e + R_i = 64 + 36 = 100\,\Omega$$

$$Q_{\text{system}} = \frac{\omega_o L}{R_e + R_i} = \frac{800}{100} = 8$$

[d] $\beta_{\text{system}} = \dfrac{\omega_o}{Q_{\text{system}}} = \dfrac{250 \times 10^3}{8} = 31.25\,\text{krad/s}$

$$\beta_{\text{system}}(\text{kHz}) = \frac{31.25}{2\pi} = 4.97\,\text{kHz} = 4973.59\,\text{Hz}$$

P 14.23 [a] Let $Z = \dfrac{R_L(sL + (1/sC))}{R_L + sL + (1/sC)}$

$$Z = \frac{R_L(s^2LC + 1)}{s^2LC + R_LCs + 1}$$

Then $H(s) = \dfrac{V_o}{V_i} = \dfrac{s^2R_LCL + R_L}{(R + R_L)LCs^2 + RR_LCs + R + R_L}$

Therefore

$$H(s) = \left(\frac{R_L}{R + R_L}\right) \cdot \frac{[s^2 + (1/LC)]}{\left[s^2 + \left(\frac{RR_L}{R+R_L}\right)\frac{s}{L} + \frac{1}{LC}\right]}$$

$$= \frac{K(s^2 + \omega_o^2)}{s^2 + \beta s + \omega_o^2}$$

where $K = \dfrac{R_L}{R + R_L}$; $\omega_o^2 = \dfrac{1}{LC}$; $\beta = \left(\dfrac{RR_L}{R + R_L}\right)\dfrac{1}{L}$

[b] $\omega_o = \dfrac{1}{\sqrt{LC}}$

[c] $\beta = \left(\dfrac{RR_L}{R + R_L}\right)\dfrac{1}{L}$

[d] $Q = \dfrac{\omega_o}{\beta} = \dfrac{\omega_o L}{[RR_L/(R + R_L)]}$

[e] $H(j\omega) = \dfrac{K(\omega_o^2 - \omega^2)}{(\omega_o^2 - \omega^2) + j\beta\omega}$

$$H(j\omega_o) = 0$$

[f] $H(j0) = \frac{K\omega_o^2}{\omega_o^2} = K$

[g] $H(j\omega) = \frac{K\left[(\omega_o/\omega)^2 - 1\right]}{\left\{\left[(\omega_o/\omega)^2 - 1\right] + j\beta/\omega\right\}}$

$H(j\infty) = \frac{-K}{-1} = K$

[h] $H(j\omega) = \frac{K(\omega_o^2 - \omega^2)}{(\omega_o^2 - \omega^2) + j\beta\omega}$

$H(j0) = H(j\infty) = K$

Let ω_c represent a corner frequency. Then

$|H(j\omega_c)| = \frac{K}{\sqrt{2}}$

$\therefore \quad \frac{K}{\sqrt{2}} = \frac{K(\omega_o^2 - \omega_c^2)}{\sqrt{(\omega_o^2 - \omega_c^2)^2 + \omega_c^2\beta^2}}$

Squaring both sides leads to

$(\omega_o^2 - \omega_c^2)^2 = \omega_c^2\beta^2$ or $(\omega_o^2 - \omega_c^2) = \pm\omega_c\beta$

$\therefore \quad \omega_c^2 \pm \omega_c\beta - \omega_o^2 = 0$

or

$\omega_c = \mp\frac{\beta}{2} \pm \sqrt{\frac{\beta^2}{4} + \omega_o^2}$

The two positive roots are

$\omega_{c1} = -\frac{\beta}{2} + \sqrt{\frac{\beta^2}{4} + \omega_o^2}$ and $\omega_{c2} = \frac{\beta}{2} + \sqrt{\frac{\beta^2}{4} + \omega_o^2}$

where

$\beta = \frac{RR_L}{R + R_L} \cdot \frac{1}{L}$ and $\omega_o^2 = \frac{1}{LC}$

P 14.24 [a] $\omega_o^2 = \frac{1}{LC} = \frac{10^6}{1} \cdot \frac{10^{12}}{4} = 0.24 \times 10^{18} = 25 \times 10^{16}$

$\omega_o = 5 \times 10^8 = 500\,\text{Mrad/s}$

[b] $\beta = \frac{RR_L}{R + R_L} \cdot \frac{1}{L} = \frac{(30)(150)}{180} \cdot 10^6 = 25\,\text{Mrad/s} = 3.98\,\text{MHz}$

[c] $Q = \frac{\omega_o}{\beta} = \frac{500}{25} = 20$

[d] $H(j0) = \dfrac{R_L}{R + R_L} = \dfrac{150}{180} = 0.8333$

[e] $H(j\infty) = \dfrac{R_L}{R + R_L} = 0.8333$

[f] $f_{c2} = \dfrac{250}{\pi}\left[\dfrac{1}{40} + \sqrt{1 + \dfrac{1}{1600}}\right] = 81.59\,\text{MHz}$

[g] $f_{c2} = \dfrac{250}{\pi}\left[-\dfrac{1}{40} + \sqrt{1 + \dfrac{1}{1600}}\right] = 77.61\,\text{MHz}$

Check: $\beta = f_{c2} - f_{c1} = 3.98\,\text{MHz}.$

[h] $Q = \dfrac{\omega_o}{\beta} = \dfrac{500 \times 10^6}{\frac{RR_L}{R+R_L} \cdot \frac{1}{L}}$

$= \dfrac{500(R + R_L)}{RR_L} = \dfrac{50}{3}\left(1 + \dfrac{30}{R_L}\right)$

where R_L is in ohms.

[i]

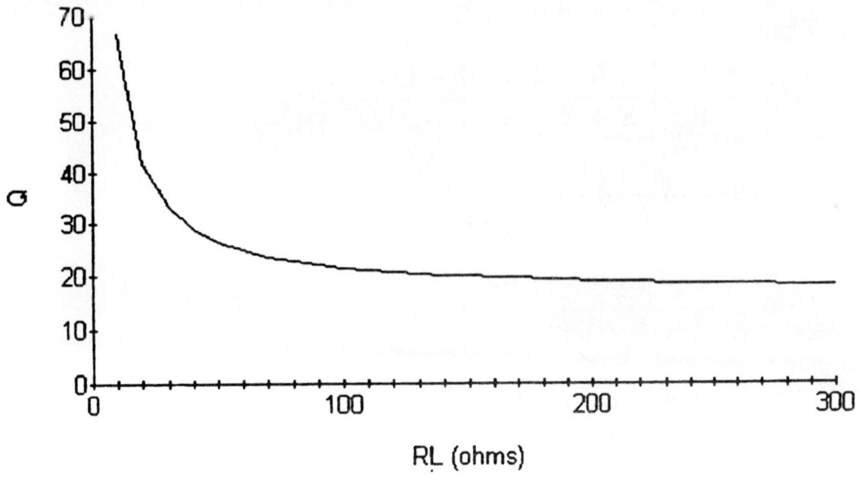

P 14.25 [a] $\omega_o^2 = \dfrac{1}{LC} = 16 \times 10^{12}$

$\therefore \quad L = \dfrac{10^{12}}{(16 \times 10^{12})(5)} = \dfrac{1}{80} = 12.5\,\text{mH}$

$\dfrac{R_L}{R + R_L} = 0.8; \qquad \therefore \quad 20 = 0.8R + 16; \qquad R = 5\,\text{k}\Omega$

[b] $\beta = \left(\dfrac{R_L}{R + R_L}\right) R \cdot \dfrac{1}{L} = 0.32 \times 10^6$

$Q = \dfrac{\omega_o}{\beta} = \dfrac{4}{0.32} = 12.5$

P 14.26 [a] In analyzing the circuit qualitatively we visualize v_i is a sinusoidal voltage and we seek the steady-state nature of the output voltage v_o.

At zero frequency the inductor provides a direct connection between the input and the output, hence $v_o = v_i$ when $\omega = 0$.

At infinite frequency the capacitor provides the direct connection, hence $v_o = v_i$ when $\omega = \infty$.

At the resonant frequency of the parallel combination of L and C the impedance of the combination is infinite and hence the output voltage will be zero when $\omega = \omega_o$.

At frequencies on either side of ω_o the amplitude of the output voltage will be nonzero but less than the amplitude of the input voltage.

Thus the circuit behaves like a band-reject filter.

[b] Let Z represent the impedance of the parallel branches L and C, thus

$$Z = \frac{sL(1/sC)}{sL + 1/sC} = \frac{sL}{s^2LC + 1}$$

Then

$$H(s) = \frac{V_o}{V_i} = \frac{R}{Z + R} = \frac{R(s^2LC + 1)}{sL + R(s^2LC + 1)}$$

$$= \frac{[s^2 + (1/LC)]}{s^2 + \left(\frac{1}{RC}\right)s + \left(\frac{1}{LC}\right)}$$

$$H(s) = \frac{s^2 + \omega_o^2}{s^2 + \beta s + \omega_o^2}$$

[c] From part (b) we have

$$H(j\omega) = \frac{\omega_o^2 - \omega^2}{w_o^2 - \omega^2 + j\omega\beta}$$

It follows that $H(j\omega) = 0$ when $\omega = \omega_o$

$$\therefore \quad \omega_o = \frac{1}{\sqrt{LC}}$$

[d] $$|H(j\omega)| = \frac{\omega_o^2 - \omega^2}{\sqrt{(\omega_o^2 - \omega^2)^2 + \omega^2\beta^2}}$$

$$|H(j\omega)| = \frac{1}{\sqrt{2}} \text{ when } \omega^2\beta^2 = (\omega_o^2 - \omega^2)^2$$

or $\pm\omega\beta = \omega_o^2 - \omega^2$, thus

$$\omega^2 \pm \beta\omega - \omega_o^2 = 0$$

The two positive roots of this quadratic are

$$\omega_{c_1} = \frac{-\beta}{2} + \sqrt{\left(\frac{\beta}{2}\right)^2 + \omega_o^2}$$

$$\omega_{c_2} = \frac{\beta}{2} + \sqrt{\left(\frac{\beta}{2}\right)^2 + \omega_o^2}$$

Also note that since $\beta = \omega_o/Q$

$$\omega_{c_1} = \omega_o \left[\frac{-1}{2Q} + \sqrt{1 + \left(\frac{1}{2Q}\right)^2}\right]$$

$$\omega_{c_2} = \omega_o \left[\frac{1}{2Q} + \sqrt{1 + \left(\frac{1}{2Q}\right)^2}\right]$$

[e] It follows from the equations derived in part (d) that

$$\beta = \omega_{c_2} - \omega_{c_1} = 1/RC$$

[f] By definition $Q = \omega_o/\beta = \omega_o RC$

P 14.27 [a] $\omega_o^2 = \dfrac{1}{LC} = \dfrac{(10^6)(10^{12})}{(625)(25)} = 64 \times 10^{12}$

$$\therefore \quad \omega_o = 8\,\text{Mrad/s}$$

[b] $f_o = \dfrac{\omega_o}{2\pi} = 1.27\,\text{MHz}$

[c] $Q = \omega_o RC = (8 \times 10^6)(80 \times 10^3)(25 \times 10^{-12}) = 16$

[d] $\omega_{c1} = 8 \times 10^6 \left[-\dfrac{1}{32} + \sqrt{1 + \dfrac{1}{1024}}\right] = 7.75\,\text{Mrad/s}$

[e] $f_{c1} = \dfrac{\omega_{c1}}{2\pi} = 1.25\,\text{MHz}$

[f] $\omega_{c2} = 8 \times 10^6 \left[\dfrac{1}{32} + \sqrt{1 + \dfrac{1}{1024}}\right] = 8.25\,\text{Mrad/s}$

[g] $f_{c2} = \dfrac{\omega_{c1}}{2\pi} = 1.31\,\text{MHz}$

[h] $\beta = f_{c2} - f_{c1} = 79.58\,\text{kHz}$

or

$$\beta = \frac{\omega_o}{2\pi Q} = \frac{500 \times 10^3}{2\pi} = 79.58\,\text{kHz}$$

P 14.28 [a] $\omega_o = 2\pi f_o = 100\pi$ krad/s

$$L = \frac{1}{\omega_o^2 C} = \frac{10^6}{10^4\pi \times 10^6(0.1)} = 101.32\,\mu\text{H}$$

$$R = \frac{Q}{\omega_o C} = \frac{8 \times 10^6}{(100\pi)(0.1 \times 10^3)} = 254.65\,\Omega$$

[b] $$f_{c2} = 50\text{k}\left[\frac{1}{16} + \sqrt{1 + \frac{1}{256}}\right] = 53.22\,\text{kHz}$$

$$f_{c1} = 50\text{k}\left[-\frac{1}{16} + \sqrt{1 + \frac{1}{256}}\right] = 46.97\,\text{kHz}$$

[c] $\beta = f_{c2} - f_{c1} = 6.25$ kHz

or

$$\beta = \frac{f_o}{Q} = \frac{50\text{k}}{8} = 6.25\,\text{kHz}$$

P 14.29 [a] $R_e = 254.65 \| 932 = 200\,\Omega$

$$Q = \omega_o R_e C = 100\pi \times 10^3(200)(0.1)10^{-6} = 2\pi = 6.28$$

[b] $$\beta = \frac{f_o}{Q} = \frac{50}{2\pi} = 7.96\,\text{kHz}$$

[c] $$f_{c2} = 50\left[\frac{1}{4\pi} + \sqrt{1 + \frac{1}{16\pi^2}}\right] = 54.14\,\text{kHz}$$

[d] $$f_{c1} = 50\left[-\frac{1}{4\pi} + \sqrt{1 + \frac{1}{16\pi^2}}\right] = 46.18\,\text{kHz}$$

P 14.30 [a] $\omega_n = 2000$

$$2\zeta\omega_n = 500, \quad \zeta = 0.125$$

$$\omega_o = \sqrt{2}\omega_p = \sqrt{2}\omega_n\sqrt{1 - 2\zeta^2} = 2783.88\,\text{rad/s}$$

$$\therefore \quad \omega = 0$$

$$\omega = 2783.88\,\text{rad/s}$$

[b] $\omega_p = \omega_n\sqrt{1 - 2\zeta^2} = 1968.50$ rad/s

[c] $A_{\text{dB}} = -10\log_{10} 4\zeta^2(1 - \zeta^2) = 12.11$ dB

$$\therefore \quad \text{ratio} = 10^{(12.11/20)} = 4.03$$

P 14.31 [a] $V_o = \dfrac{V_g(R + 1/sC)}{sL + R + 1/sC} = \dfrac{R}{L} \cdot \dfrac{s + (1/RC)}{s^2 + (R/L)s + (1/LC)}$

$$\frac{R}{L} = \frac{100}{20} \times 10^3 = 5000 \text{ rad/s}$$

$$\frac{1}{RC} = \frac{10^9}{(100)(20)} = 500{,}000 \text{ rad/s}$$

$$\frac{1}{LC} = \frac{(10^9)(10^3)}{(20)(20)} = 25 \times 10^8 = \omega_n^2$$

$$H(s) = \frac{5000(s + 500{,}000)}{s^2 + 5000s + 25 \times 10^8}$$

$$H(j\omega) = \frac{5000(5 \times 10^5 + j\omega)}{(25 \times 10^8 - \omega^2) + j5000\omega}$$

$$= \frac{1 + j(\omega/5 \times 10^5)}{-(\omega/5 \times 10^4)^2 + 1 + j(0.1\omega/5 \times 10^4)}$$

$$A_{\text{dB}} = 20 \log_{10} |1 + j(\omega/5 \times 10^5)|$$
$$-20 \log_{10} |-(\omega/5 \times 10^4)^2 + 1 + j(0.1\omega/5 \times 10^4)|$$

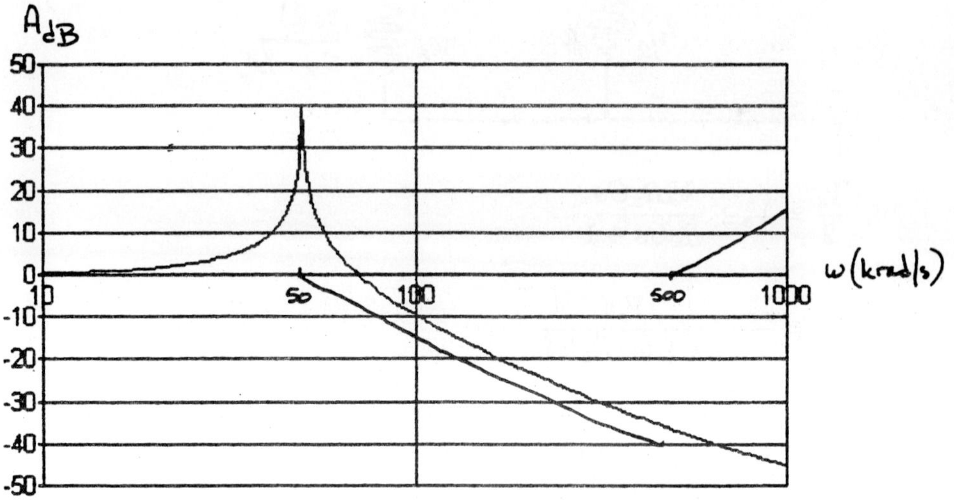

$A_{\text{dB}}(\omega_n/2) = 2.48; \qquad \omega_o = \sqrt{2}\omega_p = 70.53$ krad/s

[c] $\omega_p = \omega_n\sqrt{1 - 2\zeta^2} = 50\sqrt{0.995} = 49.87$ krad/s

[d] $A_{\text{dB}}(\omega_p) = -10 \log_{10}[0.01(0.9975)] = 20.01$ dB

Note — since the quadratic corner frequency (50 krad/s) is a decade below the simple zero (500 krad/s) we can ignore any corrections associated with the zero. Also note for graphical purposes $\omega_n = \omega_p$ and $A_{\text{dB}}(\omega_p) = A_{\text{dB}}(\omega_n) = 20$ dB.

[e] From the plot, the estimated values of ω_1 and ω_2 are

$$\omega_1 = 47\,\text{krad/s} \qquad \omega_2 = 52\,\text{krad/s}$$

[f] $\beta = \omega_2 - \omega_1 = 52 - 47 = 5\,\text{krad/s}$ or $\beta = 795.77\,\text{Hz}$

[g] $$A_{\text{dB}}(47\,\text{krad/s}) = 20\log_{10}|1 + j47/500| - 20\log_{10}|1 - (47/50)^2 + j4.7/50| = 0.04 + 16.50 = 16.54\ \text{dB}$$

$$A_{\text{dB}}(52\,\text{krad/s}) = 20\log_{10}|1 + j52/500| - 20\log_{10}|1 - (52/50)^2 + j5.2/50| = 17.63\ \text{dB}$$

P 14.32 From the circuit in Fig. P11.50 we have

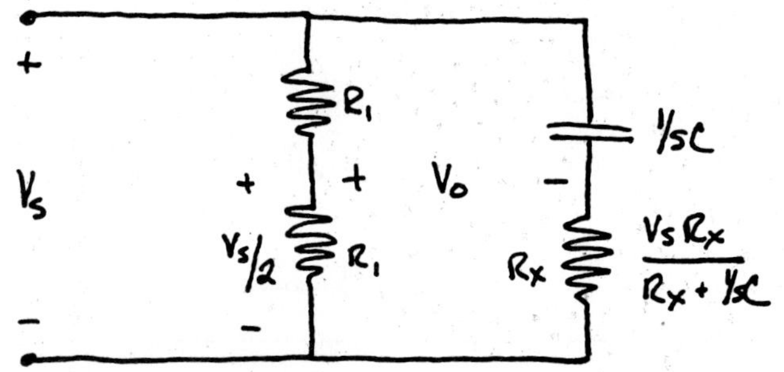

$$\frac{V_s}{2} = V_o + \frac{V_s R_x C s}{R_x C s + 1}$$

$$V_o = \frac{V_s}{2} - \frac{V_s s}{s + (1/R_x C)}$$

Let $p = \frac{1}{R_x C}$, then $V_o = V_s\left[\frac{1}{2} + \frac{s}{s+p}\right] = \frac{p-s}{2(s+p)}$

$$H(s) = \frac{V_o}{V_s} = 0.5\frac{p-s}{p+s}; \qquad H(j\omega) = \frac{0.5(1 - j\omega/p)}{1 + j\omega/p}$$

$$|H(j\omega)| = 0.5; \qquad 20\log_{10}|H(j\omega)| = -6.02\,\text{dB}$$

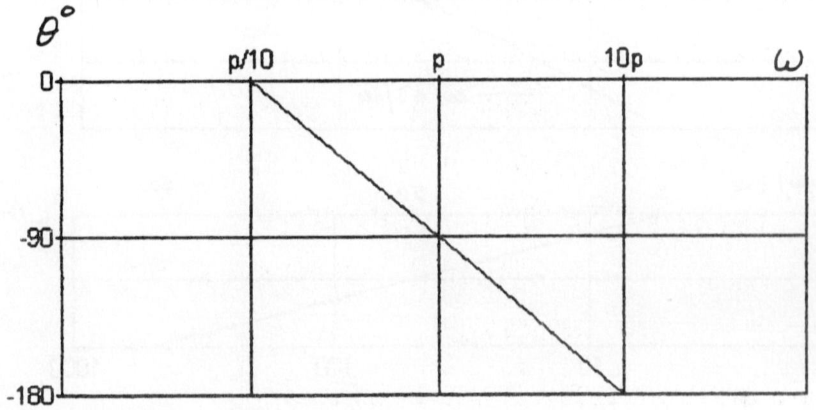

P 14.33 [a] From the solution to Prob. 13.49 we have

$$H(s) = \frac{50}{s + 50}$$

$$H(j\omega) = \frac{1}{1 + j(\omega/50)}$$

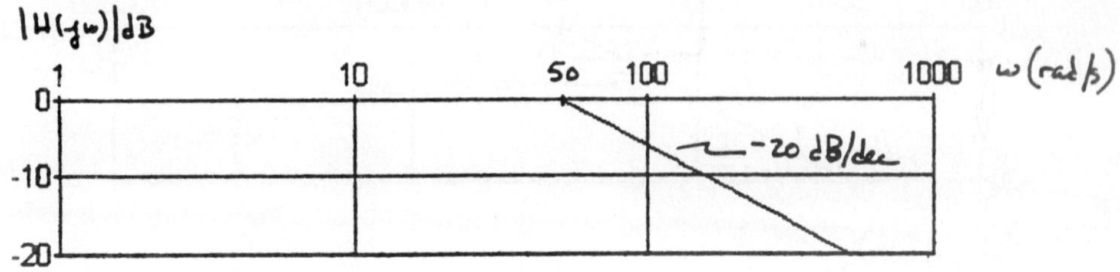

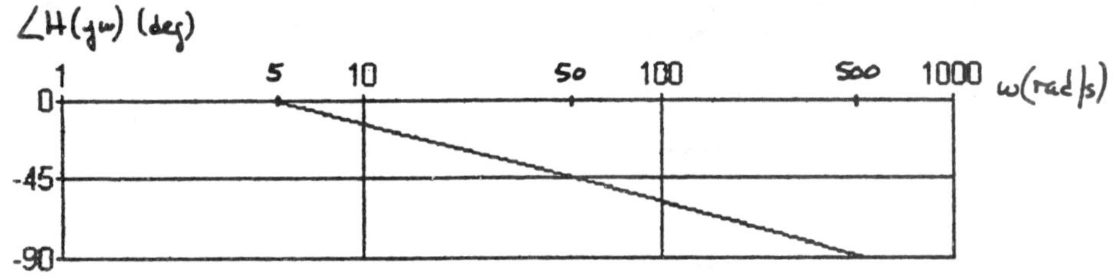

[b] $H(s) = \dfrac{s}{s + 50}$

$$H(j\omega) = \frac{j(\omega/50)}{1 + j(\omega/50)}$$

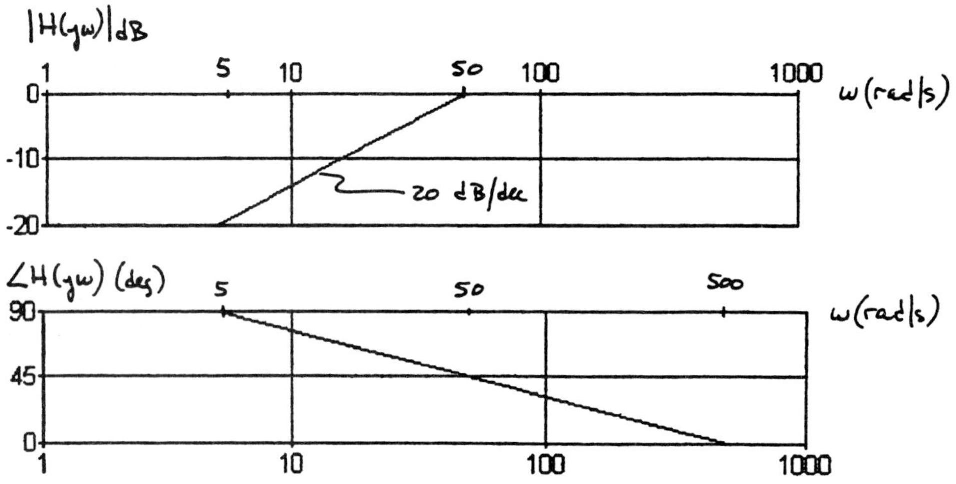

[c] $H(s) = \dfrac{s}{s + 3000}$

$$H(j\omega) = \frac{j(\omega/3000)}{1 + j(\omega/3000)}$$

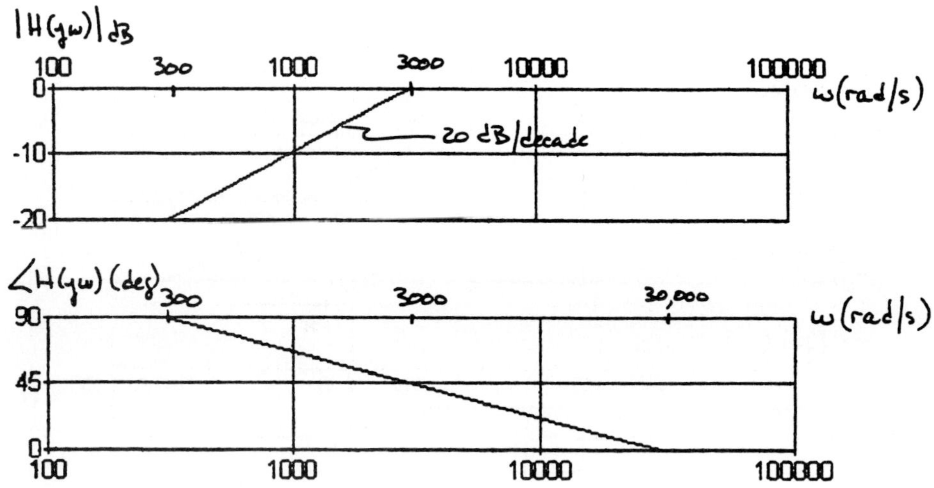

[d] $H(s) = \dfrac{3000}{s + 3000}$

$$H(j\omega) = \frac{1}{1 + j(\omega/3000)}$$

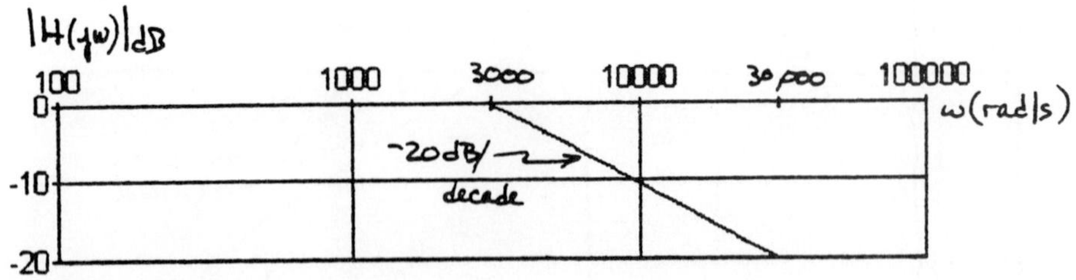

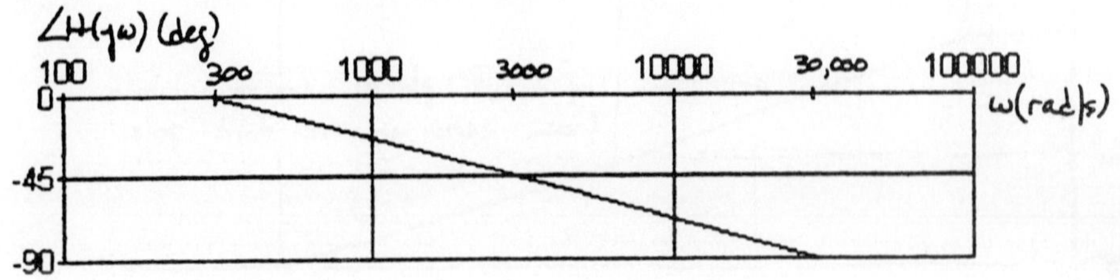

[e] $H(s) = \dfrac{100}{s + 125}$

$$H(j\omega) = \frac{0.8}{1 + (\omega/125)}$$

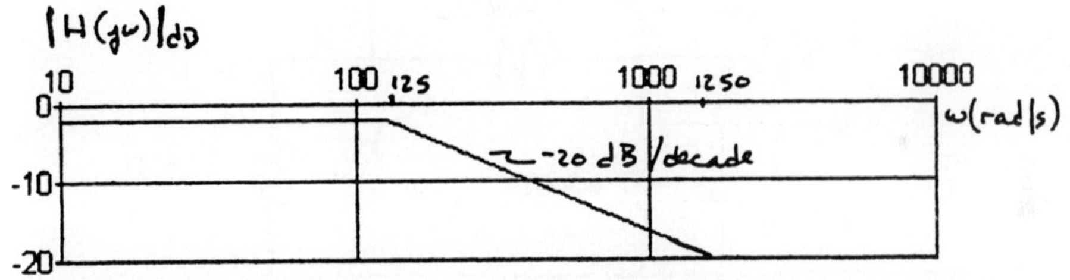

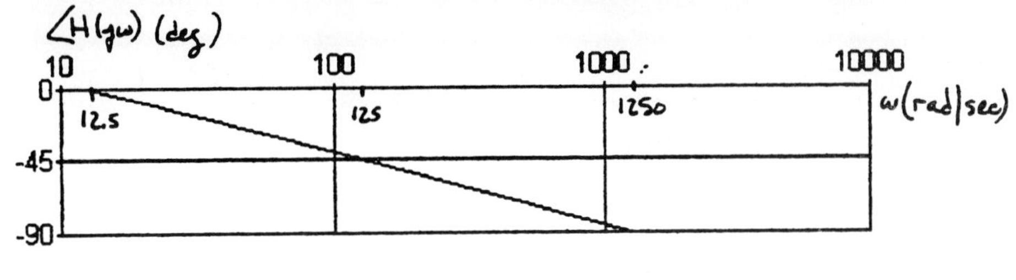

P 14.34 $\quad H(j\omega) = \dfrac{-0.5(j\omega - 20)}{(j\omega + 20)} = 0.5\dfrac{1 - j\omega/20}{1 + j\omega/20}$

$$\begin{aligned} A_{\text{dB}} &= 20\log_{10} 0.5 + 20\log_{10}|1 - j(\omega/20)| \\ &\quad -20\log_{10}|1 + j\omega/20| \\ &= -6.02 + 20\log_{10}|1 + j(\omega/20)| \\ &\quad -20\log_{10}|1 + j(\omega/20)| \end{aligned}$$

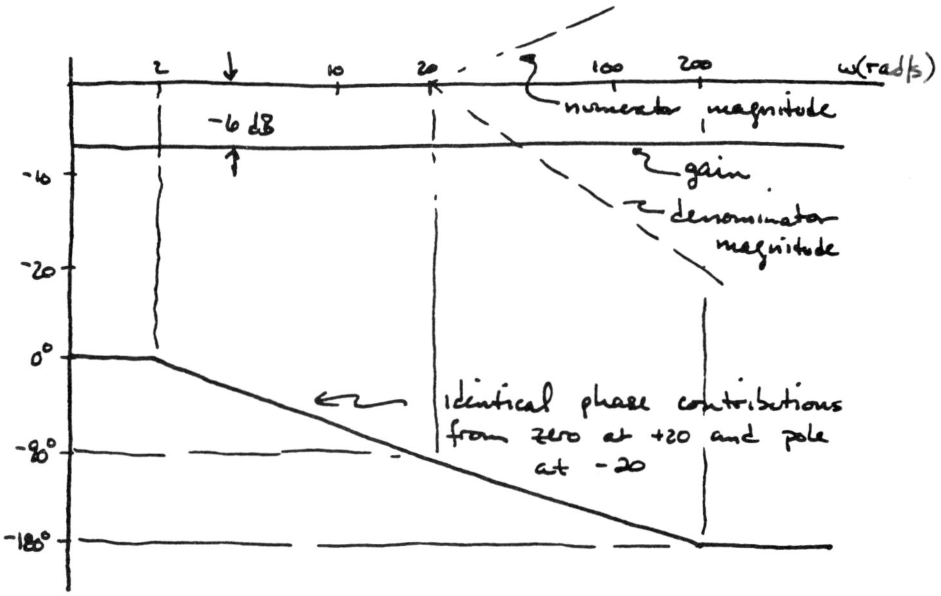

P 14.35 [a]

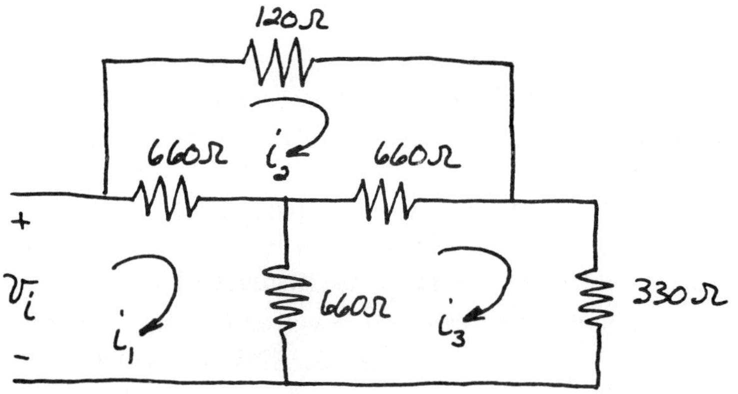

$$v_i = 1320i_1 - 660i_2 - 660i_3$$

$$0 = -660i_1 + 1440i_2 - 660i_3$$

$$0 = -660i_1 - 660i_2 + 1650i_3$$

$$\Delta = \begin{vmatrix} 2 & -1 & -1 \\ -11 & 24 & -11 \\ -1 & -1 & 2.5 \end{vmatrix} = 24.50$$

$$N_1 = \begin{vmatrix} v_i/660 & -1 & -1 \\ 0 & 24 & -11 \\ 0 & -1 & 2.5 \end{vmatrix} = \frac{49v_i}{660}$$

$$i_1 = \frac{N_1}{\Delta} = \frac{v_i}{330}; \qquad \frac{v_i}{i_1} = 330\,\Omega$$

[b] $$p_{\text{out}} = \frac{v_o^2}{330}: \qquad p_{\text{in}} = \frac{v_i^2}{330}; \qquad \therefore \quad \frac{p_{\text{out}}}{p_{\text{in}}} = \left(\frac{v_o}{v_i}\right)^2$$

$$N_3 = \begin{vmatrix} 2 & -1 & v_i/660 \\ -11 & 24 & 0 \\ -1 & -1 & 0 \end{vmatrix} = \frac{35v_i}{660}$$

$$i_3 = \frac{N_3}{\Delta} = \frac{35v_i}{(24.5)(660)}$$

$$v_o = 330i_3 = \frac{35}{49}v_i = \frac{5}{7}v_i; \qquad \frac{v_o}{v_i} = \frac{5}{7}$$

$$\text{dB} = 10\log_{10}\frac{p_{\text{out}}}{p_{\text{in}}} = 20\log_{10}\frac{v_o}{v_i} = -2.92$$

P 14.36 First find the transfer function of the system using the following arguments. $A_{\text{dB}} = 3\text{dB}$ at 1 rad/s, therefore 1 rad/s looks like a corner frequency. Assume 1 rad/s is a corner, then a straight line plot would predict 20 dB at 10 rad/s. On the plot, A_{dB} @ 10 rad/s is 17 dB, i.e., down 3 dB. Therefore, we suspect a simple pole at 10 rad/s. At this point, we have $H(s)$ is of the form $K(s+1)/(s+10)$. A straight line plot of this function would approach a constant as s increases. However, we see from Fig. 14.34 that A_{dB} drops off and is down to 17 dB @ 100 rad/s. Therefore, the transfer function has another simple pole at 100 rad/s, thus $H(s)$ is of the form $K(s+1)/(s+10)(s+100)$. Because $H(j\omega) \to 0$ dB as $\omega \to 0$, K must equal 1000.

Now since $Y(s) = H(s)X(s)$ we have

$$Y(s) = \frac{1000(s+1)}{(s+10)(s+100)} \cdot \frac{1}{s}$$

$$= \frac{K_1}{s} + \frac{K_2}{s+10} + \frac{K_3}{s+100}$$

$$K_1 = \frac{(1000)(1)}{(10)(100)} = 1; \qquad K_2 = \frac{1000(-9)}{(-10)(90)} = 10;$$

$$K_3 = \frac{1000(-99)}{(-100)(-90)} = -11$$

$$y(t) = [1 + 10e^{-10t} - 11e^{-100t}]u(t)$$

P 14.37 [a] Let $Z_1 = R_1 + \left(\frac{1}{sC_1}\right) = \frac{R_1C_1s + 1}{sC_1}$

Let $Z_2 = \frac{R_2(1/sC_2)}{R_2 + (1/sC_2)} = \frac{R_2}{R_2C_2s + 1}$

$$H(s) = \frac{V_o}{V_i} = \frac{Z_2}{Z_1 + Z_2}$$

Substituting in the expressions for Z_1 and Z_2 leads to the expression given in the text.

[b] $\frac{1}{R_1C_1} = 250; \qquad \frac{1}{R_2C_2} = 400{,}000$

$$\frac{1}{R_1C_2} = 100{,}000; \qquad \frac{1}{R_1C_1R_2C_2} = 10^8$$

Therefore $H(s) = \frac{10^5 s}{s^2 + 500{,}250s + 10^8}$

$$= \frac{10^5 s}{(s + 199.98)(s + 500{,}050.02)}$$

[c] $z = 0; \qquad -p_1 = -199.98; \qquad -p_2 = -500{,}050.02$

[d] $H(s) \cong \frac{0.20s}{s + 199.98}$

[e] $H(s) \cong \frac{10^5}{s + 500{,}050.02}$

[f] $Z_1 = \frac{R_1C_1s + 1}{sC_1}; \qquad Z_2 = R_2$

$$H(s) = \frac{Z_2}{Z_1 + Z_2} = \frac{R_2C_1s}{(R_2C_1 + R_1C_1)s + 1} = \frac{0.2s}{s + 200}$$

[g] $Z_1 = R_1; \qquad Z_2 = \frac{R_2}{R_2C_2s + 1}$

$$H(s) = \frac{Z_2}{Z_1 + Z_2} = \frac{R_2}{R_1R_2C_2s + (R_1 + R_2)} = \frac{10^5}{s + 500{,}000}$$

P 14.38 The cutoff frequencies and bandwidth are

$$\omega_{c_1} = 2\pi(1209) = 7596\,\text{rad/s}$$

$$\omega_{c_2} = 2\pi(1633) = 10.26\,\text{krad/s}$$

$$\beta = \omega_{c_2} - \omega_{c_1} = 2664\,\text{rad/s}$$

Telephone circuits always have $R = 600\,\Omega$. Therefore, the filters inductance and capacitance values are

$$L = \frac{R}{\beta} = \frac{600}{2664} = 0.225\,\text{H}$$

$$C = \frac{1}{\omega_{c_1}\omega_{c_2}L} = 0.057\,\mu\text{F}$$

At the highest of the low-band frequencies, 941 Hz, the amplitude is

$$|V_\omega| = |V_{\text{peak}}|\frac{\omega\beta}{\sqrt{(\omega_o^2 - \omega^2)^2 + \omega^2\beta^2}}$$

where $\qquad \omega_o = \sqrt{\omega_{c_1}\omega_{c_2}}$. Thus,

$$|V_\omega| = \frac{|V_{\text{peak}}|(5912)(2664)}{\sqrt{[(8828)^2 - (5912)^2]^2 + [(5912)(2664)]^2}}$$

$$= 0.344\,|V_{\text{peak}}|$$

Again it is not coincidental that this result is the same as the response of the low-band filter to the lowest of the high-band frequencies.

P 14.39 From Example 14.13 the response to the largest of the DTMF low-band tones is $0.948|V_{\text{peak}}|$. The response to the 20 Hz tone is

$$|V_{20\text{Hz}}| = \frac{|V_{\text{peak}}|(125.6)(1533)}{[(5089^2 - 125.6^2)^2 + [(125.6)(1533)]^2]^{1/2}}$$

$$= 0.00744|V_{\text{peak}}|$$

$$\therefore \quad \frac{|V_{20\text{Hz}}|}{|V_{770\text{Hz}}|} = \frac{|V_{20\text{Hz}}|}{|V_{852\text{Hz}}|} = \frac{0.00744|V_{20\text{Hz}}|}{0.948|V_{770\text{Hz}}|} = 0.5$$

$$\therefore \quad |V_{20\text{Hz}}| = 63.7|V_{770\text{Hz}}|$$

Thus, the 20Hz signal can be 63.7 times as large as the DTMF tones.

15

Active Filter Circuits

Drill Exercises

DE 15.1 $H(s) = \frac{-(R_2/R_1)s}{s + (1/R_1C}$

$$\frac{1}{R_1C} = 1\,\text{rad/s}; \qquad R_1 = 1\,\Omega, \quad \therefore \quad C = 1F_1$$

$$\frac{R_2}{R_1} = 1, \quad \therefore \quad R_2 = R_1 = 1\,\Omega$$

DE 15.2 $H(s) = \frac{-(1/R_1C)}{s + (1/R_2C)}$

$$\frac{1}{R_1C} = 20{,}000; \quad C = 5\,\mu\text{F}$$

$$\therefore \quad R_1 = \frac{10^6}{(20{,}000)(5)} = 10\,\Omega$$

$$\frac{1}{R_2C} = 5000$$

$$\therefore \quad R_2 = \frac{10^6}{(5000)(5)} = 40\,\Omega$$

DE 15.3 $\omega_c = 2\pi \times 10^4 = 20{,}000\pi\,\text{rad/s}$

$$\therefore \quad k_f = 20{,}000\pi = 62{,}831.85$$

$$\therefore \quad 0.5 \times 10^{-6} = \frac{1}{k_f k_m}$$

$$\therefore \quad k_m = \frac{10^6}{(0.5)(62{,}831.85)} = 31.83$$

DE 15.4 $\omega_o = 2\pi f_o = 400\pi \text{ rad/s}$

$$\beta = 2\pi(1000) = 2000\pi \text{ rad/s}$$

$$\therefore \quad \omega_{c_2} - \omega_{c_1} = 2000\pi$$

$$\sqrt{\omega_{c_1}\omega_{c_2}} = 400\pi$$

$$\omega_{c_1}\omega_{c_2} = 16 \times 10^4\pi^2$$

$$\omega_{c_2} = \frac{16 \times 10^4\pi^2}{\omega_{c_1}}$$

$$\therefore \quad \frac{16 \times 10^4\pi^2}{\omega_{c_1}} - \omega_{c_1} = 2000\pi$$

or $\omega_{c_1}^2 + 2000\pi\omega_{c_1} - 16 \times 10^4\pi^2 = 0$

$$\omega_{c_1} = -1000\pi \pm \sqrt{10^6\pi^2 + 0.16 \times 10^6\pi^2}$$

$$\omega_{c_1} = 1000\pi(-1 \pm \sqrt{1.16}) = 242.01 \text{ rad/s}$$

$$\therefore \quad \omega_{c_2} = 2000\pi + 242.01 = 6525.19 \text{ rad/s}$$

Thus, $f_{c1} = 38.52$ Hz and $f_{c2} = 1038.52$ Hz

$$\frac{1}{R_L C_L} = 6525.19$$

$$R_L = \frac{10^6}{(6525.19)(5)} = 30.65\,\Omega$$

$$\frac{1}{R_H C_H} = 242.01$$

$$R_H = \frac{10^6}{(242.01)(5)} = 826.43\,\Omega$$

DE 15.5 $\omega_o = 1000\,\text{rad/s}; \qquad \text{GAIN} = 6$

$\beta = 4000; \qquad C = 0.2\,\mu\text{F}$

$\omega_{c_2} - \omega_{c_1} = 4000$

$\sqrt{\omega_{c_1}\omega_{c_2}} = 1000$

$\therefore \quad \omega_{c_1}^2 + 4000\omega_{c_1} - 10^6 = 0$

$\omega_{c_1} = -2000 \pm 1000\sqrt{5} = 236.07\,\text{rad/s}$

$\omega_{c_2} = 4000 + \omega_{c_1} = 4236.07\,\text{rad/s}$

$$\omega_{c_1} = \frac{1}{R_L C_L}$$

$$\therefore \quad R_L = \frac{10^6}{(0.2)(236.07)} = 21.81\,\text{k}\Omega$$

$$\frac{1}{R_H C_H} = 4236.07$$

$$R_H = \frac{10^6}{(0.2)(4236.07)} = 1.18\,\text{k}\Omega$$

$$\frac{R_f}{R_i} = 6$$

If $R_i = 1\,\text{k}\Omega \qquad R_f = 6\,\text{k}\Omega$

DE 15.6 For a 2nd order Butterworth high pass filter

$$H(s) = \frac{s^2}{s^2 + \sqrt{2}s + 1}$$

For the circuit in Fig. 15.25

$$H(s) = \frac{s^2}{s^2 + \left(\frac{2}{R_2 C}\right) s + \left(\frac{1}{R_1 R_2 C^2}\right)}$$

For $C = 1\text{F}$

$$\frac{2}{R_2} = \sqrt{2}, \quad \therefore \quad R_2 = \sqrt{2}\,\Omega$$

$$\frac{1}{R_1 R_2} = 1, \quad \therefore \quad R_1 = \frac{1}{\sqrt{2}}\,\Omega$$

$R_1 = 0.707\,\Omega; \qquad R_2 = 1.414\,\Omega$

DE 15.7 $Q = 8, K = 5, \omega_o = 1000\,\text{rad/s}, C = 1\,\mu\text{F}$

For the circuit in Fig 15.26

$$H(s) = \frac{-\left(\frac{1}{R_1C}\right)s}{s^2 + \left(\frac{2}{R_3C}\right)s + \left(\frac{R_1 + R_2}{R_1R_2R_3C^2}\right)} = \frac{K\beta s}{s^2 + \beta s + \omega_o^2}$$

$$\therefore \quad \beta = \frac{2}{R_3C}, \quad R_3 = \frac{2}{\beta C}$$

$$\beta = \frac{\omega_o}{Q} = \frac{1000}{8} = 125\,\text{rad/s}$$

$$\therefore \quad R_3 = \frac{2 \times 10^6}{(125)(1)} = 16\,\text{k}\Omega$$

$$K\beta = \frac{1}{R_1C}$$

$$\therefore \quad R_1 = \frac{1}{K\beta C} = \frac{10^6}{5(125)(1)} = 1.6\,\text{k}\Omega$$

$$\omega_o^2 = \frac{R_1 + R_2}{R_1R_2R_3C^2}$$

$$10^6 = \frac{(1600 + R_2)10^{12}}{(1600)(R_2)(16{,}000)}$$

$$R_2 = \frac{(1600 + R_2)10^6}{256 \times 10^5}$$

$$246R_2 = 16{,}000, \quad R_2 = 65.04\,\Omega$$

DE 15.8 $\omega_o = 1000\,\text{rad/s}; \qquad Q = 4;$

$C = 2\,\mu\text{F}$

$$H(s) = \frac{s^2 + (1/R^2C^2)}{s^2 + \left[\frac{4(1-\sigma)}{RC}\right]s + \left(\frac{1}{R^2C^2}\right)} = \frac{s^2 + \omega_o^2}{s^2 + \beta s + \omega_o^2}$$

$$\omega_o^2 = 10^6; \qquad \therefore \quad \frac{1}{RC} = 1000$$

$$R = \frac{1}{1000C} = \frac{10^6}{2000} = 500\,\Omega$$

$$\beta = \frac{\omega_o}{Q} = \frac{1000}{4} = 250$$

$$\frac{4(1-\sigma)}{RC} = 250$$

$$4(1-\sigma) = 250RC = 0.25$$

$$1-\sigma = 0.0625; \qquad \sigma = 0.9375$$

Problems

P 15.1 Summing the currents at the inverting input node yields

$$\frac{0-V_i}{Z_i} + \frac{0-V_o}{Z_f} = 0$$

$$\therefore \quad \frac{V_o}{Z_f} = -\frac{V_i}{Z_i}$$

$$\therefore \quad H(s) = \frac{V_o}{V_i} = -\frac{Z_f}{Z_i}$$

P 15.2 [a] $Z_f = \dfrac{R_2(1/sC_2)}{[R_2 + (1/sC_2)]} = \dfrac{R_2}{R_2C_2s + 1}$

$$= \frac{(1/C_2)}{s + (1/R_2C_2)}$$

Likewise

$$Z_i = \frac{(1/C_1)}{s + (1/R_1C_1)}$$

$$\therefore \quad H(s) = \frac{-(1/C_2)[s + (1/R_1C_1)]}{[s + (1/R_2C_2)](1/C_1)}$$

$$= -\frac{C_1\,[s + (1/R_1C_1)]}{C_2\,[s + (1/R_2C_2)]}$$

[b] $H(j\omega) = \frac{-C_1}{C_2}\left[\frac{j\omega + (1/R_1C_1)}{j\omega + (1/R_2C_2)}\right]$

$$H(j0) = \frac{-C_1}{C_2}\left(\frac{R_2C_2}{R_1C_1}\right) = \frac{-R_2}{R_1}$$

[c] $H(j\infty) = -\frac{C_1}{C_2}\left(\frac{j}{j}\right) = \frac{-C_1}{C_2}$

[d] As $\omega \to 0$ the two capacitor branches become open and the circuit reduces to a resistive inverting amplifier having a gain of $-R_2/R_1$.
As $\omega \to \infty$ the two capacitor branches approach a short circuit and in this case we encounter an indeterminate situation; namely $v_n \to v_i$ but $v_n = 0$ because of the ideal op amp. At the same time the gain of the ideal op amp is infinite so we have the indeterminate form $0 \cdot \infty$. Although $\omega = \infty$ is indeterminate we can reason that for finite large values of ω $H(j\omega)$ will approach $-C_1/C_2$ in value. In other words, the circuit approaches a purely capacitive inverting amplifier with a gain of $(-1/j\omega C_2)/(1/j\omega C_1)$ or $-C_1/C_2$.

P 15.3 [a] $Z_f = \frac{(1/C_2)}{s + (1/R_2C_2)}$

$$Z_i = R_1 + \frac{1}{sC_1} = \frac{R_1}{s}[s + (1/R_1C_1)]$$

$$H(s) = -\frac{(1/C_2)}{[s + (1/R_2C_2)]} \cdot \frac{s}{R_1[s + (1/R_1C_1)]}$$

$$= -\frac{1}{R_1C_2}\frac{s}{[s + (1/R_1C_1)][s + (1/R_2C_2)]}$$

[b] $H(j\omega) = -\frac{1}{R_1C_2}\frac{j\omega}{\left(j\omega + \frac{1}{R_1C_1}\right)\left(j\omega + \frac{1}{R_2C_2}\right)}$

$$H(j0) = 0$$

[c] $H(j\infty) = 0$

[d] As $\omega \to 0$ the capacitor C_1 disconnects v_i from the circuit. Therefore $v_o = v_n = 0$.
As $\omega \to \infty$ the capacitor short circuits the feedback network, thus $Z_F = 0$ and therefore $v_o = 0$.

P 15.4 [a] $K = 10^{0.75} = 5.62 = \frac{R_2}{R_1}$

$$R_2 = \frac{1}{\omega_c C} = \frac{10^9}{(2\pi)(10^4)(5)} = 3.18\,\text{k}\Omega$$

$$R_1 = \frac{R_2}{K} = \frac{3.18}{5.62} = 0.57\,\text{k}\Omega$$

[b]

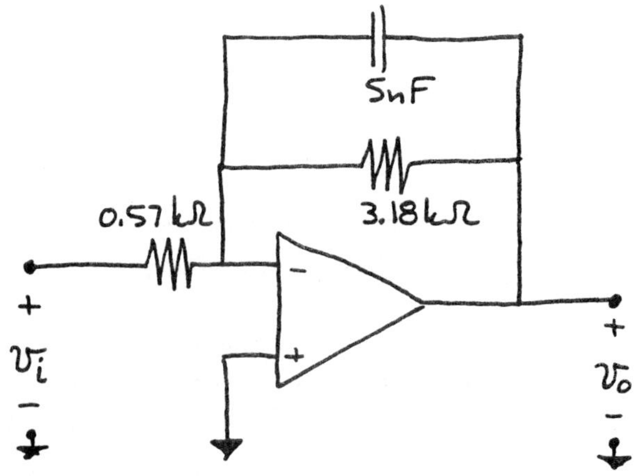

P 15.5 [a] $R_1 = \frac{1}{\omega_c C} = \frac{10^{12}}{(2\pi)(40)(10^3)(680)} = 5.85\,\text{k}\Omega$

$$K = 10^{0.6} = 3.98 = \frac{R_2}{R_1}$$

$$\therefore \quad R_2 = 3.98R_1 = 23.29\,\text{k}\Omega$$

[b]

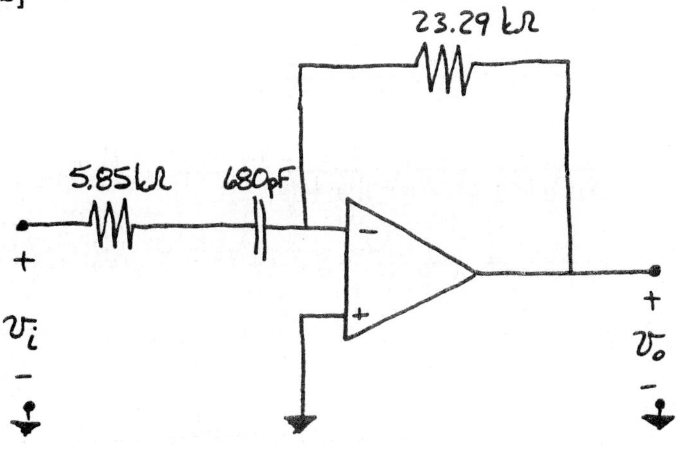

P 15.6 For the RC circuit

$$H(s) = \frac{V_o}{V_i} = \frac{(1/RC)}{s + (1/RC)}$$

$$R' = k_m R; \qquad C' = \frac{C}{k_m k_f}$$

$$\therefore \quad R'C' = k_m R \frac{C}{k_m k_f} = \frac{1}{k_f} RC = \frac{1}{k_f}$$

$$\frac{1}{R'C'} = k_f$$

$$H'(s) = \frac{(1/R'C')}{s + (1/R'C')} = \frac{k_f}{s + k_f}$$

$$H'(s) = \frac{1}{\left(\frac{s}{k_f}\right) + 1}$$

For the RL circuit

$$R' = k_m R; \qquad L' = \frac{k_m}{k_f} L$$

$$\frac{R'}{L'} = \frac{k_m R}{\frac{k_m}{k_f} L} = k_f \left(\frac{R}{L}\right) = k_f$$

$$H'(s) = \frac{(R'/L')}{s + (R'/L')} = \frac{k_f}{s + k_f}$$

$$H'(s) = \frac{1}{\left(\frac{s}{k_f}\right) + 1}$$

P 15.7 For the RC circuit

$$H(s) = \frac{V_o}{V_i} = \frac{s}{s + (1/RC)}$$

$$R' = k_m R; \qquad C' = \frac{C}{k_m k_f}$$

$$\therefore \quad R'C' = \frac{RC}{k_f} = \frac{1}{k_f}; \qquad \frac{1}{R'C'} = k_f$$

$$H'(s) = \frac{s}{s + (1/R'C')} = \frac{s}{s + k_f} = \frac{(s/k_f)}{(s/k_f) + 1}$$

For the RL circuit

$$H(s) = \frac{s}{s + (R/L)}$$

$$R' = k_m R; \qquad L' = \frac{k_m L}{k_f}$$

$$\frac{R'}{L'} = k_f\left(\frac{R}{L}\right) = k_f$$

$$H'(s) = \frac{s}{s + k_f} = \frac{(s/k_f)}{(s/k_f) + 1}$$

P 15.8 $$H(s) = \frac{(R/L)s}{s^2 + (R/L)s + (1/LC)} = \frac{\beta s}{s^2 \beta s + \omega_o^2}$$

For the prototype circuit $\omega_o = 1$ and $\beta = \omega_o/Q = 1/Q$.
For the scaled circuit

$$H'(s) = \frac{(R'/L')s}{s^2 + (R'/L')s + (1/L'C')}$$

where $R' = k_m R$; $L' = \frac{k_m}{k_f} L$; and $C' = \frac{C}{k_f k_m}$

$$\therefore \quad \frac{R'}{L'} = \frac{k_m R}{\frac{k_m}{k_f} L} = k_f\left(\frac{R}{L}\right) = k_f \beta$$

$$\frac{1}{L'C'} = \frac{k_f k_m}{\frac{k_m}{k_f} LC} = \frac{k_f^2}{LC} = kf^2$$

$$Q' = \frac{w_o'}{\beta'} = \frac{k_f w_o}{k_f \beta} = Q$$

therefore the Q of the scaled circuit is the same as the Q of the unscaled circuit. Also note $\beta' = k_f \beta$.

$$\therefore \quad H'(s) = \frac{\left(\frac{k_f}{Q}\right) s}{s^2 + \left(\frac{k_f}{Q}\right) s + k_f^2}$$

$$H'(s) = \frac{\left(\frac{1}{Q}\right)\left(\frac{s}{k_f}\right)}{\left[\left(\frac{s}{k_f}\right)^2 + \frac{1}{Q}\left(\frac{s}{k_f}\right) + 1\right]}$$

P 15.9 [a] $L = 1\,\text{H}; \qquad C = 1\,\text{F}$

$$R = \frac{1}{Q} = \frac{1}{25} = 0.04\,\Omega$$

[b] $k_f = 100{,}000; \qquad k_m = \dfrac{3600}{0.04} = 90{,}000$

Thus,

$$R' = (0.04)(90{,}000) = 3.6\,\text{k}\Omega$$

$$L' = \frac{90{,}000}{100{,}000}(1) = 0.9\,\text{H}$$

$$C' = \frac{1}{(10^5)(9\times 10^4)} = \frac{1}{9}\,\text{nF} = 0.11\,\text{nF}$$

[c]

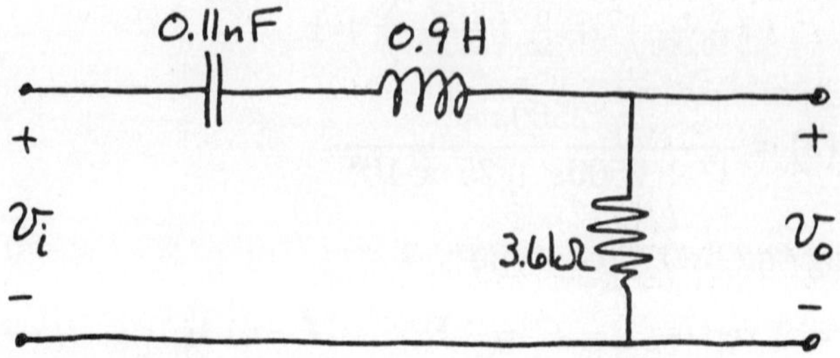

P 15.10 [a] By hypothesis, $LC = 1$; Thus,

$$C = \frac{1}{L} = \frac{1}{Q}F$$

[b] $H(s) = \dfrac{(R/L)s}{s^2 + (R/L)s + (1/LC)}$

$$H(s) = \frac{(1/Q)s}{s^2 + (1/Q)s + 1}$$

[c] In the prototype circuit

$$R = 1\,\Omega; \qquad L = 20\,\text{H}; \qquad C = 0.05\,\text{F}$$

$$\therefore\ k_m = 5000; \qquad k_f = 50{,}000$$

Thus

$$R' = 5\,\text{k}\Omega$$

$$L' = \frac{5000}{50{,}000}(20) = 2\,\text{H}$$

$$C' = \frac{0.05}{(5000)(50{,}000)} = 0.2\times 10^{-9} = 0.2\,\text{nF}$$

[d]

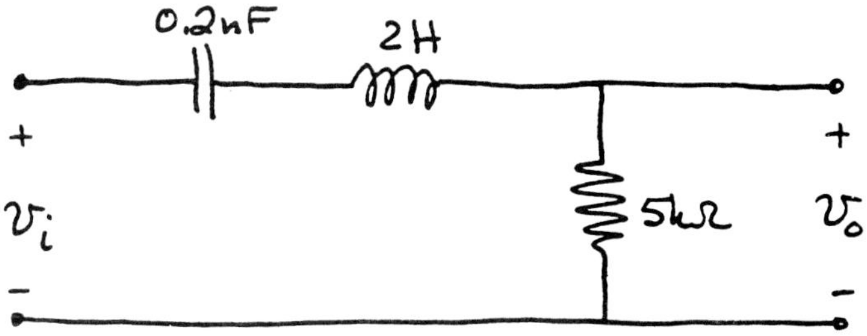

[e] $$H'(s) = \frac{\frac{1}{20}\left(\frac{s}{50,000}\right)}{\left(\frac{s}{50,000}\right)^2 + \frac{1}{20}\left(\frac{s}{50,000}\right) + 1}$$

$$H'(s) = \frac{2500s}{s^2 + 2500s + 25 \times 10^8}$$

P 15.11 [a] Using the first prototype

$$\omega_o = 1\ \text{rad/s}; \qquad C = 1\,\text{F}; \qquad L = 1\,\text{H}; \qquad R = 16\,\Omega$$

$$k_m = \frac{80,000}{16} = 5000; \qquad k_f = 80,000$$

Thus,

$$R' = 80\,\text{k}\Omega; \qquad L' = \frac{5}{80}(1) = 62.5\,\text{mH};$$

$$C' = \frac{1}{400 \times 10^6} = 2.5\,\text{nF}$$

Using the second prototype

$$\omega_o = 1\ \text{rad/s}; \qquad C = 16\,\text{F}$$

$$L = \frac{1}{16} = 6.26\,\text{mH}; \qquad R = 1\,\Omega$$

$$k_m = 80,000; \qquad k_f = 80,000$$

Thus,

$$R' = 80\,\text{k}\Omega; \qquad L' = \frac{80}{80}(6.25) = 6.25\,\text{mH};$$

$$C' = \frac{16}{64 \times 10^8} = 2.5\,\text{nF}$$

[b]

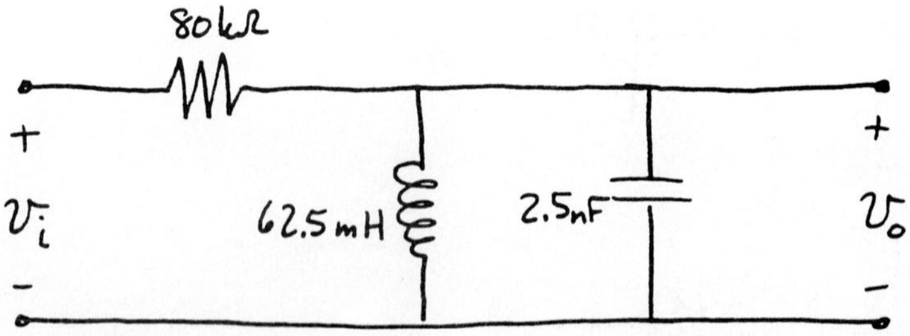

P 15.12 For the scaled circuit

$$H'(s) = \frac{s^2 + \left(\frac{1}{L'C'}\right)}{s^2 + \left(\frac{R'}{L'}\right)s + \left(\frac{1}{L'C'}\right)}$$

$$L' = \frac{k_m}{k_f}L; \qquad C' = \frac{C}{k_m k_f}$$

$$\therefore \quad \frac{1}{L'C'} = \frac{k_f^2}{LC}; \qquad R' = k_m R$$

$$\therefore \quad \frac{R'}{L'} = k_f\left(\frac{R}{L}\right)$$

It follows then that

$$H'(s) = \frac{s^2\left(\frac{k_f^2}{LC}\right)}{s^2 + \left(\frac{R}{L}\right)k_f s + \frac{k_f^2}{LC}}$$

$$= \frac{\left(\frac{s}{k_f}\right)^2 + \left(\frac{1}{LC}\right)}{\left[\left(\frac{s}{k_f}\right)^2 + \left(\frac{R}{L}\right)\left(\frac{s}{k_f}\right) + \left(\frac{1}{LC}\right)\right]}$$

$$= H(s)|_{s=s/k_f}$$

P 15.13 For the circuit in Fig. 15.31

$$H(s) = \frac{s^2 + \left(\frac{1}{LC}\right)}{s^2 + \frac{s}{RC} + \left(\frac{1}{LC}\right)}$$

It follows that

$$H'(s) = \frac{s^2 + \frac{1}{L'C'}}{s^2 + \frac{s}{R'C'} + \frac{1}{L'C'}}$$

where $R' = k_m R$; $\quad L' = \frac{k_m}{k_f} L$;

$$C' = \frac{C}{k_m k_f}$$

$$\therefore \quad \frac{1}{L'C'} = \frac{k_f^2}{LC}$$

$$\frac{1}{R'C'} = \frac{k_f}{RC}$$

$$H'(s) = \frac{s^2 + \left(\frac{k_f^2}{LC}\right)}{s^2 + \left(\frac{k_f}{RC}\right)s + \frac{k_f^2}{LC}}$$

$$= \frac{\left(\frac{s}{k_f}\right)^2 + \frac{1}{LC}}{\left(\frac{s}{k_f}\right)^2 + \left(\frac{1}{RC}\right)\left(\frac{s}{k_f}\right) + \frac{1}{LC}}$$

$$= H(s)|_{s=s/k_f}$$

P 15.14 [a] For the circuit in Fig. P15.14(a)

$$H(s) = \frac{V_o}{V_i} = \frac{s + \frac{1}{s}}{\frac{1}{Q} + s + \frac{1}{s}} = \frac{s^2 + 1}{s^2 + \left(\frac{1}{Q}\right)s + 1}$$

For the circuit in Fig. P15.14(b)

$$H(s) = \frac{V_o}{V_i} = \frac{Qs + \frac{Q}{s}}{1 + Qs + \frac{Q}{s}}$$

$$= \frac{Q(s^2 + 1)}{Qs^2 + s + Q}$$

$$H(s) = \frac{s^2 + 1}{s^2 + \left(\frac{1}{Q}\right)s + 1}$$

[b] $$H'(s) = \frac{\left(\frac{s}{10^4}\right)^2 + 1}{\left(\frac{s}{10^4}\right)^2 + \frac{1}{8}\left(\frac{s}{10^4}\right) + 1}$$

$$= \frac{s^2 + 10^8}{s^2 + 1250s + 10^8}$$

P 15.15 For prototype circuit (a):

$$H(s) = \frac{V_o}{V_i} = \frac{Q}{Q + \frac{1}{s+\frac{1}{s}}} = \frac{Q}{Q + \frac{s}{s^2+1}}$$

$$H(s) = \frac{Q(s^2+1)}{Q(s^2+1)+s} = \frac{s^2+1}{s^2 + \left(\frac{1}{Q}\right)s + 1}$$

For prototype circuit (b):

$$H(s) = \frac{V_o}{V_i} = \frac{1}{1 + \frac{(s/Q)}{(s^2+1)}}$$

$$= \frac{s^2+1}{s^2 + \left(\frac{1}{Q}\right)s + 1}$$

P 15.16 [a] $k_m = \frac{20}{4} = 5$

$$\therefore\ 100 \times 10^{-12} = \frac{5 \times 10^{-9}}{5k_f}; \qquad \therefore\ k_f = 10$$

$$L_{\text{scaled}} = \frac{5}{10}(80) = 40\,\text{mH}$$

$$R_{2\text{scaled}} = (21)(5 \times 10^3) = 105\,\text{k}\Omega$$

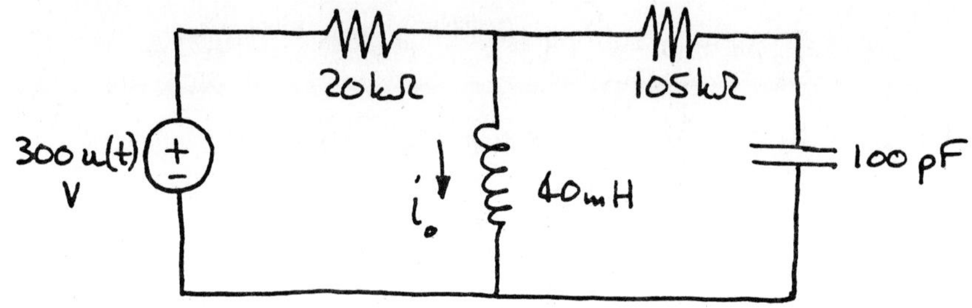

[b] From the soltion to Problem 13.32(b) we have

$$i_o = [75 + 5e^{-10{,}000t} - 80e^{-40{,}000t}]u(t)\,\text{mA}$$

Since $k_m = 5$ the amplitude of i_o in the scaled circuit will be one-fifth the original amplitude.
Since $k_f = 10$ the coefficients of t in the exponents will increase by a factor of 10. Thus,

$$i_o = [15 + e^{-100{,}000t} - 16e^{-400{,}000t}]u(t)\,\text{mA}$$

P 15.17 $k_m = \frac{1000}{10} = 100; \qquad k_f = 1000$

$$C = \frac{100 \times 10^{-3}}{10^5} = 1\,\mu\text{F}; \qquad 10\,\Omega \rightarrow 1\,\text{k}\Omega;$$

$$140\,\Omega \rightarrow 14\,\text{k}\Omega; \qquad L = \frac{100}{1000}(20) = 2\,\text{H}$$

$$0.25 \rightarrow \frac{0.25}{k_m} = 25 \times 10^{-4}$$

$$v_o = [16.8 + 722.4e^{-4000t}\cos(3000t + 91.33^\circ)]u(t) \quad \text{kV}$$

P 15.18 [a] $\frac{k_m}{k_f}(25) = 100 \times 10^{-3}; \qquad k_f = 250k_m$

$$\frac{0.02}{k_f k_m} = 0.8 \times 10^{-6}; \qquad k_m k_f = 25{,}000$$

$$250k_m^2 = 25{,}000 \quad k_m = 10, \quad k_f = 2500$$

Since the multiplier of i_ϕ must have the dimensions of impedance in the scaled circuit $20k_m = 200$

[b] Frequencies of i_o increase by k_f or 2500

$$\therefore \quad i_o = [-100 + 84e^{-2500t} + 36e^{-5000t}]u(t)\ \text{A}$$

P 15.19 $25 \times 10^{-9} = \frac{4 \times 10^{-3}}{k_f k_m}; \qquad k_f k_m = 16 \times 10^4$

$$10 \times 10^{-3} = 4\frac{k_m}{k_f}; \qquad k_f = 400k_m$$

$$\therefore \quad k_m^2 = \frac{16 \times 10^4}{400}; \qquad k_m = 20; \qquad k_f = 8000$$

From the solution to Problem 13.37 we have

$$i_o = [-300e^{-25t} + 300\sqrt{5}e^{-5t}\cos(10t + 63.43^\circ)]u(t)\ \text{mA}$$

Therefore in the scaled circuit

$$i_o = [-15e^{-200{,}000t} + 15\sqrt{5}e^{-40{,}000t}\cos(80{,}000t + 63.43^\circ)]u(t)\ \text{mA}$$

P 15.20 [a] From Eq 15.1 we have

$$H(s) = \frac{-K\omega_c}{s+\omega_c}$$

where $K = \frac{R_2}{R_1}, \quad \omega_c = \frac{1}{R_2C}$

$$\therefore \quad H'(s) = \frac{-K'\omega_c'}{s+\omega_c'}$$

where $K' = \frac{R_2'}{R_1'} \quad \omega_c' = \frac{1}{R_2'C'}$

By hypothesis $R_1' = k_mR_1; \qquad R_2' = k_mR_2,$

and $C' = \frac{C}{k_fk_m}$. It follows that

$K' = K$ and $\omega_c' = k_f\omega_c$, therefore

$$H'(s) = \frac{-Kk_f\omega_c}{s+k_f\omega_c} = \frac{-K\omega_c}{\left(\frac{s}{k_f}\right)+\omega_c}$$

[b] $H(s) = \frac{-K}{(s+1)}$

[c] $H'(s) = \frac{-K}{\left(\frac{s}{k_f}\right)+1} = \frac{-Kk_f}{s+k_f}$

P 15.21 [a] From Eq. 15.4

$H(s) = \frac{-Ks}{s+\omega_c}$ where $K = \frac{R_2}{R_1}$ and

$$\omega_c = \frac{1}{R_1C}$$

$\therefore \quad H'(s) = \frac{-K's}{s+\omega_c'}$ where $K' = \frac{R_2'}{R_1'}$

and $\omega_c' = \frac{1}{R_1'C'}$

By hypothesis

$$R_1' = k_mR_1; \qquad R_2' = k_mR_2; \qquad C' = \frac{C}{k_mk_f}$$

It follows that

$K' = K$ and $\omega_c' = k_f\omega_c$

$$\therefore \quad H'(s) = \frac{-Ks}{s+k_f\omega_c} = \frac{-K(s/k_f)}{\left(\frac{s}{k_f}\right)+\omega_c}$$

[b] $H(s) = \dfrac{-Ks}{(s+1)}$

[c] $H'(s) = \dfrac{-K(s/k_f)}{\left(\frac{s}{k_f}+1\right)} = \dfrac{-Ks}{(s+k_f)}$

P 15.22 [a] $H_{\text{hp}} = \dfrac{s}{s+1}; \qquad k_f = 4000\pi$

$\therefore \quad H'_{\text{hp}} = \dfrac{s}{s+4000\pi}$

$\dfrac{1}{R_H C_H} = 4000\pi; \qquad \therefore \quad R_H = \dfrac{10^6}{(4000\pi)(0.02)} = 3.98\,\text{k}\Omega$

$H_{\text{lp}} = \dfrac{1}{s+1}; \qquad k_f = 16{,}000\pi$

$\therefore \quad H'_{\text{lp}} = \dfrac{16{,}000\pi}{s+16{,}000\pi}$

$\dfrac{1}{R_L C_L} = 16{,}000\pi; \qquad \therefore \quad R_H = \dfrac{10^6}{(16{,}000\pi)(0.02)} = 248.68\,\Omega$

$H(j\omega_o) = \dfrac{K\omega_{c2}}{\omega_{c1}+\omega_{c2}} = 0.8K$

$20\log_{10}(0.8K) = 10; \qquad \therefore \quad K = 1.25\sqrt{10}$

$\therefore \quad \dfrac{R_f}{R_i} = 1.25\sqrt{10}$

$R_i = 10\,\text{k}\Omega; \qquad R_f = 12.5\sqrt{10} = 39.53\,\text{k}\Omega$

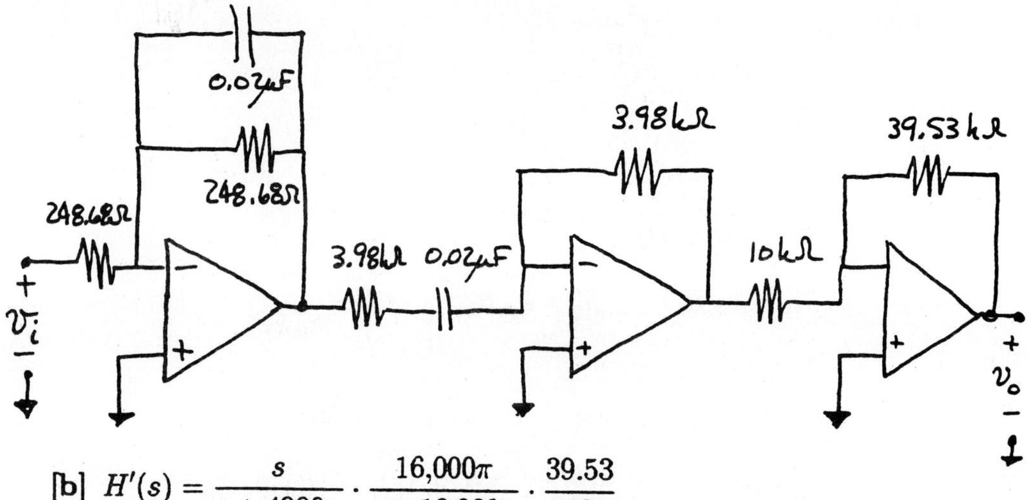

[b] $H'(s) = \dfrac{s}{s+4000\pi} \cdot \dfrac{16{,}000\pi}{s+16{,}000\pi} \cdot \dfrac{39.53}{10}$

[c] $\omega_o = \sqrt{\omega_{c1}\omega_{c1}} = 8000\pi$ rad/s

$$H'(j\omega_o) = \frac{(16{,}000\pi)(j8000\pi)}{(4000\pi + j8000\pi)(16{,}000\pi + j8000\pi)} \cdot \frac{39.53}{10}$$

$$= (0.8)(3.953) = 3.16 = \sqrt{10}$$

[d] $20\log_{10}|H'(j\omega_o)| = 20\log_{10}\sqrt{10} = 10$ dB

[e]

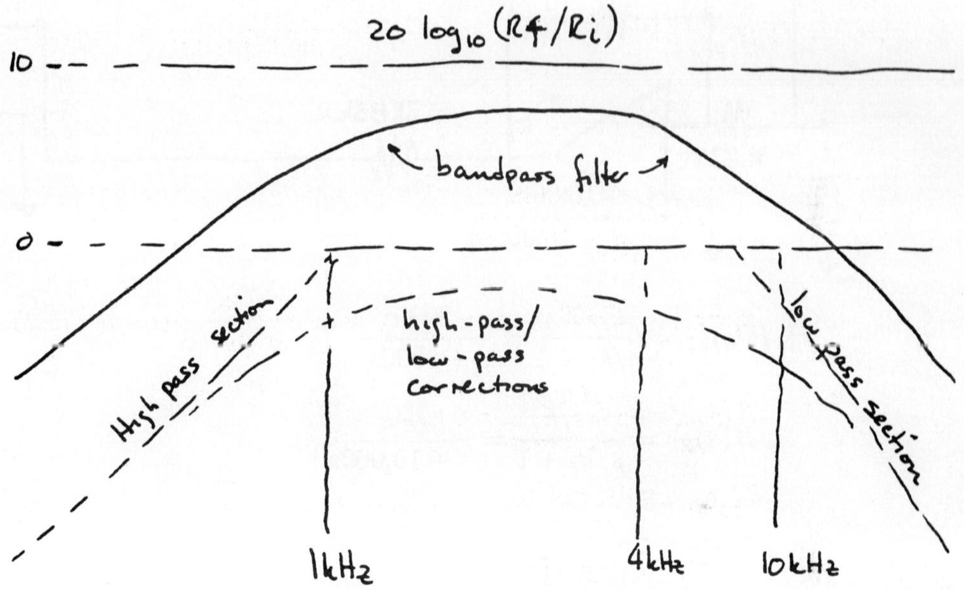

P 15.23 [a] $\omega_{c1} = \frac{1}{R_L C_L} = 2000\pi$ rad/s

$$R_L = \frac{10^9}{(2000\pi)(5)} = 31.83\,\text{k}\Omega$$

$$\omega_{c2} = \frac{1}{R_H C_H} = 10{,}000\pi \text{ rad/s}$$

$$R_H = \frac{10^9}{(10{,}000\pi)(5)} = 6.37\,\text{k}\Omega$$

$$20\log_{10}\left(\frac{R_f}{R_i}\right) = 10; \qquad \therefore\ R_f = \sqrt{10}R_i$$

Choose $R_i = 31.83\,\text{k}\Omega$; then $R_f = 100.66\,\text{k}\Omega$

[b]

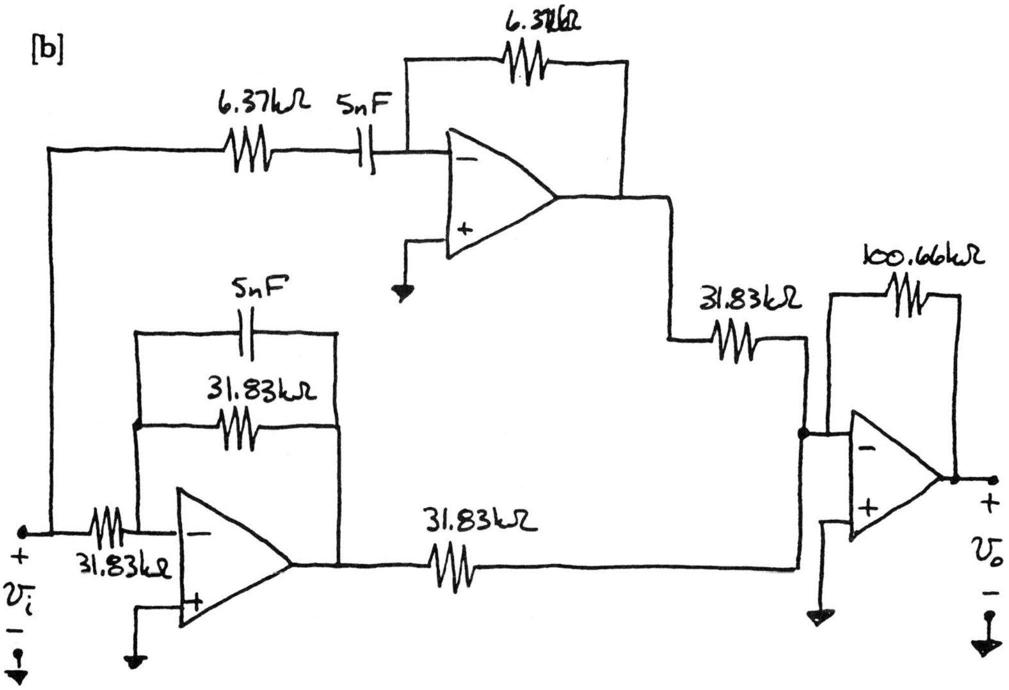

[c] $$H(s)_{\rm LP} = \frac{-1}{s/k_f + 1} = \frac{-2000\pi}{s + 2000\pi}$$

$$H(s)_{\rm HP} = \frac{-s/k_f}{s/k_f + 1} = \frac{-s}{s + 10{,}000\pi}$$

$$-\frac{R_f}{R_i} = -\sqrt{10}$$

$$H(s) = \sqrt{10}\left[\frac{2000\pi}{s + 2000\pi} + \frac{s}{s + 10{,}000\pi}\right]$$

$$= \sqrt{10}\left[\frac{s^2 + 4000\pi s + 20 \times 10^6\pi^2}{(s + 2000\pi)(s + 10{,}000\pi)}\right]$$

[d] $$\omega_o = \sqrt{\omega_{c1}\omega_{c2}} = \sqrt{20 \times 10^6\pi^2}$$

$$= 1000\pi\sqrt{20} = 2000\pi\sqrt{5}\ \text{rad/s}$$

$$H(j\omega_o) = \sqrt{10}\left[\frac{j4000\pi(2000\pi\sqrt{5})}{(2000\pi + j2000\pi\sqrt{5})(10{,}000\pi + j2000\pi\sqrt{5})}\right]$$

$$= \frac{j2\sqrt{5}\sqrt{10}}{(1 + j\sqrt{5})(5 + j\sqrt{5})} = \frac{j2\sqrt{5}\sqrt{10}}{j6\sqrt{5}}$$

$$= \frac{\sqrt{10}}{3} = 1.05$$

[e] $20\log_{10}|H(j\omega_o)| = 20\log_{10} 1.05 = 0.46$ dB

[f] $H(j\omega) = \dfrac{\left[1 - \left(\frac{\omega}{1000\sqrt{20}\pi}\right)^2\right] + j\frac{4}{\sqrt{20}} \cdot \frac{w}{100\sqrt{20}\pi}}{\left(1 + j\frac{\omega}{2000\pi}\right)\left(1 + j\frac{\omega}{10{,}000\pi}\right)}$

$$2\zeta = \frac{4}{\sqrt{20}}; \qquad \zeta = \frac{2}{\sqrt{20}}; \qquad \zeta^2 = 0.20$$

$$\omega_o = 2000\pi\sqrt{5}; \qquad f_o = 1000\sqrt{5} = 2236.07\ \text{Hz}$$

$$f_p = f_o\sqrt{1 - 2\zeta^2} = f_o\sqrt{0.6} = 1732.05\ \text{Hz}$$

$$A_{\text{dB}}(f_p) = 10\log_{10}[4\zeta^2(1 - \zeta^2)] = 10\log_{10} 0.64 = -1.94\ \text{dB}$$

$$A_{\text{dB}}(f_o/2) = 10\log_{10} 0.7625 = -1.18\ \text{dB}$$

$$A_{\text{dB}}(f_o) = 20\log_{10} 2\zeta = -0.97\ \text{dB}$$

For the quadratic term, $A_{\text{dB}} = 0$ when $f = \sqrt{2}f_p = 2449.48$ Hz.

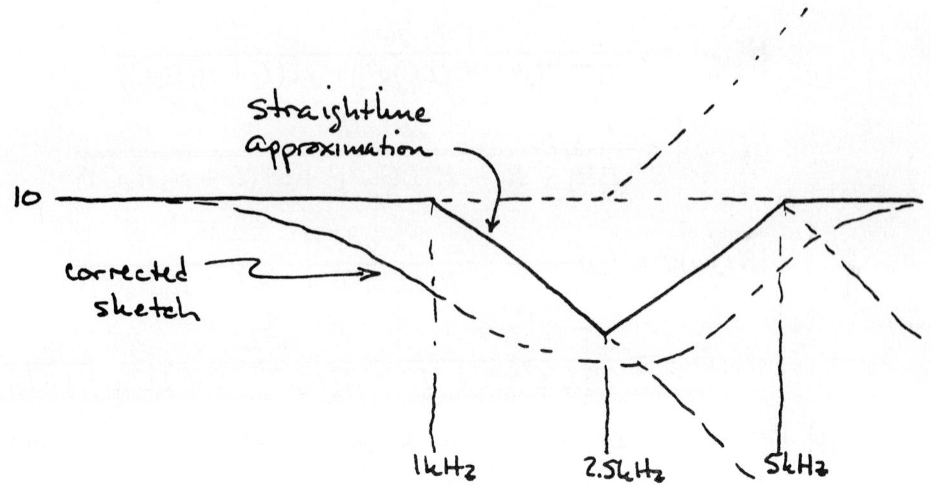

P 15.24 [a] $H(s) = \dfrac{(1/sC)}{R + (1/sC)} = \dfrac{(1/RC)}{s + (1/RC)}$

$$H(j\omega) = \frac{(1/RC)}{j\omega + (1/RC)}$$

$$|H(j\omega)| = \frac{(1/RC)}{\sqrt{\omega^2 + (1/RC)^2}}$$

$$|H(j\omega)|^2 = \frac{(1/RC)}{\omega^2 + (1/RC)^2}$$

[b] Let V_a be the voltage across the capacitor, positive at the upper terminal. Then

$$\frac{V_a - V_{in}}{R_1} + sCV_a + \frac{V_a}{R_2 + sL} = 0$$

Solving for V_a yields

$$V_a = \frac{(R_2 + sL)V_{in}}{R_1LCs^2 + (R_1R_2C + L)s + (R_1 + R_2)}$$

But

$$v_o = \frac{sLV_a}{R_2 + sL}$$

Therefore

$$V_o = \frac{sLV_{in}}{R_1LCs^2 + (L + R_1R_2C)s + (R_1 + R_2)}$$

$$H(s) = \frac{sL}{R_1LCs^2 + (L + R_1R_2C)s + (R_1 + R_2)}$$

$$H(j\omega) = \frac{j\omega L}{[(R_1 + R_2) - R_1LC\omega^2] + j\omega(L + R_1R_2C)}$$

$$|H(j\omega)| = \frac{\omega L}{\sqrt{[R_1 + R_2 - R_1LC\omega^2]^2 + \omega^2(L + R_1R_2C)^2}}$$

$$|H(j\omega)|^2 = \frac{\omega^2L^2}{(R_1 + R_2 - R_1LC\omega^2)^2 + \omega^2(L + R_1R_2C)^2}$$

$$= \frac{\omega^2L^2}{R_1^2L^2C^2\omega^4 + (L^2 + R_1^2R_2^2C^2 - 2R_1^2LC)\omega^2 + (R_1 + R_2)^2}$$

[c] Let V_a be the voltage across R_2 positive at the upper terminal. Then

$$\frac{V_a - V_{in}}{R_1} + \frac{V_a}{R_2} + V_asC + V_asC = 0$$

$$(0 - V_a)sC + (0 - V_a)sC + \frac{0 - V_o}{R_3} = 0$$

$$\therefore\ V_a = \frac{R_2V_{in}}{2R_1R_2Cs + R_1 + R_2}$$

and $V_a = -\dfrac{V_o}{2R_3Cs}$

It follows directly that

$$H(s) = \frac{V_o}{V_{in}} = \frac{-2R_2R_3Cs}{2R_1R_2Cs + (R_1 + R_2)}$$

$$\therefore\ H(j\omega) = \frac{-2R_2R_3C(j\omega)}{(R_1+R_2)+j\omega(2R_1R_2C)}$$

$$|H(j\omega)| = \frac{2R_2R_3C\omega}{\sqrt{(R_1+R_2)^2+\omega^2 4R_1^2R_2^2C^2}}$$

$$|H(j\omega)|^2 = \frac{4R_2^2R_3^2C^2\omega^2}{(R_1+R_2)^2+4R_1^2R_2^2C^2\omega^2}$$

P 15.25 [a] $y = 20\log_{10}\frac{1}{\sqrt{1+\omega^{2n}}} = -10\log_{10}(1+\omega^{2n})$

From the laws of logarithms we have

$$y = \left(\frac{-10}{\ln 10}\right)\ln(1+\omega^{2n})$$

Thus

$$\frac{dy}{d\omega} = \left(\frac{-10}{\ln 10}\right)\frac{2n\omega^{2n-1}}{(1+\omega^{2n})}$$

$$x = \log_{10}\omega = \frac{\ln\omega}{\ln 10}$$

$$\therefore\ \ln\omega = x\ln 10$$

$$\frac{1}{\omega}\frac{d\omega}{dx} = \ln 10, \qquad \frac{d\omega}{dx} = \omega\ln 10$$

$$\frac{dy}{dx} = \left(\frac{dy}{d\omega}\right)\left(\frac{d\omega}{dx}\right) = \frac{-20n\omega^{2n}}{H\omega^{2n}}\ \text{dB/decade}$$

at $\omega = \omega_c = 1\ \text{rad/s}$

$$\frac{dy}{dx} = -10\text{n dB/decade.}$$

[b] $y = 20\log_{10}\frac{1}{[\sqrt{1+\omega^2}]^n} = -10\text{n}\log_{10}(1+\omega^2)$

$$= \frac{-10n}{\ln 10}\ln(1+\omega^2)$$

$$\frac{dy}{d\omega} = \frac{-10}{\ln 10}\left(\frac{1}{1+\omega^2}\right)2\omega = \frac{-20\text{n}\omega}{(\ln 10)(1+\omega^2)}$$

As before

$$\frac{d\omega}{dx} = \omega(\ln 10); \qquad \therefore\ \frac{dy}{dx} = \frac{-20\text{n}\omega^2}{(1+\omega^2)}$$

At the corner $\omega_c = \sqrt{2^{1/n}-1}$ $\qquad \therefore\ \omega_c^2 = 2^{1/n}-1$

$$\frac{dy}{dx} = \frac{-20n[2^{1/n}-1]}{2^{1/n}}\ \text{dB/decade.}$$

[c]

For the Butterworth Filter

n	dy/dx (dB/decade)
1	−10
2	−20
3	−30
4	−40
∞	$-\infty$

For the cascade of identical sections

n	dy/dx (dB/decade)
1	−10
2	−11.72
3	−12.38
4	−12.73
∞	−12.36

[d] It is apparent from the calculations in part (c) that as n increases the amplitude characteristic at the cut off frequency decreases at a much faster rate for the Butterworth filter.
Hence the transition region of the Butterworth filter will be much narrower than that of the cascaded sections.

P 15.26 [a] $n \cong \dfrac{(-0.05)(-40)}{\log_{10}(4000/1000)} \cong 3.32$

$\therefore \quad n = 4$

[b] Gain $= 20\log_{10}\dfrac{1}{\sqrt{1+(4)^8}} = -10\log_{10}(1+4^8) = -48.16$ dB

P 15.27 [a] For the scaled circuit

$$H'(s) = \frac{1/(R')^2C_1'C_2'}{s^2 + \frac{2}{R'C_1'}s + \frac{1}{(R')^2C_1'C_2'}}$$

where

$$R' = k_mR; \qquad C_1' = C_1/k_fk_m; \qquad C_2' = C_2/k_fk_m$$

It follows that

$$\frac{1}{(R')^2C_1'C_2'} = \frac{k_f^2}{RC_1C_2}$$

$$\frac{2}{R'C_1'} = \frac{2k_f}{RC_1}$$

$$\therefore \quad H'(s) = \frac{k_f^2/RC_1C_2}{s^2 + \frac{2k_f}{RC_1}s + \frac{k_f^2}{RC_1C_2}}$$

$$= \frac{1/RC_1C_2}{\left(\frac{s}{k_f}\right)^2 + \frac{2}{RC_1}\left(\frac{s}{k_f}\right) + \frac{1}{RC_1C_2}}$$

P 15.28 [a] $H(s) = \dfrac{1}{(s^2 + 0.765s + 1)(s^2 + 1.848s + 1)}$

[b] $f_c = 1000\,\text{Hz}; \qquad \omega_c = 2000\pi \text{ rad/s}; \qquad k_f = 2000\pi$

$$H'(s) = \frac{1}{\left[\left(\frac{s}{2000\pi}\right)^2 + \frac{0.765s}{2000\pi} + 1\right]\left[\left(\frac{s}{2000\pi}\right)^2 + \frac{1.848s}{2000\pi} + 1\right]}$$

$$= \frac{(4 \times 10^6\pi^2)^2}{(s^2 + 1530\pi s + 4 \times 10^6\pi^2)(s^2 + 3696\pi s + 4 \times 10^6\pi^2)}$$

[c] $H'(j8000\pi) = \dfrac{16}{(-60 + j12.24)(-60 + j29.568)}$

$$|H'(j8000\pi)| = \frac{16}{(61.24)(66.89)} = 3.91 \times 10^{-3}$$

$$\text{Gain } = 20\log_{10}|H(j8000\pi)| = -48.16 \text{ dB}$$

P 15.29 [a] $k_m = 2000; \qquad k_f = 2000\pi$

First stage:

$$\frac{2}{C_1} = 0.765; \qquad \therefore\ C_1 = \frac{2}{0.765}$$

$$C_1' = \frac{2}{(0.765)(2000)(2000\pi)} = 208.05\,\text{nF}$$

$$C_2 = \frac{1}{C_1} = \frac{0.765}{2}$$

$$C_2' = \frac{0.765}{2(2000)(2000\pi)} = 30.44\,\text{nF}$$

Second stage:

$$\frac{2}{C_1} = 1.848; \qquad \therefore\ C_1 = \frac{2}{1.848}$$

$$C_1' = \frac{2}{(1.848)(2000)(2000\pi)} = 86.12\,\text{nF}$$

$$C_2 = \frac{1}{C_1} = \frac{1.848}{2}$$

$$C_2' = \frac{1.848}{2(2000)(2000\pi)} = 73.53\,\text{nF}$$

[b]

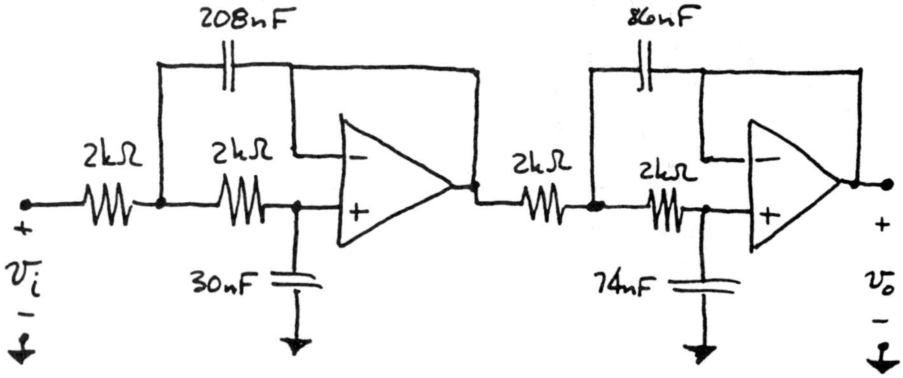

P 15.30 [a] $n \cong \dfrac{(-0.05)(-25)}{\log_{10}(5/1)} = 1.79; \qquad \therefore \quad n = 2$

$$\therefore \quad H(s) = \frac{s^2}{s^2 + \sqrt{2}s + 1}$$

$$\frac{2}{R_2} = \sqrt{2}; \qquad R_2 = \sqrt{2}\,\Omega; \qquad R_1 = \frac{1}{R_2} = \frac{1}{\sqrt{2}}\,\Omega$$

$$k_f = 10{,}000\pi$$

$$\therefore \quad k_m = \frac{10^9}{(10{,}000\pi)(25)} = \frac{4000}{\pi}$$

$$R_1 = \frac{1}{\sqrt{2}} \cdot \frac{4000}{\pi} = 900.32\,\Omega$$

$$R_2 = \sqrt{2}\left(\frac{4000}{\pi}\right) = 1800.63\,\Omega$$

[b]

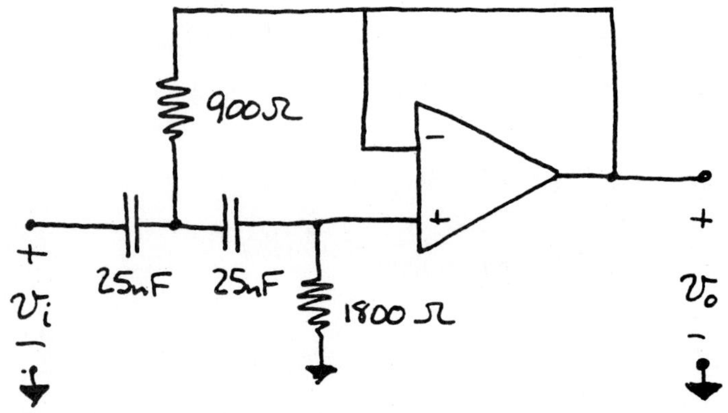

P 15.31 $n = 5$: $1 + (-1)^5 s^{10} = 0$; $s^{10} = 1$

$S^{10} = 1\underline{/0 + 360k}$

k	s_{k+1}
0	$1\underline{/0^\circ}$
1	$1\underline{/36^\circ}$
2	$1\underline{/72^\circ}$
3	$1\underline{/108^\circ}$
4	$1\underline{/144^\circ}$
5	$1\underline{/180^\circ}$
6	$1\underline{/216^\circ}$
7	$1\underline{/252^\circ}$
8	$1\underline{/288^\circ}$
9	$1\underline{/324^\circ}$

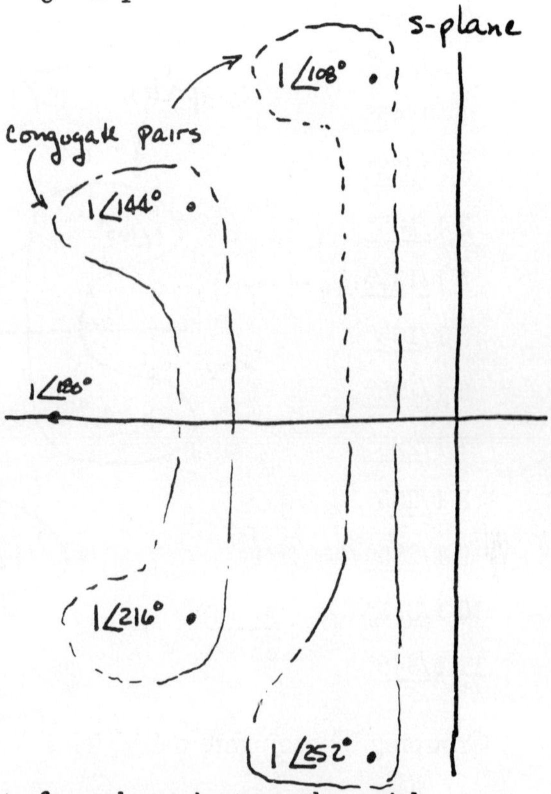

Group by conjugate pairs to form denominator polynomial.

$$(s+1)[s-(\cos 108^\circ + j\sin 108^\circ)][(s-(\cos 252^\circ + j\sin 252^\circ)]$$

$$\cdot [(s-(\cos 144^\circ + j\sin 144^\circ)][(s-(\cos 216^\circ + j\sin 216^\circ)]$$

$$(s+1)(s+0.309-j0.951)(s+0.309+j0.951)\cdot$$

$$(s+0.809-j0.588)(s+0.809+j0.588)$$

which reduces to

$$(s+1)(s^2+0.618s+1)(s^2+1.618s+1)$$

$n = 6$: $1 + (-1)^6 s^{12} = 0$ $\quad s^{12} = -1$

$s^{12} = 1\underline{/180^\circ + 360k}$

k	s_{k+1}
0	$1\angle 15^\circ$
1	$1\angle 45^\circ$
2	$1\angle 75^\circ$
3	$1\angle 105^\circ$
4	$1\angle 135^\circ$
5	$1\angle 165^\circ$
6	$1\angle 195^\circ$
7	$1\angle 225^\circ$
8	$1\angle 255^\circ$
9	$1\angle 285^\circ$
10	$1\angle 315^\circ$
11	$1\angle 345^\circ$

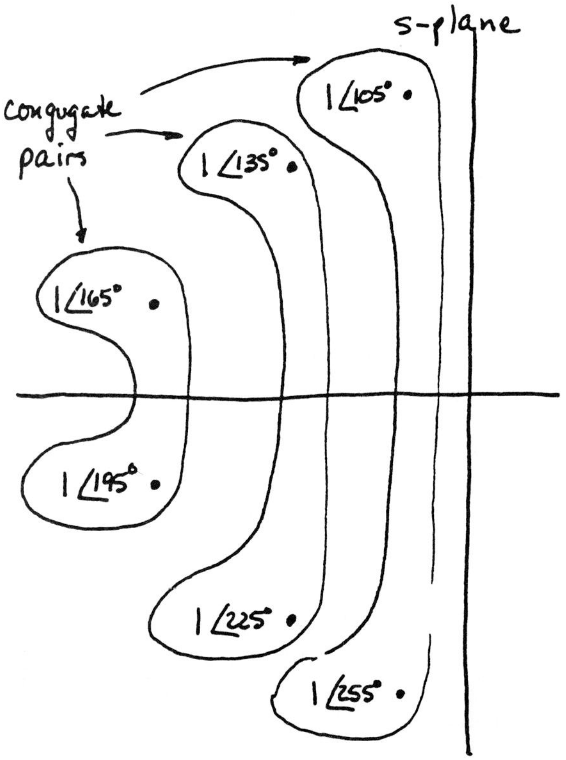

Grouping by conjugate pairs yields

$$(s + 0.2588 - j0.9659)(s + 0.2588 + j0.9659)\times$$

$$(s + 0.7071 - j0.7071)(s + 0.7071 + j0.7071)\times$$

$$(s + 0.9659 - j0.2588)(s + 0.9659 + j0.2588)$$

or $(s^2 + 0.5176s + 1)(s^2 + 1.4142s + 1)(s^2 + 1.9319s + 1)$

P 15.32 $$H'(s) = \frac{s^2}{s^2 + \frac{2}{k_m R_2 \frac{C}{k_m k_f}} s + \frac{1}{k_m R_1 k_m R_2 \frac{C^2}{k_m^2 k_f^2}}}$$

$$H'(s) = \frac{s^2}{s^2 + \frac{2k_f}{R_2 C} s + \frac{k_f^2}{R_1 R_2 C^2}}$$

$$= \frac{(s/k_f)^2}{(s/k_f)^2 + \frac{2}{R_2 C}\left(\frac{s}{k_f}\right) + \frac{1}{R_1 R_2 C^2}}$$

P 15.33 [a] $n \cong \dfrac{(-0.05)(-25)}{\log_{10}(100/20)} = 1.79; \therefore\ n = 2$

$$\therefore\ H(s) = \frac{s^2}{s^2 + \sqrt{2}s + 1}$$

$$\frac{2}{C_1} = \sqrt{2}: \qquad C_1 = \sqrt{2}\,\mathrm{F}$$

$$C_2 = \frac{1}{C_1} = \frac{1}{\sqrt{2}} = 0.5\sqrt{2}\,\mathrm{F}$$

$$k_m = 3000; \qquad k_f = 40{,}000\pi$$

$$C_1' = \frac{\sqrt{2}}{(3000)(40{,}000\pi)} = 3.75\,\mathrm{nF}$$

$$C_2' = \frac{1}{2}C_1' = 1.88\,\mathrm{nF}; \qquad R_1 = R_2 = 3\,\mathrm{k}\Omega$$

[b]

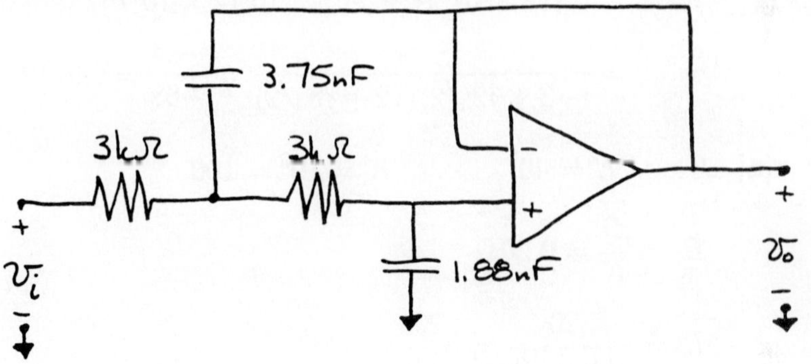

P 15.34 [a] A bandpass filter.

[b] $f_{c1} = 5000\,\mathrm{Hz}; \qquad f_{c2} = 20{,}000\,\mathrm{Hz}$

$$f_o = \sqrt{f_{c1}f_{c2}} = 10{,}000\,\mathrm{Hz}$$

$$Q = \frac{\omega_o}{\beta} = \frac{f_o}{f_{c2}f_{c1}} = \frac{10}{15} = 0.67$$

[c] $H(s)_{\mathrm{hp}} = \dfrac{s^2}{s^2 + \sqrt{2}s + 1}$

$$H'(s)_{\mathrm{hp}} = \frac{(s/10^4\pi)^2}{(s/10^4\pi)^2 + \sqrt{2}(s/10^4\pi) + 1}$$

$$= \frac{s^2}{s^2 + \pi\sqrt{2} \times 10^4 s + 10^8\pi^2}$$

$$H(s)_{\mathrm{lp}} = \frac{1}{s^2 + \sqrt{2}s + 1}$$

$$H'(s)_{\rm lp} = \frac{1}{(s/10^4\pi)^2 + \sqrt{2}(s/10^4\pi) + 1}$$

$$= \frac{16 \times 10^8\pi^2}{s^2 + 4\pi\sqrt{2} \times 10^4 s + 16 \times 10^8\pi^2}$$

$$H(s) = H'(s)_{\rm hp} \cdot H'(s)_{\rm lp}$$

$$= \frac{16 \times 10^8\pi^2 s^2}{(s^2 + \pi\sqrt{2}10^4 s + 10^8\pi^2)(s^2 + 4\pi\sqrt{2} \times 10^4 s + 16 \times 10^8\pi^2)}$$

[d] $\omega_o = 20{,}000\pi$ rad/s $= 2 \times 10^4$ krad/s

$$H(s) = \frac{16 \times 10^8\pi^2(-4 \times 10^8\pi^2)}{(-3 \times 10^8\pi^2 + j\pi\sqrt{2}10^4(2 \times 10^4\pi))}$$

$$\times \frac{1}{(12 \times 10^8\pi^2 + j4\sqrt{2}\pi 10^4(2 \times 10^4\pi))}$$

$$= \frac{-64}{(-3 + j2\sqrt{2})(12 + j8\sqrt{2})} = \frac{-64}{-68} = 0.9412$$

P 15.35 **[a]** $20\log_{10} K = 40; \quad \therefore \quad K = 10^2 = 100$

$$R_1 = \frac{Q}{K} = 0.20\,\Omega$$

$$R_2 = \frac{20}{800 - 100} = \frac{20}{700} = \frac{1}{35}\,\Omega$$

$$R_3 = 2Q = 40\,\Omega$$

$$k_f = 16{,}000\pi$$

$$\therefore \quad k_m = \frac{10^{12}}{(16{,}000\pi)(300)} = 66{,}314.56$$

$$R_1 = 0.2k_m = 13.26\,\text{k}\Omega$$

$$R_2 = \frac{1}{35}k_m = 1.89\,\text{k}\Omega$$

$$R_3 = 40k_m = 2.65\,\text{M}\Omega$$

[b]

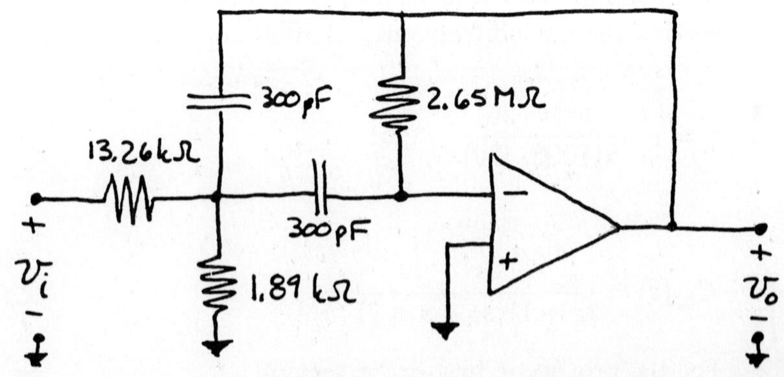

P 15.36 From Eq 15.58 we can write

$$H(s) = \frac{-\left(\frac{2}{R_3C}\right)\left(\frac{R_3C}{2}\right)\left(\frac{1}{R_1C}\right)s}{s^2 + \frac{2}{R_3C}s + \frac{R_1R_2}{R_1R_2R_3C^2}}$$

or

$$H(s) = \frac{-\left(\frac{R_3}{2R_1}\right)\left(\frac{2}{R_3C}s\right)}{s^2 + \frac{2}{R_3C}s + \frac{R_1R_2}{R_1R_2R_3C^2}}$$

Therefore

$$\frac{2}{R_3C} = \beta = \frac{\omega_o}{Q}; \qquad \frac{R_1 + R_2}{R_1R_2R_3C^2} = \omega_o^2;$$

and $K = \dfrac{R_3}{2R_1}$

By hypothesis $C = 1\,\text{F}$ and $\omega_o = 1\,\text{rad/s}$

$$\therefore \quad \frac{2}{R_3} = \frac{1}{Q} \text{ or } R_3 = 2Q$$

$$R_1 = \frac{R_3}{2K} = \frac{Q}{K}$$

$$\frac{R_1 + R_2}{R_1R_2R_3} = 1$$

$$\frac{Q}{K} + R_2 = \left(\frac{Q}{K}\right)(2Q)R_2$$

$$\therefore \quad R_2 = \frac{Q}{2Q^2 - K}$$

P 15.37 [a] First we will design a unity gain filter and then provide the passband gain with an inverting amplifier. For the high pass section the cut-off frequency is 1000 Hz. The order of the Butterworth is

$$n = \frac{(-0.05)(-20)}{\log_{10}(1000/400)} = 2.51$$

$$\therefore \quad n = 3$$

$$H_{hp}(s) = \frac{s^3}{(s+1)(s^2+s+1)}$$

For the prototype first-order section

$R_1 = R_2 = 1\,\Omega, \quad C = 1\,\text{F}$

For the prototype second-order section

$R_1 = 0.5\,\Omega, \quad R_2 = 2\,\Omega, \quad C = 1\,\text{F}$

The scaling factors are

$k_f = 2\pi(1000) = 2000\pi$

$$k_m = \frac{10^9}{50(2000\pi)} = \frac{10^4}{\pi}$$

In the scaled first-order section

$$R_1 = R_2 = \frac{10^4}{\pi}(1) = 3.183\,\text{k}\Omega$$

$C = 50\text{nF}$

In the scaled second-order section

$R_1 = 0.5k_m = 1591.55\,\Omega$

$R_2 = 2k_m = 6.366\,\text{k}\Omega$

$C = 50\,\text{nF}$

For the low-pass section the cut-off frequency is 8000 Hz. The order of the Butterworth filter is

$$n = \frac{(-0.05)(-20)}{\log_{10}(20{,}000/8000)} = 2.51; \qquad \therefore \quad n = 3$$

$$H_{lp}(s) = \frac{1}{(s+1)(s^2+s+1)}$$

For the prototype first-order section

$R_1 = R_2 = 1\,\Omega, \quad C = 1\,\text{F}$

For the prototype second-order section

$R_1 = R_2 = 1\,\Omega; \qquad C_1 = 2\,\text{F}; \qquad C_2 = 0.5\,\text{F}$

The low-pass scaling factors are

$k_m = 5 \times 10^3; \qquad k_f = (8000)(2\pi) = 16{,}000\pi$

For the scaled first-order section

$$R_1 = R_2 = 5\,\text{k}\Omega; \qquad C = \frac{1}{(16{,}000\pi)(5 \times 10^3)} = 3.98\,\text{nF}$$

For the scaled second-order section

$R_1 = R_2 = 5\,\text{k}\Omega$

$$C_1 = \frac{2}{8\pi \times 10^7} = 7.96\,\text{nF}$$

$$C_2 = \frac{0.5}{8\pi \times 10^7} = 1.99\,\text{nF}$$

GAIN AMPLIFIER

$20\log_{10} K = 10\text{ dB}, \qquad \therefore\ K = 3.16$

Since we are using 5 kΩ resistors in the low-pass stage, we will use $R_f = 15.8\,\text{k}\Omega$ and $R_i = 5\,\text{k}\Omega$ in the inverting amplifier stage.

[b]

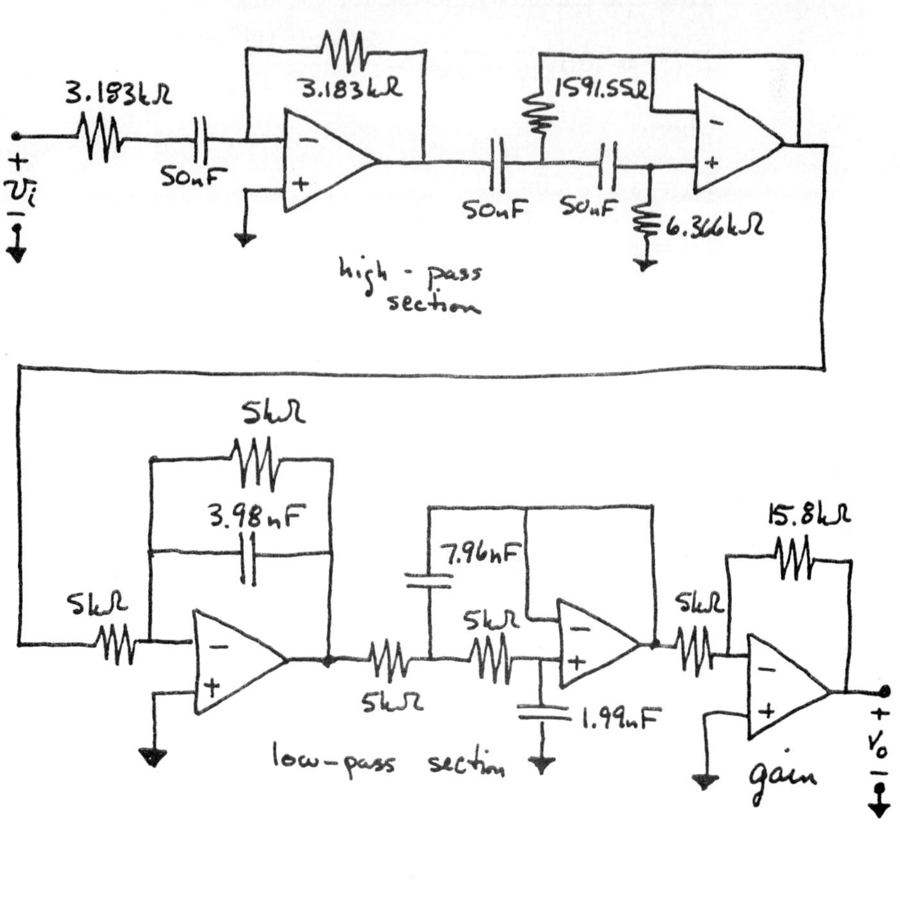

P 15.38 [a] Unscaled high-pass stage

$$H_{hp}(s) = \frac{s^3}{(s+1)(s^2+s+1)}$$

Frequency scaling factor $k_f = 2000\pi$. Therefore the scaled transfer function is

$$H'_{hp}(s) = \frac{(s/2000\pi)^3}{\left(\frac{s}{2000\pi}+1\right)\left[\left(\frac{s}{2000\pi}\right)^3 + \frac{s}{2000\pi}+1\right]}$$

$$= \frac{s^3}{(s+2000\pi)[s^2+2000\pi s + 4\times 10^6\pi^2]}$$

Unscaled low-pass stage

$$H_{lp}(s) = \frac{1}{(s+1)(s^2+s+1)}$$

Frequency scaling factor $k_f = 16{,}000\pi$. Therefore the scaled transfer function is

$$H'_{lp}(s) = \frac{1}{\left(\frac{s}{16{,}000\pi}+1\right)\left[\left(\frac{s}{16{,}000\pi}\right)^2 + \left(\frac{s}{16{,}000\pi}\right)+1\right]}$$

$$= \frac{(16{,}000\pi)^3}{(s+16{,}000\pi)(s^2+16{,}000\pi s + 256\times 10^6\pi^2)}$$

Thus the transfer function for the filter is

$$H'(s) = 10H'_{hp}(s)H'_{lp}(s) = \frac{4096\times 10^{10}\pi^3 s^3}{D_1D_2D_3D_4}$$

where

$$D_1 = s + 2000\pi$$

$$D_2 = s + 16{,}000\pi$$

$$D_3 = s^2 + 2000\pi s + 4\times 10^6\pi^2$$

$$D_4 = s^2 + 16{,}000\pi s + 256\times 10^6\pi^2$$

[b] At 400 Hz $\quad \omega = 800\pi$ rad/s

$$D_1(j800\pi) = 800\pi(2.5 + j1)$$

$$D_2(j800\pi) = 800\pi(20 + j1)$$

$$D_3(j800\pi) = 16\times 10^5\pi^2(2.1 + j1.0)$$

$$D_4(j800\pi) = 128\times 10^5\pi^2(19.95 + j1)$$

Therefore

$$D_1D_2D_3D_4(j800\pi) = 131{,}072\pi^6 10^{14}(2505.11\underline{/53^\circ})$$

$$H'(j800\pi) = \frac{(4096\pi^3 \times 10^{10})(512 \times 10^6\pi^3)}{131{,}072 \times 10^{14}\pi^6(2505.11\underline{/53^\circ})}$$

$$= 0.639\underline{/-53^\circ}$$

$$\therefore \quad 20\log_{10}|H'(j800\pi)| = 20\log_{10}(0.639) = -3.89 \text{ dB}$$

At $f = 5000$ Hz, $\qquad \omega = 10{,}000\pi$ rad/s

Then

$$D_1(j10{,}000\pi) = 2000\pi(1 + j5)$$

$$D_2(j10{,}000\pi) = 10{,}000\pi(1.6 + j1)$$

$$D_3(j10{,}000\pi) = 10^7\pi^2(-9.6 + j2)$$

$$D_4(j10{,}000\pi) = 10^7\pi^2(15.6 + j16)$$

$$H'(j10{,}000\pi) = \frac{(4096 \times \pi^3 \times 10^{10})(10^{12}\pi^3)}{2 \times 10^{21}\pi^6(2108.22\underline{/-35.35^\circ})}$$

$$= 9.71\underline{/35.35^\circ}$$

$$\therefore \quad 20\log_{10}|H'(j10{,}000\pi)| = 19.74 \text{ dB}$$

[c] From the transfer function the gain is down $19.74 + 3.89$ or 23.63 dB at 400 Hz. Because the upper cut-off frequency is eight times the lower cut-off frequency we would expect the high-pass stage of the filter to predict the loss in gain at 400 Hz. For a 3nd order Butterworth

$$\text{GAIN} = 20\log_{10}\frac{1}{\sqrt{1 + (1000/400)^6}} = -23.89 \text{ dB}.$$

5000 Hz is in the passband for this bandpass filter. Hence we expect the gain at 5000 Hz to nearly equal 20 dB as specified in Problem 15.37. Thus our scaled transfer function confirms that the filter meets the specifications.

P 15.39 [a] It follows directly from Eq 15.66 that

$$H(s) = \frac{s^2 + 1}{s^2 + 4(1 - \sigma)s + 1}$$

Now note from Eq 15.71 that $(1 - \sigma)$ equals $1/4Q$, hence

$$H(s) = \frac{s^2 + 1}{s^2 + \frac{1}{Q}s + 1}$$

[b] For Example 15.13 $\omega_o = 5000\,\text{rad/s}$ and $Q = 5$. Therefore $k_f = 5000$ and

$$H'(s) = \frac{(s/5000)^2 + 1}{(s/5000)^2 + \frac{1}{5}\left(\frac{s}{5000}\right) + 1}$$
$$= \frac{s^2 + 25 \times 10^6}{s^2 + 1000s + 25 \times 10^6}$$

P 15.40 [a] $\omega_o = 10{,}000\pi$ rad/s

$$Q = 10; \qquad C = 200\,\text{pF}$$

$$\therefore \quad R = \frac{10^{12}}{(10{,}000\pi)(200)} = 159.15\,\text{k}\Omega$$

$$\sigma = 1 - \frac{1}{4Q} = 0.975$$

$$(1-\sigma)R = \frac{R}{4Q} = 3.98\,\text{k}\Omega$$

$$\sigma R = 0.975R = 155.18\,\text{k}\Omega$$

$$\frac{R}{2} = 79.58\,\text{k}\Omega; \qquad 2C = 400\,\text{pF}$$

[b]

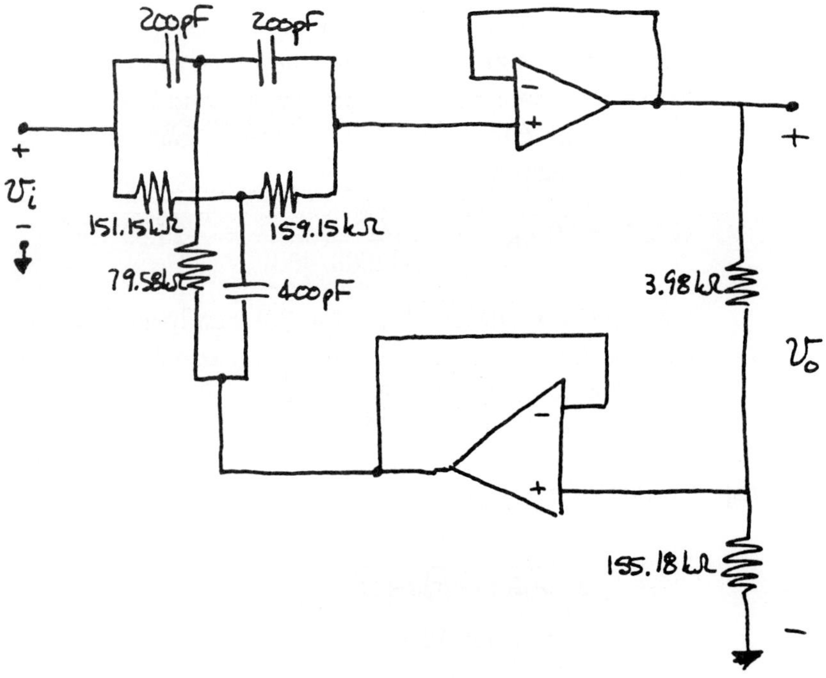

[c] $k_f = 10^4\pi$

$$H(s) = \frac{(s/10^4\pi)^2 + 1}{(s/10^4\pi)^2 + \frac{1}{10}(s/10^4\pi) + 1}$$

$$= \frac{s^2 + 10^8\pi^2}{s^2 + 10^3\pi s + 10^8\pi^2}$$

P 15.41 [a] At very low frequencies the two capacitor branches are open and because the op amp is ideal the current in R_3 is zero. Therefore at low frequencies the circuit behaves as an inverting amplifier with a gain of R_2/R_1. At very high frequencies the capacitor branches are short circuits and hence the output voltage is zero.

[b] Let the node where R_1, R_2, R_3, and C_2 join be denoted as a, then

$$(V_a - V_i)G_1 + V_a sC_2 + (V_a - V_o)G_2 + V_a G_3 = 0$$

$$-V_a G_3 - V_o sC_1 = 0$$

or

$$(G_1 + G_2 + G_0 + sC_2)V_a - G_2 V_o - G_1 V_i$$

$$V_a = \frac{-sC_1}{G_3} V_o$$

Solving for V_o/V_i yields

$$H(s) = \frac{-G_1G_3}{(G_1 + G_2 + G_3 + sC_2)sC_1 + G_2G_3}$$

$$= \frac{-G_1G_3}{s^2C_1C_2 + (G_1 + G_2 + G_3)C_1 s + G_2G_3}$$

$$= \frac{-G_1G_3/C_1C_2}{s^2 + \left[\frac{(G_1+G_2+G_3)}{C_2}\right] s + \frac{G_2G_3}{C_1C_2}}$$

$$= \frac{-\frac{G_1G_2G_3}{G_2C_1C_2}}{s^2 + \left[\frac{(G_1+G_2+G_3)}{C_2}\right] s + \frac{G_2G_3}{C_1C_2}}$$

$$= \frac{-Kb_o}{s^2 + b_1 s + b_o}$$

where $K = \dfrac{G_1}{G_2}$; $\quad b_o = \dfrac{G_2G_3}{C_1C_2}$

and $b_1 = \dfrac{G_1 + G_2 + G_3}{C_2}$

[c] Equating coefficients we see that

$$G_1 = KG_2$$

$$G_3 = \frac{b_oC_1C_2}{G_2} = \frac{b_oC_1}{G_2}$$

since by hypothesis $C_2 = 1\,\text{F}$

$$b_1 = \frac{G_1 + G_2 + G_3}{C_2} = G_1 + G_2 + G_3$$

$$\therefore\ b_1 = KG_2 + G_2 + \frac{b_oC_1}{G_2}$$

$$b_1 = G_2(1+K) + \frac{b_oC_1}{G_2}$$

Solving this quadratic equation for G_2 we get

$$G_2 = \frac{b_1}{2(1+K)} \pm \sqrt{\frac{b_1^2 - b_oC_14(1+K)}{4(1+K)^2}}$$

$$= \frac{b_1 \pm \sqrt{b_1^2 - 4b_o(1+K)C_1}}{2(1+K)}$$

For G_2 to be realizable

$$C_1 < \frac{b_1^2}{4b_o(1+K)}$$

[d] 1. Select $C_2 = 1\,\text{F}$

2. Select C_1 such that $C_1 < \dfrac{b_1^2}{4b_o(1+K)}$

3. Calculate $G_2(R_2)$

4. Calculate $G_1(R_1)$; $G_1 = KG_2$

5. Calculate $G_3(R_3)$; $G_3 = b_oC_1/G_2$

P 15.42 $b_1 = b_o = 1$

[a] $C_1 = \dfrac{1}{4(1+K)} = \dfrac{1}{36}\,\text{F}$

[b] $G_2 = \dfrac{1}{2(1+K)} = \dfrac{1}{18}\,\text{S}; \quad \therefore\ R_2 = 18\,\Omega$

$$G_1 = 8G_2 = \frac{8}{18}\,\text{S}; \quad \therefore\ R_1 = \frac{18}{8} = 2.25\,\Omega$$

$$G_3 = \frac{1}{G_2}C_1 = (18)\left(\frac{1}{36}\right) = \frac{1}{2}\,\text{S}; \quad \therefore\ R_3 = 2\,\Omega$$

[c] $f_c = 50\,\text{kHz};\qquad \omega_c = 100\pi\,\text{krad/s}$

$$k_f = 10^5\pi;\qquad 250\times 10^{-12} = \frac{1}{10^5\pi k_m};\qquad \therefore\ k_m = \frac{40}{\pi}\times 10^3$$

$$R_1 = 2.25(40/\pi)10^3 = 28.65\,\text{k}\Omega$$

$$R_2 = 18(40/\pi)10^3 = 229.18\,\text{k}\Omega$$

$$R_3 = 2(40/\pi)10^3 = 25.46\,\text{k}\Omega$$

[d] $R_1 = R_2 = k_m = \dfrac{40}{\pi}\times 10^3 = 12.73\,\text{k}\Omega$

$$C = \frac{1}{k_f k_m} = 250\,\text{pF}$$

[e]

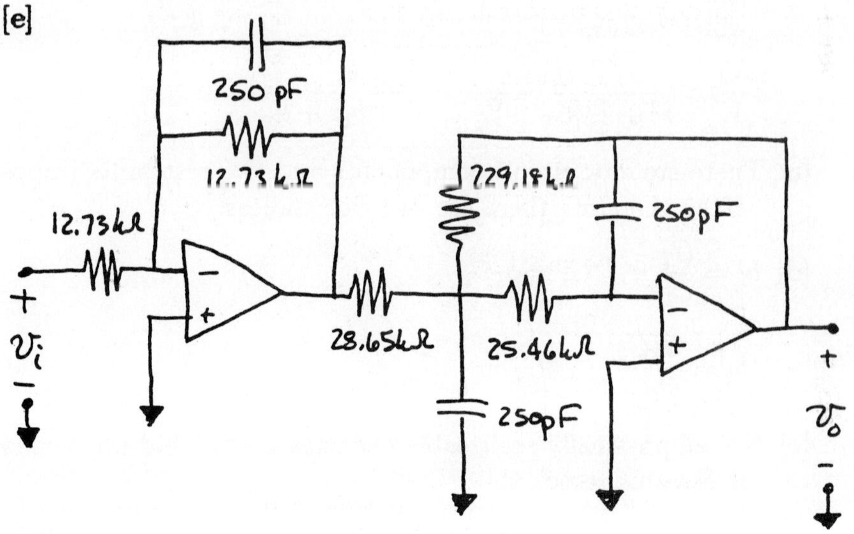

P 15.43 [a] At low frequencies the capacitor branches are open; $v_o = v_i$. At high frequencies the capacitor branches are short circuits and the output voltage is zero. Hence the circuit behaves like a unity-gain low-pass filter.

[b] Let v_a represent the voltage-to-ground at the right-hand terminal of R_1. Observe this will also be the voltage at the left-hand terminal of R_2. The s-domain equations are

$$(V_a - V_i)G_1 + (V_a - V_o)sC_1 = 0$$

$$(V_o - V_a)G_2 + sC_2V_o = 0$$

or

$$(G_1 + sC_1)V_a - sC_1V_o = G_1V_i$$

$$-G_2V_a + (G_2 + sC_2)V_o = 0$$

$$\therefore \quad V_a = \frac{G_2 + sC_2V_o}{G_2}$$

$$\therefore \quad \left[(G_1 + sC_1)\frac{(G_2 + sC_2)}{G_2} - sC_1\right]V_o = G_1V_i$$

$$\therefore \quad \frac{V_o}{V_i} = \frac{G_1G_2}{(G_1 + sC_1)(G_2 + sC_2) - C_1C_2s}$$

which reduces to

$$\frac{V_o}{V_i} = \frac{G_1G_2/C_1C_2}{s^2 + \frac{G_1}{C_1}s + \frac{G_1G_2}{C_1C_2}} = \frac{b_o}{s^2 + b_1s + b_o}$$

[c] There are four circuit components and two restraints imposed by $H(s)$; therefore there are two free choices.

[d] $b_1 = \frac{G_1}{C_1} \quad \therefore \quad G_1 = b_1C_1$

$$b_o = \frac{G_1G_2}{C_1C_2} \quad \therefore \quad G_2 = \frac{b_o}{b_1}C_2$$

[e] No, all physically realizeable capacitors will yield physically realizeable resistors.

[f] From Table 15.1 we know the transfer function of the prototype 4th order Butterworth filter is

$$H(s) = \frac{1}{(s^2 + 0.765s + 1)(s^2 + 1.848s + 1)}$$

In the first section $b_o = 1, \quad b_1 = 0.765$

$$\therefore \quad G_1 = (0.765)(1) = 0.765 \text{ S}$$

$$R_1 = 1/G_1 = 1.307\,\Omega$$

$$G_2 = \frac{1}{0.765}(1) = 1.307 \text{ S}$$

$$R_2 = 1/G_2 = 0.765\,\Omega$$

In the second section $b_o = 1, \quad b_1 = 1.848$

$$\therefore \quad G_1 = 1.848\,\text{S}$$

$$R_1 = 1/G_1 = 0.541\,\Omega$$

$$G_2 = \left(\frac{1}{1.848}\right)(1) = 0.541\,\text{S}$$

$$R_2 = 1/G_2 = 1.848\,\Omega$$

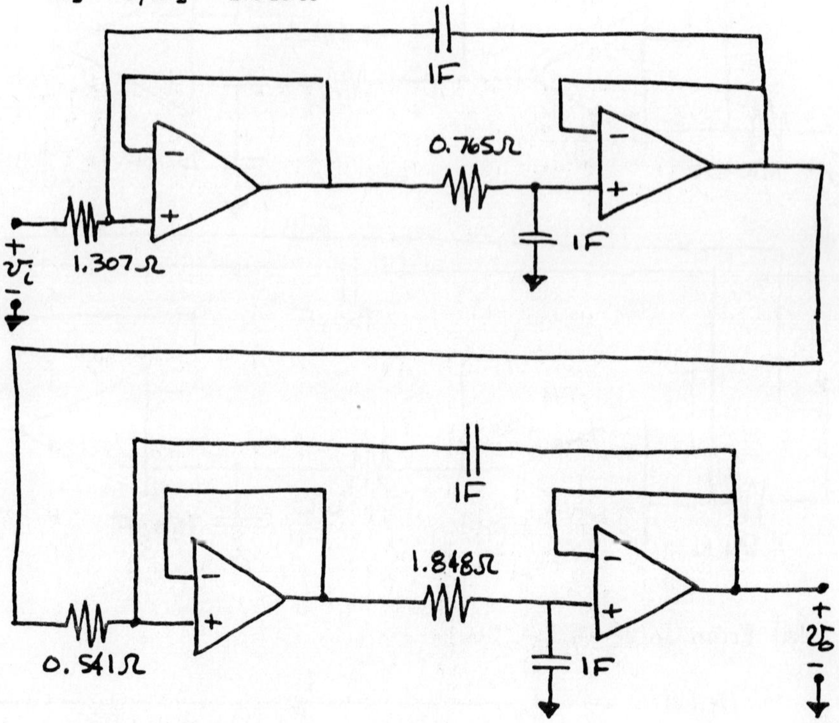

P 15.44 [a] $k_f = 2\pi(25)\times 10^3 = 50\pi\times 10^3$

$$k_m = \frac{10^{12}}{50\pi\times 10^3(750)} = \frac{80}{3\pi}\times 10^3$$

In the first section

$$R_1 = \frac{1}{0.765}\cdot\frac{80}{\pi}(10^3) = 11.10\,\text{k}\Omega$$

$$R_2 = (0.765)\frac{80}{\pi}(10^3) = 6.49\,\text{k}\Omega$$

In the second section

$$R_1 = \frac{1}{1.848}\cdot\frac{80}{\pi}(10^3) = 4.59\,\text{k}\Omega$$

$$R_2 = (1.848)\frac{80}{\pi}(10^3) = 15.69\,\text{k}\Omega$$

[b]

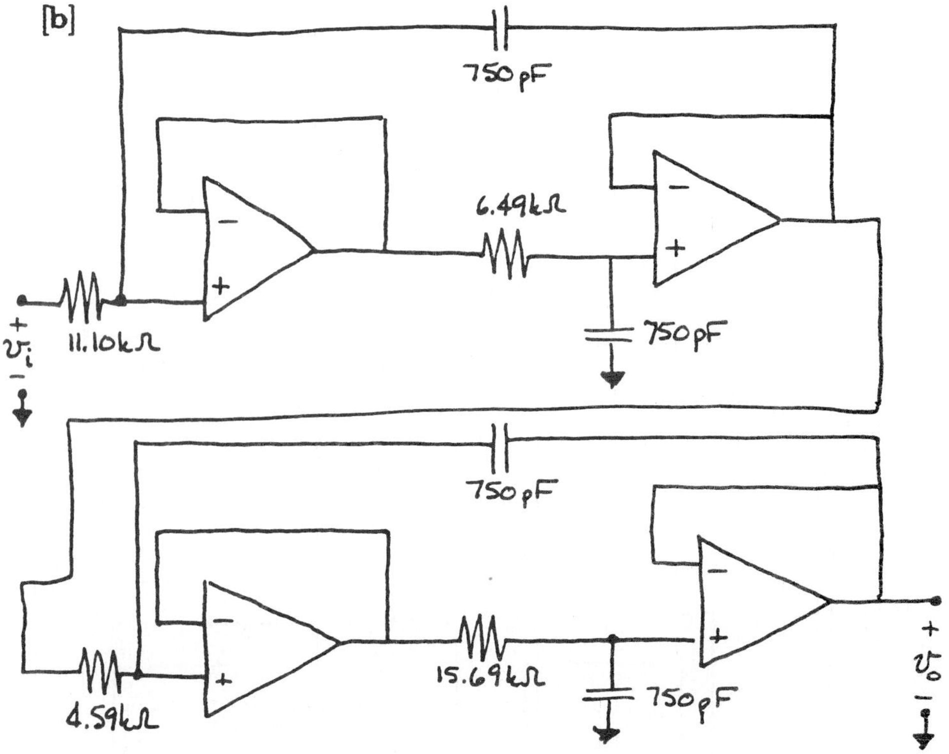

P 15.45 [a] From Table 15.1

$$H_{lp}(s) = \frac{1}{(s^2 + 0.518s + 1)(s^2 + \sqrt{2}s + 1)(s^2 + 1.932s + 1)}$$

$$H_{hp}(s) = \frac{1}{\left(\frac{1}{s^2} + 0.518\left(\frac{1}{s}\right) + 1\right)\left(\frac{1}{s^2} + \sqrt{2}\left(\frac{1}{s}\right) + 1\right)\left(\frac{1}{s^2} + 1.932\left(\frac{1}{s}\right) + 1\right)}$$

$$H_{hp}(s) = \frac{s^6}{(s^2 + 0.518s + 1)(s^2 + \sqrt{2}s + 1)(s^2 + 1.932s + 1)}$$

P 15.46 [a] $\omega_c = 2\pi(10 \times 10^3) = 2\pi \times 10^4$

$\therefore \quad k_f = 2\pi \times 10^4$

$$\therefore \quad H'(s) = \frac{(s/2\pi \times 10^4)^6}{D_1 D_2 D_3}$$

where

$$D_1 = \left[\left(\frac{s}{2\pi \times 10^4}\right)^2 + \frac{0.518s}{2\pi \times 10^4} + 1\right)$$

$$D_2 = \left[\left(\frac{s}{2\pi \times 10^4}\right)^2 + \frac{\sqrt{2}s}{2\pi \times 10^4} + 1\right)$$

$$D_3 = \left[\left(\frac{s}{2\pi \times 10^4}\right)^2 + \frac{1.932s}{2\pi \times 10^4} + 1\right) \qquad \text{or}$$

$$H'(s) = \frac{s^6}{D_4 D_5 D_5} \qquad \text{where}$$

$$D_4 = s^2 + 10{,}360\pi s + 4\pi^2 \times 10^8$$

$$D_5 = s^2 + 20{,}000\pi\sqrt{2}s + 4\pi^2 \times 10^8$$

$$D_6 = s^2 + 36{,}640\pi s + 4\pi^2 \times 10^8$$

[b] $$H'(j2\pi \times 10^4) = \frac{(j2\pi \times 10^4)^6)}{D_4(j2\pi \times 10^4)D_5(j2\pi \times 10^4)D_6(j2\pi \times 10^4)}$$

$$= 0.745 \approx \frac{1}{\sqrt{2}}$$

P 15.47 [a] Interchanging the Rs and Cs yields the following circuit.

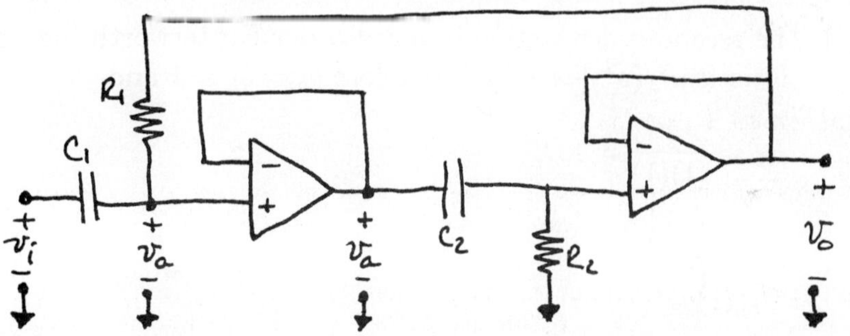

At low frequencies the capacitors appear as open circuits and hence the output voltage is zero. As the frequency increases the capacitor branches approach short circuits and $v_a = v_i = v_o$. Thus the circuit is a unity-gain, high-pass filter.

[b] The s-domain equations are

$$(V_a - V_i)sC_1 + (V_a - V_o)G_1 = 0$$

$$(V_o - V_a)sC_2 + V_oG_2 = 0$$

It follows that

$$V_a(G_1 + sC_1) - G_1V_o = sC_1V_i$$

and $$V_a = \frac{(G_2 + sC_2)V_o}{sC_2}$$

Thus

$$\left\{\left[\frac{(G_2 + sC_2)}{sC_2}\right](G_1 + sC_1) - G_1\right\} V_o = sC_1V_i$$

$$V_o\{s^2C_1C_2 + sC_1G_2 + G_1G_2\} = s^2C_1C_2V_i$$

$$H(s) = \frac{V_o}{V_i} = \frac{s^2}{\left(s^2 + \frac{G_2}{C_2}s + \frac{G_1G_2}{C_1C_2}\right)}$$

$$= \frac{V_o}{V_i} = \frac{s^2}{s^2 + b_1 s + b_o}$$

[c] There are 4 circuit components: R_1, R_2, C_1 and C_2.
There are two transfer function constraints: b_1 and b_o.
Therefore there are two free choices.

[d] $b_o = \frac{G_1G_2}{C_1C_2}; \qquad b_1 = \frac{G_2}{C_2}$

$$\therefore \quad G_2 = b_1C_2; \qquad R_2 = \frac{1}{b_1C_2}$$

$$G_1 = \frac{b_o}{b_1}C_1 \therefore \quad R_1 = \frac{b_1}{b_oC_1}$$

[e] No, all realizeable capacitors will produce realizeable resistors.

[f] The second-order section in a 3rd-order Butterworth high-pass filter is $s^2/(s^2+s+1)$. Therefore $b_o = b_1 = 1$ and

$$R_1 = \frac{1}{(1)(1)} = 1\,\Omega.$$

$$R_2 = \frac{1}{(1)(1)} = 1\,\Omega.$$

P 15.48 [a] $f_c = 40\,\text{kHz}; \qquad \omega_c = 80\pi\,\text{krad/s}; \qquad \therefore \quad k_f = 8\pi \times 10^4$

$$k_m = \frac{10^{12}}{8\pi \times 10^4(360)} = 11.05 \times 10^3$$

$$\therefore \quad R_1 = R_2 = k_m = 11\,\text{k}\Omega$$

[b] $C = 360\,\text{pF}$

[c]

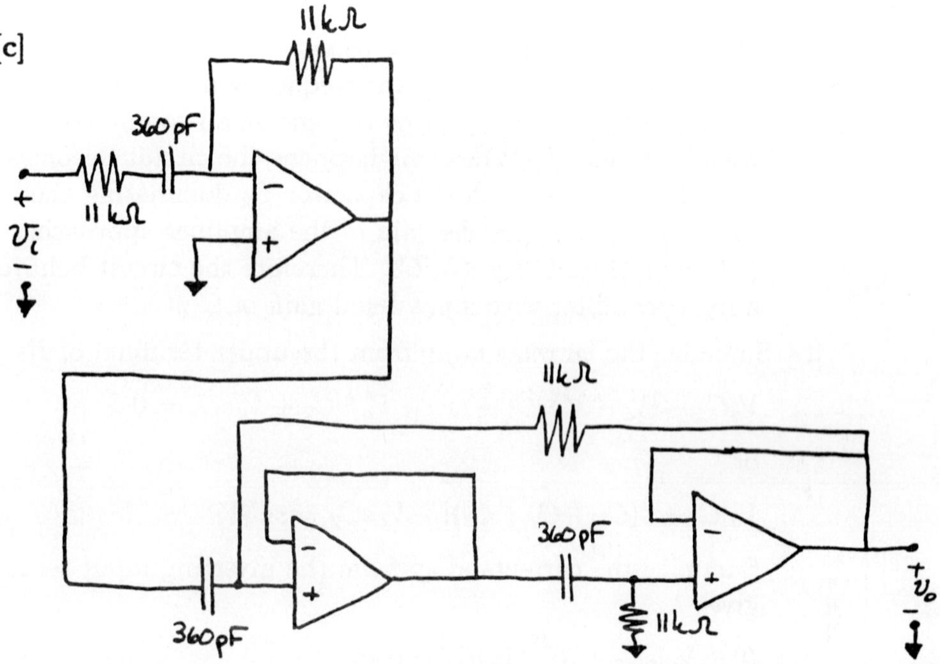

[d] $$H'(s) = \frac{(s/8\pi \times 10^4)^3}{\left[\left(\frac{s}{8\pi\times10^4}\right)+1\right]\left[\left(\frac{s}{8\pi\times10^4}\right)^2+\frac{s}{8\pi\times10^4}+1\right]}$$

$$= \frac{s^3}{(s+8\pi\times10^4)(s^2+8\pi\times10^4 s+64\pi^2\times10^8)}$$

[e] $$H'(j8\pi\times10^4) = \frac{(j8\pi\times10^4)^3}{(8\pi\times10^4+j8\pi\times10^4)(j(8\pi\times10^4)(8\pi\times10^4)}$$

$$= \frac{-j}{j(1+j1)} = \frac{1}{\sqrt{2}}\underline{/135^\circ}$$

$$\text{GAIN} = 20\log_{10}\frac{1}{\sqrt{2}} = -3.01 \text{ dB}$$

P 15.49 [a] By hypothesis the circuit becomes:

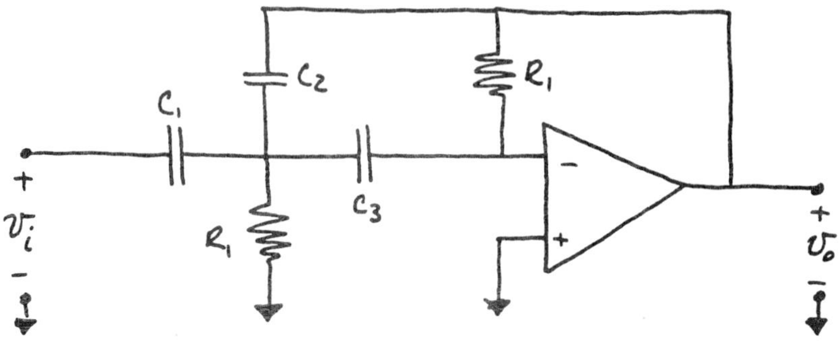

For very small frequencies the capacitors behave as open circuits and therefore v_o is zero. As the frequency increases, the capacitive branch impedances become small compared to the resistive branches. When this happens the circuit becomes an inverting amplifier with the capacitor C_2 dominating the feedback path. Hence the gain of the amplifier approaches $(1/j\omega C_2)/(1/j\omega C_1)$ or C_1/C_2. Therefore the circuit behaves like a high-pass filter with a passband gain of C_1/C_2.

[b] Summing the currents away from the upper terminal of R_2 yields

$$V_aG_2 + (V_a - V_i)sC_1 + (V_a - V_o)sC_2 + V_asC_3 = 0$$

or

$$V_a[G_2 + s(C_1 + C_2 + C_3)] - V_osC_2 = sC_1V_i$$

Summing the currents away from the inverting input terminal gives

$$(0 - V_a)sC_3 + (0 - V_o)G_1 = 0$$

or

$$sC_3V_a = -G_1V_o; \qquad V_a = \frac{-G_1V_o}{sC_3}$$

Therefore we can write

$$\frac{-G_1V_o}{sC_3}[G_2 + s(C_1 + C_2 + C_3)] - sC_2V_o = sC_1V_i$$

Solving for V_o/V_i gives

$$H(s) = \frac{V_o}{V_i} = \frac{-C_1C_3s^2}{C_2C_3s^2 + G_1(C_1 + C_2 + C_3)s + G_1G_2]}$$

$$= \frac{\frac{-C_1}{C_2}s^2}{\left[s^2 + \frac{G_1}{C_2C_3}(C_1 + C_2 + C_3)s + \frac{G_1G_2}{C_2C_3}\right]}$$

$$= \frac{-Ks^2}{s^2 + b_1s + b_o}$$

Therefore the circuit implements a second-order high-pass filter with a passband gain of C_1/C_2.

[c] $C_1 = K$:

$$b_1 = \frac{G_1}{(1)(1)}(K + 2) = G_1(K + 2)$$

$$\therefore \quad G_1 = \frac{b_1}{K + 2}; \qquad R_1 = \left(\frac{K + 2}{b_1}\right)$$

$$b_o = \frac{G_1G_2}{(1)(1)} = G_1G_2$$

$$\therefore\quad G_2 = \frac{b_o}{G_1} = \frac{b_o}{b_1}(K+2)$$

$$\therefore\quad R_2 = \frac{b_1}{b_o(K+2)}$$

[d] From Table 15.1 the transfer function of the second-order section of a third-order high-pass Butterworth filter is

$$H(s) = \frac{Ks^2}{s^2+s+1}$$

Therefore $b_1 = b_o = 1$

Thus

$$C_1 = K = 8\,\text{F}$$

$$R_1 = \frac{8+2}{1} = 10\,\Omega$$

$$R_2 = \frac{1}{1(8+2)} = 0.10\,\Omega$$

P 15.50 [a] Low-pass filter:

$$n = \frac{(-0.05)(-20)}{\log_{10}(1200/800)} = 3.66; \qquad \therefore\quad n = 4$$

In the first prototype second-order section: $b_1 = 0.765$, $b_o = 1$, $C_2 = 1\,\text{F}$

$$C_1 \le \frac{b_1^2}{4b_o(1+K)} \le \frac{(0.765)^2}{(4)(11)} \le 0.0133$$

choose $C_1 = 0.01\,\text{F}$

$$G_2 = \frac{0.765 \pm \sqrt{(0.765)^2 - 4(11)(0.01)}}{4} = \frac{0.765 \pm 0.381}{4}$$

Arbitrarily select the larger value for G_2, then

$$G_2 = 0.86\ \text{S};\therefore\quad R_2 = 1.16\,\Omega$$

$$G_1 = KG_2 = 8.6\ \text{S}; \qquad R_1 = 0.116\,\Omega$$

$$G_3 = \frac{b_oC_1}{G_2} = \frac{(1)(0.01)}{0.86} = 0.0116$$

$$R_3 = 1/G_3 = 86\,\Omega$$

Therefore in the first second-order prototype circuit

$$R_1 = 1.16\,\Omega; \qquad R_2 = 0.116\,\Omega; \qquad R_3 = 86\,\Omega$$

$C_1 = 0.01\,\text{F}; \qquad C_2 = 1\,\text{F}$

In the second second-order prototype circuit:
$b_1 = 1.848,\ b_0 = 1,\ C_2 = 1\,\text{F}$

$$\therefore\ C_1 \le \frac{(1.848)^2}{8} \le 0.427$$

choose $C_1 = 0.30\,\text{F}$

$$G_2 = \frac{1.848 \pm \sqrt{(1.848)^2 - 8(0.3)}}{4}$$

$$= \frac{1.848 \pm 1.008}{4}$$

Arbitrarily select the larger value, then

$G_2 = 0.7139\ \text{S};\therefore\ R_2 = 1.4008\,\Omega$

$G_1 = KG_2 = 7.139\ \text{S}; \qquad R_1 = 0.14\,\Omega$

$$G_3 = \frac{b_oC_1}{G_2} = \frac{(1)(0.30)}{0.7139} = 0.4202\ \text{S}$$

$R_3 = 1/G_3 = 2.3796\,\Omega$

In the low-pass section of the filter

$k_f = 2\pi(800) = 1600\pi$

$$k_m = \frac{10^9}{50k_f} = \frac{12{,}500}{\pi}$$

Therefore in the first scaled second-order section

$R_1 = 1.16k_m = 4615.5\,\Omega$

$R_2 = 0.116k_m = 461.55\,\Omega$

$R_3 = 86k_m = 342.2\,\text{k}\Omega$

$C_1 = 0.01 \times 10^{-8} = 100\,\text{pF}$

$C_2 = 10\,\text{nF}$

In the second scaled second-order section

$R_1 = 0.14k_m = 557.04\,\Omega$

$R_2 = 1.4k_m = 5570.4\,\Omega$

$R_3 = 2.38k_m = 9469.7\,\Omega$

$C_1 = 0.3 \times 10^{-8} = 3\,\text{nF}$

$C_2 = 10\,\text{nF}$

High-pass filter section

$$n = \frac{(-0.05)(-30)}{\log_{10}(13{,}500/7200)} = 3.77; \qquad n = 4.$$

In the first prototype second-order section:
$b_1 = 0.765$; $b_o = 1$; $C_2 = C_3 = 1\,\text{F}$

$C_1 = K = 1\,\text{F}$

$$R_1 = \frac{K+2}{b_1} = \frac{12}{0.765} = 15.69\,\Omega$$

$$R_2 = \frac{b_1}{b_o(K+2)} = \frac{0.765}{12} = 0.0638\,\Omega$$

In the second prototype second-order section: $b_1 = 1.848$; $b_o = 1$;
$C_2 = C_3 = 1\,\text{F}$

$C_1 = K = 10\,\text{F}$

$$R_1 = \frac{K+2}{b_1} = \frac{12}{1.848} = 6.49\,\Omega$$

$$R_2 = \frac{b_1}{b_o(K+2)} = \frac{1.848}{12} = 0.154\,\Omega$$

In the high-pass section of the filter

$k_f = 2\pi(7200) = 14{,}400\pi$

$$k_m = \frac{10^9}{(50)(14{,}400\pi)} = \frac{1388.89}{\pi}$$

In the first scaled second-order section

$R_1 = 15.69k_m = 6936.5\,\Omega$

$R_2 = 0.0638k_m = 28.2\,\Omega$

$C_1 = C_2 = C_3 = 50\,\text{nF}$

In the second scaled second-order section

$R_1 = 6.49k_m = 2869.2\,\Omega$

$R_2 = 0.154k_m = 68.08\,\Omega$

$C_1 = C_2 = C_3 = 50\,\text{nF}$

In the gain section, let $R_i = 10\,\text{k}\Omega$ and $R_f = 100\,\text{k}\Omega$.

[b]

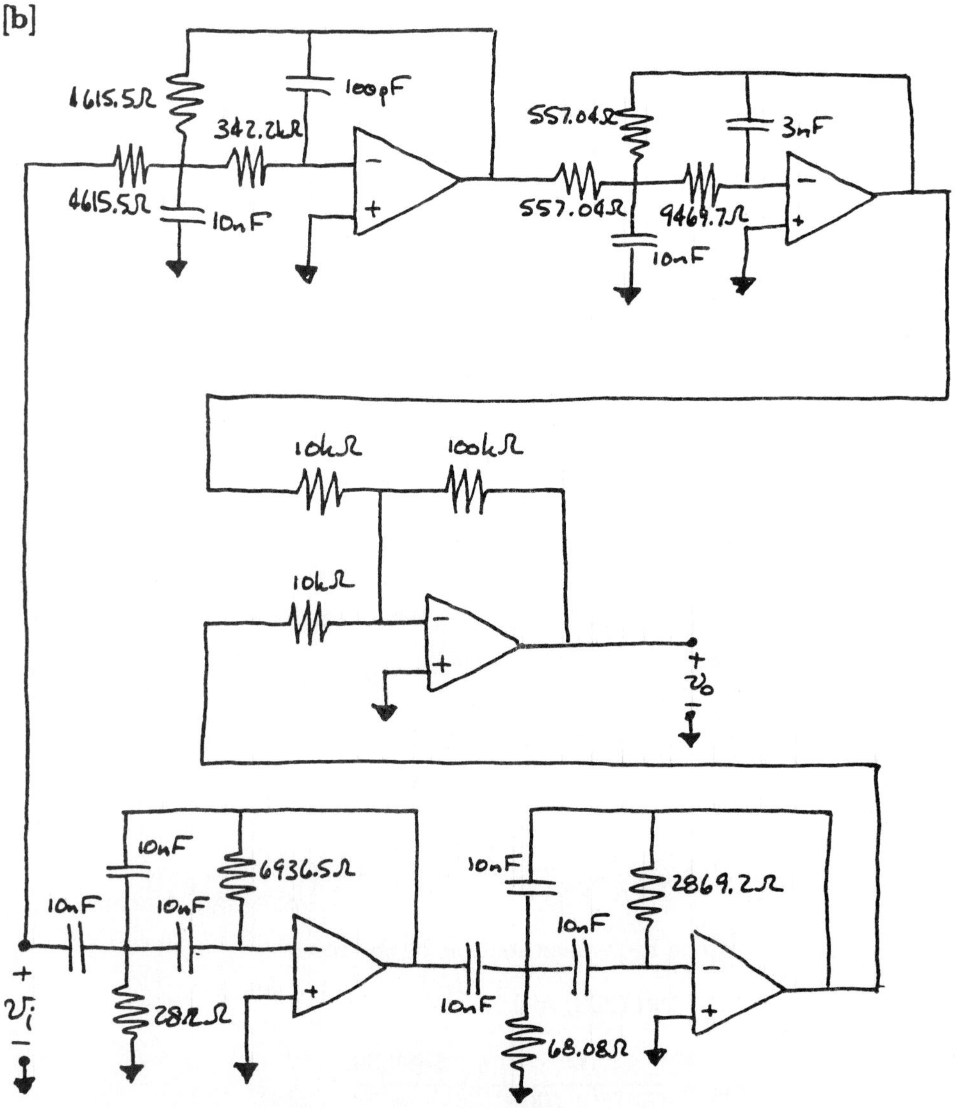

P 15.51 [a] The prototype low-pass transfer function is

$$H_{lp}(s) = \frac{1}{(s^2 + 0.765s + 1)(s^2 + 1.848s + 1)}$$

The low-pass frequency scaling factor is

$$k_{f_{lp}} = 2\pi(800) = 1600\pi$$

The scaled transfer function for the low-pass filter is

$$H'_{lp}(s) = \frac{1}{\left[\left(\frac{s}{1600\pi}\right)^2 + \frac{0.765s}{1600\pi} + 1\right]\left[\left(\frac{s}{1600\pi}\right)^2 + \frac{1.848s}{1600\pi} + 1\right]}$$

$$= \frac{65{,}536 \times 10^8\pi^4}{[s^2 + 1224\pi s + (1600\pi)^2]\,[s^2 + 2956.8\pi s + (1600\pi)^2]}$$

The prototype high-pass transfer function is

$$H_{hp}(s) = \frac{s^4}{(s^2 + 0.765s + 1)(s^2 + 1.848s + 1)}$$

The high-pass frequency scaling factor is

$k_{f_{hp}} = 2\pi(7200) = 14{,}400\pi$

The scaled transfer function for the high-pass filter is

$$H'_{hp}(s) = \frac{(s/14{,}400\pi)^4}{\left[\left(\frac{s}{14{,}400\pi}\right)^2 + \frac{0.765s}{14{,}400\pi} + 1\right]\left[\left(\frac{s}{14{,}400\pi}\right)^2 + \frac{1.848s}{14{,}400\pi} + 1\right]}$$

$$= \frac{s^4}{[s^2 + 11{,}016\pi s + (14{,}400\pi)^2][s^2 + 26{,}611.2\pi s + (14{,}400\pi)^2]}$$

The transfer function for the filter is

$$H'(s) = \left[H'_{lp}(s) + H'_{hp}(s)\right](-10)$$

[b] $f_o = \sqrt{f_{c1}f_{c2}} = \sqrt{800)(7200)} = 2400\,\text{Hz}$

$\omega_o = 4800\pi$ rad/s

$(j\omega_o)^2 = -2304 \times 10^4\pi^2$

$(j\omega_o)^4 = 5{,}308{,}416 \times 10^8\pi^4$

$$H'_{lp}(j\omega_o) = \frac{65{,}536 \times 10^8\pi^4}{[-2048 \times 10^4\pi^2 + j1224(4800\pi^2)]} \times$$

$$\frac{1}{[-2048 \times 10^4\pi^2 + j2956.8(4800\pi^2)]}$$

$$= 0.0123\underline{/50.73^\circ}$$

$$H'_{hp}(j\omega_o) = \frac{5{,}308{,}416 \times 10^8\pi^4}{[18{,}432 \times 10^4\pi^2 + j11{,}016(4800\pi^2)]}$$

$$\frac{1}{[18{,}432 \times 10^4\pi^2 + j26{,}611.2(4800\pi^2)]}$$

$$= 0.0123\underline{/-50.73^\circ}$$

$$\therefore\quad H'(j\omega_o) = -0.123(1\underline{/50.73^\circ} + 1\underline{/-50.73^\circ}) = -0.1556\underline{/0^\circ}$$

$$G = 20\log_{10}|H'(j\omega_o)| = 20\log_{10}(0.1557) = -16.15\text{ dB}$$

P 15.52 $\quad 20\log_{10}\left(\dfrac{R_1 + R_2}{R_1}\right) = 13.98$

$$\therefore\quad \frac{R_1 + R_2}{R_1} = 5; \qquad \therefore\quad R_2 = 4R_1$$

Choose $R_1 = 100\,\text{k}\Omega$. Then $R_2 = 400\,\text{k}\Omega$

$$\frac{1}{R_2C_1} = 100\pi \text{ rad/s}; \qquad \therefore\ C_1 = \frac{1}{(100\pi)(400\times 10^3)} = 7.96\,\text{nF}$$

P 15.53 [a] Combine the impedances of the capacitors in series in Fig. P15.53(b) to get

$$C_{eq} = \frac{1-\alpha}{sC_1} + \frac{\alpha}{sC_1} = \frac{1}{sC_1}$$

which is identical to the impedance of the capacitor in Fig. P15.53(a).

[b]

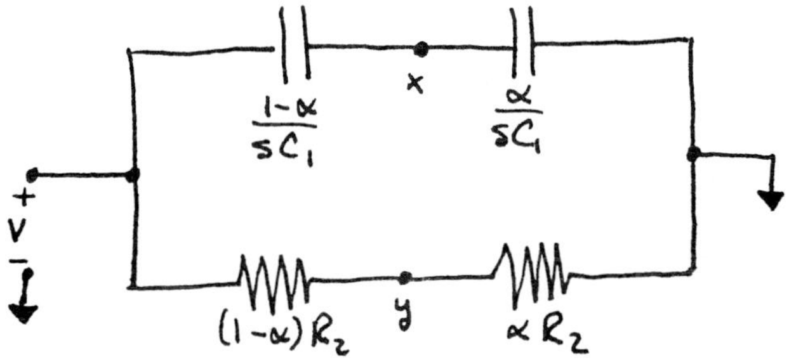

$$V_x = \frac{\alpha/sC_1}{(1-\alpha)/sC_1 + \alpha/sC_1}V = \alpha$$

$$V_y = \frac{\alpha R_2}{(1-\alpha)R_2 + \alpha R_2} = \alpha = V_x$$

[c] Since x and y are both at the same potential, they can be shorted together, and the circuit in Fig. 15.34 can thus be drawn as shown in Fig. 15.53(c).

[d] The feedback path between V_o and V_s containing the resistance $R_4 + 2R_3$ has no effect on the ratio V_o/V_s, as this feedback path is not involved in the nodal equation that defines the voltage ratio. In addition, the resistor attached to the inverting terminal has no effect on the voltage ratio, since for an ideal op amp no current flows through this resistor. Thus, the circuit in Fig. 15.53(c) can be simplified into the form of Fig. 15.2, where the input impedance is the equivalent impedance of R_1 in series with the parallel combination of $(1-\alpha)/sC_1$ and $(1-\alpha)R_2$, and the feedback impedance is the equivalent impedance of R_1 in series with the parallel combination of α/sC_1 and αR_2:

$$Z_i = R_1 + \frac{\frac{(1-\alpha)}{sC_1}\cdot(1-\alpha)R_2}{(1-\alpha)R_2 + \frac{(1-\alpha)}{sC_1}}$$

$$= \frac{R_1 + (1-\alpha)R_2 + R_1R_2C_1s}{1 + R_2C_1s}$$

$$Z_f = R_1 + \frac{\frac{\alpha}{sC_1}\cdot \alpha R_2}{\alpha R_2 + \frac{\alpha}{sC_1}}$$

$$= \frac{R_1 + \alpha R_2 + R_1 R_2 C_1 s}{1 + R_1 R_2 C_1 s}$$

P 15.54 [a] $|H(j0)| = \frac{R_1 + \alpha R_2}{R_1 + (1-\alpha)R_2} = \frac{11.1 + \alpha(100)}{11.1 + (1-\alpha)100}$

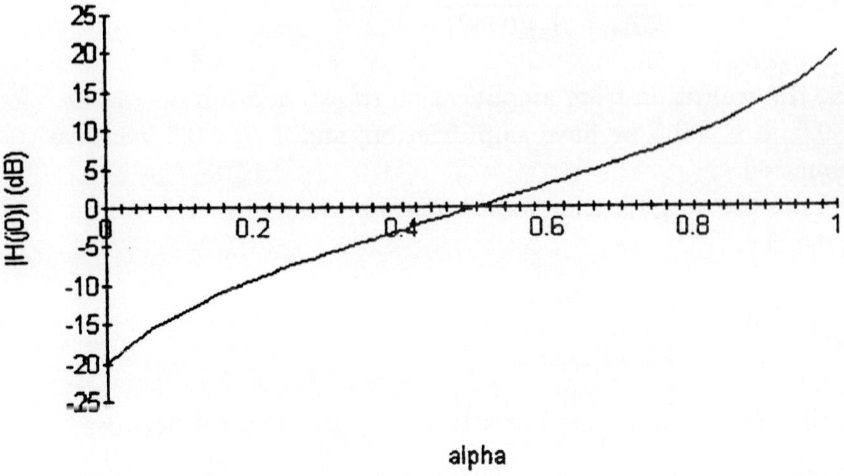

P 15.55 As $\omega \to 0$

$$|H(i\omega)| \to \frac{2R_3 + R_4}{2R_3 + R_4} = 1$$

Therefore the circuit would have no effect on low frequency signals.
As $\omega \to \infty$

$$|H(j\omega)| \to \frac{[(1-\beta)R_4 + R_o](\beta R_4 + R_3)}{[(1-\beta)R_4 + R_3](\beta R_4 + R_o)}$$

When $\beta = 1$

$$|H(j\infty)|_{\beta=1} = \frac{R_o(R_4 + R_3)}{R_3(R_4 + R_o)}$$

If $R_4 \gg R_o$

$$|H(j\infty)|_{\beta=1} \cong \frac{R_o}{R_3} > 1$$

Thus, when $\beta = 1$ we have amplification or "boost". When $\beta = 0$

$$|H(j\infty)|_{\beta=0} = \frac{R_3(R_4 + R_3)}{R_o(R_4 + R_o)}$$

If $R_4 \gg R_o$

$$|H(j\infty)|_{\beta=0} \cong \frac{R_3}{R_0} < 1$$

Thus, when $\beta = 0$ we have attenuation or "cut".
Also note that when $\beta = 0.5$

$$|H(j\omega)|_{\beta=0.5} = \frac{(0.5R_4 + R_o)(0.5R_4 + R_3)}{(0.5R_4 + R_3)(0.5R_4 + R_o)} = 1$$

Thus, the transition from amplification to attenuation occurs at $\beta = 0.5$. If $\beta > 0.5$ we have amplification, and if $\beta < 0.5$ we have attenuation.
Also note the amplification an attenuation are symmetric about $\beta = 0.5$. i.e.

$$|H(j\omega)|_{\beta=0.6} = \frac{1}{|H(j\omega)|_{\beta=0.4}}$$

Yes, the circuit can be used as a treble volume control because

- The circuit has no effect on low frequency signals
- Depending on β the circuit can either amplify ($\beta > 0.5$) or attenuate ($\beta < 0.5$) signals in the treble range
- The amplification (boost) and attenuation (cut) are symmetric around $\beta = 0.5$. When $\beta = 0.5$ the circuit has no effect on signals in the treble frequency range.

P 15.56 [a] $|H(j\infty)|_{\beta=1} = \frac{R_o(R_4 + R_3)}{R_3(R_4 + R_o)} = \frac{(65.9)(505.9)}{(5.9)(565.9)} = 9.99$

$\therefore$ maximum boost $= 20\log_{10} 9.99 = 19.99$ dB

[b] $|H(j\infty)|_{\beta=0} = \frac{R_3(R_4 + R_3)}{R_o(R_4 + R_o)}$

$\therefore$ maximum cut $= -19.99$ dB

[c] $R_4 = 500\,\text{k}\Omega$; $\quad R_o = R_1 + R_3 + 2R_5 = 65.9\,\text{k}\Omega$

$\therefore \; R_4 = 7.59R_o$

Yes, R_4 is significantly greater than R_o.

[d] $$|H(j/R_3C_2)|_{\beta=1} = \left|\frac{(2R_3 + R_4) + j\frac{R_o}{R_3}(R_4 + R_3)}{(2R_3 + R_4) + j(R_4 + R_o)}\right|$$

$$= \left|\frac{511.8 + j\frac{65.9}{5.9}(505.9)}{511.8 + j565.9}\right|$$

$$= 7.44$$

$$20\log_{10}|H(j/R_3C_2)|_{\beta=1} = 20\log_{10} 7.44 = 17.43 \text{ dB}$$

[e] When $\beta = 0$

$$|H(j/R_3C_2)|_{\beta=0} = \frac{(2R_3 + R_4) + j(R_4 + R_o)}{(2R_3 + R_4) + j\dfrac{R_o}{R_3}(R_4 + R_3)}$$

Note this is the reciprocal of $|H(j/R_3C_2)|_{\beta=1}$.

$$\therefore \quad 20\log_{10}|H(j/R_3C_2)|_{\beta+0} = -17.43 \text{ dB}$$

[f] The frequency $1/R_3C_2$ is very nearly where the gain is 3 dB off from its maximum boost or cut. Therefore for frequencies higher than $1/R_3C_2$ the circuit designer knows that gain or cut will be within 3 dB of the maximum.

P 15.57 $$|H(j\infty)| = \frac{[(1-\beta)R_4 + R_o][\beta R_4 + R_3]}{[(1-\beta R_4 + R_3][\beta R_4 + R_3]}$$

$$= \frac{[(1-\beta)500 + 65.9][\beta 500 + 5.9]}{[(1-\beta)500 + 5.9][\beta 500 + 65.9]}$$

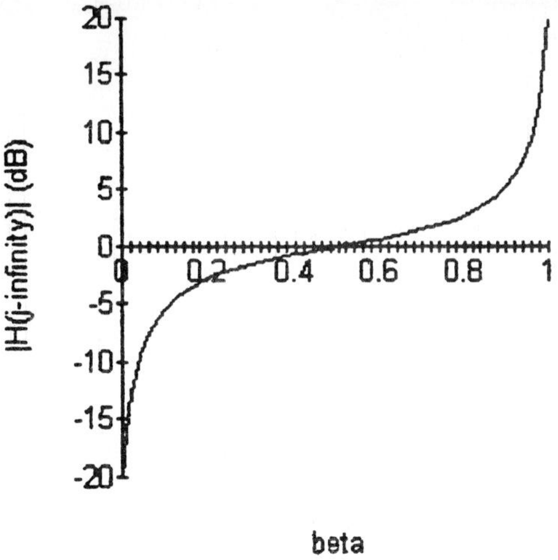

16

Fourier Series

Drill Exercises

DE 16.1 $a_v = \frac{1}{T}\int_0^{2T/3} V_m\,dt + \frac{1}{T}\int_{2T/3}^{T}\left(\frac{V_m}{3}\right)dt = \frac{7}{9}V_m = 7\pi\ \text{V}$

$$a_k = \frac{2}{T}\left[\int_0^{2T/3} V_m \cos k\omega_0 t\,dt + \int_{2T/3}^{T}\left(\frac{V_m}{3}\right)\cos\, \text{k}\omega_0 t\,dt\right]$$

$$= \left(\frac{4V_m}{3k\omega_0 T}\right)\sin\left(\frac{4k\pi}{3}\right) = \left(\frac{6}{k}\right)\sin\left(\frac{4k\pi}{3}\right)$$

$$b_k = \frac{2}{T}\left[\int_0^{2T/3} V_m \sin k\omega_0 t\,dt + \int_{2T/3}^{T}\left(\frac{V_m}{3}\right)\sin k\omega_0 t\,dt\right]$$

$$= \left(\frac{4V_m}{3k\omega_0 T}\right)\left[1-\cos\left(\frac{4k\pi}{3}\right)\right] = \left(\frac{6}{k}\right)\left[1-\cos\left(\frac{4k\pi}{3}\right)\right]$$

DE 16.2 [a] $a_v = 7\pi = 21.99\ \text{V}$

[b] $a_1 = -5.196 \quad a_2 = 2.598 \quad a_3 = 0 \quad a_4 = -1.299 \quad a_5 = 1.039$

$b_1 = 9 \quad b_2 = 4.5 \quad b_3 = 0 \quad b_4 = 2.25 \quad b_5 = 1.8$

[c] $w_0 = \left(\frac{2\pi}{T}\right) = 50\ \text{rad/s}$

[d] $f_3 = 3f_0 = 23.87\ \text{Hz}$

[e] $v(t) = 21.99 - 5.2\cos 50t + 9\sin 50t + 2.6\sin 100t + 4.5\cos 100t - 1.3\sin 200t$

$+2.25\cos 200t + 1.04\sin 250t + 1.8\cos 250t + \cdots\ \text{V}$

DE 16.3 Odd function with both half- and quarter-wave symmetry.

$$v_g(t) = \left(\frac{6V_m}{T}\right)t, \qquad 0 \le t \le T/6; \qquad a_v = 0, \qquad a_k = 0 \quad \text{for all } k$$

$$b_k = 0 \quad \text{for } k \text{ even}$$

$$b_k = \frac{8}{T}\int_0^{T/4} f(t)\sin k\omega_0 t\,dt, \qquad k \text{ odd}$$

$$= \frac{8}{T}\int_0^{T/6}\left(\frac{6V_m}{T}\right)t\sin k\omega_0 t\,dt + \frac{8}{T}\int_{T/6}^{T/4} V_m \sin k\omega_0 t\,dt$$

$$= \left(\frac{12V_m}{k^2\pi^2}\right)\sin\left(\frac{k\pi}{3}\right)$$

$$v_g(t) = \frac{12V_m}{\pi^2}\sum_{n=1,3,5}^{\infty}\frac{1}{n^2}\sin\frac{n\pi}{3}\sin n\omega_0 t \text{ V}$$

DE 16.4 [a] $A_1 = -5.2 - j9 = 10.4\underline{/-120^\circ}$; $\qquad A_2 = 2.6 - j4.5 = 5.2\underline{/-60^\circ}$

$A_3 = 0$; $\qquad A_4 = -1.3 - j2.25 = 2.6\underline{/-120^\circ}$

$A_5 = 1.04 - j1.8 = 2.1\underline{/-60^\circ}$

$\theta_1 = -120^\circ$; $\qquad \theta_2 = -60^\circ$; $\qquad \theta_3$ not defined;

$\theta_4 = -120^\circ$; $\qquad \theta_5 = -60^\circ$

[b] $v(t) = 21.99 + 10.4\cos(50t - 120^\circ) + 5.2\cos(100t - 60^\circ)$

$+2.6\cos(200t - 120^\circ) + 2.1\cos(250t - 60^\circ) + \cdots \text{V}$

DE 16.5 [a] $e^{-x} \cong 1 - x$ for small x; therefore

$$e^{-t/RC} \cong \left(1 - \frac{t}{RC}\right) \quad \text{and} \quad e^{-T/2RC} \cong \left(1 - \frac{T}{2RC}\right)$$

$$v_o = V_m - \frac{2V_m[1 - (t/RC)]}{2 - (T/2RC)} = \left(\frac{V_m}{RC}\right)\left[\frac{2t - (T/2)}{2 - (T/2RC)}\right]$$

$$= \left(\frac{V_m}{RC}\right)\left(t - \frac{T}{4}\right) = \left(\frac{V_m}{RC}\right)t - \frac{V_m T}{4RC} \qquad \text{for } 0 \le t \le \frac{T}{2}$$

[b] $$a_k = \left(\frac{-8}{\pi^2 k^2}\right)V_p = \left(\frac{-8}{\pi^2 k^2}\right)\left(\frac{V_m T}{4RC}\right) = \frac{-4V_m}{\pi\omega_0 RCk^2}$$

DE 16.6 $w_0 = \dfrac{2\pi \times 10^3}{2094.4} = 3\,\text{rad/s}$

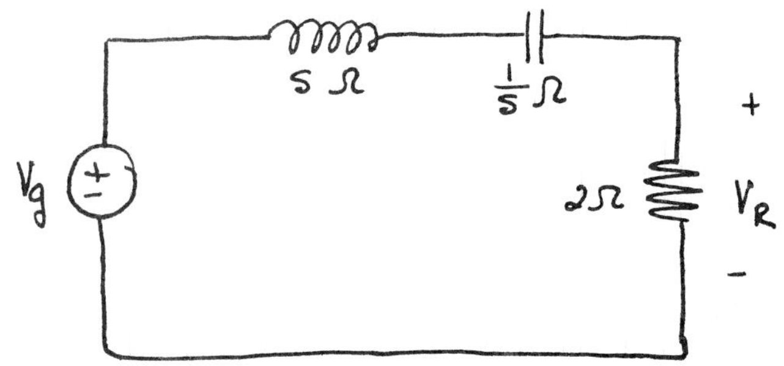

$$j\omega_0 k = j3k$$

$$V_R = \frac{2}{2+s+1/s}(V_g) = \frac{2sV_g}{s^2+2s+1}$$

$$H(s) = \left(\frac{V_R}{V_g}\right) = \frac{2s}{s^2+2s+1}$$

$$H(j\omega_0 k) = H(j3k) = \frac{j6k}{(1-9k^2)+j6k}$$

$v_{g1} = 25.98\sin\omega_0 t$ V; $\qquad V_{g1} = 25.98\underline{/0^\circ}$ V

$H(j3) = \dfrac{j6}{-8+j6} = 0.6\underline{/-53.13^\circ}$; $\qquad V_{R_1} = 15.588\underline{/-53.13^\circ}$ V

$$P_1 = \frac{(15.588/\sqrt{2})^2}{2} = 60.75\text{ W}$$

$v_{g3} = 0$, therefore $P_3 = 0$ W

$v_{g5} = -1.04\sin 5\omega_0 t$ V; $\qquad V_{g5} = 1.04\underline{/180^\circ}$

$$H(j15) = \frac{j30}{-224+j30} = 0.1327\underline{/-82.37^\circ}$$

$$V_{R_5} = (1.04\underline{/180^\circ})(0.1327\underline{/-82.37^\circ}) = 138\underline{/97.63^\circ}\text{ mV}$$

$P_5 = \dfrac{(0.1396/\sqrt{2})^2}{2} = 4.76$ mW; $\qquad$ therefore $P \cong P_1 \cong 60.75$ W

DE 16.7 [a] Area under $v^2 = A = 4\int_0^{T/6} \frac{36V_m^2}{T^2}t^2\,dt + 2V_m^2\left(\frac{T}{3} - \frac{T}{6}\right)$

$$= \frac{2V_m^2T}{9} + \frac{V_m^2T}{3}$$

Therefore $V_{\text{rms}} = \sqrt{\frac{1}{T}\left(\frac{2V_m^2T}{9} + \frac{V_m^2T}{3}\right)} = V_m\sqrt{\frac{2}{9} + \frac{1}{3}} = 74.5356\text{ V}$

[b] $v_g = 105.30\sin\omega_0 t - 4.21\sin 5\omega_0 t + 2.15\sin 7\omega_0 t + \cdots\text{ V}$

Therefore $V_{\text{rms}} \cong \sqrt{\frac{(105.30)^2 + (4.21)^2 + (2.15)^2}{2}} = 74.5306\text{ V}$

DE 16.8 Odd function with half- and quarter-wave symmetry, therefore $a_v = 0$, $a_k = 0$ for all k, $b_k = 0$ for k even; for k odd we have

$$b_k = \frac{8}{T}\int_0^{T/8} 2\sin k\omega_0 t\,dt + \frac{8}{T}\int_{T/8}^{T/4} 8\sin k\omega_0 t\,dt$$

$$= \left(\frac{8}{\pi k}\right)\left[1 + 3\cos\left(\frac{k\pi}{4}\right)\right], \quad k\text{ odd}$$

Therefore $C_n = \left(\frac{-j4}{n\pi}\right)\left[1 + 3\cos\left(\frac{n\pi}{4}\right)\right], \quad n\text{ odd}$

DE 16.9 [a] $I_{\text{rms}} = \sqrt{\frac{2}{T}\left[(2)^2\left(\frac{T}{8}\right)(2) + (8)^2\left(\frac{3T}{8} - \frac{T}{8}\right)\right]} = \sqrt{34} \cong 5.831\text{ A}$

[b] $C_1 = \frac{-j12.5}{\pi}; \quad C_3 = \frac{j1.5}{\pi}; \quad C_5 = \frac{j0.9}{\pi};$

$$C_7 = \frac{-j1.8}{\pi}; \quad C_9 = \frac{-j1.4}{\pi}; \quad C_{11} = \frac{j0.4}{\pi}$$

$$I_{\text{rms}} = \sqrt{I_{dc}^2 + 2\sum_{n=1,3,5}^{\infty}|C_n|^2} \cong \sqrt{\frac{2}{\pi^2}(12.5^2 + 1.5^2 + 1.8^2 + 1.4^2 + 0.4^2)}$$

$$\cong 5.777\text{ A}$$

[c] $\%\text{ Error} = \frac{5.777 - 5.831}{5.831} \times 100 = -0.93\%$

[d] Using just the terms $C_1 - C_9$,

$$I_{\text{rms}} = \sqrt{I_{dc}^2 + 2\sum_{n=1,3,5}^{\infty}|C_n|^2} \cong \sqrt{\frac{2}{\pi^2}(12.5^2 + 1.5^2 + 1.8^2 + 1.4^2)}$$

$$\cong 5.774\text{ A}$$

$$\%\text{ Error} = \frac{5.774 - 5.831}{5.831} \times 100 = -0.98\%$$

Thus, the % error is still less than 1%.

DE 16.10 $T = 32\,\text{ms}$, therefore 8 ms requires shifting the function $T/4$ to the right.

$$i = \sum_{\substack{n=-\infty \\ n(\text{odd})}}^{\infty} -j\frac{4}{n\pi}\left(1 + 3\cos\frac{n\pi}{4}\right)e^{jn\omega_0(t-T/4)}$$

$$= \frac{4}{\pi}\sum_{\substack{n=-\infty \\ n(\text{odd})}}^{\infty} \frac{1}{n}\left(1 + 3\cos\frac{n\pi}{4}\right)e^{-j(n+1)(\pi/2)}e^{jn\omega_0 t}$$

Problems

P 16.1 [a] $I_6 = \int_{t_o}^{t_o+T} \sin m\omega_0 t\,dt = -\frac{1}{m\omega_0}\cos m\omega_0 t\Big|_{t_o}^{t_o+T}$

$$= \frac{-1}{m\omega_0}[\cos m\omega_0(t_o + T) - \cos m\omega_0 t_o]$$

$$= \frac{-1}{m\omega_0}[\cos m\omega_0 t_o \cos m\omega_0 T - \sin m\omega_0 t_o \sin m\omega_0 T - \cos m\omega_0 t_o]$$

$$= (-1m\omega_0)[\cos m\omega_0 t_o - 0 - \cos m\omega_0 t_o] = 0 \quad \text{for all } m,$$

$$I_7 = \int_{t_o}^{t_o+T} \cos m\omega_0 t_o\,dt = \frac{1}{m\omega_0}[\sin m\omega_0 t]\Big|_{t_o}^{t_o+T}$$

$$= \frac{1}{m\omega_0}[\sin m\omega_0(t_o + T) - \sin m\omega_0 t_o]$$

$$= \frac{1}{m\omega_0}[\sin m\omega_0 t_o - \sin m\omega_0 t_o] = 0 \quad \text{for all } m$$

[b] $I_8 = \int_{t_o}^{t_o+T} \cos m\omega_0 t \sin n\omega_0 t\, dt = \frac{1}{2}\int_{t_o}^{t_o+T} [\sin(m+n)\omega_0 t - \sin(m-n)\omega_0 t]\, dt$

But $(m+n)$ and $(m-n)$ are integers, therefore from I_6 above, $I_8 = 0$ for all m, n.

[c] $I_9 = \int_{t_o}^{t_o+T} \sin m\omega_0 t \sin n\omega_0 t\, dt = \frac{1}{2}\int_{t_o}^{t_o+T} [\cos(m-n)\omega_0 t - \cos(m+n)\omega_0 t]\, dt$

If $m \neq n$, both integrals are zero (I_7 above). If $m = n$, we get

$$I_9 = \frac{1}{2}\int_{t_o}^{t_o+T} dt - \frac{1}{2}\int_{t_o}^{t_o+T} \cos 2m\omega_0 t\, dt = \frac{T}{2} - 0 = \frac{T}{2}$$

[d] $I_{10} = \int_{t_o}^{t_o+T} \cos m\omega_0 t \cos n\omega_0 t\, dt = \frac{1}{2}\int_{t_o}^{t_o+T} [\cos(m-n)\omega_0 t + \cos(m+n)\omega_0 t]\, dt$

If $m \neq n$, both integrals are zero (I_7 above). If $m = n$, we have

$$I_{10} = \frac{1}{2}\int_{t_o}^{t_o+T} dt + \frac{1}{2}\int_{t_o}^{t_o+T} \cos 2m\omega_0 t\, dt = \frac{T}{2} + 0 = \frac{T}{2}$$

P 16.2 $f(t)\sin k\omega_0 t = a_v \sin k\omega_0 t + \sum_{n=1}^{\infty} a_n \cos n\omega_0 t \sin k\omega_0 t + \sum_{n=1}^{\infty} b_n \sin n\omega_0 t \sin k\omega_0 t$

Now integrate both sides from t_o to $t_o + T$. All the integrals on the right-hand side reduce to zero except in the last summation when $n = k$, therefore we have

$$\int_{t_o}^{t_o+T} f(t)\sin k\omega_0 t\, dt = 0 + 0 + b_k\left(\frac{T}{2}\right) \quad \text{or} \quad b_k = \frac{2}{T}\int_{t_o}^{t_o+T} f(t)\sin k\omega_0 t\, dt$$

P 16.3 [a] Odd function with half- and quarter-wave symmetry, $a_v = 0$, $a_k = 0$ for all k, $b_k = 0$ for even k; for k odd we have

$$b_k = \frac{8}{T}\int_0^{T/4} V_m \sin k\omega_0 t\, dt = \frac{4V_m}{k\pi}, \qquad k \text{ odd}$$

and $v(t) = \frac{4V_m}{\pi}\sum_{n=1,3,5}^{\infty} \frac{1}{n}\sin n\omega_0 t$ V

[b] Even function: $b_k = 0$ for k

$$a_v = \frac{2}{T}\int_0^{T/2} V_m \sin\frac{\pi}{T}t\, dt = \frac{2V_m}{\pi}$$

$$a_k = \frac{4}{T}\int_0^{T/2} V_m \sin\frac{\pi}{T}t \cos k\omega_0 t\, dt = \frac{2V_m}{\pi}\left(\frac{1}{1-2k} + \frac{1}{1+2k}\right)$$

$$= \frac{4V_m/\pi}{1-4k^2}$$

and $v(t) = \frac{2V_m}{\pi}\left[1 + 2\sum_{n=1}^{\infty}\frac{1}{1-4n^2}\cos n\omega_0 t\right]$ V

[c] $a_v = \frac{1}{T}\int_0^{T/2} V_m \sin\left(\frac{2\pi}{T}\right) t\, dt = \frac{V_m}{\pi}$

$$a_k = \frac{2}{T}\int_0^{T/2} V_m \sin\frac{2\pi}{T}t \cos k\omega_0 t\, dt = \frac{V_m}{\pi}\left(\frac{1+\cos k\pi}{1-k^2}\right)$$

Note: $a_k = 0$ for k-odd, $a_k = \frac{2V_m}{\pi(1-k^2)}$ for k even,

$$b_k = \frac{2}{T}\int_0^{T/2} V_m \sin\frac{2\pi}{T}t \sin k\omega_0 t\, dt = 0 \quad \text{for} \quad k = 2, 3, 4, \ldots$$

For $k = 1$, we have $b_1 = \frac{V_m}{2}$; therefore

$$v(t) = \frac{V_m}{\pi} + \frac{V_m}{2}\sin\omega_0 t + \frac{2V_m}{\pi}\sum_{n=2,4,6}^{\infty}\frac{1}{1-n^2}\cos n\omega_0 t \text{ V}$$

P 16.4 $a_v = \frac{1}{T}\int_{t_o}^{t_o+T} f(t)\, dt = \frac{1}{T}\left\{\int_{-T/2}^{0} f(t)\, dt + \int_0^{T/2} f(t)\, dt\right\}$

Let $t = -x$, $dt = -dx$, $x = \frac{T}{2}$ when $t = \frac{-T}{2}$

and $x = 0$ when $t = 0$

Therefore $\frac{1}{T}\int_{-T/2}^{0} f(t)\, dt = \frac{1}{T}\int_{T/2}^{0} f(-x)(-dx) = -\frac{1}{T}\int_0^{T/2} f(x)\, dx$

Therefore $a_v = -\frac{1}{T}\int_0^{T/2} f(t)\, dt + \frac{1}{T}\int_0^{T/2} f(t)\, dt = 0$

$$a_k = \frac{2}{T}\int_{-T/2}^{0} f(t)\cos k\omega_0 t\, dt + \frac{2}{T}\int_0^{T/2} f(t)\cos k\omega_0 t\, dt$$

Again, let $t = -x$ in the first integral and we get

$$\frac{2}{T}\int_{-T/2}^{0} f(t)\cos k\omega_0 t\, dt = -\frac{2}{T}\int_0^{T/2} f(x)\cos k\omega_0 x\, dx$$

Therefore $a_k = 0$ for all k.

$$b_k = \frac{2}{T}\int_{-T/2}^{0} f(t)\sin k\omega_0 t + \frac{2}{T}\int_0^{T/2} f(t)\sin k\omega_0 t\, dt$$

Using the substitution $t = -x$, the first integral becomes

$$\frac{2}{T}\int_0^{T/2} f(x)\sin k\omega_0 x\, dx$$

Therefore we have $b_k = \frac{4}{T}\int_0^{T/2} f(t)\sin k\omega_0 t\, dt$

P 16.5 $$b_k = \frac{2}{T}\int_{-T/2}^{0} f(t)\sin k\omega_0 t\,dt + \frac{2}{T}\int_{0}^{T/2} f(t)\sin k\omega_0 t\,dt$$

Now let $t = x - T/2$ in the first integral, then $dt = dx$, $x = 0$ when $t = -T/2$ and $x = T/2$ when $t = 0$, also
$\sin k\omega_0(x - T/2) = \sin(k\omega_0 x - k\pi) = \sin k\omega_0 x \cos k\pi$. Therefore

$$\frac{2}{T}\int_{-T/2}^{0} f(t)\sin k\omega_0 t\,dt = -\frac{2}{T}\int_{0}^{T/2} f(x)\sin k\omega_0 x\cos k\pi\,dx \quad \text{and}$$

$$b_k = \frac{2}{T}(1 - \cos k\pi)\int_{0}^{T/2} f(x)\sin k\omega_0 t\,dt$$

Now note that $1 - \cos k\pi = 0$ when k is even, and $1 - \cos k\pi = 2$ when k is odd. Therefore $b_k = 0$ when k is even, and

$$b_k = \frac{4}{T}\int_{0}^{T/2} f(t)\sin k\omega_0 t\,dt \quad \text{when } k \text{ is odd}$$

P 16.6 Because the function is even and has half-wave symmetry, we have $a_v = 0$, $a_k = 0$ for k even, $b_k = 0$ for all k and

$$a_k = \frac{4}{T}\int_{0}^{T/2} f(t)\cos k\omega_0 t\,dt, \qquad k \text{ odd}$$

The function also has quarter-wave symmetry, therefore $f(t) = -f(T/2 - t)$ in the interval $T/4 \le t \le T/2$, thus we write

$$a_k = \frac{4}{T}\int_{0}^{T/4} f(t)\cos k\omega_0 t\,dt + \frac{4}{T}\int_{T/4}^{T/2} f(t)\cos k\omega_0 t\,dt$$

Now let $t = (T/2 - x)$ in the second integral, then $dt = -dx$, $x = T/4$ when $t = T/4$ and $x = 0$ when $t = T/2$. Therefore we get

$$\frac{4}{T}\int_{T/4}^{T/2} f(t)\cos k\omega_0 t\,dt = -\frac{4}{T}\int_{0}^{T/4} f(x)\cos k\pi\cos k\omega_0 x\,dx$$

Therefore we have

$$a_k = \frac{4}{T}(1 - \cos k\pi)\int_{0}^{T/4} f(t)\cos k\omega_0 t\,dt$$

But k is odd, hence

$$a_k = \frac{8}{T}\int_{0}^{T/4} f(t)\cos k\omega_0 t\,dt, \qquad k \text{ odd}$$

P 16.7 Because the function is odd and has half-wave symmetry, $a_v = 0$, $a_k = 0$ for all k, and $b_k = 0$ for k even. For k odd we have

$$b_k = \frac{4}{T}\int_0^{T/2} f(t)\sin k\omega_0 t\,dt$$

The function also has quarter-wave symmetry, therefore $f(t) = f(T/2 - t)$ in the interval $T/4 \leq t \leq T/2$. Thus we have

$$b_k = \frac{4}{T}\int_0^{T/4} f(t)\sin k\omega_0 t\,dt + \frac{4}{T}\int_{T/4}^{T/2} f(t)\sin k\omega_0 t\,dt$$

Now let $t = (T/2 - x)$ in the second integral and note that $dt = -dx$, $x = T/4$ when $t = T/4$ and $x = 0$ when $t = T/2$, thus

$$\frac{4}{T}\int_{T/4}^{T/2} f(t)\sin k\omega_0 t\,dt = -\frac{4}{T}\cos k\pi \int_0^{T/4} f(x)(\sin k\omega_0 x)\,dx$$

But k is odd, therefore the expression becomes

$$b_k = \frac{8}{T}\int_0^{T/4} f(t)\sin k\omega_0 t\,dt$$

P 16.8 [a] $\omega_{oa} = \frac{2\pi}{90}(10^6) = 69{,}813.17$ rad/s

$$\omega_{ob} = \frac{2\pi}{T} = \frac{2\pi}{8}(10^6) = 785{,}398.16 \text{ rad/s}$$

[b] $f_{oa} = \frac{1}{T} = \frac{10^6}{90} = 11{,}111.11\,\text{Hz}$; $\quad f_{ob} = \frac{1}{T} = \frac{10^6}{8} = 125{,}000\,\text{Hz}$

[c] $a_{va} = 0$; $\quad a_{vb} = \frac{2(50 \times 1 + 25 \times 1)}{8} = 18.75\,\text{V}$

[d] The periodic function in Fig. P16.8(a) is odd with half-wave and quarter-wave symmetry. Therefore,

$a_v = 0$; $\quad a_{ka} = 0$ for all k; $\quad b_{ka} = 0$ for k even

For k odd,

$$b_{ka} = \frac{8}{T}\int_0^{T/6} 100\sin\frac{2\pi kt}{T}\,dt + \frac{8}{T}\int_{T/6}^{T/4} 50\sin\frac{2\pi kt}{T}\,dt$$

$$= \frac{400}{T}\left\{\frac{2T}{2\pi k}\left(-\cos\frac{2\pi kt}{T}\Big|_0^{T/6}\right) + \frac{T}{2\pi k}\left(-\cos\frac{2\pi kt}{T}\Big|_{T/6}^{T/4}\right)\right\}$$

$$= \frac{-200}{\pi k}\left\{2\left(\cos\frac{\pi k}{3} - 1\right) + \cos\frac{\pi}{2}k - \cos\frac{\pi k}{3}\right\}$$

$$= \frac{200}{\pi k}\left\{2 - \cos\frac{\pi k}{3} - \cos\frac{\pi}{2}k\right\}$$

Since k is odd, $\cos \pi k/2 = 0$.

$$\therefore \quad b_{ka} = \frac{200}{\pi k}\left[2 - \cos\frac{\pi k}{3}\right], \qquad k \text{ odd}$$

The periodic function in Fig. P16.8(b) is even; therefore $b_k = 0$ for all k.

$a_{vb} = 18.75$

$$a_{kb} = \frac{4}{T}\left\{\int_0^{T/8} 50 \cos k\omega_o t\, dt + \int_{T/8}^{T/4} 25 \cos k\omega_o t\, dt + \int_{T/4}^{T/2} 0 \cos k\omega_o t\, dt\right\}$$

$$= \frac{4}{T}\left\{\frac{50}{k\omega_o} \sin k\omega_o t \Big|_0^{T/8} + \frac{25}{k\omega_o} \sin k\omega_o t \Big|_{T/8}^{T/4}\right\}$$

$$= \frac{50}{k\pi}\left\{2 \sin\frac{k\pi}{4} + \sin\frac{k\pi}{2} - \sin\frac{k\pi}{4}\right\}$$

$$= \frac{50}{k\pi}\left\{\sin\frac{k\pi}{4} + \sin\frac{k\pi}{2}\right\}$$

[e] For the periodic function in 16.8(a):

$$v(t) = \frac{200}{\pi}\sum_{n=1,3,5}^{\infty}\frac{1}{n}\left(2 - \cos\frac{n\pi}{3}\right)\sin n\omega_o t$$

For the periodic function in 16.8(b):

$$v(t) = 18.75 + \frac{50}{\pi}\sum_{n=1}^{\infty}\frac{1}{n}\left(\sin\frac{n\pi}{4} + \sin\frac{n\pi}{2}\right)\cos n\omega_o t$$

P 16.9 [a] $v(t)$ is even and has both half- and quarter-wave symmetry, therefore $a_v = 0$, $b_k = 0$ for all k, $a_k = 0$ for k-even; for odd k we have

$$a_k = \frac{8}{T}\int_0^{T/4} V_m \cos k\omega_0 t\, dt = \frac{4V_m}{\pi k}\sin\left(\frac{k\pi}{2}\right)$$

$$v(t) = \frac{4V_m}{\pi}\sum_{n=1,3,5}^{\infty}\left[\frac{1}{n}\sin\frac{n\pi}{2}\right]\cos n\omega_0 t \text{ V}$$

[b] $v(t)$ is even and has both half- and quarter-wave symmetry, therefore $a_v = 0$, $a_k = 0$ for k-even, $b_k = 0$ for all k; for k-even; for k-odd we have

$$a_k = \frac{8}{T}\int_0^{T/4}\left(\frac{4V_p}{T}t - V_p\right)\sin k\omega_0 t\, dt = \frac{8V_p}{\pi^2 k^2}$$

Therefore $v(t) = \frac{8V_p}{\pi^2} \sum_{n=1,3,5}^{\infty} \left[\frac{1}{n^2} \sin \frac{n\pi}{2}\right] \sin n\omega_0 t$ V

P 16.10 In studying the periodic function in Fig. P16.10 note that it can be visualized as the combination of two half-wave rectified sine waves, as shown in the figure below. Hence we can use the Fourier series for a half-wave rectified sine wave which is given as the answer to Problem 16.3(c).

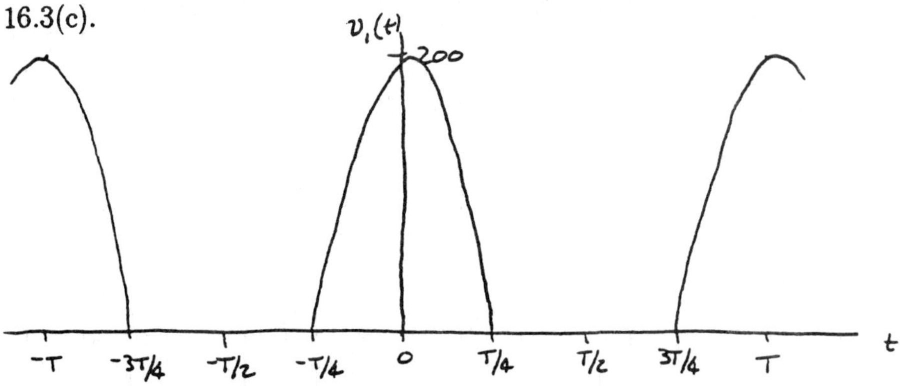

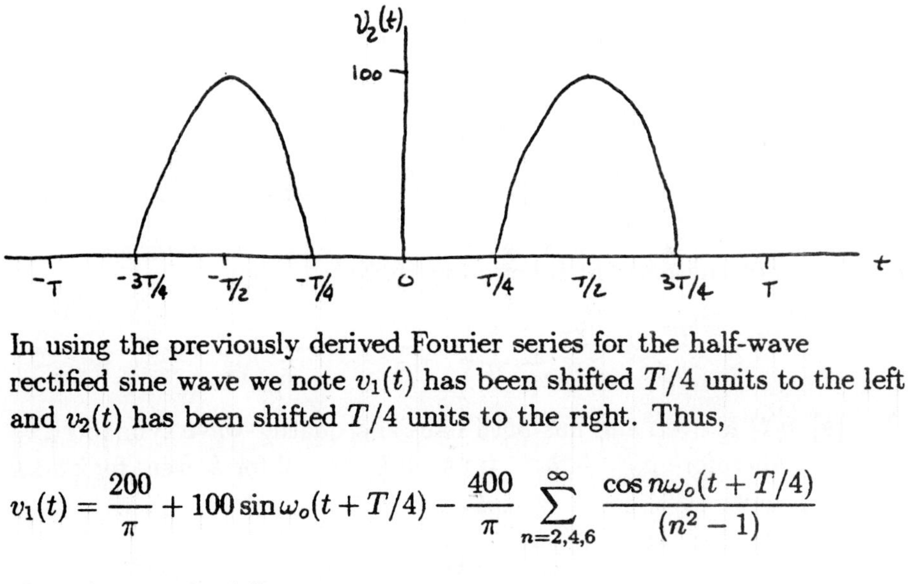

In using the previously derived Fourier series for the half-wave rectified sine wave we note $v_1(t)$ has been shifted $T/4$ units to the left and $v_2(t)$ has been shifted $T/4$ units to the right. Thus,

$$v_1(t) = \frac{200}{\pi} + 100 \sin \omega_o(t + T/4) - \frac{400}{\pi} \sum_{n=2,4,6}^{\infty} \frac{\cos n\omega_o(t + T/4)}{(n^2 - 1)}$$

Now observe the following:

$$\sin \omega_o(t + T/4) = sin(\omega_o t + \pi/2) = \cos \omega_o t$$

$$\cos n\omega_o(t + T/4) = cos(n\omega_o t + n\pi/2) = \cos \frac{n\pi}{2} \cos n\omega_o t$$

because n is even.

$$\therefore \quad v_1(t) = \frac{200}{\pi} + 100 \cos \omega_o t - \frac{400}{\pi} \sum_{n=2,4,6}^{\infty} \frac{\cos(n\pi/2)\cos(n\omega_o t)}{(n^2 - 1)}$$

$$\therefore \quad v_2(t) = \frac{100}{\pi} + 50\sin\omega_o(t - T/4) - \frac{200}{\pi}\sum_{n=2,4,6}^{\infty}\frac{\cos n\omega_o(t - T/4)}{(n^2 - 1)}$$

Again, observe the following:

$$\sin(\omega_o t - \pi/2) = -\cos\omega_o t$$

$$\cos(n\omega_o t - n\pi/2) = \cos(n\pi/2)\cos n\omega_o t$$

because n is even.

$$\therefore \quad v_2(t) = \frac{100}{\pi} + 50\cos\omega_o t - \frac{200}{\pi}\sum_{n=2,4,6}^{\infty}\frac{\cos(n\pi/2)\cos(n\omega_o t)}{(n^2 - 1)}$$

Thus: $\quad v = v_1 + v_2$

$$\therefore \quad v(t) = \frac{300}{\pi} + 50\cos\omega_o t - \frac{600}{\pi}\sum_{n=2,4,6}^{\infty}\frac{\cos(n\pi/2)\cos(n\omega_o t)}{(n^2 - 1)}$$

P 16.11 [a] $i(t)$ is even, therefore $b_k = 0$ for all k.

$$a_v = \frac{1}{2}\cdot\frac{T}{4}\cdot I_m\cdot 2\cdot\frac{1}{T} = \frac{I_m}{4}$$

$$a_k = \frac{4}{T}\int_0^{T/4}\left(I_m - \frac{4I_m}{T}t\right)\cos k\omega_o t\,dt$$

$$= \frac{4I_m}{T}\int_0^{T/4}\cos k\omega_o t\,dt - \frac{16I_m}{T^2}\int_0^{T/4} t\cos k\omega_o t\,dt$$

$$= \text{Int}_1 - \text{Int}_2$$

$$\text{Int}_1 = \frac{4I_m}{T}\int_0^{T/4}\cos k\omega_o t\,dt = \frac{2I_m}{\pi k}\sin\frac{k\pi}{2}$$

$$\text{Int}_2 = \frac{16I_m}{T^2}\int_0^{T/4} t\cos k\omega_o t\,dt$$

$$= \frac{16I_m}{T^2}\left\{\frac{1}{k^2\omega_o^2}\cos k\omega_o t + \frac{t}{k\omega_o}\sin k\omega_o t\,\Big|_0^{T/4}\right\}$$

$$= \frac{4I_m}{\pi^2k^2}\left(\cos\frac{k\pi}{2} - 1\right) + \frac{2I_m}{k\pi}\sin\frac{k\pi}{2}$$

$$\therefore \quad a_k = \frac{4I_m}{\pi^2k^2}\left(1 - \cos\frac{k\pi}{2}\right)$$

$$\therefore \quad i(t) = \frac{I_m}{4} + \frac{4I_m}{\pi^2}\sum_{n=1}^{\infty}\frac{1 - \cos(n\pi/2)}{n^2}\cos n\omega_o t$$

[b] Shifting the reference axis to the left is equivalent to shifting the periodic function to the right:

$$\cos n\omega_o(t - T/2) = \cos n\pi \cos n\omega_o t$$

Thus

$$i(t) = \frac{I_m}{4} + \frac{4I_m}{\pi^2}\sum_{n=1}^{\infty}\frac{(1-\cos(n\pi/2))\cos n\pi}{n^2}\cos n\omega_o t$$

P 16.12 [a]

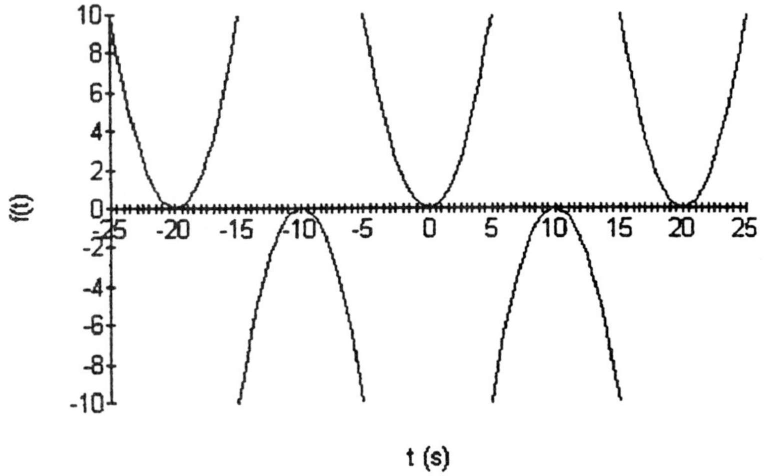

[b] even

[c] yes

[d] $a_v = 0$; $\quad b_k = 0 \quad$ for all k; the function is even

$a_k = 0, \quad k$ even, half-wave symmetry

$$a_k = \frac{8}{T}\int_0^{T/4} 0.4t^2\cos k\omega_o t\,dt$$

$$= \frac{3.2}{T}\int_0^{T/4} t^2\cos k\omega_o t\,dt$$

$$= \frac{3.2}{T}\left\{\frac{2t}{k^2\omega_o^2}\cos k\omega_o t + \frac{k^2\omega_o^2 t^2 - 2}{k^3\omega_o^3}\sin k\omega_o t\,\Big|_0^{T/4}\right\}$$

First term is 0 at both $T/4$ and 0; second term is 0 at 0, hence

$$a_k = \frac{3.2}{k^3\omega_o^3 T}\left\{\frac{k^2\omega_o^2T^2 - 32}{16}\right\}\sin\frac{k\pi}{2}$$

$$= \frac{T^2}{5k^3(8\pi^3)}(k^2 4\pi^2 - 32)\sin\frac{k\pi}{2}$$

$T^2 = 400$

$$\therefore \quad a_k = \frac{40}{\pi^3 k^3}(k^2\pi^2 - 8)\sin\frac{k\pi}{2}$$

$$f(t) = \frac{40}{\pi^3}\sum_{n=1,3,5}^{\infty}\left(\frac{n^2\pi^2 - 8}{n^3}\right)\sin\frac{n\pi}{2}\cos n\omega_o t$$

[e] $\cos n\omega_o(t - T/4) = \cos(n\omega_o t - n\pi/2)$

$= \sin(n\pi/2)\sin n\omega_o t \qquad$ since n is odd

$$\therefore \quad f(t) = \frac{40}{\pi^3}\sum_{n=1,3,5}^{\infty}\left(\frac{n^2\pi^2 - 8}{n^3}\right)\sin n\omega_o t$$

P 16.13 [a]

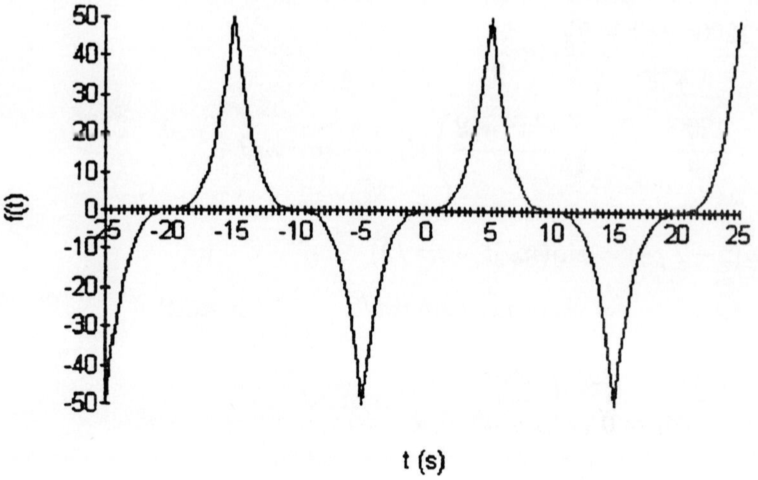

[b] odd

[c] yes

[d] $a_v = 0; \qquad a_k = 0 \quad$ for all k since the function is odd

$b_k = 0 \quad$ for k even, since the function has half-wave symmetry

$$b_k = \frac{8}{T}\int_0^{T/4} f(t)\sin k\omega_o t\,dt, \qquad k \text{ odd}$$

$$= \frac{3.2}{T}\int_0^{T/4} t^3 \sin k\omega_o t\,dt$$

$$= \frac{3k^2\omega_o^2 t^2 - 6}{k^4\omega_o^4}\sin k\omega_o t\Big|_0^{T/4} + \frac{t(6 - k^2\omega_o^2 t^2)}{k^3\omega_o^3}\cos k\omega_o t\Big|_0^{T/4}$$

Note that the first term is zero at the lower limit and the second term is zero at both limits because

$\cos k\omega_o T/4 = \cos k\pi/2, \quad k \text{ odd}$

Thus

$$b_k = \left\{ \frac{(3k^2\omega_o^2 T^2/16) - 6}{k^4\omega_o^4} \sin\frac{k\pi}{2} \right\} \frac{3.2}{T}$$

$\omega_o T = 2\pi$

$$b_k = \frac{3.2}{T}\left\{ \frac{12(k^2\pi^2 - 8)T^4}{256k^4\pi^4} \right\} \sin\frac{k\pi}{2}$$

$$= \frac{3(k^2\pi^2 - 8)T^3}{20k^4\pi^4} \sin\frac{k\pi}{2}$$

$T = 20\,\text{s}$

$$b_k = \frac{1200(k^2\pi^2 - 8)}{k^4\pi^4} \sin\frac{k\pi}{2}$$

$$f(t) = \frac{1200}{\pi^4} \sum_{n=1,3,5}^{\infty} \left(\frac{n^2\pi^2 - 8}{n^4} \right) \sin\frac{n\pi}{2} \sin n\omega_o t$$

[e] $\sin n\omega_o(t - T/4) = \sin(n\omega_o t - n\pi/2)$

$= -\cos n\omega_o t \sin n\pi/2 \qquad (n \text{ is odd})$

$$f(t) = -\frac{1200}{\pi^4} \sum_{n=1,3,5}^{\infty} \left(\frac{n^2\pi^2 - 8}{n^4} \right) \cos n\omega_o t$$

P 16.14 [a] $\omega_o = \frac{2\pi}{T} = \frac{\pi}{6}$ rad/s

[b] no

[c] yes

[d] no

P 16.15 [a] $f = \frac{1}{T} = \frac{10^3}{10} = 100\,\text{Hz}$

[b] no

[c] yes

[d] yes

[e] yes

[f] $a_v = 0,\quad$ function is odd

$a_k = 0,\quad$ for all k; the function is odd

$b_k = 0,\quad$ for k even, the function has half-wave symmetry

$$b_k = \frac{8}{T}\int_0^{T/4} f(t)\sin k\omega_o t, \qquad k \text{ odd}$$

$$= \frac{8}{T}\left\{\int_0^{T/8} 4000t\sin k\omega_o t\,dt + \int_{T/8}^{T/4} 5\sin k\omega_o t\,dt\right\}$$

$$= \frac{8}{T}\{\text{Int1} + \text{Int2}\}$$

$$\text{Int1} = 4000\int_0^{T/8} t\sin k\omega_o t\,dt$$

$$= 4000\left[\frac{1}{k^2\omega_o^2}\sin k\omega_o t - \frac{t}{k\omega_o}\cos k\omega_o t\,\Bigg|_0^{T/8}\right]$$

$$= \frac{4000}{k^2\omega_o^2}\sin\frac{k\pi}{4} - \frac{500T}{k\omega_o}\cos\frac{k\pi}{4}$$

$$\text{Int2} = 5\int_{T/8}^{T/4}\sin k\omega_o t\,dt = \frac{-5}{k\omega_o}\cos k\omega_o t\,\Bigg|_{T/8}^{T/4} = \frac{5}{k\omega_o}\cos\frac{k\pi}{4}$$

$$\text{Int1} + \text{Int2} = \frac{4000}{k^2\omega_o^2}\sin\frac{k\pi}{4} + \left(\frac{5}{k\omega_o} - \frac{500T}{k\omega_o}\right)\cos\frac{k\pi}{4}$$

$$500T = (500)(10\times 10^{-3}) = 5$$

$$\therefore\quad \text{Int1} + \text{Int2} = \frac{4000}{k^2\omega_o^2}\sin\frac{k\pi}{4}$$

$$b_k = \left[\frac{8}{T}\cdot\frac{4000}{4\pi^2k^2}\cdot T^2\right]\sin\frac{k\pi}{4} = \frac{80}{\pi^2k^2}\sin\frac{k\pi}{4}, \qquad k \text{ odd}$$

$$i(t) = \frac{80}{\pi^2}\sum_{n=1,3,5}^{\infty}\frac{\sin(n\pi/4)}{n^2}\sin n\omega_o t$$

P 16.16 [a]

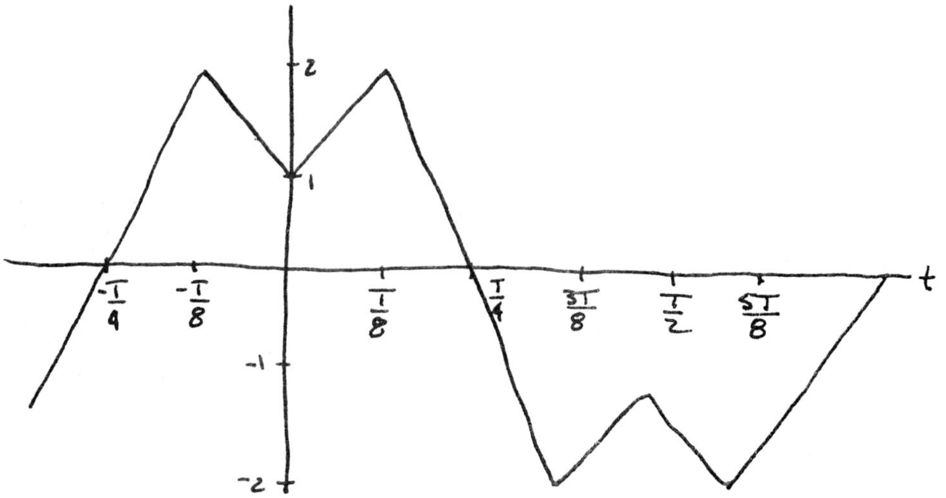

[b] $a_v = 0;\quad a_k = 0$ for all k even; $\quad b_k = 0$ for all k

For k odd, $\quad a_k = \frac{8}{T}\int_0^{T/4} f(t)\cos k\omega_o t\,dt$

$$a_k = \frac{8}{T}\int_0^{T/8}\left(1+\frac{8t}{T}\right)\cos k\omega_o t\,dt + \frac{8}{T}\int_{T/8}^{T/4}\left(4-\frac{16t}{T}\right)\cos k\omega_o t\,dt$$

$$= \text{Int1} + \text{Int2}$$

$$\text{Int1} = \frac{8}{T}\int_0^{T/8}\cos k\omega_o t\,dt + \frac{64}{T^2}\int_0^{T/8} t\cos k\omega_o t\,dt$$

$$= \frac{8}{T}\frac{\sin k\omega_o t}{k\omega_o}\Big|_0^{T/8} + \frac{64}{T^2}\left[\frac{\cos k\omega_o t}{k^2\omega_o^2} + \frac{t}{k\omega_o}\sin k\omega_o t\right]_0^{T/8}$$

$k\omega_o T = 2k\pi;\qquad (k\omega_o T)^2 = 4k^2\pi^2$

$$\text{Int1} = \frac{8}{k\pi}\sin\frac{k\pi}{4} + \frac{16}{k^2\pi^2}\left[\cos\left(\frac{k\pi}{4}\right) - 1\right] \qquad k \text{ odd}$$

$$\text{Int2} = \frac{32}{T}\int_{T/8}^{T/4}\cos k\omega_o t\,dt - \frac{128}{T^2}\int_{T/8}^{T/4} t\cos k\omega_o t\,dt$$

$$= \frac{32}{T}\frac{\sin k\omega_o t}{k\omega_o}\Big|_{T/8}^{T/4} - \frac{128}{T^2}\left[\frac{\cos k\omega_o t}{k^2\omega_o^2} + \frac{t}{k\omega_o}\sin k\omega_o t\right]_{T/8}^{T/4}$$

$$\text{Int2} = \frac{-8}{k\pi}\sin\frac{k\pi}{4} + \frac{32}{k^2\pi^2}\cos\frac{k\pi}{4} \qquad k \text{ odd}$$

$$a_k = \text{Int1} + \text{Int2}$$

$$= \frac{16}{k^2\pi^2}\left[3\cos\frac{k\pi}{4} - 1\right]$$

[c] $a_1 = \frac{32}{\pi^2}\cos\frac{\pi}{4} + \frac{4}{\pi}\sin\frac{\pi}{4} - \frac{16}{\pi^2} = 1.8178$

$$a_3 = \frac{32}{9\pi^2}\cos\frac{3\pi}{4} + \frac{4}{3\pi}\sin\frac{3\pi}{4} - \frac{16}{9\pi^2} = -0.5622$$

$$a_5 = \frac{32}{25\pi^2}\cos\frac{5\pi}{4} + \frac{4}{5\pi}\sin\frac{5\pi}{4} - \frac{16}{25\pi^2} = -0.2024$$

$$f(t) = 1.8178\cos\omega_o t - 0.5622\cos 3\omega_o t - 0.2024\cos 5\omega_o t - \cdots$$

[d] $f(T/8) = 1.8178\cos(\pi/4) - 0.5622\cos(3\pi/4) - 0.2024\cos(5\pi/4) = 1.8261$

P 16.17 Let $f(t) = v_2(t - T/6)$.

$a_v = -(2V_m/3)(T/3)(1/T) = -(2V_m/9)$ and $b_k = 0$ since $f(t)$ is even

$$a_k = \frac{4}{T}\int_0^{T/6}\left(-\frac{2V_m}{3}\right)\cos k\omega_o t dt = -\frac{4}{T}\frac{2V_m}{3}\frac{1}{k\omega_o}\sin k\omega_o t\Big|_0^{T/6}$$

$$= -\frac{8V_m}{3k2\pi}\sin\left(k\frac{\pi}{3}\right) = -\frac{4V_m}{3k\pi}\sin\left(k\frac{\pi}{3}\right)$$

Therefore, $v_2(t - T/6) = -\frac{2V_m}{9} - \frac{4V_m}{3\pi}\sum_{n=1}^{\infty}\frac{1}{n}\sin\left(\frac{n\pi}{3}\right)\cos n\omega_o t$

and $v_2(t) = -\frac{2V_m}{9} - \frac{4V_m}{3\pi}\sum_{n=1}^{\infty}\frac{1}{n}\sin\left(\frac{n\pi}{3}\right)\cos n\omega_o(t + T/6)$

Then, $v(t) = v_1(t) + v_2(t)$. Simplifying,

$$v(t) = \frac{7V_m}{9} - \frac{4V_m}{3\pi}\sum_{n=1}^{\infty}\frac{1}{n}\left[\sin\left(\frac{n\pi}{3}\right)\cos\left(\frac{n\pi}{3}\right)\right]\cos n\omega_o t$$

$$= \frac{4V_m}{3\pi}\sum_{n=1}^{\infty}\frac{1}{n}\left[\sin^2\left(\frac{n\pi}{3}\right)\right]\sin n\omega_o t$$

If $V_m = 9\pi$ then $a_v = 7\pi = 21.99$ (Checks)

$$a_k = -\left(\frac{12}{n}\right)\sin\left(\frac{n\pi}{3}\right)\cos\left(\frac{n\pi}{3}\right) = -\left(\frac{12}{n}\right)\left(\frac{1}{2}\right)\sin\left(\frac{2n\pi}{3}\right) = \left(\frac{6}{n}\right)\sin\left(\frac{4n\pi}{3}\right)$$

$$b_k = \left(\frac{12}{n}\right)\sin^2\left(\frac{n\pi}{3}\right) = \left(\frac{12}{n}\right)\left(\frac{1}{2}\right)\left[1 - \cos\left(\frac{2n\pi}{3}\right)\right] = \left(\frac{6}{n}\right)\left[1 - \cos\left(\frac{4n\pi}{3}\right)\right]$$

P 16.18 [a] The voltage has half-wave symmetry. Therefore,

$$a_v = 0; \qquad a_k = b_k = 0, \quad k \text{ even}$$

$$a_k = \frac{4}{T}\int_0^{T/2}\left(V_m - \frac{2V_m}{T}t\right)\cos k\omega_o t\,dt, \quad k \text{ odd}$$

$$b_k = \frac{4}{T}\int_0^{T/2}\left(V_m - \frac{2V_m}{T}t\right)\sin k\omega_o t\,dt, \quad k \text{ odd}$$

$$a_k = \frac{4V_m}{T}\int_0^{T/2}\cos k\omega_o t\,dt - \frac{8V_m}{T^2}\int_0^{T/2} t\cos k\omega_o t\,dt$$

$$= \text{Int1} - \text{Int2}$$

$$\text{Int1} = \frac{4V_m}{T}\int_0^{T/2}\cos k\omega_o t\,dt = \frac{4V_m}{T}\cdot\frac{1}{k\omega_o}\sin k\omega_o t\Big|_0^{T/2} = 0$$

$$\text{Int2} = \frac{8V_m}{T^2}\left[\frac{\cos k\omega_o t}{k^2\omega_o^2} + \frac{t\sin k\omega_o t}{k\omega_o}\right|_0^{T/2}$$

$$= \frac{8V_m}{T^2}\left[\frac{1}{k^2\omega_o^2}\cos k\pi - 1\right]$$

$$= \frac{-16V_m}{k^2(4\pi^2)} = \frac{-4V_m}{\pi^2 k^2}, \quad k \text{ odd}$$

$$\therefore \quad a_k = \frac{4V_m}{\pi^2 k^2}, \quad k \text{ odd}$$

$$b_k = \frac{4V_m}{T}\int_0^{T/2}\sin k\omega_o t\,dt - \frac{8V_m}{T^2}\int_0^{T/2} t\sin k\omega_o t\,dt$$

$$= \text{Int1} - \text{Int2}$$

$$\text{Int1} = \frac{4V_m}{T}\int_0^{T/2}\sin k\omega_o t\,dt = \frac{4V_m}{T}\cdot\frac{-1}{k\omega_o}\cos k\omega_o t\Big|_0^{T/2}$$

$$= \frac{-4V_m}{Tk\omega_o}[\cos k\pi - 1] = \frac{8V_m}{k\omega_o T} = \frac{4V_m}{\pi k}$$

$$\text{Int2} = \frac{8V_m}{T^2}\int_0^{T/2} t\sin k\omega_o t\,dt$$

$$= \frac{8V_m}{T^2}\left[\frac{\sin k\omega_o t}{k^2\omega_o^2} - \frac{t\cos k\omega_o t}{k\omega_o}\right|_0^{T/2}$$

$$= \frac{8V_m}{T^2}\left[0 - \frac{T}{2k\omega_o^2}\cos k\pi - 0 - 0\right] = \frac{2V_m}{k\pi}$$

$$\therefore \quad b_k = \frac{4V_m}{\pi k} - \frac{2V_m}{\pi k} = \frac{2V_m}{\pi k}$$

$$\therefore \quad A_k\underline{/-\theta_k} = a_k - jb_k = \frac{2V_m}{\pi k}\left(\frac{2}{\pi k} - j1\right)$$

$V_m = 378\pi$ mV

$$A_k\underline{/-\theta_k} = \frac{756}{k}\left(\frac{2}{\pi k} - j1\right) \text{ mV}$$

$$v(t) = \sum_{n=1,3,5}^{\infty} A_n \cos(n\omega_o t - \theta_n)$$

$$A_1\underline{/-\theta_1} = 896.20\underline{/-57.52^\circ} \text{ mV}$$

$$A_2\underline{/-\theta_2} = 257.61\underline{/-78.02^\circ} \text{ mV}$$

$$A_3\underline{/-\theta_3} = 152.42\underline{/-82.74^\circ} \text{ mV}$$

$$A_4\underline{/-\theta_4} = 108.45\underline{/-84.80^\circ} \text{ mV}$$

$$A_5\underline{/-\theta_5} - 84.21\underline{/-85.95^\circ} \text{ mV}$$

$$v(t) = 896.20\cos(\omega_o t - 57.52^\circ) + 257.61\cos(3\omega_o t - 78.02^\circ)$$
$$+152.42\cos(5\omega_o t - 82.74^\circ) + 108.45\cos(7\omega_o t - 84.80^\circ)$$
$$= +84.21\cos(9\omega_o t - 85.95^\circ) + \ldots$$

[b] $v(T/8) = 896.20\cos(45 - 57.52^\circ) + 257.61\cos(135 - 78.02^\circ)$
$+152.42\cos(225 - 82.74^\circ) + 108.45\cos(315 - 84.80^\circ)$
$= +84.21\cos(405 - 85.95^\circ) = 888.92$ mV

$$v(T/8) = 378\pi - \frac{2(378\pi)}{T}\left(\frac{T}{8}\right) = 378\pi(1 - \frac{1}{4}) = 890.64 \text{ mV}$$

The % difference based on the exact value is

$$\left(\frac{888.92 - 890.64}{890.64}\right)(100) = -0.19\%$$

P 16.19 The function has half-wave symmetry, thus $a_k = b_k = 0$ for k-even, $a_v = 0$; for k-odd

$$a_k = \frac{4}{T}\int_0^{T/2} V_m \cos k\omega_0 t\, dt - \frac{8V_m}{\rho T}\int_0^{T/2} e^{-t/RC}\cos k\omega_0 t\, dt$$

where $\rho = \left[1 - e^{-T/2RC}\right]$.

Upon integrating we get

$$a_k = \frac{4V_m}{T}\frac{\sin k\omega_0 t}{k\omega_0}\Big|_0^{T/2}$$

$$-\frac{8V_m}{\rho T}\cdot\frac{e^{-t/RC}}{(1/RC)^2+(k\omega_0)^2}\cdot\left[\frac{-\cos k\omega_0 t}{RC}+k\omega_0\sin k\omega_0 t\right]\Big|_0^{T/2}$$

$$= \frac{-8V_mRC}{T[1+(k\omega_0RC)^2]}$$

$$b_k = \frac{4}{T}\int_0^{T/2} V_m\sin k\omega_0 t\,dt - \frac{8V_m}{\rho T}\int_0^{T/2} e^{-t/RC}\sin k\omega_0 t\,dt$$

$$= -\frac{4V_m}{T}\frac{\cos k\omega_0 t}{k\omega_0}\Big|_0^{T/2}$$

$$-\frac{8V_m}{\rho T}\cdot\frac{-e^{-t/RC}}{(1/RC)^2+(k\omega_0)^2}\cdot\left[\frac{\sin k\omega_0 t}{RC}+k\omega_0\cos k\omega_0 t\right]\Big|_0^{T/2}$$

$$= \frac{4V_m}{\pi k} - \frac{8k\omega_0V_mR^2C^2}{T[1+(k\omega_0RC)^2]}$$

P 16.20 [a] $a_k^2+b_k^2 = a_k^2+\left(\frac{4V_m}{\pi k}+k\omega_0RCa_k\right)^2$

$$= a_k^2[1+(k\omega_0RC)^2]+\tfrac{8V_m}{\pi k}\left[\tfrac{2V_m}{\pi k}+k\omega_0RCa_k\right]$$

But $a_k = \left\{\frac{-8V_mRC}{T}\left[1+(k\omega_0RC)^2\right]\right\}$

Therefore $a_k^2 = \left\{\frac{64V_m^2R^2C^2}{T^2[1+(k\omega_0RC)^2]^2}\right\}$, thus we have

$$a_k^2+b_k^2 = \frac{64V_m^2R^2C^2}{T^2[1+(k\omega_0RC)^2]}+\frac{16V_m^2}{\pi^2k^2}-\frac{64V_m^2k\omega_0R^2C^2}{\pi kT[1+(k\omega_0RC)^2]}$$

Now let $\alpha = k\omega_0RC$ and note that $T = 2\pi/\omega_0$, thus the expression for $a_k^2+b_k^2$ reduces to $a_k^2+b_k^2 = 16V_M^2/\pi^2k^2(1+\alpha^2)$. It follows that

$$\sqrt{a_k^2+b_k^2} = \frac{4V_m}{\pi k\sqrt{1+(k\omega_0RC)^2}}$$

[b] $b_k = k\omega_0RCa_k + \frac{4V_m}{\pi k}$

Thus $\frac{b_k}{a_k} = k\omega_0RC+\frac{4V_m}{\pi ka_k} = \alpha - \frac{1+\alpha^2}{\alpha} = -\frac{1}{\alpha}$

Therefore $\dfrac{a_k}{b_k} = -\alpha = -k\omega_0 RC$

P 16.21 Since $a_v = 0$ (half-wave symmetry), Eq. 16.38 gives us

$$v_o(t) = \sum_{1,3,5}^{\infty} \frac{4V_m}{n\pi} \frac{1}{\sqrt{1 + (n\omega_0 RC)^2}} \cos(n\omega_0 t - \theta_n) \quad \text{where} \quad \tan\theta_n = \frac{b_n}{a_n}$$

But from Eq. 16.58, we have $\tan\beta_k = k\omega_0 RC$. It follows from Eq. 16.72 that $\tan\beta_k = -a_k/b_k$ or $\tan\theta_n = -\cot\beta_n$. Therefore $\theta_n = 90 + \beta_n$ and
$\cos(n\omega_0 t - \theta_n) = \cos(n\omega_0 t - \beta_n - 90°) = \sin(n\omega_0 t - \beta_n)$, thus our expression for v_o becomes

$$v_o = \frac{4V_m}{\pi} \sum_{n=1,3,5}^{\infty} \frac{\sin(n\omega_0 t - \beta_n)}{n\sqrt{1 + (n\omega_0 RC)^2}}$$

P 16.22 [a] Express v_g as a constant plus a symmetrical square wave. The constant is $V_m/2$ and the square wave has an amplitude of $V_m/2$, is odd, and has half- and quarter-wave symmetry. Therefore the Fourier series for v_g is

$$v_g = \frac{V_m}{2} + \frac{2V_m}{\pi} \sum_{n=1,3,5}^{\infty} \frac{1}{n} \sin n\omega_0 t$$

The dc component of the current is $V_m/2R$ and the kth harmonic phase current is

$$\mathbf{I}_k = \frac{2V_m/k\pi}{R + jk\omega_0 L} = \frac{2V_m}{k\pi\sqrt{R^2 + (k\omega_0 L)^2}} \angle -\theta_k$$

where $\theta_k = \tan^{-1}\left(\dfrac{k\omega_0 L}{R}\right)$

Thus the Fourier series for the steady-state current is

$$i = \frac{V_m}{2R} + \frac{2V_m}{\pi} \sum_{n=1,3,5}^{\infty} \frac{\sin(n\omega_0 t - \theta_n)}{n\sqrt{R^2 + (n\omega_0 L)^2}} \text{ A}$$

[b]

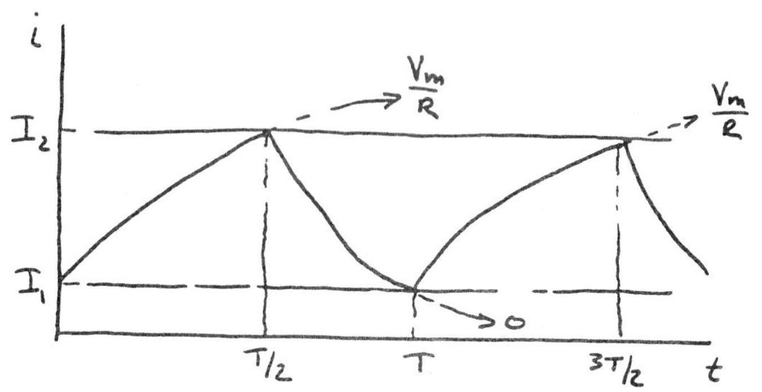

The steady-state current will alternate between I_1 and I_2 in exponential traces as shown. Assuming $t = 0$ at the instant i increases toward (V_m/R), we have

$$i = \frac{V_m}{R} + \left(I_1 - \frac{V_m}{R}\right) e^{-t/\tau} \quad \text{for} \quad 0 \le t \le \frac{T}{2}$$

and $i = I_2 e^{-[t-(T/2)]/\tau}$ for $T/2 \le t \le T$, where $\tau = L/R$. Now we solve for I_1 and I_2 by noting that

$$I_1 = I_2 e^{-T/2\tau} \quad \text{and} \quad I_2 = \frac{V_m}{R} + \left(I_1 - \frac{V_m}{R}\right) e^{-T/2\tau}$$

These two equations are now solved for I_1. Letting $x = T/2\tau$, we get

$$I_1 = \frac{(V_m/R)e^{-x}}{1 + e^{-x}}$$

Therefore the equations for i become

$$i = \frac{V_m}{R} - \left[\frac{V_m}{R(1 + e^{-x})}\right] e^{-t/\tau} \qquad \text{for} \quad 0 \le t \le \frac{T}{2} \quad \text{and}$$

$$i = \left[\frac{V_m}{R(1 + e^{-x})}\right] e^{-[t-(T/2)]/\tau} \qquad \text{for} \quad \frac{T}{2} \le t \le T$$

A check on the validity of these expressions is to show they yield an average value of $(V_m/2R)$:

$$\begin{aligned} I_{\text{avg}} &= \frac{1}{T}\left\{\int_0^{T/2} \left[\frac{V_m}{R} + \left(I_1 - \frac{V_m}{R}\right) e^{-t/\tau}\right] dt + \int_{T/2}^{T} I_2 e^{-[t-(T/2)]/\tau}\, dt\right\} \\ &= \frac{1}{T}\left\{\frac{V_m T}{2R} + \tau(1 - e^{-x})\left(I_1 - \frac{V_m}{R} + I_2\right)\right\} \\ &= \frac{V_m}{2R} \quad \text{since} \quad I_1 + I_2 = \frac{V_m}{R} \end{aligned}$$

P 16.23 $$v_i = \frac{8A}{\pi^2} \sum_{n=1,3,5}^{\infty} \left[\frac{1}{n^2} \sin\frac{n\pi}{2} \sin n\omega_o(t + T/4)\right] = \frac{8A}{\pi^2} \sum_{n=1,3,5}^{\infty} \frac{\cos n\omega_o t}{n^2}$$

$$= 3600 \sum_{n=1,3,5}^{\infty} \frac{1}{n^2} \cos n\omega_o t \text{ mV}$$

$$\frac{\mathbf{V}_o}{\mathbf{V}_i} = \frac{s}{s + (1/RC)} = \frac{s}{s + 1000}$$

$$\mathbf{V}_o = \frac{j\omega}{1000 + j\omega} \mathbf{V}_i$$

$\mathbf{V}_{i1} = 3600\underline{/0^\circ}$ mV; $\quad \mathbf{V}_{i3} = 400\underline{/0^\circ}$ mV; $\quad \mathbf{V}_{i5} = 144\underline{/0^\circ}$ mV

$$V_{o1} = \frac{j1000}{1000 + j1000}(3600\underline{/0^\circ}) = 2545.58\underline{/45^\circ}\,\text{mV}$$

$$V_{o3} = \frac{j3000}{1000 + j3000}(400\underline{/0^\circ}) = 379.47\underline{/18.43^\circ}\,\text{mV}$$

$$V_{o5} = \frac{j5000}{1000 + j5000}(144\underline{/0^\circ}) = 141.20\underline{/11.31^\circ}\,\text{mV}$$

$$v_o = 2545.58\cos(1000t + 45^\circ) + 379.47\cos(3000t + 18.43^\circ) + 141.20\cos(5000t + 11.31^\circ) + \ldots\ \text{mV}$$

P 16.24 $$v_i(t) = \frac{4A}{\pi}\sum_{n=1,3,5}^{\infty}\frac{1}{n}\sin n\omega_o(t + T/4) = 240\sum_{n=1,3,5}^{\infty}\frac{1}{n}\sin\frac{n\pi}{2}\cos n\omega_o t$$

$$\omega_o = \frac{2\pi}{T} = 2000\ \text{rad/s}$$

$v_{i1} = 240\cos 2000t$ V; $\quad \mathbf{V}_{i1} = 240\underline{/0^\circ}$ V

$v_{i3} = -80\cos 6000t$ V; $\quad \mathbf{V}_{i3} = 80\underline{/0^\circ}$ V

$v_{i5} = 48\cos 10{,}000t$ V; $\quad \mathbf{V}_{i5} = 48\underline{/0^\circ}$ V

$$H(s) = \frac{\mathbf{V}_o}{\mathbf{V}_i} = \frac{(R/L)}{s + (R/L)}$$

$$\frac{R}{L} = \frac{100}{25} \times 10^3 = 4000\ \text{rad/s}$$

$$H(j\omega) = \frac{4000}{4000 + j\omega}$$

$$H_1 = \frac{4000}{4000 + j2000} = 0.89\underline{/-26.57^\circ}$$

$$H_3 = \frac{4000}{4000 + j6000} = 0.55\underline{/-56.31^\circ}$$

$$H_5 = \frac{4000}{4000 + j10{,}000} = 0.37\underline{/-68.20^\circ}$$

$$\mathbf{V}_{o1} = (240\underline{/0^\circ})(0.89\underline{/-26.57^\circ}) = 214.66\underline{/-26.57^\circ}$$

$$\mathbf{V}_{o3} = (80\underline{/180^\circ})(0.55\underline{/-56.31^\circ}) = 44.38\underline{/123.69^\circ}$$

$$\mathbf{V}_{o5} = (48\underline{/0^\circ})(0.37\underline{/-68.20^\circ}) = 17.83\underline{/-68.20^\circ}$$

$$v_o = 214.66\cos(2000t - 26.57^\circ) + 44.38\cos(6000t + 123.69^\circ)$$
$$+ 17.83\cos(10{,}000t - 68.20^\circ) + \ldots$$

P 16.25 [a] $\omega_o = \frac{2\pi}{T} = \frac{2\pi}{0.2\pi}(10^3) = 10^4$ rad/s

$$v_g(t) = 840 \sum_{n=1,3,5}^{\infty} \frac{1}{n}\sin\frac{n\pi}{2}\cos n10{,}000t \text{ V}$$

$$= 840\cos 10{,}000t - 280\cos 30{,}000t + 168\cos 50{,}000t$$
$$- 120\cos 70{,}000t + \cdots \text{ V}$$

$\mathbf{V}_{g1} = 840\underline{/0^\circ}$ V; $\quad \mathbf{V}_{g3} = 280\underline{/180^\circ}$ V

$\mathbf{V}_{g5} = 168\underline{/0^\circ}$ V; $\quad \mathbf{V}_{g7} = 120\underline{/180^\circ}$ V

$$H(s) = \frac{V_o}{V_g} = \frac{\beta s}{s^2 + \beta s + \omega_c^2}$$

$$\beta = \frac{1}{RC} = \frac{10^9}{10^4(20)} = 5000 \text{ rad/s}$$

$$\omega_c^2 = \frac{1}{LC} = \frac{(10^9)(10^3)}{400} = 25 \times 10^8$$

$$H(s) = \frac{5000s}{s^2 + 5000s + 25 \times 10^8}$$

$$H(j\omega) = \frac{j5000\omega}{25 \times 10^8 - \omega^2 + j5000\omega}$$

$$H_1 = \frac{j5 \times 10^7}{24 \times 10^8 + j5 \times 10^7} = 0.02\underline{/88.81^\circ}$$

$$H_3 = \frac{j15 \times 10^7}{16 \times 10^8 + j15 \times 10^7} = 0.09\underline{/84.64^\circ}$$

$$H_5 = \frac{j25 \times 10^7}{25 \times 10^7} = 1\underline{/0^\circ}$$

$$H_7 = \frac{j35 \times 10^7}{-24 \times 10^8 + j35 \times 10^7} = 0.14\underline{/-81.70^\circ}$$

$$\mathbf{V}_{o1} = \mathbf{V}_{g1}H_1 = 17.50\underline{/88.81^\circ}\text{ V}$$

$$\mathbf{V}_{o3} = \mathbf{V}_{g3}H_3 = 26.14\underline{/-95.36^\circ}\text{ V}$$

$$\mathbf{V}_{o5} = \mathbf{V}_{g5}H_5 = 168\underline{/0^\circ}\text{ V}$$

$$\mathbf{V}_{o7} = \mathbf{V}_{g7}H_7 = 17.32\underline{/98.30^\circ}\text{ V}$$

$$v_o = 17.50\cos(10{,}000t + 88.81^\circ) + 26.14\cos(30{,}000t - 95.36^\circ) + 168\cos(50{,}000t) + 17.32\cos(70{,}000t + 98.30^\circ) + \cdots \text{ V}$$

[b] The 5th harmonic because the circuit is a passive bandpass filter with a Q of 10 and a center frequency of 50 krad/s.

P 16.26 [a] For the circuit in Fig. P16.26

$$H(s) = \frac{s^2 + (1/LC)}{s^2 + (1/RC)s + (1/LC)}$$

$$\frac{1}{LC} = 25 \times 10^8; \qquad \frac{1}{RC} = 5000$$

$$H(s) = \frac{s^2 + 25 \times 10^8}{s^2 + 5000s + 25 \times 10^8}$$

$$H(j\omega) = \frac{25 \times 10^8 - \omega^2}{(25 \times 10^8 - \omega^2) + j5000\omega}$$

$$H_1 = \frac{24 \times 10^8}{24 \times 10^8 + j5 \times 10^7} = 0.99978\underline{/-1.19^\circ}$$

$$H_3 = \frac{16 \times 10^8}{16 \times 10^8 + j15 \times 10^7} = 0.99563\underline{/-5.36^\circ}$$

$$H_5 = \frac{0}{j25 \times 10^7} = 0$$

$$H_7 = \frac{-24 \times 10^8}{-24 \times 10^8 + j35 \times 10^7} = 0.98953\underline{/8.30^\circ}$$

From Problem 16.25

$$\mathbf{V}_{g1} = 840\underline{/0^\circ}\text{ V}; \qquad \mathbf{V}_{g3} = 280\underline{/180^\circ}\text{ V}$$

$$\mathbf{V}_{g5} = 168\underline{/0^\circ}\text{ V}; \qquad \mathbf{V}_{g7} = 120\underline{/180^\circ}\text{ V}$$

Thus,

$$\mathbf{V}_{o1} = 840\angle 0^\circ H_1 = 839.82\angle -1.19^\circ \text{ V}$$

$$\mathbf{V}_{o3} = 280\angle 180^\circ H_3 = 278.78\angle 174.64^\circ \text{ V}$$

$$\mathbf{V}_{o5} = 168\angle 0^\circ H_5 = 0 \text{ V}$$

$$\mathbf{V}_{o7} = 120\angle 180^\circ H_7 = 118.74\angle -171.70^\circ \text{ V}$$

$$v_o = 839.82\cos(10{,}000t - 1.19^\circ) + 278.78\cos(30{,}000t + 174.64^\circ)$$

$$= +0 + 118.74\cos(70{,}000t - 171.70^\circ) + \cdots \text{ V}$$

[b] The 5th harmonic, that is, the voltage having a frequency of 50 krad/s. The circuit is a passive bandreject filter with a center frequency of 50 krad/s.

P 16.27 [a] $\omega_o = \dfrac{2\pi}{T} = 240\pi$ rad/s

$$f(t) = \frac{2(54\pi)}{\pi} - \frac{4(54\pi)}{\pi}\sum_{n=1}^{\infty}\frac{\cos n(240\pi)t}{4n^2-1}$$

$$= 108 - 216\sum_{n=1}^{\infty}\frac{\cos n(240\pi)t}{4n^2-1}$$

$$v_{g1} = \frac{216}{3}\cos 240\pi t = 72\cos 240\pi t$$

$$v_{g2} = \frac{216}{15}\cos 480\pi t = 14.4\cos 480\pi t$$

$$v_{g3} = \frac{216}{35}\cos 720\pi t$$

$$\mathbf{V}_{g1} = 72\angle 0^\circ \text{ V}$$

$$\mathbf{V}_{g2} = 14.4\angle 0^\circ \text{ V}$$

$$\mathbf{V}_{g3} = (216/25)\angle 0^\circ \text{ V}$$

$$H(s) = \frac{V_o}{V_g} = \frac{(1/LC)}{s^2 + (1/RC)s + (1/LC)}$$

$$\frac{1}{LC} = \frac{10^6}{25} = 4\times 10^4; \qquad \frac{1}{RC} = \frac{10^6}{(5000)(2.5)} = 80$$

$$H(s) = \frac{4\times 10^4}{s^2 + 80s + 4\times 10^4}$$

$$H(j\omega) = \frac{4\times 10^4}{4\times 10^4 - \omega^2 + j80\omega}$$

$$H(j0) = 1\underline{/0^\circ}$$

$$H_1(j240\pi) = \frac{4\times 10^4}{4\times 10^4 - 5.76\pi^2\times 10^4 + j1.92\times 10^4\pi}$$

$$= 0.0752\underline{/-173.49^\circ}$$

$$H_2(j480\pi) = \frac{4\times 10^4}{4\times 10^4 - 23.04\pi^2\times 10^4 + j3.84\times 10^4\pi}$$

$$= 0.0179\underline{/-176.91^\circ}$$

$$H_3(j720\pi) = \frac{4\times 10^4}{4\times 10^4 - 51.84\pi^2\times 10^4 + j5.76\times 10^4\pi}$$

$$= 0.0079\underline{/-177.96^\circ}$$

$$\mathbf{V}_{o1} = 72\underline{/0^\circ}H_1 = 5.41\underline{/-173.49^\circ}\text{ V}$$

$$\mathbf{V}_{o2} = 14.4\underline{/0^\circ}H_2 = 0.2575\underline{/-176.91^\circ}\text{ V}$$

$$\mathbf{V}_{o3} = (216/25)\underline{/0^\circ}H_3 = 0.0486\underline{/-177.96^\circ}\text{ V}$$

$$V_{odc} = (108)(1) = 108\text{ V}$$

$$v_o = 108 - 5.41\cos(240\pi t - 173.49^\circ) - 0.2575\cos(480\pi t - 176.91^\circ)$$
$$- 0.0486\cos(720\pi t - 177.96^\circ) - \cdots\text{ V}$$

[b] The circuit is a low pass filter. Hence, the harmonic terms are greatly reduced in the output voltage.

P 16.28 $$H(s) = \frac{I_o}{I_g} = \frac{(1/LC)}{s^2 + \left(\frac{1}{R_1C} + \frac{R_2}{L}\right)s + \left(\frac{R_1+R_2}{R_1}\right)\left(\frac{1}{LC}\right)}$$

where $R_1 = 800\,\Omega$ and $R_2 = 200\,\Omega$. Thus

$$H(s) = \frac{20\times 10^8}{s^2 + 60{,}000s + 25\times 10^8}$$

$$\omega_o = \frac{2\pi}{T} = \frac{2\pi}{0.2\pi}(10^3) = 10\text{ krad/s}; \qquad 5\omega_o = 50\text{ krad/s}$$

$$H(j50{,}000) = \frac{20\times 10^8}{j(60{,}000)(50{,}000)} = -j\frac{2}{3}$$

$$i_g(t) = \frac{8A}{\pi^2} \sum_{n=1,3,5,}^{\infty} \frac{1}{n^2} \sin(n\pi/2) \sin n\omega_o t$$

$$\therefore \quad i_{g5}(t) = \frac{8(30\pi^2)}{\pi^2} \cdot \frac{1}{25}(1) \sin 50{,}000t$$

$$= 9.6 \sin 50{,}000t \text{ A} = 9.6 \cos(50{,}000t - 90^\circ) \text{ A}$$

$$\mathbf{I}_{g5} = 9.6\underline{/-90^\circ}; \qquad H(j50{,}000) = \frac{2}{3}\underline{/-90^\circ}$$

$$\mathbf{I}_{o5} = (9.6)(2/3)\underline{/-180^\circ} = 6.4\underline{/-180^\circ} \text{ A}$$

$$\therefore \quad i_{o5} = 6.4 \cos(50{,}000t - 180^\circ) = -6.4 \cos(50{,}000t) \text{ A}$$

P 16.29 $\omega_o = \dfrac{2\pi}{T} = \dfrac{2\pi}{10\pi} \times 10^6 = 200 \text{ krad/s}$

$$\therefore \quad n = \frac{3 \times 10^6}{0.2 \times 10^6} = 15; \qquad n = \frac{5 \times 10^6}{0.2 \times 10^6} = 25$$

$$H(s) = \frac{V_o}{V_g} = \frac{(1/RC)s}{s^2 + (1/RC)s + (1/LC)}$$

$$\frac{1}{RC} = \frac{10^{12}}{(250 \times 10^3)(4)} = 10^6; \qquad \frac{1}{LC} = \frac{(10^3)(10^{12})}{10)(4)} = 25 \times 10^{12}$$

$$H(s) = \frac{10^6 s}{s^2 + 10^6 s + 25 \times 10^{12}}$$

$$H(j\omega) = \frac{j\omega \times 10^6}{(25 \times 10^{12} - \omega^2) + j10^6\omega}$$

15th harmonic input:

$$v_{g15} = (150)(1/15) \sin(15\pi/2) \cos 15\omega_o t = -10 \cos 3 \times 10^6 t \text{ V}$$

$$\therefore \quad \mathbf{V}_{g15} = 10\underline{/-180^\circ} \text{ V}$$

$$H(j3 \times 10^6) = \frac{j3}{16 + j3} = 0.1843\underline{/79.38^\circ}$$

$$\mathbf{V}_{o15} = (10)(0.1843)\underline{/-100.62^\circ} \text{ V}$$

$v_{o15} = 1.84\cos(3\times10^6 t - 100.62^\circ)$ V

25th harmonic input:

$v_{g25} = (150)(1/25)\sin(25\pi/2)\cos 5\times10^6 t = 6\cos 5\times10^6 t$ V

$\therefore\quad \mathbf{V}_{g25} = 6\underline{/0^\circ}$ V

$$H(j5\times10^6) = \frac{j5}{0+j5} = 1\underline{/0^\circ}$$

$\mathbf{V}_{o25} = 6\underline{/0^\circ}$ V

$v_{o25} = 6\cos 5\times10^6 t$ V

P 16.30 [a] $v(t) = \frac{480}{\pi}\{\sin\omega_o t + \frac{1}{3}\sin 3\omega_o t + \frac{1}{5}\sin 5\omega_o t + \frac{1}{7}\sin 7\omega_o t + \frac{19}{\sin}9\omega_o t + \cdots$

$$V_{\text{rms}} = \frac{480}{\pi}\sqrt{\left(\frac{1}{\sqrt{2}}\right)^2 + \left(\frac{1}{3\sqrt{2}}\right)^2 + \left(\frac{1}{5\sqrt{2}}\right)^2 + \left(\frac{1}{7\sqrt{2}}\right)^2 + \left(\frac{1}{9\sqrt{2}}\right)^2}$$

$$= \frac{480}{\pi\sqrt{2}}\sqrt{1 + \frac{1}{9} + \frac{1}{25} + \frac{1}{49} + \frac{1}{81}}$$

$$= 117.55\text{ V}$$

[b] $\%\text{ error} = \left(\frac{117.55}{120} - 1\right)(100) = -2.04\%$

[c] $v(t) = \frac{960}{\pi^2}\left\{\sin\omega_o t_{\frac{1}{9}}\sin 3\omega_o t + \frac{1}{25}\sin 5\omega_o t\right.$

$$\left. - \frac{1}{49}\sin 7\omega_o t + \frac{1}{81}\sin 9\omega_o t - \cdots\right\}$$

$$V_{\text{rms}} \cong \frac{960}{\pi^2\sqrt{2}}\sqrt{1 + \frac{1}{81} + \frac{1}{625} + \frac{1}{2401} + \frac{1}{6561}}$$

$$\cong 69.2765\text{ V}$$

$$V_{\text{rms}} = \frac{120}{\sqrt{3}} = 69.2820\text{ V}$$

$$\%\text{ error} = \left(\frac{69.2765}{69.2820} - 1\right)(100) = -0.0081\%$$

P 16.31 [a] $v(t) \approx \frac{340}{\pi} - \frac{680}{\pi}\left\{\frac{1}{3}\cos\omega_o t + \frac{1}{15}\cos 2\omega_o t + \cdots\right\}$

$$V_{\text{rms}} \approx \sqrt{\left(\frac{340}{\pi}\right)^2 + \left(\frac{680}{\pi}\right)^2\left[\left(\frac{1}{3\sqrt{2}}\right)^2 + \left(\frac{1}{15\sqrt{2}}\right)^2\right]}$$

$$= \frac{340}{\pi}\sqrt{1 + 4\left(\frac{1}{18} + \frac{1}{450}\right)} = 120.0819\text{ V}$$

[b] $V_{\text{rms}} = \frac{170}{\sqrt{2}} = 120.2082$

$$\%\text{ error} = \left(\frac{120.0819}{120.2082} - 1\right)(100) = -0.11\%$$

[c] $v(t) \approx \frac{170}{\pi} + 85\sin\omega_o t - \frac{340}{3\pi}\cos 2\omega_o t$

$$V_{\text{rms}} \approx \sqrt{\left(\frac{170}{\pi}\right)^2 + \left(\frac{85}{\sqrt{2}}\right)^2 + \left(\frac{340}{3\sqrt{2}\pi}\right)^2} \approx 84.8021\text{ V}$$

$$V_{\text{rms}} = \frac{170}{2} = 85\text{ V}$$

$$\%\text{ error} = -0.23\%$$

P 16.32 [a] Half-wave symmetry $a_v = 0$, $a_k = b_k = 0$, even k

$$a_k = \frac{4}{T}\int_0^{T/4}\frac{4I_m}{T}t\cos k\omega_0 t\,dt = \frac{16I_m}{T^2}\int_0^{T/4} t\cos k\omega_0 t\,dt$$

$$= \frac{16I_m}{T^2}\left\{\frac{\cos k\omega_0 t}{k^2\omega_0^2} + \frac{t}{k\omega_0}\sin k\omega_0 t\,\Big|_0^{T/4}\right\}$$

$$= \frac{16I_m}{T^2}\left\{0 + \frac{T}{4k\omega_0}\sin\frac{k\pi}{2} - \frac{1}{k^2\omega_0^2}\right\}$$

$$a_k = \frac{2I_m}{\pi k}\left[\sin\left(\frac{k\pi}{2}\right) - \frac{2}{\pi k}\right], \qquad k\text{—odd}$$

$$b_k = \frac{4}{T}\int_0^{T/4}\frac{4I_m}{T}t\sin k\omega_0 t\,dt = \frac{16I_m}{T^2}\int_0^{T/4} t\sin k\omega_0 t\,dt$$

$$= \frac{16I_m}{T^2}\left\{\frac{\sin k\omega_0 t}{k^2\omega_0^2} - \frac{t}{k\omega_0}\cos k\omega_0 t\,\Big|_0^{T/4}\right\} = \frac{4I_m}{\pi^2 k^2}\sin\left(\frac{k\pi}{2}\right)$$

[b] $a_k - jb_k = \frac{2I_m}{\pi k}\left\{\left[\sin\left(\frac{k\pi}{2}\right) - \frac{2}{\pi k}\right] - \left[j\frac{2}{\pi k}\sin\left(\frac{k\pi}{2}\right)\right]\right\}$

$$a_1 - jb_1 = \frac{2I_m}{\pi}\left\{\left(1 - \frac{2}{\pi}\right) - j\frac{2}{\pi}\right\} = 0.47I_m\underline{/-60.28^\circ}$$

$$a_3 - jb_3 = \frac{2I_m}{3\pi}\left\{\left(-1 - \frac{2}{3\pi}\right) + j\left(\frac{2}{3\pi}\right)\right\} = 0.26I_m\underline{/170.07^\circ}$$

$$a_5 - jb_5 = \frac{2I_m}{5\pi}\left\{\left(1 - \frac{2}{5\pi}\right) - j\left(\frac{2}{5\pi}\right)\right\} = 0.11I_m\underline{/-8.30^\circ}$$

$$a_7 - jb_7 = \frac{2I_m}{7\pi}\left\{\left(-1 - \frac{2}{7\pi}\right) + j\left(\frac{2}{7\pi}\right)\right\} = 0.10I_m\underline{/175.23^\circ}$$

$$i_g = 0.47I_m\cos(\omega_0 t - 60.28^\circ) + 0.26I_m\cos(3\omega_0 t + 170.07^\circ)$$
$$+0.11I_m\cos(5\omega_0 t - 8.30^\circ) + 0.10I_m\cos(7\omega_0 t + 175.23^\circ) + \cdots$$

[c] $$I_g = \sqrt{\sum_{n=1,3,5}^{\infty}\left(\frac{A_n^2}{2}\right)}$$

$$\cong I_m\sqrt{\frac{(0.47)^2 + (0.26)^2 + (0.11)^2 + (0.10)^2}{2}} = 0.39I_m$$

[d] $$\text{Area} = 2\int_0^{T/4}\left(\frac{4I_m}{T}t\right)^2 dt = \left(\frac{32I_m^2}{T^2}\right)\left(\frac{t^3}{3}\right)\Big|_0^{T/4} = \frac{I_m^2 T}{6}$$

$$I_g = \sqrt{\frac{1}{T}\left(\frac{I_m^2 T}{6}\right)} = \frac{I_m}{\sqrt{6}}$$

[e] $$\%\ \text{error} = \left(\frac{\text{estimated}}{\text{exact}} - 1\right)100 = \left(\frac{0.3927I_m}{(I_m/\sqrt{6})} - 1\right)100 = -3.8\%$$

P 16.33 [a] v_g has hws, qws, and is odd

$$\therefore\ a_v = 0,\ a_k = 0 \text{ all } k,\ b_k = 0\ k\text{-even}$$

$$b_k = \frac{8}{T}\int_0^{T/4} f(t)\sin k\omega_o t\,dt, \quad k\text{-odd}$$

$$= \frac{8}{T}\left\{\int_0^{T/8} V_m \sin k\omega_o t\,dt + \int_{T/8}^{T/4}\frac{V_m}{2}\sin k\omega_o t\,dt\right\}$$

$$= \frac{8V_m}{T}\left[-\frac{\cos k\omega_o t}{k\omega_o}\right|_0^{T/8} + \frac{8V_m}{2T}\left[-\frac{\cos k\omega_o t}{k\omega_o}\right|_{T/8}^{T/4}$$

$$= \frac{8V_m}{k\omega_o T}\left[1 - \cos\frac{k\pi}{4}\right] + \frac{8V_m}{2Tk\omega_o}\left[\cos\frac{k\pi}{4} - 0\right]$$

$$= \frac{8V_m}{k\omega_o T}\left\{1 - \cos\frac{k\pi}{4} + \frac{1}{2}\cos\frac{k\pi}{4}\right\}$$

$$= \frac{4V_m}{\pi k}\left\{1 - 0.5\cos\frac{k\pi}{4}\right\}$$

$$b_1 = \frac{4V_m}{\pi}\left(1 - 0.5\cos\frac{\pi}{4}\right) = 0.8231V_m$$

$$b_3 = \frac{4V_m}{3\pi}\left(1 - 0.5\cos\frac{3\pi}{4}\right) = 0.5745V_m$$

$$b_5 = \frac{4V_m}{5\pi}\left(1 - 0.5\cos\frac{5\pi}{4}\right) = 0.3447V_m$$

$$b_7 = \frac{4V_m}{7\pi}\left(1 - 0.5\cos\frac{7\pi}{4}\right) = 0.1176V_m$$

$$V_{grms} \approx \mathbf{V}_m\sqrt{\frac{(0.8231)^2 + (0.5745)^2 + (0.3447)^2 + (0.1176)^2}{2}}$$

$$V_{grms} \approx 0.7550V_m$$

[b] $\text{Area} = 2\left[2V_m^2\left(\frac{T}{8}\right) + \frac{V_m^2}{4}\left(\frac{T}{4}\right)\right] = \frac{5}{8}V_m^2T$

$$V_{grms} = \sqrt{\frac{1}{T}\frac{5V_m^2}{8}T} = V_m\sqrt{\frac{5}{8}} = 0.7906\,V_m$$

[c] $\%\ \text{Error} = \left[\frac{0.7550V_m}{0.7906V_m} - 1\right]100$

$$\text{Error} = -4.5\%$$

P 16.34 [a] Figure P16.34(b): $t_a = 0.2s$; $t_b = 0.6s$

$$v = 50t \quad 0 \leq t \leq 0.2$$

$$v = -50t + 20 \quad 0.2 \leq t \leq 0.6$$

$$v = 25t - 25 \quad 0.6 \leq t \leq 1.0$$

$$\text{Area 1} = A_1 = \int_0^{0.2} 2500t^2\,dt = \frac{20}{3}$$

$$\text{Area 2} = A_2 = \int_{0.2}^{0.6} 100(4 - 20t + 25t^2)\,dt = \frac{40}{3}$$

$$\text{Area 3} = A_3 = \int_{0.6}^{1.0} 625(t^2 - 2t + 1)\,dt = \frac{40}{3}$$

$$A_1 + A_2 + A_3 = \frac{100}{3}$$

$$V_{rms} = \sqrt{\frac{1}{1}\left(\frac{100}{3}\right)} = \frac{10}{\sqrt{3}}\ \text{V}.$$

Figure P16.34(c): $t_a = t_b = 0.4s$

$v(t) = 25t \quad 0 \leq t \leq 0.4$

$v(t) = \frac{50}{3}(t-1) \quad 0.4 \leq t \leq 1$

$$A_1 = \int_0^{0.4} 625t^2\,dt = \frac{40}{3}$$

$$A_2 = \int_{0.4}^{1.0} \frac{2500}{9}(t^2 - 2t + 1)\,dt = \frac{60}{3}$$

$$A_1 + A_2 = \frac{100}{3}$$

$$V_{\text{rms}} = \sqrt{\frac{1}{T}(A_1 + A_2)} = \sqrt{\frac{1}{1}\left(\frac{100}{3}\right)} = \frac{10}{\sqrt{3}}\,\text{V}.$$

Figure P16.34 (d): $t_a = t_b = 1$

$v = 10t \quad 0 \leq t \leq 1$

$$A_1 = \int_0^1 100t^2\,dt = \frac{100}{3}$$

$$V_{\text{rms}} = \sqrt{\frac{1}{1}\left(\frac{100}{3}\right)} = \frac{10}{\sqrt{3}}\,\text{V}.$$

P 16.35 [a] $v = 80 + 200\cos(500t + 45^\circ) + 60\cos(1500t - 90^\circ)$ V

$i = 10 + 6\cos(500t - 15^\circ) + 3\cos(1500t + 30^\circ)$ A

$$P = (80)(10) + \frac{1}{2}(200)(6)\cos(60^\circ) + \frac{1}{2}(60)(3)\cos(-120^\circ) = 1055\,\text{W}$$

[b] $$V_{\text{rms}} = \sqrt{(80)^2 + \left(\frac{200}{\sqrt{2}}\right)^2 + \left(\frac{60}{\sqrt{2}}\right)^2} = 167.93\,\text{V}$$

[c] $$I_{\text{rms}} = \sqrt{(10)^2 + \left(\frac{6}{\sqrt{2}}\right)^2 + \left(\frac{3}{\sqrt{2}}\right)^2} = 11.07\,\text{A}$$

P 16.36 [a] From Example 16.1

$$a_v = \frac{1}{2}(270\pi) = 135\pi\,\text{V}$$

$a_k = 0, \quad$ all k

$$b_k = \frac{-270\pi}{\pi k} = \frac{-270}{k} \quad \text{all } k$$

$$\therefore \quad v(t) = 135\pi - 270\sin\omega_o t - 135\sin 2\omega_o t - 90\sin 3\omega_o t - \cdots$$

$$V_{\rm rms} = \sqrt{(135\pi)^2 + \left(\frac{270}{\sqrt{2}}\right)^2 + \left(\frac{135}{\sqrt{2}}\right)^2 + \left(\frac{90}{\sqrt{2}}\right)^2} = 479.05$$

$$P = \frac{(479.05)^2}{81\pi^2} = 287.06\,\text{W}$$

[b] $V_{\rm rms} = \dfrac{270\pi}{\sqrt{3}} = 489.73\,\text{V}$

$$\therefore\quad P = \frac{(489.72)^2}{81\pi^2} = 300\,\text{W}$$

[c] $\%\ \text{error} = \left(\dfrac{287.06}{300} - 1\right)(100) = -4.31\%$

P 16.37 [a] $a_v = \dfrac{2\left(\frac{1}{2}\frac{T}{4}V_m\right)}{T} = \dfrac{V_m}{4}$

$$a_k = \frac{4}{T}\int_0^{T/4}\left[V_m - \frac{4V_m}{T}t\right]\cos k\omega_o t\,dt$$

$$= \frac{4V_m}{\pi^2 k^2}\left[1 - \cos\frac{k\pi}{2}\right]$$

$b_k = 0,\quad$ all k

$$a_v = \frac{60}{4} = 15\,\text{V}$$

$$a_1 = \frac{240}{\pi^2}$$

$$a_2 = \frac{240}{4\pi^2}(1 - \cos\pi) = \frac{120}{\pi^2}$$

$$V_{\rm rms} = \sqrt{(15)^2 + \frac{1}{2}\left[\left(\frac{240}{\pi^2}\right)^2 + \left(\frac{120}{\pi^2}\right)^2\right]} = 24.38\,\text{V}$$

$$P = \frac{(24.38)^2}{10} = 59.46\,\text{W}$$

[b] Area under v^2; $\qquad 0 \le t \le T/4$

$$v^2 = 3600 - \frac{28{,}800}{T}t + \frac{57{,}600}{T^2}t^2$$

$$A = 2\int_0^{T/4}\left[3600 - \frac{28{,}800}{T}t + \frac{57{,}600}{T^2}t^2\right]dt = 600T$$

$$V_{\rm rms} = \sqrt{\frac{1}{T}600T} = \sqrt{600} = 24.49\,\text{V}$$

$$P = \sqrt{600}^2/10 = 60\,\text{W}$$

[c] Error $= \left(\frac{59.46}{60.00} - 1\right) 100 = -0.9041\%$

P 16.38 $v_g(t) = 25 + \frac{200}{\pi^2} \sum_{n=1,3,5,}^{\infty} \frac{1}{n^2} \sin(n\pi/2) \sin n\omega_o t$ V

$$\omega_o = \frac{2\pi}{T} = \frac{2\pi}{2\pi} \times 10^6 = 1 \text{ Mrad/s}$$

$$v_g(t) = 25 + \frac{200}{\pi^2} \sin \omega_o t - \frac{200}{9\pi^2} \sin 3\omega_o t + \frac{200}{25\pi^2} \sin 5\omega_o t - \cdots \text{ V}$$

$$H(s) = \frac{(1/LC)}{s^2 + (1/RC)s + (1/LC)}$$

$$\frac{1}{LC} = \frac{(10^3)(10^{12})}{(20)(50)} = 10^{12}; \qquad \frac{1}{RC} = \frac{10^{12}}{(20 \times 10^3)(50)} = 10^6$$

$$H(s) = \frac{10^{12}}{s^2 + 10^6 s + 10^{12}}$$

$$H(j\omega) = \frac{10^{12}}{10^{12} - \omega^2 + j10^6\omega}$$

$$H(j0) = 1$$

$$H(j\omega_o) = -j1$$

$$H(j3\omega_o) = \frac{1}{-8 + j3} = 0.1170\underline{/-159.44^\circ}$$

$$H(j5\omega_o) = \frac{1}{-24 + j5} = 0.0408\underline{/-168.23^\circ}$$

$$\therefore \quad v_o = 25 + 20.26 \sin(\omega_o t - 90^\circ) - 0.2635 \sin(3\omega_o t - 159.44^\circ)$$
$$+ 0.0331 \sin(5\omega_o t - 168.23^\circ) - \cdots \text{ V}$$

Now note that the harmonic terms will have a negligible effect on the rms value of v_o, hence a good estimate of the power delivered to the 20 kΩ resistor can be obtained by assuming
$v_o \approx 25 + 20.26 \sin(\omega_o t - 90^\circ)$ V.

$$\therefore \quad V_{orms} \approx \sqrt{25^2 + \left(\frac{20.26}{\sqrt{2}}\right)^2} = 28.82 \text{ V}$$

$$\therefore \quad P \approx \frac{(28.82)^2}{20 \times 10^3} = 41.52 \text{ mW}$$

P 16.39 [a]

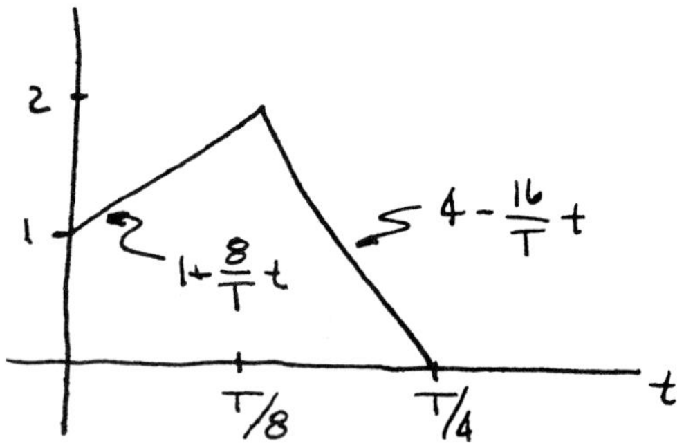

Area under i^2:

$$A = 4\left[\int_0^{T/8}\left(1+\frac{8}{T}t\right)^2 dt + \int_{T/8}^{T/4}\left(4-\frac{16}{T}t\right)^2 dt\right]$$

$$= 4\left[\frac{T}{8}+\frac{T}{8}+\frac{T}{24}+2T-4T+T+\frac{4T}{3}-\frac{T}{6}\right]$$

$$= \frac{44T}{24}$$

$$I_{\text{rms}} = \sqrt{\frac{1}{T}\left(\frac{44T}{24}\right)} = \sqrt{\frac{44}{24}} = 1.35$$

[b] $P = I_{\text{rms}}^2(54) = 99\,\text{W}$

[c] From Problem 16.16:

$$a_1 = 1.8178\text{A}$$

$$i_g \approx 1.8178\cos\omega_o t\ \text{A}$$

$$P = \left(\frac{1.8178}{\sqrt{2}}\right)^2(54) = 89.22\,\text{W}$$

[d] $\%\ \text{error} = \left(\frac{89.22}{99}-1\right) = -9.88\%$

P 16.40 $c_n = \frac{1}{T}\int_0^{T/4} V_m e^{-jn\omega_o t}\,dt = \frac{V_m}{T}\left[\frac{e^{-jn\omega_o t}}{-jn\omega_o}\Big|_0^{T/4}\right]$

$$= \frac{V_m}{Tn\omega_o}[j(e^{-jn\pi/2}-1)] = \frac{V_m}{2\pi n}\sin\frac{n\pi}{2} + j\frac{V_m}{2\pi n}\left(\cos\frac{n\pi}{2}-1\right)$$

$$= \frac{V_m}{2\pi n}\left[\sin\frac{n\pi}{2} - j\left(1-\cos\frac{n\pi}{2}\right)\right]$$

$$v(t) = \sum_{n=-\infty}^{\infty} c_n e^{jn\omega_o t}$$

$$c_o = a_v = \frac{1}{T}\int_0^{T/4} V_m\, dt = \frac{V_m}{4}$$

or

$$c_o = \frac{V_m}{2\pi}\lim_{n\to 0}\left[\frac{\sin(n\pi/2)}{n} - j\frac{1-\cos(n\pi/2)}{n}\right]$$

$$= \frac{V_m}{2\pi}\lim_{n\to 0}\left[\frac{(\pi/2)\cos(n\pi/2)}{1} - j\frac{(\pi/2)\sin(n\pi/2)}{1}\right]$$

$$= \frac{V_m}{2\pi}\left[\frac{\pi}{2} - j0\right] = \frac{V_m}{4}$$

Note it is much easier to use $c_o = a_v$ than to use L'Hopital's rule to find the limit of 0/0.

P 16.41 $c_o = a_v = \left(\frac{1}{2}(\frac{T}{4})I_m(2)\right)\frac{1}{T} = \frac{I_m}{4}$

$$c_n = \frac{1}{T}\int_{-T/4}^{0} -\frac{4I_m}{T}te^{-jn\omega_o t}\, dt + \frac{1}{T}\int_0^{T/4}\frac{4I_m}{T}te^{-jn\omega_o t}\, dt$$

$$= \text{Int1} + \text{Int2}$$

$$\text{Int1} = \frac{-4I_m}{T^2}\left[\frac{e^{-jn\omega_o t}}{-n^2\omega_o^2}(-jn\omega_o t - 1)\Big|_{-T/4}^{0}\right]$$

$$= \frac{-I_m}{(n\pi)^2}\left[1 - e^{jn\pi/2}(-jn\pi/2 + 1)\right]$$

$$\text{Int2} = \frac{4I_m}{T^2}\left[\frac{e^{-jn\omega_o t}}{-n^2\omega_o^2}(-jn\omega_o t - 1)\Big|_0^{T/4}\right]$$

$$= \frac{I_m}{(n\pi)^2}\left[e^{-jn\pi/2}(jn\pi/2 + 1) - 1\right]$$

$$\therefore\ c_n = \frac{I_m}{n^2\pi^2}[e^{-jn\pi/2}(1 + jn\pi/2) - 1 + e^{jn\pi/2}(1 - jn\pi/2) - 1]$$

$$= \frac{I_m}{n^2\pi^2}[2\cos(n\pi/2) + n\pi\sin(n\pi/2) - 2]$$

P 16.42 [a] $I_{\text{rms}} = \sqrt{\frac{1}{T}\int_0^T i^2\, dt} = \sqrt{\frac{2}{T}\int_0^{T/4}\left(\frac{16I_m^2}{T^2}\right)t^2\, dt}$

$$= \sqrt{\frac{32I_m^2}{T^3}\cdot\frac{t^2}{3}\Big|_0^{T/4}} = \frac{I_m}{\sqrt{6}} = \frac{20}{\sqrt{6}} = 8.16\,\text{A}$$

$$P = 60I_m^2 = 60\left(\frac{400}{6}\right) = 4000\,\text{W}$$

[b] From the solution to Problem 16.41

$$c_0 = \frac{20}{4} = 5\,\text{A}$$

$$c_1 = \frac{20}{\pi^2}[\pi\sin(\pi/2) - 2] = 2.31$$

$$c_2 = \frac{20}{4\pi^2}[-2 - 2] = -2.03$$

$$c_3 = \frac{20}{9\pi^2}[3\pi\sin(3\pi/2) - 2] = -2.57$$

$$c_4 = \frac{20}{16\pi^2}[2 - 2] = 0$$

$$c_5 = \frac{20}{25\pi^2}[5\pi - 2] = 1.11$$

$$I_{\text{rms}} = \sqrt{c_o^2 + 2\sum_{n=1}^{\infty}|c_n|^2}$$

$$= \sqrt{25 + 2(2.31^2 + 2.03^2 + 2.57^2 + 1.11^2)}$$

$$= \sqrt{25 + 34.62} = 7.72\,\text{A}$$

[c] $P = (7.72)^2(60) = 3577.17\,\text{W}$

$$\%\ \text{error} = \left(\frac{3577.17}{4000} - 1\right)(100) = -10.57\%$$

P 16.43 [a] $c_n = \dfrac{1}{T}\displaystyle\int_{-T/2}^{T/2} \frac{2V_m}{T} t e^{-jn\omega_o t}\,dt$

$$= \frac{2V_m}{T^2}\left[\frac{e^{-jn\omega_o t}}{-n^2\omega_o^2}(-jn\omega_o t - 1)\Bigg|_{-T/2}^{T/2}\right]$$

$$= \frac{2V_m}{4\pi^2 n^2}[e^{-jn\pi}(jn\pi + 1) - e^{jn\pi}(-jn\pi + 1)]$$

$$= \frac{-jV_m}{\pi^2 n^2}[\sin n\pi - n\pi\cos n\pi]$$

$\sin n\pi = 0 \quad$ for all n

$$c_n = \frac{jV_m}{\pi^2 n^2} n\pi\cos n\pi = j\frac{V_m}{n\pi}\cos n\pi$$

[b] $c_{-1} = j72; \qquad c_1 = -j72$

$c_{-2} = -j36; \qquad c_2 = j36$

$c_{-3} = j24; \qquad c_3 = -j24$

$c_{-4} = -j18; \qquad c_4 = j18$

[c] $\frac{V_o}{R_2} + V_o sC + \frac{V_o}{sL} + \frac{V_o - V_g}{R_1} = 0$

$$\therefore \quad H(s) = \frac{V_o}{V_G} = \frac{(1/R_1C)s}{s^2 + \left(\frac{R_1+R_2}{R_1R_2C}\right)s + (1/LC)}$$

$$= \frac{3200s}{s^2 + 4000s + 16 \times 10^8}$$

$$H(jn\omega_o) = \frac{j3200n\omega_o}{16 \times 10^8 - n^2\omega_o^2 + j4000n\omega_o}$$

$$\omega_o = \frac{2\pi}{50\pi} \times 10^6 = 40{,}000 \text{ rad/s}$$

$$\therefore \quad H(jn\omega_o) = \frac{j1.28n}{16(1-n^2) + j1.6n}$$

$H_{-1} = 0.8\underline{/0^\circ}$; $\quad H_1 = 0.8\underline{/0^\circ}$

$H_{-2} = 0.0532\underline{/86.19^\circ}$; $\quad H_1 = 0.0532\underline{/-86.19^\circ}$

$H_{-3} = 0.0300\underline{/87.85^\circ}$; $\quad H_1 = 0.0300\underline{/-87.85^\circ}$

$H_{-4} = 0.0213\underline{/88.47^\circ}$; $\quad H_1 = 0.0213\underline{/-88.47^\circ}$

$c_o = 0$

$c_{-1} = (72\underline{/90^\circ})(0.8\underline{/0^\circ}) = 57.60\underline{/90^\circ}$

$c_1 = 57.60\underline{/-90^\circ}$

$c_{-2} = (36\underline{/-90^\circ})(0.0532\underline{/86.18^\circ}) = 1.92\underline{/-3.81^\circ}$

$c_2 = 1.92\underline{/3.81^\circ}$

$c_{-3} = (24\underline{/90^\circ})(0.0300\underline{/87.85^\circ}) = 0.72\underline{/177.85^\circ}$

$c_3 = 0.72\underline{/-177.85^\circ}$

$c_{-4} = (18\underline{/-90^\circ})(0.0213\underline{/88.47^\circ}) = 0.38\underline{/-1.53^\circ}$

$c_4 = 0.38\underline{/1.53^\circ}$

[d] $V_{orms} \approx \sqrt{2\sum_{n=1}^{4} |c_n|^2}$

$$= \sqrt{2(57.6^2 + 1.92^2 + 0.72^2 + 0.38^2)} = 81.51 \text{ V}$$

$$P = \frac{(81.51)^2}{200} \times 10^{-3} = 33.22 \text{ mW}$$

P 16.44 [a] $V_{\text{rms}} = \sqrt{\frac{2}{T}\int_0^{T/2} \frac{4v_m^2}{T^2}t^2\,dt} = \frac{V_m}{\sqrt{3}} + \frac{72\pi}{\sqrt{3}} = 130.59$ V

[b] $V_{\text{rms}} \approx \sqrt{2\sum_{n=1}^{4}|c_n|^2} = \sqrt{2(72^2+36^2+24^2+18^2)} = 121.49$ V

[c] $\%\text{ error} = \left(\frac{121.49}{130.59} - 1\right)(100) = -6.97\%$

P 16.45 [a] From Example 16.3 we have:

$$a_v = \frac{40}{4} = 10\,\text{V}, \qquad a_k = \frac{40}{\pi k}\sin\left(\frac{k\pi}{2}\right)$$

$$b_k = \frac{40}{\pi k}\left[1 - \cos\left(\frac{k\pi}{2}\right)\right], \qquad A_k\underline{/-\theta_k^\circ} = a_k - jb_k$$

$A_1 = 18.01$ V $\quad \theta_1 = -45^\circ, \quad A_2 = 12.73$ V, $\quad \theta_2 = -90^\circ$

$A_3 = 6$ V, $\quad \theta_3 = -135^\circ, \quad A_4 = 0, \quad A_5 = 3.6$ V, $\quad \theta_5 = -45^\circ$

$A_6 = 4.24$ V, $\quad \theta_6 = -90^\circ, \quad A_7 = 2.57$ V, $\quad \theta_7 = -135^\circ$

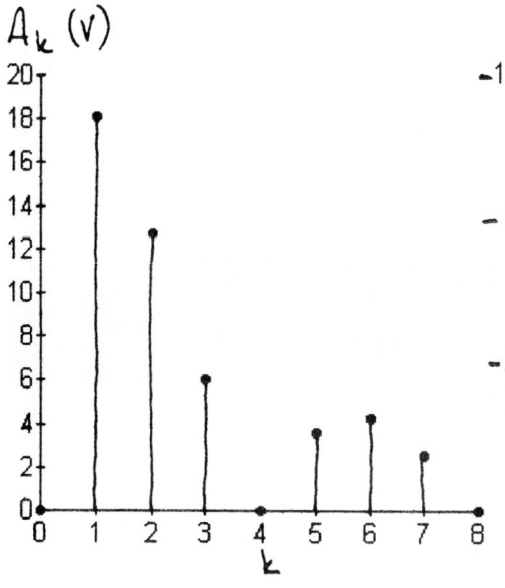

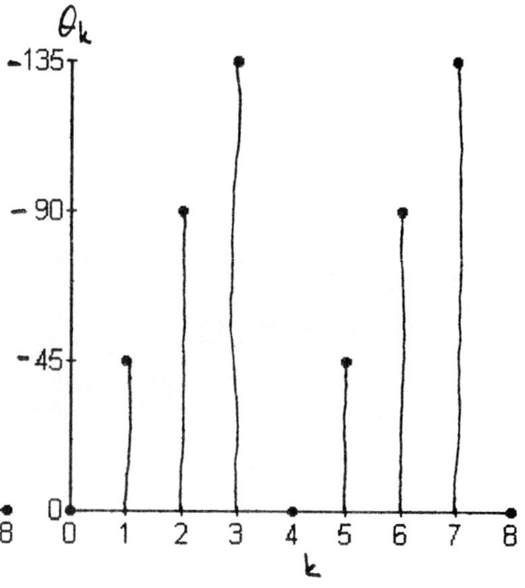

[b] $C_n = \frac{a_n - jb_n}{2}, \qquad C_{-n} = \frac{a_n + jb_n}{2} = C_n^*$

$C_0 = a_v = 10$ V $\qquad C_3 = 3\underline{/135^\circ}$ V $\qquad C_6 = 2.12\underline{/90^\circ}$ V

$C_1 = 9\underline{/45^\circ}$ V $\qquad C_{-3} = 3\underline{/-135^\circ}$ V $\qquad C_{-6} = 2.12\underline{/-90^\circ}$ V

$C_{-1} = 9\underline{/-45^\circ}$ V $\qquad C_4 = C_{-4} = 0 \qquad C_7 = 1.29\underline{/135^\circ}$ V

$C_2 = 6.37\underline{/90^\circ}$ V $\qquad C_5 = 1.8\underline{/45^\circ}$ V $\qquad C_{-7} = 1.29\underline{/-135^\circ}$ V

$C_{-2} = 6.37\underline{/-90^\circ}$ V $\qquad C_{-5} = 1.8\underline{/-45^\circ}$ V

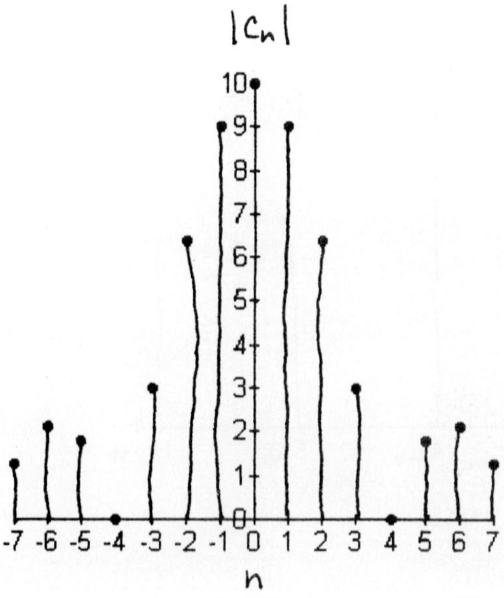

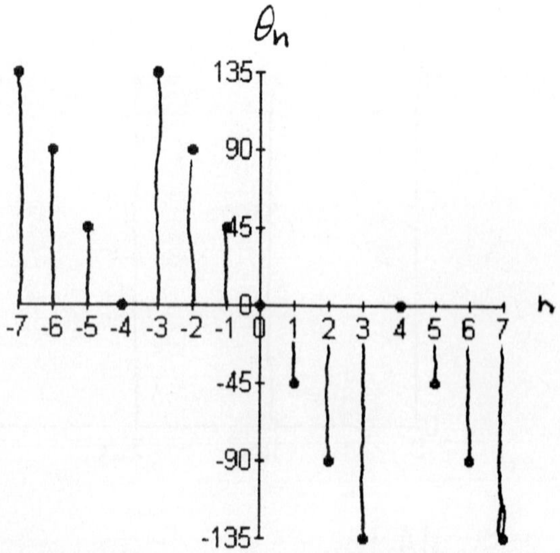

P 16.46 [a] From the solution to Problem 16.36 we have

$$a_v = 135\pi \text{ V}; \qquad a_k = 0, \quad \text{all } k$$

$$b_k = \frac{-270}{k} \quad \text{all } k$$

$$A_k\underline{/-\theta_k} = a_k - jb_k = j\frac{270}{k} = \frac{270}{k}\underline{/90^\circ}$$

$$\therefore \ \theta_k = -90, \quad \text{all } k$$

$$A_1\underline{/-\theta_1} = 270\underline{/90^\circ}; \qquad A_2\underline{/-\theta_2} = 135\underline{/90^\circ}$$

$$A_3\underline{/-\theta_3} = 90\underline{/90^\circ}; \qquad A_4\underline{/-\theta_4} = 67.5\underline{/90^\circ}$$

$$A_5\underline{/-\theta_5} = 54\underline{/90^\circ}; \qquad A_6\underline{/-\theta_6} = 45\underline{/90^\circ}$$

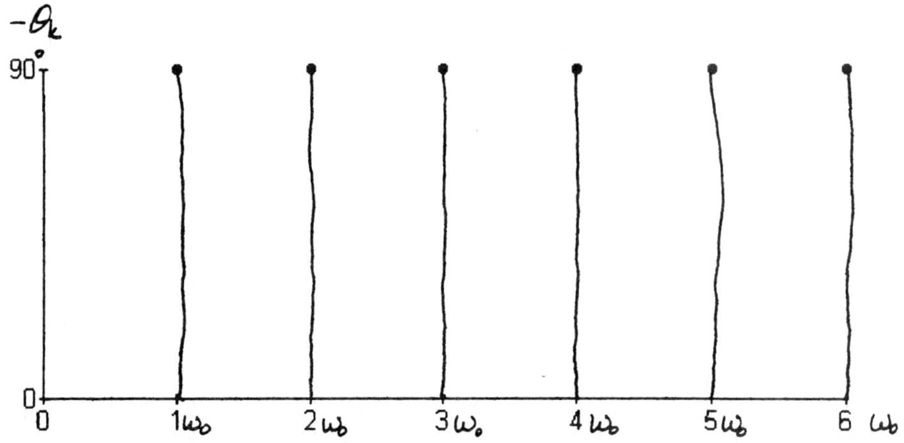

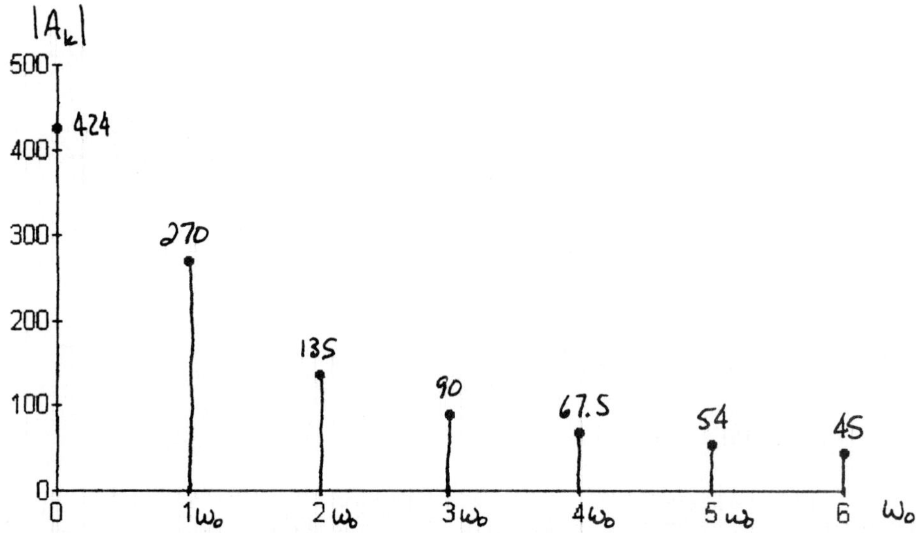

[b] $c_n = \frac{1}{2}(a_n - jb_n) = j\frac{135}{n} = c_n\underline{/\theta_n}$ (see Eq.[16.87])

$$c_{-n} = \frac{1}{2}(a_n + jb_n) = -j\frac{135}{n}$$

$c_1 = 135\underline{/90^\circ}$; $c_{-1} = 135\underline{/-90^\circ}$

$c_2 = 67.5\underline{/90^\circ}$; $c_{-2} = 67.5\underline{/-90^\circ}$

$c_3 = 45\underline{/90^\circ}$; $c_{-3} = 45\underline{/-90^\circ}$

$c_4 = 33.75\underline{/90^\circ}$; $c_{-4} = 33.75\underline{/-90^\circ}$

$c_5 = 27\underline{/90^\circ}$; $c_{-5} = 27\underline{/-90^\circ}$

$c_6 = 22.5\underline{/90^\circ}$; $c_{-6} = 22.5\underline{/-90^\circ}$

$c_o = a_v = 424.12$

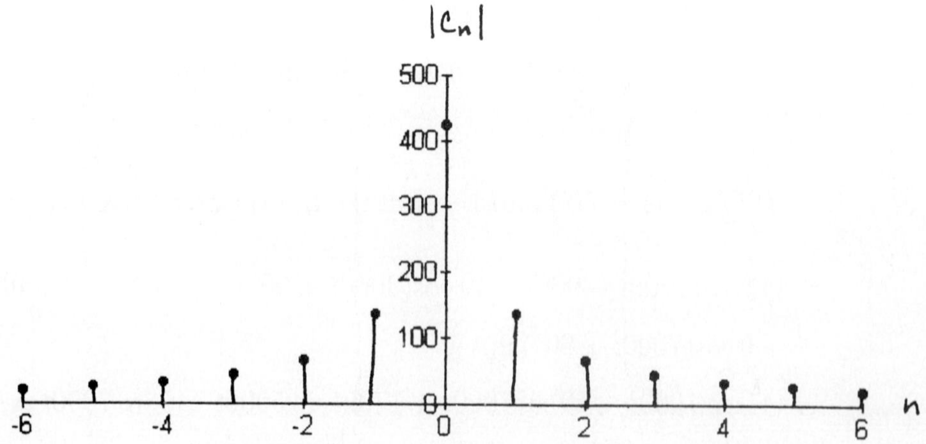

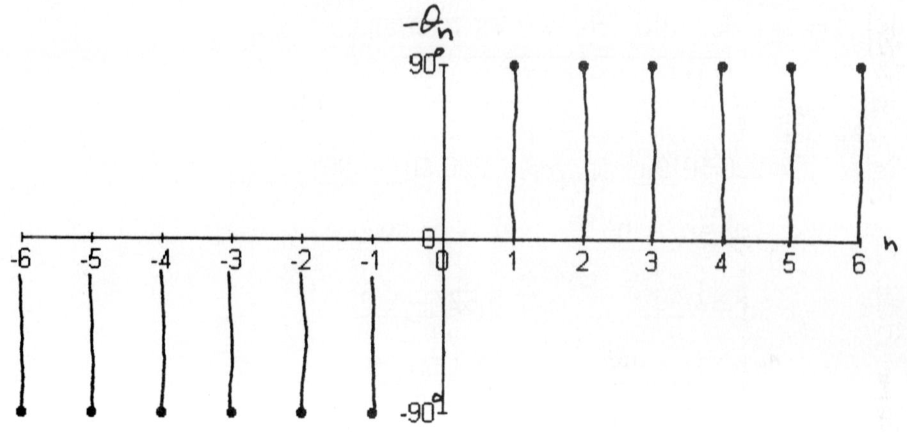

P 16.47 [a] $v = A_1 \cos(\omega_o t - 90^\circ) + A_3 \cos(3\omega_o t + 90^\circ)$

$$+A_5 \cos(5\omega_o t - 90^\circ) + A_7 \cos(7\omega_o t + 90^\circ)$$

$$v = A_1 \sin \omega_o t - A_3 \sin 3\omega_o t + A_5 \sin 5\omega_o t - A_7 \sin 7\omega_o t$$

[b] $v(-t) = -A_1 \sin \omega_o t + A_3 \sin 3\omega_o t - A_5 \sin 5\omega_o t + A_7 \sin 7\omega_o t$

$\therefore \quad v(-t) = -v(t);$ odd function

[c] $v(t - T/2) = A_1 \sin(\omega_o t - \pi) - A_3 \sin(3\omega_o t - 3\pi)$

$$+A_5 \sin(5\omega_o t - 5\pi) - A_7 \sin(7\omega_o t - 7\pi)$$

$$= -A_1 \sin \omega_o t + A_3 \sin 3\omega_o t - A_5 \sin 5\omega_o t + A_7 \sin 7\omega_o t$$

$\therefore \quad v(t - T/2) = -v(t)$, yes, the function has half-wave symmetry

[d] Since the function is odd, with hws, we test to see if

$f(T/2 - t) = f(t)$

$$f(T/2-t) = A_1 \sin(\pi - \omega_o t) - A_3 \sin(3\pi - 3\omega_o t)$$
$$+A_5 \sin(5\pi - 5\omega_o t) - A_7 \sin(7\pi - 7\omega_o t)$$
$$= A_1 \sin \omega_o t - A_3 \sin 3\omega_o t + A_5 \sin 5\omega_o t - A_7 \sin 7\omega_o t$$

$\therefore\ f(T/2-t) = f(t)$ and the voltage has quarter-wave symmetry

P 16.48 [a] $i = 441\cos(1000t - 90^\circ) + 49\cos(3000t + 90^\circ) + 17.64\cos(5000t - 90^\circ)$
$+\, 9\cos(7000t + 90^\circ)$ mA
$= 441 \sin 1000t - 49 \sin 7000t + 17.64 \sin 5000t - 9 \sin 7000t$ mA

[b] $i(t) = -i(-t)$ odd

[c] Yes $A_o = 0,\quad A_n = 0$ for n even

[d] $I_{\text{rms}} = \sqrt{\dfrac{441^2 + 49^2 + 17.64^2 + 9^2}{2}} = 314.07$ mA

[e] $c_{-1} = 220.50\underline{/90^\circ}$; $c_1 = 220.50\underline{/-90^\circ}$

$c_{-3} = 24.50\underline{/-90^\circ}$; $c_3 = 24.50\underline{/90^\circ}$

$c_{-5} = 8.82\underline{/90^\circ}$; $c_5 = 8.82\underline{/-90^\circ}$

$c_{-7} = 4.50\underline{/-90^\circ}$; $c_7 = 4.50\underline{/90^\circ}$

$$i = j4.5e^{-j7000t} + j8.82e^{-j5000t} + j24.5e^{-j3000t} - j220.5e^{-j1000t}$$
$$+\, j220.50e^{j1000t} - 24.5e^{j3000t} + j8.82e^{j5000t} - 4.5e^{j7000t} \text{ mA}$$

[f]

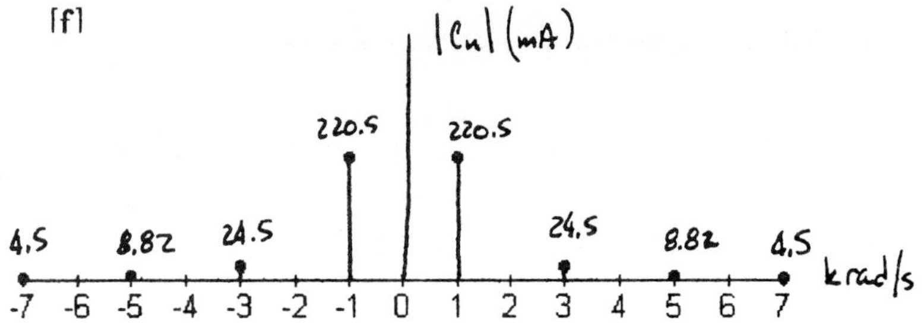

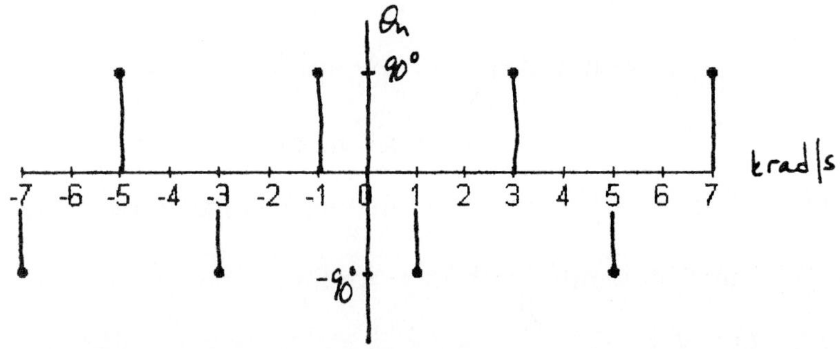

P 16.49 From Table 15.1 we have

$$H(s) = \frac{1}{(s+1)(s^2+s+1)}$$

After scaling we get

$$H'(s) = \frac{10^6}{(s+100)(s^2+100s+10^4)}$$

$$\omega_o = \frac{2\pi}{T} = \frac{2\pi}{5\pi} \times 10^3 = 400 \text{ rad/s}$$

$$\therefore \quad H'(jn\omega_o) = \frac{1}{(1+j4n)[(1-16n^2)+j4n]}$$

It follows that

$$H(j0) = 1\underline{/0^\circ}$$

$$H(j\omega_o) = \frac{1}{(1+j4)(-15+j4)} = 0.0156\underline{/-241.03^\circ}$$

$$H(j2\omega_o) = \frac{1}{(1+j8)(-63+j8)} = 0.00195\underline{/-255.64^\circ}$$

$$v_g(t) = \frac{A}{\pi} + \frac{A}{2}\sin\omega_o t - \frac{2A}{\pi}\sum_{n=2,4,6,}^{\infty} \frac{cosn\omega_o t}{n^2-1}$$

$$= 54 + 27\pi\sin\omega_o t - 36\cos 2\omega_o t - \cdots \text{ V}$$

$$\therefore \quad v_o = 54 + 1.33\sin(400t - 241.03^\circ) - 0.07\cos(800t - 255.64^\circ) - \cdots \text{ V}$$

P 16.50 Using the technique outlined in Problem 16.17 we can derive the Fourier series for $v_g(t)$. We get

$$v_g(t) = 100 + \frac{800}{\pi^2}\sum_{n=1,3,5,}^{\infty} \frac{1}{n^2}\cos n\omega_o t$$

The transfer function of the prototype second-order low pass Butterworth filter is

$$H(s) = \frac{1}{s^2+\sqrt{2}s+1}, \qquad \text{where } \omega_c = 1 \text{ rad/s}$$

Now frequency scale using $k_f = 2000$ to get $\omega_c = 2$ krad/s:

$$H(s) = \frac{4 \times 10^6}{s^2 + 2000\sqrt{2}s + 4 \times 10^6}$$

$$H(j0) = 1$$

$$H(j5000) = \frac{4 \times 10^6}{(j5000)^2 + 2000\sqrt{2}(j5000)^2 + 4 \times 10^6} = 0.1580\underline{/-146.04^\circ}$$

$$H(j15{,}000) = \frac{4 \times 10^6}{(j15{,}000)^2 + 2000\sqrt{2}(j15{,}000)^2 + 4 \times 10^6} = 0.0178\underline{/-169.13^\circ}$$

$$\mathbf{V}_{dc} = 100\,\text{V}$$

$$\mathbf{V}_{g1} = \frac{800}{\pi^2}\underline{/0^\circ}\,\text{V}$$

$$\mathbf{V}_{g3} = \frac{800}{9\pi^2}\underline{/0^\circ}\,\text{V}$$

$$V_{odc} = 100(1) = 100\,\text{V}$$

$$\mathbf{V}_{o1} = \frac{800}{\pi^2}(0.1580\underline{/-146.04^\circ}) = 12.81\underline{/-146.04^\circ}\,\text{V}$$

$$\mathbf{V}_{o3} = \frac{800}{9\pi^2}(0.0178\underline{/-169.13^\circ}) = 0.16\underline{/-169.13^\circ}\,\text{V}$$

$$v_o(t) = 100 + 12.81\cos(5000t - 146.04^\circ) + 0.16\cos(15{,}000t - 169.13^\circ) + \cdots\,\text{V}$$

P 16.51 [a] Let V_a represent the node voltage across R_2, then the node-voltage equations are

$$\frac{V_a - V_g}{R_1} + \frac{V_a}{R_2} + V_a sC_2 + (V_a - V_o)sC_1 = 0$$

$$(0 - V_a)sC_2 + \frac{0 - V_o}{R_3} = 0$$

Solving for V_o in terms of V_g yields

$$\frac{V_o}{V_g} = H(s) = \frac{\frac{-1}{R_1C_1}s}{s^2 + \frac{1}{R_3}\left(\frac{1}{C_1} + \frac{1}{C_2}\right)s + \frac{R_1+R_2}{R_1R_2R_3C_1C_2}}$$

It follows that

$$\omega_o^2 = \frac{R_1 + R_2}{R_1 R_2 R_3 C_1 C_2}$$

$$\beta = \frac{1}{R_3}\left(\frac{1}{C_1} + \frac{1}{C_2}\right)$$

$$K_o = \frac{R_3}{R_1}\left(\frac{C_2}{C_1 + C_2}\right)$$

Note that

$$H(s) = \frac{-\frac{R_3}{R_1}\left(\frac{C_2}{C_1+C_2}\right)\frac{1}{R_3}\left(\frac{1}{C_1} + \frac{1}{C_2}\right)s}{s^2 + \frac{1}{R_3}\left(\frac{1}{C_1} + \frac{1}{C_2}\right)s + \left(\frac{R_1+R_2}{R_1 R_2 R_3 C_1 C_2}\right)}$$

[b] For the given values of $R_1, R_2, R_3, C_1,$ and C_2 we have

$$-\frac{R_3}{R_1}\left(\frac{C_2}{C_1 + C_2}\right) = -\frac{R_3}{2R_1} = -\frac{400}{313}$$

$$\frac{1}{R_3}\left(\frac{1}{C_1} + \frac{1}{C_2}\right) = 2000$$

$$\frac{R_1 + R_2}{R_1 R_2 R_3 C_1 C_2} = 0.16 \times 10^{10} = 16 \times 10^8$$

$$H(s) = \frac{-(400/313)(2000)s}{s^2 + 2000s + 16 \times 10^8}$$

$$\omega_o = \frac{2\pi}{T} = \frac{2\pi}{50\pi} \times 10^6 = 4 \times 10^4 \text{ rad/s}$$

$$H(jn\omega_o) = \frac{-(400/313)(2000)jn\omega_o}{16 \times 10^8 - n^2\omega_o^2 + j2000n\omega_o}$$

$$= \frac{-j(20/313)n}{(1 - n^2) + j0.05n}$$

$$H(j\omega_o) = \frac{-j(20/313)}{j(0.050)} = -\frac{400}{313} = -1.28$$

$$H(j3\omega_o) = \frac{-j(20/313)(3)}{-8 + j0.15} = 0.0240\underline{/91.07^\circ}$$

$$H(j5\omega_o) = \frac{-j(100/313)}{-24 + j0.25} = 0.0133\underline{/90.60^\circ}$$

$$v_g(t) = \frac{4A}{\pi}\sum_{n=1,3,5}^{\infty}\frac{1}{n}\sin(n\pi/2)\cos n\omega_o t$$

$$A = 15.65\pi \text{ V}$$

$$v_g(t) = 62.60 \cos \omega_o t - 20.87 \cos 3\omega_o t + 12.52 \cos 5\omega_o t - \cdots$$

$$v_o(t) = -80 \cos \omega_o t - 0.50 \cos(3\omega_o t + 91.07^\circ)$$
$$+ 0.17 \cos(5\omega_o t + 90.60^\circ) - \cdots \text{ V}$$

17

The Fourier Transform

Drill Exercises

DE 17.1 [a] $F(\omega) = \int_{-\tau/2}^{0} (-Ae^{-j\omega t})\, dt + \int_{0}^{\tau/2} Ae^{-j\omega t}\, dt$

$$= \frac{A}{j\omega}[2 - e^{j\omega\tau/2} - e^{-j\omega\tau/2}] = \frac{-2jA}{\omega}[1 - \frac{\cos\omega\tau}{2}]$$

[b] $F(\omega) = \int_{0}^{\infty} te^{-at}e^{-j\omega t}\, dt = \int_{0}^{\infty} te^{-(a+j\omega)t}\, dt = \frac{1}{(a+j\omega)^2}$

DE 17.2 $f(t) = \frac{1}{2\pi}\left\{\int_{-3}^{-2} 4e^{jt\omega}\, d\omega + \int_{-2}^{2} e^{jt\omega}\, d\omega + \int_{2}^{3} 4e^{jt\omega}\, d\omega\right\}$

$$= \frac{1}{j2\pi t}\{e^{-j2t} - e^{-j3t} + e^{j2t} - e^{-j2t} + e^{j3t} - e^{j2t}\}$$

$$= \frac{1}{\pi t}(4\sin 3t - 3\sin 2t)$$

DE 17.3 [a] $F(\omega) = F(s)\,|_{s=j\omega} = \left.\frac{\omega_0}{(s+a)^2+\omega_0^2}\right|_{s=j\omega} = \frac{\omega_0}{(a+j\omega)^2+\omega_0^2}$

[b] $F(\omega) = \mathcal{L}\{f^-(t)\}_{s=-j\omega} = \left[\frac{1}{(s+a)^2}\right]_{s=-j\omega} = \frac{1}{(a-j\omega)^2}$

[c] $f^+(t) = te^{-at}, \qquad f^-(t) = -te^{-at}$

$$\mathcal{L}\{f^+(t)\} = \frac{1}{(s+a)^2}, \quad \mathcal{L}\{f^-(t)\} = \frac{-1}{(s+a)^2}$$

Therefore $F(\omega) = \frac{1}{(a+j\omega)^2} - \frac{1}{(a-j\omega)^2} = \frac{-j4a\omega}{(a^2+\omega^2)^2}$

DE 17.4 $\mathcal{F}\{\sin \omega_0 t\} = \mathcal{F}\left\{\frac{e^{j\omega_0 t}}{2j}\right\} - \mathcal{F}\left\{\frac{e^{-j\omega_0 t}}{2j}\right\}$

$$= \frac{1}{2j}[2\pi\delta(\omega - \omega_0) - 2\pi\delta(\omega + \omega_0)]$$

$$= j\pi[\delta(\omega + \omega_0) - \delta(\omega - \omega_0)]$$

DE 17.5 $f(t) = \frac{1}{2\pi}\int_{-\infty}^{\infty} [A(\omega) + jB(\omega)][\cos t\omega + j\sin t\omega]\,d\omega$

$$= \frac{1}{2\pi}\int_{-\infty}^{\infty} [A(\omega)\cos t\omega - B(\omega)\sin t\omega]\,d\omega$$

$$+ \frac{j}{2\pi}\int_{-\infty}^{\infty} [A(\omega)\sin t\omega + B(\omega)\cos t\omega]\,d\omega$$

But $f(t)$ is real, therefore the second integral on the right-hand side is zero.

DE 17.6 By hypothesis, $f(t) = -f(-t)$. From DE17.5, we have

$$f(-t) = \frac{1}{2\pi}\int_{-\infty}^{\infty} [A(\omega)\cos t\omega + B(\omega)\sin t\omega]\,d\omega$$

For $f(t) = -f(-t)$, the integral $\int_{-\infty}^{\infty} A(\omega)\cos t\omega\,d\omega$ must be zero. Therefore, if $f(t)$ is real and odd, we have

$$f(t) = \frac{-1}{2\pi}\int_{-\infty}^{\infty} B(\omega)\sin t\omega\,d\omega$$

DE 17.7 [a] $f'(t) = \frac{2A}{\tau}, \qquad \frac{-\tau}{2} < t < 0$

$0 < t < \frac{\tau}{2}$:

$$f''(t) = \frac{2A}{\tau}\delta\left(t + \frac{\tau}{2}\right) - \frac{4A}{\tau} + \frac{2A}{\tau}\delta\left(t - \frac{\tau}{2}\right)$$

[b] $\mathcal{F}\{f''(t)\} = \left[\frac{2A}{\tau}e^{j\omega\tau/2} - \frac{4A}{\tau} + \frac{2A}{\tau}e^{-j\omega\tau/2}\right] = \frac{4A}{\tau}\left[\cos\left(\frac{\omega\tau}{2}\right) - 1\right]$

[c] $\mathcal{F}\{f''(t)\} = -\omega^2 F(\omega)$; therefore $F(\omega) = -\frac{1}{\omega^2}\mathcal{F}\{f''(t)\}$

Thus we have $F(\omega) = -\frac{1}{\omega^2}\left\{\frac{4A}{\tau}\left[\cos\left(\frac{\omega\tau}{2}\right) - 1\right]\right\}$

DE 17.8 $v(t) = V_m\left[u\left(t+\frac{\tau}{2}\right) - u\left(t-\frac{\tau}{2}\right)\right]$

$$\mathcal{F}\left\{u\left(t+\frac{\tau}{2}\right)\right\} = \left[\pi\delta(\omega) + \frac{1}{j\omega}\right] e^{j\omega\tau/2}$$

$$\mathcal{F}\left\{u\left(t-\frac{\tau}{2}\right)\right\} = \left[\pi\delta(\omega) + \frac{1}{j\omega}\right] e^{-j\omega\tau/2}$$

Therefore $V(\omega) = V_m\left[\pi\delta(\omega) + \frac{1}{j\omega}\right]\left[e^{j\omega\tau/2} - e^{-j\omega\tau/2}\right]$

$$= \frac{2V_m}{\omega}\sin\left(\frac{\omega\tau}{2}\right) + j2\pi V_m\delta(\omega)\sin\left(\frac{\omega\tau}{2}\right)$$

$$= \frac{(V_m\tau)\sin(\omega\tau/2)}{\omega\tau/2}$$

DE 17.9 [a] $I_g(\omega) = \mathcal{F}\{10\text{sgn}\, t\} = \frac{20}{j\omega}$

[b] $H(s) = \frac{V_o}{I_g}, \qquad V_o = \frac{I_g 4s}{5+s}$

$$H(s) = \frac{4s}{s+5}, \qquad H(j\omega) = \frac{j4\omega}{5+j\omega}$$

[c] $V_o(\omega) = H(j\omega)\cdot I_g(\omega) = \frac{80}{5+j\omega}$

[d] $v_o(t) = 80e^{-5t}u(t)$ V

[e] $i_1(0^-) = \frac{1}{5}i_g = \frac{1}{5}(-10) = -2$ A

[f] $i_1(0^+) = 10 + i_2(0^+) = 10 + i_2(0^-) = 10 + 8 = 18$ A

[g] $i_2(0^-) = \frac{4}{5}(10) = 8$ A

[h] $i_2(0^+) = i_2(0^-) = 8$ A

[i] $v_o(0^-) = 0$ V

[j] $v_o(0^+) = 1i_2(0^+) + 4i_1(0^+) = 80$ V

DE 17.10 [a] $V_g(\omega) = \frac{1}{1-j\omega} + \pi\delta(\omega) + \frac{1}{j\omega}$

$$H(s) = \frac{V_a}{V_g} = \frac{1}{s+3}, \qquad H(j\omega) = \frac{1}{3+j\omega}$$

$$V_a(\omega) = \frac{1}{(1-j\omega)(3+j\omega)} + \frac{1}{j\omega(3+j\omega)} + \frac{\pi\delta(\omega)}{3+j\omega}$$
$$= \frac{1/4}{1-j\omega} + \frac{1/4}{3+j\omega} + \frac{1/3}{j\omega} - \frac{1/3}{3+j\omega} + \frac{\pi\delta(\omega)}{3+j\omega}$$
$$= \frac{1/4}{1-j\omega} + \frac{1/3}{j\omega} - \frac{1/12}{3+j\omega} + \frac{\pi\delta(\omega)}{3+j\omega}$$

Therefore $v_a(t) = \left[\frac{1}{4}e^{t}u(-t) + \frac{1}{6}\text{sgn}\, t - \frac{1}{12}e^{-3t}u(t) + \frac{1}{6}\right]$ V

[b] $v_a(0^-) = \frac{1}{4} - \frac{1}{6} + 0 + \frac{1}{6} = \frac{1}{4}$ V

$$v_a(0^+) = 0 + \frac{1}{6} - \frac{1}{12} + \frac{1}{6} = \frac{1}{4}\text{ V}$$

$$v_a(\infty) = 0 + \frac{1}{6} + 0 + \frac{1}{6} = \frac{1}{3}\text{ V}$$

DE 17.11

$$v(t) = 4te^{-t}u(t); \qquad V(\omega) = \frac{4}{(1+j\omega)^2}$$

Therefore $|V(\omega)| = \frac{4}{1+\omega^2}$

$$W_{1\Omega} = \frac{1}{\pi}\int_0^{\sqrt{3}} \left[\frac{16}{(1+\omega^2)^2}\right] d\omega$$
$$= \frac{16}{\pi}\left\{\frac{1}{2}\left[\frac{\omega}{\omega^2+1} + \tan^{-1}\frac{\omega}{1}\right]_0^{\sqrt{3}}\right\}$$
$$= 16\left[\frac{\sqrt{3}}{8\pi} + \frac{1}{6}\right] = 3.769\text{ J}$$

$$W_{1\Omega}(\text{total}) = \frac{8}{\pi}\left[\frac{\omega}{\omega^2+1} + \tan^{-1}\frac{\omega}{1}\right]_0^{\infty} = 4\text{ J}$$

Therefore $\% = 94.23$

DE 17.12

$$|V(\omega)| = 6 - \left(\frac{6}{2000\pi}\right)\omega, \qquad 0 \le \omega \le 2000\pi$$

$$|V(\omega)|^2 = 36 - \left(\frac{72}{2000\pi}\right)\omega + \left(\frac{36}{4\pi^2 \times 10^6}\right)\omega^2$$

$$W_{1\Omega} = \frac{1}{\pi}\int_0^{2000\pi}\left[36 - \frac{72\omega}{2000\pi} + \frac{36\times 10^{-6}}{4\pi^2}\omega^2\right] d\omega = 24\text{ kJ}$$

$$W_{6\text{k}\Omega} = 24 \times \frac{10^3}{6\times 10^3} = 4\text{ J}$$

Problems

P 17.1 [a] $F(\omega) = \int_{-2}^{2} \left[A \sin\left(\frac{\pi}{2}\right) t\right] e^{-j\omega t}\, dt = \frac{-j4\pi A}{\pi^2 - 4\omega^2} \sin 2\omega$

[b] $F(\omega) = \int_{-\tau/2}^{0} \left(\frac{2A}{\tau}t + A\right) e^{-j\omega t}\, dt + \int_{0}^{\tau/2} \left(\frac{-2A}{\tau}t + A\right) e^{-j\omega t}\, dt$

$$= \frac{4A}{\omega^2\tau}\left[1 - \cos\left(\frac{\omega\tau}{2}\right)\right]$$

P 17.2 [a] $F(\omega) = \int_{-\infty}^{\infty} f(t) e^{-j\omega t}\, dt$

$$= \int_{-\tau/2}^{0} \frac{-2A}{\tau} t e^{-j\omega t}\, dt + \int_{0}^{\tau/2} \frac{2A}{\tau} t e^{-j\omega t}\, dt$$

$$= \text{Int1} + \text{Int2}$$

$$\text{Int1} = \frac{-2A}{\tau}\int_{-\tau/2}^{0} t e^{-j\omega t}\, dt$$

$$= \frac{-2A}{\tau}\left\{\frac{e^{-j\omega t}}{-\omega^2}(-j\omega t - 1)\Big|_{-\tau/2}^{0}\right\}$$

$$= \frac{-2A}{\omega^2\tau}\left\{1 - [e^{j\omega\tau/2}(-j\omega\tau/2 + 1)]\right\}$$

$$= \frac{2A}{\omega^2\tau}\left\{e^{j\omega\tau/2}(1 - j\omega\tau/2) - 1\right\}$$

$$\text{Int2} = \frac{2A}{\tau}\int_{0}^{\tau/2} t e^{-j\omega t}\, dt$$

$$= \frac{2A}{\tau}\left\{\frac{e^{-j\omega t}}{-\omega^2}(-j\omega t - 1)\Big|_{0}^{\tau/2}\right\}$$

$$= \frac{2A}{\omega^2\tau}\left\{e^{j\omega\tau/2}(j\omega\tau/2 + 1) - 1)]\right\}$$

$$F(\omega) = \text{Int1} + \text{Int2}$$

$$= \frac{2A}{\omega^2 t}\left\{2\cos\frac{\omega\tau}{2} + \omega\tau\sin\frac{\omega\tau}{2} - 2\right\}$$

[b] After using L'Hopital's rule we have

$$F(0) = \lim_{\omega \to 0} \frac{2A\tau\cos(\omega\tau/2)}{4} = \frac{A\tau}{2}$$

[c]

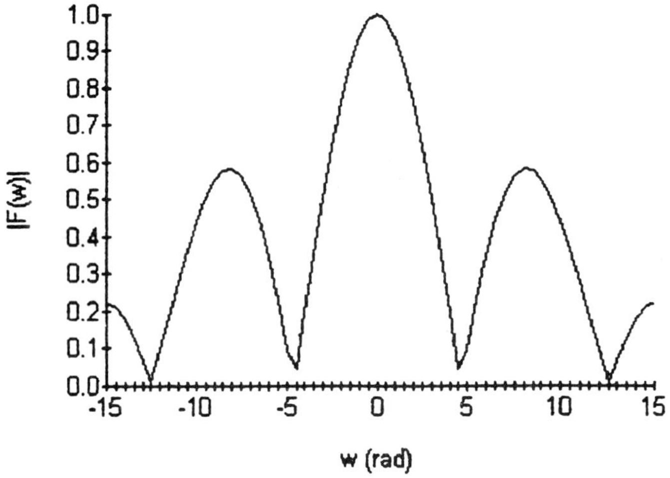

P 17.3 [a] $F(\omega = j\frac{2A}{\omega_o}\omega \qquad -\frac{\omega_o}{2} \leq \omega \leq \frac{\omega_o}{2}$

$$f(t) = \frac{1}{2\pi}\int_{-\omega_o/2}^{\omega_o/2} \frac{j2A}{\omega_o}\omega e^{j\omega t}\, d\omega$$

$$= \frac{jA}{\pi\omega_o}\left[\frac{e^{jt\omega}}{-t^2}(jt\omega - 1)\Big|_{-\omega_o/2}^{\omega_o/2}\right]$$

$$= \frac{1}{\pi\omega_o t^2}[\omega_o t\cos(\omega_o t/2) - 2\sin(\omega_o t/2)]$$

[b] $f(t) = \frac{A}{\pi\omega_o}\left[\frac{\omega_o t\cos(\omega_o t/2) - 2\sin(\omega_o t/2)}{t^2}\right]$

$$f(0) = \lim_{t\to 0}\left\{\frac{A}{\pi\omega_o}\left[\frac{\omega_o t(-\frac{\omega_o}{2}\sin\frac{\omega_o t}{2}) + \omega_o\cos\frac{\omega_o t}{2} - \omega_o\cos\frac{\omega_o t}{2}}{2t}\right]\right\}$$

$$= \lim_{t\to 0}\left\{\frac{A}{\pi\omega_o}\left[\frac{-\omega_o^2}{4}\sin\left(\frac{\omega_o t}{2}\right)\right]\right\} = 0$$

[c] When $A = 2\pi$ and $\omega_o = 2$ rad/s

$$f(t) = \frac{1}{t^2}[2t\cos t - 2\sin t]$$

$f(-t) = -f(t) \qquad$ odd function

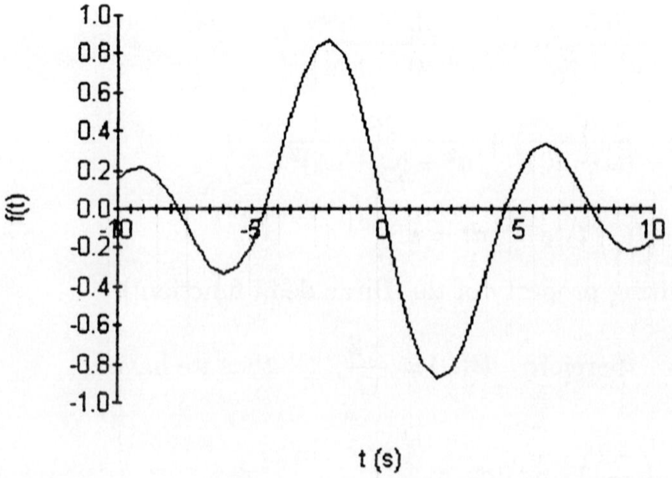

P 17.4 [a] $F(\omega) = F(s)\Big|_{s=j\omega} + F(s)\Big|_{s=-j\omega}, \qquad F(s) = \dfrac{1}{(s+a)^2}$

$$F(\omega) = \left[\frac{1}{(a+j\omega)^2}\right] + \left[\frac{1}{(a-j\omega)^2}\right]$$

$$= \frac{2(a^2-\omega^2)}{(a^2-\omega^2)^2 + 4a^2\omega^2} = \frac{2(a^2-\omega^2)}{(a^2+\omega^2)^2}$$

[b] $F(\omega) = F(s)\Big|_{s=j\omega} - F(s)\Big|_{s=-j\omega}, \qquad F(s) = \dfrac{6}{(s+a)^4}$

$$F(\omega) = \frac{6}{(a+j\omega)^4} - \frac{6}{(a-j\omega)^4} = -j48a\omega\frac{a^2-\omega^2}{(a^2+\omega^2)^4}$$

[c] $F(\omega) = F(s)\Big|_{s=j\omega} + F(s)\Big|_{s=-j\omega}$

$$F(s) = \frac{0.5}{(s+a) - j\omega_0} + \frac{0.5}{(s+a) + j\omega_0}$$

$$F(\omega) = \frac{0.5}{(a+j\omega) - j\omega_0} + \frac{0.5}{(a+j\omega) + j\omega_0}$$

$$+ \frac{0.5}{(a-j\omega) - j\omega_0} + \frac{0.5}{(a-j\omega) + j\omega_0}$$

$$= \frac{a}{a^2 + (\omega-\omega_0)^2} + \frac{a}{a^2 + (\omega+\omega_0)^2}$$

[d] $F(\omega) = F(s)\Big|_{s=j\omega} - F(s)\Big|_{s=-j\omega}$

$$F(s) = \frac{-j0.5}{(s+a) - j\omega_0} + \frac{j0.5}{(s+a) + j\omega_0}$$

$$F(\omega) - \frac{-ja}{a^2 + (\omega - \omega_0)^2} + \frac{ja}{a^2 + (\omega + \omega_0)^2}$$

[e] $F(\omega) = \int_{-\infty}^{\infty} \delta(t - t_o)e^{-j\omega t}\,dt = e^{-j\omega t_o}$

(Use the sifting property of the Dirac delta function.)

P 17.5 $F(\omega) = \dfrac{-j2}{\omega}$; therefore $B(\omega) = \dfrac{-2}{\omega}$; thus we have

$$f(t) = -\frac{1}{2\pi}\int_{-\infty}^{\infty}\left(\frac{-2}{\omega}\right)\sin t\omega\,d\omega = \frac{1}{\pi}\int_{-\infty}^{\infty}\frac{\sin t\omega}{\omega}\,d\omega$$

But $\dfrac{\sin t\omega}{\omega}$ is even; therefore $f(t) = \dfrac{2}{\pi}\displaystyle\int_{0}^{\infty}\frac{\sin t\omega}{\omega}\,d\omega$

Therefore,

$$\left.\begin{array}{ll} f(t) = \dfrac{2}{\pi}\cdot\dfrac{\pi}{2} = 1 & t > 0 \\ f(t) = \dfrac{2}{\pi}\cdot\left(\dfrac{-\pi}{2}\right) = -1 & t < 0 \end{array}\right\} \text{from a table of definite integrals}$$

Therefore $f(t) = \operatorname{sgn} t$

P 17.6 From Problem 17.4[c] we have

$$F(\omega) = \frac{\epsilon}{\epsilon^2 + (\omega - \omega_0)^2} + \frac{\epsilon}{\epsilon^2 + (\omega + \omega_0)^2}$$

Note that as $\epsilon \to 0$, $F(\omega) \to 0$ everywhere except at $\omega = \pm\omega_0$. At $\omega = \pm\omega_0$, $F(\omega) = 1/\epsilon$, therefore $F(\omega) \to \infty$ at $\omega = \pm\omega_0$ as $\epsilon \to 0$. The area under each bell-shaped curve is independent of ϵ, that is

$$\int_{-\infty}^{\infty}\frac{\epsilon d\omega}{\epsilon^2 + (\omega - \omega_0)^2} = \int_{-\infty}^{\infty}\frac{\epsilon d\omega}{\epsilon^2 + (\omega + \omega_0)^2} = \pi$$

Therefore as $\epsilon \to 0$, $F(\omega) \to \pi\delta(\omega - \omega_0) + \pi\delta(\omega + \omega_0)$

P 17.7 $A(\omega) = \int_{-\infty}^{\infty} f(t)\cos\omega t\,dt$

$$= \int_{-\infty}^{0} f(t)\cos\omega t\,dt + \int_{0}^{\infty} f(t)\cos\omega t\,dt$$

$$= 2\int_{0}^{\infty} f(t)\cos\omega t\,dt, \quad \text{since } f(t)\cos\omega t \text{ is also even.}$$

$B(\omega) = 0$, since $f(t)\sin\omega t$ is an odd function and

$$\int_{-\infty}^{0} f(t)\sin\omega t\,dt = -\int_{0}^{\infty} f(t)\sin\omega t\,dt$$

P 17.8 $A(\omega) = \int_{-\infty}^{0} f(t)\cos\omega t\,dt + \int_{0}^{\infty} f(t)\cos\omega t\,dt = 0$

since $f(t)\cos\omega t$ is an odd function.

$$B(\omega) = -2\int_{0}^{\infty} f(t)\sin\omega t\,dt, \quad \text{since } f(t)\sin\omega t \text{ is an even function.}$$

P 17.9 [a] $\mathcal{F}\left\{\frac{df(t)}{dt}\right\} = \int_{-\infty}^{\infty} \frac{df(t)}{dt} e^{-j\omega t}\,dt$

Let $u = e^{-j\omega t}$, then $du = -j\omega e^{-j\omega t}$; let $dv = [df(t)/dt]\,dt$, then $v = f(t)$.

Therefore $\mathcal{F}\left\{\frac{df(t)}{dt}\right\} = f(t)e^{-j\omega t}\Big|_{-\infty}^{\infty} - \int_{-\infty}^{\infty} f(t)[-j\omega e^{-j\omega t}\,dt]$

$$= 0 + j\omega F(\omega)$$

[b] Fourier transform of $f(t)$ exists, i.e., $f(\infty) = f(-\infty) = 0$.

[c] To find $\mathcal{F}\left\{\frac{d^2 f(t)}{dt^2}\right\}$, let $g(t) = \frac{df(t)}{dt}$

Then $\mathcal{F}\left\{\frac{d^2 f(t)}{dt^2}\right\} = \mathcal{F}\left\{\frac{dg(t)}{dt}\right\} = j\omega G(\omega)$

But $G(\omega) = \mathcal{F}\left\{\frac{df(t)}{dt}\right\} = j\omega F(\omega)$

Therefore we have $\mathcal{F}\left\{\frac{d^2 f(t)}{dt^2}\right\} = (j\omega)^2 F(\omega)$

Repeated application of this thought process gives

$$\mathcal{F}\left\{\frac{d^n f(t)}{dt^n}\right\} = (j\omega)^n F(\omega)$$

P 17.10 [a] $\mathcal{F}\left\{\int_{-\infty}^{t} f(x)\,dx\right\} = \int_{-\infty}^{\infty}\left[\int_{-\infty}^{t} f(x)\,dx\right] e^{-j\omega t}\,dt$

Now let $u = \int_{-\infty}^{t} f(x)\,dx,$ then $du = f(t)dt$

Let $dv = e^{-j\omega t}\,dt,$ then $v = \frac{e^{-j\omega t}}{-j\omega}$

Therefore,

$$\mathcal{F}\left\{\int_{-\infty}^{t} f(x)\,dx\right\} = \frac{e^{-j\omega t}}{-j\omega}\int_{-\infty}^{t} f(x)\,dx\,\Big|_{-\infty}^{\infty} - \int_{-\infty}^{\infty}\left[\frac{e^{-j\omega t}}{-j\omega}\right] f(t)\,dt$$

$$= 0 + \frac{F(\omega)}{j\omega}$$

[b] We require $\int_{-\infty}^{\infty} f(x)\,dx = 0$

[c] No, because $\int_{-\infty}^{\infty} e^{-ax}u(x)\,dx = \frac{1}{a} \neq 0$

P 17.11 [a] $\mathcal{F}\{f(at)\} = \int_{-\infty}^{\infty} f(at)e^{-j\omega t}\,dt$

Let $u = at,$ $du = adt,$ $u = \pm\infty$ when $t = \pm\infty$

Therefore,

$$\mathcal{F}\{f(at)\} = \int_{-\infty}^{\infty} f(u)e^{-j\omega u/a}\left(\frac{du}{a}\right) = \frac{1}{a}F\left(\frac{1}{a}\right), \qquad a > 0$$

[b] $\mathcal{F}\{e^{-|t|}\} = \frac{1}{1+j\omega} + \frac{1}{1-j\omega} = \frac{2}{1+\omega^2}$

Therefore $\mathcal{F}\{e^{-a|t|}\} = \frac{(1/a)2}{(\omega/a)^2+1}$

Therefore $\mathcal{F}\{e^{-0.5|t|}\} = \frac{4}{4\omega^2+1},$ $\mathcal{F}\{e^{-|t|}\} = \frac{2}{\omega^2+1}$

$\mathcal{F}\{e^{-2|t|}\} = 1/[0.25\omega^2+1]$, yes as "$a$" increases, the sketches show that $f(t)$ approaches zero faster and $F(\omega)$ flattens out over the frequency spectrum.

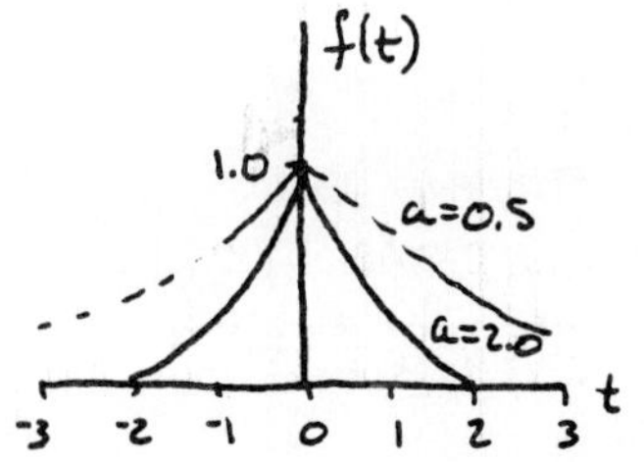

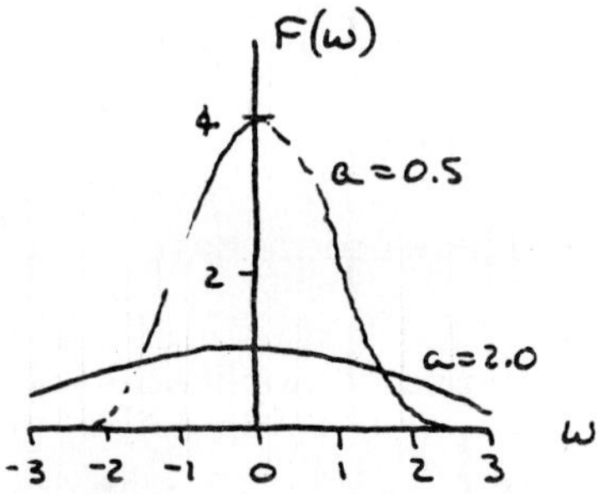

P 17.12 [a] $\mathcal{F}\{f(t-a)\} = \int_{-\infty}^{\infty} f(t-a)e^{-j\omega t}\,dt$

Let $u = t - a$, then $du = dt$, $t = u + a$, and $u = \pm\infty$ when $t = \pm\infty$. Therefore,

$$\mathcal{F}\{f(t-a)\} = \int_{-\infty}^{\infty} f(u)e^{-j\omega(u+a)}\,du$$

$$= e^{-j\omega a}\int_{-\infty}^{\infty} f(u)e^{-j\omega u}\,du = e^{-j\omega a}F(\omega)$$

[b] $\mathcal{F}\{e^{j\omega_0 t}f(t)\} = \int_{-\infty}^{\infty} f(t)e^{-j(\omega-\omega_0)t}\,dt = F(\omega - \omega_0)$

[c] $\mathcal{F}\{f(t)\cos\omega_0 t\} = \mathcal{F}\left\{f(t)\left[\frac{e^{j\omega_0 t} + e^{-j\omega_0 t}}{2}\right]\right\}$

$$= \frac{1}{2}F(\omega - \omega_0) + \frac{1}{2}F(\omega + \omega_0)$$

P 17.13 $Y(\omega) = \int_{-\infty}^{\infty}\left[\int_{-\infty}^{\infty} x(\lambda)h(t-\lambda)\,d\lambda\right]e^{-j\omega t}\,dt$

$$= \int_{-\infty}^{\infty} x(\lambda)\left[\int_{-\infty}^{\infty} h(t-\lambda)e^{-j\omega t}\,dt\right]d\lambda$$

Let $u = t - \lambda$, $du = dt$, and $u = \pm\infty$, when $t = \pm\infty$.

Therefore $Y(\omega) = \int_{-\infty}^{\infty} x(\lambda)\left[\int_{-\infty}^{\infty} h(u)e^{-j\omega(u+\lambda)}\,du\right]d\lambda$

$$= \int_{-\infty}^{\infty} x(\lambda)\left[e^{-j\omega\lambda}\int_{-\infty}^{\infty} h(u)e^{-j\omega u}\,du\right]d\lambda$$

$$= \int_{-\infty}^{\infty} x(\lambda)e^{-j\omega\lambda}H(\omega)\,d\lambda = H(\omega)X(\omega)$$

P 17.14 $\mathcal{F}\{f_1(t)f_2(t)\} = \int_{-\infty}^{\infty}\left[\frac{1}{2\pi}\int_{-\infty}^{\infty} F_1(u)e^{jtu}du\right]f_2(t)e^{-j\omega t}\,dt$

$$= \frac{1}{2\pi}\int_{-\infty}^{\infty}\left[\int_{-\infty}^{\infty} F_1(u)f_2(t)e^{-j\omega t}e^{jtu}\,du\right]dt$$

$$= \frac{1}{2\pi}\int_{-\infty}^{\infty}\left[F_1(u)\int_{-\infty}^{\infty} f_2(t)e^{-j(\omega-u)t}\,dt\right]du$$

$$= \frac{1}{2\pi}\int_{-\infty}^{\infty} F_1(u)F_2(\omega - u)\,du$$

P 17.15 [a] $f_1(t) = \cos\omega_0 t, \qquad F_1(u) = \pi[\delta(u+\omega_0) + \delta(u-\omega_0)]$

$f_2(t) = 1, \quad -\tau/2 < t < \tau/2, \qquad$ and $f_2(t) = 0$ elsewhere

Thus $F_2(u) = \dfrac{\tau\sin(u\tau/2)}{u\tau/2}$

$$F(\omega) = \frac{1}{2\pi}\int_{-\infty}^{\infty} F(u)F_2(\omega - u)\,du$$

$$= \frac{1}{2\pi}\int_{-\infty}^{\infty} \pi[\delta(u+\omega_0) + \delta(u-\omega_0)]\tau\frac{\sin[(\omega-u)\tau/2]}{(\omega-u)(\tau/2)}\,du$$

$$= \frac{\tau}{2}\int_{-\infty}^{\infty} \delta(u+\omega_0)\frac{\sin[(\omega-u)\tau/2]}{(\omega-u)(\tau/2)}\,du$$

$$+ \frac{\tau}{2}\int_{-\infty}^{\infty} \delta(u-\omega_0)\frac{\sin[(\omega-u)\tau/2]}{(\omega-u)(\tau/2)}\,du$$

$$= \frac{\tau}{2}\cdot\frac{\sin[(\omega+\omega_0)\tau/2]}{(\omega+\omega_0)(\tau/2)} + \frac{\tau}{2}\cdot\frac{\sin[(\omega-\omega_0)\tau/2]}{(\omega-\omega_0)\tau/2}$$

[b] As τ increases, the amplitude of $F(\omega)$ increases at $\omega = \pm\omega_0$ and at the same time the duration of $F(\omega)$ approaches zero as ω deviates from $\pm\omega_0$.

The area under the $[\sin x]/x$ function is independent of τ, that is

$$\frac{\tau}{2}\int_{-\infty}^{\infty}\frac{\sin[(\omega-\omega_0)(\tau/2)]}{(\omega-\omega_0)(\tau/2)}\,d\omega = \int_{-\infty}^{\infty}\frac{\sin[(\omega-\omega_0)(\tau/2)]}{(\omega-\omega_0)(\tau/2)}[(\tau/2)\,d\omega] = \pi$$

Therefore as $t \to \infty$,

$$f_1(t)f_2(t) \to \cos\omega_0 t \quad \text{and} \quad F(\omega) \to \pi[\delta(\omega-\omega_0) + \delta(\omega+\omega_0)]$$

P 17.16 [a] $F(\omega) = \int_{-\infty}^{\infty} f(t)e^{-j\omega t}\,dt$

$$\frac{dF}{d\omega} = \int_{-\infty}^{\infty}\frac{d}{d\omega}\left[f(t)e^{-j\omega t}\,dt\right] = -j\int_{-\infty}^{\infty} tf(t)e^{-j\omega t}\,dt = -j\mathcal{F}\{tf(t)\}$$

Therefore $j\dfrac{dF(\omega)}{d\omega} = \mathcal{F}\{tf(t)\}$

$$\frac{d^2F(\omega)}{d\omega^2} = \int_{-\infty}^{\infty}(-jt)(-jt)f(t)e^{-j\omega t}\,dt = (-j)^2\mathcal{F}\{t^2f(t)\}$$

Note that $(-j)^n = \dfrac{1}{j^n}$

Thus we have $j^n\left[\dfrac{d^nF(\omega)}{d\omega^n}\right] = \mathcal{F}\{t^nf(t)\}$

[b] (i) $\mathcal{F}\{e^{-at}u(t)\} = \dfrac{1}{a+j\omega} = F(\omega);\qquad \dfrac{dF(\omega)}{d\omega} = \dfrac{-j}{(a+j\omega)^2}$

Therefore $j\left[\dfrac{dF(\omega)}{d\omega}\right] = \dfrac{1}{(a+j\omega)^2}$

$$\text{Therefore}\quad \mathcal{F}\{te^{-at}u(t)\} = \frac{1}{(a+j\omega)^2}$$

(ii) $\mathcal{F}\{|t|e^{-a|t|}\} = \mathcal{F}\{te^{-at}u(t)\} - \mathcal{F}\{te^{at}u(-t)\}$

$$= \frac{1}{(a+j\omega)^2} - j\frac{d}{d\omega}\left(\frac{1}{a-j\omega}\right)$$

$$= \frac{1}{(a+j\omega)^2} + \frac{1}{(a-j\omega)^2}$$

(iii) $\mathcal{F}\{te^{-a|t|}\} = \mathcal{F}\{te^{-at}u(t)\} + \mathcal{F}\{te^{at}u(-t)\}$

$$= \frac{1}{(a+j\omega)^2} + j\frac{d}{d\omega}\left(\frac{1}{a-j\omega}\right)$$

$$= \frac{1}{(a+j\omega)^2} - \frac{1}{(a-j\omega)^2}$$

P 17.17 [a] Find the Thévenin equivalent with respect to the terminals of the inductor. Thus,

$$v_{\text{Th}} = \frac{40}{50}v_g = 0.8v_g; \qquad R_{\text{Th}} = 10\|40 = 8\,\Omega$$

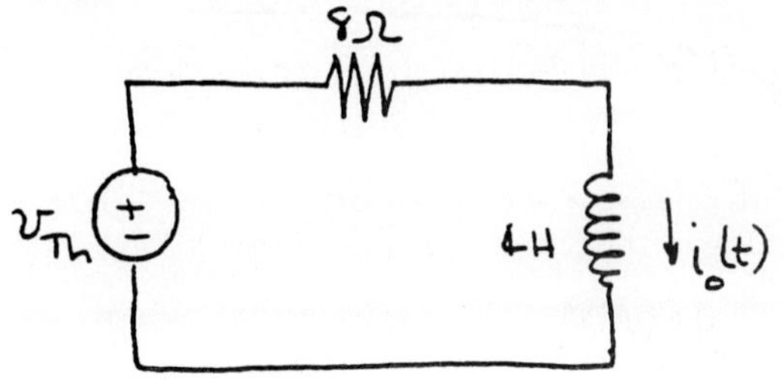

$$I_o = \frac{0.8V_g}{8+4s} = \frac{0.2V_g}{s+2}$$

$$H(s) = \frac{I_o}{V_g} = \frac{0.2}{s+2}$$

$$H(j\omega) = \frac{0.2}{j\omega+2}$$

$$V_g(\omega) = 125\left(\pi\delta(\omega) + \frac{1}{j\omega}\right)$$

$$I_o(\omega) = V_g(\omega)H(j\omega)$$
$$= \frac{25}{j\omega + 2}\left(\pi\delta(\omega) + \frac{1}{j\omega}\right)$$
$$= \frac{25\pi\delta(\omega)}{j\omega + 2} + \frac{25}{j\omega(2 + j\omega)}$$
$$= I_1(\omega) + I_2(\omega)$$

$$i_1(t) = \frac{1}{2\pi}\int_{-\infty}^{\infty} \frac{25\pi\delta(\omega)e^{j\omega t}}{2 + j\omega}\,dt = 6.25\text{ A}$$

$$I_2(\omega) = \frac{12.5}{j\omega} - \frac{12.5}{j\omega + 2}$$

$$i_2(t) = 6.25\text{sgn}(t) - 12.5e^{-2t}u(t)\text{ A}$$

$$i_o = i_1 + i_2 = 6.25 + 6.25\text{sgn}(t) - 12.5e^{-2t}u(t)\text{ A}$$

$$i_o(t) = 12.5u(t) - 12.5e^{-2t}u(t)\text{ A}$$

[b]

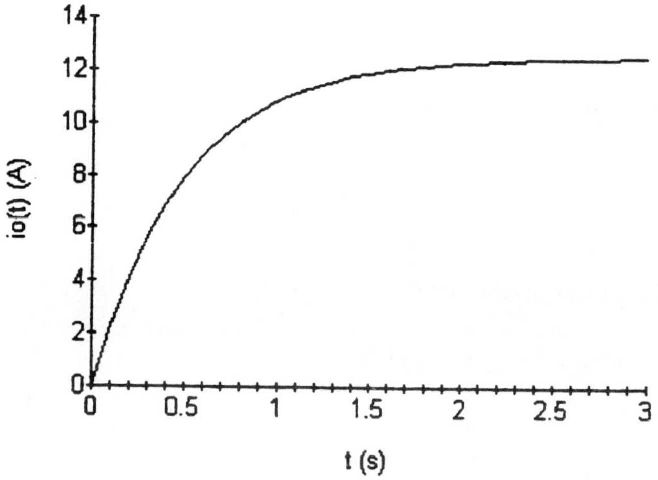

P 17.18 [a] From the solution to Problem 17.17 we have

$$H(s) = \frac{I_o}{V_g} = \frac{0.2}{s + 2}$$

$$H(j\omega) = \frac{0.2}{j\omega + 2}$$

$$v_g = 125\text{sgn}(t)\text{ V}; \qquad V_g(\omega) = \frac{250}{j\omega}$$

$$I_o = V_g H(j\omega) = \frac{50}{j\omega(j\omega + 2)} = \frac{25}{j\omega} - \frac{25}{j\omega + 2}$$

$$\therefore \quad i_o(t) = 12.5\text{sgn}(t) - 25e^{-2t}u(t) \text{ A}$$

[b]

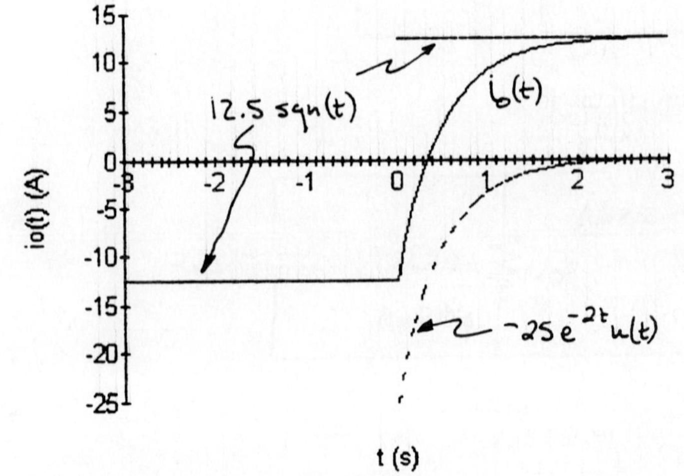

P 17.19 [a] Find the Thévenin equivalent with respect to the terminals of the capacitor:

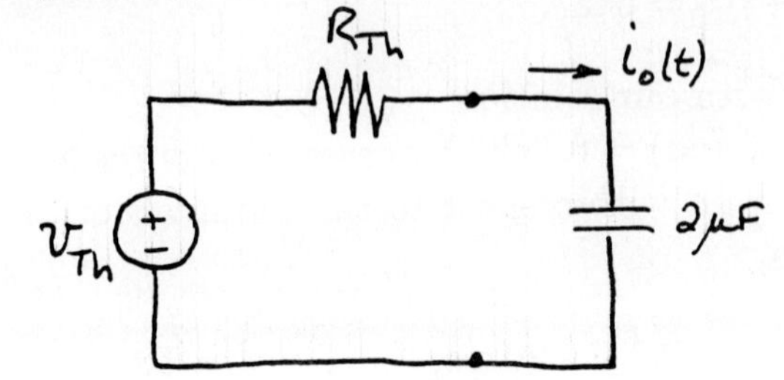

$$v_{\text{Th}} = \frac{5}{6}v_g; \qquad R_{\text{Th}} = 60\|12 = 10\,k\Omega$$

$$I_o = \frac{V_{\text{Th}}}{10{,}000 + 10^6/2s} = \frac{2sV_{\text{Th}}}{20{,}000s + 10^6}$$

$$H(s) = \frac{I_o}{V_{\text{Th}}} = \frac{10^{-4}s}{s + 50}; \qquad H(j\omega) = \frac{j\omega \times 10^{-4}}{j\omega + 50}$$

$$v_{\text{Th}} = \frac{5}{6}v_g = 30\text{sgn}(t); \qquad V_{\text{Th}} = \frac{60}{j\omega}$$

$$I_o = \left(\frac{60}{j\omega}\right)\left(\frac{j\omega \times 10^{-4}}{j\omega + 50}\right) = \frac{6 \times 10^{-3}}{j\omega + 50}$$

$$i_o(t) = 6e^{-50t}u(t)\,\text{mA}$$

[b] At $t = 0^-$ the circuit is

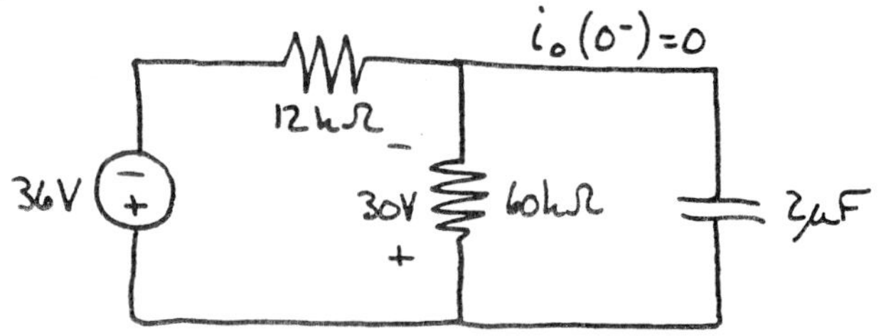

At $t = 0^+$ the circuit is

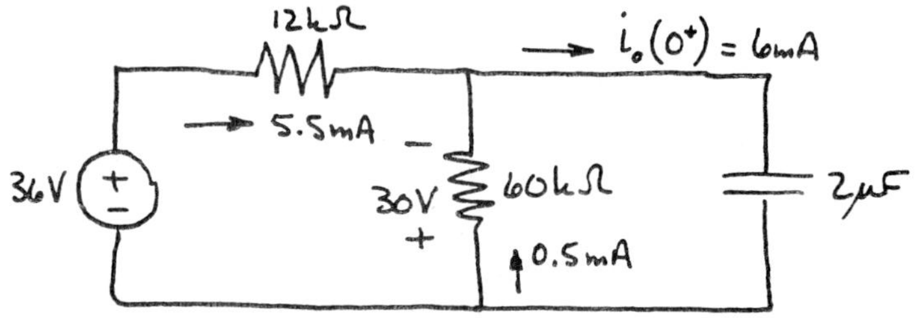

$$i_g(0^+) = \frac{30+36}{12} = 5.5\,\text{mA}$$

$$i_{60k}(0^+) = \frac{30}{60} = 0.5\,\text{mA}$$

$$i_o(0^+) = 5.5 + 0.5 = 6\,\text{mA}$$

which agrees with our solution.
We also know $i_o(\infty) = 0$, which agrees with our solution.
The time constant with respect to the terminals of the capacitor is $R_{\text{Th}}C$ Thus,

$$\tau = (10{,}000)(2 \times 10^{-6}) = 20\,\text{ms}; \qquad \therefore \quad \frac{1}{\tau} = 50,$$

which also agrees with our solution.
Thus our solution makes sense in terms of known circuit behavior.

P 17.20 [a] From the solution of Problem 17.19 we have

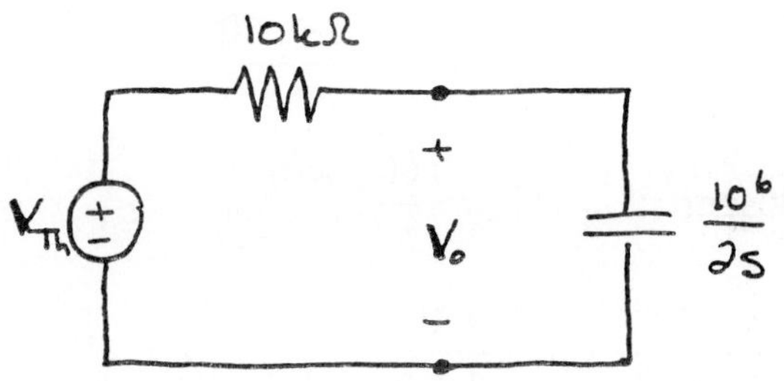

$$V_o = \frac{V_{\text{Th}}}{10^4 + (10^6/2s)} \cdot \frac{10^6}{2s}$$

$$H(s) = \frac{V_o}{V_{\text{Th}}} = \frac{50}{s+50}$$

$$H(j\omega) = \frac{50}{j\omega + 50}$$

$$V_{\text{Th}}(\omega) = \frac{60}{j\omega}$$

$$V_o(\omega) = \left(\frac{60}{j\omega}\right)\frac{50}{j\omega+50} = \frac{3000}{(j\omega)(j\omega+50)}$$

$$= \frac{60}{j\omega} - \frac{60}{j\omega+50}$$

$$v_o(t) = 30\text{sgn}(t) - 60e^{-50t}u(t)\ \text{V}$$

[b] $v_o(0^-) = -30$ V

$v_o(0^+) = 30 - 60 = -30$ V

This makes sense because there cannot be an instantaneous change in the voltage across a capacitor.

$v_o(\infty) = 30$ V

This agrees with $v_{\text{Th}}(\infty) = 30$ V.
As in Problem 17.19 we know the time constant is 20 ms.

P 17.21 [a]

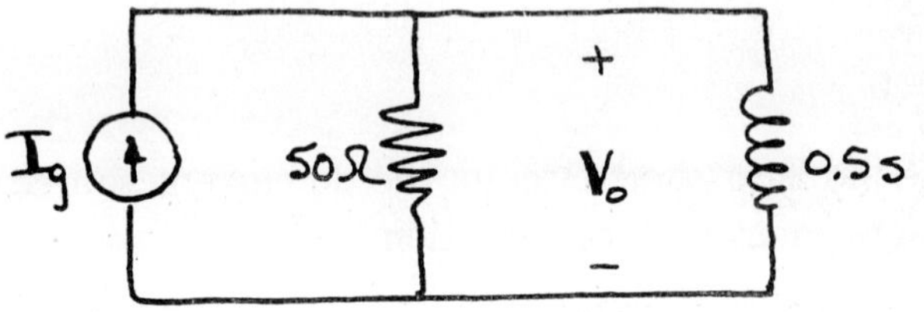

$$\frac{V_o}{50} + \frac{2V_o}{s} = I_g$$

$$V_o\left[\frac{1}{50} + \frac{2}{s}\right] = I_g$$

$$\frac{V_o}{I_g} = H(s) = \frac{50s}{s+100}$$

$$H(j\omega) = \frac{j\omega 50}{j\omega + 100}$$

$$I_g(\omega) = \frac{4}{j\omega}$$

$$V_o(\omega) = \frac{4}{j\omega} \cdot \frac{50(j\omega)}{j + 100} = \frac{200}{j\omega + 100}$$

$$\therefore \quad v_o(t) = 200e^{-100t}u(t)\text{ V}$$

[b] At $t = 0^-$ the circuit is

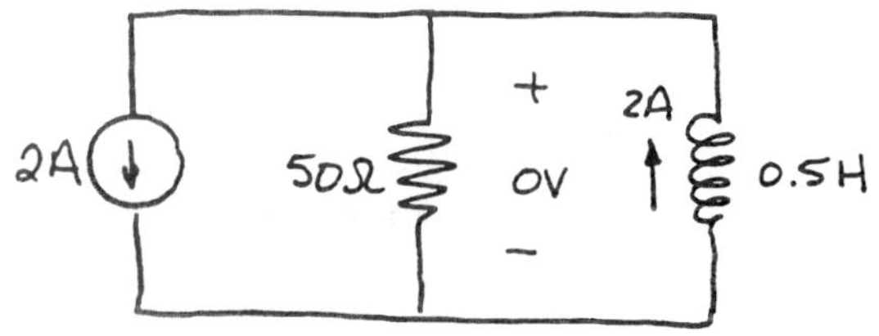

At $t = 0^+$ the circuit is

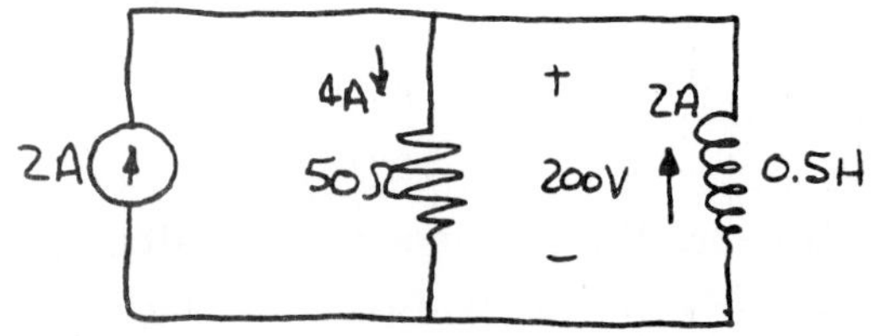

From the circuit

$$v_o(0^+) = (4)(50) = 200\text{ V}$$

which agrees with our solution.
At $t = \infty$

$$v_o(\infty) = 0$$

since the inductor short-circuits the dc current source. This is also in agreement with our solution.

$$\tau = L/R = 0.5/50 = 1/100; \qquad \therefore \quad 1/\tau = 100$$

which agrees with our solution.

P 17.22 [a] $I_o = \dfrac{V_o}{0.5s} = \dfrac{2}{s}\left(\dfrac{50sI_g}{s+100}\right)$

$$\frac{I_o}{I_g} = H(s) = \frac{100}{s+100}$$

$$H(j\omega) = \frac{100}{j\omega + 100}$$

$$I_g(\omega) = \frac{4}{j\omega}$$

$$I_o(\omega) = \frac{400}{j\omega(j\omega+100)} = \frac{4}{j\omega} - \frac{4}{j\omega+100}$$

$$\therefore \quad i_o(t) = 2\text{sgn}(t) - 4e^{-100t}u(t) \text{ A}$$

[b]
- From the solution to Problem 17.21(b) we note $i_o(0^-) = -2$ A and $i_o(0^+) = -2$ A. Our solution agrees with these results.
- From the circuit, $i_o(\infty) = 2$ A. Our solution agrees with this value.
- From the circuit, $\tau = 0.01$ s which agrees with our solution.

P 17.23 [a] $\frac{V_o}{V_g} = H(s) = \frac{4/s}{0.5 + 0.01s + 4/s}$

$$H(s) = \frac{400}{s^2 + 50s + 400} = \frac{400}{(s+10)(s+40)}$$

$$H(j\omega) = \frac{400}{(j\omega+10)(j\omega+40)}$$

$$V_g(\omega) = \frac{6}{j\omega}$$

$$V_o(\omega) = V_g(\omega)H(j\omega) = \frac{2400}{j\omega(j\omega+10)(j\omega+40)}$$

$$V_o(\omega) = \frac{K_1}{j\omega} + \frac{K_2}{j\omega+10} + \frac{K_3}{j\omega+40}$$

$$K_1 = \frac{2400}{400} = 6; \qquad K_2 = \frac{2400}{(-10)(30)} = -8$$

$$K_3 = \frac{2400}{(-40)(-30)} = 2$$

$$V_o(\omega) = \frac{6}{j\omega} - \frac{8}{j\omega+10} + \frac{2}{j\omega+40}$$

$$v_o(t) = 3\text{sgn}(t) - 8e^{-10t}u(t) + 2e^{-40t}u(t) \text{ V}$$

[b] $v_o(0^-) = -3$ V

[c] $v_o(0^+) = 3 - 8 + 2 = -3$ V

[d] For $t \geq 0^+$:

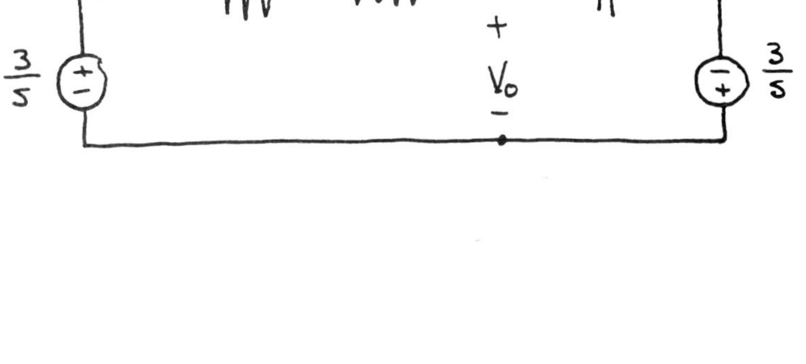

$$\frac{V_o - 3/s}{0.5 + 0.01s} + \frac{(V_o + 3/s)s}{4} = 0$$

$$V_o\left[\frac{100}{s+50} + \frac{s}{4}\right] = \frac{300}{s(s+50)} - 0.75$$

$$V_o = \frac{1200 - 3s^2 - 150s}{s(s+10)(s+40)} = \frac{K_1}{s} + \frac{K_2}{s+10} + \frac{K_3}{s+40}$$

$$K_1 = \frac{1200}{400} = 3; \qquad K_2 = \frac{1200 - 300 + 1500}{(-10)(30)} = -8$$

$$K_3 = \frac{1200 - 4800 + 6000}{(-40)(-30)} = 2$$

$$v_o(t) = (3 - 8e^{-10t} + 2e^{-40t})u(t)\text{ V}$$

[e] Yes.

P 17.24 [a] $I_o = \dfrac{V_g}{0.5 + 0.01s + 4/s}$

$$H(s) = \frac{I_o}{V_g} = \frac{100s}{s^2 + 50s + 400} = \frac{100s}{(s+10)(s+40)}$$

$$H(j\omega) = \frac{100(j\omega)}{(j\omega + 10)(j\omega + 40)}$$

$$V_g(\omega) = \frac{6}{j\omega}$$

$$I_o(\omega) = \frac{600}{(j\omega+10)(j\omega+40)} = \frac{20}{j\omega+10} - \frac{20}{j\omega+40}$$

$$i_o(t) = (20e^{-10t} - 20e^{-40t})u(t)\text{ A}$$

[b] $i_o(0^-) = 0$

[c] $i_o(0^+) = 0$

[d]

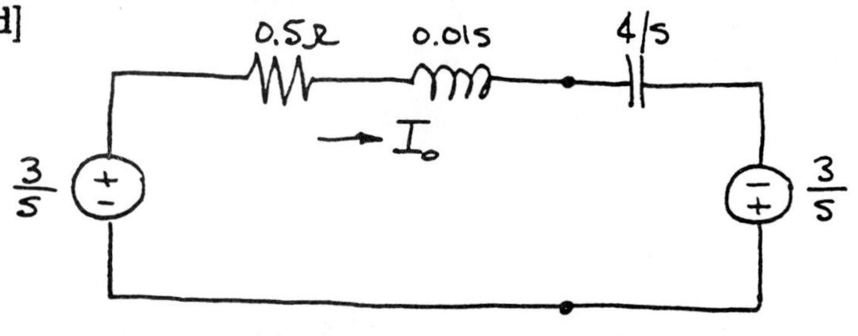

$$I_o = \frac{6/s}{0.5 + 0.01s + 4/s} = \frac{600}{s^2 + 50s + 400}$$

$$= \frac{600}{(s+10)(s+40)} = \frac{20}{s+10} - \frac{20}{s+40}$$

$$i_o(t) = (20e^{-10t} - 20e^{-40t})u(t)\ \text{A}$$

[e] Yes.

P 17.25 [a] $H(s) = \frac{V_o}{V_g} = \frac{(1/LC)}{s^2 + (s/RC) + (1/LC)}$

$$= \frac{100}{s^2 + 25s + 100} = \frac{100}{(s+5)(s+20)}$$

$$H(j\omega) = \frac{100}{(j\omega + 5)(j\omega + 20)}$$

$$v_g = 90e^{-10|t|}\ \text{V}$$

$$\therefore\ V_g(\omega) = \frac{1800}{(-j\omega + 10)(j\omega + 10)}$$

$$V_o(\omega) = \frac{180{,}000}{(j\omega + 5)(j\omega + 20)(j\omega + 10)(-j\omega + 10)}$$

$$= \frac{K_1}{j\omega + 5} + \frac{K_2}{j\omega + 20} + \frac{K_3}{j\omega + 10} + \frac{K_4}{-j\omega + 10}$$

$$K_1 = \frac{180{,}000}{(15)(15)(5)} = 160$$

$$K_2 = \frac{180{,}000}{(-15)(30)(-10)} = 40$$

$$K_3 = \frac{180{,}000}{(-5)(10)(20)} = -180$$

$$K_4 = \frac{180{,}000}{(15)(30)(20)} = 20$$

$$\therefore\ v_o(t) = (160e^{-5t} + 40e^{-20t} - 180e^{-10t})u(t) + 20e^{10t}u(-t)\ \text{V}$$

[b] $v_o(0^-) = 20\ \text{V}$

[c] $v_o(0^+) = 160 + 40 - 180 = 20\ \text{V}$

[d] $t \geq 0^+$:

$$v_o = 160e^{-5t} + 40e^{-20t} - 180e^{-10t}\ \text{V}$$

$$C\frac{dv_o}{dt} = -40e^{-5t} - 40e^{-20t} + 90e^{-10t}\ \text{A}$$

$$i_C(0^+) = -40 - 40 + 90 = 10\ \text{A}$$

$$i_R(0^+) = 20/0.8 = 25\ \text{A}$$

$$i_o(0^+) = 10 + 25 = 35\ \text{A}$$

[e] $t \geq 0^+$:

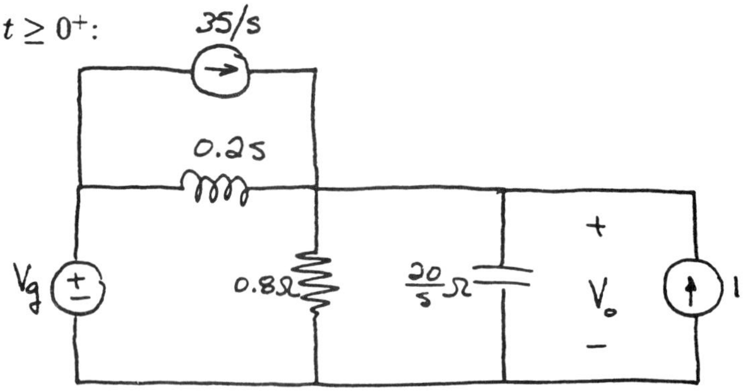

$$\frac{V_o - V_g}{0.2s} + \frac{V_o}{0.8} + \frac{V_o s}{20} = 1 + \frac{35}{s}$$

$$\therefore \quad V_o = \frac{100V_g}{(s+5)(s+20)} + \frac{20(s+35)}{(s+5)(s+20)}$$

$$v_g(t) = 90e^{-10t}u(t)\text{ V}; \qquad \therefore \quad V_g = \frac{90}{s+10}$$

$$\therefore \quad V_o = \frac{9000}{(s+5)(s+10)(s+20)} + \frac{20(s+35)}{(s+5)(s+20)}$$

$$= \frac{K_1}{s+5} + \frac{K_2}{s+10} + \frac{K_3}{s+20} + \frac{K_4}{s+5} + \frac{K_5}{s+20}$$

where

$K_1 = 120; \qquad K_2 = -180; \qquad K_3 = 60$

$K_4 = 40; \qquad K_5 = -20$

$$\therefore \quad V_o = \frac{160}{s+5} - \frac{180}{s+10} + \frac{40}{s+20}$$

$$\therefore \quad v_o(t) = (160e^{-5t} - 180e^{-10t} + 40e^{-20t})u(t)\text{ V}$$

[f] Yes.

P 17.26 [a]

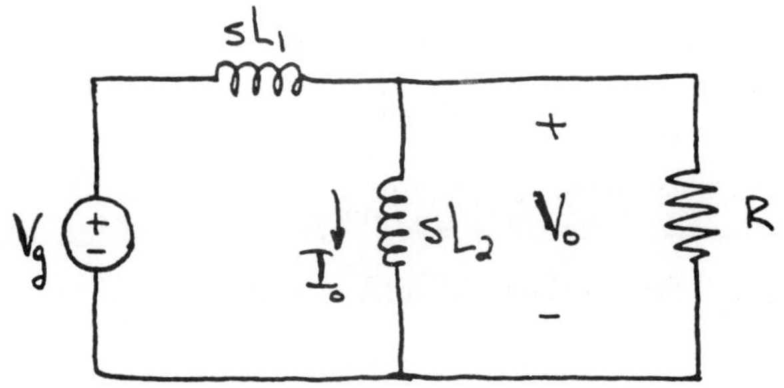

$$\frac{V_o - V_g}{sL_1} + \frac{V_o}{sL_2} + \frac{V_o}{R} = 0$$

$$\therefore \quad V_o = \frac{RV_g}{L_1\left[s + R\left(\frac{1}{L1} + \frac{1}{L_2}\right)\right]}$$

$$I_o = \frac{V_o}{sL_2}$$

$$\therefore \quad \frac{I_o}{V_g} = H(s) = \frac{R/L_1L_2}{s(s + R[(1/L_1) + (1/L_2)])}$$

$$\frac{R}{L_1L_2} = 12 \times 10^5$$

$$R\left(\frac{1}{L_1} + \frac{1}{L_2}\right) = 3 \times 10^4$$

$$\therefore \quad H(s) = \frac{12 \times 10^5}{s(s + 3 \times 10^4)}$$

$$H(j\omega) = \frac{12 \times 10^5}{j\omega(j\omega + 3 \times 10^4)}$$

$$V_g(\omega) = 125\pi[\delta(\omega + 4 \times 10^4) + \delta(\omega - 4 \times 10^4)]$$

$$I_o(\omega) = \frac{1500\pi \times 10^5[\delta(\omega + 4 \times 10^4) + \delta(\omega - 4 \times 10^4)]}{j\omega(j\omega + 3 \times 10^4)}$$

$$i_o(t) = \frac{1500\pi \times 10^5}{2\pi} \int_{-\infty}^{\infty} \frac{[\delta(\omega + 4 \times 10^4) + \delta(\omega - 4 \times 10^4)]e^{jt\omega}}{j\omega(j\omega + 3 \times 10^4)}\, d\omega$$

$$i_o(t) = 750 \times 10^5 \left\{\frac{e^{-j40{,}000t}}{-j40{,}000(30{,}000 - j40{,}000)} + \frac{e^{j40{,}000t}}{j40{,}000(30{,}000 + j40{,}000)}\right\}$$

$$= \frac{75 \times 10^6}{4 \times 10^8}\left\{\frac{e^{-j40{,}000t}}{-j(3 + j4)} + \frac{e^{j40{,}000t}}{j(3 + j4)}\right\}$$

$$= \frac{75}{400}\left\{\frac{e^{-j40{,}000t}}{5\underline{/-143.13^\circ}} + \frac{e^{j40{,}000t}}{5\underline{/143.13^\circ}}\right\}$$

$$= 0.075\cos(40{,}000t - 143.13^\circ)\ \text{A}$$

$$i_o(t) = 75\cos(40{,}000t - 143.13^\circ)\ \text{mA}$$

[b] In the phasor domain:

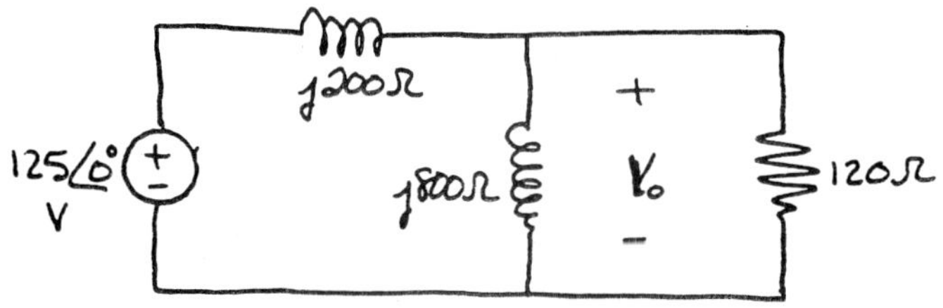

$$\frac{\mathbf{V}_o - 125}{j200} + \frac{\mathbf{V}_o}{j800} + \frac{\mathbf{V}_o}{120} = 0$$

$$12\mathbf{V}_o - 1500 + 3\mathbf{V}_o + j20\mathbf{V}_o = 0$$

$$\mathbf{V}_o = \frac{1500}{15 + j20} = 60\underline{/-53.13^\circ}\text{ V}$$

$$\mathbf{I}_o = \frac{\mathbf{V}_o}{j800} = 75 \times 10^{-3}\underline{/-143.13^\circ}\text{ A}$$

$$i_o(t) = 75\cos(40{,}000t - 143.13^\circ)\text{ mA}$$

P 17.27

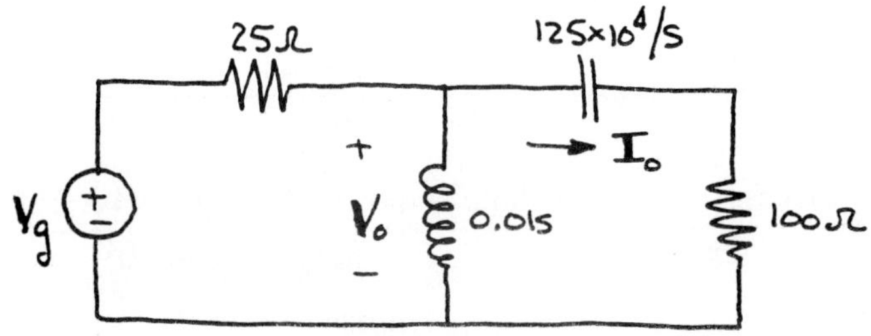

$$\frac{V_o - V_g}{2s} + \frac{100V_o}{s} + \frac{V_o s}{100s + 125 \times 10^4} = 0$$

$$\therefore \quad V_o = \frac{s(100s + 125 \times 10^4)V_g}{125(s^2 + 12{,}000s + 25 \times 10^6)}$$

$$I_o = \frac{sV_o}{100s + 125 \times 10^4}$$

$$H(s) = \frac{I_o}{V_g} = \frac{s^2}{125(s^2 + 12{,}000s + 25 \times 10^6)}$$

$$H(j\omega) = \frac{-8 \times 10^{-3}\omega^2}{25 \times 10^6 - \omega^2 + j12{,}000\omega}$$

$$V_g(\omega) = 300\pi[\delta(\omega + 5000) + \delta(\omega - 5000)]$$

$$I_o(\omega) = \frac{-2.4\pi\omega^2[\delta(\omega + 5000) + \delta(\omega - 5000)]}{(25 \times 10^6 - \omega^2) + j12{,}000\omega}$$

$$i_o(t) = \frac{-2.4\pi}{2\pi}\int_{-\infty}^{\infty} \frac{\omega^2[\delta(\omega + 5000) + \delta(\omega - 5000)]}{(25 \times 10^6 - \omega^2) + j12{,}000\omega} e^{jt\omega}\, d\omega$$

$$= -1.2\left\{\frac{25 \times 10^6 e^{-j5000t}}{-j(12{,}000)(5000)} + \frac{25 \times 10^6 e^{j5000t}}{j(12{,}000)(5000)}\right\}$$

$$= \frac{6}{12}\left\{\frac{e^{-j5000t}}{-j} + \frac{e^{j5000t}}{j}\right\}$$

$$= 0.5[e^{-j(5000t+90^\circ)} + e^{j(5000t+90^\circ)}]$$

$$i_o(t) = 1\cos(5000t + 90^\circ)\text{ A}$$

P 17.28 [a]

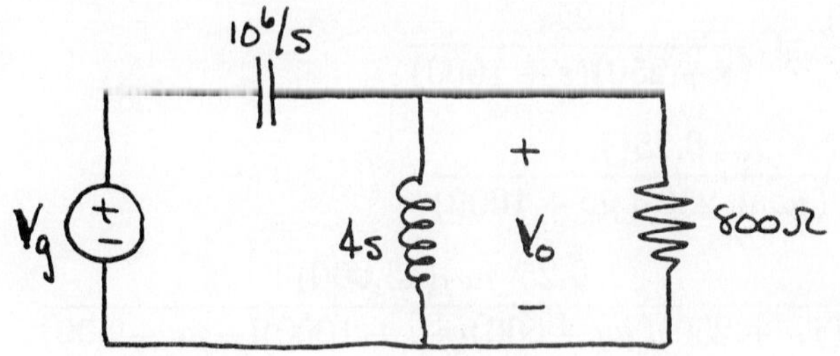

$$\frac{(V_o - V_g)s}{10^6} + \frac{V_o}{4s} + \frac{V_o}{800} = 0$$

$$\therefore\ V_o = \frac{s^2 V_g}{s^2 + 1250s + 25 \times 10^4}$$

$$\frac{V_o}{V_g} = H(s) = \frac{s^2}{(s + 250)(s + 1000)}$$

$$H(j\omega) = \frac{(j\omega)^2}{(j\omega + 250)(j\omega + 1000)}$$

$$v_g = 45e^{-500|t|}; \qquad V_g(\omega) = \frac{45{,}000}{(j\omega + 500)(-j\omega + 500)}$$

$$\therefore\ V_o(\omega) = \frac{45{,}000(j\omega)^2}{(j\omega + 250)(j\omega + 500)(j\omega + 1000)(-j\omega + 500)}$$

$$= \frac{K_1}{j\omega + 250} + \frac{K_2}{j\omega + 500} + \frac{K_3}{j\omega + 1000} + \frac{K_4}{-j\omega + 500}$$

$$K_1 = \frac{45{,}000(-250)^2}{(250)(750)(750)} = 20$$

$$K_2 = \frac{45{,}000(-500)^2}{(-250)(500)(1000)} = -90$$

$$K_3 = \frac{45{,}000(-1000)^2}{(-750)(-500)(1500)} = 80$$

$$K_4 = \frac{45{,}000(500)^2}{(750)(1000)(1500)} = 10$$

$$\therefore \quad v_o(t) = [20e^{-250t} - 90e^{-500t} + 80e^{-1000t}]u(t) + 10e^{500t}u(-t)\text{ V}$$

[b] $v_o(0^-) = 10\text{ V}; \qquad V_o(0^+) = 20 - 90 + 80 = 10\text{ V}$

$$v_o(\infty) = 0\text{ V}$$

[c] $I_L = \dfrac{V_o}{4s} = \dfrac{0.25sV_g}{(s+250)(s+1000)}$

$$H(s) = \frac{I_L}{V_o} = \frac{0.25s}{(s+250)(s+1000)}$$

$$H(j\omega) = \frac{0.25(j\omega)}{(j\omega+250)(j\omega+1000)}$$

$$I_L(\omega) = \frac{0.25(j\omega)(45{,}000)}{(j\omega+250)(j\omega+500)(j\omega+1000)(-j\omega+500)}$$

$$K_4 = \frac{(0.25)(500)(45{,}000)}{(750)(1000)(1500)} = 5\text{ mA}$$

$$i_L(t) = 5e^{500t}u(-t); \qquad \therefore \quad i_L(0^-) = 5\text{ mA}$$

$$K_1 = \frac{(0.25)(-250)(45{,}000)}{(250)(750)(750)} = -20\text{ mA}$$

$$K_2 = \frac{(0.25)(-500)(45{,}000)}{(-250)(500)(1000)} = 45\text{ mA}$$

$$K_3 = \frac{(0.25)(-1000)(45{,}000)}{(-750)(-500)(1500)} = -20\text{ mA}$$

$$\therefore \quad i_L(0^+) = K_1 + K_2 + K_3 = -20 + 45 - 20 = 5\text{ mA}$$

Checks, i.e., $\quad i_L(0^+) = i_L(0^-) = 5\text{ mA}$

At $t = 0^-$:

$$v_C(0^-) = 45 - 10 = 35\text{ V}$$

At $t = 0^+$:

$$v_C(0^+) = 45 - 10 = 35\text{ V}$$

[d] We can check the correctness of out solution for $t \geq 0^+$ by using the Laplace transform. Our circuit becomes

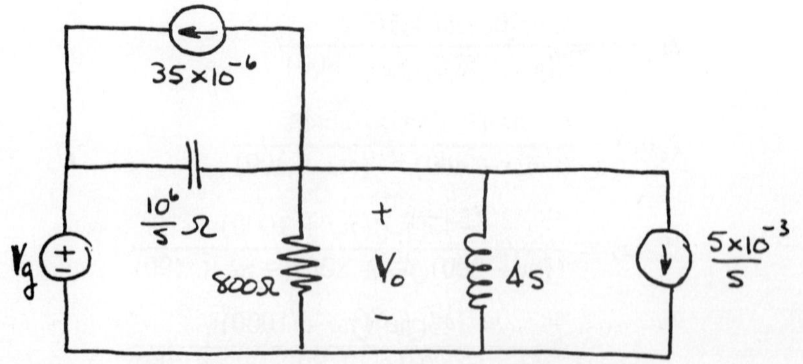

$$\frac{V_o}{800} + \frac{V_o}{4s} + \frac{(V_o - V_g)s}{10^6} + 35 \times 10^{-6} + \frac{5 \times 10^{-3}}{s} = 0$$

$$\therefore \quad (s^2 + 1250s + 24 \times 10^4)V_o = s^2 V_g - (35s + 5000)$$

$$v_g(t) = 45e^{-500t}u(t) \text{ V}; \qquad V_g = \frac{45}{s + 500}$$

$$\therefore \quad (s + 250)(s + 1000)V_o = \frac{45s^2 - (35s + 5000)(s + 500)}{(s + 500)}$$

$$\therefore \quad V_o = \frac{10s^2 - 22{,}500s - 250 \times 10^4}{(s + 250)(s + 500)(s + 1000)}$$

$$= \frac{20}{s + 250} - \frac{90}{s + 500} + \frac{80}{s + 1000}$$

$$\therefore \quad v_o(t) = [20e^{-250t} - 90e^{-500t} + 80e^{-1000t}]u(t) \text{ V}$$

This agrees with our solution for $v_o(t)$ for $t \geq 0^+$.

P 17.29 [a]

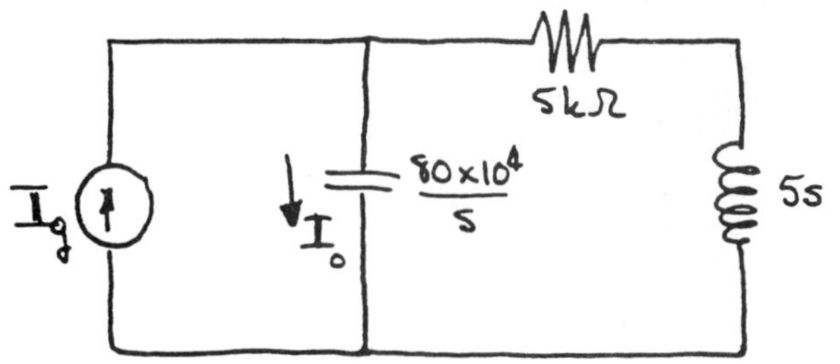

$$I_o = \frac{I_g(5000 + 5s)}{5000 + 5s + 80 \times 10^4/s}$$

$$\frac{I_o}{I_g} = H(s) = \frac{s(s + 1000)}{s^2 + 1000s + 16 \times 10^4}$$

$$H(s) = \frac{s(s+1000)}{(s+200)(s+800)}$$

$$H(j\omega) = \frac{j\omega(j\omega+1000)}{(j\omega+200)(j\omega+800)}$$

$$I_g(\omega) = \frac{-45}{(-j\omega+400)} + \frac{45}{(j\omega+400)}$$

$$I_o(\omega) = \frac{-45(j\omega)(j\omega+1000)}{(j\omega+200)(j\omega+800)(-j\omega+400)}$$

$$+\frac{45(j\omega)(j\omega+1000)}{(j\omega+200)(j\omega+800)(j\omega+400)}$$

$$= I_{o1} + I_{o2}$$

I_{o1}:

$$K_1 = \frac{-45(-200)(800)}{(600)(600)} = 20$$

$$K_2 = \frac{-45(-800)(200)}{(-600)(1200)} = -10$$

$$K_3 = \frac{-45(400)(1400)}{(600)(1200)} = -35$$

$$I_{o1} = \frac{20}{j\omega+200} - \frac{10}{j\omega+800} - \frac{35}{-j\omega+400}$$

I_{o2}:

$$K_1 = \frac{45(-200)(800)}{(200)(600)} = -60$$

$$K_2 = \frac{45(-800)(200)}{(-600)(-400)} = -30$$

$$K_3 = \frac{45(-400)(600)}{(-200)(400)} = 135$$

$$I_{o2} = \frac{-60}{j\omega+200} - \frac{30}{j\omega+800} + \frac{135}{j\omega+400}$$

$$\therefore \quad I_o = \frac{-40}{j\omega+200} - \frac{40}{j\omega+800} - \frac{35}{-j\omega+400} + \frac{135}{j\omega+400}$$

$$i_o(t) = (-40e^{-200t} - 40e^{-800t} + 135e^{-400t})u(t) - 35e^{400t}u(-t) \text{ A}$$

[b] At $t = 0^-$ we have

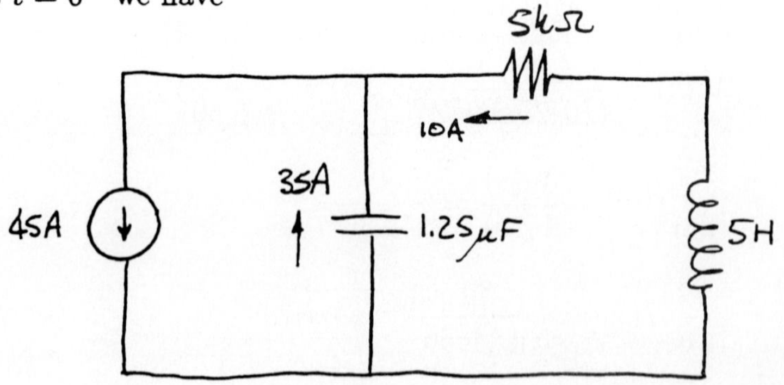

$\therefore \quad i_L(0^-) = -10\,\text{A}$

At $t = 0^+$ we have

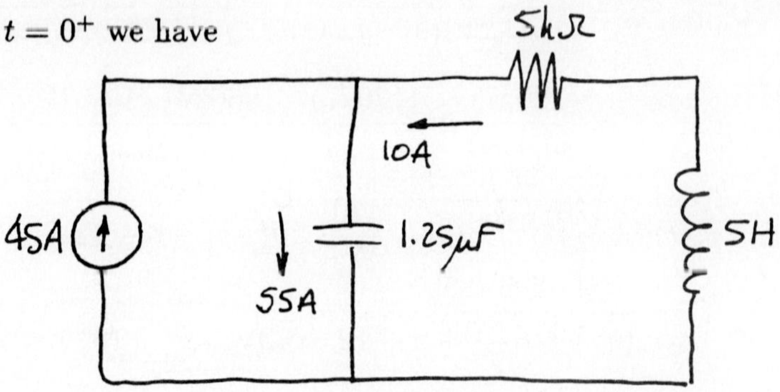

$\therefore \quad i_L(0^+) = -10\,\text{A}$

[d] Yes, there cannot be an instantaneous change in the inductor current,

$\therefore \quad i_L(0^-) = i_L(0^+)$

P 17.30 [a]

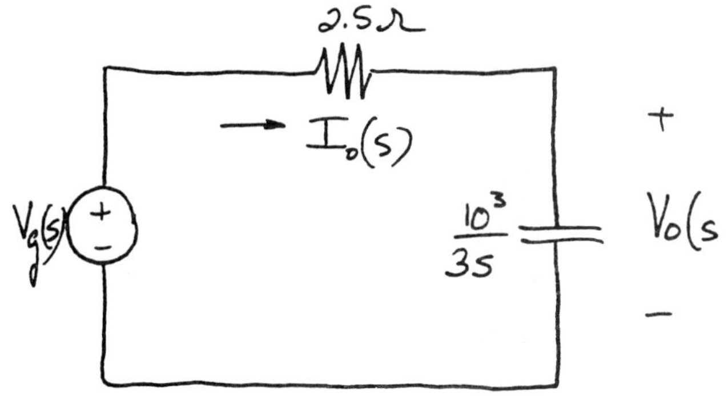

$v_g(t) = 18e^{4t}u(-t) - 12u(t); \qquad \therefore \quad V_g(\omega) = \dfrac{18}{4 - j\omega} - 12\pi\delta(\omega) - \dfrac{12}{j\omega}$

Using voltage division,

$$V_o(s) = \frac{(10^3/5s)}{(10^3/5s) + 2.5} V_g(s) = \frac{80}{s+80} V_g$$

$$\therefore \quad H(s) = \frac{V_o(s)}{V_g(s)} = \frac{80}{s+80}$$

$$\therefore \quad H(j\omega) = \frac{80}{j\omega + 80}$$

$$V_o(j\omega) = H(j\omega) \cdot V_g(\omega)$$

$$= \frac{(80)(18)}{(j\omega+80)(4-j\omega)} - \frac{(80)12\pi\delta(\omega)}{j\omega+80} - \frac{(12)(80)}{j\omega(j\omega+80)}$$

$$= \frac{(120/7)}{j\omega+80} + \frac{(120/7)}{4-j\omega} - \frac{960\pi\delta(\omega)}{j\omega+80} - \frac{12}{j\omega} + \frac{12}{j\omega+80}$$

$$v_o(t) = \frac{120}{7}e^{-80t}u(t) + \frac{120}{7}e^{4t}u(-t) - 6 - 12\text{sgn}(t) + 12e^{-80t}u(t)\text{V}$$

$$\therefore \quad v_o(0^-) = \frac{120}{7} - 6 + 12 = 13\text{V}; \qquad v_o(0^+) = \frac{120}{7} - 6 - 12 + 12 = 13\text{V}$$

The voltages at 0^- and 0^+ must be the same since the voltage cannot change instantaneously across a capacitor.

[b] $$I_o(s) = \frac{V_g(s)}{(10^3/5s) + 2.5} = \frac{0.4s}{s+80} V_g(s)$$

$$H(s) \frac{I_o(s)}{V_g(s)} = \frac{0.4s}{s+80}; \qquad \therefore \quad H(j\omega) = \frac{0.4j\omega}{j\omega+80}$$

$$I_o(j\omega) = H(j\omega) \cdot V_g(\omega)$$

$$= \frac{7.2j\omega}{(4-j\omega)(j\omega+80)} - \frac{4.8\pi\delta(\omega)j\omega}{j\omega+80} - \frac{4.8j\omega}{j\omega(j\omega+80)}$$

$$= \frac{(24/70)}{4-j\omega} - \frac{(48/7)}{j\omega+80} - \frac{4.8}{j\omega+80}$$

$$= \frac{(24/70)}{4-j\omega} - \frac{(816/70)}{j\omega+80}$$

$$i_o(t) = \frac{24}{70}e^{4t}u(-t) - \frac{816}{70}e^{-80t}u(t)\text{A}$$

$$\therefore \quad i_o(0^-) = 24/70\text{A}; \qquad i_o(0^+) = -816/70\text{A}$$

[c] $$v_o(t) = \frac{120}{7}e^{-80t}u(t) + \frac{120}{7}e^{4t}u(-t) - 6 - 12\text{sgn}(t) + 12e^{-80t}u(t)\text{V}$$

P 17.31 [a]

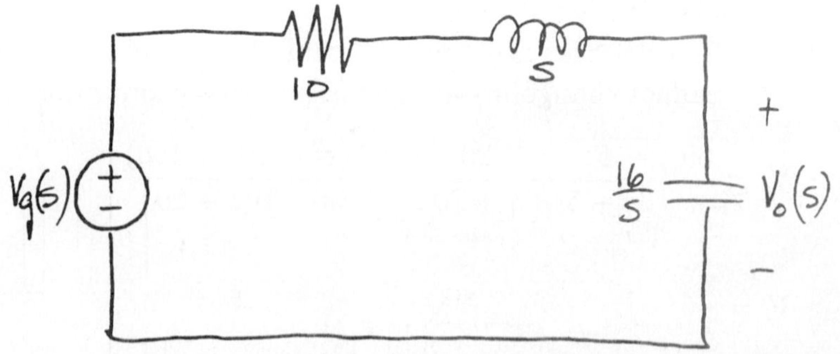

$$V_g(\omega) = \frac{36}{4 - j\omega} - \frac{36}{4 + j\omega} = \frac{72j\omega}{(4 - j\omega)(4 + j\omega)}$$

$$V_o(s) = \frac{(16/s)}{10 + s + (16/s)} V_g(s)$$

$$H(s) = \frac{V_o(s)}{V_g(s)} = \frac{16}{s^2 + 10s + 16} = \frac{16}{(s + 2)(s + 8)}$$

$$H(j\omega) = \frac{16}{(j\omega + 2)(j\omega + 8)}$$

$$V_o(j\omega) = H(j\omega) \cdot V_g(\omega) = \frac{1152j\omega}{(4 - j\omega)(4 + j\omega)(2 + j\omega)(8 + j\omega)}$$

$$= \frac{K_1}{4 - j\omega} + \frac{K_2}{4 + j\omega} + \frac{K_3}{2 + j\omega} + \frac{K_4}{8 + j\omega}$$

$$K_1 = \frac{1152(4)}{(8)(6)(12)} = 8$$

$$K_2 = \frac{1152(-4)}{(8)(-2)(4)} = 72$$

$$K_3 = \frac{1152(-2)}{(6)(2)(6)} = -32$$

$$K_4 = \frac{1152(-8)}{(12)(-4)(-6)} = -32$$

$$\therefore \quad V_o(j\omega) = \frac{8}{4 - j\omega} + \frac{72}{4 + j\omega} - \frac{32}{2 + j\omega} - \frac{32}{8 + j\omega}$$

$$\therefore \quad v_o(t) = 8e^{4t}u(-t) + [72e^{-4t} - 32e^{-2t} - 32e^{-8t}]u(t)\text{V}$$

$$v_o(0^-) = 8\text{V}$$

[b] $v_o(0^+) = 72 - 32 - 32 = 8\text{V}$

The voltages at 0^- and 0^+ must be the same since the voltage cannot change instantaneously across a capacitor.

P 17.32 $V_o = \frac{60}{s} - \frac{40}{s+5} + \frac{20}{s+20} = \frac{40(s^2+20s+150)}{s(s+5)(s+20)}$

$$V_i = \frac{8}{s}$$

$$H(s) = \frac{5(s^2+20s+150)}{(s+5)(s+20)}$$

$$H(j\omega) = \frac{5[(j\omega)^2 + 20(j\omega) + 150]}{(j\omega+5)(j\omega+20)}$$

$$V_i(\omega) = \frac{16}{(j\omega)}$$

$$V_o(\omega) = \frac{80[(j\omega)^2 + 20(j\omega) + 150]}{(j\omega+5)(j\omega+20)}$$

$$= \frac{K_1}{j\omega} + \frac{K_2}{j\omega+5} + \frac{K_3}{j\omega+20}$$

$$K_1 = \frac{(80)(150)}{100} = 120$$

$$K_2 = \frac{(80)(25-100+150)}{(-5)(15)} = -80$$

$$K_3 = \frac{(80)(150)}{300} = 40$$

$$\therefore \quad v_o(t) = 60\text{sgn}(t) - 80e^{-5t}u(t) + 40e^{-20t}u(t)\text{ V}$$

P 17.33 [a] $f(t) = \frac{1}{2\pi}\left\{\int_{-\infty}^{0} e^{\omega}e^{jt\omega}\,d\omega + \int_{0}^{\infty} e^{-\omega}e^{jt\omega}\,d\omega\right\} = \frac{1/\pi}{1+t^2}$

[b] $W = 2\int_0^\infty \frac{(1/\pi)^2}{(1+t^2)^2}\,dt = \frac{2}{\pi^2}\int_0^\infty \frac{dt}{(1+t^2)^2} = \frac{1}{2\pi}\ \text{J}$

[c] $W = \frac{1}{\pi}\int_0^\infty e^{-2\omega}\,d\omega = \frac{1}{\pi}\frac{e^{-2\omega}}{-2}\Big|_0^\infty = \frac{1}{2\pi}\ \text{J}$

[d] $\frac{1}{\pi}\int_0^{\omega_1} e^{-2\omega}\,d\omega = \frac{0.9}{2\pi}, \qquad 1 - e^{-2\omega_1} = 0.9, \qquad e^{2\omega_1} = 10$

$\omega_1 = (1/2)\ln 10 \cong 1.15\,\text{rad/s}$

P 17.34 $I_o = \frac{I_g(10)}{10+0.2s} = \frac{50I_g}{s+50}$

$$H(s) = \frac{I_o}{I_g} = \frac{50}{s+50}$$

$$H(j\omega) = \frac{50}{j\omega+50}$$

$$i(\omega) = \frac{3}{j\omega+25}$$

$$I_o(\omega) = \frac{150}{(j\omega+25)(j\omega+50)}$$

$$|I_o(\omega)| = \frac{150}{\sqrt{(\omega^2+625)(\omega^2+2500)}}$$

$$|I_o(\omega)|^2 = \frac{22{,}500}{(\omega^2+625)(\omega^2+2500)} = \frac{12}{\omega^2+625} - \frac{12}{\omega^2+2500}$$

$$W_o = \frac{1}{\pi}\int_0^\infty \frac{12d\omega}{\omega^2+625} - \frac{1}{\pi}\int_0^\infty \frac{12d\omega}{\omega^2+2500}$$

$$= \frac{12}{\pi}\cdot\frac{1}{25}\cdot\tan^{-1}\left(\frac{\omega}{25}\right)\Big|_0^\infty - \frac{12}{\pi}\cdot\frac{1}{50}\cdot\tan^{-1}\left(\frac{\omega}{50}\right)\Big|_0^\infty$$

$$= \frac{12}{25\pi}\cdot\frac{\pi}{2} - \frac{12}{50\pi}\cdot\frac{\pi}{2} = \frac{12}{50} - \frac{6}{50} = \frac{6}{50} = 120\,\text{mJ}$$

$\therefore\ W_o(\text{total}) = 120\,\text{mJ}$

$$W_o(10\text{rad/s}) = \frac{12}{\pi}\left(\frac{1}{25}\tan^{-1}(0.4)\right) - \frac{12}{\pi}\left(\frac{1}{50}\tan^{-1}(0.2)\right) = 43.06\,\text{mJ}$$

$$\% = \frac{43.06}{120}(100) = 35.88\%$$

P 17.35 [a] $V_g(\omega) = \dfrac{60}{(j\omega + 1)(-j\omega + 1)}$

$$H(s) = \frac{V_o}{V_g} = \frac{0.8s}{s+2}; \qquad H(\omega) = \frac{0.8(j\omega)}{(j\omega + 2)}$$

$$V_o(\omega) = \frac{48(j\omega)}{(j\omega + 1)(j\omega + 2)(-j\omega + 1)}$$

$$V_o(\omega) = \frac{-24}{j\omega + 1} + \frac{32}{j\omega + 2} + \frac{8}{-j\omega + 1}$$

$$v_o(t) = [32e^{-2t} - 24e^{-t}]u(t) + 8e^{t}u(-t)\text{ V}$$

[b] $|V_g(\omega)| = \dfrac{60}{(\omega^2 + 1)}$

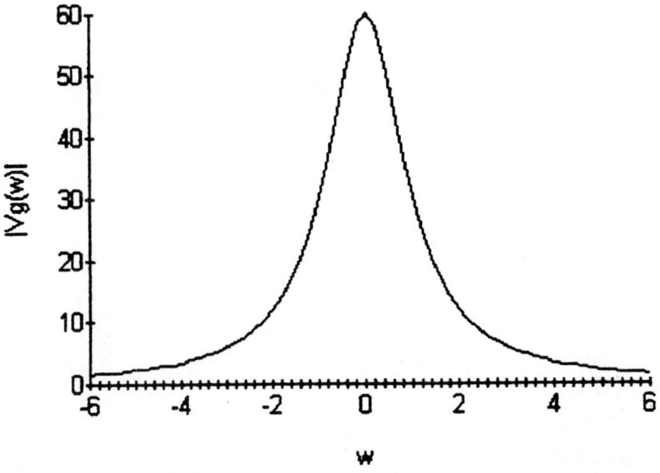

[c] $|V_o(\omega) = \dfrac{48\omega}{(\omega^2+1)\sqrt{\omega^2+4}}$

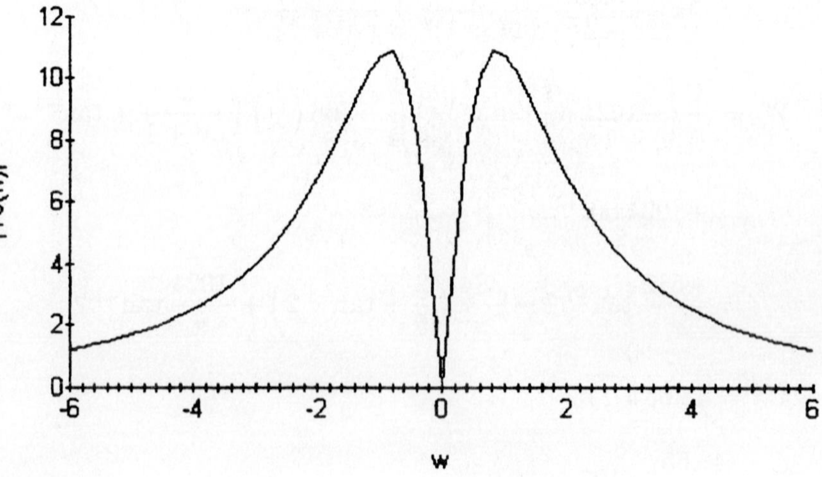

[d] $W_i = 2\int_0^\infty 900e^{-2t}\,dt = 1800\left.\dfrac{e^{-2t}}{-2}\right|_0^\infty = 900\,\text{J}$

[e] $W_o = \int_{-\infty}^0 64e^{2t}\,dt + \int_0^\infty (32e^{-2t} - 24e^{-t})^2\,dt$

$= 32\int_0^\infty [1024e^{-4t} - 1536e^{-3t} + 576e^{-2t}]\,dt$

$= 32 + 256 - 512 + 288 = 64\,\text{J}$

[f] $|V_g(\omega)| = \dfrac{60}{\omega^2+1}, \quad |V_g^2(\omega)| = \dfrac{3600}{(\omega^2+1)^2}$

$$W_g = \frac{3600}{\pi}\int_0^2 \frac{d\omega}{(\omega^2+1)^2}$$

$$= \frac{3600}{\pi}\left\{\frac{1}{2}\left(\frac{\omega}{\omega^2+1} + \tan^{-1}\omega\right)\Big|_0^2\right\}$$

$$= \frac{1800}{\pi}\left(\frac{2}{5} + \tan^{-1}2\right) = 863.53\,\text{J}$$

$$\therefore \quad \% = \left(\frac{863.53}{900}\right)\times 100 = 95.95\%$$

[g] $$|V_o(\omega)|^2 = \frac{2304\omega^2}{(\omega^2+1)^2(\omega^2+4)}$$

$$= \frac{-1024}{\omega^2+4} - \frac{768}{(\omega^2+1)^2} + \frac{1024}{(\omega^2+1)}$$

$$W_o = \frac{1}{\pi}\left\{-1024\cdot\frac{1}{2}\cdot\tan^{-1}\frac{\omega}{2}\Big|_0^2 - 768\left(\frac{1}{2}\right)\left(\frac{\omega}{\omega^2+1}+\tan^{-1}\omega\right)_0^2\right.$$

$$\left.+1024\tan^{-1}\omega\Big|_0^2\right\}$$

$$= \frac{-512}{\pi}\tan^{-1}1 - \frac{384}{\pi}\left(\frac{2}{5}+\tan^{-1}2\right) + \frac{1024}{\pi}\tan^{-1}2$$

$$= 48.65\ \text{J}$$

$$\% = \frac{48.65}{64}\times 100 = 76.02\%$$

P 17.36 $$I_o = \frac{0.5sI_g}{0.5s+25} = \frac{sI_g}{s+50}$$

$$H(s) = \frac{I_o}{I_g} = \frac{s}{s+50}$$

$$H(j\omega) = \frac{j\omega}{j\omega+50}$$

$$I(\omega) = \frac{12}{j\omega+10}$$

$$I_o(\omega) = \frac{12(j\omega)}{(j\omega+10)(j\omega+50)}$$

$$|I_o(\omega)| = \frac{12\omega}{\sqrt{(\omega^2+100)(\omega^2+2500)}}$$

$$|I_o(\omega)|^2 = \frac{144\omega^2}{(\omega^2+100)(\omega^2+2500)}$$

$$= \frac{-6}{\omega^2+100} + \frac{150}{\omega^2+2500}$$

$$W_o(\text{total}) = \frac{1}{\pi}\int_0^\infty \frac{150d\omega}{\omega^2+2500} - \frac{1}{\pi}\int_0^\infty \frac{6d\omega}{\omega^2+100}$$

$$= \frac{3}{\pi}\tan^{-1}\left(\frac{\omega}{50}\Big|_0^\infty\right) - \frac{0.6}{\pi}\tan^{-1}\left(\frac{\omega}{10}\Big|_0^\infty\right)$$

$$= 1.5 - 0.3 = 1.2\,\text{J}$$

$$W_o(0 — 100\ \text{rad/s}) = \frac{3}{\pi}\tan^{-1}(2) - \frac{0.6}{\pi}\tan^{-1}(10)$$

$$= 1.06 - 0.28 = 0.78\,\text{J}$$

Therefore, the percent between 0 and 100 rad/s is

$$\frac{0.78}{1.2}(100) = 64.69\%$$

P 17.37 [a] $|V_i(\omega)|^2 = (10 - 0.5\omega)(10 + 0.5\omega) = 100 - 0.25\omega^2$

[b] $H(s) = \dfrac{(1/RC)}{s + (1/RC)} = \dfrac{10}{s+10}$

$$H(j\omega) = \frac{10}{j\omega + 10}; \qquad |H(j\omega)|^2 = \frac{100}{\omega^2 + 100}$$

$$\therefore\ |V_o(\omega)|^2 = \frac{(100 - 0.25\omega^2)(100)}{\omega^2 + 100}$$

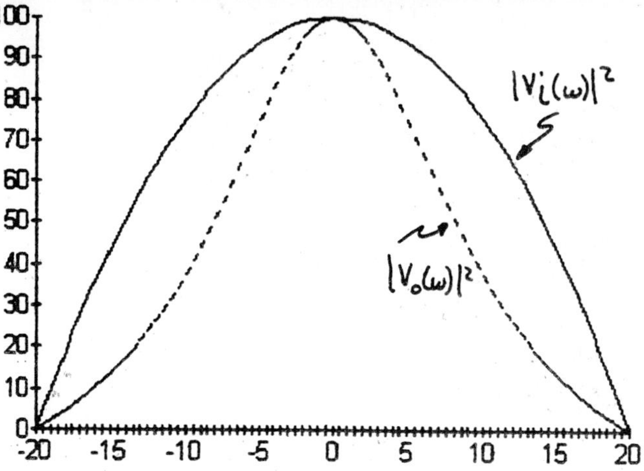

[c] $W_i = \frac{1}{\pi}\int_0^{20}(100 - 0.25\omega^2)d\omega$

$$= \frac{1}{\pi}\left[100\omega - \frac{0.25\omega^3}{3}\Big|_0^{20}\right]$$

$$= \frac{1}{\pi}[2000 - (2000/3)] = 4000/3\pi = 424.41 \text{ J}$$

[d] $W_o = \frac{1}{\pi}\int_0^{20}\frac{10^4 d\omega}{\omega^2+100} - \frac{1}{\pi}\int_0^{20}\frac{25 d\omega}{\omega^2+100}$

$$= \frac{1}{\pi}[\text{ Int1 } - \text{ Int2 }]$$

$$\text{Int1} = 10^4\left[\frac{1}{10}\tan^{-1}\frac{\omega}{10}\Big|_0^{20}\right]$$

$$= 1000\tan^{-1}(2) = 1107.15$$

$$\text{Int2} = 25\left[\omega - 100\cdot\frac{1}{10}\tan^{-1}\frac{\omega}{10}\Big|_0^{20}\right]$$

$$= 25[20 - 10\tan^{-1}(2)] = 223.21$$

$$W_o = \frac{1}{\pi}[1107.15 - 223.21] = 281.37 \text{ J}$$

P 17.38 [a] $V_i(\omega) = \frac{A}{a + j\omega}$; $\quad |V_i(\omega)| = \frac{A}{\sqrt{a^2+\omega^2}}$

$H(s) = \frac{s}{s+\alpha}$; $\quad H(j\omega) = \frac{j\omega}{\alpha + j\omega}$; $\quad |H(\omega)| = \frac{\omega}{\sqrt{\alpha^2+\omega^2}}$

Therefore $|V_o(\omega)| = \frac{\omega A}{\sqrt{(a^2+\omega^2)(\alpha^2+\omega^2)}}$

Therefore $|V_o(\omega)|^2 = \frac{\omega^2 A^2}{(a^2+\omega^2)(\alpha^2+\omega^2)}$

$W_{\text{IN}} = \int_0^\infty A^2 e^{-2at}\,dt = \frac{A^2}{2a}$; $\quad$ when $\alpha = a$ we have

$$W_{\text{OUT}} = \frac{A^2}{\pi}\int_0^a \frac{\omega^2\,d\omega}{(\omega^2+a^2)^2} = \frac{A^2}{\pi}\left\{\int_0^a \frac{d\omega}{a^2+\omega^2} - \int_0^a \frac{a^2\,d\omega}{(a^2+\omega^2)^2}\right\}$$

$$= \frac{A^2}{4a\pi}\left(\frac{\pi}{2} - 1\right)$$

$$W_{\text{OUT}}(\text{total}) = \frac{A^2}{\pi}\int_0^\infty \left[\frac{\omega^2}{(a^2+\omega^2)^2}\right] d\omega = \frac{A^2}{4a}$$

Therefore $\dfrac{W_{\rm OUT}(a)}{W_{\rm OUT}(\text{total})} = 0.5 - \dfrac{1}{\pi} = 0.1817$ or 18.17%

[b] When $\alpha \neq a$ we have

$$W_{\rm OUT}(\alpha) = \frac{1}{\pi}\int_0^\alpha \frac{\omega^2 A^2 d\omega}{(a^2+\omega^2)(\alpha^2+\omega^2)}$$

$$= \frac{A^2}{\pi}\left\{\int_0^\alpha \left[\frac{K_1}{a^2+\omega^2} + \frac{K_2}{\alpha^2+\omega^2}\right] d\omega\right\}$$

where $K_1 = \dfrac{a^2}{a^2-\alpha^2}$ and $K_2 = \dfrac{-\alpha^2}{a^2-\alpha^2}$

Therefore

$$W_{\rm OUT}(\alpha) = \frac{A^2}{\pi(a^2-\alpha^2)}\left[a\tan^{-1}\left(\frac{\alpha}{a}\right) - \frac{\alpha\pi}{4}\right]$$

$$W_{\rm OUT}(\text{total}) = \frac{A^2}{\pi(a^2-\alpha^2)}\left[a\frac{\pi}{2} - \alpha\frac{\pi}{2}\right] = \frac{A^2}{2(a+\alpha)}$$

Therefore $\dfrac{W_{\rm OUT}(\alpha)}{W_{\rm OUT}(\text{total})} = \dfrac{2}{\pi(a-\alpha)} \cdot \left[a\tan^{-1}\left(\dfrac{\alpha}{a}\right) - \dfrac{\alpha\pi}{4}\right]$

For $\alpha = a\sqrt{3}$, this ratio is 0.2723, or 27.23% of the output energy lies in the frequency band between 0 and $a\sqrt{3}$.

[c] For $\alpha = a/\sqrt{3}$, the ratio is 0.1057, or 10.57% of the output energy lies in the frequency band between 0 and $a/\sqrt{3}$.

18

Two-Port Circuits

Drill Exercises

DE 18.1 With port 2 short-circuited, we have

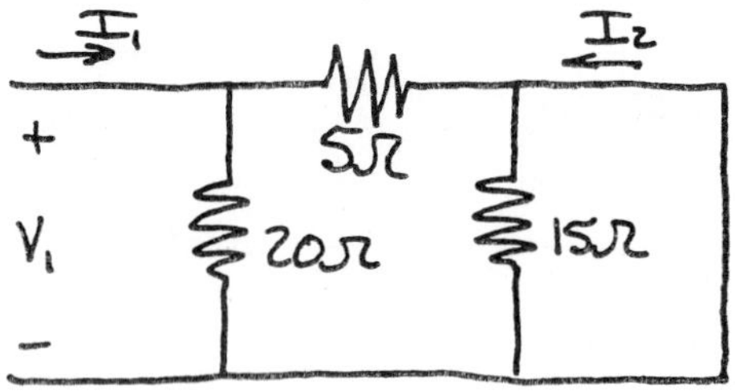

$$I_1 = \frac{V_1}{20} + \frac{V_1}{5}; \qquad \frac{I_1}{V_1} = y_{11} = 0.25\,\text{S}; \qquad I_2 = \left(\frac{-20}{25}\right) I_1 = -0.8I_1$$

When $V_2 = 0$, we have $I_1 = y_{11}V_1$ and $I_2 = y_{21}V_1$

Therefore $I_2 = -0.8(y_{11}V_1) = -0.8y_{11}V_1$

Thus $y_{21} = -0.8y_{11} = -0.2\,\text{S}$

With port 1 short-circuited, we have

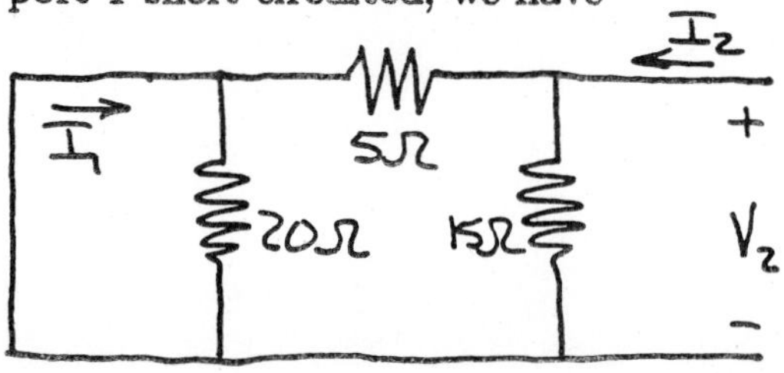

$$I_2 = \frac{V_2}{15} + \frac{V_2}{5}; \qquad \frac{I_2}{V_2} = y_{22} = \left(\frac{4}{15}\right)\,\text{S}$$

$$I_1 = \left(\frac{-15}{20}\right) I_2 = -0.75 I_2 = -0.75 y_{22} V_2$$

Therefore $y_{12} = (-0.75)\dfrac{4}{15} = -0.2\,\text{S}$

DE 18.2 $h_{11} = \left(\dfrac{V_1}{I_1}\right)_{V_2=0} = 20\|5 = 4\,\Omega$

$$h_{21} = \left(\frac{I_2}{I_1}\right)_{V_2=0} = \frac{(-20/25)I_1}{I_1} = -0.8$$

$$h_{12} = \left(\frac{V_1}{V_2}\right)_{I_1=0} = \frac{(20/25)V_2}{V_2} = 0.8$$

$$h_{22} = \left(\frac{I_2}{V_2}\right)_{I_1=0} = \frac{1}{15} + \frac{1}{25} = \frac{8}{75}\,\text{S}$$

$$g_{11} = \left(\frac{I_1}{V_1}\right)_{I_2=0} = \frac{1}{20} + \frac{1}{20} = 0.1\,\text{S}$$

$$g_{21} = \left(\frac{V_2}{V_1}\right)_{I_2=0} = \frac{(15/20)V_1}{V_1} = 0.75$$

$$g_{12} = \left(\frac{I_1}{I_2}\right)_{V_1=0} = \frac{(-15/20)I_2}{I_2} = -0.75$$

$$g_{22} = \left(\frac{V_2}{I_2}\right)_{V_1=0} = 15\|5 = \frac{75}{20} = 3.75\,\Omega$$

DE 18.3 $g_{11} = \dfrac{I_1}{V_1}\bigg|_{I_2=0} = \dfrac{5 \times 10^{-6}}{50 \times 10^{-3}} = 0.1\,\text{mS}$

$$g_{21} = \frac{V_2}{V_1}\bigg|_{I_2=0} = \frac{200 \times 10^{-3}}{50 \times 10^{-3}} = 4$$

$$g_{12} = \frac{I_1}{I_2}\bigg|_{V_1=0} = \frac{2 \times 10^{-6}}{0.5 \times 10^{-6}} = 4$$

$$g_{22} = \frac{V_2}{I_2}\bigg|_{V_1=0} = \frac{10 \times 10^{-3}}{0.5 \times 10^{-6}} = 20\,\text{k}\Omega$$

DE 18.4 First calculate the b-parameters:

$$b_{11} = \left.\frac{V_2}{V_1}\right|_{I_1=0} = \frac{15}{10} = 1.5\,\Omega; \qquad b_{21} = \left.\frac{I_2}{V_1}\right|_{I_1=0} = \frac{30}{10} = 3\,\text{S}$$

$$b_{12} = \left.\frac{-V_2}{I_1}\right|_{V_1=0} = \frac{-10}{-5} = 2\,\Omega; \qquad b_{22} = \left.\frac{-I_2}{I_1}\right|_{V_1=0} = \frac{-4}{-5} = 0.8$$

Now the z-parameters are calculated:

$$z_{11} = \frac{b_{22}}{b_{21}} = \frac{0.8}{3} = \frac{4}{15}\,\Omega; \qquad z_{12} = \frac{1}{b_{21}} = \frac{1}{3}\,\Omega$$

$$z_{21} = \frac{\Delta b}{b_{21}} = \frac{(1.5)(0.8) - 6}{3} = -1.6\,\Omega; \qquad z_{22} = \frac{b_{11}}{b_{21}} = \frac{1.5}{3} = \frac{1}{2}\,\Omega$$

DE 18.5 [a] Let V equal the voltage across the 5 A source, positive at the top; then

$$V = 5R_{eq} \quad \text{where} \quad \frac{1}{R_{eq}} = \frac{1}{12} + \frac{1}{20} + \frac{1}{30} = \frac{1}{6}\,\text{S}$$

Therefore $R_{eq} = 6\,\Omega$ and $V = 30\,\text{V}$

It follows that $V_m = \frac{5}{30}(30) = 5\,\text{V}$

[b] Let i equal the current (from left to right) in the $25\,\Omega$ resistor, then

$$i = \frac{(5)(5)}{5 + 25 + (240/32)} = \frac{2}{3}\,\text{A}$$

Now $V_m = \left(\frac{2}{3}\right)\left(\frac{240}{32}\right) = 5\,\text{V}$

DE 18.6 $z_{11} = z_{22}, \quad z_{12} = z_{21}, \quad 95 = z_{11}(5) + z_{12}(0)$

Therefore, $z_{11} = z_{22} = 95/5 = 19\,\Omega$

$$11.52 = 19I_1 - z_{12}(2.72)$$

$$0 = z_{12}I_1 - 19(2.72)$$

Solving these simultaneous equations for z_{12} yields the quadratic equation

$$z_{12}^2 + \left(\frac{72}{17}\right)z_{12} - \frac{6137}{17} = 0$$

For a purely resistive network, it follows that $z_{12} = z_{21} = 17\,\Omega$.

DE 18.7 [a] $I_2 = \dfrac{-V_g}{a_{11}Z_L + a_{12} + a_{21}Z_gZ_L + a_{22}Z_g}$

$$= \frac{-50 \times 10^{-3}}{(5 \times 10^{-4})(5 \times 10^3) + 10 + (10^{-6})(100)(5 \times 10^3) + (-3 \times 10^{-2})(100)}$$

$$= \frac{-50 \times 10^{-3}}{10} = -5\,\text{mA}$$

$$P_L = \frac{1}{2}(5 \times 10^{-3})^2(5 \times 10^3) = 62.5\,\text{mW}$$

[b] $Z_{\text{Th}} = \dfrac{a_{12} + a_{22}Z_g}{a_{11} + a_{21}Z_g} = \dfrac{10 + (-3 \times 10^{-2})(100)}{5 \times 10^{-4} + (10^{-6})(100)}$

$$= \frac{7}{6 \times 10^{-4}} = \frac{70}{6}\,\text{k}\Omega$$

[c] $V_{\text{Th}} = \dfrac{V_g}{a_{11} + a_{21}Z_g} = \dfrac{50 \times 10^{-3}}{6 \times 10^{-4}} = \dfrac{500}{6}\,\text{V}$

Therefore $V_2 = \dfrac{250}{6}\,\text{V}$; $P_{\text{max}} = \dfrac{(1/2)(250/6)^2}{(70/6) \times 10^3} = 74.4\,\text{mW}$

DE 18.8 [a] For the given bridged-tee circuit, we have

$$a'_{11} = a'_{22} = 1.25, \qquad a'_{21} = \frac{1}{20}\,\text{S}, \qquad a'_{12} = 11.25\,\Omega$$

The a-parameters of the cascaded networks are

$$a_{11} = (1.25)^2 + (11.25)(0.05) = 2.125$$

$$a_{12} = (1.25)(11.25) + (11.25)(1.25) = 28.125\,\Omega$$

$$a_{21} = (0.05)(1.25) + (1.25)(0.05) = 0.125\,\text{S}$$

$$a_{22} = a_{11} = 2.125, \qquad R_{\text{Th}} = (45.125/3.125) = 14.44\,\Omega$$

[b] $V_t = \dfrac{100}{3.125} = 32\,\text{V}$; therefore $V_2 = 16\,\text{V}$

[c] $P = \dfrac{16^2}{14.44} = 17.73\,\text{W}$

Problems

P 18.1

$$h_{11} = \left(\frac{V_1}{I_1}\right)_{V_2=0} = 20\|5 = 4\,\Omega$$

$$h_{21} = \left(\frac{I_2}{I_1}\right)_{V_2=0} = \frac{(-20/25)I_1}{I_1} = -0.8$$

$$h_{12} = \left(\frac{V_1}{V_2}\right)_{I_1=0} = \frac{(20/25)V_2}{V_2} = 0.8$$

$$h_{22} = \left(\frac{I_2}{V_2}\right)_{I_1=0} = \frac{1}{15} + \frac{1}{25} = \frac{8}{75}\,\text{S}$$

$$g_{11} = \left(\frac{I_1}{V_1}\right)_{I_2=0} = \frac{1}{20} + \frac{1}{20} = 0.1\,\text{S}$$

$$g_{21} = \left(\frac{V_2}{V_1}\right)_{I_2=0} = \frac{(15/20)V_1}{V_1} = 0.75$$

$$g_{12} = \left(\frac{I_1}{I_2}\right)_{V_1=0} = \frac{(-15/20)I_2}{I_2} = -0.75$$

$$g_{22} = \left(\frac{V_2}{I_2}\right)_{V_1=0} = 15\|5 = \frac{75}{20} = 3.75\,\Omega$$

P 18.2 $V_1 = z_{11}I_1 + z_{12}I_2$

$$V_1 = z_{21}I_1 + z_{22}I_2$$

$$z_{11} = \left.\frac{V_1}{I_1}\right|_{I_2=0} = 5\|20 + 16 = 20\,\Omega$$

$$z_{21} = \left.\frac{V_2}{I_1}\right|_{I_2=0} = 16 + (10)(5/25) = 18\,\Omega$$

$$z_{12} = \left.\frac{V_1}{I_2}\right|_{I_1=0} = 16 + (10/25)(5) = 18\,\Omega$$

$$z_{22} = \left.\frac{V_2}{I_2}\right|_{I_1=0} = 10\|15 + 16 = 22\,\Omega$$

Summary:

$z_{11} = 20\,\Omega \quad z_{12} = 18\,\Omega \quad z_{21} = 18\,\Omega \quad z_{22} = 22\,\Omega$

P 18.3 $V_2 = b_{11}V_1 - b_{12}I_1$

$I_2 = b_{21}V_1 - b_{22}I_1$

$$b_{12} = \left.\frac{-V_2}{I_1}\right|_{V_1=0}; \qquad b_{22} = \left.\frac{-I_2}{I_1}\right|_{V_1=0}$$

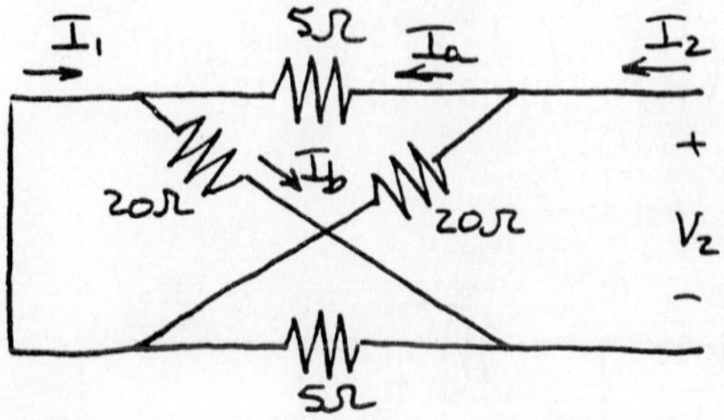

$5\|20 = 4\,\Omega$

$$I_2 = \frac{V_2}{4+4} = \frac{V_2}{8}; \qquad I_1 = I_b - I_a$$

$$I_a = \frac{20}{25}I_2; \qquad I_b = \frac{5}{25}I_2$$

$$I_1 = \left(\frac{5}{25} - \frac{20}{25}\right)I_2 = \frac{-15}{25}I_2 = \frac{-3}{5}I_2$$

$$b_{22} = \frac{-I_2}{I_1} = \frac{5}{3}$$

$$b_{12} = \frac{-V_2}{I_1} = \frac{-V_2}{I_2}\left(\frac{I_2}{I_1}\right) = 8\left(\frac{5}{3}\right) = \frac{40}{3}\,\Omega$$

$$b_{11} = \left.\frac{V_2}{V_1}\right|_{I_1=0}; \qquad b_{21} = \left.\frac{I_2}{V_1}\right|_{I_1=0}$$

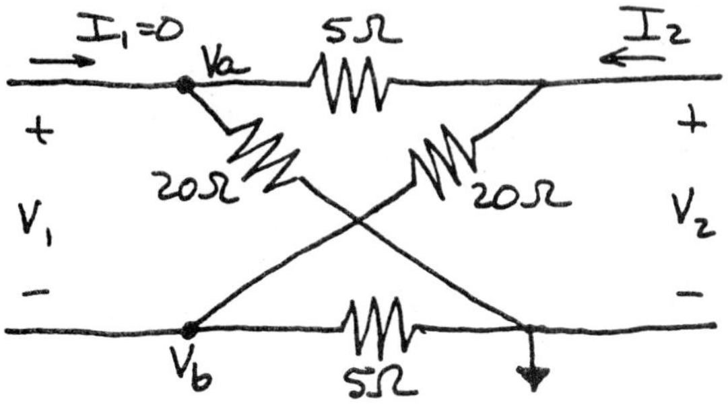

$$V_1 = V_a - V_b; \quad V_a = \frac{20}{25}V_2; \quad V_b = \frac{5}{25}V_2$$

$$V_1 = \frac{20}{25}V_2 - \frac{5}{25}V_2 = \frac{15}{25}V_2 = \frac{3}{5}V_2$$

$$b_{11} = \frac{V_2}{V_1} = \frac{5}{3}$$

$$V_2 = (20+5)\|(20+5)I_2 = 12.5I_2$$

$$b_{21} = \frac{I_2}{V_1} = \left(\frac{I_2}{V_2}\right)\left(\frac{V_2}{V_1}\right) = \left(\frac{1}{12.5}\right)\left(\frac{5}{3}\right) = \frac{2}{15}\,\mathrm{S}$$

P 18.4 $h_{11} = \left.\frac{V_1}{I_1}\right|_{V_2=0}; \qquad h_{21} = \left.\frac{I_2}{I_1}\right|_{V_2=0}$

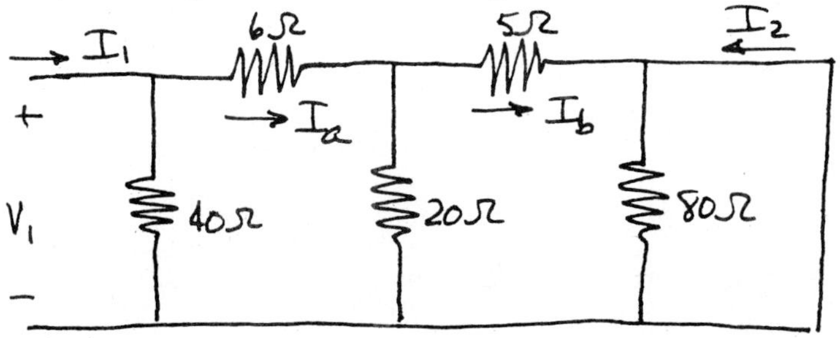

$$5\|20 = 4\,\Omega, \quad 6+4 = 10\,\Omega, \quad 40\|10 = 8\,\Omega$$

$$\therefore \quad h_{11} = 8\,\Omega$$

$$I_a = \frac{I_1(40)}{50} = 0.8I_1; \quad I_b = \frac{I_a(20)}{25} = 0.8I_b$$

$$I_2 = -I_b = -0.64I_1; \qquad \therefore \quad h_{21} = -0.64$$

$$h_{12} = \left.\frac{V_1}{V_2}\right|_{I_1=0}; \qquad h_{22} = \left.\frac{I_2}{V_2}\right|_{I_1=0}$$

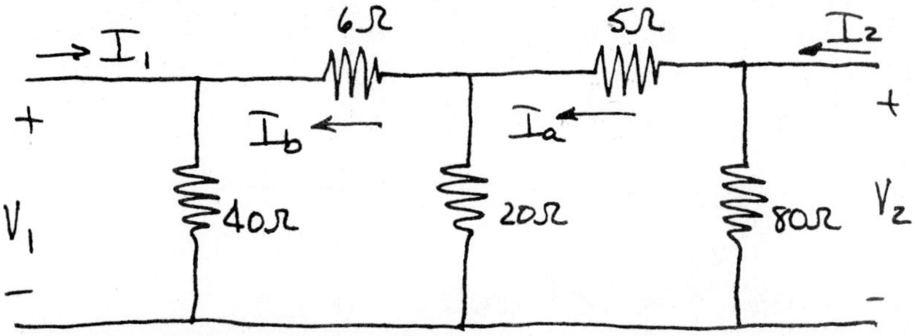

$$I_a = \frac{V_2}{5 + [(46)(20)/66]} = \frac{66V_2}{1250}; \qquad I_b = \frac{20}{66}I_a = \frac{20V_2}{1250}$$

$$V_1 = 40I_b = \frac{800V_2}{1250} \qquad \therefore \quad h_{12} = \frac{800}{1250} = 0.64$$

$$I_2 = \frac{V_2}{80} + \frac{66V_2}{1250} \qquad \therefore \quad h_{22} = 0.0125 + 0.0528 = 0.0653\,\mho$$

P 18.5 $V_1 = a_{11}V_2 - a_{12}I_2$

$I_1 = a_{21}V_2 - a_{22}I_2$

$a_{11} = \left.\frac{V_1}{V_2}\right|_{I_2=0}; \qquad a_{21} = \left.\frac{I_1}{V_2}\right|_{I_2=0}$

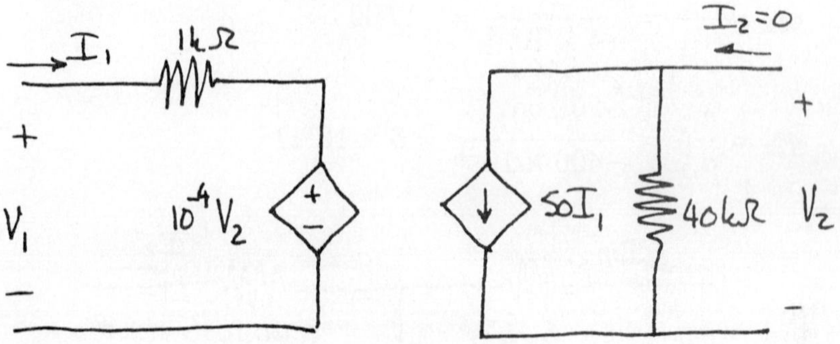

$V_1 = 10^3 I_1 + 10^{-4}V_2 = 10^3(-0.5 \times 10^{-6})V_2 + 10^{-4}V_2$

$\therefore \quad a_{11} = -5 \times 10^{-4} + 10^{-4} = -4 \times 10^{-4}$

$V_2 = -(50I_1)(40 \times 10^3); \qquad \therefore \quad a_{21} = -\frac{1}{2 \times 10^6} = -0.5\,\mu\text{S}$

$a_{12} = \left.\frac{-V_1}{I_2}\right|_{V_2=0}; \qquad a_{22} = \left.\frac{-I_1}{I_2}\right|_{V_2=0}$

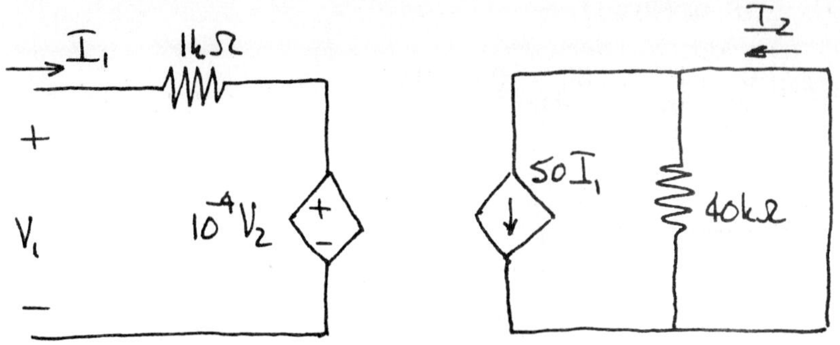

$I_2 = 50I_1; \qquad \therefore \quad a_{22} = -\frac{I_1}{I_2} = -\frac{1}{50}$

$V_1 = 1000I_1; \qquad \therefore \quad a_{12} = -\frac{V_1}{I_2} = -\frac{V_1}{I_1}\frac{I_1}{I_2} = -(1000)(1/50) = -20\,\Omega$

Summary

$a_{11} = -4 \times 10^{-4}; \quad a_{12} = -20\,\Omega; \quad a_{21} = -0.5\,\mu\text{S}; \quad a_{22} = -\frac{1}{50}$

P 18.6 $$g_{11} = \frac{a_{21}}{a_{11}} = \frac{-0.5 \times 10^{-6}}{-4 \times 10^{-4}} = 1.25\,\text{mS}$$

$$g_{12} = \frac{-\Delta a}{a_{11}} = \frac{-(-4 \times 10^{-4})(-1/50) - (-0.5 \times 10^{-6})(-20)}{-4 \times 10^{-4}} = -0.005$$

$$g_{21} = \frac{1}{a_{11}} = \frac{1}{-4 \times 10^{-4}} = -2500$$

$$g_{22} = \frac{a_{12}}{a_{11}} = \frac{(-20)}{-400 \times 10^{-6}} = 5 \times 10^{4}\,\Omega$$

P 18.7

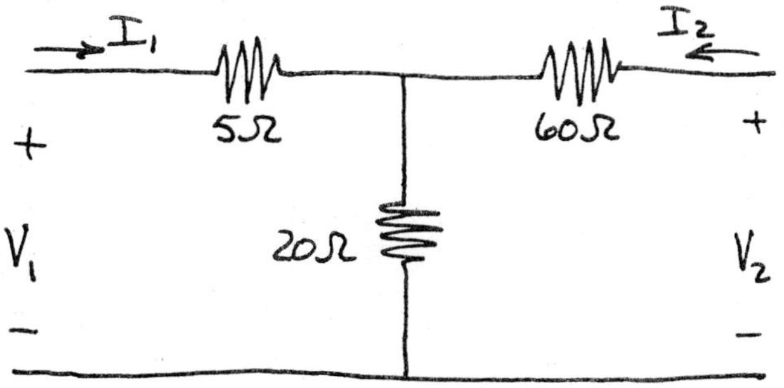

$$z_{11} = \left.\frac{V_1}{I_1}\right|_{I_2=0} = 5 + 20 = 25\,\Omega$$

$$z_{21} = \left.\frac{V_2}{I_1}\right|_{I_2=0} = 20\,\Omega$$

$$z_{22} = \left.\frac{V_2}{I_2}\right|_{I_1=0} = 60 + 20 = 80\,\Omega$$

$$z_{21} = \left.\frac{V_1}{I_2}\right|_{I_1=0} = 20\,\Omega$$

P 18.8 $$\Delta z = (25)(80) - (20)(20) = 1600$$

$$y_{11} = \frac{z_{22}}{\Delta z} = \frac{80}{1600} = \frac{1}{20}\,\text{S}$$

$$y_{12} = \frac{-z_{12}}{\Delta z} = \frac{-20}{1600} = \frac{-1}{80}\,\text{S}$$

$$y_{21} = \frac{-z_{21}}{\Delta z} = \frac{-20}{1600} = \frac{-1}{80}\,\text{S}$$

$$y_{22} = \frac{-z_{11}}{\Delta z} = \frac{25}{1600} = \frac{1}{64}\,\text{S}$$

P 18.9 $a_{11} = \left.\frac{V_1}{V_2}\right|_{I_2=0}; \qquad V_2 = \frac{V_1}{R_1 + R_3}R_3$

$$\therefore \quad a_{11} = \frac{R_1 + R_3}{R_3} = 1 + \frac{R_1}{R_3} = 1.2$$

$$\therefore \quad \frac{R_1}{R_3} = 0.2$$

$$a_{21} = \left.\frac{I_1}{V_2}\right|_{I_2=0}; \qquad V_2 = I_1R_3; \qquad \therefore \quad a_{21} = \frac{1}{R_3} = 20 \times 10^{-3}$$

$$R_3 = \frac{1000}{20} = 50\,\Omega; \qquad \therefore \quad R_1 = 0.2R_3 = 10\,\Omega$$

$$a_{22} = -\left.\frac{I_1}{I_2}\right|_{V_2=0}$$

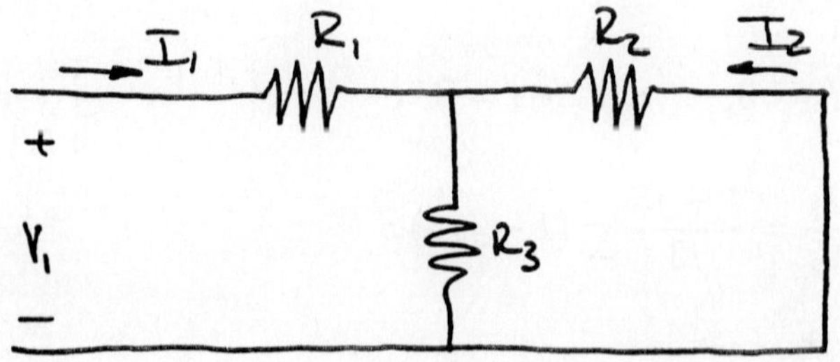

$$I_2 = \frac{-I_1R_3}{R_3 + R_2}; \qquad \therefore \quad a_{22} = \frac{R_2 + R_3}{R_3} = 1.4$$

$$\therefore \quad \frac{R_2}{R_3} = 0.40; \qquad R_2 = 0.4R_3 = 20\,\Omega$$

Summary: $R_1 = 10\,\Omega; \quad R_2 = 20\,\Omega; \quad R_3 = 50\,\Omega$

P 18.10 $h_{11} = \left.\frac{V_1}{I_1}\right|_{V_2=0}; \qquad h_{21} = \left.\frac{I_2}{I_1}\right|_{V_2=0}$

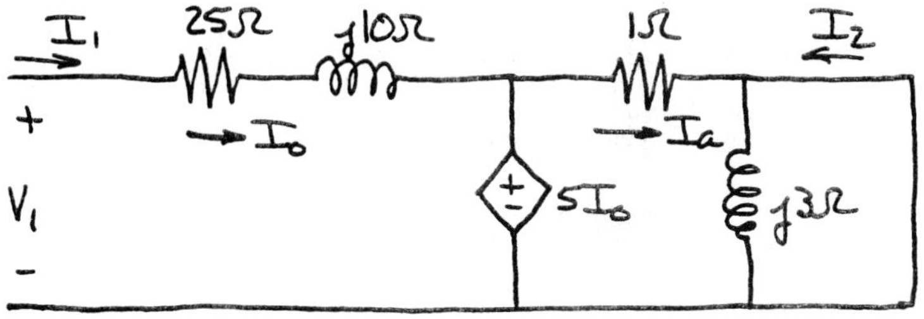

$$I_a = \frac{5I_o}{1} = 5I_1 = -I_2; \qquad \therefore \quad h_{21} = -5$$

$$V_1 = (25 + j10)I_o + 5I_o = (30 + j10)I_o = (30 + j10)I_1$$

$\therefore \quad h_{11} = 30 + j10\,\Omega$

$$h_{12} = \frac{V_1}{V_2}\bigg|_{I_1=0}; \qquad h_{22} = \frac{I_2}{V_2}\bigg|_{I_1=0}$$

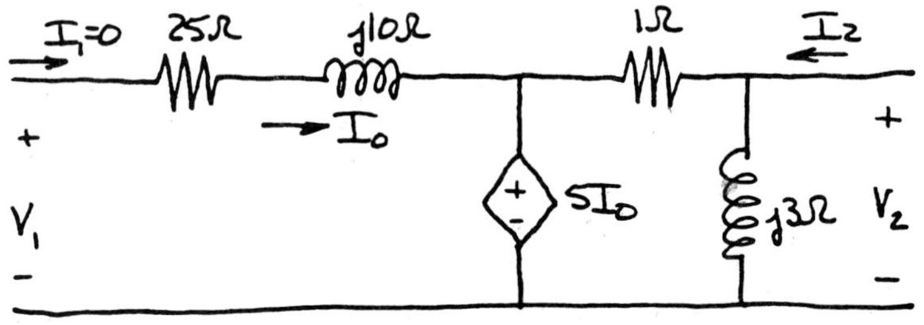

$I_o = 0 \quad$ thus $\quad 5I_o = 0 \quad$ cs is a short circuit

$V_1 = 5I_o = 0; \qquad \therefore \quad h_{12} = 0$

$$h_{22} = \frac{I_2}{V_2} = \frac{1 + j3}{j3} = (1 - j/3)\,\text{S}$$

Summary:

$h_{11} = 30 + j10\,\Omega; \quad h_{12} = 0; \quad h_{21} = -5; \quad h_{22} = 1 - j/3\,\text{S}$

P 18.11 $\quad V_1 = h_{11}I_1 + h_{12}V_2$

$I_2 = h_{21}I_1 + h_{22}V_2$

$I_1 = 0$:

$1 \times 10^{-3} = h_{12}(10); \qquad \therefore \quad h_{12} = 1 \times 10^{-4}$

$200 \times 10^{-6} = h_{22}(10); \qquad \therefore \quad h_{22} = 20 \times 10^{-6}\,\text{S}$

$V_1 = 0$:

$80 \times 10^{-6} = h_{21}(-0.5 \times 10^{-6}) + (20 \times 10^{-6})(5); \qquad \therefore \quad h_{21} = 40$

$0 = h_{11}(-0.5 \times 10^{-6}) + (1 \times 10^{-4})(5); \qquad \therefore \quad h_{11} = 1000\,\Omega$

P 18.12 [a] $V_1 = a_{11}V_2 - a_{12}I_2$

$I_1 = a_{21}V_2 - a_{22}I_2$

From $I_1 = 0$: $1 \times 10^{-3} = a_{11}(10) - a_{12}(200 \times 10^{-6})$

From $V_1 = 0$: $0 = a_{11}(5) - a_{12}(80 \times 10^{-6})$

Solving simultaneously yields

$a_{11} = -4 \times 10^{-4}$; $a_{12} = -25\,\Omega$

From $I_1 = 0$: $0 = a_{21}(10) - a_{22}(200 \times 10^{-6})$

From $V_1 = 0$: $-0.5 \times 10^{-6} = a_{21}(5) - a_{22}(80 \times 10^{-6})$

Solving simultaneously yields

$a_{21} = -5 \times 10^{-7}\,\text{S}$; $a_{22} = -0.025$

[b] $$a_{11} = -\frac{\Delta h}{h_{21}} = \frac{-[(1000)(20 \times 10^{-6}) - (1 \times 10^{-4})(40)]}{40} = -4 \times 10^{-4}$$

$$a_{12} = \frac{-h_{11}}{h_{21}} = \frac{-1000}{40} = -25\,\Omega$$

$$a_{21} = \frac{-h_{22}}{h_{21}} = \frac{-20 \times 10^{-6}}{40} = -5 \times 10^{-7}\,\text{S}$$

$$a_{22} = \frac{-1}{h_{21}} = \frac{-1}{40} = -0.025$$

Summary:

$a_{11} = -4 \times 10^{-4}$; $a_{12} = -25\,\Omega$; $a_{21} = -5 \times 10^{-7}\,\text{S}$; $a_{22} = -0.025$

P 18.13 $y_{11} = \left.\frac{I_1}{V_1}\right|_{V_2=0}$; $y_{21} = \left.\frac{I_2}{V_1}\right|_{V_2=0}$

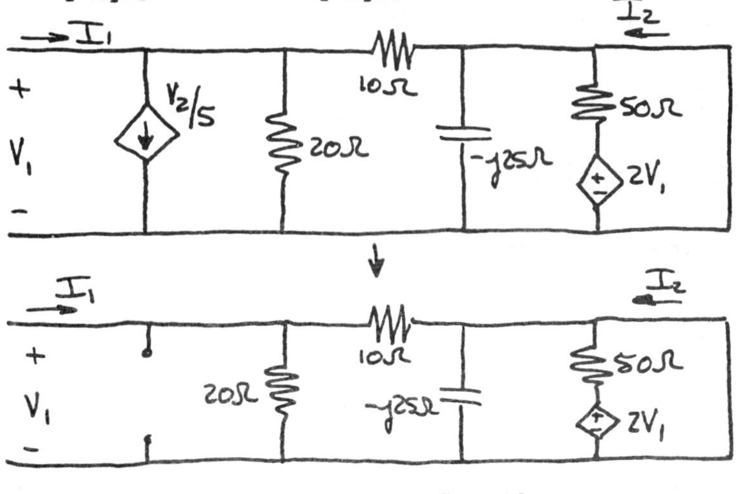

$$I_1 = \frac{V_1}{20} + \frac{V_1}{10} = \frac{3V_1}{20}; \quad \therefore\ y_{11} = \frac{I_1}{V_1} = \frac{3}{20} = 0.15\,\text{S}$$

$$I_2 = -\frac{2V_1}{50} - (I_1 - V_1/20) = -\frac{V_1}{25} - \frac{3V_1}{20} + \frac{V_1}{20} = -\frac{7V_1}{50}$$

$$\therefore \quad y_{21} = \frac{I_2}{V_1} = -\frac{7}{50} = -0.14\,\text{S}$$

$$y_{12} = \left.\frac{I_1}{V_2}\right|_{V_1=0}; \qquad y_{22} = \left.\frac{I_2}{V_2}\right|_{V_1=0}$$

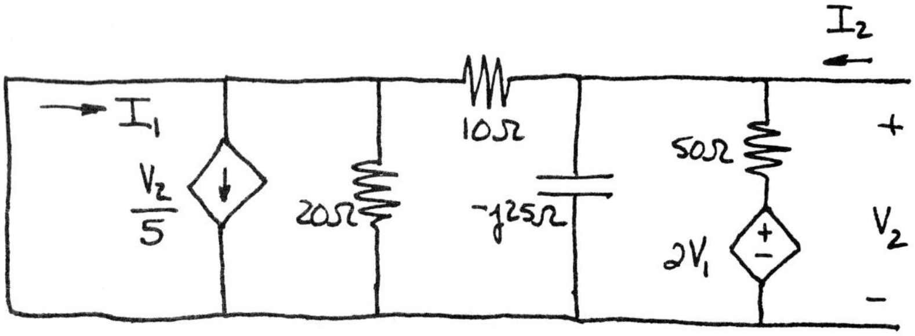

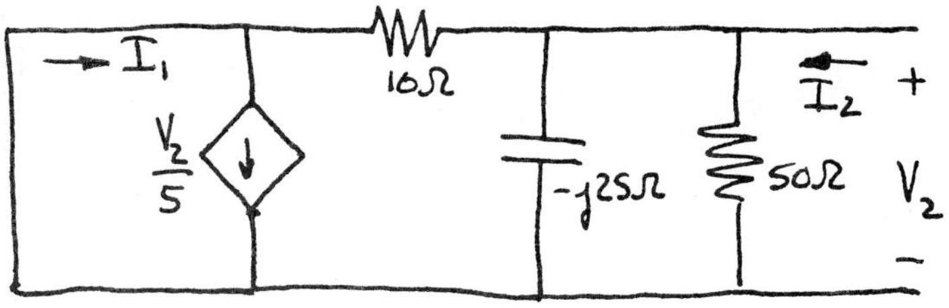

$$I_1 = \frac{V_2}{5} - \frac{V_2}{10} = 0.1V_2; \qquad \therefore \quad y_{12} = \frac{I_1}{V_2} = 0.1\,\text{S}$$

$$I_2 = \frac{V_2}{50} + \frac{V_2}{-j25} + \frac{V_2}{10} = \frac{6+j2}{50}V_2$$

$$\therefore \quad y_{22} = \frac{I_2}{V_2} = \frac{6+j2}{50} = 0.12 + j0.04\,\text{S}$$

Summary:

$y_{11} = 0.15\,\text{S}; \quad y_{12} = 0.1\,\text{S}; \quad y_{21} = -0.14\,\text{S}; \quad y_{22} = 0.12 + j0.04\,\text{S}$

P 18.14 $$b_{11} = -\frac{y_{11}}{y_{12}} = \frac{-0.15}{0.1} = -1.5$$

$$b_{12} = -\frac{1}{y_{12}} = \frac{-1}{0.1} = -10\,\Omega$$

$$b_{21} = -\frac{\Delta y}{y_{12}} = \frac{-[(0.15)(0.12 + j0.04) - (0.1)(0.14)]}{0.1} = -0.32 - j0.06\,\text{S}$$

$$b_{22} = \frac{y_{22}}{y_{12}} = \frac{0.12 + j0.04}{0.1} = -1.2 - j0.4$$

P 18.15 $h_{11} = \left.\frac{V_1}{I_1}\right|_{V_2=0}$; $h_{21} = \left.\frac{I_2}{I_1}\right|_{V_2=0}$

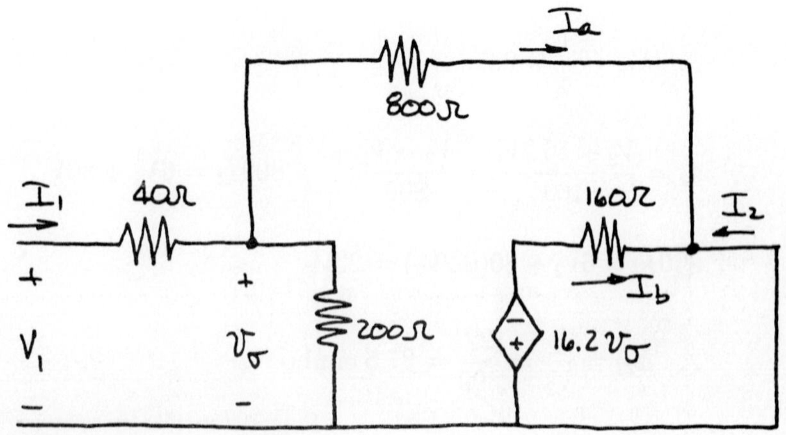

$$\frac{V_1}{I_1} = 40 + \frac{(800)(200)}{1000} = 40 + 160 = 200\,\Omega$$

$\therefore\ h_{11} = 200\,\Omega$

$$I_a = I_1\left(\frac{200}{1000}\right) = 0.2I_1$$

$16.2v_\sigma + 160I_b = 0;\qquad v_\sigma = 160I_1$

$\therefore\ 160I_b = -2592I_1;\qquad I_b = -16.2I_1$

$\therefore\ I_a + I_b + I_2 = 0;\quad 0.2I_1 - 16.2I_1 + I_2 = 0;\quad I_2 = 16I_1$

$\therefore\ h_{21} = 16$

$h_{12} = \left.\frac{V_1}{V_2}\right|_{I_1=0}$; $h_{21} = \left.\frac{I_2}{V_2}\right|_{I_1=0}$

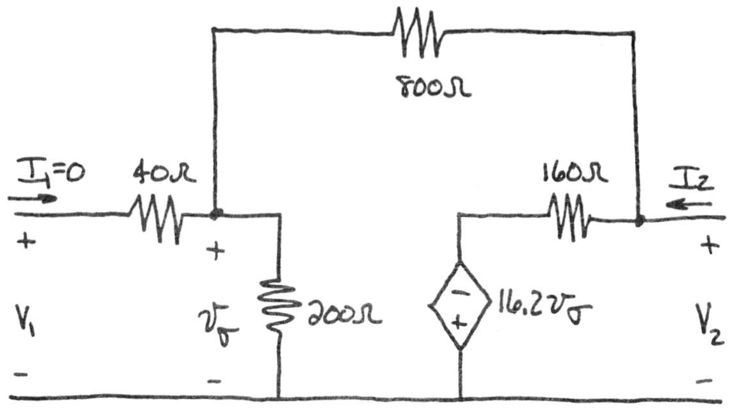

$I_1 = 0;\qquad v_\sigma = V_1$

$$\frac{V_1}{200} + \frac{V_1 - V_2}{800} = 0; \quad 4V_1 + V_1 - V_2 = 0; \quad 5V_1 = V_2$$

$$\therefore \quad h_{12} = \frac{1}{5} = 0.2$$

$$I_2 = \frac{V_2 + 16.2V_1}{160} + \frac{V_2 - V_1}{800}; \qquad 800I_2 = 6V_2 + 80V_1$$

$$800I_2 = 6V_2 + 80(0.2V_2) = 22V_2$$

$$\therefore \quad h_{22} = \frac{I_2}{V_2} = \frac{22}{800} = 27.5\,\text{mmho}$$

Summary:

$h_{11} = 200\,\Omega; \quad h_{12} = 0.20; \quad h_{21} = 16; \quad h_{22} = 27.5\,\text{mmho}$

P 18.16 $V_1 = a_{11}V_2 - a_{12}I_2; \qquad I_1 = a_{21}V_2 - a_{22}I_2$

$$V_1 = h_{11}I_1 + h_{12}V_2; \qquad I_2 = h_{21}I_1 + h_{22}V_2$$

$$V_1 = -a_{12}I_2 + a_{11}V_2; \qquad I_2 = \frac{a_{21}V_2 - I_1}{a_{22}}$$

$$\therefore \quad V_1 = -a_{12}\left(\frac{a_{21} - I_1}{a_{22}}\right) + a_{11}V_2$$

$$V_1 = \frac{a_{12}}{a_{22}}I_1 + \left(\frac{a_{11}a_{22} - a_{12}a_{21}}{a_{22}}\right)V_2$$

$$\therefore \quad h_{11} = \frac{a_{12}}{a_{22}}; \qquad h_{12} = \frac{\Delta a}{a_{22}}$$

$$I_2 = -\frac{1}{a_{22}}I_1 + \frac{a_{21}}{a_{22}}V_2$$

$$\therefore \quad h_{21} = -\frac{1}{a_{22}}; \qquad h_{22} = \frac{a_{21}}{a_{22}}$$

P 18.17 $I_1 = y_{11}V_1 + y_{12}V_2; \qquad I_2 = y_{21}V_1 + y_{22}V_2$

$$V_2 = b_{11}V_1 - b_{12}I_1; \qquad I_2 = b_{21}V_1 - b_{22}I_1$$

$$I_1 = \frac{b_{11}}{b_{12}}V_1 - \frac{1}{b_{12}}V_2$$

$$\therefore \quad y_{11} = \frac{b_{11}}{b_{12}}; \qquad y_{12} = -\frac{1}{b_{12}}$$

$$I_2 = b_{21}V_1 - b_{22}\left[\frac{b_{11}}{b_{12}}V_1 - \frac{1}{b_{12}}V_2\right]$$

$$I_2 = \frac{b_{21}b_{12} - b_{11}b_{22}}{b_{12}}V_1 + \frac{b_{22}}{b_{12}}V_2$$

$$\therefore \quad y_{21} = -\frac{\Delta b}{b_{12}}; \qquad y_{22} = \frac{b_{22}}{b_{12}}$$

P 18.18 $I_1 = g_{11}V_1 + g_{12}I_2; \qquad V_2 = g_{21}V_1 + g_{22}I_2$

$$V_1 = z_{11}I_1 + z_{12}I_2; \qquad V_2 = z_{21}I_1 + z_{22}I_2$$

$$I_1 = \frac{V_1}{z_{11}} - \frac{z_{12}}{z_{11}}I_2$$

$$\therefore \quad g_{11} = \frac{1}{z_{11}}; \qquad g_{12} = \frac{-z_{12}}{z_{11}}$$

$$V_2 = z_{21}\left(\frac{V_1}{z_{11}} - \frac{z_{12}}{z_{11}}I_2\right) + z_{22}I_2 = \frac{z_{21}}{z_{11}}V_1 + \left(\frac{z_{11}z_{22} - z_{12}z_{21}}{z_{11}}\right)I_2$$

$$\therefore \quad g_{21} = \frac{z_{21}}{z_{11}}; \qquad g_{22} = \frac{\Delta z}{z_{11}}$$

P 18.19 $g_{11} = \left.\frac{I_1}{V_1}\right|_{I_2=0}; \qquad g_{21} = \left.\frac{V_2}{V_1}\right|_{I_2=0}$

$$V_1 = 200I_1 + 800I_1 = 1000I_1; \qquad \therefore \quad g_{11} = 10^{-3}\,\text{S}$$

$$V_- = \frac{1000}{1500}V_2 = V_+; \qquad V_+ = \frac{800}{1000}V_1$$

$$\therefore \quad \frac{1000}{1500}V_2 = \frac{800}{1000}V_1; \qquad \therefore \quad g_{21} = 1.2$$

$$g_{12} = \left.\frac{I_1}{I_2}\right|_{V_1=0}; \qquad g_{21} = \left.\frac{V_2}{I_2}\right|_{V_1=0}$$

$I_1 = 0; \qquad \therefore \quad g_{12} = 0$

Also, $V_o = 0; \qquad \therefore \quad g_{22} = \frac{V_2}{I_2} = 40\,\Omega$

P 18.20 $V_2 = 0$:

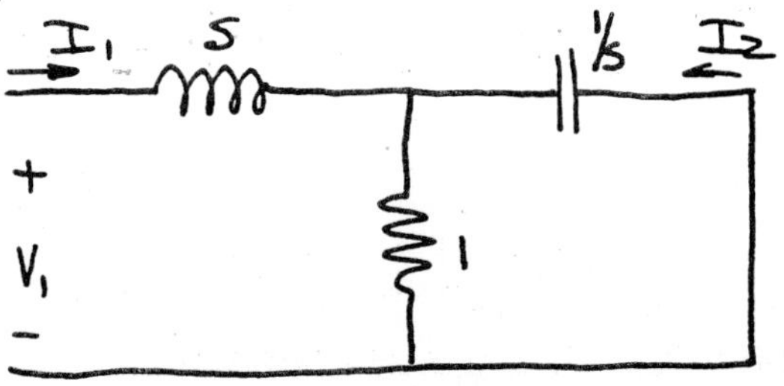

$$\frac{V_1}{I_1} = s + [1\|(1/s)] = \frac{s^2+s+1}{s+1}$$

$$\therefore \quad y_{11} = \left.\frac{V_1}{I_1}\right|_{V_2=0} = \frac{s+1}{s^2+s+1}$$

$$I_2 = \frac{-1}{1+(1/s)}I_1 = \frac{-s}{s+1}I_1 = \frac{-s}{s+1}\left(\frac{s+1}{s^2+s+1}\right)V_1$$

$$\therefore \quad y_{21} = \left.\frac{I_2}{V_1}\right|_{V_2=0} = \frac{-s}{s^2+s+1}$$

$V_1 = 0$:

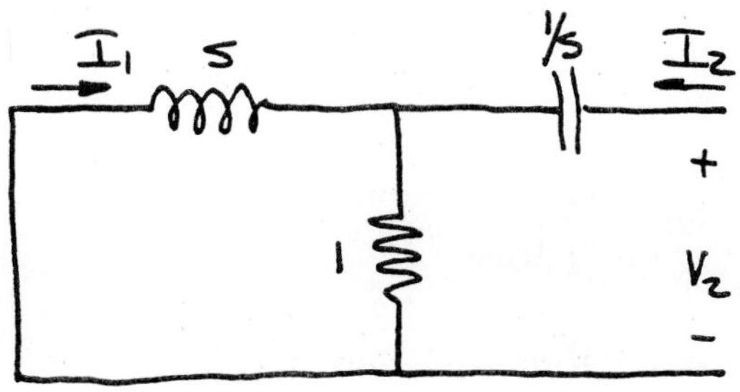

$$\frac{V_2}{I_2} = (1/s) + 1\|s = \frac{1}{s} + \frac{s}{s+1} = \frac{s^2+s+1}{s(s+1)}$$

$$\therefore \quad y_{22} = \left.\frac{I_2}{V_2}\right|_{V_1=0} = \frac{s(s+1)}{s^2+s+1}$$

$$I_1 = \frac{-1}{s+1} I_2 = \frac{-1}{s+1}\left[\frac{s(s+1)}{s^2+s+1}\right] V_2$$

$$\therefore \quad y_{12} = \left.\frac{I_1}{V_2}\right|_{V_1=0} = \frac{-s}{s^2+s+1}$$

P 18.21 First, find the y parameters:

$$I_1 = y_{11}V_1 + y_{12}V_2$$

$$I_2 = y_{21}V_1 + y_{22}V_2$$

Since the two-port is symmetric and reciprocal we only need to calculate two parameters since $y_{11} = y_{22}$ and $y_{12} = y_{21}$.

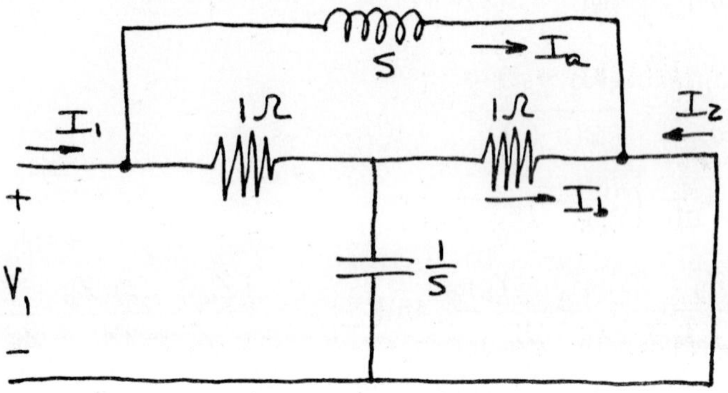

$$I_1 = \frac{V_1}{s} + \frac{V_1}{1 + \left(\frac{1}{s+1}\right)} = \left[\frac{1}{s} + \frac{1}{1+\frac{1}{s+1}}\right] V_1$$

$$\frac{I_1}{V_1} = \frac{s^2+2s+2}{s(s+2)}$$

$$y_{11} = y_{22} = \frac{s^2+2s+2}{s(s+2)}$$

$$I_a = \frac{V_1}{s}$$

$$I_b = \frac{V_1}{1+\frac{1}{s+1}} \cdot \frac{\frac{1}{s}}{1+\frac{1}{s}} = \frac{V_1}{s+2}$$

$$I_2 = -(I_a + I_b) = -\left[\frac{V_1}{s} + \frac{V_1}{s+2}\right]$$

$$\frac{I_2}{V_1} = -\frac{2s+2}{s(s+2)}$$

$$y_{12} = y_{21} = -\frac{2(s+1)}{s(s+2)}$$

Now, transform to the a parameters:

$$a_{11} = \frac{-y_{22}}{y_{21}} = \frac{s^2+2s+2}{2(s+1)}$$

$$a_{12} = \frac{-1}{y_{21}} = \frac{s(s+2)}{2(s+1)}$$

$$a_{21} = \frac{-\Delta y}{y_{21}} = \frac{-1}{y_{21}} = \frac{s(s+2)}{2(s+1)}$$

$$a_{22} = \frac{-y_{11}}{y_{21}} = \frac{s^2+2s+2}{2(s+1)}$$

P 18.22 First we note that

$$z_{11} = \frac{(Z_b + Z_c)(Z_a + Z_b)}{Z_a + 2Z_b + Z_c} \quad \text{and} \quad z_{22} = \frac{(Z_a + Z_b)(Z_b + Z_c)}{Z_a + 2Z_b + Z_c}$$

Therefore $z_{11} = z_{22}$. We also note that

$$z_{21} = z_{12} = \frac{Z_b^2 - Z_a Z_c}{Z_a + 2Z_b + Z_c}$$

Thus the network is symmetrical and reciprocal.

P 18.23 [a] $h_{11} = \left.\frac{V_1}{I_1}\right|_{V_2=0}; \qquad h_{21} = \left.\frac{I_2}{I_1}\right|_{V_2=0}$

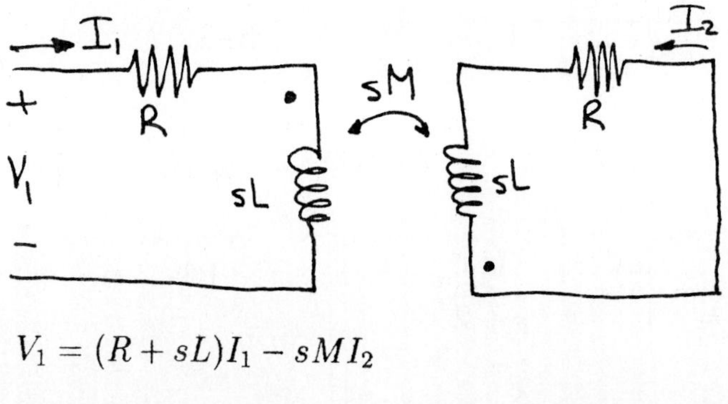

$$V_1 = (R + sL)I_1 - sMI_2$$

$$0 = -sMI_1 + (R + sL)I_2$$

$$\Delta = \begin{vmatrix} (R + sL) & -sM \\ -sM & (R + sL) \end{vmatrix} = (R + sL)^2 - s^2M^2$$

$$N_1 = \begin{vmatrix} V_1 & -sM \\ 0 & (R + sL) \end{vmatrix} = (R + sL)V_1$$

$$I_1 = \frac{N_1}{\Delta} = \frac{(R + sL)V_1}{(R + sL)^2 - s^2M^2}; \qquad h_{11} = \frac{V_1}{I_1} = \frac{(R + sL)^2 - s^2M^2}{R + sL}$$

$$0 = -sMI_1 + (R + sL)I_2; \qquad \therefore \; h_{21} = \frac{I_2}{I_1} = \frac{sM}{R + sL}$$

$$h_{12} = \left.\frac{V_1}{V_2}\right|_{I_1=0}; \qquad h_{22} = \left.\frac{I_2}{V_2}\right|_{I_1=0}$$

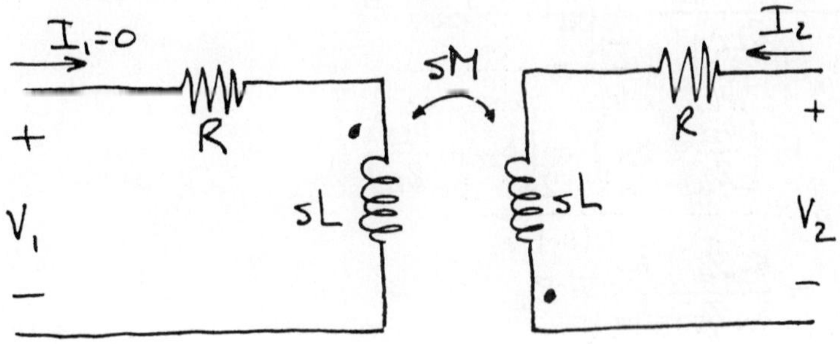

$$V_1 = -sMI_2; \qquad I_2 = \frac{V_2}{R + sL}$$

$$V_1 = \frac{-sMV_2}{R + sL}; \qquad h_{12} = \frac{V_1}{V_2} = \frac{-sM}{R_2 + sL}$$

$$h_{22} = \frac{I_2}{V_2} = \frac{1}{R + sL}$$

[b] $h_{12} = -h_{21}$ (reciprocal)

$h_{11}h_{22} - h_{12}h_{21} = 1$ (symmetrical, reciprocal)

$$h_{12} = \frac{-sM}{R + sL}; \qquad h_{21} = \frac{sM}{R + sL} \quad \text{(checks)}$$

$$h_{11}h_{22} - h_{12}h_{21} = \frac{(R + sL)^2 - s^2M^2}{R + sL} \cdot \frac{1}{R + sL} - \frac{(sM)(-sM)}{(R + sL)^2}$$

$$= \frac{(R + sL)^2 - s^2M^2 + s^2M^2}{(R + sL)^2} = 1 \quad \text{(checks)}$$

P 18.24

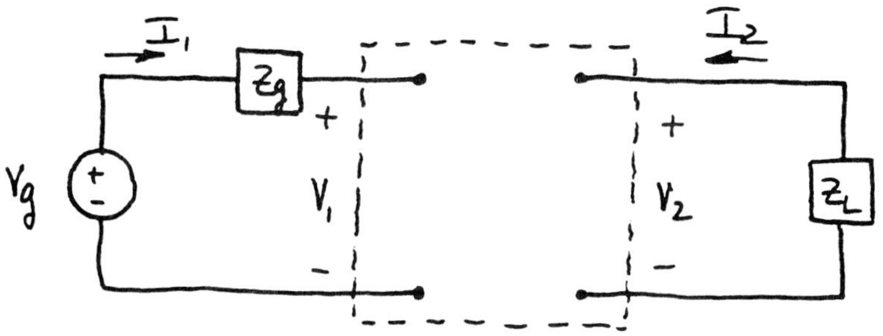

$$V_2 = b_{11}V_1 - b_{12}I_1; \qquad V_1 = V_g - I_1Z_g$$

$$I_2 = b_{21}V_1 - b_{22}I_1; \qquad V_2 = -Z_LI_2$$

$$I_2 = -\frac{V_2}{Z_L} = \frac{-b_{11}V_1 + b_{12}I_1}{Z_L}$$

$$\frac{-b_{11}V_1 + b_{12}I_1}{Z_L} = b_{21}V_1 - b_{22}I_1$$

$$\therefore \quad V_1\left(\frac{b_{11}}{Z_L} + b_{21}\right) = \left(b_{22} + \frac{b_{12}}{Z_L}\right)I_1$$

$$\frac{V_1}{I_1} = \frac{b_{22}Z_L + b_{12}}{b_{21}Z_L + b_{11}} = Z_{\text{in}}$$

P 18.25 $I_1 = g_{11}V_1 + g_{12}I_2; \qquad V_1 = V_g - Z_gI_1$

$$V_2 = g_{21}V_1 + g_{22}I_2; \qquad V_2 = -Z_LI_2$$

$$-Z_LI_2 = g_{21}V_1 + g_{22}I_2; \qquad V_1 = \frac{I_1 - g_{12}I_2}{g_{11}}$$

$$\therefore \quad -Z_LI_2 = \frac{g_{21}}{g_{11}}(I_1 - g_{12}I_2) + g_{22}I_2$$

$$\therefore \quad -Z_LI_2 + \frac{g_{12}g_{21}}{g_{11}}I_2 - g_{22}I_2 = \frac{g_{21}}{g_{11}}I_1$$

$$\therefore \quad (Z_Lg_{11} + \Delta g)I_2 = -g_{21}I_1; \qquad \therefore \quad \frac{I_2}{I_1} = \frac{-g_{21}}{g_{11}Z_L + \Delta g}$$

P 18.26 $I_1 = y_{11}V_1 + y_{12}V_2; \qquad V_1 = V_g - Z_gI_1$

$I_2 = y_{21}V_1 + y_{22}V_2; \qquad V_2 = -Z_LI_2$

$$\frac{-V_2}{Z_L} = y_{21}V_1 + y_{22}V_2$$

$$\therefore \quad -y_{21}V_1 = \left(\frac{1}{Z_L} + y_{22}\right)V_2; \qquad -y_{21}Z_LV_1 = (1 + y_{22}Z_L)V_2$$

$$\therefore \quad \frac{V_2}{V_1} = \frac{-y_{21}Z_L}{1 + y_{22}Z_L}$$

P 18.27 $V_1 = h_{11}I_1 + h_{12}V_2; \qquad V_1 = V_g - Z_gI_1$

$I_2 = h_{21}I_1 + h_{22}V_2; \qquad V_2 = -Z_LI_2$

$$\therefore \quad V_g - Z_gI_1 = h_{11}I_1 + h_{12}V_2; \qquad V_g = (h_{11} + Z_g)I_1 + h_{12}V_2$$

$$\therefore \quad I_1 = \frac{V_g - h_{12}V_2}{h_{11} + Z_g}$$

$$\therefore \quad -\frac{V_2}{Z_L} = h_{21}\left[\frac{V_g - h_{12}V_2}{h_{11} + Z_g}\right] + h_{22}V_2$$

$$\frac{-V_2(h_{11} + Z_g)}{Z_L} = h_{21}V_g - h_{12}h_{21}V_2 + h_{22}(h_{11} + Z_g)V_2$$

$$-V_2(h_{11} + Z_g) = h_{21}Z_LV_g - h_{12}h_{21}Z_LV_2 + h_{22}Z_L(h_{11} + Z_g)V_2$$

$$-h_{21}Z_LV_g = (h_{11} + Z_g)\,[V_2 + h_{22}Z_LV_2] - h_{12}h_{21}Z_LV_2$$

$$\therefore \quad \frac{V_2}{V_g} = \frac{-h_{21}Z_L}{(h_{11} + Z_g)(1 + h_{22}Z_L) - h_{12}h_{21}Z_L}$$

P 18.28 $V_1 = z_{11}I_1 + z_{12}I_2; \qquad V_1 = V_g - Z_gI_1$

$V_2 = z_{21}I_1 + z_{22}I_2; \qquad V_2 = -Z_LI_2$

$$V_{\text{Th}} = V_2\Big|_{I_2=0}; \qquad V_2 = z_{21}I_1; \qquad I_1 = \frac{V_1}{z_{11}} = \frac{V_g - I_1Z_g}{z_{11}}$$

$$\therefore \quad I_1 = \frac{V_g}{z_{11} + Z_g}; \qquad \therefore \quad V_2 = \frac{z_{21} V_g}{z_{11} + Z_g} = V_t$$

$$Z_{\text{Th}} = \left. \frac{V_2}{I_2} \right|_{V_g = 0}; \qquad V_2 = z_{21} I_1 + z_{22} I_2$$

$$-I_1 Z_g = z_{11} I_1 + z_{12} I_2; \qquad I_1 = \frac{-z_{12} I_2}{z_{11} + Z_g}$$

$$\therefore \quad V_2 = z_{21} \left[\frac{-z_{12} I_2}{z_{11} + Z_g} \right] + z_{22} I_2$$

$$\therefore \quad \frac{V_2}{I_2} = z_{22} - \frac{z_{12} z_{21}}{z_{11} + Z_g} = Z_{\text{Th}}$$

P 18.29 [a] $a_{11} = \left. \frac{V_1}{V_2} \right|_{I_2 = 0}; \qquad a_{21} = \left. \frac{I_1}{V_2} \right|_{I_2 = 0}$

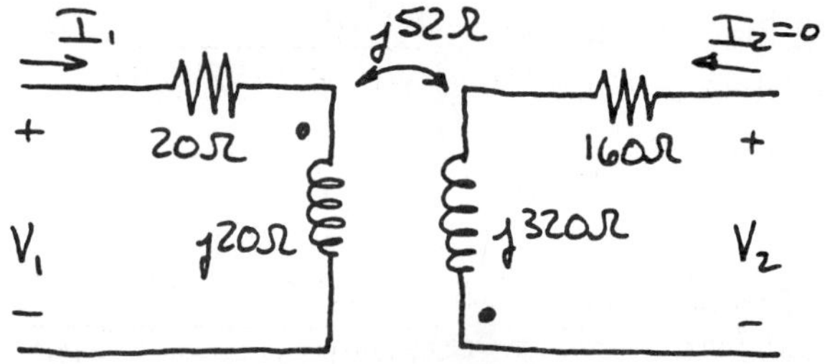

$$V_2 = -j52 I_1 = -j52 \frac{V_1}{20 + j20}$$

$$a_{11} = \frac{V_1}{V_2} = \frac{20 + j20}{-j52} = \frac{5}{13}(-1 + j)$$

$$a_{21} = \frac{I_1}{V_2} = \frac{1}{-j52} = \frac{j}{52}\,\text{S}$$

$$a_{12} = \left. \frac{V_1}{I_2} \right|_{V_2 = 0}; \qquad a_{22} = \left. \frac{V_1}{I_2} \right|_{V_2 = 0}$$

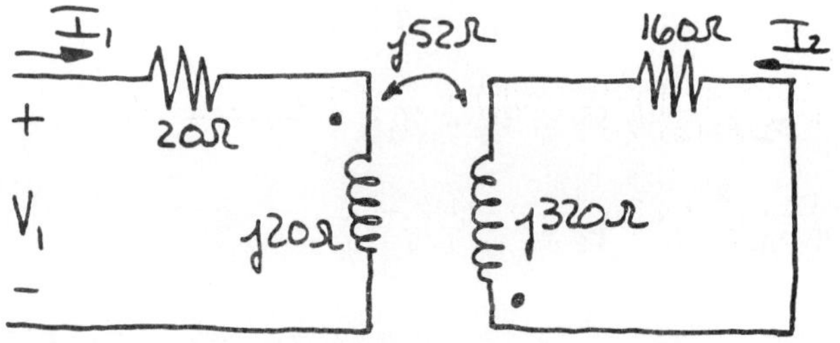

$$V_1 = (20 + j20) I_1 - j52 I_2$$

$$0 = -j52I_1 + (160 + j320)I_2$$

$$\Delta = \begin{vmatrix} 20 + j20 & -j52 \\ -j52 & 160 + j320 \end{vmatrix} = -496 + j9600$$

$$N_2 = \begin{vmatrix} 20 + j20 & V_1 \\ -j52 & 0 \end{vmatrix} = j52V_1$$

$$I_2 = \frac{j52V_1}{-496 + j9600} \quad \text{so} \quad \frac{V_1}{I_2} = \frac{-496 + j9600}{j52} = \frac{1}{52}(9600 + j496)$$

$$\therefore \quad a_{12} = -\frac{V_1}{I_2} = \frac{1}{13}(-2400 - j124)$$

$$I_1 = (160 + j320)I_2; \qquad \therefore \quad a_{22} = -\frac{I_1}{I_2} = \frac{-320 + j160}{52}$$

[b] $$V_{\text{Th}} = \frac{V_g}{a_{11} + a_{21}Z_g} = \frac{100\underline{/0^\circ}}{(5/13)(-1 + j) + (j52)(10)}$$

$$= -80 - j120 = 144.22\underline{/-123.69^\circ} \text{ V}$$

$$Z_{\text{Th}} = \frac{a_{12} + a_{22}Z_g}{a_{11} + a_{22}Z_g} = \frac{\frac{1}{13}(-2400 - j124) + \frac{-320+j160}{52}(10)}{(5/13)(-1 + j) + (j52)(10)}$$

$$= 222.4 + j278.4 = 356.33\underline{/51.38^\circ}\ \Omega$$

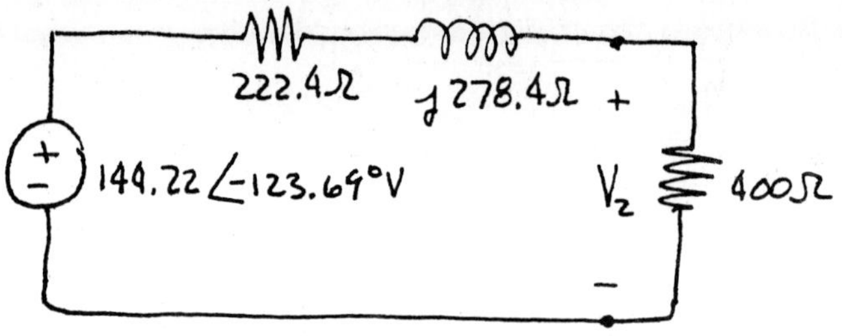

[c] $$V_2 = \frac{144.22\underline{/-123.69^\circ}}{622.4 + j278.4}(400) = 84.607\underline{/-189.59^\circ}$$

$$v_2(t) = 84.607\cos(2000t - 189.59^\circ) \text{ V}$$

P 18.30 $$\mathbf{I}_2 = \frac{y_{21}\mathbf{V}_g}{1 + y_{22}Z_L + y_{11}Z_g + \Delta y Z_g Z_L}$$

$$= \frac{-0.25(1)}{1 + (-0.04)(100) + (0.025)(10) + (-0.00125)(10)(100)}$$

$$= 0.0625\ \text{A}$$

$$P_o = \frac{1}{2}(I_2)^2 Z_L = \frac{1}{2}(0.0625)^2(100) = 0.1953\ \text{W}$$

$$\frac{I_2}{I_1} = \frac{y_{21}}{y_{11} + \Delta y Z_g} = \frac{-0.25}{0.025 + (-7.5 \times 10^{-4})(10)} = -20$$

$$\therefore\ I_1 = \frac{I_2}{-20} = \frac{0.0625}{-20} = -3.125\ \text{mA}$$

$$P_g = \frac{1}{2}(1)(-0.003125) = -1.56\ \text{mW}$$

$$\frac{P_o}{P_g} = \frac{0.1953}{-0.0015625} = -125$$

P 18.31 [a] $$Z_{\text{Th}} = g_{22} - \frac{g_{12}g_{21}Z_g}{1 + g_{11}Z_g}$$

$$g_{12}g_{21} = \left(-\frac{1}{2} + j\frac{1}{2}\right)\left(\frac{1}{2} - j\frac{1}{2}\right) = j\frac{1}{2}$$

$$1 + g_{11}Z_g = 1 + 1 - j1 = 2 - j1$$

$$\therefore\ Z_{\text{Th}} = 1.5 + j2.5 - \frac{j3}{2 - j1} = 2.1 + j1.3\ \Omega$$

$$\therefore\ Z_L = 2.1 - j1.3\ \Omega$$

$$\frac{\mathbf{V}_2}{\mathbf{V}_g} = \frac{g_{21}Z_L}{(1 + g_{11}Z_g)(g_{22} + Z_L) - g_{12}g_{21}Z_g}$$

$$g_{21}Z_L = \left(\frac{1}{2} - j\frac{1}{2}\right)(2.1 - j1.3) = 0.4 - j1.7$$

$$1 + g_{11}Z_g = 1 + 1 - j1 = 2 - j1$$

$$g_{22} + Z_L = 1.5 + j2.5 + 2.1 - j1.3 = 3.6 + j1.2$$

$$g_{12}g_{21}Z_g = j3$$

$$\frac{\mathbf{V}_2}{\mathbf{V}_g} = \frac{0.4 - j1.7}{(2 - j1)(3.6 + j1.2) - j3} = \frac{0.4 - j1.7}{8.4 - j4.2}$$

$$\mathbf{V}_2 = \frac{0.4 - j1.7}{8.4 - j4.2}(42\underline{/0^\circ}) = 5 - j6\,\text{V(rms)} = 7.81\underline{/-50.19^\circ}\,\text{V(rms)}$$

The rms value of $\mathbf{V}_2$ is 7.81 V.

[b] $\mathbf{I}_2 = \dfrac{-\mathbf{V}_2}{Z_L} = \dfrac{-5 + j6}{2.1 - j1.3} = -3 + j1\,\text{A(rms)}$

$$P = |\mathbf{I}_2|^2(2.1) = 21\,\text{W}$$

[c] $\dfrac{\mathbf{I}_2}{\mathbf{I}_1} = \dfrac{-g_{21}}{g_{11}Z_L + \Delta g}$

$$\Delta g = \left(\frac{1}{6} - j\frac{1}{6}\right)\left(\frac{3}{2} + j\frac{5}{2}\right) - \left(\frac{1}{2} - j\frac{1}{2}\right)\left(-\frac{1}{2} + j\frac{1}{2}\right)$$

$$= \frac{3}{12} + j\frac{5}{12} - j\frac{3}{12} + \frac{5}{12} - j\frac{1}{2} = \frac{2}{3} - j\frac{1}{3}$$

$$g_{11}Z_L = \left(\frac{1}{6} - j\frac{1}{6}\right)(2.1 - j1.3) = \frac{0.8}{6} - j\frac{3.4}{6}$$

$$\therefore\quad g_{11}Z_L + \Delta g = \frac{0.8}{6} - j\frac{3.4}{6} + \frac{4}{6} - j\frac{2}{6} = 0.6 - j0.9$$

$$\frac{\mathbf{I}_2}{\mathbf{I}_1} = \frac{-[(1/2) - j(1/2)]}{0.8 - j0.9}$$

$$\therefore\quad \mathbf{I}_1 = \frac{(0.8 - j0.9)\mathbf{I}_2}{-0.5 + j0.5} = \left(\frac{1.6 - j1.8}{-1 + j1}\right)\mathbf{I}_2$$

$$= (-1.7 + j0.1)(-3 + j1) = 5 - j2\,\text{A(rms)}$$

$$\therefore\quad P_g(\text{developed}) = (42)(5) = 210\,\text{W}$$

$$\%\ \text{delivered} = \frac{21}{210}(100) = 10\%$$

P 18.32 [a] $\dfrac{\mathbf{V}_2}{\mathbf{V}_g} = \dfrac{y_{21}Z_L}{y_{12}y_{21}Z_gZ_L - (1 + y_{11}Z_g)(1 + y_{22}Z_L)}$

$$y_{12}y_{21}Z_gZ_L = (-2 \times 10^{-6})(100 \times 10^{-3})(2500)(70{,}000) = -35$$

$$1 + y_{11}Z_g = 1 + (2 \times 10^{-3})(2500) = 6$$

$$1 + y_{22}Z_L = 1 + (-50 \times 10^{-6})(70 \times 10^3) = -2.5$$

$$y_{21}Z_L = (100 \times 10^{-3})(70 \times 10^3) = 7000$$

$$\frac{\mathbf{V}_2}{\mathbf{V}_g} = \frac{7000}{-35-(6)(-2.5)} = \frac{7000}{-20} = -350$$

$$\mathbf{V}_2 = -350\mathbf{V}_g = -350(80)\times 10^{-3} = -28\text{ V(rms)}$$

$$\mathbf{V}_2 = 28\underline{/180^\circ}\text{ V(rms)}$$

[b] $P = \dfrac{|\mathbf{V}_2|^2}{70{,}000} = 11.2\times 10^{-3} = 11.20\text{ mW}$

[c] $\mathbf{I}_2 = \dfrac{-28\underline{/180^\circ}}{70{,}000} = -0.4\times 10^{-3}\underline{/180^\circ} = 400\underline{/0^\circ}\ \mu\text{A}$

$$\frac{\mathbf{I}_2}{\mathbf{I}_1} = \frac{y_{21}}{y_{11}+\Delta y Z_L}$$

$$\Delta y = (2\times 10^{-3})(-50\times 10^{-6}) - (-2\times 10^{-6})(100\times 10^{-3})$$

$$= 100\times 10^{-9}$$

$$\Delta y Z_L = (100)(70)\times 10^3\times 10^{-9} = 7\times 10^{-3}$$

$$y_{11}+\Delta y Z_L = 2\times 10^{-3}+7\times 10^{-3} = 9\times 10^{-3}$$

$$\frac{\mathbf{I}_2}{\mathbf{I}_1} = \frac{100\times 10^{-3}}{9\times 10^{-3}} = \frac{100}{9}$$

$$\therefore\ 100\mathbf{I}_1 = 9\mathbf{I}_2; \qquad \mathbf{I}_1 = \frac{9(400\times 10^{-6})}{100} = 36\ \mu\text{A(rms)}$$

$$P_g = (80)10^{-3}(36)\times 10^{-6} = 2.88\ \mu\text{W}$$

P 18.33 [a] $Z_{\text{Th}} = \dfrac{1+y_{11}Z_g}{y_{22}+\Delta y Z_g}$

From the solution to Problem 18.32

$$1+y_{11}Z_g = 1+(2\times 10^{-3})(2500) = 6$$

$$y_{22}+\Delta y Z_g = -50\times 10^{-6}+10^{-7}(2500) = 200\times 10^{-6}$$

$$Z_{\text{Th}} = \frac{6}{200}\times 10^6 = 30{,}000\,\Omega$$

$$Z_L = Z_{\text{Th}}^* = 30{,}000\,\Omega$$

[b] $y_{21}Z_L = (100\times 10^{-3})(30{,}000) = 3000$

$$y_{12}y_{21}Z_gZ_L = (-2\times 10^{-6})(100\times 10^{-3})(2500)(30{,}000) = -15$$

$$1+y_{11}Z_g = 6$$

$$1+y_{22}Z_L = 1+(-50\times 10^{-6})(30\times 10^3) = -0.5$$

$$\frac{\mathbf{V}_2}{\mathbf{V}_g} = \frac{3000}{-15 - 6(-0.5)} = \frac{3000}{-12} = -250$$

$$\mathbf{V}_2 = -250(80 \times 10^{-3}) = -20 = 20\underline{/180^\circ}\text{ V(rms)}$$

$$P = \frac{|\mathbf{V}_2|^2}{30{,}000} = \frac{400}{30} \times 10^{-3} = 13.33\,\text{mW}$$

[c] $\mathbf{I}_2 = \frac{-\mathbf{V}_2}{30{,}000} = \frac{20\underline{/0^\circ}}{30{,}000} = \frac{2}{3}\text{ mA}$

$$\frac{\mathbf{I}_2}{\mathbf{I}_1} = \frac{100 \times 10^{-3}}{2 \times 10^{-3} + 10^{-7}(30{,}000)} = \frac{100 \times 10^{-3}}{5 \times 10^{-3}} = 20$$

$$\mathbf{I}_1 = \frac{\mathbf{I}_2}{20} = \frac{2 \times 10^{-3}}{3(20)} = \frac{1}{30}\text{ mA(rms)}$$

$$P_g(\text{developed}) = (80 \times 10^{-3})\left(\frac{1}{30} \times 10^{-3}\right) = \frac{8}{3}\,\mu\text{W}$$

P 18.34 **[a]** $h_{11} = \left.\frac{V_1}{I_1}\right|_{V_2=0}; \qquad h_{21} = \left.\frac{I_2}{I_1}\right|_{V_2=0}$

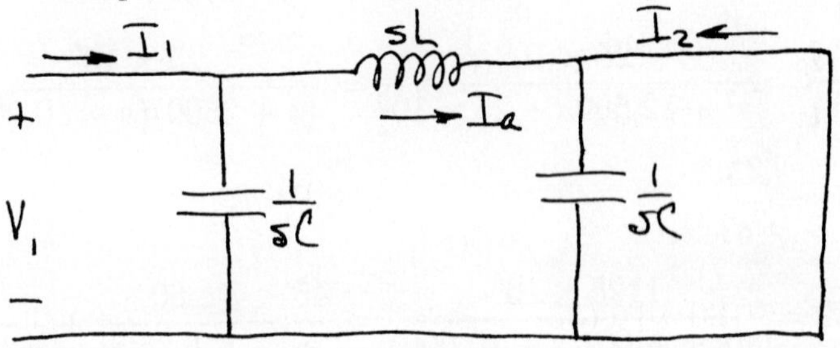

$$h_{11} = \frac{(1/sC)(sL)}{(1/sC) + sL} = \frac{(1/C)s}{s^2 + (1/LC)}$$

$$I_2 = -I_a; \qquad I_a = \frac{I_1(1/sC)}{sL + (1/sC)}$$

$$I_2 = \frac{-I_1}{s^2LC + 1}$$

$$h_{21} = \frac{I_2}{I_1} = \frac{-(1/LC)}{s^2 + (1/LC)}$$

$$h_{12} = \left.\frac{V_1}{V_2}\right|_{I_1=0}; \qquad h_{22} = \left.\frac{I_2}{V_2}\right|_{I_1=0}$$

$$V_1 = \frac{V_2(1/sC)}{sL + (1/sC)} = \frac{V_2}{s^2LC + 1}$$

$$\frac{V_2}{I_2} = \frac{(1/sC)[sL + (1/LC)]}{sL + (2/LC)} = \frac{s^2 + (1/LC)}{sC[s^2 + (2/LC)]}$$

$$\frac{I_2}{V_2} = h_{22} = \frac{Cs[s^2 + (2/LC)]}{s^2 + (1/LC)}$$

[b] $\frac{1}{LC} = \frac{10^9}{(0.1)(400)} = 25 \times 10^6$

$$h_{11} = \frac{10^7 s}{s^2 + 25 \times 10^6}$$

$$h_{12} = \frac{25 \times 10^6}{s^2 + 25 \times 10^6}$$

$$h_{21} = \frac{-25 \times 10^6}{s^2 + 25 \times 10^6}$$

$$h_{22} = \frac{10^{-7}s(s^2 + 50 \times 10^6)}{(s^2 + 25 \times 10^6)}$$

$$\frac{V_2}{V_1} = \frac{-h_{21}Z_L}{h_{11} + \Delta h Z_L} = \frac{-h_{21}Z_L}{h_{11} + Z_L} = \frac{\left(\frac{25\times 10^6}{s^2+25\times 10^6}\right)800}{\frac{10^7 s}{(s^2+25\times 10^6)} + 800}$$

$$\frac{V_2}{V_1} = \frac{25 \times 10^6}{s^2 + 12{,}500s + 25 \times 10^6} = \frac{25 \times 10^6}{(s + 2500)(s + 10{,}000)}$$

$$V_1 = \frac{45}{s}$$

$$V_2 = \frac{1125 \times 10^6}{s(s + 2500)(s + 10{,}000)} = \frac{45}{s} - \frac{60}{s + 2500} + \frac{15}{s + 10{,}000}$$

$$v_2 = [45 - 60e^{-2500t} + 15e^{-10{,}000t}]u(t) \quad \text{V}$$

P 18.35 [a] $V_1 = z_{11}I_1 + z_{12}I_2$

$$V_2 = z_{21}I_1 + z_{22}I_2$$

$$z_{11} = \left.\frac{V_1}{I_1}\right|_{I_2=0} = s + \frac{1}{s} = \frac{s^2 + 1}{s}$$

$$z_{21} = \left.\frac{V_2}{I_1}\right|_{I_2=0} = \frac{1}{s}$$

$$z_{12} = \left.\frac{V_1}{I_2}\right|_{I_1=0} = \frac{1}{s}$$

$$z_{22} = \left.\frac{V_2}{I_2}\right|_{I_1=0} = s + \frac{1}{s} = \frac{s^2 + 1}{s}$$

[b] $$\frac{V_2}{V_g} = \frac{z_{21}Z_L}{(z_{11}+Z_g)(z_{22}+Z_L) - z_{12}z_{21}}$$

$$= \frac{z_{21}}{(z_{11}+1)(z_{22}+1) - z_{12}z_{21}}$$

$$= \frac{1/s}{\left(\frac{s^2+1}{s}+1\right)\left(\frac{s^2+1}{s}+1\right) - \frac{1}{s^2}}$$

$$= \frac{s}{(s^2+s+1)^2 - 1}$$

$$= \frac{s}{s^4+2s^3+3s^2+2s+1-1}$$

$$= \frac{1}{s^3+2s^2+3s+2}$$

$$= \frac{1}{(s+1)(s^2+s+2)}$$

$$\therefore \quad V_2 = \frac{50}{s(s+1)(s^2+s+2)}$$

$$s_{1,2} = -\frac{1}{2} \pm j\frac{\sqrt{7}}{2}$$

$$V_2 = \frac{K_1}{s} + \frac{K_2}{s+1} + \frac{K_3}{s+\frac{1}{2}-j\frac{\sqrt{7}}{2}} + \frac{K_3^*}{s+\frac{1}{2}+j\frac{\sqrt{7}}{2}}$$

$K_1 = 25; \qquad K_2 = -25; \qquad K_3 = 9.45\underline{/90^\circ}$

$$\therefore \quad v_2(t) = [25 - 25e^{-t} + 18.90e^{-0.5t}\cos(1.32t + 90^\circ)]u(t)\,\text{V}$$

CHECK

$$v_2(0) = 25 - 25 + 18.90\cos 90^\circ = 0$$

$$v_2(\infty) = 25 + 0 + 0 = 25\,\text{V}$$

P 18.36 $$z_{11} = \left.\frac{V_1}{I_1}\right|_{I_2=0} = \frac{100}{1.125} = \frac{800}{9}\,\Omega$$

$$z_{21} = \left.\frac{V_2}{I_1}\right|_{I_2=0} = \frac{104}{1.125} = \frac{832}{9}\,\Omega$$

$$z_{12} = \left.\frac{V_1}{I_2}\right|_{I_1=0} = \frac{20}{0.25} = 80\,\Omega$$

$$z_{22} = \left.\frac{V_2}{I_2}\right|_{I_1=0} = \frac{24}{0.25} = 96\,\Omega$$

$$Z_{\text{Th}} = z_{22} - \frac{z_{12}z_{21}}{z_{11} + Z_g} = 96 - \frac{(80)(832/9)}{(800/9) + 0} = 12.8\,\Omega$$

$$\therefore \quad Z_L = 12.8\,\Omega$$

$$\frac{V_2}{V_1} = \frac{z_{21}Z_L}{z_{11}Z_L + \Delta z}$$

$$\Delta z = \left(\frac{800}{9}\right)96 - 80\left(\frac{832}{9}\right) = \frac{10{,}240}{9}$$

$$\frac{V_2}{V_1} = \frac{(832/9)(12.8)}{(800/9)(12.8) + (10{,}240/9)} = \frac{10{,}649.60}{20{,}480} = 0.52$$

$$V_2 = (0.52)(160) = 83.20\text{ V}$$

$$P = \frac{(83.2)^2}{12.8} = 540.80\text{ W}$$

P 18.37 $h_{11} = \left.\frac{V_1}{I_1}\right|_{V_2=0} = 25\,\Omega; \qquad h_{21} = \left.\frac{I_2}{I_1}\right|_{V_2=0} = -0.5$

From the second set of measurements we have

$$41 = 25(1) + h_{12}(20); \qquad \therefore \quad h_{12} = \frac{41 - 25}{20} = 0.80$$

$$0 = -0.5(1) + h_{22}(20); \qquad \therefore \quad h_{22} = \frac{0.5}{20} = 0.025\,\mho$$

$$R_{\text{Th}} = \frac{23 + 25}{23(0.025) + \Delta h}; \qquad \Delta h = 25(0.025) - (-0.5)(0.8) = 1.025$$

$$\therefore \quad R_{\text{Th}} = \frac{48}{1.6} = 30\,\Omega; \qquad \therefore \quad R_o = 30\,\Omega$$

$$\frac{V_2}{V_g} = \frac{-(-0.5)(30)}{(48)(1.75) + (0.4)(30)} = \frac{15}{96}$$

$$V_2 = 15\text{ V}; \qquad P = \frac{(15)^2}{30} = 7.5\text{ W}$$

P 18.38 $a'_{11} = -\frac{\Delta h}{h_{21}} = \frac{-0.02}{-0.1} = 0.2$

$$a'_{12} = -\frac{h_{11}}{h_{21}} = \frac{-150}{-0.1} = 1500$$

$$a'_{21} = -\frac{h_{22}}{h_{21}} = \frac{-10^{-4}}{-0.1} = 10^{-3}$$

$$a'_{22} = -\frac{1}{h_{21}} = \frac{-1}{-0.1} = 10$$

$$a''_{11} = \frac{1}{g_{21}} = \frac{1}{20} = 0.05$$

$$a''_{12} = \frac{g_{22}}{g_{21}} = \frac{24 \times 10^3}{20} = 1200$$

$$a''_{21} = \frac{g_{11}}{g_{21}} = \frac{0.01}{20} = 5 \times 10^{-4}$$

$$a''_{22} = \frac{\Delta g}{g_{21}} = \frac{320}{20} = 16$$

$$a_{11} = a'_{11}a''_{11} + a'_{12}a''_{21} = (0.2)(0.05) + (1500)(5 \times 10^{-4}) = 0.76$$

$$a_{12} = a'_{11}a''_{12} + a'_{12}a''_{22} = (0.2)(1200) + (1500)(16) = 24{,}240$$

$$a_{21} = a'_{21}a''_{11} + a'_{22}a''_{21} = (10^{-3})(0.05) + (10)(5 \times 10^{-4}) = 5.05 \times 10^{-3}$$

$$a_{22} = a'_{21}a''_{12} + a'_{22}a''_{22} = (10^{-3})(1200) + (10)(16) = 161.2$$

$$V_2 = \frac{Z_L V_g}{(a_{11} + a_{21}Z_g)Z_L + a_{12} + a_{22}Z_g}$$

$$= \frac{(1000)(109.5)}{[0.76 + (5.05 \times 10^{-3})(20)](1000) + 24{,}240 + (161.2)(20)} = 3.87\,\text{V}$$

P 18.39 The a parameters of the first two port are

$$a'_{11} = \frac{-\Delta h}{h_{21}} = \frac{-5 \times 10^{-3}}{40} = -125 \times 10^{-6}$$

$$a'_{12} = \frac{-h_{11}}{h_{21}} = \frac{-1000}{40} = -25\,\Omega$$

$$a'_{21} = \frac{-h_{22}}{h_{21}} = \frac{-25}{40} \times 10^{-6} = -625 \times 10^{-9}\,\text{S}$$

$$a'_{22} = \frac{-1}{h_{21}} = \frac{-1}{40} = -25 \times 10^{-3}$$

The a parameters of the second two port are

$$a''_{11} = \frac{5}{4}; \quad a''_{12} = \frac{3R}{4}; \quad a''_{21} = \frac{3}{4R}; \quad a''_{22} = \frac{5}{4}$$

or $a''_{11} = 1.25; \quad a''_{12} = 54\,\text{k}\Omega; \quad a''_{21} = \frac{1}{96}\,\text{mS}; \quad a''_{22} = 1.25$

The a parameters of the cascade connection are

$$a_{11} = -125 \times 10^{-6}(1.25) + (-25)(10^{-3}/96) = \frac{-10^{-2}}{24}$$

$$a_{12} = -125 \times 10^{-6}(54 \times 10^{3}) + (-25)(1.25) = -38\,\Omega$$

$$a_{21} = -625 \times 10^{-9}(1.25) + (-25 \times 10^{-3})(10^{-3}/96) = \frac{-10^{-4}}{96}\,\text{S}$$

$$a_{22} = -625 \times 10^{-9}(54 \times 10^{3}) + (-25 \times 10^{-3})(1.25) = -65 \times 10^{-3}$$

$$\frac{V_o}{V_g} = \frac{Z_L}{(a_{11} + a_{21}Z_g)Z_L + a_{12} + a_{22}Z_g}$$

$$a_{21}Z_g = \frac{-10^{-4}}{96}(800) = \frac{-10^{-2}}{12}$$

$$a_{11} + a_{21}Z_g = \frac{-10^{-2}}{24}\frac{-10^{-2}}{12} = \frac{-10^{-2}}{8}$$

$$(a_{11} + a_{21}Z_g)Z_L = \frac{-10^{-2}}{8}(72{,}000) = -90$$

$$a_{22}Z_g = -65 \times 10^{-3}(800) = -52$$

$$\frac{V_o}{V_g} = \frac{72{,}000}{-90 - 38 - 52} = -400$$

$$V_o = -400V_g = -3.6\,\text{V}$$

P 18.40 [a] From reciprocity and symmetry

$$a'_{11} = a'_{22}, \quad \Delta a' = 1; \qquad \therefore \; 16 - 5a'_{21} = 1, \quad a'_{21} = 3\,\text{S}$$

For network B

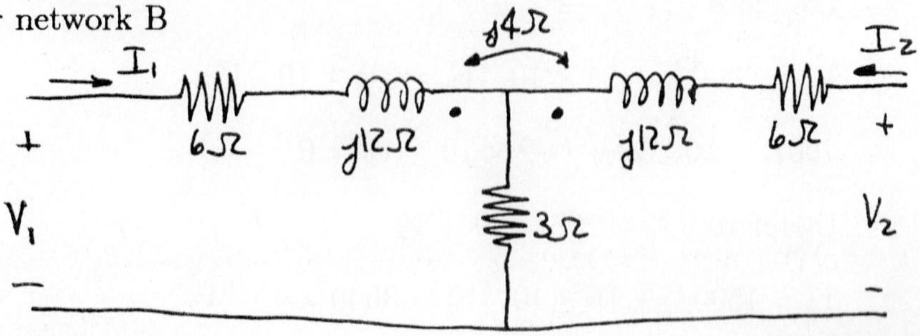

$$a''_{11} = \left.\frac{\mathbf{V}_1}{\mathbf{V}_2}\right|_{I_2=0}$$

$$\mathbf{V}_1 = (6 + j12 + 3)\mathbf{I}_1 = (9 + j12)\mathbf{I}_1$$

$$\mathbf{V}_2 = 3\mathbf{I}_1 + j4\mathbf{I}_1 = (3 + j4)\mathbf{I}_1$$

$$a''_{11} = \frac{9 + j12}{3 + j4} = 3$$

$$a''_{21} = \left.\frac{\mathbf{I}_1}{\mathbf{V}_2}\right|_{I_2=0} = \frac{1}{3 + j4} = 0.12 - j0.16\,\text{S}$$

$$a''_{22} = a''_{11} = 3$$

$$\Delta a'' = 1 = (3)(3) - (0.12 - j0.16)a''_{12}$$

$$\therefore \; a''_{12} = \frac{8}{0.12 - j0.16} = 24 + j32\,\Omega$$

[b] $a_{11} = a'_{11}a''_{11} + a'_{12}a''_{21} = 12 + 5(0.12 - j0.16) = 12.6 - j0.8$

$$a_{12} = a'_{11}a''_{12} + a'_{12}a''_{22} = (4)(24 + j32) + (5)(3) = 111 + j128\,\Omega$$

$$a_{21} = a'_{21}a''_{11} + a'_{22}a''_{21} = (3)(3) + (4)(0.12 - j0.16) = 9.48 - j0.64\,\text{S}$$

$$a_{22} = a'_{21}a''_{12} + a'_{22}a''_{22} = (3)(24 + j32) + (4)(3) = 84 + j96$$

$$\left.\frac{V_2}{V_1}\right|_{I_2=0} = \frac{1}{a_{11}} = \frac{1}{12.6 - j0.8} = 0.079 + j0.005$$

P 18.41 [a] At the input port: $V_1 = h_{11}I_1 + h_{12}V_2$;
At the output port: $I_2 = h_{21}I_1 + h_{22}V_2$

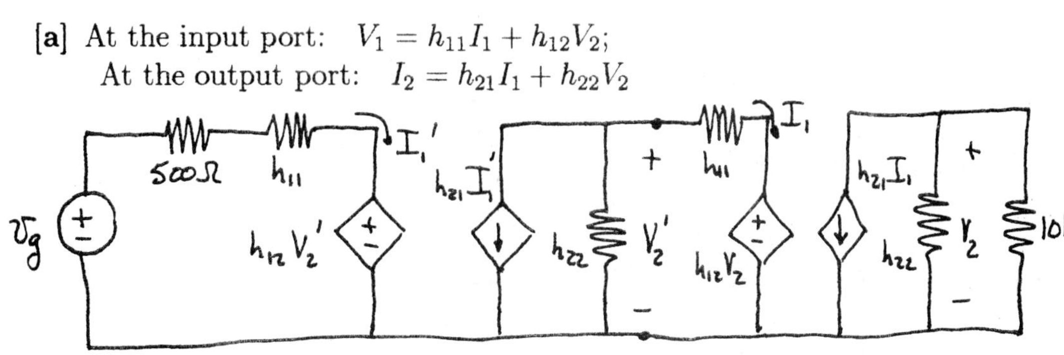

[b] $\frac{V_2}{10^4} + (100 \times 10^{-6}V_2) + 100I_1 = 0$

therefore $I_1 = -2 \times 10^{-6}V_2$

$V_2' = 1000I_1 + 15 \times 10^{-4}V_2 = -5 \times 10^{-4}V_2$

$100I_1' + 10^{-4}V_2' + (-2 \times 10^{-6})V_2 = 0$

therefore $I_1' = 205 \times 10^{-10}V_2$

$V_g = 1500I_1' + 15 \times 10^{-4}V_2' = 3000 \times 10^{-8}V_2$

$\frac{V_2}{V_g} = \frac{10^5}{3} = 33{,}333$

P 18.42 [a] $V_1 = I_2(z_{12} - z_{21}) + I_1(z_{11} - z_{21}) + z_{21}(I_1 + I_2)$

$= I_2z_{12} - I_2z_{21} + I_1z_{11} - I_1z_{21} + z_{21}I_1 + z_{21}I_2 = z_{11}I_1 + z_{12}I_2$

$V_2 = I_2(z_{22} - z_{21}) + z_{21}(I_1 + I_2) = z_{21}I_1 + z_{22}I_2$

[b] Short circuit V_g and apply a test current source to port 2 as shown. Note that $I_T = I_2$. We have

$$\frac{V}{z_{21}} - I_T + \frac{V + I_T(z_{12} - z_{21})}{Z_g + z_{11} - z_{21}} = 0$$

Therefore

$$V = \left[\frac{z_{21}(Z_g + z_{11} - z_{12})}{Z_g + z_{11}}\right] I_T \quad \text{and} \quad V_T = V + I_T(z_{22} - z_{21})$$

Thus $\frac{V_T}{I_T} = Z_{\text{Th}} = z_{22} - \left(\frac{z_{12}z_{21}}{Z_g + z_{11}}\right)\,\Omega$

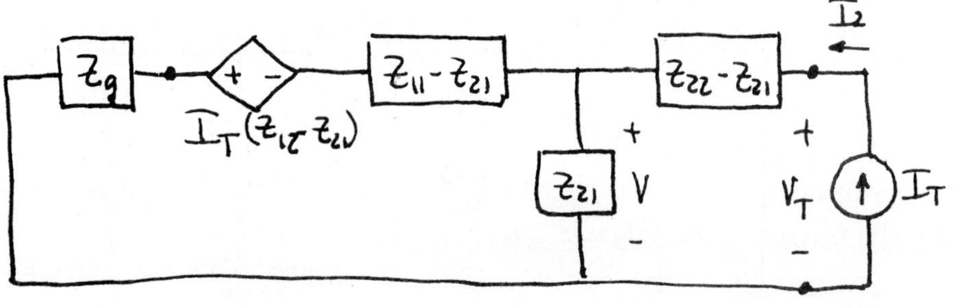

For V_{Th} note that $V_{oc} = \frac{z_{21}}{z_g + z_{11}}V_g$ since $I_2 = 0$.

P 18.43 [a] $V_1 = (z_{11} - z_{12})I_1 + z_{12}(I_1 + I_2) = z_{11}I_1 + z_{12}I_2$

$V_2 = (z_{21} - z_{12})I_1 + (z_{22} - z_{12})I_2 + z_{12}(I_2 + I_1) = z_{21}I_1 + z_{22}I_2$

[b] With port 2 terminated in an impedance Z_L, the two mesh equations are

$$V_1 = (z_{11} - z_{12})I_1 + z_{12}(I_1 + I_2)$$

$$0 = Z_L I_2 + (z_{21} - z_{12})I_1 + (z_{22} - z_{12})I_2 + z_{12}(I_1 + I_2)$$

Solving for I_1:

$$I_1 = \frac{V_1(z_{22} + Z_L)}{z_{11}(Z_L + z_{22}) - z_{12}z_{21}}$$

Therefore

$$Z_{\text{in}} = \frac{V_1}{I_1} = z_{11} - \frac{z_{12}z_{21}}{z_{22} + Z_L}$$

P 18.44 [a] $I_1 = y_{11}V_1 + y_{21}V_2 + (y_{12} - y_{21})V_2; \qquad I_2 = y_{21}V_1 + y_{22}V_2$

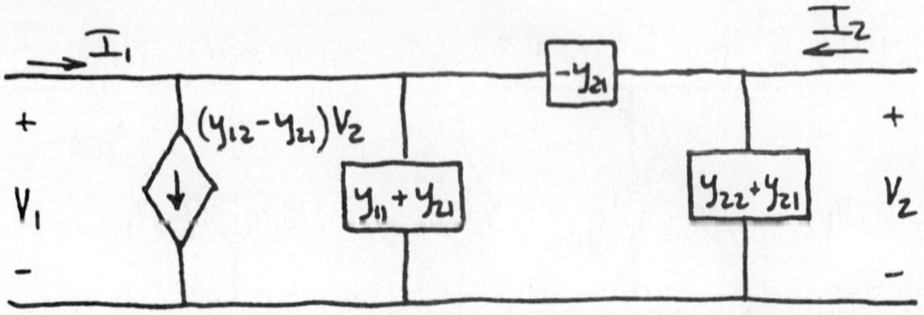

$I_1 = y_{11}V_1 + y_{12}V_2; \qquad I_2 = y_{12}V_1 + y_{22}V_2 + (y_{21} - y_{12})V_1$

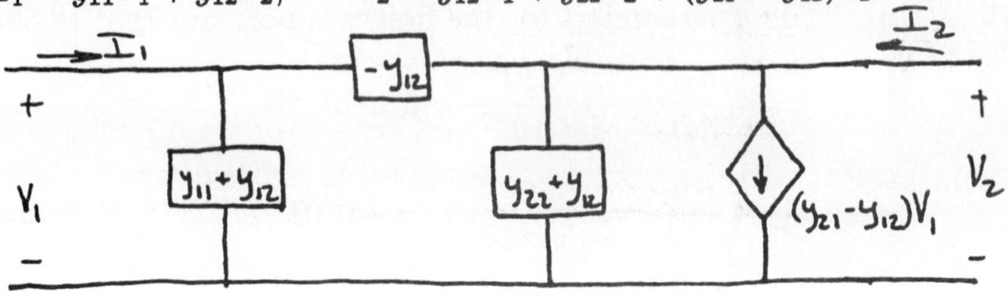

[b] Using the second circuit derived in part [a], we have

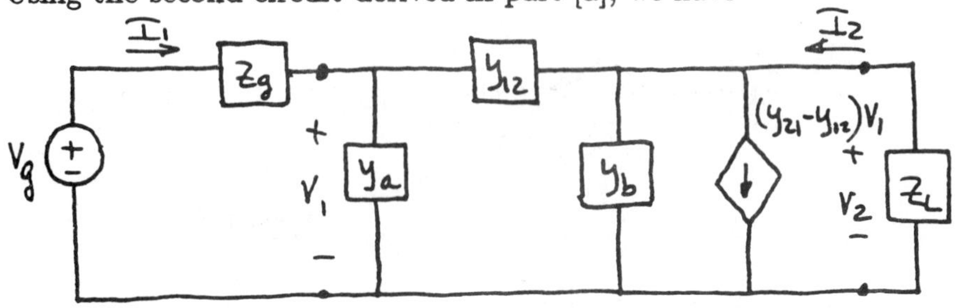

where $y_a = (y_{11} + y_{12})$ and $y_b = (y_{22} + y_{12})$

At the input port we have

$$I_1 = y_a V_1 - y_{12}(V_1 - V_2) = y_{11}V_1 + y_{12}V_2$$

At the output port we have

$$\frac{V_2}{Z_L} + (y_{21} - y_{12})V_1 + y_b V_2 - y_{12}(V_2 - V_1) = 0$$

Solving for V_1 gives

$$V_1 = \left(\frac{1 + y_{22}Z_L}{-y_{21}Z_L}\right) V_2$$

Substituting Eq. (18.2) into (18.1) and at the same time using $V_2 = -Z_L I_2$, we get

$$\frac{I_2}{I_1} = \frac{y_{21}}{y_{11} + \Delta y Z_L}$$

P 18.45 [a] The g-parameter equations are $I_1 = g_{11}V_1 + g_{12}I_2$ and $V_2 = g_{21}V_1 + g_{22}I_2$. These equations are satisfied by the following circuit:

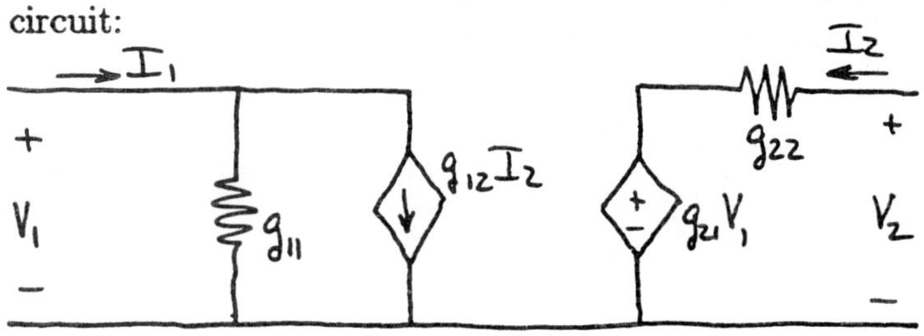

[b] The g parameters for the first two port in Fig P 18.39(a) are

$$g_{11} = \frac{h_{22}}{\Delta h} = \frac{25 \times 10^{-6}}{5 \times 10^{-3}} = 5 \times 10^{-3}\,\text{S}$$

$$g_{12} = \frac{-h_{12}}{\Delta h} = \frac{-5 \times 10^{-4}}{5 \times 10^{-3}} = -0.10$$

$$g_{21} = \frac{-h_{21}}{\Delta h} = \frac{-40}{5 \times 10^{-3}} = -8000$$

$$g_{22} = \frac{h_{11}}{\Delta h} = \frac{1000}{5 \times 10^{-3}} = 200\,\text{k}\Omega$$

From Problem 3.60 $R_{ef} = 72\,\text{k}\Omega$, hence our circuit reduces to

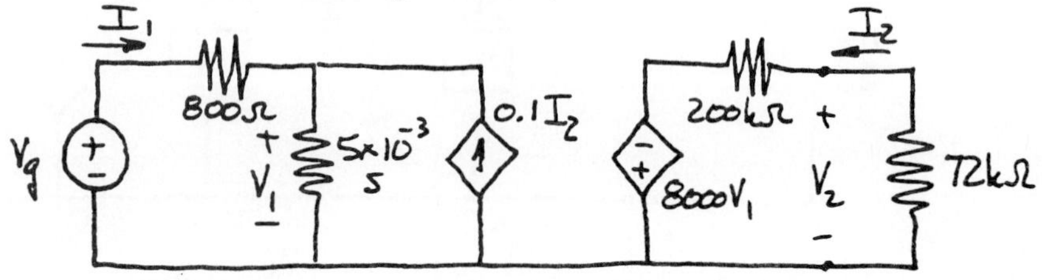

$$V_2 = \frac{-8000V_1(72)}{272}$$

$$I_2 = \frac{-V_2}{72{,}000} = \frac{8V_1}{272}$$

$$v_g = 9\,\text{mV}$$

$$\therefore \quad \frac{V_1 - 9 \times 10^{-3}}{800} + V_1(5 \times 10^{-3}) - 0.1\frac{8V_1}{272} = 0$$

$$V_1 - 9 \times 10^{-3} + 4V_1 - \frac{80V_1}{34} = 0$$

$$\therefore \quad V_1 = 3.4 \times 10^{-3}$$

$$V_2 = \frac{-8000(72)}{272} \times 3.4 \times 10^{-3} = -7.2\,\text{V}$$

From Problem 3.60

$$\frac{V_o}{V_2} = 0.5; \qquad \therefore \quad V_o = -3.6\,\text{V}$$